Mergers, Acquisitions, and Leveraged Buyouts

BUSINESS ONE IRWIN
THE LIBRARY OF INVESTMENT BANKING

Robert Lawrence Kuhn
Editor-in-Chief

Volume I: **INVESTING AND RISK MANAGEMENT**

Volume II: **CAPITAL RAISING AND FINANCIAL STRUCTURE**

Volume III: **CORPORATE AND MUNICIPAL SECURITIES**

Volume IV: **MERGERS, ACQUISITIONS, AND LEVERAGED BUYOUTS**

Volume V: **MORTGAGE AND ASSET SECURITIZATION**

Volume VI: **INTERNATIONAL FINANCE AND INVESTING**

Volume VII: **INDEX TO THE LIBRARY OF INVESTMENT BANKING**

Mergers, Acquisitions, and Leveraged Buyouts

Volume IV of the Library of Investment Banking

Robert Lawrence Kuhn
Editor-in-Chief

BUSINESS ONE IRWIN
Homewood, Illinois 60430

This publication is designed to provide accurate and authoritative information in regard to the subject matter covered. It is sold with the understanding that the publisher is not engaged in rendering legal, accounting, or other professional service. If legal advice or other expert assistance is required, the services of a competent professional person should be sought.

From a Declaration of Principles jointly adopted by a Committee of the American Bar Association and a Committee of Publishers.

Project editor: Jean Roberts
Production manager: Ann Cassady
Cover design: Tim Kaage
Compositor: Publication Services, Inc.
Typeface: 11/13 Times Roman
Printer: R.R. Donnelley & Sons Company

Library of Congress Cataloging-in-Publication Data

Mergers, acquisitions, and leveraged buyouts / Robert Lawrence Kuhn, editor.
p. cm. — (The library of investment banking; v. 4)
Includes index.
ISBN 1-55623-251-9
1. Consolidation and merger of corporations—United States. 2. Corporate reorganizations—United States. 3. Leveraged buyouts—United States. I. Kuhn, Robert Lawrence. II. Title: Mergers, acquisitions, and leveraged buyouts. III. Series.
HD2785.M46 1990
338.8′3′0973—dc20 89–7858
CIP

Printed in the United States of America
3 4 5 6 7 8 9 0 DO 6 5 4 3 2 1 0

The Library of Investment Banking *is dedicated to the investment banking community—the financial facilitator of market-driven capitalism and the economic catalyst of national and international development.*

ABOUT THE EDITOR-IN-CHIEF

Dr. Robert Lawrence Kuhn is an independent investment banker specializing in mergers and acquisitions, international corporate investments and strategic alliances, new business formation, leveraged buyouts, and the structuring of innovative financial transactions. He is a scientist, strategist, author, and scholar at home in the complementary worlds of finance, business, academe, and media.

Dr. Kuhn is Senior Research Fellow in Creative and Innovative Management, IC^2 Institute, University of Texas at Austin; and Adjunct Professor, Department of Management and Organizational Behavior, Stern School of Business, New York University. He has advised several governments on financing and commercializing technology. He is chairman of the Investment Management Institute of Japan in Tokyo. Dr. Kuhn speaks and lectures frequently and is quoted and published widely.

Dr. Kuhn has written and edited more than 20 books, including *Investment Banking: The Art and Science of High-Stakes Dealmaking* and *Investment Banking in the United States* (in Japanese). Other books include *Handbook for Creative and Innovative Managers; Deal Maker: All the Negotiating Skills and Secrets You Need; Creativity and Strategy in Mid-Sized Firms; To Flourish Among Giants: Creative Management for Mid-Sized Firms; Micromanaging: Transforming Business Leaders with Personal Computers; Frontiers in Creative and Innovative Management; New Directions for Creative and Innovative Management; Commercializing Defense-Related Technology; Commercializing SDI Technologies; Frontiers in Medical Information Sciences; The Firm Bond: Linking Meaning and Mission in Business and Religion; Corporate Creativity: Robust Companies and the Entrepreneurial Spirit; Managing Take-Off in Fast-Growth Companies; Technology Venturing: American Innovation and Risk Taking; Industrial Research and Development in Israel; and Regulatory Reform: New Vision or Old Curse*. He is a contributing editor and featured columnist for *Journal of Business Strategy*.

Dr. Kuhn has a B.A., Human Biology (Phi Beta Kappa), The Johns Hopkins University; Ph.D., Neurophysiology, Department of Anatomy and Brain Research Institute, University of California at Los Angeles; and M.S., Management, Sloan School of Management, Massachusetts Institute of Technology, where he was a Sloan Fellow and a Research Affiliate in Psychology.

THE LIBRARY OF INVESTMENT BANKING EDITORIAL ADVISORY BOARD

THE LIBRARY OF INVESTMENT BANKING CONTRIBUTORS LIST

Oliver Abel IV is Senior Vice President Kidder, Peabody & Co.

Frederick R. Adler is Managing General Partner, Adler and Company.

Edward I. Altman is Professor of Finance and Chairman of the MBA Program, Stern School of Business, New York University.

Michel Amsalem is Vice President, Citicorp.

G. Chris Andersen is Managing Director, Drexel Burnham Lambert.

Larry Anderson is Associate Director, Deutsche Bank Fixed Income Research, Deutsche Bank Capital Markets (London).

Marcelle Arak is Professor of Finance, College of Business, University of Colorado at Denver; previously she was Vice President and Head of Structured Interest Rate, Options and Guarantees Department, Citicorp North American Investment Bank.

Joseph Auerbach is the Class of 1957 Professor of Business Administration Emeritus at the Harvard Business School, Harvard University.

Robert L. Barmore, Jr. is Vice President, Asset Sales Department, Citicorp North American Investment Bank.

Alfred J. Battaglia is President, VACUTAINER Systems Division, Becton Dickinson and Company.

Andrew Bevan is Director, Fixed Interest Research WestLB UK, Ltd.; previously he was the Director of International Economics Research in the London Office office of Drexel Burnham Lambert.

Thomas C. Blum is Vice President, Financial Institutions, Salomon Brothers Inc.

Frederick Blumberg is a partner of the law firm of Pepper, Hamilton & Scheetz.

Roberta Paula Books is Vice President, Real Estate Finance, Salomon Brothers Inc.

Arthur M. Borden is a partner in the law firm of Rosenman & Colin.

Richard P. Brennan is Vice President, Thrift Asset/Liability Department, Salomon Brothers Inc.

Roberts Wyckoff Brokaw III is Managing Director, Investment Banking Division, Merrill Lynch Capital Markets.

Andrew R. Brownstein is a partner in the law firm of Wachtell, Lipton, Rosen & Katz.

G. Clyde Buck is Senior Vice President and Houston Corporate Finance Manager, Rauscher Pierce Refsnes, Inc.

James J. Burke, Jr. is President and Chief Executive Officer, Merrill Lynch Capital Partners, Inc.

George D. Caffrey is Vice President, Marine Midland Bank, N.A.

John L. Carl is Vice President/Controller, Hospital Sector, American Hospital Supply Corporation.

Leonard S. Chaikind is Administrator, Shell Provident Fund-Shell Pension Trust, Shell Oil Company.

Edward Chambliss is Managing Director and Sales Manager for High Yield Corporate Bonds, Salomon Brothers Inc.

Taeyoung Chung is a Ph.D. student in international business, School of Business Administration, University of Michigan.

Bruce M. Collins is Vice President, Shearson Lehman Hutton.

William T. Comfort is Chairman, Citicorp Venture Capital.

Thomas E. Copeland is Professor of Finance, Anderson Graduate School of Management, University of California at Los Angeles. He is currently on leave of absence while serving as Firm Consultant in finance for McKinsey & Co., Inc. He is coauthor, with J. Fred Weston, of *Financial Theory and Corporate Policy*, 3rd edition, and *Managerial Finance*.

Thomas C. Darling is Vice President, Citicorp Venture Capital.

Kenneth M. Davidson is an attorney with the Federal Trade Commission.

J. Morton Davis is Chairman and Chief Executive Officer, D.H. Blair & Co.

Jacques T. L. Delacave is Chairman, Abbeyside Group plc.

Reinaldo M. Diaz is Managing Director, PaineWebber Development Corporation.

William P. Dickey is Managing Director and Co-Head, Real Estate Finance Group, The First Boston Corporation.

Katherine E. Dietze is Vice President/Manager, Salmon Brothers Inc.

Dorothy J. Dotson is a Managing Director of the Investment Banking Group at Prudential-Bache Capital Funding, where she is head of the Private Placement Group.

Ernst-Ludwig Drayss is Abteilung Direktor, Deustche Bank Fixed Income Research, Deustche Bank A.G. (Frankfurt).

William C. Dudley is Vice President and Senior Economist, Investment Research Department, Goldman, Sachs & Co.

Gunter Dufey is Professor of International Business and Finance, School of Business Administration, University of Michigan.

Jill Dutt is the editor of *Investment Dealers' Digest*.

John Eberhardt, Jr. is Managing Director, Bear Stearns & Co., Inc.

Stephen Evans-Freke is Managing Director, PaineWebber Development Corporation.

Frank J. Fabozzi is the editor of numerous finance books and handbooks; he has been Visiting Professor, Sloan School of Management, Massachusetts Institute of Technology.

Mark Fadiman is a staff writer for *Investment Dealers' Digest*.

James L. Farrell, Jr. is Chairman of MPT Associates, an investment counseling subsidiary of Lincoln National Corporation. He is also an Adjunct Professor of Finance, Stern School of Business, New York University.

Sylvan G. Feldstein is Vice President, Securities Research & Economics, Municipal Bond Research, Merrill Lynch Capital Markets.

Carl Ferenbach is a general partner of Berkshire Partners, an investment partnership.

Michael G. Ferri holds the Edward J. and Louise E. Mellon Chair in Finance, John Carroll University.

Joseph Fichera is an independent financial consultant; previously he was Vice President, Corporate Finance Division, Smith Barney Harris Upham & Co., Inc.

Albert L. Fischetti is Vice President, Asset-Based Finance Division, Bankers Trust Company.

Warren A. Fite is Vice President, Merrill Lynch Capital Partners, Inc. and Merrill Lynch Capital Markets.

Robert Flaherty is President, Bankers Trust Company.

Steven Fletcher is an associate in the London office of Drexel Burnham Lambert.

Bruce S. Foerster is Managing Director, PaineWebber Incorporated.

James H. Fogelson is a partner in the law firm of Wachtell, Lipton, Rosen & Katz.

Martin S. Fridson is Managing Director, High Yield Research, Merrill Lynch Capital Markets; previously he was Principal and Manager of Credit Research at Morgan Stanley & Co., where he edited *High Performance: The Magazine of High Yield Bonds*.

Alan R. Friedman is a partner in the law firm of Kramer, Levin, Nessen, Kamin, & Frankel.

Emanuel Y. Friedman holds a Ph.D. in Molecular Biology from the State University of New York and a recently completed MBA at the Stern School of Business, New York University.

J. B. Fuqua is Chairman and Chief Executive Officer, Fuqua Industries, Inc.

Mario Gabelli is Chairman, Gabelli & Co. and GAMCO Investors Inc.

Glenn H. Gage is a partner in the New York Office of Ernst & Young and is senior editor of the firm's Mergers and Acquisitions Newsletter.

Ronald L. Gallatin is Managing Director of Shearson Lehman Hutton Inc., where he heads the New Product Department.

T. Dessa Garlicki is Assistant Professor of Finance, Bentley College.

Gary L. Gastineau is Vice President and Options and Futures Strategist in the Equity Options and Futures Department, Salomon Brothers Inc.

Jeffrey R. Gates is counsel to Kelso & Company, an investment banking firm specializing in ESOPs. He was counsel to the U.S. Senate Committee on Finance.

George T. Geis is Adjunct Associate Professor of Management Science, Anderson Graduate School of Management, University of California at Los Angeles. He is the co-author of *Micromanaging: Transforming Business Leaders with Personal Computers*.

Evelyn Geller is Vice President of Research and Assistant to the Chairman, D.H. Blair & Co.

Ian H. Giddy is Director of International Fixed-Income Research, Drexel Burnham Lambert. A former finance professor at Columbia and New York University, he was an economist at the International Monetary Fund.

Laurie Goodman is Vice President, Eastbridge Capital; previously she was Vice President, Goldman, Sachs & Co.

Barbara Goodstein is an associate in the law firm of Rosenman & Colin.

Michael Goroff is an associate in the law firm of Wachtell, Lipton, Rosen & Katz.

Evan Guillemin is a reporter for *Investment Dealers' Digest*.

Margaret Darasz Hadzima is Vice President, Bonds, Scudder, Stevens & Clark.

William J. Haley is Vice President, Capital Markets Service Group, Salomon Brothers Inc.

Samuel L. Hayes III is the Jacob H. Schiff Professor of Investment Banking.

James P. Heffernan is a partner in the investment banking firm of Whitman Heffernan Rhein & Co.

Jeremy Henderson is Vice President, Medium-Term Notes, Salomon Brothers Inc.

John T. Hickey is Executive Vice President and Chief Financial Officer, Motorola Inc.

Joanne M. Hill is Vice President, Futures and Options Strategies Research, Paine-Webber.

Thomas S. Y. Ho is Professor of Finance, Stern School of Business, New York University.

Arnold S. Hoffman is Managing Director, Shearson Lehman Hutton.

Carol G. Hubsch is Vice President, Investment Banking, Merrill Lynch Capital Markets.

Alastair I. Hunter-Henderson is Vice President, Morgan Guaranty Trust Company.

Charles E. Hurwitz is Chairman of the Board and Chief Executive Officer, Maxxam, Inc.

Warren J. Ingber is an attorney with the law firm of Kramer, Levin, Nessen, Kamin & Frankel.

Marko Issever is Vice President, Prudential-Bache Capital Fund.

Ann Irimia-Casella is a principal in the New York office of Arthur Anderson & Co.

Thomas Jasper is Managing Director, Capital Markets Services, Salomon Brothers Inc.

Michael D. Joehnk is Professor of Finance, Arizona State University.

Howard B. Johnson is First Vice President, PaineWebber Development Corporation.

Steven B. Jones is Research Assistant in Fixed Income Research, Morgan Stanley & Co.

Timothy P. Kane is a principal in the New York office of Arthur Andersen & Co.

Robert S. Kant is a partner in the law firm of O'Connor, Cavanagh, Anderson, Westover, Killingsworth & Beshears.

Patrick Kelly is a Director, Hedge Mangagement Department, Salomon Brothers Inc.

Stephen L. Key is New York Managing Partner at Ernst & Young, where he is in charge of its Financial Services Group and a member of its board of partners.

Byron D. Klapper is Senior Vice President and Publisher, Standard & Poor's Corp.

Frank Knowles is an associate, Prudential-Bache Interfunding Inc.

James L. Kochan is Chief Fixed-Income Strategist, Merrill Lynch, Pierce, Fenner & Smith, Inc.

Robert Kopprasch is Vice President, Salomon Brothers Inc.

George Kozmetsky is Chairman of the IC^2 Institute, Executive Associate for Economic Affairs, and the Marion West Chair Professor, University of Texas at Austin. He is the co-founder of Teledyne.

Robert Boyden Lamb is Associate Professor of Management, Stern School of Business, New York University. He is founder and editor of the *Journal of Business Strategy*, and the author of numerous works on municipal finance.

Benjamin V. Lambert is President and Chief Executive Officer, Eastdil Reality.

Jack W. Lavery is Director of Global Equities Divison and Global Research Group, Merrill Lynch & Co., Inc.

Colin Lawrence is Vice President, Currency and Foreign Security Risk Management, Citicorp NA Investment Bank; previously he was Vice President and Senior International Economist, Drexel Burnham Lambert.

Alain Lebec is Managing Director, Mergers and Acquisitions, Merrill Lynch Capital Markets.

Lawrence Lederman is a partner in the law firm of Wachtell, Lipton, Rosen & Katz.

Mark M. Lee is Associate Director, Corporate Finance, Bear Stearns & Co., Inc.

Martin L. Leibowitz is Managing Director, Bond Portfolio Analysis Group, Salomon Brothers Inc.

Donald Lessard is Professor, Sloan School of Management, Massachusetts Institute of Technology.

Ezra G. Levin is a partner in the law firm of Kramer, Levin, Nessen, Kamin & Frankel.

Arthur Lipper III is Chairman and co-founder of the New York & Foreign Securities Corporation, and is Chairman, Editor-in-Chief, and Publisher of *Venture* magazine.

Martin Lipton is a partner in the law firm of Wachtell, Lipton, Rosen & Katz.

Douglas Lister is in Mergers and Acquisitions Depratment, Kidder Peabody & Co., Inc.; previously he was an associate, Mergers and Acquisitions, Merrill Lynch Capital Markets.

John Macfarlane is a Director, Salomon Brothers Inc.

Hernando Madero is Vice President, Booz Allen & Hamilton International.

Keith M. Maillard is President, S.A.M. Associates, Inc.; previously he was Senior Vice President and Co-Head of Mortgage Finance Group, Kidder, Peabody & Co., Inc.

Joesph M. Manko is a partner in the law firm of Wolf, Block, Schorr and Solis-Cohen.

J. Steven Manolis is Managing Director, Real Estate Finance, Salomon Brothers Inc.

Brian J. Martin is Director, Prudential-Bache Capital Funding, and First Vice President, Prudential-Bache Securities.

Gilbert E. Matthews is Managing Director, Corporate Finance, Bear Stearns & Co., Inc.

Frank J. Medeiros is Department Executive, Marine Midland Bank.

David Millison is Senior Vice President, High Yield and Convertible Bonds, Drexel Burnham Lambert.

Garth L. Milne is Vice President and Director of Treasury, Motorola Inc.

Maureen Mooney is Senior/Specialist, Fixed Income, Merrill Lynch, Pierce, Fenner & Smith.

Jane Koloski Morris is Vice President, Venture Economics, Inc. and editor of *Venture Capital Journal*.

Allen D. Morton is Assistant Professor of Finance, Western Connecticut State University.

Frank Murray is a Director, Mergers and Acquisitions, Merrill Lynch Capital Markets.

Jerry K. Myers is Executive Vice President and Chief Administrative and Financial Officer, American Hospital Supply Corporation.

Robert Nabholz is an Associate, High Yields Group, Prudential-Bache Capital Fund.

Jamshid Jahm Najafi is an associate, Real Estate Finance, Salomon Brothers Inc.

Denis J. Nayden is President, Transportation and Industrial Funding Corporation, General Electric Capital.

Benjamin S. Neuhausen is a partner in the Chicago office of Arthur Andersen & Co.

Peter O'Brien is Managing Director of Equity Transactions Group, Merrill Lynch Capital Markets.

Lucille Palermo is Vice President, International Research Department, Drexel Burnham Lambert.

Gioia M. Parente is an Analyst, Bond Market Research, Salomon Brothers Inc.

Gregory J. Parseghian is Vice President, The First Boston Corporation.

Barbara Pauley is a Chartered Financial Analyst, Corporate Bond Research, Salomon Brothers Inc.

Mark Pitts is Senior Vice President, Shearson Lehman Hutton.

Claude L. Pomper is in charge of the International Corporate Finance Division of the Latin America Banking Group at Citicorp.

Stephen P. Rappaport is Manager of the Municipal Bond Research and Financial Services Department, Prudential-Bache Securities Inc.

Andrés J. Recoder is an associate in Capital Markets Research, Drexel Burnham Lambert.

Kevin B. Reilly is a principal in the New York office of Ernst & Young.

Fred B. Renwick is Professor of Finance, Stern School of Business, New York University.

C. Kirk Rhein, Jr. is a partner in the investment banking firm of Whitman Heffernan Rhein & Co., Inc.

William D. Rifkin is Managing Director and Co-Head of the Merger and Acquisition Group, Salomon Brothers Inc.

John C. Ritchie, Jr. is Professor of Finance, Temple University.

Eric S. Robinson is an associate in the law firm of Wachtell, Lipton, Rosen & Katz.

Edward J. Roncoroni, Jr. is Vice President, Beneficial Business Credit Corp.

Michael R. Rosenberg is Vice President and Manager of International Fixed Income Research Department, Merrill Lynch Capital Markets.

Daniel R. Ross is Vice President, Salomon Brothers Inc.

Jack E. Salmon is a Manager at Arthur Andersen & Co.

Anthony Saunders is Professor of Finance, Stern School of Business, New York University, and Research Advisor at the Federal Bank of Philadelphia. He is editor of the Salomon Brothers Center Monographs on Economics and Finance.

Harry C. Sauvain is University Professor Emeritus of Finance, Indiana University.

Thomas Schneeweis is Professor of Finance, School of Management, the University of Massachusetts (Amherst).

Carl W. Schneider is a partner in the law firm of Wolf, Block, Schorr and Solis-Cohen.

William A. Schreyer is Chairman and Chief Executive Officer, Merrill Lynch & Co., Inc.

Edward H. Schwallie is President, Booz Allen Acquisition Services, Booz Allen & Hamilton, Inc.

Paul Scura is a Managing Director at Prudential-Bache Securities, where he is Head of the Insurance Group and Co-Head of Financial Strategies, which contains Fixed Income Research and all of Trading and Sales Analytics.

Dexter Senft is Managing Director, Fixed Income Research, The First Boston Corporation.

Jason M. Shargel is a partner in the law firm of Wolf, Block, Schorr and Solis-Cohen.

Janet Showers is Vice President, Salomon Brothers Inc.

Andrew Silver is Senior Analyst, Moody's Investor Service; previously he was Vice President, Fixed-Income Research, Citicorp North American Investment Bank.

Evan Simonoff is a senior writer for *Investment Dealers' Digest*.

Cornelia M. Small is Managing Director, Scudder, Stevens & Clark.

David A. Smilow, Research Analyst, Drexel Burnham Lambert.

Richard L. Solar is Managing Director, Asset-Based Lending, Bankers Trust Company.

Gregory S. Stanger is an analyst at PaineWebber Development Corporation.

Francis X. Stankard is Executive Vice President and Senior Institutional Relations Officer, Chase Manhattan Bank.

John L. Steffens is President and Chief Executive Officer, Merrill Lynch Consumer Markets.

Benjamin J. Stein is an attorney and writer.

John E. Stewart is a partner in the Chicago office of Arthur Andersen & Co.

Marcia Stigum is the author of *The Money Market* and *Money Market Calculations: Yields, Breakevens and Arbitrage*, and is President, Stigum & Associates.

Valentina R. Stum is Executive Vice President and Chief Operating Officer, Merrill Lynch Specialists Inc.; she has been Vice President and Senior Counsel, Merrill Lynch Capital Markets.

Marti G. Subrahmanyam is Professor of Economics and Finance and Chairman of the Finance Area, Stern School of Business, New York University.

Kenneth H. Sullivan is Managing Director, Drexel Burnham Lambert.

Jeffrey Talbert is with Stamford Capital, Sterling, Grace & Co., Inc.; previously he was with the Real Estate Finance Group, The First Boston Corporation.

Marc D. Teitelbaum is a partner in the law firm of Spengler Carlson Gubar Brodsky & Firschling.

Rhoda F. Teters is a consultant with The Merit Group.

Robert C. Thompson is Vice President–Finance and Chief Financial Officer (retired), Shell Oil Company; he has also been Chairman, Financial Executives Institute.

Hung Q. Tran is Director, Deutsche Bank Fixed Income Research, Deutsche Bank.

Rein W. van der Does is Vice President and Director of International Portfolio Strategies, International Equities Group, Drexel Burnham Lambert.

Paul R. Van Wyck is Vice President, Chase Manhattan Corporation.

Mitchell F. Vernick is President, Capital Markets Group, Heller Financial, Inc.

N. R. Vijayaraghavan is a Vice President, Drexel Burnham Lambert.

Hubert D. Vos is President, Stonington Capital Corporation; previously he was Chief Financial Officer, Becton Dickinson and Company.

John S. Wadsworth, Jr. is Managing Director, Investment Banking Division, Morgan Stanley & Co., Inc.

Fritz Wahl is Senior Research Analyst in high yield securities, Morgan Stanley & Co., Inc.

David Walker is Managing Director and General Manager, Hong Kong, Bankers Trust Company.

Kenneth G. Walker is Executive Vice President, Lazard Fréres Property Investment Co.

Ingo Walter is Professor of Economics and Finance, Stern School of Business, New York University; and John H. Loudon Professor of International Management, INSEAD, Fontainebleau, France.

Craig M. Wasserman is an attorney at Wachtell, Lipton, Rosen & Katz.

Neil A. Wassner is a general partner in the investment banking firm of Wassner Mattingly & Company.

Robert M. Weinstein is Vice President, Salomon Brothers Inc

H Ronald Weissman is a partner in the New York office of Arthur Andersen & Co., where he heads the Financial Services Practice.

John Whitman is Chairman and Chief Executive Officer, Prudential-Bache Interfunding.

Martin J. Whitman is a partner in the investment banking firm of Whitman Heffernan Rhein & Co.

Jeremy Wiesen is a Professor of Business Law, Stern School of Business, New York University. He is a former chairman of Financial News Network.

Paul T. Wilkinson is First Vice President, Institutional Financial Futures Department, Prudential-Bache Securities, Inc.

Arthur Williams III is Managing Director, Simms Capital Management, Ltd.

Caroline Williams is Senior Vice President, Investment Banking, Donaldson, Lufkin & Jenrette, where she is director of the firm's Chicago investment banking office.

Richard S. Wilson is Vice President, Merrill Lynch Capital Markets.

Ruth Wimer is a partner in the Washington office of Ernst & Young.

Robert E. Woods is Vice President and Head of Long-term Finance Origination and Trading, Citicorp North American Investment Bank.

Robert A. Young is Vice President, Convertible Securities Reseach, Dean Witter Reynolds.

Michael D. Youngblood is Vice President and Manager of Residential Mortgage Research, Salomon Brothers Inc

PREFACE

THE LIBRARY OF INVESTMENT BANKING: STRUCTURE AND STRATEGY

The Library of Investment Banking is written by investment bankers for investment bankers. It is a professional guide for the real world; stressing practice not theory, it shows how complex financial instruments really work and how diverse financings really happen. The *Library* presents contemporary investment banking in all its dynamism, complexity, creativity, and excitement.

The Library of Investment Banking is composed of six volumes and a comprehensive index:

Volume I: INVESTING AND RISK MANAGEMENT
Volume II: CAPITAL RAISING AND FINANCIAL STUCTURE
Volume III: CORPORATE AND MUNICIPAL SECURITIES
Volume IV: MERGERS, ACQUISITIONS, AND LEVERAGED BUYOUTS
Volume V: MORTGAGE AND ASSET SECURITIZATION
Volume VI: INTERNATIONAL FINANCE AND INVESTING
Volume VII: INDEX TO THE LIBRARY OF INVESTMENT BANKING

Library chapters are basic yet complete. They begin with first principles, understandable by nonexperts. They continue with organizing frameworks and advanced techniques, each enriched by actual cases and current examples.

Library contributors are those who get things done—leading investment bankers and firing-line financiers. It is important to appreciate how these professionals think and what they do. The objective is to learn how investment bankers design financial strategies, develop financial structures, and make financial deals.

The *Library* has been conceived as a definitive reference for the finance industry, a prime resource for investment bankers and for those who use investment banking services. Investment banking today is an organic profession, rich with diversity and innovation, very different from the cookie-cutter underwriting of yesteryear. Comprehensive chapters cover all facets of the field, from broad descriptions of concepts and processes to specific delineations of products and procedures.

LIBRARY STRUCTURE

The six volumes of *The Library of Investment Banking* contain a total of 217 chapters. Each volume is divided into several parts.

The Library of Investment Banking
Volume I
Investing and Risk Management

Part 1: Industry and Profession. An overview of the industry, including globalization, regulation, and structure; and a portrait of the profession, including spreads and fees, insider trading, and ethics. (It begins with "A Philosophy of Investment Banking.")

Part 2: Organization and Personality. Attitudes and attributes of investment banking organizations and investment bankers: commitment, personality, creativity, and decision making.

Part 3: Investments. The background and applications of *relevant* finance theory, portfolio theory, security valuation, financial analysis, pension fund management, horizon and yield curve analysis, performance evaluation, risk arbitrage, and investment research; accounting services and concepts, investments, and tax; tricks and traps in financial analysis.

Part 4: Risk Management. Financial fundamentals of options, futures, and swaps with investment banking applications; mechanisms and techniques for hedging and managing interest rate risk.

The Library of Investment Banking
Volume II
Capital Raising and Financial Structure

Part 1: Capital Raising. Various financing categories: public offerings (processes and pricing), shelf registration, private placements, direct investments, partnerships, master limited partnerships, and raising foreign capital. (It begins with "The Scope of Investment Banking.")

Part 2: Venture Capital. Industry structure, venture approaches, venture transactions, and future opportunities. Investor motivations, deal structures, and handling financial crises.

Part 3: Financial Structure and Restructures. Corporate financial goals, capital structure, debt financing, dividend policy, and equity financing; rationale and approach to restructuring and recapitalizations, employee stock ownership plans (ESOPs), bankruptcies and reorganizations, and financial strategies (the "secrets" of two entrepreneurial chief executives who are well-known users of investment banking services).

Part 4: Legal and Accounting Aspects. Securities law (the going-public process and the responsibilities of a public company), relations with regulatory agencies, and the due diligence process for public offerings; accounting for public offerings; financial restructuring issues and going-private transactions.

The Library of Investment Banking
Volume III
Corporate and Municipal Securities

Part 1: Fixed-Income Analysis. Features of fixed-income securities; bond characteristics, yield measures, price volatility, duration; option-embedded bonds; zero-coupon securities. (It begins with "Financial Securities and Instruments: Classifications and Characteristics.")

Part 2: Money Market Securities. Money market instruments, commercial paper, market makers, and dealers.

Part 3: Corporate Securities. Concepts, characteristics, and classes of corporate bonds, medium-term notes, investment-grade bonds, high-yield bonds, preferred stock, and warrants; mechanisms and techniques for issuing, evaluating, and rating the securities; how the various and diverse categories of corporate instruments were developed and how they interrelate—financial innovation is a primary theme.

Part 4: Municipal Securities. Municipal securities (characteristics and categories, guidelines for investors); primary market (underwriting); secondary market (trading); comparing public and corporate finance; and corporate tax-exempt financing.

The Library of Investment Banking
Volume IV
Mergers, Acquisitions, and Leveraged Buyouts

Part 1: Mergers, Acquisitions, and Divestitures. Various facets of mergers, acquisitions, and divestitures: finding and facilitating, valuing and pricing, financing and funding, public and private companies, acquisition reviews and due diligence. (It begins with "The Strategies of Investment Banking.")

Part 2: Leveraged Buyouts. Various aspects of leveraged buyouts: concepts and development, practices and techniques, structure and strategy, difficult transactions, cashing out, and investing in leveraged buyouts.

Part 3: Legal and Accounting Aspects. Merger and acquisition law; fairness opinions; takeover and defense law (takeover techniques, defensive techniques, corporate restructuring, negotiations, liabilities, regulation). Accounting and tax considerations for mergers and acquisitions.

Part 4: The Deal-Making Process. Strategies and structures for doing deals; finding and selecting deals; elements of negotiations in formulating and implementing investment banking transactions.

The Library of Invesment Banking
Volume V
Mortgage and Asset Securitization

Part 1: Real Estate and Mortgage Finance. Development and description of real estate investment banking, real estate finance, mortgages, mortgage pass-through securities, and mortgage-backed bonds. (It begins with "How to Use Investment Bankers.")

Part 2: Asset Securitization. Concepts and applications of securitization: residential real estate, commercial real estate, non-mortgage assets, collateralized mortgage obligations, accounting for asset securitization, and tax implications.

Part 3: Asset-Based Finance. Balance-sheet financing, business value lending, finance company lending, project finance, loan distribution and multi-bank credits, and leasing.

The Library of Investment Banking
Volume VI
International Finance and Investing

Part 1: International Finance. Motivations, markets, instruments, and innovations in international debt and equities; Eurobonds; floating-rate notes; foreign exchange risks; currency swaps and synthetic securities.

Part 2: Eurocapital Markets. Description, development, and importance of the Eurocapital markets: ECU, United Kingdom, Germany, Holland, France, Italy, Austria, Denmark, Belgium, and Switzerland.

Part 3: Japanese Capital Markets. The Japanese financial system and Tokyo capital markets.

Part 4: International Investing and Risk Management. International diversification, bond investing, and portfolio management; Euro time deposits; bankers acceptances; applications of swaps and options in international finance; managing currency exposure and currency exchange warrants; international risk assessment and risk management in developing countries; bank debt restructuring; and mechanisms of capital flight.

LIBRARY STRATEGY

Professional and Practical

Library chapters describe what goes on in investment banking—on stage and behind the scenes—stressing processes and procedures as well as concepts and principles. Motivations (the "why's") are disclosed along with methods (the "how's"). Only essential theory is presented; again, the volumes of *The Library of Investment Banking* are professional guides, not academic texts. The emphasis is on practice—what actually happens when deals get made and financings get done.

Basic yet Comprehensive

Chapters are written for nonexpert professionals. They begin with simple explanations of the topics—definitions of key terms, descriptions of fundamentals, delineations of motivations, and the like. Then we step up the pace, demonstrating detailed patterns and systems so that the reader learns how the financing area works in actuality. Sophisticated examples are made plain with models and numbers (graphics and spreadsheets). The objective is to give practical meaning to general principles—to bring clarity to complexity.

The Way of Thinking

Conceptual thought, not latest trends, is what we offer. Method, not fact, is what we present. Investment banking is an organic process—ever changing, developing, and evolving. New techniques arise frequently; new instruments appear regularly. There is no way that a multivolume series, with its long production cycle, can be wholly accurate in all details. (Changes in tax considerations alone would threaten to invalidate entire categories.)

Have no illusions: We cannot claim up-to-the-minute accuracy and we do not promise state-of-the-art applications. Investment bankers keep current with *The Wall Street Journal*, various monthly publications, internal memoranda and product descriptions, and, best of all, word of mouth. For immediacy one must contact experts in each area. But our goal goes longer and larger.

The Library of Investment Banking sees a farther horizon. We want to understand *the way of thinking* in investment banking—the fundamental reasons why products are developed, how they are designed, what purposes they serve, why they change, and how they evolve. We go inside and underneath; we search deeply. By establishing the solid conceptual underpinnings of a variety of financing situations and instruments, we enable the reader to appreciate how investment bankers think. Consequently, we describe numerous financial circumstances and products, many in great detail, seeking underlying motivations and unifying mechanisms for each. Discerning the development of concepts and products is vital; the better one appreciates the past, the better one can anticipate the future. The result, we trust, will be a deepening sense of awareness of what investment banking is all about.

Perspective and Diversity

Chapters vary in size and approach. Each banker presents what he or she thinks and does best—and takes whatever space is needed to do so. Financing situations and products are presented as they actually work on Wall Street. Theory is included only where it is relevant, Practical examples are used extensively: We are great believers in using specific applications to induce general principles. One learns concepts from cases.

Chapters range from short explanations of highly specific products to lengthy descriptions of important processes (e.g., takeover defense law, deal-making negotiations). Substance dominates form: The length of chapters is determined by whatever it takes to do the job. We want you to experience the essence of the subject.

We also want you to get to know the personalities of some contributors. This may be a bit unusual for technical books (which generally promote process over people). Cold facts are sterile; method devoid of emotion just does not fully represent the reality of financial transactions. Personality is relevant in commerce, especially in investment banking. This is a people business, and personal passion cannot be ignored. We want to understand character, attitude, and demeanor as well as technique, mechanism, and algorithm. Subjective process must be an equal partner with objective content, so we have not purged the manuscript of opinions, judgments, biases, or speculations. There is spirit here, and some fire.[1]

Reader Attitude and Redundancy

Although the *Library* in general and each volume in particular proceeds linearly, you need not. Take charge! Enter and exit at any point. Select by personal interest, not numerical order. Each chapter stands alone, the best its author offers. Contributors present their favorite topics, so expect redundancy; yet similar concepts are viewed from different angles and cut from different companies, so seek insight.

Regarding redundancy, we make no excuses. With 217 chapters it is impossible to avoid overlap. But do not fear repetition. We believe that reiteration is helpful, even necessary, because it enables a reader to appreciate how different investment bankers view similar topics. Which methods are used? Which approaches are stressed? Which subjects are grouped together? Which topics are separated? Such differences are instructive. Seeing a complex subject from various angles develops perspective.

When there is overlap among chapters, look for panorama and perspective, greater dimension and deeper gain. It is important to see subjects from various viewpoints. Focused expositions, orderly instructions, and logical procedures are accented by sweeping essays, case histories, and personal opinions. Chapters are not meticulously manicured; nor do they fit together

[1] A personal note: As editor-in-chief I have written several of the organizing chapters on investment banking that introduce the volumes (e.g., philosophy, scope, strategies, finance framework, security classes, how to use investment bankers). However, my two chapters on the deal-making process (in *Volume IV, Mergers, Acquisitions, and Leveraged Buyouts*) reflect more of my true-life personality than any of the others—if a reader wants to find out about me, what I'm like to work with or be around, and what I actually *do* as an investment banker, these chapters tell the story. I was unsure whether to include such personal descriptions, whether the writing style was too flip or too cute—in fact whether the subject of deal making and negotiations is at all proper for a professional finance series. The reason I decided to flout tradition and include some "opinion" chapters is the importance of character and personality. I wanted the *Library of Investment Banking* to reflect normal daily activity, what actually goes on out there. Technical analysis is a critical part of investment banking, but it is only part, and it is not the largest part. People make the process work.

neatly as pieces in a puzzle. Real-world investment banking involves pieces too few, or pieces too many. Success in this industry is not often manicured or neat, nor is innovative progress normally tucked or trimmed.

Library Contributors

Library contributors are active investment bankers. They work as financiers and financial intermediaries. The spend their time devising financial instruments, structuring financial products, and doing financial deals. The *Library* presents the knowledge, ideas, and attitudes of these preeminent investment bankers, well-recognized names who are the industry's most knowledgeable experts. Managing directors and senior executives of more than a dozen leading investment banking houses are authors of chapters.

Library Readership

We expect that the *Library* will have broad appeal.

Primary: members of the investment banking community in the United States and worldwide.

Secondary: members of the larger financial community in the United States and worldwide (i.e., brokerage houses, commercial banks, savings and loan associations, insurance companies, financial service firms, and the like).

Tertiary: business and financial executives of corporations and institutions using modern finance techniques and investment banking services.

Quaternary: business people, students, and general readers interested in the intricacies of investment banking and high finance.

The audience, we think, is large. But never do we blur our focus: The *Library* is written by investment bankers for investment bankers.

Reference or Reading

Library chapters are intended for both reference and reading. One can look up specific ideas, say, to understand a numerical application of a particular financial instrument. Or one can read through an entire chapter, getting a full feel for the topic, learning both overall concepts and targeted examples. In either approach, easy access is facilitated by descriptive sections and subsections.

Remember, the *Library* is *not* a textbook. There is no artificial smoothness, no cosmetic harmony. Fret not. Remember our quest: real-world investment banking. To exclude either the detailed descriptions of products or the spontaneous sentiments about areas would be criminal, leaving too much good stuff a permanent prisoner of floppy disks. Seek ideas, insight, and inspiration as well as linearity, regularity, and continuity. You get raw material here, nothing less than what some truly smart heads think about all aspects of investment banking.

The *Library's* hallmark is a very large number of ideas, concepts, principles, attitudes, approaches, processes, products, instruments, mechanisms, techniques, regulations, requirements, forecasts, predictions, and opinions. This wellspring of information represents contemporary investment banking. Allow it to wash over you. Read and learn, sure, but also imbibe and experience. Develop perceptual sensitivity while honing analytical reasoning. Build inner understanding while augmenting outer knowledge. The outcome will be knowing investment banking.

TABLE OF CONTENTS

THE LIBRARY OF INVESTMENT BANKING
Volumes I through VI

Volume I INVESTING AND RISK MANAGEMENT

Volume III CORPORATE AND MUNICIPAL SECURITIES

Volume V MORTGAGE AND ASSET SECURITIZATION

PART 1

MERGERS AND ACQUISITIONS

CHAPTER 1

THE STRATEGIES OF INVESTMENT BANKING

Robert Lawrence Kuhn

Investment banks are financial intermediaries that match economic entities that need capital with those that have capital. The traditional view is that investment banks enable both issuers and investors to raise or invest capital with optimal costs-benefits.

For decades, such activities involved "gentlemen's relationships" between captains of industry and their Wall Street bankers. The markets were stable; the instruments were stable; the financings were stable; the spreads and fees were stable; the relationships were stable—all was well with the world.

The traditional investment bank structure worked just fine in the context of such stability. The traditional form and size of partnerships were quite satisfactory. Strategic planning was something that manufacturing companies had to do, but not investment banks.

But the world began to change. Markets, instruments, financings, spreads and fees, and relationships have all been transformed and have become exceedingly complex. The economic environment has shifted dramatically, and in order to prosper, even to survive, the strategies of investment banking must do likewise. It is no longer possible to take a simple, idealistic view of what investment banks should do and how they should do it.

Hence, our emphasis is on strategy. This chapter is focused on applying the principles of strategic management for investment banks. We discuss the subject in three parts. We begin with a brief description of strategy, what it is and how it works. Next, we present several strategies that investment banks should use for serving the complex needs of their clients. We conclude by presenting several strategies that investment banks should use for serving their own complex needs.

WHAT IS STRATEGY AND STRATEGIC MANAGEMENT?

Strategy is More Thinking than Doing

Strategy is an ancient term derived from warfare. It refers to the fighting plans of battlefield commanders. One can envision generals hunched over detailed relief maps, moving armies like pawns. One can visualize wars being won and lost by subtle shifts of thrust, parry, and feint. The analogy to investment banking seems apt.

Strategy defines the relationship between an organization and its environment and between the firm and its competitors. It is the critical linkage between mission and goals above and operations and functions below. It is the mechanism for arraying alternative choices and for driving the resource allocation process.

The Process of Strategy

Strategy is the process by which company longer-term mission and goals are translated into shorter-term objectives and projects. Finding effective strategies is the search for *competitive advantage*, for areas of relative strength that can coax, coddle, or coerce favorable outcomes. Competitive advantage seeks to capitalize on your *distinctive competencies*, those aspects of the business situation where your firm excels or can excel when compared with other firms.

How is corporate strategy formulated? (See Figure 1, which models the following description.) The classic process calls for mapping a firm's comparative strengths and weaknesses onto market opportunities and threats in order to accomplish long-term goals and short-term objectives.

The primary output of this strategy formulation process is the generation of a list of alternative policies, different possibilities of company direction for executive consideration. These competing policies are then subjected to rigorous strategy evaluation, using a test of consistency to help make the strategic choice.

Assessing relative strengths and weaknesses of your organization is the key to devising the best strategy. Compare your strengths and weaknesses to

FIGURE 1
Strategic Management: Layers of Thinking

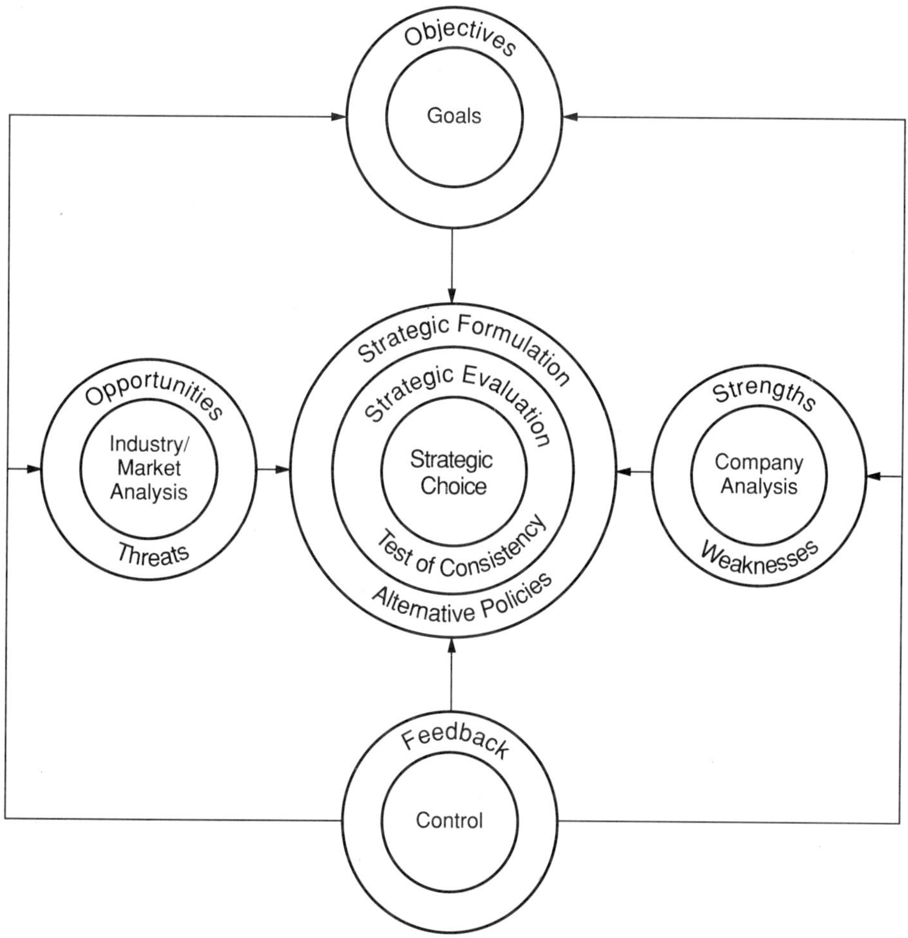

those of your competitors in the context of the current industry opportunities and threats. The result of this assessment is that list—desirably a long one—of possible strategies. These various options for strategic direction are then evaluated for probable outcomes, and the best are chosen to be put into action. Internal consistency, especially with respect to company mission and goals on the one hand and resources and capabilities on the other, is a prime test in the evaluation of each alternative strategy.

Three keys to the process follow:

- *Creativity* promotes strategy formulation.
- *Consistency* directs strategy evaluation.
- *Structure* controls strategy implementation.

There is, however, a dark side to strategy. Its presence can fool executives into thinking that they have a good grasp of a situation when they do not have much of a handle on anything. The greater the strategic sophistication, the stronger the possibility of strategic illusion. The mirage of perfection is the problem of strategy.

It has been said that corporate strategy is like a ritual rain dance. It has no effect on the weather that follows, of course, but it makes those who do it feel they are in full control. Often when we use strategic planning, we are laboring to improve the dancing, not the weather.

Strategy and Structure

The relationship between corporate strategy and organizational structure is one of the principal advances in business understanding of the past decades. Certain kinds of corporate strategies demand certain kinds of organizational structures, and conversely, if these same organizational structures are in place first, they will exert pressure to induce their complementary strategies. (The classic example is the tight relationship between a multiproduct or multinational strategy with a "division" structure. In a divisional structure, each division is an independent entity, responsible for a distinct product line or geographic area and maintaining internally its own functional departments—marketing, finance, etc.)

A Way of Thinking[1]: Incremental Versus Strategic

Strategic planning is no panacea, and it does not work under all circumstances. It is simply a way of thinking about orienting an organization. Strategic planning can be best understood in contrast to its opposite, "incremental" planning.

---

[1]Strategic thinking and strategic management are really the application of the scientific method to the world of commerce and organizations. The scientific method involves data collection and analysis, alternative hypothesis formulation, alternative hypothesis testing and eliminations, hypothesis selection, collection and analysis. Note that in science you "prove" a hypothesis to be correct by the process of elimination; you cannot prove that hypothesis "right"—you must rather prove all alternative hypotheses "wrong." (This process is called "falsification" by Karl Popper, a philosopher of science.)

The best executives function well in both modes. While the strategic process leads to original thinking in devising alternative options, the incremental mode can be fertile soil for the spontaneous sprouting of "Aha" insights.

Incremental Thinking. Operating in the incremental mode, senior executives begin *reactively* by recognizing an immediate problem or some unexpected shock, whether opportunity or threat. The person (or team) then searches selectively through a restricted variety of potential solutions, making marginal movements from the status quo, evaluating each tiny step in order. Deviations from current policy are considered sequentially and widened progressively until the first satisfactory solution is found. Such an agreeable answer is accepted immediately and all other alternatives, even if potentially better, are ignored.

Herbert Simon's idea of "bounded rationality" controls here.[2] Managers cannot ever know *every*thing; so if they want to do *any*thing, they must replace "optimizing," finding the best answer, with "satisficing," finding an acceptable answer. According to bounded rationality, problems in the real world need only be solved satisfactorily, not perfectly.

Strategic Thinking. Operating in the strategic mode, senior executives begin *pro*actively by defining general goals and setting specific objectives. They scan the industry environment seeking opportunities and threats, and analyze their own firm for relative strengths and weaknesses. The key here is to assess the specific strengths and weaknesses of their particular investment bank in the light of the opportunities and threats in the general industry. The objective is a search for competitive advantages.

What emerges from this dynamic, creative process is a set of alternatives. Each is evaluated for probable consequences. Strategic choice is made with the guideline of "internal consistency:" Which set of strategies best matches goals and strengths? Implementation (including step and time sequencing), feedback, and review complete the process.

It is a common misconception to judge incremental decision making "bad," and strategic decision making "good." Each is good, but in its own arena. One would not resolve a sudden liquidity problem in the strategic mode, just as one would not formulate a comprehensive five-year plan in the incremental mode. Learn when to stay incremental and when to jump strategic.

---

[2] Herbert Simon, *Administrative Behavior* (New York: The Free Press, 1976).

Strategy and Surprise

Strategic thinking, to be truly strategic, must deal with surprise. The unanticipated must be anticipated; the unforeseen foreseen. If everything is assumed to be known, if your organization's future is expected to emulate your organization's past, then the process is simple extension ("trending"), and strategy is playing no part.

Strategic management must be concerned with radical change—discontinuity—sharp breaks with the past and violent twists from current paths. Thoughtful leaders of investment banks must plan for the unplanned.

STRATEGIES FOR CLIENTS

Following are some strategies that investment bankers consider when contemplating how best to help clients. These are a few of the fundamentals. (See Volume I, Chapter 1 and Volume II, Chapter 1 for complementary concepts.)

Financial Optimization

Achieving the lowest overall cost of capital for issuers and the highest ratio of return-to-risk for investors is the historical objective of investment bankers. Designing and underwriting financial instruments that ever more closely optimize the opposing interests of issuers and investors has been the hallmark of the industry.

The goal of investment banking clients is often simple: Issuers seek to raise capital at the lowest possible overall (all-in) cost,[3] and investors want to achieve the highest overall return commensurate with a given level of risk. By arranging monetary transactions, exchanges, and relationships among economic entities, investment bankers make the capital markets more efficient.

Matching the highly specific profiles of myriad issuers and investors with highly specific financial instruments is the special capability that investment bankers offer.

---

[3] Whether debt or equity, all capital has a cost. The cost of debt is its interest rate, repayment schedule, covenants, and the like. The cost of equity is the dilution of current stockholders relative to the money raised. The cost of capital is directly related to the overall value of the firm as determined by the market capitalization, and to the apparent risk of the firm from both a competitive business (product-market) and financial structure (leverage, debt/equity) point of view. (See Volume I, Chapter 13 for the mathematical expression of the Weighted Average Cost of Capital.)

Financial optimization for firms has many specific expressions. Following are just five very brief examples from finance theory.

Cost of Capital. Lowering the overall cost of capital is the classic place to start (see Volume I, Chapter 13). The process of determining the lowest cost of capital (normalized for a given level of assumed risk) involves selecting, monitoring, and modifying the appropriate financial securities and instruments. The particular, tightly focused, individually unique requirements of issuers and investors—combined with the creative brilliance of investment bankers—have spawned the growing multitudes of alternative financial vehicles. (Many chapters in this *Library of Investment Banking* are devoted to the saving of less than 100 basis points through diverse financing strategies and structures.)

Leverage. Leverage is the amount of debt as compared to the amount of equity; the higher the relative proportion of debt, the higher the leverage. And the higher a company's leverage, the better its return on equity—so long as it remains profitable (and in business). The proper debt/equity ratio balances the return-on-equity benefits of high debt (high leverage) with the lower risk profile of high equity (low leverage). Though the market-approved optimum leverage ratio behaves like a roller coaster, cascading through cycles of high and low visions of what seems best, cautious investment bankers must make a long-term cost-benefit analysis for their clients—an analysis that must be personally tailored for each company. In fact, in a financial marketplace where the boundaries between debt and equity blur, the debt/equity ratio no longer dominates thinking. Ideal ratios have lost their sting and their power. Structures for specific situations are what counts. Investment bankers must therefore craft a specifically sculpted capital structure for each individual company situation.

Dividend Payouts. Studies differ on the effectiveness of dividend payouts versus retaining of the earnings. Theoretically, if the company can grow the money internally at a higher rate than the investors can externally (i.e., the investors' reinvestment rate), then the company should not pay out dividends. (This is especially true considering the double taxation on dividends.)

Pricing Considerations. The lowest cost of capital is not always the best price for issuers, nor is the highest return always the best price for investors. Risk is involved for both issuers and investors. Time is also a factor. The short-term solution may not hold for the long term. The lowest cost of capital for issuers may give investors a bad experience with the company, increasing the cost of capital in the future. Similarly, the highest price for investors may involve hidden risks (e.g., management frustration) that could jeopardize the principal itself. The market is surely complex, with uncertain and often indeterminable degrees of efficiencies and inefficiencies mingled together. In such an intricate environment, optimization is not necessarily either maximization of return or minimization of cost. It may be, but such is not required.

Offering Strategies. How much stock should be sold in an offering? Clearly, the financial strategy of structuring a public offering is a function of the number of shares and the price per share in relationship to the expected valuation of the entire company. There is always conflict here between the interests of the issuers and investors, though investment bankers can show both groups the benefits of logical analysis. It is often smart for an issuing company seeking a lower cost of capital to hold back the size of its offering, thus keeping demand greater than supply. This reduction in shares to be sold also decreases the dilution of current shareholders. The plan would be for the company to use the capital currently being raised to improve its earnings and public profile so that a subsequent offering can be made to take advantage of the expected higher market capitalizations in the future. (There is a fine line between optimizing cost of capital and being sure that the company raises sufficient capital for its current needs.[4])

Optimization, by its very essence, demands the input of qualitative insight to modulate quantitative analysis. Investment bankers must consider a myriad of issues regarding the financing situation and all proposed financing transactions. Computers could never become investment bankers.

Value Building

The ultimate goal of economic entities is to produce wealth. Investment bankers must be sure that their clients never lose sight of this fact. It is all too easy to get caught up in the glitter and excitement of aggressive acquisitions, new businesses, refurbished offices, media coverage, and all the rest of the executive high life. But corporations are enterprises whose primary task (some would argue "sole task") is to build value for their shareholders.

Consequently, every decision that is made by corporations should be governed by "value building" criteria. If acquisitions are considered, they

[4] One must also consider the expenses of the offering, some of which are constant irrespective of issue size (e.g., professional fees and printing costs).

must be considered in terms of how they will impact the value of shareholder stock. This valuation is inordinately complex and fraught with uncertainty. Nonetheless, the touchstone of "value" must always be applied. (Probabilities can be assessed, sensitivities can be tested, etc.)

"Value *creation*," a subset of value building, should always be at the forefront of a proper investment banking assessment of client companies. Value creation suggests those kinds of activities that would (or could) add incremental wealth to shareholders beyond that expected from normal operations. The obvious example is mergers and acquisitions, where, if done properly, the additional value generated should well exceed the costs and risks involved. (See Chapters 1–5.)

Growth and Development

Valuation in the market is based largely on the growth rate of earnings or cash flow (or, more accurately, the *perceived* growth rate at any given time).[5] Corporate executives are almost always striving to increase the size of their activities and operations. Investment bankers are allies in the process, supplying the necessary capital for such expansion. Cost of capital is optimized when specific liabilities with specific terms (e.g., payback periods) are carefully chosen to finance specific assets with specific uses. Matching the right kind of capital available in the market (e.g., type of equity, timing of debt, etc.) with the projected growth and development needs of the company is the special sphere where investment bankers perform their magic.

Robustness and Resiliency

Financing is most efficient for both issuers and investors when there is high confidence in a stable future. More than anything else, the market abhors uncertainty. The capacity of the company to survive economic turbulence is perhaps the prime factor in lowering the cost of its capital. Company financing costs increase as a *multiple* of any increase in uncertainty (i.e., every one unit increase in volatility triggers *more* than one unit increase in cost). Key corporate strengths are robustness, the full-bodied strength of the firm, and resiliency, the ability to spring back after any shocks. Investment bankers must be sure that all financing structures enhance robustness and resiliency.

---

[5]This anticipated growth rate is reflected in the capitalization ratios that are applied to earnings (i.e., the Price/Earnings ratios and Dividend Growth Models [see Chapter 4]).

Growth alone can be dangerous, and rapid growth without proper external positioning and appropriate internal controls is a sure recipe for disaster. The external key is competitive strength, the self-determined capacity to secure a firm's market share and margins. The internal key is administrative information and regulation, the confidence of constant awareness and rapid reaction. Companies that grow quickly are most vulnerable to environmental shocks and investment bankers must protect their client companies from exposing themselves to such heightened risks.

Robustness and resiliency are equally important in structuring financial instruments, especially those that are highly dependent on external factors. For example, securitized instruments (e.g., rolled up real estate mortgages) can be surprisingly susceptible to interest rate shifts (which change default and refinancing rates). The same is true for synthetic securities such as principal only or interest only instruments. In these cases, sensitivity testing is vital.

STRATEGIES FOR INVESTMENT BANKS

Investment bankers must never forget that theirs is a volatile industry. Stock market fads and fluctuations combine with personnel emotion and mobility to generate an erratic and unpredictable environment. Such uncertain dynamism makes life uncomfortable for investment banking executives, but it is fertile soil in which true strategic thinking and planning can flourish.

We encourage readers to use the principles of strategic management outlined above to develop alternative strategies for their firms. The idea—in one sentence—is to map an investment banking firm's strengths and weaknesses onto market opportunities and threats in order to formulate, evaluate, and implement the best of numerous alternative strategies in order to fulfill long-term goals and short-term objectives.

Following are some specific areas for strategic consideration that investment bankers should consider when contemplating how best to plan their own futures. These are a few of the fundamentals.

Strategic Constraints

There are four primary strategic constraints for investment banks:

1. **capital** (e.g., amount, allocation, relationship to strategy, growth);
2. **clients** (e.g., sector, size, industry);

3. **services** (e.g., underwriting, IPO, M&A, LBO, rate risk management, back office operations); and
4. **personnel** (e.g., traders, bankers, rainmakers, innovators).

A firm must start its strategic planning process by assessing itself with respect to all four constraints, and then must postulate where it might want to be positioned at some future date. Such an assessment must not be done in a vacuum. Investment banking is a highly competitive industry, in addition to being exceptionally volatile. Comparative and competitive analysis is essential at every stage of the process. Remember, distinctive competencies and competitive advantage—together with internal consistency[6]—are the critical criteria for evaluating all strategic alternatives.

Firm/Market Positioning

There are several ways to play the investment banking game. The key is to match the right structure with the right strategy. Several years ago the rage was to become a full financial services company, with many firms offering every conceivable function from retail brokerage to real estate services to insurance to big-money international investment banking. Of those that tried, few made it. (It is certainly possible to be a bulge-bracketed firm servicing large corporate issuers and institutional investors without having a retail distribution capability. Note Salomon Brothers and Goldman Sachs. Yet even Salomon could not do everything: Its withdrawal from municipal finance was dramatic proof of an investment bank's limitations.)

Firms must position themselves according to their assessment of the economic environment and the coming competitive pressures. Medium-sized firms, for example, seem to be particularly vulnerable to the dual crush of capital requirements and the back office costs of doing major league business. On the other hand, smaller firms that stake out strong positions in circumscribed *regions* can do very well by specializing in smaller local corporations and regional investors. Intelligence and service are the keys to success for regional investment banks.

One recent development is the formation of boutique investment banking firms. Formed around one or two name personalities (usually leaving a bulge-

---

[6] Each part of the strategy must mesh with every other part. It is remarkable how often first-rate organizations devise strategies that contain incompatible elements.

bracketed firm), these new investment banks desire to remain small so that the full energies of their partners can be devoted to the deal-making they love, not to the administration they hate. How can these boutiques compete in this capital-intensive industry? They focus on their expertise—M&A and merchant banking—and by their reputations they raise large pools of capital from financial institutions and can become real players in the great game. They focus their capital on what they do best—and they do not make markets and inventory securities.[7]

Agent or Principal

Some investment banks are having difficulty deciding whether they are agents or principals. The problem arises as a result of the enormous profits made through the ownership of companies, primarily through leveraged buyouts (see Chapters 11–16). It's enough to turn any head.

Merchant banking is the new buzzword on the Street. It involves risking the firm's capital to make bridge loans for closing fast, often hostile acquisitions (the bridge remains outstanding until the permanent financing can be put into place). Merchant banking also involves taking equity positions in companies (often in partnership with clients).

Merchant banking is clearly a hot area that can generate extraordinary returns, especially when compared with anemic returns on traditional underwriting. Yet there are major problems that arise; the most critical is a blurring of the pure professional relationship that has long characterized the industry. Merchant banking is giving investment banking an identity crisis.

Optimal Size

In some investment banks, the number of employees grew larger than the firm's current market position could support. The outcome was a ballooning organization and a bloated structure that eroded distinctive competencies and lost competitive advantage—resulting in a fast fall into oblivion.

As stated above, the most important factor in implementing a corporate strategy is designing the proper organizational structure to support it. Size

---

[7] A microcosm of the importance of market positioning and capital focus was demonstrated when Wasserstein, Parella & Company, the M&A/merchant banking boutique formed by the First Boston expatriates, leased some of the magnificent office space vacated after the forced sale of E.F. Hutton to Shearson Lehman.

is perhaps the most critical criterion here. If too small, you cannot provide the services that clients demand. If too large, you suffocate the firm with excessive costs and frustrate personnel with limited opportunity.

Capital efficiency is an important part of the optimal size analysis. Too much capital is always better than too little, but just the right amount is better than both. Investment banks should be properly capitalized to accomplish their specific business strategies (see Volume II, Chapter 1).

Competitive Advantage

Competitive advantage is the key reason why any organization survives and prospers. There must be some rationale for your firm's existence, a reason for employees to work there, and for clients to come there. What do you have that your competitors do not?

I like the definition that equates "strategy" with "rent." Rent is payment for a unique piece of real estate; there is no other plot of land, no other space *exactly* like it. You get paid because you have some place really special, someplace that no one else has. It is the same for strategy: You are being paid for occupying a unique spot in the company/market spectrum, something that no other firm has. Whether by products or personnel, there are reasons why you get every piece of business. A thoughtful executive understands these reasons. When planning the future you should examine the present.

The most important thing to remember about competitive advantage is to seek it constantly, because without advantage there is no business.

Pricing Fees and Spreads

The pricing of fees and spreads is a critical strategic decision for investment banks. Should a firm buy into a business by underpricing competitors—as the Japanese investment banks did in the Euromarkets? Should a firm back out of an industry because spreads have been squeezed—as Salomon did in municipal underwriting?

How an investment bank prices its services goes a long way towards telling its story and establishing its position. It can be tempting to cut prices in order to win business—after all, bankers must be able to show their stuff. On the other hand, the battlefield must be picked carefully. Shaving prices in the wrong underwriting can generate unacceptably large losses and produce a poor industry image. Furthermore, by offering services for lower-than-normal industry fees, a fee-cutting investment bank might inadvertently signal that its quality is lower than its peers—which, for example, would be death in the M&A business. (It is better, frankly, to charge a *higher* M&A fee for exceptional performance above an agreed level; such a request will evince strong confidence and persuade the potential corporate client that you can really deliver maximum results.)

Personnel

The importance of personnel in investment banking is so large that it demands a separate category and constant consideration. It is a truism that a firm's primary assets ride down the elevator every evening. Top personnel must be kept content or a bank cannot prosper. Granted, there are always new waves of eager, ambitious young people thrilled to get a shot at the golden ring, but an organization that experiences significant turnover is operating suboptimally.

Compensation is part of the story, but only part. Since this is the money game, a person's self-assessed worth is often colored largely in green. How to allocate bonuses is always a knotty problem. One key is to appreciate the fact that opportunity and advancement are also important for investment bankers. The capacity to make a personal impact is vital, and the firm should appreciate the importance of such recognition. Giving up-and-coming investment bankers greater responsibility, particularly the opportunity of running their own deals, is an important sign of support.

Internationalization

In the tightly wired world of international finance, the opportunities are great but the risks may be greater. It is frightfully complex to deal in foreign capital markets, as well as enormously expensive. A modern investment bank must determine its logical position in the international firmament. Many investment banks expanded dramatically into London and Tokyo, seeing the allure of Big Bang[8] and the rising Yen. Tens if not hundreds of millions of dollars in capital commitment were allocated to such expansions. Results have been spotty, and many major banks subsequently have had to curtail their operations. Investment houses considering international expansion should pick their niches and focus their activities.

---

[8] "Big Bang" is the media term for the sudden deregulation of London financial and securities firms several years ago, increasing competition and encouraging the entry of many foreign investment banks.

Strategic Alliances

One approach to several of the strategic issues discussed here is for an investment bank to form a "strategic alliance" with another, complementary firm. Such an alliance may take several forms. Often, for a United States firm, the alliance will be an investment by a foreign financial institution (e.g., Goldman Sachs and Sumitomo Bank, PaineWebber and Yasuda Mutual Life Insurance Company). The financial investment adds to the domestic firm's capital base while the strategic alliance provides international presence, visibility, and expertise with a much lower risk profile and cost exposure.

Other types of strategic alliances can be considered. When a smaller investment bank manages merchant banking money for a large financial institution (see above), this too can be a strategic alliance. The desire of the institutional investor is to be able to get an early, privileged look at an anticipated series of future transactions in which they may like to participate—in addition to earning the expected equity-level returns. The desire of the small investment bank is to have a ready source of additional financings for forthcoming deals—in addition to the profit-making opportunity of managing the initial investment.

CHAPTER 2

FINDING AND FACILITATING MERGERS AND ACQUISITIONS

William D. Rifkin
Salomon Brothers Inc

As recently as the mid-1970s, few major investment banking firms had formal merger and acquisition ("M&A") groups, and M&A transactions generally represented a small portion of total corporate finance department revenues. Today, M&A groups account for 25 to 33 percent of a typical corporate finance department's personnel and a much higher percentage of its total revenues. This fundamental change is principally due to the impact of Rule 415 on the profitability of investment grade debt underwriting, the dramatic increase in the size and number of M&A transactions, and the recent emergence of merchant banking.

According to W.T. Grimm & Co., in 1986, 3,336 acquisitions were announced and the total value of all transactions for which a purchase price was disclosed was $173.1 billion. In 1976, 2,276 acquisitions were announced, and the total transaction value disclosed was only $20.0 billion. There are many reasons for the dramatic increase in M&A activity. The most often cited is that it is often cheaper to buy assets than build them (which also avoids the problem of increasing industry productive capacity). This simplistic explanation may be appropriate in the case of the purchase of a manufacturing facility or oil and gas reserves; however, in the case of most strategic acquisitions, "building" was never a practical alternative.

One of the principal reasons chief executive officers are more receptive to M&A transactions today than in the past is the increased likelihood that if they do not maximize the value of their company, somone else will. The development of various hostile takeover techniques, the dramatic growth in the "junk bond" market (from approximately $20 billion in 1981 to over $120 billion in 1986) and the proliferation of leveraged buyout funds, have made even the largest companies vulnerable to takeover—and the universe of individuals or entities willing to put companies "in play" has grown with the financial success of highly visible raiders such as Carl Icahn and T. Boone Pickens.

Unlike underwriting and trading, the traditional M&A advisory business (as distinguished from merchant banking) requires little capital and, with due care, entails minimal risk. Fees as a percentage of transaction value have remained fairly constant, while the number and size of transactions have grown rapidly. Because fees are a small percentage of the total transaction value and, more important, because bad advice can be extremely costly, M&A has escaped the severe price competition of underwriting.

This chapter presents an overview of M&A from an investment banking perspective, addressing M&A assignments, identifying acquisition targets, structuring a transaction, approaching targets, tender offers and mergers, divestitures and takeover defense. Chapters 3–5 address the subjects of valuation and financing.

THE ENGAGEMENT LETTER

A mundane but important element of the M&A business is the engagement letter—a relatively informal contract which sets forth the understanding between an investment bank and its client in an M&A assignment. The securities industry relies so heavily on trust that investment bankers sometimes fail to pursue the negotiation of an engagement letter early in an assignment. This failure can lead to misunderstandings as a transaction evolves and can, in some cases, make it difficult for the investment bank to collect fees it believes due (such as when representing the target of a successful hostile takeover). Most important, execution of an engagement letter helps assure that the corporate officer with whom the investment bank deals has the support, both legal and moral, of the company's chief executive officer.

The typical engagement letter consists of four principal elements: (1) a description of services to be provided; (2) the fee arrangement; (3) indemnification; and (4) termination provisions.

Services

Obviously, the services to be provided will be tailored to the nature of the assignment.

Divestiture. In a *divestiture* assignment, services might include: financial analysis and valuation of the business to be sold; developing a sale strategy; identification of potential buyers; preparation of an offering memorandum; assistance in negotiations of a sale transaction; and rendering a fairness opinion with respect to the consideration received in the sale.

Acquisition. In an *acquisition* assignment, services might include: identification and valuation of acquisition candidates; development of a strategy for approaching a target company; advice with respect to the nature and terms of the consideration to be offered; assistance in the negotiations of an acquisition agreement; acting as dealer manager of a tender offer; and rendering a fairness opinion with respect to the price paid by the purchaser.

Defense. In a *defense* assignment, the financial advisor may assist in assessing its client's vulnerability to takeover and recommend corrective measures; evaluate any acquisition proposals its client receives; and assist its client in formulating an appropriate response to such proposals.

Fees

With respect to fees, the engagement letter must specify under what circumstances they are earned and how they are calculated. In general, the bulk of an M&A advisory fee is contingent upon consummation of a transaction, and is based on a percentage of the aggregate consideration paid or received. Often, a relatively small retainer fee is payable upon commencement of the assignment, and additional fees may be payable upon the occurrence of intermediate events, such as public announcement of an agreement in principal. If the fee is determined on a percentage basis, it is important to carefully define aggregate consideration to take into account the possible retention of certain assets (such as working capital) by the seller and the assumption of certain liabilities (such as debt) by the buyer that might reduce the amount of cash or stock which actually changes hands. Typically, the financial advisor will be reimbursed for its expenses regardless of whether a transaction is consummated. (See Volume I, Chapter 5.)

Indemnification

M&A transactions, particularly those involving the purchase of stock of a publicly traded corporation, often result in litigation and, in some instances, the financial advisor will be among those sued. Because the financial advisor is just that, an advisor acting as agent for a principal to a transaction, it is appropriate that the investment bank obtain indemnification from its client with respect to liabilities which might arise from the engagement. Exceptions to this indemnification will typically include bad faith, willful misconduct or gross negligence on the part of the financial advisor.

Termination

The final part of an engagement letter sets forth the entitlements and obligations of the parties thereto subsequent to its termination. The key terms of this provision are the length of time and the circumstances under which the financial advisor is entitled to a fee should its former client consummate a transaction after the engagement has been terminated.

THE ACQUISITION SEARCH

In assisting a client in the pursuit of an acquisition, it must first be determined exactly what the role of the financial advisor will be. Historically, the role of the investment banker was best described as "financial engineer" rather than business consultant. Most investment bankers will have at least a general view as to the type of acquisition which will help its client achieve its strategic objectives. It is the rare investment banker, however, who has the experience and expertise in a particular industry to know how effectively two companies can be combined from an operational standpoint and just what cost savings or synergies might result. What the financial advisor can and should do is the following: make sure that its client has carefully undertaken the self-examination and market analysis necessary in order to formulate an intelligent acquisition strategy; help identify acquisition candidates which are consistent with this strategy and which might be available on an economically justifiable basis; help develop the tactics which will be used in attempting to land a target; and assist in the structuring and financing of a transaction.

Search and Identification

Once a business strategy has been formulated, the acquisition search starts with the identification of companies which might fit this strategy. If the universe of target companies is not already known, the best place to start looking is the *Standard & Poors' Register of Corporations, Directors and Executives*, which lists 4,500 companies by standard industrial classification number (SIC code).

At this stage, the acquiror must decide whether to take an active or a passive approach toward identifying specific acquisition candidates within this universe. At a given point in time, the overwhelming majority of companies are not for sale and, as a rule, are unreceptive to such inquiries. An acquiror unwilling to pursue an acquisition on a hostile basis (which means without access to a target's detailed financial and other information) can waste a lot of time screening and analyzing companies. Such acquirors may choose to take the more passive route of responding to situations in which an appropriate target has put itself up for sale, either voluntarily or as an alternative to a hostile takeover, and will provide potential acquirors with most of the information they seek.

Active Approach: Gathering Information

The more active approach consists of taking the initiative to gather as much information as possible about the companies which might fit the acquiror's business strategy. Those companies with publicly traded securities are required to report periodically certain information to the Securities and Exchange Commission (SEC), and make such information available to the public. SEC disclosure documents include: Form 10-K, which contains a business description and audited annual financial statements (this document should be read in conjunction with the company's annual report to shareholders); Form 10-Q which contains quarterly financial information; Form 8-K, an interim period document which describes material events subsequent to the latest 10-K or 10-Q; Proxy Statements, which provide information on large stockholdings, the company's board of directors, officers' compensation, and proposed amendments to the company's bylaws or charter; and registration statements which will contain the terms (such as restrictive covenants) of publicly traded securities.

What's Available for Public Companies. Other sources of information on publicly traded companies include: company press releases; news stories (readily available through data retrieval services such as LEXIS/NEXIS); security analysts' reports (available through Investext); Spectrum's compilation of reported institutional stockholdings; and stock trading histories available from *Compustat*. Industry publications, such as *Chemical Week* or *Electronic News*, can also be excellent sources of information.

What's Not Available for Public Companies. When analyzing a publicly traded company, it is important to keep in mind what information is *not* available. Business segment data are provided in summary form only, and the individual segments do not always correspond to legal entities easily separable from the rest of the company. Corporate overhead may be allocated to the various business segments in a somewhat arbitrary manner, or it may not be allocated at all. Certain potential liabilities, such as shutdown and severance costs, may not be disclosed, and the tax basis of significant assets will certainly not be disclosed. Underfunded pension liabilities and residual medical expenses for retired employees are often a major problem for long-standing manufacturing companies. Thus, it is often quite difficult to estimate the net proceeds which might result from the sale of a subsidiary or division of a target company or to what extent costs can be cut.

Private Companies. Gathering information on privately owned companies, including subsidiaries of publicly traded corporations, is far more difficult because such companies do not file information with the SEC. At best, the financial information which is available will be in summary form, without the benefit of footnotes or management's discussion and analysis of results. In addition, the lack of publicly traded equity securities makes valuation problematic.

Valuation. If adequate information about an acquisition candidate is available, the acquiror must next determine what the target is worth (discussed in Chapter 3) and the likelihood that it can be acquired at or below that price. In the case of a publicly traded company, the answer to the latter question will depend on its shareholder profile, recent and historical stock prices, possible takeover defenses, "shark repellents," management's attitude and performance, the composition of its board of directors, and the target's appeal to other prospective purchasers.

STRUCTURING AN ACQUISITION

Before approaching a specific target, the acquiror should formulate a proposed structure for a transaction. From a financial standpoint, the key elements of structure are price, form of consideration, the acquiring company's accounting treatment of the transaction, and tax treatment at the corporate and shareholder levels. These elements, which are interrelated, affect the attractiveness of a transaction to both buyer and seller and, as discussed below under "Mergers, Tender Offers, and Share Accumulations," are of tactical significance in competitive bid situations.

Final Price

With respect to price, the first and foremost rule of M&A is that the final offer must not exceed the perceived value of the target company to the acquiror. Given the subjectiveness involved in formulating projections and discount rates, it is easy to lose sight of this rule in the heat of a battle for control or an auction—but it is a mistake from which the purchaser's stock price (and its relationship with its financial advisor) may never recover.

Initial Price

The initial offering price should be based on an assessment of the probable level of competition, the price at which the majority of shareholders are likely to sell, and the price level which the target company's board of directors will perceive as fair. It should be assumed that, even if the target company is favorably disposed toward a sale, it will be necessary to sweeten the offer to induce its board to enter into a friendly transaction.

It should be recognized that in today's world it is almost impossible to "steal" a public company from its current management—given the availability of credit for acquisitions, investment bankers' and takeover lawyers' ability to buy time against even the most determined raider, many corporations' growing comfort (or at least ability) in making rapid decisions to act as a white knight, and the increasing ability of certain targets to offer shareholders attractive alternatives to takeover, such as a leveraged recapitalization. (See Volume IV, Chapters 21–23; Volume II, Chapters 23, 24, and 36.) A "low-ball" bid is guaranteed to antagonize the target and, in general, should not be tried by a potential acquiror truly interested in completing a transaction.

Form of Consideration

If optimal capital structure were the only issue with respect to form of consideration, an acquiror could complete an acquisition with the currency most readily available or most attractive to selling shareholders (in both cases, usually cash) and, subsequent to closing, refinance such funds to achieve the desired permanent capital structure. However, in addition to having tactical implications, the form of consideration affects both the accounting and tax treatment of a business combination.

ACCOUNTING AND TAX CONSIDERATIONS

Business combinations are accounted for as either a "pooling"-of-interests or a "purchase" of stock or assets. Although the pooling rules are complex and highly technical, in general, to qualify for pooling treatment: (1) 100% of the acquisition consideration must be voting equity securities of the acquiror; (2) 100% of the target company's voting equity securities must be acquired in the transaction; (3) the acquiror and the target must not have significantly altered their respective equity interests (such as through a stock repurchase) in anticipation of or soon after the business combination; and (4) the acquiror may not make significant divestitures in the two years following the business combination. Any transaction which does not qualify for pooling treatment—the vast majority—is accounted for as a purchase. (See Chapter 28.)

Pooling-of-Interests

In a pooling-of-interests, the corresponding line items of the historical financial statements of the acquiror and the target are simply added together, with no adjustments made other than the possible conversion of any target company convertible securities into common stock. Therefore, even if the price paid for the target company exceeds its fair market value, no goodwill is created. Earnings per share is determined by dividing combined net income by the number of the acquiring company's common shares to be outstanding after completion of the merger.

Purchasing Accounting

Under purchase accounting, the target company's equity is eliminated and its assets and liabilities are adjusted to reflect their fair market value. The excess of the total purchase price over the fair market value of the target company's net assets is recorded as goodwill. Pro forma combined net income will reflect: (1) purchase accounting adjustments (such as increased depreciation resulting from the write-up of plant, property, and equipment to its fair market value); (2) an increase in interest expense, preferred dividends, or common shares outstanding as a result of the consideration issued in connection with the acquisition; (3) amortization of goodwill (a non-cash, non-tax deductible charge) over a period not to exceed 40 years; and (4) the tax effects of the above.

Taxable or Tax-free

The form and relative mix of consideration issued in an acquisition will determine whether or not the transaction is taxable to selling shareholders. Many institutional shareholders will not care; certain institutions, such as state pension funds, are tax exempt, and risk arbitrageurs rarely hold stock long enough for tax deferral to matter. On the other hand, taxability may be very important to individuals with large holdings at a low basis, such as members of a company's founding family.

In general, an acquisition will qualify as a tax-free "reorganization" under the Internal Revenue Code if at least half of the fair market value of the total consideration is in the form of equity securities of the acquiror. The equity securities can be common or preferred and need not have voting rights. Selling shareholders receiving equity securities in a tax-free reorganization recognize no taxable gain on those securities, but the historical basis of the stock they are selling carries over into the new security. Shareholders receiving consideration other than equity will recognize a taxable gain; such gain, however, shall not exceed the amount of non-equity consideration received. Tax-free reorganizations which include non-equity consideration are often structured as "cash election" mergers to give selling shareholders greater control over their tax treatment. In this case, selling shareholders may select from alternative forms of consideration, such as stock or cash; if one of the alternatives is oversubscribed, shareholders are generally treated on a pro rata basis. (See Chapter 28.)

Stock or Assets

If a company is selling a subsidiary and the transaction does not qualify as a tax-free reorganization, its tax liability may be very different depending upon whether it sells the subsidiary's stock or assets. In a taxable sale of stock, the selling corporation will recognize a gain on the difference between the fair market value of the consideration received and its tax basis in the stock sold. From the buyer's perspective, the historical tax basis of the target company's assets carries over, while its basis in the target's stock will be equal to the purchase price paid. In a taxable sale of assets, the selling corporation must allocate the consideration received to the individual assets sold based on their fair market value (this will also establish the purchaser's basis) and will recognize gain on the difference between such allocation and its tax basis in such asset. In addition, the selling corporation may be subject to recapture taxes with respect to accelerated depreciation and investment tax credits.

Tax Reform Act of 1986

Prior to enactment of the Tax Reform Act of 1986, substantially greater flexibility existed (1) to defer taxes at the corporate level in the divestiture of subsidiaries of recently acquired targets, and (2) to avoid double taxation (i.e., taxation at both the corporate and shareholder levels) in partial and total liquidations. It is therefore likely that corporations will make much greater use of tax-free spin-offs in the future than they have in the past. In order for a transaction to qualify as a tax-free spin-off, a parent company must distribute at least 80% of the common stock of a subsidiary to the parent company's shareholders and both the parent and the subsidiary must have been engaged in the "active conduct of trade or business" (although not necessarily with the present owner) for at least five years.

For example, Carson Pirie Scott agreed to a cash sale of its airline catering business, which represented roughly 60% of Carson's total market value, to Greyhound Corporation. Carson, in turn, wanted to pass the net proceeds of the sale on to its shareholders. An outright sale of the food distribution business, with a subsequent cash dividend or stock repurchase, would have resulted in double taxation. To avoid this problem, Greyhound entered into a merger agreement with Carson in which it agreed to acquire all of Carson's stock for cash (a taxable transaction at the shareholder level only) immediately *after* a tax-free spin-off of the stock of Carson's non-catering businesses. Thus, Carson completed a divestiture, the proceeds of which were distributed and taxed at the shareholder level only, and it remained a publicly traded company.

APPROACHING ACQUISITION TARGETS

Acquisition proposals are generally characterized as either "friendly" or "hostile"; in reality, these characterizations represent opposite ends of a wide spectrum.

Friendly

The truly friendly acquisition proposal begins with a private, confidential approach to the target company, and is framed in such a way as *not* to require public disclosure. Depending upon prior relationships which might exist, this approach can be made by the potential acquiror's chief executive officer, a director of the company or its investment banker. Likewise, the approach may be made directly to the target company's chief executive officer, or to one of its directors or investment bankers. Typically, the potential acquiror will not have recently acquired any of the target company's common stock, since this may be viewed as a less than friendly act. Most important, the potential acquiror will make it clear that if the target company is not interested in pursuing a business combination, it will go away without taking any further action.

There are numerous advantages to a friendly offer. First, the potential acquiror, upon signing a confidentiality and perhaps standstill[1] agreement, will be given access to material non-public information about the target company. Secondly, the potential acquiror will have the opportunity to meet and possibly negotiate employment contracts with key employees of the target company. Finally, the potential acquiror is in a better position to negotiate a favorable merger agreement, particularly with respect to representations and warranties of the seller and "lockup" provisions. Lockups include options to purchase target company equity securities, options to require "crown jewel" assets, and "bust-up" fees. These provisions may discourage competing bids for the target company and, at the very least, compensate the initial offeror if it is outbid.

Hostile

A hostile takeover attempt lacks such niceties. In its severest form, the hostile "raider" tenders for or actually purchases shares of the target company's stock without the blessing of the target company's board of directors and with little, if any, forewarning.

The principal *advantage* of a hostile takeover attempt is the fact that, while most companies' managements will be averse to almost any takeover proposal, most of their shareholders will be quite receptive. If the raider has

---

[1] A "standstill" is an agreement not to purchase any of the target company's equity securities, for a specified period of time, without its permission.

accumulated a stock position prior to launching its offer, it is likely to benefit financially even if outbid.

The obvious *disadvantages* of a hostile offer are: the raider may not gain access to non-public information; the raider is almost certain to incur the wrath of the target company's senior management, as well as other employees; the target company is likely to take whatever steps it can to avoid being acquired by the raider, at least upon the terms originally proposed; and the raider may damage its reputation in the business community at large. In recent years, the majority of raiders have been individuals (or companies acting as acquisition vehicles for those individuals) rather than industrial companies.

Bear Hug

The area of the spectrum between the truly friendly proposal and the hostile raid is broadly referred to as the "bear hug." In a bear hug, unlike a friendly offer, the potential acquiror presents its acquisition proposal to the target company in such a way that the proposal will ultimately be disclosed to the public; unlike a hostile offer, the potential acquiror does not (at least initially) commence a tender offer or substantial open market accumulations without prior notification of the target company's management.

In its mildest form, the bear hug is identical to a friendly offer, except that the terms of the proposed business combination (such as price, form of consideration, and conditions) are specific enough to require public disclosure within a reasonably short period of time. The proposal must be carefully worded to avoid a requirement, pursuant to Rule 14d-2(b) under the Securities Exchange Act of 1934, that the potential acquiror commence a proposed tender offer within five business days of public disclosure.

Although the potential acquiror may agree not to pursue a takeover without the approval of the target, the bear hug is not entirely friendly because of the market forces public disclosure sets in motion and the resulting pressure on the target company's board of directors. Unless the potential acquiror lacks all credibility as a buyer or the target has strong structural defenses against a hostile takeover, risk arbitrageurs will rapidly accumulate large blocks of the target company's stock and drive its price near to or in excess of the proposed acquisition price. This concentration of stock in speculators' hands attracts the attention of other potential raiders and increases the vulnerability of the target. Moreover, there is tremendous pressure on the target company's board of directors to maintain the recently achieved stock price level.

In a stronger variation of the bear hug, the potential acquiror makes a public announcement of its proposal simultaneous with or shortly after delivering it to the target company. The proposal and public announcement will state the potential acquiror's intention to commence a tender offer in the near future at a specific price and its desire to meet with the target company to negotiate a merger agreement acceptable to both parties. This variation eliminates any opportunity the target might otherwise have of convincing the potential acquiror to withdraw its proposal before public disclosure is made. In accordance with Rule 14d-2(b), the potential acquiror may have to proceed with or abandon its offer within five business days. It is the potential acquiror's hope that, with the threat of an imminent tender offer, the target will agree to negotiate a friendly deal, thereby gaining access to non-public information and obtaining certain representations and warranties in exchange for sweetened terms. If the target company refuses to negotiate, the potential acquiror has the flexibility to commence a tender offer or withdraw its proposal and seek other game.

In an even stronger variation of the bear hug, the potential acquiror offers to pay a certain price if the target agrees to negotiate in good faith, but threatens to commence a tender offer on less favorable terms if the target refuses to cooperate. This variation places even greater pressure on the target company's board of directors by quantifying the cost of its refusal to negotiate. In the last two years, both May Company and Interco, Inc. were able to overcome the initial resistance of their targets and successfully negotiate 100% stock-for-stock mergers by threatening cash tender offers at a substantially lower price.

While less tasteful than a friendly offer, the bear hug is much more likely to result in the sale of the target company and does keep open the possibility of a negotiated merger agreement. According to W.T. Grimm & Co., of 418 companies which received takeover proposals from 1982 to 1986, 326 (or 78 percent) were ultimately acquired. Of the 130 contested offers during the period, only 63 (or 48 percent) were successful. However, in 31 of these cases, or an additional 24 percent, the target was sold to a company other than that which made the initial offer.

MERGERS, TENDER OFFERS, AND STOCK ACCUMULATION

In the acquisition of a publicly traded company, most acquirors want to obtain 100% of its common stock, thereby avoiding the potential problem of having to deal with minority interests and gaining easier access to the target's assets. It is practically impossible to acquire all of a target's stock through a tender offer or open market purchases; therefore, it is necessary to effect a merger to achieve this goal. In a merger—which, subject to state law, must be approved by the target company's shareholders—all remaining outstanding shares of a target company's common stock are automatically converted into the merger consideration.

Mergers

Mergers are governed by both federal and state law. Federal law deals primarily with disclosure, while state law concentrates on the more substantive issues of fairness, the judiciary obligations of directors and controlling shareholders and, in the absence of a more restrictive company bylaw, the minimum stockholder vote needed to effect a merger as well as other corporate approvals.

Fairness. Fairness is an important issue because many states have historically allowed a simple majority of a target company's voting equity securities to approve a merger. Therefore, a raider can purchase 51 percent of a target company's stock through a tender offer or open market purchase and, without the support of any of the remaining shareholders, approve a merger on terms far less favorable than what it may have paid for the shares it already owns. The latest generation of state anti-takeover laws, held constitutional by the Supreme Court with respect to Indiana and therefore expected to proliferate, effectively takes such power away from controlling shareholders. (See Chapters 21–26.)

Short-Form Merger. If the acquiror owns a high percentage of the target company's stock (for example, 90 percent in Delaware and 95 percent in New York), a "short-form" merger can be approved by a simple resolution of the acquiror's board of directors.

Long-Form Merger. If the acquiror does not own sufficient shares, it must pursue a "long-form" merger, which requires the filing of a proxy statement with the SEC and a meeting of the target company's shareholders. This process takes, on average, roughly 90 days and, if the acquiror does not own a large enough percentage of the target company's voting stock, subjects the acquiror to greater risk of a competing bid. For this reason the classical "merger of equals," a stock for stock exchange with little or no premium, such as the merger of Dart Industries with Kraft in 1980 and Nabisco with Standard Brands in 1981, has almost disappeared in recent years. In 1985, Hospital Corporation of America agreed to a stock merger with American Hospital

Supply, only to have Baxter Travenol commence a cash tender offer for, and ultimately gain control of, American Hospital Supply before the merger could be completed.

As the above example illustrates, there can be advantages in quickly purchasing a large block of the target company's voting stock in friendly acquisitions as well as hostile takeovers. In general, this can only be done with cash because exchange offers (i.e., the purchase of shares with newly issued securities) must be filed with the SEC and generally take roughly 60 to 90 days to complete. Shares can be purchased for cash through tender offers, open market purchases or negotiated purchases from major shareholders.

Tender Offers

Although slower and potentially more costly than a direct purchase, a tender offer has several important advantages. First, a tender offer allows the purchaser to impose conditions which must be satisfied or waived before it is obligated to purchase shares. One of the most common and important conditions is a requirement that sufficient shares are tendered to give the purchaser effective control of the target and some assurance that a "second-step" merger can be effectuated.

Hostile tender offers often contain a condition that the offeror be able to obtain adequate financing; thus, a raider (who is certain to have already accumulated a material stock position) may be able to put a target in play without ever having to line up financing. An important condition in a hostile tender offer may be that the target company's board of directors approve the offer and disarm any "poison pills" the company may have. Another advantage of a tender offer is the flexibility it gives the purchaser. For instance, the purchaser can tender for a simple majority of the target company's stock but reserve the right to purchase any and all shares tendered.

Tender offers are governed by the Securities Exchange Act, which requires certain SEC filings by both the offeror and the target. As previously mentioned, a tender offer must commence within five business days after its principal terms have been publicly disclosed, and it must remain open for at least 20 business days.[2] If the tender offer is for less than all of the target

---

[2] In addition, in mose cases shares may not be purchased, whether through a tender offer or beyond a certain amount on the open market, prior to compliance with the Hart-Scott-Rodino Antitrust Improvement Act, which requires both the offeror and the target to submit business information to the Antitrust Division of the Department of Justice and the Federal Trade Commission. The offeror cannot purchase stock for 15 calendar days subsequent to such filing and, if additional information is requested, for 10 calendar days after submission of such additional information.

company's shares, shares may not be purchased until the offer expires and, if the tender offer is oversubscribed, shares must be purchased on a pro rata basis. If a change is made in the offer price or number of shares sought, the tender offer must remain open for at least the next 10 business days. Any increases in offer price must be paid on all shares purchased in the offer, regardless of when tendered.

Stock Accumulation

During the past few years, several companies, most notably Crown Zellerbach, SCM, TWA, and NL Industries, were taken over by raiders through massive open market purchases.

The *advantages* of open market and privately negotiated purchases can be speed, surprise, and the possibility of purchasing some shares at prices lower than what might be necessary to clear the market in a tender offer.

The principal *disadvantages* of open market purchases are the risk that an adequate number of shares cannot be obtained at an acceptable average price or that the target company's board of directors will take certain actions (such as refusal to disarm a poison pill) which make a subsequent merger difficult.

DIVESTITURES

Mergers during the so-called "go-go" years of the late 1960s through the 1970s resulted in the formation of a number of highly diversified conglomerates, such as LTV, ITT, Beatrice, and Norton Simon. In the 1980s, it became clear that the market tended to penalize diversified companies, and the sum of the value of the "parts" of these businesses exceeded the market value of the whole. The result, whether from voluntary restructurings or involuntary restructurings resulting from actual or threatened hostile "bust-up" takeovers, has been an unprecedented level of divestiture activity.

Descriptive Brochure

Once the strategic decision to sell a business has been made, the divestiture process generally begins with the preparation of a descriptive brochure. Financial information must be presented which properly accounts for the divestiture candidate as a stand-alone entity. For example, intercompany transactions on other than arm's-length terms, tax-sharing agreements, and allocation of parent company overhead must be fully accounted for and disclosed.

Public Announcement

A key issue in divestitures is whether to make a public announcement. The advantage of a public announcement is that it will attract the attention of every M&A department on Wall Street, as well as potential buyers who may not have been obvious to the seller. The disadvantages of a public announcement are the greater anxiety which will result among the divestiture candidate's employees, customers, and suppliers—and the potential embarrassment if a suitable offer is not received.

Two-Stage Informal Auction

It is both disruptive and logistically difficult to give a large group of potential buyers access to a divestiture candidate's management and facilities. Therefore, many divestitures are handled as "two-stage informal auctions." In this process, the descriptive memorandum is distributed to a large group of prospective buyers who have each signed a confidentiality agreement. Before being given access to management or facilities, each company in this group is asked to provide a preliminary indication of interest and evidence of its ability to finance the purchase. With this information, the seller will select a manageable group who will be given an opportunity to conduct a more thorough due diligence investigation.

At this point, the finalists will be provided with a draft definitive purchase agreement, which they will be asked to comment upon as part of their final bid. This helps insure that the final bids will be made on a comparable basis and allows the seller much greater control over the non-financial terms of the contract. The more explicit the seller is about exactly what is or is not included in the transaction and the desired structure for tax purposes, the lower the probability that the selected bidder will attempt to re-cut the deal at a later date.

As discussed under "Structuring an Acquisition," a divestiture can be structured as a sale of stock or a sale of assets. Under either structure, the seller will be expected to provide certain representations and warranties as to the condition of the divestiture candidate and may be asked to provide indemnification against certain potential liabilities, such as pre-existing environmental problems.

In submitting final written bids, the prospective purchasers will be asked to leave their offers open for a sufficient period of time to allow the seller to seek clarification of any aspects of the offer. During this period, the financial advisor will have an opportunity to "work the bidders" in an attempt to improve upon the offers received.

DEFENDING AGAINST HOSTILE TAKEOVERS

With the high level of hostile takeover activity in recent years, merger defense—both preemptive and reactive—has been a hot product. While little can be done to prevent a takeover by a determined, well-financed bidder prepared to make a cash tender offer for any and all shares, measures can be taken to decrease the likelihood of unfair and abusive takeover offers (such as two-tier, front-end loaded bids), to slow the takeover process down (giving the target more time to negotiate or to seek out alternatives), and to reduce a raider's incentive by narrowing the gap between a company's market price and its fundamental value.

The speed with which a hostile tender offer or open market purchase program can be completed puts a target company at a great disadvantage. A raider can plot an attack for months, with the target totally unaware. Once the attack begins, the target may have as few as 20 business days to take evasive action; this is hardly enough time in which to, for example, complete a major restructuring. The raider, on the other hand, has all the time in the world to implement a restructuring of the target *after* it has gained control. BCI Holdings, Inc., the purchaser of Beatrice Companies for $6.2 billion, was able to cut administrative costs by more than 50 percent and complete six major and several smaller divestitures raising net proceeds of $3.4 billion within 12 months after the acquisition. Thus, it is important for companies to assess their vulnerability to takeover and take appropriate corrective measures before the wolf is at the door.

Defensive Audit

A "defensive audit" should include: an analysis to determine whether the company is fairly valued by the market and if not, why not; an analysis of asset restructuring and recapitalization alternatives which might enhance the company's value; a review of state anti-takeover laws; a review of the company's charter and bylaws; a review of the company's indentures; and an analysis of the company's shareholder profile.

Preemptive defensive actions might include certain structural changes (several of which require a shareholder vote), such as: adoption of a fair price/super-majority provision; authorization of "blank check" preferred stock; adoption of a "poison pill" share purchase rights plan; creation of a staggered board of directors; creation of two classes of stock with disparate voting rights; and bylaw changes to limit the rights of shareholders to call special meetings or act by written consent. More substantive and strategic measures include: asset sales or spin-offs; a major stock repurchase program; creation of a large employee stock ownership plan; a leveraged buyout or leveraged recapitalization (discussed below and throughout this Volume); or a defensive acquisition.

Defensive Options

Once a hostile takeover offer has commenced, a target's options become greatly limited. Studies have shown that, historically, less than 10 percent of the targets of cash tender offers ultimately remained independent. Even if the target is protected by state anti-takeover laws or a poison pill which makes a second-step merger difficult in an unfriendly deal, experience has shown that boards of directors will eventually bend to the will of a majority of its shareholders. Recent defensive techniques, particularly the leveraged recapitalization, may increase a target's odds of remaining independent—but at the cost of major reconstructive surgery.

White Knights. In the absence of a legal showstopper, such as anti-trust or regulatory obstacles, the only way to overcome a hostile tender offer by a determined raider (as opposed to a "greenmail artist") is to give shareholders a more attractive alternative. The principal way of accomplishing this is to seek a better offer from a "white knight." A white knight search is, in many ways, similiar to a publicly announced divestiture. The principal difference, of course, is the time pressure involved. The target must get detailed financial information and business plans in the hands of prospective white knights as quickly as possible; it cannot afford to wait until a perfect descriptive brochure is available.

Management Leveraged Buyout. Management itself represents a potential white knight through a leveraged buyout. A number of well-funded leveraged buyout firms, such as Kohlberg Kravis Roberts & Co. and Forstmann Little and, increasingly, major investment banking firms, stand ready to assist management in evaluating this alternative. Because of an inherent conflict of interest in this situation, typically a committee of independent directors is established to represent, with the help of its own financial advisor, the best interests of the company's shareholders; this can severely limit management's role in influencing the outcome of events.

Leveraged Recapitalization. A variation of the leveraged buyout is the leveraged recapitalization. In this case, the target company borrows money and/or sells assets in order to make a large cash distribution to, or repurchase shares from, its stockholders. The company's shareholders have, in effect, provided the equity for a leveraged buyout. Moreover, many of the conflict of interest and fairness issues are reduced because the company's shareholders will have a sizeable continuing equity interest in the restructured company. Leveraged recapitalization or major stock repurchases have been undertaken in recent years by such companies as Multimedia, FMC, Colt Industries, Owens Corning Fiberglas, and Goodyear Tire & Rubber. (See Volume II, Chapters 23 and 36.)

The incremental value of a leveraged buyout or leveraged recapitalization over a hostile tender offer must be sufficient to compensate for any timing differences (such as the requirement of a shareholder vote) and any uncertainties (such as a financing condition).[3] For this reason, several major investment banks have gone into the business of providing bridge loans to companies to allow them to facilitate these sorts of transactions with greater speed and certainty. This subject is discussed in more detail in Chapter 5.

Note: See Chapters 21–26 for a thorough discussion of the legal principles and techniques in corporate takeovers and defense.

---

[3] The same is true in the case of a white knight offer which requires the registration of securities or the filing of a proxy statement with the SEC.

CHAPTER 3

VALUING AND PRICING MERGERS AND ACQUISITIONS I: CONCEPTS AND MECHANISMS

William D. Rifkin
Salomon Brothers Inc

Acquisition transactions can be quite complex, utilizing sophisticated structures and strategies and involving assorted terms and conditions. Each of these elements is important, but two factors, more so than any others, will determine whether a business combination ultimately succeeds or fails: (1) the price paid and (2) the manner in which the target company is managed by and integrated into the acquiror.

In today's merger and acquisition ("M&A") environment, the demand for quality properties far exceeds supply. Investment bankers, taking advantage of this situation, have mastered the art of developing competitive bid situations, ensuring that sellers leave little, if any, money on the table. As a result, a potential acquiror must use a sharp pencil—and a creative mind—in determining the value of an acquisition target. There are a number of methodologies that may be used for assessing value, each of which has its advantages and shortcomings. This chapter discusses the various valuation methodologies and, while not attempting to suggest how a target should be managed after it has been acquired, points out the tremendous importance of management on the derivation—and realization—of value. (See Chapter 4 for a comprehensive list of quantitative approaches and qualitative modulators of M&A pricing.)

THE PRICING PROCESS

Pricing an acquisition target is a three-step process. The first is a determination by the potential acquiror of the maximum price it can justify from an economic standpoint. The second is a determination of whether or not it can finance the acquisition. The final step is an assessment of the likely value of the acquisition target to *other* potential bidders to see if it might be possible to acquire the target at a price below that determined in step one.

Different Values to Different Buyers

The same acquisition target will have different values to different buyers, due both to perception and reality. Potential buyers will have different views on: (1) the expected financial performance of the target; (2) what can be done to enhance performance; and (3) the risk of deviation from expected results. Certain potential buyers, regardless of their perception of the future, may have a true economic advantage over others. This could be due to tax factors (such as ability to utilize net operating loss carryforwards), potential economies of scale, or opportunities to achieve synergies. Economic benefits which may result from the combination of two going concerns would not, for instance, be available to a so-called "financial buyer," such as a leveraged buyout firm. Unless a company is purchased for immediate resale, as in a "bust-up" acquisition, the potential acquiror's first step must be a determination of what the target is worth specifically to it, not others—and this requires a careful and honest assessment of what the acquiror can do with the combined company.

Affordability

The concept of affordability has changed dramatically in recent years. This is best illustrated by the April 1986 leveraged buyout of Beatrice Companies for $6.2 billion, with a common equity investment of only $410 million, and the more recent $25 billion leveraged buyout of RJR Nabisco. Nevertheless, there are still limits in this world, and there is no use in pursuing a deal that cannot be financed. (See Chapter 5 for a discussion of the financing and funding of mergers and acquisitions.)

Competitive Assessment

The final step in the pricing process, an assessment of the competition, is the most difficult, but also the least important. A potential buyer can only guess how other interested parties will perceive a target and what they think they can do with it. Moreover, the bidding process—which, in the case of a publicly traded acquisition target, often occurs even if a deal is first negotiated on a friendly basis—will quickly remove any mystery which might have previously existed. It is not unusual for multiple rounds of bidding to be employed—and the music does not stop until there is only one party left who is willing to raise its bid. What is most important is knowing at what price to stop bidding and having the self-discipline to do so.

PUBLIC VERSUS PRIVATE TARGETS

As discussed in Chapter 2, an interested buyer may only obtain detailed financial information about a privately owned company or a subsidiary of a publicly traded company if it is voluntarily provided by such company's owner. Publicly traded companies, on the other hand, must at least disclose the information required by the various securities laws.

With respect to pricing, an important difference exists between private and public target companies, even if both were to fully disclose their financial position and prospects: a public company has a quoted market value. Even if a company's stock price does not accurately reflect its fundamental economic value, stock price is an important benchmark that greatly influences the price at which a company can be acquired. For instance, it does not take a financial genius to figure out that it is difficult to purchase the stock of a publicly traded company at less than its current price.[1]

The valuation techniques discussed below apply to both public and private companies as long as adequate financial information is available. However, it is important to keep in mind how the existence of a quoted stock price can affect the price at which it is likely that a publicly traded company can be acquired.

DISCOUNTED CASH FLOW ANALYSIS

Discounted cash flow (DCF) analysis, also discussed in Chapter 4, is the most valid valuation methodology from a purely theoretical standpoint. Unfortunately, it is also the methodology that requires the greatest amount of subjectivity and greatest number of assumptions.

---

[1] An exception to this statement is the situation in which a company has been "put in play," and the market expects a higher offer which never materializes.

DCF Formula

As shown in the following formula, DCF represents the present value of an expected stream of cash flows discounted for time and risk.

$$\text{Present Value} = \sum_{t=0}^{n} \frac{CF_t}{1 + r^t}$$

where t represents time in years, zero representing the present; CF_t is the expected free cash flow generated in year t; and r represents the appropriate discount rate given the risk associated with the expected cash flows.

Present Value Methodology

There are two alternative methods for calculating present value, both of which are theoretically valid and, with certain simplifying assumptions, should yield the same result.

Return on Equity. The first is a return on equity approach in which (1) free cash flow (defined below) is net of any interest and preferred dividend expense on securities assumed by the acquiror or issued to finance the acquisition and (2) the discount rate reflects the buyer's required rate of return on equity for *this particular investment.*

Return on Total Capital. The second is a return on total capital approach in which (1) the after-tax cost of any interest and preferred dividends is added back to free cash flow and (2) the discount rate reflects the buyer's weighted average required rate of return on total capital (i.e., both debt and equity) for *this particular investment.*

Free Cash Flow

Free cash flow represents the net cash which is generated by (a positive flow), or must be invested in (a negative flow), the target company each year. From a funds flow standpoint, free cash flow is analogous to the net change in a company's cash and debt balances. With the exception of the initial cash flow which, as described below, represents the acquiror's original investment, free cash flow is equal to (1) net income *plus* (2) noncash charges (such as depreciation, amortization of intangibles and deferred taxes) *plus* (3) net proceeds from divestitures *less* (4) the net change in working capital (exclusive of cash) *less* (5) capital expenditures.

The initial cash flow, CF_O represents the net cost of the acquisition. Using the total capital approach, net acquisition cost is equal to: (1) actual cash outlays to acquire the target company's common stock, common shares resulting from convertible securities, and options and warrants (equal to the difference between the offer price per share and their respective exercise prices); *plus* (2) the fair market value of any target company debt and preferred stock which remains outstanding or is paid off by the acquiror (including prepayment penalties); *plus* (3) transaction costs; *less* (4) any excess cash on the target company's balance sheet. In the equity approach, CF_O is equal to that part of the net acquisition cost which is funded with the acquiror's common equity capital and not borrowed money.

The determination of future years' cash flows—CF_1 through CF_n—is more problematic since these cash flows represent forecasts. These forecasts should reflect the expected results of the target company *assuming* that it is integrated into and managed by the acquiror; they should not be based on the expected performance of the target if it were to remain independent. These forecasts must take into account, among other things, any expected overhead reductions; severance and shutdown costs; economies of scale or synergies; changes in competitive dynamics, such as higher prices resulting from the elimination of excess capacity; and net divestiture proceeds.

Obviously, it is difficult to forecast financial results accurately too far into the future. Yet, DCF valuation is based upon the expected cash flows of an investment over its entire life, which, for a going concern, may be forever. Since this is impossible, it is necessary to calculate a "terminal value" which represents the estimated value of the target company as of a future point in time. This value, just like the projected annual free cash flows until that time, is then discounted to the present.

Terminal Value Methodology

There are as many methodologies used for deriving terminal value as there are for determining the value of a business today. The two most common are presented below.

Perpetual Growth Model. The methodology most consistent with DCF, from a theoretical standpoint, is the "perpetual growth model." This method assumes that the free cash flow of the year in which terminal value is calculated will grow, from that point to infinity, at a fixed compound annual rate.

Terminal value can then be calculated as follows:

$$\text{Terminal Value} = \frac{CF_t}{(k - g)}$$

where CF_t represents the expected free cash flow of the year in which terminal value is calculated;
k represents the weighted average cost of capital or the cost of equity, as appropriate; and
g represents the expected growth rate of CF_t into perpetuity.

As discussed below, the results of this calculation are very sensitive to the value of "g,"which represents the expected growth rate of CF_t into perpetuity. It is important to keep in mind that a company's past or current growth rate cannot necessarily be sustained forever. If even a small company currently growing at 50 percent per annum were to sustain that rate for an extended period of time, it would soon account for the lion's share of the gross national product.

Price/Earnings Ratio. The other prevalent method used for arriving at a terminal value is simply to multiply that year's projected net income by an appropriate price/earnings (P/E) ratio. As with growth rates, high P/E ratios cannot be sustained for an extended period of time. For instance, a company's current P/E ratio may be 30× trailing twelve months' earnings because the market anticipates a doubling of earnings over the next twelve months; if this occurs, even with some appreciation in stock price, the company will have a more normal P/E ratio one year from now. (Indeed, P/E ratios should reflect the anticipated growth rate.)

Discount Rates

As mentioned earlier, the discount rate used in DCF analysis must reflect the marginal cost of capital with respect to the target company—*not* the overall cost of capital of the acquiror. If a utility is evaluating an investment in a high-technology company, the discount rate must reflect the risks inherent in the projected results of the high-technology company rather than the more reliable expectations for the utility. The cost of equity may be calculated by using the capital asset pricing model (see Volume I, Chapter 14) or may simply reflect what the acquiror deems to be an appropriate hurdle rate for this particular investment. The cost of debt (which is adjusted for its tax shelter value in deriving a weighted average cost of capital) should reflect the estimated interest rate that the target company would have to pay as a stand-alone business with the capital structure which was assumed in deriving the cost of equity.

Shortcomings of DCF Analysis

While theoretically eloquent, DCF analysis does have several major shortcomings. The first is the great difficulty of accurately projecting financial results over an extended period of time, particularly if it is necessary to rely solely upon publicly available information. Another is the tremendous sensitivity of results to the terminal value. Over a time horizon such as five years, cumulative free cash flow may be low because of capital expenditures and increases in working capital, and it is not unusual for the terminal value to represent 75 percent or more of a target company's total value. Finally, when using the perpetual growth model, the terminal value itself is highly sensitive to the assumed sustainable growth rate, which is also difficult to forecast.

Benefits of DCF Analysis

Despite these shortcomings, DCF does have great merit as a valuation technique, particularly when used in conjunction with other methodologies. The need to generate projections forces the prospective acquiror to give careful thought to what can be done in integrating and operating the target company.

It is this exercise which generally determines how attractive the target is to each of the prospective buyers and, thus, which should be willing to offer the highest price. Moreover, the theoretical validity of DCF analysis makes it an excellent test of the reasonableness of values derived from other methodologies. If it is impossible to come up with a defensible set of projections which would yield a DCF value equal to values arrived at through other methodologies, the results of such other methodologies should not be relied upon.

MARKET VALUE METHODOLOGY

A publicly traded company's stock price should reflect the market's expectations for that company's future financial performance, properly discounted for perceived risk. Thus, a company's market value is, in effect, a consensus view of its DCF value. Obviously, it is impossible to determine the specific free cash flows, terminal value or discount rate that investors use in arriving at this consensus. To deal with this problem, the "market value methodology" measures stock price against a single parameter, such as earnings, cash flow, revenues, or book value; the resulting ratios are then applied to the appropriate parameter of the target company to arrive at a *proxy* for DCF value. This methodology is particularly useful for valuing private companies and the subsidiaries of publicly traded companies.

Industry Comparables

The market value approach assumes that companies in the same industry share, more or less, a common financial outlook. A group of companies is selected, each of which, from a business and financial standpoint, is comparable to the target company. Rarely does the perfect "comparable" exist, particularly when evaluating a diversified company. In that case, several groups of comparable companies should be selected, each of which corresponds to one of the target company's principal business segments. The historical operating, financial and stock performance of the comparable companies, as well as their business prospects, are analyzed to determine an appropriate ratio value to apply to the target company.

For example, if all publicly traded dry grocery products companies happened to be valued by the market at 15× trailing twelve months' earnings, it is a safe bet that a purchase price of 15× a privately owned dry grocery products company's most recent earnings plus a "control premium" is economically justifiable. The control premium, discussed in more detail below under "Third-Party Sale Analysis," should represent the estimated present value of any cost savings or synergies expected to result from acquisition of the target company.

Three Key Elements

There are three key elements to the proper application of market value methodology: (1) "normalization" of results; (2) selection of the proper ratio for valuation purposes; and (3) emphasis on prospective rather than historical results.

Under the market value methodology, value is arrived at by multiplying just two numbers: a valuation ratio (such as a 15× P/E ratio) and the related parameter (in this case, earnings). Both numbers must be carefully selected for their product to be meaningful.

For example, if a target company were in a highly cyclical industry, such as property-casualty insurance, it would be necessary to normalize results by taking an *average* of earnings over an entire underwriting cycle and, correspondingly, an average P/E ratio. In addition to cyclicality, other factors which must be taken into consideration include: extraordinary events, such as one-time write-offs or windfall profits; differences in accounting policies among the comparable companies; purchase accounting adjustments resulting from prior acquisitions; amortization of intangibles and other non-cash charges; and recapitalizations, such as stock repurchases which reduce reported shareholders' equity.

Valuation Ratios

Price/earnings ratio is the measure most frequently used in market value methodology because of its intuitive appeal. This approach is roughly analogous to the perpetual growth model, earnings being a proxy for cash flow and the P/E multiple a reflection of anticipated growth and perceived risk. In many cases, however, earnings (even when normalized) may not be the best indicator of value. This would be the case for a start-up high-technology venture, for example, or a natural resources company with valuable assets but no reported earnings.

Companies with relatively steady results, low capital requirements and high goodwill amortization, such as broadcasters or soft drink bottlers, are often valued using multiples of cash flow. Capital-intensive smokestack companies experiencing earnings problems, such as steel mills, are often valued as a percent of their tangible book value. Companies with high operating leverage and opportunities to improve margins, such as retailers and consumer products manufacturers, are often valued as a percent of their revenues. An understanding of the fundamental economics of an industry is critical to the selection of the proper valuation ratio. A good indicator of the reliability of a particular ratio for valuation purposes is its range of values for the comparable companies. A tight range typically implies good predictive value, while a wide range brings into question the reliability of the particular ratio for valuation purposes.

Investors' Expectations

A company's market value reflects investors' expectations for its *future* performance. To the extent that a company's historical results are a good indication of what can be expected in the future, there will be some correlation between historical financial performance and the current value of relevant valuation ratios. However, this is not always the case. Changes in technology, competitive dynamics, or the regulatory environment could dramatically change a company's prospects. Therefore, when valuing a business based on its earnings, cash flow, or revenues it is necessary to determine whether or not recent results are indicative of what can be expected in the future. If not, these parameters must be adjusted to reflect more accurately what is likely to happen in the next few years.

Advantages of Market Value Methodology

While the theoretical footings of the market value methodology are not as solid as those of DCF analysis, this approach does have several advantages. First and foremost is a reliance on the market's consensus view of the financial outlook for the comparable companies (and, by deduction, that of the target company), rather than one's own projections. In addition, this methodology is simple to understand and apply, which may be important in gaining the support of the acquiror's shareholders.

THIRD-PARTY SALE ANALYSIS

The most straightforward valuation methodology is called "third-party sale" analysis. This approach, like market value methodology, derives the estimated value of a target company by analyzing values ascribed to comparable companies. Rather than looking at market value, however, third-party sale analysis evaluates the price paid in the *acquisition* of comparable companies in relation to various parameters. The principal advantage of this approach is that, unlike market value methodology, the resulting valuation ratios already include a control premium.

Valuation Ratio Approach

As with market value methodology, acquisition prices can be analyzed as a multiple or percent of earnings, cash flow, revenues, book value and, in some cases, specific assets. For example, oil company acquisitions may be looked at in terms of price paid per barrel of proven reserves, and cable television system acquisitions may be looked at in terms of price paid per subscriber.

Premium to Market

When analyzing the acquisition of publicly traded companies, an important ratio unique to third-party sale methodology is the "premium to market." This ratio measures the percentage by which the purchase price per share exceeds the acquired company's stock price immediately prior to announcement (or rumor) of the transaction. Assuming that the market is relatively efficient and has not anticipated an acquisition of the target company, and that there are more than one prospective buyer, the premium to market should represent the control premium. Thus, this methodology isolates the incremental value from cost savings or synergies which the acquiror expects to result from a particular acquisition.

The range of premiums to market, even within the same industry, can be quite wide. For instance, in 1983 Quaker Oats paid a premium to market of 107% in its acquisition of Stokely-Van Camp, while the next year Nestle paid a premium of just 32% in its purchase of Carnation. While the range of premiums to market is wide, the average premium paid for all transactions has been remarkably consistent from year to year, and is somewhat correlated to the Dow Jones Industrial Average (DJIA). For instance, according to W.T. Grimm & Co., the average premiums paid in 1983, 1984, and 1985 were 37.7%, 37.9%, and 37.1%, respectively. The DJIA low in those years was 1027.04, 1086.57, and 1184.96. From 1979 to 1982, the DJIA was lower and average premiums higher; average premiums were 49.9%, 49.9%, 48.0%, and 47.4%, respectively, while the DJIA lows were 796.67, 759.13, 824.01, and 776.92, respectively. Thus, one might conclude that (1) on average, public companies tend to trade at 30% to 40% discounts to their third-party sale value and (2) given the relationship between the DJIA and premiums to market, acquisition values are less volatile than stock prices.

In recent years, it has become increasingly apparent that premiums to market are dictated by buyers, not selling shareholders. The proliferation of entities willing and able to engage in hostile takeovers, plus court decisions which make it difficult for a target to show favoritism to a particular buyer, ensure that a target will go to the highest bidder. In addition, the general nature of stock ownership has changed in such a way that the vast majority of targets subjected to a tender offer, almost regardless of the size of the premium to market, will ultimately be taken over. Institutional investors, many of whom manage money for others, now account for over 40% of the stock ownership of the S&P 500. The performance of money managers is measured on a quarterly basis, and those who underperform will quickly lose clients. As a result, these investors often have a short investment horizon and will tender their stock even if the offer price does not represent what they deem to be the target company's long-term fundamental value. Therefore, unless a target company has a controlling shareholder who must be given special consideration, a prospective purchaser should worry more about what other bidders might be willing to pay than the price at which stockholders might be willing to sell.

Principal Shortcoming

The principal shortcoming of third-party sale analysis is that, as in the market value approach, the target company's value is derived from prices paid for similar companies, the specific circumstances of which may be quite different from those of the target. For instance, a purchaser needing a specific technology or geographic presence may be able to justify paying a high price for a certain target. This does not mean that all companies similar to that target have comparable value in the context of their being subsequently acquired. A major business combination can change the competitive dynamics of an entire industry and affect the value of all future acquisitions within that industry. This is not to say that third-party sale analysis does not provide useful benchmarks. However, as with any other valuation methodology, it is essential that a potential acquiror determine what the target is worth to *it*—not to others—in the current and foreseeable economic environment and that it pay no more than that amount.

LEVERAGED BUYOUT ANALYSIS

A leveraged buyout (LBO) is the acquisition of a business by a shell company financed almost entirely with debt. Typically, the purchaser expects to maintain private ownership of the business for three to seven years, during which time a substantial portion of the acquisition debt will be paid off with the proceeds of asset sales and free cash flow. The purchaser will then either sell the company, take it public or, possibly, leverage it up again and take out a cash dividend. (See Chapters 11–16.)

The number of major companies acquired through LBOs has skyrocketed in recent years, reaching over 75 in both 1985 and 1986. It was once thought that only noncyclical, non–capital-intensive, low-growth businesses qualified as LBO candidates. However, LBOs have now been completed in almost every industry. In addition, the multibillion dollar LBOs of RJR Nabisco, Beatrice, Safeway, and Owens-Illinois demonstrate that size is not in and of itself a constraint, and financing for LBOs remains abundant.

Pricing an LBO

The highest purchase price that can be justified in an LBO will primarily be a function of: (1) the target company's projected financial results; (2) the required rate of return of equity investors; and (3) the interest rates and projected credit ratios required by lenders. Because an LBO does not involve the combination of two operating businesses, no synergies or economies of scale can result. In addition, the transaction must be "self-financing." For these reasons, an LBO should, in theory, represent the lowest price at which a company could be sold. This will not always be the case, however, because each prospective purchaser will be working from its own set of projections, and public companies may focus more on pro forma reported earnings than on fundamental value.

Managing for Cash

The need to repay substantial amounts of debt quickly affects the way that companies purchased through LBOs will be managed, and this must be taken into consideration when formulating projections. Over the near term, these companies will generally be managed to maximize free cash flow rather than growth or return on equity. Excess working capital will be withdrawn to pay down debt, certain assets may be sold, overhead (particularly that associated with being a public company, such as investor relations) will be cut and capital expenditures may be curtailed.

Key Test: Coverage of Debt Obligations

A purchase price is assumed and an initial capital structure—typically consisting of approximately 10% common equity, 40% subordinated debt, and 50% senior debt—is overlaid on the operating projections. The LBO "works" if the resulting coverage of debt obligations is satisfactory to lenders and the estimated return on equity is acceptable to the purchaser.

As a rough rule of thumb for large LBOs, senior lenders (typically commercial banks) expect the pro forma projected financial statements to show: (1) immediate coverage of cash interest expense; (2) at least 2× coverage of total interest expense within five years; and (3) the ability to repay at least 50 percent of the senior debt within five to seven years. Subordinated lenders are sometimes willing to defer cash interest payments for up to five years, but expect to see adequate coverage at that time. Because of the financial risk inherent in an LBO, common equity investors look for a compound annual rate of return on their investment of 30 to 50 percent. To calculate this return, it is generally assumed that the company will be sold after five years at a conservative multiple of that year's earnings or free cash flow. Variations of the initial capital structure should be evaluated to determine which, subject to the constraints described above, will result in the highest justifiable purchase price.

Principal Shortcoming: Relying on Long-Term Forecasts

The principal shortcoming of LBO analysis is that, as with DCF analysis, it requires making long-range forecasts. While the prospective buyer may not have to worry about how two operating companies will perform together, it must determine, for example, what impact a cut in capital expenditures will have on the target's long-term operating results and terminal value. A number of highly publicized LBO success stories (due in large part to a favorable interest rate and stock market environment since 1982) and an abundance of capital may tend to make prospective purchasers a bit too aggressive in formulating projections.

BUST-UP ANALYSIS

In many acquisition transactions, the purchaser will quickly turn around and resell certain of the target company's assets. Reasons for this may be that the purchaser has a strategic interest in only some of the target company's operations or the purchaser needs to raise cash to pay off acquisition debt. In these cases it is necessary to evaluate the "bust-up" value of the target company—that is, the estimated net proceeds that will result from the sale of certain assets plus the value of the businesses and net assets which remain. Bust-up analysis is more an analytical approach than a valuation methodology since it relies on the techniques previously discussed for valuing the target company's component businesses.

Consolidating Financial Statements and Tax Bases

Key data needed to perform a bust-up analysis accurately are the target company's consolidating financial statements and the tax bases of its principal subsidiaries and assets. Consolidating statements break out the financials of each of the company's operating units. To arrive at consolidated statements, parent company financials are added on and intercompany transactions eliminated. This information is not publicly disclosed and therefore must be estimated if not provided by the target company; as discussed in the previous chapter, publicly reported business segment data does not necessarily correspond to readily separable operations.

Adjustments for Stand-Alone Operations

In order to value an operating unit properly it may be necessary to adjust its financial statements to reflect a truly stand-alone operation. Particular attention must be paid to the terms of any intercompany transactions and parent company cost allocations. For instance, do transfer prices reflect market rates? How dependent is a particular subsidiary on sales to or services provided by another? How, if at all, is parent company expense allocated to each subsidiary? Does this allocation overstate or understate the expenses a potential buyer might incur with respect to an independent entity instead of a subsidiary?

Once appropriate adjustments have been made, each business unit should be valued using the techniques described earlier (i.e., DCF analysis, market value methodology, third-party sale analysis, and leveraged buyout analysis). For those operations which will be sold by the acquiror, provision must then be made for estimated capital gains taxes.

Consider All Assets and Liabilities

When aggregating the value of those businesses which will be kept with the net proceeds of those which will be sold, one must be careful to ensure that all of the company's assets and liabilities (including those not shown on the balance sheet) have been taken into account. If a substantial portion of a company's assets are being sold, chances are its unallocated parent company overhead can be cut. However, cost savings may be partially offset by severance and shut-down expenses. Indentures must be analyzed to determine what, if any, restrictions exist with respect to the use of proceeds from divestitures. If outstanding debt obligations must be redeemed, bust-up value must take into account any premiums to be paid.

A Collection of Approximations

The valuation of any company is, at best, an educated approximation. A bust-up analysis is a collection of approximations, with the added complication of estimated tax and severance liabilities. Therefore, it is dangerous to assume "best case" results with respect to all of the planned divestitures. More likely than not, there will be some pleasant surprises, such as valuable excess real estate of which the buyer was unaware, and some unexpected disappointments, such as uncooperative operating company management which make a divestiture difficult.

SUMMARY

It should be obvious that each of the valuation methodologies discussed in this chapter—discounted cash flow analysis, market value methodology, third-party sale analysis, leveraged buyout analysis, and bust-up analysis—lacks scientific precision, but collectively they are more reliable than pulling a number out of thin air. Careful consideration of the results of *all* of these techniques, rather than reliance on any one, will minimize the possibility of gross error. Judgment is critical—it could be a mistake, for instance, to take the mean value of the various valuation methodologies employed. Any "outlier" values must be reevaluated and, if difficult to justify from a common sense standpoint, should be dropped from consideration.

The first rule of mergers and acquisitions is *never fall in love with a deal*—winning a competitive bid does not necessarily make the buyer a winner. Projections can be manipulated to justify any price. While too much conservatism may result in missed opportunities, too much optimism may ultimately result in a big loser—much aggravation and a diminished net worth. Acquirors can justify many of the former to avoid one of the latter.

CHAPTER 4

VALUING AND PRICING MERGERS AND ACQUISITIONS II: PRACTICES AND TECHNIQUES*

Robert Lawrence Kuhn

The valuing and pricing of business entities in merger and acquisition (M&A) transactions is both art and science. The science is founded on finance theory and models; the art on personal insight and experience. Yet there is a subtle problem emerging today. Our spectacular and increasing capacity to process data and analyze numbers on personal computer spreadsheets is undermining the art while facilitating the science (see Volume I, Chapter 12). The subliminal message emanating from the thousands of calculations involved in M&A analyses is that precision is possible, that accurate valuation and price setting is really attainable. Such unwarranted confidence is always naive and usually a mistake, even a serious one. Investment bankers specializing in M&A must retain their artistic perception as well as improve their scientific technology.

The purpose of this chapter is to survey the numerous mechanisms of M&A valuing and pricing involved in both quantitative and qualitative analysis. We present these two kinds of approaches to ascertaining M&A prices:

1. The first deals with specific models, numerical valuation techniques that establish price; these are *Quantitative Models That Determine Price*.

---

*NOTE: Sections of this chapter have been derived from "Merger and Acquisition Prices: Creativity Through Multiple Mechanisms," by Robert Lawrence Kuhn and Brian Saffer, from *Handbook for Creative and Innovative Managers*, Robert Lawrence Kuhn, editor in chief (New York: McGraw-Hill), 1988.

2. The second lists general "modifiers," non-numerical elements that affect price; these are *Qualitative Factors That Modify Price*.

A primary point is the considerable variety and diversity in practice and technique. No one system or method is inherently more appropriate or more valid under all conditions. Each mechanism and model has its own special slant on M&A transactions and as such has its own special application in specific circumstances. Never assume that numbers are inviolate; they may be precise without being accurate. Everything in business is contingent.

THE NEED FOR MULTIPLE MECHANISMS

The academic literature on valuing companies for acquisition largely stress *discounted cash flow* (DCF) analysis as the methodologically "correct" route to the "right" answer. DCF calculates the net present value or internal rate of return using the stream of expected cash flow outputs from the business over time as compared to the initial cash investments into the business (i.e., acquisition payment). It is a highly quantitative, apparently rigorous methodology, and is thus proffered as inherently more valid as an economic model of the firm.

But the problem is that companies as complex organizations operating in an even more complex environment are not given to such simplistic portrayal. (Indeed, the apparent sophistication of DCF is in itself deceiving.) Experience proves that no single method of valuing acquisition targets is always proper or truly comprehensive. The M&A process thrives in the real world where multiple forces interact on so many levels as to almost defy analysis; M&A is not sheltered by the highly stylized, well-controlled, idealized models of academic theorists and computer programs.

We will see how the "softer," less numerical methods can work better than the "harder," more numerical methods. While academic business scholars must prefer methods which are grounded in finance theory (i.e., discounted cash flow analysis), pragmatic investment bankers know from experience that the assumptions necessary to perform such rigorous procedures can generate an impractically broad band of possible outcomes. In such situations—which are not uncommon—the results of the more quantitative techniques become virtually useless and one must engage other techniques to value and price the deal.

Irrespective of DCF's pure economic soundness, the real world uses additional practices and models for evaluating investments. And when such practices and models produce results that differ from those produced by DCF, they must not be ignored. To deny the existence of other models, techniques, or avenues of analysis is to repudiate potential sources of value or ignore potential areas of risk that must be included in a thorough M&A pricing analysis. It is a fundamental error not to employ multiple mechanisms to assess valuation and price.

IMPORTANCE OF PRICE

How often we have heard someone say that everything has been worked out in a deal "except the price." That's like saying that you like everything about the philosophy of Buddhism except the teachings of Buddha.

Price is the quintessential part of M&A transactions. The key to every merger, acquisition, and divestiture is the amount and nature of consideration changing hands. (See Appendix II for a discussion of how investment bankers evaluate and compare diverse kinds of consideration in M&A offers.)

To make good deals, you have to *find* the right price, that exquisitely fine line interfacing between the maximum the buyer can pay and the minimum the seller can accept. Finding that interface, from either buy or sell side, is a creative, exhaustive process.

Creativity is enhanced when options are multiplied, when choices are expanded, and when issues are addressed from diverse viewpoints. Thus we provide numerous ways, numerical and judgmental, for valuing a business. Each offers its own angles and its own cut of the problem. Choosing the right models, and deciding which modifiers apply and how, is part of the requisite insight.

Seeing a problem from multiple perspectives is the essence of creativity in business. All relevant models and factors should be considered as components of a broadly comprehensive analysis that blends all forces determining price. Used effectively, the combination of these quantitative models and qualitative factors can go far in pricing mergers and acquisitions. Such blending portrays the investment banker's art.

QUANTITATIVE MODELS THAT DETERMINE PRICE

Quantitative models focus on generating a hard numerical output to specify price; they determine what businesses are worth and how to value companies. What methods are used, when are they used, how are they used, how do they work, where do they work, and where do they fail? (We do not focus on terms and conditions. The type, timing, features, and constraints of consideration used—such as cash, notes of all kinds, stock of all kinds, earn-outs, participations, personal contracts, etc.— are beyond the scope of this chapter. See other chapters in this Volume.)

The following models for assessing business value are listed in approximate order of usage or importance. The large number of models and mechanisms is designed to stimulate the art of M&A thinking. Though some are similar, consider the nuances that differentiate among them and under what circumstances might such differences prove helpful.

Discounted Cash Flow

As stated above, DCF is generally considered the most theoretically valid model for valuing and pricing enterprises whose economic life is a description of streams of cash flows going in and coming out. Its application in M&A is derived from its original usage in evaluating capital budgeting proposals. DCF is discussed much in the M&A world, though as most investment bankers would admit, it is used less.

The internal mechanism of DCF is simple. It works, as we've seen, by weighing the amount of cash invested for the acquisition against the amounts and timing of all future net free cash generated over the life of the investment (net of depreciation, capital expenditures, working capital needs, etc.). This calculation derives an *internal rate of return* (IRR) (which is actually the implied discount rate when the present value of the cash flows going in are set equal to the present value of the cash flows going out).

Alternatively, the future cash flows can be discounted to present value (using an appropriately selected, though rather arbitrary, discount rate) and compared to the initial investment. This calculation yields a *net present value* (NPV), the difference between what you paid and what you expect to make (in present value terms).

Note that the key difference between the IRR and the NPV is that the IRR calculates the implied discount rate by setting the present value of the in-going (negative) and out-coming (positive) cash flows equal to zero, while the NPV uses independently chosen discount rates in order to compare the net present values of these same cash flows.

Using either internal rate of return or net present value, DCFs require that a terminal value be estimated (using various growth models—see Appendix I), normally about seven to ten years out, which is then discounted back to the present. This logic is similar to the salvage value of a capital asset.

DCF analysis is highly dependent on the choice of the discount rate.[1] A difference in one percentage point can be critical. There are four normal approaches for determining the appropriate discount rate:

1. Select the acquiring company's current weighted cost of capital (debt and equity) as the base discount rate and then factor it up by several percentage points (since new projects should require a higher hurdle rate than current operations).
2. Select the acquiring company's historic return on assets as the base discount rate and then factor it up as by several percentage points as above.
3. Utilize current estimates of future interest rate expectations as the base discount rate, which is then increased by a risk factor related to the industry, company, financial structure, and the like.
4. Utilize current estimates of similar companies' weighted cost of capital (from public data) as the base discount rate, which is then increased by a risk factor as above.

The major problem with the DCF, of course, is the inherent uncertainty in estimates and projections. The future is still the future and forecasts are still forecasts. So many assumptions must be made regarding markets, products, pricing, competition, management, the economy, interest rates, and the like that confidence becomes severely eroded. In this matrix of multiplied uncertainty, the numerical elegance of the method can be its greatest danger—the gloss of sophistication and the illusion of control can be both deceptive and intoxicating. DCF can be precise (i.e., replicable) without being accurate (i.e., not conforming to reality). This distinction between precision and accuracy is vital to appreciate.

Nonetheless, one should use DCF in every M&A situation. The process itself is important since it focuses attention on the critical assumptions and uncertainties. Results are important as well, especially when defining the maximum pricing for buyers. For example, if a potential buyer's analysis would show that even if actual results would track estimated projections (which they never do) and rates of return are still only modest, the price is surely too high.

Sensitivity analysis is a necessary exercise in all analytical evaluations. Here various scenarios are explored by assessing how "sensitive" your valuation model is to various changes in input. As stated above, the choice of

---

[1]See Appendix I: Merger and Acquisition Formulas for additional discussion of this issue.

discounts rate makes enormous impact on the outcome of the analysis. In fact, one often finds that the largest variations in the sensitivity analysis is produced by testing alternative discount rates.

In addition, since DCF is fundamentally based on the time value of money, it is exceedingly dependent on the timing of cash inflows and outflows. Due to the compounding effect, no mathematical symmetry will be obvious: A simple decrease of 15 percent in margins will not, you can be sure, cause a simple 15 percent decrease in value.

One must be aware of the strange peculiarities of time in determining rates of return; the compounding curve accelerates benefits and costs. In almost every M&A analysis, anticipated rates of return decline drastically after the first few years, irrespective of business operations—this is more a conceptual shortcoming of the method than an actual loss of value. It is virtually impossible to maintain excessively high rates of return over extended periods of time since the corporate bases (i.e., the denominator in the equation) swells large as is custom with most projections. Professional corporate financiers would much rather attain a 25 percent compounded annual rate of return for ten years than a 40 percent return for three years.

Price/Earnings (P/E) Ratio

The price/earnings ratio reflects the earning power of the company capitalized by an appropriate discount rate. The formulation is expressed as the P/E "multiple," which is the inverse of the discount rate. An industry appropriate income statement number—such as earnings before interest and taxes (EBIT) or net profits after tax (NPAT)— is multiplied by an appropriate P/E factor to calculate price. (EBIT is considered a reflection of the *operational* earning power of the company irrespective of financing and financial structure, while NPAT embeds all current factors including financing and financial structure.)

The P/E multiple is determined by both industry and company characteristics, with anticipated growth rate being the key variable. Indeed, the P/E ratio is virtually a surrogate for anticipated growth rate modulated by an assumed risk factor. P/E ratios for acquisition purchases are usually applied to average earnings over a period of time, say 3 to 5 years. This will not work, of course, for young companies. Here, the P/E may be applied to current or even projected earnings. Higher P/Es (or lower discount rates) can be justified (using strict financial criteria) only by higher anticipated growth in earnings. P/Es work best when assessing steady-state companies in industries with similar public firms (so that an average P/E ratio can be determined).

We note that the use of P/E multiples to evaluate and compare company valuations is what has engendered Wall Street's obsession with earnings per share (EPS), since EPS times P/E multiple equals selling share price.

Market Value

For public companies, the stock market gives a daily assessment of value. The current market capitlization of publicly traded companies is central to M&A pricing—share price times number of shares outstanding, factored up by an appropriate premium (generally ranging from 20 to 100 percent or more) is what it generally takes to acquire a public company with a relatively liquid float. (Thinly traded companies generate distortions.)

Premiums are paid by investors acquiring control positions; such stock dominance (not necessarily more than 50 percent) overcomes foot-dragging by incumbent owners or managers and thwarts potential rivals from cranking up competing offers. Market price is obviously a necessary model for pricing a public company— since it is almost impossible to buy a company below its market price given the need for independent "fairness opinions" by investment bankers (see Chapters 18–19).

But market price alone is usually not sufficient. The share pricing mechanism is grounded on the efficient market theory: that the market is continuously evaluating all information about each company and expressing its current conclusions in up-to-the-minute cash bids and offers for the company's shares.

Yet for acquisition analysis, there is a fatal flaw here. Stock market investors and M&A activists are not conceptually grounded on the same financial foundation and as such should require assymmetrical analyses. Stock market investors are not buying whole companies; they are purchasing small, highly liquid, minority interests. The investor hopes to gain from market forces, not personal managerial influences, and can close out the position at any time. On the other hand, M&A activists who do buy whole companies cannot enjoy such liquidity and flexibility but can, conversely, dictate future operations through managerial control. These are different concepts requiring different models.

The fruits of control usually command a hefty premium, but that premium may be more or less than the "real" value of the company. Hence the need for other techniques to be used in parallel and conjunction. Market value obviously applies to public companies but can be used to assess non-public companies by comparison (see Merger Market Value).

Merger Market Value

In merger market valuation models, we compare prices among similar companies, much like comparison shopping for a consumer item among similar retail stores. Merger market value arrays reasonably similar transactions (i.e., similar industry, company size, financial structure, time frame, etc.) and uses these prices to judge the relative worth of the target company. Investment bankers favor this technique, generating long lists of comparable transactions to advise clients on both buy and sell sides.

In theory, the M&A market is the true reflection of current interaction between willing sellers and willing buyers. In the real world, however, this is rarely the case. Corporations are not yellow pencils, quickly stacked and easily matched; it is difficult to make true comparisons of complex situations—in one way or another virtually every M&A sale can be considered special or extraordinary. Furthermore, the M&A market often evinces aberrations—companies selling too low when suffering distressed conditions and companies selling too high when faddish or foolish buyers are over-eager to acquire. The feeding frenzy of M&A in recent years—the search for synergy and the hostile takeover battles—have bid up many M&A prices to unrealistic levels.

Book Value

Book value is the classic accounting determination of net worth. It is a definitive, time-locked, "snapshot" number reflecting a firm's accounting value at a particular time. Book value is important because it is produced by standarized generally accepted accounting principles (GAAP) and prepared by independent third parties. Yet it is just this apparent precision that makes book value so deceptive and therefore so dangerous.

Book value often means nothing; worse, it can be terribly deceptive. When Maxxam Group bought the Pacific Lumber Company, the value of the latter's world-dominant position in old growth redwood trees was carried on its books for less than 5 percent of real worth. (Historical cost at decades-ago prices—the GAAP principle—was far less than current market value.) On the other hand, many companies maintain ancient plants and worthless inventories, fearing the consequences of large writedowns. In this case, book value would be highly inflated over real value.

Book value may occasionally be used to add tax benefits to a transaction; for example, if the purchase price can be structured below book, additional cash may be generated through tax loss carrybacks or carryforwards—the economic value of the transactions to the seller may then be sweetened in other ways (such as consulting contracts). (*Book Asset Value* takes initial cost minus accumulated depreciation for all real assets; it is used to get a standardized assessment of hard assets.)

Breakup Value

A breakup valuation model assesses the cumulative net worth resulting from selling off all divisions and hard assets of a company (generally in multiple transactions) and netting the proceeds against all remaining liabilities. A breakup valuation is used in two general ways. First, it is considered as downside protection in case the anticipated strategy does not work out. Second, it can be the specific, preplanned strategy of the acquiror (usually in hostile takeovers).

Some companies are indeed worth more dead than alive. The value of the individual parts is higher than the combined sum. This often occurs when companies have little or no business synergies among divisions and mediocre track records for generating healthy returns. Many conglomerates fall into this category.

Breakup value models estimate anticipated prices one could get if the various subsidiaries or divisions were sold off independently as viable businesses. Often these business are highly desirable to potential acquirors who would pay a substantial premium for them (but would not be interested in buying the entire company). The ideal goal of some acquirors is to recover most or all of the full purchase by selling off parts of the target company, and thereby to wind up keeping some desirable parts for a nominal investment.

Real Asset Value

Real asset value determines the market value of all "hard assets" of the company—what you could get for the plant, property and equipment, any natural resources or reserves, and the like. This does not include the "business premiums" for earning power or divisions. Real asset value defines a baseline, or a floor, on which the liquidation value model can be estimated.

Liquidation Value

A liquidation valuation model can be used as a pricing benchmark, the lowest realistic value for any target company. The key factor here is the company's realizable net asset value judged according to the following procedure: All assets are sold individually to generate best obtainable prices, and all liabilities are paid off as they are due—with both sale of assets and payment of liabilities assumed to be conducted in an orderly, businesslike fashion. (Note that the difference between "orderly sales" and "firesales" can be shocking.) What remains, theoretically, should approximate book value—but variance is wide, and one should not be surprised if there is great disparity.

Often the analysis does not assume maintenance of any division or subsidiary as a going concern. The company is simply liquidated for its raw assets: Receivables are collected, inventories are sold off, fixed assets (including advantageous leases) are given to brokers for sale or auction—all assets are converted to cash. (Don't forget intangibles such as patents, trademarks, etc.)

Debts are then netted against the likely gross cash generated to determine a floor for the purchase price. Don't forget hidden liabilities such as underfunded pension plans, retiree medical benefits, and other contingencies. Also, never underestimate the costs and problems of liquidation—running the company as it is being closed down—from poor collections of receivables (people just won't pay) to managing unmotivated personnel. (Watch the vultures circle.) Remember: Debts are sure; assets are not.

It is essential to ascertain the liquidation value when estimating the downside—especially when acquiring troubled companies. It's a worthwhile exercise when evaluating all companies to give some sense of the ultimate floor. DCF and other going concern techniques do not contemplate sale of assets and therefore provide no sense whatsoever of liquidation value. Liquidation analysis often requires the assistance of appraisers, brokers, and actuaries.

Perceived Growth

Perceived growth differs from actual growth. In this model, forecasts and projections are crucial—and here's where anxious acquirers can really fool themselves. In these situations, the acquiror must pay a price higher than historic or current earnings can support. What is the worth; what is the justification; and what price can be offered? Assumptions are key; numbers on computer screens mean nothing of themselves. Numerous possibilities must be considered: market growth, competitive position, potential substitutes, and changing technology, to name just a few.

Synergy Value

Buying a company for its potential synergy value is dangerous. Many a stratospheric price has been lavished on a pipedream. The assessment process evaluates the operational and financial impact of the proposed acquisition on the acquiring company's current business.

Ask if the combination can yield benefits to either acquiror or target or both. Can the target's sales force sell the acquiror's products? Can the customers of one buy the products of the other? Can the acquiror's plants produce the target's products? Can our overhead support their needs? Can our management help them, their management help us? Will "2 + 2 = 5"—or "3," as often happens?

Such *anti*synergy is the autoimmune disease of the M&A body. All too frequently, especially when many acquisitions are made by one acquiror, the headstrong attempt to achieve an unrealistic or impossible level of synergy can destroy the original health of both companies.

Investment Value

An investment value model takes a more passive look at the acquisition and evaluates the target company as if it were merely a small stock purchase to be put into a large investment portfolio. Though the analysis will use many of these same techniques, the *attitude* and *approach* will be different. Passion will be less, as will assumptions of managerial magic. Here the acquiror forgets about synergy value on the one hand and breakup value on the other.

Going Concern Value

A going concern valuation model is a hybrid. First it takes net asset expectations (whether break up or liquidation value) and then adds any excess rates of return anticipated for operating the business. This techniques hedges assets and earnings.

Competitive Value

The competitive valuation model assesses how much the target company might be worth to competitors. What would be the amount that a company would be willing to pay in order to lessen competition, to gain share, and to shore up prices—to thwart you? For example, magazines are occasionally bought by competitors and immediately closed—the point being to fold in acquired subscription lists in order to enhance the acquiror's existing properties. Competitive valuation is generally applied to industrial, not financial players (though financial players can use the competitive model to assess potential resale values, especially given some operational and market share improvement).

Replacement Value

The replacement value model estimates the cost of replacing the target company with *all new* plant, equipment, materials, and the like—which is obviously more expensive than the next two similar valuation models. Replacement valuation only applies to industrial companies requiring the target's facilities and/or contemplating entrance into the target company's business.

There are two kinds of replacement value analyses: (1) only assets (fixed and current) are considered; and (2) the entire conduct of the current business is assessed, including hiring and training personnel, designing and producing products, establishing markets, building customer lists and service operations, installing control systems, and the like. This analysis is similar to the "make or buy" decisions of industrial manufacturers.

Reproduction Value

Reproduction valuation estimates the cost of totally replicating the target company in exactly its present form. Similar plant and equipment are assumed to be bought in their current condition; personnel must be hired and trained; new product names must be established; and the like. This technique, as the previous and following ones, are used primarily by industrial buyers who are considering entering the target's industry.

Build-or-buy analyses should accompany all corporate acquisition programs and determine the relative advantages of buying ongoing companies or starting similar businesses from ground up. Time delays, asset availability, personnel training, and market recognition are often the most important factors in the cost comparisons.

Substitution Value

The substitution value model estimates the cost of buying the same *output* as the target company currently produces without having to purchase any of its specific elements. Ends not means are judged—a decidedly less expensive proposition.

Rules of Thumb for Multiple Values

Each of the above Quantitative Models That Determine Price are used in conjunction with prevailing "rules of thumb" which convert numerical output into actual pricing values. These rules, almost by definition, are creatures of the market to be discerned by common knowledge and constant monitoring.

Rules of thumb are generally expressed in multiples—industry-specific integer multipliers of operational data such as net profits after tax (NPAT), earnings before interest and taxes (EBIT), and net free cash flow; or industry-specific integer multipliers of unit values such as price per barrel of oil reserves, price per bed for a health care company, or price per subscriber for a cable television concern.

Rules of thumb are tricky, perhaps unreliable. Procedures and fingers differ and so do multiples, and one must keep attuned to the latest notions. Even more important, not all companies in a given industry are equal. Differences in market share, brand name, reputation, management, cost structure, and a myriad of other elements are critical, so that the same multiple paid willingly for an industry leader would yield an absurdly excessive price for a follower. The bottom line is that numerical techniques are necessary to get some sense of the situation, but inadequate to fix a final price. For that, we must look beyond numbers.

Estimating Earnings Projections

Estimating future earnings is vital in M&A valuation and pricing. After all, multiples in the above quantitative models must multiply *something*. One should work with five-year financial data, normalized to adjust for changes in accounting principles, mergers and acquisitions, nonrecurring events, and the like. Percentages should be calculated so that trends become easier to spot.

Critical trends and deviations from those trends should be noted, over the five years in general and the most recent two years in particular. Special attention should be paid to sales growth (by product line), gross margins, general and administrative costs, and all the traditional ratios of liquidity, leverage, activity, and profitability.[2]

By trending the previous five years, one can make a first estimate on what the next five years might be like. The fundamental assumption, of course, is that the future will emulate the past—a dangerous decision under the best

[2]Example ratios for trending and deviation analysis: *Liquidity*: current ratio, quick ratio; *leverage*: debt-to-total assets, debt/equity, times interest earned, fixed charge coverage; *activity*: inventory turnover (cost of goods sold to average inventory), average collection period, sales to fixed assets turnover, sales to total assets turnover; *profitability*: gross margin on sales, net margin before interest and taxes on sales, net margin after interest and taxes on sales, return on total assets, and return on net worth.

of circumstances.[3] With earnings estimates made, growth rates and discount rates can be calculated (see Appendix), which are then transformed into the proper multiples to use in the quantitative models (e.g., for P/E ratio models, the growth rate surrogate is applied to the net income; for DCF models, the discount rate is applied to the yearly cash flows).

QUALITATIVE FACTORS THAT MODIFY PRICE

Valuing and pricing M&A transactions cannot be done independent of the context in which the deal is being done. Knowing why a certain deal is desired facilitates knowing which quantitative models and qualitative factors to consider. For example, industry and financial buyers would have different motivations to do the same deal, would make different assessments, and would be willing to pay different prices. Client motivation, therefore, is important for investment bankers to assess.

Client motivations for doing M&A are many:

1. *Financial M&A*—stock enhancement, balance sheet/earnings improvement, leveraged buyout, management buyout, going private).
2. *Strategic M&A*—horizontal integration, vertical integration, market share growth, product-market protection, plant utilization, overhead amortization, technology leaps, diversification.
3. *Managerial M&A*—company restructure, desired growth, chief/senior executive interest, personal ambition.

Price is the universal currency of the international M&A economy. A "too high" or "too low" price, even though calculated by microprocessor and printed by laser, does not generate exceptional value for M&A activists on either side of the buy or sell.

In general, there are two categories of qualitative factors which affect value—operational factors and transactional/financial factors. The two are interrelated, and in most transactions acquirors look for both sets of benefits.

---

[3]For mature companies in mature industries this assumption is less speculative than for early-stage ventures in young industries. One's confidence in making five-year projections for, say, a large furniture or pipe manufacturer would be considerably higher than for a start-up firm in superconductivity or expert systems.

Operational factors—such as market position and presumed synergy—tend to relate to specific companies at specific times and are less susceptible to general rules. Consequently we focus on transactional/financial factors.

Following are transactional/financial factors that impact M&A valuation and pricing. Each must be evaluated in the specific context of acquiror and target.

Do-Ability

This is my first choice—the top of the list. Can the deal get done? No matter how attractive a situation, no matter how right the price, the deal has to be "do-able." There are virtually an infinite number of reasons that make a deal *un*-doable—even after terms and conditions are generally agreed.

How to unhinge a deal? Anything can slam the door—from bad chemistry and personal piques to over-eager lawyers and potential lawsuits to changing business conditions and interest rates. Deals bust up, even at the last moment. It is much easier to uncover a dozen attractive situations than to consummate one of them.

How to assess do-ability? There is no cookbook list of secret recipes and special ingredients. The best advice is to optimize benefits for both sides, strive for simplicity, assess major sticking points (deal breakers)—and use your nose (does the deal "smell" right?). (See Chapter 29.)

Financibility

The ability to finance an acquisition is usually dependent on two factors: the general creditworthiness of the acquiring company and its credibility with lenders and/or security holders; and the specific confidence of financial institutions that the proposed deal is a good one. (If equity interests in the acquiror and/or seller paper are the consideration being used, this problem becomes less important and perhaps moot.)

The initial financial strength of both acquiror and target are critical. Factors to consider include history of earnings, quality of assets, and absence of encumbrances. Projected streams of income, from which cash coverage of interest and amortization of principal will be derived, must be scrutinized. (Always remember that debts are paid with cash not earnings, so cash flow is always more important than accounting income.) "Haircuts" (reductions) will be taken on company projections so that lenders can be confident that their loans are safe even under almost-worst case conditions.

Financial Structure

Acquisition price, independent of financial structure, may be misleading. How deals are financed can greatly affect appropriateness of price. For example, an all-cash payment financed entirely with three-year senior debt would constrain a very low price from the perspective of the buyer, while the use of owner-carried notes, zero coupon bonds, and preferred stock would support a much higher price for the same transaction.

Sometimes a deal is actually worth more than the acquiring company can afford to pay. In a well-known billion dollar acquisition of a natural resource company, interest charges in the highly leveraged structure amounted to twice the preacquisition cash flow. The deal could not have been done without substantial use of zero coupon notes which would mature as the target's assets could be converted to cash over a 15-year period.

Much of the advance in modern M&A involves the creative development of novel financial instruments that match company cash flow with debt requirements and balance risk and return for various levels of lenders and investors. The three traditional levels—senior debt, mezzanine, equity—are often segmented into a dozen or more "strips" in larger and more complex transactions.

Tax Considerations

Tax is a massive concern in all M&A transactions, fraught with opportunity and threat—and incurring high professional costs. (See Chapter 28.)

Tax issues for the buyer include: how do anticipated taxes impact the net free cash available for operating the company and amortizing debt? What will the new tax basis of the acquired assets be and how will they be allocated? Are there any special tax considerations in the industry or company? Any hidden tax liabilities? Any recapture? Any net operating loss carryforwards?

Tax issues for the seller include: What is the after-tax, realizable, net free cash generated? What is the most efficient structure to minimize tax liability? What about tax-free exchanges, taxable transactions that generate losses, installment structures, capital gains treatment, contingent payouts, consulting arrangements, liquidations, spin-offs, and blanket tax exemptions? It is usually important to control timing, such as when taxes would become payable on exercise of options or on constructive receipts of dividends; the worst case is to mismatch the receipt of cash and income so that a tax liability is incurred without producing money to pay it.

The key to many deals is to find the win-win structure that minimizes the collective tax liabilities for both the acquiring company and the selling shareholders. In this manner, more value will be available to allocate between the parties.

Cost of Capital

A company's cost of capital is one of its key characteristics, in which the weighted cost of debt and equity are embedded. Required rates of return must be evaluated in light of the acquiror's cost of capital, factoring in such additional returns above the cost of capital as a new, more risky project must command.

Hurdle rates differ. A company selling for a high P/E in the market can afford to pay a higher price (in cash as well as stock) than a comparable company selling at a low P/E. The higher P/E company has, by definition, a lower cost of capital. (The implicit assumption, not wholly valid, is that the pooled future earnings will be capitalized by the public markets with the same high multiples.) Conversely, if corporate or investment fund money is languishing in low-return, short-term instruments, hurdle rates for a potential acquisition might be lower.

Liquidity

Liquidity factors for the buyer include two types, operational and transactional. Operational liquidity issues are: What are the immediate cash requirements for operating the business, including working capital (seasonality) and capital expenditures? Many new owners have found themselves desperately short of operating cash the day after closing, having calculated only the direct acquisition costs. Transactional liquidity issues includes: What are prospects for turning the business into cash? Can it be sold easily? Taken public? Refinanced? (Liquidity issues for the seller are only meaningful if they were not paid fully on closing.)

Competitive Bidding

Competitive bidding factors for the buyer include: How strong are competitive bidders? How serious? What are their primary motivations? If the M&A interests of a competitor's company are complementary with those of your own company's, might there be some cooperative effort—such as agreeing to break up the target so that each partner would obtain a desired division while keeping the overall price within reason? If competitors' interests are not complementary, how likely are they to remain interested (and hence be available to buy the business should the acquiror change its mind or seek a quick profit)? What about risks of getting outbid after incurring high costs, primarily in a contested public arena? Can you get a "lockup" on some stock or key asset of target?

Competitive factors for the seller include: Can the price be jacked up by competitive bidding? Is a formal auction appropriate? How can all bidders be encouraged to participate in the process?

Defensive

Defensive factors for the buyer include: Would purchasing the target make the acquiring company *less* risky, say by becoming countercyclical, by protecting key markets and customers, or by securing sources of supply? Or would the acquisition create a *more* risky company with higher operational costs and exposure to a given market (in addition to the greater financial strain)? Would the target be dangerous if acquired by a competitor?

Control

Control factors for the buyer include: Are there any special positions that target controls—such as stock of other companies, market share, key customer relationships, long-term supply contracts, key real estate? Is there any value of buying a control position in the target company, but not buying the entire company? (For example, preserving a net operating loss carryforward [NOL]—which becomes severely attenuated with more than a 50 percent change of ownership.[4]) If only a control position is sought—not the entire company—a different analysis is required. Control of any kind is valued highly, and control premiums are common.

Understandability

It is shocking how often acquirors do not understand the business they have just bought. Hundreds if not thousands of hours of time will have been lavished on doing the deal while only a small fraction of that on appreciating the business. Understandability factors for the buyer include: How well do you know the

[4]There are many technical facets for determining NOL utilization and its limitations. It is a minefield requiring expert assistance.

industry, from the nature of the business to the key people in it? Could your management take over the target if their current management walked? The history of M&A is littered with good deals going bad because the acquiror just was not aware of the critical issues in an unfamiliar industry or organization.

Desirability

We delude ourselves if we think that personal desire does not wield substantial influence on M&A decisions. Owning a new company is one of the great ego boosts in modern society, not only for the chief executive but for the entire management team. Never underestimate the importance of enhanced power and prestige.

Desirability factors for the buyer include: How strongly is the target wanted or needed? How far will your company reach to get it? How important for business position? How important for CEO/executive interests?

Synergy

Synergy factors for the buyer include: What are benefits to the current company if combined with the intended target? What are the procedures, timeframes, roadblocks, and dangers of generating the planned-for synergies between acquiror and target? What could happen to destroy such hoped-for incremental benefits? Should the deal be done even if the expected synergies do not materialize? (This is especially critical if synergistic increases in revenues or decreases in costs are part of the projections that support the purchase price and its financing.)

Business Timing

Business timing factors for the buyer include: Is this the right part of the cycle to acquire this company? If at the top of the cycle, are you paying top dollar? If at the bottom of the cycle, what are the target firm's immediate business prospects? What are trends? What is likely to happen to target's relative cost of doing business over time? For example, will labor become progressively more expensive relative to foreign competition?

Payment Timing

Payment timing factors for the seller include: How important is cash upfront? Are you willing to take back notes? Even when equating price with market rate interest, a seller who waits for full payment can demand a higher (present value) price due to the assumption of inherent risks.

Acquisition Timing

Acquisition timing factors for the buyer include: How fast *must* you move? How fast *can* you move? Must money be raised from new third parties, or is it currently available with established credit facilities?

Acquisition timing factors for the seller include: How quickly should the transaction be completed? Who is under more time pressures—buyer or seller?

General Risk

General risk factors for the buyer include: What is the likelihood that business and financial expectations may not be met? How volatile is the industry and company? What are the environmental and competitive threats? How important is management; what is their attitude; and what happens if they walk?

General risk factors for the seller include: What is the likelihood of a better offer coming in? Conversely, what is the likelihood of the current best offer vanishing? If the transaction is not all cash, what is the probability of not receiving full payment? In any case, what is the likelihood of closing?

INTEGRATION OF VALUATION AND PRICING PRACTICES

Do not be misled: there is no simple formula for valuing and pricing M&A. In determining the "best price" for a business, from either buyer's or seller's side, a wide-ranging, creative analysis is prescribed. Such an analysis must reflect responses to a wide variety of stimuli; only a cyclical, looping, systems oriented, organic approach can protect against simplistic or deceptive conclusions.

For example, an acquiring company could do a discounted cash flow analysis based on best-guess forecasts for the target. But should an astute buyer be tied to the price that emerges from the computer model? Not necessarily. The DCF value may be twice the stock market value—so why offer double upfront? On the other hand, the DCF may be far less than the breakup value (other companies may put strategic premiums on various divisions)—so why lose the deal?

Alternative valuation approaches can be correlated to assess acquisition pricing strategies and concomitant risks. An "if/then" analysis seeks an array of recommended actions based on generally known conditions. Consider the following logic: If comparable M&A market prices are below liquidation value, acquisition risks are minimal; but if market prices are above DCF and break up values, acquisition risks are substantial.

If/thens are not new and not magic. They rather reflect the complex process that goes on among acquirors examining a potential transaction. Serious buyers will always use sophisticated quantitative techniques—but the canny ones will not be bound by them. They will always plug a diversity of intuitive qualitative factors into the valuation process.

It is good practice for both buyer and seller to assess the other side's position with a series of scenario planning exercises—absolute worst case, probable minimal requirements, desired deal level, and realistic best case. Other companies should be included in the analysis. The buyer can evaluate what competitors might pay for target (and why), as well as what other companies might make a better alternative candidate for acquisition. The seller should do likewise, exploring all possible suitors. (Having alternative possibilities for M&A transactions, even if questionable, makes both buyers and sellers better negotiators—See Chapters 29–30.)

A thorough and effective valuation and pricing analysis would include using many of the *Quantitative Models That Determine Price* and *Qualitative Factors That Modify Price* in various combinations. Matrices can be developed by mapping one onto the other, the Models against the Factors, so that each cell of intersection has the potential for generating new thinking. Then multi-dimensional matrices can be designed so that cells include several Models and Factors working together (or fighting against one another).

Sensitivity analysis should be conducted across many models and factors, testing what happens under various scenarios (e.g., sales down 20 percent; margins eroded by 15 percent; interest rates jump up to 17 percent; etc.) Such computer-based analysis should analyze the cross-impact of various factors working together (or fighting against one another). In this manner, a fuller appreciation for price can be determined. Additional insights into the business will also be gleaned.

To sum up, valuing and pricing M&A demands multiple levels of attitude and approach. It is a mistake to allow one methodology to dominate thinking. Conversely, it is impractical to calculate every quantitative model and weigh every qualitative factor in every transaction. Pick only those most appropriate and explore them in depth. Good judgment, honed by experience, will enable investment bankers to assess which models and factors to use and how to use them. Yet it is always advised to test a few of the more obscure Models and Factors in order to expand horizons. You never know what you might find. (A list of the largest corporate mergers and acquisitions in history, as of mid 1989, is presented in Figure 1.) (See Chapters 29–30 for a detailed discussion of the deal-making process.)

FIGURE 1
The Largest Corporate Mergers and Acquisitions
(as of July 12, 1989)

Target Company	*Acquiring Company*	*Merger and Acquisition Value (in billions)*	*Year Completed*
RJR Nabisco	Kohlberg, Kravis, Roberts[1]	$24.5 billion	1989
B.A.T. Industries	Hoylake Investments[2]	$21.0	Pending[3]
Warner Communications[4]	Time, Inc.	$14.0	Pending[3]
Gulf Oil	Standard Oil	$13.4	1984
Kraft Foods	Phillip Morris	$13.4	1988
Time, Inc.[4]	Paramount[5]	$12.2	Pending[3]
Getty Oil[6]	Texaco Oil	$10.1	1984
Dome Petroleum	Amoco Canada	$9.0	1988
SmithKline Beckman	Beecham Group	$7.8	Pending[3]
Conoco Oil	DuPont	$7.4	1981
Federated Department Stores	Campeau	$7.4	1988
Marathon Oil	USX[7]	$6.5	1982

[1] Kohlberg, Kravis, Roberts (KKR) is the most famous leveraged buyout (LBO) firm. They have completed many successful LBOs, from Houdaille Industries (the first major LBO in 1979) to Beatrice Foods, making enormous profits (and spectacular returns on equity investments) for themselves and their partners.

[2] Hoylake Investments is a partnership lead by Sir James Goldsmith, Jacob Rothschild, and Kerry Packer. Although the outcome is far from clear as we go to press, the situation exemplifies the contemporary M&A game for large investment partnerships led by entrepreneurial financiers (or, depending on one's view, corporate raiders).

[3] Pending transactions are subject to change. As we go to press (August 12,1989), Paramount has withdrawn its offer for Time, while Time is moving ahead with its acquisition of Warner.

[4] In this well-known corporate battle, Time and Warner originally announced a merger. Paramount then made an unsolicited acquisition offer for Time, following which Time made a friendly acquisition offer for Warner. Although the outcome is far from clear as of July 12, 1989, the situation exemplifies the contemporary M&A game for large corporations.

[5] Paramount is the former Gulf & Western Corporation.

[6] This is the famous (or infamous) case whether Pennzoil sued Texaco for disrupting Pennzoil's own acquisition of Getty. Pennzoil was awarded $10 billion, Texaco filed Chapter 11 bankruptcy, and a settlement was eventually reached at $3 billion.

[7] USX is the former United States Steel Corporation.

APPENDIX I: MERGER AND ACQUISITION FORMULAS

Earnings Growth Formula

The formula for determining the earnings growth rate is

$$(1 + g)^t = \frac{e_t}{e_i}$$

where g represents the growth rate through the forecast period t (say five years),

e_t represents the after-tax net income in the t_{th} period (say in the fifth year), and

e_i represents the after-tax net income in the ith time period (the first year).

Solving for g, we find that if trended earnings are doubled over the five years, this is the equivalent of a compounded annual rate of earnings growth of about 15%; if earnings are tripled, about 25%; if increased four fold, about 32%; if five fold, about 38%; if six fold, about 43%; if seven fold, about 48%.

Discount Rate Formula

The appropriate discount rate for calculating DCF reflects the risk profile of the acquisition. The general formula is:

$$d = r_f + r_p$$

where d is the appropriate discount rate,

r_f is the "risk-free" rate of return (normally indexed by the highest return on currently available Treasury bills), and

r_p is the "risk premium," the incremental rate of return (above the risk-free rate) that the acquiring company must earn in order to accept the risk inherently involved in making the acquisition.

The critical issue is to determine r_r, the risk premium, the required incremental rate of return. Various theoretically-founded methods can be employed; these usually relate to the capital asset pricing model and/or the Stock Market beta:

1. The capital asset pricing model relates the risk premium to the expected value of return and standard deviations of return for the current portfolio of corporate assets.

2. A beta-weighted adjustment relates the risk premium to the stock market beta, which defines the relationship between the excess returns on the common stock of the target company and the excess returns of a market portfolio. ("Excess returns" is simply the difference between the expected return and the risk-free rate.) Beta is simply a representation of the systematic risk of the target company, the risk that is intrinsically related to the company itself and cannot be diversified away.

As discussed in the text, most companies in the real world do not employ these theoretically more rigorous but less practical methods. Rather, they set an artificial hurdle rate related to their current cost of capital or historic return on assets, adjusting both upward for the inherently higher risk of new projects.

Acquisition Valuation Formula

There are numerous formulas for valuing a business. Most are based on discounting and/or capitalization rates of streams of cash flow and/or income. (Variations relate to the specific variables chosen and how they interrelate.) Following is the model I prefer (at least currently).

The acquisition value of a company (present value), AV_{PV}, equals the present value of its stream of net free cash flow, CF_{PV}, plus the present value of its terminal value, TV_{PV}, at the end of the cash flow period:

$$AV_{PV} = CF_{PV} + TV_{PV}$$

where

$$AV_{PV} = \text{Present value of the Acquisition Value}$$

$$CF_{PV} = \text{Present Value of the Cash Flows}$$

$$= \sum_{1}^{t} \frac{\text{Net Free Cash Flow in Time Period } t}{(1.0 + \text{Discount Rate } [d_1])^t}$$

$$TV_{PV} = \text{Present Value of the Terminal Value at the End of the Cash Flows}$$

$$= \frac{\left(\dfrac{\sum_{t+1}^{\infty} \text{Earnings Before Interest and Taxes in Year } t}{(1.0 + \text{Discount Rate } [d_2]]^{t+1}}\right) - \text{Debt}}{(1.0 + \text{Discount Rate } [d_3]]^t}$$

$$= \frac{\left(\dfrac{\text{Earnings Before Interest and Taxes in Year } t}{\text{Discount Rate } [d_2]}\right) - \text{Debt}}{(1.0 + \text{Discount Rate } [d_3])^t}$$

Note that d_1, d_2, and d_3 are the appropriate discount rate in each term and time period—and should differ. Certainly the rate discounting (d_2) the pre-interest-pre-tax earnings in determining the terminal value (TV_{PV}) will be higher than the rate discounting (d_1) the after-interest-after-tax net free cash flow (CF_{PV}).

The acquisition formula values the target company strictly from the perspective of the acquiror. Thus the first term (CF_{PV}) uses the net free cash flow generated, representing the actual cash that would be available for the acquiror to upstream during the term of ownership.

The second term (TV_{PV}) assesses a terminal valuation at the end of the period of cash flows (usually when the company is sold or assumed sold), and then discounts this terminal value back to present value. The terminal value is based on the earnings (not cash flows), since the multiples-of-income method is used to evaluate companies in the public markets and in third-party sales. I prefer to use earnings before interest and taxes (EBIT), rather than earnings after interest and taxes, since EBIT factors out the financial structure of the company and focuses on the business operations. Since we assess terminal value using EBIT, we must subtract out the balance sheet debt (compensating for interest) and choose a higher discount rate (compensating for interest and taxes).[5]

APPENDIX II: EVALUATING MERGER AND ACQUISITION OFFERS

Since many tranactions involve consideration other than all cash at closing, investment bankers for the target company are required to evaluate the absolute and comparative values of the consideration (especially in a competitive situation where alternative offers usually have different characteristics). The basic technique is to equate all consideration to *present value cash equivalents*.

Evaluating cash is easy—cash is cash, and so all payments of cash are valued at 100% (unless there are contingencies).

Notes and other interest-bearing instruments must be evaluated as to their term, stated coupon, payment schedules (interest and principle), covenants,

[5]We could arrive at the same valuation by using a similar discount rate—but we would then have to factor out the taxes. We would do this by multiplying the pre-interest-pre-tax cash flow by a term that subtracts out the effective taxes (not forgetting the tax shielding effect of the interest). Such a factor—one minus the effective tax rate $(1 - t)$—is often used in similar equations.

seniority, security, default likelihood, insolvency likelihood, remedies, and ratings (if applicable). This analysis yields an independently evaluated market rate for the note. If this market rate is below the stated coupon on the note, then the note must be discounted by the difference and is thus valued below par.

Common stock is evaluated according to similar principles. If the stock is of a large public company and is not restricted, it will be assessed close to market but a bit below it. (Even the most blue-chip stock cannot be valued exactly at market, since the market can change at any moment, and even though the share price may just as easily go up as down, it is this volatility itself that demands a discount.) If the stock taken as consideration in an M&A transaction is not publicly traded, or is thinly traded, or if there are restrictions of any kind, then appropriately larger discounts are made.

Contingent payments (which are often used as consideration elements when private companies are acquired) are the most complicated to assess since they are based on future events uncertain by definition. Investment bankers make reasonable assumptions regarding the key industry, business and operating criteria and then discount the resulting numbers rather heavily to compensate for the substantial uncertainty and risk.

CHAPTER 5

FINANCING AND FUNDING MERGERS AND ACQUISITIONS

William D. Rifkin
Salomon Brothers Inc

The preceding two chapters discuss how to determine the value of an acquisition candidate and the lowest price at which it might be acquired successfully. This chapter addresses the form, structure and sources of consideration (e.g., cash, debt and stock) which can be used to make up that price.

TWO EVALUATION LEVELS

The financing of a significant merger and acquisition (M&A) transaction must be evaluated on two levels: *tactical* (how to get the deal done) and *strategic* (how to live with it).

Tactics

Tactical considerations, among other things, include: the speed with which an acquisition can be consummated; the attractiveness of the form of payment to the seller(s); the coercive nature of an offer; and vulnerability to defensive measures which may be taken by an unreceptive target, such as a proposed leveraged recapitalization or adoption of a "poison pill."

Strategy

Strategic issues with respect to the buyer include such things as: its "optimal capital structure"; tax implications; impact on and importance of its credit ratings; future access to capital; financial flexibility; market timing; and its own vulnerability to takeover.

When tactical and strategic considerations are in conflict, the financing of an acquisition becomes a multiple-step process. For instance, cash paid to a seller may be funded with a short-term loan, which will subsequently be replaced with more permanent capital. It is not uncommon today for companies to undertake massive recapitalization programs, such as extraordinary dividend distributions, stock repurchases or exchange offers; therefore, sacrifices made with respect to optimal capital structure for tactical reasons are not necessarily irreparable.

SPECIAL CONSIDERATIONS

In reading this chapter, please keep in mind that certain generalizations made with respect to the various forms of acquisition consideration may not be applicable in all cases. For example, if a target company is insignificant in size relative to its acquiror, the availability of credit to fund a cash purchase may not be an issue. On the other hand, if the target is significantly larger than the acquiror, as in a leveraged buyout, the availability of credit is a critical issue.

Ownership Profile of Target

It is important to analyze the ownership profile of a target company when selecting a specific form of consideration. What percent of the shareholders are taxpayers? What are the likely tax bases of the larger taxpaying shareholders? What percent of the target company's stock is likely to end up in the hands of risk arbitrageurs? The tactical considerations of speed and vulnerability to competing offers obviously take on greater importance when the target is a publicly traded company than when it is private. Likewise, the seller of a private company may have certain tax considerations which would not be relevant when the target is a broadly held publicly traded company.

Consideration Capability

Certain acquirors may not have access to all forms of merger consideration. For instance, it may or may not be practical for a foreign or private company to use its securities as consideration in acquiring the common stock of a domestic corporation, depending upon the buyer's ability to comply with Securities and Exchange Commission (SEC) disclosure requirements.

Market Reaction

Regardless of the form of consideration used, the acquiror must make a determination as to how the market will react to its pro forma financial results. While it is dangerous to generalize, it is fair to say that, in most cases, investors prefer less dilution in earnings per share to more, so long as the acquiror's pro forma capital structure is deemed appropriate under the circumstances. (See Chapters 2 and 28 for a discussion of accounting for M&A transactions.)

CASH CONSIDERATION

With few exceptions, cash is the acquisition currency of choice from a tactical standpoint.

Speed

From the buyer's perspective, the principal advantage of cash, whether used to purchase shares on the open market or through a tender offer, is speed—minimizing the time that competing purchasers or a reluctant target will have to react. As discussed in Chapter 2, a target company's shares may be purchased pursuant to a cash tender offer, and effective control obtained, in as few as 20 business days. The registration of securities to be used in an exchange offer, on the other hand, may take four to six weeks to get through the SEC, and the offer must then remain open for an additional 20 business days.

Two-Tier Front-End Loaded Offers

In the early 1980s, a cash tender offer for some but not all of a target's shares, to be followed by a squeeze-out merger with securities of lesser value, was sometimes used to "stampede" shareholders into tendering their stock. This tactic, known as a "two-tier front-end loaded offer," is far less effective today because of various "poison pill" plans which can be put in place by target companies to protect minority shareholders.

Liquidity and Hard Value

From the seller's perspective, cash is generally preferable to securities because there are no questions as to liquidity or hard value. The net proceeds which will be realized upon the sale of a security depend on: (1) market conditions (e.g., have interest rates risen or fallen?); (2) market depth (i.e., what amount of securities can be sold at a given time without driving its price down?); (3) any changes in the issuer's creditworthiness or business prospects; and (4) transaction costs. Obviously, none of these issues exist with respect to cash.

Drawbacks of Cash

The possible drawbacks of cash consideration from the seller's standpoint are (1) an inability to defer recognition of gain for tax purposes and (2) lack of a continuing equity interest in the combined company. In general, however, these issues are only important in certain negotiated transactions in which the target has a controlling shareholder, such as a largely family-owned company. Short-term investors, such as arbitrageurs, and tax exempt institutions, such as state pension funds, gain nothing from a tax-deferred transaction.

Refinancing Issues

Assuming that the cash used to purchase shares is borrowed on a short-term basis, the key strategic issue is whether such a loan can be refinanced on an acceptable basis. This will depend on market conditions at the time of the refinancing and on certain important constraints. For instance, the market for equity securities is generally more limited than the market for debt securities, and there is a practical limit on the dollar amount of any security sold. If market depth is not an issue, the acquiror should eventually be able to refinance the acquisition loan in a manner so as to achieve its target capital structure; however, until such time, the acquiror will be at risk with respect to changes in interest rates and its stock price.

SOURCES OF ACQUISITION CASH

There are four general sources of "quick" cash to finance a tender offer or open market purchase program. We discuss three in this section: commercial banks; the private placement market; and investment banks which provide bridge loans. The fourth, shelf offerings of registered debt, is discussed in Volume II, Chapter 5.

Commercial Banks

The terms of a bank loan, as with any borrowing, will depend on the creditworthiness of the borrower, taking into account the pro forma effect of the acquisition, and the structure of the acquisition transaction. In general, commercial bank term loans will: (1) be senior to any other acquisition financing and, in the event of a tender offer, secured by the stock to be purchased; (2) have a floating interest rate at some spread over an index such as the prime rate or LIBOR; (3) have a maturity of no more than seven years and an average life of no more than four or five years; and (4) in certain cases, have highly restrictive covenants with respect to additional debt issuance and the payment of dividends.

The Federal Reserve Board, through the "margin rules," regulates the extension of credit by banks and other lending institutions for the purchase of most publicly traded equity securities if the loan is secured by such stock. Presently, bank loans may not exceed 50 percent of the market value of the collateral. There is no limit on the amount that banks may lend on an unsecured basis, but such terms are hard to come by. Beginning in 1986, the Board of Governors of the Federal Reserve extended the margin rules to apply to tender offers made by certain highly leveraged shell companies whose borrowings, while not technically secured, are for all practical purposes "indirectly secured."

Drexel's "Highly Confident" Letters

Drexel Burnham Lambert Inc. (Drexel), beginning in 1984, developed a means of quickly tapping a segment of the private placement market for acquisition financing. An under-capitalized acquiror, in many cases a corporate raider such as Carl Icahn or T. Boone Pickens, would enhance the credibility of its bid by obtaining a letter stating that Drexel was "highly confident" that a specified amount of money could be raised to help finance a tender offer. Drexel would then attempt to obtain commitments from a group of investors to purchase non-registered securities immediately prior to the acquiror's take-down of shares pursuant to the tender offer. As quickly as practicable after their issuance, such securities would be registered with the SEC and become freely tradeable. These securities would typically consist of various levels of subordinated debentures and, in some cases, increasing rate notes which the issuer would intend quickly to pay off with the proceeds of asset sales.

Investment Bank Bridge Loans

In order to compete with Drexel's extraordinarily effective approach, a number of investment banks lacking its track record have begun to use their own capital to provide the balance of funds needed to complete a tender offer. These so-called "bridge loans" are intended to be interim financing, and their terms are designed to induce the borrower to obtain permanent financing as quickly as possible. A typical bridge loan might mature in 180 days, but may be extended for an additional 180 days upon the payment of, say, a 2 percent fee. Its interest rate would float at prime plus 500 basis points for the first six months, increasing to prime plus 700 basis points if the maturity is extended. The bridge loan would be subordinate to any bank debt, and its covenants designed accordingly. The borrower pays a commitment fee for the bridge loan, typically 1 percent, and an additional fee, also typically 1 percent, on any funds actually drawn down.

Bridge loans, particularly those used in leveraged buyouts, can be highly risky, and individual loans are often large relative to even a well-capitalized investment bank's net worth. Because investment banks are themselves highly leveraged, their financial performance is very sensitive to their cost of funds. This effectively limits the size of the bridge loan market since excessive exposure of this nature by an investment bank could lead to a downgrade in credit rating and a commensurate increase in its cost of borrowed funds. A rough estimate of the current potential capacity of bridge loans by all investment banks combined is $5 to $10 billion outstanding at any one time.

COMMON STOCK

The tactical and strategic characteristics of using common stock to gain control of a target company are, for the most part, directly opposite those of cash.

Issuing Mechanisms

Common stock may be issued to the target company's shareholders through an exchange offer or by means of a statutory merger—both of which can be time-consuming processes. In either case, the issuer must have a sufficient number of authorized but unissued shares of stock for use in the transaction, and a registration statement must be filed with the SEC.

If the issuer does not have a sufficient number of authorized but unissued shares, it must obtain its shareholders' consent for an increase. Depending upon the company's charter and by-laws, this can take as long as three months. In the case of a merger, a joint proxy statement can be used to seek simultaneously the following: an increase in the number of the issuer's authorized shares of common stock; registration of such shares; and approval of the merger by the target company's shareholders.

Assuming that no lengthy regulatory approvals are necessary, this process will take approximately three months, comprised of the time needed by the SEC to declare the proxy statement "effective" and the time needed by each company to conduct a shareholder vote. In most cases, a merger would take this long even if the acquiror had sufficient authorized but unissued shares because of the time needed for the target company's shareholders to approve the merger. As previously mentioned, a first-step exchange offer can be completed in approximately eight to ten weeks if the acquiror already has sufficient authorized but unissued shares.

The New York Stock Exchange (NYSE) requires that shareholders of a listed company approve the issuance of common stock in an acquisition transaction when such issuance would result in an increase of 18.5 percent or more in the number of the issuer's shares outstanding. Companies which do not comply with this rule run the risk of being delisted by the NYSE.

Thus, not only is the issuance of common stock to gain control of a target company a lengthy process—increasing vulnerability to competing offers and to defensive measures by the target—but it may also give the acquiror's shareholders an opportunity to waylay a transaction with which they are unhappy. This can be a real possibility since, for reasons described below, the issuer's stock price will typically fall upon the announcement of a stock for stock acquisition.

Price Volatility

In stock for stock acquisitions, risk arbitrageurs will attempt to lock in a profit, subject only to the successful completion of the transaction, by purchasing shares of the target company and selling short shares of the acquiror; if the acquisition is completed, the arbitrageurs will exchange their target shares for shares of the acquiror, which they will then use to cover their short position. This selling pressure can cause a potential acquiror's share price to fall by as much as 5 to 10 percent in a relatively large acquisition. The acquiror's share price might also fall because of concerns with respect to dilution of its earnings per share.

Obviously, the acquiror is taking a risk if it offers to exchange a fixed dollar value of its stock as of some date in the future for each share of the target company's stock; the acquiror will have to issue proportionately more or less stock for any decrease or increase in its price. To deal with this problem, the issuer can fix or put a "collar" on the number of shares it will issue in exchange for the target company's stock (the "exchange ratio").

If the exchange ratio is fixed at, say, 1.2, at the closing, the acquiror will issue exactly 1.2 of its shares for each target company share whether the acquiror's stock price rises or falls subsequent to announcement of the offer. If a collar is used, the initial exchange ratio will be adjusted upward or downward, *within limits*, if the acquiror's stock price falls or rises between the day of announcement and a date on which the final exchange ratio will be determined. A typical collar might allow the initial exchange ratio to vary by no more than 5 percent and, to discourage market manipulation, will be based on the acquiror's average stock price for the 20 days prior to the target company's special shareholder meeting.

In certain cases, a target company's owner(s) may desire a tax-free transaction and/or a continuing interest in the combined company. A transaction will qualify as a tax-free reorganization if at least 50 percent of the total acquisition consideration is in the form of equity securities. (See Chapters 2 and 28.) In the case of most broadly held corporations, however, the vast majority of shareholders will discount the value of securities relative to cash due to transaction costs, questions of liquidity, market volatility, and the time value of money. Therefore, the market value of a common stock offering must exceed a competing cash offer by a material amount to appeal to selling shareholders.

New Classes of Stock

General Motors (GM), through the creation of new classes of stock in connection with two acquisitions, has achieved a unique form of continuity of interest for selling shareholders, as well as certain other tactical and strategic advantages. As part of the consideration used in its acquisitions of Electronic Data Systems and Hughes Aircraft, GM created new classes of stock whose dividend policies are tied to the performance of each of these companies, respectively, rather than the performance of GM as a whole.

To avoid being delisted by the NYSE, the voting and liquidation rights of the new classes of stock were structured so as to be proportionate to those of the existing GM stock. These new classes of stock: (1) appealed to selling shareholders who were reluctant to give up entirely their interest in the future of the target company; (2) helped to preserve management incentives tied to stock performance; and (3) allowed the market to value certain of the diversified company's lines of business separately and more directly. The creation of this type of stock requires that the acquiror maintain the integrity of and deal at "arms length" with the acquired company. In addition, this type of stock does not qualify for pooling-of-interest accounting treatment.

Strategic Considerations

Though scoring poorly on a tactical basis, common stock does have several redeeming characteristics from a strategic standpoint. The new issue market for common stock is limited in depth and can be quite volatile. There is no guarantee that a company will be able to issue common stock on favorable terms at a time of its choosing to refinance debt incurred to fund an acquisition. If a company is unable or unwilling to take this risk, the target company's shareholders may represent a "captive" market for the acquiror's common stock at or near its current price. Under certain circumstances, such as a second-step squeeze-out merger, the acquiror can force the target company's shareholders to accept its stock, and liquidity may not be a major issue.[1]

A 100 percent common stock for common stock exchange offer can, under certain circumstances, qualify for pooling-of-interests accounting treatment and thereby avoid the creation of goodwill in the acquisition. (See Chapters 2 and 28.) In this case, if the acquiror's price/earnings multiple exceeds the price/earnings multiple paid for the target company, its pro forma earnings per share will increase as a result of the transaction. In the late 1960's a number of companies, such as LTV, ITT, Litton, and Gulf & Western played this "earnings per share" game by using their highly valued stock

[1]In a squeeze-out merger, the acquiror will obtain an opinion from an investment bank that its offer (which may include the price paid for shares already purchased) is fair to the selling shareholders from a financial point of view. However, the investment banker will tend to focus on the fundamental economic value of the target company, and may not take transaction costs and liquidity into consideration. In these cases, the security to be issued in the merger is typically valued on a "fully distributed" basis.

to acquire companies with low p/e ratios. Today, investors appear to show greater sophistication in analyzing the value of a company and are giving greater weight to cash flow (which adds back noncash charges such as amortization of goodwill) and less to reported earnings per share. Nevertheless, in two recent transactions, May Department Store's acquisition of Associated Dry Goods and Interco's acquisition of Lane, the buyers were willing to pay substantially higher prices per share in a pooling transaction than in a cash tender offer.

Fairness Opinions

In rendering a fairness opinion to the buyer or the seller in an acquisition involving common stock consideration, the investment banker must take into account the value of both parties to the transaction. Before it can determine whether or not the offering price is fair, the banker must evaluate whether the acquiring company's current stock price truly reflects its fundamental value and how that value will be affected by the proposed acquisition. (See Chapters 18 and 19.)

CONVERTIBLE PREFERRED STOCK

In the early 1980s, when common stock prices were generally depressed and the junk bond market had not yet developed into a major source of acquisition financing, convertible preferred stock was often used as acquisition consideration. Examples of this include Allied Corporation's acquisitions of Bunker Ramo and Fisher Scientific, and Allegheny International's acquisition of Sunbeam.

These and similar transactions were in many ways the precursors of the coercive two-tier front-end loaded acquisition, as roughly half of the target's shares were purchased in a cash tender offer, with the lower value convertible preferred stock issued in a second-step squeeze-out merger.

From a tactical standpoint, convertible preferred stock is very similar to common stock: (1) registration with the SEC is necessary; (2) if it comprises at least 50 percent[2] of the acquisition consideration, the transaction qualifies

---

[2]In Allegheny International's acquisition of Sunbeam, convertible preferred stock accounted for only 40 percent of the total consideration, but the proxy statement stated that various courts have sustained tax-free reorganization treatment in comparable situations.

as a tax-free exchange; (3) the selling shareholder maintains an equity interest in the combined entity; and (4) selling shareholders may discount its value due to concerns about liquidity.

From a strategic standpoint, convertible preferred stock is a hybrid between a nonconvertible subordinated fixed-income security and common stock. Rating agencies will generally treat convertible preferred stock at least partially as equity if it has a sufficiently long average life.

Acquirors wishing to issue common equity but concerned about their current stock price may prefer a convertible security; the exercise price of the convertible will typically be a premium of roughly 20 percent over the common's current market value. However, this premium must be weighed against the increased interest or dividend payout of a like amount of common stock.

As discussed earlier, "poison pills" have been developed which are an effective defense against unsolicited two-tier front-end loaded offers. In addition, the availability of junk bond financing has, in many cases, eliminated the need to use so-called "cram down" securities in squeeze-out mergers. As a result, convertible preferred stock is rarely used as acquisition consideration today.

DEFERRED PAY SECURITIES

A deferred pay security is a debt or preferred stock instrument which pays no cash interest or dividends for a specified period of time, typically two to five years, after which cash interest or dividends are paid at a determined fixed rate until maturity. Deeply subordinated deferred pay securities are frequently used in highly leveraged acquisitions to (1) reduce the cash debt service burden on the acquiror in the early years after the transaction and (2) make it easier for the acquiror to raise more senior funds from banks and other lenders. Deferred pay securities can be sold through private placements or underwritten public offerings or issued directly to the target company's shareholders (commonly referred to as "cram down" securities). In the latter two cases, registration with the SEC is necessary.

Because cram down securities are effectively forced upon the target company's shareholders, the issuer will often have a reasonable degree of flexibility in establishing their terms. As a result, there is somewhat less uniformity of terms in the universe of deferred pay securities than with other fixed-income instruments. Nevertheless, two general models have evolved: (1)

zero to full coupon subordinated debt (ZTFs); and (2) pay-in-kind debentures or preferred stock (PIKs).

Zero to Full Coupon Subordinated Debt

As its name connotes, a ZTF begins as a zero coupon bond which, after a certain period of time, turns into a traditional current pay bond. Generally, the cash interest rate to be paid in the future roughly approximates the current market rate for a security of comparable creditworthiness and maturity. Thus, if the market and the company's risk profile were not to change, the ZTF would be expected to trade at par when it begins to accrue cash interest (the "accrual date"). Its value at issuance would then be determined by applying an appropriate discount rate to par value for the non–interest paying period. Due to heavy selling pressure immediately after issuance, cram down securities usually begin trading at a substantial discount to their theoretical fully distributed value.

Pay-In-Kind Securities

PIKs are similar to ZTFs except that, in the years prior to the payment of cash dividends, interest or dividends are paid in the form of additional securities. Assuming a market dividend rate, this means that the fully distributed value of the PIKs at issuance will be close to par. This does not mean, however, that a PIK will be less expensive to the issuer than a ZTF; if their fully distributed market values are identical at issuance, their principal amounts should be identical as of the cash accrual date. Many PIK preferreds give the issuer the right to exchange the preferred stock for subordinated debentures with identical terms at some point in the future, at which time the acquiror might be a taxpayer and would benefit from the deductability of interest.

Expensive Pricing

Deferred pay securities issued in highly leveraged transactions are very expensive, yielding as much as 300 basis points more than comparable current pay securities. Therefore, the non–pay period should be as short as is acceptable to senior lenders who, in addition to seeking adequate coverage of cash interest charges, expect their principal to be repaid prior to that of junior securities. For these reasons, deferred pay securities are, from the issuer's perspective, usually preferable to zero coupon bonds.

CONTINGENCY PAYMENTS

In certain negotiated acquisitions, the parties to the transaction agree that a business combination would be beneficial but, because of honest differences of opinion as to the target company's financial prospects, cannot agree on price.

Earn-Out: Sharing the Risk

In these situations, a contingency payment, often referred to as an "earn-out," may be used to bridge the gap between the bid and ask. In a typical earn-out, the acquiror agrees to make a future payment to the seller should the target company achieve certain financial objectives. In this way, both parties share in the financial risk that their respective views as to the target company's prospects will or will not be realized.

Private Companies

Contingency payments are most often found in private transactions, particularly when the target company is a family-owned and run business. In these cases the earn-out may serve the dual purpose of (1) getting the deal done and (2) placing "golden handcuffs" on the owner/manager of the target company. If the owner of the target company is critical to its success, the acquiror will want to ensure that he is properly incentivized to remain with and work hard for the company. A long-term management contract may not be sufficient because the seller's new found liquidity could affect his motivation. Therefore, the buyer will want to tie a significant portion of the selling price to the target company's performance over an extended period of time.

Structure of Formula and Strategy of Company

Earn-out formulas, particularly those which extend over a number of years, must be carefully constructed to ensure that: (1) the buyer retains sufficient flexibility with respect to the overall disposition of its investment; (2) the seller is not encouraged to manage the business in a less than optimal way from the buyer's perspective; and (3) both buyer and seller are treated fairly.

If the contingency payment is tied strictly to the performance of the target company, opportunities to consolidate its operation with those of the acquiror may be limited, and all intercompany transactions must be arm's length. In certain cases, it may be more appropriate to tie the contingency payment to consolidated results. If the acquiror thinks it may want to sell parts or all of the target company during the pendency of the earn-out, appropriate provisions must be made.

If the contingency payment is tied to, say, reported earning, it may not be in the seller's best interests to manage the business the way the buyer would want. For example, R&D or capital expenditures might be deferred to maximize near-term earnings at the expense of the long term. These issues must be taken into consideration when establishing the proper financial objectives. If the target company's business is cyclical, it might be appropriate to base the contingency payment on average results over a typical business cycle rather than on a single year's results.

Troubled Companies

In recent years, contingency payments have also been used in the acquisition of troubled public companies, particularly regional commercial banks facing the possibility of massive loan write-offs. The first such transaction was BankAmerica Corporation's acquisition of Seafirst Corporation in 1983, in which approximately half of the merger consideration was cash and half a new series of BankAmerica preferred stock. Both the face amount and the dividend rate of the preferred stock are subject to adjustment if, in the five years subsequent to the merger, the write-off of certain pre-existing Seafirst loans, net of recoveries, exceeds a specified amount. BankAmerica and Seafirst jointly selected "umpires" to review each write-off and, if inappropriate, disallow them.

In Chemical New York Corporation's acquisition of Texas Commerce BankShares (TCB) in 1987, a new class of Chemical common stock whose dividend (and ultimate conversion ratio into Chemical common stock) in five years is based upon TCB's retained earnings subsequent to the merger. In order to ensure that TCB was operated on a stand-alone, arm's-length basis, its bylaws required that the majority of its board members not be affiliated with Chemical. In Republic Bank Corporation's acquisition of InterFirst Corporation, the merger consideration included a new class of Republic common stock whose dividend and conversion ratio is based on consolidated earnings because of a planned integration of the two banks' operations. (See Volume I, Chapter 21.)

SUMMARY

The financing and funding of transactions is one of the most dynamic and creative aspects of mergers and acquisitions. Innovations such as the leveraged buyout, two-tier front-end loaded offers, and deferred pay securities have been largely responsible for the dramatic increase in M&A activity in recent years.

Such creativity, however, must be tempered by an appreciation of the limitations imposed (or opportunities created) by the ever changing capital markets. "Black Monday" and the resultant temporary closure of the new issue junk bond market was a painful reminder that, at least with respect to the financing of M&A transactions, the past is not always prologue to the future. Success in the practice of M&A requires state-of-the-art knowledge of the relevant legal issues, valuation techniques, takeover tactics and, particularly today, the financing opportunities available under current market conditions.

CHAPTER 6

DO MEGAMERGERS MAKE SENSE?

Kenneth M. Davidson

For over a decade we have witnessed a spectacular increase in megamergers. What began as a trickle of $100 million acquisitions in the 1970s (14 in 1975, 80 in 1978) became a flood in the 1980s (200 in 1984, 346 in 1986). Once rare billion-dollar transactions have now become almost commonplace. There were only four acquisitions valued at more than $1 billion in 1980, but twelve in 1981, eighteen in 1984, and in 1985 the total doubled to thirty-six. By themselves those thirty-six transactions accounted for more than half of the $180 billion paid for all acquisitions in that year.

Despite the evident growth and persistence of these megamergers, there have been repeated suggestions (hopes) that this merger wave might be ended as a result of changes in the legal environment. The Federal Reserve banned junk bond financing (for certain corporate structures). The Tax Reform Act of 1986 eliminated preferential rates for capital gains. The Supreme Court upheld state anti-takeover laws. State courts upheld "poison pill" defenses. And acquisition transactions have been the prime substrate of insider trading scandals.

Yet there has been no slowdown in mergers and acquisitions. Instead, the wave has continued to roll. But even if the total were to decline, the phenomenon of megamergers is unlikely to disappear. The source of these

---

This chapter is derived from *The Journal of Business Strategy*, Volume 7, Number 3 (Winter 1987), pages 40–48. The author is an attorney with the Federal Trade Commission. The chapter reflects the personal opinions of the author and not necessarily those of the Federal Trade Commission.

giant transactions now seems embedded in the structure of the U.S. capital markets if not the entire economy.

This wave of takeovers began with two large diversification acquisitions in 1974: Mobil's $1.6 billion acquisition of Marcor and the bidding war that resulted in International Nickel's takeover of ESB. These two transactions changed the takeover rules for investment banking and established a new mainstream for megamergers. First, these basically hostile transactions were strongly resisted, initially, by the target companies. Second, that hostility was overwhelmed by the unprecedented size of the cash premium offered for the target's stock. Third, the targets were large, apparently well-run companies. Fourth, the acquiring companies were well-known, successful blue-chip firms.

These characteristics were in direct contrast to the conglomerate mergers of the 1960s. Then, the acquirors tended to be smaller companies (e.g., Textron, Ling-Tempco-Vought, Litton, Gulf & Western, and ITT) that achieved their size and reputations as a result of acquisitions. They made many more and much smaller acquisitions. Gulf & Western alone made 67 between 1961 and 1968. In contrast to 1985's 3,000 merger total, W.T. Grimm recorded a total of 6,107 mergers for 1968, the peak year of the conglomerate wave. In addition, the acquisitions of the 1960s were more likely to be friendly deals and more often for stock than cash.

From their increasing popularity, one might think that megamergers have been profitable and that the biggest deals were even more so. Experience does not provide support for such conclusions. If anything the reverse appears to be more true (See Figure 1).

How, then, can one explain this merger trend that has continued to grow during stock market highs and lows, economic expansion and recession, stagflation and disinflation? Megamergers are the product of a small number

FIGURE 1
Divested or Economically Disappointing Megamergers

Acquiring Firm	*Target*
Mobil	Marcor
General Electric	Utah International
Arco	Anaconda
R.J. Reynolds	Sea-Land
Coca-Cola	Taylor Wines
Phillip Morris	7-Up
Exxon	Reliance Electric
RCA	CIT Financial
Kennecott	Carborundum

of precedent-setting business transactions which, once accomplished, opened new possibilities for takeovers. Collectively, these precedents produced defensive mergers, greenmail, leveraged buyouts, golden parachutes, and other forms of acquisition activity.

The acquisitions by the largest, best-known, most successful corporations in the United States have shaped the megamerger wave in two ways. They established the financial and stock market precedents that made large takeovers technically feasible, thus opening the way for other acquirors. Subsequently, the evident economic failure of these mainstream megamergers helped set in motion a cycle of aftershock acquisitions—divestitures or takeovers of firms that could not manage their targets. And, unless corporate managers learn from these merger mistakes, more profitless acquisitions and more takeovers of acquiring firms can be expected.

If managers are to avoid repeating the mistakes of the past fifteen years, they must appreciate the reasons mainstream megamergers arose and better alternatives that exist. Over the past decade, the stock market has developed a distinguishable reaction to these flawed acquisitions. Corporations formed by megamergers have become vulnerable to takeovers, apparently because they have become too complex to be managed effectively.

WHY MEGAMERGERS?

During the 1970s, some of the United States' largest and most successful firms faced a problem. They were accumulating, and expected to continue to accumulate, more revenues than they could invest in their traditional lines of business. Megamergers provided a logical investment solution to this problem for the reasons described below.

Accumulating Profits

For some firms, and especially those in oil, automobiles, cigarettes, liquor, and soft drinks, this overabundant accumulation of profits, this free cash flow, was a new problem. Throughout the post-World War II economic boom, these companies grew through internal expansion of their primary business by exploiting the growing affluence in North America and followed that economic expansion to Europe and then to the Third World.

They were exceptional in confining their growth to a single dominant business. Most U.S. companies had diversified. In 1949, 70 percent of the 500 largest industrial firms in the United States earned 95 percent of their revenues from one business. By 1969, as a result of acquistions and internal investment, 70 percent of the largest firms no longer had a dominant business.

Because of the great success of their dominant business, these exceptional firms grew dramatically. Thus, when they perceived that they had reached the frontier of the world's economy, when they began to bump into other multinationals abroad and found themselves challenged at home, they were forced by accumulating profits to look beyond their established patterns of business.

Alternative Choices for Using Profits

Apart from overinvestment in their basic business, they had five major options:

- Distributing the profits to shareholders
- Starting new businesses
- Investing in securities
- Giving the profits to employees
- Making acquisitions

Whereas all were undertaken, acquisitions (i.e., megamergers) had a special attraction for firms with the greatest accumulation of profits. Unlike the alternatives, there was no limit on the amount of funds that could be absorbed by acquisitions.

Each of the other options quickly reached an obvious limit. The oil industry reached a point in the 1970s where, even with record crude oil prices, the companies were drilling for new reserves in doubtful places at even more dubious prices. Liquor, soft drink, and cigarette companies reached a saturation point where further advertising could only raise costs and diminish profits.

Distributing Profits

Distribution of profits to shareholders, although theoretically the appropriate disposition of earnings, runs contrary to federal income tax incentives and against the inclinations of corporate managers. Federal tax laws have encouraged corporations to retain earnings by taxing dividends at higher rates than capital gains. Consequently, a shareholder was better off leaving untaxed profits in the corporation to be reinvested. He could later realize the increased value of his investment by selling his corporate stock and then being taxed at the lower capital gains rate. Managers thereby obtained significant discretion in reinvesting corporate earnings.

Starting New Businesses

Using profits to start up new businesses is often unsatisfactory in several ways. New businesses are very risky ventures. Because they are new, it is difficult to develop hard data to persuade a board of directors that production cost objectives can be met or market share projections can be achieved. Moreover, prudence usually requires new ventures to be started on a scale that does not approach the billion-dollar amounts that have become typical of megamergers. Most of all, however, the risk of a failure that must be completely written off is most acute for new ventures. Exxon's ten-year, $ 2 billion excursion into office automation systems is a lesson for those who believe otherwise.

Buying Securities

Buying securities poses different kinds of risks. Too large a percentage of passive investments could result in punitive tax rates if earnings are accumulated "beyond the reasonable needs of the business."[1] But long before the tax authorities become interested in those earnings, they are likely to attract the attention of other companies. Those companies can use a target's liquid assets to pay off takeover costs. Consequently, to maintain a large portion of assets in that form can jeopardize a corporation's independence.

Paying Employees

There is little doubt that line employees as well as top executives routinely capture a portion of a company's profits. Evidence from the auto, steel, and deregulated airline industries shows when competitive forces change, employees' compensation may have to be lowered to maintain a viable business. But even during more stable, profitable times, compensation levels of individual firms are normally in accord with an industry standard that does not absorb accumulating profits.

Making Acquisitions

Megamergers generally avoid the difficulties of directing accumulating profits posed by these alternatives. The acquisition target has an established production process and a market share from which earnings and thus value can be projected. As a consequence, even acquisition blunders such as Exxon's $1.6 billion takeover of Reliance Electric do not normally have the potential to be completely written off (unlike Exxon's office automation systems venture). Acquisitions benefit from favorable tax treatment by cashing out the target company shareholders at capital gains rates. And acquisitions dispose of liquid assets that make firms immediately vulnerable to takeovers.

Although it is likely that megamergers were viewed as profitable investments, rather than merely as safe repositories for retained earnings, they frequently failed to achieve even that lesser status. Figure 1 includes a group of early megamergers where the target firm was subsequently divested or economically disappointing for the acquiring firm. All of these mergers occurred before the annual merger totals took off in 1981 and their poor results were well-known long before the record-shattering megamerger years of 1984 and 1985.

REACTIONS TO MAINSTREAM MEGAMERGERS

One reaction to these mainstream megamergers was to induce imitation. After all, it seemed giant takeovers could not be a silly idea if Mobil, General Electric, R.J. Reynolds, Coca-Cola, and Exxon were all buying large firms in unrelated businesses. The Boston Consulting Group cash-box matrix provided a popular framework for thinking about diversification and a plausible theory of how to manage the resulting more complex corporation. So the megamerger movement was able to create its own momentum.

Defensive Megamergers

It is clear that momentum quickly caused fear in the corporate community. As early as 1978, when there were a scant eighty mergers valued at $100 million or more, 40 percent of the nation's largest businesses identified themselves as potential takeover targets. By 1982, more than 1,500 companies had amended their corporate charters or bylaws to provide income-protecting "golden parachutes" for their managers. And, more recently, hundreds of firms have also adopted "fair price" or supermajority provisions to make takeovers more difficult. (Chapters 21–26).

In its early phase, it seemed that larger firms could fend off takeover attempts. Mead Corporation fought off Occidental Petroleum's 1978 billion-dollar tender offer. McGraw-Hill defeated American Express's 1979 attempt. As a consequence, some firms may have tried to grow to an indigestible size; Carrier Corporation, for example, tried (unsuccessfully) to avoid a takeover by buying Jenn-Air. But as hostile takeover tactics and billion-dollar acquisitions became more common, it became clear that large size would not deter takeovers.

Nevertheless, defensive takeovers helped swell the merger totals. Firms with liquid assets made acquisitions, sometimes very quickly, to avoid takeovers. Hiram Walker and the Disney Corporation both deflected attempted takeovers, in part, by stripping themselves of cash reserves through acquisitions that cost hundreds of millions of dollars. Others such as Kennecott, Seagram, and McDermott made major acquisitions to forestall takeover attempts by spending their liquid assets. And once a firm like Bendix, under William Agee, amassed funds to finance a takeover, it thereby became committed to making some takeover if it wanted to avoid becoming a target as a result of its own cash reserves. And, as Agee found to his chagrin, a target might also avoid takeover by buying the firm trying to acquire it. As a consequence, in contested takeover battles, the contending firms frequently became acquirors for defensive reasons.

Leveraged Buyouts

A more direct defensive tactic is the self-tender offer—a bid by the target for its own shares at a price higher than that offered by the acquiring firm. The tactic, successfully used as early as 1975 by the Hi-Shear Corporation, gained great prominence in 1985 when it was the centerpiece of the effective defenses mounted by Phillips Petroleum, Unocal, CBS, and Union Carbide.

For the incumbent management of the target, the ultimate defense is to take the company private. The use of leveraged buyouts for this purpose (and for future profits) was pioneered by the merchant banking firm of Kohlberg, Kravis, Roberts & Co. (KKR) but was quickly followed by others. KKR started by taking smaller companies private, such as the 1979 buyout of Houdaille Industries, for hundreds of millions of dollars. With experience, and as their reputation and financial contacts grew, they were able to raise $6.2 billion in 1985 to take the Beatrice Corporation private and then in 1988 $25 billion to take RJR Nabisco private! Along the way, many other large companies went private, including Metromedia, Macy's, Uniroyal, Levi's, Dr Pepper, Mary Kay Cosmetics, and Wometco.

If management was attracted to leveraged buyouts partly as a way of avoiding takeovers, KKR, Forstmann, Little & Co., and other investors have been attracted partly by the substantial tax savings from switching equity to debt. Because interest payments are deductible from corporate profits and dividends are not, the buyer can come out ahead on the same cash flow. Using debt, the buyer can afford to pay a premium to those lending the money and still end up with higher profits because as much as half the interest costs are borne by the U.S. Treasury. (Of course the greater debt also makes the company more vulnerable to bankruptcy if the cash flow diminishes.)

Leveraged Takeovers

There was what incumbent managers must have viewed as a parallel darker side of mirror image in the development of leveraged acquisitions. While KKR was developing means to join management in taking their companies private, Carl Icahn was doing the same for his investment partners to take over public companies. Like KKR, he started with smaller companies, but by 1985 he made a multibillion-dollar failed (but profitable) attempt to buy Phillips Petroleum, and later that year succeeded in gaining control of TWA.

Icahn, Sir James Goldsmith, T. Boone Pickens, and others have been viewed with special hostility by incumbent management, because frequently their takeover attempts have been for the purpose of obtaining quick profits—

either from greenmail for dropping the takeover bid or, after gaining control, from breaking up and reselling the company in pieces. In the 1970s, Carl Icahn broke from the ranks of risk arbitrageurs who speculate on merger transactions by refusing to wait for takeover attempts. He sought out undervalued or mismanaged companies, invested in their shares and then provoked a takeover or corporate breakup. He hired the merger lawyers who developed takeover tactics for large corporations and enlisted the capital of investors by the lure of large profits earned by risk arbitrageurs.

When Icahn tapped into the Drexel, Burnham & Lambert "junk bond" network in an assault on Phillips Petroleum, corporate size ceased to be a takeover barrier. Anyone, it seemed, with personal credibility and a plausible profit story had the potential to mount a major takeover attempt, at least until the Federal Reserve Board limited junk-bond financing of takeovers.

The potential profits from breaking up these leveraged takeovers is substantial. Forstmann, Little & Co., for example, acquired Dr Pepper in 1984 for $623 million, all but $30 million of which was borrowed. By selling the bottling plants and Canada Dry division, that debt was reduced to $170 million. Thus, in 1986, when a group including Cadbury-Schweppes purchased Dr Pepper for $416 million, Forstmann, Little stood to earn $250 million from its $30 million investment. Similarly, John Kluge, who took Metromedia private in 1984 for $1.6 billion, realized $2 billion on the sale of its television stations alone and another $1.6 billion from the sale of its mobile phone and paging services. Other divestitures brought in another $1 billion.

Conglomerate Megamergers

There have been growing numbers of acquisitions of large conglomerate corporations. Esmark bought Norton Simon. Esmark was bought by Beatrice. Beatrice itself was bought in a leveraged buyout. R.J. Reynolds bought Heublein and Nabisco. Bendix tried to buy RCA and Martin Marietta, but instead Bendix was bought by Allied, which also bought Signal Corporation. General Electric bought RCA.

These transactions, unlike the conglomerate mergers of the 1960s, are very large acquisitions. Rather than growing by adding a number of small single-line businesses, these transactions join together already large, highly diversified companies. In terms of size, they resemble the mainstream megamerger transactions, but their purpose seems distinct.

Unlike most megamergers, these transactions are less frequently an outlet for an overabundant cash flow. More often, the takeover of these conglomerates is based in part on an expectation of profits from breaking up the targets. In this, the objectives are closer to the breakup premise of many leveraged buyouts and the Icahn/Pickens takeover strategies.

The Bendix offer for RCA, for example, assumed that much of the cost could be recouped by selling off poorly performing divisions such as CIT Financial and Hertz to managers with more experience relevant to those businesses. And, indeed, RCA sold both divisions to firms in more closely related businesses in an effort to bolster its share price to remain independent. RCA provided further evidence that conglomerates are vulnerable targets if they become too diversified to be managed effectively. When it was taken over by General Electric, RCA Chairman Thornton Bradshaw conceded that a higher price might have been obtained if he had been willing to split divisions "up into little pieces and parcel them out to the highest bidder."

The histories of Allied, Dart & Kraft, and General Electric also suggest overdiversification through acquisition. After buying Bendix and Signal, Allied quickly spun off business units worth more than $3 billion in an effort to create two companies, each with a more coherent focus. Dart & Kraft, in contrast, tried for five years to run its combined operations before spinning off in 1986 a $2 billion company that included Tupperware, West Bend, Hobart, and Wilsonart. And General Electric, prior to buying RCA, sold off a $5 billion chunk of its enterprise, including Utah International (for $2.4 billion), Family Financial Services, and several radio and television stations. GE claimed the $6 billion merger with RCA would build on their strengths in the electronics and defense industries.

These acquisition-divestitures are part of a larger trend among conglomerates to reduce the diversity of their enterprises. ITT, for example, has sold 85 of its business ventures. Gulf & Western has divested 50 operations. International Harvester (Navistar) sold its farm equipment division. Singer spun off its sewing machine business (before being taken over itself by Paul Bilzerian). All of these actions reflect the growing belief that there are limits to the number of businesses managers can understand and that businesses are worth more to managers that understand them because they can run them better.

Acquiring Competitors

The trend away from programs of broad corporate diversification is also reflected in a resurgence of intraindustry acquisitions. The two largest megamergers in history occurred in 1984 between competing firms: Chevron's $13 billion acquisition of Gulf Oil and Texaco's $10 billion acquisition of Getty Oil. Since the passage of the Celler-Kefauver Amendments to the Clayton Antitrust Act in 1950, mergers of large competitors had virtually disappeared. But beginning in the late 1970s, it began to appear that the antitrust laws were no longer an insurmountable barrier.

At first, these large mergers seemed to reflect only established exceptions to otherwise stringent antitrust standards. The 1960s' Penn Central merger of competing New York-Chicago railroads presented a compelling example of one such exception: the acquisition of a failing company that would otherwise go out of business. Combining Youngtown Sheet & Tube with Jones & Laughlin to form LTV Steel in 1982 may also have fit that model. The giant railroad mergers of the 1970s and 1980s, however, were rationalized on two other theories. The railroads operated in different geographic markets and thus did not compete with each other. Also, because they both competed in a transportation market against trucks, barges, and airplanes, it could be argued that the railroads had only a small share of that total market that was not significantly increased by the mergers.

The "different geographic market" exception was more clearly applicable to the print media mergers of Gannett, Newhouse, and Rupert Murdoch. The wave of financial company mergers that combined banking, brokerage, insurance, credit cards, and real estate were plausibly justified as exempt on the ground that they combined different businesses. And the oil mergers, which led the way in establishing new size records in 1979 when Shell acquired Belridge Oil for $3.6 billion, successfully argued that there were so many multibillion-dollar oil companies combining that even the largest would not significantly reduce competition.

If permitting all of the above mergers was consistent with antitrust enforcement policies developed after 1950, the same could not be said of a series of merger announcements beginning in 1985. These included mergers between leading dishwasher manufacturers, tire makers, soft drink companies, and airlines. These were all industries that appeared to have relatively few competitors, therefore it would have been assumed that mergers between major competitors would be challenged.

However, from the outset, the antitrust agencies and judges appointed under the Reagan Administration have expressed a different attitude toward antitrust. Although the agencies continue to condemn anticompetitive practices, they have emphasized a companion concern that enforcement of the antitrust laws not inhibit efficient business practices. Mergers between direct competitors are, for example, more likely to create efficiencies than mergers between unrelated businesses, both because there is a greater potential for eliminating duplicate facilities and because the management of the acquiring firm is more likely to understand the business of the target. The agencies became, therefore, less ready to presume that mergers between competitors are anticompetitive. They required some greater indication that competition would be reduced before they would prevent a merger that might enhance efficiency.

Given the shift in enforcement emphasis, it was only a matter of time before some firms began to explore how far the new antitrust line had moved. The courts and the antitrust agencies both declined to oppose Whirlpool's acquisition of Kitchen Aid. Ultimately, the antitrust agencies permitted Texas Air to buy Eastern Airlines after divesting landing rights at Washington's National Airport, but challenged Coca-Cola's and Pepsi's attempts to swallow Dr Pepper and 7-Up.

What is most significant for this discussion is that these acquisitions fit the pattern of corporate actions away from diversification. Like the conglomerate divestitures and leveraged acquisition plans, the trend toward acquisitions of competing firms seems to reflect managers' misgivings about their ability to operate many unrelated businesses. In some instances, they may seek to acquire competitors for the prospect of monopoly profits. But obtaining obvious monopoly profits by merger must still run the time-consuming antitrust gauntlet, and lesser mergers contain no guarantee of great financial reward even if the acquisition is permitted. Consequently, it seems likely that much of this trend toward intraindustry mergers is based as much on a conscious decision by firms to stay with businesses they know.

ARE MEGAMERGERS WORTHWHILE?

Whether megamergers are worthwhile depends, to a great extent, on which mergers and what alternatives are compared. It surely made more sense for R.J. Reynolds to pour its profits into Heublein or Nabisco than it would have to invest in more intensive cigarette advertising. From the standpoints of both public health and corporate profits, more advertisements are likely to have been more harmful. But would a stock buyback or a different kind of an acquisition have made more sense? Is there any justification (other than the inevitability of some errors) for billion-dollar misacquisitions, such as Exxon's purchase of Reliance Electric or Sohio's purchase of Kennecott? Was the unsuccessful management of Montgomery Ward department stores by Mobil foreseeable or avoidable?

Mergers Generally Suffer

The evolution of megamergers suggests answers to at least some of these questions. It seems clear that the pure diversification mergers are extremely risky ventures. Perhaps because the stock market places lower values on overly diversified firms, economic studies show that the price of acquiring a firm's shares tends to drop following a takeover. Other studies have shown that the profitability of merged firms declines and that targets grow less rapidly after being acquired. The conclusion that mergers can weaken firms is also demonstrated by the support and credibility the stock markets have given to leveraged takeover efforts premised on breaking up the firm. And it explains why a firm like Union Carbide can beat off a takeover attempt by promising to break itself up.

It is not that all megamergers are doomed to failure. They may succeed. Occasionally, even a purely conglomerate corporation will sustain an outstanding success over a long period of time. But F.M. Scherer and David Ravenscraft's longitudinal study of merged firms shows that although Teledyne has been spectacularly successful, the performance of most businesses suffer as a result of being acquired (Federal Trade Commission Working Paper, 1986).

Predicting is Difficult

Predicting which few mergers will be profitable is difficult for many reasons. The most important reasons relate to unforeseeable economic forces, such as consumer demand or cost of inputs, that affect all businesses in that industry. But beyond generic economic factors, the prospects for integrating targets into the acquired firm is often equally unpredictable. The economic theories of Richard Nelson and Sidney Winter explain why managers lack the necessary information: To a high degree, large corporations operate on the basis of routine acquisition, production, and distribution procedures that are never made explicit, that are not known or even knowable by any single individual. Consequently, it is always possible that changes associated with a takeover will adversely disrupt those routine operations. And it is certain that no one can specify in advance how two complex organizations in similar businesses, such as GE and RCA, will be able to integrate their operations.

In addition to undermining forecasts of profits, the uncertainty associated with takeovers also weakens the case that acquisitions (i.e., the market for corporate control) can act as a discipline on inefficient managers. The market discipline theory holds that the price of shares in poorly managed firms will fall to a point where more able managers will be induced to buy the firms because they can run them more efficiently. But because of uncertainty, the general proposition that acquiring firms can project the usefulness of managerial changes, other than very gross ones, is not plausible.

An acquiring firm could plan, for example, to provide a different source of capital or decide to replace one existing distribution system with another existing system. However, the firm could not confidently expect to improve existing systems of a large organization as a result of takeovers.

CEOs of acquiring firms have repeatedly denied that their takeovers are premised on revitalizing an existing business. Harry Gray of United Technologies, for example, stated, "We never go for a turnaround situation. . . . Maybe somebody can do that but we can't." Royal Little, founder of Textron, was more specific on the reason for not trying to buy firms to improve them: "It's fantastic the number of things you can do that don't work out."

Breakup Takeovers and Leveraged Buyouts

Although the general takeover discipline theory seems unlikely to be relevant to most acquisitions, two narrower subsets of takeovers have greater promise: breakup takeovers and leveraged buyouts by divisional or plant managers. In both instances, it is assumed that the value of shares in the target corporation has fallen because its executives cannot effectively manage operations that have become too diverse. The higher takeover price is justified by the breakup. The new managers of the smaller or less diversified company are presumed to understand the business better and, consequently, it is believed they will profit by avoiding mistakes that are currently being made.

The general idea is that the Beatrice leveraged buyout was the logical consequence of Esmark's buying Norton Simon and Beatrice's buying Esmark. The problems of operating the businesses of these diverse conglomerates are more likely to be increased than solved when one conglomerate took over another. Unlike production or marketing problems, excessive diversity and complexity can be addressed by making changes solely at the top. That remedy does not necessarily depend on altering complex operating routines. Manufacturers Hanover Trust Co., may be able to understand better the problems of CIT Financial and to make better capital allocation decisions for it than RCA would because Manufacturers Hanover is in the financial industry. United Airlines might have managed Hertz better than RCA did because it is a transportation company. But look what happened to United's so-called business "synergies"—"Allegis" had a short life, selling Hertz to Ford and Hilton International to the Ladbroke Group.

When corporate problems can be addressed by making changes at the top, then some firm or person—a KKR, a Carl Icahn, a Sir James Goldsmith—can make a profit by buying a company and selling it off in pieces to more appropriate managers. Or managers may offer a premium price directly for that portion of an overly diverse firm that fits their capabilities.

No Letup in Megamergers

Experience therefore confirms the common sense that megamergers are risky, although more likely to be successful if the target is in the same or a related business. That experience, however, is not very helpful to the type of firms that initiated megamergers. For various reasons, these companies find they can no longer invest substantial amounts of their earnings in their own or related businesses.

There is no indication of any letup in these giant retained-earnings acquisitions. In the past five years, General Motors has bought Hughes Aircraft and EDS. Ford bought Nationwide Savings & Loan. Philip Morris bought General Foods, and R.J. Reynolds bought Nabisco. Even General Electric's $6 billion acquisition of RCA did not exhaust its reserves of cash and marketable securities. These transactions, which are among the largest ever consummated, cannot help but have a profound effect on the future of these firms.

The question for firms with accumulating profits is whether they will devise strategies to grow by merger or whether a succession of mergers will make them vulnerable to a subsequent breakup or takeover. The answer remains in doubt.

New Business Focus

Some companies, such as R.J. Reynolds, seem to have made a serious effort in the past decade to establish a separate business focus through their acquisitions. Reynolds has built its food-related products division from Chun King and Hawaiian Punch by the acquisitions of Del Monte, Heublein, and Nabisco. At the same time, it has divested the Sea-Land containerized shipping business and its oil and gas interests. Although the new constellation of acquisitions has neither a sharp business focus nor a profit potential that approaches current earnings in cigarettes, the related nature of many of the newer product lines may make the group more manageable. The learning associated with one may be transferable to managing the others. Similarly,

U.S. Steel has continued to make major oil and gas purchases following its acquisition of Marathon Oil.

For other companies, the prospect is much more uncertain. They seem to cast their acquisition net in one direction and then another in the hope of a lucky strike. Exxon failed with its acquisition of Reliance Electric, but did no better with its even more costly internal attempt to develop an automated office systems division. Coca-Cola tried with Taylor and Mogen David Wines and then tried again with Columbia Pictures. Perhaps these very large companies can afford to speculate one at a time on large new business ventures.

Growing to Unmanageability

The danger for the corporate entity and its stockholders is that managers will continue to add on businesses until the entire company becomes unmanageable. For example, is General Motors, which is struggling to compete in the automobile business about which it knows a great deal, likely to become a stronger company by adding Hughes and EDS, which compete in fields in which it has no expertise? Is General Electric, with the addition of RCA and Kidder Peabody, likely to be more or less manageable? Will these companies become tomorrow's vulnerable conglomerates that need to be dismembered?

Stock Buybacks

The argument that these firms must make acquisitions if they are to avoid takeovers is not persuasive. As Union Carbide, CBS, and Phillips Petroleum have shown, even in the context of takeover battles, a stock buyback program can raise the price of the target's stock over a takeover bid by cashing out target stockholders (at capital gains rates) who value the stock at a lower level. Exxon's $2.3 billion buyback of its shares in 1985 was surely a better bet for its shareholders than its earlier investments in electric motors and office systems. IBM, Ford, and other large corporations have all made major buybacks that bolstered their stock prices. These seem preferable to a directionless acquisition program.

In the aftermath of the 1960s' conglomerate merger wave, there developed a consensus that these organizations were too complex to run efficiently. By the early 1980s, a similar appraisal was made of mainstream megamergers. Although there seems to be an attempt by some to incorporate those assessments in designing megamergers, overall large, successful companies with overabundant profits continue to include as targets businesses about which they know nothing. That is unfortunate.

Mainstream megamergers are unlikely to benefit shareholders, managers, or the public. Shareholders of unmanageable corporations lose as the value of their stock declines. The public loses because of higher costs from inefficient business operations and because of disruption to communities when corporate entities are acquired, only to be resold after decline. And for managers, this acquisition policy aimed at corporate growth and independence can be self-defeating. Acquisitions using excess cash flow may provide only the illusion of safety from takeovers. If the breakup value exceeds the selling price of the corporation's shares, the managers will continue to find themselves under seige.

It is time to break this cycle of megamergers. One does not need to have acquisitions followed by divestiture or dismemberment followed by more acquisitions. Managers need not buy blindly in a frenetic takeover market. They can follow the leads of those who have made only acquisitions of businesses related to their current operations and those which have pursued a consistent acquisition policy to develop a new business focus. If these options are not available, managers should shrink the size of their corporation by buying back a portion of its shares.

ENDNOTES

1. See I.R.C. §§ 532 et seq.

CHAPTER 7

MERGERS AND ACQUISITIONS FOR PRIVATE COMPANIES

Robert Lawrence Kuhn

The merger or sale of a private company differs in style and substance from the merger or sale of a public company.[1] Such a transaction is usually a unique event in the life of the owners of that private company, who are often the entrepreneurial founders or their families. Most likely, the entrepreneur will never have sold his or her business before and the prospects are both bitter and sweet. On the one hand, it is time to enjoy the financial rewards after years of hard work. On the other hand, selling your company feels like selling your baby.

Our orientation in this chapter is that of investment bankers representing sellers or buyers of privately held companies. With the increased activity in entrepreneurial ventures, there is a growing market for mergers and acquisitions (M&A) among private companies. Investment bankers should be sensitive to the special issues involved and not assume that "M&A is M&A."

In most respects, private company M&A is not much different from traditional M&A. Virtually all of the issues involved in finding, facilitating, valuing, pricing, strategizing, and structuring M&A transactions apply equally well to private companies as to public companies (Chapters 1–4). What we

[1] Note that we define "private company" to mean those nonpublic companies whose shareholder/owners or their families are active members of management or at least members of the board of directors. We do not include in this definition subsidiaries or divisions of public companies, though technically they are also private.

stress in this chapter are the exceptions (i.e., those areas where private company M&A *differs* from traditional M&A: personal motivations for selling, personal motivations when selling, business analysis, financial analysis, and structuring the deal). These differences may seem subtle, but whether or not the deal gets done often depends on whether or not such subtleties get sensed. We conclude with some thoughts about the role of investment bankers in private company transactions.

PERSONAL MOTIVATIONS FOR SELLING

From the viewpoint of a private business owner, there are four primary driving motivations for merging or selling his or her business: personal liquidity, expansion capital, personal liability, and generation transition.

Personal Liquidity

First, clearly, is the desire to liquify one's personal holdings. In many cases, the seller is the founder of the company and his or her personal wealth is virtually 100 percent tied up in the business. Here is the first opportunity to reap the financial fruit of one's labor, to diversify one's portfolio ("taking some chips off the table"), to enjoy the material benefits of building a successful business.

In many cases, achieving security and confidence rather than making maximum monies is most important. Many entrepreneurs have been living on the edge for years—their risk/reward profile has skewed far toward high risk—and they look forward to reducing the incessant pressure.

Expansion Capital

The second reason for sale is the recurring need for expansion capital. The only thing more financially taxing than a stagnant business is a growing business. Growth demands capital—for research and development, plant and equipment, inventory and receivables, distribution and service, and a host of administrative necessities.

Oftentimes, good growth companies outrun their internal financial capabilities (even supported by commercial banks), and the public markets are either not available or not desirable. Suddenly, these small and medium-sized companies find themselves competing against larger players in larger markets. Success has catapulted them into a different league, and competing in the new league requires new strengths. Many companies have discovered, to their chagrin, that success at one size does not guarantee success at another size.[2]

Personal Liability

The desire for financial reward and the need for expansion capital are not the only motivations for private company merger or sale. The elimination of personal liabilities can be a powerful stimulant.

The most common kind of personal liabilities are personal guarantees of company debt.[3] Many owners of private businesses are required to support their company's credit with commercial banks by giving their own commitments; this pledge means that they are legally obligated to use their own private assets to pay back any bank debt that the company is unable to pay for any reason whatsoever. (The owners' signatures may even be required for real estate mortgages.) In many cases, such personal guarantees originated years before in the early, risky days of the business and just were never removed. (There are few things harder to do in business than to take away security from a bank once they have it.)

Successful entrepreneurs are self-confident to a fault and may not give those guarantees a thought or a worry. That is a serious mistake: Such guarantees may put at risk a family's entire net worth. In business, there is no certainty. You can never control the future. Eliminating personal guarantees and liabilities is an entirely appropriate motive for selling a business.

Generational Transition

Generational transition is another reason that owners of privately held businesses seek to sell. Private businesses are often sold as part of the estate planning or settlement process. They are also sold to resolve family disputes, generally occurring when the founders' progeny encounter fundamental disagreements (both personal and professional).

---

[2] Robert Lawrence Kuhn, *Creativity and Strategy in Mid-Sized Firms* (Englewood Cliffs, NJ, Prentice-Hall, 1989).

[3] Other forms of personal liability include tax obligations (e.g., employee withholding taxes), product liability (on occasion), and personal damages.

Motivations of Acquirors

From the viewpoint of potential acquirors of privately held companies, motivations are more traditional. Good private companies may have proprietary products or technology. They may have a solid position in a small market niche and enjoy strong customer loyalty. Often such companies have product lines that can be expanded dramatically when supported by adequate resources, organizational and financial. There can be high market leverage in privately held companies.

PERSONAL MOTIVATIONS WHEN SELLING

In most cases involving the sale of private companies, emotions run high. When it comes to their businesses, owners of closely held businesses usually think beyond dollar signs. Their motivations encompass more than the simple maximization of purchase price.

Broad Concerns

Consideration to founder/owners takes on broader meaning, expressing itself in nonfinancial terms as well as financial numbers. For example, a continuing involvement in the business is desired by many selling entrepreneurs. In these situations, remuneration may play a more minor part. Participating in the business and assuring its continuing success are the things that count.

The nonfinancial concerns of selling shareholder/managers frequently reach beyond themselves and involve their employees and even their customers and vendors. The company founder feels a sense of family for those with whom he or she has long worked. Loyalty is a typical trait that entrepreneurs value in employees and associates, and at the time of the sale many come to realize that loyalty should be a two-way street.

Comfort with New Owners

It is important for founder/owners to feel comfortable with the new management and owners. Will they do right by the company and its people? Will they preserve what the founder built? Private company transactions often fall apart when the founders or their families "just didn't feel right" about the prospective buyers. (For example, this hesitation might develop if part of the new owner's plans would involve plant relocations and employee layoffs or a cheapening of the quality image of the company's products.) Conversely, more than a few private company transactions were made in which the new buyers were not the highest bidder but were the "best people."

BUSINESS ANALYSIS

Due diligence is critical to all mergers and acquisitions, and there are standard systems of "business reviews" that are an essential part of the process (Chapter 10). We assume that such detailed analysis has been done successfully. The key criterion to assess when doing due diligence of privately held companies is the personal importance of the owner or owners (i.e., the selling shareholders).

How important are the current owners to the continuing operations of the business? Are they involved actively in management, and if so, in which aspects? (Sales is generally the most sensitive area.) There are some serious traps here. Assume that retaining the previous management/owner is critical for business success, at least for the short term. A long-term consulting contract with the former owner is no guarantee of his or her continued participation. Nor is a contingent payout based on performance for part of the purchase price. (The difference between no million dollars and one million dollars in purchase price is far greater than between one million and ten million.) There are psychological factors at work here, some outside of the owner's control, intent, or even awareness.

When Owner/Managers Are No Longer Owners

What happens when the entrepreneur puts real money into his or her pocket for the first time? The fact is that no one can predict what will happen. Work habits may not change an iota, or on the other hand a penchant for exotic travel and strange companions may suddenly emerge.

Another factor is the diminished sense of personal ownership. The realization of loss has a slow but insidious impact on the performance of many former owners. Identity is blurred and estrangement breeds, and the work product becomes severely depressed. Said one entrepreneur so afflicted, "What seemed to be my normal job on the outside was bothering me terribly on the inside. It was something like being asked to continue living with my wife after she had just married another man."

Entrepreneurial founders of companies are a feisty lot, and are not accustomed to working for anyone. Organizational structure and bureaucratic procedures are not things with which they can identify. Taking direction is not something they can do well. There are too many things to rub them the wrong way. It is a simple historical fact that most arrangements for entrepreneurial founders to work with their companies after its sale will terminate, for one reason or another, short of the original contract date.

Business Importance of Owner/Managers

Consequently, it is vital for investment bankers representing buyers or sellers of privately held companies to appreciate the business importance of the selling shareholders. The more important they are for the continuing prosperity of the company, the less that company should be worth. This means that the business significance of the owner/managers is a vital modulating force on the normal quantitative techniques and qualitative factors in valuing and pricing mergers and acquisitions (Chapter 4).

When considering the importance of the selling shareholders to the business, the following areas of potential concern should be considered: relationship with customers; relationship with suppliers; technology and product development; management and labor relations. For example, how much of the company's revenues do the shareholders/managers generate or influence strongly? Are there particular customers with whom they have a special relationship? Are they the vital force behind new product development? Might there be labor problems without their paternal or maternal guidance?

On the other hand, some companies may be more valuable *without* the former owners involved. (Witness the stock jump of some public corporations when the founder/chief executive retires or dies.) Sometimes founders cannot see beyond their own prejudices and once-wonderful ways of thinking. For example, when the old guard is no longer holding the reins, younger executives may be inspired to do better work ("to bring the company into the modern world," as one liberated manager put it); freedom from the shackles of fear can stimulate creative and innovative thinking. For another example, unprofitable lines of business may be closed since new owners will have no emotional attachment to them.

Noncompete Clauses

Noncompete clauses are an essential part of virtually all purchases of privately held companies. It would be the height of folly to buy a company only to have its key people go out and start a competitive company. Noncompete clauses normally run from three to seven years and are usually related to a contemporaneous consulting contract.[4]

FINANCIAL ANALYSIS

There are three general ways in which the particular financial analysis of privately held companies may differ from the general financial analysis of all M&A companies: (1) differences in financial reporting motivations (e.g., tax minimization procedures); (2) personal compensation and benefits for the owners and their families; and (3) business changes that should or might be made. Investment bankers must be attuned to these issues and, whether representing buyers or sellers, use them to best service their clients in the requisite financial analysis.

Reconstructed Income Statements

The normal procedure for conducting a financial analysis of privately held companies is to prepare a *reconstructed* income statement, giving effect to all changes that would be immediately instituted (or could be easily implemented) once new buyers take over.

It is commonly acknowledged that privately held companies have different financial reporting objectives than public companies. Nonpublic firms have no incentive to maximize reported earnings—there are no stock prices to worry about and no financial analysts with which to bother.[5] In fact, there is a major *disincentive* for showing high earnings—taxes. The higher the earnings a company shows, the higher the taxes a company pays. The more money that appears as income, the more money that is paid out to the government—with the paradoxical results that the more a company shows in earnings the less it is actually worth!

Consequently, private companies do everything legally appropriate to diminish profits for tax purposes (and sometimes that fuzzy line between legal and illegal is shaved rather closely). There are two primary methods that private companies use to reduce earnings: compensation to owners and their families, and evaluations of inventories.

---

[4] One problem with noncompete clauses is that they are difficult to enforce. Courts are reluctant to deprive an individual of his or her only means for making a living. So although noncompete clauses are critical and essential, be aware that they may be unenforceable.

[5] Of course, financial institutions and creditors are concerned with the financial status of the company—but they are used to dealing with private companies.

Compensation to Owner/Managers

High compensation of owner/managers is virtually universal in all profitable private companies. For owners to draw low salaries and take out their profits as dividends, they must pay a double taxation—first at the corporate level and second at the personal level. That hardly makes sense, especially to aggressive entrepreneurs.

What to do? Owners of mature profitable businesses seek to take money out of the business in tax deductible form—salary and expenses. Salaries are often higher than comparable salaries in public companies. (Note: The Internal Revenue Service [IRS] will challenge "excess compensation"). There may be numerous ways in which general expenses are charged to the business (e.g., travel and entertainment, automobiles, and the like) with questionable benefits for operating the business. (Note: The IRS has become much stricter in disallowing personal expenses as business deductions).

Nepotism

Nepotism, the employment of family members, is a common custom in private companies. And although the word connotes an activity somewhat shady, there is nothing intrinsically wrong with families working together to build a business and make it prosper.

We do not suggest that nepotism is merely a circuitous route for reducing taxes. Family members are often very hard workers, feeling a great sense of commitment to the business. Indeed, the business becomes in many cases an extended family, with the positive results beneficial for all.[6] Nonetheless, a new owner may not feel the need to employ so many members of the family, and perhaps those jobs could be replaced at lower pay scales.

Pitfalls of Income Reconstruction

In reconstructing an income statement for a privately held company, be aware of the pitfalls. It is clear that the salaries of owners and their families can often be added back to income. What is easily forgotten is that most of those jobs must be done by someone. Other people–new people– must be hired

---

[6] Studies suggest that there may be some special benefits of family-run companies. There seems to be more commitment to the company and more pride in its success. For example, employees seem to prefer the working environment.

to do those jobs. The reconstruction needs to make provisions for the new compensation packages required for the replacements.

Inventory Evaluations

Regarding the evaluation of inventories, private companies can be tempted to understate their values—for example, taking aggressive write-offs to reduce profits and hence taxes. (Such write-offs might be praised in a public company as conservative management.) Although inventory should be valued at market, market is often difficult to estimate, and value judgments are almost always required.

There is an interesting trap in inventory evaluations for unwary buyers. Private companies may choose to "let out" the built-up "cushion" in their inventories in preparation for a merger or sale (or going public). In these cases, profits in the last year or so might appear *greater* than they would normally be.

How to assess the numbers and get at the truth? The key is to compare the gross margin percentages. If this margin has jumped up in the last year, though there may be other explanations, suspicion should be aroused. (Making comparisons with industry averages is one method of corroboration.)

New Operating Strategies

Potential buyers should evaluate M&A candidates in the light of how new owners might run the business. This analysis takes on added weight when appraising privately held companies since there are often rather obvious business decisions that the original owners were just unprepared to make. (Often the old owners tell the new owners exactly what they should do.) These decisions are usually unpleasant ones disappointing employees, customers, and/or vendors—dropping unprofitable product lines long associated with the company, closing inefficient plants, getting competitive bids for supplies, transferring lackluster executives, firing unproductive staff, and the like.

There is also the stagnancy factor. Many founders like to keep doing business the way they have always been doing business. The power structure considers change uncomfortable, if not downright dangerous. It is hard to be creative and innovative in such an environment. Founders of companies can exhibit high inertia to fresh ideas. The challenge of the new appears to be an attack on the old—and the old is what made the business successful in the first place. Some founder/managers act as if all new ideas are a personal affront.

In such stifling situations, new owners can come in, do what has to be done, and improve the business substantially. Yet it is difficult to project up front, before the deal is made, the impact of such benefits. Consequently, buyers should not count on making significant improvements in the company—but should rather consider the potential opportunities as incremental profits.

STRUCTURING THE DEAL

Making deals with privately held companies is often more complex than making similar deals with publicly held companies. The number of elements and options of consideration, financial and nonfinancial, can be greater. When acquiring public companies, cash must be, by far, the primary consideration. It is possible to use stock in mergers with large companies, and sometimes debentures can play a part, but cash is almost surely king.

When acquiring private companies, investment bankers on both buy and sell sides have more with which to work. Cash, of course, is still king. Indeed, many entrepreneurs will have an inherent distrust of anything else. Nonetheless, there is more flexibility here. In fact, there has to be room for structural elasticity, since it is often more difficult to harmonize price.

To find any overlap between the lowest price the founder is willing to accept and the highest price the buyer is willing to pay is a formidable task. After all, the founder is giving up his or her life's work, and the buyer is incurring severe risk when purchasing a relatively unknown business. Often, there is no chance whatsoever of overlap if the purchase price must be paid all in cash.

How to bridge the gap between sellers and buyers? Frequently it is the noncash portions of the consideration that work the harmonizing magic. In a typical case, perhaps 50 to 75 percent of the purchase price may be paid in cash or highly liquid securities (see below). The remainder may be composed of the following elements.

Seller Paper

Seller paper is where the former owner takes back debt as part of the purchase price (much as in real estate transactions). This debt can be structured with great variety and creativity. It usually pays a market rate of interest (or slightly less) and has an acceptable amortization schedule, say, five to seven years.

Seller debt is often subordinated to any senior financing that is part of the buyout. Though owners and their bankers may squawk, subordination is usually the rule in leveraged buyouts (but not in sales to corporate acquirors). Occasionally, there may be a "grace period," in which the amortization of the seller's principal is postponed for several years and/or the seller's interest is accrued but not paid, thus giving the new owners some cash flow breathing room.

If the sellers agree to take back paper in order to assist the buyers in financing the transaction, the sellers always seek to maximize the likelihood of getting their money. Sellers desire guarantees for their debt. Ideal are third-party guarantees, such as irrevocable bank letters of credit or insurance company guarantees—but such security is rarely achieved. More customary is that the sellers take a second position on the assets and stock of the company behind the senior debt. This would mean that, in the worst case, the sellers would have a chance of getting their company back if the buyers would default on the debt.

Earn-out Contingent Compensation

Earn-out contingent compensation is the trick that gets impossible deals done; it is the vehicle that spans the unbridgeable gaps in private company transactions. In earn-outs, the additional compensation is related directly to some future performance or events, thereby harmonizing the disparate interests of sellers and buyers. The contingent formula for the additional purchase price is often based on financial performance, which is preset by formula and payout schedule.[7] An earn-out can take many forms, though it is most often figured as a percentage of earnings.[8]

Stock of the Acquiring Company

There are two general conditions when shareholders of privately held companies will take the stock (preferred or common) in the acquiring company as consideration in the transaction. First, stock can be used as additional com-

---

[7] Earn-outs could also be based on nonfinancial criteria, such as the commercialization of a technology (e.g., triggered by federal approval to bring a new drug to market) or the number of subscribers to a magazine or cable television system.

[8] Experienced M&A specialists representing a private company seller are usually uncomfortable with profit-based contingency formulas since the new owners have full control of the company (and the books) and can alter the profit picture significantly. Even if a major accounting firm is doing the audit, there are too many ways in which profits in any given year can be severely depressed—such as increasing managerial bonuses, R&D, advertising, and capital expenditures and consequent depreciation. To make matters more complicated, many of these decisions may be in the best long-term interests of the firm. Furthermore, sellers do not want to be forced to delve into the books of the buyer. Better for many sellers is to devise a formula based on operational information, such as gross revenues or numbers of items sold.

pensation—as a mechanism of reaching a mutually acceptable price. (Stock is often used as the medium for paying the earn-out contingency compensation.) Second, there are occasional tax considerations that make it desirable for founder/owners to take all stock (less likely when there is no distinction between capital gains and ordinary income). But whenever a seller agrees to take all the consideration in stock, it is essential that the stock must be in a well-capitalized public company whose shares are highly liquid and traded daily on a major exchange. (In all cases, the float should be very large relative to the seller's total position.)

Note that when some companies give their stock as consideration in the acquisitions of other companies, they may require certain restrictions to be placed on that stock. Such restrictions would decrease its value, perhaps substantially. Private companies are ill-advised to take restricted stock as a major part of their consideration when selling. If the transaction is a merger in which they have or share control, it may be a different story.

Assumption of Liabilities

When a buyer accepts a selling company's liabilities, this kind of consideration can be just as important as if that buyer were paying cash for assets (all the more so if some of those debts are personally guaranteed by the owners). Though it is often hard for founder/owners to accept, the fact is that sometimes the assumption of liabilities is even more important than being paid cash (e.g., when all seller responsibilities for ongoing lawsuits are eliminated). A private company's bankers will strive to eliminate all possible legal and financial responsibilities of the previous owners in any M&A transaction.

Related-Party Transactions

Owners of private companies often have various relationships with their business. For example, they or their family members may own the land on which the factories are built or the buildings in which the retail stores are leased. These relationships give opportunity for more creative structuring, taking advantage of win-win tradeoffs such as tax benefits. The entrepreneur can be allowed to keep ownership of these properties, and long-term contracts can be signed, assuring the former owner and family of long-term income and relieving the new owner of having to finance a larger purchase price.[9]

[9] Such an arrangement is similar to an automatic, pre-existing sale-leaseback.

Employment Agreements

Employment agreements are common when founder/owners sell their business. After all, the buyer wants to assure continuity, and the seller is looking for additional consideration (and probably meaningful work). Pending the precise situation, it may be mutually beneficial to put more dollars into the employment agreement and less into the purchase price. The term of employment contracts are often tied to the payment of final obligations; for example, the contract can be structured to last until the *later* of either five years or the final payout of the seller's debt.

Consulting Contracts

Multiyear consulting contracts are common in the sale of privately held companies. Such contracts normally last as long as the necessary noncompete clauses and may involve other members of the family as well as the founder/owners themselves. The amount of actual work done under these consulting contracts is usually minimal.

Fringe Benefits

Offering fringe benefits, though the amount is minimal compared to other elements in the merger consideration, can be an important psychological assist in doing a deal with a founder/owner. Continuing to maintain an office or provide health insurance can be a powerful incentive to someone who has never had another corporate home other than this company.

Employee Benefits

Finally, founder/owners will likely bring their employees into the deal. They might have given some stock to personnel at very low values. They might require pledges of employment. They might insist on contracts for key people. They might even opt to go for an Employee Stock Ownership Plan (ESOP) when selling their business, even if it doesn't generate the most money with the best security (see Volume II, Chapters 25–26).

ROLE OF INVESTMENT BANKERS

Most entrepreneur/founders of small and medium-sized companies never have worked with an investment banker in their lives and the prospect probably does not thrill them. All they know about these Wall Street Wolves they have learned from the mass media. Talk about starting out with two strikes against you!

What benefits can investment bankers bring to private companies seeking merger or sale and, how can these be communicated? First of all, the inexperience of entrepreneurs should be stressed—especially in relationship to potential acquirors who are almost always highly experienced in negotiating acquisitions (whether large industrial corporations or financial investment groups). Entrepreneurs understand expertise: They are experts in their business and should appreciate that investment bankers are experts in mergers and acquisitions.

Next is the matter of secrecy and discretion. It is vital to respect the confidentiality of clients. This is a central ethic of investment banking (Volume I, Chapter 7) but it takes on special significance in private company M&A. There is often some reticence, if not ambivalence, on the part of the seller. Any premature disclosures may disrupt the entire process. Unauthorized exposure may cause personal and professional embarrassment and could damage the client company's business relationship with customers and vendors. Frankly, investment bankers provide a buffer between the company's manager/owners and the public. If there is an accidental leak (often from the manager/owners themselves), the "blame" can be placed on the firm's "overly aggressive investment bankers." (It is easy to blame investment bankers for their over-anxious rapacity; everyone will believe the excuse and belt the scapegoat.)

Selling a business is a sophisticated process, demanding the highest professional standards. Investment bankers should be able to fulfill the following services for private companies.

Understand the Business

First of all, the investment banker should really get to know the company—its products and people and the reasons that make it all work. Examine all facets of the business—market, products, product development, manufacturing, distribution, service, reputation with customers, image, advertising, management, organization, finances, and the like. Go for the jugular issues, the critical success strategies—what makes this company special, what are its distinctive competencies, what are its comparative advantages and competitive strengths?

Since the company is private, getting inside (figuratively speaking) will be more difficult than with public companies. Manager/owners will be reluctant to talk openly—even though they have invited the investment bankers to come in. After all, a private company is not used to confiding in outsiders (a public company, remember, deals continuously with the insistent and incessant questions of shareholders and analysts). Patience is needed, as are interpersonal skills such as sincere human interest and warm human compassion. Conducting due diligence on a privately held company is much like running a group therapy session for first-time patients.

But don't go milquetoast and forget about the weaknesses—the product/market soft spots, company defects, and organizational problems. You do not want to appear negative (or a boor), but finding the truth is your responsibility. Explain that, as their representative, you are professionally bound both to confidentiality and to presenting them in the best possible manner. In the M&A process, it is best to assume that investment bankers who represent potential buyers will uncover all skeletons, so investment bankers who represent the seller must be ready with all answers and explanations.

Understand Owner Priorities

As M&A representatives, the investment bankers must know what their client/owners want to achieve. Not everyone's objective is similar. In fact, not everyone's objective is logical.[10]

Some owners want to get their money and get out totally. Others desperately want to stay in the company and remain a part of their life's work. Still others want to enable their family members to continue in the business in some way. It is even possible to develop a transaction in which owners can cash out most of their value in their company and still maintain control (whether themselves or through their families). Deals can be structured to accomplish virtually all interests.

Business Presentation

Investment bankers are known for the professionalism of their presentations. They generally prepare a "book" portraying the company in the best possible light, which would include a description of the business and industry, products and markets, competitive positioning and market share, management and organization, operating history, financial history and current condition, future

---

[10] I once knew an owner who was not happy unless he was personally guaranteeing the company's indebtedness. Such risk gave him the feeling of total commitment—which was what he required to remain highly motivated and energized. Talk about a risk-seeking personality, this was the pinnacle! (The end of the story was not a happy one—and emphasizes the importance of *eliminating* personal guarantees for owners of privately held companies.)

opportunities, and the like. (The book is presented quite elegantly, with thick dividers, embossed lettering, and perhaps a hard cover.[11])

Special attention should be focused on recasting the financial statements to reflect properly how a traditional business would appear without the special owner benefits. Such a recasting should not include the hypothetical results of assumed business decisions—such as curtailing unprofitable product lines or closing inefficient plants—no matter how obvious or easy. The effect of implementing such cost efficiencies as well as developing growth opportunities should be described in a different section and can include appropriate financial estimates of what the company would look like if the stated changes were made.

Buyer List Development

First-rate investment bankers can interact with a large universe of potential buyers, calling on the experience of its internal team and the information of its external network. In addition, investment banks have access to sophisticated public and private databases with enormous amounts of data on industries and companies.

From these vast resources, investment bankers should be able to bring dozens of potential candidates to the table, international as well as domestic. In addition, they should be able to develop lists of comparative transactions that give ballpark estimates of values and general categories of structures. Such unbiased data helps bring both buyers and sellers closer to the real world.

There are various factors to consider in evaluating a long list of potential buyers. Degree of interest in the client's business is obviously first, and the financial capacity to complete the deal is a close second. But other factors should also be involved. For example, suppose that the founder/owner insists on retaining a minority share (say 20 percent) of the company for his son; such a demand would eliminate many potential buyers, but not all. The corporate culture of potential purchases could be another important factor in that most owners want their employees to be happy in their future home.

Buyer Contact and Evaluation

Minimum interference with business operations is vital in the early stages of all M&A situations, and this is especially true for smaller, privately held companies. It is highly disruptive to have waves of potential buyers stomping

[11] Not infrequently the covers and dividers are much thicker than the papers and documents.

through the offices and arousing uncertainty and worry. (After many years of working for the founder or his family, most employees would needlessly fear for their jobs.) Why allow the merely curious to agitate your people? Investment bankers have a responsibility to minimize such disruptions.

Negotiating the Deal

How a deal is negotiated depends on company conditions. Sometimes it is best to evaluate buyer interest and then work with the two or three most serious candidates. At other times, a controlled auction makes the most sense. This is where potential buyers submit one round of bids based only on the "book" prepared by the investment bankers—and then only the few leading bidders are invited to participate in the next round which involves on-site analysis and interviews. (See Chapters 29–30.)

The negotiating stage is where many founder/owners begin to get nervous. They imagine they are losing control of their businesses (and their lives). They seem surrounded by swirling, simultaneous meetings of multiple buyers on a feeding frenzy. It may appear that all decision making has passed to these fast-talking, fancy-dressed, hot-shot investment bankers whom they barely know.

Investment bankers working with private companies must be sensitive to the special concerns of manager/owners. Care must be taken never to slight their clients, no matter how irrelevant their questions or how pressing the situation. Investment bankers must always be cognizant of the fact that they are agents, not principals. Owners should never lose control of the process and it is the responsibility of their bankers to give such assurances.

Legal, Accounting, and Tax

Here is where the professionalism of investment bankers should shine. The places for possible pitfalls in structuring a deal are innumerable. For example, the simple decision whether to sell stock or assets is fraught with complex ramifications involving tax, continuing liabilities, and future plans of both buyers and sellers. Since this sale is probably the most important transaction that the owner will ever make, and since most of his or her net worth is probably tied up here, nothing less than the best professional advice must be used.[12]

---

[12] This is another example of investment bankers being far better equipped to handle mergers and acquisitions than "business brokers," who are often just glorified matchmakers. Investment bankers bring an integrated, professional approach to the most important decision of a company's life.

Investment Banking Fees

You get what you pay for. Investment banking fees are calculated as a percentage of the transaction size. They are normally set as a sliding scale downwards as the transaction increases in size (Volume 1, Chapter 5).[13]

Since investment banking fees are a percentage of the entire deal, they can become quite large. Such numbers can only be justified if they are a very small percentage of the incremental value that the investment bankers add in a transaction. (Value added is most often reflected in a higher purchase price—derived through attracting better buyers and negotiating better deals. It is also reflected by a smarter structure for both sides, a greater likelihood of closing a transaction, and a lesser likelihood of legal and tax foul-ups.)

Many investment bankers currently seek an up front retainer before they begin M&A work with a company, especially a privately held company where owners have been known to change their minds halfway through the process (or just before the end). Should such retainers be charged, or should the only fees be contingent on the successful conclusion of a transaction? (Out of pocket expenses, from travel to computer time, are always billed to the client company, irrespective of transaction outcome.)

There are two sides to the issue: On the one hand, a retainer seems coercive and not in keeping with industry tradition where only success is rewarded and failure means failure for the banker as well as the client. On the other hand, a retainer separates the serious from the curious. An enormous amount of work is involved, and opportunity costs are high; consequently, an investment bank must be assured that, should a reasonable deal materialize, its client is committed to close the transaction.

Investment Banking Attitudes

It is important that investment bankers treat their private company clients properly. The fact that the deal may be small should not affect the work product at all. Even the appearance of a condescending or patronizing atti-

---

[13] The traditional "Lehman Formula" is the standard on which most fees are based: five percent on the first million, four percent on the second million, three percent on the third million, two percent on the fourth million, and one percent on the fifth million and thereafter. However, as with everything else in M&A, many modifications are made. In small, hard-to-do deals, the five percent may extend for several millions or for the entire deal. In very large deals, the total fees will amount to less than one percent. Innovative, incentive-based fee structures may offer investment bankers a lower amount, say one percent, below a certain trigger and a higher amount, say two percent, above that trigger. Such an incentive fee structure really encourages the bankers to "top out" the price.

tude must be avoided. Granted, the entrepreneur/founder is not financially sophisticated. But, he or she is a significant success (and is probably worth *more* than the banker!) Unless investment bankers are going to do their best possible job, they should not take the assignment.

Each transaction should be given the attention of a senior investment banker, one with significant experience handling either private companies or firms in the specific industry (or both). Although the proverbial young MBAs will be doing much of the work, they must be continuously guided by an experienced dealmaker.

Indeed the fundamental difference between investment bankers and business brokers is that the bankers must be able to provide significantly more services and expertise. Private company M&A is generally not the grist for page one news or even the inside pages of *The Wall Street Journal*. Some investment bankers, accustomed to the megamerger spotlight, cannot get themselves up for smaller deals. However, these are the exceptions.

To true investment bankers the deal itself is the thing, its size being of little matter. Most M&A specialists just love doing deals and doing them well. Indeed, some bankers enjoy doing smaller, private company deals more than larger, public company ones. It is in the private company deals that investment bankers can take more personal responsibility and thus gain greater satisfaction from a job well done.

CHAPTER 8

DIVESTITURES I: MOTIVATIONS AND MECHANISMS*

Arnold S. Hoffman
Shearson Lehman Brothers, Inc.

Divestiture can offer management a unique tool for raising capital. While the concept of divestiture (or sell-off, as it is often called) is not entirely new, only since the early 1970s has it become an accepted practice for the astute operator. A successful sell-off of a company, division, or product line not only produces cash for the corporate treasury without equity dilution, but in those cases where the sale is of a troubled unit, it improves the overall performance of a company by directly eliminating losses and allowing management to focus quality time on more profitable business segments.

In the 1960s, the goal of the management of most conglomerates was to build a multimarket company that could profitably withstand changes in the economic cycle. In concept, the more widely diversified a company, the better able it is to take advantage of both up and down economic cycles. In practice, most management groups found themselves spending an inordinate amount of time trying to turn around losers and having almost no time available to expand and improve healthy operations. This caused considerable concern to most companies from a strategic viewpoint, since management was always putting out fires but was never able to rebuild after the damage. In the late 60s the issue was not which companies were acquired and how they fit in with existing operations, but rather how many companies could be acquired and how big volume and profits could grow.

*This chapter was originally published in *Handbook for Raising Capital: Financing Alternatives for Emerging and Growing Businesses*, Lawrence H. Chimerine, Robert F. Cushman, and Howard D. Ross, editors; Homewood, IL: Dow Jones-Irwin, 1986.

By the early 1970s it became apparent that conglomerates would have to develop a portfolio management strategy. The goal of these organizations could no longer be pure expansion through acquisitions, but would have to include spinning off or selling divisions or product lines that either did not fit long-term strategy, had no growth potential, or were damaging the other operations of the company. In the days of active acquisitions, most managers of conglomerates felt that selling off a unit or two was a sign of failure in their aggressive buying programs and felt a deep concern that a selected divestiture program would result in a lower stock price. In order to avoid risking a reversal of the upward trend in stock prices, they patched, fixed, regrouped, restocked, and retooled, but despite these efforts, often failed to turn around and solve their problems.

Though conglomerates in general realized that divestiture in concept was needed as an additional management tool, it was not until the mid-70s that certain managers defied accepted practice and began to restructure their companies. To everyone's surprise, the stock market welcomed restructuring by divestiture, and those managements that pursued this course were looked upon as properly serving their shareholders. Divestiture is now an accepted and welcomed management tool and should be utilized on a regular basis in reviewing an organization's business units.

An ongoing task of management now involves recognizing the need that exists within a company to redirect a portion of its portfolio of assets in order to take advantage of the opportunities that might exist if this redirection were to include the sale of a division or product line. In order to ensure its effectiveness over time, the practice of systematizing management's review of its company's portfolio is critical.

Divestiture cannot only cure a failing situation and offer a good profit opportunity, but a timely sell-off, whether planned or forced, does in fact put capital into a company's treasury without dilution of equity. The following factors, some of which are internal, some external, should be considered as management reviews its company's holdings to determine whether divestiture opportunities exist and, in the case of a losing situation, whether divestment is mandatory to help redirect a company toward a new course that is consistent with long-term strategy.

DIVESTMENT DECISION CONSIDERATIONS

Figure 1 provides an overview of a number of the factors that come into play in making divestment decisions. These factors are grouped under three general categories: (1) opportunistic, (2) planned, and (3) forced. The opportunistic

FIGURE 1
Divestiture Considerations

Categories	*(1) Opportunistic*	*(2) Planned*	*(3) Forced*
Economic		Never be a factor at any investment level	
		Continual failure to meet goals	
	Tax considerations	Tax considerations	Tax considerations
		Shrinking margins	
	Better alternative use of capital	Better alternative use of capital	
	Profit motivation	Profit motivation	
		Marginally profitable	
		Recover some capital	Recover some capital
		Unprofitable division	Unprofitable division
		Liquidity problems	Liquidity problems
Psychological		Eliminate psychological effect of a loser	
		Bad apple theory	
Operational		Lack of intercompany synergy	
		Labor considerations	Labor considerations
		Competitive reasons	Competitive reasons
		Management deficiencies	
		Concentration of management efforts	Concentration of management efforts
		Eliminate ineffciencies	
Strategic		Change in corporate goals	
		Change in corporate image	
		Technological reasons	Technological reasons
	Poor business fit	Poor business fit	Poor business fit
		Market saturation	
	Takeover defense	Takeover defense	Takeover defense
Governmental		Government-directed divestitures	Government-directed divestitures

NOTE: Some considerations may fall under more than one category. For example, shrinking margins and better alternative use of capital may also be strategic considerations.

considerations in column 1 are totally optional and are meant to be implemented in a reactive manner. An example might involve profit motivation. A division that was operating successfully receives an unsolicited cash bid from a suitor that translates into an extraordinary profit, and while there may be no immediate use for the cash, the profits from selling off this division are such that management cannot in good conscience turn down the offer. This consideration is slightly different from profit motivation in column 2, planned considerations. Under this scenario, a company may have a profitable, well-run division, but may decide to divest in order to raise the necessary capital to invest in something new, or if there is concern about the division's long-term future. While in both instances profit motivation is the same, it is clearly different circumstances that lead to the divestiture decision.

Another example of the fine line between these categories is shown in column 2, the planned sell-off scenario, when the seller recovers some capital. Clearly this consideration refers to a faltering situation wherein, as a result of an ongoing portfolio review, the division is sold off in time to "recover some capital." Conversely, under column 3, the forced scenario, the extent of capital recovered would generally be much less, since a forced liquidation of assets would probably occur only after a greater erosion of assets than if a divestiture were implemented as part of an ongoing planning review.

While there is understandably some overlap between the three basic scenarios that trigger or motivate a divestiture, there is also interchangeability among the individual factors.

In order to simplify the use of these factors, they can be easily divided into five categories: (1) economic, (2) psychological, (3) operational, (4) strategic, and (5) governmental or legislative. Naturally, many of these subjects overlap, but they have been split into the above categories in an attempt to isolate their primary meaning in relation to the overall divestment or spin-off situation.

Economic

Never Be a Factor at Any Investment Level

In many situations, the market the company is dealing in is too narrow. Regardless of the dollars and corporate muscle put into the particular division, it will be impossible for management to realize an adequate return. It is the old case of throwing good money after bad, and generally occurs in situations where the company is faced with impossible goals of achieving market share in the face of competition that is either too well entrenched, tough, or numerous to make it worth investment at any particular dollar level. RCA Corporation faced this situation when it abandoned its mainframe computer business after attempting to compete directly with IBM.

Continual Failure to Meet Goals

The frustration faced by most corporate managers when a division continually fails to make quarterly or yearly projections is an excellent rationale for divesting. Patience with meeting predefined or predetermined goals is certainly a virtue. However, continual losses or continuing shortfalls from overestimating the potential of a division can be very costly to any company.

Tax Considerations

Tax considerations as a justification for divestment come into frequent play, given the complexities of our tax laws. A company can often take advantage of changes in the tax law by selling a division or product line at an opportune time, and deriving the benefits from losses or other quirks allowed by the existing tax laws. This rationale is somewhat unique in that tax laws continually change, and therefore divestment should be considered on a regular basis, as an opportunity that can quickly be lost by a change in law. As an example, when net operating losses (NOLs) could easily be sold and utilized by the acquiror, many companies took advantage of this temporary tax benefit by selling loss-plagued divisions.

Shrinking Margins

Reduced profit margins should be reviewed in all divisions and product lines and are often the primary reason for a divestiture. Typical of companies that have run large divestiture programs because of shrinking margins are G. D. Searle and American Can. While the divestment programs for both of these companies were part and parcel of a strategic plan, the short-term reason for initiating them was the continual softening in the profit margins of the divisions the companies sold.

Better Alternate Use of Capital

Here again is a combined economic and strategic reason for considering divestment. This factor should be a key to the rationale for beginning any divestment program. The list of companies that have begun divestment programs to make better use of capital reads from A to Z in corporate America. Companies that have used in-depth divestment programs to reinvest proceeds into other areas of existing businesses or into new acquisitions have been extremely satisfied.

Profits

Profits are still the ultimate motivator. Lack of profits, on the other hand, is the most noted and visible reason for corporations to begin divestment programs. The marginally profitable divisions, those divisions not in line with the financial performance of other divisions in the company, are certainly divestment targets. Unless they satisfy some strategic requirement, such as a research and development unit, divisions that continue to be unprofitable and lose money year in and year out certainly should be divested. A corporation exists at the pleasure of its stockholders, and for the most part, the best way to satisfy stockholders is to perform well and produce generous profits. Divisions and product lines that erode profits and cannot be restructured and reshaped to turn a substantial and acceptable return on investment within the range of the corporation's goals should be prime candidates for divestiture.

Psychological

Eliminate Psychological Effect of a Loser

No one wants to be associated with a loser. Nothing is more depressing psychologically than to know that you are working for or are associated with a company that is losing money and has very little future ahead of it. The effects of a loser can be as contagious as the effects of a winner, and having a losing company over a long term is something that every management should try to avoid. If it cannot be fixed, sell it.

Bad Apple Theory

Unfortunately, losers have a way of creating other losers. The faster a company gets rid of a loss division, the better off all its other divisions will be. Employees have a difficult time understanding the rationale of trying desperately to turn around an operation year after year. Losers should be eliminated quickly before they infect the company's management teams at its other, more profitable divisions.

Operational

Lack of Intercompany Synergy

Prime targets for sell-offs are product lines or divisions that were originally acquired or begun in order to add synergy to the company's other divisions, but failed to do so. In cases where one plus one equals two rather than three, these operations should be considered divestment candidates. If management is not able to consolidate operations to increase profitability, then liquidation or divestment is an alternative.

Labor Considerations

In many cases, companies are divested because of unusual labor situations. These situations might consist of labor unrest in a particular plant, the lack of an adequately skilled labor pool, or outside economic and political factors causing a shortage of labor at competitive prices. If the situation cannot be remedied by moving or consolidating the operation, divestiture might be an alternative.

Competitive Reasons

Certainly competition is the basis of a capitalistic system. However, when competition is intense, and the competition is of a nature that it is so large and effective that it is impossible to compete, withdrawing from a market can be accomplished by divesting an ongoing division. International Harvester has recently been involved in several markets where the competition was too intense, much larger, and more able to compete in terms of productivity, research and development, and new facilities. Instead of remaining in these market segments as an ineffective also-ran, management chose to sell off one of its staple old businesses to a larger, more financially capable company. Separating emotions from reality in terms of competitive ability is often the key to properly making this decision.

Management Deficiencies

Oftentimes, for one reason or another, a company has not been able to put together the right management team to run a division. This problem does not generally speak well of management's ability to recruit, hire, and even provide, internally, the proper management to run its companies, and if the situation exists and cannot be corrected, divestitures should be considered. An example of a divestment yet to happen for this reason is Mobil Oil Corporation's Montgomery Ward & Co. division.

Concentration of Management Efforts

Perhaps the key element underlying all of the operational factors is the need to focus management's efforts where they will be most productive for the company. It is often hard to measure the total losses absorbed by a corporation when one or several of its divisions are losing money and management has to concentrate its efforts on trying to turn around the losers. When problem divisions are divested quickly, management has ample time to return to its normal and important functions of promoting the solid and strategically important units of its company.

Eliminate Inefficiencies

Many companies will operate marginal divisions indefinitely as long as these units do not encounter significant losses. However, marginally profitable units tend to get caught in the trap where management will starve them for growth capital. Over a period of time those units become more inefficient and less competitive and eventually begin to lose important money. It is mandatory to spot these trends early and to try to sell these units before they become big losers and start gathering significant downward momentum. If divestiture can be accomplished within a reasonable time frame, not only are future losses eliminated, but the sale of the unit will inject more capital into the corporate treasury than if the sell-off was delayed too long. Many times, these situations occur in vertically integrated firms, where various operations can no longer be conducted efficiently. Ford Motor Corporation's divestiture of its basic steel operations is an excellent example.

Strategic

Change in Corporate Goals

This factor is probably the most visible reason for companies to begin divestment programs. Oftentimes a company's motivation to divest itself of bad divisions, or any division, is masked by the statement that the corporation is changing its strategic goals and wishes to divest one or several of its divisions. Perhaps the best example of a total commitment to a change in corporate strategic goals was Gould Inc.'s efforts several years ago to get out of the electrical equipment and equipment-support business and upgrade technologically into the electronics business. Over several years, the company divested all of its more technologically mundane divisions and used those funds to acquire companies in the electronics business, thereby moving several steps up the technological ladder. In beginning a divestment program as a result of a change in corporate strategy, the key to the divestments is not only getting out of the businesses that are not wanted, but estimating and projecting how much capital will be raised by selling off these divisions and how much this capital will assist in either acquiring or starting up new ventures that are more in line with newly stated corporate strategic goals.

Change in Corporate Image

In addition to the change in corporate goals mentioned above, some companies feel that in order to effect a "new" image, certain divisions must be divested. While the divestments are not necessarily segments that are failing, or even segments that have limited long-term potential, the businesses might be in areas that are not to the liking of management. For example, Gulf & Western has been involved in a total restructuring and has utilized divestiture of several of its large divisions to move out of mundane manufacturing areas and become more visible in the fast-moving, aggressive financial and entertainment businesses.

Technological Reasons

Many companies have begun divestment programs to technologically upgrade operations. Litton Industries goes through a continual year-to-year upgrading of its companies, regardless of profitability, to maximize the potential of growth companies in higher and higher technological areas. On the other hand, companies downgrade technologically when they are not able to adapt to the fast-moving nature of technology-oriented businesses. Many companies that have decided to withdraw from the high tech areas have retreated to their core businesses and have used divestment strategies to accomplish these goals. Warner Communications, with the sale of its Atari division, provides an excellent example.

Poor Business Fit

Many times, divisions make no sense at all strategically and just do not fit with other divisions of the company. Acquiring companies sometimes use strange rationale for justifying an acquisition, and oftentimes the new management that inherits these businesses take the course of divesting quickly. One of the first management initiatives of Western Union Telegraph Co.'s newly appointed chairman was the divestiture of E. F. Johnson Company, an operation that fit only marginally with Western Union's core business.

Market Saturation

From a strategic standpoint, a division or product line in which the investment required to maintain market share is greater than the cash it generates is a divestiture candidate. This situation is simply a case of a cash cow becoming a dog.

Takeover Defense

In the recent wave of takeovers, divestitures have become one of a number of key defense mechanisms. Typical of these maneuvers is the sale of a "Crown Jewel" to deter an aggressive takeover artist from going forward with his plans. An example of the use of this tactic was Brunswick Corporation's sale of its medical division, the best operating division of the company, to American Home Products in order to stave off an unsolicited takeover attempt by Whitaker Corporation. Shortly after that event took place, Whitaker withdrew its takeover bid for the company. Divestment has become a classic takeover defense mechanism in the last couple of years and has been used successfully to thwart many of these bids.

Governmental

Government-Directed Divestitures

These often occur as a result of major mergers or acquisitions where the merger of two like companies creates antitrust problems. In order to avoid antitrust litigation on the part of the government, the companies are either directed to, or voluntarily, divest certain divisions. The rash of oil combinations that has taken place over the last few years has resulted in major oil companies selling off large parts of their merged companies. The Gulf/Standard Oil of California, and Texaco/Getty transactions are good examples of government-directed divestitures.

As a result of government-enacted environmental laws and practices, companies are forced to evaluate offending operations, and in many cases, either decide to sell a plant, convert to an alternate method of operation, or shut down the offending operation to meet government regulations.

While the above is a fairly comprehensive listing of the factors to be considered when making divestment plans, there are obviously other factors that may come into play. Outside pressure from stockholders, the economic conditions at any given time, and political considerations can certainly have a direct bearing on divestment strategy. Any combination of the factors described above plus these additional macroconsiderations should be reviewed before the divestment decision is made.

IMPLEMENTING A DIVESTMENT PROGRAM

Choose In-House Staff or Outside Professionals

Once the decision has been made that divestiture is necessary to stop losses, to raise additional capital, to strategically redirect a company's focus, or to accommodate a multitude of other reasons, implementing that strategy becomes paramount. A company can choose either to handle the divestitures in-house or to retain an outside professional. This decision depends on the size, structure, and workload of each particular case and relationships with the outside investment banking community. Larger companies that have corporate planning or development departments, or a large financial staff, have the ability to accomplish these divestitures internally. Medium to smaller-sized companies or, in some cases, large corporations that are overloaded in certain administrative areas, may want to retain outsiders to do their divestiture work.

There are a number of alternatives available to companies that prefer to take advantage of outside professionals. There are several independent merger, acquisition, and divestiture firms with the needed expertise that have had excellent results in directing effective divestiture programs. Most of the large regional and national investment banking firms have either special departments or considerable expertise in assisting companies with a total divestment program or with particular individual divestitures as they arise. Both methods, either the use of in-house staff or retaining professional help, have been utilized successfully by many companies. If a company has an active mergers and acquisitions department that is constantly in the mergers and acquisitions marketplace, handling divestments on an in-house basis can make sense. However, if a company is not familiar with the process, and would have to find someone to assign to a particular program or project regarding divestitures, it should strongly consider the use of outside professional help to implement divestment plans. In addition to investment bankers and independent business brokers, many large national accounting firms, management consulting firms, and even some banking institutions perform divestment services. It is best to retain a professional who is knowledgeable about divestitures in general and preferably one who is knowledgeable about the industry within which the division operates.

Retain Key Management Personnel and Current Course

Generally, there are two major items to keep in mind while doing either a divestiture or a spin-off of an operation. The first is to keep key management in place throughout the divestment cycle. It is imperative that the chief executive officer and the chief financial officer of the company or department that is being divested stay on board throughout the entire divestment process. As incentives to these individuals, bonuses upon sale can be promised, and employment contracts should be entered into to prevent them from leaving during this period. Stable management often is critical to getting the divestiture accomplished properly and can provide great comfort to the employees and also to the potential buyers as a source of knowledge and, particularly, the continuity so much needed during the transition process from one corporation to another. It is most difficult to keep divestiture plans private, as much as management might try, and therefore the presence of the CEO and the CFO are key to the success of any divestiture program undertaken. If they leave or are dismissed before the divestiture is complete, the process becomes traumatic to the unit and could cause irreparable damage.

Secondly, corporate management must continue to operate the divestiture candidate in the normal course of business as though the decision to divest had not been made. Decisions cannot be made based on projecting what a new owner would want, but on what current management believes is the correct course.

Prepare a Selling Memorandum

Once the decision to divest has been made, the actual divestment process in either case is started by the preparation of a complete selling memorandum describing the company. This memorandum is usually written either by internal staff or by an outside professional. Those topics discussed are company motivation for the sale; the company history; its present condition; its future potential; its product line (if it is a manufacturing facility); its service capability (if it is in the service business); its people, plant facility, physical facilities, and real estate; and a comprehensive financial overview of the company. The financial presentation should consist of a three- to five-year profit and loss statement, a current balance sheet, cash flow projections, and a short-range forecast.

Target Potential Buyers

In-house staff or outside counsel will then develop a list of target buyers to consider. At this point a decision must be made whether to directly market the company through a negotiated basis or to effect an auction. This choice is an individual decision and depends on the inherent characteristics of the business being sold, how quickly management would like to dispose of the company, and what effect a wide open, broad-range marketing thrust will have on the continuity of the business. Again, these are decisions that have to be made and evaluated with each individual divestiture. There is no basic formula to do a divestiture. Each one has to be handled like any other major business decision, on an individual basis, where all the facts and circumstances are weighed before making a decision on how to proceed.

Negotiated Format

Under the negotiated format, companies are contacted directly on a controlled basis—perhaps three to five companies at a time. The essence of a negotiated divestiture is the proper targeting of prospective buyers so as to enter into substantive negotiations with a qualified buyer until a satisfactory agreement can be reached. If it becomes obvious that an agreement cannot be reached, the seller must quickly move to another viable buyer. A negotiated sale is employed when management wants to maintain secrecy, keep employment unrest to a minimum, avoid a competitive reaction, and control the market reception.

Auction

An alternative method of selling a company is the use of an auction. This tool has evolved during the past few years and is used very effectively with high visibility companies. The M&A (Merger and Acquisition) auction is generally limited to divestitures of divisions of public companies, both large and small. Like any other methodology employed in the sale of a business, there are a number of factors in utilizing this technique of which sellers should be aware before committing to its use. In theory, the auction offers the following advantages to the seller: (1) efficacy, (2) simplicity, (3) control, and (4) visibility.

Efficacy. The auction is able to draw the greatest number of interested parties into the activity within the shortest time span, at the lowest possible selling cost, and with minimal business interruption.

Simplicity. The process eliminates the slower, more complicated method of seeking a buyer by approaching selected target buyers as stated above.

Control. By virtue of the nature of an auction (take it or leave it), the seller can better control the momentum of the particular transaction. Time deadlines are set early, and if the seller meets its target for the dissemination of information to the buyers (the confidential memorandum as discussed above), he can control the timing and response in a competitive atmosphere, which eliminates bidder delays. The bidder either responds on time or loses not only the investment opportunity, but the time, effort, and dollars he has put forth to examine this opportunity.

Visibility. Companies committed to a specific divestiture often go "public," which generally opens up the market potential and allows the seller to reach the largest buyer universe within the shortest period of time.

While the seller seeks to reach the greatest number of people in the shortest time frame, it sometimes reaches too many potential buyers, including a combination of real players and casual opportunists as well as competitors whose motives may be clouded by the process. The sheer volume of interested parties can lead to the virtual elimination of one of the primary motives for using the M&A auction—speed. Unfortunately, it is difficult to limit early participants and maintain the aura of a true auction process. Indiscreet control of the number of bidders tends to destroy the whole process and ultimately leads to an arm's-length negotiation with several bidders. This process is time-consuming and difficult to orchestrate without turning off bidders who originally would not have made the investment in due diligence if they knew a protracted negotiated auction was going to take place. The M&A auction also eliminates buyers who will not come to the table at all without having an exclusive (30/45/60-day) period to negotiate a purchase.

Further complicating the bid process is the complexity of trying to negotiate a "purchase agreement" before the business issues are resolved. While business issues seem to be consistent from buyer to buyer in the main, the legal issues tend to reflect the individual style of each buyer's attorney, which creates a complex of legal questions that ultimately requires writing individual contracts with each prospective buyer. These negotiations slow the process down to a crawl while drastically increasing legal costs. The promise of speed and simplicity sometimes backfires by using the M&A auction and instead becomes a nightmare of accommodation to each buyer's individual goals.

There are also other serious negatives associated with the process: (1) secrecy, (2) employee unrest, (3) competitive reaction, and (4) market perception.

Secrecy. Surely a company with technical and proprietary information to protect will find it almost impossible to use the M&A auction as a means of divesting a division, since full disclosure to all interested parties is a must in effectively utilizing this process.

Employee Unrest. All divestitures cause both management and labor force unrest by virtue of the cloud of uncertainty hanging over the business. Many times, key players panic and leave the company or attempt to hold up the new owners for lucrative contracts that can cause a buyer to pass. The constant presence of strangers in offices and plants slows productivity, engenders low morale, and often causes negative feedback that can severely damage the process by raising a caution flag to the buyer interested in retaining management and maintaining normal relations with all other employees.

Competitive Reaction. Competitors usually have a field day when they find out about a public divestiture. Furthermore, if the seller runs a fair M&A auction, it will usually get a large number of competitors at its doorstep to take a look. As mentioned before, their motives are not always the same as those of other buyers, yet in many cases where the M&A auction has been successful, a direct competitor has often been the successful high bidder. It is still difficult to properly orchestrate the selling of a division to a direct competitor, and it always causes great consternation and unrest during the process. Not only do competitors get to look into the bowels of a company but they will have that advantage over the new owner, if not a competitor, which may leave the auction buyer queasy enough to drop out or pass on the auction situation as a matter of policy.

Market Perception. If the divestment decision is correct for the parent, the perception of the market should be positive. For the most part, especially during the past five to eight years, selling of divisions has been a strategy usually welcomed by the investment community. On the other hand, the perception within the specific industry in which the divestiture candidate operates can be cause for concern. Customers worry about maintaining an uninterrupted flow of products or services during the process, and begin to look at the competition as an alternative, since they are never sure who will eventually buy the division and how the new owner's policy and philosophy will affect their past relationship.

SUMMARY

Divestiture, as with any major corporation decisions, can result from a multitude of factors. As a management tool, it is somewhat unique in its implications and far-reaching effects. Though it should not be used cavalierly, or viewed as a universal elixir for what ails a company, management should not avoid divestiture when its appropriate use can benefit the corporation and its stockholders. In conclusion, the following short poem might sum up the essentials of this chapter.

Buyers are winners, the track record shows
They flash brilliance with numbers in charts and cash flows
The target once landed is turned over to staff
The brilliance may fade which is no cause to laugh
Some fight it with money and people and such
Some look for a saviour with a magical touch
When momentum heads south you must face up to the test
If you can't solve your problem, it's time to divest.

—Arnold S. Hoffman

CHAPTER 9

DIVESTITURES II: PROCESS AND TECHNIQUES*

Paul R. Van Wyck
Chase Manhattan Bank

The decision to divest a business, like the decision to acquire one, represents a very significant strategic action and critical corporate undertaking. Acquisitions and divestitures derive from fundamental decisions about the future strategic direction of the corporation. For the emerging, growth-oriented corporation, the acquisition or divestiture of a business may well be the single most critical event in determining the future success or failure of the enterprise. While acquisitions are almost always exciting corporate events, surrounded by much glamour, divestitures very often take place in a much more subdued environment.

Acquisitions bring with them a sense of accomplishment and positive corporate visibility along with great expectations of future growth, profits, and size. While these expectations do not always work out, everyone in the acquiring corporation wants to be part of the triumph, and few corporate resources are spared in assuring that the transaction is professionally managed and staffed.

Divestitures, on the other hand, are often corporate events with which few in the corporation wish to be associated and for which the primary objective often tends to be getting the transaction consummated as quickly as possible. While the corporate psychologist may find the attitudinal difference between the manner in which acquisitions and divestitures are approached quite under-

*This chapter was originally published in *Handbook for Raising Captial: Financing Alternatives for Emerging and Growing Businesses*, Lawrence H. Chimerine, Robert F. Cushman, and Howard D. Ross, editors; Homewood, IL: Dow Jones-Irwin, 1986.

standable, the management, directors, and stockholders of the corporation should not. The thesis here is very simple. In order to maximize the benefits or minimize the losses associated with a divestiture, these transactions must be professionally managed and supported in the corporation with the same type and level of commitment given acquisitions. Like acquisitions, divestitures are not business-as-usual transactions. They require not only professional management but also specialized functional skills and experienced negotiating capability. These skills should be brought together in a dedicated team and, where necessary, supplemented with outside professional advisers.

This chapter addresses the steps required to complete a successful divestiture. These steps include:

- Assembling the divestiture team.
- Preparing the divestiture.
- Valuing the business.
- The selling process.

ASSEMBLING THE DIVESTITURE TEAM

Divesting a business requires a team of functional experts under the direction of an experienced project manager. Selection of the project manager is the first and one of the most important actions taken after reaching the decision to divest. In addition to general project management skills, the project manager must be knowledgeable in the tasks and techniques necessary to consummate a successful divestiture. Within the corporation, people with these types of skills most often reside in the corporate development function. Those corporations that do not have a formal corporate development activity may find qualified divestiture managers within the financial, legal, or corporate planning organizations. Even in those instances where the corporation elects to engage an investment banker or some other intermediary to assist in the divestiture, the appointment of an internal project manager and core team is absolutely critical.

The project manager's first task is to assemble the core team. While the makeup of the core team will vary depending on the specific nature of the divestiture, it generally includes someone extremely knowledgeable about the business being sold and someone from the corporate financial function. Where practical, a member of the corporate legal staff should be closely associated with the activities of the core team from the very beginning of the project. This will facilitate the preparation of the offering memorandum, the negotiations, and the writing of the letter of intent and definitive purchase agreement.

The core team will also need assistance from time to time during the project from other functional areas of the corporation. These often include the tax department, human resources, corporate communications, and the corporate controller.

Having assembled the core team, the project manager should draw up a definitive project plan and obtain approval of the approach to be utilized from corporate management. The project plan will include:

1. Identification of the core team and supplementary internal resource requirements.
2. The specific tasks to be performed and the responsibilities of each project participant.
3. Identification of outside resource requirements such as investment bankers, their specific tasks, and the anticipated costs of these services.
4. The timetable for each major phase of the project.
5. An overall project budget.

A critical element in assembling the project team and preparing the project plan is the decision regarding the use of outside resources. Some corporations may not have the breadth of resources and talent internally to effect a successful divestiture. These types of organizations often turn to investment bankers, outside law firms, or other intermediaries for professional assistance. This is a perfectly appropriate decision because, as indicated earlier, selling a business is a highly specialized activity. In addition to providing the necessary professional expertise that may be lacking in the selling corporation, investment bankers can be particularly helpful in a number of other areas important to a successful divestiture. These are:

1. Identification of potential purchasers.
2. Approaching potential purchasers on an anonymous basis.
3. Assisting in the structuring of the deal.
4. Assisting in the negotiating process.

The process of engaging outside resources must be carefully planned and executed. Both investment bankers and outside law firms receive substantial compensation for their services. While these services are generally worth their cost, it is important to be very specific as to the services to be rendered and the billing methodology to be used. For divestitures, like acquisitions, investment bankers generally bill on the basis of a percentage of the selling price. Before engaging an investment banker, it is worthwhile to do some research on deals of comparable size and complexity as preparation for discussions of the fee arrangements. Investment banking fees are negotiable even with those firms that profess to have policy-directed fee structures. Since fees for deals of this type are generally based on a percentage of the price, small deals are by definition less attractive to the most senior people in the firm than are large deals. Therefore, part of the negotiations in engaging an investment banker should include a discussion of specifically who in the firm will be assigned to the project. The well-known investment banking firms all have very talented young people, but experience can be worth substantial dollars in the ultimate price received for the business being sold. Therefore, when engaging an investment banker, it is important to get the best talent available in the firm assigned to the project.

Outside law firms generally bill on the basis of time and expenses. Here again the best law firms have large numbers of very bright young lawyers, and as with the investment bankers, these people are often assigned to the smaller deals. While this will save some money since the billing rates for these people are considerably lower than those of the partners, the value of experience should not be underestimated. The real value of the larger law firms is in the breadth of legal specialization available. Divestitures often involve technical legal issues ranging from tax matters to complex licensing agreements. It is always comforting for the selling corporation to know that the lawyer preparing the contracts of sale has, at his or her disposal for consultation, lawyers with specialized knowledge in almost every aspect of the law.

PREPARING THE DIVESTITURE

One of the earliest tasks for the project team is to determine exactly what is to be sold. No two divestitures are exactly the same. Some divestitures involve the sale of assets, others the sale of legal corporate entities. For example, the sale of a division of a company or part of a division usually results in the transaction taking the form of an asset sale. There are cases where for tax, legal, or other reasons the selling company may find it beneficial to package the assets being sold within a legal corporate entity prior to sale. In those cases where an existing corporate entity is to be sold, the selling corporation may find the marketability and, therefore, the financial return on the divestiture to be better if the transaction is converted into a sale of assets. When determining specifically what is to be sold, there are tax and legal as well as business implications to be considered from both the buyer's and seller's perspective.

In addition to the form of the transaction, there are a number of other issues to be considered in preparing the divestiture. The cleanest divestitures are those involving totally stand-alone businesses that after the sale have no ongoing relationship with the selling corporation. However, often divestitures do involve some sort of continuing business relationship. The selling corporation may be a supplier of products and or services to the business being sold. These may be critical to the future success of the business and the purchaser will expect to negotiate a service agreement as part of the transaction. In other instances, there may be marketing or distribution dependencies between the selling corporation and the business being divested. Here again, the purchaser will want to develop operationally viable and economically feasible agency agreements as part of the transaction. These types of interdependencies must be carefully analyzed at the outset of the divestiture project. Failure to understand them and to prepare for their resolution as part of the overall transaction can often cause major problems in completing the divestiture successfully. Discovery of critical interdependencies late in the negotiating process can, at a minimum, seriously impact the selling price or deal structure, and may cause the buyer to walk away from the deal.

Another important matter in preparing the divestiture is the resolution of management and human resources issues. These aspects of a divestiture may affect the nature, timing, and valuation of the business. If key members of management are critical to the future success of the business or if staff expertise is a valuable asset of the enterprise, these people must be retained and motivated to assure a successful sale. The needs and desires of these people must be understood and dealt with early in the divestiture process. In some instances, special compensation and employment contracts are useful tools to be considered in order to assure management and staff cooperation in the divestiture process. The manner in which employees are handled can affect the price a buyer is willing to pay for a business and the net value of the deal to the seller.

The major effort in preparing the divestiture is the gathering of the data and information necessary to present the business to prospective purchasers. This data-gathering exercise serves several purposes. It will enable the selling corporation to make some of the policy-type decisions identified above. It is the basis on which the initial selling document or offering memorandum is developed and it is the foundation for the business reviews that will be held with serious prospective buyers later in the selling process. In this regard, it has been observed that often as a result of preparing a business for sale, the project team ends up knowing more about the business being sold than either the management of the business or the selling corporation. This is simply another way of saying that successful divestitures depend on careful preparation and intimate knowledge of the business being sold.

In order to address the types of data and information that must be gathered in preparing a divestiture, it may be helpful to look at these requirements in the context of a typical offering memorandum. While all divestitures do not require the preparation of a formal offering memorandum, the data and information necessary to start the selling process tend to be the same. The decision whether or not to prepare a formal offering memorandum is generally driven by the type of selling process elected. If the business being sold is to be offered to a number of potential buyers, either sequentially or on a competitive bidding basis, a formal offering memorandum is essential. In those instances where the selling corporation has a high degree of confidence that it knows the buyer and that the deal will be done with that one party, the formality of an offering memorandum may not be necessary; however, the same level of information will have to be made available to the prospective buyer.

One final comment is in order before moving to the contents of a typical offering memorandum. The offering memorandum must provide a sufficient level of detail for prospective buyers to determine if they are seriously interested in acquiring the business. Its contents must be accurate in every respect. Errors or misstatements about the business that appear in an offering memorandum will almost without exception be identified by prospective buyers during the negotiating process or later during due diligence. This can cause serious difficulties in consummating the transaction and may cause discussions to be terminated completely. Although anything short of complete accuracy in an offering memorandum puts the transaction at risk and should be avoided, this document from the sellers perspective should be viewed, and therefore prepared, as a selling tool. It should emphasize the strengths of the business and position these, where possible, in the context of the strategies or potential strategies of prospective buyers.

CONTENTS OF THE OFFERING MEMORANDUM

Executive Summary

This is one of the most important parts of the document. In addition to summarizing the key points about the business, including specifically what is for sale and the reasons the business is being offered for sale, it should stress the strengths and advantages of the business. This is the key selling chapter of the document.

Buyer Procedure

This section lays out the rules of the sale as set by the selling corporation. It indicates if competitive bidding or another process is being used. It sets the dates for indications of serious interest and for initial bid submission. It stipulates when and where detailed business reviews will be held, and it sets the date for submission of final bids. It describes the methods of payment that the seller will accept as well as outlining both acceptable and unacceptable deal structures. Finally, it indicates specifically who at the selling corporation prospective purchasers are authorized to contact.

Background

This section introduces the business by providing a historical perspective and by highlighting key events in its evolution to date.

Important elements of this section are:

- The history of the business, date of founding or acquisition, identification of minority stockholders, if any.
- Past and current strategic objectives.
- Background on why the business is being sold.
- Summary financial history.
- Geographic locations, legal entities, and states of incorporation.
- Organization chart.
- Background on key officers and employees.

The Market

This chapter presents a comprehensive picture of the industry in which the business participates and provides information that emphasizes the strengths of the business being sold. This is done using the following types of data and information:

- Market size, major products/services, historic growth rates.
- Industry's current position in its life cycle.
- Product/Service life-cycle position.
- Projected growth rate of market and major segments.
- Barriers to entry.
- Importance of product/service to customers.
- Purchase frequency.

- Customer concentration.
- Market saturation.
- Market share of business being sold.
- Major competitors and their market shares.
- Market strengths and weaknesses.
- Domestic and international factors.
- Product/service analysis by major competitors.

Products/Services

In describing the products/services of the business being offered for sale, the following types of information are helpful to prospective buyers:

- Quality objectives.
- Pricing policies and schedules.
- Technical specifications of the product/service.
- Operating and/or production processes.
- Descriptions of differentiating features.
- Customer profiles by product/service.
- Customer turnover by product/service.
- Trademarks and patents.
- New product development history and current activities.

Facilities and Fixed Assets

Specific lists of facilities and fixed assets to be included as part of the sale should be shown on separate exhibits. Facilities and fixed assets are broken down in terms of owned versus leased, by location, and by key activities. Contractual obligations are indicated. An analysis of the adequacy of both facilities and equipment for future growth is included.

Systems and Operations

Complete descriptions of the systems and operations of the business are included. Those systems and operations capabilities to be included as part of the sale are separated from any not included in the sale. This section addresses the adequacy of the systems and operations included as part of the sale for both current and future production and delivery of the product/service.

Organization, Management, and Personnel

This section describes the key human resource elements of the contemplated transaction. Where management and/or personnel are believed critical to the business, this is so stated. The numbers and categories of employees to be made available are listed. All employee benefits are described.

Key Financial Information

Prospective purchasers will expect to receive sufficient financial information necessary to make a preliminary judgment as to their interest in acquiring the business. Generally, a five-year financial history of the business is provided. Often this five-year history is shown in pro forma terms in order to accurately reflect the specific nature of the business being sold. Items that are often left out of the profit and loss statement include intercompany charges for services that the selling corporation no longer intends to provide, overhead allocations from the selling corporation, and federal and state taxes. Prospective purchasers are advised of these adjustments and instructed to insert their own estimates of these expenses when valuing the business. Similar adjustments are often made to the balance sheet, again to reflect specifically what is being sold.

Listed below are the types of data and information that might be included:

- I. Balance sheet and income statement (past five years).
- II. Revenue analysis.
  - A. By product or service.
    - 1. By customer.
    - 2. By geography.
    - 3. By month.
    - 4. By location.
  - B. Seasonality factors.
  - C. Sales policies.
- III. Expense analysis.
  - A. By business segment.
  - B. By product or service.
  - C. Fixed versus variable cost.
  - D. Break-even levels.
  - E. Growth rates for major expense items.
- IV. Other specific financial items.
  - A. Loans or other financial assets.
  - B. Receivables analysis (turnover, bad debts).
  - C. Prepaid expenses and deferred charges.
  - D. Purchase contracts.

VALUING THE BUSINESS

Prospective purchasers can be expected to utilize one or more of several basic valuation techniques in developing their offering price for the business. The divestiture team should conduct a similar analysis. This effort will serve a number of purposes. First, it will provide the selling corporation with an estimate of the market value of the business. Second, it will assist in the identification of prospective buyers. Third, in those instances where more than one offer is received, it will assist in comparing the values of the different offers. Finally, it will provide the foundation for negotiating the price later in the selling process.

Some of the basic valuation methodologies that might be used follow. (See Chapter 4 for a complete discussion of valuation methodologies.)

1. Book value: The accounting value of the items on the balance sheet.
2. Comparables: Public market values and price earnings multiples of similar firms, or prices paid for recent acquisitions of similar firms.
3. Discounted cash flow (net present value): The after-tax cash flows discounted at a risk-adjusted cost of capital results in a net present value.
4. Payback: The length of time necessary to generate cash flows equal to the purchase price.
5. Replacement cost: Estimated cost of replicating the business on a de novo basis.

It is important to recognize that these are basic valuation methodologies and that they must be modified to reflect the special circumstances of each prospective purchaser. For example, different prospective buyers will assume different purchase price adjustments. These include the method of acquisition (tax free or taxable), purchase price allocation assumptions, tax assumptions, and the application of accounting policies. These adjustments can have a very significant impact on the valuation of the business and on the price a purchaser is willing to pay. Furthermore, the price that a prospective purchaser is willing to pay will be affected by considerations of market forces, competition, and the effect of the acquisition on the buyers' base business. Prospective purchasers will evaluate the impact of the acquisition on current and future earnings, return on investment, financing capability, and balance sheet considerations.

The valuation and pricing of a business are not, therefore, precise activities. The outcome of these activities is influenced by business, market, financial, and other assumptions. Successful divestitures often depend on the seller's knowledge and understanding of these as they apply to specific purchasers.

THE SELLING PROCESS

There are four key elements of the selling process: (1) identification of prospective buyers, (2) selection of the type of selling process to be utilized, (3) business reviews, and (4) negotiating the transaction and closing the deal.

Identifying Potential Buyers

The selling process begins when the project team starts to identify potential buyers. Prior to this step, the decision to divest, the organization of the project team, and the preliminary work in preparing the divestiture have all been activities internal to the selling corporation. The identification of potential buyers is the beginning of the external process that hopefully will lead to the successful consummation of the divestiture transaction.

At this stage in the divestiture process, the decision to engage or not to engage an investment banker or other intermediary is often considered or reconsidered. The decision to use an intermediary to identify prospective buyers is often made based on the selling corporation's experience with divestitures, the confidence it has in its divestiture team, and the knowledge it has in-house regarding potentially interested buyers. As indicated earlier, investment bankers can be helpful in identifying prospective buyers. They know the types of businesses their clients are seeking to acquire, they often know the kinds of businesses their competitors are seeking, and they have the capability to identify potential acquirers who have not been active in the market, but for whom a particular business may be a good strategic fit. Since, almost without exception, selling corporations do not enjoy the prospect of having the business they are divesting characterized as having been widely "shopped," investment bankers can also often qualify potential leads anonymously.

Potential buyers can be identified by evaluating the assets of the business being sold and matching these against the strategies or apparent strategies of others. Often it is possible to consider the assets of the business to be sold and to create a strategic rationale for the acquisition of these assets by another company. In other words, as part of the selling process, it may be possible to create the strategy for the potential acquirer by demonstrating that a good strategic fit does exist between the business being sold and other things a particular company may be doing or planning to do.

Potential buyers tend to fall into several general categories:

Competitors

Direct competitors are the most obvious potential buyers. They have the most to gain and, therefore, they are generally in a position to pay the highest price. For potential buyers who are direct competitors, the acquisition will increase market share, provide both marketing and operational economies of scale, and should result in a significant increase in earnings. If the business being sold is operating at a loss or break-even point, selling to a competitor may be the only viable option since only a competitor has the leverage to turn the business around quickly.

While a direct competitor can be expected to pay the best price for a business for the reasons summarized above, there are some definite disadvantages in selling to a competitor. The direct competitor will usually plan to reduce the expense base of the business being acquired by combining the acquisition with his current business. Therefore, the residual costs of the divestiture to the selling corporation can be very high and must be factored against the selling price to determine the net value of the deal. If the form of the transaction is the sale of assets, the selling corporation is often left with significant shutdown costs in the form of personnel severance, lease obligations, and the need to sell fixed assets at below book value. If the form of the transaction is a stock sale, these same costs can be left with the selling corporation or, if the entity is to be sold intact to a competitor, the purchase price can be significantly reduced in anticipation of these costs by the buyer.

Companies in Similar Types of Businesses

These types of potential buyers tend to have some of the characteristics of direct competitors, but not all. The trick here is to identify companies that might see marketing leverage or operational synergies that could be gained through the acquisition. The following are some examples of these types of potential buyers.

Buyers Who Want to Broaden Their Product Lines. If the business being divested is a provider of specialized information based on a proprietary data base, potential buyers may be other information companies who provide data base services and see the benefits of adding the information service of the company being sold to their product line. In this example, the buyer is able to broaden his product line and possibly leverage his existing distribution system.

Buyers Looking for Operational Economies of Scale. If the business being sold is a transaction processing organization, it is often productive to look for potential buyers who are also transaction processors. The acquisition may enable the acquiring company to achieve operational economies of scale and will generally fit with the management style and culture of these types of acquirers.

In attempting to identify these types of potential buyers, it is important to understand their strategies and views of their business without judging their correctness. In other words, the selling corporation should not disregard potential buyers by imposing its own strategic or operational philosophy while screening them. In the second example above, the selling corporation may see no operational efficiencies and may even see risks in combining two different transaction processing activities, and therefore eliminate a particular potential buyer from consideration. That same potential buyer may see the situation quite differently, and therefore may be willing to pay handsomely for the business.

Suppliers and Customers

Depending on the nature of the business being sold, both suppliers to that business and customers of the business may be potential buyers. Good candidates in both these categories are relatively easy to identify and assess since the business being sold has had an association with them.

Others

Companies seeking diversification, holding companies, investment groups, and venture capitalists all may be potential buyers. These types of buyers are often more difficult to identify and screen. They are generally identified by the management or directors of the selling corporation who have personal knowledge of the investment objectives of certain of these types of organizations. Investment bankers and business brokers are other sources of information on these types of buyers. Often the management of the business being sold will identify and introduce these types of buyers as part of a management buyout plan.

Selecting the Selling Process

There are basically four different methods of selling a business. Each has its advantages and disadvantages. The selection of the process to be utilized depends largely on the nature of the business being sold and the objectives of the selling corporation. The four methods are:

- Competitive bidding.
- Sequential selling.
- One buyer.
- Going public.

Competitive Bidding

In most instances this process, if managed correctly, will produce the highest price and best deal structure for the selling corporation. By definition, it suggests that more than one prospective purchaser has been identified. This process is usually most effective when 5 to 10 potential buyers have been identified and when diverse strategic objectives are present in the potential buyer list. The process begins when the divestiture manager contacts each identified prospective purchaser to determine if there is initial interest. Those indicating interest are then requested to sign a confidentiality letter prior to receiving a copy of the offering memorandum. As indicated earlier, the offering memorandum will state the rules to be followed by potential bidders, including the date for preliminary bids, and the individual at the selling corporation to be contacted for any necessary clarification prior to the bid date.

To maximize the effectiveness of competitive bidding, the selling corporation must carefully control the process and information flow. Upon receipt of preliminary bids, the prospective buyer list will usually be reduced. Some may not bid at all. Others may bid low or present an apparently unacceptable deal structure. In any event, all bidders should be contacted in order to clarify their bids and their bidding philosophies. At this point, it is important to understand that the highest bidder may not be the winner and that the lower bids may not be losers. It is, however, necessary to determine which are the serious bidders and which are not. Those considered serious should then be scheduled for business reviews (see below).

Final bids are generally scheduled for receipt a short time after the completion of the business reviews. Upon receiving the final bids, the project team will conduct what is often referred to as an apples-to-apples analysis. This is the process in which the similarities and differences in the bids are identified, and it is the basis on which the apparent winner is selected. This is the most critical point in the use of competitive bidding from the selling corporation's perspective. It is at this point that the project manager notifies the bidders of the results. This should be done in reverse order, that is, from the least attractive bid to the most attractive. Often during this process, when a bidder is advised that his bid has been unsuccessful, he will ask what it will take to win. These discussions can result in the revision of one or more bids and often lead to a transaction considerably more attractive than any of the so-called final bids.

The potential disadvantages of utilizing competitive bidding generally derive from the unlikely possibility of an unsuccessful sale. If the business, for whatever reason, is not sold, the use of competitive bidding can impair the value and near term viability of the business. Customers see a lack of commitment to the business on the part of the selling corporation. Employees feel that lack of commitment as well. Competitors turn this to their advantage. If a competitor has been a prospective buyer, it will have gained significant knowledge about the business that can be used against that business in the marketplace. Unsuccessful divestitures, in general, usually result from poor initial planning of the divestiture or, in some cases, from badly managed selling processes.

Sequential Selling

Having identified prospective purchasers, the selling corporation can elect to offer the business to what is believed to be the most likely potential buyer and, if unsuccessful, move down the pre-established priority list. If successful with the first potential buyer, this is obviously a much easier process to manage than competitive bidding. However, the price and deal structure that is negotiated will have no market frame of reference. The seller will never know if a better deal could have been made with someone else. If the primary objective is to get out of the business, with price and deal structure secondary, this is an acceptable selling method. Should the pre-established priority list prove faulty, requiring the business to be offered to a number of prospective purchasers in sequence, the business will quickly become known as one that has been "shopped" and rejected, and its value potentially impaired.

One Buyer

If, in the identification of prospective buyers, only one candidate can be identified, the seller will be in a position with little negotiating leverage. Even in those instances where the selling corporation has been approached on numerous occasions by the apparent single buyer, the seller's negotiating position will be weak, and therefore the resulting transaction most probably will not meet all of the seller's objectives. In those instances where there is a known anxious buyer, the seller should carefully consider the value this buyer sees in the business and attempt to identify others who might see it as well. If successful, a one-buyer divestiture might be turned into a competitive bidding transaction, thereby shifting the negotiating leverage away from the anxious buyer. The result will be significantly better price and terms than could have been expected in a one-buyer transaction.

Going Public

Taking a division or a subsidiary public as a means of divesting that business is considerably different than selling an entity through a private transaction. First, the entity to be sold must have an established history of profits and growth or at least a proprietary product or service on which a public market price can be based. Second, market conditions must be favorable in terms of an appetite for initial public offerings and for those in the industry in which the proposed new issue operates. Unlike private transactions, even the most sophisticated selling corporations require the assistance of investment bankers when contemplating the divestiture of a business through an initial public offering.

Business Reviews

Where the selling process involves the use of competitive bidding, business reviews are held for all prospective buyers who are considered serious after receipt of initial bids and clarifying discussions. In a sequential sale, a business review is held only for the top-priority prospective buyer, and no one else, unless discussions with that buyer are terminated, in which case the process is started over with the next potential buyer on the priority list. The same is true in a one-buyer transaction; however, in this instance, should discussions terminate, the selling corporation's only alternatives are to keep the business or, as mentioned earlier, perhaps try to turn it into a competitive bidding deal by finding other prospective buyers who can be shown the value of the business originally only seen by the one buyer.

During the business reviews, which generally last one or two days, prospective buyers are given detailed presentations on all aspects of the business. It is during the business reviews that prospective buyers are able to meet the key members of management of the business being sold and to obtain a level of detail about the business that reaches well below the general type of information contained in the offering memorandum. Also, during the business reviews, prospective purchasers are often given the opportunity to visit the company's facilities.

The primary purpose of business reviews is to provide prospective purchasers with sufficient information necessary for the preparation of firm offers for the business. In those instances, where the selling process utilized is competitive bidding, prospective purchasers will often want to significantly refine their initial bid after the business reviews. This will enable the selling corporation to better understand the offers and will facilitate the selection of the winning bidder. If the process being utilized is sequential selling, the business reviews will either reinforce the interest of the priority purchaser, thereby significantly increasing the probability of consummating the transaction with that party, or they will result in less interest, causing the selling corporation to consider moving to the next potential purchaser on the priority list. In a one-buyer type selling process, the business reviews will tend to blend with the negotiating process. While the same, detailed level of information will be provided in this instance, since both parties are generally aware that there is only one potential purchaser, the information exchange will invariably combine discussions of the deal structure and purchase price.

Negotiating and Closing the Transaction

Negotiating and closing a divestiture transaction requires a diverse set of skills and very thorough preparation. Facts and information alone are not sufficient. The chief negotiator must be a consummate actor, and the other members of the negotiating team must know their roles. Good negotiators know when to be tough and when to give on a specific point. Furthermore, they know how to effectively link negotiating points so that if they must retreat from a position on one point they can maintain or improve their position on another. Even in those rare instances where businesses almost sell themselves, the objective of good negotiators is to maximize price and optimize the deal structure.

Preparing for Negotiations

As stated above, the chief negotiator must be an accomplished actor, and the other members of the negotiating team must know their roles. Like successful plays, effective negotiations require a good script, trained players, and sufficient rehearsal. Prior to beginning negotiations, the negotiating team should identify all major points to be discussed. Each of these points should be carefully evaluated in the context of the overall objective of the divestiture. For each negotiating point, the team should prepare its opening position, preferred position, fallback position, and the deal breakers. While the negotiations will generally be led by the chief negotiator, other members of the team may be assigned to take the lead on specific points. This should be determined in advance. It is also helpful sometimes to designate a "hero" and a "villain." There will certainly be some difficult points during the negotiations. Often a position on a point can be preserved if it can be made to appear that while one member of the team is working toward a compromise, another member of the team is very unhappy. For this technique to be effective, the point being negotiated must have been established as a critical one and the individual playing the villain must have been positioned as a person of sufficient authority to upset the deal.

Prior to beginning negotiations, and where possible, it is often helpful to role-play the forthcoming negotiations. This will often identify weaknesses in the positions established for each point and will enable the members of the negotiating team to polish their roles.

Conducting the Negotiations

Actual negotiations usually take place in several steps. The first step usually deals with reaching an agreement in principle. This is the process where the seller and the buyer meet to discuss and negotiate each of the key points of the transaction as they see them. In some cases, this process results in what is simply a term sheet to be used as the basis for negotiation and preparation of the definitive purchase agreement. In other cases, the parties may agree to sign a formal agreement in principle once all major points are believed to have been resolved. (See Chapter 30 for a complete discussion of the negotiations process.)

Due Diligence Examinations

Having reached and documented agreement on the major points of the transaction, the purchaser will expect to conduct a due diligence examination of the business. This requires the seller to make available to the purchaser all appropriate books, records, and facilities of the business for verification of financial statements and other information. Any misrepresentations discovered by the purchaser can void the agreement or cause renegotiation of price and deal structure.

The due diligence inspection will include examination and verification of:

Accounting records.

Physical inventory.

Accounts receivable.

Current liabilities and long-term obligations.

Contracts.

Systems and operations.

Insurance coverage.

Contingent liabilities and litigation.

Employment contracts.

Other pertinent issues.

Upon completion of the due diligence examination, negotiations will address the resolution of any issues that may have arisen as a result of that process. (See Chapter 10 for a complete discussion of the due diligence process.)

The Purchase Agreement

The next step in the conduct of negotiations is the preparation of the definitive purchase agreement and any supplementary agreements that may be required. The extent and depth of negotiations required to finalize the purchase agreement will generally depend on the level of detail included in the agreement in principle and the extent to which major new issues have developed as part of the due diligence examination. If few or no major new business issues are outstanding at this point in the process, negotiation of the definitive purchase agreement will tend to focus on legal matters.

The final step is the actual preparation of the definitive purchase agreement and any necessary supplementary agreements. These agreements generally go through numerous drafts and revisions prior to the closing. If the divestiture was planned well by the selling corporation and the business issues were negotiated in good faith by both parties, the preparation of agreements and closing documents will be greatly facilitated.

Closing the Transaction

The actual closing should be nothing more than the signing of agreements, the exchanging of the proceeds of the transaction, and perhaps a glass of champagne to celebrate a successful deal for both buyer and seller. A word of caution, however, is in order. The best way to state this caution is to quote Yogi Berra, who is reputed to have said, "It ain't over 'til it's over." Stated in more traditional terms, a seller can never relax until the documents are signed and proceeds change hands. A high confidence level after reaching an agreement in principle is a sure prescription for disaster. A comfortable feeling about the last draft of the purchase agreement can bring great disappointment, and insufficient attention to detail in preparing the closing documents can result in a deferred closing or no closing at all.

SUMMARY

The decision to divest a business represents a significant strategic action and critical corporate undertaking. While divesting a business is one of a number of alternative methods of raising capital, it is one of the most complex, and therefore requires specialized skills and professional management. Divestitures are not business-as-usual transactions. They should not be undertaken by, or assigned to, individuals with little or no experience in successfully completing transactions of this type. Successful divestitures are those that are carefully planned, cleverly sold, and competently negotiated.

CHAPTER 10

A BUSINESSMAN'S REVIEW INVESTIGATION FOR MERGERS AND ACQUISITIONS

Arthur Andersen & Co.

If a business combination is to have a reasonable chance of succeeding, it must be properly planned and the acquisition candidate thoroughly investigated. The purpose of this chapter is to assist in designing and performing a thorough due diligence investigation, particularly one type of investigation commonly referred to as a "Businessman's Review." The chapter is divided into two sections:

- An Overview of the Investigation Process
- The Businessman's Review Checklist

The first section discusses the various types and stages of a purchase investigation, together with some common problems and exposure areas. The second section contains a model Checklist for a Businessman's Review, which is usually performed during the preliminary negotiations. The purpose of the Businessman's Review is to obtain a general understanding of an acquisition candidate and whatever information is required without verification before deciding to proceed with the negotiations.

To decide whether a deal is as good as it appears, the acquiror should conduct an investigation, and verify the representations the seller has made to strike the deal. We broadly refer to this effort as the "purchase investigation." It is an ongoing activity that begins even before there is a general understanding. It may involve fact gathering, review, analysis and verification, or only some of these activities depending on the circumstances.

Why is the investigation so important? Because the risks inherent in acquisitions increase dramatically without it. Buying a business without adequate information, or with half-truths, can lead to a significant financial loss. Although this may sound simplistic, this basic principle is frequently violated.

In some instances, purchase investigations can be ineffective, and may not provide the information necessary to properly evaluate the candidate and make a sound decision. The cause may be poor communication, misunderstandings, lack of careful planning, failure to fix responsibilities and coordinate the effort and, perhaps most important, the fact that the investigation often focuses on the quantity of information it can obtain, rather than on the quality. Important information either gets lost in a sea of paper or the right information never gets collected.

For example, with respect to marketing information, acquirors should focus not just on market share or growth statistics, but on data that help them evaluate why the acquisition candidate has been successful in the marketplace and whether its competitive strategy will continue to be viable. With respect to financial information, acquirors should focus on major exposure areas, trends and unusual financial characteristics—not on every item in the financial statements.

NATURE AND SCOPE OF A PURCHASE INVESTIGATION

Depending on their experience and time availability, a company's personnel can perform a purchase investigation with or without the help of outside consultants (e.g., accountants, investment and merchant bankers, lawyers, special industry consultants, actuaries, appraisers). We recommend that management play a major role in the investigation. This permits them to obtain information that is important to the ultimate decision to proceed, and can be helpful in the successful operation of the business after acquisition.

The scope of an investigation may range from a minimal effort (such as a review of available financial information, visits to company facilities, and discussions with management concerning representations made or other matters) to a comprehensive effort (involving a detailed investigation and/or purchase audit). The type of investigation depends on management's need for information, the size and relative significance of the acquisition candidate, the availability of audited and internal financial information, the degree of inherent risk, the time allowed, etc. For example, in the case of a tender offer, the ability to analyze internal information on the target company may be limited. Consequently, the acquiror and its professional advisers may not be able to do much more than gather, compile, and analyze available public information. However, in the case of a private company, the need for a full-scale investigation is much greater and is more difficult to perform. This would also apply to a divestiture by a company.

Frequently, an acquiror performs more than one type of investigation on the same candidate or performs its investigation in stages as the acquisition process moves forward. For example, it may be advisable to perform a preliminary investigation before the general agreement is reached or before the contract is signed. As noted earlier, this preliminary investigation is a "Businessman's Review." It is usually performed without independent verification or audit, and is designed to obtain and analyze information needed before deciding to proceed with the negotiations.

Later, after a general agreement is reached, it is wise to extend the investigation and audit the seller's financial statements and/or verify the representations made by its management. Whether this later investigation involves a complete purchase audit or only limited verification procedures depends on the degree of assurance required.

Once a definitive agreement or contract is signed, a purchase audit may be required to verify the closing date financial statements. If a purchase audit was already performed before the contract signing, updating procedures may be all that is required to detect material changes occurring between the date of the purchase audit and the closing.

THE ROLE OF THE BUSINESSMAN'S REVIEW

At a fairly early stage, the acquiror needs to obtain sufficient information about the seller's operations to make a decision whether or not to proceed with the acquisition. The Businessman's Review fulfills this need.

This Review involves fact gathering and analysis, usually without independent verification, of an acquisition candidate's financial and accounting records or other information obtained. The acquiror's management may or may not participate in this Review, and the Review may be performed in one or several stages at various points during the negotiations. The Businessman's Review provides a broad understanding of all aspects of the company's business, including:

- Industry information.
- Marketing methods.
- Manufacturing and distribution methods.
- Financial reporting systems and controls.
- Industrial relations.
- Comprehensive understanding of the company's financial statements, accounting data, and tax posture.
- Research and development programs.
- Regulatory reporting requirements.
- International operations.
- Legal matters.

Besides obtaining information on the seller, the Businessman's Review may also include a detailed review and analysis of the information obtained. The scope of this part of the Review usually depends on the nature of the transaction and the particular needs of the acquiring company. Usually, however, accounting and tax principles and practices are reviewed in depth, with special emphasis on the problems related to the intended acquisition. The acquiror and its independent accountants must agree at the outset on the scope of this part of the Review, and the acquiror must understand its objectives and limitations.

Because the Businessman's Review normally generates a great deal of information, management should prepare a checklist of questions for the seller in advance. This will ensure that the buyer gets the right kind of information from the seller. The Checklist contained in the second section of this chapter can be used as a model; it can be used in its present form, or sections can be added or deleted to suit a particular situation. For example, the *Industry Analysis* section can be deleted if an analysis is already available on the seller's particular industry. Also, the section on *Research and Development* activities may be omitted if it is not relevant. A section on international factors can be added if the company is engaged in international activities.

The Checklist focuses primarily on financial and accounting matters, particularly in the review and analysis phase. Generally, the buyer has focused on nonfinancial or operating matters during its own investigation (e.g., quality of products, reputation with customers, manufacturing efficiency, management capabilities, etc.). However, the independent accountant can be helpful in obtaining this information as well, which explains why the Checklist contains sections on nonfinancial and operating matters.

PURCHASE AUDIT AND OTHER VERIFICATION PROCEDURES

In some cases, review and analysis may not be enough. The buyer may require an audit of the seller's financial statements and/or verification of the representations made by its management. These requirements depend on the desired degree of assurance, the seller's past audit history and the time permitted. These verification procedures may involve a comprehensive purchase audit or specially designed auditing procedures applied to specific accounts and/or exposure areas. For example, inventory is such a significant item to manufacturing and distribution enterprises that auditors are frequently asked to observe and test the physical inventories and audit the valuation, with particular emphasis on excess and obsolete inventory and valuation practices.

These procedures often turn up undisclosed problems, particularly in today's environment. Although management may not wish to incur the cost of an audit, it does provide an additional level of assurance.

When the seller has a history of audits done by a reputable accounting firm (which also may have prepared its tax returns), and the audited financial statements are reasonably current, a purchase audit may not be necessary, except in areas normally not covered by the annual audit (e.g., quality of the seller's products, its reputation with customers, and other nonfinancial areas). However, at a minimum, the seller's auditors' workpapers should be reviewed in detail to identify potential problems and exposure areas. This review may eliminate the need for independent verification.

AREAS OF INVESTIGATION

The Businessman's Review, whether performed alone or in conjunction with verification/auditing procedures, should accumulate a portfolio of basic information about the seller. Depending on the extent of the particular Review, it should investigate and analyze the areas noted below. If, after the Review, the reliability of the information is suspect or if the buyer wants greater assurance, a full purchase audit or other verification procedures may be necessary.

Company Background and History

The general nature of the business, principal locations and facilities, history, and similar information should be collected in the early phase of the investigation. In addition, information is usually obtained on management, directors, and outside advisers. Whenever possible, information on recent developments in the company, plans for the future, and major problems (e.g., lawsuits, government restrictions, environmental considerations, and sensitive transactions) should be covered.

Industry Analysis

When a proposed acquisition is in an industry new to the buyer, a detailed industry review is prudent. This review normally is performed prior to the investigation of a particular company.

Factors usually included in the industry analysis are:

- Competition—within the industry and from other industries—and relative market share.
- Industry growth rates in sales and profits (past and projected), and external factors affecting industry growth and profitability.
- Mergers and acquisitions in the industry—to determine if a business combination is crucial for survival or growth in the industry.
- Government regulations—degree and trends.
- Patents, trademarks, copyrights, etc.—important to the companies within the industry.
- Key factors of success, barriers to entry and threats.

In many instances, companies may engage industry experts and consultants to assist in the analysis.

Financial and Accounting Data

It is useful to compare financial ratios by major business segments for a period of years to determine important trends. These ratios usually include, as a minimum, return on assets and stockholders' investment, gross profit, profit margin, fixed charge coverage, current ratio, net quick ratio, and debt-to-equity ratio. Information concerning the impact of inflation or cyclicality on operations and the company's ability to operate in such an environment, together with current value and/or replacement cost data and future capital requirements, also should be obtained.

It also is useful to obtain and analyze the prior years' balance sheets, statements of income and statements of changes in financial position, as well as budgets and forecasts for the future. Understanding projected cash flow and the underlying assumptions used in such projections is extremely important. In addition, it is important to understand any differences in, or questionable aspects of, accounting principles and practices followed by the seller. The most important differences and questionable aspects usually relate to bad debt reserves, inventory valuation, depreciation, accounting for long-term contracts, accounting for pensions and employee benefits, reserves, and special industry practices.

In the inventory valuation area in particular, questionable practices are often uncovered such as valuing production overruns, excess stock, or returned goods at full cost.

Taxes

The tax returns and status of tax examinations of the acquisition candidate should be reviewed. This review normally will serve a dual purpose. A review of the seller's tax status should satisfy the buyer that the tax liabilities of the business being acquired are properly stated on the seller's books. In addition, the tax review should focus on the buyer's ability to monetize a portion of its investment through proper tax planning strategies, tax attributes of the seller, etc.

The tax liability review essentially asks the question, "Has the seller paid all its tax liabilities on a current basis, and has a reasonable reserve been accrued for known and anticipated adjustments likely to arise on in-progress and future audits by various taxing authorities?" Although the procedures used to satisfy these questions will vary depending on the size of the candidate, complexity of the seller's particular tax situation, etc., generally they will entail a review and analysis of the tax returns filed for a minimum of three prior years with special emphasis on the reconciliation between financial statement and taxable incomes, together with a review of the most recent report of adjustments made by the various taxing authorities, relating the nature of the adjustments to years still open for examination. The results of this review then are compared to the reserve for taxes, or so-called "cushion," to determine whether the seller has provided adequately for any tax exposures.

Historically, these reviews focused primarily, if not exclusively, on federal income tax issues that could result in a permanent tax cost. Recent developments indicate that an expansion of scope probably is warranted in many situations in the areas of state and local income taxes and the interest cost of tax "timing items." Focusing on permanent disallowances or adjustments measures a seller's liability for past taxes in absolute dollars. In recent years, however, several countries, including the United States, have escalated dramatically the interest imposed on assessments for past taxes and most recently have adopted a compound versus simple interest methodology. Thus, although timing differences such as capitalization of repairs or a disallowance of financial statement reserves will result in no additional tax over time, the shifting of deductions to later years or acceleration of income to earlier years can result in a very substantial interest cost.

State and local taxes also should be considered in this review process. For example, in the United States, many states have become extremely aggressive in taxing multistate enterprises. Some of those states are actively pursuing collection of additional taxes for prior years. With the advent of accelerated cost recovery in the United States, state taxes for many enterprises are becoming an increasingly greater share of the overall corporate tax bite. Accordingly, the buyer should consider a detailed review of the seller's state and local taxes. Multinational companies present unusual problems in this area and, depending on the size of the international operations, may warrant tax reviews on a country-by-country basis.

Succession of the seller's tax attributes also is an important area to review. Because of recent tax legislation in the United States, many companies today have tax net operating loss carryforwards, unutilized investment tax and other credits. Depending on the type of acquisition structure, these tax attributes can represent significant cash savings to the buyer after the acquisition. Therefore, quantifying these attributes is an important step in the review process. Quantification must go beyond merely copying numbers from the tax returns. The buyer must get behind the numbers and adjust the attributes for potential softness due to aggressive tax positions that could be challenged successfully by the tax authorities. If the buyer is purchasing a company's stock from an existing consolidated group, an important part of this phase of the review is advising the buyer on how to protect against the loss of tax benefits associated with postacquisition net operating losses or excess credits that can be carried back for tax purposes to the pre-acquisition tax years of the seller. This involves arranging the proper tax-sharing agreement with the seller tailored to the specifics of the transaction.

Depending on the type of transaction, the tax review should also include a tax basis analysis and an evaluation of potential "step-up" opportunities. If the buyer is considering financing a potential acquisition by selling off certain assets of the acquired company, it should make a careful review of the potential taxes due on the sale of those assets, taking into account the fact that tax basis of assets is usually less than the book value. An evaluation of the seller's "step-up" potential and recapture tax costs associated with this "step-up" starts with an allocation of the purchase price to the various assets of the seller. From there, the recapture costs associated with the allocation are quantified and compared to the tax savings derived from "stepping up" the tax basis of the seller's assets. Because the recapture taxes are required to be paid within a short time after the acquisition and, typically, the "step-up" will be realized over a number of years to arrive at a true comparison, it is necessary to discount the future tax savings using a reasonable interest rate. Unfortunately, recent tax law changes in the United States have increased the potential for recapture tax liability, thereby making a "step-up" of the tax basis of the assets less attractive unless a major portion of the "step-up" can be allocated to inventories or similar short-lived assets.

Investment tax credits, depreciation, international and DISC earnings and profits and LIFO inventory reserves are just some of the types of recaptures that could arise if a "step-up" is elected in the United States. To combat these higher recapture costs, the buyer should look for intangible assets of the seller that can be assigned value and for which a useful life can be developed (e.g., patents, customer lists, etc.).

Human Resources and Industrial Relations

The buyer must appraise the capabilities of the seller's management, particularly when buying a company in an unrelated industry. The buyer should interview key officers and managers, review their prior business experiences, investigate their backgrounds, and compare compensation benefit levels and plans because changes often will result from the transaction.

The buyer should review union contracts, strike history, and related factors to determine any existing problems. Many planned personnel savings may not be possible because of labor agreements. Pension, profit sharing and other employee benefit plans also must be reviewed to determine the effect of the future operations of the combined business. If the seller has many long-term employees, the buyer's cash flow will be depressed when unfunded pension benefits must be paid upon retirement. On the other side of the equation, many pension funds now have surpluses, making acquisitions less expensive.

Marketing

The buyer should obtain information on and analyze various product and marketing factors concerning:

- Sales, profit, and backlog by product line.
- Descriptions of major products and new product developments.
- Annual and monthly sale histories (long-term trend and seasonal or cyclical fluctuations).

- Government sales.
- Major customers.
- Marketing and sales organization, including special compensation arrangements.
- Sales planning and forecasting methods.
- Advertising and promotion expenditures and methods.
- Distribution channels and strategy.
- Customer satisfaction and buying power.
- Market shares of key competitors.
- Product life cycles and technological obsolescence.
- Pricing strategy.
- Competitive strategy.
- New product development.

The trends should be compared to industry averages to determine the company's relative performance. Competitive and potentially competitive new products should be investigated because of their possible negative impact on the seller's future results.

The marketing intelligence and present product sales trend information should be compared to an analysis (aging and usage by item) of inventory to detect excess and obsolete inventory. Scrapping of inventory after the company is acquired can be very costly.

Manufacturing and Distribution

A review of the manufacturing and distribution areas should include:

- Each production facility (name, location, owned/leased, book value, fair market value, capacity, employees, present condition, present utilization, alternative uses, etc.).
- Manufacturing processes.
- Suppliers of major raw materials.
- Physical distribution methods (purchase, intracompany transfers, final sales to customer).
- Manufacturing efficiency.

Research and Development

The buyer should analyze past R&D programs (cost and actual or estimated benefits), current and planned programs (estimated cost and benefits), personnel and facilities utilized in R&D, and the method of accounting for R&D.

Financial and Management Control Systems

Understanding a seller's internal reporting and control systems is always important, particularly when the seller is in a different industry. The acquiring company probably will rely heavily on the seller's existing systems, since it is normally not possible to install identical systems in both companies because of differences in operations or management philosophy or because of the cost involved in conjoining systems. Production and material control systems and order systems are particularly important since deficiencies can seriously affect the company. However, basic accounting controls are also important because of their potential impact on the accuracy of reporting and employee fraud.

Regulatory Reporting Requirements

Reporting requirements promulgated by various regulatory authorities should be given special attention because they can have a profound effect on the future of the business. Ignoring them may result in substantial fines and embarrassment. The buyer should be satisfied that the seller's facilities are in compliance with the various regulatory authorities, such as the Environmental Protection Agency (EPA) and Occupational Safety and Health Administration (OSHA) in the United States.

International Factors

If the target company is engaged in international trade or has other international activities, the acquiror should have a good understanding of these international operations and how they affect the overall operation. Questions concerning the international country's investment climate, trade and investment restrictions, exchange controls, inflation rates and reporting requirements should be addressed. Repatriation of earnings may be necessary to repay acquisition debt, but may be impeded by exchange controls or the seller's international tax credit limitation status.

Discretionary Expenses

The seller can defer certain expenses, such as research and development costs and repair and maintenance costs, for the short term with adverse long-term effects. A careful review of these discretionary expenses can avoid possible future unanticipated outlays of capital, which effectively increase the cost of the acquisition.

COMMON PROBLEMS OR EXPOSURE AREAS

Following are some of the common financial and accounting problems frequently uncovered in Businessman's Reviews or other types of investigations:

- *Undervaluation of inventory* by private companies to minimize taxes, which can lead to distorted earnings trends and potential tax assessments—This undervaluation usually is accomplished through conservative pricing, excessive obsolescence writedowns, or failure to count inventory on hand accurately.
- *Overvaluation of inventory* due to unrecorded inventory obsolescence or over-costing—This may be caused by product overruns, sales returns and allowances, changing technology, new product development, and maturing or discontinued products. This may occur even when a substantial LIFO reserve exists.
- *Litigation*—Few firms are totally free from litigation. The most common litigation results from product liability, which frequently doesn't surface until after the acquisition is completed.
- *"Dressing up" financial statements* before selling a company—This tactic can include deferral of R&D expenses and repairs and maintenance, "release" of inventory reserves, inadequate reserves, faulty estimates or changes in estimates or assumptions (e.g., for bad debt reserves, pension accounting, sales returns and allowances, warranties, slow-moving and excess inventory, etc.), and undisclosed changes or aggressive accounting principles or methods.
- *Receivables not collectible* at recorded amounts—Doubtful accounts, cash and trade discounts, dated receivables and sales returns and allowances may not be adequately reserved.
- *Certain investments may not be realizable*—Investments accounted for using the equity method and nonmarketable investments are required to be written down only for "permanent impairment" in value, not for temporary declines. Liberal judgments may have been applied to avoid recognition of permanent impairment.
- *Credibility and integrity of management*—Often a private investigation is needed to obtain sufficient information and background on management to determine if they are right for the job and trustworthy.
- *Inclusion of personal expenses* in the financial statements of a private company—These expenses usually decrease reported net income; however, this practice also can be used to yield a favorable result when one does not exist, i.e., to change historical trends (by decreasing personal expenses, profits can appear to be increasing).

- *Tax contingencies*—One of the more important problem areas in an acquisition. Most companies tend to be very aggressive when preparing tax returns. A careful review of current and prior years' returns and Revenue agents' reports should be made, and any unusual items should be noted.
- *Unrecorded liabilities*—May include vacation pay, sales returns, allowances and discounts (volume and cash), pension liabilities, claims, items resulting from poor cutoffs, loss contracts and warranties, among others.
- *Related-party transactions*—Most often found in private companies, these can have a material effect on the company under new ownership or on the historical trends presented.
- *Inadequate financial controls,* including poor pricing and costing policies, and weak budgeting systems and controls.
- *Major customers or contracts*—Usually loss of one has a material effect on operations.
- *Need for significant future expenditures*—These could include plant relocation or expansion, replacement of aging property, plant and equipment and new product development.
- *International operations*—These present multiple problems of their own including labor, management and operating difficulties, as well as those of a financial nature.
- *Unusual transactions and extraordinary items,* such as sales of assets—These often improve the trend presented and should be identified and evaluated carefully.

The foregoing are some of the common financial and accounting problems that a Businessman's Review and/or other type of investigation can uncover.

CONCLUSION

A purchase investigation should provide the acquiror with a thorough understanding of the seller's business, particularly concerning aspects that are not readily known and/or are critical to the ultimate acquisition decision. Accordingly, the investigation should be designed to obtain and verify predetermined essential elements of information that the acquiror needs to evaluate the candidate properly. It also should provide for verification of the information obtained whenever the reliability of that information is important and/or suspect.

The Businessman's Review is the first step in the investigation process, and often the most critical. The following section contains a Checklist that can be used for such Reviews. This Checklist provides a standardized, fact-finding approach, eliminating the initial start-up time and cost of designing information-gathering and review procedures.

The importance of management's participation in the investigation cannot be overemphasized. Management should be the prime mover, scope-setter and leading edge of the investigation, in both financial and nonfinancial areas. Too often management delegates the entire investigation to outside accountants or industry experts, and important information is overlooked. In addition, the "feel" for the seller, its management and qualitative considerations so necessary in making the "buy" decision often are lost when management does not take a primary role in the investigation.

APPENDIX: THE BUSINESSMAN'S REVIEW CHECKLIST

As discussed in the preceding section, this Checklist can help the buyer obtain a broad understanding of all aspects of the seller's business before independent verification is required. Verification or auditing procedures frequently are employed at a later point in the negotiations to substantiate the information obtained from using this Checklist.

The breakdown by area allows different members of management with pertinent functional responsibility to review specific areas, with or without the assistance of outside consultants.

The sections on *Financial and Accounting Data, Financial Reporting System and Accounting Procedures and Controls* and *Taxes* are more detailed than the other sections because they frequently are reviewed with the assistance of independent public accountants. The other sections normally are reviewed by company personnel with the occasional assistance of accountants or other outside specialists (engineers, employee benefit specialists, actuaries, industry and marketing experts, etc.). Therefore, these other sections are somewhat general because they are intended to provide only a broad overview.

It is essential at the outset that management agree on the scope of the review, its objectives and limitations, and the persons responsible for reviewing each area. This will ensure that the right type of information is obtained to properly evaluate the acquisition candidate.

This Checklist is intended only as a guide. Although the Checklist can be used in its entirety, sections should be added or deleted to suit the particular circumstances and information needs for each case.

The Checklist is composed of the following parts:

I. Company Background
II. Industry Analysis
III. Financial and Accounting Data
IV. Financial Reporting System and Accounting Procedures and Controls
V. Taxes
VI. Organization, Human Resources, and Industrial Relations
VII. Marketing and Products
VIII. Manufacturing and Distribution
IX. Research and Development
X. Financial Ratios

I. COMPANY BACKGROUND

A. Company Name

______

B. Address

______

C. Telephone Number

______

D. Other Principal Locations (Describe)

1. Sales ______
2. Manufacturing ______
3. Other ______

E. Date of Incorporation

______

F. State of Incorporation

______

G. Ownership

______

1. Public or private ______
2. Exchanges on which traded ______
3. Type of securities outstanding (common stock, preferred stock, etc.) ______
4. Principal stockholders and percentage of ownership ______

H. Directors

List all Directors Name	Years as Director	Other Affiliations

Identify board committee participants and chairperson, i.e., audit committee, etc.

I. Outside Experts

	Name	Years Employed	Description of Relationship
1. Attorneys			
2. Auditors			
3. Bankers			
4. Other—describe			

J. Brief Description of Business—Attach detailed description, if available. Include all significant business segments, organizational structures, products or services the company has developed, etc.

K. Brief History of Company—Attach detailed description, if available. Include any recent significant changes in ownership and business operations.

L. Selling Objectives of the Company and Related Information

1. Why is the company for sale? ______

2. Who are the individuals responsible for the sale of the company? ______

3. Are there any minority or dissenting shareholder rights that may affect the sale transaction? ______

4. What are the proposed terms and conditions of the acquisition (e.g., cash/stock/combination thereof, etc.)? ______

5. Is there an anticipated time frame to consummate the transaction? ______

6. What are the tax objectives of the seller and its shareholders? ______

7. What are the tax consequences to the seller and its shareholders? ______

8. What is the anticipated accounting and tax treatment? ______

9. Who is responsible for payment of brokers' fees (buyer/seller responsibility)? What is the amount, terms, and when payable?

M. Management

1. What is the reputation of major shareholders, directors and management?
2. Will they continue after the sale with or without employment contracts?
3. Have the company's officers, directors or major shareholders been involved in criminal or other legal proceedings?
4. Will the sale trigger severance or other employee benefit obligations, loss of key customers or contracts, employee resignations, etc.?
5. Have obvious management actions been taken to make the company look more attractive, i.e., deferral of bonuses, research and development, advertising and capital improvement expenditures, etc.?

N. Recent Major Developments and Trends

1. Have there been any major trends or developments within the company?
2. Have there been any major trends or developments within the industry and competition?

O. Plans for the Future—Obtain corporate minutes for the past ______ years and any operating plans (including those pertaining to contemplated discontinued operations), forecasts, budgets, etc., that are available.

P. Related Parties—Are the operations of the company significantly impacted by related-party transactions? If so, list the parties and describe the relationship and transactions.

Q. Major Litigation, Pending or Potential—Describe and obtain letters from attorneys assessing litigation.

R. Governmental Restrictions and Regulation—Describe impact on business.

S. Cyclical Factors—Describe any affecting the industry.

T. Credit and Securities Rating—Obtain Dun & Bradstreet Report and securities analyst research reports (if a public company).

U. Major External Forces That Affect the Company—Describe and note the source.

V. Political and Social Attitudes Toward the Company—Describe and note the source.

W. Related Industry Perception—Describe the general perception of suppliers and customers toward the company. Specific supplier and customer checks should be performed as part of Section II (*Industry Analysis*), Section VII (*Marketing—Products*), Section VIII (*Manufacturing—Distribution*) or as part of subsequent verification procedures.

X. Other Comments

II. INDUSTRY ANALYSIS

A. Industry Structure

1. Number of companies by size category
2. Degree of industry concentration
3. Merger and acquisition trends
   a. Vertical
   b. Horizontal
   c. Other
4. Business failures/successes
   a. Trends
   b. Causes
5. Industry structure
   a. Geographic location
   b. Product lines
   c. Channels of distribution
   d. Pricing policies
   e. Degree of integration
   f. Type of customer
6. Barriers to entry by new companies

B. Industry Growth

1. Estimated Annual Growth Rate—Last _______ Years

	Total $	% Increase	Variation Analysis*
a. Sales	_____	_________	_________________
b. Profits	_____	_________	_________________
c. Market Share	_____	_________	_________________

2. Estimated Annual Growth Rate — Next _______ Years

	Total $	% Increase	Variation Analysis*
a. Sales	_____	_________	_________________
b. Profits	_____	_________	_________________
c. Market Share	_____	_________	_________________

*This should include major reasons for growth or lack thereof, including demand changes, cyclicality, trends, market share changes, competitive changes, etc.

3. Factors Affecting Growth

	Major	Minor	Describe
	(check one)		
a. Demographic trends ____________________	_____	_____	_______________
b. General economic trends ____________________	_____	_____	_______________
c. Disposable income ____________________	_____	_____	_______________
d. Interest rates ____________________	_____	_____	_______________
e. Industry composition and trends ____________________	_____	_____	_______________
f. Market size ____________________	_____	_____	_______________

	Major	Minor	Describe
	(check one)		
g. Market share ____________________	_____	_____	_______________
h. Technological innovation ____________________	_____	_____	_______________
i. Production design ____________________	_____	_____	_______________
j. Economies of scale ____________________	_____	_____	_______________
k. Product pricing and differentiation ____________________	_____	_____	_______________
l. Imports/Exports ____________________	_____	_____	_______________
m. Advertising or marketing developments ____________________	_____	_____	_______________

n. Government factors ______ ___ ___ ______

- ☐ Demand ______ ___ ___ ______
- ☐ Fiscal Policy ______ ___ ___ ______
- ☐ Regulation ______ ___ ___ ______

o. Customer buying power ______

______ ___ ___ ______

p. Environmental considerations ______

______ ___ ___ ______

q. Other (describe) ______

______ ___ ___ ______

C. Competition

1. Other companies in industry and their strategy ______
2. Competition from other industries, i.e., substitute products ______
3. Nature and extent of trade practices and cooperation ______
4. Key factors for success, barriers to entry and major threats to success ______

D. Customers/Suppliers by Industry

1. List major industries to which products are sold.

	Total Industry Sales/ % Growth Rate/Market Share		
Description	**Last ( ) Years**	**Next ( ) Years**	**Source**

2. Has there been significant growth of new customers/suppliers in the last five years? ______
3. Has there been a trend in forward integration of suppliers and reverse integration of customers? ______
4. Is there a dependence on a few key customers/suppliers? ______

E. Labor—Overall industry and regional analysis

1. Are adequate community services and skilled labor available? ______
2. Are the local pay rates industry competitive? ______
3. Have there been recent union negotiations and/or labor contract renewals? What were the results and settlements of union negotiations?

4. What is the degree of unionization in the industry?

F. Government Regulations

1. To what extent is the company regulated by the government? (describe)
2. What regulatory agencies are responsible?
3. Is there a trend to increased regulation?
4. Are there any unique reporting requirements?

G. Patents, Trademarks, Copyrights, etc.

Are patents, trademarks, copyrights, etc., important in the company's line of business? If so, describe major patents; indicate expiration dates and discuss any recent patent litigation.

H. Other Information—Obtain and attach, if available, current periodicals, newspaper clippings, trade association releases, company-prepared documents (including annual reports, projections, budgets and business plans, public filings and brochures), Standard & Poor's Reports, Value Line Surveys, Moody's Manual extracts, securities research reports, government data including IRS publications and census studies, etc., that provide additional background on the particular industry and competition therein. This should include, wherever possible, the opinion of suppliers, customers, distributors, competitors, lending institutions and other involved parties. The material should include, but not necessarily be limited to, what is being done by the leaders within the industry in terms of product, processes, marketing, pricing, organization, financing and performance trends in terms of volume, market share, profitability and growth.

III. FINANCIAL AND ACCOUNTING DATA

A. Financial Statements—Obtain:

1. Balance Sheets—Annual and interim for last ______ years.
2. Income Statements—Annual and interim for last ______ years.
3. Statements of Changes in Financial Position and Cash Flow—Annual and interim for last ______ years.
4. Comparative financial statements for major business segments, product lines and geographical locations (include a breakdown of sales, gross profit, operating profit and net assets as a minimum).
5. Prospectuses and Registration Statements (if any)
6. Most recent Proxy Statement
7. Interim Financial Statements and Form 10-Q—Most recent

8. Dun & Bradstreet, Standard & Poor's and/or Value Line Reports ______

9. Other SEC Filings—Forms 10-K, S-1, etc. ______

10. Financial and operating projections, budgets, business plans, etc. ______

11. Federal, state and local tax returns and Internal Revenue Service, state and local agent reviews for last ______ years.

B. Assets

1. Cash
   a. Name and number of major disbursement accounts. ______
   b. Average cash balance for last ______ years.
   c. Have all bank accounts been reconciled on a timely basis and all unusual reconciling items been properly explained? ______
   d. Are there any restrictions due to compensating balances? ______
   e. Is cash in other than local currency, and, if so, is it subject to restrictions? ______

2. Receivables—Describe the recognition policy for recording revenues and establishing receivables.
   a. Accounts Receivable

   ☐ Credit Terms—Describe collection, discount and return policies. ______

   ☐ List receivables that are discounted/factored—With whom, cost, terms, purpose, etc. ______

   ☐ List all major receivables segregating trade, employee and other for amounts over ______ %, ______ %, ______ % of respective balances. Also segregate and highlight accounts receivable that represent conditional sales. ______

Name	Current Amount Receivable	Terms	Age	%	Explanation*

*Explain any trade receivables over ______ days old, and employee/officer or other unusual receivables over $ ______.

b. Notes Receivable—List *all* notes over $ ________.
Indicate if any collateral is held.

Name	Amount Receivable	Interest Rate	Date Due	Explanation-Description

c. Obtain a description of the company's bad debt reserve policy.

d. Obtain a summary of bad debt experience for the last ________ years and most recent interim period.

e. Obtain support for and determine reasonableness of general and specific reserve balances.

f. Obtain a summary of the reserve for returns and allowances for the last ________ years. Discuss any unusual trends and variations with management.

g. Obtain receivable aging and turnover analyses for last ________ years.

3. Investments

a. Marketable securities—List all holdings.
(Segregate current and long-term portfolios.)

Description	Date Acquired	Effective Yield	Market Value	Original Cost	Carrying Value

b. Other investments—List all other investments.

Description	Date Acquired	% of Ownership	Effective Yield	Estimated* Value	Original Cost	Carrying Value

*Indicate source of estimates for all significant investments. Attach financial information, and determine if more detailed review is required.

4. Inventories—Obtain breakdown for each major component and product line. Determine location of inventory (on hand, in transit, at outside warehouses, etc.), ownership vs. "bill and hold" or on consignment and whether pledged as collateral for outstanding borrowings. Obtain specifics.

Category By Product Line	Age or Turnover Rate*	Latest Date	Beginning of Year	Beginning of Previous ( ) Years	Valuation Method	Estimated Replacement Cost	Estimated NRV
Raw materials							

Work in process							
Finished goods							
Total							

NOTE: Include a breakdown of labor, material and overhead content by category.
*Disclose how calculated and details.

a. Describe physical inventory and cutoff procedures. ______

b. Describe inventory accounting records (e.g., do perpetual inventory records exist?; is the gross profit method used to determine interim inventories?).

c. Dates of last ______ physical inventories; amount and nature of adjustments. Obtain book-to-physical reconciliations and analyses.

d. Date of next physical inventory. ______

e. Describe inventory reserve policy (excess, slow-moving, obsolete, etc.), and procedures to identify such inventory.

f. Describe procedures used to determine net realizable value. ______

g. Analyze reserves and writedowns for past ______ years and most recent period.

h. Compare trends in product line sales, new product development and changing technology to inventory levels by product.

i. Analyze seasonal inventory requirements/fluctuation. ______

j. Describe the inventory and production cost system. Is a standard or actual cost system used? What are the accounting implications?

- ☐ How is job or process costing accomplished? ______
- ☐ What costs are included in overhead, and what overhead allocations are made? List overhead rates for past ______ years and most recent period.
- ☐ What assumption is made about practical capacity for purposes of absorbing overhead costs? Is it conservative?
- ☐ How are returns, overruns and scrap costed?

- ☐ Have variances been significant if a standard cost system is used? If so, obtain an analysis of variances by product line for the last ______ years.

k. Describe inventory valuation procedures and assess degree of reliability.

____

____

l. List open long-term contracts, including name and type of customer, price, terms, profit recognized, total estimated cost, costs incurred to date and estimate to complete, progress billings to date and scheduled, subcontractors, details and the method of recording income or loss. Obtain an analysis of historical variations and open contracts. Inquire about procedures used and their reliability. Note: A separate investigative work program may have to be designed if the seller produces under long-term contracts due to the inherent lack of accounting precision normally attributable to such contracts.

____

____

5. Plant, Property and Equipment

a. Land—Obtain for each major holding

				Estimated Value		
Location	**Description**	**Date Acquired**	**Cost**	**Amount**	**Basis of Valuation**	**Liens**

b. Plant and Equipment—Obtain for each major facility

Location	**Description**	**Age**	**Original Cost**	**Book Value***	**Estimated Value****	**Replacement Cost**	**Accumulated Depreciation***	**Depreciation Method***	**Estimated Remaining Life**	**Liens**

*For tax and book purposes.
**Describe method of valuation, i.e., liquidation, going concern, etc.

c. Obtain a list of any significant plant, property and equipment additions or retirements for the past ______ years, and of projects currently under construction or committed to.

d. Obtain a summary of all significant leasehold improvements, including original cost, accumulated amortization, the period of amortization and related lease expiration dates.

e. Describe the accounting policies for capitalization of plant, property, equipment, construction costs, interest during construction, start-up or preoperating costs, recognition of gains and losses upon retirement/disposal and maintenance and repairs. Also describe the depreciation and amortization policies.

____

____

f. Obtain a summary of changes in policy or estimates over the past ______ years.

6. Other Assets—Obtain a description and analysis, including nature, how they arose, capitalization and amortization policy, rights of use, liens, threats to loss in value, appreciation, etc.
   a. Goodwill ____________________
   b. Deferred charges ____________________
   c. Research and development ____________________
   d. Organization costs ____________________
   e. Contract rights ____________________
   f. Patents ____________________
   g. Trademarks/Trade Names ____________________
   h. Other ____________________

C. Liabilities

1. Accounts Payable
   a. List all companies that constitute ______% or more of the total accounts payable balance, or that account for ______% or more of annual purchases during the past ______ years.

Name	Current Amount Payable	Last Year $ Amount of Purchases	Description of Materials/ Services Purchased

   b. Describe any unusual credit terms or relationships that exist with the companies listed, e.g., volume discounts, extended terms, commitments, etc.

   ____

   ____

   c. Describe normal credit terms—Are discounts taken, etc.? ____________________

   ____

2. Accrued Liabilities—Obtain an analysis of the current balance and the balance at the past ______ years. Explain significant variations.
   a. Have all required items been properly accrued, i.e., professional fees, employee benefits, payroll, taxes, vacation pay, claims, probable contingencies, severance and retirement benefits, warranty costs, pension liabilities, planned move or facility shutdown costs, utilities, unvouchered purchases, etc.?

   ____

   b. Have other potential unrecorded liabilities been considered? — See D.

   ____

3. Notes Payable—List *all* notes over $ ______.

Payee	Description*	Interest Rate	Date	Amount		
				Original	Current	Payment Schedule

4. Long-term Liabilities—List.

Payee	Description*	Interest Rate	Date	Amount Original	Amount Current	Payment Schedule

*Include conversion rights, warrants, other equity features, prepayment premiums, sinking-fund requirements, effects of ownership changes, and credit ratings by outside sources.

5. Banking Relationships—List all banks with whom the company maintains a borrowing relationship.

Bank Name	Location	Line of Credit Terms/ Unused Balance	Letters of Credit	Commitment Fees	Interest Costs	Borrowing History

6. Obtain Loan Agreements and Indentures—Can all debt be assumed in the case of an asset purchase or liquidation? State restrictions on debt assumptions, if any.

___

___

7. Describe financial covenants, and attach latest compliance computations and auditor's/officers' certification.

___

8. What assets, if any, are pledged as collateral against the liabilities? ___

___

9. Obtain an analysis of short-term borrowing patterns for past ___ years (minimum and maximum levels, average amount, weighted average interest rate, etc.), and compare to the cyclical nature of sales, inventory and production levels. Indicate interest rate and security required, if any.

___

10. Describe any "off-balance-sheet" financing and obtain a summary of terms and restrictions.

___

D. Potential Unrecorded Liabilities—Is an overall review for unaccrued and unrecorded liabilities regularly performed by the seller? How?

___

Have the following been considered?

1. Product and sales related:
   a. Product safety or truth-in-advertising problems.
   b. Product liability claims—Obtain a summary of reserves for warranties for the past _______ years and discuss warranty policy, reserve requirements and unusual trends with management.
   c. Service guarantees.
2. Employee related:
   a. Obtain recent compliance reports or deficiency letters issued by governmental agencies or other regulatory authorities.
   b. Describe any OSHA, EEO or other violations, and actions the company has taken to resolve them.

      ____

   c. Are there any occupational diseases inherent to the industry? _______________
   d. What other unusual employee obligations exist? _______________
   e. Is the company a member of a multiemployer pension plan, and have the related funded and unfunded accumulated benefits been calculated?

      ____

   f. Do unions have the right to veto planned facility shutdowns or be compensated as a result?

      ____

3. Environmental problems—Have there been any environmental regulation violations or warnings given to the company? If so, what actions does the company plan to take to resolve them, and what will the related cost be?

   ____

   ____

4. Sensitive transactions—Describe the nature, extent and action taken with respect to any sensitive transactions or irregularities.

   ____

E. Contingent Liabilities and Commitments

1. Leases
   a. List all leases for which the company is obligated by category (capital or operating).

Description	Minimum Annual Amount	Years Remaining Non-cancellable	Years Remaining Total	Description of Escalation/ Adjustment Terms	Description of Renewal/ Purchase Options

   b. List the aggregate minimum capital lease payments for the next _______ years, and the related imputed interest (in the aggregate) to derive the present value of such future lease payments. Has such amount been reflected as a liability? How has the related asset been reflected?

      ____

c. How does the present value of capital leases compare to their fair market value? ______

______

d. Describe major sublease terms. ______

______

e. Has the availability/cost of entering into new lease agreements been assessed?

______

2. Litigation

a. Has the company been involved in any significant litigation in the past ______ years, or is it threatened by pending or unsettled claims? If so, list and describe the nature of those claims and the current status. Attach legal opinions and representation letters provided to the company's auditors, if available.

b. Are there any legal problems or potential litigation presently facing the industry, and if so, what effect might this have on the company?

______

c. Are there any potential antitrust problems, and have they been considered in connection with the proposed acquisition?

______

3. Loan Guarantees

a. List any loans for which the company is a guarantor, and assess the financial condition of the related companies. Do subsidiary loans, guarantees or exchange laws restrict dividend payments to the parent company?

______

4. Open Contracts

a. List all open contracts. Describe the nature and potential cost, including informal agreements (i.e., consultants, severance, death, pension, etc.).

______

F. Stockholders' Equity—Net Worth

1. Summarize for all classes of stock:

a. Type ______

b. Shares Authorized ______

c. Shares Outstanding ______

d. Voting Rights ______

e. Liquidation Preferences ______

f. Dividends ______

g. Terms of Warrants and Options Outstanding ______

h. Major Owners ______

i. Date Acquired by Major Owners ______

j. Major Owner Cost Basis ______

k. Market Price Range ______

l. Special Terms, Conversion Features ______

2. Obtain a shareholders' list.

3. Obtain a list of treasury stock activity for the past ______ years.

4. List any stock option or purchase plans, and attach details concerning each.

____

G. Accounting Policies

1. Obtain a summary of significant accounting policies and procedures.

2. Obtain auditor's report and management's representation letters for the past ______ years. Are there any issues or events that resulted in other than an unqualified opinion?

3. Describe any significant changes in accounting principles, policies or estimates over the past ______ years.

____

4. Describe any accounting policies that are unique to the company's industry.

____

5. Describe any accounting policies that differ from industry practice, represent alternative methods where other preferable methods exist, or are excessively conservative or aggressive.

____

6. Determine if the interim financial statements are prepared on a basis consistent with that of the annual report. Describe any differences.

____

7. Describe any proposed accounting pronouncements or government regulations that may have a significant impact on the company.

____

8. Describe major accounting policy differences from that of the buyer.

____

9. Have the financial statement effects of the above been quantified, where appropriate, and have financial ratios been adjusted accordingly?

____

H. Financial Statement Ratio Analysis

See Exhibit I for key ratios frequently used to help evaluate a proposed acquisition.

1. Future Operating Results and Pro Forma Estimates
   a. Has support for projected financial statements been obtained? ______________
      - ☐ What methodology is the forecasted growth based upon (e.g., regression analysis, trend projection and extrapolation, economic and/or industry indicators, market studies, management estimate)?

        ____

      - ☐ Are the assumptions concerning sales growth (volume and price), gross margins, working capital requirements, operating expenses, capital expenditures, financing requirements and terms, etc., reasonable based on historical results, trends, industry and overall business expectations, etc.?

        ____

   b. Do the basic financial ratios (i.e., profit to equity and sales, sales to assets and others in Exhibit I) indicate that projected levels of growth are feasible without significant infusions of outside capital or changes in historical financial ratios? If not, how will increased financing, faster asset turnover, improved profit margins and dividend increases be accomplished?

c. Identify and describe any factors that could impact the pro forma financial statements significantly and that are not readily apparent from a review of the historical financial statements. The following items may not be recorded at their current fair market value. The extent to which these and other factors affect the pro forma statements will depend on whether the acquisition is accounted for as a pooling of interests or purchase and whether it is taxable or nontaxable.

Items that may not be recorded at fair market value—

- ☐ Lease agreements
- ☐ Long-term receivables/obligations
- ☐ Plant, property and equipment
- ☐ Inventory
- ☐ Intangible assets, patents, copyrights, computer software
- ☐ Distribution agreements, customer lists, licenses
- ☐ Pension obligations and assets
- ☐ OSHA, EPA and other regulatory deficiencies and related expected obligations
- ☐ Severance costs (anticipated layoffs)
- ☐ Customer lists, licenses, franchises, air rights, easements
- ☐ Net of tax valuation adjustments (resulting from different tax vs. accounting valuations)
- ☐ Other

Potential future earnings adjustments

- ☐ Excessive expenses incurred to reduce tax liability, i.e., personal expenses, excessive owner compensation, etc.
- ☐ Functions performed by parent for which no cost has been allocated
- ☐ Salary adjustments required for a more competitive wage; other employee benefit requirements
- ☐ Expected changes in material or other costs
- ☐ Incremental depreciation and amortization charges resulting from expected asset/liability revaluation; other effects of asset/liability revaluations
- ☐ Different tax provision due to new ownership structure and tax basis
- ☐ Cost savings from elimination of duplicate facilities, overhead and "synergy"
- ☐ Reduction in interest income from excess cash
- ☐ Expected sales of facilities
- ☐ Other

Accounting Policies

- ☐ Changes required to conform to the buyer's accounting principles
- ☐ Anticipated industry changes/trends in accounting principles, and effect upon present and future operations

I. Impact of Inflation on Operations and Financial Position

Provide additional information that will aid the buyer in determining the current and future value of the business operations in view of possible inflation/deflation including the following:

1. Impact on Financial Statements

a. If FIFO is used to value inventory, has the company prepared an estimate of the impact of restating costs for current prices (i.e., elimination of "inventory profit") for each product line to determine real gross profit?

b. Have sales price increases during the last year (and projected for the next year) offset the increase in costs? Has the gross profit percentage been maintained?

____

____

c. If depreciation or rental expense were calculated on the estimated replacement cost of property, plant and equipment and leases, what impact would this have on reported and budgeted net income?

____

____

d. Assuming interest on all long-term debt was at a current rate, what impact would this have on net income?

____

____

e. After adjusting for each of the above factors, what is the return on capital? Is it still acceptable? Does it exceed the cost of capital?

____

____

2. Review of Company's Ability To Operate in an Inflationary Environment—How does the company manage each of the following to assure current inflation is taken into account?

a. Sales price increases to pass through increased costs

b. Receivables
- ☐ Speed in billing
- ☐ Use of lock boxes in key geographical areas
- ☐ Discount policy
- ☐ Collection efforts

c. Fixed assets
- ☐ Financing methods
- ☐ Major replacement or expansion needs
- ☐ Appropriation procedures
- ☐ Increasing/decreasing fuel costs on older, less efficient facilities

d. Accounts payable and accrued liabilities
- ☐ Deferral of payments
- ☐ Cash discount policy
- ☐ Pension and tax payment timing

e. Financing
- ☐ Type
- ☐ Timing
- ☐ Cyclical requirements

f. Labor costs
- ☐ Competitiveness of wages
- ☐ Influence of unions
- ☐ Pension funding assumptions
- ☐ Impact of possible relocation

g. Budgeting and planning
- ☐ Availability of accurate cash-flow projections
- ☐ Assumptions used in long-range planning

- ☐ Taxes

h. Impact of inflation on foreign operations
- ☐ Impact on exchange rates—Use of hedging contracts

i. Insurance coverage
- ☐ Frequency of review

IV. FINANCIAL REPORTING SYSTEM AND ACCOUNTING PROCEDURES AND CONTROLS

A. Management Reports

1. Obtain copies of key management reports.
2. Describe each as follows:

Description	Prepared By	Period Covered/ Issue Date	User	Reason for Report

3. Are performance reports prepared for all major areas of accountability? Do these reports relate actual performance to plans and budgets? Is adequate information provided to manage effectively and make informed judgments?

____

____

B. Reporting Structure

1. Describe the interface of subsidiaries, divisions and departments with corporate headquarters concerning centralized reporting requirements.

____

2. Describe how the financial and management reporting systems work.

____

C. Internal Controls

1. Obtain the corporate policies and procedures manual, if any, and broadly assess comprehensiveness. Determine how compliance with these policies and procedures is enforced.
2. Obtain independent accountants' memorandum on accounting procedures and internal controls for past ________ years.
3. Describe the composition, policies and procedures of the internal audit department, and obtain internal audit department reports for past ________ years and management response thereto.
4. Obtain any other significant documentation concerning internal control.
5. Obtain Audit Committee minutes.
6. Based upon the information obtained in 1-5, and discussions with management, describe and broadly assess the overall internal control environment, noting any significant weaknesses.

D. Computer Facilities

Type of Machine	Ownership	Date Installed	Location	Applications

1. List outside computer services utilized. ______

2. How do users perceive the EDP function? How do user and EDP department perceptions differ? How effective is communication between EDP and user personnel?

3. Obtain any recent evaluations of the EDP function and note significant weaknesses, problems and/or opportunities.

E. Insurance

1. Property—List policies and describe significant conditions, benefits and frequency of review. Also list and describe any self-insurance plans. Summarize significant claims filed over past ___ years. Compare coverage to estimated replacement cost of assets held and contingent liabilities.

   a. Are there significant unaccrued costs on open or incurred but not reported claims? ______

   b. Are increased premiums anticipated as a result of unfavorable trends or the need for increased coverage? ______

   c. Are significant retroactive premium adjustments anticipated? ______

2. Obtain information on other insurance policies in force, e.g., product liability, officer life, medical, etc., as noted above.

F. Long-Range and Budgetary Planning

1. Describe the process employed and objectives. Note the personnel responsible.

   a. Do the individuals within the organization help develop the objectives and plans for their area of accountability, and are plans communicated to the appropriate personnel?

   b. Does the budgeting system continually monitor the accuracy of forecasts? Are there procedures established to explain major variations (actual versus budget) on a current basis? Have explanations for significant variations over the past ______ years been provided?

   c. Does the company develop and maintain contingency plans in the event actual results vary significantly from budget?

   d. How is profitability of individual business units and product lines monitored? Are financial ratios, controllable expense analyses, contribution to overhead analyses, direct costing and other financial evaluation techniques employed?

____

____

G. Procedures and Organization Manuals

Provide a brief description, including the use of manuals and personnel responsible for preparation.

____

____

H. Other Significant Areas

Describe other significant aspects of the company's operations as they relate to financial reporting and accounting procedures and controls.

____

____

V. TAXES

A. Applicable Taxes — Describe, including federal, state and local income, property, excise and other taxes paid by the company:

1. Federal ____
2. State ____
3. Local ____

B. Federal Income Taxes

1. Examinations conducted by local tax authorities, i.e., the Internal Revenue Service (IRS) in the United States:
   a. Last year examined ______________________________
   b. Amount of deficiencies and nature of adjustments in last ________ years examined.
   c. Have the results of the above reviews been reflected in the current reserve for taxes for both the years examined and the years subsequent to the examination? ______________

      ____
   d. Status of the current examinations ______________________________

      ____
   e. Tax years open and closed to future tax authority examination ______________
2. Tax carryforwards — Amounts by year of expiration and type (i.e., net operating loss, capital loss, ITCs, FTCs, R&D credit, etc.).

   ____
3. Describe any special industry considerations — including depletion allowances, special credits or deductions, etc.

   ____
4. Obtain a reconciliation of the effective income tax rate to the statutory tax rate for the past ________ years. Obtain an analysis of the deferred tax provision for the past ________ years.
5. Obtain an analysis of the current income tax requirements and compare the total of those requirements to the current income tax reserve. Obtain an analysis of the components of the deferred income tax reserve, and assess the reasonableness and future cash requirements.

C. State and Local Taxes

1. Have all applicable state and local tax returns been filed? ______
2. Have there been any state tax audits or disputes? ______
3. List the amount of deficiencies and nature of adjustments in the last ______ years examined.
4. Have the results of the above reviews been reflected in the current reserve for taxes for both the years examined and the years subsequent to the examination?
5. Have federal deficiencies been reflected in state and local tax reserves? ______
6. Tax carryforwards — amounts by year of expiration and type. Note that not all states permit carryover of losses.
7. Is the company complying with regulations regarding sales and payroll tax collection and remittance?

D. Tax Planning and Preparation

1. Is the company's tax planning and compliance performed internally or by outside accountants and/or attorneys?
2. Has the company taken advantage of all potential tax savings? Are aggressive interpretations adequately reserved for?
3. Does the company maintain adequate tax basis records? ______

E. Other Considerations — Describe any other significant tax planning considerations of interest to the buyer; include potential tax savings not currently achieved but that could be achieved by the buyer, e.g., LIFO, accelerated depreciation, installment sales, FSC, accelerated pension or other expensing, etc., or proposed legislation that may adversely affect the company to be acquired.

F. Factors Affecting Purchase Structure and Price

1. Obtain an analysis of the tax basis of assets being acquired and an estimate of the fair value of the assets being acquired and liabilities assumed; estimate the recapture tax liability assuming that such is triggered; consider the following:
   a. Depreciation — machinery and equipment and buildings
   b. Investment and other tax credits
   c. LIFO inventory reserves

d. Research and development

e. International, FSC or DISC earnings and profits

f. Previously expensed items, e.g., supplies, tools and dies, etc.

g. Other

2. Determine if there are deferred intercompany gains or nondeductible writeoffs that may result in additional taxes.
3. Determine the existence of "golden parachute"-type arrangements.
4. Determine the expected transaction effect on net operating loss and tax credit carryovers.
5. What are the expected benefits of a taxable vs. nontaxable transaction? Has the present value of step-up benefits been compared to the recapture and related tax liability cost?

____

VI. ORGANIZATION, HUMAN RESOURCES, AND INDUSTRIAL RELATIONS

A. Organization Chart—Obtain the most recent chart, or describe the organization.

1. Are job descriptions updated as required to meet changing conditions? Do they define reporting relationships, responsibility, authority and basis for performance measurement?

   ____

2. Is the organization structure consistent with short- and long-range business requirements?

   ____

3. Are potential savings available through consolidation, realignment and other restructuring actions?

   ____

4. Are key personnel policies compatible? ______________________________

B. Key Executive Personnel—Provide the following information (attach resumes, if available), and highlight recent and/or anticipated key personnel losses:

Name	Title/ Position	Age	Years in Present Position	Years with Co.	Prior Business Experience	Education	Compen- sation	Written/ Unwritten Employment Agreements

1. Are successful and proven management personnel available to carry out plans, or does everything depend on one key person? What happens if an employee is not available for an extended period?

   ____

2. Is there a blend of youth and experience, or are most employees in the same age or experience bracket?

3. Are there cohesive lines of authority and communication? Do all parts of the unit work closely together? Is there an integrated approach to all major problems?

4. Is there excessive domination of operations and planning by any one individual?

5. Have development plans been established for key managers and high-potential employees?

6. What is the strategy for filling key positions? Can internal development alone meet requirements or will intercompany transfer or outside hiring be required? Are outside consultants used? What has been past experience?

7. Are local laws prohibiting discriminatory hiring and advancement practices being complied with?

8. Is the compensation plan being administered so as to attract and retain top-quality personnel? Are salary levels competitive with industry norms?

9. Have any of the company's key management personnel or directors been involved in:
   a. Criminal proceedings?
   b. Regulatory commission violations?
   c. Significant civil court litigation?
   d. SEC or IRS investigations?

10. Key nonexecutive personnel by department.

Department	Total Male	Total Female	Age	Years with Company	Education	Training Program	Turnover	Sick Days	Compensation

a. Are the critical functions staffed with well-qualified people?

b. Are there special personnel or skill needs, e.g., related to technology, marketing, manufacturing (short- or long-term)?

c. What are the plans to respond to skill needs or technical obsolescence?

d. Is there or will there be an excess of manpower in some functional areas?

e. Can excess people be retrained for other positions within the organization if the need arises?

C. Employee Benefits—Review accounting treatment, including amounts, personnel covered and eligibility:

1. Describe pension plan, how funded and amount of unfunded or overfunded vested benefits. Extract key pension plan provisions (e.g., effect of employee terminations on vested benefits) and actuarial assumptions. Include amount of unrealized gains and losses in portfolio. In the United States, attach latest ERISA financial statement filings and actuarial studies.
2. Describe profit sharing, bonus, incentive and deferred compensation plans.
3. Describe other benefit, retirement, social and severance plans, including escalation clauses, if any.
4. Describe medical and sick leave benefits and policies. Also determine the number, type and cost of claims over the past ______ years, and specifically identify any significant open claims.
5. Describe vacation/holiday policies.
6. Describe stock option or related equity incentives.
7. Describe policies related to travel and entertainment expenses.
8. Describe policies related to use of automobiles, airplanes, limousines, boats, etc.
9. Comment on escalation clauses or expectations, if any, within current fringe benefit programs. Expected higher levels of benefits and/or inconsistencies with the buyer should be highlighted.
10. Obtain a summary of the company's rating for unemployment and workmen's compensation.
11. Determine if either buyer or seller would need to upgrade its benefits programs or salaries as a result of the acquisition to effect uniformity.
12. What are medical and life insurance costs for postretirement, and when are they provided?
13. Other—Describe.

D. Union Contracts (Attach significant contracts):

1. Name(s) of union(s)
2. Control of membership (i.e., local or national)
3. Employees covered
4. Length of contract(s)
5. Expiration date(s)
6. Other significant terms—Describe (i.e., escalation clauses, regular rate increases, productivity clauses, promotions, retirement and other benefits, hiring and firing, hours/work week, etc.)

E. Labor Relations

1. Strike History—Include all in past ______ years:

Date	Union	Duration	Cause	Settlement
______	______	______	______	______
______	______	______	______	______
______	______	______	______	______
______	______	______	______	______

2. List of grievances filed and arbitration awards. ______
3. Are labor contract problems anticipated? ______
4. If there is no union, are organizing efforts taking place that might change that status? Are changes likely to occur after acquisition? ______
5. Are significant increases anticipated for contracts nearing expiration? ______

F. Labor (Payroll) Ratio Analysis

See Exhibit I for key ratios frequently used to help evaluate a proposed acquisition.

VII. MARKETING AND PRODUCTS

A. Product Lines—Describe major products or product lines within the segments identified in the "*Financial and Accounting Data*" section. Include all that constitute ___% or more of total company sales. Summarize the following:

		Sales/Operating Income Gross Profit*			
Name of Line	**Description**	**Last ( ) Year**	**Year to Date**	**Current-Year Estimate**	**Total Order Backlog****
______	______	______	______	______	______
______	______	______	______	______	______
______	______	______	______	______	______
______	______	______	______	______	______
Total Product Line		______	______	______	______
Total Company		______	______	______	______

*Detail by geographic region, distribution channel and type of customer, as available.

**Include the following information:

- ☐ Age of significant backlog orders
- ☐ Delivery date quoted customers on significant current orders, and actual performance expected relative to dates promised
- ☐ Expected profitability of backlog

B. Major Products—This section should be prepared for each of the major products listed above. Also attach descriptive literature (e.g., product brochures):

1. Name ______
2. Description ______
   a. Components/key raw materials ______
   b. Price ______
   c. Quality ______
   d. Customer service ______
   e. Product life ______
   f. Market size ______
   g. Market share ______
   h. Franchising protection ______
   i. Warranty terms ______
   j. Patent/trademark protection ______
   k. Technological sensitivity ______
   l. Competitive strategy and assessment ______
   m. Future plans ______
3. Date introduced ______
4. Significant modifications ______
5. Amount in inventory and turnover (historical and projected) ______
6. Distribution methods ______

7. Return history ________________
8. Annual production capability ________________
9. Advertising—Promotion methods ________________
10. Customers ________________
    a. List all that account for ___% or more of total product sales. Indicate any special pricing policies, product warranties, return privileges, contractual agreements (terms, expectation of renewal), customer complaints and relationships dependent on a specific individual within the company. Obtain available financial information for significant customers.

	Total Sales					
	Last ( ) Years		Year to Date		Next Year's Budget	
Customer Name/Location	**$**	**% of Total Product**	**$**	**% of Total Product**	**$**	**% of Total Product**
Total All Other						
Total Product Line*						

*Amount from VII-A

b. What industry purchases the products, and how are the products used?

____

c. Why do companies and individuals purchase the products? What differentiates the products from others in the industry (i.e., price, quality, service, availability, etc.)?

____

11. Monthly sales history by segment and/or major product line

	Last ( ) Years		This Year*		Next Year's Budget	
	$	**% of Total**	**$**	**% of Total**	**$**	**% of Total**
January						
February						
March						
April						
May						
June						
July						
August						
September						
October						
November						
December						
Total		100%		100%		100%

*Actual to date plus estimate for remainder of year.

12. Product line comparison to industry (last ____ years and next ____ years). Describe key assumptions.

	Sales			Gross Profit %
Name of Product Line	Product Total	Industry Total	Market Share %	Company/ Industry Average

13. Competitors' history and projections (last ______ years and next ______ years). Obtain Standard & Poor's, Value Line and Dun & Bradstreet Reports. Also obtain descriptions of the overall strategies and goals for these companies, and the specific strengths and weaknesses of their products.

Company Name/Location	Product Sales	Market Share Estimate	% Gross Profit Estimate

14. Amount of sales, if any, subject to renegotiation. List all open contracts, terms, conditions, etc.

15. Summary of intracompany/intercompany sales.

	Total Sales			
	Last ( ) Years		Current Year	
Description	$	% of Total Product	$	% of Total Product

16. Unit Pricing

a. Obtain the following:

- ☐ Description of how prices and discount policies are developed by the company and its competitors.
- ☐ List average unit prices of major products (last ______ years and next ______ years).

Product	Year	Price Company/Competition

b. What has been the price movement in relation to frequency of occurrence, magnitude of occurrence, elasticity of demand and sales promotion?

☐ What is the industry's ability to meet current and future product demand?

☐ Does management believe cost increases could be passed on? Why?

☐ Is the company sensitive to industry price changes?

☐ Is there a price leader? Which company? Describe circumstances.

C. Other Products—Less than ___% of total company sales.

		Sales				
Name	**Description**	**Last Year**	**Year to Date**	**Est. Current-Year Total**	**Backlog Total**	**Current-Year Gross Profit %**
	Total					

D. Marketing and Sales Organization

1. Obtain a description of the company's marketing and sales strategy.
2. Obtain organization chart. If not available, describe or flow-chart the organization.

E. Personnel

1. Describe key personnel (i.e., experience, age, training, etc.).
2. Describe how marketing and sales personnel are compensated (i.e., salary, commission, incentive plans, etc.). List and describe any contractual agreements.
3. Describe training programs, if applicable.
4. Are empioyees aware of corporate objectives?
5. Are bonus incentive plans, quotas, etc., used to increase sales initiative?

F. Sales Planning

1. How are plans formulated? Is there a general consistency between geographic locations and market segments?

   ____

2. Who is responsible? Are there account or territorial coverage plans?

   ____

3. Describe use of sales reports and external information.

   ____

G. Advertising Expenditures—Obtain an analysis of the last ______ years and next ______ years projections.

Type	Amount	% of Sales	Description
a. Media	______	______	______
b. Point of sale	______	______	______
c. Other	______	______	______
Total Advertising Expenditures	======	======	______

1. Does the company use an advertising agency, and are the results of advertising evaluated? How do expenditures and results compare to competitors? To industry norms?

   ____

H. Public Relations

1. Does the company have a public relations department or utilize outside public relations consultants?

   ____

2. Is there a planned public relations program and, if so, at whom is it directed (i.e., stockholders, press, customers, financial community, etc.)?

   ____

I. Describe the company's philosophy on new product promotion and advertising. Have specific programs been undertaken to create new markets, enlarge existing markets, obtain new accounts or improve sales to existing accounts? Compare current with prior programs and highlight any deferral of advertising/promotion efforts to increase current earnings at the expense of future earnings and product development.

____

____

J. Competitive Position

Has an assessment of the company's position and projected future position in the industry vis-a-vis the competition been made? Discuss with management how they perceive the company's strengths and weaknesses relative to its competition and what factors they attribute to helping or preventing them from achieving their objectives. What are the key factors for success, barriers to entry and threats to success?

____

____

K. Marketing Ratio Analysis

See Exhibit I for key ratios frequently used to help evaluate a proposed acquisition.

VIII. MANUFACTURING AND DISTRIBUTION

A. Production Facilities

Describe each production facility as follows:

	Facility			
	No. 1	**No. 2**	**No. 3**	**No. 4**
1. Name				
2. Location				
3. Date Constructed				
4. Owned/Leased				
5. Cost				
6. Book Value				
a. Method				
b. Years				
7. Estimated Remaining Life				
8. Capacity				
a. Floors				
b. Square Feet				
c. Production Units				
9. Shifts				
10. Employees				
11. Present Condition				
12. Capacity Utilization				
13. Alternative Uses				

B. Machinery and Equipment—List principal machinery and equipment, including cost, age, accumulated depreciation, depreciation rates, condition, replacement cost, location, production use, specific or general nature and capacity utilization.

C. Manufacturing Processes—Obtain description of the manufacturing processes/operations that take place at each of the facilities listed previously. Have plant visits been made where significant operations exist? Have the following been considered in assessing the nature of the process?

1. What kind of manufacturing process exists?
   a. Mass production or job shop oriented
   b. Product or process structured flow
   c. Production to order or for stock
2. Have the key components of the manufacturing process been identified?

   ____

3. Nature of operations:
   a. What are the major operations and their sequence (e.g., component fabrication and machining, component assembly, final assembly and testing)?

      ____

b. What is the relationship of the cost of each operation to total product cost?

____

c. What percentage of total factory floor space is used for each major operation?

____

d. What is the degree of mechanization and automation for each major operation (highly automated machinery, semiautomatic, etc.)?

____

4. To what extent are finished products and components standardized?

____

5. What programs exist for increasing standardization and ensuring quality control?

____

6. What are the major components of total production cycle time?

____

a. Lead time—resource acquisitions, production engineering, planning and scheduling.

b. Manufacturing time—volume effects (e.g., can several units be in process at the same time?) and product mix effects.

7. Are subcontractors utilized?

____

8. Productivity:

a. What are the current trends in manufacturing productivity?

____

b. Are there indications of technical obsolescence?

____

c. Does product design restrict the selection of the manufacturing process?

____

d. Is the design conducive to an efficient manufacturing process (safety, degree of accuracy, etc.)?

____

e. What degree of integration exists between product and manufacturing engineering?

____

9. Has the efficiency of this process been compared to competitors in the industry?

____

10. Does the plant layout appear efficient?

____

D. Purchasing

1. Procedures

a. Obtain a copy of the company's purchasing procedures or, if not available, determine through discussion with management informal procedures that may exist.

2. Suppliers

a. List the basic raw materials used in the manufacturing process.

b. List all suppliers who furnish ______% or more of the total material purchases for any of the facilities listed previously for the last ______ years and next ______ years:

Facility	Supplier Name	Supplier Location	Type of Material	Unit Price and Total Purchased Amount	Special Terms

c. Determine (through discussion with management, etc.) the economic condition of the suppliers' industry, including competitive structure, and the related possibility of significant raw material shortages, interruption of deliveries or price fluctuations.

d. List and describe any long-term supply contracts and/or reciprocal buying agreements.

e. Summarize intracompany/intercompany purchases:

	Total Purchases			
	Last __ Years		Current Year	
Description	$	% of Total	$	% of Total

E. Maintenance

1. Capitalization vs. expense policies and scheduled maintenance and repair expense for the past ______ years and next ______ years; explain inconsistent trends or unusual expenditures.

   ______

2. List any maintenance facilities, and describe the company's program for maintenance and repairs.

   ______

3. Determine if the company is following its regular maintenance program. (Has maintenance been deferred?) Highlight deferral of preventive maintenance to increase current earnings at the expense of future earnings.

   ______

F. Distribution

1. Describe physical distribution methods and transportation facilities utilized. Estimate costs where possible.

	Company		Competition	
	$	% of Sales	$	% of Sales
a. Raw material purchases				
b. Intracompany transfers				
c. Finished goods to customers				

G. Does the company use any of the following techniques to operate efficiently in the manufacturing and inventory management areas:

1. Control of inventory using "ABC," zero inventory and/or "just in time" inventory techniques. ______
2. Setup and production line time reduction studies ______
3. Plant utilization and layout studies ______
4. Obsolescence reviews ______
5. Long-term supplier contracts ______
6. Responsibility accounting for inventory and scrap ______
7. Value engineering (input from purchasing into decisions made by engineering regarding the components of new products) ______
8. Parts standardization ______
9. Establishment of a cycle counting program ______
10. Reduction of ECNs (Engineering Change Notices) ______
11. Purchasing reviews (e.g., usage vs. substitution, competitive bidding, approved vendor list, etc.) ______
12. Vendor evaluation procedures (quality, timeliness, price) ______
13. Establishment of a routing system ______
14. Time and motion studies ______
15. In-line vs. batch manufacturing ______
16. Make or buy analyses ______

H. What is management's plan for capital expansion and investment over the next five years, and have any commitments been made? Analyze that plan to determine if future capital investment is (1) merely to maintain present capacity or (2) to increase present production capabilities that will increase future profitability. Are these plans consistent with present condition of facilities, production needs based on projections and anticipated technological changes?

______

______

I. Obtain a summary of historical capital expenditures, and comment on significant variations contained therein. Highlight current deferrals and expenditure programs to improve liquidity and comment on the future impact thereof.

______

______

J. Productivity/Efficiency Ratio Analysis

See Exhibit I for key ratios frequently used to help evaluate a proposed acquisition.

IX. RESEARCH AND DEVELOPMENT

A. Major Programs

1. Completed in last 5 years

Description	Cost	Estimated Benefits

2. Currently in process

Description	Cost		Est. Time To Complete	Estimated Benefits
	To Date	Est. To Complete		

3. Proposed for future

Description	Estimated		Estimated Benefits
	Cost	Time	

B. List any significant products recently developed and/or under development by competition.

C. What attempt has been made to develop new or improved products to satisfy current customers' needs in existing and potential markets, and customer needs currently being met by other products?

____

D. Personnel

Name	Salary	Background

1. Review for current and proposed staffing

____

2. Evaluate technical competence

____

E. Facilities—Laboratories (Describe) ______________________________

____

____

F. Discuss current vs. historical levels of R&D and highlight variations thereof, particularly with respect to any apparent deferral of R&D effort to increase current earnings and the effect of this policy on future product development and earnings and in comparison to industry trends. Are budgets sufficient to maintain or improve the company's competitive position?

____

____

G. Compare industry expenditures for R&D to that of the company and its competitors. Review the percentage of expenditures for R&D costs to sales for the last ______ years, and explain major variations.

H. What is status of patents, trademarks, etc.? ______________________________

____

I. Are proprietary rights protected by the company for all R&D projects in the United States as well as international markets?

____

____

X. FINANCIAL RATIOS

Introduction

The ratios presented in this exhibit are frequently used to help evaluate a proposed acquisition. If the buyer desires these ratios, the following should be performed with respect to them:

1. Compute (or request management to compute) the ratios for ______ years;
2. Identify and explain significant trends and variations between years;
3. Compare the ratios to industry averages and key competitors; obtain explanations for significant variations;
4. Review the calculations to ensure that significant, unusual or nonrecurring items have been considered and/or disclosed.

A. Financial Statement Ratio Analysis

Sales/Profitability Factors		Equation	Purpose
Gross Profit Margin	=	$\frac{\text{Gross Profit}}{\text{Net Sales}}$	Measures gross profit margin and, by comparing to prior periods, can be used to determine trends
Pretax Profit Margin	=	$\frac{\text{Income before Taxes}}{\text{Net Sales}}$	Measures profit per sales dollar after all expenses (except income taxes)
Net Return on Sales	=	$\frac{\text{Net Income}}{\text{Net Sales}}$	Indicates net profitability of each dollar of sales
General Income Statement Analysis		Various	Measures relationship of major expense categories as percent of sales; cost of sales to operating and selling, general and administrative expenses; major components of cost of sales as percent of total; profitability of sales by division, location or product line, and to other income and expenses
Return on Total Investment	=	$\frac{\text{Net Income}}{\text{Total Capital}}$	Measures profitability on the total capital invested
Return on Equity	=	$\frac{\text{Net Income}}{\text{Total Shareholder Equity}}$	Measures the return on invested capital
Return on Assets	=	$\frac{\text{Net Income}}{\text{Average Total Assets}}$	Indicates return on each average dollar of assets
Price/Earnings Ratio	=	$\frac{\text{Market Price}}{\text{Earnings}}$	Measures the future expectation of the trading public and potential dilutive effect on buyer's equity or earnings per share

Liquidity Factors			
Current Ratio	=	$\frac{\text{Current Assets}}{\text{Current Liabilities}}$	Measures ability to pay short-term obligations
Quick Ratio	=	$\frac{\text{Current Assets—Inventories}}{\text{Current Liabilities}}$	Measures ability to pay short-term obligations without utilizing inventory funds
Stockholders' Equity Ratio	=	$\frac{\text{Stockholders' Equity}}{\text{Total Assets}}$	Measures long-term liquidity; measures financial strength and cushion for creditors
Working Capital to Total Assets	=	$\frac{\text{Working Capital}}{\text{Total Assets}}$	Indicates net liquid assets relative to total capitalization
Overall Liquidity Ratio	=	$\frac{\text{Total Assets}}{\text{Total Liabilities}}$	Measures the overall liquidity of the company

Working Capital and Debt Factors		Equation	Purpose
Working Capital Turnover	=	Net Sales / Average Working Capital	Measures how effectively working capital is used to generate sales and whether a company has a high proportion of fixed or slow assets
Asset Utilization	=	Net Sales / Average Total Assets	Indicates the efficiency with which total resources are used
Cash Flow to Total Assets	=	Net Cash Flow / Total Assets	Measures cash generated in relationship to assets
Debt-to-Equity Ratios	=	Debt / Stockholders' Equity	Measures debt levels of the company in comparison to owners' equity
Total Liabilities to Stockholders' Equity	=	Total Liabilities / Stockholders' Equity	Measures the relative "ownership" of the company's assets by owners and creditors
Debt Coverage Ratio	=	Earnings before Interest and Taxes / Annual Debt Service	Measures the ability to pay off debt
Times Interest Earned	=	Earnings before Interest and Taxes / Interest Charges	Measures the extent to which earnings could decline before resulting in an inability to pay annual interest charges
Ratio of Earnings to Fixed Charges	=	Earnings before Interest and Taxes plus Fixed Charges / Fixed Charges	Measures the extent to which earnings can decline without affecting the ability to meet fixed costs

Realizability and Cash Management Factors			
Cash Cycle	=	Receivables + Inventory / Average Cost of Goods Sold	Measures the number of days in the cash cycle
Receivables Turnover	=	Net Credit Sales / Average Trade Receivables (net)	Indicates efficiency of receivable collections and effectiveness of credit policies
Past-Due Index	=	Total Receivables Past-Due / Total Receivables	Used to indicate trends in collection activity
Bad Debt Expense as a Percentage of Sales	=	Bad Debt Expense / Total Credit Sales	Measures bad debt trends
Inventory Turnover	=	Cost of Goods Sold / Average Inventory	Measures number of times average inventory "turned over" or was sold during the period

B. Labor (Payroll) Ratio Analysis

Labor (Payroll) Analysis Factors		Equation	Purpose
Sales per Employee	=	Net Sales / Number of Employees	Measures the efficiency of employee utilization
Average Salary per Employee by Division or Class of Employee	=	Total Payroll Expense for Division or Class / Number of Employees in Division or Class	Measures overall salary levels
Total Payroll and Benefits as a Percentage of Sales	=	Total Payroll and Benefits Expense / Net Sales	Measures labor costs relative to sales
Benefits as a Percentage of Payroll	=	Benefits / Total Payroll Expense	Measures level of benefits relative to payroll
Employees Per Supervisor	=	Number of Employees / Number of Supervisors	Helps identify top-heavy supervisory structures
Employee Turnover	=	Number of Employees That Quit or Were Terminated / Average Number of Employees	Measures employee stability and satisfaction

C. Marketing Ratio Analysis

Marketing Analysis Factors		Equation	Purpose
Returns as a Percentage of Sales	=	Returns / Sales before Returns but after Discounts	Measures customer satisfaction and/or product quality
Marketing Expense as a Percentage of Sales	=	Marketing Expense / Sales	Measures the cost of marketing programs relative to sales generated
Gross Profit per Marketing Dollar	=	Gross Profit / Marketing Expense	Measures marketing effectiveness
Discounts as a Percentage of Sales	=	Discounts / Gross Sales	Indicates the level of discounts given
Selling Expense as a Percentage of Sales	=	Selling Expense / Sales	Measures the level of selling efforts expended for the current level of sales
Sales per Salesman	=	Net Salesmen's Sales / Number of Salesmen	Measures salesmen's efficiency and productivity
Sales Salaries and Commissions as a Percentage of Sales	=	Sales Salaries and Commissions / Sales	Measures the sales payroll cost relative to sales

D. Productivity / Efficiency Ratio Analysis

Productivity/Efficiency Analysis Factors		Equation	Purpose
Direct Labor Utilization	=	Available Direct Labor Hours — Idle Time / Available Direct Labor Hours	Measures efficiency of employees
Production per Direct Labor Hour	=	Units Produced / Direct Labor Hours (including overtime)	Measures employee productivity
Percentage of Hours Worked on Overtime	=	Overtime Hours Worked / Total Hours Worked	Measures overtime and capacity utilization
Labor Cost to Total Production Cost	=	Labor Cost / Total Product Cost	Measures proportion of labor cost to total production cost
Material Costs to Total Production Costs	=	Cost of Material / Total Product Cost	Measures proportion of material to total production cost
Manufacturing Overhead to Total Production Cost	=	Manufacturing Overhead / Total Product Cost	Measures proportion of manufacturing overhead to total production cost
Machine Utilization	=	Productive Machine Hours / Total Available Machine Hours	Measures efficiency of equipment and scheduling
Scrap Rate	=	Number of Units Scrapped / Total Units Produced	Measures how efficiently materials are used
Direct Labor Hours as a Percentage of Total Factory Hours	=	Direct Labor Hours / Total Hours of Factory and Production Personnel	Measures the level of production support personnel
Warehouse and Delivery Expense per Order	=	Warehouse and Delivery Expense / Number of Orders	Measures the cost of filling an order

PART 2

LEVERAGED BUYOUTS

CHAPTER 11

LEVERAGED BUYOUTS I: STRUCTURE AND RESTRUCTURE

Robert Lawrence Kuhn

How to overpay and get rich? It is simple if you know what to buy and how to buy it, and when to sell and how to sell it. Mix financial leverage, managerial ownership, clever structure, and cleverer restructure. It's called a "leveraged buyout" (LBO), and what it does is cure the healthy.

Take a sound company strong with equity. Sell it. Make it sick, laden heavy with debt. Make it better by rebuilding equity—redeploy assets, cut overhead, pay back debt (not too much), and perhaps improve earnings.[1] Sell it again. Count your money.

How can ordinary mortals offer $6.1 billion for Beatrice Companies, the food and consumer products giant; $1.6 billion for Metromedia, Inc., the broadcasting chain; or $648 million for Dr Pepper, the soft drink company—and hope to make a profit?

An LBO looks like it's done with mirrors. Remember one of the first barn burners? It was when William Simon (Westray) made a $50+ million bonanza in a period so short he might have been caught for ordinary income, not capital gains. Simon simply bought Gibson Greeting Cards from a tired RCA and then sold part of it back to a ravenous public at a much higher

[1]Note that improving P&L earnings is generally *not* critical for leveraged buyouts to succeed. Some LBOs have been known to "lose money" every year on the income statement until the time they were sold for an enormous profit. (Such P&L loses were due to huge depreciation and amortization as well as accrued interest on the highly leveraged balance sheet.) Cash flow, you can be sure, was quite positive.

price/earnings multiple. Simon's timing was good, but his structure was better. What did the former Secretary of the Treasury put up? Only a few hundred thousand dollars, which, if you look closely, was hardly put up at all. (Would that he had performed such miracles with the national debt!)

STRUCTURE

How do LBOs work? To begin with, investors chip in preciously little cash—not much real money is ever put at risk. This equity (the cash contribution) is then "leveraged," 10, 20, even 50 times with debt. Leverage, that's part of the secret. (Management, as we will see, is the other part.)

Where does all this debt come from, and how can conservative bankers take such risks? First of all, the debt is arrayed into multiple layer or strips, with higher levels in the capital structure (up toward the senior debt) yielding lower risks and lower returns, and lower levels in the capital structure (down toward the equity) yielding higher risks and higher returns. (See Volume I, Chapter 13 regarding the relationship between risk and return and its importance in analyzing the capital structure of enterprises.)

Senior debt is normally *secured* in LBOs. This means that the assets of the acquired firm are pledged to support the debt. (Such asset-based financing is essential in LBOs—see Volume V, Chapters 19–21.) Lending limits, for example, might be 80 percent of receivables, 50 percent of inventories, and 25 percent of plant and equipment. Mortgages of real estate and saleleaseback of plant and equipment can raise additional cash. (Note that no matter how large the debt, the acquirors take no risks other than their equity investment.)

Often middle layers of subordinate debt are needed to make the financing work. Such subordinate debt is called "mezzanine" money since it stands *between* the senior bank debt and the investor equity.

Who finances the subordinated debt? It can be taken back by the seller (common in LBOs of private companies—see Chapters 12–16) or it can be bought by third parties. Such third-party subordinated debt can be sold as private placements (e.g., to insurance companies—see Volume II, Chapter 7) or as public offerings (i.e., high yield debt—see Volume III, Chapters 18–22). If bought by a third party, this mezzanine money demands a piece of the equity, called a "kicker," in addition to a fixed rate of return higher than that of the senior debt, which is appropriate considering the higher risk. An example capital structure, showing sources and uses of cash in a stylized LBO, is shown in Figure 1.

FIGURE 1
Example Capital Structure of a Leveraged Buyout (In $ Million)

Sources of Cash	
Revolving line of credit	$ 200 million
Mortgage/sale-leaseback debt	100 million
Senior term loan[1]	600 million
Increasing rate notes[2]	250 million
Senior subordinated debt[3]	100 million
Junior subordinated debt[4]	75 million
Junior zero coupon notes[5]	50 million
Preferred (pay-in-kind)[6]	50 million
Preferred (convertible)[7]	50 million
Common equity	25 million
Total sources of cash	$1,500 million
Uses of Cash	
Acquisition of common stock	$ 815 million
Acquisition of preferred stock	50 million
Refinancing of existing debt	460 million
Transactional fees and expenses	50 million
Working capital support	125 million
Total uses of cash	$1,500 million

[1]A senior term loan is usually structured for five to seven years, with a regular amortization schedule.

[2]Increasing rate notes are usually designed to be a bridging facility for asset disposition. The increasing rate, say 25 basis points per quarter, encourages speedy sale of the assets/divisions and rapid retirement of the notes.

[3]Senior subordinated debt may have a rate about 200 basis points over the senior term loan. It would pay interest currently but not require principal repayment for several years, say equal payments in years six, seven and eight (after the senior debt is completely repaid). The senior subordinated debt could only be called (i.e., paid off and retired) by the company by paying a premium (say 108 percent of par) to investors (this premium would decline in later years). After all, the investors took a significant risk in purchasing this piece of paper and should not be penalized for a successful company.

[4]Junior subordinated debt would have a rate slightly higher (say 50 basis points) than senior subordinated debt. It, too, would only pay interest currently and have an amortization schedule later than the senior subordinated debt, say equal payments in years seven, eight and nine. Likewise, the junior subordinated debt could only be called (i.e., paid off and retired) by the company by paying a premium (say 108 percent of par) to investors (this premium would decline in later years). Again, the investors took a significant risk in purchasing this piece of paper and should not be penalized for a successful company.

[5]Zero coupon notes accrue interest over the life of the note, with all interest and principal paid at the end. Zero coupon notes are structured as deeply discounted original issue, with the implied interest rate being the accrual rate that brings the initial cash payment up to the face value at the maturity date. This maturity date might be just subsequent to the payment of all senior indebtedness, in this case say the tenth year. Naturally, the interest rate on zeros is higher (say 100 basis points) than the current-pay junior subordinated debt.

[6]Pay-in-kind preferred stock offers a high rate of dividends (15 to 20+ percent), with the understanding that for a period of years, the interest can be paid "in kind" (i.e., with additional pay-in-kind prefered). Redemption of this preferred would not be mandated for many years, probably not until after all senior indebtedness, including the zero coupon bonds, are retired.

[7]Convertible preferred would pay a lower dividend rate than the pay-in-kind preferred but would expect an ultimately higher annual return (in the 25 to 40 percent range) as a result of its convertibility into a healthy amount of equity (say 15 to 30 percent of the company ownership).

INSTITUTIONAL SUPPORT

Who is supplying this huge mountain of LBO debt? Equity players like talking about "OPM" (Other People's Money), but who are all these "other people"? Suckers they are not, of this you can be assured.

In fact, many of the largest and more astute financial institutions in the country are the primary suppliers of LBO debt[2]—and they get very well compensated for taking these risks. This is premium lending, with banking returns far outdistancing their typical commercial loans. By earning several hundred basis points over alternative investment opportunities for their assets,[3] LBO lenders give a tremendous boost to their own return on equity, since these financial institutions are themselves highly leveraged[4].

CASH FLOW

The touchstone of LBOs is cash flow. Almost nothing else matters. Profit and loss statements, surprisingly, are almost irrelevant. All that counts is whether, when, and with what safety you can meet interest coverage in the near term and can pay back principal in the long term. Payment schedules can be staged, with endless variation, to meet anticipated forecasts. The creative use of various layers and terms of debt, as discussed above and shown in Figure 1, is essential for many deals to succeed.

A nice feature in calculating cash flow is tax payments, or, more accurately, the lack thereof. Paying an inflated price can thus present minimal problems. Interest is tax deductible, and if depreciation is high, that too becomes an effective tax shield. The acquiror could merely write up company assets and generate higher write-offs for depreciation—far easier to do

---

[2]For example, banks such as Citibank, Chemical Bank, Bankers Trust, Security Pacific, and Manufacturers Hanover, and insurance companies such as The Prudential, are large LBO lenders. (In the early days of LBOs, such lending was viewed as "fringe"—certainly not befitting the blue-chip institutions. The enormous returns eliminated such snobbery and, today, the blue-chippers are fierce competitors for the LBO business.)

[3]Overall returns for the financial institutions include up front fees (perhaps 3 percent on the entire deal) plus participations in the equity layers by being issued warrants to purchase common stock and/or by making direct investments in the higher return instruments. Such structure generates a very healthy blended rate of return for the LBO lenders.

[4]For example, a bank leveraged 20 to 1 (assets to equity) would earn a 20 percent incremental return on equity (before direct expenses) for every one percent incremental return on assets.

under the pre-1986 tax law—in addition to already hefty interest deductions. Similarly, companies with net operating loss carryforwards (NOLs) have a competitive edge in LBO acquisitions. NOLs generate a powerful engine of payback power, dramatically shortening the time period of debt repayment, which serves to both increase return and decrease risk.

SENSITIVITY

You only have to watch the windows. Downdrafts in this business cause quick pneumonia. Sensitivity analysis is critical. "What if" games are not games. LBO investors had better be awfully sure they can weather any storm. Default sits directly overhead in those low-altitude rain clouds, especially during the first few years. A slight change in market, pricing, margins, overheads, and especially interest rates cause the banks to blow in with their liens in one hand and auction blocks in the other. (Or do they? When you owe small money, you have a creditor; when you owe big money, you have a partner.)

Sensitivity analysis is required to assess and compare the alternative capital structures in order to determine which is most effective in financing the LBO. Which layers of debt, with what terms and conditions, have the greatest likelihood of initial appeal to investors and ultimate success for the issuer? The optimum capital structure improves robustness since the multiple layers of debt enhance flexibility.

RESTRUCTURE

LBOs work, notwithstanding the extraordinary debt, because of the restructure. Assets not being properly employed, such as current inventory, are shrunk down, thus making the operation more efficient. Conserving cash is the touchstone that evaluates all business decisions. Long-term thinking is a nice luxury; short-term cash management is an absolute necessity. Subsidiary businesses may be sold off for values far in excess of their cash-generating potential.

The key is to sell all assets, divisions, or subsidiaries whose price/earnings multiples (or, better yet, price/cash flow multiples) exceed the original multiples paid for the entire company. Those assets, divisions, or subsidiaries that generate a high degree of cash relative to the acquisition price (and possible sale price) should be kept. These "cash cows" will generate the dollars required to pay off the debt and build rapid shareholder value.

The restructuring process often reveals hidden assets in LBO acquisitions that have been long ago written off the books, such as real estate, lease values well in excess of lease costs, and smaller divisions that have significant potential. It is amazing how frequently these assets emerge, especially when mature public companies (e.g., conglomerates assembled years before) are taken private in management-led LBOs.

CASHING OUT

LBO financiers always think about the "exit" before they walk through the entrance. "How do we get out?" is a question they must answer before investing their cash. (See Chapter 15.)

There are really only two alternatives for cashing out. One is the public markets. It is the dream of every LBO investor to take the company public in a relatively short period of time (three years, say, but no longer than five) and reap the enormous rewards of financial leverage. But the public markets are not always available: The "market window" may not be open and/or the company itself may not be ready.

A second option is a private sale to a new buyer. The new buyer may be another LBO investor group that seeks to purchase the entire company in a manner similar to the way the original LBO group did it. The new buyer may be current management seeking to own all of their own company. Or the new buyer may be a corporate acquiror, seeking a market or operational fit with its overall strategy. From an American perspective, foreign corporations have been eager buyers of restructured LBOs, especially since the fall of the dollar.[5]

From the standpoint of the LBO financiers, corporate acquirors are often the most desirable, (even if a public offering would appear to generate higher

---

[5]Foreign corporations are buyers for many restructured LBOs. Cheap dollars are surely one reason but there is also another. Many foreign corporations seek entry into the American market, often as a channel of distribution for their other products. They have long wanted to purchase various American public companies—*but*, by culture and custom, they would never have approached such a company when it had been traded on the stock market (prior to the LBO) and certainly would never have considered taking any hostile action. Here, then, may be the first opportunity for these foreign corporations to buy many long-sought companies. Foreign corporations will pay a healthy price to acquire access to the American market.

profits on *paper*.)[6] Mergers with large corporations are most efficient; they are easier to structure and quicker to close. Consideration is normally all cash (or highly liquid securities) and generally the shareholders get it all at once. Furthermore, if a large corporation really wants the company it will not be afraid to pay top dollar.

EVALUATING RETURNS ON EQUITY (ROE)

Everyone speaks about returns on equity (ROE). It is LBO lingo personified. It is the "holy grail" of the LBO game. But there is more to ROE than is immediately obvious. Understanding the nature of returns on equity is fascinating: The leverage appears to create miracles.

Assume an LBO financing of $100 million, structured with $90 million in debt supported with $10 million (or 10 percent) in equity. Now assume the company is sold four years later for $130 million, after having paid back only $20 million of the debt. Seems like a rather mediocre performance? Well, watch what happens.

The absolute after-debt value of the deal is $60 million (the $130 million sale price minus the remaining debt of $70 million). But ROE, remember, is calculated on the original equity investment, $10 million. So the payback is 600 percent—[$60 million divided by $10 million (60/10)], which equals a compound annual rate of return of about 56 percent (pretax) over the four years. Not bad in any financial scheme.

Evaluating returns on equity is usually considered the key criterion in determining the viability and desirability of any LBO transaction. However, there is an inherent complexity, perhaps even a fallacy, that crops up in such analyses—the factor of time.

Almost always, the spreadsheet-calculated returns decrease as the time frame of evaluation increases. This means that the ROE might look best two years out and thereafter it declines progressively (and precipitously) as you look three, four, five, six, etc., years into the future.

Such a decline does *not* mean that the company is becoming less valuable. After all, the company is continuing to generate cash and pay down debt.

---

[6]From the standpoint of the operational managers of the LBO company, a corporate acquiror is often *not* the best alternative. Granted, the managers get their profit out—but now they are back working for others and suddenly the future becomes less certain and they become less good.

The problem is that the rate of growth is far less than would be required to maintain the excessive returns. (The initial high returns are the product of the leveraged structure.) So a declining ROE should be expected and it should not discourage the potential acquiror. Nor should the decline suggest that the company be sold after two years to lock in those higher returns! Frankly, it is far better to earn a compounded ROE of 30 percent for ten years than a compounded ROE of 50 percent for two years.

MANAGEMENT

The key to successful LBOs is management. LBO financiers insist that operating executives take part of the action. The folks with the bucks require that management go at risk—making great gain on the upside and suffering painful loss on the downside. (Not known for their generosity, financiers seek only to solidify their own success.) Savvy investors never bankroll an LBO unless those who run target companies get a good hunk of the equity, generally 10 to 20 percent, and put up hard cash to buy it.

The critical transition, then, occurs inside the heads of these executives. Previously employees, they are suddenly owners. Professional managers with company-paid club memberships change mystically into personal entrepreneurs who scrutinize every expense. Participation and commitment grab the essence of motivation. It is a most remarkable transformation.

To be a general manager of a conglomerate division managing public money is one thing. To be president of an independent company building personal wealth is quite another. Take the decision-making process. Which will it be, a new corporate aircraft or an upgraded manufacturing facility? The decision is made in a microsecond. Care is exercised over every facet of the business. No cost savings are too minor. Dollar signs are seen everywhere. Lights are turned off and spirits are turned on. Think of the enhanced effort and reduced waste. When management is galvanized, the company is rejuvenated.

PUBLIC POLICY

Debate about the socio-economic value of leveraged buyouts continues to rage. LBOs have become a whipping post for the mass media. It is easy to attack businesses where a few people make so much money so quickly—

seemingly without doing, well, *anything*. Nothing new has been produced, it is argued, except untold stacks of paper have been shuffled and unseemly amounts of legal bills have been paid.

There is another side to the issue, and it focuses on the remarkable success rate of LBOs and the equally remarkable amount of money now committed to LBO funds. As of mid-1988, it was estimated that $25 billion had been invested in LBO funds ready to do deals. At least six firms controlled more than $1 billion each, with several more getting close.[7] The investors in these funds were some of the strongest and smartest institutions in the world. And considering a typical 10 to 1 leverage structure, this meant that $250 billion worth of deals could be completed. (Roughly $40 billion worth of LBOs were consummated in each of the years 1986 and 1987—see Figure 2).

The danger is competition. The intense rivalry on the buy side generates wild prices on the sell side. What will so many high-powered LBO funds do with so much cash? Those institutional investors do not want their money languishing in Treasury Bills—they expect a very healthy return on their investment. The result is predictable: with too much money chasing too few deals, prices get bid up and the risk escalates geometrically.

LBO investors would like to pay between four to five times cash flow. Deals work quite well at those levels; debt service is comfortable and the financial structure is robust enough to withstand aberrations and shocks. But those days are gone, perhaps forever. It becomes hazardous, even perilous, to pay eight to twelve times cash flow (unless there is a clear opportunity to sell off available assets at even higher multiples). But such risk is precisely what current LBOs must absorb.

The first major LBO failure, the $1.5 billion collapse and Chapter 11 bankruptcy of Revco, the drug discount chain, exemplifies the problem. Even the initial, pre-deal (usually optimistic) projections showed that the company would have to sustain healthy, profitable growth in a highly competitive industry just to tread water (i.e., service its debt and pay its interest). It seemed uncertain, even in those heady days prior to the transaction.[8]

---

[7]Kohlberg Kravis Roberts (KKR), $5.6 billion; Forstmann Little, $2.7 billion; Morgan Stanley Group, $1.6 billion; Merrill Lynch Capital Appreciation Fund II, $1.5 billion; Shearson Lehman, $1.3 to 1.5 billion; Prudential-Bache, $800 million (capital) plus $500 million–$1.5 billion (fund); Wasserstein Perella, $750–$1 billion; Blackstone, $750 million; Gibbons Green van Amerongen, $600+ million.

[8]As a matter of uncertain interest, the author, representing an institutional investor, rejected an opportunity to invest in Revco.

FIGURE 2
Value of Leveraged Buyouts

Value of leveraged buyouts completed, in billions of dollars.
In parentheses are the number of deals completed each year.

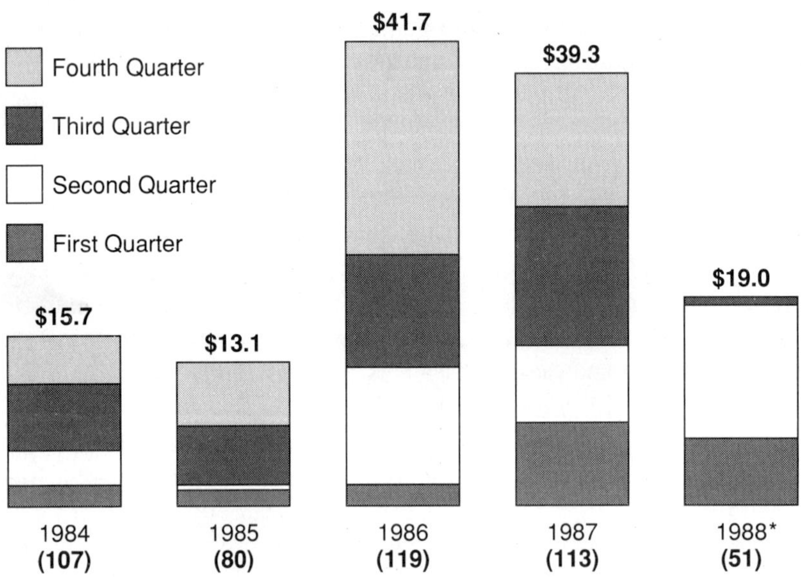

*1988 third quarter data is July only
Source: IDD Information Services

How do so many of these highly leveraged companies survive and indeed prosper? They sparkle, operationally and financially. Why? How is it that, even with all that debt, many LBOs perform better as highly leveraged companies than they had ever performed as unleveraged companies?

The answer, as we have seen, is management—their spectacular change in attitude and increase in commitment. Businesses are not democratic organizations, and it is the executives and managers that make them successful. This fact may not resonate with some folks' idealized sense of social structure, but it's the way the world really works.

One can argue that those equity-owning executives and managers should have been doing the same good things pre-LBO as they are now doing post-LBO. Should have done, sure. But didn't do, sorry.

Managers and executives are people, not gods, and it is unreasonable to expect that they would act the same when they are owners with cash invested (post-LBO) as they did when they were just representing the stockholders' interests with no personal investment (pre-LBO). People are people, and no political philosophy will alter the powerful motivation of self-interest.

There is a new and growing factor in the LBO world, and it maximizes both the impact of active ownership and the sensitivities of public policy. Employee Stock Ownership Plans (ESOPs) are complex structures where *all* the employees of a company participate in the new ownership. ESOPs have been enjoying an increasing level of congressional support and hence evince substantial and fascinating tax benefits. ESOP-led LBOs are the wave of the future (see Volume II, Chapters 25 and 26).

Thus, from a public policy point of view, LBOs can be seen as the refresher of capitalism. They enhance efficiency, raise productivity, and reward creativity. One can make the case that the surge in LBOs is returning the economy to the early days of entrepreneurship and rugged individualism, when managers were owners and owners were managers—and when these corporate leaders worked best for themselves, the system worked best for everyone.[9] Given the American way of thinking, the managerial ownership of enterprise is vital.[10]

---

[9]When we say that "the system worked best for everyone," the reference is to relative economic growth and productivity compared to other nations, not necessarily to social fairness or political equality. We would be well advised to allow the economy to function as efficiently as possible on its own terms (i.e., with management- and employee [ESOP]-led LBOs), and then cure social unfairness and political inequality through wealth reallocation policies (i.e., taxes) and entitlement programs.

[10]There are obvious exceptions. For example, LBOs are much less appropriate in industries requiring substantial investment in research and development that will not generate commercial products for many years. Nonetheless, for these companies as for all companies, the principal of managerial ownership is indeed vital.

CHAPTER 12

LEVERAGED BUYOUTS II: CONCEPTS AND DEVELOPMENT

John Whitman
Frank Knowles
Prudential-Bache Interfunding

The term leveraged buyout, or LBO, has evolved to encompass any acquisition of a company in which a major portion of the purchase is financed by debt of the company being acquired. However, the "self-LBO," or leveraged recapitalization (recap), has many of the same characteristics, and much of this chapter would apply equally to both an LBO and a recap. (See Volume II, Chapters 23, 24, and 36.)

In this chapter we discuss the spectacular rise of the LBO concept during the 1980s. We explore the reasons that LBOs began to occur, and look at some of the history of their development. We then discuss valuation and pricing, which are really subsets of the structuring of LBOs. Finally we describe two transactions in which the authors of this chapter have participated.

HISTORY AND DEVELOPMENT

In order to understand the development of the LBO in the 1980s, one must first look at the growth within the U.S. economy of the conglomerates in the 1960s and 1970s. Conglomerates were built up primarily in response to a set of accounting rules which allowed an acquisitive company to purchase a number of operating entities during a year and include (for the most part) their full earnings in the conglomerate's reported financial results. The result was a number of companies that indiscriminately bought a variety of operating entities with no view to synergistic savings or operating efficiencies from the transactions. The larger conglomerates consequently developed very sophisticated reporting and accounting systems which required large staffs in both the operating entities and the corporate headquarters in order to provide management the kind of current financial information needed to control reported operating income, earnings per share, and public perceptions of their stock. These systems, and the constant need to promote the professional managers both within the operating subsidiaries and from the operating subsidiary to the headquarters, built up in the '70s an inefficient bureaucracy in the conglomerates' head office staffs. By 1985, in the case of one major chemical conglomerate, there had developed *six* layers of management in the corporate headquarters between the highest ranking operating manager and the chairman of the board.

As the Accounting Standards Board changed its rules on accounting for acquisitions, and as the U.S. economy went into hyperinflation at the end of the 1970s, the cost to the conglomerates of managing their subsidiaries became staggering and their ability to do so was questioned. The conglomerates began to realize that they could improve their reported earnings by taking gains on the sale of these assets to other parties, while at the same time eliminating the need for expensive working capital, capital expenditures, and overhead associated with those assets. (See Volume II, Chapter 30.)

As the 1980s dawned, therefore, there were many properties in the hands of major companies which were ripe to be divested.

The Rise of the Leveraged Buyout

While, as we have seen, there were a large number of potential acquisition candidates available, the economic conditions in the late 1970s and early 1980s were less than conducive to the LBO as we know it today. Interest rates in this period reached their all-time high, with the prime rate hitting 20 percent in 1981.

At the same time real company earnings, corrected for inflation, were at depressed levels. As we will see, the price of an LBO is primarily a function of company cash flow and interest rates; during this period both of these factors were working against the completion of many transactions. However, even as early as 1979, there began to be a number of deals recognized to be LBOs.

Figures 1 and 2 present the number of deals and the aggregate dollar volume of those deals from 1979 to 1987. It is our intention to explore the causes of the significant increases seen in both of those figures.

FIGURE 1
Leveraged Buyouts: Number of Deals

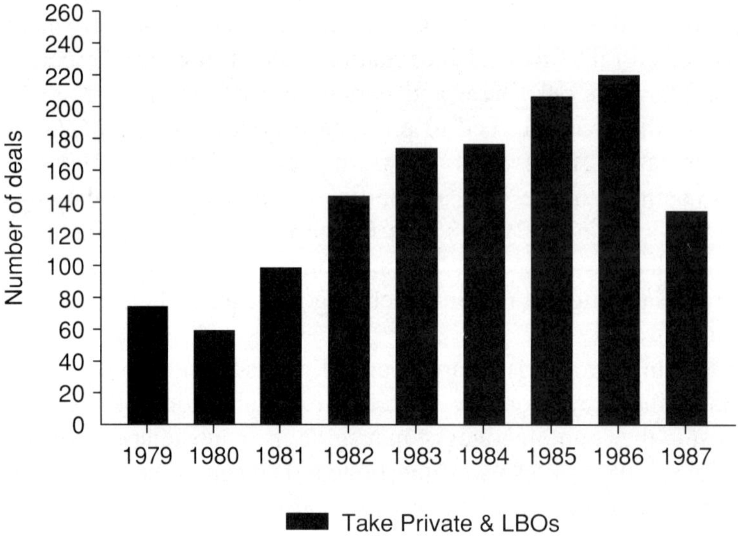

Source: W.T. Grimm

FIGURE 2
Leveraged Buyouts: Aggregate Dollar Volume ($bn)

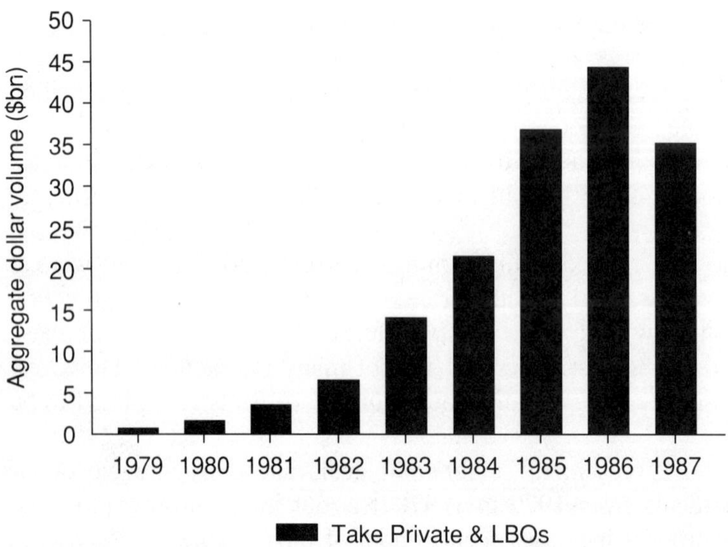

Source: W.T. Grimm

The first LBOs in 1979 and 1980 were completed in an environment of depressed earnings and high interest rates. These transactions were completed at multiples of approximately five times earnings before interest and taxes (EBIT), or operating cash flow, where depreciation and capital expenditures were not about equal. The typical LBO at this time took three to six months to complete, and the purchase price was financed at closing with 60 percent to 70 percent bank debt, approximately 20 percent by the private placement of subordinated debt, and 10 percent with equity. Negotiations with all the lenders and all the equity holders were completed before the transaction closed and there was a high mortality rate of individual transactions because they required so many people to agree on so many things at the same time. Furthermore, there was no guarantee that another buyer might not come in at a higher price during the protracted negotiating period.

While these early transactions were extremely tedious to complete, they became extraordinarily profitable. Enormous returns were generated because of low multiple purchase prices in a high interest rate environment, and the unparalleled success stimulated a feeding frenzy.

In 1982, interest rates declined substantially from their highs of 1981. The economy began to pick up, and with it, corporate earnings rose. This was the first year of the five-year bull market, which did not end until October 19, 1987. There was a large jump in the number of transactions and the aggregate dollar volume of transactions increased substantially. However, the LBO marketplace was still in its infancy. The financing of these transactions was still on a completed deal basis and still took a three to six month period.

The "Highly Confident" Concept

LBOs took off in 1983. The critical change in the marketplace was the development by Drexel Burnham Lambert (DBL) of the High-Yield "junk" bond market. (See Volume III, Chapters 18–22.) At this time DBL's innovative West Cost trading operation (Beverly Hills), under the direction of Michael Milken, developed the concept of the "highly confident letter." A DBL highly confident letter, which virtually promised a seller that the funds would be available for the transaction, significantly shortened the time that it took to complete transactions, and increased the certainty of that completion to both buyers and sellers. At the same time as the high-yield bond market began to develop, the economy was taking off, interest rates continued their downward spiral, and corporate earnings improved (reflecting the improvements in the economy).

The highly confident letter provided the first true change in the LBO market. The banks were called upon to issue only 40 percent to 50 percent of the total funds required to complete a transaction, with the subordinated debt or junk bond market providing 30 percent to 40 percent of the required purchase price, and the remainder coming from equity. The time required to close transactions decreased from three to six months to one to three months, and purchase price multiples took off. While purchase price multiples had been at the five times EBIT level in 1979 and 1980, by 1983 they had increased to six to eight times. Figures 3 and 4 indicate the tremendous growth since 1981, both in the number of high-yield securities issued and their dollar volume.

The LBO Funds

The marketplace continued, after 1983, to be driven by the availability of quick and cheap subordinated financing from the high-yield market, low interest rates, and an ebullient economy. Multiples continued to increase and the successes of the various LBO groups attracted more and more money to the marketplace. During this time Kohlberg Kravis & Roberts (KKR) raised the first leveraged buyout fund, and were rapidly followed into the marketplace by other groups who raised substantial money for the express purpose of investing in LBOs. The availability of this money drove up both the number and size of the deals, and the multiples paid for them.

Because of the large capital availability, the LBO market expanded from divestitures out of conglomerates and medium-sized private transactions to transactions in which large public companies were purchased in their entirety, undervalued assets were divested, and attendant overhead eliminated. The prime example was the Beatrice transaction.

The Bought Deal

In 1986 the concept of the "bought deal" became a reality. The reason was the huge amount of capital sitting in LBO funds and the fierce competition among buyers for good deals.

With the highly confident letter, transactions still took one to three months to complete and were vulnerable to overbids from other equally voracious, extremely liquid LBO funds. In order to gain control over their transactions, the major LBO funds began to commit to close transactions with their own capital, not subject to raising third-party financing. This concept—the "bought deal"—quickened the process of committing to and, in some cases, closing transactions in as short a time as one week (if required). By 1986 the EBIT multiples paid for businesses had overheated to a stratospheric eight to twelve times. In spite of low interest rates and high earnings, at these multiples the companies could not afford to carry enough debt to finance the purchase.

FIGURE 3
Leveraged Buyouts vs High-Yield Issues: Total Number of Deals

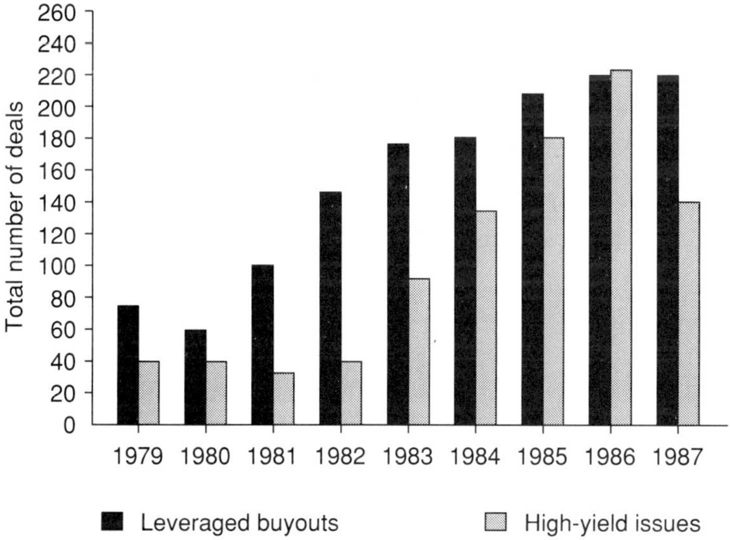

Source: Prudential-Bache Capital Funding

FIGURE 4
Leveraged Buyouts vs High-Yield Issues: Aggregate Dollar Volume ($bn)

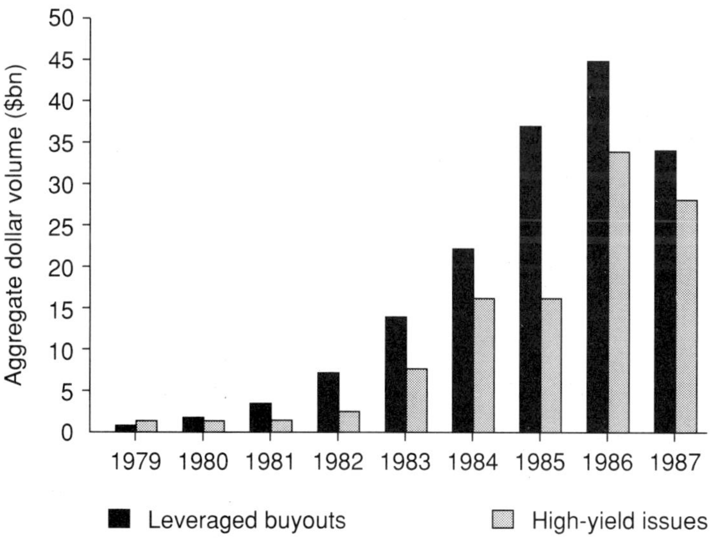

Source: Prudential-Bache Capital Funding

This inability to service debt in the early years of an LBO led to the development of two new types of securities for the LBO market—the pay in kind (PIK) security, and the zero coupon bond, both of which were designed to provide debt financing in transactions that could not carry the current interest burden on their full debt load. Both of these securities were to be regarded as debt, although in many cases no payments were required to be made on them in either principal or interest for three to five years. Essentially, these securities were equity securities that were sold to the public on the basis of a return normally associated with low ranking subordinated indebtedness. They represented, in fact, the overpayment made by acquirors at the eight to twelve multiple of EBIT levels required to secure transactions at that time.

The Bull Market

In 1987 even more money flooded the marketplace, driving purchase multiples even higher. During the summer of 1987, major LBOs were being completed in the nine to twelve times operating income range, with the investment banks and the LBO funds committing tremendous amounts of money very quickly. The investment banks had discovered that if they wanted to be able to place the junk bonds for a transaction and to buy equity in them, they had to be willing to put their own money at risk in the transactions in the form of bridge loans and/or equity investments. In 1986 and early 1987 many of these firms made tremendous profits on the fees connected with LBOs and by refinancing them through junk bonds. The values of equity investment grew on paper to many multiples of their original investment and the marketplace continued to mushroom.

The Bear Market

On October 19, 1987, the overheated market finally took a cold shower. The transactions that had been funded out prior to October 19, and which had PIKs and zeros as part of their financing package, saw these securities drastically decline in market value. The investment banking firms that had not refunded their outstanding bridges by October 19 for transactions that had been completed prior to that date, found it almost impossible to place the PIKs and zeros required to repay bridge loans. The high yield market for such securities virtually closed down for several months after October 19. The most notable example was the Southland transaction which had to be restructured at least twice in order to be sold after October 19.

The equity marketplace on the whole suffered a 30 percent drop in value in the October crash. While this drop in value was obvious for publicly traded companies, the owners of private companies or divisions were slow to change the aspirations they had for the sale prices of their properties. While transactions similar to those that had been completed in the nine to twelve times EBIT multiple range prior to October 19 could have been completed in the seven to nine range, almost no transactions were completed between October 19 and the end of 1987.

Future Direction

In the first quarter of 1988 there was a new vibrancy in the acquisition marketplace. Interest rates did not rise substantially, the well-touted U.S. recession was yet again delayed and corporate earnings countinued to increase. A number of well-publicized transactions were negotiated in which the original offer had been at depressed market values but the final purchase price was at or close to pre-October 19 multiples. The amount of money looking for transactions, if anything, increased and the competition once again bid up acquisition prices. In addition, because of the drop in the value of the dollar abroad, foreign acquirors became serious and active in purchasing companies or assets in the United States. Even at high purchase multiples, American companies and/or their assets were surprisingly cheap for Japanese or European acquirors.

As of the middle of 1988, there appeared to be few potential clouds on the horizon spelling the demise of the LBO. While the sources of financing may vary considerably depending on both U.S. and foreign marketplaces, the increasingly liquid market in U.S. corporate assets appear to be here to stay.

LBO VALUATION AND PRICING

We have seen that when interest rates decline, there is an opposite reaction in the multiples paid for companies. Unlike the conglomerates looking for reported earnings, LBOs are driven primarily by cash flow. Purchase prices are a function of how much you can borrow based on how much cash you can generate. Figure 5 demonstrates the inverse correlation between interest rates and purchase multiples.

While the figure uses P/E multiples (the ratio of purchase price to after-tax earnings) and not multiples of EBIT or operating cash flow, they provide a reasonable proxy for the cash-generating capabilities of companies. For pricing and financing LBOs, the critical factors are the actual and potential level and the stability of cash generation in the entity, and the current interest rate environment.

FIGURE 5
Public Leveraged Buyouts: Purchase Multiples vs Interest Rates

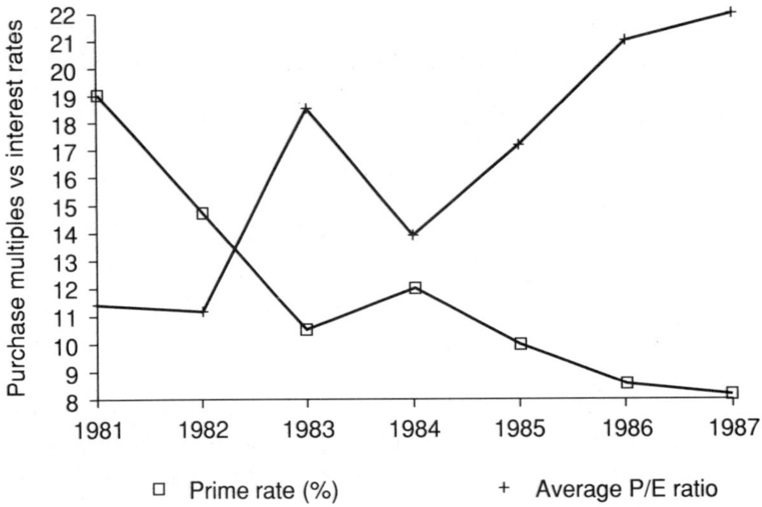

Sources: W.T. Grimm
Prudential-Bache Capital Funding

In general, the lower the interest rate environment, the higher the purchase price an investor would be willing to pay, because he would be able to afford to support a higher level of debt. In addition, many LBOs have been based upon the potential of improved operating cash flow from improvements in operating efficiency, synergy, or sales of unprofitable assets. Obviously all these things must be considered carefully when pricing an LBO.

Levels of Financing

Central to the financing of the modern LBO is the concept of "relative" position on the balance sheet as opposed to designation as a particular kind of security. While everyone in the business understands the difference between bank debt, subordinated debt, and equity, the marketplace has required structuring of numerous different securities at different levels of seniority within each of these main categories of financing. Because of these distinct layers of financing, or strips of paper, each of these securities has its own unique overall rate of return expectation. Some are interest rate driven; others have interest rate and equity components; and still others have equity components only. Typically the structure used for any specific deal will be tailored to the cash flow forecasts of that deal.

As we have noted, PIKs and zeros are used when cash flow is insufficient to service subordinated debt on a current basis. Buyers of these securities will typically require equity, often in the form of detachable warrants. These securities would often trade in the aftermarket without the attached equity. After October 19, many PIKs and zeros were trading at substantial discounts with yield in excess of 20 percent.

The public high-yield bond market is typically driven by cash flow coverage of interest. Unlike commercial bank lenders, bond buyers do not look for principal repayment from company cash flow; rather they rely on a company's ability to refinance based upon increased earnings and senior debt paydown. In the worst event, they derive comfort from the liquidity of the high-yield market to provide a second way out. This desire for liquidity has led (in part) to the increasing size of LBOs, since the larger the bond offering, the more willing the buyers are to participate.

Cram Down Paper

In addition to these multiple levels of securities, which are usually sold to third parties, one concept that has helped support the high price levels of transactions has been seller paper, commonly called "cram down" paper. This type of financing takes the form of very junior subordinated debt or senior preferred stock. It usually carries a lower-than-market rate and requires a lower total return than securities at the same level sold to third parties. In an environment where it is difficult to sell PIKs and zero bonds to third parties, seller financing may have no current return for years and may have to rely on improvements in operations for its ultimate repayment. When the seller's motivation is to recognize a book gain, and not necessarily the full cash payment, seller paper is often a successful inducement to buyers, as it allows a smaller equity commitment with a more easily finaceable subordinated debt piece.

Equity Investments and Participations

The ultimate goal of LBO investors is to purchase as much of the "cheap" common equity of the entity for as little cost as possible. The common equity in these transactions is usually a very small percentage of the total financing, but owns nearly all of the upside (and the downside) after the rest of the financing is paid off. The rate of return on these small LBO investments can be astronomical. Many LBO groups, and particularly investment banks, will collect fees at closing in excess of their equity investment, thus owning substantial upside for no real net investment.

Operating managers of LBO companies are usually given or allowed to buy between 5 and 20 percent of the common equity of the LBO company. This equity stake encourages managers to think as owners rather than employees, and it has been fundamental in changing the way they look at their businesses.

The incentive of actual ownership for operating managers is crucial to LBOs. These equity participations, which have given managements the chance to share in the great wealth generated by LBOs, have been instrumental in making LBOs succeed. Managements with major equity stakes in their businesses focus on every operating and spending decision, because it directly affects the value of their own stock. This motivation has proven time and again to be the most dominating factor in the improvement of operating earnings and the reduction of wasteful expenditure in LBO companies. It is not uncommon for breakeven levels to drop by 20 to 40 percent below those which existed prior to the LBO when the management owned little or none of the stock in the company.

EXAMPLES OF LEVERAGED BUYOUTS

In this section we discuss two LBOs that were completed by the authors. While two examples cannot encompass all of the many varieties of LBOs, they represent two extremes of LBOs; one was a turnaround and the other an asset sale.

The Seven-Up Company

During the summer of 1986, Philip Morris, Inc. decided to sell its wholly owned subsidiary, the Seven-Up Company (7-Up). Initially, Philip Morris negotiated a sale of 7-Up with Pepsico, but this sale was contested by the Federal Trade Commission and ultimately dropped, with Pepsi buying only 7-Up's foreign operations. Philip Morris then retained Morgan Stanley, Inc. to sell the domestic operations of 7-Up. Morgan Stanley held an auction and ultimately awarded the transaction to a group led by Hicks & Haas (H&H); Donaldson, Lufkin & Jenrette (DLJ); and Citicorp Venture Capital, Ltd. (CVC). H&H was a partnership made up of two Texas entrepreneurs who had, just prior to purchasing 7-Up, purchased the Dr Pepper Company from Forstmann Little and Company, and A&W Beverages from CVC.

The purchase price for 7-Up was $240 million and, together with fees and expenses of the transaction, required a total financing of $260 million. 7-Up was expected to report a small operating cash flow surplus for 1986 but had lost money on a GAAP earnings basis for each of the prior four years while it had been owned by Philip Morris. Morgan Stanley had required that each of the bids for 7-Up be fully financed in order to be considered. Therefore, H&H had secured bank commitments for $80 million from Bankers Trust, subordinated bridge commitments for $140 million from DLJ, and preferred and common equity commitments for $45 million from CVC, management, and others. While the purchase price as a multiple of operating cash flow was almost infinite, the investor group had determined during its due diligence investigation that if 7-Up could be run in conjunction with another soft drink company, significant savings could be made in the areas of staffing, inventory, production, and plant and equipment.

The investors concluded that if 7-Up could be run in conjunction with Dr Pepper's operations (H&H had just purchased Dr Pepper two months earlier), the financial performance could be improved to generate at least $30 million of annualized operating cash flow in a short period of time. In addition, the investment group relied on the fact that the soft drink industry had a 20-year pattern of greater than 5 percent growth in revenues and that unit volume itself had grown faster than the population growth of the country over that period.

Therefore, because of the savings available from operating with Dr Pepper, the investor group was confident that a purchase, which was considered to be an outrageous price at the time, would in fact turn out to be an attractive transaction. At closing, the bridge notes and $40 million of senior preferred stock were sold to third parties by DLJ. The Dr Pepper management team, operating under a management agreement with 7-Up, immediately began to rationalize 7-Up's operations. 7-Up's headquarters was moved from downtown St. Louis to Dallas, and the corporate headquarters was put up for sale. Plans were made to move Dr Pepper's concentrate production facility from Dallas to 7-Up's facility in St. Louis. Many of Dr Pepper's senior managers took on similar responsibilities for 7-Up, as well as their own. As a result, 7-Up's management staffing level rapidly decreased from its high under Philip Morris of over 600 people to approximately 300. The office building was sold for a $14 million gain and the inventory levels at 7-Up were reduced from $35 million to $18 million.

As these improvements began to be reflected in the company's operating performance, 7-Up issued a high-yield bond through DLJ to replace the bridge financing. (See Figure 6.) The high-yield offering closed on April 1, 1987 at a yield to maturity of approximately 12¼ percent, reflecting the market's understanding of and belief in both the business and management's ability to

FIGURE 6
The Seven-Up Company Prospectus
March 26, 1987

$155,781,000
The Seven-Up Company
12⅛% Senior Subordinated Notes Due May 15, 1997
Donaldson, Lufkin & Jenrette
Securities Corporation

The following table presents summary historical combined financial data of the U.S. Franchise Operations of the Company for the fiscal years ended December 31, 1982, 1983, 1984, and 1985 and for the period from January 1, 1986 to November 11, 1986 and summary historical consolidated financial data for the Company for the period from November 12, 1986 to December 31, 1986. Prior to the Acquisition, Philip Morris sold the Company's international franchise operations to PepsiCo, Inc. and transferred all divisions and subsidiaries not associated with the U.S. Franchise Operations to another wholly-owned subsidiary of Philip Morris. Accordingly, the Company, as acquired by the Holding Company, consists soley of the U.S. Franchise Operations.

	U.S. Franchise Operations					*Company*
	Years Ended December 31,				*Period from January 1, 1986 to November 11, 1986*	*Period from November 12, 1986 to December 31, 1986*
	1982	*1983*	*1984*	*1985*		
	(In thousands, except ratios)					
OPERATING DATA:						
Net sales	$220,876	$274,552	$300,689	$291,402	$233,446	$38,180
Cost of sales	86,000	105,984	123,801	121,117	99,752	13,640
Gross profit	134,876	168,568	176,888	170,285	133,694	24,540
Marketing and administration expenses	143,017	169,270	173,614	168,710	132,017	22,648
Amortization of goodwill and other intangible assets	5,306	5,306	5,306	5,309	4,557	666
Other income (expense):						
Interest	41	35	32	8	(16)	(3,976)
Other	12	(27)	(45)	498	156	—
Loss before income taxes	(13,394)	(6,000)	(2,045)	(3,228)	(2,740)	(2,750)
Income tax benefit (expense)	5,425	748	(1,270)	(891)	(921)	(103)
Net loss	$ (7,969)	$ (5,252)	$ (3,315)	$ (4,119)	$ (3,661)	$(2,853)

Pro Forma Condensed Combined Statement of Operations

The following unaudited Pro Forma Condensed Combined Statement of Operations of the Company gives effect to the Acquisition (and the borrowings in connection therewith) and the issuance of the Notes by the Company and the application of the estimated net proceeds therefrom as if such transactions had occurred on January 1, 1986. The Pro Forma Condensed Combined Statement of Operations should be read in conjuction with the historical combined financial statements of the U.S. Franchise Operations of the Company as of dates and for periods ended prior to November 12, 1986 and the historical consolidated financial statements of the Company

FIGURE 6—*Continued*

as of December 31, 1986 and for the period from November 12, 1986 to December 31, 1986, and the related notes thereto, appearing elsewhere in this Prospectus. The pro forma information is not necessarily indicative of the results that would have been reported had such events actually occurred on January 1, 1986, nor is it indicative of the Company's future results.

The Seven-Up Company Pro Forma Condensed Combined Statement of Operations (In thousands, except ratios)

	Historical			
	Period from January 1, 1986 to November 11, 1986	*Period from November 12,1986 to December 31, 1986*	*Pro Forma Adjustments(1)*	*Pro Forma Combined Year Ended December 31, 1986*
Net sales	$233,446	$38,180	$ —	$271,626
Cost of sales	99,752	13,640	—	113,392
Gross profit	133,694	24,540	—	158,234
Marketing and administrative expenses	132,017	22,648	—	154,665
Amortization of goodwill and other intangible assets	4,557	666	(365)	4,858
Management fee	—	—	7,000	7,000
Operating income (loss)	(2,880)	1,226	(6,635)	(8,289)
Interest:				
Credit Agreement borrowings	—	889	5,411	6,300
Increasing Rate Notes	—	2,100	(2,100)	—
Senior Subordinated Notes including amortization of original issue discount	—	—	17,241	17,241
Amortization of loan fees	—	987	3,647	4,634
Other	16	—	—	16
Total interest	16	3,976	24,199	28,191
Other income	156	—	—	156
Loss before income taxes	(2,740)	(2,750)	(30,834)	(36,324)
Income tax expense (benefit)	921	103	(1,024)	—
Net loss	$ (3,661)	$(2,853	$(29,810)	$(36,324)
Ratio of earnings to fixed charges (Note g)				—

[1]Reflects adjustments to the historical financial data for the period from January 1, 1986 to November 11, 1986.

Use of Proceeds

The Notes will provide gross proceeds of approximately $140 million. The net proceeds of this offering, together with additional borrowings of approximately $9 million under the Credit Agreement, will be used to pay the principal of, and all accrued and unpaid interest on, the Increasing Rate Notes, which will total approximately $142.2 million at the estimated date of payment. The company issued the Increasing Rate Notes to fund a portion of the purchase price of the Acquisition. The Increasing Rate Notes will mature on November 12, 1988 and currently accrue interest at the rate of 12% per annum. See "The Company—Acquisition—The Increasing Rate Notes." As of the date hereof, affiliates of the Underwriter hold approximately $26.3 million aggregate principal amount of the Increasing Rate Notes.

effect a turnaround. (Note in Figure 6 that at the time of the offering 7-Up not only had had a long history of operational losses but also that the pro forma financials, giving effect to the costs of the proposed financing, showed losses of over $36 million. Investors sure had to have confidence in the new management.)

In addition to the operating improvements, which had been foreseen by the investors, management decided to introduce a new product at 7-Up to extend its product range. In mid-1987, the company introduced Cherry and Diet Cherry 7-Up. These products were an instantaneous success and provided substantial incremental revenue and profit in 1987.

As a result of these improvements and the new product introduction, 7-Up's operating cash flow increased to $48 million in 1987. The purchase price of $260 million thus came to represent a 5.4 multiple of cash flow—quite a low price considering 7-Up's strong national franchise. This level of performance can only be described as outstanding and almost unprecedented. It is an example of the ability to pay a perceived very high price for an entity and make it work because the synergistic effects were extraordinary.

On April 13, 1988, Dr Pepper and 7-Up announced a merger plan, in conjunction with a sale of 49 percent of the combined entity to Prudential-Bache Interfunding, the merchant banking arm of Prudential-Bache Securities Inc., for $600 million. This sale would value the companies at approximately $1.3 billion, almost doubling their stated worth in 1986. While this valuation, representing a multiple of cash flow of approximately 10 ×, is a full one, the value of companies such as 7-Up and Dr Pepper lies in their value as national franchises. While the soft drink market in the U.S. is dominated by Coca-Cola (40 percent) and Pepsi Cola (31 percent), Dr Pepper/7-Up has a share of approximately 11 percent, and is the only major company in the domestic industry not held by a large corporation. In addition, the exceptionally stable real growth of the domestic soft drink industry, the cash flow generation of the combined entities, and the likely decline in the cost of aspartame, a major cost component, as it nears the end of its patent, indicate that this is a supportable price level. In Figures 6 and 7, we show the financials and pro formas of Dr Pepper and 7-Up at the times of the various transactions. Note the required investor confidence in the ability of new management to support the heavy debt.

CBS Magazine Division

In July 1987, several units of The Prudential Insurance Company of America and management purchased the magazine division of CBS, Inc. Management of the division had been brought by an intermediary to The Prudential with

FIGURE 7
Dr Pepper Company Prospectus
November 14, 1986

$218,000,000
Dr Pepper Company
12¾% Senior Subordinated Debentures due November 30, 2001
Shearson Lehman Brothers, Inc.

Pro Forma Condensed Statement of Operations (In thousands of dollars, except for ratio data) (Unaudited)

	Year Ended December 31, 1985		
	Historical	*Adjustments*	*Pro Forma*
Net sales	$173,838		$173,838
Cost of sales	25,314		25,314
Gross profit	148,524		148,524
Administrative, marketing and general expenses	108,239	$ 16,265 (5,429)	119,075
Operating profit	40,285	(10,836)	29,449
Interest:			
Existing debt at acquisition	26,178	(25,230)	948
Credit agreement borrowings		18,900	18,900
Senior subordinated debentures (including amortization of original issue discount)		24,750	24,750
Amortization of loan fees		1,251	1,251
Total interest	26,178	19,671	45,849
Other income (expense)	226		226
Income (loss) before income taxes	14,333	(30,507)	(16,174)
Income taxes	10,129	(10,129)	
Net income (loss)	$ 4,204	$(20,378)	$(16,174)
Ratio of earnings to fixed charges	1.54		—

the idea of making an offer for the division. Based on management's reports, The Prudential's own due diligence review, and the valuations of two outside consultants, The Prudential group agreed to provide management with a $700 million financing package. Management approached the board of CBS and ultimately was given a 4-day window in which to complete a definitive purchase agreement. Because of the high price to be paid for the division, management and The Prudential group agreed that several of the division's magazines would have to be sold postclosing to reduce the interest burden of the debt required to complete the transaction.

During the period between the signing of the purchase agreement at the beginning of August and the closing date of October 1, 1987, management and The Prudential assessed which properties would be sold and prepared to approach potential purchasers as soon as possible after the closing. As part of the $700 million financing package for the newly formed acquisition company, named Diamandis Communications, Inc. (after the CEO), a tranche of $120 million of junior subordinated notes was structured as a bridge financing to be repaid out of the proceeds of the expected sale of some of the magazines. The permanent financing for the company was provided by The Prudential group in strips of senior and senior subordinated debt. Management and The Prudential group together owned in excess of 95 percent of the stock.

In doing its diligence on the magazine division, The Prudential group determined that each of the 21 magazines which made up the group was a national monopoly and that it would be virtually impossible for another company on a start-up basis to attack any of those franchises. (See Figure 8.) As a result it was felt that certain magazines could be sold to certain buyers at multiples of operating income far higher than the average multiple paid for the entire company. Potential industry buyers should be willing to pay high multiples of the preoverhead contributions of individual magazines which could be incorporated into their own overhead structure.

Immediately after closing, management approved a predetermined group of buyers and, almost immediately, negotiated a sale of five of the magazines to one industry player at a premium price. While this price was negotiated prior to October 19, the purchaser completed the deal in December, without renegotiation. During the same time frame, two other magazines were sold, which also closed prior to the end of 1987. The proceeds from the sale of these magazines fully retired the bridge financing which had been put up to cover them. The Company, renamed DCI subsequent to closing, was left with a vastly reduced level of debt, and as a result had sufficient cash flow generated by the remaining magazines to cover debt service on a current basis. While this short-term strategy was successful in reducing debt, management was simultaneously engaged in eliminating significant excess overhead costs associated with both the magazines that were sold and the corporate staff that had been required as a part of the CBS group.

On April 13, 1988, DCI announced a sale of the whole company to Hachette S.A., one of the world's largest magazine publishers based in

FIGURE 8
Diamandis Communications (Purchase and Sale of Magazines)

	Magazines Originally Purchased from CBS	*Divested Prior to Sale of Company*	*Company Sold to Hachette*
	American Photographer		American Photographer
	Audio		Audio
	Automobile Quarterly	Automobile Quarterly	
	Backpacking	Backpacking	
	Boating		Boating
	Car and Driver		Car and Driver
	Cycle		Cycle
	Cycle World		Cycle World
	Field and Stream	Field and Stream	
	Flying		Flying
	Home Mechanix	Home Mechanix	
	Modern Bride	Modern Bride	
	Popular Magazines		Popular Magazines
	Popular Photography		Popular Photography
	Road and Track		Road and Track
	Skiing	Skiing	
	Stereo Review		Stereo Review
	Woman's Day		Woman's Day
	Yachting	Yachting	
Purchase Price:	$700 million	$235 million	$712 million

France, for $712 million. Together with the prior sale of seven of the magazines for approximately $235 million, and the reduction of debt through cash flow, this sale represented a gain of approximately $300 million to The Prudential and DCI management. Once again, this LBO realized the value of national monopolies, in this case the individual magazine franchises. In addition, the company reduced overhead and sold assets quickly enough to alleviate the high initial debt load required to finance the initial transaction.

Figure 8 lists the magazines DCI bought from CBS and their subsequent dispositions.

IMPLICATIONS OF LBOs

In the early 1980s the financial press, bankers and corporate executives typically looked upon LBOs as a manipulation by entrepreneurs to enrich themselves at the expense of shareholders or owners. This view persisted for a number of years and culminated in an entire issue of Forbes magazine in 1983 which caricatured the whole LBO process in a cartoon on its front cover.

In recent years, however, experience has afforded a better understanding of the mechanisms of operating efficiency, asset utilization, and management incentives—and LBOs have proved to be a powerful source of improved productivity for the United States economy. Many companies are now restructuring themselves, providing shareholders with value that in the past they never would have seen; in fact, it is very difficult to find a public LBO where the shareholders have not received far in excess of the price at which their shares were trading before the LBO was initiated.

But, in the end, it is really the change of management's status from employee to owner that has generated the tremendous efficiency and individual benefits that have been realized in the LBOs of the 1980s. (This is not to say that there have not been some egregious examples of LBOs entered into for the sole purpose of enriching the participants with little regard for the enhancement of the company's operations. Some well publicized "corporate raiders" have specialized in acquiring companies in hostile takeovers and liquidating the companies' assets in order to achieve quick profits. Nonetheless, these "asset stripping" transactions represent a small proportion of buyouts.)

Another criticism of LBOs which is often made is that the need to use available cash flow to service debt starves the company of capital required to be invested in plant and equipment and research and development for the long-term health of the company.

However, similar pressures to maximize short-term results are often applied by the marketplace to publicly traded companies, and it can be argued that operation under the constraints of high leverage imposes upon a company the need to justify the optimal utilization of cash for capital expenditures and development programs in a way that would not be present where management were acting merely as employees. Furthermore, the "deconglomeratization" of corporate America since the early 1970s, largely a result of the increase in leverage buyout activity, has eliminated to a large extent multiple levels of bureaucracy which historically did not create value within the economy. By allowing management to share in the ownership and the upside of their companies, the LBO has blurred the distinction between owners and employees which in the past spawned much of the fat and corporate "empire-building" inherent in pre-LBO corporations.

Nonetheless, many of the LBOs consummated in the 1980s have yet to experience a recessionary economy, and it remains to be seen whether the effects of leverage, which heretofore have so enriched LBO participants, will undermine the value of recent LBO investments under a less beneficial enconomic environment. But whatever the economy, LBOs have forever changed the concept of companies and the landscape of corporate America.

CHAPTER 13

LEVERAGED BUYOUTS III: PRACTICES AND TECHNIQUES

James J. Burke, Jr.
Warner A. Fite
Merrill Lynch Capital Partners, Inc.

In recent years, leveraged buyouts have received a great deal of attention both within the financial community and in the national media. Leveraged buyout activity has increased in a rapid and visible fashion. In 1981, fewer than $2 billion in transactions, mainly acquisitions of mature industrial businesses, were completed. By 1986, five years later, over $100 billion in transactions had been completed ($35 billion in 1986 alone), and many companies with household names (such as Avis, Beatrice and Denny's) had been the subject of leveraged buyouts.

OVERVIEW

Generally speaking, a leveraged buyout is any acquisition of a business financed primarily with debt capital. In most cases, these acquisitions are accomplished by "shell" companies established by a leveraged buyout sponsor or other investor group solely for the purpose of the transaction. The acquiring vehicle is financed with a relatively small amount of equity capital, and uses the assets and cash flow of the acquired company to secure, service, and repay the debt it has incurred to finance the acquisition.

Leveraged buyouts can be complex and difficult transactions. Their completion requires the confidence and enthusiasm of a variety of sophisticated financial participants who scrutinize every aspect of a potential transaction.

The ultimate success of a leveraged buyout—which is not established until a large portion of the debt is repaid and the value of the equity investment is realized (most likely a number of years after the closing)—depends upon sound investment judgment and credit decisions, company performance, and economic and market conditions.

This chapter cannot cover all aspects of this complex topic in detail. Rather, it focuses upon management leveraged buyouts from the perspective of the sponsor (or organizer) of these transactions. It discusses the economics and history of leveraged buyouts as well as criteria used to assess potential buyout candidates. It also covers the analysis, structure, and completion of transactions. Particular attention is given to the objectives and criteria of the various financial participants in a leveraged buyout.

Structure and Uses of Leveraged Buyouts

The most common use of the leveraged buyout has been management-led transactions. In a management buyout, a group of equity investors, working with a company's management, proposes to acquire the company on a friendly basis, with the terms negotiated between the acquiring group and the selling company's board of directors. Characteristic of these transactions is the "promoted" equity participation of company management, (i.e., equity ownership in excess of pro rata investment percentage, or "sweat equity"). Those who provide the cash equity in management buyouts are generally financially rather than operationally oriented. Thus, they depend upon management to make the transaction a success through the creation of equity appreciation. All equity participants expect to realize gains through the sale of the acquired company's equity after a significant holding period. During that time, a meaningful portion of the acquisition debt should have been repaid through internally generated funds or through the divestiture of noncore assets or businesses.

The Market for Leveraged Buyouts

Leveraged buyouts have gained sufficient credibility to be considered by management, boards of directors, and controlling shareholders in virtually every instance in which a company changes control or undergoes a significant recapitalization.

The market for leveraged buyouts can be divided into three segments: public companies that are acquired in "going private" transactions; privately held companies in which the ownership is recognized as part of a recapitalization of the company; and divested divisions or subsidiaries of larger corporations (both public and private) that are acquired through a leveraged buyout.

Public Companies

In the case of public companies, leveraged buyouts are employed both as a strategy for maximizing shareholder wealth and as a defensive response to unwelcome overtures from third parties. Public securities markets may not fully reflect a public company's intrinsic value. Often the public markets reward (through higher price-earnings multiples) companies that are considered to have the potential for rapid growth while penalizing (through lower price-earnings multiples) those that have more modest short-term growth potential. Accordingly, the improvement of earnings over the short term can become the overriding management consideration. The public markets, therefore, may undervalue the financial capabilities of those companies that have only a moderate near-term expectation of earnings growth. A leveraged buyout, providing shareholders with a premium to the public market value of their shares, offers a strategic approach to maximizing shareholder values. Public companies such as Metromedia, Levi Strauss, and R.H. Macy & Co. have gone private for such strategic reasons.

A leveraged buyout can also represent an attractive alternative in cases of public companies that receive unsolicited acquisition proposals from hostile third parties. By participating in a leveraged buyout proposal, management can take a proactive role in assuring that the shareholders receive the maximum value for their interests. Since the management group should be intimately familiar with the operations and prospects of a company, a management proposal can often reflect the highest value while providing an attractive opportunity for new lenders and investors. Leveraged buyouts completed as defensive maneuvers in cases in which hostile transactions were attempted or believed imminent include Safeway Stores in 1986 and Borg-Warner Corporation and Supermarkets General Corporation in 1987.

Private Companies

A leveraged buyout often represents an attractive alternative in the case of private companies whose shareholders are seeking liquidity. Owners of privately held companies who wish to sell all or part of their holdings may be faced with a difficult choice. They may offer stock publicly, in which case only partial liquidity can be obtained. Alternatively, the owners may sell their business to another, generally larger, corporation, which is often a competitor. In such situations, a leveraged buyout provides the private shareholders, who may include trusts, management, and family groups, with an opportunity to achieve maximum liquidity while maintaining the independence of the company. The flexibility of equity ownership in a leveraged buyout also allows different shareholder groups to achieve varying objectives. Some groups, such as management shareholders, can retain a significant continuing interest in the business while achieving meaningful net liquidity. At the same time, other shareholders can realize an attractive value for their entire interests. Therefore, leveraged buyouts may present particularly appealing opportunities for the sale and recapitalization of privately held companies. Management buyouts of private companies have been successfully completed in many instances, including Ithaca Industries and Clinton Mills.

Divestitures

Leveraged buyouts have also proved appealing to companies wishing to divest themselves of divisions or subsidiaries for strategic reasons. When a unit is chosen for divestiture, operating management is often well-positioned (with a financial partner) to acquire the business because of intimate understanding of its values. A management buyout allows the parent company to conduct the sale of its division or subsidiary discreetly and to achieve for itself an attractive price with a minimum of publicity and business disruption. Management's disadvantage is its inability to benefit from any synergies created by a combination with a competitor or by integration. Management-led leveraged buyouts of divisions or subsidiaries have been successful in many instances, including Gibson Greeting Cards, National Rent-A-Car, and Converse.

HISTORICAL BACKGROUND AND RECENT DEVELOPMENTS

Large institutional leveraged buyouts are a recent phenomenon, having become common only since 1979. Prior to then, from about 1960, leveraged buyouts, or "bootstrap" transactions, as they were then known, were mostly quite small and involved the acquisition of private companies. In most cases, the acquirors were either the managers of the business or well-to-do individual investors. In these transactions, a secured senior lender typically advanced funds against the fixed assets and working capital of the business. The equity investor provided whatever additional capital was required. Because the debt financing was generally available only on a "borrowing base" formula—sufficient to provide a 100 percent collateralized loan in the event of the company's failure—leveraged acquirors were, for the most part, unable to pay a significant premium to book value. For this reason, bootstraps accomplished during the 1960s were often acquisitions of troubled businesses whose acquisition value might be a discount to book value.

In the late 1960s, subordinated debt became available for leveraged buyouts. In addition to senior creditors, transactions came to include subordinated creditors who were willing to lend without the same asset protection enjoyed by the senior lender. In addition to a higher yield, subordinated lenders often required an equity participation in the transaction to compensate for the increased risk. When subordinated debt became available, leveraged buyouts became more flexible. Values in excess of book value could be paid and larger transactions could be accomplished. During the 1970s, investment banking firms became involved as financial intermediaries in leveraged buyouts, and a number of boutique firms were established to engage solely in sponsoring leveraged buyouts. Gibbons, Green & Rice, the first of these firms, acquired Syracuse China in 1975 for $7.7 million.

A milestone in leveraged buyout activity was reached in 1979. Kohlberg Kravis Roberts & Co., a group which had been formed in 1976, completed the $370 million leveraged buyout of Houdaille Industries, Inc. Houdaille was the first large institutional leveraged buyout of a significant public company. The acquisition, which was financed with four layers of debt and two of equity, demonstrated that leveraged buyouts could be accomplished in the public arena and that the securities created in financing such a transaction could prove attractive for institutional investors. The lenders and investors in the Houdaille transaction included some of the largest banks and insurance companies in the U.S., as well as a number of retirement funds.

Growth in Numbers and Size

Since the Houdaille transaction, the number and size of management leveraged buyouts has grown rapidly, as shown in Figure 1. In 1981, 15 transactions in excess of $25 million were announced, with an aggregate value of $3.1 billion; in 1988, approximately 190 such transactions were announced, with an aggregate value of $143.9 billion.

The size of individual buyouts has also increased. In 1980, the largest buyout to date was Congoleum Corporation, at $448 million; two years later, Signode Corporation ranked as the largest at $485 million. At the end of 1984, the Metromedia buyout was the largest to date, valued at $1.7 billion, and at the end of 1986, the Beatrice Companies transaction, valued at $7.7 billion, ranked as the largest ever done. In 1989, the $29.5 billion leveraged buyout of RJR Nabisco was completed.

FIGURE 1
Leveraged Buyout Market Activity (a) Total Value and Number of Transactions (b) Number of Transactions above $25 Million

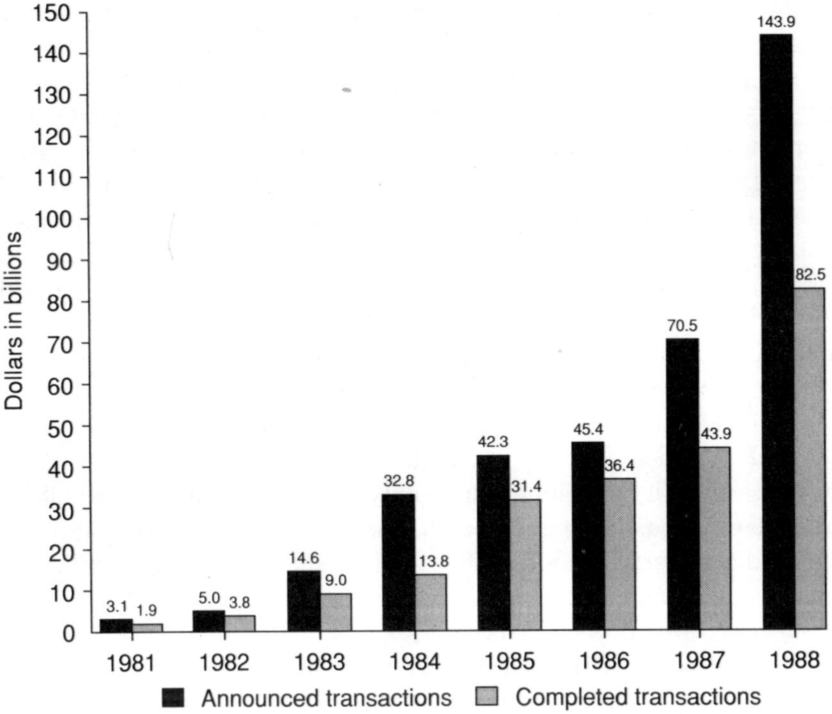

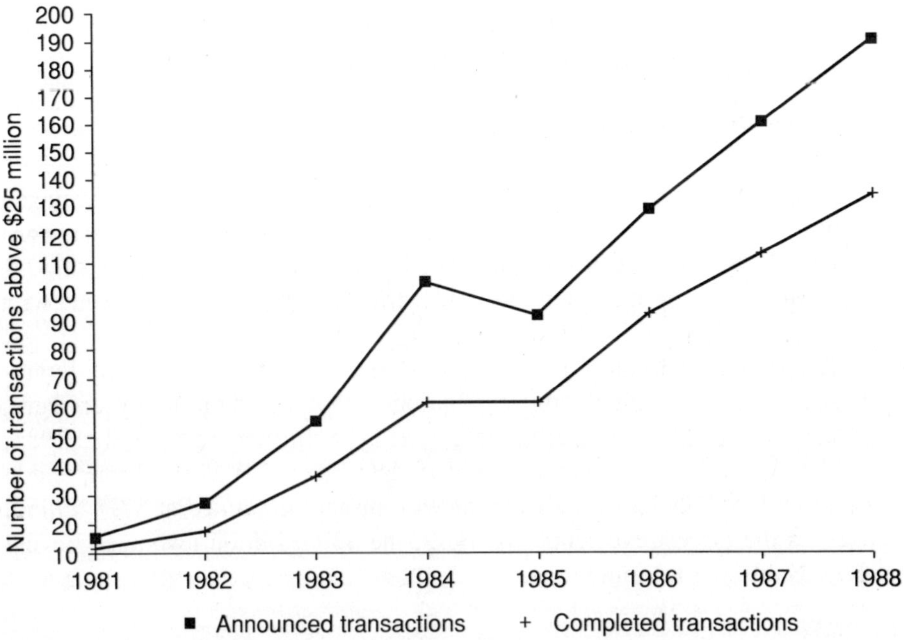

Reasons for Rapid Growth

The rapid growth in the leveraged buyout marketplace that has occurred in recent years is attributable to a number of factors.

Excellent Returns Elicit Pools of Capital

The record of excellent returns has encouraged investors to participate in the pooled equity funds managed by leveraged buyout sponsors. Both leveraged buyout boutiques and investment banking firms have assembled pools of capital with contributions from insurance companies, commercial banks, corporate and governmental pension and retirement plans, and individual investors. The availability of these funds allows the major leveraged buyout sponsors to commit significant financing to even the largest transactions.

Private Debt Markets

The second factor contributing to the enormous increase in leveraged buyout activity is the development of both the private and public debt markets. On the private side, both commercial banks and insurance companies have become increasingly sophisticated and experienced in evaluating leveraged buyout opportunities. Many large banks have turned to leveraged buyout financing as an attractive source of income. Large insurance companies, often providers of subordinated debt and equity in leveraged buyouts, continue to be drawn to leveraged buyout financing due to the generally excellent performance of investments in these transactions. Many of the leading institutions have dedicated specialized units to leveraged buyout financing in recent years.

Public High-Yield Debt ("Junk Bonds")

The growth in the public market for high-yield debt (junk bonds) and the recent development of merchant banking capabilities among the leading investment banking firms has also contributed to the increase in leveraged buyout activity. The public market for below-investment-grade debt has grown rapidly in recent years as many sophisticated investors have come to believe that the additional return on such debt more than compensates for its additional risk. The growth in the public high-yield market, in fact, has largely corresponded with the increase in the number and volume of leveraged buyouts, and this alternative source of subordinated debt has been crucial to the successful completion of many large transactions.

Capital Commitment as Bridge Loans

The recent willingness of investment banking firms to commit their own capital to leveraged buyouts has served to increase the competitiveness of leveraged buyout proposals in contested or potentially contested situations. Typically, the investment banking firm advances subordinated capital to complete the acquisition in the form of a bridge loan; the proceeds of a subsequent public debt offering are then used to repay the bridge loan. This willingness to purchase leveraged buyout debt outright, pending its final public distribution, can be important in giving leveraged buyout proposals full financial credibility against competing offers for control of a company.

Hostile and Unsolicited LBOs

In the past several years, leveraged acquisition activity has expanded beyond management buyouts. The leveraged buyout structure has been adopted by corporate acquirors willing to proceed on an unsolicited and unfriendly basis. This development is directly related to the development of the high yield bond market since few traditional (private) subordinated lenders will become involved in hostile transactions. Almost every hostile leveraged buyout bid has been financed through public subordinated debt. The watershed event in hostile leveraged acquisitions occurred in early 1984, when Drexel Burnham Lambert arranged $2 billion in financing for Mesa Petroleum's bid for Gulf Oil Corporation. Mesa did not succeed in acquiring Gulf, but did force its sale to Standard Oil of California. Notable hostile leveraged acquisitions that have been completed include Revlon, AMF, Ponderosa, Scovill, and Warnaco. Each of these transactions was financed with a limited amount of equity capital from the acquiror and a large amount of debt capital raised in the public markets and from commercial banks.

The definition of leveraged buyout has been further expanded to include leveraged acquisitions by other types of financial buyers. These buyers are willing to attempt to make an acquisition on an unsolicited and unfriendly basis when they believe that the public markets do not fully value a company. An example of this approach was Paul Bilzerian's bid for Hammermill Paper Company in July 1986. When Bilzerian launched his unsolicited tender offer for the shares of Hammermill Paper, he employed the techniques of the management buyout sponsors, with two notable differences. His offer was made without the support of management (and, therefore, without access to internal financial information and forecasts) and the offer was not negotiated.

In other respects, the offer was a leveraged buyout proposal. Bilzerian and his partners committed approximately $90 million in equity capital to the $900 million transaction. The remainder of the capital came from a group of commercial banks and an investment banking firm committed to bridging the subordinated debt portion of the capital structure. Moreover, in contrast to prior hostile bids in which prospective acquirors castigated management for the performance of its business, Bilzerian praised Hammermill's incumbent management and offered to retain them in their positions and to provide them with an equity participation in the transaction.

Private Sales and Divestitures as LBOs

Leveraged buyouts are becoming increasingly common in private sale situations as well. In their efforts to realize the greatest possible values, private sellers and their advisors are turning more and more to financial buyers not affiliated with management. In many cases, the private sale process is being designed to prevent management from forming an alliance with any one possible acquiror who could prove detrimental to the auction process. Financial buyers are bidding for—and acquiring—companies without specific support or assistance from management. In these cases, the buyer and management reach a specific understanding concerning the management's participation (if any) only subsequent to the acquisition.

Public LBOs

The most recent development which expands the definition of leveraged buyout is the advent of the leveraged recapitalization—or "public LBO." In a leveraged recapitalization, a company raises debt as it would in a traditional leveraged buyout. Because there is no new equity capital in a leveraged recapitalization, the amount of debt that can be raised in this type of transaction is generally less than can be raised in a leveraged buyout. The proceeds of the debt offering are distributed to existing shareholders, either pursuant to a shareholder-approved plan of recapitalization or through a special dividend. Instead of selling equity (and, therefore, the company) to a private investor group, the company allows shareholders to retain an equity interest in the highly leveraged enterprise. In effect, shareholders receive a continuing equity interest in lieu of a portion of the consideration that they would have received in a traditional leveraged buyout. Significant leveraged recapitalizations have included FMC Corporation, Colt Industries, Owens-Corning Fiberglass, Holiday Corporation, and Union Carbide Corporation. (See Volume II, Chapters 23–24.)

THE BUYOUT PROCESS AND THE ROLE OF THE SPONSOR

The impetus for a management leveraged buyout can come from a number of sources. In a public company, a management buyout might be initiated as a response to an unfriendly takeover bid (possibly a leveraged buyout itself). A company's management also might independently initiate a buyout as a means to increase shareholder value. Management or shareholders of private companies often consider a leveraged buyout to provide liquidity. Managers of subsidiaries and divisions of larger companies initiate buyouts, as do financial buyers who attempt to acquire these operations.

Importance of the Sponsor

Unless the potential transaction has been initiated by a sponsor, or unless the group initiating the transaction has experience in structuring leveraged transactions and enjoys access to a significant amount of capital, the first step is the selection of a sponsor for the transaction. This is not a casual decision, for it marks the establishment of a partnership that is likely to last several years and that will determine the ultimate success of the transaction. In the case of those sponsors who manage equity funds, the sponsor often is the majority acquiror of the business.

The sponsor is one of the most important participants in the leveraged buyout process. The sponsor manages the transaction and is responsible for the success of its every aspect. The sponsor structures the financing of the transaction, secures commitments for the financing, negotiates the terms of the transaction with the company's board of directors or other seller and, in most cases, invests in the equity of the transaction.

Leveraged buyout sponsors generally fall into two groups: boutique firms and investment banking houses. The boutique firms are relatively small groups whose sole activity is the sponsorship of leveraged buyouts. In recent years, a large number of smaller boutique firms have been created as many individuals with financial backgrounds have attempted to become part of the leveraged buyout boom. Many investment banking firms have also become active as leveraged buyout sponsors. These firms have established specialty groups within their corporate finance departments to concentrate on these transactions.

Selection of the Sponsor

Management groups often evaluate several possible sponsors before making a selection. While only a handful of firms can compete for and complete the very largest transactions, a larger number of firms are capable of completing medium and small-sized buyouts. Management groups tend to focus on the potential sponsor's financial credibility, the management participation in the transaction offered, and the sponsor's approach to the management of the company after the transaction. In some cases, such as contested public takeovers and some private sell or divestiture situations, management's ability to select a sponsor can be constrained by fiduciary responsibilites.

Access to Capital

When management selects a partner, the prospective sponsor's access to capital usually ranks among the most important criteria. The completion of the transaction depends upon the sponsor's ability to raise capital and its own financial resources. In the current competitive acquisition environment, corporate sellers—be they public boards of directors or private shareholders—are unlikely (and often unable) to be indulgent of acquisition proposals that appear financially suspect. The potential acquiror must have financial credibility. In the case of leveraged buyout sponsors, this credibility is partially demonstrated by the ability to commit capital directly. Most management groups receive only one opportunity to complete a leveraged buyout and are willing to become involved with only credible partners.

Managed Pools of Funds

Nearly all of the leading sponsors have raised equity funds for investment in their transactions. As discussed in more detail below, these funds are pools of institutional capital, mainly contributed by insurance companies, commercial banks and pension funds. The funds have proliferated to the extent that the capability to commit equity capital in this manner is virtually a requirement for leveraged buyout sponsorship. These equity commitments serve as the foundation for raising the other layers of capital required in a transaction.

Certain sponsors have raised "mezzanine" funds, either in the place of or in addition to equity funds. These funds draw upon many of the same investors as the equity funds and make investments in both equity and subordinated debt of buyouts. Mezzanine funds can reduce or eliminate a sponsor's need to seek subordinated debt from a third party, possibly broadening the capital base upon which to build the financing.

Network of Financial Relationships

To successfully complete a transaction, the would-be sponsor also must enjoy a wide access to other sources of capital. Commercial banks and public and private lenders provide senior and subordinated debt, as described below. A sponsor's relationship with these financing sources is an important element in his overall ability to raise capital quickly. The most successful sponsors have built a network of relationships which provide them with ready access to these financing sources. Reputation and the success of past transactions are important elements in a sponsor's ability to elicit rapid and aggressive responses to financing proposals.

Management Participation

Management groups consider a number of factors besides financing abilities when choosing a sponsor. The financial participation that the sponsor is prepared to provide the management group is important. Because few sponsors participate in the operational management of their investments, they want management to invest and participate meaningfully in the transaction; indeed, management's reluctance to do so will preclude many sponsors from becoming involved with a potential transaction. Most sponsors incorporate a promoted interest into management's participation. This incentive can take the form of loans, stock options, and incentive compensation programs, usually ranging from 5 to 15 percent of the total equity in the transaction, provided that performance expectations are met over time.

Corporate Governance

In selecting a partner, management also considers corporate governance after the completion of the transaction. Because in many cases the fund managed by the sponsor acquires a controlling interest in the company, the sponsor's approach to the management of the enterprise plays an important role in its overall profile. Sponsors vary in their orientation from the largely passive financial buyers to the management-oriented turn-around investors, with most sponsors falling between the two extremes. It is important for the management group to become comfortable with the sponsor's approach at an early stage in order for the transaction to proceed smoothly.

How Sponsors Evaluate Transactions

Just as the management group evaluates prospective sponsors, so do the sponsors evaluate the potential transaction with which they are presented. On the average, the more active sponsors decline 90 percent or more of the opportunities they receive. In many cases, the businesses involved do not lend themselves to long-term leverage. In other cases, the sponsor cannot become comfortable with the management group and its objectives. For this reason, success as a major sponsor of leveraged buyouts requries access to a steady stream of prospective transactions. The corporate client bases and institutional relationships of investment banking firms provide them with a source of opportunities. The boutique firms draw upon relationships with financing sources, other management groups, and investment and commercial banking firms as a source of potential transactions.

Planning the Transaction

Once a sponsor has been selected, management and the sponsor work together to formulate a comprehensive business plan for the company. Often this plan is extended as far as ten years into the future. In many cases, management develops such plans in the normal course of its activities; in other cases, the sponsor is instrumental in focusing management upon the future and prospects of its business. The plan, and the financial projections based upon it, provide the basis for determining the feasibility of the transaction and the structure of the financing.

The business plan and forecasts should be basically conservative. Because the financing of the leveraged buyout is based on these expectations of company performance, failure by the company to meet its plan after the closing of the transaction can prove disastrous. Projections should take into account the likelihood of economic downturns during the term of the plan. The business plan must also reflect the fact that the company will be highly leveraged going forward, and therefore must not depict growth based upon large capital spending or significant acquisitions.

The experience and judgment of the sponsor is critical in determining the maximum value for a company in a leveraged buyout and in structuring the financing necessary to complete the transaction. In a leveraged buyout, value and financial structure are inseparable. The major factors contributing to the valuation and structure are stability of future earnings, prospects for real earnings growth, working capital and fixed capital requirements, and current and anticipated interest rates. The main criteria employed to evaluate these factors are interest coverage, timeliness of debt amortization, and projected returns to equity investors—all based upon the requirements of the various anticipated financial participants. An example of the type of analysis undertaken by a sponsor in structuring a leveraged buyout appears later in this chapter.

Financing the Transaction

When the management group and the sponsor believe that they have developed an attractive and realistic financing structure, they begin the process of raising the capital necessary to complete the transaction. The first solicitations will be made to those financing sources with whom the management and the sponsor enjoy the best relationships. This will often include the company's line banks as well as any insurance companies or other private financing sources that have lent money to the company. The sponsor would also be likely to approach those institutions, both among banks and other institutions, that had demonstrated their desire to participate in leveraged buyouts through significant commitments to past transactions. If the sponsor were a boutique firm, an investment banking firm might be approached concerning public financing for the transaction.

As soon as prospective financing sources begin to indicate their interest in participating in the transaction, the sponsor attempts to commence serious discussions with the board of directors or other seller of the company. Management's role in these discussions varies according to the situation. In the case of the leveraged buyout of a private company or of a divestiture from a larger company, management is likely to be very active in these discussions, whereas in a contested public situation, management must be more circumspect in light of their fiduciary obligations and those of the other directors to current stockholders.

Assuming that the outcome of the financing efforts and the ongoing dialogue with the board of directors is favorable, the sponsor moves to complete the transaction as rapidly as possible. Financing commitments are firmed up and the agreement to acquire the company is formalized.

Completing the Transaction

The actual closing of the leveraged buyout of a public company can take two forms: a merger vote or a tender offer followed by a merger. Most public transactions that have been completed to date have taken the form of mergers of the subject company into an acquisition vehicle approved by vote of the existing shareholders. When the sponsor has reached a definitive agreement with the board of directors and received commitments for the financing, the company distributes proxy materials to its shareholders. When they have approved the exchange of their interest for the leveraged buyout consideration, the transaction is completed. Except in the face of a competing offer, there is no known instance of shareholders voting down a leveraged buyout.

LBO Tender Offers

Since 1985, leveraged buyout sponsors have been able to obtain the financing necessary to complete tender offers. In these transactions, the sponsor commences a tender offer immediately after reaching an agreement with the board of directors. Although the financing for the transaction must be virtually complete before the sponsor can propose such a transaction, the tender offer is frequently conditional upon the final documentation of the financing. After receiving sufficient shares to control the company in the tender offer, a merger of the company with the acquisition vehicle is accomplished. Shareholders who either did not tender or who were pro-rated out of a portion of the tender offer receive the merger consideration at this time.

The major advantage of a tender offer over the merger vote structure is timing. A tender offer requires 20 business days for completion. Proxy materials, however, require Securities and Exchange Commission review in addition to the 20 business day voting period. The review process requires several weeks at a minimum, increasing the time between the announcement of the transaction and its completion. This longer period of exposure increases the likelihood that a competing offer to acquire the company will be made prior to the completion of the leveraged buyout.

The tender offer structure can involve a greater degree of risk to the acquiror. In cases in which a portion of the final financing is to be raised in the public markets, a bridge loan must be obtained in order to complete the tender offer without the delay created by public registration of securities. This means that the final cost of financing cannot be known until after the company has been acquired through the tender offer.

FINANCIAL PARTICIPANTS

The completion of a leveraged buyout requires the confidence and enthusiasm of a variety of financial participants. Despite the great increase in the number and size of leveraged buyouts successfully completed in recent years, they remain complex transactions. Most leveraged buyouts rely upon at least three types of financing: senior lenders (most often commercial banks), subordinated lenders (usually either large insurance companies or the public debt markets), and equity investors. To be ultimately successful, the transaction must be structured to strike balance and compromise among the participants.

Senior Lenders

Senior lenders provide the greatest portion of the financing in most leveraged buyouts. Commercial banks are the largest providers of senior debt, although savings and loan associations, commercial finance companies, and insurance companies play a role in some transactions.

In the 1960s and 1970s, banks made leveraged buyout loans solely on a collateral basis. They insisted upon receiving a security interest in the assets of the acquired company which would adequately protect their principal in almost any foreseeable circumstance. In addition, senior lenders generally required a prospective debtor to demonstrate the ability to repay its borrowings out of operating cash flow within a period of five to six years.

Bank Aggressiveness

As the other markets in which commercial banks operated became more competitive (short-term corporate lending) or more risky (foreign credits), and as leveraged buyout financing became more tested and understood, banks became more aggressive. Large leveraged buyout credits today frequently are not secured loans in the traditional sense. Security in recent large transactions has often been limited to pledges of subsidiary stock and limitations on indebtedness. Lenders are more willing to focus upon a company's future cash flow as the source of debt repayment. The increasing amount of subordinated debt and equity financing available, and the overall increased liquidity of corporate assets, has given banks a type of asset protection which they had not enjoyed previously. Maturities have also been extended in these credits up to a maximum of seven to ten years, depending upon market conditions.

Bridging Divestitures

As banks and other senior lenders have gained a greater degree of sophistication in leveraged transactions, they have become more willing to finance transactions that require or contemplate asset divestitures as part of the overall financing program. This is particularly significant in the larger public leveraged buyouts of diversified enterprises, which are often characterized by high acquisition multiples. In these cases, it is often necessary to downsize the company through selected divestitures of assets (businesses) that are not suited to leverage or carry particularly high acquisition multiples relative to operating earnings and cash flow.

In many cases, a bank group provides all or a portion of the financing required to bridge the divestiture of the assets to be sold. The bank credit is structured to include a short-term loan to be repaid with the proceeds from asset sales and a longer-term credit to be repaid from ongoing operating cash flow. Several factors have been important in the development of this form of financing. First, the great increase in mergers and acquisitions activity in recent years has given business units the liquidity characteristic of financial assets. This provides lenders the assurance that asset sales can be successfully accomplished. The investment banking firms and the other sponsors of leveraged buyouts have also become much more sophisticated and accurate in their analysis and prediction of divestiture values. This allows lenders to become comfortable with the debt reduction that can occur through divestitures.

Levels of Bank Involvement

As in other bank loans, there are usually three levels of bank involvement in a leveraged buyout senior credit: agents, syndicate members, and loan participants.

Agent Banks. The agent bank (sometimes there is more than one) is responsible for structuring the bank credit and is typically the largest lender in the transaction. Specialized expertise is required to reconcile the credit concerns of a commercial banking institution with the aggressiveness required to succeed in the competitive leveraged buyout environment. The agent bank must create a credit that will both prove attractive to other banks and allow the investor group to proceed with its acquisition proposal. Several of the large money center wholesale banks, in particular, have devoted significant resources to the development of this expertise and have been willing to commit large amounts to leveraged buyout transactions. As the largest financing commitment in most transactions, the agent bank's capital commitment is a major element in the financial credibility of the overall acquisition proposal. Increasingly, the large agent banks are coming to act as distribution agents for the credit to a large group of syndicate and participant banks, retaining modest amounts of the loans for their own accounts.

Syndicate Banks. In most larger transactions, the commitments made by the agent bank(s), although substantial, do not represent the entirety of the required bank financing. Additional banks are usually invited on a selective basis to participate directly in the syndicate. Invitations are made, in most cases, on the basis of a bank's relationship with the company, the sponsor or the agent bank. Even in cases in which the agent's commitment provided for the entirety of the bank financing, other banks are often invited into the credit prior to closing to reduce the agent's exposure and to provide a broader group of lenders.

Loan Participants. Both agent banks and syndicate members often sell down their positions just as they would with any other loan. This most often takes the form of the sale of participations to correspondents that do not include the voting rights of direct lenders. Assignments, in which the correspondent does receive those rights, are sometimes allowed, although often only to some limit which ensures that control of the bank group does not change over time. (See Volume V, Chapters 24–25.)

Fees and Income

The fees and income received by the banks vary with their level of participation. The agent bank receives an agency fee for its efforts in structuring, negotiating, and marketing the bank credit. This fee decreases proportionately as the credit size increases. In small transactions, bank agency fees can equal as much as 2 1/2 percent of the total bank credit. These fees represent very significant income to commercial banks, particularly on a return-on-assets basis. By the time bank debt is funded, the syndication process has usually reduced the agent's loan to a fraction of the original commitment, before giving effect to any participations or assignments to correspondents.

Syndicate members, as well as agent banks, receive commitment fees with respect to the participation in the transaction. These fees, which also decrease proportionately in the case of large transactions, can be as high as 1 percent of a commitment. In many transactions, proportionately larger fees are paid to those banks willing to make larger commitments to the credit.

The actual interest rate, which is paid to all eventual holders of the debt, is generally priced at a premium to most other commercial loans. The loans generally bear interest at a margin over the prime rate (generally 125 to 150 basis points) or LIBOR. The lenders also receive an ongoing fee for the maintenance of their commitments.

Loan Structure

Bank credits in leveraged buyouts generally take the form of some combination of a serial term loan and a revolving credit facility. The revolving credit feature gives the borrower the ability to obtain working capital when required without the cost of maintaining cash balances. The term loan feature, whose maturities are tailored to the timing of the company's anticipated cash flows or asset divestitures, allows the acquisition indebtedness to be repaid on an even and predictable basis for which the borrower can plan.

Restrictive Covenants

Bank credit agreements in buyouts usually contain fairly restrictive covenants concerning the operations of the company until some debt repayment has taken place. Covenants contained in senior credit agreements are designed to serve two purposes: to prevent the company from taking financial action detrimental to the interests of the senior lenders and to provide a mechanism for the early detection of the company's potential inability to service its debt. Covenants are determined through negotiation, and should provide a comfortable cushion to the borrower's expectations of future performance while assuring at least the minimum level of performance rerquired to guarantee repayment of the borrowed funds.

The first set of covenants take the form of limitations on capital spending, the making of investments, and the payment of dividends. Senior lenders are insistent upon receiving all of the borrower's available cash flow paid as principal against their loans. These covenants force the company to channel excess cash flow toward the repayment of debt, at least until some meaningful amount of debt repayment has occurred.

The second set of covenants is designed to provide the senior debtors with advance notice of the impending inability of the borrower to meet its financial obligations. These covenants, which require certain minimum levels of financial performance, measure the borrower's net worth, fixed charge coverage, and debt-to-net-worth ratio. Lenders realize that the mere existence of these covenants does little to influence corporate performance. Rather, these covenants are intended to provide the senior lenders with a degree of leverage against other creditors in the event of the borrower's inability to meet its obligations. If performance falls below the agreed-upon level (but still remains above the levels required to minimally service interest and principal), the senior lenders have the ability to call a default and accelerate their indebtedness. This ability to "pull the trigger" through acceleration, whether exercised or not, provides the senior creditors with leverage in negotiating a favorable resolution of the situation with the borrower and with other creditors.

Subordinated Lenders

Leveraged buyout subordinated debt can be placed either privately (usually with large insurance companies or "mezzanine" funds) or publicly (in the high yield bond market). As these two markets have evolved, they have responded differently to the risk and return profiles of subordinated debt. The private financing sources lend under restrictive financing arrangements and generally require an equity participation in the transaction. In the public markets, the debt is sold under a less restrictive public indenture, and equity participation is not always required.

Leveraged buyout subordinated debt carries a longer maturity than does the senior financing. In virtually every case, the senior credit agreement prohibits the borrower from making principal payments on the subordinated debt prior to the complete repayment of the senior debt. Typical maturities for subordinated debt range from eight to fifteen years, and often have required amortization prior to final maturity.

Private Subordinated Debt

Until 1984, the private debt markets were the only significant source of subordinated debt financing for leveraged buyouts. The large life insurance companies pioneered the financing of large leveraged buyouts through their participation in transactions such as Houdaille Industries and Coca-Cola Bottling Co. of New York in the late 1970s and early 1980s. These institutions remain very active in leveraged buyout lending and in some cases have raised pools of outside capital for these investments. While they are no longer the only source of subordinated debt, the insurance companies continue to be an important and competitive financing source.

Private subordinated debt can also be provided by the so-called mezzanine funds. These pools have been raised by leveraged buyout sponsors from institutional sources, largely corporate pension funds. These funds are used, as are equity funds, to invest in and promote the transactions sponsored by their managers. In a limited number of cases, institutional investors (rather than buyout sponsors) have created mezzanine funds.

The interest rate on private subordinated debt is often determined at the time the lender makes a financing commitment. This rate generally does not change during the pendency of the transaction. Recently, in transactions with both private and public subordinated debt, the private lenders have been reluctant to finalize pricing until the actual offering of the public debt. Private subordinated lenders sometimes receive a "placement" or "structuring" fee of 1 to 2 percent of the financing provided, which is a significant incentive for their participation in buyouts.

The borrower of private subordinated debt can expect to be required to enter into a credit agreement that contains a variety of negotiated covenants similar to those contained in the senior credit agreement. These covenants exist to protect the private lender who has no market for the sale of his debt instrument and who has therefore made a long-term commitment to the transaction. The lender will also negotiate to keep the provisions related to subordination to other lenders as loose as possible so as to have as strong a position as possible in case of financial difficulty on the part of the borrower.

Private subordinated lenders generally require an equity participation in the transaction, which augments their overall return to compensate for the risk of taking a subordinated debt position. Frequently this equity participation takes the form of a nonvoting common stock that is purchased along with the debt securities. Thus, the subordinated debt-and-equity "strip" has come to be the form of financing most frequently provided by insurance companies and other private sources. They generally seek an overall blended rate of return equal to approximately 1000 basis points over Treasuries on the combined investment.

The insistence upon an equity participation on the part of the private financing sources has both advantages and disadvantages. On the positive side, private subordinated lenders can be a significant source of equity financing. While the growth in equity funds has lessened this advantage, insurance companies and private subordinated lenders remain an important source of equity capital in very large transactions and in smaller transactions where a sponsor with an equity fund is not involved. On the negative side, the private lenders often do not separate the decision to provide debt financing from the decision to make an equity investment, nor is the one form of financing generally available without the other in the private market.

Public Subordinated Debt

As has been previously discussed, the emergence of the high-yield debt market has been an important factor in the growth of the leveraged buyout market. Prior to approximately 1984, there was no public market for leveraged buyout debt securities. In recent years, however, the availability of public subordinated debt financing has increased greatly.

Public subordinated debt is largely the same as private debt in term and rate. Equivalent maturities are generally available, both markets require roughly equal spreads over Treasuries in terms of current yield, and both carry fixed rates. There is a significant difference in the timing of the determination of the yield, however. While in the private market pricing can be determined at the time of financing commitment to the transaction, the pricing on any public issue is based on market conditions at the time of the actual sale of the securities. In a typical transaction, this latter date could be as much as 90 days or more after a private financing commitment would otherwise have been obtained, which increases the risk to the transaction of a sudden increase in interest rates.

Whereas a private issue is placed directly with the ultimate lender, public debt issues are placed through an underwriter. This structure requires the preparation of a registration statement and the public offering of the debt securities thereunder. The gross underwriting spread for a subordinated debt offering usually approximates 3.5 percent of the gross proceeds, somewhat more expensive than the up front fees charged in the private markets. However, as part of the distribution process, most underwriters commit to make a market in the issue being sold after the offering. This provides the debt buyers with an assurance of the issue's aftermarket liquidity.

The buyer of public debt in a leveraged buyout therefore takes less risk than a private buyer of the same debt. The public debt is traded publicly, and the underwriter of the issue, in maintaining a market, is almost always prepared to repurchase the instrument at some price. Thus, public buyers are not making the same long-term commitment as are the private buyers.

The public investor, therefore, does not receive the same covenant protection as does the private investor. Public investors receive greater liquidity, while modification of a publicly held debt instrument is difficult and expensive. The indenture under which the public security is issued does not contain the breadth of covenants that the private subordinated credit agreement contains, nor are its terms as restrictive. Covenants are generally limited to limitations on dividends, the incurrence of additional debt, and the merger or liquidation of the company. The indenture also subordinates the public debt more deeply to senior creditors than a private instrument. Similarly, there is often no equity participation provided to buyers of public leveraged buyout debt except during difficult market conditions or in marginal transactions.

Bridge Financing

Recently, a number of leading investment banking firms have undertaken to strengthen their leveraged buyout capabilities through the commitment of their own capital to transactions. Bridge financing is designed to hasten the transaction, making it more attractive to the seller and less susceptible to outside interference. Public subordinated debt, a common feature of large leveraged buyouts, must be registered under the securities laws before it can be offered. With time added for marketing, ten weeks or more may pass between the decision to proceed with the offering and the availability of the proceeds. In certain other instances, the timing of a transaction does not allow the marketing of debt or equity to private buyers.

Bridge financing eliminates the impact of these delays. The investment banking firm advances funds equal to the proceeds of the entirety of the issue(s) in question. The availability of the bridge capital, plus the equity contributed by the sponsor and others, and senior debt provided by a group of commercial banks allows the leveraged buyout group to acquire sufficient shares in the target company to assure the completion of the transaction. In this way, the sponsor and a merchant banking partner act almost as a mezzanine fund in completing a transaction. The proceeds of the public debt offering (which is generally accomplished concurrently with the actual merger finalizing the transaction) are used to repay the bridge financing.

Equity Investors

The equity financing in most leveraged buyouts comes from some combination of senior and subordinated lenders, pure equity buyers (most often funds) and company management. Occasionally other investors are brought directly into the equity in a transaction, but this is rare. The equity in a leveraged buyout is highly prized and is usually only available to participants who play an important role in the transaction.

Sponsors Who Control Funds

The most significant equity investors in the leveraged buyout market are those sponsors who control equity funds. The evolution of the market has acted to concentrate capital earmarked for leveraged buyout equities under the control of a limited group of boutique firms and investment banking houses. Many of the institutions that desire to make these investments (such as insurance companies, commercial bank holding companies, and pension funds) are not well-positioned to make specific investments. For the most part, they do not have access to the stream of potential transactions that the successful sponsors have developed. Similarly, many of these institutions have generally not chosen to dedicate the required resources to distinguish the desirable opportunities from the undesirable ones. These institutions have, therefore, come to funnel their equity investments through the sponsors who have both developed networks for identifying prospective transactions and dedicated the resources necessary to build expertise in identifying and completing attractive transactions.

Even those institutions with the resources and commitment to assess individual opportunities have, in many cases, chosen to invest in equity funds. Often, these institutional investors view their participation as a source of investment opportunities. Nearly all sponsors give investors in their funds a preferential opportunity to participate in other financing layers of a transaction. Commercial bank participants might receive an early chance to propose the senior financing while the insurance companies might be able to lead the subordinated portion of the financing.

Institutions have also found the pooled-investment approach the best method in which to build a balanced and diversified portfolio of leveraged buyout equities. Despite the success stories of recent years, these securities remain very risky investments. Even the largest investors commit only very moderate amounts of their total equity portfolios to leveraged buyouts. This fact, coupled with the importance of having a significant control position when making leveraged buyout investments, serves to prevent the prudent investment of large amounts in many deals. Through investing in a fund, which takes major positions in a number of leveraged buyouts, investors enjoy both diversification and a significant level of control on a pooled basis.

Control of Corporate Assets

Another impetus toward the rising size and number of funds has been the increasingly competitive nature of the market for control of corporate assets.

As the mergers and acquisitions market, for legal and other reasons, has come to require rapid capital commitments, those potential acquirors—including leveraged buyout groups—with the greatest access to capital have come to enjoy an advantage. Leveraged buyout sponsors, who once allocated months to complete a transaction, now must be able to provide fully financed transactions within days or weeks. Except for a small number of the most sophisticated insurance companies, most sources of leveraged buyout equity are not positioned to focus upon individual transactions on an immediate basis. Thus, in order to actually make investments in completed transactions (rather than commitments to failed ones), institutions invest through the funds.

Investment Objectives

Leveraged buyout equities are illiquid, long-term investments made in companies with high degrees of financial leverage. Sponsors commit their funds' capital only when they believe that they will earn superior returns in return for assuming these risks. In most cases, the anticipated returns—based upon conservative analysis—must exceed 30 percent on an annual compound basis over a period of several years for a transaction with "average" risk characteristics.

Most experienced leveraged buyout investors view 5 to 7 years as the appropriate investment horizon for a straight "cash flow" transaction. Generally, this period of time allows a successful transaction to repay a significant portion of its debt and to generate a meaningful return in absolute dollars. Investors are usually willing to sell their investments prior to this period for proper consideration, but when investments are held longer than this, the declining leverage reduces incremental returns to marginal levels.

Investors can realize the value of their investment in a number of ways. The process is not fundamentally different from that of the shareholders of any private company seeking liquidity. The objectives and positions of different parties play a role in determining the "cash out" strategy, as do the values achievable at any time under the various alternatives. (See Chapter 15.)

In the first instance, some (but not complete) liquidity may be sought. This is the case when either certain investors desire liquidity but others wish to retain their positions, or when the investors as a group wish to realize the value of a portion of their investment. An initial public offering is often an attractive mechanism by which to sell a portion of the investors' holdings. Public offerings of the stock of leveraged buyout companies have been completed successfully in many cases. Recapitalizations and second leveraged buyouts have been completed in a number of cases to provide partial liquidity. Recapitalizations are used most often to provide liquidity to outside investors in cases in which management desires to retain its investment and increase its ownership.

In the second instance, complete liquidity may be sought by all investors. Here, in addition to the other strategies, the complete sale of the company to a third party is often considered. In some cases, companies have gone public (with original investors selling only a portion of their holdings) as a first step in the realization of equity values. The second step has been the complete sale of the company, with the public markets having provided a minimum valuation level.

CHARACTERISTICS OF AN LBO CANDIDATE

Because of the financial risk created in a leveraged buyout, a candidate company should have a stable and strong core business and a limited level of business risk. This foundation is required for the prudent long-term leveraging of the company. The discussion that follows highlights a number of the characteristics most indicative of a business likely to be suitable for a leveraged buyout. It portrays a company with steady and predictable profitability and operating performance. There are also a number of financial traits that tend to signify that the leveraged buyout structure might prove advantageous, and they will be discussed as well.

While no company is likely to possess all of the characteristics enumerated below, it is unlikely that a company which does not possess some number of them would make an attractive leveraged buyout candidate. Each potential candidate possesses a different set of positive and negative attributes. The appropriate evaluation does not determine whether a company has a majority of the following characteristics, but rather whether the company's overall level of business risk is such as to allow a high degree of financial risk. A determination and weighing of the various factors must be made in each case to determine the overall risk profile of the enterprise. In addition, the financial structure of the transaction must be designed with the candidate company's business characteristics in mind.

Product and Market Attributes

Leading Market Share

An attractive buyout candidate should enjoy a leading market share in the manufacture or sale of a number of relatively mundane products or services. This provides for steady cash flow and limited business risk, allowing the prudent assumption of a large debt burden. Strong market share serves to insulate the company from predatory pricing by competitors. Strong brand or trade names and customer franchises prove very desirable in this respect. Such market strength helps to ensure that the company's operations will remain competitive in downturns and times of industry contraction.

Product or Market Diversification

A leveraged buyout candidate should also display a degree of product or market diversification. Heavy reliance upon one product is usually not consistent with low business risk since the faltering or collapse of the single product or market would render the company unable to service its debt. Similarly, a company's products or services should be relatively mundane and well-established in nature. This reduces the risk of technological or market obsolescence and eliminates risky research and product development expenditures which constitute a drain on cash flow.

Minimal Economic Cyclicality

The prototypical leveraged buyout candidate also enjoys relative immunity from economic cyclicality. This is important in allowing the company to service its debt through downturns while maintaining values for equity investors. Similarly, the business of a potential leveraged buyout company should demonstrate a resistance to the negative impacts of inflation. As borrowers with some amount of fixed rate debt, leveraged buyout companies can benefit from inflation and the corresponding reduction in real borrowing costs. However, it is important for the company to be able to pass cost increases to customers, otherwise its real margins become compressed at a time when the cost of floating rate debt is increasing. This characteristic is also important in helping the business enterprise itself to retain value across economic cycles.

Domestic Orientation

A candidate for leveraged buyout financing in the U.S. should possess a heavy domestic weighing of its sales and operating profit. In a case where a significant portion of a company's total value is attributable to foreign earnings, it is unlikely that the domestic operations can support the debt necessary to complete a leveraged buyout. To achieve a competitive valuation, the foreign operations would have to be leveraged. However, unless the company has previously built a sizeable reserve of foreign tax credits, moving the proceeds of the borrowings to distribute to U.S. shareholders creates a prohibitive tax burden. Furthermore, reliance upon foreign operations creates risk for lenders and investors, which is often difficult to overcome. Foreign exchange risk and the uncertainty of a foreign government's stability, regulation, and taxation are issues not easily resolved in the context of a highly leveraged enterprise. Foreign-source earnings are also difficult to leverage efficiently because of the workings of the U.S. tax code, which allows foreign-source income to be taxed at a total rate of 60 percent or more after repatriation by an American parent. Offshore borrowing, while sometimes available, often cannot be structured to take full advantage of the tax aspects of a leveraged acquisition.

Minimal Governmental Regulation

In keeping with limiting business risk, a significant degree of governmental regulation is highly undesirable. Regulation, or a heavy reliance upon government contracts, can make a company's operations overly susceptible to changes in the political climate. Lenders and investors seek to profit by assuming a prudent amount of financial risk, not by wagering upon future government policy.

Strong Management Team

Finally (and perhaps most important), a leveraged buyout candidate must possess a strong and cohesive management team. Few (if any) equity investors in the larger transactions have the expertise or resources to manage operating companies. The performance of the business after the completion of the transaction and the success of their investment depends upon management's talent and dedication. The transition to private ownership and to an operating emphasis on cash flow over reported earnings is not always an easy one. In order for a leveraged buyout to be completed, sophisticated lenders and investors must be able to develop confidence in the management team's skills and resources.

Recently, a number of leveraged buyout sponsors have entered transactions in support of specific executives not associated with the subject company. This has occured mostly in contested or in auction situations and reflects the sponsors' attempts to add value to their competitive efforts through additional operational expertise.

Financial Attributes

Financial Growth With Minimal Investment

The ideal leveraged buyout company is one that can achieve an increase in revenues and earnings without the investment of large amounts of additional capital. Therefore, the company should have a high margin of profitability to working capital and fixed asset intensity. Underutilization of manufacturing capacity or the recent completion of an expansion or modernization program is an attractive feature. This suggests the potential for an expansion in business volume without additional capital spending. Operations with limited capital expenditure requirements in the intermediate term (which tend to be those companies with relatively mundane products) are attractive candidates due to their high free cash flow.

High Tax Rate and Dividend-to-Earnings Payout Ratio

Other financial indicators that can serve to indicate a company's suitability for a leveraged buyout include a high effective tax rate and a high dividend-to-earnings payout ratio. A high historical tax rate suggests that a leveraged acquisition can create value through the tax shield created by interest payments. Funds that would otherise leave the company can be used to finance acquisition indebtedness. Similarly, a high dividend payout ratio indicates another source of cash flow that can be used to service debt. Rather than pay shareholders on an ongoing after-tax basis, the company can use the funds to service debt and repay debt, thereby contributing to equity values on a longer-term (and tax-deferred) basis.

STRUCTURING LEVERAGED BUYOUTS AND VALUE REALIZATION STRATEGIES

The leveraged buyout structure is intended to optimize the relationship between a company's capital structure and the equity values realizable by its current shareholders and prospective future shareholders. Current shareholders receive an acquisition value that reflects the financial capabilities of the company and its ability to assume a significant debt burden. New investors bear the risk of the ownership of the leveraged company with the expectation of receiving an excellent return on their investment as compensation for the financial risk being assumed.

Leveraged buyouts can be broadly divided into three categories depending upon the prospective mechanism for debt repayment and realization of equity values.

Bust-up LBOs

One type of buyout relies upon the sale of assets of the acquired company to generate returns for the equity investors. The general public often associates this type of transaction with leveraged buyouts because hostile acquirors in several well-publicized instances have sought to profit by disaggregating diversified companies. The "bust-up" leveraged buyout is usually seen in acquisitions of diversified public companies where the equity markets may not fully value the companies' component pieces. The acquiror in such a circumstance usually seeks a relatively short-term return based upon a rapid sale of the individual components to exploit the markets' failing to recognize (or imposing a discount upon) the full value of a diversified business.

The economics of a bust-up transaction depend upon the values of the assets that comprise a diversified entity. In this respect, values provided by the mergers and acquisitions markets are central to the financing of these transactions. Lenders and investors must become comfortable with minimum asset values. The greater these minimum values, the less equity is required to accomplish the transaction, providing greater returns when the individual assets are sold at a premium to the leveraged buyout price. Investors will be willing to acquire a corporation at a discount to the aggregate values of its components sufficient to create a return that compensates them for the risk of having overestimated values.

Despite the popular press' view that all leveraged buyouts are bust-up transactions, this form of transaction accounts for the smallest portion of all leveraged transactions. In fact, the 1986 tax reform revisions, particularly in the area of the General Utilities provisions, have made most bust-up transactions uneconomic.

Cash Flow LBOs

The second category of leveraged buyout, most common in management-led transactions, is a transaction that calls for the repayment of acquisition financing through operating cash flow. In this type of transaction, referred to as the "cash flow" leveraged buyout, equity investors receive returns through the replacement of debt capital with equity and through any increase in the total market value of the company (the value of outstanding debt and equity). In this sense, the cash flow leveraged buyout is analogous to the purchase of income-producing real estate property with mortgage financing and equity. Returns are created when the overall value of the property increases with escalating rents (operating income) and when equity capital replaces debt as the income from the property is used to retire debt.

In a cash flow transaction, just as in a bust-up leveraged buyout, the issues of valuation and capital structure are inseparable. The amount of leverage lenders are willing to provide has an upper limit, as does the amount of equity invested. A capital structure that includes too much equity reduces investors' returns. The acquisition value realizable in a leveraged buyout depends on the limits of the financial structure of the transaction.

Selective Bust-up/Cash Flow LBOs (Hybrid)

The third type of leveraged transaction is a hybrid of the bust-up and cash flow techniques. The hybrid structure entails the purchase of a somewhat diversified company and the subsequent divestiture of selected units to retire a portion of the acquisition debt. The acquiror comes to control a smaller group of assets, those chosen as best-suited for longer-term leverage, and has hopefully captured a premium on the assets which have been sold. The remaining assets form the operations of a cash flow leveraged buyout.

The financing of this type of transaction is also a combination of the bust-up and cash flow structures. The final capital structure is derived as in a cash flow transaction, while the additional financing required pending the divestitures is based upon asset valuations as in the pure bust-up situation.

Proposal Tension and Optimizing Leverage

In structuring a leveraged buyout, there exists a tension between designing a conservative and relatively safe transaction and assembling a successful proposal. The conservative transaction, able to easily withstand any conceivable adverse development, provides the maximum security for the equity investors. Yet such a transaction, which does not leverage the company to the greatest prudent extent, will generally create above-market returns on leveraged equity. This is all well and good—if the conservative proposal becomes the winning proposal. But in a highly competitive buyout environment, successful proposals must often be aggressive proposals. By raising the additional debt which the company can prudently assume and contributing a greater amount of equity (thus reducing equity returns to the "market" level), a competing acquiror can offer greater value to the company's current stockholders while still structuring an attractive transaction for itself.

The structuring of a potential transaction must focus upon finding the optimum compromise between conservative capitalization and maximum acquisition values. Extensive analysis of the company's operations and sensitivity analyses based upon a range of forecasting assumptions are the core of the structuring exercise.

TAX CONSIDERATIONS

An important element in the economics of leveraged acquisitions is the value created through tax savings at both the corporate and shareholder levels. At the corporate level, the deductibility of interest expense allows income, which would otherwise be paid in taxes, to be used to finance the acquisition. The higher the tax rate, the greater the impact of the value created through leverage.

At the shareholder level, the leveraged buyout structure allows for the conversion of ordinary income into long-term capital gains. In the current tax environment, this principally means that by realizing any return on investment in the form of one-time capital gains, rather than as a stream of dividend payments over time, the leveraged buyout investor receives a two fold benefit. First, by not realizing gains in the form of dividends, he is not taxed on the periodic appreciation of the investment. Second, because there are no periodic distributions, gains compound within the company (as debt is repaid) on a tax-deferred basis until the investment is liquidated.

It should be mentioned that the 1986 Tax Reform Act revisions reduced the tax advantages of leveraged buyouts at both the corporate and shareholder levels. On the corporate level, two changes occurred. The lowering of the corporate tax rate from 46 percent to 34 percent proportionately reduced the value of leverage relative to market valuations. Furthermore, the repeal of the General Utilities provisions eliminated an additional tax shield available to acquirors of corporations. Under former Sections 337 and 338, acquirors were able to achieve tax savings in certain circumstances through the deduction of the amortization of the purchase price premium paid in the transaction (achieved by "writing up" the acquired assets). While not always possible (due to the recapture tax associated with such tax treatment), in a great many cases these benefits proved quite significant.

The levelling of ordinary income rates and capital gains rates at the shareholder level has reduced the value of the tax-deferral feature of leveraged buyout investments. Previously, an investor paid up to 50 percent tax on dividends. Through a leveraged buyout, he could eliminate the 50 percent (or 46 percent) annual tax in favor of a 20 percent (or 18 percent) tax paid only after tax-free compounding had occurred. Under the new tax code, the rate advantage in the recharacterization of the gain no longer exists, although the deferral and compounding benefits remain.

A DETAILED, FINANCIAL EXAMPLE

The following example, an analysis of the potential acquisition of the fictional Sample Manufacturing Company, serves to demonstrate the structuring and economics of the cash flow leveraged buyout. The analysis and structuring of a transaction is an iterative process requiring careful review of a company's financial characteristics, prospects, and of conditions in the financing markets. Valuation and structure are developed simultaneously and a balance is reached between financial conservatism and aggressive valuation.

Uses of Capital

As shown in Figure 2, the total uses of capital in the acquisition of Sample Manufacturing Company amount to $1,384 million. This amount takes into consideration the funds required to purchase the stock from the shareholders, to refinance the company's existing debt, and to pay accrued taxes and transaction expenses. In this example, Sample's shareholders receive $66.00 for each of the 17.85 million shares outstanding, $56.00 in cash and $10.00

FIGURE 2
Sample Manufacturing Company: Hypothetical Transaction Structure (Dollars in Millions)

Uses of Funds			
Purchase of Common Stock			
17.85 million shares	$56.00 per share cash	$1,000	
	$10.00 per share debentures	178	
Refinancing of existing debt		130	
Payment of income tax accrual and transaction expenses		77	
Total uses of funds		$1,385	
Sources of Funds			
Senior bank credit @ 10.00%		666	48.1%
Senior subordinated notes @ 13.50%		400	28.9%
Junior discount debentures @ 14.00%		179	12.9%
Common equity		140	10.1%
Total sources of funds		$1,385	100.0%

in value in a junior discount debenture. This debenture, which is common in large leveraged buyouts, is issued at a discount to its face amount and pays no cash interest for a period of five years. The $10.00 of value which the shareholders receive has an actual face amount of $19.21, assuming a 14.00 percent yield to the first cash interest payment.

Sources of Capital

A number of sources provide the $1,384 million of capital required in the hypothetical transaction. The largest source of financing is senior debt amounting to $666 million provided by a group of banks. The capital structure also includes $400 million of senior subordinated debt, placed publicly or privately, and the $179 million of junior discount debentures, which were received by the shareholders in the acquisition. Finally, equity financing of $140 million is provided by a combination of the management group, the transaction's sponsor, and subordinated lenders.

Historical Statements and Projections

In this example, it is assumed that the leveraged buyout takes place on December 31, 1989. Figures 3, 4, and 5 provide a summary of Sample's historical and financial statements and projections based upon a hypothetical conservative business plan. In this case, a recession is assumed to occur three years after the completion of the transaction. The projected financial statements have been adjusted to give effect to the leveraged buyout financing. The construction and analysis of these statements is central to structuring a transaction.

There are three major quantitative factors to consider in designing the capital structure for the transaction: *interest coverage*, *debt amortization*, and *equity returns*. The requirements that the transaction must satisfy depend upon the specifics of the company and its industry, as well as upon market conditions at the time of the financing. Leveraged buyouts of companies with extremely low degrees of business risk do not require as high interest coverage, as rapid debt amortization, or as high equity returns as those of companies that are less stable or predictable.

Interest Coverage

Interest coverage, defined here as earnings before interest and taxes (EBIT) divided by interest expense, provides a measure of the company's ability to

FIGURE 3
Sample Manufacturing Company: Historical and Projected Statements of Income
(Dollars in Millions)

	Historical Fiscal Years Ended December 31,						
	1983	*1984*	*1985*	*1986*	*1987*	*1988*	*1989*
Net sales	$1,002	$930	$1,045	$1,180	$1,322	$1,467	$1,618
Cost of sales	683	653	716	801	892	996	1,099
Depreciation & amortization	32	36	39	40	48	50	57
Gross profit	287	241	291	339	382	421	463
Selling, general & admin. expense	165	160	172	194	219	241	265
Operating income	122	81	119	145	163	180	197
Other expense (income)	8	14	16	18	20	22	24
Earnings before interest & taxes	113	67	102	127	143	158	173
Interest expense							
Existing debt	15	22	23	24	20	17	15
Senior bank credit	—	—	—	—	—	—	—
Senior subordinated debt	—	—	—	—	—	—	—
Junior discount debentures	—	—	—	—	—	—	—
Interest income on cash	—	—	—	—	—	—	—
Total interest expense (income)	15	22	23	24	20	17	15
Earnings before taxes	98	45	79	103	123	141	158
Provision for income taxes							
Current U.S. income taxes	41	21	31	43	49	56	49
Deferred U.S. income taxes	6	2	7	9	11	12	14
Total provision for income taxes	47	23	38	52	60	68	63
Net income	51	22	41	51	63	73	95
Common stock dividends	14	14	15	16	17	18	21
Increase in retained earnings	$37	$8	$26	$35	$46	$56	$74

FIGURE 3—*Continued*

Projected Fiscal Years Ended December 31,

1990	*1991*	*1992*	*1993*	*1994*	*1995*	*1996*	*1997*	*1998*	*1999*
$1,780	$1,926	$1,811	$1,983	$2,177	$2,373	$2,587	$2,819	$3,073	$3,350
1,207	1,291	1,244	1,332	1,456	1,590	1,733	1,889	2,059	2,244
68	72	73	74	79	82	84	92	100	109
505	564	494	576	641	701	769	839	914	996
292	312	299	323	353	384	419	454	492	536
213	252	195	253	289	317	350	385	422	461
21	23	24	26	27	29	31	33	35	37
192	229	171	227	261	288	320	352	388	424
0	0	0	0	0	0	0	0	0	0
65	58	50	43	32	23	14	5	0	0
54	54	54	54	54	54	54	54	41	20
25	28	32	37	42	42	42	42	42	42
(3)	(2)	(2)	(2)	(2)	(2)	(2)	(2)	(4)	(4)
141	138	135	132	126	117	108	97	80	58
51	91	36	96	135	171	212	255	308	366
9	23	4	26	44	60	76	93	113	135
9	8	8	7	4	0	(2)	(4)	(5)	(7)
18	32	13	33	47	60	74	89	108	128
33	59	23	62	88	111	138	166	200	238
0	0	0	0	0	0	0	0	0	0
$33	$59	$23	$62	$88	$111	$138	$166	$200	$238

FIGURE 4
Sample Manufacturing Company: Historical and Projected Balance Sheets
(Dollars in Millions)

	Historical Fiscal Years Ended December 31,							
	1983	*1984*	*1985*	*1986*	*1987*	*1988*	*1989*	*Pro Forma 12/31/89*
Assets								
Operating cash and equivalents	$20	$15	$21	$28	$30	$31	$31	$31
Accounts receivable	155	163	173	198	209	232	261	261
Inventories	241	253	273	300	330	371	411	411
Other current assets	10	8	14	11	18	19	19	19
Total current assets	427	439	481	537	588	653	722	722
Property, plant & equipment	475	521	574	634	703	777	858	858
Accumulated depreciation	(215)	(251)	(290)	(330)	(378)	(428)	(484)	(484)
Net property, plant & equip.	260	270	284	304	326	350	374	374
Other assets	67	56	64	72	79	86	90	90
Purchase price premium (a)	—	—	—	—	—	—	—	728
Total assets	$754	$765	$829	$913	$993	$1,089	$1,185	$1,914
Liabilities and Shareholder's Equity								
Notes payable & CP-LTD	$15	$15	$16	$15	$20	$23	$21	$0
Accounts payable	133	139	142	152	174	200	214	214
Accrued liabilities	117	106	119	133	151	167	186	205
Accrued income taxes	13	6	10	16	14	19	17	17
Total current liabilities	279	265	287	316	359	409	437	416
Existing long-term debt	157	171	177	186	157	131	108	0
Acquisition financing								
Bank revolving credit	—	—	—	—	—	—	—	666
Senior subordinated notes	—	—	—	—	—	—	—	400
Discount debentures	—	—	—	—	—	—	—	179
Total long-term debt	157	171	177	186	157	131	108	1,244
Deferred income taxes	6	8	15	24	35	47	61	61
Other non-current liabilities	39	37	40	40	46	50	52	52
Total liabilities	480	481	518	565	597	636	659	1,774
OLDCO common equity	274	284	311	348	396	453	527	0
NEWCO common stock	—	—	—	—	—	—	—	140
NEWCO retained earnings	—	—	—	—	—	—	—	0
Total equity	274	284	311	348	396	453	527	140
Total liabilities & equity	$754	$765	$829	$913	$993	$1,089	$1,185	$1,914

(a) Does not comform to GAAP accounting; Purchase Price Premium will be allocated according to fair market value of assets under purchase accounting.

FIGURE 4—*Continued*

Projected Fiscal Years Ended December 31,

1990	*1991*	*1992*	*1993*	*1994*	*1995*	*1996*	*1997*	*1998*	*1999*
$27	$19	$16	$18	$20	$21	$23	$25	$28	$30
281	293	290	305	331	356	388	423	461	502
436	460	447	466	501	546	595	648	707	770
21	21	18	20	22	24	26	28	31	33
766	794	771	809	873	947	1,302	1,125	1,226	1,337
949	1,032	1,104	1,184	1,284	1,380	1,477	1,587	1,708	1,845
(552)	(624)	(697)	(771)	(850)	(932)	(1,016)	(1,108)	(1,208)	(1,316)
396	408	407	414	434	448	461	479	501	528
95	99	104	109	114	119	125	131	138	144
728	728	728	728	728	728	728	728	728	728
$1,985	$2,029	$2,011	$2,060	$2,149	$2,243	$2,347	$2,463	$2,593	$2,737
$0	$0	$0	$0	$0	$0	$0	$0	$0	$0
240	268	259	278	305	332	362	395	430	469
222	208	228	250	273	297	324	353	385	
3	8	1	9	14	20	25	31	37	45
448	497	469	514	570	625	685	750	821	899
0	0	0	0	0	0	0	0	0	0
633	528	480	372	268	190	92	0	0	0
400	400	400	400	400	400	400	377	233	64
204	232	264	302	344	344	344	344	344	344
1,236	1,160	1,144	1,073	1,012	934	836	721	576	408
70	78	86	93	97	97	95	91	86	79
57	62	56	61	65	71	78	82	89	94
1,811	1,796	1,755	1,742	1,743	1,693	1,643	1,573	1,479	
0	0	0	0	0	0	0	0	0	0
140	140	140	140	140	140	140	140	140	140
33	92	116	178	265	376	514	680	880	1,118
173	232	256	318	405	516	654	820	1,020	1,258
$1,985	$2,029	$2,011	$2,060	$2,149	$2,243	$2,347	$2,463	$2,593	$2,737

(a) Does not comform to GAAP accounting; Purchase Price Premium will be allocated according to fair market value of assets under purchase accounting.

FIGURE 5
Sample Manufacturing Company: Historical and Projected Statements of Cash Flow
(Dollars in Millions)

	Historical Fiscal Years Ended December 31,						
	1983	*1984*	*1985*	*1986*	*1987*	*1988*	*1989*
Earnings before interest and taxes	$113	$67	$102	$127	$143	$158	$173
Depreciation	32	36	39	40	48	50	57
Cash flow before interest expense	145	103	141	167	191	208	230
Interest expense							
Existing debt	15	22	23	24	20	17	15
Senior bank credit	—	—	—	—	—	—	—
Senior subordinated debt	—	—	—	—	—	—	—
Junior discount debentures	—	—	—	—	—	—	—
Interest income on cash	—	—	—	—	—	—	—
Total interest expense (income)	15	22	23	24	20	17	15
Cash flow before income tax	130	81	118	143	171	191	215
Current U.S. income tax expense	41	21	31	43	49	56	49
Cash flow before discretionary items	89	60	87	100	122	135	166
Discretionary items							
Capital expenditures	—	46	53	60	69	74	80
Incr. in adj. working capital	—	23	20	25	9	23	36
Incr. in other working capital	—	3	1	2	(1)	(7)	4
Increase (decr.) in other assets	—	(10)	5	8	1	3	2
Common stock dividends	—	14	15	16	17	18	21
Total discretionary items	—	76	93	112	94	111	144
Cash flow before financing	—	(16)	(6)	(11)	28	24	22
Financing activities							
Repay. (inc.) of existing debt	—	—	—	—	—	—	—
Repayment of bank credit	—	—	—	—	—	—	—
Repayment of sr. subord. debt	—	—	—	—	—	—	—
Repayment of jr. disc. debt	—	—	—	—	—	—	—
Total financing activities	—	—	—	—	—	—	—
Net cash flow	—	—	—	—	—	—	—

FIGURE 5—*Continued*

Projected Fiscal Years Ended December 31,									
1990	*1991*	*1992*	*1993*	*1994*	*1995*	*1996*	*1997*	*1998*	*1999*
$192	$229	$171	$227	$261	$288	$320	$352	$388	$424
68	72	73	74	79	82	84	92	100	109
260	301	244	301	341	370	404	444	488	533
0	0	0	0	0	0	0	0	0	
65	58	50	43	32	23	14	5	0	0
54	54	54	54	54	54	54	52	41	20
0	0	0	0	0	42	42	42	42	42
(3)	(2)	(2)	(2)	(2)	(2)	(2)	(2)	(4)	(4)
116	110	103	95	84	117	108	97	80	58
144	191	141	206	256	253	296	347	408	474
9	23	4	26	44	60	76	93	113	135
135	168	137	180	213	193	220	254	295	340
91	83	72	80	99	97	97	109	122	136
3	(9)	3	(2)	13	22	29	31	34	37
9	(12)	3	(6)	(4)	(4)	(3)	(4)	(4)	(4)
(1)	(0)	10	(0)	1	(0)	(1)	2	(1)	2
0	0	0	0	0	0	0	0	0	
102	62	89	72	109	115	122	139	151	171
33	105	48	108	104	78	98	115	144	169
0	0	0	0	0	0	0	0	0	0
33	105	48	108	104	78	98	92	0	0
0	0	0	0	0	0	0	23	144	169
0	0	0	0	0	0	0	0	0	0
33	105	48	108	104	78	98	115	144	169
$0	($0)	$0	($0)	$0	$0	$0	$0	(0)	$0

service a given level of debt. Generally, the minimum total coverage must exceed 1.1 to 1.2:1 on a pro forma basis. In the Sample example, total interest coverage for 1988, the year immediately subsequent to the transaction, is 1.37:1. EBIT coverage of cash interest (which excludes the accretion of the discount debentures) is 1.67:1. It is particularly helpful to the financing efforts if the company has generated earnings for a number of years historically that are sufficient to cover the interest expense created in the transaction.

Debt Amortization

The financing must be structured so as to demonstrate an ability to repay acquisition financing. Assuming that all cash flow after interest, taxes, working capital, and capital expenditure requirements is used to repay debt, the forecasts show that the company is able to repay its bank financing in approximately seven and one-half years despite the recession assumed in 1992. The senior subordinated debt can nearly be repaid within ten years based upon the forecasts. Were no refinancings or acquisitions to take place, at the end of ten years the company's only debt would be $64 million of subordinated debentures and the $344 million of discount debentures.

Equity Returns

Equity appreciation represents the third consideration in structuring a transaction. The financial structure of a leveraged buyout creates equity appreciation in two ways. First, as the leverage is reduced equity capital takes the place of debt. Figure 6 depicts the replacement of debt with equity in the case of Sample Manufacturing. At the time of the transaction, $1,244 million of debt (89.9 percent of the total *financial* capitalization) and $140 million of equity (10.1 percent) comprises the capital structure of the company. After five years, the debt has been reduced by $238 million to $1,006 million (71.2 percent of the total financial capitalization at that time). During the same period, retained earnings have increased the total equity to $408 million (28.8 percent), without giving effect to purchase accounting adjustments that would be made as a result of the transaction.

Assuming that the overall value (*market* capitalization—which initially equals financial capitalization) of the company has not increased or decreased in the five years, its outstanding debt and equity is worth $1,384 million. After deducting the outstanding debt of $1,006 million, the value of the equity is $378 million. The replacement of debt capital with equity alone in this

FIGURE 6
Sample Manufacturing Company: Pro Forma Projected Financial Capitalization

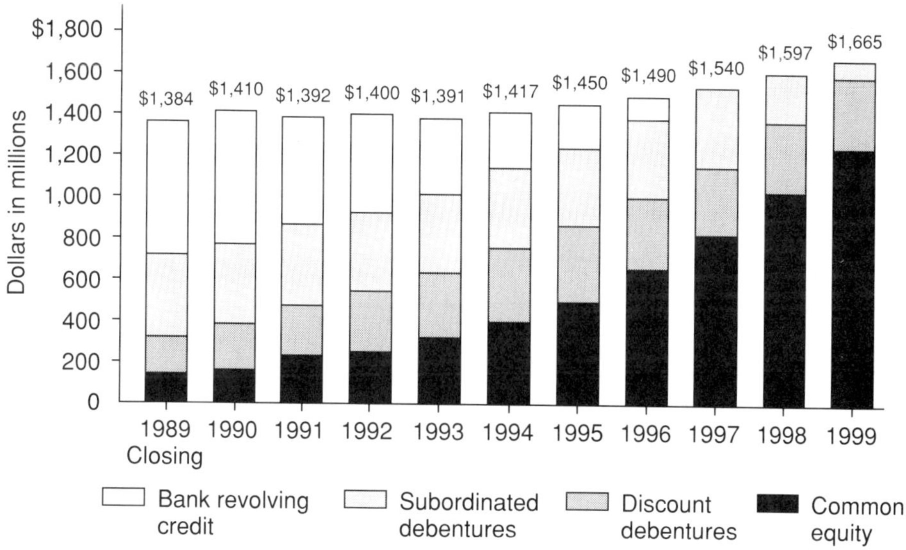

example has resulted in an increase in equity values of 170 percent over five years in this example.

An increase in the earnings of the company also creates value of the equity investors. As earnings and total market capitalization increase, and as debt is repaid, the market value of the equity rises rapidly. This increase occurs more rapidly than the increase in financial capitalization. Figures 7 and 8 depict this increase over time. From 1989 to 1994, for example, Sample's EBIT is assumed to increase by approximately 50 percent, from $173 million to $261 million. The capitalization multiple paid in the 1989 leveraged buyout was 8 times ($1,384 million total capitalization divided by EBIT of $173 million). Assuming that company is worth the same 8 times multiple after five years, its total capitalization amounts to $2,089 million at that time. After deducting the $1,073 million of debt, the value of the equity amounts to $1,016 million, an increase of over six fold in five years. This gain gives effect to both debt repayment and the increase in value of the company.

Figure 8 also displays a hypothetical calculation of equity returns based upon various cash out multiple assumptions. Like all equity investors, leveraged buyout participants rely upon market multiples to generate returns. The fact that the equity is a small piece of the total capitalization in a leveraged buyout serves to magnify the effects of even small changes in the market

FIGURE 7
Sample Manufacturing Company: Pro Forma Projected Market Capitalization

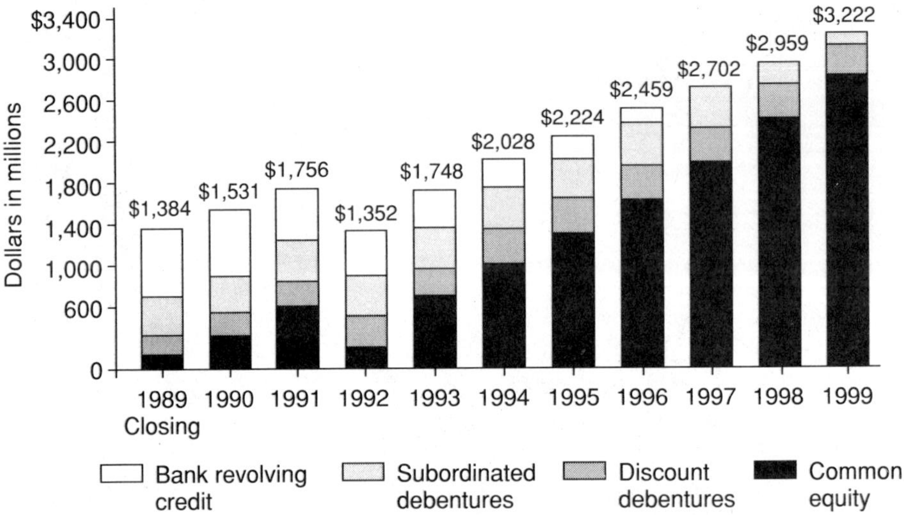

multiple. In the case of Sample Manufacturing, as shown in Figure 8, a decrease of the capitalization multiple from 8 times to 7 times would reduce the total equity value after five years by $261 million, or nearly twice the original total equity investment. An increase in the multiple to 9 times would increase equity values by the same amount.

CONCLUSION AND PROSPECTS

The 1980s saw an enormous growth in the size and number of leveraged buyouts attempted and completed. Reflecting the growth of leveraged buyout transactions in recent years, an infrastructure within the financing markets has been built. Commercial banks, insurance companies, mutual funds and pension funds, as well as investment banking firms and specialized leveraged buyout boutiques, have devoted resources and expertise to the completion of these transactions.

Leveraged buyouts have played an increasingly important role in the ongoing restructuring of American industry. In the case of public companies, management buyouts have allowed many corporations to leave the public markets and restructure away from the short-term earnings orientation by

FIGURE 8
Sample Manufacturing Company: Hypothetical Rates of Return to Investors (Dollars in Millions)

			Projected Fiscal Years Ended December 31,									
Market Capitalization			1990	1991	1992	1993	1994	1995	1996	1997	1998	1999
At market value of	7 x EBIT		$1,346	$1,603	$1,196	$1,592	$1,828	$2,014	$2,238	$2,465	$2,715	$2,967
	8 x		1,539	1,832	1,367	1,819	2,089	2,302	2,557	2,817	3,103	3,391
	9 x		1,731	2,061	1,538	2,047	2,351	2,589	2,877	3,169	3,491	3,815
Less total debt and pfd.			$1,244	$1,236	$1,160	$1,144	$1,073	$1,012	$934	$836	$721	$576
Equity value at	7 x EBIT		$102	$367	$37	$448	$755	$1,002	$1,304	$1,629	$1,995	$2,391
	8 x		294	596	207	675	1,016	1,290	1,623	1,981	2,383	2,814
	9 x		487	825	378	903	1,277	1,578	1,943	2,333	2,770	3,233
Initial Common Stock Investors												
Investment		$140.0										
Percent ownership		100.0%										
Pre-tax IRR at	7 x EBIT		NA	61.9%	NA	33.7%	40.1%	38.8%	37.5%	35.9%	34.3%	32.8%
	8 x		110.2%	106.3%	14.0%	48.2%	48.7%	44.8%	41.9%	39.3%	37.0%	35.0%
	9 x		247.6%	142.8%	39.3%	59.4%	55.6%	49.7%	45.6%	42.1%	39.3%	36.9%

which these markets judge corporate performance. In public and private situations, as well as in divestitures from larger companies, leveraged buyouts have given operating management new incentives for the performance of their businesses. Well-conceived and properly structured leveraged buyouts, as well as other forms of corporate restructuring, serve an important market function by providing an allocation mechanism for corporate assets and promoting their efficient use.

CHAPTER 14

LEVERAGED BUYOUTS IV: JOINT VENTURES FOR DIFFICULT ACQUISITIONS OR DIVESTITURES

Stephen L. Key
Arthur Young

While leveraged buyouts (LBOs) have become increasingly popular forms of acquisitions for funds or management groups involved in buying private companies, divisions of public companies, or public companies in "going private" transactions, the LBO is seldom used as an M&A device by the publicly held corporation. However, in situations where there are volatile market conditions or where the transaction size is so great that the resulting leverage makes an acquisition seemingly unaffordable, the LBO technique can be used by public companies to make acquisitions that might otherwise not be possible. The use of the leveraged joint venture as an M&A technique makes this possible.

From the acquiring company's point of view, the joint venture leveraged buyout is an acquisition structure that resolves a number of problems. In addition, the divesting company may want to explore the attributes of a leveraged sellout.

Before embarking on a discussion of these two structures, let's briefly review how an LBO works (see Chapters 11–13).

HOW LEVERAGED BUYOUTS WORK

In a typical LBO, an investor group (often including management) will put up a small amount of equity and use the assets of the acquired business or its future cash flows as collateral for a loan to finance the purchase. As the post-acquisition cash flow of the purchased business pays down the debt, the value of the equity position can often rise dramatically. Once the acquisition debt is reduced to a more manageable level, the company can be taken public, sold, or releveraged to provide for further expansion.

HOW A JOINT VENTURE LBO IS STRUCTURED

A joint venture LBO attempts, often successfully, to overcome a major disadvantage of a public company using an LBO to acquire a target company. The public company, in concert with a partner, acquires another business through an LBO but does not have to show the related debt on its balance sheet. Yet it is still free to operate the business, turn it around, and ultimately purchase and consolidate the entire operation when the debt declines to a manageable level. As a result, the joint venture LBO is attracting increasing interest as its advantages become more widely recognized and appreciated.

In a typical joint venture LBO, one partner is a corporation—usually publicly owned—which owns up to 50 percent of the acquired company's voting stock and sometimes owns a large block of preferred stock as well. In these deals the preferred stock is usually nonvoting. The other partner is a leveraged buyout firm, fund, or an investment bank—some type of relatively passive financial partner—owning the remainder of voting stock. In some instances, management of the acquired firm may also own some of the common stock.

In many cases, the preferred stock capitalization exceeds the aggregate common stock equity of the two venture partners. However, in all other respects, the venture appears to be a true corporate joint venture, except that the leveraged buyout target usually is managed and operated by the corporate partner. A fee for management services and/or elective services usually is paid to the corporate partner. The payment of such a fee often can lend credibility to the existence of a 50/50 relationship between the venture partners.

If the corporate partner owns directly and indirectly more than 50 percent of the voting rights, the company would not, for accounting purposes, be considered a joint venture and therefore would be consolidated by the corporate partner. From an accounting standpoint, this is what the corporate partner wishes to avoid. If the joint venture were consolidated, the debt arising from the LBO would find its way onto the corporate partner's balance sheet and any goodwill arising from the acquisition would be shown separately.

HOW A JOINT VENTURE LBO WORKS

Let's examine briefly how a typical joint venture LBO would work. The first step in a successful joint venture LBO is for the corporate partner and the passive financial partner to agree on the essential terms of the partnership arrangement. After agreement has been reached on issues such as the buyout arrangement for the eventual unwinding of the venture, who would operate the business on a day-to-day basis, how the board would be structured, and what the board would be required to vote on, the next step is to agree on a target.

In the event that the acquisition is a friendly one, typically a new corporation would be established that would buy the target company in a negotiated transaction. Ownership of the new corporation would be 50/50 as described above. Afterwards, the venture partner would arrange for extensive financing and take out whatever short-term indebtedness has been utilized to make the acquisition. In the event that the acquisition is a hostile acquisition, typically the corporate partner will have to make the initial acquisition and tender for the target. Afterwards, the 50/50 venture will be established, and the venture will buy the target from the corporate partner for corporate partner cost, and will arrange for extensive debt including possibly the registration and sale of high-yield bonds.

Immediately, the venture will effect a plan to emphasize cash generation to reduce the indebtedness. In other words, this acquisition will be treated exactly like a traditional leveraged buyout, rather than a normal corporate acquisition emphasizing earnings. That plan may include plans for disposition of unwanted businesses of the target to reduce venture debt.

After an appropriate period in which the corporate partner has had an opportunity to effectively evaluate the business and to reduce the acquisition indebtedness, the corporate partner has a separate decision to make with respect to the remaining 50 percent interest held by the financial partner—that is, it can buy out the financial partner, it can sell its 50 percent interest, or it can hold its investment, causing the financial partner to sell its 50 percent interest to another party—generally the public. This subsequent investment decision should be evaluated independently of the first investment decision, and depends on the initial agreement between acquiring partners.

ADVANTAGES OF JOINT VENTURE LBOs

The advantages of using a leveraged joint venture in effecting a corporate acquisition of this nature are several:

1. The leveraged joint venture will not be consolidated. As a result, there is little short-term impact on the corporate partner balance sheet, and the debt and goodwill will not be shown separately.

2. The investment will require a small amount of cash. The equity portion of this type of acquisition will be equivalent to the amount required in a leveraged buyout.

3. The acquisition is financed on a "stand alone" basis. That is to say, the cash flows or asset values of the target are utilized to finance the acquisition, not the corporate partner's general borrowing power. The corporate partner's line of credit otherwise remains untapped.

4. The corporate partner effectively controls and manages the business on a day-to-day basis.

DISADVANTAGES OF JOINT VENTURE LBOs

On the other hand, there are some disadvantages to this structure which must be considered before commencement of the venture:

1. Partnerships can be cumbersome. Typically, in the event that the acquisition is an economic success, there will be no unusual problems between the partners. However, in the event that the acquisition does not do as well as the original projections indicated, there may be some difficulty between the partners in deciding what courses of action need to be taken to correct the situation.

2. This structure requires a careful balance between the need for synergy with the corporate partner and the need for the entity to be run on a "stand alone" basis. For this type of acquisition to be successful, the corporate partner should be contributing something other than cash—otherwise, the acquisition could be done in a straight leveraged buyout form just as efficiently. The corporate partner, therefore, should either be bringing management or some form of comparative advantage or competency to add value to the acquisition. On the other hand, since the financing will be done on a "stand alone" basis, and management will normally be compensated on the results of the venture, there is a need for the venture to be somewhat autonomous and "stand alone."

3. The marginal financing cost will usually be higher as a result of the fact that the venture is financed on a "stand alone" basis and is highly leveraged.

4. The financial partner is paid a high return. Equity capital is not cheap, and accordingly this adds to the effective overall costs of the acquisition for the corporate partner—if the corporate partner is looking at the acquisition from the perspective of eventually buying all of the target.

5. The venture will be a separate taxpayer. In the event that the venture is projected to run tax losses in the early years, these may have to be carried forward and not consolidated with the corporate partner's profits.

6. There is little short-term impact on a corporate partner's income statement. Since little equity capital is being infused into the investment, it is unusual that an investment of this nature would produce early dramatic earnings results.

ACCOUNTING QUESTIONS

There are numerous accounting questions regarding these structures that must be addressed, but two of the most common ones are: What is the consolidation threshold for the public corporate partner in these LBO ventures? And, how is income recognized by the public corporate partner?

Consolidation Thresholds

With respect to the first question, accounting literature indicates that unless a company is majority-owned (an investment of greater that 50 percent of voting stock), consolidation usually is not necessary or appropriate. However, this literature was written in 1959 and is in the process of being revised. Moreover, the concept has been eroded by some Enforcement Releases of the Securities and Exchange Commission. On occasion, the SEC has indicated that it believes consolidation is mandatory in situations where actual control exists, whether or not there is immediate voting control.

Without attempting to define "control" or advising on how to "walk the tightrope," it is important to note that careful structuring is required to ensure that the LBO joint venture won't have to be consolidated by the corporate partner. Note that if the corporate partner owned less than 50 percent of the voting stock, the consolidation question would be mitigated. It is essential that the 50/50 voting aspect of the partnership be maintained in all respects.

This generally means that each of the partners in the joint venture should be entitled to elect an equal number of board members and have an equal say in important matters such as approval of transactions between the LBO company and the corporate partner, selling the business, merging, or dissolution.

Usually the corporate partner will want an option or right of first refusal to buy the LBO partner's shareholdings in the future. It's important that the device the corporate partner ultimately will use to buy the interest held by the financial partner be perceived as a true option. The risks and rewards of owning the equity held by the financial partner should not reside with the corporate partner. Clearly, bargain purchase options, puts and calls at the same price, and similar devices seem to be a sham by giving the appearance of a "temporary lack of control." A defensible structure of a 50/50 venture can be maintained by using rights of first refusal at fair market value, calls at their fair market value, or similar devices that keep such a transaction at arm's length.

It is important to note that an operating management agreement does not in and of itself mandate consolidation. However, such an agreement certainly is a factor to be considered. Above all, the joint venture must maintain the appearance of a 50/50 relationship in order to avoid consolidation.

Income Recognition

Now let's turn to the second frequently asked question: How does the corporate venture partner recognize income on its investment? To calculate the amount of earnings or loss to be recognized, there must be a determination of the capital structure—how much of the investment was put into common stock and how much went into preferred stock. Also, keep in mind that the aggregate income of the economic entity (in this case the leveraged buyout target) should not be increased by any change in the amount of common and preferred stock outstanding.

Accordingly, to determine the equity in earnings to be recognized by the corporate venture partner, one must first calculate the earnings attributable to common stock. This is done by determining the net income of the leveraged buyout target company on a "pushdown" basis (i.e., reflecting an allocation of the corporate partner's purchase price), and subtracting the preferred dividend requirement. The earnings or loss attributable to the corporate venture partner is determined with respect to the common stock interest by multiplying the percentage of the common stock owned by the corporate venture partner times the earnings (or loss) attributable to common stock. The application of this calculation and the calculations to follow are illustrated in Figure 1.

FIGURE 1
Income Recognition in an LBO

To illustrate, let us look at the following hypothetical example. Assume that Company A is a company acquired in a leveraged buyout by leveraged buyout firm L and corporate partner B, with the following equity capitalization:

Common Stock—L	$10 million
Common Stock—B	10 million
Preferred Stock—B	100 million
Total equity	$120 million

Assume that the preferred stock has a dividend requirement of 10 percent per year, which is payable in redeemable preferred stock bearing a market dividend rate. Company A is projected to show the following results:

Year	*Income (loss)*
1	$(10) million
2	$(10) million
3	$(10) million
4	$ 30 million

Using these facts, the loss attributable to common stock in Year 1 is $20 million ($10 million of loss and $10 million for the preferred dividend requirement). Company B's ownership percentage is 50 percent; accordingly, B's interest in the common equity loss is 50 percent × $20 million, or $10 million. Common equity at the end of Year 1 is $20 million beginning equity less the entire loss attributable to common stock of $20 million, or zero. Thus the entire preferred dividend requirement is recognized as income, and the income on Company B's holdings in A is:

	Income (loss)
Common Stock	$(10) million
Preferred Stock	10 million
Total	$ 0

In Years 2 and 3 it is not necessary to calculate income attributable to common stock since there is no longer any common stockholders' equity and the result for the year is a loss. Rather, the entire loss is borne by the preferred stockholders, or Company B. Accordingly, the results for both Years 2 and 3, as reported by Company B, are losses of $10 million in each year.

In Year 4, the first $20 million of the $30 million of Company A income is allocated to restore the deficiency from the prior two years on the preferred. The remaining $10 million of income is also allocated to preferred stockholders to recognize the preferred dividend requirement of Year 2. Accordingly, in Year 4, all $30 million of income is allocated to Company B's holdings in its preferred stock.

The more difficult calculation is determining the amount of income attributable to preferred stock. This calculation begins with the preferred stock dividend requirement (plus any accretion required for a redeemable preferred stock). That number must then be adjusted for any losses or catch-up earnings attributable to the preferred stockholders. Such losses should be calculated by allocating to the common stockholders' equity the loss attributable to common stockholders. As long as there is positive common stockholders' equity, none of the loss is allocated to the preferred stock holdings; therefore, the preferred stock income is the dividend requirement plus any accretion on redeemable preferred stock.

If the common stockholders' equity is reduced to zero, any remaining losses are then allocated to reduce preferred stockholders' equity. On that basis, such losses should be subtracted from the preferred dividend requirement to calculate the loss attributable to preferred stockholders. If the leveraged buyout target company should become profitable in subsequent years, such profits are first allocated to the preferred stockholdings until such time as earlier losses attributed to the preferred have been reduced to zero (this is the so-called "earnings catch-up"). Profits are then allocated to the preferred on the basis of the preferred stock dividend requirement, with additional profits allocated to the common stockholders' interest (see Figure 1).

One additional caveat is required. Care should be taken with respect to the structuring of the preferred stock dividend requirements. Preferred dividends that are payable in cash or a monetary liability should always be included in a calculation of income attributable to preferred stockholders. However, in many cases the preferred dividend requirement may be structured as a stock dividend or a dividend in kind for a period of time. "Payment-in-kind" preferred stocks, or PIKs, may be exchangeable for debt at the option of the holder, which helps the income recognition. Careful analysis is required as to whether the stock dividend is, in substance, income, or whether income recognition should be postponed until a later date.

Now that we have looked at the advantages of the joint venture LBO for the investing parties, let's explore an advantageous LBO technique from the divesting party's standpoint.

THE LEVERAGED SELLOUT

The leveraged buyout has provided companies with tremendous flexibility in divesting themselves of businesses that don't fit into their strategic plans.

However, some LBOs have proven to be too successful, at least from the standpoint of the selling companies. Many businesses divested in LBO transactions in recent times have been resold or taken public at prices significantly exceeding what was originally paid for them. Understandably, this has caused considerable chagrin in many executive suites. No CEO likes to be seen as having underpriced assets he is selling.

In order to avoid missing out on the opportunity to cash in on the future appreciation of the equity of a divestiture candidate, some companies are turning to the technique of the leveraged sellout, or LSO. Like the LBO divestiture, the LSO enables a company to raise cash from the sale of a business unit. It differs, however, from the traditional LBO in that it lets the divesting party retain an interest in the equity of the divested business.

Structuring a Leveraged Sellout

Proper structuring of an LSO is important if the goals of the divesting party are to be attained. A typical structuring plan is as follows.

A company decides to sell 50 percent or more of a subsidiary. The company, as a corporate partner, enters into an agreement with a financial partner—most likely an LBO fund or an investment bank—to restructure the subsidiary and obtain the necessary buyout financing. Next, the subsidiary declares a dividend, in an amount approaching the fair value of the subsidiary, to the corporate partner in the form of a note payable. The subsidiary then sells new common shares to the financial partner, so that after the sale the corporate and financial partners each own 50 percent of the entity. The amount of cash required by the financial partner to purchase its 50 percent interest is relatively small, since the equity of the subsidiary is diminished by the dividend declared to the corporate partner. A plan may also be put into place to allow the subsidiary's management to obtain an interest in the business, either through an option plan or a purchase.

The company would then raise cash through the issuance of bank debt or high-yield securities, and use the proceeds to satisfy the dividend liability to the corporate partner. This debt is generally not guaranteed by either of the partners. In this respect, the LSO is much like a standard LBO, in that the venture is financed on a stand-alone basis.

The final step is the same as in most leveraged buyout transactions: The subsidiary implements an operating plan that stresses cash generation and debt reduction through asset disposals and other means. At some later date, the company can be sold to a third party or be taken public.

Advantages of Leveraged Sellouts

The principal advantage of this transaction is, of course, that it enables the corporate partner to retain an interest in the company and yet realize a substantial amount of cash through the sale of part of its equity in the subsidiary. It also provides a side benefit. As discussed earlier, if the corporate partner owns only a 50 percent interest in the company after the LSO has been completed, it will generally no longer have to consolidate the subsidiary for accounting purposes. See Figure 2 for an example of an LSO.

Accounting Issues for Leveraged Sellouts: Consolidation

The consolidation issue is a difficult one, and care must be taken in structuring the LSO venture if deconsolidation by the corporate partner is desired. If the subsidiary is no longer consolidated, the equity method of accounting is used by the corporate partner to account for its investment in the subsidiary. Under this method, 50 percent (assuming that is the percentage retained by the corporate partner) of the future profits reported by the subsidiary will be reflected in the corporate partner's income statement. According to APB Opinion 18, which governs equity accounting, "the investor should ordinarily discontinue applying the equity method when the investment and any loans

FIGURE 2
Leveraged Sellout

To date, the leveraged sellout technique has not been widely used. However, the prospectus for a common stock offering completed by Union Texas Petroleum Holdings, Inc. (UT) provides a good example of how effectively the technique can be utilized. In mid-1985 UT, a wholly-owned subsidiary of Allied-Signal, made a $2.2 billion distribution to Allied in the form of cash, redeemable preferred stock, and the forgiveness of an intercompany loan. For UT, the distribution created a common shareholder's deficiency of approximately $318 million. Allied then sold approximately 50 percent of its interest in UT to Kohlberg, Kravis, Roberts & Company (KKR) for $250 million in cash, recognizing a pretax gain of approximately $308 million on the entire transaction. Although Allied was subsequently required to purchase $200 million of UT redeemable preferred stock under the terms of a shareholders' agreement, it was able to take a significant amount of cash out of UT (some analysts say it was as much as Allied would have recieved for the entire company in a conventional sale) and still retained approximately 50 percent of the UT common equity.

To top it off, UT recently issued 18 million shares of common stock to the public at $14/share, which reduced Allied's interest in UT from approximately 50 percent to 39.2 percent. However, using the offering price as a benchmark, the 39.2 percent interest has an aggregate market value of $430 million.

made to the investee are reduced to zero, and should not provide for additional losses unless the investor has guaranteed the obligations of the investee." Thus, if losses are initially reported, 50 percent of such losses should not be recorded by the corporate partner since recording them would reduce its investment below zero.

Disadvantages of Leveraged Sellouts

The LSO structure is not without some disadvantages. As in many LBO divestitures, financing the new venture on a stand-alone basis may be difficult. In addition, the corporate entity and the LBO fund or other financial party involved in the LSO transaction will essentially be "partners" in the venture, and, as in the LBO situation, this can prove cumbersome in some instances. However, the ability of the corporate partner to participate in any postbuyout equity appreciation, coupled with the receipt of a significant amount of cash at the buyout date, may represent an opportunity too good to pass up. Consequently, the LSO technique will probably become an increasingly popular means of effecting a disposition for corporations.

CHAPTER 15

LEVERAGED BUYOUTS V: CORPORATE STRUCTURE AND CASHING OUT STRATEGIES

Carl Ferenbach
Berkshire Partners

When considering a leveraged buyout (LBO), among the most important questions for which the investor group seeks an answer is what will be the long-term value of its investment and how and when will it be realized. One response has been a significant number of public offerings of common stock or sales of control of LBO companies. Both exiting strategies were used frequently during the 1986–1987 bull market, often for companies acquired in a leveraged buyout during the prior two or three years. The *New York Times* described this trend as "Reverse LBOs." It also emphasized the enormous returns; for example, those achieved by the purchasers of Western Auto Supply Co.—Wesray Corp. and Western's executives—from a $338 million divestiture by Beneficial Corp. in December 1985. The buyer's equity investment of $5 million was worth $102 million on the basis of market prices for Western stock in late April 1987, about four months after the chain had gone public.

LBO CASHOUT CASES

Additional successful initial public offerings of companies that previously had been through LBOs included J. Baker (formerly National Shoes), Sterling Inc. (jewelry retailing), and Leslie Fay Inc. (apparel). Other companies, divested by corporate parents and subsequently offered to the public, included Western Publishing Group (divested by Mattel Inc. in February 1984 for $71 million) and Wearever-Procter Silex (a housewares firm merged by Wesray after buying units from SCM Corp. in September 1983 for $56 million and Aluminum Co. of America in November 1982 for an undisclosed price). J. Baker was acquired in July 1985 for $31.5 million; Sterling in June 1985 for approximately $30 million; and Leslie Fay in April 1982 for $58 million. Typically, 10 to 15 percent of the purchase price of these companies was funded with equity. Following their public offerings these companies had market values as follows: J. Baker, $89.8 million; Sterling, $60.5 million; Leslie Fay, $84.6 million; Western Publishing, $400 million; and Wearever-Procter Silex, $72.9 million.

But initial public offerings have been only one means to investor liquidity. Kohlberg Kravis Roberts & Co., which acquired Amstar Corp. in February 1984 for $438.6 million, sold the company two and a half years later to an investor group organized by Merrill Lynch for approximately $640 million. Signode Corp., a 1982 LBO valued at $430 million, was sold to Illinois Tool Works Inc. in September 1986 for approximately $522 million; Blue Bell Inc., a $470.9 million LBO in November 1984, was sold to VF Corp. in January 1986 for $732 million; and Forstmann Little & Co. sold Dr Pepper to an investment consortium for $435 million in August 1986, 30 months after buying the soft drink company for $627 million and executing several profitable divestitures (e.g., Canada Dry).

One should note that the gain in the value of the equity achieved in all of these LBOs is substantially larger than may be readily apparent . Each of these prices represents an enterprise value, or the cost of purchasing both debt and equity. As approximately 10 to 15 percent of the original purchase price was equity, any gain in value plus any debt reduction went to the benefit of the equity holders. The entire gain, therefore, should be compared to the original, relatively small, highly leveraged equity investment. The returns have often been extremely attractive.

THE LBO FORM OF CORPORATE GOVERNANCE

What follows is a description of how the typical investor group analyzes the expected value of an enterprise, including the value of its equity, which so-called exit alternatives to consider, and why one such alternative is selected and when. Since the makeup and financial goals of a typical investor group are critical to this analysis, an LBO investment group is described in some detail, along with the means by which the investors and managers develop a commonality of interests for the purpose of successful corporate governance. Because most leveraged buyouts are of operating subsidiaries or divisions of diversified companies, or of closely held companies, the analysis assumes this focus rather than that of transactions where success is directly dependent upon the sale of the various parts of the business at values greater than the whole.

THE LBO INVESTOR GROUP

For the most part, the American corporation has been owned by some combination of entrepreneurs/founders, their heirs, and the public through public equity distributions. The entrepreneur either had absolute control of the company or shared it with venture capitalists, who in turn intended to share it with the public at the earliest opportunity.

Publicly owned companies have forms of governance focused on a board of directors, which, in the American system, has come to mean membership by people outside company management. Because outside directors cannot be affiliated with competitors, and because the typical board rarely meets more than 12 times a year, independent directors often do not know much about the operations of the businesses they govern. What they do know, they see through the eyes of management. Hence, their ability to contribute beyond the conceptual level has been somewhat limited by the standards imposed by this system of governance.

The LBO structure of ownership provides a relatively new form of corporate governance which combines professional owners and professional manager/owners. To understand how it functions, one must first understand the nature and purpose of an LBO group. The LBO community of the 1980s has included major investment banks, certain wealthy individuals, and some so-called corporate raiders, but for the most part, the typical LBO sponsor has had the following characteristics:

- *Structure:* A partnership staffed by five to ten professionals, including partners.
- *Capital Resources:* A fund, organized as a limited partnership, in which the investors are pension funds, insurance companies, bank holding companies, investment management firms on behalf of certain clients, and wealthy individuals.
- *Investments:* Five to fifteen companies in the portfolio at any one time.

- *Objective Standards:* To organize and invest in acquired companies, to be the primary shareholder of such companies, and to earn a substantial rate of return on such investments. (The target internal rate of return is typically greater than 35 percent.)
- *Structure of Typical Investment:* An acquired company is capitalized with various layers of debt (about 80–90 percent) and equity (about 10–20 percent). The LBO group typically purchases a majority of the equity and arranges for management to purchase or earn a meaningful interest in the company (from 5 to 25 percent depending on size and personal resources). The LBO group arranges the balance of the financing or engages an investment bank to do so. Of the lenders, those that are subordinated generally also purchase equity.
- *Basis for Investment:* A detailed five-year plan for operation of the company, including any new investment, debt reduction, restructuring, improvements in market position, changes in operations, and contingency plans for a business downturn or large business risks. The plan will have been thoroughly researched, and both management and investors will have agreed upon it.
- *Relationships:* An LBO group typically forms alliances with major investment and commercial banks and insurance companies, with general managers capable of operating acquired businesses, with other sources of potential acquisitions (the "deal stream"), and with various professional firms that provide legal, accounting, and consulting services.

If described in terms of an operating company, the LBO firm's customer is its institutional limited partner. Its supplier is an investment bank or other deal source. Its task is to purchase products—transactions and financing—from its suppliers at the best value it can find for its various customers.

The customers have bought:

- A ten-year limited partnership interest.
- A commitment to invest their money over a five-year period.
- An expected rate of return well in excess of those available in other markets.
- A professional staff capable of meeting these commitments.

For these services, the investors (or limited partners) usually pay:

- An annual management fee, which varies from 1.5 to 2.5 percent of capital commitments.

- A percentage of their profits once their capital has been returned (typically 20 percent or higher if the limited partners' capital gets a preferential return).

Hence, the LBO firm is providing investment services to a group of institutional and individual clients.

THE LBO GROUP vs. THE CORPORATE PARENT

Some have suggested that it is possible to look at the LBO firm as the parent company of a conglomerate. Although each company in which the LBO firm invests is in fact a free-standing company, the LBO firm provides many of the same services—financing, policy and direction, management, and compensation—as would a conglomerate headquarters. What, then, makes it different from any other investment firm? And how is its ownership of a company different from corporate ownership or entrepreneur/family ownership?

Unlike the entrepreneur/family, the LBO firm is a professional owner. It arranges the purchases and financing of operating businesses, invests the funds under its management and controls a significant equity investment (typically 35–75 percent), and it oversees those operations without participating in management. It determines when to seek liquidity for its investment and typically does so rather dispassionately. Unlike the conglomerate, the LBO firm shares ownership with management, with its financing sources and, of course, with its limited partners. Hence, while the LBO firm is providing investment services and investment banking services, it is also providing management services through its oversight function. Its ownership interests, accomplished through both direct investment and participation in its limited partners' profits, provide it with a meaningful incentive to create value for all investors. Of these differences, by far the most meaningful is sharing ownership with management.

In monitoring operations, the LBO firm is focused on two objective criteria: the production of cash to retire debt; and continued investment in the operations of the business over its investment period to ensure future growth and development. By contrast, the traditional investment manager's focus on quarterly results has become legend. The entrepreneur/family is known for hanging on too long. The conglomerate has often been guilty of both.

The LBO firm, therefore, is an owner of a business over which it has the ability to exercise considerable control. Its ultimate objective is to realize a high rate of return on its investment—an objective thoroughly consistent with that of its limited partners since neither will have achieved financial success if the investment is only an average one. This objective is also consistent with that of management since as a group it is a meaningful owner of the company. (It is important that the LBO model invariably provides an ownership stake to management. The LBO firm negotiates this management participation, and it is essential to the LBO firm that this negotiation be concluded such that management's interests are thoroughly parallel with those of the LBO firm and its limited partners.)

PLANNING THE LBO

Prior to actually contracting to organize a leveraged buyout, the LBO group, with management's assistance, will undertake a thorough "due diligence" investigation of the business. A significant portion of this investigation is keyed to developing a detailed budget for the next 12 months and a five-year operating plan. The budget and the plan will be driven by business strategies that recognize that the company will be operating with abnormal financial risk for at least two years because of its leveraged capital structure. The budget and the plan, therefore, will reflect tight management of working capital and a thorough review of capital expenditures.

With this understanding of operations, the LBO group will then determine a price range it is willing to pay and impose a financial structure based upon its knowledge of financial markets and upon the company's ability to service debt. As noted earlier, about 10 percent of the financing required will be in the form of equity. Of the balance of funds, banks typically provide the senior credit based upon their standards for interest coverage and asset protection, and the company's need for seasonal funds. Subordinated notes or debentures placed privately or sold publicly will generally fill out the capital structure.

To determine the hypothetical return on its equity investment based upon this plan, the LBO group will analyze the likely progress of the company in retiring this debt, both from operations and asset sales, for the five to seven years presented in the plan. Projecting operations at the end of this period, the LBO group will value the enterprise based upon a multiple of earnings before interest, taxes, and depreciation. The multiple or multiples applied will reflect historical market pricing, the price paid to acquire the business, such other factors as remaining goodwill and/or a relatively low book value, and the expected form of sale (e.g., public or private, assets or stock). From this number, the remaining debt will be subtracted to determine the value of the equity. A simple calculation of the internal rate of return over the investment period enables the investor group to make a judgment about its interest in the acquisition based upon this hypothetical rate of return.

The investor group must at this time make some judgments about the form of exit. Will the target company be appropriate for a public offering? Are there logical strategic acquirors for the company? Do its cash flow characteristics lend themselves to a recapitalization or management buyout of the investor group?

CASHOUT STRATEGY I: PUBLIC OFFERING

Timing is also important. An early public offering to reduce financial risk and to enable the company to take on new opportunities can be an interesting strategy. Yet, although there have been periodic markets for initial public offerings through much of the 1980s, there was only a limited window during the 1970s, and the crash of October 1987 pointedly demonstrates that a pure public offering strategy is unreliable. Further, except for the hottest markets, the investor group rarely is able to sell more than 20 percent of its holdings in any one offering, making the public offering a relatively long-term exit strategy.

A study published by Kidder, Peabody during 1987 suggests, however, that investor perception of LBO companies that have been offered to the public, while initially skeptical, has been generally favorable. This has been reflected in their superior aftermarket performance, when the new investors have concluded that management's demonstrated ability during the LBO period to tighten operating costs and undertake new initiatives would be continued for their benefit.

Many of the IPOs undertaken within a year or two of the buyout have denominated the equity at values well in excess of the price paid by the investors. The Kidder, Peabody study suggests that this appreciation has come about because management has successfully executed the plan that it, the investor group, and all the lenders agreed upon at the time of the leveraged buyout.

Hence, the principal reasons to pursue an initial public offering are to reduce the company's financial risk by raising additional equity capital, to enhance its operating strategies by employing these new funds, to denominate the value of the business, and to enable the investors to realize some cash return on their investment. The timing of the offering will be dependent on markets, need for capital, and the personal preferences of the investor group.

CASHOUT STRATEGY II: PRIVATE SALE

The timing of sale of control, recapitalization, or a management buyout is more commonly motivated by the desires of the investors to realize the gains they believe they have achieved. The market for corporate control, like the common stock market, experiences phases of expansion and contraction with commensurately higher and lower valuations placed on businesses. The LBO firm generally has the additional need (and financial motivation) to produce gains for its limited partners. A record of gains will ensure its future access to equity capital as well as its continued favorable participation in its partners' profits. The LBO group, therefore, will consider the markets for control as well as the evolution and development of the company in its exit strategy decision.

It is not uncommon for management to initiate a sale of control. Management's interests in so doing often will be both strategic and personal. The personal reason, of course, will be to diversify portfolios and estates. Often the strategic reason will be based upon a belief that an alliance will improve their position in the marketplace. Unlike the board of a public company, once it has made the decision to sell, the private, professionally owned corporation can choose to negotiate a sale rather than open an auction to all bidders. It is not uncommon for management to use its gains to organize its own buyout, and professional owners often will forego the better price that an auction might bring in favor of the management deal. If management is not a buyer, the owners can still forego an auction in favor of negotiating with a limited group of strategic buyers; this approach can bring about both a favorable price and long-term strategic development.

It is often asked whether high value creation for an investor group is truly consistent with such goals as new investment, growth, and research and development, and whether it is inconsistent with the interests of such other constituents of the enterprise as employees, customers, and suppliers. In other words, are the investors determined to reap financial rewards at the expense of the employees and others? This is important because the concerns of these constituents are critical to prospective buyers as well as to politicians. A sound case can be made that if the owners' intent is to operate the enterprise for both long-term growth and financial efficiency—as is the case with most LBOs—then there are considerable parallel interests among all constituents.

PARALLEL INTERESTS: THREE LBO CASES

The reasons that parallel interests exist in a leveraged buyout are the common ownership of management and the investor group, the clear need to retire debt, and the agreement on the plan. In operating the enterprise, management must discard earnings as an objective and adopt three goals.

1. It must increase free cash available for debt reduction through both better operations and more efficient asset utilization (e.g., working capital).
2. It must reduce its operating costs through better staffing, purchasing, and production practices while eliminating redundant general and administrative costs.
3. It must make commitments to the future of its existing business through new investments—in both productivity and growth.

Pursuit of these goals will improve the job content for current employees, lead to new jobs as the enterprise grows, and focus the organization on an understandable future. Three examples of companies that have prospered as leveraged buyouts are Sterling Inc., the jewelry chain; Signode Corp., the nation's largest manufacturer of strapping for industrial packaging; and Corhart Refractories Incorporated, a leading producer of high-intensity refractory bricks.

Sterling, Inc.

At the time the acquisition of Sterling was arranged, there were three national jewelry chains. Although privately owned, Sterling was not among these. It was putting in place the industry's best management and control systems. To expand from its 70-store base it needed to invest in middle-level management, in new store openings, and in strategically located acquisitions. Two years after its LBO, Sterling had expanded its operations to 117 stores. During this period, revenues grew to $100.4 million from about $47 million, and operating income climbed to $14.4 million from $4.7 million. But while expanding, Sterling retired a significant portion of its debt. Sterling made two public offerings of its stock, in 1986 and 1987, and in mid-1987 it was acquired by Ratners Group PLC, a large British-based jewelry chain, for $210 million. Sterling went public because having put the structure in place to manage a bigger company, it needed to grow both by acquisition and by opening new stores. Its subsequent acquisition was the result of an unsolicited proposal.

Signode Corporation

Signode Corporation was the nation's major producer of steel and plastic strapping systems for packaging and distribution purposes at the time of its 1982 LBO. It had also diversified into the fastener industry and into some smaller packaging activities. While Signode had invested in the development of its existing businesses, the markets for its products were maturing quickly and its R&D function had not been focused on additional diversification. Approximately 18 months after its buyout, and after a concerted and successful effort to manage working capital efficiently and to retire debt, Signode recruited a highly qualified person to head up R&D and designated him an executive vice president, one of the company's most senior titles. This was followed by creation of venture teams, staffed by people within the organization who were charged with developing creative new products based on an existing Signode technology. The company invested significantly in these new opportunities. Several were successful and became important new businesses to Signode. In 1986, Signode was acquired by Illinois Tool Works, Inc., with its shareholders enjoying a substantial gain.

Signode's successes could not have been realized without the owners' commitment to corporate development. In fact, management had the alternative of not investing new capital in the enterprise, expecting that short-term, cost-related measures that would temporarily improve earnings would also produce a quick killing. Yet it seemed unlikely that cost reduction alone could provide for the future of the company, and in fact it would have represented a more risky business strategy than most buyout groups could afford to pursue.

Corhart Refractories, Inc.

Corhart Refractories, a subsidiary of Corning Glass Works, was engaged in producing refractory bricks used in the high sections of glass and steel-making furnaces at the time of its LBO. Corning was interested in divesting Corhart in order to redeploy funds into other developing businesses.

Both Corning and Corhart had long-standing relationships, including technology agreements, with such leading non–U.S. multinational corporations as Saint-Gobain and its refractories subsidiary SEPR. At the time of the divestiture of Corhart by Corning, SEPR was unable to acquire Corhart, at least in part because of concerns about the policies of the Socialist government of France and concerns about U.S. government antitrust policy. This created the opportunity for management and a leveraged buyout group to acquire Corhart with possible changes in government policy anticipated in the purchase agreement.

Following the leveraged buyout, Corhart made the decision to redeploy some of its assets. This involved withdrawing from the steel industry, where Corhart's business had been declining. This restructuring would have been more difficult had Corhart been owned by either Corning or SEPR. Two and one half years after the buyout, SEPR was able under a new government to make the acquisition of Corhart. With the restructuring, the transaction was a successful one for all parties.

MANAGING THE LBO

In each of these cases, the board of directors consisted of the investors —management and the LBO group—and two or more outsiders with relevant operating experience to contribute to the development of the company. Although board meetings were conducted following an orderly agenda, they also provided an open forum in which major issues facing the company were discussed at length. There also were frequent interim conversations among management, the investors, and the other directors regarding various operating considerations. Because all the investors had undertaken an in-depth due diligence investigation before making their investment, they fully understood the companies, their operations, and the issues facing them. With that knowledge, they could understand the need to provide support for the companies' growth through new investment, the financial leverage notwithstanding.

As noted, a key ingredient in the development of the parallel interests that enable an LBO company to develop is the business plan. The plan is the basis for management's participation in the equity. It is also the basis for annual compensation programs, for lender participation in the acquisition, and, of course, it is the basis for the investor group's participation. Hence, the business plan is a program committed to by all parties. All participants consider unleveraging strategies at the time of investment as well as equity valuation and realization strategies. Since the investors most often conclude that continued investment and corporate development are critical to future valuation, funding the company's future becomes a necessary component of the plan. With the agreement that cash flow be dedicated to both debt reduction and corporate development, management's tasks are clearly focused.

As a professional owner representing the interests of institutional investors as well as its own, the LBO group is by definition a transitional owner, typically with a five-year time horizon. Notwithstanding the claims of creditors on a leveraged company's cash flow, the LBO form of corporate goverance is often a required catalyst for new development of the business. Without such commitments the investor group may not have a means of creating exit value for its equity. The ability of the LBO group to pursue value-creating development or growth depends on the upfront agreement between management and investors. It is the joint commitment to this plan that often leads to public offerings or mergers when they are needed to support the firm's future growth.

CHAPTER 16

ANALYSIS OF LEVERAGED BUYOUTS, TAKEOVERS, AND ASSET VALUE INVESTMENTS*

Mario J. Gabelli
Gabelli & Company, Inc. and GAMCO Investors, Inc.

PORTFOLIO MANAGEMENT TECHNIQUES

Before I detail our analytical methodology, allow me to briefly describe our basic philosophy, goals, research procedures, and portfolio management techniques. We invest primarily in common stocks selling at a significant discount to the underlying company's private market value. We define private market value (PMV) as the price an informed industrialist would be likely to pay to acquire the company's assets. Simply stated, our philosophy is that assets purchased in the stock market at 50 to 60 cents on the dollar can eventually be sold to other investors for a significantly higher price. In many instances, these "other investors" will be leveraged buyout (LBO) specialists or corporate acquirors who use the same criteria we do in evaluating an investment.

To limit the time horizon in which private market values are likely to be realized, we look for situations in which a catalyst is working to help surface value and attract investment attention. Catalysts include: (1) changes in a regulatory environment; (2) increasing merger and acquisition activity within an industry; (3) management succession questions such as the death

*This chapter was originally published in *The Financial Analyst's Handbook,* Sumner Levine, editor; Homewood, IL: Dow Jones-Irwin, 1988.

of a founder; (4) share repurchases and other restructuring activities such as the sale of a division; and (5) substantial stock purchases by outside interests. Acknowledging that even with catalysts present it can take time for private market values to be realized, we favor companies whose values will grow at least at the rate of inflation.

We invest in a stock only if we see the realistic potential for 50 percent appreciation within two years irrespective of the broad stock market environment. We maintain an awareness of the economic, political, and psychological factors that affect the market; however, under normal circumstances, the direction of the broad market should not be the dominant influence on our stock's appreciation potential. Our goal is to consistently achieve an annual 10 percent real rate of return (after tax and in excess of the prevailing inflation rate). This goal appears modest, and, in fact, we've comfortably exceeded this objective every year we've been in business. Over the longer term, however, achieving this goal will mean superior investment performance.

In tandem, Gabelli & Company, Inc. and GAMCO Investors, Inc. form an independent research organization. Other than broad-based economic and industry studies, we do not use outside sources for ideas or analysis. We subject each and every investment candidate to intensive analysis, applying our own asset-oriented criteria to identify opportunities. Once a stock has passed a rigorous examination and is included in a portfolio, it is monitored daily and held only as long as it continues to represent value by our standards. When a stock becomes fully priced relative to our private market value estimates, it is liquidated and replaced by another qualifying equity.

Our strategy is to be 100 percent invested at all times with the exception of periods in which we cannot find stocks that offer value. We are willing to take very substantial positions in stocks we favor because in buying one share we are expressing our belief that our clients would be well served by owning the entire company. We view stocks as pieces of a company and are willing to buy as many pieces at the right price as is feasible. In addition, I believe large positions are often more liquid than smaller positions when there may be a leveraged buyout specialist or corporate acquiror seeking a large block of stock.

I've described our basic philosophy and how we work. Now, I'll detail the conceptual and fundamental cornerstones of private market value investing. There are four exogenous methods for private market values to be realized: leveraged buyouts; takeovers; liquidations; and corporate restructurings. Perhaps the best way to illustrate private market value analysis is to describe our experiences with some of the stocks we have recommended and owned whose PMV has surfaced via these four methods.

IDENTIFYING LEVERAGED BUYOUT CANDIDATES

Let's start with the leveraged buyout, a transaction which is still not thoroughly understood by many sophisticated investors. The term *leveraged buyout* (LBO) generally refers to the acquisition of an existing company or a division of a company by a new corporation formed by the acquiror for that sole purpose and funded simultaneously with substantial amounts of institutional debt relative to contributed equity. The amount of leverage employed depends upon the nature of the business acquired and the level of confidence the acquiror and the lending institutions have in the cash-generating capability of the target company. The benefits to the acquiring group, which almost always consists of the financial partners and company management, are as follows.

1. The company becomes owned by management and a limited number of sophisticated and supportive investors with common goals and objectives.
2. Management has strong additional incentives through meaningful equity participation.
3. Dividends subject to double taxation are converted into tax-deductible interest payments.
4. Through partnerships or S corporations the investors can take advantage of noncash tax benefits created through stepped-up depreciation and other techniques.
5. If successful, the investors in the new company achieve a rate of return that is substantially greater than that which can be earned from most other alternative investments.

Leveraged buyout opportunities in publicly held companies are created when the stock market fails to accurately appraise the productive value of assets. Many public companies are managed for short-term earnings-per-share results rather than long-term return-on-capital, cash flow, and return-on-asset goals. The securities markets tend to penalize companies that operate to achieve these longer-term objectives and thus undervalue these companies on a long-term fundamental basis. An LBO generally provides the public shareholders of the company with a cash price for their shares at a substantial premium over the public market and more closely in line with the real or private market value of their security holdings.

Thinking like leveraged buyout specialists, we try to locate undervalued stocks of companies that qualify on most, but not necessarily all, of the following criteria:

- Cash flow in excess of debt service, capital, improvements and working capital requirements (free cash flow).
- A history of profitable operations.
- A committed and conservative management team, with depth and stability.
- Relatively low cyclicality.
- Moderate unit growth.
- A high current asset base and inventory values in excess of book value.
- Undervalued and salable nonoperating assets.
- Off-balance-sheet assets.
- An efficient, modern asset base which is not single-purpose equipment.
- Products and processes that are not subject to replacement due to technological changes.
- A relatively low debt level.
- An excessive cash position.
- Limited off-balance-sheet liabilities.

Growth companies rarely meet these qualifications. In most instances, prospective LBO targets have passed their growth phase and are well along in what could be described as their golden years. These are not the kind of companies that excite earnings growth-oriented investors; consequently, the stock market pays them little tribute. Yet, these are established, profitable enterprises with management in place, a predictable income stream, and minimal capital needs. By recasting the balance sheet via a leveraged buyout and using operating income to service debt rather than pay dividends and taxes, the LBO partners controlling a small, highly leveraged equity base can get an exceptional return on their investment. So, too, can the public shareholder who is bought out at a price usually significantly higher than the public market value of the shares. In the cradle-to-grave life cycle of a public company, LBO candidates are closer to the grave. As is illustrated in Figure 1, we try to buy them just before the leveraged buyout specialists begin to prepare the plot.

LBO CRITERIA

The key fundamental criterion in evaluating an LBO candidate is free cash flow, which we define as pretax, preinterest, predepreciation, operating income minus debt service, and any capital expenditures needed to sustain

FIGURE 1

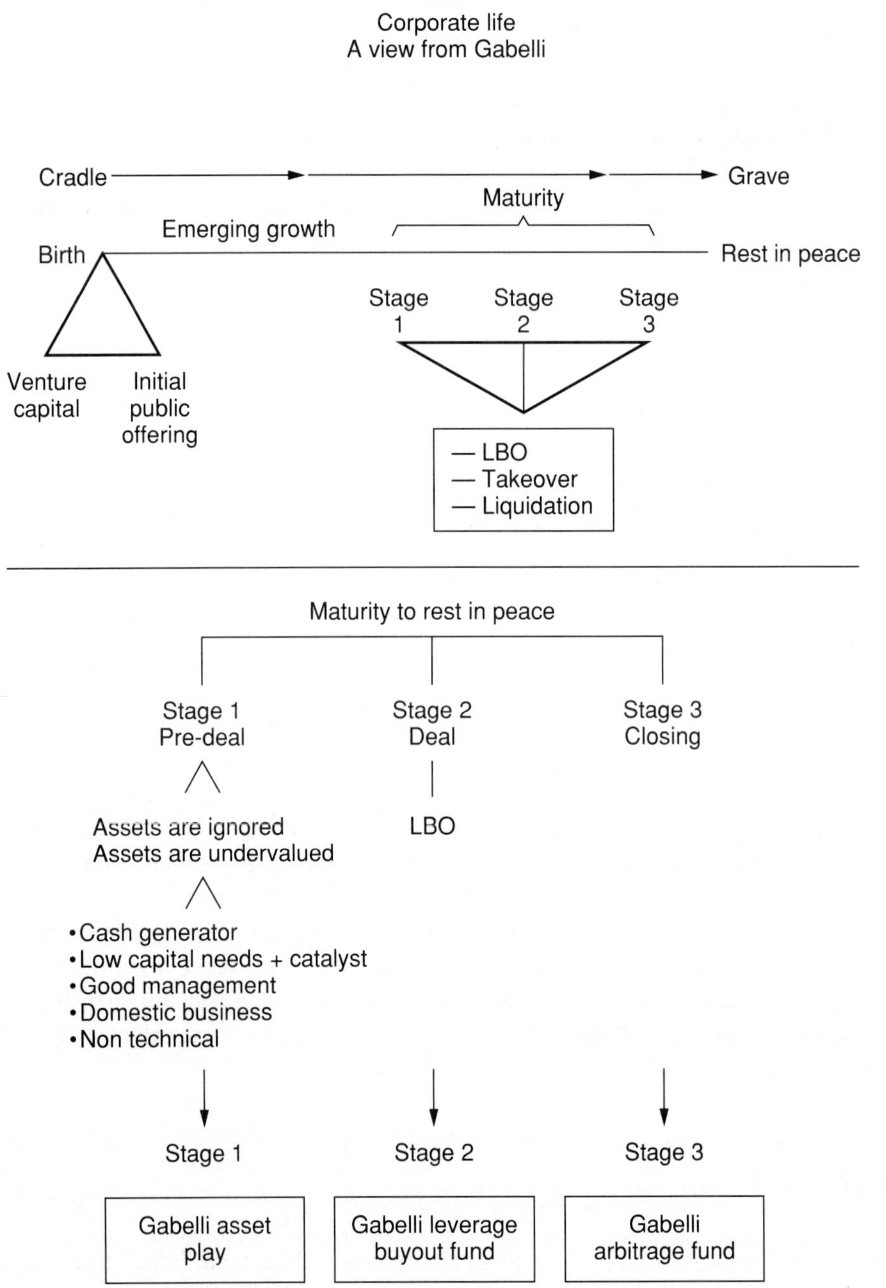
Corporate life
A view from Gabelli
Cradle
Grave
Maturity
Emerging growth
Birth
Rest in peace
Stage 1
Stage 2
Stage 3
Venture capital
Initial public offering
— LBO
— Takeover
— Liquidation
Maturity to rest in peace
Stage 1 Pre-deal
Stage 2 Deal
Stage 3 Closing
Assets are ignored
Assets are undervalued
LBO
•Cash generator
•Low capital needs + catalyst
•Good management
•Domestic business
•Non technical
Stage 1
Stage 2
Stage 3
Gabelli asset play
Gabelli leverage buyout fund
Gabelli arbitrage fund

operating income. Since the price an LBO specialist will be willing to pay to take a company private will largely be determined by how much cash the company can generate to service debt, free cash flow is generally the most important consideration in our private market value estimates. Consequently, to a large extent, private market value (PMV) analysis is free cash flow analysis. In making our PMV estimates, we are also cognizant of other cash-generating factors such as the prospective sale of marginally profitable businesses or other passive assets, cash on the balance sheet producing investment income, and/or any marketable securities that could be sold to produce cash. Of course, the cost of debt must also be factored into the PMV equation.

EXAMPLES OF PRIVATE MARKET VALUE ANALYSIS

I've given you the theory. Now let me give you a few real-life examples of how our private market value analysis has identified leveraged buyout situations. I'll begin by reviewing our experience with Houdaille Industries, Inc., a company I first wrote up while still employed as an analyst with William D. Witter, Inc., and on which I continued to report after founding Gabelli & Company, Inc., in 1977.

Houdaille was a diversified manufacturer of industrial goods, auto parts, machine tools, and construction materials; in short, a somewhat boring company in somewhat mundane industries. Coupled with its lack of "sex appeal" was a lackluster earnings record that turned off most investors. I was attracted to Houdaille because of its steady growth in book value, large cash position, stable revenue stream, declining capital expenditures, and accelerating free cash flow. At the time, I was confident management would be able to translate these asset-oriented strengths into increasing profitability. I believed institutional investors would appreciate it. Over the three-year period I recommended the stock, earnings did not develop as I anticipated. I stuck with it, however, because free cash flow and book value were still accelerating and I remained convinced that sooner or later either earnings would follow suit or another corporate entity would spot the big discrepancy between stock price and asset value and buy the company. In my final (October 20, 1978) research report on Houdaille, I concluded, ". . . $35 to $40 per share is the price any eventual suitor would pay to own this company."

In early 1979, a unique investment partnership, Kohlberg Kravis Roberts & Co. (KKR) took Houdaille private at approximately $40 per share via a still somewhat novel transaction, the leveraged buyout. When I looked at the deal closely, I realized that not only did my clients (the shareholders) make money, but KKR and Houdaille management also did very well. I reasoned that since the economics of LBOs made dollars and sense, there would be many more in the future. I wanted to recommend and own the stocks of companies likely to be targets. Thus, private market value investing became my primary focus.

Since Houdaille, we have recommended and owned positions in more than a dozen companies that have been LBO'd. Our research on these companies provides excellent examples of private market value analysis at work. The following is a Gabelli & Company research report on Cowles Broadcasting, Inc., a stock our GAMCO clients inherited with the liquidation of its parent, Cowles Communications.

Gabelli & Company, Inc.

Asset Play No. 12: December 28, 1982

Cowles Broadcasting, Inc.

Current Price: 16

(CWL-NYSE)

The Company

Cowles Broadcasting was spawned from the liquidation of Cowles Communications, our first Asset Play. In addition to other assets, each former shareholder of Cowles Communications will receive one share of Cowles Broadcasting, with such shares distributed on or about January 14, 1983. As background, we initially recommended Cowles Communications on April 5, 1977, at $14. Since then, we re-recommended it in seven separate Abstracts. Its last trade on the NYSE was %51.00 on December 16, 1982.

We refer to the new company as the "son" (daughter, if you prefer) of Cowles. It has two main assets: two television stations—WESH-TV, the NBC affiliate in Daytona-Orlando, Florida, and KCCI-TV, the CBS affiliate in Des Moines, Iowa—and about $4 million in cash with no debt. We place the private market value of CWL during the early 1980s at around $22.50 to $26.25 per share. We believe these values will rise over time. We believe accumulation of the shares at current levels is timely for investors seeking long-term capital gains.

Private Market Value of Cowles—Our Assumptions

Our assumptions for the private market value of CWL (as of the early 1980s) were as follows:

- Rule of 7 (currently the FCC restricts TV station ownership to seven stations) is modified, permitting group operators with more mature properties to bid on CWL.
- Revenue for CWL's stations over the next five years should grow as follows:

	Spot		
	National	*Local*	
Des Moines	10%	8%	
Daytona	11	13	
Total			108.%

- Private market value in 1985 would be derived as follows:
  The broadcast properties:

	Operating Profit ($ million)	*Multiple Cash Flow*	*Private Value ($ million)*
Des Moines	$ 4.0	9–10	$ 36–40
Daytona-Orlando	6.0	11–13	66–78
Total	$10.0		$102–118
Per shares			$25.75–$30.00

  Cash, which we estimate will be roughly $4.0 million at the end of 1982, will be close to $10 million or $2.50 per share at the end of 1985.

- This would place total private market value at $28 to $33 per share then.
- No shares are repurchased, though we would suggest that management pursue "aggressive cap shrink" now that the company is no longer hobbled by Investment Company Act considerations.
- License renewal question will be out of the way by June 1983.

Our Rate of Return Model

If we are correct, a total return to investors who bought the stock at various prices might be determined from the following matrix:

If CWL's Purchase Price	and Realized Value*		Annual Rate of Return (percent)	
	18 Months	3 Years	18-Month Workout	3-Year Workout
$12	$26.00	$34.00	77.8%	61.1%
14	26.00	34.00	57.1	47.6
16	26.00	34.00	41.7	37.5
18	26.00	34.00	29.6	29.0
20	26.00	34.00	20.0	23.3

* We are assuming payout ratio of 50 percent, or an average of about $0.50 per share over the next three years. Sale of assets completed by either July 1984 at $25.00 (18-month workout) or December 1985 at $32.50 per share (three-year workout).

Source: Gabelli & Company, Inc., calculations.

In sum, we believe that long-term equity-oriented investors should purchase Cowles Broadcasting. If a deal is completed within 18 months from today, the annualized rate of return would be over 40 percent. If the time frame is stretched out because litigation proves sticky, which we do not believe will be the case, we believe values will continue to grow, providing a still attractive 37.5 percent return in a three-year workout.

You will note that Cowles's TV stations are appraised at different multiples of operating cash flow.

The Des Moines station, located in a slower growth market, is valued at 9 to 10 times cash flow and the Orlando station, in the fast-growing Florida market, is appraised at 11 to 13 times cash flow. The compounded annualized growth rate of a broadcast property, or any franchise-type business, is an important consideration in determining the cash flow multiple used to determine PMV.

As the box (below) and Figure 2 prepared by GAMCO Vice President Douglas Jamieson reveal, there is a wide swing in the compounded annualized growth rate of broadcast properties in different markets.

FIGURE 2
Growth in Operating Income: Six Scenarios (A–F)

		Year							*Compound Growth Rate (percent)*
		0	*1*	*2*	*3*	*4*	*5*	*6*	
Case A:									
Revenue growth	= 8%	$20.00	$21.60	$23.33	$25.19	$27.21	$29.39	$31.74	
Cost growth	= 8%	10.00	10.80	11.66	13.60	14.69	15.87		
Operating profit		$10.00	$10.80	$11.66	$12.60	$13.60	$14.69	$15.87	8.0%
Case B:									
Revenue growth	= 10%	$20.00	$22.00	$24.20	$26.62	$29.28	$32.21	$35.43	
Cost growth	= 9%	10.00	10.90	12.95	14.12	15.39	16.77		
Operating profit		$10.00	$11.10	$12.32	$13.67	$15.17	$16.82	$18.66	11.0
Case C:									
Revenue growth	= 12%	$20.00	$22.40	$25.09	$28.10	$31.47	$35.25	$39.48	
Cost growth	= 10%	10.00	11.00	12.10	13.31	14.64	16.11	17.72	
Operating profit		$10.00	$11.40	$12.99	$14.79	$16.83	$19.14	$21.76	13.8
Case D:									
Revenue growth	= 14%	$20.00	$22.80	$25.99	$29.63	$33.78	$38.51	$43.90	
Cost growth	= 11%	10.00	11.10	12.32	13.68	15.18	16.85	18.70	
Operating profit		$10.00	$11.70	$13.67	$15.95	$18.60	$21.66	$25.20	16.7
Case E:									
Revenue growth	= 16%	$20.00	$23.20	$26.91	$31.22	$36.21	$42.01	$48.73	
Cost growth	= 12%	10.00	11.20	12.54	14.05	15.74	17.62	19.74	
Operating profit		$10.00	$12.80	$14.37	$17.17	$20.48	$24.38	$28.99	19.4
Case F:									
Revenue growth	= 20%	$20.00	$24.00	$28.80	$34.56	$41.47	$49.77	$59.72	
Cost growth	= 14%	10.00	11.40	13.00	14.82	16.89	19.25	21.95	
Operating profit		$10.00	$12.60	$15.80	$19.74	$24.58	$30.51	$37.77	24.8

Cases A Through F

Assumption

The television station in our model has $20 million in revenues and $10 million in operating expenses, generating operating income of $10 million.

The Cases

Case A: Toledo-type market. Case A could be a station in a low-growth market, where revenues and costs grow in line at 8.0 percent. The result is an 8 percent compounded annual growth rate in operating income.

Cases B–E: Atlanta-type market. In Cases B through E, we assume growth rates in revenues at incrementally higher levels, from 10 to 16 percent. Costs are assumed to grow at a slower pace than revenues, from 9 to 12 percent. The results are compounded annual growth rates ranging from 11.0 percent to 19.4 percent.

Case F: Phoenix-, Orlando-, Tampa-type market. Case F would be a typical Sunbelt station, where revenue growth is at 20 percent while the costs are growing at 14 percent. The resulting annualized compounded growth rate is 24.8 percent.

The moral of the story is that analysts must consider compound growth in formulating a value model based on a multiple to operating cash flow. Cowles Broadcasting's Des Moines station located in a Case B 10 to 16 percent annual operating cash flow growth market is not worth as much as its Orlando station in a Case F 20 percent plus annual operating cash flow growth market.

In updates on Cowles Broadcasting, we raised our PMV estimates from the initial $22.50 to $26.25 figure to more than $40 per share. In January 1985, Cowles Broadcasting went private via a leveraged buyout at $46.05 per share, returning almost 300 percent on our investment in less than three years.

Wometco Cable TV, Inc.

For another example of our private market value analysis leading us to an LBO, I've included the following Gabelli & Company report on Wometco Cable Television, Inc., a spinoff from Wometco Enterprises, at one time one of our largest portfolio holdings. I've chosen Wometco Cable TV because it is an excellent example of both free cash flow analysis and the effect of catalysts in surfacing private market value.

Wometco Cable TV, Inc.

	March 1983
Current Price:	
(WCTV–OTC)	17 bid
1983 Price Range	18–13
Operating Income per Share:	
1984P	$ 4.00
1983E	3.30
1982A	2.42
Private Market Value per Share:	
1985P	$38.00
1984P	30.80
1983E	25.50

The Company

Wometco Cable TV, Inc. (WCTV-17-OTC) was spawned from Wometco Enterprises, Inc. (WOM-32-NYSE) when, in a public underwriting led by Drexel Burnham Lambert and E. F. Hutton & Company, Inc., in May 1981, 1,170,000 shares of new stock were sold to the public at $16.00 per share. About $17 million was raised for WCTV. Based on its roughly 240,000 basic subscribers at April 30, 1983, Wometco ranks as the 22nd largest MSO (or multiple system cable TV operator).

Wometco Cable Internal Attributes

- All of its 240,000 basic subscribers are served by 20 or more channel systems.
- Growth prospects, based on the geographic location of its systems, are *favorable*. Even if no new franchises are acquired, we project 330,000 basic subscribers by the end of 1985:

	1980	*1981*	*1982*	*1983E*	*1984P*	*1985P*
Number of basics (000)	142	195	229	265	300	350

- Capital expenditures are trending down.

	1980	1981	1982	1983E	1984P	1985P
Outlays ($ million)	$23.5	$33.7	$29.3	$23.0	$18.0	$18.0

- Operating margins are exploding upwards.

	1 Qtr.	2 Qtr.	3 Qtr.	4 Qtr.	Year
1981	31.3%	31.6%	30.5%	31.8%	31.4%
1982	33.8	36.0	38.5	40.4	37.6
1983	41.3	—	—	—	41.0E

- Private market values are not $25 to $30 per share and rising rapidly.

	1983E	1984P	1985P	1986P
PMV/share	$22.50	$30.80	$38.00	$45.00

The Assets

As of January 1, 1983, Wometco had 46 cable TV systems located in eight states. Certain industry trends should influence the value of cable systems. In turn, they provide an underpinning to the growth in the private market of WCTV we envision. Thus, even if the two-year time frame we allow for surfacing of values in our asset play is stretched out, we think investors will be compensated by a commensurate increase in the private market value of WCTV. These factors include:

Improving governmental regulation, notably S.66. This bill provides assurances that a cable operator who lives up to his franchise agreement can expect a renewal of his franchise. The bill would curtail state and local authority to regulate cable television. The measure also grants cable systems full control over the rates they charge subscribers for basic service in large markets, calls for timely consideration of a cable system's renewal application, and establishes a renewal test that prevents cities from arbitrarily refusing franchise renewal.

- Investors will refocus on the free and clear cash flow that will be generated by companies such as Wometco one year hence.
- Industry fundamentals will be aided by addressable two-way converters and pay per view.

The Catalyst

Wometco Enterprises, Inc., the parent of Wometco Cable, Inc., is now controlled by the children of its founder, Mitchell Wolfson. We were particularly privileged to have known Mr. Wolfson for close to 14 years. He was a terrific patriarch. When he died on January 28, 1983, we believe a series of opportunities for the existing shareholders were set in motion. Simply stated, we believe that Wometco, which we have been recommending for the past 18 months and which we also believe is a superb asset play, will be the envy of many corporate types. Corporate America is casting about for cash generating entities, of which Wometco Enterprises has three: (1) broadcasting, (2) coke bottling, and (3) cable TV.

- Legislation is increasingly favorable for stepped-up merger activity in the broadcasting area.
- New entrants are appearing in broadcasting, notably, Kohlberg Kravis Roberts & Co. (New York), Rockefeller (Outlet), and Forstmann-Little.
- New financial techniques are surfacing, in particular, the purchase of Ziff Davis TV stations by the management through a leveraged buyout accomplished through a "retail syndicate."

Value Matrix

Without trying to be precise in an accounting sense, we believe the data in Figure 3 should help investors answer such questions as:

- What happens if average revenues rise $1 per subscriber per month?
- What if 10,000 more basic subscribers are added?
- What if the operating margin changed by 1 percent?

FIGURE 3
Value Matrix

	10,000 Basic Subscribers	*$1.00 Monthly Basic Charge*	*$1.00 Monthly Pay Charge*	*1% Margin*
Operating Cash Flow/Share	$0.13	$0.40	$0.20	$0.08
PMV/Share	$1.30	$4.00	$2.00	$0.80

Source: Gabelli & Company, Inc., estimates.

How Do These Values Surface?—Several Alternatives

There are many ways for investors to realize both the present and future values that we see in Wometco Cable TV. Among the possibilities are:

• Growth in cash flow and higher multiple of cash flow. The higher cash flow would stem from the internal analysis we did on Wometco. The higher valuation is likely as investors focus attention on the industry's rising "free and clear" cash flow. Also favorable legislation would bring more corporate buyers, particularly coincident with the passage of legislation with language similar to S. 66. Thus, the company has to do nothing but continue to manage its affairs as well as it has done in the past and we should make our investment hurdle rates.

• Swap of Wometco for Wometco Cable TV. Wometco might offer to its shareholders the right to receive two shares of WCTV for each of its own shares. This would result in approximately 3.5 million shares of Wometco common being exchanged for Wometco Cable. This would give a broader market to WCTV and allow it to pursue its own destiny or, in turn, to be pursued more freely by outside entities. From Wometco's point of view, this action would help improve its own private market value, simplify its asset base, and make itself easier to acquire.

Wometco Parent	*Shares o/s*	*WOM PMS**
Before swap	17.5 million	$45
After swap	14.0 million	$48

* Private market value of Wometco Enterprises based on Gabelli & Company, Inc., estimates.

• Wometco Enterprises might consider repurchasing outstanding shares of WCTV. The reasons that Wometco spun off the WCTV in the past no longer seem justified. Perhaps a purchase price of $25 in cash might be forthcoming. This would represent a slight discount from our perceived private market value, but the "cleanness and quickness" of the deal would support this discount. It would cost cash generating Wometco only $30 million to pursue this option.

• Sale of Wometco Cable to another entity. Obviously, this is the easiest of all alternatives and would be part of a larger program within the arena of Wometco Enterprises that would surface.

We don't care to place probabilities as to which alternative will be the one to surface the values.

In this situation there were two powerful catalysts at work: the unfortunate death of founder Mitchell Wolfson and government Regulation S.66 which freed the cable TV industry from pricing restraints and arbitrary license renewal standards, which clouded the future of all cable TV enterprises.

On March 1, 1984, Wometco Cable TV was merged into Wometco Cable Acquisition Corp., a private company controlled by preeminent leveraged buyout specialists Kohlberg Kravis Roberts & Co. (KKR). WCTV shareholders received $29.50 per share, slightly less than my 1984 private market value estimate of $30.80 per share, but significantly more than KKR's initial $25.00 bid. The dissolution of WCTV within less than a year of our recommendation and at a price approximating our PMV estimate teaches two lessons. First, when powerful catalysts are at work, private market values surface rapidly. Second, investors should not automatically accept the first buyout bid. If enough investors know what the fair price of the stock is and stick to their guns, the bid is likely to increase.

Storer Broadcasting, Inc.

In the case of Storer Broadcasting (later Storer Communications), our private market analysis put us into a profitable leveraged buyout and a unique opportunity to participate in the equity portion of the deal. We first recommended Storer at $22 per share in March 1978. In our initial Storer report, I estimated the company's PMV at approximately $65 per share. I continued to recommend and to buy the stock through 1985 even though the stock had climbed significantly and exceeded my initial private market value estimate. The reason? Due to accelerating operating cash flow from the company's broadcast properties and cable TV operations, our PMV estimate rose even more dramatically than Storer's stock price. Following is a private market value model we did on Storer in early 1983 (Figure 4).

Basing value on 10 times Storer's broadcasting operating earnings (operating cash flow) plus $1,000 per cable subscriber minus declining debt paid by excess cash flow divided by the outstanding shares, I saw Storer's per share private market value growing from $72 in 1983 to $167 in 1988. Kohlberg Kravis Roberts & Co. bought us out of Storer at $91 cash per share and a warrant to buy a share of SCI Holdings, the new private company, in January 1986. I was pleased to see that KKR shared my opinion of Storer's true worth—on a cash basis they paid $1 less than my $92 PMV estimate—and I was also happy to receive my SCI Holdings warrant, the subject of the following Gabelli & Company report.

Special Situation

SCI Holdings, Inc. New Warrants Trading When Issued 11/21/85

Son of Storer.

Storer Communications, a long-standing favorite of ours, and still the largest investment position for our clients, has scheduled a special shareholders' meeting for this Friday, November 22, 1985. At that time, shareholders will approve a merger with a newly organized company created by the preeminent leveraged buyout specialist, Kohlberg Kravis Roberts & Co. The transaction calls for payment to each shareholder of $91 cash and a warrant to purchase one share of stock in the new privately owned company, SCI Holdings, Inc.

The Concept

The ownership of Storer warrants represents the first opportunity for the public investor to participate in the equity of a deal created by Kohlberg Kravis Roberts & Co. Stated another way, ownership of the warrant represents a call on KKR's exit strategy. Since KKR makes money only when they realize profits on their carry in private deals (bah!), the public shareholders may make money because KKR has motivation to sell the assets in SCI at a financially opportune time.

The Time Frame

The shareholders are scheduled to approve a merger on Friday, November 22nd. The FCC has yet to approve the license transfers, but, in light of recent decisions, notably Murdoch/Metromedia, ABC/CapCities, we do not anticipate any insurmountable structural barriers. However, a minor glitch may unfold. A gadfly, named Traylor, may attempt to disrupt the transfer. He is the same individual who attempted to interfere in the sale of Wometco to KKR. While the functionings of due process may delay the closing, we assume that the transaction will close by mid-December/early January. Thus, a purchase of Storer common today at $92 will create the new Storer warrant for $1 plus cost to carry the investment for 45 days.

Why Storer?

Why are we interested in Storer? Obviously, not solely because of KKR. The new Storer wil emerge almost as a pure play in cable. For example, we estimate that by 1988, roughly three quarters of Storer's operating cash flow will be generated by its cable operations. Moreover, we anticipate that KKR might capitalize on the current voracious appetite for broadcast properties by selling off one or several television stations to increase the return on their investment, as well as provide greater financial flexibility. This would make it even more of a cable play.

FIGURE 4
Storer Communications—Estimated Private Market Value

	Broad-casting Operating Earnings ($million)	*Prevailing Acquisition Price (10 × cash flow) ($million)*	*Cable Subscribers (million)*	*Prevailing Acquisition Price ($1,000/ subscriber) ($billion)*	*Oustanding Debt ($million)*	*Shares Outstanding (million)*	*Estimated Private Market Value (per share)*
1988	$89.0	$890.0	1.9	$1,900	—	21.2	$167.00
1987	81.0	810.0	1.8	1,800	$ 75.0	21.2	146.00
1986	74.0	740.0	1.6	1,600	400.0	21.2	110.00
1985	67.0	670.0	1.5	1,500	530.0	21.2	92.00
1984	61.0	610.0	1.5	1,500	666.0	21.2	80.00
1983	53.2	532.0	1.4	1,400	628.0	21.2	72.00

THE MATH—WHAT WILL THE PRIVATE MARKET VALUE OF SCI HOLDINGS BE IN 1995?

In Figure 5, we depict the financing of the merger. In this regard, we wish to note the initial capitalization.

In Figure 6, we track the pro forma ownership of the new company. Yes, there will be 212 million shares outstanding.

Finally, in Figure 7, we find management's projected operating data through 1990.

FIGURE 5

Financing the Merger

The Financing

General. SCI Holdings has entered into agreements with the banks and expects to enter into agreements with the partnership and two limited partnerships of which KKR Associates is the general partner, with the Management Investors and with the purchasers of Debt Securities, and Scipsco expects to enter into agreements with the purchasers of the Preferred Stock, to provide the Financing in the approximate amount of $2.48 billion. The sources and applications of the funds constituting the Financings are estimated to be as follows:

Source of funds:	
Bank debt (7½ year senior revolving credit	$ 740,000,000
Working capital line of credit	50,000,000
Issuance of the notes	600,000,000
Issuance of the senior subordinated debentures	600,000,000
Issuance of the preferred stock	261,100,000
Issuance of the holdings common stock	227,264,000
Issuance of the warrants	5,000,000
Total	$2,483,364,000
Application of funds:	
Payment of cash for shares of Storer common stock	1,929,200,000
Available for payment of fees and expenses incurred in connection with the consummation of the merger, repayment of certain indebtedness of Storer and for working capital	554,164,000
Total	$2,483,364,000

Source: Storer Communications, Inc., October 23, 1985, p. 26.

FIGURE 6
Ownership of SCI Holdings Common Stock after the Effective Time

After completion of the Financing and consummation of the Merger, SCI Holdings Common Stock is expected to be beneficially owned as follows:

			Fully Diluted (1)	
Name and Address	*Number of Shares*	*Percent*	*Number of Shares*	*Percent*
KKR Associates (2) 9 West 57th St., Suite 4170 New York, NY 10019	107,696,000	97.2%	107,696,000	50.3%
SCI Partners (2) 9 West 57th St., Suite 4170 New York, NY 10019	—	—	67,340,000	32.0
Management Investors (3) (approximately 25 persons) c/o Storer Communications, Inc. 12000 Biscayne Boulevard Miami, FL 33131	3,052,300	2.3	15,264,000	7.2
Storer common stockholders (4)	—	—	21,200,000	10.0
	110,743,300	100.0	212,000,000	100.0

FIGURE 7
SCI Holdings—Six-Year Consolidated Operating Projection 1985–1990 (in thousands)

	Actual	*Projected*					
	1984	*1985*	*1986*	*1987*	*1988*	*1989*	*1990*
Net revenues	$536,324	$602,793	$661,796	$743,259	$823,190	$907,420	$999,625
Expenses, including depreciation	468,354	496,662	514,536	547,215	586,805	629,009	672,727
Operating income	67,970	106,131	147,260	196,044	236,385	278,411	326,898
Income (loss) before extraordinary items	(16,742)	1,459	78,600	73,760	113,507	145,418	179,937
Extraordinary items:							
Tax benefit of net operating loss carryforward	0	6,092	10,145	0	0	0	0
Net income (loss)	$ (16,742)	$ 7,551	$ 88,745	$ 83,760	$113,507	$145,418	$179,937

Source: Storer Proxy, p. 42.

In analyzing the data, we concluded that the operating numbers are achievable.

- Cash flow from cable will represent 80 percent of the 1990 money.
- We are optimistic with cable reflecting industry dynamics, and the maturity of Storer Systems.
- The franchised nature of the business and the discreet nature permits a series of "mini-exit" windows.

THE RATE OF RETURN—OUR NUMBERS—OUR METHODOLOGY

In Figure 8, we unfold our approach both as to arriving at a private market value for Storer in 1995 and a value for the warrant at that time.

In Figure 9, we walk you through our model regarding cash flow and its impact on debt. The driving force to calculating the 1990 and 1995 values of the merger warrants is estimating the private market value (PMV) of SCI Holdings, Inc., by those dates.

Assumptions underlying our projections are:

- Operating cash flow to 1990 is projected by management to increase 15 percent per annum, a projection with which we agree.
- Operating cash flow from 1990 to 1995 increases at 10 percent per annum.
- PMV valuation of 10X operating cash flow.
- Debt reduction as scheduled by SCI Holdings in proxy material and our data.

Figure 10 is our "workout matrix" of the merger warrants' value to 1995, given the above assumptions. In looking at the numbers, we point out that our projections do not include any "time value" premium which might build up in the warrants. In addition, they do not reflect an "earlier exit strategy" by KKR, which would likely enhance the return.

When looking at the numbers, they should be viewed not for their "accounting" precision, but rather as a springboard for reflection on various price/purchase points. For example, if one were to purchase a warrant for $3 in December 1985, the internal rate of return would be 21.8 percent to 1995. If one were to purchase the warrant at $4 per share, the rate of return would be 18.4 percent.

In sum, the combination of purchasing Storer warrants to achieve a 20 percent compounded rate of return, which on its own is attractive, coupled

FIGURE 8
Storer LBO Analysis—Merger Warrant Valuation, 1986 Estimated–1995 Projected

($million)	*1986E*	*1987P*	*1988P*	*1989P*	*1990P*	*1991P*	*1992P*	*1993P*	*1994P*	*1995P*
Operating cash flow	$ 262.0	$ 312.0	$ 356.0	$ 405.0	$ 458.0	$ 503.8	$ 544.2	$ 609.6	$ 670.6	$ 737.6*
Valuation multiple	10×	10×	10×	10×	10×	10×	10×	10×	10×	10×
Total	$2,620.0	$3,120.0	$3,560.0	$4,050.0	$4,580.0	$5,038.0	$5,542.0	$6,096.0	$6,706.0	$7,376.0
Less: (LTD + Preferred Stock)	(2,339.1)	(2,443.3)	(2,540.0)	(2,614.0)	(2,527.9)	(2,540.8)	(2,273.8)	(2,061.0)	(2,061.0)	(2,061.0)
Plus: Warrant exercise†	—	—	—	—	—	—	—	—	—	$ 265.0†
Estimated PMV	$ 280.9	$ 676.7	$1,020.0	$1,436.0	$2,052.1	$2,497.8	$3,268.2	$4,035.0	$4,645.0	$5,580.0
Shares o/s (million)	212.0	212.0	212.0	212.0	212.0	212.0	212.0	212.0	212.0	212.0
PMV per share	$1.30	$3.20	$4.80	$6.80	$9.70	$11.80	$15.40	$19.03	$21.91	$26.30
Less: Warrant exercise price	(4.72)	(4.72)	(4.72)	(4.72)	(4.72)	(4.72)	(4.72)	(4.72)	(4.72)	(4.72)
Est. warrant value	—	—	$0.10	$2.10	$5.00	$7.10	$10.70	$14.90	$19.40	$21.60

*Internal projections are about 5 percent lower.
†Includes merger warrants and warrants held by Drexel Burnham and Storer management group.

Source: Storer Communication, Inc., Proxy, October 23, 1985 and Gabelli & Company, Inc. estimates.

FIGURE 9
SCI Holdings, Inc.—LTD Schedule ($ million)

($ million)	*1985*	*1986*	*1987*	*1988*	*1989*	*1990*	*1991*	*1992*	*1993*	*1994*	*1995*
Bank debt	$ 740.0	$ 715.0	$ 615.0	$ 490.0	$ 365.0	$ 200.0	$ 120.0	$ 40.0	—	—	—
Zero notes	600.0	685.0	783.0	894.0	1,022.2	1,017.8	1,012.9	757.0	$ 465.0	$ 131.0	—
Senior subordinated debentures (at face falue)	600.0	600.0	600.0	600.0	600.0	600.0	600.0	600.0	600.0	600.0	$ 400.0
Storer 10% Subordinated debentures due 2003 (at face value)	138.0	138.0	138.0	138.0	138.0	138.0	138.0	138.0	127.7	117.3	107.0
Preferred stock	261.1	305.4	357.3	418.0	489.0	572.1	669.3	738.8	742.0	742.0	742.0
New financing required (balance)	—	—	—	—	—	—	—	—	126.3	470.7	812.0
Total LTD and preferred	$2,339.1	$2,443.4	$2,493.3	$2,540.0	$2,614.2	$2,527.9	$2,540.2	$2,273.8	$2,061.0	$2,061.0	$2,061.0

Source: Storer Communications, Inc., Proxy; 1984 Annual Report; Gabelli & Company, Inc., projections.

FIGURE 10
Storer Merger Warrants—Annualized Return on Investment to 1995 (1995 warrant value = $21.60)

Workout Matrix Warrant Price	*12/31/85*	*6/30/86*	*12/31/86*	*6/30/87*	*12/31/87*	*6/30/88*	*12/31/88*
$2.00	26.90%	28.50%	30.30%	32.30%	34.60%	37.30%	40.50%
2.50	24.10	25.50	27.10	28.90	30.90	33.30	36.10
3.00	21.80	23.10	24.50	26.10	28.00	30.10	32.60
3.50	20.00	21.10	22.40	23.90	25.50	27.50	29.70
4.00	18.40	19.40	20.60	21.90	23.50	25.20	27.20
5.00	15.80	16.70	17.70	18.80	20.10	21.50	23.20
6.00	13.70	14.40	15.30	16.30	17.40	18.60	20.10
7.00	11.90	12.60	13.30	14.20	15.10	16.20	17.50
8.00	10.40	11.00	11.70	12.40	13.20	14.20	15.20

Source: Gabelli & Company, Inc., calculations.

with an opportunity to participate in KKR's LBO make us recommend this highly speculative and somewhat unique financial instrument.

It's too early to tell whether our SCI Holdings warrants recommendation will bear fruit long term. As of this writing, the warrants are selling at 3½ bid, 3⅝ ask. My confidence in the idea is reflected in the fact that GAMCO clients still own all the warrants received from the Storer buyout. Our continuing faith in what we've nicknamed Son of Storer reflects our characteristic willingness to hold onto stocks as long as they remain private market value bargains. I am a postage stamp investor. I stick to stocks as long as I believe they can deliver profits.

Our "Rest in Peace" List

Three of the four examples I've presented have been broadcast and/or cable TV companies. Although these industries do lend themselves to private market value analysis, they are not the only industries in which we've owned and recommended stocks that have been retired from public life—some by LBO transactions. Figure 11, which shows a list of transition of major GAMCO client holdings, indicates that we've identified LBO candidates in a range of industries.

FIGURE 11
Transition of Major Holdings (1977-1984)

Investment	*Name of Company*	*Acquiring Concern*
Broadcasting & CATV	Combined Communications	Gannett
	Cowles Broadcasting	H & C Communications
	Cox Communications	*Private firm*
	Gross	Going private
	Kingstrip	Lin Broadcasting
	Metromedia	*Private firm*
	Outlet	Rockefeller Center
	Rust Craft	*Private firm*
	Sonderling Broadcasting	Viacom
	Starr Broadcasting	*Private group*
	Storer Communications	*Private firm*
	Teleprompter	Westinghouse
	Wometco	*Private firm*
	+ Various CATV & Newspapers	
Motion pictures	Columbia Pictures	Coca Cola
	Twentieth Century Fox	*Private firm*

FIGURE 11—Continued

Investment	*Name of Company*	*Acquiring Concern*
Service companies	Avis	Norton Simon
	Baqker Industries	Borg-Warner
	Brinks	Pittston
	Burns Int'l	Borg-Warner
	International Courier	Gelco
	Loomis	Mayne Nickless
	Pacific Holdings	*Private firm*
Other	ACF	Carl Icahn
	Cadence	*Private firm*
	Esquire	Gulf & Western
	Stokely-Van Camp	Quaker Oats
Auto parts: Distribution	APS	Gulf & Western
	Crtiss-Noll	Congoleum
	General Automotive	Genuine Parts
	Whitlock	LCP Holdings
Manufacturing	Altamil	*Private firm*
	American Mfg.	Allied
	Anderson Co.	Champion Spark Plug
	Bendix	Allied
	Budd Co.	Tyssen
	CR Industries	IFI
	Globe-Union	Johnson Controls
	Houdaille	*Private group*
	Maremont	Alsuisse
	McCord	Ex-cello
	Monroe Auto	Tenneco
	Moog	IFI
	Norris Industies	*Private group*
	Raybestos	Echlin
	STP	Esmark
	Texstar	Hillman
	Weatherhead	Dana
	Wix	Dana

In today's market, leveraged buyouts no longer seem to be limited in scope or size. Kohlberg Kravis Roberts & Co.'s $6.2 billion leveraged buyout of Beatrice, and subsequent $25 billion LBO of RJR Nabisco indicates there is virtually no company too big to be LBO'd provided it qualifies via the criteria I listed earlier. With the federal government and the Federal Reserve contemplating and enacting regulations regarding the financing of leveraged buyouts, one must concede that LBO activity is likely to slow. However, as long as the stock market undervalues public companies' assets and as long as capital remains free to seek its highest rate of return, leveraged buyout transactions will take place. Analysts who learn to spot the qualifiers will continue to be rewarded.

IDENTIFYING TAKEOVER CANDIDATES

The corporate takeover is the best known and most frequent method for private market values to be realized. We have owned many more stocks that have been taken over than have been LBO'd, but I prefer to analyze a company from the perspective of a leveraged buyout specialist rather than a potential corporate acquiror. LBOs are usually achieved at lower premiums to public market prices than takeovers because the value of the target's assets alone determines the economics of the deal. Corporate acquirors have additional resources such as stock and/or cash to finance a takeover. Since we don't always know who a prospective corporate acquiror may be, it is often difficult to factor in the impact of these resources on a company's private market value or likely takeover price. By using the more conservative PMV estimate derived from a leveraged buyout perspective, I feel more secure. The financial considerations such as cash, free cash flow, and salable assets are similar for LBOs and takeovers. So, if you buy a stock on the basis of its value to a leveraged buyout specialist, the higher premium you receive from a takeover is pure gravy.

Having said this, I will mention that in the analysis of takeovers, an investor does benefit from several sources of information frequently not present in a prospective LBO situation. The most obvious is the ability to monitor significant corporate purchases of the stock. I receive a service that alerts me to all 13d filings. A 13d is required by the SEC whenever any investor purchases more than 5 percent of a publicly owned company. An amendment must be filed any time there is a material change in this position, which is defined as a change exceeding 1 percent.

When I come upon an intriguing 13d filing, I try to answer numerous questions. Why is one corporation investing in the stock of another? Will the businesses complement each other? Might the acquiror be looking for entry into a business which is cheaper to buy than to build? Does it need a cash cow to support its other businesses? The next step is to determine how difficult and expensive an acquisition would be. How much stock does the management of the target company own? Is management in the mood to "make love" or will it respond to an offer by putting up the obstacles to a takeover bid? Can the prospective acquiror afford to pay a fair price for the target company? If adding substantial debt is necessary to make an acquisition, what will the capital costs be? Are there any potential regulatory problems? Finally, how is the 13d filer accumulating the stock? Is it being purchased patiently and consistently on the bid side of the market or aggressively in large blocks on the offering side? If I can come up with logical answers to these questions and if the target company qualifies as a true private market value by our standards, I may buy a stock as a pure takeover play.

In industries which are already experiencing increased merger and acquisition activity, the analyst benefits from prevailing takeover formulas such as multiples of revenues, earnings, or cash flow. You should be aware, however, that these formulas are not static. They will vary with supply and demand as is the case with what I refer to as a buffalo group like the cable TV and group broadcasters in the last several years. For example, when Taft Broadcasting acquired Gulf Broadcast in one of the first shots fired in the group broadcaster takeover wars, it paid approximately 12 times calendar 1985 cash flow. In some of the ensuing deals for Cox Communications' broadcast properties, hungry acquirors bid the multiple to cash flow price up to 15.

Economic forces may also affect prevailing merger and acquisition formulas. For example, today the multiple to cash flow equation for broadcast acquisitions may be coming down due to weakening of the broadcast advertising market. We own Taft Broadcasting because it is selling at a deep discount to our private market value estimate of $137 per share. As the PMV model in Figure 12 indicates, we are valuing Taft's TV stations, most of which are in the top 40 growth markets, at just 10 times cash flow even though there is some takeover flavor (via San Francisco Partners, Robert Bass of the infamous Bass Brothers owns 11 percent of Taft stock), and recent takeovers in the industry have been at higher multiples to cash flow.

The Crayon Explosion

Another thing to consider in analyzing takeover candidates is that what didn't happen yesterday may still happen tomorrow. Consider our experience with Binney & Smith. As the following report indicates, we viewed Binney & Smith as a demographic play with some takeover flavor.

Demographic Play No. 1 — Update No. 4

Binney & Smith, Inc.—(BYS-24-NYSE)—AGGRESSIVE BUY

Year	*EPS*	*P/E*		*Current*
1982P	$3.10	7.7	Dividend	Return: 4.3%
1981E	$2.40	10.0	3,532,000 shares	
1980	$1.68	14.3	Range (1980–1981):	29-19

FIGURE 12
Private Market Value Model

	Prepared March 1984		*Updated August 1985*	
	Fiscal 1984	*PMV*	*Fiscal 1986*	
Broadcasting:				
TV station at 10 × Cash flow	$613(*)		$770	
Radio station at 8 × Cash flow	72		96	
	$685		$866	
5 TV stations	–0–		750	
Total TV		$685		$1,616
Taft Entertainment Co.:				
Hanna Barbera				
Cy Fisher				
World Vision				
Miscellaneous	$125–$150		$150–200	
Miscellaneous assets:				
Equity in Kings Ent. Co. (⅓ ownership)	$ 10		$ 15	
Equity in CATV with T COMA	20		40	
Philadephia Phillies at cost	15		15	
R. E. in King Island	20		20	
Golf Course				
Kings Diner				
Winter Wonderland (Toronto, Can.)	50		70	
Other	20		20	
		$135		$ 180
		970		1,946
Less: Debt		45		700
By 9.1 shares o/s		$925		$1,246
PMV per share	$100(†)		$137	

*TV station now (10 × CF before); Radio now at 8 (6 × CF before).
Comments:†Based on 9.2 shares outstanding.
Prepared by: Mario J. Gabelli, 8/27/85.

The Company

Binney & Smith, a small but highly profitable company with estimated revenues of $118 million in 1981, is best known for its Crayola brand of crayons, a market which it dominates. In our last published report (Abstract—November 29, 1979—For Sale), we indicated that "accounts that were willing to speculate on a change in management's position toward making love" should retain positions. All others should sell. We now recommend aggressive purchase. To review the fundamentals on which we base our recommendations:

Demographics

- We have written reports about the trends in live births in previous reports and recent developments continue to unfold favorably for the company.
- Again, our case is that there will be a 2 percent per annum gain in children in the three-to-nine-year-old age bracket in the early 1980s versus a decline for most of the past 15 years. (Incidentally, from our own observations in the Gabelli household, we have concluded that children consume—not use—crayons at an age earlier than three, and that parents are a prime market for the "survival" kits that Binney is now marketing.)

Management Change

- Jack K. Kofoed (age 54) assumed the role of chief executive officer on January 1, 1981. While he is not new to the company, events since he has assumed the helm have pointed to a more aggressive pursuit of both revenues growth and profit improvement:

  Price increases have been accelerated.
  Low growth product lines are being weeded out.
  Crayola brand awareness is being capitalized on.
  Crayola markers are finally profitable.
  Marketing channels are being broadened.
  New product development is accelerating.

Earnings Breakout

- Refer to Figure 13.
- Revenues and earnings appear to be in a breakout phase which we believe is sustainable.
- For 1981 we are projecting revenues of $118 million, up 25 percent over the $94 million reported for 1980 and earnings of $2.40 to $2.50 per share, up nearly 50 percent from the depressed $1.68 per share earned in 1980.
- Beyond this year, we project revenues growth in excess of 14 percent from internal sources. Figure 13 depicts our growth model for revenues through 1985. Reflecting better operating efficiency, declining financial costs, and lower tax rates, earnings gains should approach

FIGURE 13
Binney & Smith Inc.—Sales by Product, 1974–1983P

Area of Activity	*1974*	*1975*	*1976*	*1977*	*1978*	*1979*	*1980*	*1981P*	*1982P*	*1983P*	*Percent of Total 1981P*	*Expected Growth 1981–1985P*	*Total Expected Growth 1981–1985P*
Artists' materials:													
Crayons and chalks	$27.1	$30.8	$33.5	$35.4	$38.3	$40.1	$47.0	$ 59.0	$ 67.0	$ 77.0	50.0%	13.0%	6.5%
Paints, brushes, and other	20.0	21.0	21.5	23.3	27.0	26.8	31.0	36.0	40.0	47.0	30.5	12.0	3.6
Activities	3.0	3.4	4.8	8.0	9.8	11.0	16.0	23.0	30.0	36.0	19.5	20.0	3.9
Other:													
Total revenues	$50.1	$56.0	$59.8	$66.7	$75 0	$78.7	$94.0	$118.0	$137.0	$160.0	100.0%		14%
Percent change	12.5%	11.9%	6.7%	11.5%	12 4%	4.9%	19.4%	26.7%	16.1%	16.8%			

Source: Gabelli & Company, Inc., estimates.

20 percent per annum. However, we note that earnings will remain seasonal and quarterly results somewhat erratic on a year-to-year basis.

Financial Position is Excellent:

- Long-term debt of $10.5 million represented only 16 percent of total capitalization at September 30, 1981.
- Book value is estimated at $15.50 per share at December 31, 1981.
- Future growth financed internally.

Sell-out Always Possible:

- In this regard, a little history might prove helpful. It was on September 7, 1979, that the Kellogg Company offered to acquire B&S for $36 per share for 45 percent of the stock and 1.75 shares of Kellogg for the balance. While the board of directors rejected that offer, perhaps the board is reexamining its fiduciary duty to provide public (i.e., nonfamily) shareholders the option of accepting a premium bid. At the time Kellogg's offer was made, we observed that it was at 3 times book value and 18 times our earnings estimate.
- New lower long-term capital gains tax rate, high (versus inflation) reinvestment rates, and new estate tax laws might combine to spark renewed merger fever from major family holders who own 1,284,542 shares of common stock, or 36.9 percent of the total. (In addition, another 10 percent is closely held.) Externally, interest in the company could be whetted again by declining cost of capital and perceived brighter dynamics.

The fact that no one appeared willing to follow up on Kellogg's original takeover bid eliminated Binney & Smith as a takeover candidate in the minds of most investors. We stuck with the stock because it continued to qualify as a decent private market value discount, earnings prospects were favorable, and there was a hunger developing in consumer nondurable industries for brand names. Our patience paid off when Binney & Smith was acquired by Hallmark for $56 per share in August 1984.

The Thunderbolt Stock Story

Occasionally, we've been taken out of portfolio companies that we couldn't honestly qualify as well-documented takeover candidates. I always have a list and, in some cases, positions in what I call thunderbolt stocks. These are undermanaged companies that have failed to properly utilize assets to create good operating results, and thus sell at significant discounts to PMV. There are no catalysts present to give me any great faith that private market value is likely to surface in the foreseeable future. The hope is that someone or something will appear like a thunderbolt and either turn these companies around or take them over.

Transway International Corp. was one thunderbolt stock that did get hit by lightning. The following comments made in a June 1984 Stock Market Innovators interview illustrated by thoughts on Transway.

INNOVATORS:

Anything interesting at the moment?

GABELLI:

I've always got some stocks. Let me give you situations that I didn't develop in my recent *Barrons* interview. The first is Transway Int'l (NYSE, TNW). At $30 7/8 a share, Transway is currently selling at about its accounting book value. Private market value is much higher. For your $30 7/8 you get Great Dane, the largest manufacturer of refrigerated trailers in the U.S. Good market niche, efficient manufacturer . . . Great Dane was the only player in the game which remained profitable at the bottom of the last business cycle. I see a few good years ahead. Cash flow should be $45 million next year. I think this business alone is worth the full price of Transway stock.

On top of Great Dane, you get a propane distribution business which should produce a cash flow of $10 to 15 million next year. I figure this is worth another $16 per share. Add $5 per share of cash, and you get a private market value somewhere in the $50 per share range. This isn't even counting Transway's other two divisions, a transportation company and a freight forwarding business. You could liquidate these businesses and wipe out all of Transway's $68 million debt.

So far no catalyst has surfaced. However, I would mention that management owns very little stock and doesn't appear to be the kind of folks who would stand in the way of their shareholders making some money. I'm buying the stock right now.

Transway was acquired by International Controls for cash and stock valued at $48.15 per share in December 1985.

IDENTIFYING LIQUIDATION CANDIDATES

The most straightforward way for private market values to be realized is through a pure liquidation of a public company. Since a liquidation involves disposing of assets usually in the private market, our brand of analysis lends itself to identifying liquidation candidates. In fact, Gabelli & Company's first official asset play, Cowles Communications, also became the first stock we recommended and owned that was liquidated. The following Gabelli & Company research report tells the story.

Gabelli & Company, Inc. **April 15, 1977**
Asset Play No. 1
Cowles Communications, Inc.
Current Price: 14
(CWL-NYSE)
We recommend Cowles on the basis of:

- *Dividends.* The present $0.16 per share quarterly rate is likely to jump to $0.20 per share during the second half of this year. We envisage annual dividends growth of 10 percent beyond.
- *Assets.* The stock is selling at over a 30 percent discount from the $20 per share valuation we place on the company's assets.

	Private Market Value per Share
Cash at year-end	$ 1.30
Two TV stations (our estimate)	7.50
Ownership of 23% of *The New York Times* ($17-ASE)	11.20
	$20.00

- No long-term debt on the balance sheet at year-end.

We believe that Cowles's assets are of above-average interest. First, the company's two TV stations are in rapidly growing markets, are handily capable of enjoying revenues growth of 8 to 10 percent and pretax profits growth of 12 percent, and generate what we describe as "free and clear" cash flow, which is "domestic" in nature. Second, while we don't hold ourselves out as experts on *The New York Times*, our examination of the just released 1976 annual report points to an improving financial posture there. This could lead to higher dividends, and just as important, "inflation indexed" growth in asset value for *The Times*.

The question arises, "What will Cowles do with itself?" To understand all the alternatives we must first discuss what we perceive to be the main obstacle to some form of "surfacing" of the assets. This involves continued legal jousting over the license renewal of Cowles' Florida TV station. Almost seven years ago, a challenge against WESH-TV was initiated by a group seeking the license. The issue centered on whether the station's studio was out of the "city of license." The FCC, in a 4–1 decision, voted to renew the license on January 5, 1977. However, the challenger applicant has filed an appeal with the U.S. Court of Appeals. We doubt any actions regarding the disposition of corporate assets will be pursued until this issue is resolved. Based on our observation of somewhat similar proceedings (e.g., *Carter v. Maxwell*), we conclude it is reasonable to expect resolution of this within the next 12 months.

The Company

We do not wish to repeat history here. Let it suffice to say that since October 1971, Cowles has operated as a closed-end, nondiversified management investment company. From 1971 to the present, the company has been pruning its corporate base to where it presently has only two assets: two television stations and the stock position in *The New York Times*.

The TV Stations

In Figure 14 we depict financial highlights of the two markets. Note the growth rate versus the national average.

FIGURE 14
Market Growth—Five-Year Compound Growth 1969–1974, Spot Advertising

	*Ranking—1975**	
Market	*By Revenues*	*By Profit*
Orlando-Daytona, Florida	47	45
Des Moines-Ames, Iowa	66	67

	National	*Local*	*Total*
Orlando-Daytona	9.3%	8.2%	8.9%
Des Moines-Ames, Iowa	14.8	18.2	16.5
Industry total—U.S.	3.6	13.6	7.1

*Latest available data.

Source: FCC

FIGURE 15
TV Operating Performance ($ million)

	1974	*1975*	*1976*	*1977E*	*1980E*
Revenues	7.7	8.5	10.8	12.3	16.5
Operating profit	1.1	1.8	2.6	3.4	5.0
Station value ($ million):					
At 8 × Operating profit	$ 8.8	$14.4	$20.8	$27.2	$40.0
At 10 × Operating profit	11.0	18.0	26.0	34.0	50.0

In 1975 Orlando enjoyed a 14.4 percent growth in National Spot, while Des Moines was up 18.2 percent—both above the national average. While FCC data is not available, we expect 1976 results were good.

In Figure 15 we depict the stations' recent operating performance and our projections. We also depict our approach at arriving at approximate market values for the properties.

Precise split-up of revenues for each of the Cowles properties is not available, but we suspect that WESH-TV generates significantly more profits than does KCCI-TV for Cowles.

Since Cowles changes all management's salaries against its operating properties (such costs were $507,218 in 1976), the use of the industry's historical rule of thumb of valuing a station (8 to 10 times operating profits) appears to provide conservative values for the two stations. Also, we observe that the expected prices paid for TV stations are likely to climb in light of Combined Communications' recent proposed purchase of WMAL-TV in Washington, D.C.

The License Challenge

The renewal application of Cowles Florida Broadcasting, Inc., for the license to operate WESH-TV is still being contested. On December 7, 1973, Federal Communications Commission Administrative Judge Chester F. Naumowicz, Jr., released an initial decision in which he granted renewal of the license. This decision was appealed to the FCC and oral arguments were heard in November 1974.

Regarding KCCI-TV, the FCC released a memorandum opinion and order granting the motion of the company to dismiss the petition to deny the renewal of the license on January 26, 1976, filed by the U.S. Department of Justice. The FCC unanimously granted the renewal application for KCCI-TV subject to whatever action the FCC may deem appropriate as a result of the matters pending involving the renewal application of WESH-TV. The FCC found on review of the application of KCCI-TV that the company is legally, technically, financially, and otherwise qualified to remain an FCC licensee. The most recent license renewal application for KCCI-TV for a three-year period beginning February 1, 1977, and ending January 31, 1980, was granted by the commission on January 20, 1977.

On July 2, 1976, the FCC announced a decision granting the renewal of the license application of Cowles Broadcasting, Inc., the licensee of WESH-TV. Three of the seven commissioners dissented from the decision by the majority of the commission granting the renewal. *However, after reconsideration, on January 5, 1977, the commission clarified its earlier decision and after such clarification the final vote of the commission was 4–1 in favor of renewal.*

The challenger-applicant, which had applied for a construction permit to operate WESH-TV, has filed an appeal with the U.S. Court of Appeals for the District of Columbia and proceedings attendant to this matter may continue for an indefinite period.

If we were to assume an end to the legal imbroglio over the licenses, then we would speculate that Cowles could:

- Buy more TV stations.
- Spin-off the extant stations to its shareholders.
- Sell the stations and pay a tax on the profit.
- Keep the stations in Cowles and sell off or spin-off the other assets to its shareholders.
- Sell off the entire company or merge into *The New York Times*.

We believe that the last option is the most probable alternative. If we were to speculate that the license challenge were terminated, which might take one year, and that a merger would be pursued, we have calculated that *The New York Times* could pay $25 per share in cash for Cowles, finance the $100 million purchase at 10 percent, and enjoy an enlargement of its earnings base.

Other Comments

Finally, we observe that earnings for the first quarter of 1977 from the TV stations may be flat from year to year. This is traceable to strong political advertising in first quarter of 1976 in Florida, which is absent this year.

The New York Times (ASE-NYT.A-$17)

Market Value. Cowles owns 2.6 million shares of *The New York Times* Class A stock, or 23 percent. Thus, for each share of Cowles owned, an investor indirectly obtains approximately .66 shares of *The New York Times*.

Market Value

If Price of N.Y. Times	*Then Value/Share of CWL*
$14	$ 9.25
16	10.85
18	11.85
20	13.20
22	14.50

Dividends. *The New York Times* pays a $0.60 per share dividend. Under present tax law 85 percent of dividends received by one corporation from another corporation are excludable from taxable income. Thus, Cowles only pays a 7.2 percent tax on such dividends received from *The Times*. Assume that:

If annual dividends—N.Y.T	$0.60	$0.80	$1.00
Total cash received on 2.6 million shares	$1,560,000	$2,080,000	$2,600,000
Less taxes at 7.2%	112,000	150,000	187,000
Net available cash	$1,448,000	$1,930,000	$2,413,000
Available/CWL share	$0.37	$0.49	$0.60

Thus, if *The Times* were to increase its dividend rate, as some have speculated, we would expect Cowles to pass through this dividend increase to its shareholders, particularly as it has no debt, extra cash, and a large untapped "borrowing power."

In Sum

We believe that Cowles represents a sound investment on the basis of rising dividends and a sizable discount from replacement cost of its assets. If we were to assume no change in price in *The New York Times* from the current \$17.00 per share price, an end to the legal hassle at WESH-TV, a liquidation of the company, the return to Cowles' shareholders over the next three years could be derived as follows:

	1977	*1978*	*1979*	*Total*
Expected dividends	\$0.72	\$0.82	\$0.96	\$ 2.50
Expected value of assets				22.00
				\$24.50

If CWL Bought at	*Annual Return Would Be*
\$12	35%
13	29
14	25
15	21
16	17

Cowles Communications took much longer to work out than we first anticipated. We owned and continued to recommend Cowles Communications through December 16, 1982, at which time it was formally liquidated. In mid-January 1983, Cowles shareholders received \$2.25 in cash, two thirds of a share of *The New York Times* stock, which after a 3-for-1 split effectively became two shares, and one share of a new company, Cowles Broadcasting which traded initially at 16. Add it all up and it was a \$64 value for a stock we first bought at about \$14 per share, or about 4½ times our original investment over 5¾ years. We are satisfied with that rate of return.

REALIZING PRIVATE MARKET VALUES THROUGH CORPORATE RESTRUCTURING

A prevailing misconception about asset value investing is that you only make money when the stocks are taken over, LBO'd, or liquidated. This is hardly the case. There are numerous examples of private market value discounts we have owned and recommended that have survived and prospered because assets have been redeployed to produce greater profitability or to fund restructuring and/or substantial share repurchases. The moral of the story is that undervalued assets can be and often are used to benefit shareholders.

Our experience with GenCorp, the former General Tire, is a good example. Our firm has been following GenCorp for quite a while. It was managed, or I should say undermanaged, by the founding O'Neil family for as long as we've known it. GenCorp had been in decent businesses, but was never able to produce profits comparable to the quality competition, or in some cases even the industry average. The company was characterized by a lot of excess fat in its operating divisions, participation in many marginal businesses, and family management too stubborn or lethargic to change anything. We had never owned GenCorp stock, but it had long been on my thunderbolt list. I became an active buyer last year when a catalyst emerged in the form of new CEO Bill Reynolds. I was familiar with Mr. Reynolds from his management role at TRW and felt he was a guy who could change GenCorp's destiny and surface its \$110 to \$120 private market value. The change in the FCC Rule of 7 which allowed broadcast companies to own more than seven TV stations was another catalyst. GenCorp's RKO division owned TV stations in New York and L.A., two flagship markets. The stations had miserable operating records, but were worth a great deal of money to any group broadcaster looking for an entry into these heretofore closed markets.

I began accumulating GenCorp stock in the mid-30s per share in the fall of 1984. Mr. Reynolds did not disappoint. He dumped Frontier Airlines, a consistent money loser; closed the Akron, Ohio, tire plant; and eliminated half the capacity of the big Waco, Texas, plant. He also put the L.A. and New York television stations up for bid. Both are in the process of being sold for a combined total of almost \$600 million, part of which we believe will be used for a major share repurchase program. In the process of Reynolds's restructuring, GenCorp stock has climbed to the mid-70s as I write.

In an October 14, 1984 interview in *Barron's*, I portrayed GenCorp as a likely takeover or leveraged buyout candidate.[1] With the stock now in the mid-70s versus 47 at the time of this interview, the prospects for an exogenous event have narrowed along with the spread between stock price and private market value. I now view a major share repurchase program and rapidly rising earnings as the primary factors that will push GenCorp stock significantly higher. Am I disappointed it wasn't taken over or LBO'd? No, we've already doubled our money from our initial investment in GenCorp and expect to make even more money in the future on the basis of the cap shrink and continuing redeployment of assets.

---

[1] Reprinted here by courtesy of *Barron's National Business and Financial Weekly*

Q: . . . . What else do you like, Mario?

A: The other great value that should not be ignored is General Tire, now known as GenCorp. GenCorp is an outstanding takeover play. If I were going to spot one for you and be a bird dog on it, and one that I want to hammer away on because of its broadcast assets, I would pick on GenCorp. I think the investors should own GenCorp.

Q: Why should they own GenCorp?

A: There are 23 million shares of stock. We think that their non-RKO assets—that is, their tire business, their aerojet business, and their industrial products business, minus all the liabilities, plus some minor other assets—is worth about $45 a share. Then, the investor picks up through RKO, which is 100 percent owned by GenCorp, a bottling business—Pepsi Cola Bottling—which is worth about $13 to $14 a share.

Q: You got hit by lightning on that offer for Frontier, which Gencorp owns a piece of.

A: No, no. We were always of the opinion that the company would sell out their investment in Frontier. It took longer than we thought, true. They had a great problem getting $17 to $20, and now apparently—whatever the reasons—they are going to get $24 a share. So it is an extra $5 times 5 million shares—it is $25 million. That is only $1 per share incrementally of GenCorp—that extra $5. But what it does is all of a sudden it tells the world: "My God, look they are getting $125 million in cash." And that buys a lot of chopped liver.

Q: And the rye bread to put it on.

A: They have got three or four other cash assets that are worth another $25. In addition to that, the company has a television license in New York—WOR—and in L.A.—KHJ—and one in Memphis, and some other radio stations. They are No. 1 in the radio market in New York. And I think those broadcast properties are worth another $40 a share. So an investor today is getting New York and L.A. for nothing. The O'Neils have moved on. They are retiring. They have professional management. Bill Reynolds has moved in, and he is doing a marvelous job.

Q: Is that hassle with the government over?

A: No. But it is not with the government these days. A bunch of people in L.A. decided that the company did a no-no back about 10 years ago, and they pooled their resources, and challenged the license. I believe that this company committed major violations of the rules and their character was impugned; however, I believe the shareholders suffered a penalty—the loss of their license in Boston. I think they took their punishment for the violations. I think that any standards of fair play for the shareholders will indicate that, yes, there were problems, and yes, they got caught and were guilty, and yes, they took a penalty. And I believe that when this comes under examination again by the full Federal Communications Commission that the shareholders will not lose more value. The stock is worth $110 to $120 a share.

Q: You're talking about it as an asset play.
A: Well, that is all that counts. But earnings are going to improve dramatically. You have terrific management. Book value on a historical basis is nothing but accounting. And that is not an important number. But I am mentioning it: It is close to $50. They are going to earn $5 for the year ending Nov. 30.
Q: So the only thing that is hanging over the company is this dispute.
A: No, there are lots of little glitches in every story. But I think that those glitches should not be focused on. The entire forest of the company, the value, the virtues of the company, should be focused on. And I think that at $47, GenCorp offers outstanding value for the patient investor, and particularly in this environment. You have a management change. The O'Neils are all retiring. The company is improving internally, dramatically. I think the shareholders of GenCorp who have been frustrated for a long time, are now going to enjoy a major upside opportunity.
Q: But just what, Mario, if we dare ask, will make the stock go higher?
A: It could happen one of several ways. They could buy back their own shares, which they should. They could do a leveraged buyout. They could be taken over in a hostile way. I mean, why shouldn't Carl Icahn, after doing Uniroyal, focus on this one, because he understands the tire business now.

EXPERT ANALYSIS

I've provided numerous examples of our private market value analysis, including free cash flow value models, and reflections on many of the conceptual considerations we employ in our asset-oriented stock picking process. I haven't yet mentioned the role that outside experts play in our evaluation methodology. I'm not referring to investment experts, but to the true experts in any business—the brilliant people working in the industries we follow. I would be remiss if I didn't credit these experts with some of our success. Through my years in the investment business, I've become an expert at knowing the real experts in a variety of industries. Today, I can call up a half dozen of the people I know in a particular industry, list the assets of a competitor, and ask what they would pay for them in a sealed bid, winner-take-all auction. I usually get some interesting answers and novel perspectives that help me accurately evaluate an investment candidate's private market value. Analysts shouldn't be shy about consulting with industry professionals who often have a better feel for what's happening within their industry than do the people on Wall Street.

PART 3

LEGAL AND ACCOUNTING ASPECTS

CHAPTER 17

MERGER AND ACQUISITION LAW

Arthur M. Borden
Barbara Goodstein
Rosenman & Colin

In general, there are three alternative means of acquiring ownership of the entire business of another company: (1) acquisition of stock, (2) acquisition of assets, or (3) merger between the acquiring company and the company being acquired. In determining which structure is used, tax consequences, state procedural and fairness requirements, federal securities law disclosure rules, stock exchange restrictions, and potential liabilities of the acquired business, among other items, must all be considered.

In addition, other factors relating to the characteristics of the parties involved, such as whether the parties are friendly or unfriendly, and whether the acquired business is widely or closely held, often dictate the choice of transactional structure. Since takeover defenses, strategies and techniques in the context of an unfriendly acquisition are treated at length elsewhere (see Chapters 21–26), this chapter will deal with acquisitions generally in the context of a friendly transaction.

OBJECTIVES OF LEGAL STRUCTURE

In determining the appropriate legal structure for a transaction, five important objectives must be kept in mind.

Conformity to Intent

The first is to ensure that the business being acquired conforms to what the purchaser thought it was acquiring when it negotiated the price.

Legal Title

The second is to ensure that the purchaser receives good legal title to what it is buying.

Liability Protection

Third, the purchaser must protect itself against unknown or contingent liabilities in the acquired business and may wish to limit to some extent the assumption of known liabilities.

Efficiency

Fourth, the transaction should be consummated efficiently and expediently, and at minimal cost to both sides.

Tax Considerations

The fifth objective is to accomplish the transaction with minimal tax liability to all parties, especially, of course, to your client. (Tax considerations are dealt with in Chapters 27–28.)

OTHER LEGAL CONSIDERATIONS

The items to consider in a business acquisition obviously do not end with determination of the legal structure. Significant business and legal issues often emerge during the course of negotiations between the parties as they engage in discussions over the extensive representations and warranties in regard to, among other things, the financial condition, operating results, and contractual and other obligations of the business being sold usually contained in the initial drafts of the acquisition agreement.

In addition, during such period of negotiations the acquiring corporation will normally conduct a due diligence investigation of the business to be acquired, including review by its accountants of the books and records of the business, examination by its attorneys of the material contracts of the business, on-site inspections of the assets of the business and interviews with key employees (see Chapter 10 and Volume II, Chapter 34). Often, items discovered in such a due diligence review will become a major issue at the negotiating table; thus, it is important to complete a due diligence investigation prior to execution of a definitive acquisition agreement.

STOCK ACQUISITION VERSUS ASSET ACQUISITION

As noted above, the three primary means of acquiring a company are acquisition of stock, acquisition of assets, and merger.[1] An acquisition of stock differs in several significant respects from an assets acquisition or merger. In a stock purchase, the acquiring corporation does not directly acquire the business being transferred; rather, it acquires ownership of the corporation that owns the business being transferred. As a result, there is no effect, by virtue of the transaction itself, on the target corporation's assets, rights, liabilities and obligations, other than the accounting changes required as a result of the acquisition.[2] The owners of the target corporation have simply sold their ownership interest in the target corporation for whatever consideration they individually or as a group could negotiate.

Conveyance and Assignability

A stock sale, therefore, leaves the corporate structure intact, thus averting many of the conveyance and assignability problems associated with transferring property. On the other hand, in an asset sale, the conveyance of all

---

[1]Two other forms of transactions available in certain jurisdictions are *consolidations* and *share exchanges*, although these formats are used so infrequently in general corporate practice as not to warrant detailed treatment here. Briefly, a *consolidation* is a transaction in which the "resulting corporation" is a new entity within which all of the constituent corporations are consolidated. It is distinguishable from its nearest relative, a merger, in that the corporation which "results" from a merger is one of the constituent corporations and is therefore often referred to as the "surviving corporation." In a *share exchange*, a corporation, by approval of its Board of Directors and shareholders and the Board of Directors and shareholders of the target corporation, may acquire all of the stock of a target corporation. The share exchange permits an acquisition of stock by the same procedure as required in a merger except that, as opposed to a merger, the corporation being acquired does not cease existing but rather becomes a subsidiary of the acquiring corporation.

[2]Under prevailing accounting principles, every business combination must be accounted for as either a "purchase" or a "pooling" of interests. Discussion of the rather complex rules dealing with this subject is set forth in Chapter 28.

assets being sold must be documented. In the case of intangible rights, such as copyrights and trademarks, assignments can often be time-consuming and expensive. In many instances, assets, such as contract rights (leases are a common example), may not be assignable without the consent of the other contractual party. While certain nonassignability provisions sometimes specifically preclude a sale of stock without such consent, more often than not these provisions will be triggered by the sale of assets but not the sale of the stock of a company.

Liability Issues in Stock Sales

Generally, the view is that a purchaser of stock (as opposed to assets) of a corporation is subject to all undisclosed liabilities of the business being acquired. Upon closer examination, however, this distinction becomes less apparent. A stock purchase, at least in the context of a friendly acquisition, clearly has means for allowing the parties to shift the risk of loss for undisclosed liabilities. In addition, as discussed below, statutory and decisional law creating "successor liability" for certain purchasers who acquire the assets of a business has further blurred this traditional difference between asset and stock purchases.

Typically, in an assets sale, the parties determine through assumption of liability provisions in the contract which liabilities are passed on to the purchaser and which are retained by the seller. In the case of a stock sale of a closely-held company, or even in the acquisition of a public company where the purchaser, through negotiation, may acquire blocks of stock privately, indemnification provisions in the contract enable the parties to shift the risk of paying for an undisclosed liability from the purchaser to the seller. The real risk of a stock purchaser with regard to unknown liabilities is that from the creditor's standpoint the acquired corporation will continue to bear these liabilities at least in the first instance. At that point, the purchaser must seek reimbursement from a seller, who may be unable (or unwilling) to pay him. Although an escrow arrangement may adequately shield a purchaser from this risk, an escrow may or may not be a feasible solution in the context of a particular transaction.

Advantages of a Stock Sale

On the other hand, the stock sale presents several advantages. State regulatory restrictions are generally fewer than with an assets sale or merger, thus furthering the objectives of expediency and minimal cost. Other practical considerations in choosing a stock purchase as the form of transaction are the number of stockholders (in the case of a public company, a tender offer, with its concomitant expenses, may be required; on the other hand, tender offers avoid recalcitrant management and an often long and hard negotiation process, even with friendly management); the selling stockholders' willingness, in the case of a closely-held corporation, to sign the stock purchase agreement (in many businesses, for example, there have been stockholders inactive in management who will be reluctant to provide representations and warranties in regard to the business being sold or to share liability in the event of a breach); and the ability of the purchaser to acquire 100 percent of the stock (needless to say, a minority stockholder who refuses to sell can be a continual source of antagonism in the future operation of an acquired business), although it may be possible to avoid this problem when the acquisition is by share exchange.

Advantages of an Asset Sale

In certain situations, an assets acquisition may be the only viable way of consummating the purchase of the business of a target corporation. Often a purchaser may seek to acquire a division of a corporation or only specified assets of the seller. An assets acquisition may be the recommended format when the acquiring corporation is not assuming any liabilities of the business being acquired. Asset sales are advantageous to the extent that they can be molded by the parties in a manner that reflects their underlying needs.

Liability Issues in Asset Sales

As noted above, generally an assets purchaser does not acquire the liabilities of the selling corporation, although the transaction may be structured through negotiation to transfer those liabilities to the purchaser. Usually, a purchaser will be willing to assume balance sheet liabilities, subsequent liabilities that occur in the ordinary course of business, and obligations under specified contracts. The seller is left with the unassumed liabilities. Nevertheless, liabilities have been imposed upon an assets purchaser for liabilities of the seller in certain circumstances.

The first exception is when the bulk transfer provisions of the Uniform Commercial Code apply (these provisions require notice to creditors of the seller in certain assets sales) and these provisions have not been complied with. Creditors of the seller may in that situation have recourse to the purchaser with respect to transferred assets.

Second, if the sale was not for bona fide and adequate consideration, a creditor may be able to attach the assets as fraudulently conveyed.

Finally, in areas where statutes or case law have indicated a strong public policy against certain conduct, such as in product liability cases and governmental proceedings involving release of hazardous waste materials, many courts or other tribunals have held a purchaser liable for claims against the seller where the purchaser acquired the line of business of the seller, continued substantially the same business as the seller, and the seller discontinued operations. Several courts which have recently considered product liability claims have adopted either a "continuity of product line" or a "continuity of enterprise" exception to the general rule of nonliability of a successor corporation for liabilities of a predecessor. Under the product line theory, the courts have looked to whether the products or product line that result from the use of the acquired assets are substantially identical to those produced by the acquired assets prior to the transaction. To test for the existence of continuity of enterprise, the courts have looked for a continuation of management, personnel, physical location, assets, and general business operations.

Problems of Asset Sales

Assets sales, on the other hand, present difficulties when there are numerous items of personal or real property to convey—since these conveyances must be documented—and when there are restrictions on the assignability of these items. In addition, in many jurisdictions a sales tax on items such as real estate, fixtures, and furniture is payable in an asset acquisition but not in a merger or stock sale. In certain instances this tax can significantly affect the price of a transaction. Finally, where substantially all of the assets of the seller are being acquired, the seller's stockholders must approve the transaction under state law, thus increasing the cost of the transaction, as compared to a stock sale where no such approval is required.

MERGERS

A merger is a transaction created entirely by state law. By definition, a merger is a combination of two or more corporations in which one of the constituent corporations survives and the other corporation's existence, as a matter of state law, is terminated. The effect of a merger is that the surviving corporation is automatically vested with title to the assets, tangible or intangible, and is subject to all of the liabilities of the acquired company—in other words, the same result as would occur with a stock purchase. Unlike a stock purchase (other than by share exchange), however, the Boards of Directors for both the acquired and acquiring corporations must approve the transaction and, in certain instances, the stockholders of both corporations must approve the transaction as well.

Advantages of Mergers

A distinct advantage to a merger is that it avoids the necessity for getting consent to the transaction from holders of all of the outstanding shares. Once the Board of Directors of the target company, in the due exercise of its business judgment, recommends to the stockholders that a merger be approved, and the requisite percentage (usually, but not always, 66 2/3 percent) of stockholders approve the transaction, even though the remaining one-third may object, the merger will be consummated. In most states, the sole recourse of an objecting stockholder will be to seek the fair value of his shares under state appraisal statutes (see below).

Flexibility of Mergers

There is a substantial amount of flexibility in shaping a merger transaction. Shares of all constituent corporations can be changed or converted into shares of the surviving corporation or into cash, other securities, or property. Mergers also have the advantage of generally preserving intact the contracts, franchises and existing legal relationships of all participants, and they avoid the possibility of a mistake in a complicated asset conveyance, as well as the cost and contractual restrictions which are sometimes applicable to such transfers.

STATE REGULATORY ISSUES

Acquisitions are generally regulated at the state level through the state business corporation acts. These statutes often impose certain procedural requirements in connection with a transaction, including Board of Director and stockholder approval, to try to ensure that such a transaction is both appropriately considered at the corporate level and viewed by at least a majority (and, in many states, more than a majority) of the corporation's directors and stockholders as being in their best interests. In addition to state corporate laws, various state statutes may affect a proposed acquisition, as for example, the New

Jersey Environmental Cleanup Responsibility Act or statutes which regulate various industries such as banking, insurance, and on occasion, state antitrust statutes.

Stock Purchase

Assuming that stock is purchased for cash, state restrictions on the sale of stock of a corporation are few. In general, the acquiring corporation need only obtain approval of the transaction from its Board of Directors. The acquired corporation is not a party to the transaction, and thus no approval is needed from its Board of Directors or stockholders. The only exceptions arise in the case of a share exchange, which generally requires Board and stockholder approval of both the acquired and acquiring corporations, and in the case of a purchase of stock for other securities. The issuance of securities as consideration for the stock to be purchased triggers the applicability of several state law requirements which are discussed below (see "Cash or Stock as Payment - State Regulatory Issues").

Recently, in their renewed attempt to regulate tender offers (the first attempt having been thwarted by the Supreme Court's invalidation of state takeover statutes in *Edgar v. Mite*), state legislatures have been enacting what are referred to as "control stock acquisition statutes" and "business combination statutes." Buoyed by the Supreme Court's affirmation of the constitutionality of control share acquisition statutes in *CTS Corp. v. Dynamics Corp.*, this new generation of state takeover defense statutes typically regulates tender offers through state corporation law rather than, as with the prior generation of these statutes, through state securities laws.

Control Stock Acquisition Statutes

Control stock acquisition statutes generally prevent a stockholder who acquires voting power of a specified percentage (usually in the range of 20 to 33 1/3 percent) from exercising that voting power subject to giving certain notice of its acquisition to the corporation and to approval by a vote of disinterested shareholders.[3] Under certain circumstances, if that notice is not given or that approval is not obtained, such purchaser's shares may be subject to redemption by the corporation. Further, many, though not all, of these statutes provide that if full voting rights are accorded to the acquiring person, and that person thereafter acquires a majority of the voting power, then all other holders have

[3]See Ind. Code § 23-1-42-1 et seq.; Fla. Gen. Corp. Act § 607.109; Mass. Gen. Laws. Ch. 110D, § 1-8; Ch. 110E § 1-7; Mich. Bus. Corp. § 21.200 (7990) et seq.

appraisal rights and may, in effect, put their shares to the issuer at their fair value as determined under the state's appraisal statute.[4]

Business Combination Statutes

The "business combination statutes" generally prohibit any merger or other business combination for a period of three to five years between a 20 percent (although in some states this is as low as 10 percent) stockholder and a corporation without a disinterested stockholder vote, or, in certain instances, a vote of the Board of Directors, and, in certain states (such as New York), also require that the ultimate purchase price satisfy a statutory fairness formula.[5] Under the Delaware business combination statute, for example, which departed from the theretofore common format for these statutes, a stockholder who, without Board approval, acquires at least 15 percent of a company's stock cannot acquire additional stock for three years unless (1) the Board of Directors and at least two-thirds of the disinterested stockholders approve such acquisition or (2) the buyer, at the point at which he crosses the 15 percent threshold, acquires at least 85 percent of the outstanding stock (excluding stock held by certain company insiders).

"Business combination" is broadly defined to include mergers, sales, and other dispositions of 10 percent or more of the assets of the subject corporation, any transaction increasing the stockholdings of the acquiring person, or receipt by the acquiring person of any other financial benefit. The statute applies only to companies whose stock is listed on an exchange or quoted on a quotation system or which have more than 2,000 stockholders.[6]

As is the case with most "business combination" jurisdictions, a company, generally by shareholder approval, may elect to opt out of the statute, although not retroactively and with the opting-out period effective only after some considerable delay. Although Federal legislators have proposed several bills which would limit or preempt the effect of control share acquisition and business combination statutes, and the constitutionality of the latter has not been established, for the time being these statutes are a necessary consideration in any stock acquisition of a company.

---

[4]See Ind. Code § 23-1-42-11; Fla. Gen. Corp. Act § 607.109 (11); Mass. Gen. Laws. Ch. 110D § 7; Mich. Bus. Corp. Act. § 21.200 (799).

[5]See Indiana Code § 23-1-43-1 et seq; New York Bus. Corp. Law § 912; 8 Delaware Code Annotated § 203.

[6]Most business combination statutes do not apply to corporations with less than 100 shareholders. See Ind. Code § 23-1-43-1 et seq; Mich. Bus. Corp. Act § 21.200(775) et seq.; Ga. Bus. Corp. Code § 14-2-232 to 14-2-238.

Asset Purchase

State corporation law uniformly requires shareholder approval for the sale of all or substantially all of a corporation's assets and, in almost all states, Board of Directors approval as well. In some states, the favorable vote of a majority of outstanding shares will suffice (e.g., Delaware and Pennsylvania), in some the percentage is two-thirds (e.g., New York and Massachusetts) and in some a higher percentage is required (e.g., Hawaii, where the vote of three-fourths of the outstanding shares is required with respect to corporations formed before July 1, 1987). In almost all states, shareholders who appropriately dissent from the proposed sale have the right to have a determination of the appraised value of their shares and to receive that value in cash, with exceptions, as in Delaware, if the target company meets certain public ownership criteria; the theory of the exception is that the dissenting shareholder may realize the cash value of his shares on the market rather than accept the sale consideration.

Asset sales raise bulk sale issues which the buyer normally waives since the purchaser, at least of a public company, will usually assume all of its outstanding liabilities of any nature.

On the other hand, the purchasing corporation in an asset sale transaction can normally act by vote of the Board of Directors, whether the consideration be cash or securities, unless the corporate charter does not authorize the kind or amount of securities to be issued, in which event shareholder action to amend the charter is required.

In approving an asset sale, the target's Board of Directors will have the protection of the business judgment rule (see Chapter 22), so long as it acts with due care, except if the transaction places the Board in a conflict of interest, in which case other procedures are normally invoked to protect the Board in sustaining the burden of establishing the fairness of the transaction (see Chapter 18).

Mergers

Like asset sales, mergers are subject to a state law requirement of shareholder approval and in almost all cases to Board of Directors approval as well. As in asset sales, the percentiles vary from a majority to supermajorities, and again, as in asset sales, appraisal is ordinarily available, with exceptions in some states, if the target company meets certain ownership criteria.

If the acquiring company is a public company and elects to merge directly with the target, a vote of its shareholders will of course be required. On the other hand, almost all acquisitions effected through the merger technique are effected between the target and a subsidiary of the acquiring corporation. Since the parent is the sole shareholder of the subsidiary, the requisite corporate action is represented by the written consent of the parent.

FEDERAL REGULATORY ISSUES—GENERAL CONSIDERATIONS

Generally, except as noted below, Federal requirements are not a major factor in an acquisition of a private company, although Rule 10b-5, the well-known antifraud rule issued under the Securities Exchange Act of 1934, applies to any sale or purchase of a security involving any means or instrumentality of interstate commerce or the mails. In addition to the Federal securities laws, other federal statutes may have to be considered, such as those governing banks, insurance companies, utilities, broadcasters, antitrust matters, and the like. However, Federal securities laws and regulations do play a material part in any transaction in which stock is issued as consideration. Specifically, the Securities Act of 1933 requires an issuer to register under that act any securities that it issues, unless it qualifies for an exemption from such registration.

Generally, registration is a complicated and costly process (even for companies that are already public), except where certain short form registration forms are available, and will rarely be used by a private company in an acquisition. Even certain exemptions, should the companies qualify for them, such as Regulation D (a limited offering exemption), will require in various circumstances the compilation and dissemination to stock purchasers of information approximate in scope and amount to what would be required under a full-blown registration. Failure to comply with the federal securities laws could result in dire consequences for an issuer, including civil damages, criminal penalties, a Securities and Exchange Commission enforcement action or rescission of the stock purchase.

Once stock is registered under the Securities Act of 1933, the issuer must register such shares under, and become subject to, certain reporting requirements of the Securities Exchange Act of 1934. In addition, registration of any class of securities listed on a national securities exchange is required under the Exchange Act as well as any equity security held by more than 500 stock holders, if the issuer of that security has total assets exceeding $5,000,000. Exchange Act registration subjects an issuer to additional requirements, including short-swing profit restrictions and a comprehensive set of proxy regulations. Moreover, stock acquisitions of Exchange Act registered companies (i.e., public companies) bring into play that part of the Exchange Act which was the Congressional answer to the corporate raiders of the 1960s, namely, the Williams Act.

Public Companies—Tender Offers

The Williams Act (Sections 13 and 14 of the Exchange Act) provided the Securities and Exchange Commission with a framework for regulating tender offers. Congress' primary concern, as embodied in the Williams Act, was to provide stockholders in a tender offer situation with sufficient time and information to make an informed investment decision.

Section 13 of the Williams Act

Section 13 of the Exchange Act contains the beneficial ownership reporting requirements of the Williams Act. Disclosure is required from any persons or groups at the point at which they own 5 percent or more of the outstanding shares of a public company. Currently, such disclosure must be made within 10 days of crossing the 5 percent threshold, although the SEC has proposed that such period be reduced to two days. Section 13 is designed to alert the marketplace to an accumulation of stock in the hands of a purchaser which might presage a shift in control of an issuer.

Section 14 of the Williams Act

Section 14 contains the provisions of the Williams Act governing acquisition (other than by the issuer) of stock of a public company by tender offer. Although the term "tender offer" is never defined (the SEC in 1979 proposed a definition of tender offer that was never adopted), decisional law has characterized a tender offer as "a general, publicized bid by an individual or group to buy shares of a publicly-owned company, the shares of which [are] traded on a national securities exchange, at a price substantially above current market price."[7]

---

[7] [774 F.2d 47, 54–55 (2d Cir. 1955) (citing H.R. Rep. No. 1711, 90th Cong.; 2d Sess. 2 (1968); S. Rep. No. 550, 90th Cong. 1st Sess. 2 (1967).]

Tender Offer Tests

The SEC and the judiciary have generally relied upon an eight factor test in determining whether a proposed acquisition constitutes a tender offer. These factors are:

1. an active and widespread solicitation is made for shares of an issuer;
2. the solicitation is made for a substantial percentage of the issuer's stock;
3. the offer to purchase is made at a premium over the prevailing market price;
4. the terms of the offer are firm rather than negotiable;
5. the offer is contingent on the tender of a fixed minimum number of shares and often subject to a ceiling of a fixed maximum number of shares to be purchased;
6. the offer is open for only a limited period of time;
7. the offerees are subject to pressure to sell their stock; and
8. public announcements of an acquisition program precede or accompany the accumulation of stock.

Tender Offer Rules

A purchase plan that constitutes a tender offer must comply with the detailed requirements of the rules promulgated under Section 14. As a general rule, a tender offer is deemed to commence when the material terms are first published by the bidder or otherwise sent or given to stockholders. Concurrently with such commencement, the bidder must file a Tender Offer Statement on Schedule 14D-1 with the SEC and target company, disclosing, among other things, the material terms of the offer. Third-party tender offers must remain open for at least 20 business days from the date the tender offer is commenced. Any change in the number of securities being sought or consideration being offered will require the bidder to maintain its offer for at least 10 business days from such change. The SEC has taken the position that any other material changes may require a bidder to maintain its offer at least 5 business days from such change.

The rules require that the tender offer be made to all security holders of that class and that no holder be paid less consideration than any other holder. Commission rules also permit any person who has tendered his shares to withdraw them during the offering period. A bidder who makes a partial tender offer must accept all of the shares tendered on a pro rata basis.

The target company must disclose certain information when it becomes the subject of a tender offer. Within 10 business days of commencement of the tender offer, the target must file and disseminate a Schedule 14D-9 disclosing, among other things, the target's position on the tender offer and whether any negotiation is being undertaken by the target in response to the tender offer that would result in an extraordinary transaction or material change in the target's capitalization or dividend policy.

Although separate rules apply to issuer tender offers (Rule 13e-4), these requirements, which also apply to affiliate offers, are generally the same as the requirements under the Section 14 rules. The issuer tender offer rules contain filing, disclosure, and dissemination requirements and specific antifraud provisions.

Tender Pros and Cons

Tender offers as a means of acquiring a public company are useful to the extent that they circumvent uncooperative management or preempt competing offerors. However, because tender offers are consummated without the benefit of negotiation, adequate due diligence or the protections to a purchaser normally built into a contract, a tender offeror is in a position of greater risk in acquiring a business than a purchaser who acquires a business through other means.

Tender Structure

Stock in a tender offer may be purchased for cash or securities. If purchased for securities, the tender offer will take the form of an exchange offer prospectus which must be filed with the SEC like any other registration statement. The considerations for determining which method of payment is preferable are the same as for any other stock acquisition (see "Cash or Stock as Payment" below).

Tender offers are often conducted as multistep transactions in which the cash offer is preceded by a purchase, either privately or through the open market, or a large block of shares, and then is succeeded by a cash merger or part-cash part-stock merger. The cash offer may also involve different pricing: a higher price for shares tendered immediately and a lower price for shares purchased in the succeeding cash-out merger. However, two-tier pricing has been attacked as inherently coercive and may, if the pricing is sufficiently disparate, raise a question of the fiduciary obligations of the majority shareholder.

Target responses to tender offers and other tender offer defensive measures are a specialized and rapidly evolving area of the law (see Chapters 21–26).

Public Companies—Going Private

Going private transactions, that is to say, transactions in which the interest of voting public shareholders are eliminated, either for cash or for a nonvoting security such as a nonvoting preferred stock or a debenture, may be effected in one or more steps, but the last step is invariably either a merger or a reverse split, which serves to ultimately freeze out the last of the public stockholders. If the transaction is accomplished in more than one step, the first step is usually a tender offer, either by a new corporation formed by the proponents of the corporation or a self-tender by the subject company itself.

A reverse split transaction is, in effect, an amendment to the charter, with all outside stockholdings being converted into a fraction of a share, which is redeemed for a cash consideration. By lumping all of the shares held by the proponents of the transaction into one certificate (as for instance in the name of a new corporation), which then becomes the largest registered holder of shares on the record date, a reverse split under which that number of shares becomes one share and all other shares become a fraction of a share, to be paid out in cash, will eliminate all other outstanding stockholders.

Going private transactions are regulated by SEC Rule 13e-3, which is described in detail in Volume II, Chapter 37.

Hart-Scott-Rodino

The Hart-Scott-Rodino Antitrust Improvements Act, administered by the U.S. Department of Justice and the Federal Trade Commission, regulates virtually all significant business acquisitions, regardless of whether implemented through stock purchase, asset purchase, or merger. The rules promulgated under the Hart-Scott Act prohibit, without prior notice to these two governmental entities and the expiration of the waiting period specified under the Act, the consummation of any merger or acquisition where more than 15 percent of voting securities or assets would be acquired or where the aggregate total amount of voting securities and assets to be acquired is in excess of $15 million and where one side of the transaction has total assets or annual net sales of at least $100 million and the other side has total assets or annual net sales of at least $10 million. Where a purchaser acquires 15 percent of a company's voting stock or assets, and the value of the stock and assets is less than $15 million, filing is necessary only if the acquisition confers control of a company with at least $25 million in total assets or annual net sales.

Securities Act Disclosure Requirements

Whatever form the transaction takes, whether a tender offer, a proxy statement, or a registration statement, it must necessarily comply with the pertinent disclosure requirements of the federal securities laws for that form of transaction, and if it is a going-private transaction subject to Rule 13e-3, it must also comply with the disclosure requirements of that rule. In the early days of tender offers there was considerable litigation as to the adequacy of tender offer disclosure, but as the practice has developed, disclosure litigation has tended to confine itself almost exclusively to issues relating to value or conflict of interest, or, on occasion, when the bidder is not itself a public company, to required financial disclosures or other financial issues.

CASH OR STOCK AS PAYMENT—TAX AND OTHER CONSIDERATIONS

A cash transaction clearly has advantages for the purchaser. Assuming financing is not required or is available on reasonable terms, a cash transaction frees the purchaser, especially the purchaser of a publicly-owned company, from compliance with federal and state regulations and stock exchange restrictions governing the issuance of stock. Such compliance can be costly, burdensome, and time-consuming. A cash transaction also avoids the dilution of value of the outstanding shares of a company associated with issuing additional stock.

Cash may also be preferred by the sellers, who may not wish to assume the risk of being stockholders in the combined business. On the other hand, nonrecognition of taxable gain may be a nonnegotiable item in a seller's offer. Tax considerations relating to the form of payment of the purchase price in an acquisition are discussed in Chapter 28.

State Regulatory Issues

State securities laws (or "Blue Sky" laws, as they are commonly referred to) must always be considered in an acquisition where stock is issued as payment. State Blue Sky restrictions are, to put it simply, always an administrative obstacle course and, at their worst, are a trap for the unwary. Failure to comply, for example, with the New York Real Estate Syndication Act, which applies in circumstances where one normally would not think it pertinent, can have such disastrous consequences, as an unrestricted right of rescission.

Under some Blue Sky statutes, rescission is available not only against the offending corporation but also against its officers and directors.

Federal Regulatory Issues

As discussed above, federal securities laws are a major consideration where stock or other securities are issued as payment of a purchase price in an acquisition. By virtue of complicated provisions, the Securities Act of 1933, in effect, restricts the resale of shares not issued in registered transactions. Normally the governing rule here is the famous SEC Rule 144, which generally provides that so-called restricted securities (those sold in a private placement or in a series of transactions, none of which involved a public offering) may only be sold into the market after they have been held for two years after being fully paid for, and then only subject to the available public information and in accordance with the so-called leakage provisions of that rule. On the other hand, an amendment of some years ago provides freedom from the resale restrictions of the rule if the securities have been held for more than three years and the seller has not for 90 days been a controlling person of the issuer. The rules are technical, and counsel should be consulted on their application.

STOCK EXCHANGE REQUIREMENTS

When an acquisition involves the issuance of securities of a listed company, shareholder approval is required if the securities represent, in the case of the New York Stock Exchange, more than $18\frac{1}{2}$ percent of the outstanding shares, and, in the case of the American Stock Exchange, more than 20 percent, and shareholder approval is also required in certain interested-party transactions, such as the granting of options or adoption of special remuneration plans for directors, officers, or key employees of a listed company.

In addition, both exchanges have so-called back door listing policies which govern the issuance of shares in such quantity as to transfer the control of the listed company, thus effecting a listing via the back door. Generally, these standards are that the company seeking back door listing status should, but for the public flotation, have satisfied the exchange's original listing criteria.

For the New York Stock Exchange, the current criteria are that there be at least 1,100,000 publicly-held shares (excluding shares held by insiders and concentrated holdings of 10 percent or more), an average monthly trading volume of at least 100,000 shares, an aggregate market value of the publicly-held shares of at least $18,000,000 (although the Exchange will also look to net tangible assets as an alternative measure of satisfying this criterion), and at least 2,000 holders of lots of 100 shares or more *or* at least 2,200 shareholders in total.

For the American Stock Exchange, the general listing criteria currently are stockholders' equity of at least $4,000,000 and pretax income of at least $750,000 in the last fiscal year or in two of the last three fiscal years. Companies unable to satisfy the pretax income requirement may be able to satisfy alternative numerical criteria, which include at least three years of operations, an aggregate market value of publicly-held shares of at least $15,000,000 and a minimum of 500,000 publicly-held shares (excluding insiders and concentrated holdings), together with a minimum of 800 public holders or a minimum of 1,000,000 publicly-held shares with at least 400 public holders.

Both the New York Stock Exchange and the American Stock Exchange have additional criteria that apply, depending upon whether the securities being listed are common stock, preferred stock, bonds, debentures, or warrants.

CHAPTER 18

FAIRNESS OPINIONS AND COMMON STOCK VALUATIONS

Gilbert E. Matthews
M. Mark Lee
Bear, Stearns & Co. Inc.

A fairness opinion is a special form of valuation report, usually a letter, that is often viewed as a "shield" against potential legal damages. It states that, in the view of the investment banker, based upon certain procedures followed and assumptions made, a specific transaction at a specific price is fair, from a financial point of view, to specific parties.

This chapter is organized in two major parts, (1) the definition of the engagement, and (2) valuation methodology. In most assignments, defining the valuation takes far less time than doing it. Nevertheless, a misunderstanding at the beginning of the engagement can lead to wasted time and effort. At worst, it can cost the client millions of dollars and tarnish an investment banker's reputation.

LEGAL IMPLICATIONS OF FAIRNESS

What is fair is not necessarily obvious, especially to contending parties in a lawsuit. Fairness depends on the facts and circumstances, in each case interpreted through financial and legal precedents. A fairness opinion by a reputable investment banker, backed with a thorough and proper study, can provide a potential party to a litigation with protection against a materially adverse result by showing that such party had a reasonable basis for approving the transaction.

Lack of a fairness opinion can be devastating. Directors can be held liable for millions of dollars in damages as a result of deciding upon a corporate transaction. For example, in *Smith v. Van Gorkom* (1985), the Supreme Court of the State of Delaware held that the Board of Directors of Trans Union Corporation, all reputable individuals acting without fraud or malice, did not act with informed business judgment in approving a cash-out merger of the company into the Marmon Group, despite the fact that they relied on the chairman of the company in determining the financial fairness of the transaction, and even though the merger price of $55 per share represented a substantial premium over the market price of the company's stock. The directors were forced to agree to a settlement in which $23.5 million in damages was paid the stockholders of Trans Union by insurance, the Marmon Group and *the directors themselves*. (Fortunately for the directors, the Marmon Group agreed to pay the entire settlement for the directors.)

In evaluating the conduct of the board in this matter the Delaware Supreme Court wrote: "Representation of the financial interests of others imposes on a director an affirmative duty to protect those interests and to proceed with a critical eye in assessing information. . . . Despite the foregoing facts and circumstances, there was no call by the Board . . . for any valuation study or documentation of the $55 price per share as a measure of the fair value of the Company in a cash-out context."

While the court went on to state that it did "not imply that an outside fairness study is essential to support an informed business judgment" and did not "state that fairness opinions by independent investment bankers are required as a matter of law," it is clear from the opinion that had the directors obtained such an opinion they could have been better protected.

DEFINING THE ENGAGEMENT

The key to the opinion process is stating precisely the circumstances on which the investment banker must opine. Defining the engagement is the critical phase of the job. The values of companies and their securities are always dependent on the specific situation. Before an assignment can begin, the following questions must be answered:

1. What is being valued?
2. What is the date of the opinion?
3. What is the standard of value and how is it applied?
4. What are the limitations imposed, if any?

Small changes in the answers to any of these questions may have a major impact on the cost and content of the opinion.

The Property Being Valued

The value of common stock is dependent on its income, assets, and appreciation potential, as well as its voting power and marketability.

Income, Assets, and Appreciation Potential

The source of the equity's economic value determines the emphasis given to the valuation methods employed. The economic value of an equity interest in a business is either its share of the company's earning power as a going concern or its share of the company's collection of assets, or a combination of both, as compared to alternative investments.

In theory, the value of common stock is the present value of all of its future income, discounted at an appropriate rate of return. This income can result either from the firm's operations, from liquidation distributions of the firm's assets, or from a combination of both. As a company grows, the value of its income and assets increases, causing the value of its stock to appreciate. Most investors expect to sell the stock to realize the shares' appreciation.

If the company has little or no earning power, but has asset value, the techniques for evaluating asset value on a disaggregation or liquidation basis will be emphasized. If a corporation is profitable and has prospects of continuing to generate income, its value is dependent on earning power, and the techniques valuing earning power will be emphasized in the opinion. Value based on income may be enhanced by the value of assets which are not contributing to operating income. In this case, both sets of techniques must be used.

Voting Power and Marketability

Voting power and marketability are both material factors in determining value. Generally, all common stock valuations can be classified as either (1) valuations of freely marketable minority blocks, (2) enterprise or control block valuations, or (3) valuations of closely-held or restricted minority blocks.

Freely marketable minority blocks of common stock are those that are legally salable in the open market, either on an exchange or over-the-counter. Normally, their market value can be determined simply by looking up contemporaneous market quotations. The value of these blocks of stock reflects that they are passive investments in concerns managed by others. Value is dependent upon the potential for price appreciation and dividends, based upon the prospects of the corporation as run by its current management. However, the size of the block of stock may have a material effect on its value. If the block is large relative to either the trading volume of the common stock of the company or the amount of common stock in public hands, the value of the block may be reduced in the hands of a seller as a result of selling pressure on the market and the need to induce additional buyers. This reduction in value is known as the *blockage discount*. Conversely, the value of the same block to a potential buyer may be increased over the prevailing market price as a result of upward pressure needed to induce additional sellers.

Control blocks are active ownership interests. Depending on the size of the block held, an owner of a control block may have the power to select the Board of Directors of a corporation and thereby to direct day-to-day operations of the corporation, to liquidate or redeploy assets, or to sell, merge, or liquidate the entire corporation. To the extent that these powers represent the potential for added income or capital appreciation, the value of control blocks on a per share basis will be greater than the value of minority interests and approach or even exceed the pro rata share of *enterprise value*—the value of 100 percent ownership of the equity of the corporation. Depending on the situation, the per share value of control blocks can be substantially more than the value of freely traded minority interests. This increment in value is known as the *control premium*. The reverse of this premium, in moving from enterprise value to freely traded value, is the *minority interest discount*.

Minority interests in closely-held corporations or restricted minority interests in public corporations legally cannot be sold in the open market, but can only be sold in private placements. These blocks have the added risk of lack of ready marketability, which means that their owners may not be able to sell quickly enough to take advantage of high prices or to avoid expected price declines. This added risk often causes these shares to be valued 30 to 50 percent below the market price of equivalent freely-traded minority shares. This discount is the *discount for lack of marketability*.

Legal rights and stockholder agreements also can have a major impact on the property being valued. In some states, such as New York, it takes two-thirds of the voting power of common stockholders either to liquidate, to merge, or to sell the assets of a corporation. In Delaware, a simple majority can accomplish the same task. A corporation's articles of incorporation or charter can also limit or enhance the voting power of different sized blocks of stock by requiring supermajority votes to accomplish certain actions, or by providing for special allocation of voting rights. Corporate charters may also contain special allocations of dividends, assets, and earnings, or may limit the transferability of a class of shares. Each of these can have a significant effect on value. While these unusual charter provisions were once mainly found in the charters of closely-held corporations, some of these provisions are now used by public corporations to ward off unfriendly takeovers. Special consideration may have to be given to *high vote securities* or *poison pill preferred stocks* in the valuation process as they may affect value. Side agreements by stockholders, whether in the form of buy-sell agreements, voting trusts, or estate planning devices, can have much the same effect of increasing or reducing the value of common stock by altering its rights to assets, income, appreciation, marketability, or corporate control. Therefore, any unusual agreements should be reviewed.

The Opinion Date

The value of common stock may be quite different, depending on the effective date of the opinion. Stock prices will vary depending upon economic conditions, interest rates, and outlook as perceived by investors at any given time. During periods of strong stock prices, economic expansion, or low interest rates, values will be higher; conversely, during period of a depressed stock market, economic contraction, or high interest rates, common stock prices will be lower. Moreover, changes in the company's earnings and prospects may affect the value of the shares. The result can be that, while an acquisition or "going-private" transaction may be fair during the planning stage, it may become unfair several months later because of changed economic or corporate circumstances. The investment banker may have to consider withdrawing his opinion when circumstances change.

THE STANDARD OF VALUE AND ITS APPLICATION

The question, "What is it worth?" put to a jury seems to call for a precise answer. The implicit assumption is that value is a fixed and absolute standard. This is not the case. Depending on the valuation's purpose, the financial standard can range from pragmatic economic judgments for business planning decisions to complex legal formulas that differ depending on the jurisdiction and context of the litigation. Despite an opinion's accuracy from an economic or financial point of view, a court can accept or reject it *as a matter of law* because of the valuation standard used or the valuation methodologies prescribed in the jurisdiction.

An important standard of value for fairness opinions in the United States is fair value, as used in dissenting shareholder actions. It is usually considered a minimum condition of fairness.

Fair Value as Defined in Delaware

This standard of value is important because of its use in corporate control questions, both for Delaware corporations and the corporations of other states that use Delaware's corporate law as a model. Under Delaware law, the primary remedy of a stockholder dissenting from corporate actions in which there is an extinguishment of the dissenters' interests in a going concern, such as sales, cash mergers, and going-private transactions, is the dissenters' right to receive the *fair value* of their shares, known as the *right of appraisal*.

The fair value standard in Delaware is described in *Tri-Continental Corp. v. Battye* (1950):

> The basic concept of value under the appraisal statute is that the stockholder is entitled to be paid for that which has been taken from him, viz., his proportionate interest in a going-concern. By value of the stockholder's proportionate interest in the corporate enterprise is meant the true or intrinsic value of his stock which has been taken by the merger. In determining what figure represents this true or intrinsic value, the appraiser and the courts must take into consideration all factors and elements which might enter into the fixing of value. Thus, market value, asset value, dividends, earnings prospects, the nature of the enterprise, and any other facts which were known or which could be ascertained as of the date of merger and which throw any light on future prospects of the [acquired] corporation are not only pertinent to an inquiry as to the value of the dissenting stockholders' interest, but must be considered by the agency fixing value.

The court must determine the fair value of the shares exclusive of any element of value arising from the accomplishment or expectation of the merger.

Prior to the Weinberger decisions discussed below, *the Delaware block approach* had been the traditional basis for determining fair value of common stock sold for cash or for cash and securities. The appropriate pricing analysis in this approach is to develop, based upon all the relevant qualitative and quantitative factors, three values: (1) market value, (2) asset value, and (3) earnings or going concern (investment) value, and then to weigh them to determine the final fair value of the shares.

Market Value

Market value, if a corporation's common stock was publicly traded at the acquisition date, generally, is the trading price of stock in the marketplace excluding any impact of the transaction from which the stockholder is dissenting. Thus, if the dissent stems from a sale of the company or a going-private transaction, which typically causes an increase in the price of the stock, such increase in value would be factored out.

If the corporation's stock is not publicly traded, or has been influenced by the pending transaction, a reconstructed market value sometimes is developed by using the procedure that typically determines fair market value, that is, using the market prices of similar companies.

Fair Market Value

Fair market value is the most common standard of value for United States law. It is used principally in federal and state tax matters, as well as in corporate control questions in some jurisdictions. The definition of fair market value is:

> [T]he price at which the property would change hands between a willing buyer and a willing seller when the former is not under any compulsion to buy and the latter is not under compulsion to sell, both parties having reasonable knowledge of relevant facts.

This definition of value is found in United States Internal Revenue Code and in Internal Revenue Service Revenue Ruling 59-60. When the market price of a company or its securities is not available or is unreliable, a valuation for fair market value requires the analysis of at least the following factors:

1. The nature of the business and the history of the enterprise from its inception.
2. The economic outlook in general and the condition and outlook of the specific industry in particular.
3. The book value of the stock and the financial condition of the business.
4. The earnings capacity of the company.
5. The dividend-paying capacity.
6. Whether or not the enterprise has goodwill or other intangible value.
7. Sales of the stock and the size of the block to be valued.
8. The market price of stocks of corporations engaged in the same or similar line of business having their stocks actively traded in a free and open market, either on an exchange or over-the-counter.

The above is only a partial listing. All relevant factors that are known or knowable at the valuation date should be considered.

The valuation process is essentially one of *developing a hypothetical market price by analogy* for the securities in question. The closer the hypothetical market transaction is to an actual unaffected market transaction, the more weight is given to such transaction in determining value. However, if no such transaction is available reasonably proximate to the valuation date or if a transaction is significantly different, then the pricing analogy is based upon an analysis of transaction prices for similar securities and comparisons of their business and financial profiles with that of the company and securities in question. In Delaware, a discount for lack of marketability generally is not appropriate if the common shares have transfer restrictions or are interests in a closely-held corporation. (This differs from valuations for tax purposes where such a discount is generally appropriate.)

Fair *market* value is only one component of fair value under Delaware law. The market value determined is generally a minority interest value unless the shares being valued are a control block.

Asset Value

Asset value, or net asset value as described above, is the market value of the firm's assets less the liabilities that have to be paid. The value of the assets should be determined on a going-concern basis (that is, the value of the assets in use). Book value is seldom equal to asset value, and therefore must be used with caution.

Holding/Investment Company Discount

The holding company discount or investment company discount is a factor used in the determination of the fair market value of minority blocks of common stock in companies that either are primarily investment companies or have very low earning power in relation to the market value of the firm's assets. This discount reflects the relationship of the market value of the firm's equity on a going-concern basis to the value of the firm's net assets. It is a proper deduction from net asset value in computing the fair market value of a minority interest block when liquidation of the company is not contemplated. Under the fair value standard, however, no holding company or investment company discount is allowed in the determination of net asset value.

Earnings or Investment Value

Earnings or investment value reflects the value of the shares on a going-concern basis. In this approach historical earnings are capitalized, generally using price/earnings ratios based on the capitalization rates of the common stocks of similar companies to develop the value. The process is similar to determining fair market value. As the capitalization rate is developed independent of the subject company's historic market price in relation to its earnings, this value is distinct from market price. Prospective increases or decreases in earnings typically are handled by adjusting the capitalization rate. However, they may be capitalized separately.

Weighting the Values

In the weighting of these three values, market value generally gets substantial weight if the market price is reliable; earnings or investment value gets substantial weight if the corporation is expected to remain as a going concern with little prospect of liquidation or sale of its assets; and asset value is important if the corporation has little or no earning power and liquidation or asset sales are clearly in prospect. The following is a sample of the values that might apply in an appraisal proceeding in which is the result of a minority interest's dissent from a going-private transaction:

Basis	*Indicated Value*
Market value	15.00
Asset value	30.00
Earnings value	10.00

Obviously, even assuming that both sides agreed with the above values, one side might give greater weight to asset value, in this case, and the other give greater weight to market value or earnings value. The Delaware Court of Chancery would set the final value depending on its views of the relative merits of the case.

The Weinberger v. UOP, Inc. Cases

There has been considerable discussion about whether dissenting stockholders should be paid, as a minimum, their full proportionate share of enterprise value (also known in this debate as "third party sale value") in going-private transactions instead of minority interest value plus, possibly, some premium. The difference in the two values can be enormous. In addition, there has been considerable concern over the use of market value, asset value, and earnings value as the sole bases for determining fair value. These questions were addressed in a series of five landmark Delaware cases known as *Weinberger v. UOP, Inc.*, the first two heard in the Court of Chancery, the next two heard in the Delaware Supreme Court, and finally, on remand, the last heard in the Court of Chancery.

In the second case (the first did not deal with valuation) in the Court of Chancery (1981), the plaintiff contended, among other things, that The Signal Companies, Inc., which owned 40.5 percent of UOP Inc., unfairly used its majority stock ownership position in UOP to cash out UOP's minority at a grossly inadequate price per share of $21.00, and abused its position by causing UOP to disseminate proxy information which misrepresented how the merger price had been established. The plaintiff advocated the fairness standard of third party sale value, contending that, in evaluating the fairness of the merger terms to the majority, one must look to the reasonable worth to the majority shareholder of being rid of all the other shareholders and becoming the sole owner of the enterprise. Plaintiff's expert determined fair value using two approaches, (1) acquisitions of comparable companies, and (2) discounted cash flow analysis determining enterprise value.

Defendants' expert used the Delaware block approach, as well as considering UOP's dividend record, and the premium offered over the market price of UOP's stock on the day preceding the announcement of the merger. The Court of Chancery rejected plaintiff's valuation as being contrary to logic and to Delaware law, and ruled for the defendants on all counts.

This decision was first approved by the Delaware Supreme Court, but then reversed by the Delaware Supreme Court, sitting *en banc* (1983), primarily for two reasons—the failure of Signal to deal fairly with UOP's minority stockholders, and the Court of Chancery's rejection of plaintiff's expert's discounted cash flow valuation as a matter of law.

The Supreme Court wrote that the discounted cash flow method that the lower court had rejected as a matter of law was the method used by two UOP directors in evaluating the merger, and stated that, to the extent that the Delaware block approach excluded other generally accepted techniques used by the financial community, it was clearly outmoded. The Court continued:

> Accordingly, the standard 'Delaware block' or weighted average method of valuation, formerly employed in appraisal and other stock valuation cases, shall no longer exclusively control such proceedings. We believe that a more liberal approach must include proof of value by any techniques or methods which are generally considered acceptable in the financial community and otherwise admissible in Court."

The Court did not rule that the discounted cash flow approach determined the value of the UOP minority shares or even that it was an appropriate technique to use in this situation. It simply ruled that it could not be excluded as a matter of law.

On remand, the Court of Chancery considered the discounted cash flow analysis determining enterprise value and rejected it because it "did not provide a realistic measure for the value that which was possessed by a minority shareholder prior to the merger and which was taken from him by merger." The Chancellor's emphasis, using the *Tri-Continental v. Battye* appraisal standard in rejecting discounted cash flow, was the phrase, "'what is meant by the stockholder's proportionate interest in corporate enterprise' is the 'true or intrinsic value of *his* stock which has been taken by the merger.'" He focused on the difference between (a) the value of a share to a minority interest and (b) the value that the same share to Signal as the 100% owner of UOP. The Chancellor "did not think that the two were the same since the minority shareholder, because of his status as a member of the minority, could never have possessed as his proportionate interest in the corporate enterprise that which Signal could possess by virtue of its ability to become sole owner of the entire corporation," i.e., control over the cash flow of UOP. This decision appeared to refute the concept of third party sale value as the appraisal standard of fairness in Delaware. The Court did award $1.00 per share in damages because of the procedural wrongdoing found by the Supreme Court.

Cavalier Oil v. Hartnett

A recent Delaware case, *Cavalier Oil v. Harnett* (1988), affirmed by the Delaware Supreme Court in 1989, summarized some well-established Delaware appraisal concepts: (1) liquidation value is not appropriate under Delaware law, as value must be determined on a going-concern basis; (2) a lack-of-marketability discount is improper; (3) post-merger data may be considered only if it is "known or susceptible of proof as of the date of the merger and is not the product of speculation". In addition, unlike the final *Weinberger* case, the Vice Chancellor in Cavalier (1) accepted the discounted cash flow approach (which was used by experts for both sides) as a valid valuation technique in this case, though susceptible to a wide range of error; and (2) indicated that no minority discount from going-concern value was permitted under Delaware law.

It appears that the Vice Chancellor and the Delaware Supreme Court did not view going-concern value necessarily as third party sale value. Both noted that, for investment companies, it was appropriate to apply a discount to asset value to determine going-concern value.

However, the Vice Chancellor also wrote: "That a stockholder might happen to own a significant block of stock will not, for that reason, entitle him to a premium above the appraised fair value of his shares. Similarly, that a dissenting stockholder may own a minority interest (which is the case in all appraisal proceedings) will not diminish his right to receive fair value by subjecting him to penalty in the form of a minority discount."

Sterling v. Mayflower Hotel Corp.

The landmark case describing the standard of value (and therefore the minimum condition of fairness) in common stock mergers for Delaware corporations is *Sterling v. Mayflower Hotel Corp.* (1952). In this decision the Supreme Court of Delaware wrote: "A merger ordinarily contemplates the continuance of the enterprise and of the stockholder's investment therein, though in an altered form. . . . In [this] case the stockholder of the merged corporation is entitled to receive directly securities substantially equal in value to those held before the merger."

There is no premium requirement in this type of merger. The primary issue in the pricing analysis is the *fairness of the exchange ratio,* that is, the value contributed by each share to the merger versus the value received in view of all relevant qualitative and quantitative factors. If the merging companies are similar, and have similar capitalization rates, the exchange ratio computation compares the constituent companies on a per share basis. For example, the exchange ratios in the case of ABC Corporation merging into XYZ, Inc., could be computed as follows:

Basis (Per Share)	*ABC Corporation ($)*	*XYZ Inc. ($)*	*Exchange Ratio (Times)*
Market value	10.00	15.00	0.67
Asset value	30.00	20.00	1.50
Historical earnings			
Five-year average	1.00	1.50	0.67
Latest 12 months	0.50	1.50	0.33
Projected earnings	1.20	1.75	0.69
Dividends	0.50	0.80	0.63

In this case, the bases of value tend to indicate an exchange ratio of one share of ABC Corporation for about 0.67 shares of XYZ Inc. Stockholders of ABC in this case would get about the same market value, dividends, average historical earnings, and projected earnings. They would also receive a somewhat higher share of current earnings, but a lower share of net asset value.

Occasionally, plaintiffs contend that an exchange such as the one above is unfair because the $10.00 per share market value received by the common stockholders of ABC is less than the $30.00 per share asset or liquidation value given up. This argument usually is not correct. As stated in the *Sterling v. Mayflower Hotel Corp.* opinion: "On its face, this proposition is unsound, since it attempts to equate two different standards of value. In the case of many industrial corporations, and also in the instant case, there is a substantial gap between market value and the liquidation value of the stock; and to apply to the merger of such corporations the proposition advanced by plaintiffs would be to bestow upon the stockholder of the subsidiary something which he did not have before the merger and could not obtain—the liquidation value of his stock."

In practice, stockholders of merged corporations are given some premium in terms of market value to induce them to vote for the merger.

In the above merger case involving ABC Corporation and XYZ Inc., both companies had similar ratios, and it was possible to make direct comparisons of earnings and dividends. In some mergers the capitalization rates of the merging companies will be different and the analysis focuses primarily on comparing the market value received in the combined firm in exchange for the market value given up.

Application of the Standard of Fair Value

The appropriate methodology, under this standard of value, is to conduct three types of analyses:

1. A *qualitative analysis* of the subject company and/or securities in question—which describes the history, nature, operations, and outlook of the corporation as well as its environment, and the rights and privileges of the securities in question.
2. A *quantitative analysis* of the subject company and/or securities in question—which consists of a financial analysis of the Company's financial statements and forecasts as well as the income and asset claims of the securities in question.
3. A *pricing analysis* to determine the fair value of the subject company or the securities in question—in which value is determined by analyses of:

a. Historical market prices, prior sales, and arm's-length bids.
b. Comparable market values and acquisition values of similar companies and/or securities in relation to performance.
c. Net asset value—the fair market value of underlying asset claims less all liabilities that must be paid.
d. Other appropriate methodologies.

Important concepts for the pricing analysis under the fair value standard in Delaware include:

1. The determination of fair value in an appraisal proceeding and sale of stock for cash and/or nonconvertible securities should consider factoring in the Delaware block approach, but they are not the exclusive means of determining value.
2. The determination of fair value in a common stock for common stock merger should compare merger exchange ratios and the value of common stock received in comparison to the value of common stock given up.
3. To the extent that other valuation methods are probative of value, they should be considered.
4. Value that arises from the action to which the dissenter objects must be excluded in the appraisal.
5. Fair value should be considered as the result of a bargained transaction; this transaction should consider the potential benefits to the actual parties involved.
6. Fair value is determined on a going-concern basis, not on a liquidation basis.

These concepts are the *minimum,* but not necessarily sufficient, conditions for fairness. An investment banker may determine that, in a given transaction, a higher value is warranted as a matter of equity. For example, if, in the sale of a company, alternate buyers are readily available at higher prices or one group of sellers is getting a disproportionately preferential price, these factors should be considered as part of the overall fairness of the transaction even though they might not be considered in an appraisal proceeding. Moreover, the investment banker should consider whether liquidation value is relevant to the overall fairness of the transaction.

The fairness standard in other jurisdictions, particularly California, can be significantly different from either the fair market value or fair value standards discussed above. Moreover, different standards may apply for different purposes, such as dissolution, bankruptcy, or ERISA. It is best, in all engagements, for the investment banker to discuss with counsel the minimum valuation or fairness standard applicable in the jurisdiction governing the transaction.

Limitations Imposed on The Valuation Process

It is not unusual in the initial phase of the valuation process for the party requesting the valuation to try to limit either the scope of the investment banker's investigation or the time required to produce the opinion, with the thought of either reducing the fee or quickening the completion of the contemplated transaction. While opinions might be produced within these limitations, the utility of the opinions may be greatly reduced. Any material reduction in the investigation would have to be noted in the investment banker's opinion letter, and courts do not look favorably upon opinions completed in record time. Generally the minimum period required to complete the valuation process for a fairness opinion is between one and two weeks.

VALUATION METHODOLOGY

Once the engagement has been defined, the next step is to perform the qualitative, quantitative, and pricing analyses necessary to determine either an appropriate value or the fairness of the proposed transaction. Each of these phases of the process is discussed below.

Qualitative Analysis

Purpose

The purpose of the qualitative analysis is to understand the history, nature, operations, and outlook of the subject company as well as its environment, and the rights, privileges and restrictions of the securities in question. This understanding provides a framework for (1) analyzing the risks and potential of the enterprise and the specific securities in question, (2) analyzing the company's financial statements, and (3) pricing the securities in comparison to other transactions. This phase also includes the review of the terms of the proposed transaction to determine their impact on the valuation process.

Factors Considered

Figure 1 lists factors and data (in addition to the specifics of the assignment) that are often reviewed in the qualitative phase of the valuation process.

FIGURE 1
Common Stock Valuation—Qualitative Factors of the Subject Company

1. Legal Rights of Ownership
   a. State of incorporation
   b. Voting rights
   c. Other rights and limitations of equity securities
   d. Special agreements
2. Equity Ownership
   a. Significant Equity Ownership by Class
      (1) Relationships
      (2) Institutional ownership
   b. Impact of options, warrants, convertibles
      (1) Terms of exercise
      (2) Potential dilution of earnings and assets per share
      (3) Additional payments to Company on exercise
   c. Recent appraisals, transactions, or offers
3. Nature and Business of the Company
   a. Nature
      (1) Going concern dependent on earning power
      (2) Going concern dependent on asset values
      (3) Start-up
      (4) Not a going concern
   b. Business Description
      (1) History of Company
         (a) Changes over the years
         (b) Recent expansions, discontinued operations, or other changes
         (c) Operating methods and policies
      (2) Principal divisions, subsidiaries and affiliates
      (3) Major lines of business
         (a) Description
         (b) Revenues
         (c) Profits
         (d) Cash Flow
   c. Facilities
      (1) Brief discription of:
         (a) Location
         (b) Size, age, use, utilization
      (2) Ownership
         (a) If leased, significant lease terms
         (b) If owned, recent appraisals, if any
      (3) Insurance, including contents and business interruption
      (4) Excess assets
         (a) Description
         (b) Approximate market value—appraisal may be necessary
   d. Preparation of goods and services for sale, and sources of supply
      (1) Manufacturing methods and procedures
      (2) Cyclical and/or seasonal patterns
      (3) Major raw material requirements
      (4) Key suppliers and alternates
      (5) Important contractual arrangements
      (6) Key capital assets
      (7) Key patents, licenses, processes, copy rights, permits, etc.
      (8) Backlog compared to prior years
      (9) Research and development budget and contribution
      (10) Quality control

FIGURE 1—*Continued*

(11) Regulatory relationships
(12) Capacity constraints

e. Marketing
(1) General statement of goals and strategy
(2) Geographic market served
(3) Nature of end users
(4) Importance of repeat customers
(5) Price vs. quality vs. brand competition, etc.
(6) Leader or follower role in marketplace
(7) Market share—goal vs. actual
(8) Methods and costs of generating business (e.g., advertising, promotion, etc.)
(9) Sales terms including warranties, if any
(10) Sales people—kind, number, location, compensation
(11) Important contracts
(12) Methods of delivery including distribution centers or delivery equipment, if any
(13) Use of market research
(14) Names and volume of percent of business with customers accounting for 5 percent or more of sales

f. Competition and Industry Outlook
(1) Names and approximate market share of competitors
(2) Public competitors or comparables
(3) Comparative strengths and weaknesses
(4) Industry outlook

g. Management
(1) Organization Chart
(2) Key management
(a) Name, age, duties, etc.
(b) Compensation, benefits and agreements
(c) Provision for succession, training programs
(d) Key man insurance

h. Employees
(1) Number
(2) Union relationships, contracts, etc., if any
(3) Work stoppages, turnover, etc.
(4) Availability
(5) Status of management-employee relations
(6) Benefit plans

i. Regulation and litigation
(1) Compliance with federal regulations (e.g. OSHA, EEOC, SEC, etc.)
(2) Compliance with state regulations
(3) Summary of significant litigation to which company, directors, officers, or employees have been a party
(4) Pending or threatened actions.

j. Outlook
(1) Expansion plans
(a) Capital expenditures
(b) Acquisitions
(c) Financing
(d) Assumptions
(2) Divestiture or liquidation plans, status
(3) Sale or merger plans, status
(4) Special risks, opportunities, contingency plans

However, these points are merely representative and are not intended to be exhaustive. Not all of the above factors are needed in any individual analysis. The factors reviewed must be tailored to individual assignments.

Sources

The sources of information for this phase of the study include (1) written company materials, (2) publicly available secondary sources, (3) due diligence at the company, and (4) other information required for the specific study.

Written Company Materials

Normally, the important descriptive materials about a public company are its Securities and Exchange Commission Filings, its annual and interim reports to stockholders, and its proxy statements. Filings include:

1. *Form 10-K*. The company's annual report to the SEC which includes not only the company's financial statement, but also descriptions of its history, business and competition by major product lines as well as management's discussion of a firm's profitability and financial resources.
2. *Form 10-Q*. The company's interim report to the SEC.
3. *Form 8-K*. The company's disclosure of significant events to the SEC.
4. *Rule 13e-3 Transaction Statement*. The SEC filing statement for an issuer or an affiliate for a going-private transaction.
5. *Schedule 13D*. This is required of any person or group who acquires beneficial ownership of five percent or more of any class of equity security.
6. *Schedule 14D-1*. This is required of any person or group who makes a tender offer which would result in the ownership of five percent or more of any class of equity security.
7. *Schedule 14D-9*. This is issued as a response to the Schedule 14D-1 filing.
8. *Registration Statements and Prospectuses*. These are issued by the company in public offerings of securities and which contain detailed descriptions of the company and the securities sold.
9. *Proxy Statements*. These are issued by the company in connection with shareholder votes and describe shareholder ownership and the composition of the Board of Directors. Proxy statements issued in connection with mergers are particularly informative.

Drafts of the above documents not yet filed with the SEC should also be reviewed. Other written company data include press releases, reports to regulatory agencies, sales material, important engineering and consultants reports, critical agreements, and in the case of closely-held companies, the charter and bylaws of the corporation. Obviously, if a proxy statement or other document is to be distributed, it should be reviewed as well.

Other Available Public Data

Other sources of data include Standard & Poor's *Corporation Records, Stock Reports,* and *Industry Survey,* Moody's *Manuals,* Value Line's *Investment Survey,* and *The Wall Street Journal,* any of which may provide useful factual company and industry data. Industry and economic data may also be found in government and industry publications as well as in trade association documents. Reports of securities analysts should not be overlooked as a source in the case of a public company. Typically, a public company keeps a file of analysts' reports and press articles.

Due Diligence at Company

This part of the study usually consists of two phases: tours of the facilities and key management interviews. Tours of facilities are visits to significant manufacturing facilities, or other facilities, and include discussions with appropriate operating personnel with a view toward reviewing the suitability, orderliness, general condition and utilization of the facilities, management depth and quality, general employee morale, and the condition and quality of inventories and other assets. The investment banker should be alert to material negatives, potential problems or questions which elicited contradictory, angry or negative responses as well as potentially hidden values or opportunities. However, the investment banker is not expected to be an expert on the operations of the company. Interviews with key management are detailed discussions about the history, operations, environment, and outlook for the company. Although often not possible, these discussions should take place after the qualitative analysis of the business and the quantitative analysis of the firm's financial statements and projections are well under way. Follow-up interviews should be conducted if important questions subsequently develop.

Other possible sources of information for a particular engagement include: (1) customers and suppliers, (2) auditors, (3) appraisers, (4) commercial bankers, (5) investment bankers, (6) credit agencies, and (7) special experts such as actuaries or pension consultants.

Quantitative Analysis

Purpose

The purpose of the quantitative analysis is to analyze the firm's financial statements and projections to determine its income generation potential, the nature of its assets and liabilities, its financial condition, and its risks.

Standard Analyses of Historical Financial Statements

Generally five years of annual historical financial statements of the subject company as well as the latest interim comparative financial statement are reviewed and the following comparative ratios may be calculated.

1. Profit margins on revenues, such as gross profit margin, operating margin, earnings before interest and taxes (EBIT) margin, and after-tax margin, which show on a comparative basis the profitability of the corporation after various expenses have been paid.
2. Trends and growth rates in revenues and income, which show how the revenues and income of the corporation have changed under different economic and industry conditions.
3. Capital structure ratios, such as (1) percentage composition of invested capital or total liabilities, normally computed based on the latest available balance sheet, which shows the relative composition of the firm's liabilities and equities, (2) interest, fixed charges, and preferred dividend coverage ratios, and (3) analysis of funds available for debt service, all of which show the degree of leverage in the corporation which can increase both the financial risks and earning returns of the common stockholders.
4. Liquidity ratios, generally computed based on the latest available balance, such as (1) current ratio, (2) quick or acid test ratio, and (3) accounts receivable and inventory turnover ratios, which show the adequacy of the firm's current operating capital to meet the needs of its operating cycle.
5. Return on total assets or invested capital, which show how well the corporation has been able to generate a profit, given the total funds (debt and equity) invested in the company.
6. Return on common stockholders' equity, which shows how well the corporation has generated a profit on sales and used financial leverage to generate a profit on the common stockholders' investment in the firm.

7. Industry-specific ratios, such as sales per square foot in retailing, advertising lineage in newspaper and magazine publishing, or the interest spread in commercial banking, which show the performance of the company based on standard industry statistics.

These ratios and statistics are analyzed and compared to the company's management's comments to stockholders and in personal interviews.

Pro Forma Financial Statements

Sometimes the financial statements of the company must be adjusted to determine the recurring earning power of the corporation. Possible causes of restatements include discontinued operations, acquisitions, refinancings, nonrecurring events, and changes in accounting methods. If the company has excess assets that do not contribute to the value of the firm on an operating basis, pro forma financial statements may be created excluding the income and expense associated with these assets from the income statement and excluding the assets and their financing, if any, from the balance sheet. This procedure shows more clearly the earning power and risk of the firm's operations, the value of which then can be combined with the value of the excess assets. Similarly, if the firm is multidivisional based upon product lines and the divisions are run relatively autonomously, it is useful to have divisional financial statements for valuing each division separately to determine the aggregate value of the total corporation.

For a closely-held concern, additional adjustments may be necessary. Public companies are generally run to maximize reported profit so as to maximize stock values. Private companies do not maximize taxable profit but tend to stress cash flow; furthermore, owners of closely-held companies often take perquisites not given to the management of public companies. Both of these factors could conceal earning power. Thus, the financial statements of private companies often are recast.

Other Accounting and Financial Matters

Important in all valuations is a "qualified opinion" by the auditor of the firm's financial statements. This opinion indicates that the auditor was concerned about a specific condition and that the reader of the financial statements should review the impact of the condition carefully.

Other accounting and financial matters that may be important in particular situations include: (1) the status of and accounting for receivables and inventories (e.g. LIFO vs. FIFO) (2) revalued assets, (3) the nature of the firm's intangibles and their amortization, (4) depreciation and depletion policies,

(5) contingent assets and/or liabilities, (6) covenants in existing debt and their effect on financial and operating policies, (7) sale-leaseback arrangements, (8) debt maturity schedules and other cash flow requirements, (9) dividend restrictions and arrearages on preferred stock, and (10) the company's tax position, including unusual problems and tax loss carry forwards.

Budgets and Projections

The company's current operating budgets and projections express management's view of the recurring earning power of the firm. They are credible if their key underlying assumptions incorporate the company's historical performance and current economic conditions, and the projections are the result of an ongoing operating control and reward system which has been a relatively accurate predictor of corporate performance in the past. Any financial projections given to secure financing should be carefully reviewed. Management should explain any significant deviations from past performance. If forecasts are not available, the investment banker should know management's general expectations for revenues and earnings.

Pricing Analyses

Any pricing analysis that is appropriate may be used to test the fairness of a transaction as long as the technique is standard and acceptable in the investment banking community. Nonstandard techniques should be used sparingly, as they may be rejected as a matter of law. The following is a discussion of the three major pricing analyses for Delaware law—market value, investment or comparable company value, and asset value, as well as two other approaches to common stock valuation.

Market Value

One of the major indicators of common stock value for fairness opinions are common stock prices in arm's-length sales, unaffected by the pending transaction.

Typically, in fairness opinions for freely marketable common stock of public companies, the value of the consideration offered is compared to the annual price range of the common stock for about three years prior to the announcement of the transaction, and the interim period preceding the transaction. Weekly or daily stock prices and share volume for several months prior to the offer are also reviewed, and the offer price is related to the price of the stock at the time of particular company events, and the price of the stock to one day prior and one month prior to announcement.

An offer is presumptively fair based on a market value if the value is significantly higher than the price of the stock one day prior and one month prior to the announcement and also is higher than the market price in the preceding few years. An offer is unfair if the value of the consideration offered is below the market price or bid price for the stock prior to announcement and the stock is traded in reasonable volume.

If the value of the consideration offered is equal to or only somewhat higher than the unaffected price of the stock during the month preceding the offer and/or is below the market prices in the preceding periods, then the price trends, volume trends, price/earnings ratio trends, and price performance comparisons may become important aspects of establishing the fairness of the transaction. When the price decline in the stock occurs with reasonable trading volume and mirrors either a decline in stock prices generally and in the company's industry, or a decline in the company's economic performance, then the price of the stock at the time of the offer may be representative of the market value of the stock. If the decline takes place with low trading volume and is unrelated to either the stock market's or the company's performance, then the market price at the time of the offer merits further investigation.

Investment Value and Comparable Company Analysis

Two kinds of investment (or comparable company) value can be computed for the subject company's common shares, viz. (1) their value in the hands of existing shareholders on a minority interest basis, and (2) their value to a potential acquiror of 100 percent of the common stock of the corporation. The valuation process for each is pricing by analogy.

Selection of Comparable Group. The first step in the process is the selection of the comparable group of publicly traded companies for the minority valuation, and of acquisitions for the majority or controlling interest valuation. The following list contains some of the typical criteria for selection.

1. Line of business, often with minimum percentages of revenue or income from particular predefined product or service categories (e.g. using Standard Industrial Classification [SIC] codes, Securities and Exchange Commission codes, Standard & Poor's *Stock Guide* codes, etc.).
2. Geographic areas served.
3. Adequacy of financial and pricing information.
4. Minimum or maximum size in terms of revenues or assets.
5. Profitability.
6. In the case of acquisitions, the date of the announcement of the transaction and its outcome.

The group should be selected on objective criteria, but this should not preclude the investment banker from using professional judgment for including or excluding specific companies if the situation warrants it. For example, named competitors may be included even if they are not in the appropriate business classification, or specific acquisitions may be included because of some particular aspect of the transaction. Nevertheless, the group of comparables selected should be reasonably complete and defensible. In trying to discredit a fairness opinion, a plaintiff may allege that comparable companies were omitted or that the selection was biased.

Comparables' Financial Performance Ratios. The second step in the process is computing many of the same financial performance ratios for the comparables as were computed for the subject company in the quantitive analysis (e.g. the profit margin ratios, trends, capital structure ratios, etc. listed above). Care should be taken to note any significant or unusual financial statistics of the comparable companies. Generally, because more financial information is available for publicly traded companies than for acquisitions, the comparative analysis of the former is conducted in more detail. Based on these computations, the relative performance of the subject company is determined either by ranking the subject company with the comparables or by comparing the company's performance ratios to the group's average or median statistics. If an average is used, care must be taken that it is not distorted by extraordinarily high or low ratios.

Comparables' Pricing Ratios. The next step in the process is developing the pricing ratios of the comparables. The pricing ratios may be based on either the value of common equity or the value of the total market capitalization (often computed as common stockholders' equity at market value or acquisition price plus the sum of senior equity capitalization at either book liquidation value or market value less the sum of cash and marketable securities). The ratios often used are presented in Figure 2.

All of the ratios in Figure 2 do not have to be computed. Market quotations of common stock, or the prices of common stock in acquisitions, are used for calculation of equity value. Pricing based on the total market capitalization of the comparables and acquisitions results in the value for the total capitalization of the firm; the firm's senior equity capitalization and debt must be subtracted from this value, and the firm's excess cash and marketable securities must be added back to determine the market value of the common equity.

The equity values determined by both of these methods should be roughly similar if the subject company has a similar capital structure to the

FIGURE 2
Developing Pricing Ratios for the Comparable Group

Pricing Rations Based on Common Equity Value

1. Price/historical earnings based on:
   a. Latest available 12-month earnings.
   b. 5-year average or 3-year average, often used for cyclical companies;
2. Price/projected earnings based on:
   a. Current year's earnings;
   b. Following year's earnings.
3. Price to book value based on:
   a. Book value;
   b. Tangible book value.
4. Dividend yield based on indicated dividend rate.
5. Price to historical or projected cash flow, usually used when the subject company has little or no earnings, or is in an industry which typically generates substantial noncash charges for investment in new projects (such as oil and gas, real estate, and broadcasting) and uses the ratio as a customary standard of value.

Pricing Ratios Based on Market Capitalization

1. Total market capitalization to historical operating income
   a. 5-year average or 3-year average, often used for cyclical companies;
   b. Latest year or latest 12-month earnings.
2. Total market capitalization to projected operating income
   a. Current year's earnings;
   b. Following year's earnings.
3. Total market capitalization to revenues, usually used when the subject company has little or no earnings.
4. Total market capitalizaiton to operating cash flow (operating income plus operating depreciation and amortization, usually used when the company has little or no earnings or is in an industry which typically generates substantial noncash charges for investment in new projects.

---

comparables. If the capital structures are different, the results may be drastically different because debt and equity often have different pretax capitalization rates. For example, while the debt of companies in an industry may require a yield of 10 percent, the pretax yield requirement of equity based on a price/earnings ratio of 10 may be 16.7 percent (calculated as the inverse of the price/earnings ratio, adjusted for a 40 percent tax rate.)

If the subject company is highly leveraged and the comparable group is only moderately leveraged, the calculated value of the equity of the subject company based on total market capitalization may be small or negative despite substantial earnings.

Harmonic Mean. Pricing the subject company by either approach requires using either the statistics of individual comparable companies or the group as whole. Arithmetic means may produce significant distortions because of unusually high or low multiples. The median, i.e., the number that is in the middle of the group, is usually a much better measure; however, it has the disadvantage of discarding the information contained in all remaining comparable company multiples. In many instances, the best measure is the harmonic mean (H), calculated based on the arithmetic mean of the reciprocals of the multiples as follows:

$$H = \frac{n}{\sum (1/x)}$$

where

H = harmonic mean
n = the number companies for which ratios are computed
$\sum (1/x)$ = the sum of the reciprocals of the individual comparable company ratios

With respect to P/E ratios, the harmonic mean calculates an average based on the *earnings/price* ratios. This is identical to the method of calculating an average yield on a group of securities, as the yield is simply the dividend/price ratio. Another way of describing the harmonic mean is that it gives equal weight to equal dollar investments in the securities whose ratios are being averaged. The harmonic mean is usually the best and most reliable average of ratios in which price is in the numerator.

The following should clarify the concept of the harmonic mean:

1. Assume that Company A sells at $20 per share, earns $2 per share and pays a $2 dividend, and Company B sells at $25 per share, earns $1.25 per share and pays a $1.25 dividend. They yield 10 percent and 5 percent respectively; the "average" yield (i.e., the arithmetic mean) is 7.5 percent. Their P/E ratios are 10 and 20, respectively. An arithmetic mean of these two numbers is 15. The harmonic mean is calculated by taking the reciprocals of 10 and 20 (0.10 and 0.05), averaging them (0.075) and taking the reciprocal of 0.075, (i.e., a harmonic mean P/E of 13.3).
2. One can look at this a different way. If one has an equal amount invested in each stock, what is the P/E ratio of the portfolio? If one spends $1,000 to buy 50 shares of Company A, the underlying earnings would be $100 (50 times $2); if one spends $1,000 to buy 40 shares of Company B, underlying earnings would be $50 (40 times $1.25). With $2,000 invested in a portfolio earning an aggregate of $150, the P/E ratio of the portfolio would be 13.3 (i.e., equal to the harmonic mean).

3. If, instead, one wished to purchase $100 of underlying earnings in each company, one would still buy 50 shares of Company A for $1,000, but it would be necessary to spend $2,000 to buy 80 shares of Company B. Then the portfolio would cost $3,000 for earnings of $200, giving a P/E ratio of 15 (i.e., the arithmetic mean).

Thus, it is clear that the harmonic mean gives *equal weight* to *equal dollar investments,* while the arithmetic mean gives a greater weight to stocks with higher P/E ratios.

Acquisition Premium. Sometimes people attempt to determine the value of a corporation by adding an average acquisition premium to the freely-traded value of the company's common stock. This average premium is often calculated by averaging acquisition premiums in an industry over a specific period of time. This procedure is usually unsound. An acquisition premium is the result of factors unique to each transaction, and of the degree of market undervaluation prior to the transaction.

Asset Value

This approach appraises the common stock of the subject company by valuing its assets, subtracting the liabilities that must be paid and the senior equity, and dividing the result by the number of common shares. The asset value can be determined on several different bases.

Value of Assets in Use

Value of assets in use focuses on value of the company's assets as part of a profitable going concern. There may be only a small writedown, if any, of receivables and inventory. Fixed assets are valued at either (1) depreciated replacement cost including costs of assemblage, that is, the cost of putting the plant and equipment together and the costs of making them ready for operation or (2) inplace revenue producing ability. Using this approach the value of the company's plant, property, and equipment may approximate or exceed book value. This valuation method is not realistic unless the business has significant revenue and profit producing ability.

Liquidation Value

Liquidation value focuses on the value of the company broken up and liquidated piecemeal. There may be major writedowns of receivables and inventory. It is not unusual to write down receivables by 15 percent or more and inventories by 50 percent or more, depending on their marketability in bulk or on their condition. Fixed assets are valued based on auction value.

This value may be materially different from recorded book value. To provide for the time value of money, expenses, and risks of the liquidation process, these values may be further discounted by an additional 15 percent or more.

Disaggregation Value

Disaggregation value focuses on the "break-up" value of the company. Some operations are valued using operating approaches such as comparable company analyses, while other operations are valued on a liquidation basis. It is usually appropriate to provide for the time, tax effects, expenses, and risks of breaking up and selling the company. This method is suitable for larger multidivisional operations. It is seldom realistic for smaller single product line concerns.

In all approaches, excess assets and investments such as marketable securities are valued at their net realizable value, net of tax effect.

Net Operating Loss Carryforwards (NOLs)

NOLs may be an additional source of value if the net asset value approach used assumes the continuation of the firm without a material change in ownership. The valuation of the carryforward is based upon its magnitude and time to expiration, the corporate tax rate in effect, the forecasted profitability of the firm, and an appropriate discount rate to reflect both the timing and uncertainty of realizing the tax savings. Assuming some projected profitability for the firm, it is not unusual for carryforwards to be valued at 5 to 15 percent of their face value. (Note that a $1,000 cost carryforward is worth a maximum of $340 if the tax rate is 34 percent, before discounting it further to present value.)

Tax Liabilities

With the *elimination of tax-free liquidations,* an additional factor to consider, if the net asset value of the company is based upon a complete or partial liquidation approach, is the payment of income taxes on any gains and the possibility of tax refunds if the liquidation creates any losses. Recapture of investment tax credits should also be considered.

Off-balance Sheet or Contingent Assets and Liabilities

Off-balance sheet or contingent assets and liabilities also may have an impact on net asset value. Factors to consider include excess or deficient pension funding, medical liabilities, litigation by or against the company, product warranties, and loan guarantees.

Convertible Securities and Options

Convertible securities, warrants, and options may also affect the net asset value per share of the company. If the conversion price or the exercise price is less than the expected value per share, the incremental shares should be reflected pro forma. The proceeds from the exercise or conversion should be added to the net asset value of the company, and the total then should be divided by the new number of shares to calculate the net asset value per share.

Other Approaches to Valuation

Besides the three standard approaches to value used in the Delaware block approach, there are at least two other approaches to value that are used with mixed degrees of success—formula pricing and discounted cash flow.

Formula Pricing

Formula values, in some industries, are often the basis of buying or selling a business, such as a specific dollar amount per subscriber in the publishing and cable television industries. In some industries, however, these formulas are primarily used as negotiating points or short cuts to a more complete financial and economic analysis. These formulas can be useful indications of value if they have an economic basis applicable to the specific situation and if the formulas are often used, with limited variability in price, in transactions in the industry.

Discounted Cash Flow

Discounted cash flow, which has gained widespread acceptance both in business and academia, is based directly on the concept that the value of common stock in a corporation is the present value of expected future cash flows from distributions of available annual net free cash flow, from the sale of underlying assets, from the sale of the common stock held, or a combination of all these sources. Essentially, an investment banker using the approach relies on forecasts of net free cash flow for a number of years, determines a "terminal value" at the end of the forecast period, and then, based on a selected discount rate for both time and risk, calculates a present value of the forecasted annual cash flow and the terminal value.

Minority Interest Valuations. Annual cash flow for minority interest valuations consists of the expected annual dividend payments to the shares involved and the terminal value consists of a forecasted selling price for the stock or the result of the perpetual capitalization of the projected dividend in the final year. Usually, both projections assume the continued operation of the firm by existing management following existing dividend policies. The discount rate is usually based on the rate of return required, or cost, for common equity.

Control Valuations. For control valuations, these procedures are more complex. The forecasted cash flow and terminal value may be computed either on a "debt-free" or "post-debt" basis. Annual debt-free cash flow is computed as net funds generated by operations before interest expense but after provision for taxes, plus net additional funds provided by other assets after taxes, less net funds required for additions to working capital, capital expenditures and other fund requirements excluding financing. Post-debt cash flow, in addition to the preceding factors, provides for the subtraction of projected annual interest expense and debt amortization. Both cash flows are known as *net free cash flow*. If the debt-free approach is used, the current value of the firm's debt must be subtracted from the present value of the cash flow and terminal value to calculate the value of the firm's equity. The second approach determines this value directly.

Volatility. Cash flows, at best, tend to have greater volatility and are less predictable than dividends. Furthermore, in situations involving the sale of the company, cash flow projections may tend to incorporate some untested actions to increase sales, cut costs, or provide for asset sales or synergistic benefits. As in evaluating all business projections, to the extent that the cash flow forecast is internally consistent, consistent with the business' historical operations, developed by experienced operating management, and consistent with the current and expected economic environment, the forecasted cash flow is more credible; to the extent that the forecast is based on untested or speculative assumptions, credibility and reliability is reduced.

The Forecast Horizon. The forecast horizon, i.e., the number of years for which the forecast is made, can have a significant impact on the value determined. If both limited annual net free cash flow and limited growth in cash flow are projected in a forecast and the number of years in the projection is increased, then the discounted cash flow value will decrease as a result of the impact of the discount rate on the terminal value.

Terminal Value Choices. Terminal value choices may have a major impact on the computed discounted cash flow value. Typical terminal value computations are based on: (1) the projected book value of the firm at the end of the period (this choice should not be used, but often is), (2) the projected net asset value of the firm at the end of the period, computed on a liquidation basis, (3) capitalization of projected earnings, cash flow, etc., based on anticipated future market or acquisition multiples, or (4) the Dividend

Discount Model, which capitalizes the projection's final dividend or net free cash flow as a perpetuity according to the following formula:

$$P = \frac{D(1 + G)}{K - G}$$

Where:

P = The value of equity
D = Final year's dividend or net free cash flow
K = Cost of capital or discount rate
G = The long-term growth rate in D

Each of these terminal value choices can result in a different terminal value and, thus, a different valuation based on the discounted cash flow approach.

Discount Rate Choices. Discount rate choices can also have a major impact on the final value determined. For a post-debt cash flow projection, the discount rate should be based on the rate of return required for common equity. For debt-free cash flow, the discount rate should be based on the required rate for the firm's capital structure, also known as the weighted cost of capital. In determining the weighted average cost of capital, it may be necessary to consider not only the existing capital structure, but also the appropriate capital structure, and to calculate the required rates of return on other sources of long-term financing as well.

Advantages and Disadvantages of Discounted Cash Flows. The advantages of the discounted cash flow method for fairness opinions include its focus on future performance, its conceptual simplicity, and its use by business, academia, and increasingly the Courts. However, in most fairness situations these advantages are usually outweighed by the method's disadvantages, including (1) the reliance on forecasts, which often tend to be quite optimistic, (2) the myriad of assumptions, many of which can be highly speculative, and the high degree of sensitivity to such assumptions, (3) the tendency to ignore past performance, (4) the horizon problem, and (5) the lack of appropriateness of the methodology in many fairness situations. Even in those situations where the method might be appropriate, it is often easy in litigation to challenge the forecasts, the discount rate, and terminal value assumptions.

The viability of valuations based on discounted cash flow is dependent upon the assumptions on which they are based. The inaccuracy of earnings forecasts limits the usefulness of discounted cash flow as a valuation technique in fairness opinions (See Chapter 4).

THE OPINION

Development of the Conclusion

The final determination of fairness is a subjective assessment by professionals of all the facts and circumstances of the values developed and the standards to be applied. It is the result of informed judgment and common sense. Fair value in an appraisal proceeding provides some guidance as to the minimum consideration for the fairness of a proposed transaction. Often, however, this standard is not enough. In terms of fairness, these cases often focus too heavily on what shareholders have, excluding the impact of a proposed transaction, and give too little weight to the shareholders' economic contribution to the success of it. Furthermore, the courts often have used a weighting procedure that can be unfair to minority shareholders.

At Bear, Stearns we often use what we call the "silver dollar analogy" in determining fairness to a seller. If one has a silver dollar that is worth $1 as currency, $5 in silver content, and $10 to a coin collector, its value is not $5. It is worth $10 less provision for the time, effort and ability to sell it. Similarly, fairness to outside shareholders for a pending transaction requires that predominant weight be given to the highest reasonable, realizable value for common stock considering the transaction.

Delivery of the Opinion

After internal review, the investment banker's opinion is usually presented orally at a meeting of the Board of Directors or the Independent Directors' Committee requesting the opinion. The discussion usually is about the investment banker's assignment, the procedures followed, and the factors considered important in formulating the opinion. An undated form of the opinion letter may be presented to the Board and its counsel.

The final opinion letter usually contains the following sections:

1. The date—unless otherwise specified, which is usually the date of opinion and the date of the document to shareholders in which the opinion letter appears.
2. The addressee—which is usually either the Board of Directors or the Independent Directors' Committee.
3. The description of the transaction—a short description of transaction for which opinion is required.
4. The definition and scope of the investment bankers' assignment.

5. The description of the procedures used and factors considered, including:
   a. Materials reviewed.
   b. People interviewed.
   c. Facilities seen.
   d. Review of stock market prices and volume data.
   e. Consideration of comparable public company data.
   f. Review of comparable acquisition data.
   g. Review of appraisals.
   h. Other factors.
6. The scope and limitations of the assignment, including:
   a. The use of unaudited annual financial statements, if any.
   b. Access to personnel and information.
   c. Material time constraints, if any.
   d. Reliance on management.
   e. Reliance on others.
   f. Other limitations and qualifications.
8. The opinion statement—which includes the opinion and its date if it is other that the date of letter.
9. The signature.

The Appendix contains a representative opinion letter for a Bear, Stearns engagement.

APPENDIX: SAMPLE OPINION LETTER

BEAR STEARNS

BEAR STEARNS & CO. INC.
245 PARK AVENUE
NEW YORK, NEW YORK 10167
(212) 272-2000

ATLANTA • BOSTON
CHICAGO • DALLAS • LOS ANGELES
NEW YORK • SAN FRANCISCO

AMSTERDAM • GENEVA • HONG KONG
LONDON • PARIS • TOKYO

November 21, 1988

Veeco Instruments
515 Broad Hollow Road
Melville, NY 11747

Attention: Board of Directors

Dear Sirs:

We understand that Veeco Instruments Inc. ("Veeco") has received an offer from VII Acquisition Corporation ("Purchaser"), an indirect wholly-owned subsidiary of Unitech plc, pursuant to which the stockholders of Veeco would receive $26.50 per share in cash (the "Transaction") in accordance with an Agreement and Plan of Merger, dated as of November 16, 1988, by and among Veeco, Unitech plc, Purchaser and VII Merger Corporation ("Merger Sub"), a wholly-owned subsidiary of Purchaser, which provides, among other things, that Purchaser will promptly commence a tender offer (the "Tender Offer") for all the outstanding shares of Veeco. Following completion of the Tender Offer, Veeco and the Merger Sub will be merged (the "Merger") and each Veeco Common Share not purchased in the Tender Offer will be converted into the right to receive $26.50 in cash pursuant to the Merger. You have provided us with the Offer to Purchase and related documents, all in substantially the form to be sent to the stockholders of Veeco (the "Tender Offer Documents").

You have asked us to render out opinion as to whether the Transaction is fair, from a financial point of view, to the stockholders of Veeco.

In the course of our analyses for rendering this opinion, we have:

1. reviewed the Tender Offer Documents;

2. reviewed Veeco's Annual Report to Stockholders and its Annual Reports on Form 10-K for the fiscal years ended September 30, 1983 through 1987; and its Quarterly Reports on Form 10-Q for the periods ended January 3, April 3, and July 3, 1988;

3. reviewed certain appraisals and operating and financial information, including projections, provided to us by management;

4. met with certain members of Veeco's senior management to discuss its operations, historical financial statements and future prospects;

5. visited certain of Veeco's facilities;

6. reviewed factors relating to the Japanese securities market and Japanese mergers and acquisitions;

7. reviewed historical stock prices and trading volumes of the common shares of Veeco;

8. reviewed publicly available financial data and stock market performance data of other public companies which we deemed generally comparable to Veeco;

9. reviewed the terms of recent acquisitions of companies which we deemed generally comparable to Veeco; and

10. conducted such other studies, analyses, inquiries and investigations as we deemed appropriate.

In the course of our review we have relied upon and assumed, without independent verification, the accuracy and completeness of the financial and other information provided to us, and we have further relied upon the assurances of management that they are unaware of any facts that would make the information provided to us incomplete or misleading. In arriving at our opinion, we have not performed any independent appraisal of the assets of Veeco.

Based on the foregoing, it is our opinion that the Transaction is fair, from a financial point of view, to the stockholders of Veeco who tender their shares pursuant to the Tender Offer.

Very truly yours,

BEAR, STEARNS & CO. INC.

By: /s/ G.E. Matthews

Managing Director

CHAPTER 19

AN OPINION ON FAIRNESS OPINIONS

Martin J. Whitman
Whitman Heffernan Rhein & Co., Inc.

Fairness opinions by investment bankers are a sacred cow—virtually unattacked by anyone in scholarly literature or in legal courtrooms. There tends to be blind reliance by the judiciary on the integrity of investment bankers and on their competence to render fairness opinions. Virtually all boards of directors now insist on investment banking opinions, thus paying millions of dollars in fees while at the same time indemnifying the investment bankers against all costs and liabilities. Court decisions encourage—indeed insist—that boards of directors be protected against stockholder suits in cases of mergers, acquisitions, takeovers, and the like, by relying on investment bankers' opinions (see Chapters 21–24 on the Van Gorkhom decisions in Delaware).

It is high time that someone examined what these investment banking opinions are—and what they should be. The two key issues, we will see, are *competence* and *integrity*.

A FINANCIAL VIEWPOINT?

In almost every case, an investment banker's fairness opinion talks of fairness "from a financial point of view." But what does "from a financial point of view" mean?

- A premium over market?
- A range of fairness with investment bankers deeming a price fair even if stockholders are paid a price equal to the lowest part of a range of fairness?

- As a practical matter, does "financial point of view" conflict with deriving fairness by considering "all relevant factors?" I think it does.

CONFLICTS OF INTEREST

The primary reason for hiring investment bankers to render a fairness opinion is to have them represent and protect public security holders against buyers who typically are insiders with the power to force a transaction (often going private). There is an immediate conflict of interest here: The investment bankers are paid by the buyers to protect the sellers in an area in which there are no standards of behavior for the investment banker, and no discipline whatever to which the investment banker is subject.

This "no standards, no discipline" contrasts sharply with other areas in which insiders hire a financial professional to protect public security holders, specifically auditors and indenture trustees.

WHAT IS "FAIRNESS?"

Fairness is that price and those terms that would be arrived at after negotiations between a willing buyer and a willing seller, both with knowledge of the relevant facts and neither under any compulsion to act.

The investment bankers' job is to determine what that willing buyer-willing seller price and terms would be, if in fact there was a willing buyer-willing seller environment. In actuality there is often no willing buyer-willing seller, but rather a coercive buyer-forced seller situation in which the buyer also happens to be a fiduciary, quasi-fiduciary, informed control, active insider, while the seller most often is a beneficiary, quasi-beneficiary, less well-informed, noncontrol, passive outsider. For an investment banker to do his job he has to abstract from the real world and simulate a willing buyer-willing seller environment. Probably not many bankers do this; few even realize that this is what they are supposed to do.

Many corporate control blocks and their investment bankers seem to think that all an investor is entitled to is the price at which he could sell his stock in the open market; and that any premium over market is fair per se (see several Delaware Statutory Appraisal valuation decisions). This is antithetical to the willing buyer-willing seller concept, because one of the elements to be considered in arriving at fairness is what the equity security being valued is really worth to the buyer.

On the other hand, many attorneys representing stockholder-plaintiffs think that in a fiduciary-beneficiary situation, the fiduciary-insider buyer has to pay to the beneficiary-outsider seller that price that represents *full* value to the buyer. This, too, is antithetical to the willing buyer-willing seller concept in which a transaction has to appear attractive to *both* sides. If the buyer has to pay full value, he would not buy in the first place. This is not good for public security holders or their portfolios. A premium over market is an important, though not necessarily decisive, element making a transaction attractive for a seller of a publicly held security. There is no sense in removing incentives for fiduciaries to pay premium over market by requiring them to pay full value. Fairness typically lies in the middle to the upper end of a range of value, but not at the very top.

In truth, investment bankers cannot arrive at fairness unless they consider certain factors.

1. Premium over market prices.
2. Reasonableness of price based on comparative analysis with other issuers, and/or discounted cash flows, and/or ability of the buyer to finance the proposed transaction.
3. Benefits to buyer as a result of the transaction.

COMPETENCE, INTEGRITY, AND ACCOUNTABILITY

Valuation of equity securities of corporations will always lack the precision one can bring to other financial services and appraisals. In these other valuations, there are either well-developed or codified standards or only a limited number of variables that need be examined (e.g., audited financials, tax accounting, credit analysis, and MAI appraisals of income producing real estate).

Thus, as a matter of necessity in giving fairness opinions, investment bankers have to be given wider latitude than exists for other financial professions performing related functions.

This being so, and as a matter of public policy, I think that investment bankers who command huge multimillion dollar fees should no longer be indemnified. If they err, they should pay. But if investment bankers continue to collect without risk, then courts should place little reliance or weight on their opinions.

What, then, should investment bankers do to strengthen public confidence in their opinions? There are, as I have said, two qualities on which we should rely: competence and integrity.

In terms of *competence*, many investment bankers—even those from the most prestigious houses—do poor quality work (e.g., when a top-tier firm only considered public information in its fairness opinion of a major oil company).

In terms of *integrity*, many investment bankers seem to owe their first loyalties to those who are paying them (i.e., the insiders) rather than those they are supposed to protect from the insiders (i.e., the outsiders). No checks exist to require these renderers of fairness opinion to act with integrity. In contrast, there are meaningful constraints on boards of directors, accountants, managements, and attorneys.

Unless the system is changed, minority stockholders will continue to get shortchanged. Investment bankers must be held accountable for the consequences of their highly paid opinions.

CHAPTER 20

PURCHASE PRICE CONSIDERATIONS WHEN SELLING A BUSINESS

Ezra G. Levin
with
Warren J. Ingber
Kramer, Levin, Nessen, Kamin & Frankel

The determination of a satisfactory purchase price, combined with peace of mind regarding the method and reliability of receipt, are usually the most important factors for sellers of businesses. This chapter addresses some of the issues involved, especially with respect to asset sales (e.g., inventories) and contingent earn-outs. There are three sections:

1. An outline of purchase price issues when selling a business. This gives a framework for the evaluation of options.
2. Sample contract excerpts and associated comments for an asset-based purchase price (given in *purchaser*-oriented form).
3. Sample contract excerpts and associated comments for a contingent earn-out (given in *seller*-oriented form).

The latter two sections demonstrate how such contractual provisions regarding price can be *skewed* to benefit either the purchaser or the seller, depending on the terms of the agreement (and the way they are drafted). The text presents the sample sections from the (biased) contracts and the footnotes give the explanatory comments from the viewpoint of either purchaser or seller.

 The assistance of Michael R. Becker is gratefully acknowledged.

OUTLINE OF PURCHASE PRICE ISSUES WHEN SELLING A BUSINESS

1. The form of payment

a. Cash, New York clearing house, or federal funds

(1) Immediate availability of funds, especially if weekend or holiday intervenes.

(2) No opportunity for Purchaser to back out after closing.

(3) Appraisal rights (Delaware G.C.L. Section 262; New York B.C.L. Section 910). Consider setting maximum, e.g. 5%.

b. Common stock or warrants

(1) Valuation problems—time of fixing; trading ranges; minima/maxima.

(2) Potential discount for blockage—may create large block of Purchaser's stock. Request registration rights.

(3) Defining antidilution rights for warrantholder—voting power; economics.

(4) Purchaser's uncertainty as to whether warrant will be exercised.

c. Preferred stock

(1) Mandatory or discretionary, cumulative or noncumulative dividends. Pay-in-Kind (PIK) permits deferral of cash dividend for period.

(2) Right to elect directors in case of arrearages.

(3) Convertible/Non-convertible

d. Redeemable preferred stock

(1) At option of issuer (may permit buyer to avoid appraisal rights); exchangeability for debt (buyer may later seek deduction for interest payments).

(2) At option of holder—tax and accounting issues:

(a) Reorganization provisions of Internal Revenue Code Section 368 (may defeat nontaxable reorganization).

(b) Regulation S-X, Article 5, paragraph 28 (potential exclusion from stockholders' equity; impact on debt covenants). Importance of defining "equity" for purposes of required ratios.

e. Debt

(1) Will subject Purchaser to covenants and risk of acceleration upon default.

(2) Gives Seller no active control over Purchaser.

(3) May require granting of security interest.

(4) Review provisions of other debt instruments. Various levels: senior, senior subordinate, subordinate, etc.

- *f.* Payment in installments
  - (1) Protects Purchaser in event of claims against Seller.
  - (2) Application of offsets to installments in reverse order. (But buyer would prefer to defer earlier rather than later payments).
  - (3) Consider tax impact of monetization and pre-acquisition §351 reorganization so that subsidiary owes parent debt, which remains outstanding after the transaction is consummated.

2. Elements of value: maintenance mechanisms for noncash aspects of transactions

- *a.* Guaranties with makeup (in cash, stock, or debt)
- *b.* Reset of dividend or interest after period of months/years
  - (1) Reset to cause instrument to sell at par.
  - (2) Redeemability at option of holder if not satisfied with reset.
- *c.* Dividends tied to postacquisition performance of seller's business; So-called alphabet stock permits diversified company with low PE ratios to capture value of subsidiary with higher PE multiple without losing control or deconsolidating; Confirm tax treatment.
- *d.* Use of industry index (e.g., a commodity index)
- *e.* Plan for protection of seller in event of delayed closing.

3. Asset-based valuation

- *a.* Arriving at a purchase price formula
  - (1) What assets are to be counted toward the price?
  - (2) Basis of valuation.
  - (3) Inventory discounts.
  - (4) Bad debt reserve.
  - (5) Concept of "Cushion"—recover excess above pre-designated sum, or entire short-fall?
- *b.* Investigation of Seller's assets
  - (1) Providing Purchaser adequate access to Seller's facilities.
  - (2) Providing Seller adequate protection from disruption.
  - (3) Preparing final balance sheet in advance of closing as an alternative.
  - (4) Examine carefully: maintenance; R & D; inventory accumulation.
- *c.* Unsatisfactory inventory
  - (1) Slow-moving or obsolete inventory. Concept of Base Period against which to measure turnover.
  - (2) Defective inventory.
- *d.* Taking of closing inventory
  - (1) Conducted by Seller.
  - (2) Purchaser's right to participate.
- *e.* Closing

f. Preparation of closing date balance sheet by Seller
g. Initial adjustment of amount paid at closing
(1) Adjustments to reflect resolution of inventory-related disputes.
(2) Accounts receivable holdback.
h. Treatment of accounts receivable
(1) Purchaser's collection responsibilities.
(2) Application of amounts collected.
(3) Payment to Seller of excess amounts collected.
(4) Allowances.
i. Post settlement

4. Contingent earn-out
a. Consideration: form and timing
(1) If Purchaser's stock, when to value. Set floor on value to protect against dilution.
(2) Additional consideration to include interest at stipulated rate.
(3) Annual payments versus lump sum payment.
(4) Complicated because it addresses future. Frequently useful in bridging gap. Be mindful of preliminary discussions as basis for later negotiations ("What do you expect to earn?")
b. Determining net earnings: general considerations
(1) Whose accountants make initial application of GAAP?
(2) Definition of "division" should track the business sold.
(3) Account for division as if a freestanding corporation.
(4) Before- versus after-tax earn-out formula. Deter Purchaser's temptation to compromise on tax audits with multiple issues.
(5) Percentage of profits versus excess of earnings over agreed amount.
c. Exclusions from the computation of net earnings
(1) Transaction costs, goodwill and other incidents of the sale affecting net earnings.
(2) Extraordinary gains and losses.
(3) Other gains and losses not in the ordinary course.
(4) Results of expansion of the business.
(5) Transactions in the ordinary course.
(6) Home office overhead.
(7) Compensation of Seller's representative.
(8) Cost of replacement capital.
(9) Intercompany transactions.
d. Operation of the division during the payout period
(1) Representation on the board and in management.

(2) Differing interests of Seller and Purchaser.
(3) Procedures for resolving differences.

5. Purchase price based on earnings prior to closing as opposed to earnings after closing

a. Similarities

(1) Need to make certain exclusions (e.g., extraordinary gains/losses, differences in overhead, etc.).
(2) Treating business as a freestanding corporation rather than as belonging to a particular group.

b. Contrasts

(1) Seller rather than Purchaser has better claim to accounting role.
(2) Seller has no interest in participating in future operations of the business.
(3) No need for Seller to control Purchaser's actions after closing.
(4) Seller has no need to control accounting practices with respect to the business after closing.

ASSET-BASED PURCHASE PRICE PROVISIONS—EXCERPTS OF PURCHASER-ORIENTED FORM

2. Computation and Payment of Purchase Price

(a) In consideration of the sale, transfer, conveyance, assignment and delivery of the Division's Assets by Seller to Purchaser, and in reliance upon the representations and warranties made herein by Seller, Purchaser will, in full payment hereof, pay to Seller a total purchase price (the "Purchase Price") equal to the difference between (1) the Net Book Value (as hereinafter defined), of the Division's Assets and (2) the sum of $3,000,000 (the "Inventory Discount") provided, however, that the Purchase Price shall be subject to reduction as provided in subsection 2(a)(iii) hereof and as otherwise hereinafter provided.[1]

(i) The term "Net Book Value" as used herein as applied to the Division's Assets shall mean the excess of (A) the aggregate net book value of the tangible assets of the Division over (B) the aggregate of all liabilities of

[1]The basic formula "Purchase Price equals Net Book Value less Inventory Discount" is structured to provide, at least initially, only for downward adjustments from Seller's book values. Purchaser has provided, before all else, that at least $3,000,000 will be deducted from Net Book Value, which itself reflects certain exclusions from Seller's asset accounts. The provision could readily be rewritten to provide for a premium above book value (i.e., a Purchase Price "equal to the sum of (i) the Net Book Value . . . plus (ii) $3,000,000").

the Division, as reflected on the Closing Date Balance Sheet (as hereinafter defined) prepared in accordance with the provisions set forth in subsection 2(a)(ii) hereof, it being understood and agreed that (x) tangible assets shall not include any goodwill, and shall not include any capitalized costs or any other intangible assets except to the extent expressly set forth in Exhibit B annexed hereto,[2] (y) accounts receivable shall be reflected net after deduction of a reserve for bad debts determined in a manner consistent with the prior practices of the Division (the "Bad Debt Reserve") and (z) inventory (1) shall be valued on the Closing Date Balance Sheet on the basis of the lower of cost or market in a manner consistent with the prior practices of the Division[3] after the deduction therefrom of an inventory reserve in the amount of $150,000 (the "Inventory Reserve")[4] and (2) shall in no event include the book value of any Defective Inventory (as hereinafter defined) in excess of the Inventory Reserve; provided, however, that in computing the sum of Net Book Value for the purposes of this Agreement, the aggregate net book value of all of the inventory of the Division on the Closing Date which is to be reflected in the Closing Date Balance Sheet (before the amount of any Defective Inventory is deducted therefrom) shall not exceed [$7,500,000].[5]

(ii) The term "Closing Date Balance Sheet" as used herein shall mean a balance sheet of the Division, to be prepared by Seller as of the close of business on the business day immediately preceding the Closing Date, which, except as otherwise provided in Exhibit B annexed hereto, shall be prepared from the books and records of Seller in accordance with generally accepted accounting principles, and all inventory and supplies reflected thereon shall

---

[2]The Purchase Price will not reflect intangible assets or capitalized costs except as expressly provided, leaving it for Seller to propose exceptions. The assets to be factored into the Purchase Price will depend on the nature of the business and are subject to negotiation.

[3]Assuming rising costs, Purchaser would also want to require valuation of inventory under the LIFO method if the Division's prior practices do not already require use of this method. Seller would prefer valuation of inventory at current replacement cost. Notice that under the "lower of cost or market" basis of valuation, Purchaser need not pay the full cost of slow-moving, obsolete, or defective inventory that may have a market value below cost, even if such inventory is not excluded (pursuant to Sections 2(a)(i)(z)(2) or 2(a)(iii)) from the computation of Net Book Value.

[4]At least $150,000 is deducted in respect of Defective Inventory regardless of how much inventory is subsequently determined to be defective, but there is no cap on the amount of inventory that may be so deducted. In the event of a shortfall below the stated amount, however, Seller receives a credit against slow-moving or obsolete, inventory (see footnote 7) so that Seller would not be conceding this full amount without regard to the amount of defective inventory Seller is carrying if Seller anticipated sufficiently high amounts of slow-moving or obsolete inventory.

[5]The [$7.5 million] cap on inventory is designed to limit Purchaser's risk of either an overstatement or an overaccumulation of inventory on the Closing Date Balance Sheet regardless of whether Purchaser is able to achieve any specific adjustments to the initial count.

be so reflected on the basis of a complete physical count taken on the three-day holiday weekend beginning after the close of business on February 12, 1990 and shall be valued at the lower of cost or market in accordance with Seller's prior practices. Purchaser's representatives shall have the right to participate in the taking of such physical inventory and the valuation thereof, and Seller shall have access to the books and records of the Division in connection with its preparation of the Closing Date Balance Sheet.[6] To the extent that Purchaser shall utilize such of the Division's personnel as may be necessary or useful for the prompt preparation of the Closing Date Balance Sheet, such employees shall be made available to Seller, consistent with their primary duties and responsibilities to the Purchaser in connection with the business of the Division, but shall remain under the direction and supervision of Purchaser. Purchaser agrees to direct such personnel to proceed expeditiously and to cooperate with Seller in the preparation of the Closing Date Balance Sheet, subject, however, to such primary duties and responsibilities. In addition, Seller may utilize its own employees, agents or other representatives in connection with the preparation of the Closing Date Balance Sheet, which persons shall be under the direction and supervision of Seller, provided that they do not interfere with the normal operations of the Division's business.

(iii) The Purchase Price shall be reduced (by increasing the Inventory Discount) by an amount equal to the lesser of (A) $500,000 or (B) the aggregate net book value of all Final Exclusion Inventory (determined as provided in subsection 2(b) hereof) in excess of the Available Inventory

---

[6]Seller prepares the Closing Date Balance Sheet. In addition to Purchaser's right (pursuant to Section 2(b)(i)) to inspect Seller's inventory at any time prior to Closing, Purchaser is given the opportunity to participate in the pre-Closing taking of inventory. Since the Division changes hands at Closing, by which time Seller will not have completed the Closing Date Balance Sheet, Seller is given rights of access to books and records, and to the employees and other representatives of the Division, after the Closing. Purchaser, in the interest of continuing the operations of the Division, is given primary control over such persons and the extent to which Seller's activities through its own personnel may interfere with such operations. As a general matter, since Seller is responsible for preparation of the Closing Date Balance Sheet (from which Net Book Value is derived), and since Purchaser is able only to secure such reductions in the Purchase Price as it will be able to establish just prior to and just after the Closing, Purchaser will want to ensure that Seller makes a firm representation (e.g., without knowledge exceptions and/or with language importing a high standard of care) as to the accuracy of the Closing Date Balance Sheet.

The timetable of this transaction, as structured in the Agreement, envisions that a significant, if estimated, portion of the Purchase Price will be paid at a Closing to take place immediately after the taking of inventory on which the Closing Date Balance Sheet will be based. Many sellers and purchasers would be unwilling to enter into an arrangement in which the Purchase Price would be so uncertain. In lieu of the structure reflected in the Agreement, many parties would schedule the Closing only after the final balance sheet is available. Such a schedule would anticipate Seller's operating the Division on and after the date of the final balance sheet for the benefit of Purchaser, and would require negative covenants on the part of Seller (e.g., with respect to extraordinary transactions, compensation levels and the like).

Reserve. The term "Available Inventory Reserve" as used herein shall mean the amount, if any, by which the $150,000 Inventory Reserve exceeds the aggregate net book value of all Defective Inventory.[7]

(b) (i) At any time and from time to time prior to the Closing Date, Purchaser and its representatives, employees, and agents shall have the right, upon reasonable notice to Seller, to inspect the inventory of the Division at the various locations where such inventory is located; provided, however, that Purchaser's representatives shall not spend more than a total of _________ full business days (whether or not consecutive) at any one such location. Purchaser shall have the right to give, not later than the Closing Date (as the same may be postponed as provided below), a written notice (a "Designation Notice") to Seller designating (A) each Inventory Class (as hereinafter defined), that may be included in the Closing Date Balance Sheet which Purchaser, in its sole discretion, deems to be slow-moving, obsolescent or obsolete (all of which items of inventory included in such Inventory Class being hereinafter collectively referred to as "Preliminary Exclusion Inventory")[8] and

---

[7]An amount of no greater than $500,000 is deducted from the Purchase Price for "Final Exclusion Inventory," which is inventory determined to be slow-moving or obsolete. Seller should insist upon a cap on the deduction to the extent Seller is unwilling to sell at less than a floor amount. Purchaser may receive a lesser deduction if a lower figure is reached after deducting from the Final Exclusion Inventory the "Available Inventory Reserve," which is the excess, if any, of $150,000 over the amount of inventory identified as defective. Whereas Seller accepts a minimum of $150,000 as a deduction for defective inventory, Purchaser is agreeing that, to the extent defective inventory is not so identified, Purchaser will receive no deduction for slow-moving or obsolete inventory and that in any case such deduction will not exceed $500,000. Purchaser is protected against the advent of substantial amounts of defective inventory, while Seller is protected against the possible discovery of large amounts of slow-moving or obsolete inventory and gets relief if less than $150,000 of defective inventory is discovered. Notice that, under Section 2(b)(i), any inventory that is both defective and slow-moving or defective and obsolete is deemed to be defective only, so that any overlap between categories is treated in Purchaser's favor.

If Purchaser is unable to get Seller to agree upon a mechanism, such as the one provided in Sections 2(a)(iii) and 2(b), for reducing the Purchase Price as slow-moving, obsolete, or defective inventory is discovered, Purchaser would have even greater reason to obtain from Seller a firm representation (see footnote 6) to the effect that the amount of such inventory is immaterial. Within such a framework Seller could propose a "cushion" below which Purchaser would be prohibited from bringing a claim against Seller based upon a shortfall in the actual value of the inventory as compared to the value specified in Seller's representation. If the shortfall were to exceed the amount of the cushion, Purchaser could, in one variant, seek to recover only amounts in excess of the cushion amount. In a second variant, Purchaser could recover the full amount of the shortfall if it exceeded the cushion amount. Alternatively, the cushion could relate to the Division's assets as a whole, or exclusively to one element such as receivables.

[8]Purchaser is given complete discretion in designating inventory as slow-moving or obsolete or as defective, subject only to general contractual standards of good faith and fair dealing. Some criteria for defectiveness are provided, but none for what constitutes slow-moving or obsolete inventory. This contrast is somewhat offset by the facts (1) that there is a cap on the deduction for slow-moving or for obsolete inventory but none on the deduction for defective inventory and (2) that Seller is afforded, in Section 2(b)(iii), an objective procedure for rebutting exclusion of inventory as slow-moving or obsolete.

(B) those items of inventory that are defective items because they (x) bear an expiration date prior to the Closing Date (or fail to bear any expiration date where such type of inventory is ordinarily dated) or (y) are broken, inoperative, or otherwise physically defective to the extent that they are unsuitable for their intended purpose or are unsalable other than at a price of 50 percent or less of the replacement cost thereof (such items being hereinafter collectively referred to as "Defective Inventory")[8]; provided, however, that Purchaser shall have the right to postpone the Closing by not more than two business days in the event that Purchaser has failed for any reason to deliver a Designation Notice to Seller at or prior to the then scheduled Closing.[9] The term "Inventory Class" shall mean a particular class of inventory item described as a type of merchandise, identified by catalogue number appearing in Seller's catalogue or by similar means. Where substantially identical items are described by more than one such catalogue number, such substantially identical items shall be treated as falling within a single Inventory Class for the purposes of this subsection 2(b). Any items of inventory which are ultimately determined to be both Defective Inventory and Final Exclusion Inventory shall be deemed to constitute Defective Inventory and not Final Exclusion Inventory for all purposes of this Agreement.

(ii) Seller may, within ten days after receipt of a Designation Notice, give a written notice (a "Dispute Notice") to Purchaser disputing the propriety of Purchaser's designation of any one or more items of Defective Inventory. If such dispute cannot be resolved between the parties within ten days after the giving of the Dispute Notice, the matter shall be determined by arbitration as provided in subsection 13(j) hereof.[10]

(iii) Seller may, within 30 days after receipt of the Designation Notice, give a written notice (a "Removal Notice") to Purchaser seeking to disqualify any portion of the Preliminary Exclusion Inventory included in one or more Inventory Classes from constituting Final Exclusion Inventory on the ground that the quantity of Preliminary Exclusion Inventory included in each such Inventory Class on the Closing Date is less than or equal to 110 percent of the quantity of items of such Inventory Class that were sold other than at a loss by the Division during the six-month period ended December 31, 1989 (such quantity of items of such Inventory Class so sold during such six-

[9]Since Purchaser is uncertain what it will find upon examining Seller's inventory before Closing, Purchaser has obtained the right to a two-day extension to prepare its findings as to slow-moving, obsolete and defective inventory. This provides Seller with an incentive to facilitate Purchaser's inventory review.

[10]Seller may attempt to rebut Purchaser's contentions as to defective inventory within ten days.

month period being hereinafter referred to as the "Base Period Quantity").[11] Such Removal Notice shall be signed by an officer of Seller, shall set forth the number of items and the value of the Preliminary Exclusion Inventory which Seller seeks to disqualify as Final Exclusion Inventory hereunder, shall identify each Inventory Class in which such items are included, and shall certify the amount of the Base Period Quantity of such Inventory Class. In the event it is determined that any quantity of Preliminary Exclusion Inventory is disqualified as aforesaid, only that quantity of Preliminary Exclusion Inventory which exceeds 110 percent of the Base Period Quantity shall constitute Final Exclusion Inventory hereunder. Any dispute as to whether any Preliminary Exclusion Inventory should be disqualified from constituting Final Exclusion Inventory that cannot be resolved by the parties within ten days after the giving of the Removal Notice shall be determined by arbitration as provided in subsection 13(j) hereof.

(iv) If or to the extent Seller does not give a Dispute Notice or a Removal Notice as provided above with respect to any inventory items designated in Purchaser's Designation Notice as Preliminary Exclusion Inventory or as Defective Inventory, Seller shall conclusively be deemed to have approved the classification of such inventory items as Final Exclusion Inventory or as Defective Inventory, as the case may be.

(v) Although all items of Defective Inventory and all or a portion of any Final Exclusion Inventory shall be excluded from the computation of Net Book Value for purposes of determining the Purchase Price hereunder, Purchaser shall nevertheless retain all right, title, and interest in and to all items of Defective Inventory and Final Exclusion Inventory.[12]

(c) (i) At the Closing, Purchaser will pay to Seller on account of the Purchase Price the sum of $15,000,000 by wire transfer of federal funds to Seller's account at _________ Bank.

(ii) At the Settlement, Purchaser will pay to Seller on account of the Purchase Price the excess, if any, of (A) the Purchase Price over (B) the sum of (x) $15,000,000, (y) the Accounts Receivable Holdback (as defined

---

[11] Seller may remove from Purchaser's exclusion list inventory of a given Inventory Class to the extent of 110 percent of the turnover during a recent six-month reference period of items in such Inventory Class. Although Seller bears the burden of proof in this procedure, Seller has greater familiarity than Purchaser with the relevant facts about the business. The procedure thus affords Purchaser a way of flushing out such facts and provides Seller a procedure within which to rebut charges or overstating.

[12] Purchaser does not want to refuse unsatisfactory inventory but only to receive a discount for having purchased it. This contrasts with the ultimate disposition of uncollected accounts receivable, which after 120 days following the Closing revert to Seller under Section 2(d)(i).

in subsection 2(d)(ii) hereof) and (z) any reduction in the Purchase Price pursuant to the provisions of subsection 2(a)(iii) hereof, which excess amount, if any, shall be paid by wire transfer of federal funds to Seller's account at _________ Bank.[13] In the event that the Purchase Price as of the Settlement Date shall be less than the sum of items (x), (y) and (z) above, Seller shall pay to Purchaser at the Settlement an amount equal to such deficiency by wire transfer of federal funds to Purchaser's account at _________ Bank or as Purchaser may otherwise designate.[14]

(d)(i) For a period of 120 days after the Closing Date, Purchaser will attempt to collect the accounts receivable of the Division reflected on the Closing Date Balance Sheet (the "Purchased Receivables") in accordance with the Division's prior reasonable commercial practices (but without resort to litigation or the use of collection agencies or similar efforts).[15] Any payment made by an account debtor to Purchaser with respect to an account receivable shall be applied to the Purchased Receivables before they are applied to any outstanding account receivable from such account debtor arising from sales made by the Division after the Closing Date; provided, however, that if an account debtor specifies that any one or more of the payments made by such account debtor is being made with respect to a particular outstanding account receivable of such account debtor to Purchaser, such payment shall be applied as such account debtor so specifies.[16] On the later of (A) the first Friday following the thirtieth day after the Closing Date or (B) the first Friday that is at least five business days after the first day on which

---

[13]Purchaser pays $15 million at the Closing and afterward, at the Settlement, pays the amount, if any, by which this sum falls short of the Purchase Price (as adjusted downward after the Closing to reflect slow-moving, obsolete, or defective inventory) and the "Accounts Receivable Holdback." The Accounts Receivable Holdback is defined in Section 2(d)(ii) as the sum of (a) the portion of overdue receivables over 15 percent of the aggregate amount of Purchased Receivables plus (b) $_________. In this particular Agreement the amount of the Accounts Receivable Holdback will depend on the amount of overdue receivables (see footnote 20).

[14]If the Purchase Price as reduced for unsatisfactory inventory and overdue receivables is less than $15 million, Seller pays Purchaser at the Settlement, as Purchaser will in such case have received a business worth less than the amount paid at Closing.

[15]Purchaser must attempt to collect the Purchased Receivables for 120 days but (since the account debtors are largely persons with whom Purchaser and not Seller will be dealing in the future) Purchaser will not want to be required initially to use aggressive collection methods. The extent to which Purchaser may be required to employ such methods is subject to negotiation.

[16]Seller is entitled to apply any amounts received from an account debtor to the Purchased Receivables rather than receivables arising from post-Closing sales, unless the account debtor otherwise specifies.

the amount of the Accounts Receivable Holdback exceeds the net amount of the uncollected Purchased Receivables (after deduction of the Bad Debt Reserve), and on every second Friday thereafter until the last Friday that is not more than 120 days after the Closing Date (the "Post Settlement Date"), Purchaser shall deliver to Seller a schedule setting forth (x) the name of each person who was an account debtor as of the Closing Date and who has made any payment on account of any Purchased Receivable since the most recent such schedule (and, with respect to the first such schedule, since the Closing Date), (y) the remaining balance of such account debtor's account outstanding at the Friday of the preceding week, and (z) the aggregate amount of all uncollected Purchased Receivables as of the Friday of the preceding week.[17] Within one week after the first day on which the amount of the Accounts Receivable Holdback exceeds the net amount of the uncollected Purchased Receivables (after deduction of the Bad Debt Reserve), Purchaser shall pay to Seller any such excess Accounts Receivable Holdback. Any Purchased Receivables in excess of the Bad Debt Reserve remaining uncollected by Purchaser on the Post Settlement Date shall be transferred on such date, without recourse, to Seller for Seller's own account, and Purchaser shall retain from the Accounts Receivable Holdback the amount of such uncollected Purchased Receivables as a reduction in the Purchase Price hereunder.[18] If the net amount of the uncollected Purchased Receivables on the Post Settlement Date (after deduction of the Bad Debt Reserve) exceeds the amount of the

[17] As Purchased Receivables are collected, the amount of the Accounts Receivable Holdback may come to exceed the amount of uncollected Purchased Receivables (net of the Bad Debt Reserve). Purchaser is required to pay Seller such excess amounts as they accrue every other week until 120 days after Closing. Uncollected Purchased Receivables are turned over to Seller on the 120th day after the Closing, with Purchaser retaining a portion of the Accounts Receivable Holdback equal to the amount of such receivables. If the net uncollected receivables exceed the Accounts Receivable Holdback on such 120th day, Seller must pay the excess to Purchaser as a further reduction in the Purchaser Price.

[18] Since Seller prepares the Closing Date Balance Sheet, Seller has control over the amount of the Bad Debt Reserve. Understating this amount will result in a higher payment from Purchaser (or a lower refund to Purchaser) up front at the Settlement, although by increasing the amount of net Purchased Receivables Seller will decrease the amounts refunded later on from (or increase the amounts paid later on in excess of) the Accounts Receivable Holdback. Seller in effect has timing incentives to understate the Bad Debt Reserve. However, Seller's allowance can be challenged through enforcement of Seller's representations as to the accuracy of the Closing Date Balance Sheet.

As a corollary to what was noted in footnote 7, note here that if Seller does not agree to some mechanism, such as a holdback, for adjusting amounts paid for receivables, Purchaser would have even greater reason to obtain from Seller a firm representation that there are no material inaccuracies (or, alternatively, no inaccuracies above a specified amount) either in the amount of receivables or in the Bad Debt Reserve as reflected in the final balance sheet.

Accounts Receivable Holdback, Seller shall promptly pay to Purchaser an amount equal to such excess as a further reduction of the Purchase Price. All payments made pursuant to this subsection 2(d) shall be made by check (subject to collection) drawn on a bank located in __________.[19]

(ii) The term "Accounts Receivable Holdback" as used herein shall mean an amount equal to the sum of (A) that portion, if any, of the Purchased Receivables more than 90 days overdue which exceeds 15 percent of the aggregate amount of the Purchased Receivables (the "Excess Overdue Receivables") plus (B) $__________.[20]

(e) At reasonable times and upon reasonable notice to Purchaser between the Closing Date and the Post Settlement Date, Seller shall have the right to audit (at Seller's expense) the Division's books and records to confirm the accuracy of Purchaser's schedules and remittances in respect of collections of Purchased Receivables.[21] Purchaser shall have the right to grant or allow reasonable credits, returns, discounts, or other allowances (collectively, "Allowances") on any Purchased Receivable to facilitate the partial collection of any Purchased Receivables, such Allowances to be granted or allowed by Purchaser in its reasonable discretion.[22] Not later than ten business days after Purchaser grants any such Allowances, Purchaser shall give Seller a written notice (an "Allowance Notice") of its decision to grant such Allowance. If Seller disputes the reasonableness of any such Allowances, Seller shall, within ten days after receipt of the Allowance Notice with respect thereto,

---

[19]Provision for payment by check reflects the anticipated amount of the final settlement.

[20]As written, Purchaser is acknowledging, in (A), that a certain portion of the Division's receivables will be more than 90 days overdue and that Purchaser will not be entitled to "hold back" any portion of the Purchase Price therefor. An additional "cushion" is provided to the Seller in (B). Both the concept of a "holdback" and its particulars are negotiable.

[21]Although Purchaser is responsible for collection until the 120th day after Closing, Seller has the right to confirm the accuracy of Purchaser's biweekly statements.

[22]Purchaser is given reasonable discretion in settling or in making other allowances with respect to Purchased Receivables, subject to a dispute resolution procedure. Seller may have interests adverse to Purchaser on this score. Any uncollected amounts are to be collected by Seller after the 120th day following the Closing, when Purchaser turns over uncollected receivables. By virtue of its status as owner of the business Purchaser may be better able to persuade debtors to settle. But Seller may have its own assessment of the reasonableness of Purchaser's allowance under circumstances. Also, Purchaser will not lose any amounts compromised by its allowances, as such amounts are treated as uncollected Purchased Receivables, whereas Seller will of course be unable to collect such amounts after the Purchased Receivables are turned over to it. Whether and to what extent Purchaser is permitted to settle with account debtors are subject to negotiation.

give a written notice (an "Allowance Dispute Notice") to Purchaser. If such dispute cannot be resolved within ten days after the giving of the Allowance Dispute Notice, the matter shall be determined by arbitration in accordance with the terms of subsection 13(j) hereof; provided, however, that in any arbitration relating to the reasonableness of any Allowance, there shall be no presumption of the reasonableness or unreasonableness thereof in favor of either party. As a condition of its right to dispute the reasonableness of any Allowance granted by Purchaser pursuant to this subsection 2(e), Seller shall give Purchaser written notice of its intention to contest any such grant within ten days after receipt of Purchaser's Allowance Notice with respect thereto, failing which Seller shall conclusively be deemed to have approved such Allowance. In the event Purchaser accepts the return of any merchandise which gave rise to any Purchased Receivable in connection with any return Allowance granted hereunder, Seller shall be entitled to obtain such returned merchandise from Purchaser ("as is" and "where is"). Any portion of the Purchased Receivables reduced by Allowances shall be deemed uncollected Purchased Receivables for purposes of this Agreement.

(f) At the Closing Date or as promptly thereafter as practicable, the parties shall adjust the annualized or periodic items as of the Closing Date, with Seller being responsible therefor up to the Closing Date, and Purchaser being responsible therefor from and after the Closing Date. Such adjustable items shall include electric, gas, telephone, and utility charges of the Division and payroll expenses and taxes in respect of employees of the Division, either paid or accrued; provided, however, that nothing contained in this Section 2(f) shall increase the liabilities and obligations of Seller assumed by Purchaser pursuant to the Liabilities Undertaking referred to in subsection 2(g) hereof.

(g) In addition to the payment of the Purchase Price as provided above, Purchaser will execute and deliver to Seller at the Closing a Liabilities Undertaking in the form of Exhibit C annexed hereto.

CONTINGENT EARNOUT PROVISIONS—EXCERPTS OF SELLER-ORIENTED FORM

2.1 Additional Consideration

(a) On or before April 30, 1994, Purchaser will deliver to Seller aggregate additional consideration (the "Additional Consideration") equal to 85 percent of ten (10) times the amount by which (x) the average annual net pretax earnings of the Division during the four-year period from January 1, 1990 through December 31, 1993 (the "Payout Period") exceeds (y) $2,000,000.[23,24] Any such Additional Consideration shall be paid in cash[25] and shall be deemed to consist of interest compounded semiannually at the applicable federal midterm rate as determined in accordance with the provisions of Section 1274(d) of the Internal Revenue Code of 1986, as amended.[26]

(b) As used in this Section 2.1, the term "Division" shall include the Division and its subsidiaries as well as any business or businesses conducted

---

[23]Seller's proposed earn-out formula is expressed as a multiple of the excess of average annual earnings during the Payout Period over a fixed sum (which sum may represent earnings during an agreed base period). Alternatively, an earn-out formula could be expressed in terms of a fixed percentage of profits earned during the Payout Period (with the additional consideration payable either annually or in a lump sum at the end of the Payout Period), for example, if Seller and Purchaser are unable to agree on a base figure.

[24]The formula is based on pretax earnings. Seller thereby eliminates the temptation of Purchasers to compromise a claim in respect of taxes attributable to the Division by agreeing to pay such taxes while taking a tax benefit in respect of a disputed item relating to another business that is part of Purchaser's consolidated group, or to reduce the amount of the earn-out by making income-suppressing elections under the tax code.

[25]If the consideration to be paid for the business were Purchaser's stock rather than cash, the issue would arise of when to value the stock. Seller could propose either the date of the Closing (or whatever other date is agreed to for valuation of the shares to be delivered at the Closing) or the date on which the Additional Consideration is to be paid. Seller's decision may depend largely upon Seller's assessment of whether or not Purchaser's stock is likely to appreciate in value over time. Both parties should, in any case, seek to ensure that, if such a valuation is based on trading, it is based on a reasonably representative trading period (customarily not less than 10 days), although, as events of October 1987 attest, it may be difficult to predict whether any particular period will be representative. If the valuation is to take place at the end of the Payout Period and if this period is relatively long, additional risks may arise for Seller and Purchaser. A significant decline in the stock's value may require Purchaser to issue to Seller more shares than it wants to issue. A sharp increase in value may leave Seller with fewer shares than it considers worth acquiring. To address this and similar concerns, the parties might wish to define a range of share prices, or of aggregate numbers of shares, outside of which Purchaser and/or Seller (depending on the circumstances) could pay or receive, as the case may be, cash in lieu of Purchaser's stock. In addition, Seller may want to include provisions for registration rights with respect to any shares it receives of Purchaser's stock. Such provisions are beyond the scope of the current discussion.

[26]Under Section 1274(d) of the Internal Revenue Code of 1986, interest will be imputed in respect of deferred payments under an installment sale agreement at a rate based on the term of the agreement unless the agreement stipulates a rate of interest at or above a formula amount. Under current tax law, Seller is indifferent as to the imputed rate of interest since income to Seller will receive the same treatment whether it is interest or capital gain. Seller does, however, have a reason for keeping interest at a minimum: the possibility of a restoration of the more favorable treatment of capital gains under the tax code. Although Purchaser will prefer as high a rate of interest as is legally permissible (since interest payments are deductible as paid) and can be expected to argue that Seller's point is tenuous, Seller is leaving it to Purchaser to propose a rate above the statutory minimum.

by Purchaser, or by any subsidiary or affiliated corporations of Purchaser, that represent a succession to and a continuation of the business or businesses conducted by the Division and its subsidiaries, as the same may be expanded as provided in Section 10 hereof.[27]

(c) As used in this Section 2.1, the term "net pretax earnings of the Division" shall mean the consolidated net earnings (or losses), before all taxes, of the Division, computed on the accrual basis of accounting in accordance with generally accepted accounting principles consistently applied (and consistent with the accounting principles applied by Seller in respect of the Division in its prior fiscal years) except that the following provisions shall govern the computation of the net pretax earnings of the Division for purposes of this Section 2.1:[28]

(i) Any extraordinary nonrecurring items of income, gain, loss, or expense shall be excluded from such computation.[29]

(ii) Any loss, charge, or expense (A) not related to the ordinary business operations of the Division, or (B) paid, incurred, or charged in connection with expansion of the business operations presently conducted by the Division as a

---

[27]Seller has included this provision to ensure that it is the business sold, rather than the particular entity operating the business on the closing date, whose earnings are taken into account during the Payout Period. Purchaser can have little objection to such a provision.

[28]Requiring the use of GAAP on a basis consistent with prior years helps ensure that the contingent price will reflect the realization of the Division's earnings potential as Seller has assessed it. The additional guidelines that follow in Section 2.1(c)(i) through (ix) are intended to provide for matters whose inclusion or exclusion, as the case may be, under GAAP consistently applied might not accord with this objective. Requiring the use of GAAP consistently applied will not protect Seller anywhere near as well as would a requirement that Seller's own accountants assume responsibility for computing net pretax earnings of the Division. Seller's inability to challenge Purchaser's accounting decisions unless they can be shown to represent a departure from GAAP, even as modified by the guidelines under Section 2.1(c)(i) through (ix), is a serious drawback. Section 2.1(c)(x) is a further attempt to channel in Seller's favor any discretion allowed under GAAP as so modified, while Seller's access to the books and records of the Division under Section 2.1(d) may enable Seller to raise during the Payout Period any concerns it may have about Purchaser's accounting decisions rather than require Seller to await Purchaser's final statement and invoke the dispute procedure provided for under Section 2.1(e).

[29]Under Section 2.1(c)(iii) of Seller's draft, Seller, by refusing to consent to Purchaser's proposal to obtain insurance coverage against certain casualty losses, may exclude the expense of such coverage from the computation of net pretax earnings. Purchaser should request that the exclusion in Section 2.1(c)(i) be narrowed to provide that casualty losses against which Purchaser had proposed to insure (but that were not insured against because Seller objected pursuant to Section 2.1(c)(iii)) be included in the computation of net pretax earnings. As a compromise, Seller could agree provided that at the time of Purchaser's proposal such insurance was customary within the Division's industry or was commercially available and, as an administrative matter, that Purchaser refer to Section 2.1(c)(i) in connection with any proposal to obtain insurance coverage.

result of the making of acquisitions or the opening and staffing of new offices, or any income or revenues directly derived therefrom, shall be excluded from such computation.[30]

(iii) Any loss, charge, or expense related to the ordinary business operations of the Division initiated by Purchaser or any of its affiliates and not covered by the Provisions of subparagraph (ii) above shall be excluded from such computation unless _________ ("Seller's Representative") initiates or consents in writing to the transaction giving rise to, or the payment or assumption of the obligation to pay, such loss, charge, or expense.[31]

(iv) Any charge or expense for the amortization of goodwill arising out of the fact that Purchaser has purchased the stock of the Division, pursuant hereto or otherwise, or that the purchase price thereof is in excess of the net worth thereof, shall be excluded from such computation.[32]

(v) In the event of an election with respect to the Division pursuant

---

[30]If Purchaser objects, Seller may counter that Section 2.1(c)(ii) already reflects a concession from the position that the Division should not expand or depart at all during the Payout Period from its ordinary business operations. A further compromise would require Seller to object to a proposed transaction within a stated time after notice or knowledge thereof in order for Seller to exclude from the computation of net pretax earnings the losses, if any, that eventually result from the transaction and, in addition, would deem Seller's failure so to object to constitute approval of the transaction.

[31]Seller's inclusion of such a seemingly harsh provision derives from Seller's desire not to risk losses, charges, or expenses attributable to Purchaser's ideas about how to operate the Division, which are at odds with Seller's concept about how to maximize Seller's earn-out. As discussed earlier, Section 2.1(c)(iii) does not give Seller's Representative a veto over expenditures by Purchaser, but would exclude such expenditures in computing net pretax earnings. This veto procedure provides Purchaser an incentive to give Seller discretion in operating the Division during the Payout Period, since it is only those expenditures initiated or consented to by Seller's Representative that will count in computing net pretax earnings.

As with Section 2.1(c)(ii), Purchaser would want to provide that failure to object before a transaction is entered into is tantamount to consent. Seller should then insist that prior notice be a condition for so treating a failure to object. Assuming Purchaser agrees to some such mechanism, Purchaser may propose as a counter that gains resulting from the Division's entering into a transaction over the veto of Seller's Representative not be included in the computation of net pretax earnings. (Note that Section 2.1(c)(ii) already so provides in respect of new business operations of the Division.) Purchaser should request that Seller be required to object within a stated period of time after notice of a proposed transaction in order to be able to have the results thereof excluded from the computation of net pretax earnings, as discussed in footnote 30.

In addition, Purchaser should secure in advance the consent of Seller and Seller's Representative to certain classes of activities of the Division, objection to which on Seller's part would unduly disrupt the operations of the Division, such as the filing of documents with regulatory agencies and the preparation of monthly operating statements of the Division on the basis of which net pretax earnings of the Division are to be computed.

[32]Purchaser can do little but concede this exclusion, since the amortization of goodwill incurred in acquiring the Division bears no true relation to the expense of operating the acquired business.

to Section 338 of the Internal Revenue Code of 1986, as amended, such computation shall be made as though no such election had been made.[33]

(vi) Any payments, charges, or expenses for allocation of home office, executive, general, and administrative expenses, or other payments, charges, or expenses of Purchaser and/or its affiliates shall be excluded from such computation, except that there shall be included for the purposes of such computation a charge to the Division equal to the normal management fee or home office fee which Purchaser charges its subsidiaries generally; provided, however, that the maximum annual amount of such charge for management and home office fees shall not exceed the lesser of (A) 1 percent of the net revenues of the Division for such year or (B) $________.[34]

(vii) The deduction for salary paid or payable to Seller's Representative shall be limited to $80,000 per annum, regardless of the amount actually paid, and there shall be no deduction for any other compensation paid or payable to him which he rejects in advance thereof.[35]

(viii) Any interest expenses or charges shall be excluded from such computation to the extent they relate to funds furnished to the Division in replacement of any Present Funds (as defined in Section 10(a) hereof) withdrawn from the Division (by way of loans, dividends, or otherwise) by Purchaser or any affiliate thereof.[36]

---

[33]With this provision, Seller seeks to ensure that Seller's consent to a Section 338 election proposed by Purchaser will not be deemed to be a consent (pursuant to Section 2.1(c)(iii)) to a write-up of assets in connection with such election.

[34]Negotiations over this provision will likely center on whether or not a cap on home office overhead acceptable to both Purchaser and Seller will be set. Purchaser may insist that Seller's proposed cap be removed and that any "normal" fees be included in computing net pretax earnings. If so, Seller must insist on curbing Purchaser's discretion in this area, which becomes considerable in the absence of well-defined limits if the Division will be part of a large group of businesses.

[35]Seller's provision seeks to enable Seller's Representative to receive salary increases above the stated amount without compromising Seller's interest in maximizing earnings or, alternatively, to further this interest by refusing compensation. Assuming that Seller's Representative is to receive a portion of the Additional Consideration, Purchaser may object to any special treatment of compensation of Seller's Representative on the basis that the Division's earnings would be distorted under a formula that excludes from net earnings calculations part of the cost of obtaining managerial services and, in addition, creates an incentive to render such services at little or no expense.

[36]Seller seeks to guard against Purchaser's reducing pretax net earnings by replacing the Division's own available funds or other capital with interest-bearing loans from Purchaser or any of its affiliates or with other replacement capital for which additional amounts will be paid. If it appears to Purchaser that the Division is more than adequately capitalized, Purchaser may request that it be entitled to receive a specified or formula amount of dividends or other distributions from present amounts without having interest on loans to the Division excluded from net pretax earnings if such loans should become necessary. Note the relationship between this provision and that of the immediately following Section 2.1(c)(ix), which compensates Seller in the event Purchaser withdraws Present Funds from the Division.

(ix) For the purposes of such computation, interest shall be credited to and deemed earned by the Division at a rate equal to 1.2 times the prime interest rate for short-term borrowings as from time to time published by _______ Bank (the "Intercompany Rate") on any Present Funds withdrawn (by way of loans, dividends, or otherwise) from the Division by Purchaser or any affiliate thereof and not replaced as provided herein, such interest to be computed on a daily basis. For the purposes of such computation, interest shall be deducted and deemed paid to Purchaser or such affiliate by the Division at the Intercompany Rate on any amounts in excess of the Present Funds loaned to the Division by Purchaser or such affiliate, such interest to be computed on a daily basis.[37]

(x) Consistent with generally accepted accounting principles (and consistent with the accounting principles applied by Seller in respect of the Division in prior fiscal years), all available accounting elections (including, without limitation, those relating to methods of depreciation, useful lives of depreciable items, the capitalizing of charges and the setting up of reserves) shall be made in such a manner as to reflect the highest possible net pretax earnings of the Division.

(xi) Such computation (including, without limitation, the determination of the basis for depreciation and the reflection of intercompany transactions) shall be made as though all of the outstanding shares of capital stock of the Division (the "Shares") were not sold to Purchaser hereunder and the Division were a single corporation with all of the Shares owned by persons who are neither directly nor indirectly related to or affiliated with Purchaser or any of its affiliates.[38]

(xii) Any and all expenses paid or incurred by the Division (other than those expressly permitted by the above provisions) which would not have been so paid or incurred if not for the sale of the Shares and the other transactions contemplated hereby, shall be excluded from such computation.[39]

---

[37]Seller's position is that interest on any intercompany advance should be calculated as if the parties to such advance were engaged in an arm's-length transaction. Purchaser will be able to dispute this position if and to the extent that Seller has itself in the past advanced funds to or withdrawn funds from the Division on a non-arm's-length basis.

[38]The requirement to account for operations of the Division as if the Division were a single freestanding corporation may help ensure that revenues and charges reflect the performance of the Division as represented by Seller rather than prevailing accounting practices within Purchaser's group; although, as noted under footnote 37, Seller's own practices may undercut the position being advanced. Disregarding the sale of the Division's shares for purposes of determining depreciation precludes a write-up of assets in connection with computation of the earn-out (though not, obviously, for other of Purchaser's purposes in its acquisition of the Division).

[39]The transaction costs of the sale of the business should not reduce net pretax earnings of the Division.

(xiii) Except as otherwise expressly provided above, all amounts determined in accordance with subparagraphs (i) through (xii) of this Section 2.1(c) shall be determined in accordance with generally accepted accounting principles consistently applied (see footnote 28)

(d) During the Payout Period Seller shall have free and unrestricted access to the financial books and records of the Division.

(e) As soon as may be practicable after December 31, 1993, but not later than April 30, 1994, Purchaser will deliver to Seller a statement setting forth in reasonable detail its calculation of the average annual net pretax earnings of the Division during the Payout Period and the amount of any Additional Consideration to be paid to Seller pursuant to this Section 2.1, which statement shall be accompanied by payment to Seller, by wire transfer of federal funds to Seller's account at _______ Bank (or to such other account as Seller may designate), of the Additional Consideration as shown thereon. If within 30 days after delivery of such statement Seller has not given written notice to Purchaser disputing such statement and indicating the basis of such dispute, Purchaser shall thereafter have no further liability to Seller under this Section 2.1. In the event Seller gives Purchaser such notice of dispute within such 30-day period, Seller and Purchaser will use their best efforts to settle the dispute within 30 days after the giving of such notice.[40] Any dispute unresolved after such 30-day period shall be submitted to a national public accounting firm satisfactory to Seller and to Purchaser, or, in the absence of agreement on such firm, to a panel of three public accounting firms, one designated by Seller, one designated by Purchaser and one jointly designated by the other two firms. The decision of such accounting firm or such panel of accounting firms, as the case may be, with respect to such dispute shall be final and binding on the parties hereto. Purchaser shall make any further payments to Seller required in order to comply with such decision within 10 days after such decision is rendered.

10. Operations of the Division Following Closing

(a) Seller's Representative shall, from January 1, 1990 until the end of the Payout Period (or until such earlier time as he shall have voluntarily resigned

---

[40]In most bargaining situations, Seller will have no choice but to concede that Purchaser's accountants will initially be determining net pretax earnings (see footnote 28). Seller has provided that Purchaser deliver the amount of Additional Consideration payable pursuant to such initial determination at the conclusion thereof rather than at the conclusion of the entire dispute resolution procedure provided for in Section 2.1(e). Purchaser may request that delivery await the conclusion in order to keep pressure on Seller.

or his employment has been terminated for good cause), be a director and the principal executive officer of the Division, and Purchaser shall cause him to be so elected. Subject to the ultimate control and responsibility of the Board of Directors of the Division and of Purchaser as a majority stockholder, during the Payout Period Seller's Representative shall have the right to manage the business and affairs of the Division and shall direct the formulation and execution of both shortand long-term corporate plans, including, without limitation, the hiring, retention or termination of employees, the setting of compensation and fringe benefits of employees other than himself, the expansion of the business and the making of commitments for capital expenditures. Purchaser shall cooperate with Seller's Representative in maintaining and increasing the Division's profitability, but this Agreement shall not be construed as a commitment on the part of Purchaser to invest in or make available to the Division any particular amount of additional capital, or to incur any particular expense or obligation on behalf of the Division, whether or not Purchaser is to be reimbursed by the Division for any such expense or obligation, other than to the extent of an amount equal to the assets and funds available to the Division immediately prior to the Closing, as the same may be adjusted by the amount of any increase or decrease thereof by reason of the operations of the Division from and after the Closing (the "Present Funds").[41]

---

[41] Seller is proposing that its representative be given the maximum day-to-day and long-term management responsibilities for the Division consistent with Purchaser's ownership of the Division, and that Seller be represented on the Division's board of directors. Seller is conceding that it is in Purchaser's discretion to invest in or otherwise make funds and other capital available to the Division in exchange for Purchaser's commitment not to provide any lesser amounts than are currently available. (Under Section 2.1 (c)(viii), any interest and other charges that may be payable in connection with substitute capital are excluded from the calculation of net pretax earnings.) Seller will insist to Purchaser that "we are in this together" during the Payout Period and that Seller's expertise would be invaluable to the advancement of their mutual interests. Whether or not Purchaser agrees to Seller's proposal will depend on the relative positions of the parties and other factors, such as Purchaser's independent willingness to rely on the expertise of Seller's Representative during the Payout Period.

CHAPTER 21

TAKEOVER AND DEFENSE LAW I: THE TAKEOVER ENVIRONMENT

Martin Lipton
James H. Fogelson
Andrew R. Brownstein
Craig M. Wasserman
Wachtell, Lipton, Rosen & Katz

During the past several years, takeover battles have not only increased in number but also in scope and intensity. This year, in particular, has witnessed an enormous surge in activity, and there are no signs that it will abate. Philip Morris' $13 billion bid for Kraft and the fierce competition to take RJR Nabisco private in a $25 billion transaction indicate the apparently limitless capacity of this marketplace for takeovers.

The takeover process is fundamentally a process of bargaining and negotiation. As bidders develop new and more aggressive techniques to make any corporation a potential target and to increase their ability to consummate the acquisitions they attempt, target corporations counter with new defensive techniques designed, for the most part, to increase the bargaining position of the board of directors. No takeover defense technique, other than concentrating the voting securities in friendly hands, has ever made a corporation acquisition-proof. Defensive techniques have, however, increased the leverage of the board of directors in finding a better deal.

 This chapter is current through November 18, 1988 (with modifications made through July 1989). David A. Katz and David M. Silk, associates of the firm, and many other members of Wachtell, Lipton, Rosen & Katz assisted in the preparation.

While defensive techniques, such as shareholder rights plans and state business combination statutes, have effectively forced bidders and would-be acquirors to negotiate with the target board of directors, takeovers continue to play a significant and fundamental role in corporate America. After 15 years of world-wide growth of takeovers spanning periods of changing economic, market, and tax environments, one conclusion is inescapable: takeovers are not a temporary aberration. Takeovers have become a major aspect of the free-world economies.

The following six chapters attempt to provide an overview of certain aspects of the continuously evolving area of takeover law.

Chapter 21 presents an overview of the current takeover environment—the factual backdrop against which the business judgment of target company directors must be addressed.

Chapter 22 provides an analysis of basic legal principles in the area, including an analysis of recent case law addressing a board of directors' duties in selling the company.

Chapter 23 addresses developments in takeover defenses, with a focus on the various defensive strategies available to a target.

Chapter 24 presents an analysis of developments concerning disclosure obligations in the takeover context.

Chapter 25 addresses the crisis with respect to the availability of directors' and officers' liability insurance along with statutory responses to the crisis.

Chapter 26 discusses federal and state regulatory initiatives designed to address some of the same perceived abuses that underlie directors' responses in the current environment.

I. OVERVIEW OF THE TAKEOVER ENVIRONMENT

Hostile takeovers have gone through numerous permutations over the past decade. Not long ago, the most powerful takeover tactic was the 100 percent cash offer for the entire target company made on the basis of financing commitments in place at the time of the offer. With the advent of junk bond financing in the early 1980s, however, raids began to be structured as partial two-tier offers with junk bonds imposed on shareholders in the second step squeeze-out transaction. Then, with the enormous increase in the size and liquidity of the junk bond market, all cash deals were initiated by takeover entrepreneurs, financed by private placements of junk bonds sold on the basis of the target's cash flow and asset base.

Many bids were (and still are) initiated without financing in place, based on a mere commitment from an investment bank that it was "highly confident" it could arrange the financing necessary to consummate the proposed transaction. More recently, as an alternative to junk-bond-financed deals, more and more investment banks have evidenced a willingness to write checks for enormous sums of their own money in order to finance all-cash deals, which are later refinanced by the sale of junk bonds. Investment banks have also taken equity positions in acquiring entities and have operated as joint bidders. We have also witnessed the use by raiders of "market sweeps," which are designed to accumulate a large—or even a controlling—position from market professionals. And, as takeover defenses and state takeover statutes have reduced (though far from eliminated) the strategic advantages enjoyed by hostile tender offerors, proxy fights have resurfaced as a means to garner shareholder support for acquisition proposals.

Over time, attitudes too have changed, adding a whole new dimension to the takeover environment. There is no longer any cultural barrier to a hostile takeover bid. Corporate raiders are glorified on the covers of magazines and on television and, as a result, the unwritten rules of hostile takeovers have been rethought. We have seen Morgan Guaranty act for a Swiss company, Hoffman-LaRoche, in a tender offer for Sterling Drug, a long-time Morgan banking client; Shearson Lehman Hutton join as an equity partner with a British company to make a hostile bid for Koppers; General Electric, pillar of the Business Roundtable and the corporate establishment, make a hostile bid for a small appliance manufacturer, Roper; Emhart, a major company in Hartford, Connecticut, become the first company in a close business community like Hartford to make a hostile bid for another company in the same community; KKR, the preeminent merchant bank, make an unsolicited offer for Kroger and an unsolicited bid for RJR; the spread of takeover activity to continental Europe and the concomitant willingness of European companies to make hostile bids in the U.S.; and the beginning of Japanese participation with the Bridgestone white knight bid of $80 per share ($2.6 billion) for Firestone after a hostile bid of $58 per share ($1.9 billion) by Pirelli and Michelin.

As public perceptions have changed, boardroom attitudes have changed too. Management is no longer restrained by fear that directors will look askance at a proposal to make a hostile bid. Many companies believe that if they are not taking over other companies and not increasing their size and leverage, they too will become targets. To remain independent, companies have become raiders.

Managers themselves are taking over companies through leveraged buyouts. The LBO gives management a greater equity stake than the customary stock incentives in most public companies. For professional managers there is great attraction in getting away from worrying about quarter-to-quarter earnings performance and instead focusing on the objective of maximizing cash flow. Many managers today believe that there is no good reason not to preempt a possible hostile bid with a management-led LBO. With the huge amount of LBO capital available, there is great momentum behind the LBO movement. It has become a major factor in the rationalization of American business and continues to grow at a very rapid pace. And, as the $25 billion buyout of RJR illustrates, there is almost no limit to the size of an LBO candidate.

Investors have also changed their views, thus giving rise to sustained take over growth. The market encourages highly leveraged companies. The standards for the ratio of debt to equity have reversed so substantially that where once it was thought too risky to have debt greater than half of equity, today debt ten times equity is applauded. The highly leveraged company is accorded a premium price in the market. The stub shares of highly leveraged, restructured companies sell at prices not based on earnings or assets, but as calls on what the earnings might be in five years or more. The premium for leverage is a major factor in promoting takeovers. Indeed, the market today so deeply discounts unleveraged future growth that there is a significant disincentive to invest in research and development and new plants and equipment.

Institutional investors control such a majority of the market that they fundamentally influence the direction and speed of today's takeover activity. Takeover premiums play a central role in boosting institutional stock portfolio returns and, as a result, institutions are an important force catalyzing sustained takeover growth. Simply put, the institutions have become activists in opposing takeover defenses, voting for corporate raiders in proxy fights and forcing companies to auction themselves to the high bidder. Today, institutional investors are not just insisting on a takeover premium when a company is put in play, they are taking on a new role by actively promoting takeovers. Institutional investors have shown little restraint in their pursuit of short-term profits.

The strategic buyer is also back. The 1987 change in the tax law eliminating devices that allowed a raider to liquidate a target on a tax-favored basis has reduced the incentive for bust-up takeovers and, in many cases, results in a price advantage to a buyer who does not plan to resell a significant part of the acquired assets. Moreover, the October 1987 market correction, the cheap dollar, and the overall resilience of the U.S. economy have also served to fuel takeover activity. Domestic acquirors are encouraged to strengthen their core operations in order to compete more effectively in the increasingly globalized economy, and the cheap dollar has made U.S. companies extremely attractive takeover targets for foreign buyers.

Permissive attitudes of regulators and courts also account for the ongoing explosion of takeovers. The SEC, FRB, ICC, FCC, and Republican administrations all generally favor takeovers and disapprove of anti-takeover legislation. It is also clear that many courts are reluctant to interfere with the takeover process, and view the process as one that should be resolved in the marketplace.

With all this attitudinal change, it is not surprising that a complex takeover infrastructure has developed. Almost every large company has an acquisition staff. All the major law firms and accounting firms have merger and acquisition departments. Takeovers are the most profitable investment banking activity. In fact, takeovers are so profitable that the major commercial banks have developed large merger and acquisition departments to compete with the investment banks. Moreover, boutique investment banking firms are springing up and, large and small, all the firms want to become merchant bankers with direct equity participation in takeovers. The expanding infrastructure itself is a driving force in expanding takeover activity.

Fueling the entire takeover phenomenon is the virtually unlimited funding available to finance corporate acquisitions. While the junk bond market has from time to time faced temporary setbacks, it has proven extremely resilient, and junk bonds remain a potent tool for the corporate bidder. Moreover, following First Boston's lead, notwithstanding some occasional difficulty in refinancing, all the investment banks are now providing enormous bridge loans to facilitate an acquisition until it can be funded with junk bonds. And, the major commercial banks are competing with the investment banks to provide takeover financing.

Financing for acquisitions is also available from insurance companies, and there is an enormous pool of acquisition financing available through numerous LBO equity funds, estimated to have at least $25 billion of capital commitments, with some estimates ranging much higher (estimates of the total amount in LBO funds range as high as $60 billion). At a 10 to 1 debt to equity ratio, typical of most leveraged buyouts, these commitments could finance deals worth at least $250 billion. Funds for LBO junk bond and senior debt financing have also been established. Manufacturers Hanover Trust recently created a $1 billion dollar senior bridge loan fund for LBOs, the first LBO fund for a major commercial bank. With all this money looking for deals—like Pirandello's actors in search of a play—it is no wonder that the takeover boom continues unabated.

II. JUNK BONDS AND TENDER OFFER FINANCING

A. Junk Bonds

The advent of junk bond financing has resulted in a significant change in the nature of takeovers. Takeover entrepreneurs have felt free to accumulate large positions through open market transactions, knowing that, if they so desire, they would be able to finance a bid for all of a company's shares using junk bonds. Although the accumulation of large stock positions has been limited to some extent by provisions in certain state takeover statutes and the flip-in provisions of shareholder rights plans, junk bond financing has allowed takeover entrepreneurs to put the company into play and profit through a bust-up of the target—a white knight transaction, a restructuring at a price higher than the bid or a repurchase of their position at a profit—"greenmail." The enormous size and liquidity of the junk bond market also means that there is almost no deal that is too big to finance.

Junk bonds are typically high yield, below investment grade bonds or preferred stocks, frequently with variable rate or exchangeability options and with detachable warrants or other equity "kickers." The high yields associated with junk bonds attract a variety of investors, including mutual funds, insurance companies, pension funds, savings and loans, foreign investors, individuals, and corporations. Early junk bond issues tended to carry relatively few restrictive covenants, but since the October 1987 market correction, more and more junk bond buyers have been looking for stricter financial covenants. Prudential Insurance Co., the nation's largest institutional investor, has indicated that it will not purchase junk bonds unless they contain change of control covenants to protect bondholders in the event of a takeover. In addition, bondholders have started to file lawsuits against issuers, based upon contract rights and disclosure issues.

The size of the market for junk bonds has increased dramatically over the past few years as many investment banks, attracted by the high fees and broadening base of junk bond issuers, have entered the market. Junk bonds have become a major source of takeover financing. They are used for direct tender offer financing, refinancing bridge loans, and refinancing bank debt used in tender offers to satisfy the Federal Reserve Board's margin requirements. Junk bonds have also promoted increased leverage through leveraged buyouts, recapitalizations, and other corporate restructurings, as well as providing general corporate financings. In addition, the junk bond market has been a source of blind pools of funds for a number of takeover entrepreneurs, such as Carl Icahn and Ronald Perelman, and for arbitrageurs seeking to make quick profits from takeover activity.

Junk bonds permit a raider to facilitate a bust-up, bootstrap takeover of a target much larger than the raider itself. Based on experience garnered from leveraged buyouts, bootstrap acquirors can sell junk bonds specifically designed to finance a takeover. With the cash proceeds of the sale of junk bonds, financial entrepreneurs have been able to obtain sufficient bank financing to make a cash offer for 100 percent of a target's stock. Such financing is often predicated on the acquiror's plan to "bust-up" the target company.

In such a bust-up transaction, following the takeover, a significant portion of the target's assets are sold to retire part of the acquisition financing. Junk bond, bust-up takeovers are particularly effective against targets for which there are a limited number of white knights interested in purchasing all of the target's business, but a large number of prospective buyers of individual pieces of the target in the postacquisition bust-up. Changes in the tax treatment of bust-up transactions, most notably the uncertainty during most of 1987 concerning the availability of the so-called "mirror image" technique and the elimination of that technique and related devices for selling assets without corporate level gain since December 15, 1987, have somewhat deterred bust-up transactions. Where the viability of the bust-up depends upon avoiding corporate level tax, the attractiveness of the transaction has decreased. Companies with a high tax basis in their assets or a large net operating loss, however, are still attractive bust-up candidates. Moreover, junk bonds remain a potent tool for bootstrap takeovers financed with the target's own cash flows.

B. Bridge Financing

The ability of raiders to finance hostile tender offers has also been enhanced by a financing technique known as bridge financing, in which investment bankers provide raiders with the funds needed to finance their raid by making short-term borrowings of the investment bank's own capital. With bridge financing a raider can launch a tender offer for a target without the delay of arranging long-term financing. In the past few years, billion dollar bridge loans have become common.

Bridge financing has enabled a raider teamed with an investment banker to buy now and refinance later. There is great risk for the investment bank, for which it is highly compensated. First Boston reportedly received more than $100 million in advisory and commitment fees in connection with a bridge loan and other investment banking services it provided to Campeau Corp. in its bid for Allied Stores Corp.

1. Risk and Reward

Bridge loans usually carry interest rates at up to 500 basis points over prime, escalating even higher if the loan remains outstanding for more than 90 days. Typically, the investment bank commits to refinance the bridge loan in the junk bond market, sometimes at a specified interest rate, as quickly as possible after the acquisition is consummated. Bridge loans may also be paid down with the proceeds of asset divestitures. Due to the escalating interest rate on the bridge loan and the investment bank's understandable concern with having its firm's capital exposed to such high risk for an extended period, the borrower may be forced to take drastic steps to pay down his debt upon acquiring the target.

The potential risk of bridge loans was illustrated by the delay in the closing of the second-step acquisition of The Southland Corporation by the Thompson family due to the upheaval in the junk-bond market following the October 1987 market correction. Goldman Sachs and Salomon Brothers each provided $300 million in bridge loans to finance the first-step tender offer. These loans were intended to be refinanced with public junk bond financing at the time of the second-step merger. After a delay of several weeks, the acquisition was closed. The bridge loans were refinanced in December 1987 following a restructuring of the terms of the public junk bond financing, including the addition of warrants as an equity kicker.

In structuring a bridge financing transaction, care must be taken to deal with the potential conflicts that can arise from the investment bank's dual role as advisor and lender, both in the initial stages of the transaction and at the time of refinancing the bridge loan. The special problems that arise when an investment bank acts as financial advisor and bridge lender in a problem loan or work-out situation have yet to be fully explored. At a minimum, investment banks should be prepared to field two "teams" to handle the situation.

2. Investment Banker as "Bidder"

A further wrinkle in bridge financing was developed by Shearson Lehman in the successful bid by Beazer PLC for Koppers Company, Inc. In that deal Shearson Lehman agreed to provide bridge financing via an equity investment in Beazer's acquisition vehicle. The structure chosen was influenced by Hart-Scott considerations, since the partnership form permitted Beazer to accumulate more than $15 million of Koppers' stock without review by the FTC and the Department of Justice. This was the case because Beazer's partnership interest was 49 percent, Shearson Lehman's was 46.1 percent and NatWest's

(Beazer's other financial advisor and its principal lender) was 4.9 percent. The District Court for the Western District of Pennsylvania determined that Shearson Lehman was a "bidder" for Williams Act purposes because of its equity interest in the bidding entity. *Koppers Co.* v. *American Express Co.*, 689 F. Supp. 1371, 1387–90 (W.D. Pa. 1988). Upon close analysis, Shearson Lehman's participation is different only in form from that of other bankers who provide bridge financing for tender offers. The decision is a warning to bankers as to the structuring of bridge financing for hostile tender offers and an opportunity for targets to defend against such offers.

In *City Capital Associates Ltd. Partnership* v. *Interco, Inc.*, 860 F.2d 60 (3d Cir. 1988), a divided panel of the Third Circuit held that Drexel Burnham was not a "bidder" for Interco stock for Williams Act purposes. Drexel was going to own up to 36 percent of the equity of the shell vehicle making the tender offer, had committed to provide a substantial amount of the preferred equity financing, and was entitled to a percentage of the profits on any sale of Interco stock if the offer was unsuccessful and to substantial fees if the offer was successful. The majority held that Drexel was not a "bidder". Placing its principal reliance on an interpretation of the SEC's instruction to Item 9 of Schedule 14D-1 regarding financial disclosure, the majority held that a shareholder of a nominal entity making a tender offer need not make disclosure unless it controls the acquisition entity. (The majority did not, for procedural reasons, consider the fact that Drexel was itself providing financing.)

Judge Weis in dissent rejected the majority analysis, arguing that the instruction to Item 9 must be read in conjunction with the statutory language which prohibits "any person, directly or indirectly" from making a tender offer without complying with the Act. To hold otherwise, said Judge Weis:

> [t]he formation of a shell corporation for the purpose of making a tender without disclosing who or what is behind the legal facade would be a blatant device to circumvent the express congressional prohibitions against an undisclosed party "indirectly" acquiring beneficial ownership.

860 F.2d at 69. Finding that Drexel was a "critical player in the Interco tender offer," Judge Weis likened the instant case to the *Koppers* case. In light of Judge Weis' dissent and the *Koppers* opinion, an investment banker that has a significant equity stake and other financial interests in a tender offer cannot be assured that it will not be deemed to be a "bidder" under the Williams Act.

In *MAI Basic Four Inc.* v. *Prime Computer, Inc.*, [Current] Fed. Sec. L. Rep (CCH) ¶94,317 (D. Mass. Dec. 29, 1988), *aff'd*, 871 F.2d 212 (1st Cir. 1989), the court continued a preliminary injunction previously issued against MAI's bid for Prime Computer. The injunction was based on the failure of Drexel, which was held to be a "bidder" within the meaning of the Williams Act, and MAI to make sufficient disclosure regarding Drexel's ability to provide the financing necessary for consummation of the offer, in light of Drexel's recent acknowledgment of violations of the securities laws and agreement to pay at least $650 million in fines and civil damages. The court also held that further disclosure was necessary regarding the bidders' likely violation of Federal margin requirements or alternate financing plans not involving such a violation, and the bidders' plan to increase the price of its offer in response to the decision of the Delaware Chancery Court in related litigation. On March 29, 1989, the First Circuit Court of Appeals affirmed, stating:

> In this case we cannot say that, as a matter of law, an active advisor-broker-financier-participant who owns less than a majority interest in the surviving entity is not a bidder where, as here, there has been a history of close association, equity sharing, board representation and involvement from the beginning of the present offer, and where there is the possibility of the advisor-broker being the indispensable key to the offer's success. Nor can we say that while a 46 percent stockholder qualifies as a bidder, a 14 percent direct stockholder with other indirect equity interests cannot qualify. At a minimum it is evident that Drexel has "act[ed] as a partnership, limited partnership, . . . or other group for the purpose of acquiring, holding, or disposing of securities of an issuer," 15 U.S. § 78n(d)(2). We are not convinced that the district court erred in determining that Prime demonstrated a likelihood of success on the merits, and therefore affirm the court's ruling that Drexel is a bidder.

MAI Basic Four, Inc. v. *Prime Computer, Inc.*, 871 F.2d 212, 221 (1st Cir. 1989).

The SEC has issued a release containing proposals to revise Schedules 13D, 13E-3, 14B, and 14D-1 in order to provide shareholders with material information concerning significant equity participants in limited partnerships, closely held corporations, and similar entities engaging in control transactions. The amendments would require additional disclosure by persons engaging in substantial acquisitions of securities, tender offers, proxy fights, and going-private transactions who contribute more than 10 percent of the equity capital or would have the right to receive, in the aggregate, more than 10 percent of the profits or assets in such transactions. See *Disclosures of Equity Participants in Control Transactions*, Exch. Act Rel. No. 34-26599 (March 6, 1989).

C. The Federal Reserve Board Ruling

In the Unocal and Revlon bids, highly leveraged junk bond financing schemes were attacked under the margin rules on the theory that the junk bond debt was indirectly secured by stock pledged to the banks as part of the financing package by virtue of cross-default provisions and covenants in the bank loans. Although there was no final judicial resolution in either of the court challenges, the courts' concern about the abuse of the margin regulations is evidenced by the decision in the District of Delaware in *Revlon, Inc.* v. *Pantry Pride, Inc.*, 621 F. Supp. 804 (D. Del. 1985). While refusing to contradict the Federal Reserve Board's then-existing interpretation that the margin rules do not apply to publicly issued debt when the minimum investment in the debt was $2.5 million, the court commented:

> [A]s a matter of public policy, there is much to commend Revlon's position. It is apparent that the Pantry Pride Group has taken advantage of a possible oversight on the part of the [Federal Reserve] Board in formulating the public offering exception to the margin regulations. However, it is not the role of this Court to engage in the rulemaking activities delegated by Congress to the Federal Reserve Board (*Id.* at 815).

By late 1985 several bills had been introduced in Congress to curb the use of junk bonds. When legislative efforts stalled, the Federal Reserve Board stepped in and proposed regulations of its own. On January 10, 1986, the Federal Reserve issued an interpretation of Regulation G (Securities Credit by Persons Other Than Banks, Brokers or Dealers) that applies the margin rules to the sale of debt securities by a shell corporation, the proceeds of which are used to purchase stock of a public company. The interpretation applies to debt issued by a corporation that "has virtually no operations and no significant business function other than to acquire and hold stock of a target company and substantially no assets or cash flow to support credit extended to it other than the stock it has acquired or intends to acquire" because such debt would be presumed to be indirectly secured by the target's stock. The margin rules, however, do not apply where there is specific additional evidence that the acquisition debt is being secured in a different manner, such as by a guarantee of the parent of the shell corporation, or where there is a merger agreement between the shell corporation and the target or where the acquisition of target stock is contingent on obtaining sufficient stock to do a short form merger without target company approval.

While the interpretation applies the margin rules to junk bond financed tender offers when the raider is unprepared to commit a sufficient amount of its own assets to support the debt financing, it apparently does not change existing rules with respect to debt financings by a target company in connection with a leveraged buyout. The interpretation does not restrict junk bond financing by raiders currently in control of operating companies. Thus, for example, Carl Icahn (ACF Industries and TWA), Irwin Jacobs (AMF), and

T. Boone Pickens (Mesa Petroleum) would not be affected by the rule if they financed the transaction through their companies. The interpretation is not applicable to preferred stock, although a Federal District Court has applied the interpretation to exchangeable preferred stock, which it concluded was actually a debt instrument, "due to the underlying and ultimate intentions of the issuer and the purchasers to create a creditor-debtor relationship." *Caesars World, Inc.* v. *Sosnoff*, CV 87-1622 WJR (C.D. Cal. June 8, 1987) (order granting plaintiff's motion for preliminary injunction); see also *Koppers Co.* v. *American Express Co.*, 689 F. Supp. 1371, 1402-3 (W.D. Pa. 1988) ("reasonable probability" that preferred stock together with bank financing would violate margin regulations); *Duro-Test Corp.* v. *TCA-IV Ltd. Partnership,* No. 87-4418 (D.N.J. Dec. 10, 1987) (although plaintiff was likely to succeed on argument that preferred stock is actually debt, such possibility was adequately disclosed in tender offer documents, and there is no private right of action under margin rules); *West Point-Pepperell, Inc.* v. *Farley, Inc.*, No. 88-cv113-GET (N.D. Ga. Nov. 14, 1988) (same).

The Federal Reserve Board ruling has had little impact on the aggregate use of junk bonds in takeover financing. The rule, which only affects acquisitions by shell companies, has been easily circumvented by new acquisition techniques. According to a January 1987 study conducted by the Investor Responsibility Research Center, the ruling has encouraged some acquirors to issue investment grade debt and preferred stock themselves or to obtain bank loans as the initial source of tender offer financing, rather than issuing junk bonds through shell corporations. Not surprisingly, however, much of the equity and high grade debt financing is converted into junk bond financing after the tender offer is completed or a merger agreement is reached. The study concludes that "the ruling appears to have altered the timing of junk bond issuance more than the absolute amount of junk bonds issued to finance takeovers." Investor Responsibility Research Center, *Junk Bonds and Tender Offer Financing*, 19 (January 1987).

D. The Continuing Policy Debate

Concerns over the impact of junk bond financing continue. In July 1986 the junk bond market was jolted by the bankruptcy of LTV Steel placing $375 million of LTV junk bonds into default. Then the October 1987 market correction sent shock waves through the junk bond market. And, in July 1988, Revco became the first billion dollar leveraged buyout to file for bankruptcy. Even in October 1988, a junk bond offering for Federated was withdrawn and reformulated, due to lack of investor interest. Many public policy analysts worry that the risk of large scale defaults associated with junk bonds is dangerously high. They note that banks, savings and loans and pension funds along with other institutional investors have become the predominant investors in the LBO and junk bond market and that a major correction in the market could cause serious shock waves through the banking, savings and loan and pension industries, and the economy as a whole. *See, e.g.*, Liscio, The Buyout Bubble When It Bursts, There'll be Fallout Aplenty, *Barrons*, Oct. 31, 1988, p. 6; Uchitelle, Pushing the Stakes to New Heights, *The New York Times*, Oct. 30, 1988, p. D1. Recognizing the risks associated with the tremendous debt loads that have been generated by recent takeover activity, Federal Reserve Chairman Alan Greenspan advised Congress in October 1988 that it should consider action that would limit takeover borrowing. However, Treasury Secretary Brady, testifying before the House Ways and Means Committee hearings on LBOs, stated that although he had "a growing feeling that we are headed in the wrong direction," he thought that LBO activity might be "leveling off" and advised Congress to defer any legislative solutions. Basky, Brady Sees No Urgency to Put Curbs on Buyouts, *The New York Times*, Feb. 1, 1989, p. D2.

The growth in junk bond financed takeovers has rekindled the public debate over the efficacy of takeovers in general and the effect such transactions may have on the economy through an explosive leveraging of America's capital structure. Some financial and legal analysts argue that these over-leveraged acquisitions take advantage of a loophole in our tax system and that, as a practical matter, high-risk junk bonds should be treated as equity for tax purposes. See Canellos, The Over-Leveraged Acquisition, 39 *Tax Law.* 91 (Fall 1985) at 115-119. Others argue that the explosive growth in the junk bond market coupled with the extreme volatility in the stock market caused by speculation in takeovers—both actual and rumored—undermines investor confidence in the nation's financial markets and thereby adversely affects their liquidity and efficiency. (See Sterngold, Deep-Pocketed Deal Makers, *The New York Times*, Apr. 14, 1987, p. D1, col. 3; Rohatyn, Junk Bonds and Other Securities Swill, *The Wall Street Journal*, Apr. 18, 1985, p. 30, col. 3; Lipton, Takeover Abuses Mortgage the Future, *The Wall Street Journal*, Apr. 5, 1985, p. 16, col. 4; Greenspan, Takeovers Rooted in Fear, *The Wall Street Journal*, Sept. 27, 1985, p. 28, col. 4.) Following the takeover of RJR Nabisco, Congress has again become interested in the issues surrounding highly leveraged transactions. The 101st Congress is having a number of hearings on the issues surrounding LBOs, and several prominent congressmen have suggested that interest payments on debt in highly leveraged transactions should no longer be deductible.

Arguments that takeover financings represent only a small portion of total corporate borrowings are no longer valid, as the level of takeover-induced debt continues to escalate. The unprecedented levels of takeover borrowings, illustrated most starkly by the $25 billion leveraged buyout of RJR Nabisco, have fueled investor concerns about the creditworthiness of corporate debt, as almost all corporate debt must now be discounted for the effects of a potential change of control or contain poison pill provisions. (See Winkler and Herman, "Takeover Fears Rack Corporate Bonds," *The Wall Street Journal*, October 25, 1988, p. C1; "The Fear Gripping Bond Buyers," *Business Week*, Nov. 14, 1988, p. 133.) Increased leverage has forced American companies to focus on short-term results at the expense of long-term investment strategies, and as more and more companies are forced to replace their equity with debt, the real costs of borrowing continue to rise, thus increasing the discount on future growth opportunities.

While not all junk bond financing is bad, the combination of huge commitment fees, easy access to financing, and the rise of financial entrepreneurs interested in pursuing short-term speculative returns on highly leveraged investments causes a great rise in the level of takeover activity and, as some argue, a rise in takeover abuses, which are harmful to corporations and their shareholders, non-shareholder constituencies—such as employees, customers, suppliers, local communities—and the economy as a whole.

E. Is There a Duty Owed to Bondholders?

Courts have consistently refused to recognize the existence of fiduciary duties owed by a company to its creditors. *See Simons* v. *Cogan*, 549 A.2d 300 (Del. Supr. 1988) (no fiduciary duty owed to holders of convertible debentures until after they convert their securities); *see also Metropolitan Securities* v. *Occidental Petroleum Corp.*, 705 F. Supp. 134 (S.D.N.Y. 1989) (no disclosure duty owed to convertible bondholders in a tender offer for the underlying securities). Bondholders, upset over the erosion of their credit, have turned to other legal theories for possible relief. Metropolitan Life and ITT Corp. each filed suit against RJR based on the decrease in value of RJR bonds following the announcement of the RJR buyout proposal, claiming respectively that RJR violated a contractual duty of good faith and fair dealing and that RJR violated the securities laws in failing to disclose its consideration of buyout plans when the bonds were sold in April 1988, but failed in their attempt to block consummation of the transaction. *Metropolitan Life Insurance Co.* v. *RJR Nabisco, Inc.*, Civ. No. 88-8266 (S.D.N.Y. June 1, 1989).

III. SECRET ACCUMULATIONS

Although some state takeover statutes (such as Delaware's business combination statute), and flip-in provisions of shareholder rights plans limit the number of shares that may be purchased by a raider or other investor without potentially serious consequences, these limits are really just ceilings that still allow substantial stock accumulation. Current securities and antitrust regulations permit a raider to acquire significant share positions before making any public disclosure concerning its purchases and its intentions with respect to the target. As such, a raider can reap tremendous profit simply by acquiring a large stake and then putting the target "into play." Moreover, once a substantial stock position is obtained, the raider is in a position to attempt a tender offer for the target company or to force a significant corporate restructuring of the company through a proxy contest.

A. Section 13D

A raider can quietly begin buying a target company's stock up to a level just short of 5 percent of the outstanding shares, the point at which the SEC requires public disclosure. The actual purchases are typically made through obscure corporations and partnerships in order to keep secret the identity of the raider. Before crossing the 5 percent level, at which point the raider has 10 days to make a public disclosure of its target company holdings, the raider firms up its group and obtains the financing required for its planned stock purchases. Once set, it crosses the 5 percent threshold, commencing a vigorous open market purchase program. Often an acquiror will be able to accumulate up to 10 or 20 percent of the target's shares before disclosing such purchases in a Schedule 13D filing. A number of legislative proposals have been put forward that would close the 10-day window period under §13(d) of the Exchange Act. Some of these proposals would also reduce the 5 percent threshold. However, these proposals have been lost in the broader debate over takeover reform legislation.

In *SEC* v. *First City Financial Corp.*, 688 F. Supp. 705 (D.D.C. 1988), the SEC, in a civil proceeding, charged the defendants with deliberate attempts to disregard the mandatory disclosure requirements of Section 13(d) of the Exchange Act in failing to reveal the extent of their purchases of shares of Ashland Oil prior to an attempted takeover. The defendants were charged with "parking" their stock by making purchases through third party nominees, thus allowing such defendants to purchase their shares at prices far below what they would have been had proper disclosure been made. In finding that the defendants violated the disclosure requirements under Section 13(d), the court fashioned two forms of relief: (i) it issued an injunction against future violations of the Exchange Act; and (ii) it required the defendants to disgorge their entire profits ($2.7 million) resulting from the failure by defendants to properly disclose the required information (with the amount of profits determined by the difference in purchase price of shares at the time disclosure should have been made and the price of shares when disclosure was in fact made). The court noted the deterrent effect the disgorgement of profits would have on future violations. *See also SEC* v. *Levy*, Civ. 88-0131 (D.D.C. Feb. 2, 1989).

In *Torchmark Corp.* v. *Bixby*, 708 F. Supp. 1070 (W.D. Mo. 1988), a federal district court held that a group was not formed for Williams Act purposes where related shareholders who owned more than 50 percent of the target's common stock "individually and separately" advised the target's Board of Directors in writing that they had no intention to sell their shares in response to an acquisition proposal. The court stated:

> The mere fact that defendants were related through blood, marriage, business or social relationships is insufficient to warrant the finding that a "group" existed within the definition of § 13(d) of the Act. There is no evidence proving any defendants entered into any expressed or implied agreement with respect to the disposition of their stock prior to the November 21, 1988 Stockholders' Agreement.

708 F. Supp. at 1083. When most of the same shareholders signed an agreement not to tender their shares in response to a tender offer by the same bidder or anyone else for six months, a Williams Act group was formed, requiring the filing of a Schedule 13D.

On March 2, 1989, The Commission announced a release containing proposals that would amend the rules relating to the reporting of beneficial ownership in public companies. The Commission stated that "[t]he proposals are intended to improve the effectiveness of the beneficial ownership disclosure scheme, while at the same time reducing the reporting obligations of passive investors." The release proposes significant amendments to Exchange Act Rules 13d-1, 13d-2, and 13d-7, as well as changes to Schedules 13D and 13G. *See Reporting of Beneficial Ownership*, Exch. Act Rel. No. 34-26598 (March 6, 1989).

B. Filings Under the HSR Act

The Hart-Scott-Rodino Antitrust Improvements Act of 1976 (the "HSR Act") generally requires an acquiror to notify the Federal Trade Commission and the Antitrust Division of the Department of Justice (and the target) and wait 30 days (unless there is early termination) before acquiring $15 million of the target's stock.

The HSR Act, however, is not primarily concerned with the full and fair disclosure of an acquiror's accumulation of the target's shares and thus, provides incomplete protection against secret share accumulations. First, an acquiror can accumulate in excess of $15 million of a target's shares up to a 10 percent stake if it can establish that the acquisition "is solely for the purpose of investment." Then, subject to FTC scrutiny (and possible sanctions) if the change occurs too quickly, the acquiror can change its subjective intent and file for HSR clearance at a higher threshold level. Moreover, a loophole in the HSR filing requirements has permitted raiders to avoid the filing requirements by forming partnerships to accumulate target shares.

Effective July 3, 1987, the FTC promulgated a new rule that partially closed the "partnership loophole." The new rule requires HSR Act filings in connection with acquisitions by newly-formed partnerships where one of the partners has the right to 50 percent or more of (1) the profits of the entity or (2) the assets of the entity upon its dissolution. While the new rule does not apply to partnerships in which no partner satisfies the 50 percent standard, the FTC takes the position that a partnership that is formed for the purpose of avoiding the obligation to comply with the HSR Act filing requirements will be disregarded. In an early application of the new rule, the FTC reportedly launched an investigation of T. Boone Pickens' role in the purchases by Ivanhoe Partners of Newmont Mining shares; no action has been taken to date. The FTC also deadlocked (by a 2–2 vote) on bringing a preliminary injunction action against the Rales brothers' acquisition of shares in Interco for violations of the HSR Act's requirements; however, the FTC has voted to request that the Justice Department bring suit against the Rales brothers for "profit disgorgement" for such violations. Such a proceeding would represent the first time that the FTC has taken action (despite repeated threats to do so) that would result in significant penalties for violations of the HSR Act. In the largest civil penalty ever for violation of the HSR Act, the Great Atlantic & Pacific Tea Co. has agreed to pay a $3 million civil penalty to settle government charges of failing to comply with pre-merger notification requirements in connection with its acquisition of Waldbaum securities in 1986. No HSR filing was made until November 1988.

In September 1988, the FTC issued a notice of proposed rulemaking in which it proposed three alternative rule amendments that would raise the initial reporting threshold under the HSR Act to 10 percent. According to the FTC, the principal motivations behind the proposed rule change are to (1) reduce the non-antitrust-related incentive to avoid HSR filing obligations; (2)

eliminate any unnecessary burden on the parties; and (3) avoid unnecessary interference with the securities laws' disclosure requirements and the market for corporate control.

IV. STREET SWEEPS

A. Overview

Market and legal developments have led to a pronounced increase in the ability of a raider to "sweep the street" to accumulate large and sometimes controlling blocks of a target's shares while depriving shareholders of the procedural protections of the Williams Act. In several situations, large accumulations of stock through open market purchases were made by the raider immediately following the termination of a previously announced tender offer.

The ability of raiders to "sweep the street" for large amounts of a target's stock results primarily from the activities of arbitrageurs and certain specialized securities firms who buy-up a substantial portion of a target's shares once the target is put in play. Public shareholders who sell their shares to the arbitrageurs do so without the benefits of the Williams Act protections as to disclosure, timing, withdrawal rights, and best price. Once assembled, these blocks can be sold to the highest bidder, whether that bidder is a raider, the target, or a third party. And, as discussed below, the courts have generally been reluctant to hold that such stock accumulations constitute a de facto tender offer within the meaning of the Williams Act.

Hostile Transactions

Open market purchases have been utilized by hostile acquirors to gain control in the following contexts.

1. TWA

In early May 1985 rumors surfaced that Carl Icahn was purchasing shares of Trans World Airlines. The rumors proved to be true when Icahn disclosed in a 13D filing that ACF Industries, a company he controlled, along with 10 investment partnerships also controlled by Icahn, owned 20.5 percent of the outstanding shares of TWA. Icahn had purchased the bulk of those shares in the 10 days prior to the filing after his holding had reached the 5 percent threshold. Icahn continued to accumulate shares in the open market raising his stake to 25 percent. Finally, on May 21, 1985, Icahn delivered a letter to the TWA board proposing an offer at $18 per share for the 75 percent of

TWA he did not already own. The TWA board, deciding to put the company up for sale, instructed management to seek out alternatives superior to the Icahn proposal. On June 4, Icahn announced that he had increased his stake to 32.7 percent. The following week TWA announced that Texas Air had agreed to acquire the Company at $23 per share in cash and debt. Icahn, however, with the support of the TWA pilots union, raised his bid to $24 per share in cash and preferred stock and continued to purchase shares in the open market. Additional attempts by Texas Air and the board to structure an alternative transaction were unsuccessful and on August 22 Icahn boosted his stake to over 50 percent, thus gaining control of TWA without ever having launched a tender offer.

2. Crown Zellerbach

In Sir James Goldsmith's takeover of Crown Zellerbach, Goldsmith began his most aggressive open market purchases just as management was conducting a "road show" for its restructuring program. Notwithstanding the fact that the Crown Zellerbach "road show" was well received by stock market analysts, Goldsmith continued to buy stock in the open market. During the week after the Crown Zellerbach restructuring prospectus was filed with the SEC, he increased his ownership of the company's outstanding shares from approximately 26 percent to approximately 50.7 percent, which placed him in a position to frustrate the transaction. As in the *SCM* case, Goldsmith had started and then stopped a highly conditional tender offer prior to proceeding with his open market purchases.

3. NL Industries

In his takeover of NL Industries, Harold Simmons, in a single trade for over 23 percent of the shares of NL Industries, acquired control of that company. Simmons was able to make this purchase soon after terminating his tender offer because the Second Circuit, which had prohibited any purchases under the offer pending the appeal of the NL Rights Plan decision, refused to expand its order to cover open market purchases.

4. Anderson Clayton

On September 19, 1986, shortly after the court enjoined Anderson Clayton's $60 self-tender, Anderson Clayton announced that it had begun negotiations with Ralston Purina Company concerning a possible white knight transaction. The Quaker Oats Company, however, bought approximately 2.9 million Anderson Clayton shares, or 23.4 percent of the outstanding shares, in the open market at $64 per share. On September 27, 1986, after negotiations between Ralston and Quaker, Quaker agreed to acquire Anderson Clayton for $66 per share. Quaker's ability to sweep the street for almost a quarter of Anderson Clayton's stock gave Quaker the toehold it needed to resist the white knight transaction with Ralston.

5. Other Examples

See also *SCM*, *Allied Stores*, and *Pay 'N Pak* as other examples of hostile street sweeps discussed in Chapters 21.IV.B and 21.IV.C.

Friendly Transactions

Open market purchases have also been utilized in friendly transactions and by targets defending against a hostile bid:

6. Cyclops

In late March 1987, when only 54 percent of the outstanding shares of Cyclops Corp. had been tendered to Dixons Group PLC pursuant to a board-supported tender offer at $90.25 per share, Dixons attempted to waive its 80 percent minimum condition and purchase the shares that had been tendered. At the SEC's insistence, Dixons agreed to extend its offer for 10 days and, due to a rival tender offer by Audio/Video Affiliates and Citicorp Capital Investors at $92.50 per share, more than half the shareholders who had previously tendered their shares pursuant to Dixons' offer withdrew their shares. Shortly following the termination of its tender offer, and in the face of the competitive offer at $92.50 per share, Dixons purchased nearly 2.5 million Cyclops shares (approximately 60 percent of the outstanding shares) from Jefferies Group Inc. for $233 million (approximately $95 per share) bringing its total holdings to approximately 83 percent of the outstanding shares and announced its intention to proceed with a second-step merger in which the remaining shareholders would receive $95 per share.

7. Other Examples

See also *Carter Hawley Hale* and *Newmont Mining* as examples of friendly street sweeps discussed in Chapters 21.IV.B.2 and 21.IV.C.2.

B. What Constitutes a Tender Offer?

1. The Wellman Eight-Factor Test

The SEC has suggested an eight-factor test to determine whether a stock accumulation constitutes a tender offer. The test was applied by the court in *Wellman* v. *Dickinson*, 475 F. Supp. 783, 823-24 (S.D.N.Y. 1979), *aff'd on other grounds*, 682 F.2d 355 (2d Cir. 1982), *cert. denied*, 460 U.S. 1069 (1983), and has come to be known as the Wellman eight-factor test. The eight factors are:

1. Active and widespread solicitation of public shareholders for the shares of an issuer,
2. Solicitation made for a substantial percentage of the issuer's stock,
3. Offer to purchase made at a premium over the prevailing market price,
4. Terms of the offer are firm rather than negotiable,
5. Offer contingent on the tender of a fixed number of shares, often subject to a fixed maximum number to be purchased,
6. Offer open only for a limited period of time,
7. Offeree subject to pressure to sell his stock,
8. Public announcements of a purchasing program concerning the target company precede or accompany rapid accumulation of large amounts of the target company's securities. 475 F. Supp. at 823-24.

SEC attempts, however, to gain judicial support in regulating street sweeps have met with little success.

2. Carter Hawley Hale

In 1984, Carter Hawley Hale Stores responded to a partial tender offer by The Limited by selling a new series of preferred stock to General Cinema Corporation (with 22 percent of the voting power of the then outstanding stock) and allocating up to $500 million for the repurchase of up to 15 million (later increased to 18.5 million) shares of the approximately 35.7 million then-outstanding shares of Carter Hawley common stock in the open market or in privately negotiated transactions. On April 17, Carter Hawley purchased 6.5 million shares (approximately 18 percent of the outstanding stock) within a two-hour period at an average price of $25.88. By the close of business on April 24, Carter Hawley had acquired approximately 50 percent (17.9 million shares) of the shares outstanding prior to the commencement of the repurchases. Immediately following Carter Hawley's announcement of the open market repurchase program, The Limited unsuccessfully sought to enjoin the purchases. *Carter Hawley Hale Stores, Inc.* v. *The Limited, Inc.*, C.A. No. 84-2200 AWT (C.D. Cal. Apr. 17, 1984).

The SEC filed suit alleging that Carter Hawley's open market repurchase constituted an illegal tender offer in violation of the Williams Act. The U.S. District Court for the Central District of California denied the SEC's motion for a preliminary injunction citing the Wellman eight-factor test and finding that only two of the eight factors were present. *SEC* v. *Carter Hawley Hale*

Stores, Inc., 587 F. Supp. 1248 (C. D. Cal. 1984), *aff'd*, 760 F.2d 945 (9th Cir. 1985).

3. SCM

In Hanson Trust PLC's acquisition of SCM, Hanson purchased a total of 33 1/3 percent of SCM's outstanding stock—25 percent in six transactions following Hanson's termination of its tender offer—in order to frustrate SCM's announced leveraged buyout transaction, which under New York law required a two-thirds vote. The announced tender offer had the effect of moving large amounts of SCM's stock into the hands of arbitrageurs, thus assuring the effectiveness of an aggressive open market purchase program following the termination of the tender offer in which purchases could be made without compliance with the procedural protections of the Williams Act. Notwithstanding this effect, the Second Circuit Court of Appeals ruled that Hanson Trust's purchase of 25 percent of SCM's outstanding stock following the termination of a tender offer was not a violation of the federal securities laws. *Hanson Trust PLC* v. *SCM Corp.*, 774 F.2d 47 (2d Cir. 1985). The court rejected the Wellman eight-factor test in favor of a test that looks to the sophistication of, and information available to, the solicitees.

4. Allied Stores

On October 24, 1986, faced with a tender offer from white knight ASC Acquisition Corp. at $67 per Allied Stores share, Campeau terminated its own $66 per share tender offer and, within 30 minutes of termination, was able to purchase 48 percent of Allied Stores' shares in the open market (giving Campeau a 52 percent stake). The Federal District Court for the Southern District of New York granted a temporary restraining order prohibiting Campeau from, among other things, paying for or settling the open market purchases until the court could hold a hearing on the issue of whether these purchases constituted an illegal tender offer. *Allied Stores Corp.* v. *Campeau Acquisition Corp.*, 86 Civ. 7841 (S.D.N.Y. Oct. 24, 1986). On October 29, 1986, the court vacated this portion of the TRO, subject to the restrictions, however, that Campeau not vote the shares or seek to influence Allied Stores' activities based upon ownership of the shares, and that Campeau give Allied Stores at least eight business hours notice before taking any action that might affect Allied Stores' legal or financial interests or the ability of Allied Stores' Board of Directors to influence or control Allied Stores. *Allied Stores Corp.* v. *Campeau Acquisition Corp.*, 86 Civ. 7841 (S.D.N.Y. Oct. 29, 1986). Allied Stores had little choice but to enter into negotiations with Campeau, with Allied agreeing to be acquired by Campeau for a package of cash and securities valued at $69 per share. As a result of the agreement to drop all litigation, the legality under the Williams Act of Campeau's open market purchases was never resolved by the court.

5. GM/EDS

In *In re General Motors Class E Stock Buyout Securities Litigation*, 694 F. Supp. 1119 (D. Del. 1988), the Federal District Court for Delaware held that the repurchase by GM of the GM Class E stock held by H. Ross Perot and three other EDS officers was not a Williams Act tender offer. In so doing, the Court rejected the Wellman eight-factor test and accepted the Second Circuit's *Hanson Trust* test to the effect that the tender offer rules are inapplicable where the sellers are sophisticated and well-informed and do not need the protection of the Williams Act.

C. Other Issues in Cases Involving Street Sweeps

1. Pay 'N Pak

In the course of a competitive bidding process for Pay 'N Pak Stores, Inc., Pay 'N Pak provided confidential information to Paul Bilzerian, who owned 9.99 percent of Pay 'N Pak's stock, pursuant to a confidentiality agreement limiting Bilzerian's right to purchase shares other than pursuant to a tender offer. Rosewood Holdings Corporation, an investor group that included Pay 'N Pak's management, outbid Bilzerian and commenced a tender offer at $21 per share pursuant to a merger agreement with the company.

Two days before the expiration of the Rosewood tender offer, Morgan Stanley & Co. Inc., acting on Bilzerian's behalf, arranged to purchase a 4.1 million share block, representing 41 percent of the outstanding shares, from approximately 20 holders at $21.25 per share. The purchase was made on a next-day closing basis and would have given Bilzerian a majority of the Pay 'N Pak shares. Pay 'N Pak sought a temporary restraining order to prevent the consummation of the purchase, citing the confidentiality agreement entered into by Bilzerian, and the Federal District Court for the Western District of Washington granted the TRO. *Pay 'N Pak Stores, Inc.* v. *Bilzerian*, No. C87-925C (W.D. Wash. July 8, 1987). Two days later, following a hearing, the court issued a preliminary injunction against any purchase of Pay 'N Pak stock by Bilzerian. *Pay 'N Pak Stores, Inc.* v. *Bilzerian*, No. C87-925C (W.D. Wash. July 10, 1987).

Prior to the entry of the TRO, Morgan Stanley, citing "significant legal questions under the tender offer rules," had canceled the transaction. The

New York Stock Exchange, however, subsequently determined that the trade would stand in its records although no action would be taken unless Morgan Stanley was challenged by one of its customers.

2. Newmont Mining

In Ivanhoe Partners' attempted takeover of Newmont Mining, Consolidated Gold Fields plc, which had owned 26 percent of Newmont stock, increased its ownership to 49.67 percent through open market purchases on September 21 and 22, 1987 (including purchases of Newmont shares on September 22, 1987 at an aggregate price of $1.53 billion). On September 22, 1987, Ivanhoe Partners sought a TRO in the Delaware Chancery Court against the closing of these trades, which had been made on the customary five-day settlement basis. On September 23, 1987, the Court declined to enjoin payment for these trades, but entered a TRO against Gold Fields purchasing any additional shares pending a decision on Ivanhoe Partners' motion for a preliminary injunction.

At a September 25 hearing on Ivanhoe Partners' motion to modify the TRO to restrain Gold Fields from consummating its purchases, the New York Stock Exchange and the National Securities Clearing Corporation intervened to urge the Court not to block the closing of the trades, stating that such action "would result in immediate and irreparable harm to N.Y.S.E. and N.S.C.C., including both harm and severe injury to public confidence in the securities markets." On September 28, 1987, the Court denied Ivanhoe Partners' motion to expand the September 23rd TRO to enjoin the closing of the trades. *Ivanhoe Partners* v. *Newmont Mining Corp.*, C.A. No. 9281 (Del. Ch. Sept. 28, 1987). Expressly following the approach taken in *SCM* and *Allied Stores*, the Court amended the restraining order, pending the hearing and decision on Ivanhoe Partners' motion for a preliminary injunction, to enjoin Gold Fields to refrain from voting and to hold separate the Newmont shares purchased on September 21 and 22, 1987, provided that Ivanhoe Partners' agree not to seek consents or take any further action with respect to its tender offer other than to extend the duration or complete the financing arrangements.

On October 15, 1987, the Chancery Court dissolved the TRO and denied Ivanhoe Partners' motion for a preliminary injunction. *Ivanhoe Partners* v. *Newmont Mining Corp.*, 533 A.2d 585 (Del. Ch.), *aff'd*, 535 A.2d 1334 (Del. Supr. 1987). The court found that Gold Fields' purchases were, standing alone, legally proper (*id.* at 606) and did not violate any Delaware law or fiduciary principle (*id.* at 589). The court rejected the claim that the sellers in the street sweep were coerced by some wrongful act by Gold Fields, finding that any pressure to sell was the result of "market forces," including the "economic merits of the Gold Fields purchases."(*Id.* at 604-06).

On November 18, 1987, the Delaware Supreme Court affirmed the Chancery Court's decision that the street sweep was not wrongfully coercive. *Ivanhoe Partners* v. *Newmont Mining Corp.*, 535 A.2d 1334 (Del. Supr. 1987). The Court viewed the street sweep as "an essential part of Newmont's defensive plan, which enabled Newmont to maintain its independent status for the benefit of its other stockholders" (*Id.* at 1344).

3. Best-Price Rule

In several recent cases, courts have found that the best-price rule might be violated if successive tender offers were integrated. *See Field* v. *Trump*, 850 F.2d 938 (2d Cir. 1988), *cert. denied*, 109 S. Ct. 1122 (1989); *Feder* v. *McFadden Holdings, Inc.*, 698 F. Supp. 47 (S.D.N.Y. 1988). This may raise issues in street sweeps if a mere announcement is held to be insufficient to terminate an outstanding tender offer.

D. Regulatory Initiatives

1. Proposed Rule

In September 1987, the SEC announced that it was seeking public comment on proposed Rules 13e-2 and 14d-11 to require, with certain exceptions, that acquisitions by persons seeking an increase in their ownership of 10 percent or more of a class during, and for the ten business days following the scheduled expiration of a tender offer for securities of such class, must be made through a tender offer. The proposed street sweep rules would apply to the target and bidder as well as third parties and would cover offers, arrangements or understandings to purchase or solicitations of offers to sell. See *Acquisitions of Substantial Amounts of Securities and Related Activities Undertaken During and Following a Tender Offer for Those Securities*, Exch. Act Rel. No. 24976, (1987 Transfer Binder) Fed. Sec. L. Rep. (CCH) ¶84,160 (Oct. 1, 1987). A bidder who commenced a tender offer by public announcement pursuant to Rule 14d-2(b) would be restricted from the time of such announcement and, if he withdrew his offer within the five business day period, would be restricted until the expiration of 30 business days after the withdrawal announcement.

There would be exemptions from the proposed rules for (1) purchases of blocks of 5 percent or more if the ownership had been reported on Schedule 13D or Schedule 13G for at least one year prior to purchase, (2) purchases pursuant to a binding contract between the purchaser and the owner of securities entered into prior to the announcement of the tender offer, (3) transactions such as recapitalizations and mergers approved by stockholders of the issuer and (4) purchases by third parties from the issuer.

The SEC also proposed to repeal Rule 13e-4(f)(6), which prohibits an issuer from purchasing the securities subject to its issuer tender offer for 10 business days following termination of the offer, if the proposed rules are adopted. The SEC sought comments on whether stockholders should be allowed to vote to "opt in" to or "opt out" of the proposed rules. The SEC disclosed that its economics staff had concluded, based upon the empirical evidence of the limited number of street swaps by hostile bidders over the last few years, that nonprofessional stockholders generally have not been harmed. In December 1987, the Chairman of the Council of Economic Advisors, the Director of the Office of Management and Budget, and the Chief of the Justice Department's Antitrust Division filed comments opposing the proposed rule, generally on the grounds that there was no evidence of harm to stockholders and that the proposed rule favored incumbent management. (See Ricks, Three Top Administration Aides Oppose SEC Ban on a Takeover-Related Tactic, *The Wall Street Journal*, Dec. 29, 1987, p. 4.) No action has been taken.

2. Legislative Proposals

A variety of legislative proposals have also been introduced that would limit the ability of an acquiror to accumulate control share positions through open market purchases (see Chapter 26.II).

V. TENDER OFFER STRATEGIES

A. Two-tier, Front-end Loaded Bids

In a two-tier, front-end loaded takeover bid, the bidder makes a first step cash tender offer for over 50 percent of the target's shares and then "squeezes out" the remaining shareholders in a lower priced "back-end" merger. Two-tier bids can be highly coercive because they stampede shareholders into tendering (in the first step) out of the fear of receiving only the lower back-end consideration in the second-step merger. While from 1981 to 1984 the two-tier, front-end loaded tender offer in many situations displaced the any-and-all cash offer as the tactically stronger bid, the availability of junk bond takeover financing and the general receptiveness of courts to defenses against hostile two-tier offers has resulted in a resurgence of the any-and-all cash bid.

Like junk bond financing, two-tier bids enable small companies and takeover entrepreneurs to bootstrap the financing for acquisition of large companies. Mesa Petroleum, for example, borrowed $500 million to bid $40 per share for half the shares of General American Oil Company, stating that upon getting control it would merge with General American, issuing Mesa equity or subordinated debt (with a value of less than $40 per share) for the remaining half of the shares. The banks financing Mesa were assured of two dollars of asset coverage for each dollar loaned to Mesa. Without the two-step technique or junk bond financing, such bootstrap bids could not be financed.

B. Conditional Bids

It has become common for raiders to launch tender offers conditioned upon, among other things:

1. obtaining sufficient financing for the offer,
2. obtaining necessary regulatory approvals,
3. having the target's rights plan redeemed or the rights invalidated, or
4. having the target's board take other actions necessary to neutralize other defensive measures the target may have adopted.

By launching a conditional offer, the raider seeks to start the clock running on the 20-business day period under the Williams Act so that, once financing is obtained or the other conditions are satisfied, the raider can move quickly to purchase shares under the offer. Conditions tied to the target's defensive measures are designed to pressure the target's board to remove such defenses either in connection with a negotiated transaction with the raider or an auction sale of the company. However, the SEC has made it clear that material changes in the offer, including changes in conditions, require that the tender offer remain open for at least five business days after the change. See *Interpretative Release Relating to Tender Offer Rules*, Exch. Act Rel. No. 21,375, 3 Fed. Sec. L. Rep. (CCH) ¶24,284J (April 3, 1987); see also Chapter 21.IV.C.

C. Conditional Financing

In *Warnaco, Inc.* v. *Galef*, C. No. B-86-146 (D. Conn. Apr. 13, 1986), *aff'd by sum. order*, 800 F.2d 1129 (2d Cir. 1986), the court sustained the legality of launching a tender offer with no financing in place and thus permitted an offer to proceed contingent on financing to be obtained in the junk bond market. The court rejected the argument that the Williams Act requires a bidder to have at least some of its financing in place in some form prior to making a tender offer. Under the court's holding, a letter from an investment banker to the effect that it is "highly confident" that the financing can be obtained is all the financing necessary for a legal tender offer by a shell acquisition corporation.

The Ninth Circuit and the Fourth Circuit have reached similar conclusions. *Newmont Mining Corp.* v. *Pickens*, 831 F.2d 1448 (9th Cir. 1987); *IU International Corp.* v. *NX Acquisition Corp.*, 840 F.2d 220 (4th Cir. 1988), *aff'd per curiam*, 840 F.2d 229 (4th Cir. 1988 *en banc*). In each case, the SEC filed an amicus curiae brief, in which it argued that the Williams Act does not require that a bidder have firm financing in place before commencing a tender offer, but that when the bidder's financing is subsequently arranged, the bidder will have to amend its tender offer filings and may have to extend its offer depending upon the significance of the new financing information. See also *Damon Corp.* v. *Nomad Acquisition Corp.*, [1988–89 Transfer Binder] Fed. Sec. L. Rep. (CCH) ¶94,041 (D. Mass. Sept. 16, 1988) (revised Sept. 20, 1988) holding that the Williams Act does not require that financing be in place prior to commencement of a tender offer; *Cities Service Co.* v. *Mesa Petroleum Co.*, 541 F. Supp. 1220 (D. Del. 1982) rejecting attack on "tender now, finance later" bid where the bidder had obtained the financing for the 15 percent tendered for and stated its intent to seek additional financing to purchase a greater percentage.

In the Maxxam/Pacific Lumber takeover fight, a raid was initiated on the basis of advice from an investment banker that it was highly confident it could raise the financing if it were asked by the raider to do so—in other words, the target was put in play in a situation where the raider had not even asked its investment banker to seek financing.

In connection with the bidding contest for Federated Department Stores in early 1988, the SEC announced its view that obtaining commitments for all or substantially all of the financing necessary to purchase shares under a tender offer constitutes a material change in the offer, requiring that the tender offer remain open for at least 5 business days after dissemination of such information. Letter from SEC General Counsel to Judge Sand in *CRTF Corp.* v. *Federated Department Stores, Inc.* See, reprinted in, [1988–89 Transfer Binder] Fed. Sec. L. Rep. (CCH) ¶84,224 (Mar. 28, 1988). The extension of the offer upon obtaining firm financing commitments would be required notwithstanding the bidder's prior disclosure of the anticipated terms of the financing, the receipt of a "highly confident" letter and the expressed willingness of the parties providing the financing to enter into commitments.

There is a question whether a bidder could avoid the requirement to extend its offer by delaying its acceptance of commitments until promptly after the expiration of its offer. The SEC side-stepped the issue, finding that "as a practical matter, a tender offeror will obtain financing commitments before it concludes its offer." However, in view of the SEC's position that the bidder "should not be allowed to shift to shareholders the burden of guessing whether and when financing will be obtained," such an attempt to avoid adequate dissemination could be challenged as a violation of the Williams Act.

D. Changes Requiring Extension of Offer

In 1986, the SEC adopted amendments to Rule 14e-1 under the Exchange Act which provide that a tender offer must remain open for a minimum of 10 business days from the date of an increase or decrease in the percentage of securities being sought or the consideration offered by the offeror. See Exchange Act Release No. 23,421 (July 11, 1986). In *Allied Stores Corp.* v. *Campeau Acquisition Corp.*, 86 Civ. 7837 (S.D.N.Y. Oct. 10, 1986) the court granted a temporary restraining order against the closing of a tender offer because the bidder had announced over the Dow Jones tape, on the morning of the day its offer was scheduled to expire, that if shareholders tendered in sufficient numbers, the bidder would vote its proxies in the target to give the target's shareholders a $3 dividend. The court found a likelihood that this announcement constituted an increase in the tender offer price, and thus required the offer to be extended for 10 business days.

In April 1987, the SEC issued an interpretation of the Williams Act rules to the effect that the waiver of a minimum condition near or at the end of a tender offer is a material change in the terms of the offer that requires extension of the offer. See Exchange Act Release No. 24, 296 (April 3, 1987). While the Release does not specify the number of business days the offer must be extended, it makes clear that the extension must be for at least 5 business days and perhaps as long as 10 business days. The Release specifically states that an offeror may not avoid the extension requirement by reserving the right to extend the offer without further notice. The catalyst for the Release apparently was the tender offer by Dixons for Cyclops in which Dixons attempted to drop an 80 percent condition just prior to the expiration of its offer when only 54 percent of Cyclops's shares had been tendered. The theory of the SEC's position is that the Williams Act provisions and rules are designed to insure that shareholders have the opportunity, after a material change, to effectively consider the new information and factor it into a decision whether to tender, withdraw shares that may already have been tendered, sell shares into the market, or hold shares. And as discussed in Section C above, in connection with the bidding contest for Federated Department Stores, the SEC announced its view that obtaining commitments for all or substantially all of the financing necessary to purchase shares under a tender offer constitutes a material change in the offer, requiring that the tender offer remain open for at least 5 business days after dissemination of such information.

E. The Two-Price Bid

Some acquirors have made bids where the offer price, but not the offer itself, was conditioned upon the target board's agreement to enter into a friendly transaction. For example, Unilever, Inc. stated in its offer for Richardson-Vicks, Inc. that it would pay $56 per share if the Richardson-Vicks' board accepted the offer, but that it would only pay $48 per share if its offer was rejected. Similarly, in its bid for Sperry Corporation, Burroughs Corporation initially offered $70 cash per share in a hostile offer, but later informed the Sperry board that it would be willing to "meaningfully increase" that offer if the board would enter into an acquisition agreement and agree to support the deal. Ultimately, the Sperry board entered into such an agreement, providing for the acquisition of Sperry for a combination of cash, preferred stock, and debt valued at $76.50 per share. Dart Group, in its hostile bid for Safeway Stores, offered to increase its bid from $58 to $64 per share if Safeway agreed to a friendly merger.

By holding out the incentive of an increased price through negotiations, this tactic is designed to increase the pressure on the target's board to negotiate with the bidder and deter the board from undertaking radical defensive measures. It can be particularly successful in large, complicated transactions where the target may have difficulty finding a white knight in the limited time available to it. Its effectiveness is more limited in situations where there is a white knight available, as in the Richardson-Vicks and Safeway Stores transactions where Procter & Gamble and Kohlberg Kravis Roberts & Co. entered the respective fights with topping bids, or in situations where a white knight leveraged buyout can be effected, as in the Supermarkets General transaction.

F. The Decreasing Bid

In several notable transactions, buyers have made proposals or signed acquisition agreements only to substantially reduce their offer prior to consummating the transaction. While each of the situations listed below may be explained by its unique circumstances, other interpretations are possible. One explanation is that the financing for the acquisitions was difficult to obtain because purchasers of junk bonds were examining transactions more carefully out of fear that higher interest rates and an economic downturn might impair the targets' ability to service their LBO debt. Alternatively, some of the buyers may have bid very aggressively in order to ensure that their offer was the winner, then used a "problem" to reduce the price. After the deal was first announced other bidders could lose interest or become involved in other transactions, reducing the risk that a competing bid would challenge the reduced offer and putting the target in the position of accepting the lower, but still above market, offer or terminating the transaction entirely.

1. MGM/UA

Ted Turner agreed to acquire MGM/UA for $29 per share in cash, or $1.45 billion, with the United Artists subsidiary to be sold to Kirk Kerkorian for $470 million. After Drexel Burnham Lambert reportedly had difficulty raising financing, which included junk bonds, for the transaction, Turner offered to pay $25 in cash and one share of a new series of Turner Broadcasting System (TBS) preferred stock, to be worth $4. When the revised proposal encountered trouble, Turner again revised his offer to $20 in cash and one share of TBS preferred with a stated value of $10.33 per share. Security analysts valued the package at $25 per MGM/UA share, for a total of $1.25 billion.

2. R.H. Macy

Macy accepted a leveraged buyout offer from a management group to take the company private at $70 per share in cash, for a total value of $3.6 billion. Financing difficulties led the group to reduce the price to $68 per share in cash.

3. Beatrice

A group led by Kohlberg Kravis Roberts & Co. offered to take Beatrice private in an LBO for $43 in cash and $7 market value of preferred stock per share. After entering into a definitive merger agreement with Beatrice, KKR revised its price to $40 in cash and $10 liquidation preference (but at that time a lower market value) in stock, with dividends on the stock payable in the first six years in cash or additional stock. Subsequent declines in interest rates in general restored the value to $50 per share by the time the deal closed.

4. TWA

Carl Icahn initially proposed a leveraged buyout of TWA at $19.50 in cash and $4.50 in TWA preferred stock per share, with the cash to be raised through the sale of junk bonds. In the second half of 1985, however, TWA lost over $125 million, causing Icahn first to renegotiate for $13 in cash and $11 in preferred stock and then to withdraw his offer entirely.

VI. STOCK REPURCHASES/"GREENMAIL"

A. Overview

Technically speaking, "greenmail"—stock accumulation coupled with threats of takeover attempts or proxy fights in order to force a buyback at a premium—is not a takeover method. The greenmailer's goal is not to acquire the company but to be bought out at a good price. To this end, the greenmailer uses the threat of a takeover—a threat which is made credible, however, by the availability of junk bond financing and of the two-step takeover technique. Greenmail is particularly effective because even if the greenmailer does not desire to take over the target company, the greenmailer, by holding 10 percent or more of the outstanding shares of the target, can (1) sell its shares at a premium to a bidder who does want to take over the target and (2) preempt the ability of the target's board of directors to determine the price, form and timing of an acquisition transaction.

Many companies have become less willing to engage in greenmail because of the phenomenon of "double-dipping" whereby the inevitable drop in a company's market price after paying off one greenmailer brings on another. Because paying greenmail does not solve the problem, many companies have been reluctant to engage in the practice. Some companies have adopted antigreenmail charter amendments.

In December 1985, the Financial Accounting Standards Board issued a technical bulletin that provides that if a company repurchases shares at a price significantly over the then current market price in consideration of the receipt of certain rights or agreements, then only the amount representing the fair value of such shares can be accounted for as the cost of the shares, and the rest of the purchase price has to be accounted for as expenses and charged against earnings in the period paid.

B. New Stock Repurchase Techniques

In light of the aversion to being perceived as either paying or receiving greenmail, several new sophisticated greenmail techniques have evolved. One greenmail technique that has evolved is the company's repurchase of the greenmailer's block at market value, coupled with a purchase of an unwanted division or subsidiary of the raider at a higher price than would be warranted in a stand-alone sale. In this variation, the greenmail premium is factored into the purchase of the raider's unwanted division or subsidiary. Carl Icahn apparently employed this technique when he resold his shares to Chesebrough-Ponds. In that situation, at the same time that Chesebrough-Ponds repurchased a 5 percent block from Icahn at the market price, it also purchased the Polymor division of ACF Industries, a company controlled by Icahn, at a price that was perceived by the marketplace to be well in excess of the value of that division and thus to represent a greenmail payment. See Chesebrough Buys Icahn Stake, *The New York Times*, Apr. 10, 1984, p. D3, col. 6.

In settlement of a suit brought by Coniston Partners in connection with its 1988 proxy fight for control of Gillette, in which Gillette's proxy contest advertisements were found to be "deliberately false and misleading" and a new meeting was ordered to be called, Gillette agreed to spend $720 million to buy back 16 million of its 112 million shares at $45 per share (when the market price was approximately $33). By giving all shareholders an opportunity to sell shares, Gillette protected itself against charges of a second greenmail payment (its first payment being to Ronald Perelman in 1986). The stock buy back, however, was designed to help facilitate Coniston's sale of a large portion of its shares back to Gillette. Instead of purchasing shares in the market or making a cash self-tender, Gillette issued "share repurchase rights" which entitled shareholders to sell or "put" one share to the corporation for every seven shares held. Coniston was able to purchase the put rights in the market and was thus able to "put" a large portion of its shares to Gillette at a premium. If a simple self-tender had been conducted, Coniston would not have been able to successfully tender all of its shares, due to the prorationing requirements under the Williams Act. As a greenmail mechanism, the put program was less than perfect, since Coniston had to pay for the rights in the market, increasing its average cost per share. Nonetheless, it was a means by which Gillette was able to circumvent the antigreenmail provisions in its charter and the tax code, and at the same time pay Coniston a premium for the shares it had acquired before the proxy contest. Gillette was able to obtain a standstill agreement in return.

C. Greenmail Excise Tax

The Revenue Act of 1987 imposes a 50 percent nondeductible excise tax on any entity that realizes any gain (whether or not recognized) or realizes any income with respect to the receipt of greenmail. The excise tax would result in an 84 percent effective tax rate for a corporate shareholder who receives a greenmail payment. For these purposes, greenmail is defined as any consideration paid by a corporation (or any person acting in concert with such corporation) directly or indirectly to acquire its stock if (1) such stock has been held by the shareholder for less than two years, and (2) the shareholder (or any related person or persons acting in concert with the shareholder) made or threatened a "public tender offer" for stock in the corporation during that period. "Public tender offer" is defined as any offer to purchase or otherwise acquire stock or assets, if such offer would be required to be filed or registered with any Federal or state securities agency. The greenmail excise tax does not apply if, prior to the acquisition, the acquiror offers to acquire the stock of other shareholders on the same terms (including, presumably, similar rules as to proration for all shareholders). For the purposes of the preceding sentence, payments made in connection with or in transactions related to an acquisition of stock (e.g., expense payments) are treated as being made in the acquisition.

Acquirors may consider making an election under the Internal Revenue Code to capitalize (rather than deduct) carrying costs relating to target company stock so as to avoid taxable gain on a redemption that would be subject to the excise tax and that arises solely from the reimbursement for the cost of carrying target stock.

As was the case in the Tax Reform Act of 1984 when Congress subjected "golden parachute" payments to regulation through the Internal Revenue Code, this provision is vague and could be interpreted broadly. Therefore, until regulatory guidance is available, a potential acquiror who holds or may acquire more target stock that might be redeemed by the target company must carefully monitor all public and private statements of its intentions regarding the target company to avoid "threatening" a tender offer. In this regard, any standard disclosure of a litany of potential future actions with respect to a target company in Securities and Exchange Commission filings (such as Schedule 13D) should be carefully scrutinized.

The scope of the greenmail tax was extended by the Technical and Miscellaneous Revenue Act of 1988 to reach consideration transferred by any person acting "in concert" with a target corporation to directly or indirectly acquire stock. This provision could conceivably extend the scope of the greenmail tax to purchases by successful competing bidders in situations where such purchase is sanctioned—formally or informally—by the target corporation and the losing bidder receives additional consideration in the form of expense reimbursement or a "break-up" fee or otherwise receives special treatment (such as not being subject to proration).

VII. PROXY FIGHT AND CONSENT SOLICITATIONS

A. Overview

As the share purchase rights plan and takeover statutes have provided target boards of directors with additional negotiating leverage and time to respond to hostile takeover attempts, more and more acquirors have turned to proxy and consent solicitations in attempts to dismantle a target's defenses, to gain precatory support for their proposal, or to gain control of the target's board in order to implement their proposal. In some states control share acquisition statutes have helped facilitate proxy contests by enabling acquirors to obtain a shareholder vote on their takeover proposal within a 50 day period.

In theory, a shareholder referendum represents the most democratic and least coercive means of deciding the fate of a target company once a contest for control has begun. Unlike tender offers, proxy contests provide shareholders with an opportunity to determine collectively who should govern the corporation and what broad policies should be pursued. Control share acquisition statutes and other state and federal rules governing proxy and consent solicitations, however, often favor the raider by facilitating a short deadline for the shareholder vote. The ability of a raider to demand a vote on its proposal within a short time frame denies the target a meaningful opportunity to realize its long-term potential by convincing shareholders that they will be best served if the target remains independent and unrestructured, or even a meaningful opportunity to structure a competing proposal to the hostile bid. Moreover, the ability of an acquiror to accumulate a significant stake in the target before announcing its intention to commence a proxy solicitation enables the acquiror to profit simply by putting the target into play through a proxy contest. And, by accumulating a large stake, the acquiror reduces the number of shareholders he needs to convince of the merits of his proposal in order to be successful in the solicitation.

The referendum process incorporated in the second generation share purchase rights plan, discussed in Chapter 23.II.E, and the proposed uniform third generation state takeover statute, discussed in Chapter 26.III.G, establishes an appropriate and balanced forum for determining the future of a target corporation. The referendum establishes a 90 to 120 day period to enable the target to evaluate its situation, assess the restructuring of white knight alternatives, and determine what course of action would be in the best interests of the shareholders. It provides time for an informed and rational debate on the issues presented, free from the extraordinary pressures created in the tender offer process. The referendum process addresses the collective action problem inherent in a tender offer—even an all cash offer for all shares—by removing the incentive for the shareholder to tender into an inadequate offer for fear of holding a minority position in a corporation controlled by the bidder. It provides shareholders with ample time to evaluate the complex issues posed by competing proposals and creates a forum in which diversity of shareholder opinions can be expressed. While much power is still left in the hands of the institutional investors, the referendum process offers the promise that some institutions can be persuaded to forego an immediate premium for an attractive long-term prospect. Diversity of opinion among institutions would thus provide for a system of checks and balances, assuring victory to the most attractive business strategy and the people who are believed most capable of implementing it.

Recent proxy seasons have illustrated that when corporate control issues are presented to shareholders through a referendum process, a more reasoned debate is possible than in the context of a hostile tender offer in which shareholders purportedly vote with their feet. When faced with a tender offer at an above market price, a majority of the shareholders will always tender, fearful that they will be disadvantaged if other shareholders tender and they do not. However, as illustrated in the Texaco/Icahn proxy contest, when shareholders are permitted to vote on whether it is the proper time to sell the company, sound arguments against putting the company on the auction block can prevail. The defeat of shareholder proposals seeking rescission of share purchase rights plans (see Chapter 23.II.D), also illustrates that shareholders are willing to support management efforts to rationalize the takeover process.

Not all proxy contests, however, provide for rational debate. Too often a raider or dissident shareholder views the process as an expeditious means of acquiring control or forcing an extraordinary transaction on the target. Acquirors can creep up on targets by buying a stake in their stock, and then launch a proxy contest to force a deal on the target. In some cases the acquiror is interested in buying the target, and views the proxy mechanism as a means of gaining a quick referendum on its proposal. In other cases, the acquiror just wishes to put the target into play in order to profit on the stake it has accumulated.

The speed with which a dissident can strike can be startling, especially when a target's annual meeting is approaching. In 1982, Alan E. Clore, a British investor, having accumulated a 15 percent block, commenced a proxy fight 18 days prior to the annual meeting of Gulf Resources and Chemical Corporation and succeeded in electing 12 of the 14 directors by promising to consider "redeployment of some or all" of the company's assets. As discussed below, in 1986, both Leaseway Transportation and Fruehauf found themselves the victims of similar surreptitious proxy strikes. Consent solicitations, where permitted, can be concluded as rapidly as an acquiror can clear proxy materials and solicit consents from a majority of the target's shareholders.

B. Case Studies

The following summaries of some proxy fights and consent solicitations illustrate the various contexts in which such contests can arise in the course of a contest for control.

1. Leaseway

In the Leaseway situation, barely three weeks before the 1986 annual meeting, family members and associates controlling approximately 30 percent of the company's stock announced a proxy fight in opposition to the company's slate of directors. However, when it appeared that they would be defeated, they quickly changed tactics and pledged, if elected, to put the company up for sale. Fearing that institutional holders seeking a quick takeover profit would shift support from the company to the dissidents, and thus allow control of the company to pass without a control premium being paid to all Leaseway shareholders, the board decided that it was in a better position to maximize values for all shareholders and pledged to find a buyer for the company. Thus, in a matter of days, the issue changed from who was better able to run the company to who was in a better position to consummate a sale. Though the company's slate prevailed by a wide margin, the price for that victory was a commitment to put the company up for sale. In late 1986 the board approved a $51 per share leveraged buyout by an investor group led by Citicorp Capital Investors.

2. Fruehauf

In Fruehauf, Asher Edelman surfaced less than six weeks before the company's May 1, 1986 annual meeting with over 5 percent of the stock and a conditional proposal to acquire the company at $41 per share. When his proposal was rejected by the Fruehauf board as inadequate, he commenced a proxy fight for control. Less than two weeks before the meeting he announced that he owned 9.5 percent of the stock and sweetened his offer to $42 per share. The offer apparently was still conditioned on receiving financing and was an apparent ploy to further the prospects of the Edelman slate. This offer was also rejected. At the annual meeting the Edelman slate was overwhelmingly defeated. Notwithstanding his defeat, Edelman announced that he would commence a tender offer for $44 in cash, signaling his continued intent to force a change of control of the company.

3. CTS

Dynamics Corporation of American (DCA), a longtime dissident shareholder of CTS Corporation, commenced a proxy contest for control of CTS based on a platform that challenged several prior acquisitions by CTS. Unlike the Leaseway and Fruehauf situations, DCA/CTS did not involve a transaction for the whole company but rather related to a fight to force CTS to effect a change in its overall business strategy. DCA also commenced a tender offer for approximately 17.9 percent of CTS's outstanding stock which, together with the approximately 9.6 percent already owned by DCA, would have virtually assured DCA's victory in a proxy contest. CTS responded by adopting a rights plan having a "flip-in" feature that would be triggered if DCA acquired more than 15 percent of CTS's stock and would, if so triggered, substantially dilute DCA's interest in CTS. In *Dynamics Corp. of America* v. *CTS Corp.* (*CTS I*), 637 F. Supp. 406 (N.D. Ill.), *aff'd*, 794 F.2d 250 (7th Cir. 1986), *rev'd on other grounds*, 481 U.S. 69 (1987), the court enjoined the CTS rights plan noting that, unlike the rights plan upheld by the Delaware Supreme Court in the *Household* case (see Chapter 23.II.F.1) which was carefully designed, and found by the Delaware courts not to interfere with proxy contests, the CTS rights plan was apparently designed to obstruct a DCA proxy contest. The *CTS I* decision, together with the emphasis placed by the *Household* court on noninterference with voting rights, suggest that a target's defensive response may be more carefully scrutinized by the courts if a proxy fight is involved as well as a tender offer.

4. USG

In October 1987, Desert Partners, which is owned by persons who had previously been involved in some of T. Boone Pickens' takeover attempts and had made takeover bids of their own, announced that it owned approximately 9.84 percent of USG's common stock. After Desert Partners' attempts at pressuring USG into a transaction with it failed, Desert Partners, in February 1988, launched a partial tender offer for USG's common stock and commenced litigation to compel the board to approve a transaction with Desert Partners and to redeem a rights plan that USG had adopted in March 1986. On March 11, 1988, Desert Partners initiated a proxy contest to elect its own slate to the board of USG with the intent of having this new board redeem the rights and approve a transaction with Desert Partners. Desert Partners amended its tender offer several times in an attempt to make it more attractive. Even though

Desert Partners was denied a preliminary injunction to compel the board to redeem the rights, the board decided to propose a recapitalization of USG as an alternative to the Desert Partners offer and to persuade shareholders to reelect the USG board, which they did at USG's annual meeting. In the context of this takeover battle, even though a proxy fight was involved, the court refused to order redemption of the rights, and it did not reach the issue of whether the rights interfered with Desert Partners' ability to wage a proxy fight.

5. Atlas

In December 1987, Blasius, a 9.1 percent shareholder of Atlas, proposed a recapitalization plan for Atlas that would have involved the incurrence by Atlas of a substantial amount of debt in order to pay a special dividend of cash and "7 percent Secured Subordinated Gold-Indexed Debentures" to Atlas shareholders. Blasius also commenced a consent solicitation intended to expand the size of the Atlas board from seven to fifteen members (the maximum number permitted by Atlas' charter) and to fill the eight newly created vacancies with Blasius' nominees. The Atlas board of directors was advised that if the restructuring proposal was implemented, (1) a severe drain on operating cash flow would result, (2) Atlas would "have no chance of repaying its debt" and could end up in bankruptcy, (3) the common stock of Atlas would have little or no value, (4) the debentures proposed to be issued could have a value of only 20 to 30 percent of their face amount and (5) if Atlas (a goldmining company) made a meaningful commercial discovery of gold it would not have the resources to develop the discovery. The Atlas board therefore rejected Blasius' proposals. In addition, the Atlas board added two new members to its seven-member board, thus assuring that, even if Blasius succeeded in increasing the number of directors to fifteen and filling the newly created vacancies, the incumbent directors would constitute a majority of the board. In *Blasius Industries, Inc.* v. *Atlas Corp.*, [1988–89 Transfer Binder] Fed. Sec. L. Rep. (CCH) ¶93,965 (Del. Ch. July 25, 1988), the court found that, in adding these two new members, the Atlas board had been chiefly motivated by a desire to forestall the election of a majority of directors sympathetic to Blasius' proposal. (*Id.* at 90,483). Even though the court also concluded that the Atlas board had not acted selfishly, but rather in a good faith effort to thwart implementation of a restructuring plan that it reasonably believed would cause great injury to the company, the court concluded that the board's action constituted an unintended violation of the duty of loyalty that the board owed to the shareholders. (*Id.* at 90,483, 90,487). In reaching this decision, however, the court rejected the plaintiff's argument for a *per se* rule invalidating every board action taken for the sole or primary purpose of thwarting a shareholder vote. Rather, the court concluded only that the board was not justified in taking such an action in the situation presented by this case, where

> The board was not faced with a coercive action taken by a powerful shareholder against the interests of a distinct shareholder constituency (such as a public minority). . . . Moreover, here it had time (and understood that it had time) to inform the shareholders of its views on the merits of the proposal subject to stockholder vote. ¶93,965, at 90,486.

6. B.A.T./Farmers Group

In January 1988, a unit of B.A.T. Industries offered $60 per share for Farmers Group's stock. The board of directors of Farmers Group rejected this offer, as well as B.A.T.'s overtures at negotiations, and on March 3, 1988, B.A.T. launched a tender offer for Farmers Group at $63 per share. Farmers Group responded with a vigorous campaign of legal challenges to the B.A.T. offer, both in the courts and before state insurance regulators without whose approval B.A.T. could not acquire Farmers Group, an insurance company. Beginning in March, B.A.T. solicited proxies from Farmers Group shareholders on a proposal requesting the incumbent board to negotiate with B.A.T. on the basis of B.A.T.'s $63 per share offer.

The vote at Farmers Group's May 21, 1988 annual meeting of shareholders was very close, with both sides claiming victory. On June 9, when the preliminary count was released, Farmers Group said the report of the judges of election showed about 27.8 million votes in favor of the B.A.T. resolution, 26.8 million votes opposed and 2.4 million votes abstained. On the basis of this count, Farmers Group announced that since the B.A.T. resolution had failed to win a majority of the votes cast, including abstentions, the resolution had not been passed. On June 14, B.A.T. claimed that the "proper" final count should have been at least 28 million votes cast in favor of the resolution, no more than 25.6 million opposed, and about 300,000 abstaining.

Following the inconclusive proxy contest, B.A.T. continued to press its takeover. In August 1988, Farmers Group agreed to a transaction with B.A.T. at $75 per share.

7. Gillette/Coniston Partners

Coniston Partners, which held a 6 percent stake in Gillette, began the 1988 season promising to sell or break up the company, but Coniston lost its bid to elect four out of 12 directors to the Gillette board and put the company up for sale by a 52–48 percent vote. Although Coniston's slate was defeated by a narrow 4 percent margin, a court held that, in the proxy fight, Gillette had published a "deliberately false and misleading" advertisement which misinformed its shareholders. *Gillette Co.* v. *RB Partners*, 693 F. Supp. 1266 (D. Mass. 1988). The judge ordered that the annual meeting be reheld. However, because there were also serious allegations of misleading disclosures by Coniston, the court stated that rather than immediately invalidating the results of the shareholder meeting, it would consider accelerating the next annual meeting and having the contest involve eight rather than four directors, if the allegations against Coniston were proved. Although Coniston's partial court victory was widely viewed as significantly improving the likelihood that Coniston would be successful in a subsequent contest, Coniston backed down. The suit was ultimately settled, and Gillette remained independent. In settling the suit, Gillette agreed to spend $720 million to buy back a portion of its stock.

8. Texaco/Icahn

One of the most publicized proxy contests of 1988 was Carl Icahn's attempt to win five seats on Texaco's 14-member classified board. Icahn had accumulated a large stake in Texaco when the company was in bankruptcy and took an active role in encouraging a settlement with Pennzoil. After the settlement, Icahn began discussing how the company should proceed following its emergence from bankruptcy. After negotiations between Icahn and Texaco management broke down on May 25, Icahn launched a proxy fight, proposing a competing slate of directors. Icahn pledged he would withdraw his slate if the company put itself up for sale at $55 per share; later, he announced his own bid for $60 a share. Texaco's management vigorously sought the support of institutional shareholders to fend off Icahn's offer. The company quickly began implementing its $5 billion reorganization plan, which included many of Icahn's proposals. Texaco's efforts paid off—management's nominees were elected by a margin of 58.6 to 41.4 percent. All but one of the shareholder's rights resolutions that Texaco agreed to propose as part of the reorganization plan also passed.

In 1989, Texaco reached separate agreements with both Icahn and Texaco's large institutional shareholders. Icahn signed a seven-year standstill agreement after increasing his stake in Texaco to over 16 percent of the shares outstanding and threatening to launch a second proxy fight in 1989, in conjunction with Texaco's agreeing to sweeten its special dividend. In addition, Texaco agreed to add John Brademas, the President of New York University, to its Board of Directors in response to pressure from its large institutional shareholders, who wanted a greater voice in corporate policymaking. In June 1989, Icahn disposed of his entire Texaco holdings.

9. BNY/Irving

On February 25, 1988, the Bank of New York (BNY) received conditional approval from the Federal Reserve Board to proceed with its previously announced attempt to acquire Irving Bank Corp. That same day, BNY notified Irving of its intention to nominate a slate of directors for election at Irving's upcoming annual shareholders meeting. BNY's stated purpose was to elect nominees who were committed to the BNY transaction and who would vote to approve the BNY transaction and to redeem the Irving Rights Plan so BNY's offer could go forward as planned.

As a result of Irving's effort to come up with an alternative proposal to the BNY offer, Irving and Banca Commerciale Italiana S.p.A. (BCI), announced in April that they had entered into an agreement providing for a BCI cash tender offer at $65 per share for 51 percent of Irving's common shares. Irving would also pay a special dividend of up to $10 per Irving share to its shareholders. On April 20, BCI revised and increased its offering price to $75 cash for 45 percent of the shares, and on April 21, 1988, the Irving board approved the revised offer.

An intense proxy contest was waged. The contest was, in essence, a referendum between the BNY merger proposal and the ongoing auction process favored by the Irving directors. On May 3, as a result of that process, BCI agreed to further increase its bid, offering to pay $75 in cash for 51 percent of the outstanding Irving stock and 7 percent interest on the tender price from May 31, 1988 to the date of consummation of the offer. Irving's shareholders voted on May 6. As certified by the inspectors of election, the Irving slate won by a margin of 7.72 million to 7.16 million.

BNY disputed the results of the election in the courts. In July, however, after discovery, a hearing before a referee and a trial court review of the referee's findings, the trial court finally upheld the vote as tabulated by the inspectors.

Irving also unsuccessfully waged a proxy contest against BNY's authorization for issuance of the BNY stock necessary to accomplish the transaction.

On August 19, the Federal Reserve Board issued an unexpected order, reversing its previous position and holding that the Italian government agency which controlled BCI would be required to file an application with the Federal Reserve Board. On August 29, BCI withdrew its offer to acquire Irving. The Irving board reiterated its commitment to find the best available financial transaction for Irving shareholders, and in early October, after BNY revised the terms of its proposed offer, Irving approved the BNY offer.

10. Farley/West Point-Pepperell

On October 30, 1988, Farley, Inc. announced a tender offer for West Point shares at $48 per share. At the time of the offer, West Point-Pepperell, a Georgia corporation and a leading textile and apparel manufacturer, had in force a shareholders' rights plan with a flip-in provision that would be triggered if a raider accumulated over 10 percent of the outstanding stock. West Point did *not* have a staggered board.

West Point's directors concluded that Farley's $48 offer was inadequate, and decided to fight the takeover attempt. In the ensuing litigation, the U.S. District Court for the Northern District of Georgia declined to invalidate the Georgia takeover statute, but preliminarily enjoined the operation of the "flip-in" feature of the rights plan.

Farley began a solicitation of consents to call a special meeting of shareholders, which under Georgia law could be called with the concurrence of 25 percent of the voting stock. Farley's solicitation (which was not affirmatively opposed by West Point) was successful, and a special meeting was scheduled. As the date for the special meeting approached and it became apparent that a Farley slate could be elected and agree to a deal at $48, West Point decided to put the Company up for sale. In February 1989, Farley emerged as the highest bidder in the auction, with a $58 offer. The special meeting of shareholders was canceled.

11. Pennwalt

Centaur Partners, a 12.6 percent shareholder of Pennwalt, bid $100 per share for Pennwalt and requested a meeting with Pennwalt's board of directors. After watching the price of Pennwalt's shares rise well above its offer price and being rebuffed by Pennwalt's board, Centaur commenced a solicitation of demands to call a special meeting of shareholders to replace Pennwalt's board of directors. Pennsylvania law requires the demand of holders of at least 20 percent of the outstanding voting stock to call a special meeting; therefore, Centaur required consents of holders of at least an additional 7.4 percent of Pennwalt's voting stock. A Pennsylvania district court denied Pennwalt's motion for a temporary restraining order against Centaur's solicitation, and Centaur was able to solicit more than 34 percent of the outstanding Pennwalt shares to demand a special meeting of shareholders. When Pennwalt did not respond to the demand, Centaur unilaterally set a date for the special meeting, announced its slate of nominees for the board, and raised its bid.

Pennwalt responded by lobbying Congress and the Pennsylvania legislature for hearings on the hostile bid and the adoption of certain legislative protections. In *Pennwalt Corp.* v. *Centaur Partners*, 710 F. Supp. 111 (E.D. Pa. 1989), a federal district court found that Centaur's consent solicitation was void by its own terms, and granted a preliminary injunction against the solicitation since Centaur sought to avoid the application of Pennsylvania's "fair value" statute.

C. Disclosure Issues

The SEC has indicated that when a proxy or consent solicitation accompanies a tender offer, additional disclosure requirements may arise. Tender offer materials may be considered proxy solicitation materials requiring compliance with the proxy rules, including the filing of preliminary materials, if the tender offer materials include information relevant to the proxy solicitation beyond that required by either Schedule 14D-1 or Schedule 14D-9. Where a person commences a tender offer and also initiates a proxy contest to elect a slate of nominees to the target's board of directors, the SEC staff has found that materials disseminated to shareholders by the bidder, the target, or a competing white-knight bidder constitute solicitation materials requiring compliance with the proxy rules. In particular, a target must be sensitive to the possible applicability of the proxy rules to press releases or other public statements made in response to the bidder's takeover proposal. *See ConAgra, Inc.* v. *Tyson Foods, Inc.*, 708 F. Supp. 257 (D. Neb. 1989) (white knight's press release, apparently issued to respond to certain of the raider's statements, found to be a proxy solicitation with respect to white knight's proposed merger with target, even though no shareholder meeting had been scheduled). *See also Data Probe Acquisition Corp.* v. *Datatab, Inc.*, 568 F. Supp. 1538, 1556, n.7 (S.D.N.Y. 1983) (letter purportedly disseminated as a statement of position under Rule 14e-2 may serve as a proxy solicitation with respect to competing merger agreement), *rev'd on other grounds*, 722 F.2d 1 (2d Cir. 1983), *cert. denied*, 465 U.S. 1052 (1984). The staff has also indicated that it will require compliance with Regulation 14A with respect to tender offer materials that include statements that are reasonably calculated to result in the procurement, withholding, or revocation of a proxy or a consent. The staff has noted that to avoid inadvertent violations, materials to be disseminated to shareholders during a proxy contest should be filed in advance with the SEC. *See generally* D. Goelzer & L. Quinn, *Recent Developments in Tender Offer Regulation* 49-50 (Jan. 7, 1989).

Proxy solicitation materials that recommend acceptance or rejection of the tender offer may be required to be filed as amendments to Schedule

14D-1 or Schedule 14D-9. According to the SEC, a target's early response to commencement of a proxy contest may require the filing of a Schedule 14D-9 prior to the expiration of 10 business days from the commencement of the tendar offer. The SEC has also indicated that the interrelationship of the tender offer and the solicitation, including the bidder's anticipated recourse if the solicitation is unsuccessful, must be fully disclosed in both the tender offer and proxy materials. *Id.* at 51.

According to the SEC, management's opposition to a proxy or consent solicitation on the basis that the offering price in the tender offer is inadequate must be substantiated by disclosure of the basis for such belief. This may require the disclosure of any material projections, appraisals, or reports that relate to the value of the company as well as appropriate disclosure of the underlying assumptions for such materials.

In *CNW Corp.* v. *Japonica Partners, L.P.*, [874 F.2d 193] (3d Cir. 1989), the Third Circuit Court of Appeals, reversing the district court, held that Japonica Partners violated Section 14(a) of the Exchange Act by failing to disclose in its solicitation materials the identity of its limited partners and the contents of its co-investor agreements. Japonica and CNW were in the midst of an intense proxy fight. The court found that the proposed SEC rule changes relating to the reporting of equity ownership in control transactions did not relieve Japonica of its disclosure obligations under the current proxy rules.

CHAPTER 22

TAKEOVER AND DEFENSE LAW II: BUSINESS JUDGMENT AND LEGAL PRINCIPLES

Martin Lipton
James H. Fogelson
Andrew R. Brownstein
Craig M. Wasserman
Wachtell, Lipton, Rosen & Katz

I. LEGALITY OF DEFENSIVE TACTICS: THE BUSINESS JUDGMENT RULE

A. Overview

It is no longer controversial that the business judgment rule is applicable to director conduct in the takeover context or that directors have no absolute legal duty to explore an acquisition proposal or to accept a bid that offers shareholders a premium over market price. The Delaware Supreme Court has described the business judgment rule in the context of a takeover battle:

> Under the business judgment rule, directors' decisions are presumed to have been made on an informed basis, in good faith, and in the honest belief that the action taken was in the best interests of the company. This presumption

 This chapter is current through November 18, 1988 (with modifications made through July 1989). David A. Katz and David M. Silk, associates of the firm, and many other members of Wachtell, Lipton, Rosen & Katz assisted in the preparation.

> and its underlying fiduciary duties are equally applicable in a takeover context. When directors oppose a hostile takeover there arises "the omnipresent specter that a board may be acting primarily in its own interests, rather than those of the corporation and its shareholders . . ." (*Unocal* 493 A.2d at 954). This Court has addressed the potential for conflict by placing upon the directors the burden of proving that they have not acted solely or primarily out of a desire to perpetuate themselves in office, that the threatened takeover posed a danger to corporate policy and effectiveness, and that the defensive measures adopted are reasonable in relation to the threat posed. The target directors must satisfy these prerequisites by showing good faith and reasonable investigation before enjoying the presumptions afforded by the business judgment rule.

Ivanhoe Partners v. *Newmont Mining Corp.*, 535 A.2d 1334, 1341 (Del. Supr. 1987) (citations omitted); see also *Panter* v. *Marshall Field*, 646 F.2d 271, 293–95 (7th Cir.), *cert. denied*, 454 U.S. 1092 (1981); *Treadway Cos.* v. *Care Corp.*, 638 F.2d 357, 382–83 (2d Cir. 1980); *Johnson* v. *Trueblood*, 629 F.2d 287, 292–93 (3d Cir. 1980), *cert. denied*, 450 U.S. 999 (1981); *Unocal Corp.* v. *Mesa Petroleum Co.*, 493 A.2d 946, 955 (Del. Supr. 1985).

Thus, by way of example, courts have upheld a variety of defensive tactics under the business judgment rule: a self-tender offer that excluded the shareholder-raider, *Unocal Corp.* v. *Mesa Petroleum Co.*, 493 A.2d 946, 955 (Del. Supr. 1985); a share purchase rights plan that would substantially dilute an unwanted acquiror's holdings in the target, *Moran* v. *Household International, Inc.*, 500 A.2d 1346 (Del. Supr. 1985); a $2.2 billion dividend that facilitated a "street sweep" by a 26 percent stockholder to increase its ownership to 49.7 percent, coupled with a standstill agreement, *Ivanhoe Partners* v. *Newmont Mining Corp.*, 535 A.2d 1334 (Del. Supr. 1987); the use of "springing warrants," *Gearhart Industries, Inc.* v. *Smith International, Inc.*, 741 F.2d 707 (5th Cir. 1984); initiating substantial purchases of its common stock, while issuing a new preferred stock and granting an option on a subsidiary, *Carter Hawley Hale Stores, Inc.* v. *The Limited, Inc.*, C.A. No. 84-2200-AWT (C.D. Cal. Apr. 17, 1984); a counter-tender offer for the raider's stock, *Martin Marietta Corp.* v. *Bendix Corp.*, 549 F. Supp. 623 (D. Md. 1982); a sale of the target's "crown jewel" asset, *Whittaker Corp.* v. *Edgar*, 535 F. Supp. 933 (N.D. Ill.), *aff'd*, Nos. 82–1305, 82–1307 (7th Cir. Mar. 5, 1982); entering into a standstill agreement whereby a prospective offeror agreed not to make a tender offer, *Enterra Corp.* v. *SGS Associates*, 600 F. Supp. 678 (E.D. Pa. 1985); making acquisitions for the purpose of creating an antitrust obstacle to a takeover, *Panter* v. *Marshall Field & Co.*, 646 F.2d 271, 297 (7th Cir.), *cert. denied*, 454 U.S. 1092 (1981); approving a merger agreement with a no-shop provision, thereby forgoing competing offers, *Jewel Cos.* v. *Pay Less Drug Stores Northwest, Inc.*, 741 F.2d 1555, 1564 (9th Cir. 1984); *cf. ConAgra, Inc.* v. *Cargill, Inc.*, 222 Neb. 136, 382 N.W.2d 576 (Neb. Supr. Ct. 1986) ("best efforts" clause in merger agreement does not preclude a board of directors from recommending a subsequent superior offer to the shareholders).

Having firmly established that the business judgment rule is applicable to director conduct in the takeover context, the courts have begun to grapple with a host of new and subtle limitations on directorial actions in the takeover context. While still recognizing a large area for directorial discretion, the courts have nonetheless stepped in and upset a target's defensive plans in an increasing number of cases.

The courts have stressed the importance of the procedures followed by a board of directors when evaluating a takeover bid or a defensive response thereto, and have closely scrutinized the bases upon which directorial decisions in the takeover context are made. The courts have generally supported efforts designed to thwart inadequately priced and coercively structured bids when a proper record is established that the steps taken were reasonable in relation to the threat posed and that actions did not interfere with the shareholders' voting rights. Courts have also supported structural defenses, such as the shareholders rights plan, designed to give the target leverage to thwart inadequate and coercively structured bids, and give the target added time to seek economic alternatives to a hostile bid. Once a decision to sell the company has been made, however, the courts have closely scrutinized directorial action to make certain that it was designed to maximize shareholder values.

In considering a takeover bid, the board of directors may consider "the inadequacy of the bid, the nature and timing of the offer, questions of illegality, the impact on constituencies other than shareholders, the risk of nonconsummation, and the basic stockholder interests at stake, including the past actions of the bidder and its affiliates in other takeover contests." *Ivanhoe Partners* v. *Newmont Mining Corp.*, 535 A.2d 1334, 1342 (Del. Supr. 1987).

Application of the business judgment rule in these varying contexts reflects the view that the decisions required by directors faced with a takeover attempt are *business* decisions; the existence of a takeover offer at a premium over market does not create a disabling conflict of interest and should not render the directors incapable of acting; the questions raised by a takeover offer are *business* decisions that must be addressed, and should be decided, in the boardroom and not in the courtroom. Some example questions follow:

> Is this the time to sell the company?
>
> Will the stockholders who remain be participants in a viable economic enterprise?

What risks do the stockholders face in a company controlled by the raider?

What are the company's prospects if it remains independent?

Does the raider have the ability to run the company?

If the plaintiff is able to show that the directors appeared on both sides of a challenged transaction, or that the directors derived a personal financial benefit which did not devolve upon the corporation and its shareholders generally, the court will not review the transactions under the presumptions of the business judgment rule but will instead require the directors to show the intrinsic fairness of the challenged transactions to the company and its shareholders. See *Ivanhoe Partners* v. *Newmont Mining Corporation*, Nos. 341, 345, slip op. at 14 (Del. Supr. November 18, 1987), which rejected applying the "intrinsic fairness" analysis in lieu of the business judgment rule, notwithstanding Newmont's entering into a standstill agreement.

In *Paramount Communications Inc.* v. *Time Incorporated*, C.A. No. 10866 (Del. Ch. July 14, 1989), *aff'd*, No. 279 (Del. Supr. July 24, 1989), the Delaware Chancery Court reaffirmed its long-standing deference to the business judgment of a board of directors and its adherence to the principle that the board need not maximize short-term stock prices, but may manage the company to achieve the long-term goals the board sets. The Court said:

> Reasonable persons can and do disagree as to whether it is the better course from the shareholders' point of view collectively to cash out their stake in the company now at this (or a higher) premium cash price. However, there is no persuasive evidence that the board of Time has a corrupt or venal motivation in electing to continue with its long-term plan even in the face of the cost that course will no doubt entail for the company's shareholders in the short run. In doing so, it is exercising perfectly conventional power to cause the corporation to buy assets for use in its business. Because of the timing involved, the board has no need here to rely upon a self-created power designed to assure a veto on all changes in control.
>
> The value of a shareholder's investment, over time, rises or falls chiefly because of the skill, judgment and perhaps luck—for it is present in all human affairs—of the management and directors of the enterprise. When they exercise sound or brilliant judgment, shareholders are likely to profit; when they fail to do so, share values likely will fail to appreciate. In either event, the financial vitality of the corporation and the value of the company's shares is in the hands of the directors and managers of the firm. The corporation law does not operate on the theory that directors, in exercising their powers to manage the firm, are obligated to follow the wishes of a majority of shares. In fact, directors, not shareholders, are charged with the duty to manage the firm. *See Smith* v. *Van*

Gorkom, Del. Supr., 488 A.2d 858 (1985); *Sealy Mattress Co. of New Jersey, Inc.* v. *Sealy, Inc.*, 532 A.2d 1324 (1987).

In the decision they have reached here, the Time board may be proven in time to have been brilliantly prescient or dismayingly wrong. In this decision, as in other decisions affecting the financial value of their investment, the shareholders will bear the effects for good or ill. That many, presumably most, shareholders would prefer the board to do otherwise than it has done does not, in the circumstances of a challenge to this type of transaction, in my opinion, afford a basis to interfere with the effectuation of the board's business judgment.

B. Preplanned Strategies

Courts have recognized that the business judgment rule is applicable to preplanned strategies as well as to responses to a particular offer. "[P]replanning for the contingency of a hostile takeover might reduce the risk that, under the pressure of a takeover bid, management will fail to exercise reasonable judgment. Therefore, in reviewing a pre-planned defense mechanism, it seems even more appropriate to apply the business judgment rule." *Moran* v. *Household International, Inc.*, 500 A.2d 1346, 1350 (Del. Supr. 1985); see also *Warner Communications, Inc.* v. *Murdoch*, 581 F. Supp. 1482, 1490–91 (D. Del. 1984) (corporations frequently develop "preplanned" defensive strategies which "may serve a positive function" and are unlawful only if adopted for the "primary purpose of entrenchment"); *Gelco Corp.* v. *Coniston Partners*, 652 F. Supp. 829, 850 (D. Minn. 1986), *aff'd in part and vacated in part*, 811 F.2d 414 (8th Cir. 1987); *Desert Partners, L.P.* v. *USG Corp.*, 686 F. Supp. 1289 (N.D. Ill. 1988); *cf. Packer* v. *Yampol*, C.A. No. 8432 (Del. Ch., Apr. 18, 1986) (enjoining voting of supervoting preferred stock issued in midst of proxy context and relying on fact that company previously considered issuing such stock but did not do so until a particular takeover threat surfaced); *Dynamics Corp. of America* v. *CTS Corp.*, 637 F. Supp. 406 (N.D. Ill.) (court contrasts preplanned defensive measures with those adopted in the heat of a hostile acquisition contest which it implies were adopted for the sole purpose of defeating the unwanted bid), *aff'd* 794 F.2d 250 (7th Cir. 1986), *rev'd on other grounds*, 481 U.S. 69 (1987). See also Chapter 23.III.A for a discussion of the importance of adopting golden parachute and other benefit protection arrangements before any takeover threat exists.

Defensive tactics such as staggered boards and charter provisions regulating the ability to call a special shareholder meeting and eliminating action by written consent without a shareholders meeting are examples of preplanning devices that are within that ambit of the business judgment rule. In structuring these devices however, care must be taken not to run afoul of other statutory proscriptions.

The recent *Polaroid* and *Time* decisions illustrate the importance of long-term business planning as a preplanned strategy. In *Polaroid*, the court found that the company's establishment of an ESOP in the face of a hostile bid was "entirely fair" even though it had a significant anti-takeover effect because the ESOP had been planned prior to the hostile bid, served long-term profit maximizing goals, and, because of its confidential and pass-through voting provisions, did not appear to be primarily a device designed to affect or secure control. See Chapter 23.VI.D.7. In *Time*, the court upheld Time's cash tender offer for Warner in the face of a hostile bid by Paramount, stating that Time's achievement of its long-term strategic plan of combining with Warner was "a most important corporate policy." The court stated that "Delaware law does recognize that directors, when acting deliberately, in an informed way, and in the good faith pursuit of corporate interests, may follow a course designed to achieve long-term value even at the cost of immediate value maximization." The court was influenced heavily by the documented history of Time's long-term business and acquisition strategies, including the fact that Time had determined that Warner was the optimal merger partner long before Paramount had made its hostile bid, as well as Time's previous consideration and rejection of Paramount as a merger partner. See Chapter 22.II.H.8.

C. Directors' Consideration of a Takeover Bid; The Duty of Care

The current case law emphasizes the importance of the procedures followed by the board of directors of a target company when evaluating a takeover bid—an emphasis that is underscored by the enhanced attention given the duty of care following *Smith* v. *Van Gorkom*, 488 A.2d 858 (Del. Supr. 1985).

1. Trans Union

In *Smith* v. *Van Gorkom*, the Delaware Supreme Court found directors of Trans Union Corporation personally liable for approving the sale of the company to Marmon Group. In its initial form, the merger agreement had been approved at a directors' meeting held a week after the initial discussion between the parties. The Court found that the directors had been grossly negligent, citing, among other things, its view that (1) the Company's directors relied entirely upon an oral presentation and had no written documentation with respect to the proposal or the adequacy of the offer price; (2) the directors acted hastily, without prior consideration of the proposal and had no prior knowledge of the subject of the meeting; (3) the premium over market price in the proposal was accepted without sufficient valuation information (such as a "fairness opinion" by an independent investment banker) and the market price of Trans Union's stock was an insufficient basis from which to measure the appropriateness of the premium price; (4) the directors did not sufficiently provide for competing offers to be obtained; (5) the directors did not make sufficient inquiry of members of management who presented the proposals to them; and (6) the actions of the directors following approval of the merger agreement, including certain amendments made to the agreement, did not cure the directors' inappropriate act in approving the acquisition. The Court also held that the shareholders' vote approving the merger did not preclude liability in that the shareholders had not been appropriately informed by the proxy material relating to the transaction.

Smith v. *Van Gorkom* was based upon the duty of care: the requirement that the directors' decision be an "informed one." The Court held that the "proper standard for determining whether a business judgment . . . was an informed one" was "gross negligence" (488 A.2d at 873). The Court stated that the determination of whether the business judgment is an "informed one" turned on "whether the directors have informed themselves 'prior to making a business decision, of all material information reasonably available to them" (*Id.* at 872). The Court nonetheless found the directors liable. It made no difference that there were no allegations of fraud, bad faith, or self-dealing on the part of the directors, who included heads of major companies.

Smith v. *Van Gorkom* has caused great concern and has been criticized as a major departure from the traditional application of the business judgment rule. The decision in *Van Gorkom*, coupled with the crisis in directors' and officers' liability insurance, has prompted legislative initiatives aimed at reducing director liability, including a Delaware statute that permits corporations to eliminate directors' liability for duty of care violations. See Chapter 25. However, the *Van Gorkom* opinion may be read to complement the broad discretion granted to the board of directors in the takeover context. The Court's holding, in effect, is that if a board of directors has the power to formulate strategies that will determine the fundamental structure of the corporation's existence, it must act only after a thorough and reasoned analysis. And, as the opinion indicates, this responsibility cannot be transferred to the shareholders: "[A] director may not abdicate [his] duty by leaving to the shareholders alone the decision to approve or disapprove" proposed corporate action. *Id.* at 873.

The Court also clearly reaffirmed that a board acting within the ambit of the business judgment rule faces no ultimate liability for rejecting a premium takeover bid. Thus, the decision reinforces the principle that a well-informed board of directors may, after careful consideration, legitimately reject and take steps to prevent a takeover proposal that is not in the best interests of all shareholders. *Id.* at 881. See also *Gelco Corp.* v. *Coniston Partners*, 652 F. Supp. 829, 849–50 (D. Minn. 1986.) ("The mere fact that the Coniston bid represented a premium above prevailing market values is not alone sufficient to require a merger"), *aff'd in part and vacated in part*, 811 F.2d 414 (8th Cir. 1987.)

The essential point of *Smith* v. *Van Gorkom* is that an offer at a premium over market does *not* suspend the usual rules governing director conduct that require the exercise by the directors of business judgment in good faith and on an informed basis. While no director has ever been held liable for *opposing* a premium takeover offer, the Trans Union directors were held liable for *accepting* a premium takeover offer.

2. SCM

In *Hanson Trust PLC* v. *ML SCM Acquisition Inc.*, 781 F.2d 264 (2d Cir. 1986), the Second Circuit invalidated a lock-up option granted to induce a higher bid on the ground of lack of due care, albeit the court also referred to the directors' "duty of care" as requiring their ensuring "the shareholders' fundamental right to make the 'decisions affecting [the] corporation's ultimate destiny" *Id.* at 277. The court stated that "while directors are protected to the extent that their actions evidence their business *judgment*, such protection assumes that courts must not reflexively decline to consider the content of their 'judgment' and the extent of the information on which it is based" (*Id.* at 275, emphasis in original). The court found a lack of due care, although noting that the directors' actions "do not rise to that level of gross negligence found in *Smith* v. *Van Gorkom*," *id.*, based on the directors' "paucity of information and their swiftness of decision-making" (*Id.*).

3. CTS I and II

In *Dynamics Corp. of America* v. *CTS Corp.*, 794 F.2d 250 (7th Cir. 1986), *rev'd on other grounds*, 481 U.S. 69 (1987) (*CTS I*), the court, in enjoining a rights plan adopted by CTS Corporation in response to a partial tender offer by Dynamics Corporation of America (DCA), was critical of the fact that CTS failed to evaluate the DCA tender offer in a "dispassionate and thorough fashion." The court also questioned how much weight could properly be placed on the fairness opinion of CTS's financial advisor Smith Barney, when Smith Barney had been promised a bonus of $75,000 if CTS was successful in defeating DCA's efforts to gain control of CTS. In *Dynamics Corp. of America* v. *CTS Corp.*, 805 F.2d 705 (7th Cir. 1986) (*CTS II*), the court expressed concerns regarding the procedure by which a back-end plan designed to provide the CTS board with time to shop the company was adopted. The court was concerned that the $50 exercise price for the rights was unreasonably high and that the compensation of Smith Barney, the investment banker upon whose advice the exercise price was set, might have been structured so as to bias the advisor's analysis in reaching the $50 price. The court was also troubled by the fact that Smith Barney never independently validated management's earnings projections upon which its analysis was based. The court's willingness to look beneath the surface of Smith Barney's analysis, questioning the price earnings multiple and earnings forecasts upon which Smith Barney's analysis was based, is a clear indication of the degree of heightened scrutiny to which investment banker opinions may be subject. See also *Buckhorn, Inc.* v. *Ropak Corp.*, 656 F. Supp. 209 (S.D. Ohio), *aff'd by sum. ord.*, 815 F.2d 76 (6th Cir. 1987); *City Capital Associates Ltd. Partnership* v. *Interco Inc.*, 551 A.2d 787 (Del. Ch. 1988) (since the investment banker's fee arrangement called for a substantial contingent payment in the event the target's restructuring was successful, there was "a rather straightforward and conventional conflict of interest when it opine[d] that the inherently disputable value of its restructuring is greater than the all cash alternative offered by the [raider]").

4. Procedural Checklist

The SEC's tender offer rules highlight the need for timely consideration of a takeover bid through their requirement that a target's board consider and respond to a tender offer and that the target disclose the reasons for the board's decision within 10 business days of the offer (Rules 14d-9 and 14e-2).

As noted in Lipton, *Takeover Bids in the Target's Boardroom*, 35 Bus. Law. 101, 121–24 (1979):

a) Management (usually with the help of investment bankers and outside legal counsel) should make a full presentation of all of the factors relevant to the consideration by the directors of the takeover bid, including:

1. Historical financial results and present financial condition.
2. Projections for the next two to five years and the ability to fund related capital expenditures.
3. Business plans, status of research and development and new product prospects.
4. Market or replacement value of the assets.
5. Management depth and succession.
6. Can a better price be obtained now.
7. Timing of a sale; can a better price be obtained later.
8. Stock market information such as historical and comparative price earnings ratios; historical market prices and relationship to the overall market, and comparative premiums for sale of control.
9. Impact on employees, customers, suppliers and others who have a relationship with the target.

10. Any antitrust and other legal and regulatory issues raised by the offer.
11. An analysis of the raider and its management and, in the case of a partial offer or an exchange offer, pro forma financial statements and a comparative qualitative analysis of the business and securities of both companies.

b) An independent investment banker or other expert should opine as to the adequacy of the price offered and management's presentation.

c) Outside legal counsel should opine as to the antitrust and other legal and regulatory issues in the takeover and as to whether the directors have received adequate information on which to base a reasonable decision.

d) If a majority of the directors are officers or otherwise might be deemed to be personally interested, other than as shareholders, a committee of independent directors, although not in theory necessary, may be desirable from a litigation strategy standpoint. The exigencies and pressures of a takeover battle are such that it is desirable to avoid proliferation of committees, counsel and investment bankers. The target will be best served if it is advised by one investment banker and one outside law firm.

D. "Good Faith and Reasonable Investigation"

As indicated above in the *Unocal* case the Delaware Supreme Court, applying the business judgment rule to an exclusionary self-tender, placed the initial burden on the directors to show that application of the business judgment rule is appropriate in a change of control context. The court stated that:

> When a board addresses a pending takeover bid it has an obligation to determine whether the offer is in the best interests of the corporation and its shareholders. In that respect a board's duty is no different from any other responsibility it shoulders, and its decisions should be no less entitled to the respect they otherwise would be accorded in the realm of business judgment. There are, however, certain caveats to a proper exercise of this function. *Because of the omnipresent specter that a board may be acting primarily in its own interests, rather than those of the corporation and its shareholders, there is an enhanced duty which calls for judicial examination at the threshold before the protections of the business judgment rule may be conferred.*
>
> . . . In the face of this inherent conflict directors must show that they had reasonable grounds for believing that a danger to corporate policy and effectiveness existed because of another person's stock ownership. *Cheff* v. *Mathes*, Del. Supr., 199 A.2d 548, 554–55 (1964). However, they satisfy that burden "by showing good faith and reasonable investigation . . . ." Furthermore, such

> proof is materially enhanced, as here, by the approval of a board comprised of a majority of outside independent directors who have acted in accordance with the foregoing standards *Unocal Corp.* v. *Mesa Petroleum Co.*, 493 A.2d at 954–55 (citations omitted) (emphasis added).

As indicated in *Unocal*, a showing of good faith is materially enhanced if the Board's actions are approved by a majority of independent directors. See also *Moran* v. *Household International, Inc.*, 500 A.2d 1346, 1350 (Del. Supr. 1985); *Revlon, Inc.* v. *MacAndrews & Forbes Holdings, Inc.*, 506 A.2d 173 (Del. Supr. 1986); *Polk* v. *Good*, 507 A.2d 531, 537 (Del. Supr. 1986) ("the presence of the 10 outside directors on the Texaco board, coupled with the advice rendered by the investment banker and legal counsel, constitute a *prima facie* showing of good faith and reasonable investigation" in the decision to repurchase stock at a premium from a disruptive shareholder); *Ivanhoe Partners* v. *Newmont Mining*, 535 A.2d 1334, 1343 (Del. Supr. 1987).

If the plaintiff is able to show that the directors appeared on both sides of a challenged transaction, or that the directors derived a personal financial benefit which did not devolve upon the corporation and its shareholders generally, the court will not review the transactions under the presumptions of the business judgment rule but will instead require the directors to show that the intrinsic fairness of the challenged transactions to the company and its shareholders. See *Ivanhoe Partners* v. *Newmont Mining Corp.*, 535 A.2d 1334, 1341 (Del. Supr. 1987); see also *AC Acquisitions Corp.* v. *Anderson, Clayton & Co.*, 519 A.2d 103, 111 (Del. Ch. 1986) ("where a self-interested corporate fiduciary has set the terms of a transaction and caused its effectuation, it will be required to establish the entire fairness of the transaction to a reviewing court's satisfaction"); *Blasius Industries, Inc.* v. *Atlas Corp.*, [1988–89 Transfer Binder] Fed. Sec. L. Rep. (CCH) ¶ 93,965, at 90,483, 90,487 (Del. Ch. July 25, 1988) (actions by board after a consent solicitation had begun, designed to thwart the dissident shareholder's goal of obtaining majority representation on the board, violated the board's duty of loyalty).

In evaluating a proposal for a management buyout, it is thus essential that the board establish adequate procedures to assure that any transactions with the buyout group are not tainted by the conflicts presented by management's participation in the buyout. As the court cautioned in *SCM*:

> We do not say that the independent directors of SCM were required to appoint an independent negotiating committee of outside directors to negotiate with [the buyout group], as the court suggested in *Weinberger* v. *UOP, Inc.*, 457 A.2d 701, 709 n.7 (Del. Supr. 1983), though that certainly would have constituted one appropriate procedure under the circumstances.

781 F.2d at 277; see also *Freedman* v. *Restaurant Associates Industries, Inc.*, [1987 Transfer Binder] Fed. Sec. L. Rep. (CCH) ¶ 93,502, at 97,219–20 (Del. Ch. Oct. 16, 1987) (stressing the importance of the role of special committees under Delaware law when courts are asked to review transactions that involve elements of self dealing); *In re Fort Howard Corp. Shareholders Litigation*, Civ. No. 9991 (Del. Ch. Aug. 8, 1988) slip op. at 30–31 (criticizing procedures followed in selecting a special committee and its advisors to evaluate a management buyout proposal).

Management's conduct during an auction will be closely scrutinized when a management buyout group is one of the competing bidders. See *Mills Acquisition Co.* v. *Macmillan, Inc.*, [Current] Fed. Sec. L. Rep. (CCH) ¶94,401 (Del. Supr. May 3, 1989) (conduct of auction violated principles of fair dealing).

The entire fairness standard will not be applied if the board of directors can demonstrate that it acted independent of any of the bidders or management, in good faith, and with due care. For example, in *In re RJR Nabisco, Inc. Shareholders Litigation*, [1988–89 Transfer Binder] Fed. Sec. L. Rep. (CCH) ¶94,194 (Del. Ch., Jan. 31, 1989), the Delaware Chancery Court refused to grant a preliminary injunction against the closing of a pending tender offer for up to 74 percent of outstanding RJR common stock, an order declaring invalid a $1 per share "topping fee" in the merger agreement between RJR and KKR, and an order for the Special Committee to revive the auction by informing the management group which had submitted an opposing bid that the Committee would consider any bid that the group wished to make. The plaintiffs had asserted that the Special Committee did not act in good faith and did not exercise due care, and that even if it had, its actions should be enjoined because it failed to conduct a fair and effective auction as required by *Revlon* v. *McAndrews & Forbes Holdings, Inc.*, 506 A.2d 173 (Del. Supr. 1986). Analyzing the case under the structure of the business judgment rule, the court rejected the plaintiffs' factual assertions of bad faith and uninformed decisions, and determined that when a disinterested board acts in good faith and upon the exercise of due care, the decisions of the board are not subject to any heightened review. *But compare In re Holly Farms Corp. Shareholders Litigation*, [1988–89 Transfer Binder] Fed. Sec. L. Rep. ¶94,181 (Del. Ch. Dec. 30, 1988).

E. "Reasonable in Relation to the Threat Posed"

Current expressions by the Delaware courts of the business judgment rule in the takeover context require that defensive measures be "reasonable in relation to the threat posed."

1. Unocal

This doctrinal element was first introduced by the Delaware Supreme Court in its *Unocal* opinion upholding a defensive self-tender offer that excluded the raider, where the Court stated:

> A further aspect is the element of balance. If a defensive measure is to come within the ambit of the business judgment rule, it must be reasonable in relation to the threat posed. This entails an analysis by the directors of the nature of the takeover bid and its effect on the corporate enterprise. Examples of such concerns may include: inadequacy of the price offered, nature and timing of the offer, questions of illegality, the impact on "constituencies" other than shareholders (i.e., creditors, customers, employees, and perhaps even the community generally), the risk of nonconsummation, and the quality of securities being offered in the exchange. See Lipton and Brownstein, *Takeover Responses and Directors' Responsibilities: An Update*, p. 7, ABA National Institute on the Dynamics of Corporate Control (December 8, 1983). While not a controlling factor, it also seems to us that a board may reasonably consider the basic stockholder interests at stake, including those of short term speculators, whose actions may have fueled the coercive aspect of the offer at the expense of the long term investor. Here, the threat posed was viewed by the Unocal board as a grossly inadequate two-tier coercive tender offer coupled with the threat of greenmail.
>
> Specifically, the Unocal directors had concluded that the value of Unocal was substantially above the $54 per share offered in cash at the front end. Furthermore, they determined that the subordinated securities to be exchanged in Mesa's announced squeeze out of the remaining shareholders in the "backend" merger were "junk bonds" worth far less than $54. It is now well recognized that such offers are a classic coercive measure designed to stampede shareholders into tendering at the first tier, even if the price is inadequate, out of fear of what they will receive at the back end of the transaction. Wholly beyond the coercive aspect of an inadequate two-tier tender offer, the threat was posed by a corporate raider with a national reputation as a "greenmailer." 493 A.2d at 955–56 (footnotes omitted).

The heightened standard under *Unocal* is only invoked in evaluating defenses against a potential takeover. In *Doskocil Cos.* v. *Wilson Foods Corp.*, Civ. No. 10,095 (Del. Ch. Aug. 18, 1988) the Delaware Chancery Court recently addressed the question of when a board's action should be viewed as a response to a potential takeover. The court held that after a raider had filed a Schedule 13D indicating that the raider might seek to acquire the company, actions by a target's board to authorize the issuance of a preferred stock containing a "poison put," was not a response to the potential takeover bid. The target had been considering for some time the possibility of issuing the preferred for financing purposes and had been previously advised by its investment banker that the poison put would be necessary to make the preferred marketable. Applying the traditional business judgment rule, the court found that the directors were not grossly negligent and that the plaintiff had failed to establish that the directors did not act with due care or had acted in bad faith in authorizing the "poison put" preferred. After the raider's tender offer was announced, the target's board decided not to proceed with the preferred offering, having been advised by the target's investment banker that institutions would not purchase the preferred while the tender was pending. The target did state it was considering issuing a preferred in defense of the raid. The court stated that any decision to issue a preferred would be subject to the enhanced *Unocal* business judgment rule, but refused to enjoin in advance the placement of a preferred by the target. The court stated that the raider would have the ability to litigate the appropriateness of any such transaction when and if it were announced. See also *Nomad Acquisition Corp.* v. *Damon Corp.*, [Current] Fed. Sec. L. Rep. (CCH) ¶ 94,040, at 90,873 (Del. Ch. Sept. 16, 1988) (revised Sept. 20, 1988) (court refused to enjoin "white squire" defense or require 5 days' notice prior to the private placement of securities, since this "would impinge on the Board's managerial functions").

In *In re J.P. Stevens & Co. Shareholders Litigation*, 542 A.2d 770, 780 (Del. Ch. 1988), the Delaware Chancery Court held that a decision approved by a special committee of the board to sign a merger agreement containing a bust-up fee in order to induce a bidder to submit a higher bid in an auction was not subject to the *Unocal* standard. The court reasoned that the case did not involve "corporate measures designed to defeat a threatened change in control."

In *Gilbert* v. *El Paso*, Civ. No. 7075 (Del. Ch. Nov. 21, 1988), the court rejected the application of the heightened *Unocal* standard to the director's actions in entering into a negotiated transaction with an initially hostile bidder, reasoning that such actions were not antitakeover defenses.

In *Torchmark Corp.* v. *Bixby*, 708 F. Supp. 1070 (W.D. Mo. 1988), the court held that a self-tender offer commenced two months after the target's rejection of the initial acquisition proposal but prior to the tender offer was part of a pre-existing open market purchase program "not taken in apprehension of a challenged takeover" and apparently not subject to the enhanced business judgment rule analysis mandated by *Unocal* in respect of takeover defenses.

In *TW Services, Inc.* v. *SWT Acquisition Corp.*, [Current] Fed. Sec. L. Rep. (CCH) ¶94,334 (Del. Ch. Mar. 2, 1989), the court applied the business judgment standard (and not *Unocal*) to determine whether the TW Services board could refuse to redeem its stock purchase rights in the face of a hostile bid. The court's ruling was predicated on its finding that SWT's tender offer was subject to the condition, among others, that the TW Services board enter into a satisfactory merger agreement with SWT. TW Services took the position that, until SWT dropped the merger agreement condition, the rights had no effect upon SWT's ability to purchase shares pursuant to the offer, and the board had no reason, or duty, to consider SWT's request that the board redeem the rights. Noting that the board's authority to determine whether to enter into a merger agreement derived from the Delaware General Corporation Law, rather than from a share purchase rights plan that the board had itself enacted, the court held that the board's rejection of the tender offer, based upon its view that the offer was not a "real" offer but was merely an invitation to negotiate, should be evaluated under the business judgment standard. The court found that the *Unocal* standard did not apply because of the statutory merger requirement. *Id.* at 92,178–92,182. The court framed the issue as a question of whether the board had breached a duty owed to the corporation and the shareholders by concluding, at this stage of the proceedings and under the present circumstances, that it was not required to deviate from its management of the corporation in a "long term" mode and maximize the short-term values for shareholders. The court distinguished this situation from the *Pillsbury* and *Interco* cases on the grounds that in each of those cases the board had elected to pursue a defensive restructuring that "in form and effect was (so far as the corporation itself was concerned) a close approximation of and an alternative to a pending all cash tender offer for all shares." *Id.* at 92,181. Chancellor Allen noted that in this situation, the board decided in good faith to "continue managing the enterprise in a long term mode and not to actively consider an extraordinary transaction of any type." *Id.* To the extent that the offer constituted a proposal to negotiate a merger, the board was entitled to consider the long-term functioning of the company and could reject the offer in the good faith pursuit of legitimate corporate interests. The court noted, however, that concern with long-term implications becomes illegitimate once the board is required to focus upon the maximization of current share value. *Id.* at 92,182.

2. Application of the Standard—Takeover Defenses Upheld

The "reasonable in relation to the threat posed" element subsequently has been invoked by the courts to uphold a variety of defenses including the following:

(a) In the Delaware Supreme Court's decision in *Revlon*, where the court cited *Unocal* in stating that "the directors must analyze the nature of the takeover and its effect on the corporation in order to insure balance—that the responsive action taken is reasonable in relation to the threat posed," and, more specifically, in ruling that consideration of corporate constituencies other than shareholders is permissible "provided there are rationally related benefits accruing to the stockholders" (506 A.2d at 180, 182).

(b) In the Delaware Supreme Court's decision in *Polk* v. *Good*, 507 A.2d 531 (Del. Supr. 1986), affirming the approval of the settlement of the stockholder litigation arising out of the Texaco/Bass Brothers greenmail matter, where the Court refused to alter long-standing Delaware principles requiring deference to director judgments as to such repurchases; the Court cited *Unocal* in stating that "[u]nless the primary or sole purpose was to perpetuate the directors in office, such an acquisition will be sustained if, after reasonable investigation, a board has a justifiable belief that there was a reasonable threat to the corporate enterprise" (*Id.* at 536–37). The Court concluded that "the payment of a premium of approximately 3 percent over market seems reasonable in relation to the immediate disruptive effect and the potential long-term threat which the Bass group posed" (*Id.* at 537).

(c) In the Delaware Supreme Court's opinion in *Household* upholding a flip-over rights plan/"poison pill" where the court held that the threat of a boot-strap, bust-up and two-tier takeover rendered the Rights Plan reasonable.

(d) In the Delaware Supreme Court's opinion in *Newmont Mining*, where the court found that the declaration of a $2.2 billion dividend by Newmont, which facilitated a street sweep by a 26 percent shareholder was reasonable in response to a coercive two-tier partial tender offer by Ivanhoe Partners at an inadequate price. The court also applied the *Unocal* standard to Newmont's response to the threat posed by Gold Fields, finding that it was reasonable for Newmont to have declared the dividend while obtaining a standstill agreement from the 26 percent shareholder to protect Newmont's public stockholders.

(e) In the Delaware Chancery Court's opinion in *Grand Metropolitan PLC* v. *Pillsbury Co.*, Civ. No. 10323 (Del. Ch. Nov. 7, 1988) (letter opinion), where the court held that the Pillsbury board had met its *Unocal* duties in rejecting a hostile bid by Grand Met as inadequate and in standing behind its rights plan as it explores available alternatives.

(f) In the District Court for the Northern District of Illinois' decision in *Desert Partners, L.P.* v. *USG Corp.*, 686 F. Supp. 1289 (N.D. Ill. 1988), where the court found that USG's refusal to redeem the company's rights and to negotiate with a raider that had made a coercive and inadequate offer for the company was reasonable in relation to the threat to USG's corporate effectiveness presented by the hostile bid.

(g) In the Delaware Chancery Court's opinion, in *MAI Basic Four, Inc.* v. *Prime Computer, Inc.*, [1988–89 Transfer Binder] Fed. Sec. L. Rep. (CCH) ¶94,179 (Del. Ch. Dec. 20, 1988), where the court held that the

Prime board had met its *Unocal* duties in rejecting a hostile bid by MAI as inadequate and adopting a number of takeover defenses—including a rights plan, an employee severance plan, an employee pension plan, an employee retention plan, a stock appreciation rights plan, and granting stock options—with the court noting that each of the defenses could be rescinded without major cost to the target, that only a short time had passed since the offer had commenced, and that without the defenses, the bidder would have no incentive to increase its bid.

(h) The Delaware Chancery Court, in *Shamrock Holdings, Inc.* v. *Polaroid Corp.*, Civ. No. 10,075 (Del. Ch. Mar. 17, 1989) upheld the sale of a block of stock to a white squire and an accompanying self-tender offer under the *Unocal* standard even in the face of a proxy fight and previously issued 14 percent ESOP. The court found that an all-cash offer for all shares could be coercive and found a reasonable threat to the corporation given Shamrock's inability to adequately value the outstanding Kodak judgment due to be paid to the target. The court found this was a significant enough threat to satisfy the "reasonable in relation to" test.

(i) In *Amanda Acquisition Corp.* v. *Universal Foods Corp.*, 708 F. Supp. 984 (E.D. Wis. 1989), *aff'd on other grounds*, 1989 U.S. App. LEXIS (7th Cir. May 24, 1989), a federal district court in Wisconsin, applying local law that looked to Delaware, upheld under the *Unocal* standard a decision by the board of directors not to redeem the rights in the face of a hostile all-cash tender offer for all shares. The court allowed the target to "just say no" to the offer when it faced an inadequate offer that could be seen as a serious threat to the corporation. The court was bolstered by the fact that only 27 percent of the target's shareholders had tendered in an offer that was three and one-half months old.

(j) In the Delaware Chancery Court's opinion in *Paramount Communications Inc.* v. *Time Incorporated*, C.A. No. 10866 (Del. Ch. July 14, 1989), *aff'd*, No. 279 (Del. Supr. July 24, 1989), the court held that Time's achievement of its long-term strategic plan of consolidating with Warner provided sufficient justification for Time to alter the form of its proposed combination with Warner from a stock merger to a cash tender offer in response to the threat posed to the Warner combination by Paramount's hostile tender offer for Time.

3. Application of the Standard—Takeover Defenses Overturned

The courts have also found defensive strategies adopted by target boards of directors "unreasonable" in relation to the threat posed by the hostile bid. These cases often involve situations where the defensive action interferes with shareholder voting rights or unreasonably restricts shareholder choice, as in the following examples:

(a) In *Phillips* v. *Insituform of North America, Inc.*, C.A. No. 9173 (Del. Ch. Aug. 27, 1987), the Delaware Chancery Court applied *Unocal* to enjoin a board's issuance of stock designed to dilute the voting power of a controlling shareholder. Synthesizing the traditional Delaware abhorrence of board action impeding stockholder voting rights with "the flexible *Unocal*-style analysis," the court cited *Canada Southern Oils* v. *Manabi Exploration Co.*, 96 A.2d 810 (Del. Ch. 1953), and *Condec Corp.* v. *Lunkenheimer Co.*, 230 A.2d 769 (Del. Ch. 1967), concluding:

> In applying the teachings of these cases, I conclude that no justification has been shown that would arguably make the extraordinary step of issuance of stock for the admitted purpose of impeding the exercise of stockholder rights reasonable in light of the corporate benefit, if any, sought to be obtained. Thus, whether our law creates an unyielding prohibition to the issuance of stock for the primary purpose of depriving a controlling shareholder of control or whether, as *Unocal* suggests to my mind, such an extraordinary step might be justified in some circumstances, the issuance of the Leopold shares was, in my opinion, an unjustified and invalid corporate act (*Id.*, slip op. at 24).

But cf. *Freedman* v. *Restaurant Associates Industries, Inc.*, [1987 Transfer Binder] Fed. Sec. L. Rep. (CCH) ¶ 93,502 at 97,221 (Del. Ch. Oct. 16, 1987) (board might be justified in issuing an option that would dilute the voting power of a majority shareholder in an attempt to achieve the highest price for the shareholders in a sale).

(b) In *AC Acquisition Corp.* v. *Anderson, Clayton & Co.*, 519 A.2d 103 (Del. Ch. 1986), the court held that the Board had acted properly in seeking to provide the shareholders an economic alternative to a hostile tender offer by Bear Stearns & Co. and Gruss & Co. ("B/S/G"), but that the specific means it employed to achieve that objective were not appropriate. Therefore, the court enjoined consummation of the Anderson Clayton self-tender because, according to the court, the defense was not structured in a manner to assure shareholders a realistic choice between the B/S/G deal and the Anderson Clayton deal and "no rational shareholder could afford not to tender into [Anderson Clayton's] self-tender offer at least if that transaction were viewed in isolation." *Id.* at 113. The court reached this conclusion on the bases that Anderson Clayton's financial adviser had not opined that either alternative was economically superior to the other, the B/S/G offer had a 51 percent minimum condition and if the self-tender were successful, the value of the common stock of Anderson Clayton would fall to a level substantially below the current market price. While the court acknowledged the legitimacy of a board-created competitive alternative that generates an immediate cash distribution while permitting the stockholders to remain as equity participants in the ongoing company, it ruled that in the face of an all cash offer at a concededly fair price, an alternative that is not economically superior must allow the shareholders the ability to choose between the alternative and the raider's offer.

(c) In *Dynamics Corp. of America* v. *CTS Corp.* ("CTS I"), 637 F. Supp. 406 (N.D. Ill.), *aff'd*, 794 F.2d 250 (7th Cir. 1986), *rev'd on other grounds*, 107 S. Ct. 1637 (1987), the court enjoined the CTS rights plan, noting that, unlike the rights plan upheld by the Delaware Supreme Court in the *Household* case, which was carefully designed and found by the Delaware courts not to interfere with proxy contests, the CTS rights plan was apparently designed to obstruct a proxy contest by Dynamics. The *CTS I* decision, together with the emphasis placed by the *Household* court on noninterference with voting rights, suggest that a target's defensive response may be more carefully scrutinzed by the courts if a proxy fight is involved as well as a tender offer.

(d) In *Robert M. Bass Group, Inc.* v. *Evans*, 552 A.2d 1227 (Del. Ch. 1988), the board of directors of the target company, Macmillan, Inc., adopted a complex restructuring plan that involved splitting the company into two parts as a defense against a hostile bid by the Bass Group. The restructuring took the form of a dividend and, as such, no shareholder vote was required. Macmillan argued that the restructuring was reasonable because (1) it allowed shareholders to realize immediate value while retaining their equity interest, (2) it created a structure designed to result in higher market value for each separate component, and (3) it created incentives for management to efficiently manage the companies. The court held, however, that the restructuring plan—under which management's ownership of the more valuable piece of the company would be "rolled up" to 40 percent—offered less value to shareholders than the Bass Group's offer and that "these rationales, even if accepted, do not justify forcing shareholders to accept an economically inferior transaction while, at the same time, precluding them from considering an economically superior one" (*Id.* at 90,200). The court found that the restructuring effectively "takeover proofed" the company.

(e) In the Delaware Chancery Court's opinion in *City Capital Associates Ltd. Partnership* v. *Interco Inc.*, 551 A.2d 787 (Del. Ch. 1988), discussed in Chapter 22.IV.F.5, the court held that, given the closeness in values between the hostile tender offer and the target's recapitalization plan, the threat from a cash tender offer for 100 percent of the target's shares, which the board had determined was inadequate, was too mild to justify keeping the target's rights plan in place indefinitely and precluding shareholders from choosing between the hostile offer and the target's proposed recapitalization.

(f) In the Delaware Chancery Court's opinion in *Grand Metropolitan PLC* v. *Pillsbury Co.*, 558 A.2d 1049 (Del. Ch. 1988), the court held that the target's refusal to redeem the rights in the face of an offer that the court determined to be adequate was not reasonable in relation to the threat posed. The court found that the offer presented no danger to corporate policy or effectiveness and that the "real threat" was that of the bidder withdrawing its bid and the stock price falling to its pre-offer levels. It is important to note that in both *Pillsbury* and *Interco* there was no finding of bad faith on the part of the directors. In addition, both cases were decided in situations where the directors were to implement some type of restructuring as an alternative to a pending tender offer.

4. Analysis of Trends

The *Unocal* test has been defined as "a flexible intermediate form of judicial review," situated between two poles. *AC Acquisitions Corp.* v. *Anderson, Clayton & Co.*, 519 A.2d 103 (Del. Ch. 1986). At one side, courts will decline to evaluate the wisdom or merits of business decisions made by directors with no financial interest in the transaction adverse to the corporation. In such circumstances, the traditional "any rational business purpose" test effectively removes the courts from the fray. At the opposite side is the exacting "entire fairness" review that comes into play when the challenged decision has been made by a board of directors that predominantly has a financial interest in the transaction. The creation of the *Unocal* intermediate test gave the courts the freedom to apply a standard whose mere invocation did not decide the outcome of the case, and reestablished a role for the courts to play in policing defensive conduct.

The full significance of the "reasonable in relation to the threat posed" element is unclear. At one extreme, this new doctrinal element can be utilized by the courts as a rubric under which to exercise their own "business judgment" and, in effect, second guess directors' decisions, or perhaps adopt a kind of "least restrictive alternative" analysis under which the courts can invalidate any defensive conduct that goes beyond what is necessary to counter the particular threat that is being confronted. Under *Unocal*, the emphasis is on the *objective* reasonableness of the board's response, not the good faith of the directors. Every case is therefore scrutinized on its facts, and few general principles may be derived. This is particularly clear where the defensive tactic implicates voting rights as in *Insituform* and *Blasius, supra*. It also explains the Delaware Supreme Court's careful analysis of the possible impact of the shareholder rights plan on proxy contests in the *Household* case. It is therefore prudent to devise defensive strategies while keeping in mind their impact on voting rights and proxy solicitations, as has been done with the newer Second Generation Rights Plan.

At a minimum, it appears that the Delaware courts have created greater room for flexibility in their review of defensive conduct while leaving intact the other traditional elements of business judgment analysis. Under the *Unocal* standard, the courts have generally supported efforts by target boards to thwart coercive two-tier offers or to obtain the time and leverage needed to structure economic alternatives to inadequate bids. Yet, as demonstrated by the *Interco* decision, the *Unocal* standard can be utilized by a court to deprive the board of the traditional deference due business judgments made in good faith and on a fully informed basis. In any event, the *Unocal* standard requires that an additional effort be made by the board to articulate the rationale for particular defensive conduct in terms of its relation to a perceived threat.

Several states have concluded that the *Unocal* standard represents an unwarranted encroachment by the courts on the business judgment of the board and have proposed or adopted legislation explicitly rejecting the heightened standard. *See, e.g.*, Indiana Code § 23-1-35-1 (1989).

F. Constituencies

While it is generally accepted that a corporation should be managed primarily in the interest of its shareowners, courts and legislatures have recognized that constituencies beyond shareholders are a proper concern of directors and have attempted to fashion rules accordingly. See *Herald Co.* v. *Seawell*, 472 F.2d 1081 (10th Cir. 1972) (upholding the Denver Post's defensive maneuvers against a bid by a newspaper publisher with a history of labor difficulties).

1. Unocal

In *Unocal*, 493 A.2d at 954–55, the Delaware Supreme Court suggested that the target's directors could legitimately consider a takeover bid's effect on constituencies other than stockholders:

> [T]he board's power to act derives from its fundamental duty and obligation to protect the corporate enterprise, which includes stockholders, from harm reasonably perceived, irrespective of its source.
>
> . . . If a defensive measure is to come within the ambit of the business judgment rule, it must be reasonable in relation to the threat posed. This entails an analysis by the directors of the nature of the takeover bid and its effect on the corporate enterprise. Examples of such concerns may include: inadequacy of the price offered, nature and timing of the offer, questions of illegality, the impact on "constituencies" other than shareholders (i.e., creditors, customers, employees, and perhaps even the community generally), the risk of nonconsummation, and the quality of securities being offered in the exchange. See Lipton and Brownstein, *Takeover Responses and Directors' Responsibilities: An Update*, p. 7, ABA National Institute on the Dynamics of Corporate Control (December 8, 1983).

2. *GAF/Union Carbide*

Similarly, in *GAF Corp.* v. *Union Carbide Corp.*, 624 F. Supp. 1016 (S.D.N.Y. 1985), the court—in the course of rejecting a raider's attacks on a target's defensive program that included a self-tender for cash and debt securities (which contained restrictive covenants) and the vesting of surplus in its retirement plan to prevent the raider's use of such funds—stated that:

> What the plaintiff plainly fails, or wishes not, to recognize is that shareholders might well decline its cash buyout offer and prefer instead either to remain with the Company as stockholders or to accept the position formulated by the Directors. In addition, even accepting the Company's self-tender offer, they might wish to assure fair and equitable recognition and treatment for its relationships with pensioners, employees and management.
>
> The Directors are not to be faulted for their caution in not leaving to chance the resolution of questions settled by the actions complained of. The protection of loyal employees, including managers, of the organization is not anathema in the Courthouse. To be compared are the situations in which similar protection to the well-being and security of employees, pensioners, and loyal members of management is regularly accorded when a business is moved or substantially liquidated; they are similarly directly affected by unfriendly raids on control. 624 F. Supp. at 1018–19.

3. *Revlon*

In *Revlon, Inc.* v. *MacAndrews & Forbes Holdings, Inc.*, 506 A.2d 173 (Del. Supr. 1986), the Delaware Supreme Court, referencing its statement in *Unocal*, stated that nonstockholder interests may be considered if "there are rationally related benefits accruing to the stockholders." However, the court held that it was impermissible to consider the interests of noteholders in granting a lock-up option to one bidder who had pledged to support the par value of the notes which had been jeopardized by the leveraged nature of the proposed transaction:

> The original threat posed by Pantry Pride—the break-up of the company—had become a reality which even the directors embraced. Selective dealing to fend off a hostile but determined bidder was no longer a proper objective. Instead, obtaining the highest price for the benefit of the stockholders should have been the central theme guiding director action. Thus, the Revlon board could not make the requisite showing of good faith by preferring the noteholders and ignoring its duty of loyalty to the shareholders. The rights of the former already were fixed by contract *Wolfensohn* v. *Madison Fund, Inc.*, Del. Supr., 253 A.2d 72, 75 (1969); *Harff* v. *Kerkorian*, Del. Ch., 324 A.2d 215 (1974). The noteholders required no further protection, and when the Revlon board entered into an auction-ending lock-up agreement with Forstmann on the basis

of impermissible considerations at the expense of the shareholders, the directors breached their primary duty of loyalty.

The Revlon board argued that it acted in good faith in protecting the noteholders because *Unocal* permits consideration of other corporate constituencies. Although such considerations may be permissible, there are fundamental limitations upon that prerogative. A board may have regard for various constituencies in discharging its responsibilities, provided there are rationally related benefits accruing to the stockholders (*Unocal*, 493 A.2d at 955). However, such concern for nonstockholder interests is inappropriate when an auction among active bidders is in progress, and the object no longer is to protect or maintain the corporate enterprise but to sell it to the highest bidder (506 A.2d at 182, 184).

4. Newmont Mining

In *Ivanhoe Partners* v. *Newmont Mining Corp.*, 535 A.2d 1334 (Del. Supr. 1987), the Delaware Supreme Court stated that in considering a takeover bid, the board may consider "the inadequacy of the bid, the nature and timing of the offer, questions of illegality, the impact on constituencies other than shareholders, the risk of nonconsummation, and the basic stockholder interests at stake, including the past actions of the bidder and its affiliates in other takeover contests" (*Id.* at 1342). The Court concluded that

> [t]he series of Ivanhoe maneuvers, including the secret acquisition of shares, the 'bear hug' letter, the coercive partial tender offer and inadequate bid were all viewed by the defendants as classic elements of Mr. Pickens' typical *modus operandi*. Thus, the Newmont board could properly conclude that the Ivanhoe tender offer was not in the shareholders' best interests or those of their company. *Unocal*, 493 A.2d at 952, 956–57 (*Id.* at 1342).

5. Gelco

In *Gelco Corporation* v. *Coniston Partners*, 652 F. Supp. 829 (D. Minn. 1986), *aff'd*, 811 F.2d 414 (8th Cir. 1987), the U.S. District Court of Minnesota, relying on *Unocal*, held that in determining the adequacy of a bid, a board of directors may rightfully consider factors such as the timing of the offer and the impact on constituencies other than shareholders (652 F. Supp. at 850).

6. Universal Foods

In *Amanda Acquisition Corp.* v. *Universal Foods Corp.*, 708 F. Supp. 984 (E.D. Wis. Mar. 18, 1989), *aff'd on other grounds*, 1989 U.S. App. LEXIS (7th Cir. May 24, 1989), the court looked at the effect of an inadequate unsolicited offer on the corporation itself (besides the shareholders) and other constituencies as well, including customers, suppliers, and employees. The court found that the highly leveraged aspect of the unsolicited offer was a cause for alarm to nonshareholder constituencies.

7. Macmillan

In *Mills Acquisition Co.* v. *Macmillan, Inc.*, [Current] Fed. Sec. L. Rep (CCH) ¶92,401 (Del. Supr. May 3, 1989), the Delaware Supreme Court, broadening the factors that directors may consider in addressing competitive bids, held:

> In assessing the bid and the bidder's responsibility, a board may consider, among various proper factors, the adequacy and terms of the offer; its fairness and feasibility; the proposed or actual financing for the offer, and the consequences of that financing; questions of illegality; the impact of both the bid and the potential acquisition on other constituencies, provided that it bears some reasonable relationship to general shareholder interests; the risk of nonconsummation; the basic stockholder interests at stake; the bidder's identity, prior background and other business venture experiences; and the bidder's business plans for the corporation and their effects on stockholder interests.

Id. at 92,597 n.29 (citations omitted). The Court's footnote was to the Court's statement that "[t]he proper objective of Macmillan's fiduciaries was to obtain the highest price reasonably available for the company, *provided that it was offered by a reputable and responsible bidder*." *Id.* at 92,597 (emphasis added).

8. Time

In *Paramount Communications Inc.* v. *Time Incorporated*, C.A. No. 10866 (Del. Ch. July 14, 1989), *aff'd*, No. 279 (Del. Supr. July 24, 1989), Chancellor Allen held that a corporation's long-term strategic plans can take precedent over short-term maximization of share prices. The court characterized Time's achievement of its long-term strategic plan of combining with Warner as "a most important corporate policy" and indicated that it was within the business judgment of the board, as opposed to the wishes of the majority of the shareholders, that the duty of achieving that policy lay. The court stated that

> under Delaware law, directors are under no obligation to act so as to maximize the immediate value of the corporation or its shares, except in the special case in which the corporation is in a "Revlon mode." Thus Delaware law does recognize that directors, when acting deliberately, in an informed way, and in the good faith pursuit of corporate interests, may follow a course designed to achieve long-term value even at the cost of immediate value maximization. (citations omitted)

It is this recognition, the court noted, that permits a corporation to make reasonable charitable contributions or to take other actions that will not have a direct or immediate positive impact upon the financial performance of the firm.

The court also indicated that in certain circumstances "the law might recognize as valid a perceived threat to a 'corporate culture' that is shown to be palpable (for lack of a better word), distinctive and advantageous."

9. Analysis of Trends

The restriction in *Revlon* that nonstockholder interests may be considered if "rationally related" to stockholder benefits would seem to turn, in many cases, on whether the overall goal is independence or a sale of the company: if the former, consideration of various constituencies would seem appropriate since in the case of an ongoing enterprise the stockholders depend upon all of the other constituencies and consideration of them will thus generally be related to stockholder benefit; if the company is to be sold and the stockholders' equity interest terminated, it is less likely that consideration of nonstockholder constituencies will be related to stockholder benefit since the stockholders' interest is thus not the continued prosperity of the enterprise but solely the receipt of the highest price obtainable. But see *Dynamics Corp. of America* v. *CTS Corp.*, 794 F.2d 250, 256 (7th Cir.) (refusing to sanction a rights plan designed to protect the target and its many constituencies against a junk-bond, bust-up takeover, applying the sole criterion of whether the plan advanced "the goal of stockholder wealth maximization"), *rev'd on other grounds*, 481 U.S. 69 (1987).

Legislation has been enacted in several states authorizing directors to consider nonshareholder interests when evaluating a takeover bid (see Chapter 25.IV.G). Many companies have themselves sought to broaden the base of directorial responsibility. For example, in 1986 the shareholders of Dow Jones & Company approved a charter amendment that requires the directors, in the event of a takeover, to take into consideration noneconomic factors such as "the independence and integrity of the corporation's publications and services and the social and economic effects of such action or transaction upon the corporation's stockholders, employees, subscribers, readers, advertisers, customers, and suppliers." Companies having similar charter or by-law provisions include McDonald's Corporation and Control Data.

II. DIRECTORS' DUTIES IN SELLING THE COMPANY

Once it is decided that the company is to be sold, the directors' overriding duty is to seek the highest price for the stockholders. A disinterested board, however, maintains the right to exercise its business judgment in seeking to maximize shareholder value. Thus, the board may in good faith determine to enter into a merger agreement in an arm's-length negotiated transaction, as opposed to placing the company on the "auction block," if it determines that such a process is in the best interest of the company's shareholders. Moreover, even once a competitive bidding contest has begun, a board may, under proper circumstances, favor one bidder over another "if in good faith and advisedly it believes shareholder interests would be thereby advanced." *In re Fort Howard Corp. Shareholder Litigation*, Civ. No. 9991 (Del. Ch. Aug. 8, 1988); see also *In re J.P. Stevens & Co. Shareholders Litigation*, 542 A.2d 770, 781–82 (Del. Ch. 1988).

A. *Revlon, SCM* and *Fruehauf*—Auctions and Level Playing Fields

In 1986, in three cases decided by the Delaware Supreme Court, the United States Court of Appeals for the Second Circuit, and the United States Court of Appeals for the Sixth Circuit, respectively, courts began to speak of directors' duties once a decision to sell the company has been made in terms of "auctions" and "level playing fields." The *Revlon, SCM* and *Fruehauf* cases set the stage for subsequent debate and analysis of the complex issues involved in contests for corporate control. As numerous courts interpreting the *Revlon* standard have now accepted, resort to simple concepts of "auctions" and "level playing fields" should not be utilized to deprive directors of their proper role in determining what course of action is in the best interest of the corporation and its shareholders. See *In re J.P. Stevens & Co. Shareholders Litigation*, 542 A.2d 770, 783–84 (Del. Ch. 1988) (rejecting the level playing field metaphor). The courts have created some room for directors to exercise their business judgment in structuring the auction process and even to favor one bidder over another if necessary to induce that bidder to enter the bidding contest. Yet the courts continue to closely scrutinize directors' conduct under the applicable standards of duty of loyalty and duty of care, and imperfections in the record or deviations from equal treatment of competing bidders that cannot be supported by an articulable business basis lead a court to substitute its judgment for that of the board in overturning the board's actions.

1. Revlon

In *Revlon, Inc.* v. *MacAndrews & Forbes Holding, Inc.*, 506 A.2d 173 (Del. Supr. 1986), the Delaware Supreme Court upheld a preliminary injunction against a lock-up option and no-shop provision. The Court held that the directors' duties changed significantly once a sale of the company, rather than independence, became the goal:

> The Revlon board's authorization permitting management to negotiate a merger or buyout with a third party was a recognition that the company was for sale. The duty of the board had thus changed from the preservation of Revlon as a corporate entity to the maximization of the company's value at a sale for the stockholders' benefit. This significantly altered the board's responsibilities under the *Unocal* standards. It no longer faced threats to corporate policy and effectiveness, or to the stockholders' interests, from a grossly inadequate bid. The whole question of defensive measures became moot. The directors' role changed from defenders of the corporate bastion to auctioneers charged with getting the best price for the stockholders at a sale of the company.
>
> . . . Selective dealing to fend off a hostile but determined bidder was no longer a proper objective. Instead, obtaining the highest price for the benefit of the stockholders should have been the central theme guiding director action.
>
> . . . Market forces must be allowed to operate freely to bring the target's shareholders the best price available for their equity (506 A.2d at 182, 184).

The Court voided a lock-up option granted by Revlon to white knight Forstmann Little in exchange for a $1.00 increase in the per share offer price and Forstmann Little's promise to support the notes issued as part of Revlon's earlier defensive exchange offer. The notes had declined substantially in value after Revlon's independent directors exercised their right to waive the protective covenants restricting the company's ability to incur further debt in order to facilitate Forstmann Little's bid. The Court held that when the board entered into an "auction-ending lock-up agreement," for what the Court construed to be impermissible considerations regarding noteholders at the expense of the stockholders, the directors breached their duty of loyalty.

The Court suggested, however, that the result might have been different if the lock-up had been granted initially to induce Forstmann's white knight bid rather than to induce the modest increase in the bid.

> Current economic conditions in the takeover market are such that a 'white knight' like Forstmann might only enter the bidding for the target company if it receives some form of compensation to cover the risks and costs involved. However, while those lock-ups which draw bidders into the battle benefit shareholders, similar measures which end an active auction and foreclose further bidding operate to the shareholders' detriment. . . .The Forstmann option had a . . .destructive effect on the auction process. Forstmann had already been drawn into the contest on a preferred basis, so the result of the lock-up was not to foster bidding, but to destroy it. *Id.* at 183 (citations omitted).

Similarly, the Court held that the no-shop provision in the Forstmann-Revlon merger agreement, while not illegal *per se*, "is impermissible under the *Unocal* standard when a board's primary duty becomes that of an auctioneer responsible for selling the company to the highest bidder" (*Id.* at 184). The

Court also upheld the Chancery Court injunction against payment of a $25 million cancellation fee to Forstmann Little, pending resolution of the case on the merits. The Chancery Court had acknowledged that cancellation fees were not unusual in transactions of the magnitude of the Forstmann-Revlon transaction but noted that the placing of the cancellation fee in escrow at the time the lock-ups were granted was disturbing. The dispute over the cancellation fee was later settled with Forstmann receiving $24.4 million in a settlement of all claims.

2. SCM

Revlon found support for its holding in *Hanson Trust PLC* v. *ML SCM Acquisition, Inc.*, 781 F.2d 264 (2d Cir. 1986). There, the Second Circuit invalidated a lock-up, holding that the directors breached their fiduciary duties because "[t]he effect was to preclude shareholders from achieving any value higher than that agreed upon by SCM management and Merrill [the locked-up bidder]. In short, the Board appears to have failed to ensure that alternative bids were negotiated or scrutinized by those whose only loyalty was to the shareholders" (*Id.* at 277). The Second Circuit so held notwithstanding that, under the applicable New York law, the burden of proving the directors' fiduciary breach rests with the plaintiff (*id.* at 273); the use of a lock-up option is not illegal *per se* (*id.* at 273–73); and the SCM board of directors consisted largely of independent, outside directors with no personal interest in the challenged acquisition proposal (*id.* at 267).

The court concluded that Hanson had made a *prima facie* case that the SCM board, by its lack of due care in considering the fairness of the lock-up option price and the effect exercise of the option would have on SCM, had breached its duty of care.

The lock-up option had been granted to white knight Merrill Lynch in exchange for Merrill Lynch's increasing its leveraged buyout offer to $74 per share (a price $2 per share higher than Hanson's then competing bid). The option entitled Merrill Lynch to purchase two of SCM's businesses in the event a third party acquired more than one-third of SCM's common stock. The court found that the directors had not properly considered the fairness of the lock-up option price and the effect exercise of the option would have on SCM. Specifically, the court seemed to base its decision on: (1) the directors' reliance on "conclusory" opinions of their financial advisors that the option prices were "within the range of fair value" when no specific range had been calculated; (2) the absence of a written opinion on the value of the optioned businesses; (3) the lack of adequate discussion of the likelihood of the option trigger being pulled; (4) the lack of discussion of what the company would look like if the option were exercised; (5) the directors' failure themselves to read the various offers and agreements, instead relying on the advisors' description; (6) the directors' failure to seek any documents in support of the financial advisors' opinion; and (7) the directors' consideration of the lock-up option having consisted solely of a single, three-hour, late-night meeting.

The court was also concerned that the lock-up option might foreclose bidding and thus have the effect of depriving the stockholders of the best offer available in the free market:

> Although the SCM independent directors have not been shown to have acted out of self-interest or to have been fraudulent or self-dealing in breach of their duty of loyalty, they do not appear to have pursued adequately their obligation to ensure the shareholders' fundamental right to make the "decisions affecting [the] corporation's ultimate destiny," *Id.* at 276–77 (citing *Norlin Corp.* v. *Rooney, Pace, Inc.*, 744 F.2d 255, 258 (2d Cir. 1984)).

3. Fruehauf

In *Edelman* v. *Fruehauf Corp.*, 798 F.2d 882, 886–87 (6th Cir. 1986), the court, applying Michigan law, stated:

> Once it becomes apparent that a takeover target will be acquired by new owners, whether by an alleged "raider" or by a team consisting of management and a "white knight," it becomes the duty of the target's directors to see that the shareholders obtain the best price possible for their stock. . . . When, in violation of this duty, directors take measures that are intended to put an end to the bidding, those measures may be enjoined.

The court concluded that the Fruehauf board failed to carry its burden of establishing that the granting of certain inducements to a management leveraged buyout group along with other actions taken to defeat a hostile offer made by Asher Edelman was fair and reasonable in light of the circumstances. The court stated that the fact that Fruehauf was on the auction block was not in dispute. Citing *Revlon*, the court stated that the board's duty was thus to obtain the best price for the stockholders in a sale of the company. The court concluded that the Fruehauf board had apparently decided to make a deal with management no matter what other bidders might offer.

The court was critical of the fact that the special committee of the board that approved the Merrill offer had refused to talk to Edelman or promote an open bidding contest prior to entering into the agreement with Merrill that provided Merrill with significant competitive advantages, including among other things: payment of approximately $30 million to Merrill for loan commitment and advisory fees, a pension parachute worth $70 to $100 million, a "break-up" fee and a "no-shop" clause.

The court criticized the directors' actions stating that:

> They acted as interested parties and did not treat the Fruehauf managers and the Edelman group in an even handed way but rather gave their colleagues on the Board, the inside managers, the inside track and accepted their proposal without fostering a real bidding process (*Id.* at 885).

To ensure an open bidding process and a level playing field the court ordered the Fruehauf board:

> . . . to refrain from taking any corporate actions which are intended to or have the effect of favoring or advantaging any particular bidder over any other bidder . . .[and] to make available upon reasonable notice to any potential bidder for Fruehauf all information concerning Fruehauf's business and properties (subject to such bidder agreeing to reasonable provisions to keep such information confidential) and to meet on mutually agreeable and reasonable terms with any potential bidder in good faith (*Id.* at 890-91).

It is noteworthy that the court was concerned not that the board actively shop the company, but rather that it treat all bidders that entered the bidding contest equally.

B. Lock-up Options and Bust-up Fees After Revlon

Lock-up options and bust-up fees are designed to provide friendly acquirors and white knights with some assurance that their planned transaction will be consummated without interference from a hostile bidder and/or that they will be compensated if the deal is not consummated. Without such assurances, many bidders are unwilling to enter into a negotiated transaction. Financial buyers are typically unwilling to become stalking horses for the hostile bidder and wish to be compensated for the expenses and risks associated with making a white knight bid. Corporate buyers may face the additional risk that if their proposed transaction is not consummated, having announced their willingness to engage in an extraordinary transaction, they will themselves become the target of a hostile bid.

For a long time, lock-ups and bust-up fees were generally accepted as a means of inducing a friendly acquiror to enter into a merger agreement in a negotiated transaction; courts had repeatedly upheld the grant of lock-ups as within the proper exercise of the board of directors' business judgment. *See, Thompson* v. *Enstar Corp.*, 509 A.2d 578 (Del. Ch. 1984). The *Revlon, SCM* and *Fruehauf* cases cast doubt on the use of lock-ups in certain defensive situations. Recent decisions, however, have indicated that lock-up options are acceptable even in a competitive bidding situation where a proper record is established. Courts have recognized that lock-ups and bust-up fees are often necessary to induce white knights to enter the bidding contest. When a bidding contest arises, the courts will closely scrutinize the auction process to see whether a lock-up is appropriate. *See Mills Acquisition Co.* v. *Macmillan Inc.*, [Current] Fed. Sec. L. Rep. (CCH) ¶94,401 (Del. Supr. May 3, 1989); *In re Holly Farms Corp. Shareholders Litigation*, [1988–89 Transfer Binder] Fed. Sec. L. Rep. (CCH) ¶94,181 (Del. Ch. Dec. 30, 1988); *In re RJR Nabisco, Inc. Shareholders Litigation*, [1988–89 Transfer Binder] Fed. Sec. L. Rep. (CCH) ¶94,194 (Del. Ch. Jan. 31, 1989).

1. Lock-up Options and Bust-up Fees in Competitive Bidding Situations

Courts have examined lock-up options and bust-up fees granted after a competitive bidding contest has begun in the following contexts:

(a) Lock-up Options and Bust-up Fees Upheld

(1) Burlington Industries. In *Samjens Partners I* v. *Burlington Industries, Inc.*, 663 F. Supp. 614 (S.D.N.Y. 1987), the court denied the request of a hostile bidder controlled by Asher Edelman and Dominion Textile, Inc. for a preliminary injunction against a merger agreement between Burlington Industries and a white knight LBO group led by Morgan Stanley. The court, interpreting *Revlon*, stated that it was permissible for a target to enter into a negotiated merger agreement with a white knight containing a bust-up fee and no-shop provision, provided the transaction is approved on a proper record:

> [A]lthough Morgan might have been Burlington's white knight, it was not Burlington's patron saint. . . .[I]t wanted a response to its bid quickly, it wanted compensation for the risk it was undertaking in tying up its capital, and it did not want to serve as a "stalking horse" and have its bid shopped around (*Id.* at 625).

The court also rejected the hostile bidder's claim that the board had an obligation to offer it a break-up fee of the sort offered to Morgan Stanley, noting that:

> [The bidder] has purchased approximately 13 percent of Burlington shares in the pre-tender offer market at an average price of $50 per share. Thus, [the bidder] enters the bidding process with a nearly $80 million advantage over other prospective bidders who must pay at least $78 per share for all outstanding shares. Denying [the bidder] a break-up fee thus helps to even the playing Field (Id. at 626)

(2) West Point-Pepperell. In *In re J.P. Stevens & Co. Shareholders Litigation*, 542 A.2d 770 (Del. Ch. 1988), the Delaware Chancery Court rejected the argument that the decision of the Delaware Supreme Court in the *Revlon* case prohibits the grant of bust-up fees, topping fees, or other advantages to one of the competing bidders for a company that is for sale. Instead, the court confined *Revlon* to cases where it is shown that the board of the target was not acting in good faith. Where the board is not so shown, the court held that the business judgment rule applies. In such a case the court will not second guess the directors' decision that the grant of an advantage to one bidder was an appropriate means to obtain the best price for the shareholders. The court recognized that the grant of an advantage to a bidder may be the way to get a better price. While the case did not involve stock or crown jewel lock-up options, the reasoning and result should be the same.

(3) Storer Communications. In *Cottle* v. *Storer Communication, Inc.*, 849 F.2d 570 (11th Cir. 1988), the court upheld crown-jewel asset lock-ups granted to KKR at the end of a competitive auction. The court stated that in determining the validity of the lock-ups "[t]he question is whether Storer conducted a fair auction, and whether KKR made the best offer" (*Id.* at 576). The court noted that in exchange for the lock-ups, Storer received a cash price of $91 per share, $16 more per share than KKR's previous offer and $7.50 more per share than the competing offer by Comcast. This improvement, the court stated, distinguished the case from *Revlon* and *SCM* "where there was . . . 'very little improvement' in the subsequent bid" in exchange for the lock-up (*Id.* at 576–77). The court also noted that, unlike *SCM*, there was no allegation that the option price was outside of the range of fair value for the optioned assets.

(4) RJR. In *In re RJR Nabisco, Inc. Shareholders Litigation*, [1988–1989 Transfer Binder] Fed. Sec. L. Rep. (CCH) ¶94,194 (Del. Ch. Jan. 31, 1989), the court refused to grant an order declaring invalid a $1 per share "topping fee" granted to the winning bidder at the end of an auction that the court concluded had been conducted by an independent board acting in good faith.

(b) Lock-up Options Overturned

(1) Macmillan. In *Mills Acquisition Co.* v. *Macmillan, Inc.*, [Current] Fed. Sec. L. Rep. (CCH) ¶ 94,401 (Del. Supr. May 3, 1989), the Supreme Court of Delaware invalidated an asset lock-up and a $70 million break-

up fee and expenses (2.5 percent of the total transaction price) granted by Macmillan to KKR at the end of an auction for Macmillan in which Maxwell Communications Corp. was the losing bidder. Looking to *Revlon* for guidance, the court distinguished between lock-up options that draw bidders into an auction, and therefore benefit shareholders, and those that end an active auction and foreclose further bidding, thereby harming shareholders. *See id.* at 57. The court ruled that the KKR lock-up was intended to foreclose further bidding, and, comparing the value received by shareholders to the value received by KKR, noted that the increased price offered by KKR (from its previous offer of $89.50 per share to $90.05 per share; $1.05 [face value] higher than Maxwell's bid) was a *de minimus* justification for the lock-up. *Id.* at 92,600.

The court stated:

> Even if [a] lock-up is permissible, when it involves "crown jewel" assets careful board scrutiny attends the decision. When the intended effect is to end an active auction, at the very least the independent members of the board must attempt to negotiate alternative bids before granting such a significant concession.

Id. at 92,600–601 (footnote omitted). Finding that the board did not attempt to negotiate an alternative bid despite a record showing Maxwell's willingness to increase its price, the court invalidated the lock-up.

The court also clarified the relationship between the enhanced duties of directors, mandated by *Unocal*, when issues of corporate control are at stake and the altered responsibilities of directors, imposed by *Revlon*, when a company is to be sold. The court stated:

> When *Revlon* duties devolve upon directors, this Court will continue to exact an enhanced judicial scrutiny at the threshold, as in *Unocal*, before the normal presumptions of the business judgment rule will apply. However, as we recognized in *Revlon*, the two-part threshold test, of necessity, is slightly different.
>
> At the outset, the plaintiff must show, and the trial court must find, that the directors of the target company treated one or more of the respective bidders on unequal terms. It is only then that the two-part threshold requirement of *Unocal* is truly invoked, for in *Revlon* we held that "[f]avoritism for a white knight to the total exclusion of a hostile bidder might be justifiable when the latter's offer adversely affects shareholder interests, but . . . the directors cannot fulfill their enhanced *Unocal* duties by playing favorites with the contending factions."
>
> In the face of disparate treatment, the trial court must first examine whether the directors properly perceived that shareholder interests were enhanced. In any event the board's action must be reasonable in relation to the advantage sought to be achieved, or conversely, to the threat which a particular bid allegedly poses to stockholder interests.

> If on the basis of this enhanced *Unocal* scrutiny the trial court is satisfied that the test has been met, then the directors' actions necessarily are entitled to the protections of the business judgment rule. The latitude a board will have in responding to differing bids will vary according to the degree of benefit or detriment to the shareholders' general interests that the amount or terms of the bids pose. We stated in *Revlon*, and again here, that in a sale of corporate control the responsibility of the directors is to get the highest value reasonably attainable for the shareholders. Beyond that, there are no special and distinct "Revlon duties." Once a finding has been made by a court that the directors have fulfilled their fundamental duties of care and loyalty under the foregoing standards, there is no further judicial inquiry into the matter.

Id. at 92,602 (citations omitted).

(2) Holly Farms. In *In re Holly Farms Corp. Shareholders Litigation*, [1988–89 Transfer Binder] Fed. Sec. L. Rep. (CCH) ¶ 94,181 (Del. Ch. Dec. 30, 1988), the Delaware Chancery Court preliminarily enjoined effectuation of the lock-up, termination fees, and reimbursement of expenses provisions of a merger agreement between Holly Farms and ConAgra. The court determined that although the Holly Farms board of directors properly negotiated with ConAgra (a "white knight") to maximize shareholder values, it failed to inform Tyson Foods (a "hostile" bidder) of its decision to sell the company. The court accepted Tyson's argument that Tyson was prepared to make a higher bid on the night that the board decided to enter into a merger agreement with ConAgra, and that Tyson would have bid more than the discounted value of the ConAgra merger transaction, which involved an exchange of stock. The court found that the decision to enter into a common stock merger with ConAgra constituted a decision to "sell" the company, which required the board to assume the role of auctioneer, and that the failure of the board to inform Tyson of its decision to sell, or to in any way encourage an improved bid from Tyson, violated the *Revlon* standard. The court concluded that the lock-up, termination fees, and reimbursement provisions of the merger agreement were not necessary to obtain ConAgra's bid, but were instead "showstoppers" designed to preclude a genuine auction.

In May of 1989, the Holly Farms board again attempted to auction the company, setting a bidding deadline of May 13. Tyson, however, argued that the bidding guidelines imposed by Holly Farms unduly favored ConAgra at the expense of Tyson, and sought to enjoin the auction. Among other things, the guidelines included a provision that required Tyson essentially to bear the cost of any negotiated settlement of the dispute concerning the validity of the lock-up. The Delaware Chancery Court agreed that the guidelines unfairly favored ConAgra, but nevertheless refused to enjoin the auction. The court held that Tyson's only claim of irreparable harm was that it would be required to return to court to seek to enjoin any merger agreement resulting from the tainted auction and that, in any event, the lack of assurances that either (1) any bids would be submitted in the auction or (2) the tainted guidelines would not be changed caused the controversy to not be ripe. *See In re Holly Farms Shareholders Litigation*, [Current] Fed. Sec. L. Rep. (CCH) ¶ 94,443 (Del. Ch. May 19, 1989).

Over the weekend of May 19–21, Holly Farms conducted another auction for the company and accepted an improved bid from ConAgra. Tyson then sought to enjoin the merger agreement. Despite the fact that the court found that Tyson was again not treated equally with ConAgra, the Delaware Chancery Court refused to enjoin the merger agreement. *See In re Holly Farms Shareholders Litigation*, [Current] Fed. Sec. L. Rep. (CCH) ¶ 94,486 (Del. Ch. June 14, 1989). The court followed the decision of the Delaware Supreme Court in *Macmillan* and ruled that the merger agreement could be set aside only if the directors did not properly perceive that shareholder interests were advanced. *Id.* at 93,110. The court found that because of the existence of a justifiable reason to believe that Tyson and ConAgra would reach a settlement that would cause ConAgra's bid to be withdrawn, thereby costing the shareholders at least $2.50 per share, the directors properly perceived the merger agreement to enhance shareholder interests. The court found that accepting the higher offer before it could be withdrawn "seem[ed] to have been 'reasonable in relation to the advantage sought to be achieved, or conversely, to the threat which a particular bid allegedly poses to the stockholder interests.'" *Id.* at 93,111 (quoting *Macmillan* at 64). The actions of the directors were therefore entitled to the protections of the business judgment rule. The court also noted that Tyson failed to demonstrate that (1) a failure to grant the injunction would cause irreparable harm and (2) the harm it would grant if the injunction were not granted would outweigh the harm that would be caused to shareholders if the injunction were granted. Finally, the court refused to force Holly Farms to redeem its share purchase rights plan, finding that such a redemption, at a time when Tyson had presumably not yet made its best offer (*see id.* at 93,113), would not enhance the best interest of the shareholders of Holly Farms.

2. Lock-up Options and Bust-up Fees Provisions in Negotiated Transactions

Courts have upheld lock-up options and bust-up fees granted to acquirors in negotiated transactions in the following contexts:

(a) Texas Air

In *Hastings-Murtagh* v. *Texas Air Corp.*, 649 F. Supp. 479 (S.D. Fla. 1986), a case arising from the Texas Air/Eastern Air Lines merger, the court dismissed the Eastern unions' challenge to the merger agreement, which contained a lock-up option and no-shop provision, which Eastern had entered into without soliciting competing bids. The court, applying Delaware law, distinguished the *Revlon* case stating that lock-ups and no-shop provisions are valid when they serve to attract a bidder and result from arm's-length negotiation and are impermissible "only if they are adopted in a situation where there is a live auction with competing bidders."

(b) Commonwealth National

In *Keyser* v. *Commonwealth National Financial Corp.*, 644 F. Supp. 1130 (M.D. Pa. 1986), the court upheld the granting of a stock option to a purchaser in a negotiated bank merger. According to the court's opinion, in connection with a merger, Commonwealth granted Mellon Bank Corporation an option to purchase approximately 25 percent of its common stock under certain circumstances. The conditions to exercise principally related to activities of third parties designed to thwart the merger. At the time of the granting of the option, a prior bidder for Commonwealth (whose offer price was less than the Mellon offer price) had withdrawn its bid. The option exercise price was the market price of a share of Commonwealth common stock on the last trading day preceding the execution of the merger agreement, which was slightly more than \$5 less than the merger consideration of \$40 per share. The plaintiffs charged that the granting of the option was done in a "hasty" manner without independent evaluation by Commonwealth's board, was designed to prevent competitive bids and was in breach of the directors' fiduciary duty of care. In upholding the validity of the bank's action, the court noted that lock-up provisions are "very common in bank mergers." It found that were it not for the lock-up, Commonwealth would not have been able to keep Mellon as a competitive bidder. In upholding the exercise of business judgment and finding no breach of the directors' fiduciary duty of care, the court held:

> The warrant and option price were fully negotiated and were a necessary and integral part of a merger agreement with Mellon. A merger with Mellon was considered by the directors to be in the best interests of Commonwealth and its shareholders. Further, the essence and the effects of the [lock-up] were fully disclosed to shareholders, who ultimately voted to approve the merger agreement. *Id.* at 1147 (citations omitted).

The court's opinion makes no reference to the *Revlon* or *SCM* decisions.

(c) Scientific Leasing

In *Yanow* v. *Scientific Leasing, Inc.*, [Current] Fed. Sec. L. Rep. (CCH) ¶ 93,660 (Del. Ch. Feb. 8, 1988), the court upheld a stock option for 16 percent of the company's shares at the offer price granted in a negotiated transaction after the company had been partially shopped. The court held that the option was a proper means of inducing a premium offer, stressing that the option in this case was not sufficiently costly to an interloper as to preclude higher bids. The court noted with approval that the "window shop" clause in the merger agreement allowed the seller to cooperate with a bona fide higher bidder.

(d) Sea-Land

In *Hecco Ventures* v. *Sea-Land Corp.*, No. 8486 (Del. Ch. May 19, 1986), a case arising out of CSX's agreement to acquire Sea-Land at $28 per share—which included an alleged "lock-up" stock option—the Delaware Chancery Court denied a temporary restraining order against the pending tender offer. The court noted that the option was granted at the conclusion of the auction process and that there was no bidder other than CSX; there was no bid other than CSX's; and there was no showing that an injunction would cause a different bidder or a higher bid to materialize (Slip op. at 13, 14).

Plaintiffs were unable to support claims of breach of fiduciary duty by Sea-Land's board, by Harold Simmons (who controlled 39.5 percent of the Sea-Land stock and for $5 per share had sold CSX an option to purchase his position for $28 per share), or by CSX as a conspirator in the Sea-Land board's and Simmons' alleged breaches. The court found that Sea-Land had actively searched for a buyer, had invited Simmons to top CSX, had provided him with the same information given to CSX, had not participated in the Simmons-CSX transaction, and had sold to the highest and only bidder remaining at a price deemed fair by its investment banker.

(e) Time

In *Paramount Communications Inc.* v. *Time Incorporated*, C.A. No. 10866 (Del. Ch. July 14, 1989), *aff'd*, No. 279 (Del. Supr. July 24, 1989), the court held that a stock for stock merger of Time and Warner (with Warner shareholders receiving 62 percent of the combined company's shares) did not constitute a sale of either Time or Warner within the meaning of *Revlon* since control of both companies "remained in a large, fluid, changeable and changing market." The grant of lock-up options in this context may thus be easier to sustain than in the context of a sale of the company.

C. No-Shop and "Fiduciary Out" Termination Provisions

1. No-Shop Provisions

Before entering into a merger agreement, a white knight will often request a covenant by the target company not to solicit or encourage anyone to make a competing bid or to engage in any negotiations with or supply any information to any other person who expresses an interest in acquiring the target company.

(a) Revlon

In *Revlon*, the court held that a no-shop provision, while not illegal *per se*, "is impermissible under the *Unocal* standard when a board's primary duty becomes that of an auctioneer responsible for selling the company to the highest bidder." The court stated that:

> Favoritism for a white knight to the total exclusion of a hostile bidder might be justifiable when the latter's offer adversely affects shareholder interests, but when bidders make relatively similar offers, or dissolution of the company becomes inevitable, the directors cannot fulfill their enhanced *Unocal* duties by playing favorites with the contending factions. Market forces must be allowed to operate freely to bring the target's shareholders the best price available for their equity. Thus, as the trial court ruled, the shareholders' interests necessitated that the board remain free to negotiate in the fulfillment of that duty. 506 A.2d at 184.

(b) Texas Air

In the *Texas Air* decision, discussed in Chapter 22 II.G.1, the court, distinguishing *Revlon*, held that no-shop provisions are valid when they serve to attract a bidder and result from arm's-length negotiation. 649 F. Supp. 479 (S.D. Fla. 1986).

(c) Becor Western

In *Rosenfield* v. *Becor Western Inc.*, No. 87-C-0988 (E.D. Wis. Nov. 5, 1987), the court upheld a no-shop provision in a merger agreement for a management leveraged buyout entered after the company had been extensively shopped, stating that "[t]he directors were justified in deciding to accept what they deemed to be the most favorable offer available, close the bidding process, and permit . . .shareholders to decide for themselves whether they want to approve the Merger" (Slip op. at 23).

(d) Macmillan

In *Macmillan*, [Current] Fed. Sec. L. Rep. (CCH) ¶ 94,401 (Del. Supr. May 3, 1989), The Delaware Supreme Court invalidated a no-shop clause, stating that "[a]bsent a material advantage to the stockholders from the terms or structure of a bid that is contingent on a no-shop clause, a successful bidder imposing such a condition must be prepared to survive the careful scrutiny which that concession demands." *Id.* at 92,601.

2. Fiduciary Out Provisions

It is becoming more common for directors upon entering into a merger agreement to reserve the right to terminate the merger agreement if a more favorable offer is received at a later date. Even lacking such a clause, there are limits to the degree that a merger agreement can bind the board to take actions that are inconsistent with the directors' fiduciary duties to shareholders.

(a) Jewel

In *Jewel Cos.* v. *Pay Less Drug Stores Northwest, Inc.*, 741 F.2d 1555 (9th Cir. 1984), the Ninth Circuit Court of Appeals, applying California law, reversed a Federal District Court's grant of summary judgment for Pay Less Drug Stores Northwest "Northwest" on Jewel's claim of tortious interference with a merger agreement between Jewel and Pay Less Drug Stores "Pay Less".[1] In *Jewel*, Jewel and Pay Less entered into a merger agreement pursuant to which the two companies would engage in a tax-free merger in which each outstanding share of Pay Less stock would be exchanged for .652 shares of Jewel stock. The merger agreement contained a so-called "best efforts" clause pursuant to which each company's board of directors was obligated to "use its best efforts to fulfill those conditions . . .over which it has control or influence and to consummate the merger." The merger agreement also obligated Pay Less to forbear from selling or transferring any of its properties or assets, or agreeing or committing to make any such sale or transfer, and from entering into or terminating any contract other than in the ordinary course of business.

Subsequently, Northwest purchased over 12 percent of Pay Less' stock in the open market and commenced a tender offer at $22.50 per share of Pay Less stock. Two weeks later, Northwest increased its tender offer to $24 per share, Pay Less' board recommended that shareholders accept the

[1] Pay Less and Northwest were entirely unrelated parties prior to the events described in *Jewel*, despite the similarity of their names.

Northwest offer, and Northwest and Pay Less, through Pay Less' board, entered into an agreement pursuant to which, among other things, (1) the Pay Less board agreed to abandon the Jewel merger if the merger was not approved by Pay Less' shareholders and (2) Northwest agreed to indemnify Pay Less and its directors against any alleged breach of the merger agreement with Jewel. On the same date, the Pay Less board signed a merger agreement with Northwest. The Jewel merger agreement was subsequently rejected at a Pay Less shareholders' meeting.

The court concluded that under California law the board of directors of a corporation could agree in a merger agreement to forbear from entering into competing and inconsistent agreements until the shareholders vote on the merger. Having entered into such an agreement, the Pay Less board was bound by it, and the board's breach of the agreement could not be justified on the basis of its fiduciary duties:

> It is nowhere written in stone that the law of the jungle must be the exclusive doctrine governing sorties into the world of corporate mergers. The legitimate exercise of the right to contract by responsible boards of directors can help bring some degree of much needed order to these transactions 741 F.2d at 1568–69.

The court noted, however that:

> Even after the merger agreement is signed a board may not, consistent with its fiduciary obligations to its shareholders, withhold information regarding a materially more attractive offer. While the board can bind itself to exert its best efforts to consummate the merger under California law, it can only bind the corporation temporarily, and in limited areas, pending shareholder approval. *Id.* at 1564 (citations omitted).

The court declined, however, to address the question of whether a merger agreement could bind the board, in the event of an unsolicited receipt of a more favorable offer after signing the agreement, to continue to recommend to its shareholders that they approve the initial proposal.

(b) ConAgra

In *ConAgra, Inc.* v. *Cargill, Inc.*, 222 Neb. 136, 382 N.W.2d 576 (Neb. Sup. Ct. 1986), the Court held that a "best efforts" clause in a merger agreement does not preclude a board of directors from recommending a subsequent superior offer to the shareholders. ConAgra had entered into a definitive merger agreement to acquire MBPXL. The agreement contained a "best efforts" clause requiring both corporations' directors and officers to "take all such further action as may be necessary or appropriate in order to effectuate the transactions contemplated hereby including recommending to their respective shareholders that the merger be approved." The clause then continued: "provided, however, nothing herein contained shall relieve either Board of Directors of their continuing duties to respective shareholders." Subsequently, after negotiations initiated by a target company director/shareholder and then participated in by other directors, Cargill determined to make a tender offer for MBPXL. MBPXL's board ultimately determined that this offer was superior to the ConAgra merger agreement; refused to recommend the merger to the shareholders; and, instead, recommended Cargill's tender offer.

ConAgra sued Cargill for tortiously interfering with the merger agreement and MBPXL for breach of contract and conspiracy with Cargill. ConAgra prevailed in the lower court. The Nebraska Supreme Court reversed. First, the Court read the "fiduciary out" proviso to the "best efforts" obligation as expressly countenancing the course taken by the target board. But in language that makes clear that the result would have been the same regardless of the terms of the particular merger agreement, the Court stated:

> This court should not sanction "agreements which have the effect of removing from directors in a very substantial way their duty to use their own best judgment on management matters."
>
> The directors of MBPXL could not agree to assist ConAgra by pledging their best efforts if, by doing so, the directors of MBPXL violated their legal duties to the MBPXL shareholders.
>
> Once the directors of MBPXL learned of the competing Cargill offer, the 'best efforts' clause in the ConAgra proposal could not relieve the MBPXL directors of their duties to act in the shareholders' best interests (382 N.W.2d at 587, 588).

The Court expressly noted that it was not deciding whether the directors of MBPXL might be personally liable for breach of an agreement with ConAgra. See *id.* at 587.

D. No Duty to Shop the Company When Company Is to Be Sold

The decision to sell the company is firmly within the business judgment of the board and, absent a competitive bidding situation, courts have indicated that a board need not affirmatively shop the company before entering into a negotiated transaction.

1. Texas Air

In the *Texas Air* case, the court stated that the board had no obligation to solicit or help to arrange a competing bid prior to entering into a negotiated merger agreement. The court noted that plaintiffs (the Eastern Air unions) failed to cite "any legal authority that obligates a board of directors to jeopardize one bid in order to give a group of employees or anyone else an indefinite amount of time in which to develop and finance an acquisition proposal" [649 F. Supp. 479, 484 (S.D. Fla. 1986)]. See also *In re Anderson Clayton Shareholders' Litigation*, 519 A.2d 694 (Del. Ch. 1986) (directors have no duty to delay an otherwise appropriate transaction merely because a competitor shows up at the last minute).

2. Scientific Leasing

In *Yanow* v. *Scientific Leasing, Inc.*, [Current] Fed. Sec. L. Rep. (CCH) ¶ 93,660 (Del. Ch. Feb. 8, 1988), the Delaware Chancery Court held that the "specific methods corporate directors may use to elicit bids from potential acquirors" is a matter within the business judgment of the board "that necessarily must vary with each case." The court concluded that the "directors had valid reasons to proceed discretely [sic] in carrying out their strategy for marketing the company, and that they had no motive to obtain less than the best available price." The fact that a 26 percent shareholder with board representation, with interests identical to those of the other shareholders, supported the negotiated transaction, provided added proof that the board had negotiated a fair price.

3. Interco

In *City Capital Associates Ltd. Partnership* v. *Interco Inc.*, 551 A.2d 787 (Del. Ch. 1988), Chancellor Allen stated:

> *Revlon* should not, in my opinion, be interpreted as representing a sharp turn in our law. It does not require, for example, that before every corporate merger agreement can validly be entered into, the constituent corporations must be "shopped" or, more radically, an auction process undertaken, even though a merger may be regarded as a sale of the Company. But mergers or recapitalization or other important corporate transactions may be authorized by a board only advisedly. There must be a reasonable basis for the board of directors involved to conclude that the transaction involved is in the best interest of the shareholders. This involves having information about possible alternatives. The essence of rational choice is an assessment of costs and benefits and the consideration of alternatives (Slip op. at 40–41).

4. TW Services

In *TW Services, Inc.* v. *SWT Acquisition Corp.*, [Current] Fed. Sec. L. Rep. (CCH) ¶ 94,334 (Del. Ch. 1989), Chancellor Allen stated his view that the *Revlon* duty

> is not necessarily a duty to conduct an "auction" or to keep "a level playing field" when the firm is for sale or, indeed, to proceed in any prescribed way; rather it is the duty to exercise judgment (in good faith and prudently) in an effort to maximize immediate share value. When a corporation is in a "Revlon mode," legitimate concerns relating to the claims of other constituencies are absent and, indeed, concerns about the corporation as a distinct entity become attenuated.

Id. at 92,179 (footnotes omitted). He stated that this duty arises when a board decides to sell a company, and, as in *Interco* and *Pillsbury*, where a board, responding to its own view of its duties to shareholders, proposes an alternative transaction that, realistically viewed, constitutes a functional alternative to a resisted tender offer. *Id.* at 92,179–92,180. Chancellor Allen stated, however, that the Delaware Courts have not yet addressed "the question when, if ever, . . . a board's duty to 'the corporation and its shareholders' require[s] it to abandon concerns for 'long-term' values (and other constituencies) and enter into a current share value maximizing mode." *Id.* at 92,180.

E. "Market Checks" and Leveraged Buyouts

Where a company has not been shopped prior to the board's entering into a merger agreement, especially in the context of a management leveraged buyout, some courts have indicated that the absence of a lock-up or no-shop provision helps assure that the price received by shareholders is fair.

1. Trans Union

In *Trans Union*, the Delaware Supreme Court found that the stock lock-up granted to Marmon effectively eliminated the practical utility of the market test. The court noted that its review of the record compelled "a finding that confirmation of the appropriateness of the [Marmon] offer by an unfettered or free market test was virtually meaningless in the face of the terms and time limitations of Trans Union's Merger Agreement with [Marmon]" (488 A.2d at 885).

2. Beatrice

In *In re Beatrice Cos. Litigation*, Civ. No. 8248 (Del. Ch. Apr. 14, 1986), the court approved the settlement of stockholder litigation arising out of the leveraged buyout agreement between Beatrice and Kohlberg, Kravis, Roberts & Co. ("KKR"). The court stated that important benefits had been conferred on Beatrice stockholders due to the fact that the merger agreement between KKR and the company had been revised to exclude a no-shop clause and the company had subsequently canvassed alternatives to the KKR offer. The court noted that while no alternatives to the KKR offer arose, the stockholders at least had the comfort of knowing that no higher offer from a third party was overlooked.

3. Fort Howard

In *In re Fort Howard Corp. Shareholders Litigation*, Civ. No. 9991 (Del. Ch. Aug. 8, 1988), the Delaware Chancery Court denied a motion brought by a shareholder for a preliminary injunction against a management buyout that was approved by the board without shopping the company. The court expressed some concerns about the procedures followed by the company in establishing the special committee to evaluate the buyout offer, namely, that the CEO handpicked the members of the special committee and chose the special counsel for the committee. The court concluded, however, that the inclusion of the provisions in the merger agreement permitting an effective "market check" before the LBO offer could close provided a sufficient basis to conclude that the board had acted in good faith in seeking the best available transaction for the shareholders. The elements establishing the effective market check in the court's view were that (1) the buyout group's tender offer would remain open for 30 business days (as opposed to the minimum required 20 business days); (2) although the special committee could not actively solicit alternative bids, it could entertain alternative bids and cooperate in the development of alternative bids (and this fact was made clear in the press release announcing the buyout); and (3) the $68 million bust-up fee (approximately 2 percent of the transaction value) did not provide a meaningful impediment to competing bidders.

4. Amsted

In *In re Amsted Industries Inc. Litigation*, Civ. No. 8224 (Del. Ch. Aug. 24, 1988) (letter opinion), the court approved a settlement of shareholder litigation challenging an ESOP-LBO transaction in which no effort to shop the company had been made. The court stated that it was "deeply troubled" as to why, in a transaction as important to shareholder interests as this one, "did the independent committee of the board—if it was motivated in good faith to achieve the best transaction for the shareholders—not check [the investment banker's fairness] opinion by shopping the company, or at least negotiating for a period in which it could publicly encourage any interested party to come forward" (*Id.* at 18–20). Nonetheless, the court approved the settlement, stating that it was "far from clear that the highest price was not achieved" and that there was little in the record to establish that the board acting through the special committee was grossly negligent in failing to negotiate for a market check or that it was not acting in good faith when it negotiated the ESOP-LBO. One factor weighing in favor of the board's actions was that the ESOP transaction had tax advantages that arguably placed the ESOP in the most advantageous position to pay the highest price.

5. KDI Corp.

In *In re KDI Corp. Shareholders Litigation*, Civ. No. 10278 (Del. Ch. Nov. 1, 1988), the court refused to enjoin a management–LBO for KDI. The Special Committee solicited bids and received over 40 inquiries although no bids other than management's. A foreign corporation held 49.5 percent of KDI's stock and agreed in the merger agreement to sell its stock to the management group; however, KDI retained the right to terminate the merger agreement (which would, in turn, terminate the 49.5 percent stock purchase agreement), upon acceptance of a more favorable unsolicated offer. The court found that this agreement did not constitute an impermissible lock-up, and in any case higher bids were not foreclosed under the merger agreement.

6. Formica

The Delaware Chancery Court has held that a 30-day market test following execution of a merger agreement with a management-led LBO group was a valid method for testing the board's judgment as to price. *In re Formica Corp. Shareholders Litigation*, [Current] Fed. Sec. L. Rep. (CCH) ¶ 94,362 (Del. Ch. Mar. 22, 1989). The court upheld the decision of the Formica special committee to enter into an $18 per share transaction despite the fact that the board had rejected six months previously a $20 per share proposal. The court upheld the board's business judgment for concluding, after a reasonable investigation, that the prior $20 per share proposal was not a bona fide offer but rather was simply an effort to put Formica "in play."

The market test provided for in the merger agreement required the tender offer to remain open for 30 business days (47 calendar days) as opposed to the minimum 20 days required by SEC rules. During this period, Formica would conduct a market search and actively solicit higher bids. If a higher bid emerged, the management investment group would receive a $5 million break-up fee and up to $5.5 million for its expenses. The court noted that the special committee's financial advisor had contacted more than 125 potential acquirors during the market-test period and, citing *Fort Howard*, found "that the auction procedures being employed here are adequate to 'effectively probe the market for alternative possible transactions.'" ¶ 94,362 at 92,393. The court also noted that the Formica market test was more compelling than *Fort Howard* since here Formica could actively solicit potential acquirors and the market test period was one week longer than in *Fort Howard*.

7. Envirodyne

In *In re Envirodyne Industries, Inc. Shareholders Litigation*, Civ. No. 10702 (Del. Ch. Apr. 20, 1989), the Delaware Chancery Court rejected the shareholders' claim that Envirodyne's directors breached their fiduciary duty by failing to conduct a market test or advertise an auction prior to entering into a merger agreement. The court's decision was dependent on the fact that the directors had made a concerted effort to find a bidder for the company eight months earlier and the absence of any other interested bidders showed that a further search was unnecessary. In addition, the court found that the merger agreement did not foreclose discussions with other interested parties, and even though negotiations were highly publicized, no other bona fide offers emerged.

F. No Duty to Raider

Given that the raider is seeking to arrogate to itself and its stockholders the underlying values of the target, arguably the palpable conflict of interest is not between the target directors and the target stockholders, but rather between the raider and the target stockholders. As noted in *GAF Corp.* v. *Union Carbide Corp.*, 624 F. Supp. 1016 (S.D.N.Y. 1985), the target directors owe no duty to the raider to fashion their response so as to aid the hostile bid. And, as the Delaware Supreme Court held in *Unocal*, the target directors may deal selectively with the raider qua stockholder and deny it the economic benefits of a self-tender if that discrimination fulfills the directors' "supervening" duty to protect the corporation and its other stockholders from a takeover determined to be inadequate or unfair. (*Unocal*, 493 A.2d at 958);[2] see also *In re J.P, Stevens & Co. Shareholders Litigation*, 542 A.2d 770, 781 (Del. Ch. 1988) ("It is the shareholders to whom the board owes a duty of fairness, not to the persons seeking to acquire the Company").

---

[2] Interestingly, *Unocal* pointed to the fact that the Delaware corporate statute required prior director approval before a merger or other fundamental corporate change could be put before the shareholders— a requirement that is inconsistent with the proposition that directorial passivity in the face of a takeover should be the legal norm. (*Unocal*, 493 A.2d at 954 n.8).

G. No Duty to Sell the Company or to Negotiate When the Company is Not for Sale

1. Buckhorn

In *Buckhorn, Inc.*v. *Ropak Corp.*, 656 F. Supp. 209 (S.D. Ohio), *aff'd by sum ord.*, 815 F.2d 76 (6th Cir. 1987), the court, applying Delaware law, held that a board may engage in preliminary negotiations with one party concerning the potential sale of the company or its assets without committing itself to sell the company.

On November 24, 1986, after preliminary discussions concerning a possible business combination between Buckhorn, Inc. and suitor Ropak Corporation broke down, Ropak launched a hostile tender offer for Buckhorn shares. Although the Ropak bid was a cash offer for all shares, due to concerns regarding Ropak's ability to secure financing for the entire acquisition, the Buckhorn directors treated the offer as a two-tiered bid. The Buckhorn board responded by adopting a back-end rights plan and other defensive measures, and authorized management to explore alternatives to the Ropak offer, including a restructuring of the company, a sale of a significant portion of Buckhorn's assets, a business combination with another company or an acquisition of another company. Management and the company's financial advisors explored several such alternatives including the sale of the company's crown jewel.

Ropak sued, claiming, among other things, that the Buckhorn board had decided to sell the company, either in whole or in part, and thus had a fiduciary duty to negotiate with Ropak while pursuing negotiations with other companies. The court concluded that the Buckhorn board had not inevitably committed itself to sell the company, even though it had authorized management to continue negotiations concerning a sale of the company's crown jewel, noting that the directors had simply maintained a policy of evaluating potential sales on a case-by-case basis along with other strategic alternatives. The court concluded that throughout the Ropak tender offer the directors' primary objective had been to maintain Buckhorn as a going concern, and therefore the directors did not breach a fiduciary duty by refusing to negotiate with Ropak.

2. Newmont Mining

In *Ivanhoe Partners* v. *Newmont Mining Corp.*, 535 A.2d 1334 (Del. Supr. 1987), the Delaware Supreme Court held that a street sweep by a 26 percent shareholder to increase its ownership to 49.7 percent, together with a 10-year standstill agreement that limited such shareholder to 49.9 percent of the stock and a maximum of 40 percent of the board, did not constitute an inevitable sale of the company that required the board to become an auctioneer or negotiate with the hostile bidder:

> First, Newmont was never for sale. During the short period in which these events occurred, the Newmont Board held fast to its decision to keep the company independent. Ultimately, this goal was achieved by the standstill agreement and related defensive measures.
>
> Second, there was neither a bidding contest, nor a sale. The only bidder for Newmont was Ivanhoe. Gold Fields was not a bidder, but wished only to protect its already substantial interest in the company. It did so through the street sweep. Thus, the Newmont Board did not "sell" the company to Gold Fields. The latter's purchases were from private sellers. While Gold Fields now owns 49.7 percent of the stock, its representation on the Board is only 40 percent because of the restrictions of the standstill agreement. These facts do not strip the Newmont Board of the presumptions of independence and good faith under the business judgment rule. Even though Newmont's declaration of the dividend facilitated the street sweep, it did not constitute a "sale" of the company by Newmont (*Id.* at 1345). (citations omitted)

Thus, leaving no doubt that reasonableness does not mean ineffectiveness, the Supreme Court sanctioned under *Unocal* strong action to maintain independence: "The Newmont board acted to maintain the company's independence and not merely to preserve its own control. It succeeded in that goal. Thus, the Newmont directors have satisfied their burden under *Unocal* . . ." (*Id.* at 1344). Indeed, indicating that it views *Unocal* as providing greater leeway than did the Chancery Court, the Supreme Court further held that even the original Newmont/Gold Fields standstill—which the Vice Chancellor had thought went "too far"—was proper. The Supreme Court held that because the standstill guaranteed continued independent directors on the Newmont Board, its transfer restrictions and voting provisions were not objectionable.

3. USG Corporation

In *Desert Partners, L.P.* v. *USG Corp.*, 686 F. Supp. 1289 (N.D. Ill. 1988), the U.S. District Court for the Northern District of Illinois, applying Delaware law, upheld the refusal of USG management to negotiate with Desert Partners over the terms of Desert Partners unsolicited, two-tier bid to acquire USG and USG's refusal to redeem its rights plan to allow Desert Partners' offer to proceed. The court used the test laid out in *Newmont Mining* in evaluating the actions of the USG Board of Directors. First, the court determined that the USG Board was reasonable to perceive Desert Partners' actions as threatening to "USG's corporate policy and effectiveness." The court noted that "the USG

Board undertook a careful analysis of USG's performance potential in relation to Desert Partners' offer. Consequently, this court will not interfere with the Board's conclusion that Desert Partners' offer is coercive and inadequate and therefore presented a threat to USG's corporate effectiveness" (*Id.* at 1300).

Second, the court concluded that "the Board fashioned a defensive strategy which was reasonable in relation to the threat" (*Id.*) The court stated that:

> The Board decided that the company's continued independence would result in greater value to shareholders than Desert Partners' $42 offer. Consequently, because it reasonably concluded that Desert Partners' offer was inadequate and coercive, the Board concluded that "USG's shareholders are entitled to and require the continued protection of the Company's Rights plan."
>
> The Board did not breach its fiduciary duty by refusing to negotiate with Desert Partners to remove the coercive and inadequate aspects of the offer. USG decided not to bargain over the terms of the offer because doing so would convey the image to the marketplace "that (1) USG was for sale—when, in fact, it was not; and (2) $42/share was an 'in the ballpark' price—when, in fact, it was not." Once a Board decides to maintain a company's independence, Delaware law does not require a board of directors to put their company on the auction block or assist a potential acquiror to formulate an adequate takeover bid. In this case, the Board has neither put the company up for sale nor entertained a bidding contest. It therefore had no duty to negotiate with Desert Partners over the terms of its offer. *Id.* at 1300 (citations omitted).

Finally, the court found that Desert Partners was unable to "rebut the directors' good faith and reasonable investigation by showing that the board acted in order to entrench themselves" (*Id.*)

4. TW Services

In *TW Services, Inc.* v. *SWT Acquisition Corp.*, [Current] Fed. Sec. L. Rep. (CCH) ¶ 94,334 (Del. Ch. 1989), the court applied the business judgment standard (and not the heightened *Unocal* standard) to the board's decision to refuse to enter into a merger agreement with a bidder who had an outstanding tender offer that was explicitly conditioned upon execution of a satisfactory merger agreement.

5. Universal Foods

In *Amanda Acquisition Corp.* v. *Universal Foods Corp.*, 708 F. Supp. 984 (E.D. Wis. 1989), *aff'd on other grounds*, 1989 U.S. App. LEXIS (7th Cir. May 24, 1989), the court, in applying the *Unocal* standard under Wisconsin law, upheld the decision of the board not to redeem the rights. The court stated:

> [The raider] challenges the board's actions in failing to negotiate with [it], or to do anything other than "just say no" to the offer, such as finding potential purchasers including a "white knight" or pursuing a management LBO or recapitalization. . . . I find no support in the case law that a company must negotiate with a tender offeror. This is especially true where, as here, the offeror has not approached the company prior to commencing the offer and related litigation. I also disagree . . . that *Unocal* and its progeny require a target company, faced with a hostile tender offer, to place itself on the auction block or burden itself with debt in an amount such as would reasonably threaten its continued existence.

708 F. Supp. at 1013.

H. The Limits on Rights Plans and the "Just Say No" Defense

Courts have not required a board to accept a takeover proposal that the board determines is inadequate, but there is an open issue as to the length of time a shareholders rights plan may remain in place to protect shareholders from bids determined by the board to be inadequate. Several courts have forced redemption of outstanding rights when there is an all-cash bid that either is not determined to be inadequate or is only marginally inadequate and the target has taken some affirmative steps to restructure the company in a manner such that the offer could not be consummated. In *TW Services*, Chancellor Allen recognized that because each proposed some form of restructuring, neither *Pillsbury* nor *Interco* were "just say no" cases. In *Universal Foods,* a federal district court in Wisconsin, applying Wisconsin law which looks to Delaware, upheld the use of the "just say no" defense against an inadequate offer, finding that an all-cash tender offer could still be coercive.

It is important to note that all of the decisions applying Delaware law to order redemption of rights have been made by lower courts—the Delaware Supreme Court has not yet addressed the issue. Moreover, the lower courts have not come to terms with the Delaware Supreme Court's decision in *Revlon*, which stated that a rights plan might be used to resist hostile offers, or *Newmont*, where the Delaware Supreme Court recognized the right of a board of directors to choose a course of action that allowed a company to remain independent.

The recent *Polaroid* and *Time* decisions illustrate that the courts are willing to support a board's efforts to pursue strategic long-term business plans in the face of a hostile tender offer when it does so through the exercise of conventional powers, such as causing the corporation to buy assets or to establish an ESOP.

1. Moore McCormack

In *Southdown, Inc.* v. *Moore McCormack Resources, Inc.*, 686 F. Supp. 595 (S.D. Tex. 1988), a Federal District Court in Texas, stating that it was applying Delaware law, enjoined Moore McCormack from pursuing a restructuring plan and ordered it to redeem its poison pill in order to facilitate a hostile cash tender offer for all its shares. Apparently the court was influenced by the value of the restructuring plan being slightly less than the bid, by the absence of any effort by the target to use the pill to encourage white knights, and by the fact that the board did not have an inadequacy opinion. The court implies that a pill may not be used to stop an all cash bid and may only be used against two-tier bids. The court said that in deciding to issue a preliminary injunction it was applying the standard "whether a fully informed, wholly disinterested, reasonably courageous director would dissent from the board's act in any material part." It seems unlikely that other courts will follow this standard in the future.

2. Interco

In *City Capital Associates Limited Partnership* v. *Interco Incorporated*, 551 A.2d 787 (Del. Ch. 1988), the Delaware Chancery Court held that the target of a $74 per share all cash offer could not stand behind its rights plan to thwart the bid and implement a recapitalization that the target and its investment banker valued at $76 per share at least, but that the market and other investment bankers had valued at lower than $74 per share.

The court stated that there are two types of threats to shareholder interests posed by hostile offers: "threats to the voluntariness of the choice offered by the offer, and threats to the substantive, economic interest represented by the stockholding." The court noted that in the *Unocal, Household,* and *Newmont* cases, the Delaware Supreme Court had upheld structural defenses aimed at thwarting structurally coercive bids. The court assumed, however, that a tender offer for all shares was not coercive and that the only threat to shareholder interests from such a bid "relates to the 'fairness' or 'adequacy' of the price." But see Bebchuk, *The Pressure to Tender: An Analysis and a Proposed Remedy*, 12 Del. J. Corp. L. 911, 926 (1987) ("The problem of distorted choice is in no way limited to . . .partial bids and two-tier bids. . . .The pressure to tender is rooted in the consequences that the shareholder might suffer if he does not tender. . . .As long as the expected value of minority shares is lower than the bid price, this fear introduces a pressure to tender.") Operating under the debatable premise that inadequate offers for all shares are not coercive, the court still recognized that structural defenses may be employed to preclude a hostile offer at an inadequate price:

> Even where an offer is noncoercive, it may represent a 'threat' to shareholder interests in the special sense that an active negotiator with power, in effect, to refuse the proposal may be able to extract a higher or otherwise more valuable proposal, or may be able to arrange an alternative transaction or a modified business plan that will present a more valuable option to shareholders. If [a determination that a bid is inadequate] is made in good faith . . . it alone will justify leaving a poison pill in place, even in the setting of a noncoercive offer, for a period while the board exercises its good faith business judgment to take such steps as it deems appropriate to protect and advance shareholder interests. *Interco*, (citations omitted).

The court concluded, however, that at least where the threat from the inadequate offer was "mild" the rights plan could not be utilized to defeat the bid once the board had decided on its preferred course of action.

> [Once] it is apparent that the board does not intend to institute a *Revlon*-style auction, or to negotiate for an increase in the unwanted offer, and that it has taken such time as it required in good faith to arrange an alternative value-maximizing transaction, then, in most instances, the legitimate role of the poison pill in the context of a noncoercive offer will have been fully satisfied. . . .
>
> Perhaps there is a case in which it is appropriate for a board of directors to in effect permanently foreclose their shareholders from accepting a noncoercive offer for their stock by utilization of the recent innovation of 'poison pill' rights. If such a case might exist by reason of some special circumstance, a review of the facts here show this not to be it. The 'threat' here, when viewed with particularity, is far too mild to justify such a step in this instance (*Id.* at 27, 28).

Although the court concluded that Interco could not stand behind its rights plan, it did not enjoin the restructuring. The court stated that raiders had "no right to demand that their chosen target remain in status quo while their offer is formulated, gradually increased and, perhaps, accepted." The court held that Interco could proceed with its proposed auction sale of its Ethan Allen division. The court also held that a proposed pro rata cash dividend would be permissible, but that any restrictive covenants offering anti-takeover protection in the debt securities issued to finance the dividend would have to be reviewed to determine whether the creation of such covenants was a reasonable step in relation to the threat posed by the hostile offer.

Interco's appeal of this decision to the Delaware Supreme Court became moot when the bidder withdrew its tender offer while the Chancery Court's decision was stayed pending appeal.

3. Pillsbury

In *Grand Metropolitan PLC* v. *Pillsbury Co.*, Civ. No. 10323 (Del. Ch. Nov. 7, 1988), the Delaware Court of Chancery endorsed a "just say no" response to a cash tender offer for all shares that the target's independent board, acting in good faith and on a reasonable basis, determined to be inadequate. The court cautioned, however, that "a 'just say no' posture may not justify keeping a Pill in place [indefinitely] when its only purpose is to bar all stockholders from having an opportunity to consider an all-cash, all-shares offer to sell their shares."

Following developments in the five weeks since its initial decision in *Grand Metropolitan PLC* v. *Pillsbury Co.*, 558 A.2d 1049 (Del. Ch. 1988), the Delaware Chancery Court held that a target could not stand behind its rights plan to prevent shareholders from electing to tender into an all-cash offer that the court considered adequate, despite the fact that the target's board of directors, acting upon the advice of its investment bankers, determined the bid to be inadequate. Grand Met had increased its tender offer to $63 per share, while Pillsbury argued that the present minimum value of its long-term plan (which included a sale of the company, in pieces, over a 2.5- to 5-year period) was $68.

The court found no showing that the target's board of directors failed to act in good faith or failed to make a reasonable investigation into the tender offer. It also noted that, pursuant to *Unocal*, the target's proof as to the *Unocal* requirements was "materially enchanced" by the fact that "independent" directors constituted a majority of its board. *Id.* at 91,193. Despite those findings, the court examined the reasonableness of the board's refusal to redeem the rights in relation to the threat posed. It found that the offer presented no threat to corporate policy and effectiveness because Grand Met had committed not to dismember Pillsbury and to keep its headquarters intact in Minneapolis, *see id.* at 91,192, and found that the only threat was to shareholder values. Noting the testimony of a holder of 16.5 percent of the target's stock, the absence of other bidders, the fact that 87 percent of such stock had been tendered, and the optimistic forecasts of the financial alternative put forth by Pillsbury and the assumptions necessary to get there, the court determined that the record contained substantial evidence that the price offered was fair. The court, finding that the "real" threat posed was that of the bid's being withdrawn and the stock price's falling to its pre-offer levels, held that the refusal to redeem the rights was not reasonable in relation to the threat posed. *Id.* at 91,915.

The court concluded that the only propose served by the rights plan under the facts of this case was to preclude shareholders from accepting the tender offer, and the rights must therefore be redeemed. It also enjoined the target from completing a spin-off of the Burger King subsidiary planned as a response to the offer.

4. Prime

The Delaware Chancery Court, in an opinion rendered after the *Pillsbury* decision, denied a bidder's motion to require redemption of a rights plan where the board had rejected the all-cash, all-shares bid but had not proposed or sought to effect any alternative. *MAI Basic Four, Inc.* v. *Prime Computer, Inc.*, [1988–89 Transfer Binder] Fed. Sec. L. Rep. (CCH) ¶ 94,179 (Del. Ch. Dec. 20, 1988). The decision came in the context of the target board's position that it was continuing to review alternatives to maximize shareholder value and that the hostile bid was financially inadequate. The decision distinguished *Interco* and *Pillsbury* from *Prime* on the grounds that those decisions came at the end of takeover struggles in which the target was seeking to use the rights plan to protect a board-approved restructuring. In particular, the court pointed to the facts that the offer had been pending for only a little over one month, the bidder had not increased its offer, the board had not taken any steps to change the company, and the board had accelerated the annual meeting date to a time prior to the expiration of the bidder's financing commitments.

5. TW Services

In *TW Serrvices* v. *SWT Acquisition Corp.*, [Current] Fed. Sec. L. Rep. (CCH) ¶ 94,334 (Del. Ch. 1989), the court distinguished the TW situation from the *Pillsbury* and *Interco* cases on the grounds that in each of those cases the board had elected to pursue a defensive restructuring that "in form and effect was (so far as the corporation itself was concerned) a close approximation of and an alternative to a pending all-cash tender offer for all shares." *Id.* at 92,181. Chancellor Allen (the author of *Interco*) noted that in this situation, the board decided in good faith to "continue managing the enterprise in a long term mode and not to actively consider an extraordinary transaction of any type." *Id.* To the extent that the offer constituted a proposal to negotiate a merger, the board was entitled to consider the long-term functioning of the company, and could reject the offer in the good faith pursuit of legitimate corporate interests.

6. Church's

In *A. Copeland Enterprises* v. *Guste*, 706 F. Supp. 1283 (W.D. Tex. 1989), a federal district court, applying Texas law, held that under the directors' duty of loyalty the rights did not have to be redeemed during an auction where non-stockholder interests had been put aside and the object was to sell the company to the highest bidder. The court noted that, once the auction was completed, any increase in market price achieved by blocking the outstanding tender offer would disappear once the offer was withdrawn. Under the Texas duty of loyalty, the board could not act in its own interest, which would include director entrenchment: "If at the conclusion of the auction, when all of the benefits of the pill are gone, the pill is not redeemed, it will be clear that the Defendant Directors are keeping the pill in place for the sole purpose of entrenching themselves as [target]'s directors." Slip op. at 21. Therefore, the court stated that if the rights plan was not redeemed at the conclusion of the auction, it would issue a preliminary injunction ordering that the rights be redeemed.

7. Universal Foods

Applying Wisconsin law, which it held would follow the Delaware *Unocal* standard, the court in *Amanda Acquisition Corp.* v. *Universal Foods Corp.*, 708 F. Supp. 984 (E.D. Wis. 1989), *aff'd on other grounds*, 1989 U.S. App. LEXIS (7th Cir. May 24, 1989), ruled that a board of directors could under appropriate circumstances "just say no" to a hostile all-cash tender offer—the board need not negotiate with a hostile bidder, and the target corporation is not required to restructure itself or put itself on the auction block. Universal had not proffered any short-term alternative to the offer, which began on December 2, 1988, other than to stick to its highly successful long-term business plan. Moreover, according to the court, the board of directors has the obligation to protect the corporation from bids that it reasonably believes to be serious threats to the corporation and its constituencies, and it may use a Rights Plan to do so. The court stated:

> In the opinion of Universal management, they are not "just saying no," but are instead saying yes—yes to the future prospects of the company. I find no support in the case law that a company must negotiate with a tender offeror. . . .
>
> I also disagree . . . that *Unocal* and its progeny require a target company, faced with a hostile tender offer, to place itself on the auction block or burden itself with debt in an amount such as would reasonably threaten its continued existence. If faced with a tender offer which the board reasonably believes to be a serious threat to the corporation and its shareholders, then the board should take measures to alleviate that threat.

708 F. Supp. at 1013. The district court rejected the assertion that all-cash, all-shares offers are noncoercive, stating "[t]here is an element of coercion or risk even in an all cash, all shares offer." *Id.* The district court stated that it was not concluding that a board "may in all instances preclude shareholder choice on the basis of *its own* perception of the inadequacy of the offer." *Id.* at 92,804 (emphasis added). Rather, "[i]f *no other threat* is posed to the corporation and its shareholders, a board must at some point allow shareholders to choose between the offer and some alternative." *Id.* (emphasis added).

In the Universal situation, however, the district court found that several threats existed providing a reasonable basis for the board's refusal to redeem the Rights: (1) the threat of an offer that Universal's board had reasonably determined to be inadequate (the court also held that the Universal board had not breached its fiduciary duties by not seeking an investment banker's inadequacy opinion); (2) the threat created by misleading disclosures contained in the offering documents and by doubts concerning the offeror's compliance with the margin regulations; (3) the threat to non-tendering shareholders; (4) the threat created by launching the offer at a time when Universal was in the midst of realizing the full potential of a recent restructuring; and (5) the threat to corporate policy and effectiveness, and to the corporation's constituencies, created by the highly leveraged structure of the transaction.

In sum, the *Universal Foods* district court decision is strong support for a board's decision to use a Rights Plan to defeat an inadequate, highly leveraged offer and instead advocate the "just say no" defense.

8. Time

In *Paramount Communications Inc.* v. *Time Incorporated*, C.A. No. 10866 (Del. Ch. July 14, 1989), *aff'd*, No. 279 (Del. Supr. July 24, 1989), the Delaware Chancery Court characterized the *Pillsbury* and *Interco* cases as cases where "management was seeking to 'cram down' a transaction that was the functional equivalent of the very leveraged 'bust up' transaction that management was claiming presented a threat to the corporation." In contrast, the court viewed Time's cash tender offer for Warner (following Paramount's hostile bid for Time) as a transaction that had "its origin and central purpose in *bona fide* strategic planning, and not in questions of corporate control," and upheld the transaction under the *Unocal* standard. The court stressed that the Time-Warner transaction was not the functional equivalent of a sale to Paramount and that Time's tender offer for Warner did not legally preclude (or even necessarily practically preclude) the successful prosecution of a hostile tender offer. The court noted that because of its timing advantage, Time did not need to rely on its rights plan to successfully deter the Paramount bid and stated that a decision by Time not to redeem its rights plan in the same setting might present distinctive considerations.

I. Does a Recapitalization Constitute a Sale?

In *Newmont Mining*, the Delaware Supreme Court held that a substantial cash dividend followed by a street sweep by a 26 percent shareholder to increase its ownership to 49.7 percent of the outstanding stock, together with a 10 year standstill that limited such shareholder to 49.9 percent of the stock and a maximum of 40 percent of the board, did not constitute an inevitable sale of the company. Recent cases have expanded on the issue of when a recapitalization does constitute a sale of the company.

1. American Standard

In *Black & Decker Corp.* v. *American Standard, Inc.*, 682 F. Supp. 772 (D. Del. 1988), the court held that a sale of control amounts to a sale of the company under the *Revlon* doctrine and that a proposed recapitalization in which management and certain employee stock plans would increase their percentage ownership from 7.4 percent of the outstanding voting stock prior to the recapitalization to 55.5 percent of the outstanding voting stock after the recapitalization constituted a sale of control. The court distinguished *Newmont* because, among other things, the standstill in *Newmont* limited Gold Field's to 49.9 percent of the outstanding shares and 40 percent board representation.

2. Gelco

In *Gelco Corp.* v. *Coniston Partners*, 652 F. Supp. 829 (D. Minn. 1986), *aff'd in part and vacated in part*, 811 F.2d 414 (8th Cir. 1987), the U.S. District Court of Minnesota held that Gelco's proposed restructuring transaction involving a self-tender and sale of preferred stock to Merrill Lynch did not constitute an irreversible shift of control of the company. The court rejected Coniston's argument that the exchange offer, combined with the sale to Gelco's investment banker of a block of voting preferred stock, constituted an irreversible shift of control of Gelco, noting that the preferred stock was redeemable by Gelco at any time, that it would in all likelihood be redeemed in the near future, and that the banker was under no obligation to vote the stock in any particular way.

The court rejected the argument that merely because Coniston Partners made an all-cash offer, Gelco's board was required to assume the role of auctioneer. The court, citing *Revlon*, noted however that "to the extent the bidding war continues, with offers steadily increasing in value, the transition from corporate defender to auctioneer becomes inevitable." *Gelco*, 652 F. Supp. at 847.

3. HBJ

In *British Printing & Communication Corp. plc* v. *Harcourt Brace Jovanovich, Inc.*, 664 F. Supp. 1519 (S.D.N.Y. 1987), the court denied a raider's motion for a preliminary injunction against implementation of the recapitalization. The court held that the issuance of stock to First Boston (in connection with certain bridge financing provided by First Boston) and to an ESOP did not foreclose a successful bid for control of HBJ since there was no restriction on how First Boston voted its shares and a "pass-through" provision on the ESOP shares ensured that those shares would be voted by HBJ's employees, not by management. The court found that:

> [N]one of these aspects of the recapitalization plan prohibit an acquisition of HBJ by an entity with sufficient capital and determination. That they might discourage less well-equipped suitors, while providing immediate value to HBJ's shareholders, does not constitute the sort of irreparable harm that the Court ought to protect through injunctive relief. *Id.* at 1529.

The court found that the payment of the special dividend itself did not cause irreparable harm to the bidder as a shareholder, because it merely allowed shareholders to realize the value of their investment more fully.

While the court did not believe the directors were truly self-interested, the court placed the burden of demonstrating the fairness of the recapitalization on HBJ's directors as if the directors were self-interested, because of the importance of the recapitalization to HBJ and its shareholders, and because of the preliminary nature of the court proceeding. The court found that the directors had satisfied their duty of care. There was a substantial record of the board's careful consideration of the proposal. The court said that the board had no obligation to approach the bidder for negotiations since it "was reasonable to conclude from the terms of the [bidder's] proposal and the manner in which it was made and publicized that the [bidder] did not intend to negotiate in good faith toward a purchase of HBJ at a fair price." *Id.* at 1530. The court also concluded that the bidder had failed to demonstrate that the recapitalization was improperly motivated by a desire to entrench the present management of HBJ.

4. Evans

In *Robert M. Bass Group, Inc.* v. *Evans*, 552 A.2d 1227 (Del. Ch. 1988), the court held that a restructuring that would result in management's owning

39 percent of one of two pieces of the restructured company constituted a sale of effective control of the company. The court was clearly influenced by the fact that previous permutations of the restructuring had management owning over 50 percent of the restructured company. "That was the plan up until the last moment . . . [and] [t]he change . . . was one of form, not substance." Finding that the restructuring involved a transfer of effective control, the court suggested that the shareholders were entitled to the control premium that normally accompanies such a transfer, and was critical of the fairness opinions upon which the board relied, because they were expressly grounded on the assumption that control would not pass.

5. *Interco*

In *City Capital Associates Ltd. Partnership* v. *Interco Inc.*, 551 A.2d 787 (Del. Ch. 1988), the court held that implementation of a restructuring, in which voting control was not being consolidated in management hands, did not constitute a sale of the company requiring the company to conduct an auction of the company (Slip op. at 39). The court, however, invoked a broad interpretation of *Unocal* in its scrutiny of the directors' conduct in implementing the recapitalization (see Chapter 22.I.E.1).

See also Chapter 23.V.C.2., discussing cases involving self-tenders.

6. *Time*

In *Paramount Communications Inc.* v. *Time Incorporated*, C.A. No. 10866 (Del. Ch. July 14, 1989), *aff'd*, No. 279 (Del. Supr. July 24, 1989), the court held that a stock for stock merger of Time and Warner (with Warner shareholders receiving 62 percent of the combined company's shares) did not constitute a sale of either Time or Warner within the meaning of *Revlon*. The court stated that

> where . . . the shares of both constituent corporations are widely held, corporate control can be expected to remain unaffected by a stock for stock merger. . . . [A]side from legal technicalities and aside from arrangements thought to enhance the prospect for the ultimate succession of Mr. Nicholas, neither corporation could be said to be acquiring the other. Control of both remained in a large, fluid, changeable and changing market. . . . [E]ffectuation of the merger would not have subjected Time shareholders to the risks and consequences of holders of minority shares. This is a reflection of the fact that no control passed to anyone in the transaction contemplated. The shareholders of Time would have 'suffered' dilution, of course, but they would suffer the same type of dilution upon the public distribution of new stock.

J. The Auction Process and the Business Judgment Rule

1. Structuring the Auction

Courts have recognized that a board's decisions in conducting an auction are protected by the business judgment rule and that the interests to be served by the auction process are those of the shareholders and not those of the bidders.

(a) Federated Department Stores

In *CRTF Corp.* v. *Federated Department Stores, Inc.*, 683 F. Supp. 422 (S.D.N.Y. 1988), the District Court for the Southern District of New York held that a target need not redeem its rights plan once a *Revlon* type auction is underway, but rather that the rights provide "the directors with a shield to fend off coercive offers, and with a gavel to run an auction . . . . We believe . . . that with respect to a poison pill, the teachings of *Revlon* require directors to enhance the bidding in an auction as best they can." *Id.* at 439, 441. The court stated that the teaching of *Revlon* is that the directors must sell the company at the highest attainable price for the stockholders' benefit and that the case "must be read to emphasize the goal of the 'best price available' rather than the means of 'market forces' " used to achieve that price. *Id.* at 441. The court did not reach the issue of selective revocation of the rights at the end of the auction.

(b) West Point-Pepperell

In *In re J.P. Stevens & Co. Shareholders Litigation*, 542 A.2d 770 (Del. Ch. 1988), the court, in approving a $17 million break-up fee and $8 million topping fee representing approximately 2.2 percent of the total deal price, held that the board may favor one bidder over another in an auction in the service of shareholder interests. The court stated that:

> *Revlon* recognizes that once a change in control is concededly in the works, the responsibility of the board is limited to facilitating and achieving the best possible transaction for the shareholders. *Revlon*, however, does not purport to restrict the powers of a disinterested board from entering into agreements of the kind here under attack if, in doing so, the board acts in good faith and with appropriate care. While it is true that once agreements of this kind are in place, they do have the effect of tilting the playing field in favor of the holder of such rights, that fact, alone, does not establish that they necessarily are not in the best interest of shareholders. It is the shareholders to whom the board owes a duty of fairness, not to persons seeking to acquire the Company. To continue with the metaphor, the board may tilt the playing field if, but only if, it is in the shareholders' interest to do so [*Id.* at 781–82 (footnote omitted)].

(c) Becor Western

In *Rosenfield* v. *Becor Western, Inc.*, No. 87-C-0988 (E.D. Wis. Nov. 5, 1987), a Wisconsin federal court affirmed (under Delaware law) that a board of directors' decisions in conducting an auction for its company are protected by the business judgment rule. The Becor board had announced that it would hold an open auction for the company, published the criteria that it would use to assess the offers, and set a deadline for the receipt of bids. After the board agreed in principle to a proposal from management for a leveraged buyout of the company, the bidders submitted additional offers. Those offers were then considered at a second Board meeting. At that meeting, the board determined to accept the management proposal and to terminate the auction until shareholders could vote on that offer.

After this decision was made, one of the bidders submitted another acquisition proposal. The court rejected the claim that the board had to reopen the bidding process, finding that "[t]he directors were justified in deciding to accept what they deemed the most favorable offer available, close the bidding process, and permit Becor shareholders to decide for themselves whether they want to approve the merger." Slip op. at 23.

(d) Fairchild Camera

In *Citron* v. *Fairchild Camera and Instrument Corp.*, [Current] Fed. Sec. L. Rep. (CCH) ¶ 93,915 (Del. Ch. May 19, 1988), the Delaware Chancery Court further clarified the duties of target company directors. In the *Fairchild Camera* case the court declined to find fault with a target board that had opted for an all-cash offer for less than a part-paper offer. Some people had read the *Trans Union* and *Revlon* cases to mean that the directors of a company who had determined to sell the company had an absolute duty to get the highest possible price and that, in this circumstance, there was no room for the exercise of discretion. In the *Fairchild Camera* case the Delaware Chancery Court said that:

> [It] is certainly incorrect to assert that [*Revlon*] recognized a duty on the part of directors when a corporation is "for sale," to get the highest available price. Rather, the duty can only be to try in good faith, in such a setting to get the best available transaction for the shareholders. Directors are not insurers (*Id.* at 90,102–03, n.17).

The *Fairchild Camera* court went further and laid to rest the fear that the *Trans Union* case undercut the business judgment rule, by saying,

> In my opinion, where a disinterested board in good faith considers the significance of the decision called for, the available information of which it and its

> advisors are aware, and the time constraints imposed upon it, and in those circumstances, the board makes a decision that it *is* in the best interests of the corporation to act, that decision itself is entitled to the benefits of the business judgment rule. *Id.* at 90,104.

(e) Wilson Foods

In *Doskocil Cos.* v. *Griggy*, C.A. No. 10095 (Del. Ch. Oct. 7, 1988) (Berger, V.C.), the court held that Wilson Foods, the target, did not have to redeem its rights for a $14.50 per share hostile bid even though it had earlier agreed to redeem the rights to facilitate a $13.50 per share white knight deal, while the Wilson board was continuing to seek higher bids. The court accepted that the directors, despite possible personal desires to avoid a sale to the hostile bidder, were "'confronting' their fiduciary duties" in seeking to maximize shareholder value. The court cautioned, however, that "[i]t is difficult to imagine that Wilson Foods will continue to block the [$14.50] offer if no higher bid is forthcoming." Ultimately, the court was correct.

In summarizing recent decisions addressing the "*Revlon* auction process," the court affirmed that the following principles apply once a decision to sell the company has been made:

> First, a target board is not required to redeem the rights in the face of a noncoercive all cash tender offer. Where the board has determined that the offered price is inadequate and has decided to conduct an auction for the company, it may be appropriate to keep the rights in place in order to allow time for higher bids to be made. *Facet Enterprises, Inc.* v. *Prospect Group, Inc.*, Del. Ch., Civil Action No. 9746, Jacobs, V.C. (April 15, 1988). See also *Nomad Acquisition Corp., et al.* v. *Damon Corp., et al.*, Del. Ch., Civil Action No. 10,173, Hartnett, V.C. (September 16, 1988). Second, even if the offered price is not inadequate, it may be appropriate to maintain the rights in order to promote the continuation of the auction. *CRTF Corp.* v. *Federated Department Stores, Inc.*, 683 F. Supp. 422 (S.D.N.Y. 1988). Third, when conducting a *Revlon* auction, the target board may favor one bidder over another "if in good faith and advisedly it believes shareholder interests would be thereby advanced." *In re Fort Howard Corp. Shareholder Litigation*, Del. Ch., Civil Action No. 9991, Allen, C. (August 8, 1988). It is important to note, however, that these decisions did not involve findings of bad faith by the target board. Slip op. at 49–50.

(f) Holly Farms

In *In re Holly Farms Corporation Shareholders Litigation*, [1988–89 Transfer Binder] Fed. Sec. L. Rep. (CCH) ¶ 94,181 (Del. Ch. Dec. 30, 1988), the Delaware Chancery Court preliminarily enjoined the effectuation of provisions of a merger agreement between Holly Farms and ConAgra granting a lock-up, termination fees, and reimbursement of expenses. The court noted that the Holly Farms board of directors neither informed Tyson Foods of its decision to sell the company nor attempted to obtain an increased bid from Tyson. In addition, Holly Farms' financial advisor testified that he did not consider his role to be that of an "auctioneer," and depositions of three of Holly Farms' directors indicated that the board did not believe that the merger constituted a "sale" of the company and did not conduct an auction. The court concluded that "[e]ven if the Board thought it was acting in good faith, the sale process itself was so substantially flawed that the Board's actions . . . were not likely to have maximized the value of the corporation for its shareholders and, therefore, its actions cannot be viewed as being rational." *Id.* at 91,644. The court thus held that the board did not meet the *Revlon* standard of obtaining the best price for the company. *But see In re RJR Nabisco, Inc. Shareholders Litigation*, [1988–89 Transfer Binder] Fed. Sec. L. Rep. (CCH) ¶ 94,194 (Del. Ch. Jan. 31, 1989) (*Holly Farms* can be read as finding a breach of the duty of good faith, and not creating separate *Revlon* duties outside of the business judgment analysis).

(g) RJR Nabisco

The decision of the Delaware Chancery Court in the shareholder litigation that attacked the RJR Nabisco auction not to enjoin the KKR tender offer provides important guidance with respect to the conduct of an auction. *In re RJR Nabisco, Inc. Shareholders Litigation*, [1988–89 Transfer Binder] Fed. Sec. L. Rep. (CCH) ¶ 94,194 (Del. Ch. Jan. 31, 1989).

The court held that although a Special Committee of independent directors that is in the process of auctioning a company is obligated to be informed of "all material information reasonably available" (¶ 94,194 at 91,713 (quoting *Aronson* v. *Lewis*, 473 A.2d 805, 812 (Del. 1984))), the Special Committee may exercise its business judgment to determine what information is reasonably necessary to best conduct the auction, and it is not required to return to the bidders to seek higher bids even when the current round is close. In *RJR*, the Special Committee of independent directors had returned to the bidders four times to seek higher bids and testimony indicated that at least one of the two competing bidders was "outraged" by the final request. *Id.* at 91,707. The KKR bid, which was accepted by the Special Committee, was valued at $108 to $108.50 per share, and the competing Management Group bid was valued at $108.50 to $109 per share, which, under the market conditions existing at the time, was considered "substantially equivalent." *Id.* at 91,708.

The court declined to apply a "super" *Revlon* rule, holding that if a board of directors satisfies its duty of care and duty of loyalty obligations under the business judgment rule, there is no further obligation to ensure a "fair auction." Citing *Fairchild*, the court stated that the board's duty is not to get the best price but to strive in good faith to get the best available transaction. *Id.* at 91,715. "Effectiveness cannot mean perfection." *Id.* In so holding, the court acknowledged that its decision might be inconsistent with *Holly Farms*, where the court concluded that even if a board thinks it is acting in good faith, the board can be criticized if the court believes the process was such that it was not likely to maximize value. Here, the court states: "Assuming [the board] does exercise a business judgment, in good faith and advisedly, concerning the management of the auction process, it has, in my opinion, satisfied its duty."

A board will breach its duty of loyalty if it selects a bid for a reason unrelated to pursuit of the corporation's best interests. Here, the court concluded that the Special Committee acted in good faith throughout the process. The Special Committee concluded in good faith with the help of its financial advisers that the management bid was not superior and that the bids were substantially equivalent; it acted properly in so concluding. Further, since KKR had placed a 30-minute fuse on its bid, the Special Committee acted properly in not seeking to break the tie, which would have meant risking the loss of the KKR deal and leaving RJR with the management deal which, while of substantially equivalent value, had some less appealing terms. It was appropriate to select the KKR deal:

> Nor can the decision to prefer KKR's bid with $3 less cash and with less nominal or face value per share be seen as so beyond the bounds of reasonable judgment as to raise an inference of bad faith in my opinion. The larger equity stub, the different future business plans of the two bidders, and the superior reset provision of KKR's proposed converting debentures, all provide a basis to support the notion that the choice was a rational one. That KKR as an acquiror presented antitrust questions or offered a somewhat lower proportion of cash simply presents an occasion for the exercise of judgment; the judgment reached does not, as indicated, appear so far afield as to raise a question of the motivation of the board.

Id. at 91,713.

The Special Committee did not breach its duty of care in deciding not to attempt to break the tie. The Committee was obligated to obtain all information reasonably available to it, but whether it has sufficient information is itself a business judgment "of a type that courts are institutionally poorly equipped to make." The *RJR* court concluded that is was appropriate for the Special

Committee to conclude not to ask the bidders if they would increase their bids, particularly since KKR had issued its ultimatum and would have received a $0.20 per share expense reimbursement if it walked. The decision was a risk/reward decision that the court found the Special Committee addressed with due care:

> It is the case that that decision was made under extreme time pressure. But where an arm's-length negotiating adversary imposes time limits, a board is forced to contend with that circumstance. If it exercises informed judgment in the circumstances, considers the risks posed by the deadline imposed, and concludes that it is prudent to act and acts with care, it has satisfied its duty.

Id. at 91,714. In addition, the court did not criticize the Special Committee's agreeing to KKR's condition of an expense reimbursement provision and a topping fee. *Id.* at 91,706 n.7.

The *RJR* court justifies judicial examination of the wisdom of a board's decision as a review of whether the board has acted in bad faith. The court accepts that it is not appropriate for a court to act as a "super-director" and to review the substance of a business judgment decision for "fairness," "reasonableness," or "rationality" where the decision is made in good faith, with appropriate care and by "truly disinterested directors." *Id.* at 91,710 n.13. Although this is an interesting intellectual exercise, it nonetheless involves the courts in a second-guessing process, whether under the rubric of good faith, due investigation, or otherwise. It was important to the court's decision that the CEO had no role in the selection of the members of the Special Committee or its financial advisers and legal counsel, and that management was in no way involved in the auction process.

(h) Macmillan

The Delaware Supreme Court's opinion in the *Mills Acquisition Co.* v. *Macmillan, Inc.*, [Current] Fed. Sec. L. Rep. (CCH) ¶ 94, 401 (Del. Supr. May 3, 1989), where the Court found that management had improperly tipped one of the bidders during the auction, embraces the general propositions that there is no standard formula to conduct an auction, and that disparate treatment of bidders may be appropriate to advance the purpose of seeking the highest price. The Court applied the entire fairness standard after it found that "the board's own lack of oversight in structuring and directing the auction afforded management the opportunity to indulge in the misconduct which occurred." *Id.* at 92,595. However, the opinion confirms the extreme skepticism of the Delaware courts to lock-ups and no-shop clauses. While the opinion reaffirms that lock-ups and no-shops are not *per se* illegal, even though they often foreclose further bidding, it also cautions that such agreements will be upheld only if they are found to confer a significant benefit upon the stockholders. The opinion holds that the asset lock-ups must be justified by a material price increase and the independent directors must attempt to negotiate alternative bids before agreeing to the lock-up.

Broadening the factors that directors may consider in addressing competitive bids, the Court held:

> In assessing the bid and the bidder's responsibility, a board may consider, among various proper factors, the adequacy and terms of the offer; its fairness and feasibility; the proposed or actual financing for the offer, and the consequences of that financing; questions of illegality; the impact of both the bid and the potential acquisition on other constituencies, provided that it bears some reasonable relationship to general shareholder interests; the risk of nonconsummation; the basic stockholder interests at stake; the bidder's identity, prior background and other business venture experiences; and the bidder's business plans for the corporation and their effects on stockholder interests.

Id. at 92,597 n.29.

The Supreme Court's opinion also makes a number of more specific points about an auction process in the context of a potential management buyout. The opinion criticizes having management select the financial and legal advisors to the Special Committee of independent directors. Similarly, the decision criticizes allowing management access to information about the ongoing bidding and condemns the tipping by management of one side's bid to the other bidder.

2. Duty to Provide Confidential Information to Hostile Bidder in Auction

(a) Burlington Industries

In *Samjens Partners I* v. *Burlington Industries, Inc.*, 663 F. Supp. 614, 625 (S.D.N.Y. 1987), the court rejected a raider's claim that the target had acted improperly in denying the raider confidential information once an auction for the company had commenced. The court held that the target was entitled to request that the raider, like all other interested bidders, sign a confidentiality agreement. The court concluded that the board did not deal selectively with the raider. Instead, the raider dealt selectively with the board.

(b) West Point-Pepperell

In *In re J.P. Stevens & Co. Shareholders Litigation*, 542 A.2d 770, 784 (Del. Ch. 1988), the court held that where nonpublic information was offered to all bidders on the same terms (i.e., conditional upon their signing a confidentiality agreement containing a standstill), a competing bidder had no equitable grounds to complain that it was denied fair access to the information.

(c) Business Strategy Privilege

Bidders may try to obtain information concerning a target's plans or prospects through discovery in connection with litigation challenging the target's refusal to negotiate or redeem its rights. In *Grand Metropolitan PLC* v. *Pillsbury Co.*, [1988–89 Transfer Binder] Fed. Sec. L. Rep. (CCH) ¶ 94,096 (Del. Ch. Nov. 21, 1988), the court ruled that Grand Met and the Pillsbury shareholders were entitled to test the validity of Pillsbury's decision to reject Grand Met's bid in favor of its planned restructuring and thus to obtain documents relevant to that decision. Chancellor Allen required Pillsbury to disclose analyses of LBO and recapitalization alternatives that were conducted prior to the Board's adoption of the restructuring plan and the names of potential white knights that had been contacted but who no longer had any active interest. Chancellor Allen ruled, however, that Delaware recognizes a "white knight" or "business strategy" qualified immunity to discovery and allowed Pillsbury not to disclose the identity of potential white knights with whom discussions were still ongoing.

III. THE BROADER POLICY ISSUES RELATING TO TAKEOVER ACTIVITY

The courts have expressly eschewed taking sides in the public debate over whether takeovers are good or bad in terms of national policy and whether the "leveraging of corporate America" is a desideratum. In *Norlin Corp.* v. *Rooney, Pace, Inc.*, 744 F.2d 255, 269 (2d Cir. 1984), the Second Circuit took care to note that while it had ruled against director action to effectively give voting control to themselves in response to an undesired stock purchase program, its holding should not be read as reflective of any general views on the takeover debate:

> Although we are cognizant that takeover fights, potentially involving billions of dollars, profoundly affect our society and economy, it is not for us [the courts] to make the policy choices that will determine whether this style of corporate warfare will escalate or diminish. Our holding here is not intended to reflect a more general view of the contests being played out on this and other corporate battlefields.

The Delaware Supreme Court in *Polk* v. *Good*, 507 A.2d 531 (Del. Supr. 1986), similarly declined to overturn long-standing doctrine on stock repurchases or greenmail in light of the public policy debate on that particular defensive response.

In the *CTS* opinion, the Supreme Court of the United States, upholding the constitutionality of the Indiana Control Share Acquisitions Act, declined to second guess the judgments of the Indiana Legislature regarding the utility of the Indiana Act, noting that "the Constitution does not require the States to subscribe to any particular economic theory" (107 S. Ct. at 1651). The Court noted, however, that "the potentially coercive aspects of tender offers have been recognized by the Securities and Exchange Commission . . .and by a number of scholarly commentators," (*id.*), and that "the divergent views in the literature—and even now being debated in Congress—reflect the reality that the type and utility of tender offers vary widely." *Id.* n.13.

IV. "THE LAW OF THE MARKETPLACE"

In dealing with target requests for judicial relief against a raider's tactics, the courts have similarly been extremely reluctant to intervene and have expressed the view that the outcome of takeover battles should be determined by the marketplace, not the courts. See *Hanson Trust PLC* v. *SCM Corp.*, 774 F.2d 47, 60 (2d Cir. 1985) (preliminary injunctive relief to target "must be used with great care, lest the forces of the free marketplace, which in the end should determine the merits of takeover disputes, are nullified."); *Warnaco, Inc.* v. *Galef*, Civ. No. B-86-146 (PCD) slip op. at 20 (D. Conn. Apr. 3, 1986) ("The law of the marketplace should thus prevail."), *aff'd by sum. order*, 800 F.2d 1129 (2d Cir. 1986).

V. PROGNOSIS

The common law of business judgment in the *Unocal* generation continues to grind slowly. The challenge of that process continues—for counseling, in the face of the inevitably shifting directions that come with common law developments; and for the courts, in exercising their increased power of review under *Unocal* without second guessing the fundamental business decisions that directors faced with takeovers are obliged to make.

CHAPTER 23

TAKEOVER AND DEFENSE LAW III: TAKEOVER DEFENSE

Martin Lipton
James H. Fogelson
Andrew R. Brownstein
Craig M. Wasserman
Wachtell, Lipton, Rosen & Katz

I. CHARTER AND BYLAW PROVISIONS

Most of the recently adopted charter and bylaw provisions are not "shark repellants" in the classic sense, since they are not designed to prevent takeovers. These amendments do, however, protect shareholders from some of the abusive takeover tactics. Moreover, obtaining control of the target's board prior to crossing the applicable ownership threshold will empower a bidder to effect the redemption of a target's shareholder rights plan or approval of his proposed transaction pursuant to a New York or Delaware type business combination statute. Commonplace charter provisions, such as those described below, are not takeover deterrents in the strictest sense, but they can give the target board of directors leverage in dealing with these threats.

 This chapter is current through November 18, 1988 (with modifications made through July 1989). David A. Katz and David M. Silk, associates of the firm, and many other members of Wachtell, Lipton, Rosen & Katz assisted in the preparation.

A. Fair Price and Staggered Board Provisions

Many companies have sought shareholder approval of charter amendments designed to deter two-tier, front-end loaded takeovers and bust-up proxy fights. "Fair price" provisions mandate that shareholders receive equivalent consideration at both ends of a two-tier bid, thus deterring coercive two-tier, front-end loaded tender offers. Many companies that adopt fair price provisions have also adopted "staggered boards."

"Staggered board" provisions establish continuity for the board of directors by staggering the directors' terms and by providing for a longer term of service (usually 3 years), so that an acquiror who seizes control must wait for more than one year before being able to effectuate its plans. These provisions, which will prevent a bidder from acquiring control in one election, have proven effective against creeping acquisitions, partial bids and bust-up proposals not accompanied by an actual bid, but they will not, as a practical matter, deter an all-cash bid for all shares. Under Delaware law, if a corporation has a staggered board, directors may only be removed for cause unless the charter provides otherwise (But see *Roven* v. *Cotter*, this chapter 23.I.A.3).

1. Result of Voting and Effects on Stock Prices

A November 1988 survey by the Investor Responsibility Research Center showed that institutional opposition to staggered board and fair price provisions is significant and that, as a result, fewer companies have been proposing such provisions in recent years. Those companies who have submitted such proposals to a shareholder vote, however, have with a few exceptions received shareholder approval.

Little evidence has been offered on the effects of fair price, staggered board, and other anti-takeover amendments on either shareholders or the corporations that have adopted them. Four studies examining the effects of such amendments on the stock prices of companies adopting them have reached conflicting conclusions.

2. Effects on Takeover Fights

Staggered board and fair price charter provisions are not designed to be, and are not, effective against an any-and-all tender offer. However, staggered board charter provisions, as a final bargaining chip, have provided boards of directors with a degree of leverage to negotiate protections for shareholders, employees, and other corporate constituencies, even after a raider has acquired a majority of the company's stock. For example, following Harold Simmons' acquisition of a majority of NL Industries stock, NL's board of directors was able to negotiate continued board representation of the minority shareholders as well as protections against self-dealing and for the holders of the preferred stock redeemable for shares of NL Chemicals before handing over control to Simmons. This agreement provided that, prior to the 1991 annual meeting of NL shareholders, certain transactions with the Simmons group, including tender and exchange offers, mergers, and consolidations, must be approved by directors who are not designees or affiliates of Simmons and determined by an independent investment banker to be fair to NL's minority shareholders from a financial point of view. The agreement also stated that, subject to NL's right to redeem the preferred stock for cash and unless a buyer for NL Chemicals could be found prior to November 1, 1986, the preferred stock would be redeemed for shares of Common Stock of NL Chemicals as soon as it was determined by NL that such redemption is not likely to result in a significant tax liability to NL or NL Chemicals. Similarly, Crown Zellerbach's board was able to negotiate protections against self-dealing and a commitment to undertake steps to enhance the financial interests of Crown Zellerbach's minority shareholders before handing over control to Sir James Goldsmith.

3. Removal of Directors

In a recent case interpreting classified board provisions, *Roven* v. *Cotter*, 547 A.2d G03 (Del. Ch. 1988), the Delaware Chancery Court held that shareholders of a Delaware corporation may amend the corporation's certificate of incorporation to eliminate classified board provisions and thereafter remove directors without cause. The court rejected the argument that directors on a classified board have a vested right to serve their full term. In light of *Roven* v. *Cotter*, Delaware corporations should make sure that the classified board and removal provisions in their charters are protected by supermajority amendment provisions.

4. Contingent Cumulative Voting Provisions

An innovation in 1985 was the proposal to authorize a staggered board in combination with a charter amendment providing for cumulative voting in the event a person or group acquires a significant percentage (e.g., 35 percent) of the outstanding common stock. Diamond Shamrock, Martin Marietta, and Burlington Industries, Inc., among others, adopted such provisions. Cumulative voting, when combined with a staggered board, can further delay a majority shareholder or proxy contestant from gaining control of the board of directors, even if the holder or contestant controls a majority of the outstanding shares. Contingent cumulative voting provides an advantage over ordinary cumulative voting to the extent that contingent cumulative voting does not allow a holder of only 5 percent or 10 percent of the outstanding shares to threaten to, or actually, elect a director to the board.

B. Antigreenmail Provisions

Following the lead of International Minerals & Chemicals and Perkin-Elmer in the fourth quarter of 1984, a number of companies, including Mobil Oil Corporation, adopted provisions designed to restrict the payment of greenmail. Antigreenmail amendments are most effective when combined with charter provisions designed to protect shareholders against two-tier or bust-up bids. For example, antigreenmail amendments have been proposed in conjunction with fair price charter provisions. See Chapter 21.VI.C for a discussion of the greenmail excise tax.

C. Elimination of Action by Consent, Limitation of Shareholder Ability to Call a Special Meeting

These provisions will ensure that formal proxy contests only occur at an annual meeting, unless the target board otherwise agrees. While a bidder can still attempt to seek a shareholder referendum outside the proxy process, solicitations on this basis are rare.

1. Consent Bylaws

In *Datapoint Corp.* v. *Plaza Securities Co.*, 496 A.2d 1031 (Del. Supr. 1985), the Delaware Supreme Court struck down a bylaw adopted by the board to regulate shareholder action by written consent as arbitrary and unreasonable. The Chancery Court opinion in that case casts doubt on whether a board of directors could adopt any bylaw to regulate action by written consent.

However, in *Empire of Carolina, Inc.* v. *Deltona Corp.*, 514 A.2d 1091 (Del. Supr. 1985), the Delaware Supreme Court held that pursuant to Section 213(a) of the Delaware General Corporation Law, the board of directors, in the exercise of its business judgment, may fix the record date for any action by written consent unless a shareholder (1) executes the first written shareholder consent to the proposed action and (2) delivers the consent and communicates the substance of the action to the company. The court held that this power was express in Section 212(a) and thus was unaffected by *Datapoint*, which involved a board's authority to impose restrictions on the written consent process beyond those expressly provided by the DGCL.

Sections 213 and 228 of the DGCL were amended in 1987. The amendments authorize the board of directors to establish a record date for determining shareholders entitled to act by written consent, which date shall not be more than ten days from the date of such board action. If no record date has been fixed by the board of directors, the record date shall be the first date on which a signed written consent is delivered to the corporation. The amendments also clarify the procedures by which written consents must be delivered to the corporation and provide that no written consent shall be effective unless and until consents sufficient to take such action are delivered to the corporation within 60 days of the date of the earliest consent so delivered.

In *Allen* v. *Prime Computer, Inc.*, 540 A.2d 417 (Del. Supr. 1988), a case decided after the 1987 amendments to Sections 213 and 228, the Delaware Supreme Court again struck down a bylaw adopted by the target of a hostile tender offer that regulated shareholder action by written consent. Prime Computer had launched a tender offer for any or all of the shares of Computervision Corporation. In order to effect a redemption of Computervision's poison pill, Prime announced that it intended to solicit stockholder consents to install its nominees on Computervision's board. In response, Computervision adopted a bylaw that provided that any action effected by written consent pursuant to Section 228 could not take effect for a period of at least 20 days, and made such actions subject to a fairly elaborate procedure of inspection and challenge.

Prime sued for a preliminary injunction against the effectiveness of Computervision's bylaw. In ruling that such an injunction was appropriate, the Delaware Supreme Court reaffirmed *Datapoint*'s position holding that "a bylaw which imposed 'minimal essential provisions for ministerial review of the validity of the action taken by shareholder consent' would serve the purposes of § 228." *Id.*at 420 (quoting *Datapoint*). However, the Court went on to conclude that Computervision's bylaw "did more than 'defer consummation of shareholder action until a ministerial review of the validity of the consents' has occurred." *Id.*(quoting *Datapoint*). Instead, the Court concluded that the minimum twenty-day delay provision in Computervision's bylaw was impermissibly long. The Court announced a three-part test for determining the reasonableness of bylaws "which purport to establish ministerial review of the validity of consents" (*id.*):

> First, a court must determine the purpose to be served. A bylaw whose real purpose is delay of shareholder action is *per se* unreasonable. Second, the court should consider the impact of the bylaw upon the effective exercise of the power conferred under § 228. Finally, the bylaw should contain only the minimal requisites for a reliable and prompt ministerial review to ensure the

> orderly function of corporate democracy. Such ministerial review must not be unduly elaborate, should contain reasonable time periods only necessary to the circumstances, and should be one which, when administered in good faith, is reasonable and balanced. *Id.*.

Also in the context of a consent solicitation, the Delaware Court of Chancery held, in *Blasius Industries, Inc.* v. *Atlas Corp.*, [Current] Fed. Sec. L. Rep. (CCH) ¶ 93,965 (Del. Ch. July 25, 1988), that the broad reach of the business judgment rule does not extend to board action designed for the primary purpose of interfering with the effectiveness of a stockholder vote. Blasius, which owned 9 percent of Atlas, commenced a consent solicitation that requested Atlas' board to develop and implement Blasius' restructuring proposal, sought to amend the bylaws to expand the seven-member board to 15 (the maximum number permitted under the Atlas charter), and to elect Blasius' eight nominees to fill the vacancies so created. The board responded by increasing its size by two and filling the vacancies with its own nominees, thus precluding Blasius, were it to be successful in its consent solicitation, from obtaining a majority of the board. Atlas' charter created staggered terms for directors.

The court concluded that, even though the board had acted in good faith in order to thwart implementation of a recapitalization plan that it reasonably believed would adversely affect the company, its action was not entitled to the "formidable" protections of the business judgment rule. "The shareholder franchise," said the court, "is the ideological underpinning upon which the legitimacy of directorial power rests." In Chancellor Allen's view, the question raised was not one of the corporation's power over its property, or one concerning its right to governance of the corporation. "That," he said, "will not be left to the [board's] business judgment." The court did not go so far as to adopt a *per se* rule invalidating, in equity, every board action taken for the sole or primary purpose of thwarting a shareholder vote, observing that some set of facts might justify such extreme action. It did hold, however, that a board bears a heavy burden of demonstrating a compelling justification for such action.

In *Nomad Acquisition Corp.* v. *Damon Corp.*, [Current] Fed. Sec. L. Rep. (CCH) ¶ 94,040 (Del. Ch. Sept. 16, 1988) (revised Sept. 20, 1988), the Delaware Court of Chancery upheld two bylaw amendments that were adopted at a board meeting held shortly after the accumulation of a 10 percent stake in Damon by a shareholder group. One of the bylaws regulated the setting of a record date for shareholder action by written consent. This bylaw required both that the board act, within ten days of receiving a written request, to set a record date, and that the record date be set within ten days of the board's response to the written request. The court found this bylaw was a "reasonable mechanism" to aid the corporation in its ministerial review of consents without unreasonably delaying the effectiveness of any consents.

2. Notice of Business and Nominations

Bylaw provisions requiring a shareholder to provide advance notice of business proposed to be brought before, and of nominations of directors to be made at, shareholder meetings have become common. Such provisions generally set a date by which a shareholder must advise the corporation of his or her intent to seek to take action at a meeting, and stipulate the contents of the notice, which can include beneficial and record ownership information. Failure to deliver proper notice in a timely fashion usually results in denial to the shareholder of the right to propose such action at the meeting. These provisions help target boards regulate shareholder meetings, but are not intended to be, and are not, takeover deterrents. *See also Nomad Acquisition Corp.* v. *Damon Corp.*, [1988–89 Transfer Binder] Fed. Sec. L. Rep. (CCH ¶ 94,040 (Del. Ch. Sept. 16, 1988) (revised Sept. 20, 1988) (upholding bylaw that required a shareholder to give at least 60 days' notice prior to nominating any person for election to the board of directors). *But see International Banknote Co.* v. *Muller*, [Current] Fed. Sec. L. Rep. (CCH) ¶ 94,418 (S.D.N.Y. May 2, 1989) (striking down nomination bylaw adopted after announcement of intention to commence proxy fight, because board violated duties of care and loyalty).

D. Precatory Referendums

If unable to obtain control of the target's board because of, for example, a staggered board provision, a bidder may seek to commence a proxy solicitation to attempt to influence the target's board to dismantle a defense or approve a transaction. Although these precatory resolutions are nonbinding, as a practical matter they can have a powerful effect on a target board. (It should be noted that such a shareholder referendum does not absolve the board from exercising its fiduciary duties.) The provisions described in the preceding section are as useful in limiting exposure to precatory resolutions as to election contests.

E. Dual Class Capitalization

1. One Share/One Vote

In the past, companies have adopted dual class capitalization, scaled voting provisions, or duration of ownership provisions in order to make it more difficult for an outside stockholder or group to exercise a controlling vote on matters to be approved by the stockholders of a corporation. In July 1988, however, the SEC adopted Rule 19c-4, designed to prohibit the adoption of such measures.

Rule 19c-4 prohibits national securities exchanges and associations from listing or authorizing for quotation the common stock or other equity security of a domestic company that "issues any class of security, or takes other corporate action, with the effect of nullifying, restricting, or disparately reducing the per share voting rights of holders of an outstanding class or classes of common stock." The rule specifically prohibits scaled voting provisions; duration of ownership provisions, the issuance of stock having greater voting rights per share than those of any outstanding class of common stock, and exchange offers in which the securities issued have voting rights greater or lesser than the per share voting rights of any outstanding class of common stock.

The rule specifically permits corporate action taken in compliance with state takeover statutes, such as the Indiana statute, that condition voting rights of the holders of a specified threshold percentage of the corporation's voting stock on the approval of the corporation's independent shareholders, and permits the issuance of securities, regardless of voting rights or restrictions, in an initial public offering. In addition, the rule excludes from its coverage the issuance of preferred stock or debt securities having voting rights that only become effective as a result of specified events, not relating to an acquisition of common stock of the corporation, which reasonably can be expected to jeopardize the issuer's financial ability to meet its payment obligations. The rule may require that the voting rights of preferred stock issued to a "White Squire" be proportionate to the equity interest in the corporation represented by the preferred (see Chapter 23.VI.B). Dual class voting schemes in effect as of July 7, 1988, are grandfathered by the rule. Therefore, dual class capitalization will generally be an effective measure to retain control only for corporations having such stock issued before July 7, 1988, or issuing such stock after that date in an initial public offering.

2. Examples of Companies That Have Instituted Dual Class Capitalization

Most of the companies that have adopted dual class capitalization have had large blocks of stock held by members of a single family or by other sympathetic shareholders. General Cinema Corp., The Coastal Corp., Hershey Foods Corp., Dow Jones, Inc., Chris-Craft Industries, Inc., Kaufman and Broad, Inc., Tyson Foods, United Artists Communications, Wm. Wrigley Jr. Co. and Rockwell International, among others, have authorized an additional class of high vote common stock. The high vote common stock is generally designed to be retained by management or major shareholders (such as founding families or charitable trusts). Dual class capitalization is particularly beneficial for significant shareholders who want the flexibility to sell some of their common equity in an initial public offering while still maintaining control.

The Office of the SEC Chief Economist initially issued a study in June 1987 of 63 companies that had adopted dual class capitalizations, which concluded that there was no statistically significant decline in the stock market prices of such companies upon their announcement. One month later, the same office issued an updated study that added 34 companies to the sample and found "significant and negative" abnormal stock declines at the time of announcement.

A variation on the dual class capitalization structure provides that a shareholder will have normal voting rights for each share owned up to a specified percentage (e.g., 10 percent). Each share owned above that percentage will only have a fractional vote per share (e.g., 1/100 of a vote) or no vote. When combined with fair price and/or supermajority provisions, a scaled voting provision is a substantial deterrent to partial or two-tier, front-end loaded offers. Under scaled voting, a stockholder proposal requires the broad-based support of the stockholders in order to be adopted, and no single stockholder or group can have a substantially disproportionate influence over the outcome of any stockholder vote.

Duration of ownership provisions provide that each share of common stock will have a stated number of votes (e.g., 5 votes). If beneficial ownership changes, the share will carry only one vote until it has been held by the same beneficial owner for a specified number of years (e.g., 3 years). Like the dual class capitalization structure, this type of provision allows a family to retain control of the company while permitting sales of stock when necessary.

3. Challenges to Dual Class Capitalizations

In *Barris Industries, Inc.* v. *Bryan*, 686 F. Supp. 125 (E.D. Va. 1988), the court rejected Burt Sugarman's attempt to circumvent Media General's dual class capitalization. Media General's charter provides that both classes of the company's stock will vote together on proposals involving the acquisition of stock or assets of any other company *if* any holder of more than 10 percent of the voting securities of Media General has an interest in the company to be acquired. This provision was included in Media General's charter originally because of a listing requirement of the American Stock Exchange. In his quest for control of Media General, Sugarman, who had acquired more than

10 percent of the company's stock, proposed that Media General merge with a shell company he controlled and that Media General would *survive* that merger. Media General shareholders would receive cash in the merger. Thus, although Media General could be said to "acquire" the shell company, in reality the shell company's owner would gain control of Media General. Sugarman argued, however, that his proposal that Media General "acquire" a company he owned required all Media General shareholders to vote on his proposal without regard to the supervoting powers of the company's class B stock. The court rejected Sugarman's literalistic characterization of the transaction he proposed as being an acquisition by Media General and concluded that "under this version of a reverse triangular merger, no one can fairly say that Media General is acquiring anything in the transaction. Instead, 'Media General shareholders acquire cash, Sugarman acquires Media General, and Media General acquires nothing.'" *Id.* at 130. For good measure, the court pointed out that Sugarman's "merger proposal is not the type of deal that the equal voting provision was designed or intended to safeguard against." *Id.* at 131.

In the Griffin-Trump fight for Resorts International, Griffin used a novel technique to force Trump to the bargaining table. Although Trump had clear voting control of Resorts due to his ownership of the supervoting Class A shares, Griffin suggested that the board of directors of Resorts sell to him sufficient authorized but unissued shares of the Class A stock to dilute Trump below the control level, so that he could then offer a premium price to the holders of the Class B shares. The theory that the board had an obligation under *Revlon* to take such a step was never tested in court, and practitioners doubted whether it would have proven viable. However, Bergen Brunswig Corporation, another company with two classes of common stock, issued a dividend of all of its unissued supervoting stock to avoid a potential problem in a future situation.

In *Providence & Worcester Co.* v. *Baker*, 378 A.2d 121 (Del. Supr. 1977), the Supreme Court of Delaware upheld a scaled voting provision in Providence and Worcester's charter under which each stockholder was entitled to one vote for every share of common stock held not exceeding 50 shares, one vote for every 20 shares more than 50, and in no event could a stockholder vote more than one fourth of the whole number of shares issued and outstanding. The Court construed the scaled voting restriction as a limitation upon the voting rights of the stockholder and not as a variation in the voting powers of the stock *per se*. As such, the Court concluded that the provision was valid under Delaware. See also *Dynamics Corp. of America* v. *CTS Corp.*, 805 F.2d 705 (7th Cir. 1986) (citing *Providence & Worcester* for the proposition that Delaware law distinguishes between "discrimination among shares" and "discrimination among shareholders," allowing corporations to engage in the latter form of discrimination).

In *City Federal Savings & Loan Ass'n* v. *Mann*, C.A. No. 84-4010 (D.N.J. Aug. 2, 1985), the court refused to enjoin preliminarily the issuance of a preferred stock dividend that would have provided scaled voting rights.

In *Williams* v. *Geier*, C.A. No. 8456 (Del. Ch. May 20, 1987), the Delaware Chancery Court dismissed a claim that a charter amendment by Cincinnati Milacron, which granted 10 votes per share to holders prior to the charter amendment and those who thereafter acquire shares and hold them for at least three years, was invalid under Delaware law, on the basis of *Providence & Worcester Co.* v. *Baker*, because the amendment did not provide differing voting rights for the stock *per se* but affected the personal right of stockholders to exercise voting power.

II. SHARE PURCHASE RIGHTS PLANS

The device most frequently associated with the term "poison pill" is the Share Purchase Rights Plan. As of July 1989, over 1,000 companies had adopted Share Purchase Rights Plans, including 41 percent of the *Business Week* 1000 companies, 46 percent of the *Fortune* 500 companies, and 54 percent of the *Fortune* 200 companies.

The key provisions of the Share Purchase Rights Plan are the flip-over provision coupled with the ability of the board of directors to redeem the rights issued pursuant to the Rights Plan for a nominal amount prior to a 20 percent acquisition. These provisions are designed to encourage an acquiror to negotiate with the board of directors of the target company rather than proceeding unilaterally with a takeover, and to dissuade the acquiror from employing abusive takeover tactics. If the acquiror purchases in excess of a specified percentage of the target's stock (e.g., 20 percent), and then acquires the remaining target common stock in a business combination transaction, the flip-over provision entitles the holder of a share purchase right to purchase the *acquiror's* common stock at half price. Because the flip-over provision does not operate unless the acquiror attempts to acquire all of the target company's common stock by merger or similar transaction, flip-over plans do not prevent acquisitions of a controlling, but less than 100 percent, interest in a company. Normally, however, an acquiror desires to acquire all of the target's common stock in order to gain unrestricted access to the target's earnings, cash flow, and assets to service the acquisition debt.

In addition, an increasing percentage of Rights Plans permit the holders of rights, other than the acquiror, to purchase shares of the target company at half price if the acquiror either (1) purchases more than some specified percentage (generally 20–50 percent) of the stock of the target or (2) purchases more than some specified percentage of the stock of the target and then engages in certain "self-dealing" transactions. A variation of the status "flip-in" provision permits the target's board of directors to reduce the 30 percent ownership trigger to 15 percent, or from 20 percent to 10 percent. To the extent that a "flip-in" provision based merely on ownership of a stated percentage of stock adversely affects an acquiror who has purchased his shares through noncoercive transactions, the provision raises legal questions not addressed by the *Household* court, and most of the cases in which Rights Plans were invalidated involved flip-in plans. In response to these concerns, it has been recommended that the most aggressive flip-in plans contain provisions requiring redemption of the Rights in certain circumstances with a shareholder vote.

A. Applications of the Rights Plans

Share Purchase Rights Plans do not interfere with negotiated transactions since the Rights are typically redeemable until a specified ownership threshold (usually 20 percent) is crossed. Furthermore, Rights Plans have not acted to preclude all unsolicited takeovers. A study performed by Wachtell, Lipton, Rosen & Katz in November 1988 indicated that, as of that date, at least 110 companies that had Rights Plans had been acquired or were parties to agreements to be acquired, including at least 85 companies that were acquired after receiving an unsolicited bid or having a substantial percentage of its stock acquired by a party seeking control. Although Rights Plans have not precluded all hostile takeover attempts, such plans have achieved their desired effect—acquirors launching hostile bids against companies with Rights Plans in almost all cases initially condition their bids on the Rights being redeemed or nullified. Furthermore, in 72 of the 75 acquisitions in the November 1988 study that were initiated by unsolicited bids, the price ultimately received by shareholders was higher than the initial bid, including 27 cases in which the premium over the initial bid exceeded $100 million. The aggregate premium paid to shareholders over the initial bids in these 27 cases was over $13.3 billion. Furthermore, a March 1988 study by Georgeson & Company Inc. found that companies with Rights Plans received substantially higher premiums than companies without Rights Plans. Georgeson analyzed hostile takeovers that were commenced after January 1, 1986 and completed by October 19, 1987 having a value over $100 million. After adjusting for changes in the Standard & Poor's 500-stock index, Georgeson found that the 27 companies with Rights Plans received final offers that exceeded their stock price six months before the takeover contest began by an average of 52.7 percent in excess of the S & P Index, compared with an average gain relative to the S & P Index of only 31.3 percent by the 21 companies without Rights Plans that were acquired during the survey period. Thus, the evidence suggests that the Rights Plans have indeed served their intended purpose of increasing the bargaining power of the target's board of directors—even in situations where the board accedes to the demands of the initial bidder.

B. Effect on Market Price

All of the investment banking firms that have studied the issue have concluded that adoption of a Share Purchase Rights Plan does not have an effect on the long-term market value of a company's stock. A March 5, 1986 study by the Office of the Chief Economist of the SEC concluded, based on analyses of stock prices of companies in the two-day period consisting of the day of and the day before the announcement of the adoption of a Rights Plan, that there was no statistically significant reduction of market prices for the entire group of companies sampled. However, the SEC study did find a statistically significant reduction of stock prices, in the two-day period, of companies that were the subjects of takeover speculation. The SEC study did not address the long-term impact, if any, of adoption of the Share Purchase Rights Plan. The SEC admits that this study "is not a sufficient basis on which to judge right or wrong in a public policy context."

A second SEC study, dated October 23, 1986, based on an expanded sample of 245 companies adopting Rights Plans, found that adoption of Rights Plans had no statistically significant effect on the stock market prices—even within the artificially limited window period (measured from the day before to the day after announcement of the Rights Plan) chosen by the SEC. Further, there was no statistically significant effect on the stock market prices of companies that were not the subject of takeover speculation. Finally, the SEC was unable to find, under any set of assumptions within the sample, a statistically significant negative impact on stock prices resulting from adoption of the type of plan that was the subject of the *Household* case. The study did, however, find a statistically significant negative return during the two-day window of approximately 2 percent for companies that adopted plans with "discriminatory" flip-in provisions at a time when their stock was subject to takeover speculation. It should be noted, though, that this result was obtained only by eliminating all of the companies—consisting of 50 percent of this subsample—that released important news (usually good) simultaneously with the announcement of the plan's adoption.

A Georgeson study, dated October 31, 1988, concluded that the market prices of companies with Rights Plans during the period December 31, 1985 to September 30, 1987 outperformed a control group of comparable companies without Rights Plans by 9.6 percent. This study also found that appreciation in shareholder value for companies with Rights Plans exceeded that of the S&P 500, while those without such plans experienced less appreciation than the S&P 500. The biggest performance differential occurred in situations where an acquisition was involved, where the average gain for deals involving companies with Rights Plans was almost twice the gain for the deals involving companies without Rights Plans.

C. SEC Concept Release

On July 31, 1986, the SEC issued a concept release requesting comments on, among other things, poison pills. See Exch. Act Rel. No. 23486 (July 31, 1986). Noting the substantial controversy surrounding Rights Plans and that over 190 companies had adopted Rights Plans, with more expected to do so in the future, the SEC requested comment regarding the extent to which the incidence of Rights Plans is increasing, the costs and benefits of Rights Plans and the investor protection issues raised by Rights Plans, including whether their adoption should be subject to shareholder approval. The SEC also sought comment on whether a government response to Rights Plans is appropriate, whether state or federal action is more appropriate, and, if at the federal level, what response would be most appropriate. Of the 81 commentators expressing views on poison pill plans, 23 favored prohibition of poison pills while 15 others favored shareholder approval of such plans. See *Summary of Comments Relating to Takeovers and Contests for Corporate Control*, [1987 Transfer Binder] Fed. Sec. L. Rep. (CCH) ¶ 84,112 (Mar. 1987). The SEC subsequently expressed its view that it "does not believe that federal regulation of poison pills is appropriate at this time." See Exch. Act Rel. No. 24976 (October 1, 1987) at n.2; see also Exch. Act Rel. Nos. 25891 and 25891A (July 7 and 13, 1988) (adopting Rule 19c-4 and stating that shareholder Rights Plans should generally not be covered by Rule 19c-4).

D. Shareholder Proposals

In the 1987 proxy season, the $38 billion College Retirement Equities Fund (CREF) and the $58 billion California Retirement System submitted resolutions to some 30 companies, generally those with institutions holding a majority of the outstanding shares, requesting rescission of their Rights Plans unless submitted to a shareholder vote and approved by a majority of the shares.

These proposals received the support of an average of only 20 percent of the outstanding shares and failed to attract a majority of the shares voting at any company that considered them.

Two Illinois insurance companies, Arthur J. Gallagher & Co. and Old Republic International, elected to have their shareholders vote at their 1987 annual meetings on whether to adopt Rights Plans. The plans were approved by 89 percent and 78 percent of the shares voted, respectively. Insiders hold 48 percent and 35 to 40 percent of the outstanding shares of the respective companies. See Corporate Governance Bulletin, p. 166 (September/October 1987).

During the 1988 proxy season, opponents of Rights Plans were similarly unsuccessful in their efforts to achieve support. According to a study undertaken by Georgeson, the percentage of votes against rights plans was actually lower in 1988 than in 1987. This was so despite a selective targeting of companies where the 1987 effort had been most successful. The only exception to the general trend in 1988 was the voting with respect to Sante Fe Southern Pacific's Rights Plan. In that case 49.1 percent of the shares outstanding, or 59.1 percent of the shares voted on the issue, were voted against the rights plan. However, the Sante Fe situation was unusual because more than 35 percent of the outstanding shares were owned by The Henley Group and Olympia & York, shareholders more or less committed to a fundamental restructuring of Sante Fe's operations. Excluding such shares on the assumption they were cast in favor of the rescission proposal, less than the average vote at other companies targeted by opponents of the Rights Plan was achieved. One shareholder proposal was withdrawn after the company agreed to redeem its rights by 1991. Texaco, as part of its settlement in emerging from bankruptcy, recently adopted a new rights plan, responsive to its institutional holders, that would not act to hinder certain tender offers. The rights plan was found to be fair by an independent investment banking firm.

E. Second Generation Share Purchase Rights Plan

The second generation Share Purchase Rights Plan, which was first adopted in an early form by MCA Inc. in July 1987, combines the flip-over and flip-in features at a 20 percent threshold with a provision for a special meeting of shareholders to vote on redemption of the rights where a cash offer for all the target's shares is proposed at a fair price. The flip-in at a 20 percent threshold was designed to provide greater protection against current takeover abuses, while the special meeting procedure provides an avenue for the raider to pursue its takeover if the target's board refuses to redeem the rights. Thus, prior to a bidder crossing the 20 percent threshold, the rights issued under this Rights Plan are redeemable at a nominal cost by the directors and, where the offer meets fairness standards, the shareholders can, by a vote of a simple majority of the outstanding shares, override a decision by the directors not to redeem.

To avail itself of the special shareholder meeting, a bidder, at the time it requests the meeting, cannot own more than 1 percent of the target's shares and in the prior 12 months cannot have owned more than 1 percent at a time when it disclosed or caused the disclosure of an intent to acquire or influence control of the target. The 1 percent threshold limits the profit potential to a level that makes it unlikely that the bidder is attempting to put the target in play for the purpose of greenmail or to profit from the target being forced to seek a white knight or pursue a drastic restructuring. In addition, to avail itself of the special meeting, the bidder must have financing or financing commitments; furnish an opinion, addressed to the target's shareholders, of a recognized national investment banking firm that the price the bidder is proposing is fair; and agree to bear half of the costs of the special meeting.

The special shareholder meeting is required to be held no later than 120 days nor earlier than 90 days after the bidder's request. If a majority of the company's outstanding shares are voted in favor of the resolution at the special meeting, the rights would be redeemed so as to permit consummation of the bidder's proposal or a competing better proposal. If following an approving vote the company does not enter into a cash merger agreement with the bidder—and there would be no obligation to do so—the bidder could consummate a tender offer unaffected by the plan, provided that the tender offer is for all the shares at a price not less than the price voted upon by shareholders.

This rights plan provides that, if the flip-in is triggered, the target's board of directors may elect to exchange each outstanding right (other than rights held by the raider, which become void upon the flip-in) for one share of common stock of the target. This provision gives the shareholders the equivalent of the flip-in in circumstances where an acquiror may otherwise be able to avoid the full impact of the plan. This Rights Plan also permits the board of directors to reduce the 20 percent flip-in trigger to 15 percent or 10 percent to meet specific threats. The availability of the protections of the flip-in at these levels makes the second generation rights plan a powerful tool for boards of directors. In deference to legal and institutional concerns about shareholder rights, the special referendum procedure is believed to provide support for application of the flip-in at the lower threshold. Without the referendum procedure, it is recommended that the threshold should be set at a 30 percent level reducible to 15 percent.

F. Share Purchase Rights Plans in the Courts

1. Household

On November 19, 1985, the Delaware Supreme Court upheld the validity of a Share Purchase Rights Plan adopted by Household International. *Moran* v. *Household International, Inc.*, 500 A.2d 1346 (Del. Supr. 1985). Although the Household plan had not been adopted during a takeover battle, but rather as a preventive mechanism to ward off future raiders, the court stated that "preplanning for the contingency of a hostile takeover might reduce the risk that, under the pressure of a takeover bid, management will fail to exercise reasonable judgment. Therefore, in reviewing a preplanned defensive mechanism it seems even more appropriate to apply the business judgment rule." *Id.* at 1350. The approval of a Rights Plan as a preplanned takeover defense was reaffirmed by the Delaware Supreme Court in the *Revlon* case.

The Court noted that the plan would not deter all hostile tender offers, pointing to the takeover of Crown Zellerbach, which had adopted a Rights Plan similar to Household's, by Sir James Goldsmith, as well as other methods of mounting a hostile takeover, such as making an offer conditioned on the board redeeming the rights, or on the tender of a high minimum number of shares and rights, or forming a group holding up to 19.9 percent of the outstanding shares and soliciting proxies for consents to remove the board and redeem the rights. *Id.*

Reflecting the concern motivated by the *Unocal* standard that defensive devices do not reasonably interfere with voting rights, the Court carefully analyzed whether the Rights Plan restricts proxy contests. On this point the Court said:

> We conclude that there was sufficient evidence at trial to support the Vice Chancellor's finding that the effect upon proxy contests will be minimal. Evidence at trial established that many proxy contests are won with an insurgent ownership of less than 20 percent, and that very large holdings are no guarantee of success. There was also testimony that the key variable in proxy contest success is the merit of an insurgent's issues, not the size of his holdings. *Id.* at 1355.

The Court found that the standard of conduct enunciated in *Unocal* for the application of the business judgment rule was satisfied in *Household*, since there were no allegations of bad faith or entrenchment by the directors, the directors evidenced concern about "bootstrap," "bust-up," and two-tier takeovers and were aware of overtures being made by a potential acquiror. Under such circumstances, the Court concluded, "the Directors reasonably believed Household was vulnerable to coercive acquisition techniques and adopted a reasonable defensive mechanism to protect itself." *Id.* at 1357. The *Household* Court further stated that:

> When the Household Board of Directors is faced with a tender offer and a request to redeem the Rights, they will not be able to arbitrarily reject the offer. They will be held to the same fiduciary standards any other board of directors would be held to in deciding to adopt a defensive mechanism, the same standard as they were held to in originally approving the Rights Plan. *Id.* at 1354 (citation omitted).

2. Subsequent Cases

A listing and brief summary of all known cases to date involving the legality of Rights Plans or situations where the board of directors may be required to redeem outstanding rights is set forth below. It appears that most courts will follow *Household*, and there now is relatively little doubt as to legality of the basic Rights Plan, although a court may find that the corporate law of a particular state does not permit the specific Rights Plan in issue in a particular case. This has been the case with the decisions striking down certain flip-in plans. Indeed, no court has struck down a Rights Plan containing only those features contained in the Household Plan. Furthermore, the *Gelco, CTS II,* and *Harvard Industries* decisions, and the more recent *Santa Fe, Federated, Staley, Koppers,* and *Facet* decisions, illustrate that the validity of Rights Plans containing discriminatory "flip-in" features is widely recognized by the courts. (But see *Irving* and *West Point-Pepperell* discussions below.)

As a general matter, most litigation concerning Rights Plans now focuses on the decision by a board of directors whether to redeem the rights in response to a particular bid, as opposed to their inherent legality, which shift in focus was contemplated by the *Household* decision. Courts applying Delaware law have upheld the determination not to redeem rights in response to two-tier offers (*USG*) or inadequate 100 percent cash tenders offers (*Koppers, Damon*), as well as to protect an auction or permit a company to explore alternatives (*Federated, Facet Enterprises, Staley Continental, Doskocil, Prime*). However, certain recent decisions have held that the rights may not interfere with shareholder choice at the conclusion of an auction (*Macmillan*) or at the "end stage" following an opportunity to search for alternatives (*Interco, Pillsbury*) where the value of the competing bid was higher than or relatively close to the alternative supported by the target's board of directors. The Delaware Chancery Court held that the Pillsbury board would be required to redeem rights in the face of a fully financed 100 percent cash bid that the court deemed adequate, following a 2½-month period to explore alternatives, where the only threat posed by the hostile bidder was to shareholder values and not to the corporate entity or other constituencies. The recent court decision in *TW Services* (which was decided by the same judge who decided *Interco*) points out that *Interco* and *Pillsbury* were both cases where the target company had embarked on a restructuring plan and that those decisions did not rule out the "just say no" defense. *TW Services* holds that the traditional business judgment rule, as opposed to the heightened *Unocal* standard, applies to a board's decision to reject a merger proposal.

a. Upheld Rights Plans

1. *Moran* v. *Household International, Inc.*, 500 A.2d 1346 (Del. Supr.), *aff'g* 490 A.2d 1059 (Del. Ch. 1985) (flip-over plan).
2. *Horwitz* v. *Southwest Forest Industries, Inc.*, 604 F. Supp. 1130 (D. Nev. 1985) (flip-over plan; court denied injunction relying on Delaware Chancery Court decision in *Household*).
3. *APL Corp.* v. *Johnson Controls, Inc.*, 85 Civ. 990 (E.D.N.Y. March 25, 1985) (flip-over plan with self-dealing flip-in applying Wisconsin law; court denied injunction relying on Delaware Chancery Court decision in *Household*).
4. *Revlon, Inc.*v. *MacAndrews & Forbes Holdings, Inc.*, 506 A.2d 173 (Del. Supr. 1986), *aff'g* 501 A.2d 1239 (Del. Ch. 1985) (back-end plan).
5. *Edelman* v. *Phillips Petroleum Co.*, C.A. No. 7899 (Del. Ch. June 3, 1986) (flip-over plan with self-dealing flip-in, substituted for back-end plan in connection with court approved settlement of class action litigation).
6. *Dynamics Corp. of America* v. *CTS Corp.*, 635 F. Supp. 1174 (N.D. Ill.) *aff'd in part and vacated in part*, 805 F.2d 705 (7th Cir. 1986) (*CTS II*) (back-end plan applying Indiana and Delaware law; District Court refused to enjoin plan; Seventh Circuit remanded for further consideration as to whether the procedure by which the rights plan had been formulated and recommended for adoption met the requisite standards of reasonableness and good faith, but held that the basic concept of the rights plan is valid and legal under Indiana and Delaware law and that the discrimination against certain

large shareholders is discrimination among shareholders, not among shares, and, therefore, is not in violation of the statutory prohibition against discrimination among shares).

7. *Allied Stores Corp.* v. *Campeau Acquisition Corp.*, 86 Civ. 7841 (PNL) (S.D.N.Y. Oct. 29, 1986) (back-end plan applying Delaware law; court refused to grant TRO).
8. *N.V. Homes* v. *Ryan Homes*, Civ. No. 86-2139 (W.D. Pa. Oct. 24, 1986) (back-end plan; court refused to preliminarily enjoin plan).
9. *Gelco Corp.* v. *Coniston Partners*, 652 F. Supp. 829 (D. Minn. 1986), *aff'd in part and vacated in part*, 811 F.2d 414 (8th Cir. 1987) (flip-in plan; court specifically rejected the *NL* decision and held that adoption of a Rights Plan was not *ultra vires*).
10. *Harvard Industries, Inc.* v. *Tyson*, [1986–87 Transfer Binder] Fed. Sec. L. Rep. (CCH) ¶ 93,064 (E.D. Mich. Nov. 25, 1986) (flip-in plan; court denied request for preliminary injunction, holding that discrimination was among shareholders, not among shares, and therefore was not prohibited).
11. *Spinner Corp.* v. *Princeville Development Corp.*, [1986–87 Transfer Binder] Fed. Sec. L. Rep. (CCH) ¶ 93,058 (D. Haw. Oct. 31, 1986) (*Spinner*) (flip-over provisions of rights plan applying Colorado law; court refused to enjoin such provisions on the grounds that they did not discriminate among shareholders).
12. *The Henley Group, Inc.* v. *Santa Fe Southern Pacific Corp.*, C.A. No. 9569 (Del. Ch. March 11, 1988) (court refused to enjoin enforcement of flip-in plan).

b. Upheld Refusal to Redeem Rights

1. *CRTF Corp.* v. *Federated Department Stores, Inc.*, 683 F. Supp. 422 (S.D.N.Y. 1988) (flip-in plan under Delaware law; court refused to preliminarily enjoin flip-in plan, finding that it "provides the directors with a shield to fend off coercive offers, and with a gavel to run an auction"; court held that target's board was not required to redeem Rights Plan in the course of an auction with respect to plaintiff's two-tiered bid although it had removed plan as impediment to a white knight's bid that board reasonably believed was superior).
2. *BNS, Inc.* v. *Koppers Co.*, 683 F. Supp. 458 (D. Del. 1988) (flip-in plan; court refused to preliminarily enjoin plan, finding that the refusal to redeem the rights in response to an inadequate 100 percent cash offer was not unreasonable, and that plaintiff had failed to

show that the board's decision was undertaken solely or primarily for entrenchment purposes or was otherwise a breach of their fiduciary duties).

3. *Facet Enterprises, Inc.* v. *The Prospect Group, Inc.*, C.A. No. 9746 (Del. Ch. April 11, 1988) (flip-in plan; court refused to issue preliminary injunction requested by tender offeror to redeem rights plan, finding that target should be permitted to keep rights in place until the auction process that it had announced has reasonably run its course).
4. *Desert Partners, L.P.* v. *USG Corp.*, 686 F. Supp. 1289 (N.D. Ill. 1988) (self-dealing flip-in applying Delaware law; court refused to issue preliminary injunction requested by tender offeror to redeem Rights Plan, finding that the Board of Directors acted reasonably in response to coercive, two-tier offer).
5. *Tate & Lyle PLC* v. *Staley Continental, Inc.*, [1987–88 Transfer Binder] Fed. Sec. L. Rep. (CCH) ¶ 93,764 (Del. Ch. May 9, 1988) (flip-in plan in which 40 percent threshold had been reduced to 20 percent following takeover threat; court refused to issue preliminary injunction requested by tender offeror to redeem Rights Plan, finding that Rights Plan was serving a useful purpose in allowing board to seek a higher offer and for the board "[t]o do otherwise could conceivably subject the Board to actions predicated upon their failure to earnestly seek the highest bidder").
6. *Bank of New York Co.* v. *Irving Bank Corp.*, No. 10217/88 (N.Y. Sup. Ct. July 25, 1988) (order; *see* July 6, 1988 transcript), *aff'd without opinion*, Nos. 34387 & 34388 (N.Y. App. Div. October 4, 1988) (court refused to order redemption of flip-over provisions of rights plan while target was conducting an auction).
7. *Nomad Acquisition Corp.* v. *Damon Corp.*, [Current] Fed. Sec. L. Rep. (CCH) ¶ 94,040 (Del. Ch. Sept. 16, 1988) (revised Sept. 20, 1988) (flip-in plan; court refused to order redemption of Rights Plan, finding Board acted reasonably in finding offer inadequate; court held that Board "had both the duty and responsibility to oppose inadequate offers . . . even if the tender offer is for all cash.").
8. *Doskocil Cos.* v. *Griggy*, C.A. No. 10095 (Del. Ch. Oct. 7, 1988) (flip-in plan; court held that in order to promote an auction rights plan could be used to delay a hostile bidder which had increased its bid over a white knight bid even though the target had already agreed to redeem the rights to facilitate the white knight bid).

9. *Grand Metropolitan PLC* v. *Pillsbury Co.*, C.A. 10323 (Del. Ch. Nov. 7, 1988) (flip-in plan; court refused to order redemption of Rights Plan while the company continued to explore alternatives, finding that an all-cash, all-shares offer may be a threat to stockholders' economic interests if it is inadequate; rehearing granted following Pillsbury's announcement of spin-off defense).
10. *Garland's Inc. Profit Sharing Plan* v. *Pillsbury Co.*, Civ. No. 88-17834 (Minn. Dist. Ct. Nov. 10, 1988) (flip-in plan; court refused to order redemption of rights where company was exploring financial alternatives in the diligent exercise of its fiduciary duties).
11. *MAI Basic Four, Inc.* v. *Prime Computer, Inc.*, [1988–89 Transfer Binder] Fed. Sec. L. Rep. (CCH) ¶ 94,179 (Del. Ch. Dec. 20, 1988) (refused to order redemption of rights which the target was continuing to review alternatives to maximize shareholder value; distinguished from *Interco* and *Pillsbury* on the grounds that those decisions came at the end of takeover struggles in which the target was seeking to rely on the rights to protect a board-approved restructuring).
12. *In re Holly Farms Corp. Shareholders Litigation*, [1988–89 Transfer Binder] Fed. Sec. L. Rep. (CCH) ¶ 94,181 (Del. Ch. Dec. 30, 1988) (flip-in plan; court refused to order redemption of rights where there was no evidence that the target was using the rights plan for any improper purpose and where the court found that the plan may still have a role in maximizing values in the context of a bidding contest).
13. *TW Services, Inc.* v. *SWT Acquisition Corp.*, Civ. No. 10427 [Current] Fed. Sec. L. Rep. (CCH) ¶ 94,334 (Del. Ch. Mar. 2, 1989) (flip-in plan; court held that the board had no duty to consider whether to redeem the rights where it made a good faith determination to continue its long-term business plan and the bidder had conditioned its tender offer on board approval of a merger agreement; court applied a traditional business judgment standard, not a heightened *Unocal* standard, in reviewing the board's decision not to pursue a merger opportunity).
14. *A. Copeland Enterprises* v. *Guste*, 706 F. Supp. 1283 (W.D. Tex. 1989) (flip-in plan; court held that duty of loyalty under Texas law not breached by keeping plan in place during auction, but court noted that after the auction there would be no reason to keep the plan in

place, which would serve only to entrench current board; court noted that if rights were not redeemed at conclusion of auction, it would issue a preliminary injunction).

15. *Amanda Acquisition Corp.* v. *Universal Foods* 708 F. Supp. 984 (E.D. Wis. 1989(*aff'd on other grounds*, 1989 U.S. App. LEXIS (7th Cir. May 24, 1989) (flip-in plan with shareholder referendum; court found that rights need not be redeemed in the face of a coercive all-cash tender offer for all shares the board found to be inadequate, finding that the offer posed numerous threats to the corporation and various constituencies).
16. *In re Holly Farms Corp. Shareholders Litigation* [Current] Fed. Sec. L. Rep. (CCH) ¶ 94,486 (Del. Ch. June 14, 1989) (flip-in plan; court refused to order redemption of rights when one offer was economically superior but would take longer to complete and could be blocked by an inferior offer that could be completed more quickly).

c. Invalidated Rights Plans

1. *Dynamics Corp. of America* v. *CTS Corp.*, 637 F. Supp. 406 (N.D. Ill.), *aff'd*, 794 F.2d 250 (7th Cir. 1986), *rev'd on other grounds*, 481 U.S. 69 (1987) ("*CTS I*") (flip-in plan applying Indiana and Delaware laws; court enjoined plan on basis that the CTS directors had not satisfied the requirements of the business judgment rule, and questioned the validity of the flip-in provisions on the basis of mere ownership of 15 percent of the common stock).
2. *Amalgamated Sugar Co.* v. *NL Industries, Inc.*, 644 F. Supp. 1229 (S.D.N.Y. 1986) (flip-over plan with self-dealing flip-in applying New Jersey law; court held that self-dealing flip-in provision discriminated against large shareholders in violation of New Jersey law).
3. *R.D. Smith & Co.* v. *Preway Inc.*, 644 F. Supp. 868 (W.D. Wisc. 1986) (flip-in plan; court denied injunction for failure to show irreparable harm, but, in *dicta*, said that plaintiffs have a good chance of succeeding on the merits, citing *NL*) (Wisconsin has subsequently amended its statute to eliminate this problem).
4. *Spinner* (flip-in and back-end plans applying Colorado law; court enjoined self-dealing flip-in provisions because of discriminatory features but left intact flip-over provisions; *see* above).
5. *Buckhorn Inc.* v. *Ropak Corp.*, 656 F. Supp. 209 (S.D. Ohio), *aff'd by sum. ord.*, 815 F.2d 76 (6th Cir. 1987) (back-end plan applying Delaware law; while adoption of the back-end plan was a

"reasonable response to the threat perceived," the particular plan was invalidated due to the board's failure to exercise due care in setting the exercise price for the plan, citing several flaws in the financial analysis presented to the board).

6. *The Bank of New York Co. Inc.* v. *Irving Bank Corp.*, 528 N.Y.S. 2d 482 (N.Y. Sup. Ct. 1988), *aff'd without opinion*—A.D.2d—(1st Dep't Oct. 4, 1988) (court enjoined flip-in provision under New York law because it discriminated among shareholders, citing *NL*).
7. *West Point-Pepperell, Inc.* v. *Farley Inc.*, 711 F. Supp. 1088 (N.D. Ga. 1988) (flip-in plan with exchange provisions; court enjoined flip-in and exchange provisions under Georgia law because they discriminated among shareholders).
8. *Topper* v. *Emhart Corporation*, Civ. Act. No. 89-00110-R. (E.D. Va. Mar. 23, 1989) (flip-in plan applying Virginia law; court granted preliminary injunction against rights plan as *ultra vires* under Virginia law).
9. *Policemen and Firemen Retirement System of the City of Detroit* v. *Income Opportunity Realty Trust*, Case No. C 89 1152 AJZ (N.D. Cal. May 16, 1989) (flip-in plan by a real estate investment trust ("REIT") under California law; court granted plaintiffs' motion for summary judgment that the flip-in provision of the Rights Agreement violated the Declaration of Trust of the REIT, which provided that "any Share or security shall have the same characteristics and entitle the registered holder thereof to the same rights as any identical securities of the same class or series issued separately by the Trust" and did not reach issue of legality under California law).

d. Ordered Redemption of Rights

1. *Southdown, Inc.* v. *Moore McCormack Resources, Inc.*, 686 F. Supp. 595 (S.D. Tex. 1988) (flip-in plan applying Delaware law; court forced redemption of rights to eliminate impediment to 100 percent cash tender offer, suggesting that plan may only be used to deter two-tier bids or to facilitate auction; court also suggested that a flip-in plan may be invalid under Delaware law or preempted by the Williams Act).
2. *Mills Acquisition Co.* v. *Macmillan, Inc.*, [Current] Fed. Sec. L. Rep. (CCH) ¶ 94,071 (Del. Ch. Oct. 17, 1988), *rev'd on other grounds*, [Current] Fed. Sec. L. Rep. ¶ 94,072 (Del. Supr. Nov. 2, 1988) (bench ruling) (flip-in plan; lower court ordered redemption of rights at conclusion of auction to permit shareholders the opportunity

to consider a competing tender offer for a fair (indeed higher) price, provided the higher bidder determined to proceed with its offer, either by waiving its condition that an asset lock-up option be declared invalid, or by successfully invalidating the option on appeal).

3. *City Capital Associates Ltd. Partnership* v. *Interco Inc.*, 551 A.2d 787 (Del. Ch. 1988) (flip-in plan; court ordered redemption of rights to eliminate impediment to 100 percent cash tender offer after the target had had a reasonable opportunity to explore alternatives or attempt to negotiate; court found refusal to redeem, even in response to an offer the board reasonably concluded was inadequate, was unreasonable in relation to the threat posed, particularly in view of the relative closeness of values between the target's recapitalization plan and the bidder's tender offer price; injunction subsequently mooted by termination of tender offer).
4. *Grand Metropolitan PLC* v. *Pillsbury Co.*, [1988–89 Transfer Binder] Fed. Sec. L. Rep. (CCH) ¶ 94,104 (Del. Ch. Dec. 16, 1988) (flip-in plan; court ordered redemption of rights to eliminate impediment to 100 percent cash tender offer that the court determined to be adequate where the only threat posed by the hostile bidder was to shareholder values and not to the corporate entity or other constituencies).
5. *A. Copeland Enterprises* v. *Guste*, 706 F. Supp. 1283 (W.D. Tex. 1989) (flip-in plan; court, although upholding refusal to redeem rights during auction, stated that it would issue a preliminary injunction ordering redemption of rights if the rights were not redeemed at the conclusion of the auction).

e. Other Issues

1. *Young* v. *Colgate-Palmolive Co.*, 790 F.2d 567 (7th Cir. 1986) (court held that cause of action for breach of fiduciary obligation occurred where a rights plan was adopted for purposes of the Illinois long-arm statute).
2. *Holstein* v. *UAL Corp.*, 662 F. Supp. 153 (N.D. Ill. 1987) (Rights Plan not actionable as a tender offer under the Williams Act at least until the rights become exercisable).
3. *Williams* v. *Geier*, C.A. No. 8456 (Del. Ch. May 20, 1987) (reaffirmed, in context of common stock with different voting rights depending upon length of time shares are owned, that differential treatment among stockholders, rather than among the shares of stock *per se*, is permitted under Delaware law). But see 23.I.E.1 (one share/one vote).

4. *CRTF Corp.* v. *Federated Department Stores, Inc.*, 683 F. Supp. 422 (S.D.N.Y. 1988) (court denied target's motion to dismiss bidder's claims against Rights Plan for lack of standing based on the absence of financial commitments; court held that issue of standing depended upon whether the tender offer was made in good faith by a bidder with a realistic financial capacity to consummate its bid, based upon all of the facts and circumstances relating to the bidder's past history, its current financing capability and the extent of its investment in its bid).
5. *Bank of New York Co.* v. *Irving bank Corp.*, 528 N.Y.S.2d 482 (N.Y. Sup. Ct. Apr. 18, 1988) (applying New York law to strike down rights plan provision, adopted during proxy fight, that limited redemption of rights).
6. *Heil* v. *Morrison Knudsen Corporation*, 863 F.2d 546 (7th Cir. 1988) (court dismissed a shareholder's action against an amended rights plan for lack of personal jurisdiction since the holding of a board meeting for the original adoption of a rights plan in Illinois was insufficient for "doing business" under the Illinois long-arm statute and, furthermore, the challenged conduct related to an amendment adopted in a board meeting held in New York).
7. *Seidel* v. *Allegis Corp.*, 702 F. Supp. 1409 (N.D. Ill. 1989) (applying Delaware law to claim that adoption of rights plan deprived shareholders of right to vote or sell shares, court found only a derivative action claim based on mismanagement).
8. *Davis Acquisition Inc.* v. *NWA Inc.*, C.A. No. 10761 (Del. Ch. Apr. 25, 1989) (flip-in plan with provision that delays ability of a board of directors not nominated by the incumbent board to redeem the rights for 180 days following its election in order to facilitate a transaction with an "interested person"; court refused to enjoin deferred redemption provision prior to annual meeting on condition that the defendants agree to notify stockholders that the validity of this provision has been challenged in litigation and that the court intended to finally determine its validity within 45 days of the annual meeting).

G. Suggested Corporation Law Amendments

Judicial decisions in a few jurisdictions outside Delaware have found the discriminatory feature of the standard flip-in rights plan to violate provisions of state corporation laws. Other recent decisions, focusing primarily on the question of when a rights plan must be redeemed, have created uncertainty as to the proper role of a board of directors in responding to an acquisition proposal and the proper considerations that a board of directors may take into account in that context.

These decisions may effectively deprive boards of directors of one of the few available counterbalances to the takeover abuses that are prevalent in the current environment. They are likely to have an undesirable chilling effect on boards of directors, creating situations where directors will feel compelled to look only to the short-term economic interests of shareholders.

The passage of two amendments to state corporation laws could alleviate the problems created by these decisions and help restore the ability of boards of directors to respond meaningfully to, and represent their companies in the face of, today's acquisition attempts.

In validating flip-in rights plans and clarifying the fiduciary duties of a board of directors, the amendments would take the better view of recently decided cases that a corporation need not always be for sale, and that a board may consider all the corporation's interests, may determine that any particular acquisition proposal is not in the best interest of the corporation, and may take effective steps to implement that determination. This clarification is necessary if a board is to have the ability to deal with takeover abuses and represent meaningfully the corporation's interests in the takeover context.

1. Amendment to Validate Flip-in Rights Plans

This amendment would specifically validate the discriminatory feature of the flip-in rights plan. Similar provisions have already been added to the corporation laws of several states, including Illinois, Indiana, Florida, Ohio, New York (interim provision), Pennsylvania, Wisconsin, and Hawaii (these provisions were generally added to the existing sections authorizing creation of rights and options rather than by adding a new section).

> Section ____. The terms and conditions of rights or options issued by the corporation may include, without limitation, restrictions or conditions that preclude or limit the exercise, transfer or receipt of such rights or options by any person or persons owning of offering to acquire a specified number or percentage of the outstanding common shares or other securities of the corporation, or any transferee or transferees of any such person or persons, or that invalidate or void such rights or options held by any such person or persons or any such transferee or transferees.

2. Amendment Regarding Consideration of Constituencies and Responses to Acquisition Proposals

This amendment would make clear that the fiduciary duties of directors under the state's corporation law permit directors to take into consideration factors beyond the short-term economic interests of the corporation's shareholders, including the interests of the corporation's employees, suppliers, creditors, and customers; the communities in which the corporation operates; and the long-term interests of the corporation and its shareholders. It would also allow a board of directors, after considering such factors, to reject an acquisition proposal, and would provide that a board of directors that has rejected an acquisition proposal has no duty to facilitate, remove any barriers to, or refrain from impeding the acquisition proposal. Sections 23-1-29-2 and 23-1-35-1 of the Indiana Code have recently been amended to reflect these concerns.

> Section ____. *Consideration of Interests in Addition to Shareholders' Interests; Duties in Response to Acquisition Proposals.* (1) In discharging his duties to the corporation and in determining what he reasonably believes to be in the best interests of the corporation, a director may, in addition to considering the effects of any action on shareholders, consider any of the following:
>
> (a) The effects of the action on the corporation's employees, suppliers, creditors and customers;
>
> (b) The effects of the action on the communities in which the corporation operates; and
>
> (c) The long-term as well as short-term interests of the corporation and its shareholders, including the possibility that these interests may be best served by the continued independence of the corporation.

(2) If on the basis of the factors described in paragraph (1) above, the board of directors determines that any proposal or offer to acquire the corporation is not in the best interests of the corporation, it may reject such proposal or offer. If the board of directors determines to reject any such proposal or offer, the board of directors shall have no obligation to facilitate, to remove any barriers to, or to refrain from impeding the proposal or offer.

H. Note Purchase Rights Plans

While Share Purchase Rights Plans focus on the second step in an acquisition and provide protection only in the event of a second-step or certain selfdealing transactions, Note Purchase Rights Plans, also known as "back-end plans," provide protection even if there is no second step and, indeed, may be thought of as providing a second step for shareholders. The note purchase right, which gives the holder a right to "put" his stock to the issuer in exchange for a specified package of securities if a specified percentage (e.g., 30 percent) of the company is acquired by a third party, in essence "puts a price" on the company. The securities for which the stock becomes exchangeable may also contain provisions designed to make a bidder's financing more difficult or unobtainable, such as seniority, restrictions upon sales of assets or incurrence of debt, and maintenance of certain financial ratios. There is great flexibility in tailoring a back-end plan, and such plans can be designed to meet specific and changing situations. The terms of the Plan, and in particular the exercise price and the terms of the securities to be received upon exercise of the rights, must be reasonable and must be determined by the issuer's board of directors in good faith. The SEC has taken the position, however, with respect to certain Note Purchase Rights Plans, that the new rules regarding self-tenders (all-holders and best-price rules) become applicable once the Rights are triggered.

As a general matter, back-end rights plans, if adopted after a hostile takeover attempt has begun, can be a valuable protection for shareholders against partial or two-tier tender offers, open-market accumulation programs and other coercive takeover techniques. If adopted before such an attempt has begun, however, they may place the board of directors of the target in the position of seeming to pick a price for the company at a time when the company is not for sale. In the event a takeover attempt does occur, the board will be able to implement a back-end rights plan, if the board considers it appropriate to do so.

Back-end rights plans have been upheld in *Revlon Inc.* v. *MacAndrews & Forbes Holdings, Inc.*, *Allied Stores Corp.* v. *Campeau Acquisition Corp.*, *NV Homes* v. *Ryan Homes*, *Buckhorn Inc.* v. *Ropak*. But see *Princeville* and *CTS II*.

The value assurance plan is a modification of the back-end rights plan. It was employed by the Mayflower Group as one of its defenses to an all-cash tender offer for all shares by Laidlaw Transportation. The company issued, as a dividend to shareholders, "contingent unsecured notes" having a two-year term. The notes automatically detached and traded separately from the common stock. The plan had two components, the second of which became effective only after Laidlaw withdrew its offer. First, in the event of a non-negotiated acquisition of 30 percent or more of the common stock, the principal amount of the notes became fixed at the difference between $33 (a price which Mayflower's Board had been advised could reasonably be expected to be obtained in an orderly auction process within a reasonable period of time if the company actively sought a sale) and the weighted average price paid in the acquisition. All shares not purchased by the acquiror within six months after the acquisition would be treated as having been acquired at their market price. Second, if there is no such acquisition, the principal amount of each note would be equal to an amount reflecting the amount by which the average market price (plus dividends) of a Mayflower share at some point in the future is less than a valuation of the Laidlaw offer with interest and other adjustments. The plan provides that any attempt to require the transfer of the notes as a condition to the purchase of shares by a bidder would cause the record holder of the notes before the tender to be deemed the payee under the notes.

Other variations of the Note Purchase Rights Plan have been adopted by TRE Corporation (Investor Protection Plan or Contingent Subordinated Obligations Plan, November 4, 1986), ChemLawn (Interim Safeguard Rights Plan, March 5, 1987) and Newmont Mining (Equal Value Rights Plan, September 23, 1987).

In the *Allied Stores* matter, the SEC took the position with respect to the Allied Stores back-end rights plan that the self-tender offer rules, including the all-holders rule, would become applicable once the rights were triggered. The discriminatory features of most back-end plans would violate the all-holders rule if it were deemed to apply upon triggering of the rights.

I. Supervoting Rights Preferred Stock Dividend Plans

While the economic-type plans referred to above frequently have been upheld, plans that change voting rights have (with at least one exception) fared less well in court. Most of the cases addressing the propriety of defensive tactics which shift voting power whether through the issuance of supervoting rights preferred stock dividends or placement of voting stock in the hands of management or the board of directors can be rationalized on the basis that the courts are extremely reluctant to allow a shift of voting power without a shareholder vote approving such shift. See *Asarco, Inc.* v. *MRH Holmes A Court*, 611 F. Supp. 468 (D.N.J. 1985); *Unilever Acquisition Corp.* v. *Richardson-Vicks, Inc.*, 618 F. Supp. 407 (S.D.N.Y. 1985); *Minstar Acquiring Corp.* v. *AMF, Inc.*, 621 F. Supp. 1252 (S.D.N.Y. 1985). But see *City Federal Savings & Loan Ass'n* v. *Mann*, C.A. No. 84-4010 (D.N.J. Aug. 2, 1985) (court refused to enjoin preliminarily the issuance of a preferred stock dividend that would have provided scaled voting rights). For a discussion of one share/one vote, (see Chapter 23.I.E.1); for cases applying the *Unocal* standard to defensive actions interfering with shareholder voting rights (see Chapter 22.I.E.3).

III. CHANGE OF CONTROL CONTRACTS

A. Golden Parachutes

In recent years, golden parachute agreements have become an important consideration in executive compensation planning. Generally, the term "golden parachute" refers to a contract between an executive and an employer, or a provision in an executive compensation plan that provides additional compensation or benefits to an executive upon the occurrence of a change in control or ownership of the employer or upon the termination of the executive's employment following such a change in control. As part of the Tax Reform Act of 1984, as amended by the Tax Reform Act of 1986, Congress imposed penalties on certain golden parachute payments in an effort to curb perceived abuses associated with the use of golden parachutes. The rules governing the application of the golden parachute tax penalties are complex.

If the total amount of change of control compensation payments to an employee equals or exceeds three times the employee's "base amount" (the average annual taxable compensation of the employee for the five years preceding the year in which the change of control occurs), the payments are considered "parachute payments," and the excess of the total amount of parachute payments over the greater of (1) one times the employee's base amount or (2) the amount of such payments considered "reasonable compensation" for services actually rendered prior to the change of control will be considered "excess parachute payments." Excess parachute payments are subject to a 20 percent, nondeductible excise tax (payable by the employee) and are not deductible by the employer.

Three approaches to dealing with golden parachute tax penalties are possible:

1. Payments can be "grossed-up" so that the employee is in the same after-tax position as if there were no excise tax.
2. Payments that are contingent on a change of control can be "cut-back" to 299.9 percent of the base amount, so that no payments are considered parachute payments.
3. Payments can be scaled down only if the result is to give the employee a larger after-tax return than if the payment were not scaled down.

Golden parachutes are primarily a mechanism for compensating a company's key officers for the risk that they may be displaced in a change of control transaction, a risk which if uncompensated might encourage some executives to seek other employment opportunities. Some commentators have also claimed that golden parachutes are useful in aligning management and shareholder interests in a takeover scenario. Golden parachutes are not a takeover defense. The size of the parachute payments does not typically constitute a significant economic barrier for a potential acquiror.

In *Orin* v. *Huntington Bancshares, Inc.*, Nos. 61129, 61392 (Ohio Ct. Comm. Pleas, Sept. 30, 1986), *aff'd*, No. 52861 (Ohio Ct. App. Nov.

25, 1987), an Ohio trial court upheld the enforceability of golden parachute contracts in connection with a change of control, provided that the conditions precedent to the creation of the obligations thereunder are satisfied. The court stated that the contracts were "legal and binding" and that the "interests of . . . shareholders were served in retaining . . . management and in encouraging their faithful performance during negotiation with those attempting to assume control . . . ." The court also noted that payments required under the contracts were "comparable to severance pay provided employees in other contexts." In a related appeal, *Worth* v. *Huntington Bancshares*, No. 52861 (Ohio Ct. App. Nov. 25, 1987), the court upheld Worth's golden parachute noting that the parachute benefited the target by preventing Worth from "jumping ship" during a crisis "and accepting employment elsewhere." Slip op. at 24.

In *Buckhorn, Inc.* v. *Ropak Corp.*, 656 F. Supp. 209 (S.D. Ohio), *aff'd by sum. ord.*, 815 F.2d 76 (6th Cir. 1987), the District Court, applying Delaware law, held that the adoption of golden parachutes for six key employees in the face of a hostile tender offer by Ropak Corporation was reasonable in relation to the threat posed. The court concluded that the parachute provisions "reasonably [advance] the shareholders' interest in retaining key management personnel in their present positions during a critical transition period, without unduly entrenching management or overburdening Ropak." *Id.* at 232–33. The court concluded, however, that amendments to the CEO's employment contract to extend the agreement for six additional years and to accelerate his salary and pension upon change of control were not reasonable in relation to the threat posed. The court was most troubled by the fact that the CEO could trigger the parachute payments at will upon a change of control. The court also concluded that the grant of new stock options to key employees and the amendment of existing stock options to allow vesting upon a change of control were not reasonable in relation to the threat posed. The court noted that such actions did little to add to the job security of such employees, given the golden parachutes, and caused demonstrable harm to the shareholders, because the actions diluted shareholder equity.

In a decision of potentially far reaching application, a federal district court in Delaware, applying Delaware law, applied a stringent standard of review to severance and employee benefit protection arrangements adopted while a hostile tender offer was pending *and* target company management was planning a defensive restructuring to thwart the takeover; and the court enjoined the restructuring *Black & Decker Corp.* v. *American Standard, Inc.*, 682 F. Supp. 772 (D. Del. 1988). The court's reasoning stemmed from its conclusion that the restructuring planned by the target, American

Standard, amounted to a sale of the company. Among the facts that the court considered were: that management and employees would acquire a greater than 50 percent equity interest following the recapitalization; and that the raider was being discriminated against because of the triggering of the severance arrangements upon the raider acquiring control of American Standard, while the recapitalization would not have triggered the severance arrangements.

The result of *Black & Decker* might have been different had American Standard adopted golden parachute and other benefit protection arrangements while a hostile takeover was pending but before a decision to "sell" (or recapitalize) the company had been made. However, the result would almost certainly have been different if such measures were adopted before any threat of takeover was present.

In *Tate & Lyle PLC, et al.* v. *Staley Continental, Inc.*, [1987–88 Transfer Binder] Fed. Sec. L. Rep. (CCH) ¶ 93,764 (Del. Ch. May 9, 1988), the Delaware Chancery Court enjoined the funding of a trust for several employee compensation plans and a nonemployee directors retirement plan. Although the Court was troubled by several aspects of the employee plans, it held that "the defendants seem to have shown that the plans were adopted in a good faith response to possible future hostile tender offer advances and that the directors were not misinformed or uninformed and were not grossly negligent." *Id.* at 98,585. However, because all of the plans that were to benefit from the trust were approved by directors having "a direct personal interest in one or another of the compensation plans [being] funded," the court held that the board had to show the entire fairness of the transaction, which it was able to do. *Id.* 98,586.

During the course of Nomad's acquisition of a substantial stake in Damon Corporation, and prior to a hostile tender offer by Nomad, Damon's Board of Directors amended the corporation's severance agreements and benefit plans, increasing Damon's severance liability by approximately $4 million. The Delaware Chancery Court rejected Nomad's claims that these were entrenchment devices. The court sustained the informed, good faith business judgment of the Damon Compensation Committee—comprised of independent directors—in amending the agreements and plans. See *Nomad Acquisition Corp.* v. *Damon Corp.*, [Current] Fed. Sec. L. Rep. ¶ 94,040 (Del. Ch. Sept. 16, 1988) (revised Sept. 20, 1988).

A federal court in Florida has found that the decision by a board of directors to adopt golden parachutes was protected by the business judgment rule even though payments under the plan were not dependent upon the officer's or director's termination. *International Insurance Co.* v. *Johns*, 685

F. Supp. 1230 (S.D. Fla. 1988). The plan's purpose was to maintain management intergrity during an important period of corporate development, and the plan was viewed as achieving its purpose. In addition, because the adoption of the plan was a lawful exercise of the directors' business judgment, an insurer was required to indemnify the directors under an officers' and directors' liability policy for amounts paid in settling a corporate waste claim against the officers and directors.

B. Rabbi Trusts

A "rabbi trust" is a trust established to provide a pool of funds for the payment of employee benefits due in the future, whether or not related to a change of control. In order to avoid taxation of the employees upon the creation of the trust, the employer must make sure that it is a grantor trust, the assets of which remain subject to the claims of creditors of the employer. Companies with large amounts of deferred compensation obligations or other unfunded employee benefits should consider creating a rabbi trust. While not a completely secure arrangement (it is subject to claims of the employer's creditors), the rabbi trusts provide employees some level of assurance that the benefits will be paid. The rabbi trust often contains a change of control provision that states when actual funding will occur.

C. Tin Parachutes

A "tin" parachute is a variation of a golden parachute which provides for severance payments for certain salaried employees who are terminated during an interim period (typically two years) following a "change in control." Such benefits are generally less generous than golden parachutes and apply to a broader range of employees. Such plans are designed to provide employees with additional protection against termination in the event of a hostile takeover and are intended to approximate the protections that management would secure for such employees in a friendly negotiated transaction. Depending upon the size of the potential tin parachute payments, such provisions may or may not provide an economic impediment to a hostile bid. Note that no costs are incurred by a hostile acquiror upon triggering a tin parachute unless the acquiror terminates target employees following the change of control. In the *AMF* decision (below), the court enjoined a tin parachute along with a pension parachute and poison pill adopted by the target company in the face of a hostile tender offer.

D. Pension Parachutes

Several companies have adopted amendments to their pension plans (so-called "pension parachutes") to provide for the immediate allocation and vesting of excess pension funds upon a change of control, often defined as the acquisition of a certain percentage of the company's shares (e.g., 20 percent). Most pension parachutes provide that the allocation and vesting of excess pension funds will not occur if the company's board of directors approves the acquisition in advance. Pension parachutes are designed to ensure that the target's pensioners are protected in the event of a hostile takeover. Unlike golden parachutes, however, pension parachutes typically have a significant anti-takeover effect. Assuming the overfunding in the target's pension plan is substantial, a pension parachute will provide an economic impediment to a hostile bid and will thus encourage potential acquirors to negotiate with management prior to crossing the trigger threshold. Recent amendments to the Code and ERISA have potentially lessened the need for a pension parachute. The Code now provides for an excise tax of 15 percent on most reversions from qualified plans on or after October 21, 1988. Furthermore, under ERISA, no reversion of excess assets may occur under a pension plan that has been amended within the 5 previous years to allow for such a reversion. Pension parachutes raise legal questions that go beyond those raised by the standard Share Purchase Rights Plan. Unlike the percentage flip-in provision contained in some rights plans, which dilutes a raider's economic interest in a target company by allocating an economic benefit to all shareholders excluding the raider, a pension parachute dilutes a raider's economic interest by allocating an economic benefit to the target's employees. The courts that have considered the issue are divided over the legitimacy of such an allocation. See *Edelman* v. *Fruehauf Corp.*, 798 F.2d 882 (6th Cir. 1986) (enjoining pension parachute); *Minstar Acquiring Corp.*v. *AMF, Inc.*, 621 F. Supp. 1252 (S.D.N.Y. 1985) (same); *GAF Corp.*v. *Union Carbide Corp.*, 624 F. Supp. 1016 (S.D.N.Y. 1985) (upholding pension parachute). The courts have isolated two separate issues that must be considered in determining the validity of a pension parachute: (1) whether the parachute is a legitimate defensive tactic and (2) whether the decision to vest the overfunding in the pension plan upon a change of control constitutes a legitimate exercise of the directors' business judgment. Furthermore, in an active bidding situation the courts may require that the impact of the pension parachute be equal for all bidders. See *Edelman* v. *Fruehauf Corp.*, 798 F.2d at 890.

IV. POISON PUTS

A company may agree to clauses in loan agreements or other material contracts permitting the lender to call the loan or the other contracting party to cancel the contract in the event of a change in control. The efficacy of such provisions is highly doubtful unless necessary to secure attractive financings. Such clauses can backfire in the event that target management seeks to expedite a transaction with a white knight which the lender or other contracting party does not favor. However, with the current surge in large leveraged transactions, including the $25 billion buyout of RJR, more and more lenders have been seeking poison put protection (See "Harris, Williams Cos. Unit Are First to Offer Super 'Poison Put,'" *The Wall Street Journal*, Nov. 16, 1988, p. C1), and borrowers may have no choice but to offer such protections in order to obtain desired funds.

Investors in convertible debt issues have also been seeking broad changes in covenant language because of the takeover climate. These changes include: (1) put rights in the event of certain changes of control; (2) net worth restrictions that trigger a sinking fund; and (3) restrictions on distributions to common shareholders. See "Investors Want Big Changes in Convertible Debt Securities," *Corp. Fin. Week*, Mar. 21, 1988.

Bondholders have turned to contractual protections as the courts have made it clear that no general fiduciary duties are owed to them. *See, e.g.*, *Simons* v. *Cogan*, 549 A.2d 300 (Del. Supr. 1988); *Metropolitan Securities* v. *Occidental Petroleum Corp.*, 705 F. Supp. 134 (S.D.N.Y. 1989).

V. RESTRUCTURING DEFENSES

Corporate restructurings have proven to be an effective defense, especially against two-tier and junk bond bust-up takeovers. Corporate restructurings often enable a target company to provide shareholders with economically superior value to that offered by the raider. This is often possible since the raider has designed his bid to achieve substantial economic returns for himself, while a restructuring is designed to maximize shareholder value. Unlike a white knight transaction, a restructuring does generally not involve a sale of the company; shareholders retain a continuing equity in the company and thus can benefit from the company's future growth and profitability. However, if significant voting power is consolidated in the hands of management through the restructuring, courts may view the restructuring as a sale of effective control, which under Delaware law would trigger the *Revlon* doctrine and thus require the board of directors to act as auctioneers seeking to obtain the best possible price for the company.

Although self-tenders, large-scale open market repurchases, and recapitalizations are not always accompanied by sales or spin-offs of assets, a financial restructuring that is sufficiently dramatic to forestall a raider often entails sales of assets or reorganization of the corporate hierarchy to reduce costs. Restructuring defenses can also be implemented before a company is even rumored to be potentially a target for a raid.

In structuring self-tenders, exchange offers, and recapitalizations, the restrictions of SEC Rule 19c-4 ("one-share one-vote") should be examined to determine whether the rule has any application to the proposed transaction. *See* Exch. Act Rel. No. 34-26390 (Dec. 20, 1988) (proposed NYSE rule change concerning Rule 19c-4).

A. Sales of Attractive Assets

A target may try to discourage the bidder by selling off those assets which are most attractive to the bidder. This tactic may be effective if the bidder values some aspect of the target's assets more highly than does the target itself.

Courts presented with challenges to this tactic have applied the business judgment rule. See *GM Sub Corp.* v. *Liggett Group, Inc.*, C.A. No. 6155, slip op. at 3–5 (Del. Ch. Apr. 25, 1980) (rejecting Grand Metropolitan's motion for a preliminary injunction against the sale of Austin Nichols by the Liggett Group); see also *Carter Hawley Hale Stores, Inc.* v. *The Limited, Inc.*, C.A. No. 84-2200 AWT (C.D. Cal. Apr. 17, 1984) (upholding Carter Hawley's grant of an option to purchase its subsidiary Waldenbooks to deter a hostile bid by The Limited); *Whittaker Corp.* v. *Edgar*, 535 F. Supp. 933, 951 (N.D. Ill.), *aff'd*, Nos. 82-1305, 82-1307 (7th Cir. Mar. 5, 1982) (upholding target Brunswick Corp.'s sale of one of its divisions to defend against an offer by Whittaker); *City Capital Associates Ltd. Partnership* v. *Interco Inc.*, 551 A.2d 787 (Del. Ch. 1988) (upheld auction sale of Ethan Allen division as part of a proposed recapitalization). Asset lock-ups granted to white knight bidders will be scrutinized under the *Revlon* standard (see Chapter 22.II.A.1. and II.B).

B. Corporate Split-ups and Spin-offs

One alternative means of focusing stock market attention on a company's underlying assets is to place crown jewel assets in a corporation and sell off some of the shares in an initial public offering. As with a master limited partnership (see 23.V.E), the shares of the new corporate entity could be distributed to shareholders in the event of a takeover of the parent corporation. Another means of boosting the share price of a company is to deconglomerate—sell off businesses that no longer fit the company's strategic plans or split the company into logically related units. In either case, a company tries to focus the market's attention on its individual businesses which, viewed separately, may enjoy a higher market valuation than when viewed together. In the Lucky Stores restructuring and reincorporation several years ago, a spin-off constituted but one element of a comprehensive business and financial restructuring in which the company sold three of its operating units and spun-off a fourth in an effort to refocus the company on its core food business and to enhance shareholder values. In 1988, a restructured Lucky Stores was acquired at a substantial premium to the value placed on its prior restructuring and the tender offer by Edelman.

A split-up or spin-off may be accomplished free of tax to the corporation and its shareholders, provided that the highly technical requirements of Section 355 of the Income Revenue Code are met. If the transaction so qualifies, stockholders will not recognize gain or loss on the receipt of shares of the spun-off entity, and the company will not recognize any gain or loss on the distribution. One of the requirements under Section 355 is that the spin-off not be a device for the distribution of earnings and profits of the distributed or the distributing company. Current and proposed Treasury Regulations under Section 355 of the Code provide, among other matters, that under certain circumstances post-spin-off sales of the stock or securities of the distributed or distributing company are evidence that a spin-off was a device to distribute earnings and profits. Thus, if such companies were acquired in a taxable transaction soon after the spin-off, it is possible that the IRS could successfully contend that the spin-off would fail to qualify as a tax-free transaction. The possibility of such adverse tax consequences may discourage an acquiror from attempting to acquire the separately traded companies in the period following the spin-off. In the contemplated NL spin-off of its chemical business (see below), the chemical business indemnified NL for any tax liability which would accrue to NL as a result of any NL tax triggered by a party purchasing the chemical business and disqualifying the tax-free nature of the spin-off transaction. Similar arrangements have been contemplated in the attempted spin-off by Pillsbury of its Burger King subsidiary (*see* p. 593).

Spin-offs have been utilized as part of a defensive restructuring in the following contexts:

1. NL Industries

NL Industries, as part of a settlement agreement with Coniston Partners, agreed to set up a new corporation to hold its chemical business and to sell 20 percent of the shares to the public. The purpose of this plan was to let the market recognize NL's position as a chemical company rather than just as an oil field services company, which should have boosted NL's stock price. After this plan was announced and before the public offering had taken place, Harold Simmons launched a tender offer for all of the shares of the parent company at a price that the Board of Directors considered inadequate. The Board rejected Simmons' offer and approved a spin-off of the company's chemical business to the shareholders hoping to achieve a market valuation that better reflected the value of NL than Simmons' offer. Under SEC rules, the parent normally would have been unable to complete the spin-off in time to allow the market to decide whether the company as divided was worth more than Simmons' offering price. To avoid this dilemma, the company decided to distribute a new series of preferred stock which was exchangeable for shares in the new chemical company upon completion of the spin-off and in the interim was entitled to the free cashflow of the chemicals company. Simmons' request for a temporary restraining order against distribution of the preferred stock was denied.

Although Simmons eventually did acquire control of NL and the chemicals subsidiary (NL Chemicals) by purchasing NL common shares on the open market, he was unable to take full advantage of the acquisition for another two years and NL's shareholders ultimately realized more value than Simmons' tender offer price.

2. Diamond Shamrock

In response to an offer by T. Boone Pickens, which the board viewed as inadequate and coercive, Diamond Shamrock developed a restructuring plan designed to maximize shareholder value by creating two separate entities, each clearly focused on one of the company's two core businesses. The principal elements of the restructuring plan included (1) a cash self-tender for up to 20 million common shares at $15 per share; (2) the sale of a new issue of convertible preferred stock to The Prudential Insurance Company of America; and (3) the spin-off of the company's refining and marketing business as a result of which the company would be primarily engaged in the exploration and production of hydrocarbons. No shareholder vote was required for the implementation of the restructuring plan. The spin-off was structured so as to qualify as a tax-free transaction under Section 355 of the Code.

In response to the announcement of the restructuring plan, Pickens made a proposal to the Board for an all-cash deal and requested that the Board let the shareholders choose between the merger proposal and the restructuring. The Board concluded that the restructuring was preferable to the Pickens merger proposal, rejected the proposal as inadequate, and reaffirmed its commitment to pursue the restructuring. The Board stated that since it determined the merger proposal was inadequate, there was no basis to submit such proposal to the shareholders and that to do so would be inappropriate under Delaware law. Upon commencement of the self-tender, Pickens dropped its partial offer.

3. Carter Hawley Hale

As part of the restructuring by Carter Hawley Hale to fend off a hostile bid by The Limited and the Edward J. DeBartolo Corporation, Carter Hawley Hale spun off its specialty store chains. Under the restructuring plan, General Cinema, a major shareholder of Carter Hawley Hale, received a 60 percent equity and 44 percent voting interest in the new company.

4. Pillsbury

Pillsbury, in response to a hostile tender offer from Grand Metropolitan, proposed to spin off its Burger King subsidiary to its shareholders on a tax-free basis. Part of this distribution would have involved cash obtained by leveraging some of the assets of its Burger King subsidiary. The plan was not viewed favorably by the market or the Burger King franchisees, who for the most part opposed the spin-off and any leveraging of Burger King. In addition, Grand Metropolitan stated that it would continue its tender offer, but that if the spin-off occurred, it would calculate the negative tax effects in formulating a new lower price for the Pillsbury shares.

A Minnesota state court, in *Garland's Inc. Profit Sharing Plan* v. *Pillsbury Co.*, No. 8817834 (Minn. Dist. Ct. Dec. 16, 1988), enjoined the Burger King spin-off pending a decision in Delaware on Pillsbury's rights plan. The Delaware Chancery Court, in addition to ordering redemption of the Pillsbury rights, enjoined the Burger King spin-off for a number of reasons, including (1) the chaos it might cause for Pillsbury, its shareholders, and third parties; (2) the permanent change in Pillsbury's capital structure that would result from the spin-off and the formation of two separate companies; (3) that the spin-off would necessarily reduce the price offered for Pillsbury's shares in the pending Grand Met tender offer, with the court noting that more than 80 percent of the outstanding shares had already been tendered in response to Grand Met's current offer; (4) the creditor-debtor relationship which, under

Delaware law, might be created between Pillsbury and its shareholders on the record date of the spin-off; (5) the fact that trading of the Burger King shares after the spin-off would bring additional third parties into the controversy; and (6) the "significant tax implications" that might result if various other actions were taken in the near future. *Grand Metropolitan PLC* v. *Pillsbury Col*, [1988–89 Transfer Binder] Fed. Sec. L. Rep. (CCH) ¶ 94,104 (Del. Ch. Dec. 16, 1988).

C. Self-tenders; General

When faced with a hostile tender offer, a target may implement a self-tender (i.e., offer to purchase its own shares) for cash and/or securities with a value per share in excess of the value of the bidder's offer. The value per share of the target's offer may approximate the board of directors' view of the fair value of a share, in which case the self-tender has the advantage of affording shareholders the choice between obtaining cash and/or securities pursuant to the self-tender and remaining shareholders in a company that management believes will provide higher returns over time. Alternatively, the value per share of the target's offer may substantially exceed the value of a share, in which case the self-tender enables eligible shareholders to obtain a premium price for a portion of their shares while retaining their proportionate interest as shareholders. A self-tender may form an important component of a corporate restructuring involving a split-up or spin-off, a defensive recapitalization or a leveraged buyout led by management, or a white knight. In *Lowenschuss* v. *Option Clearing Corp.*, C.A. No. 7972 (Del. Ch. Mar. 27, 1985), the Chancery Court rejected the argument that directors have no power to authorize a self-tender without shareholder approval because of its fundamental effect on the corporation's capital structure. Street sweeps can also be utilized as a defensive measure (see Chapter 21.IV.B).

Large scale self-tenders are generally possible only when a target has sufficient unrestricted assets to support large borrowings or has the ability to sell equity securities quickly to friendly purchasers, because, even though a debenture or preferred stock exchange offer may be an alternative to a cash self-tender, it also requires that the target have adequate borrowing power or the ability under existing debt convenants to pay significant preferred dividends. Finally, if a self-tender does not destroy the raider's ability to finance a takeover or result in the creation of a management-controlled control block of target shares, it has no real defensive impact other than possibly to increase the price paid to the target's shareholders, which may be sufficient. Even if the raider's ability to finance a takeover is destroyed, other potential acquirors may accumulate substantial positions in the market as arbitrageurs try to get rid of the stock. For example, as a result of Ted Turner's bid for CBS, Loews acquired a substantial position in CBS and the Chairman of the Board of Loews subsequently became the Chief Executive Officer of CBS.

1. Applications

The following case histories are illustrative of the possibilities made available by self-tenders:

(a) SCM. In SCM's defense against a hostile tender offer by Hanson Trust PLC for all SCM shares at $72 in cash per share, SCM combined a white knight tender offer with a self-tender. The self-tender was designed to protect shareholders in the event neither white knight Merrill Lynch nor raider Hanson was able to consummate its tender offer for the company. The Merrill Lynch offer was conditioned on, among other things, the tender of two-thirds of SCM's common stock, calculated on a fully diluted basis. Because Hanson's approximately one-third position in SCM left consummation of the Merrill Lynch offer in doubt, the SCM offer was a predominant factor supporting SCM's stock price. Shortly after the Second Circuit Court of Appeals invalidated certain lock-up options granted by SCM to Merrill Lynch, Hanson purchased over seven million shares pursuant to its tender offer, raising Hanson's stake to approximately 91.6 percent of SCM's outstanding common stock (see Chapter 21.IV.B.3).

(b) Revlon. An early step in Revlon's defense against Pantry Pride's raid was a self-exchange offer of $57.50 of subordinated debt and preferred stock for approximately 26 percent of its stock. The objective of the self-tender was to give shareholders an immediate premium for some of their shares and permit them to retain their equity interest in the company. The securities issued in the exchange offer contained covenants designed to interfere with Pantry Pride's financing. Pantry Pride responded with a reduced bid that purportedly took into account the exchange offer and indicated that it could finance around the covenants in the exchange offer securities (although Pantry Pride was never tested on this point). The combination of the self-tender and the Revlon Note Purchase Rights Plan provided Revlon with sufficient time to put together a complicated transaction with Forstmann Little & Co. This development prompted a bidding war that ultimately led to approximately $900 million in increased value for Revlon's shareholders.

(c) Phillips. After the Phillips recapitalization plan was defeated by shareholders, Phillips proposed an enriched, and more highly leveraged, recapitalization plan to be accomplished through a self-exchange offer. This exchange offer persuaded Carl Icahn to abandon his two-tier bid for Phillips. The exchange offer contained provisions requiring a tendering shareholder to forgo any rights to sell his shares to Phillips through other arrangements. This provision was designed to prevent Mesa Petroleum Co., which had attempted to gain control of the company, from having some of its Phillips shares purchased in the exchange offer for $62 in debt securities and having the remainder of its shares purchased at $53 in cash (which would be a substantial premium to market in the recapitalized company) pursuant to the settlement agreement between Mesa and Phillips.

(d) Lucky Stores. In the Lucky Stores restructuring and reincorporation, an integral component of the restructuring was a self-tender for 27 percent of the company's shares at a significant premium over the market price.

(e) Diamond Shamrock. Diamond Shamrock was able to defeat a hostile takeover attempt by T. Boone Pickens by implementing a corporate restructuring consisting of a self-tender for 18 percent of the company's shares, a sale of preferred stock to The Prudential Insurance Company of America (see 23.VI.A.1), and a spin-off of the company's refining and marketing division (see 23.V.B.2). The self-tender, which matched the partial offer that had been made by Pickens, was designed to provide shareholders with cash for a portion of their shares along with an opportunity to retain a continuing equity interest in the company.

(f) GenCorp. GenCorp was able to defeat a junk bond bust-up takeover bid by Wagner and Brown and AFG Industries by implementing a self-tender for over half of the company's shares to be financed by substantial asset sales. In response to a hostile bid at $100 per share which the GenCorp Board rejected as inadequate, GenCorp announced a self-tender at $130 per share for 54 percent of its shares, to be financed by the sale of the company's tire and soft-drink bottling operations and the consummation of the previously announced sales of certain broadcasting properties. Following the announcement of the self-tender, GenCorp shares traded at $118 per share.

(g) Pennwalt. Pennwalt attempted to disarm a threatened hostile bid by Centaur Partners by employing a preemptive restructuring plan through which it sold two divisions and used most of the proceeds from those sales to purchase approximately 37.6 percent of its outstanding shares through a self-tender. Pennwalt's "dutchauction" self-tender, which was commenced over four months after Centaur's first announcement, offered shareholders a price range of between $85 and $97 per share; 72 percent of the outstanding shares were tendered to Pennwalt at $85, and the self-tender was completed at that price. Less than two weeks after the expiration of the buyback offer, Centaur launched its own bid for all the outstanding shares of Pennwalt at $100 per share, which it later raised to $112 per share. Eventually, Pennwalt accepted a $132 white knight bid from Elf Aquitaine.

(h) Polaroid. In response to an unsolicited tender offer from Shamrock Holdings and on the eve of an impending proxy fight, Polaroid, after creating an ESOP, sold $300 million of convertible preferred stock to an investor willing to make a substantial equity investment in the company. This sale was combined with a stock repurchase program, the first step of which was a self-tender at $50 per share while the competing tender offer was at $45 per share. The self-tender and the stock issuance were upheld by the Delaware Chancery Court. *Shamrock Holdings, Inc.* v. *Polaroid*, Civ. No. 10,075 (Del. Ch. Mar. 17, 1989).

2. Cases Involving Self-tenders

(a) Revlon. In *Revlon*, the Delaware Supreme Court upheld Revlon's defensive exchange offer under the *Unocal* standard. *Revlon, Inc.* v. *MacAndrews & Forbes Holdings, Inc.*, 506 A.2d at 181. The Court decided that the directors' conclusion that Pantry Pride's $47.50 offer was grossly inadequate was made in good faith, and on an informed basis, with reasonable grounds to believe that there existed a threat of harm to the corporate enterprise and that the adoption of the exchange offer was reasonable in relation to the threat posed.

(b) GAF/Union Carbide. In the *GAF/Union Carbide* decision, the court specifically endorsed the right of directors to offer the shareholders a superior economic alternative to a takeover attempt that would have ended their investment in the company. Judge Pollack approved the resolve of a company faced with a tender offer to foster its continued existence by leveraging the company in order to offer a superior economic alternative to its shareholders. See 624 F. Supp. at 1017–18, 1020. Judge Pollack stated:

> Deterring an unfair offer is entirely legitimate. GAF is not entitled to have the terms of an exchange offer dictated by GAF, free of competition.
>
> Self-appointed potential acquirors of control are not a protected species in corporate law. The hostile offeror is not entitled to have a Board of Directors smooth his path to control. *Id.* at 1020.

(c) Anderson Clayton. In *AC Acquisitions Corp.* v. *Anderson, Clayton & Co.*, 519 A.2d 103 (Del. Ch. 1986), the court held that the Board had acted properly in seeking to provide the shareholders an economic alternative to a hostile bid, but that the specific means it employed to achieve that objective were not appropriate. Therefore, the court enjoined consummation of the Anderson Clayton self-tender because, according to the court, the defense was not structured in a manner to assure shareholders a realistic choice between the competing deal and the Anderson Clayton deal and "no rational shareholder could afford not to tender into [Anderson Clayton's] self-tender offer at least if that transaction were viewed in isolation." *Id.* at 113. A factor influencing the court's decision was that Anderson Clayton's financial adviser had not opined that either alternative was economically superior to the other. While the court acknowledged the legitimacy of a Board-created competitive alternative that generates an immediate cash distribution while permitting the stockholders to remain as equity participants in the ongoing company, it ruled that in the face of an all cash offer at a concededly fair price, an alternative that is not economically superior must allow the shareholders the ability to choose between the alternative and the raider's offer.

During the course of its opinion, the court observed that the raider could have eliminated the coercive element of the Anderson Clayton self-tender by eliminating its 51 percent condition, but that the raider had "no legal duty to extend an unconditional offer whereas the Board does have a legal duty to its shareholders to exercise its judgment to promote the stockholders' interests" *Id.* at 114 n.12. The relief granted by the court permitted Anderson Clayton to proceed with its self-tender but prohibited it from purchasing shares for about two weeks.

(d) Gelco. In *Gelco Corp.* v. *Coniston Partners*, 652 F. Supp. 829 (D. Minn. 1986), *aff'd in part and vacated in part*, 811 F.2d 414 (8th Cir. 1987) (see 23.II.C.8.), the District Court refused to preliminarily enjoin the purchase by Gelco of its common stock pursuant to an exchange offer. Prior to the commencement of the hostile tender offer for Gelco by Coniston Partners, Gelco had announced a restructuring plan, including the sale of four of its divisions, a cash self-tender, and the sale of a new series of voting preferred stock to Gelco's financial advisor, as a form of bridge financing for the self-tender. After Coniston submitted to Gelco's Board a bid to purchase Gelco for the equivalent of $22.50 in cash per share, Gelco withdrew the self-tender and announced the exchange offer. If Gelco were to buy six million shares pursuant to the exchange offer and to complete the sale of the voting preferred stock to Merrill Lynch, management and Merrill Lynch together would have about 53 percent of the voting power of Gelco's voting capital stock, although there was ostensibly no voting agreement between Gelco and Merrill Lynch.

In refusing the injunction, the court noted that (1) Gelco's investment banker had advised the Board that Coniston's offer was inadequate from a financial point of view, (2) the Gelco Board had determined in good faith that Gelco's restructuring program promised greater long term value to shareholders and (3) the restructuring program had first been undertaken prior to Coniston's initial bid to Gelco's Board and the exchange offer had been commenced prior to the commencement of Coniston's tender offer.

(e) Chicago Milwaukee. In *Eisenberg* v. *Chicago Milwaukee Corp.*, 537 A.2d 1051 (Del. Ch. 1987), the Delaware Court of Chancery enjoined a post-October 19th any-and-all self-tender for preferred shares on grounds of inadequate disclosure and "coercion."

The Court held that boilerplate-type disclosure of purpose (to acquire the shares at an attractive price and to reduce costs) was misleading where the purpose was to take advantage of the October 1987 market correction that drove the price of the preferred shares to an unprecedented low level. The court further held that boilerplate-type disclosure on fairness of the offer (that "the current range of market prices was among the factors in the Board of Directors' determination") was misleading, because the current market level was the primary, if not predominant, motivating factor.

On the "coercion" point, the court held that the statement in the offer that the company intends to request delisting of the preferred shares following the offer rendered the offer "unequitably coercive." The court did indicate, however, that the fact that the offer was made at a time of an historical low trading price for the preferred shares did not make the offer "coercive."

(f) Polaroid. In *Shamrock Holdings Inc.* v. *Polaroid Corp.*, [1988–89 Transfer Binder] Fed. Sec. L. Rep. (CCH) ¶ 94,185 (Del. Ch. Jan. 30, 1989), the Delaware Chancery Court refused to grant a temporary restraining order to Shamrock, the unsolicited offeror, against Polaroid's sale of $300 million of preferred stock, which was convertible into 6 million shares of common stock and had voting rights on an "as converted" basis (amounting to approximately 12.5 percent of the outstanding voting power after the company's repurchase program). In addition, Polaroid granted seven-year warrants for 635,000 shares to the same party and had given such party the right to name directors to the Polaroid board. Shamrock had made an $45 per share tender offer and had announced its intention to commence a proxy fight to elect its nominees to Polaroid's board. In response, Polaroid had also announced a program to repurchase approximately $1.1 billion of Polaroid stock at $50 per share. These actions by Polaroid were in addition to the earlier sale of approximately 14 percent of its outstanding shares to an ESOP, which had been validated by the Delaware Chancery Court. The court declined to grant a temporary restraining order against either the stock sale or the repurchase program. In *Shamrock Holdings, Inc.* v. *Polaroid Corp.*, Civ. No. 10,075 (Del. Ch. Mar. 17, 1989), the court, applying the *Unocal* standard, upheld the stock issuance and self-tender, finding them to be reasonable responses to the threat posed, even though there was an impending proxy fight.

3. Exclusionary Self-tenders

In *Unocal Corp.* v. *Mesa Petroleum Co.*, 493 A.2d 946 (Del. Supr. 1985), the Delaware Supreme Court vacated a preliminary injunction against Unocal's proposed "discriminatory exchange offer" (i.e., the Mesa shareholder group was excluded from participating in the offer). The Court found that the Board acting in good faith had determined the Mesa proposal to be "grossly inadequate," and deferred to the Board's choice of tactics to defend against Mesa's two-tier takeover bid. An exclusionary self-tender was also utilized by Union Carbide in response to a hostile bid by GAF.

On July 14, 1986, however, the SEC amended the tender offer rules to prohibit exclusionary tender offers and to require that the same price be made available in a tender offer to all holders of the same class of stock (the so-called "all holders" rule). The new Rules 14d-10 and 13e-4(f)(8) through (11) state that no bidder may make a tender offer unless the tender offer is open to all security holders of the class of securities subject to the tender offer (except that a tender offer may exclude residents of a state in which the offer is prohibited).

The rules also provide that the consideration paid to any security holder pursuant to a tender offer must be equal to the highest consideration paid by the offeror to any other security holder during the tender offer. The rules would not prohibit an offeror from decreasing the price originally offered in the tender offer, so long as the highest consideration actually paid is paid to all tendering security holders. If more than one type of consideration is offered, the new rules require only that tendering security holders be given an equal right to elect among each of the types of consideration offered and that the highest consideration of each type paid to any security holder be paid to any other security holder electing that type of consideration. The alternative forms of consideration are not required to be equivalent in value. If any state prohibits the offer or sale of securities in that state pursuant to an exchange offer, the offeror may offer alternative consideration to security holders in that state without offering the alternative consideration to security holders in any other states.

The new rules would not apply to an open market purchase program that is not a tender offer. However, the SEC has taken the position with respect to certain Note Purchase Rights Plans that the new rules regarding self-tenders become applicable once the Rights are triggered.

D. Recapitalizations

Recapitalizations have emerged as an important variation on leveraged buyouts. The development is due both to changes in the corporate debt and equity markets over the last several years and to the perceived success of a number of leveraged buyouts. Indeed, the potent ability of recapitalizations to respond to the public's appetite for the equity of highly leveraged companies indicates that recapitalizations can effectively compete with LBOs as a form of corporate restructuring. (See Volume II Chapters 23 and 36.)

In a recapitalization, each share of a company's stock held by its public shareholders is exchanged for a substantial payment of cash (and in some cases debt securities), while shareholders retain a substantial equity interest in the recapitalized company. The cash (or cash and debt) portion of the consideration is, in a typical case, approximately equal to or greater than the market price of the stock immediately prior to the announcement of the transaction. The value of the retained equity represents, in most cases, the premium or a significant portion of the premium over the market price prior to announcement of the transaction. Members of the company's management usually do not exchange their shares and stock options for cash (or cash and debt), but instead acquire, tax-free, additional equity and options for the value of the cash and debt that they would have received had they participated ratably with the public shareholders, thereby increasing their proportionate equity interest in the company.

A recapitalization transaction, like an LBO, represents a powerful means of increasing management's equity participation and addressing the dilemma faced by many managers of mature, slow-growth companies. Such companies often find themselves acquisition targets in the current takeover environment, primarily because they generate large amounts of cash without having adequate opportunities to reinvest such cash or make acquisitions and are unwilling to undertake extensive stock repurchase programs. Both an LBO and a recapitalization address this problem through a radical restructuring of a company's capitalization in the form of a large-scale substitution of debt for equity. Both transactions also represent effective and appropriate defensive responses, in the event of a takeover bid (whether the takeover bid is by tender offer, market accumulation, or proxy fight), that will provide shareholders with a meaningful alternative to the third-party bid and that may induce an auction for the company. In the acquisition of Kraft by Philip Morris, Kraft was able to get Philip Morris to raise its bid by almost $2 billion by announcing its intention to structure a recapitalization of the company.

A recapitalization, however, is different from an LBO in that a recapitalization is not a going-private transaction: Public shareholders substantially retain their percentage equity interest in the company. This difference has highly significant financial, legal, and strategic implications.

Recapitalizations are financially compelling because they allow a company to take advantage of both the low cost of debt financing and the high multiples at which equity securities are now trading. In this respect, a recapitalization may be able to offer public shareholders, largely through the value of the new equity given to the public, significantly greater consideration than a comparable LBO. This is because public shareholders often will demand lower returns than those sought by private investors in leveraged buyouts. Recaps can also be structured in connection with tax free spin-offs, and thus may have significant tax advantages over LBOs contingent on significant asset sales. Second, recapitalizations can be structured so as to create efficiency gains analogous to those created by LBOs. Third, recapitalizations are not serious self-dealing transactions, and if properly structured, need not run the risk of an appearance of impropriety or potential conflicts of interest. Compare Chapter 22.II.I. discussing whether a recapitalization is a "sale of the company."

In addition, recapitalizations are a potent response to the current hostile takeover environment. Announcement of a recapitalization need not necessarily place a company in as vulnerable a position with respect to unsolicited acquisition proposals as it would be in an LBO transaction. However, the recapitalization could be considered a sale of the company. See Chapter 22.II.I. Rule 19c-4 has also limited the type of protective provisions which may be adopted following a recapitalization, since scaled voting provisions and voting caps, which were adopted in previous recapitalizations, are prohibited by the new rule. Moreover, the *Interco* decision has cast doubt on whether a rights plan can be used to assure implementation of a recapitalization in a competitive bidding situation.

One limitation on the initiation of recapitalizations will be the willingness of boards of directors to be stewards of publicly held, highly leveraged companies. In certain situations, faced with the issuance of high-risk securities, a knowledgeable board of directors may prefer to pursue an LBO transaction, which has the effect of shifting the risk of a company's future performance onto insiders and sophisticated investors. On the other hand, in any case in which an LBO is proposed, the independent committee and the board should consider, in their evaluation of an LBO proposal, the alternative of a recapitalization, which would meet many of the goals of an LBO without terminating the equity interest of the public.

1. Structure

Under Delaware law, a recapitalization can be structured as either a merger or a reclassification. Under a merger structure, a shell corporation is merged into the company, with the company as the surviving corporation. In the merger, each share of the company's stock is converted into cash (or cash and debt) plus a new share, and each share of the shell corporation's stock is converted solely into new shares. The shell corporation stock is received by management immediately prior to the merger in exchange for their shares of the company's stock. Any amendments to the company's charter are included in the merger agreement, which is approved by shareholders. Under a reclassification structure pursuant to Delaware law, shares are reclassified into new shares and a new class of preferred shares that immediately converts into cash (or cash and debt) pursuant to a plan of recapitalization approved by stockholders. Immediately prior to the transaction, management exchanges its shares into shares of another new series of preferred stock, which in turn is reclassified and converted solely into new shares. Any charter amendments to be enacted in connection with the recapitalization may be presented to shareholders as part of the plan in a unified proposal. In contrast to a merger structure, under Delaware law shareholders are not entitled to appraisal rights in a reclassification structure.

A recapitalization may also be structured as an exchange offer in which the company offers to purchase a certain number of its shares in exchange for cash and debt securities. The transactions involving Phillips Petroleum, Unocal, and Union Carbide are the most celebrated examples of this structure. Recapitalizations can also be achieved through dividends as in the HBJ transaction. Notably, these structures have been used largely in response to hostile tender offers.

Care must be taken in structuring a recapitalization in response to a hostile cash tender offer for all shares, to avoid a legal challenge that the recapitalization has been structured coercively and precluded shareholder choice. See *Anderson Clayton* discussed in Chapter 23.V.C.2.; *Evans*, discussed in Chapter 22.I.E.3.

2. Accounting and Fraudulent Conveyances Issues

Unlike an LBO, a recapitalization is accounted for as a redemption of shares rather than as a purchase of a company. In consequence, a company cannot use a recapitalization to write up its assets to their fair market value. Assuming there is a substantial difference between the book value and the fair market value of a company's assets, a company will have a negative net worth for financial reporting purposes for several years after completion of a recapitalization. This fact has no particular legal significance in jurisdictions such as Delaware where, for corporate law purposes, the board of directors can revalue assets and liabilities to their fair market value to effect a redemption. The prospect of a negative net worth has also been accepted by the New York Stock Exchange in listing new shares following a recapitalization, and by lenders that face fraudulent conveyance issues.

In *Warnaco, Inc.* v. *Galef*, C. No. B-86-146 (PCD) (D. Conn. Apr. 13, 1986), the court denied the W Acquisition Corp. motion for a preliminary injunction against the recapitalization. W Acquisition Corp. contended that the recapitalization would violate both the Connecticut statutory prohibitions on distributions that would render the corporation insolvent and the statutory requirement that distributions be made out of surplus. Warnaco had revalued assets to achieve the requisite surplus. The court found there to be substantial issues as to the propriety of such revaluation but denied the motion on balance of hardship grounds.

A recapitalization may constitute a fraudulent conveyance under state law if, among other things, following the distribution of cash (or cash and debt) to shareholders, the fair market value of the company's assets would be less than the fair market value of the company's liabilities, or the company's ability to pay its obligations as they become due would be impaired. This test is not, however, governed by the accounting treatment of the transaction. Rather, the company's board of directors can, in an exercise of its business judgment, make a determination with respect to the fair market value of the company's assets and the existence of a sufficient surplus to support the recapitalization. This judgment should be, and typically is, supported by a formal third-party appraisal of the company's assets. Lenders will now require that such "solvency letters" be obtained prior to any financing.

3. Tax Issues

Although recapitalization transactions are taxable to shareholders, the amount of gain recognized does not exceed the cash and fair market value of the debt securities received. One primary objective in a recapitalization transaction has often been to have the shareholders' taxable income taxed at capital gain rates and not dividend rates.

In recapitalizations, shareholders generally receive shares in the new company, cash and/or debt securities in exchange for all of their shares. Such an exchange is tested for dividend equivalency under the rules of Section 302 of the Code governing redemptions. Generally, under Section 302(b) of the Code, redemptions are taxed as dividends to the extent of the corporation's earnings and profits, unless the redemption (1) is not essentially equivalent to a dividend, (2) is substantially disproportionate with respect to the selling shareholder, or (3) terminates the shareholder's interest in the corporation.

A primary objective in structuring recapitalization transactions has been to meet the safe-harbor "substantially disproportionate" test. To meet this test, public shareholders must have their equity interest in the company reduced, so that after the transaction they hold less than 80 percent of the voting power and common stock held prior to the recapitalization. There are two principal means to achieve this result. Either some group of the existing shareholders can substantially increase its equity interest in the business and forgo the cash or debt securities offered to other shareholders in the recapitalization, or new investors must be found to acquire equity in the recapitalized company.

The importance of ensuring capital gains treatment for shareholders was reduced beginning in 1988, when capital gains and ordinary income became subject to the same rate of tax. Corporate shareholders will continue to prefer to receive dividends rather than capital gains, because such shareholders will continue to be eligible for the dividends-received deduction, subject, however, to the newly tightened extraordinary dividends provisions that require corporate recipients to decrease their stock basis to reflect the dividends-received deduction on unusually large dividends or non-pro rata dividends. However, if a recapitalization is structured as a self-tender, a transaction which meets the tests of Section 302(b) set forth above will result in a shareholder's gain being limited to the difference between the amount such shareholder receives and his tax basis in the shares sold. A transaction taxed as a dividend results in ordinary income up to the cash received (assuming sufficient earnings and profits).

E. Master Limited Partnerships

Recent experience with respect to the natural resource industries has proven that placing crown jewel assets in limited partnerships can be an effective means of enhancing shareholder values and—in the event of a takeover—

of ensuring that a company's shareholders, and not the raider, realize the long-term value of these assets. Diamond Shamrock, International Paper, Borden, Transco, Unocal, and Mesa have utilized this approach. Typically, the limited partnership is managed by the general partner, which may be a subsidiary of the former parent corporation or may be controlled by the former managers of the division or subsidiary placed in the partnership. Assets that are undervalued by the stock market in the context of a large corporation but that have the potential to generate a significant and steady cash flow are ideal candidates for distribution to a limited partnership. The transfer of such assets, in certain circumstances, to a limited partnership provides a vehicle for shareholders to realize the benefits of the earnings stream generated by such assets unencumbered by corporate-level taxation of such earnings. In addition, many limited partnerships have been structured so that early distributions to limited partners are treated as returns of capital that offset basis.

These tax benefits are obtained at the cost of the significant added complexity involved in the taxation of partnerships, particularly those whose units are publicly traded.

Furthermore, under the Revenue Act of 1987, generally effective December 17, 1987, publicly traded limited partnerships are generally taxed as corporations for federal income tax purposes. As a result, the principal tax advantage of the partnership structure—avoidance of corporate level taxation—is unavailable. An exception to this rule is provided for a publicly traded partnership if 90 percent or more of its gross income is "qualifying income." For these purposes qualifying income includes:

1. Certain interest and dividends.
2. Real property rents.
3. Gain from the sale of real property.
4. Income and gains from the exploration, development, mining, production, refining and transportation of any mineral or natural resource.
5. Any gain from the sale or other disposition of a capital asset or certain assets described in paragraphs (1) through (4) above.
6. In certain circumstances, income and gains from commodities and futures.

Moreover, under the Revenue Act of 1987, income from publicly traded partnerships that are not treated as corporations is generally treated as portfolio income for purposes of the passive loss rules of the Internal Revenue Code. As a result, a limited partner will be unable to utilize passive losses against such income. Furthermore, under the 1987 Act, losses from such publicly traded limited partnerships are generally treated as passive losses and tax-exempt organizations are subject to taxation on any income from such publicly traded partnerships. The Treasury Department has been directed by Congress to continue studying the rules applicable to publicly traded partnerships, and further developments are possible.

In transferring assets of a "crown jewel" to a partnership that is taxed as such, the corporation will recognize no taxable gain unless the liabilities also transferred exceed the tax basis of the transferred property or the corporation receives property other than partnership units. The corporation's basis in the partnership units will equal its basis in the property transferred to the partnership. Distribution of the partnership units to shareholders will generally cause the corporation to recognize taxable gain to the extent that the fair market value of the partnership units so distributed exceeds their basis in the hands of the corporation. This problem can be mitigated to some extent, if the corporation contributes high-basis, low-value assets to the partnership.

Units in the partnership holding the crown jewel assets can be either fully distributed initially to a corporation's shareholders or held by the corporation and distributed over time. In the latter instance, it could be provided that the partnership units will automatically be distributed to shareholders in the event of a takeover of the parent corporation. Thus, a raider would be deprived of the opportunity to liquidate the crown jewel for his own account. If only a small portion of the partnership units are to be distributed initially, a company may wish to conduct a simultaneous public offering of some of the partnership units. This would focus market attention on the company's underlying assets and could improve the company's stock price. Subsequent distributions of partnership units could be made from time to time at the discretion of the company or according to a prearranged plan, such as at an established annual dividend rate. Any pro rata distribution of partnership units to shareholders will be taxed as a dividend to the shareholders.

F. Strategy, Tactics, and Issues

One problem with restructuring defenses generally is that they are possible in many cases only if there has been careful preparation by the company and by its investment bankers and counsel. Arranging for a friendly buyer of a particular asset, for example, and restructuring one's business to accommodate the loss of the asset, are time consuming, complicated, and costly endeavors. In the case of the self-tender defense, the money must be raised quickly and the assets that are to be mortgaged or sold should be carefully chosen.

The use as defensive measures of self-tenders, open market repurchases, leveraged buyouts, and recapitalizations, which result in highly leveraged corporate entities, like the use of junk bond financing in general, has increased the public debate over the efficacy of takeover transactions. Similarly, questions have been raised when companies have sold or spun-off properties that may have been their most promising assets. For example, it is not at all clear whether companies that have adopted radical restructuring plans have sufficient financial flexibility to deal with unforeseeable changes in economic conditions. On the other hand, defensive restructurings have often represented the only viable alternatives to inadequate bids. Restructurings often are most effective as a preplanning measure rather than as a defense to an actual bid.

VI. "WHITE SQUIRE" AND WHITE KNIGHT ARRANGEMENTS

A. Issuance of Stock to a Friendly Holder

In many cases, a company that has become the target of a hostile takeover attempt determines that its independence can be maintained only by selling a large block of voting securities to a "big brother" or "white squire." Typically, the target and the white squire enter into a standstill agreement delineating various restrictions on the white squire's ability to vote securities held by it and/or to acquire additional voting securities. Such transactions should be upheld when a target properly determines that the takeover is not in the best interests of shareholders or when the issuance is not for the sole or primary purpose of entrenching management. See *Chris-Craft Industries, Inc.* v. *Piper Aircraft Corp.*, 480 F.2d 341, 365 (2d Cir.), *cert. denied*, 414 U.S. 910 (1973).

The courts have generally upheld the issuance of stock to a white squire as a defensive measure when the result was not to consolidate voting control in management's or employee's hands. See *Gearhart Industries, Inc.* v. *Smith International, Inc.*, 741 F.2d 707 (5th Cir. 1984); *News International* v. *Warner Communications Inc.*, C.A. No. 7420 (Del. Ch. Jan. 12, 1984); *Gelco*, 652 F. Supp. at 850; *cf. Consolidated Amusement Co.* v. *Rugoff*, [1978 Transfer Binder] Fed. Sec. L. Rep. (CCH) ¶ 96,584 (S.D.N.Y. 1978) (management not entitled to place a block of stock in friendly hands where there was no independent legitimate business purpose for the transaction); *Shamrock Holdings, Inc.* v. *Polaroid Corp.*, [Current] Fed. Sec. L. Rep. (CCH) ¶ 94,430 (Del. Ch. Mar. 17, 1989).

White squire arrangements may be especially useful in Delaware, where a 15 percent block in friendly hands could make it difficult for a hostile acquiror to avoid the restrictions of the Delaware business combination statute.

1. Diamond Shamrock

As part of the restructuring plan implemented by Diamond Shamrock, the company sold 3 million shares of a new series of preferred stock (the $9.75 Cumulative Convertible Preferred Stock) to The Prudential Insurance Company of America for $300 million. Prudential, as long as it holds a majority of the $9.75 Preferred Shares, is entitled to elect three directors to the Company's Board and can veto certain self-dealing transactions between the Company and a 5 percent shareholder and certain amendments to the Company's charter. The $9.75 Preferred Shares are not convertible until 1990 and contain certain restrictions on transfer. Prudential received a $2.25 million structuring fee (which included a $1.5 million commitment fee) in connection with the preferred stock sale.

2. Allegis Corp.

In the face of heightened takeover speculation resulting from the proposal by the United Airlines' pilots to acquire the airline from its parent, Allegis Corp., Allegis sold $700 million principal amount of its convertible notes due 1992 to Boeing Aircraft Corp. The sale of the notes to Boeing was presented by Allegis as an integral part of a $2.1 billion order for new planes by United, but was widely perceived primarily as an anti-takeover measure. The financial and other terms of the notes appear to confirm this perception. The notes are repayable in equal installments commencing 1990 and carry a coupon of 7.52 percent; however, the coupon increases to 9.5 percent in the event a person makes a tender offer resulting in its ownership of 40 percent or more of Allegis' common stock and does not, within three months thereafter, complete a second step for the same kind and amount of consideration as was paid in the first step. The notes are convertible at any time at Boeing's option into common stock at $70.62 per share (slightly in excess of Allegis' stock price at the time the notes were sold) or a new series of convertible preferred stock, also convertible into common stock. The financial terms of the preferred stock generally mirror those of the notes, including the interest "kickup" and the terms of the conversion. Boeing has the option on one occasion only, commencing 30 and ending 150 days after issuance of the notes, to reset the conversion price (for both the notes and the preferred stock) at 125 percent of a 20-day average market price determined during that period; the conversion price as reset is subject to a "collar" of $65.125–$76.125. The reset option would presumably only be exercised by Boeing if it believed the 20-day average would be approximately $52 or less, an unlikely event in the circumstances. Both the notes and the preferred stock contain various negative covenants, such as prohibitions on the creation of liens and transactions with subsidiaries, minimum net worth and borrowing restrictions, and a prohibition on the sale of subsidiaries. The preferred stock also prohibits any "self-dealing transaction" with an "interested stockholder" (5 percent) without the approval of a majority of the preferred stock voting as a class. For its part, Boeing agreed not to sell the notes or the preferred stock at any time, not to sell any common stock prior to 1990, and thereafter until 1997 to sell common stock only in a registered public offering. The common stock may be sold at any time in a tender offer not opposed by Allegis' board or in a merger. Boeing also agreed to various standstill provisions for a 10-year period, including not to acquire more than 30 percent of Allegis' common stock and not to execute a written consent (Allegis' charter does not prohibit stockholder action by written consent).

3. Phillips-Van Heusen

On July 9, 1987, Rosewood Financial, Inc., which owned approximately 19 percent of the outstanding shares of Phillips-Van Heusen Corporation, proposed to acquire the remaining shares at $22 per share. On July 29, 1987, Phillips-Van Heusen approved a restructuring program consisting of (1) the disposition of the company's tailored clothing manufacturing subsidiary and traditional men's specialty retail store chains (which dispositions had been authorized prior to the receipt of the Rosewood proposal), (2) the acquisition of G.H. Bass & Co. and certain related entities for $79 million, (3) the commencement of a tender offer for up to 5,200,000 of its shares (representing approximately 34 percent of the outstanding shares) at $28 per share, and (4) the sale of $77.2 million in Senior Notes and $72.8 million in convertible preferred stock to The Prudential Insurance Company of America. Phillips-Van Heusen has a charter provision requiring the affirmative vote of 80 percent of the outstanding stock of the Company to enter into any merger or other extraordinary transaction with a 5 percent or larger stockholder, unless such transaction is approved by the Board prior to the time such person acquires 5 percent of the outstanding shares.

The preferred shares carry an annual dividend of 11.25 percent and become convertible on August 1, 1989 into 2,600,000 common shares (constituting approximately 22.4 percent of the common shares then outstanding after completion of the tender offer) at a conversion price of $28 per share. The preferred shares are entitled to cast a number of votes, voting together with the common shares as a single class, equal to the product of .66 and the number of common shares into which they are convertible, or approximately 16 percent of the votes entitled to be cast by holders of the company's voting securities outstanding following consummation of the tender offer. The voting rights of the preferred shares were subject to the expiration of any applicable waiting periods under the HSR Act. The preferred shares and the common shares issuable upon conversion thereof are subject to certain restrictions on transfer. Prudential agreed to certain standstill provisions until the earlier of the expiration of (1) seven years or (2) one year after it no longer owns any preferred shares or common shares subject to the purchase agreement, provided that Prudential may vote its shares in its discretion. The notes and the preferred shares contain various negative covenants, such as limitations on the amount of long-term debt, annual capital expenditures, dividends and the sale during any 12-month period of capital assets representing more than 10 percent of the company's tangible assets or operating revenues.

Prior to the expiration of the Company's tender offer, Rosewood sold substantially all of its shares.

4. Polaroid

In January 1989, Polaroid, in the midst of the prolonged battle against a $45 per share tender offer by Shamrock (which owned 3 million Polaroid shares and had announced its intention to commence a proxy fight), announced a $1.1 billion common stock repurchase program at $50 per share and the sale of $300 million of convertible preferred stock to Corporate Partners, an investment group. The preferred stock, which is convertible into 6 million shares of common stock and has voting rights on an "as converted" basis, was also accompanied by the grant of seven-year warrants for an additional 635,000 shares of Polaroid common stock. Corporate Partners was also given the right to name directors to Polaroid's board.

The stock repurchase and preferred stock sale were in addition to the prior issuance of 14 percent Polaroid's outstanding common stock (approximately 10 million shares) to an ESOP. As a result of the repurchase, Polaroid would end up with approximately the same number of common shares outstanding as prior to the issuance of stock to the ESOP. Corporate Partners has discretion on how its shares will be voted, and the ESOP provides for confidential voting by the underlying employees.

One result of the issuance and sale of stock combined with a stock repurchase is the effect it may have on an acquiror who is constrained by the Delaware takeover statute (§ 203). Since § 203 restricts business combinations for three years when a hostile acquiror fails to obtain 85 percent of the nonmanagement shares, the leveraging of the ESOP percentage of shares outstanding through share repurchases may be significant.

In *Shamrock Holdings, Inc.* v. *Polaroid Corp.*, [Current] Fed. Sec. L. Rep. (CCH) ¶ 94,430 (Del. Ch. Mar. 17, 1989), the Delaware Chancery Court, applying *Unocal*, upheld the slae of stock to Corporate Partners and refused to enjoin the self-tender despite the effect the two transactions (plus the ESOP) might have on the impending proxy fight. The court refused to apply *Blasius*, which required a "compelling justification" for actions that interferred with the electoral process. The court found that the transactions undertaken by Polaroid made it only more difficult for Shamrock to win the proxy fight, not impossible. Applying *Unocal*, the court found that the stock issuance and self-tender were "reasonable in relation to the threat posed" given that, in Polaroid's view, the Shamrock tender offer did not offer full value for the Kodak judgment, was highly leveraged, highly conditional, and opportunistically timed. The court found that, under limited circumstances, an inadequate all cash, all shares tender offer with a back-end commitment at the same price could be a continuing threat under *Unocal*; the special circumstances surrounding the Kodak judgment and the fear that a vanquished Polaroid might diminish the opportunity for a full recovery from Kodak were such appropriate circumstances. The court found that the stock issuance was an advantageous form of financing for a self-tender, which would offer immediate value to those shareholders interested in cash while increasing the equity interest held by remaining shareholders.

5. White Squire Funds

Lazard Freres has formed a large equity fund to act as a white squire by taking sizable minority stakes in potential takeover targets and providing funds for friendly acquisitions. The fund is designed to make three-to-five year investments of $20 million to $200 million for a 20 percent to 30 percent stake. See "Lazard Freres Marketing $2 Billion 'White Squire' Fund," *Corporate Financing Week*, p. 1 (August 24, 1987). In October 1987, the Blackstone Group raised $630 million in capital which they announced would be available for a variety of purposes, including funding white squire investments. Other major investment banking firms are also setting up similar investment partnerships. Warren Buffett has acted as a white squire investor in Salomon and Gillette.

6. Debt with Warrants

A variation on the defensive stock placement involves the sale of debt with warrants. In *Gearhart Industries, Inc.* v. *Smith International, Inc.*, 741 F.2d

707 (5th Cir. 1984) the Fifth Circuit affirmed a lower court's ruling that the business judgment rule protected the Gearhart Board's determination, in the face of a market accumulation of Gearhart stock by Smith, to sell $100 million principal amount of discount coupon subordinated debentures with attached "springing warrants" to a small group of institutional investors. The warrants to purchase Gearhart shares were designed to be exercisable by the debenture holders at a lower price in the event of a change of control than if no change of control occurred. In holding that the Gearhart Board had acted fairly and had not breached any fiduciary duty, the court ruled that the District Court had properly considered, among other things, the failure of Smith to present any evidence that any of the directors had authorized the debenture/warrant transactions in order to entrench himself, the fact that six of the seven directors were outside directors and the directors owned 7 percent of Gearhart's stock, and that the Board had retained well-respected financial advisors and counsel. The court noted with approval the District Court's observation that "merely because one of Gearhart's reasons for the transaction was to discourage Smith's impending tender offer does not make the transaction inherently illegal." *Id.* at 724.

B. Rule 19c-4—One Share/One Vote

In 1988, the SEC promulgated Rule 19c-4, prohibiting national securities exchanges or associations from listing or authorizing for quotation the common stock of a domestic company that issues any class of securities with the effect of reducing the per share voting rights of holders of an outstanding class of common stock. Recognizing that there exist legitimate uses for disparate voting rights stock, the SEC excluded from the rule's coverage the issuance of preferred stock or debt securities having voting rights that only become effective as a result of specified events not relating to an acquisition of common stock of the corporation, which reasonably can be expected to jeopardize the issuer's financial ability to meet its payment obligations (see 23.I.E.1).

As applied to the per share voting rights of preferred stock issued to a white squire, the rule may require the voting rights to be proportionate to the equity interest in the corporation represented by the preferred. See "New SEC Rule Helps Define One Share/One Vote," *The National Law Journal*, p. 19 (September 19, 1988). However, the provision of class voting rights designed to protect the economic interests of the preferred stock, including class votes with respect to waivers of financial covenants triggered by highly leveraged takeover transactions, are not specifically covered by the text of the rule and may be considered, by the SEC, to have valid business and economic purposes. See *id*. The full effects of and the limits imposed by Rule 19c-4 will become more apparent in the future as it is applied by the SEC.

C. New York Stock Exchange

The New York Stock Exchange restricts the ability of a corporation to issue securities without shareholder approval where the issuance involves a change of control or the acquisition of a business (NYSE Listed Company Manual ¶ 312.00). In July 1988 the threshold percentage that a company was permitted to issue without a shareholder vote was raised from 18 1/2 percent to 25 percent. The American Stock Exchange and NASD have adopted similar provisions. In addition, the New York Stock Exchange objects to certain typical provisions of standstill agreements including rights of first refusal with respect to the newly issued shares (NYSE Manual ¶ 308) and requirements that the holder vote the block in accordance with management's direction. NYSE Manual ¶ 308, 313.00(B).

In The Limited/Carter Hawley Hale contest, the New York Stock Exchange responded to Carter Hawley Hale's issuance and sale of convertible preferred stock representing 22 percent of the outstanding voting power to General Cinema by threatening to commence delisting proceedings against Carter Hawley Hale common stock (the limit was 18 ½ percent at the time). The convertible preferred stock was originally to be voted on all matters in accordance with the recommendation of a majority of the Carter Hawley Board of Directors. After negotiations with the NYSE, Carter Hawley agreed that (1) the preferred would be voted on matters other than the election of directors either at General Cinema's discretion or proportionately with the other votes cast by Carter Hawley shareholders, as Carter Hawley might elect, and (2) Carter Hawley would seek, and it subsequently obtained, shareholder approval of the issuance and sale of the convertible preferred stock at an upcoming shareholders' meeting.

D. Issuance of Stock to an ESOP

As the cases below indicate, the sale of stock to an Employee Stock Option Plan (ESOP) during the heat of a takeover battle will be closely scrutinized by the court to determine whether the board's actions were in good faith and were reasonably related to the threat posed to shareholder interests by the pending hostile bid. Confidential voting and tendering provisions are suggested to counter arguments that management controls the ESOP shares. In *Shamrock Holdings, Inc.* v. *Polaroid Corp.*, [1988–89 Transfer Binder] Fed. Sec. L. Rep. (CCH) ¶ 94,176 (Del. Ch. Jan. 6, 1989), the court upheld an ESOP with greater than 5 percent dilution under the entire fairness test.

Companies considering establishing an ESOP as a means of building a loyal shareholder base and taking advantage of tax incentives that make an ESOP an attractive vehicle for compensating employees and aligning employee and corporate interests, should do so as a preplanned action before the company becomes the subject of a takeover attempt.

ESOP investments can also be used to help facilitate a white knight leveraged buyout, as in the AMSTED transaction.

The creation of an ESOP may make it more difficult for a hostile bidder to obtain the needed 85 percent of a target's shares to avoid the prohibition on business combinations under the Delaware business combination statute.

1. Norlin

In *Norlin Corp.* v. *Rooney, Pace, Inc.*, 744 F.2d 255 (2d Cir. 1984), the Norlin Board of Directors responded to purchases of large blocks of Norlin's stock by issuing new common and voting preferred stock to its wholly owned Panamanian subsidiary and a recently created employee stock ownership plan. As a result, the Norlin Board effectively assured itself voting control over the company. The Second Circuit Court of Appeals upheld a preliminary injunction barring Norlin from voting the newly issued shares. *Norlin* may stand for the proposition, at least in the Second Circuit, that the actions of a target's board of directors in issuing new shares which result in the board's effectively assuring its own voting control will not normally be entitled to the protection of the business judgment rule. In reaching that conclusion, the court stressed a number of facts, including the fact that no rationale had been offered for the stock transfers other than the "determination to oppose, at all costs" the threat of a takeover. *Id.* at 265. The court reasoned that "[t]he duty of loyalty requires the board to demonstrate that any actions it does take are fair and reasonable. We conclude that Norlin has failed to make that showing." *Id.* at 266. This decision has had implications for other defensive tactics that have the effect of altering voting rights without a shareholder vote. See *Unilever Acquisition Corp.* v. *Richardson-Vicks, Inc.*, 618 F. Supp. 407 (S.D.N.Y. 1985).

2. EAC

In *Frantz Manufacturing Co.* v. *EAC Industries, Inc.*, 501 A.2d 401 (Del. Supr. 1985), the Delaware Supreme Court upheld a preliminary injunction against a target company's issuance of treasury shares to an ESOP in an attempt to dilute an acquisition of 51 percent of its stock. The court stated:

> Although the directors generally act under the protection of the business judgment rule both in prospective measures and in reactive measures seeking to ward off a threatened hostile takeover, corporate action which seeks to undo a takeover bid *after* control has already passed to another group is not protected by the business judgment rule. *Id.* at 408 (emphasis in original).

The Chancery Court had found that the "hastily-called directors meeting" at which an attempt was made to ratify by executive committee action the transfer of shares to the ESOP did not satisfy the requirement that board members be adequately informed and act after sufficient deliberation. In the court's view, the "improvised fairness opinion" presented to the Board, the absence of discussion at the meeting and the limited knowledge of all but two directors of the events surrounding the transfer of stock strongly suggested that "the attempted ratification . . . was mere window dressing." *EAC Industries, Inc.* v. *Frantz Manufacturing Co.*, C.A. No. 8003, Walsh, V.C., slip op. (Del. Ch. June 28, 1985).

3. Anderson Clayton

In connection with its self-tender restructuring defense discussed in 23.V.C.2., Anderson Clayton proposed to sell over 10 percent of its currently outstanding shares (representing over 25 percent of the shares that would be outstanding after the self-tender) to a newly created ESOP. The court indicated that the sale of stock to the ESOP should be enjoined until shareholders had had an opportunity to tender their shares to the B/S/G offer.

4. Chicago Pneumatic Tool

In *Danaher Corp.* v. *Chicago Pneumatic Tool Co.*, 633 F. Supp. 1066 (S.D.N.Y. 1986) (New Jersey Corporation), a federal district court rejected a hostile bidder's challenge to Chicago Pneumatic Tool's 1 million share ESOP that was authorized four months before the hostile bid was launched, but that was not funded until shortly prior to the commencement of the hostile tender offer.

5. Buckhorn

In defending against a hostile takeover attempt by Ropak Corporation, the directors of Buckhorn, Inc., in connection with other defensive measures, established an ESOP to which a small percentage of the company's shares would be sold. In *Buckhorn, Inc.* v. *Ropak Corp.*, 656 F. Supp. 209 (S.D. Ohio), *aff'd by sum. ord.*, 815 F.2d 76 (6th Cir. 1987), the court enjoined the sale of shares to the ESOP, concluding that the directors had adopted the ESOP in order to defeat the hostile bid and "to entrench Buckhorn's management." *Id.* at 232. The court noted that "while it is certainly permissible for directors to adopt measures for the benefit of its employees during the midst of a corporate control struggle, the directors must show that 'there are rationally related benefits accruing to the stockholders' from adopting such measures." *Id.* at 231, citing *Revlon*, 506 A.2d at 182.

6. Harcourt Brace Jovanovich

In connection with its recapitalization defense, Harcourt Brace Jovanovich (HBJ) proposed to issue a new series of convertible preferred stock to an existing ESOP and offer the ESOP HBJ common shares repurchased in the open market. In *British Printing & Communication Corp. plc* v. *Harcourt Brace Jovanovich, Inc.*, 664 F. Supp. 1519 (S.D.N.Y. 1987), the court accepted HBJ's justification that the contribution to the ESOP was necessary to provide employees with an incentive for increased productivity that would be essential for the success of the recapitalization. The court held that the "pass-through" voting provisions for the shares held by the ESOP, whereby shares allocated to participants would be voted by them and unallocated shares would be voted proportionally with the directed votes of the allocated shares, rebutted BPCC's argument that these measures entrenched HBJ management.

7. Polaroid

In *Shamrock Holdings, Inc.* v. *Polaroid Corp.*, [1988–89 Transfer Binder] Fed. Sec. L. Rep. (CCH) ¶ 94,176 (Del. Ch. Jan. 6, 1989), the Delaware Chancery Court upheld Polaroid's issuance of approximately 14 percent of its outstanding shares to an ESOP. The decision is an endorsement of ESOPs for Delaware corporations. The court questioned whether the directors' decision in adopting the ESOP was fully informed and thus entitled to the protection of the business judgment rule. Specificially, the court criticized the fact that at the board meeting where the ESOP was adopted, the directors did not discuss that: (1) there was strong opposition to the proposed employee give-backs that were funding the ESOP; (2) Polaroid is subject to the Delaware takeover statute (§ 203) and the 14 percent ESOP would have significant implications in light of the statute's restriction on business combinations where a hostile acquiror fails to obtain 85 percent of the nonmanagement shares; and (3) management viewed the ESOP as an important defensive measure. The court was also critical of the fact that the board did not explicitly consider whether the creation of the ESOP was reasonable in relation to the takeover threat facing the company.

In the face of such concerns, one would have expected that the Polaroid directors would have had a virtually impossible burden to meet. Nevertheless, the court upheld the ESOP under the exacting "entire fairness" standard under Delaware law. The court found that the ESOP structure was entirely fair to the corporation and its shareholders. It stressed that (1) the ESOP was "shareholders neutral" because it was being funded by the employees and not the corporation and its stockholders; (2) ESOPs are widely recognized as an effective means of improving employee productivity; and (3) the ESOP provided for confidential voting and tendering as directed by the employees, with unallocated shares being voted and tendered in the same proportion as the allocated shares.

In light of the pass-through voting and confidentiality provisions, the court refused to hold that the 14 percent ESOP block of stock constituted an absolute deterrent to a takeover. Thus it rejected the argument that the ESOP was not entirely fair because it might deter a takeover. The court held that the slight (5 percent) dilution caused by the issuance of shares to the ESOP was justified and that the price at which the shares were sold to the ESOP, namely, the market price at the time of the ESOP was adopted, was not unreasonably low, notwithstanding the fact that the subsequent takeover attempt by Shamrock raised the market price.

Following a remand from the Supreme Court because of later developments concerning the sale of the significant block of stock to a third party and the announcement of a self-tender, the Chancery Court affirmed its early opinion upholding the ESOP under the entire fairness standard. *Shamrock Holdings, Inc.* v. *Polaroid Corp.*, [Current] Fed. Sec. L. Rep. (CCH) ¶ 94,430 (Del. Ch. Mar. 17, 1989). the court noted that the ESOP now explicity required confidential voting, which made the court's conclusions stronger. *Id.* at 92,225.

E. Tax Treatment of ESOP White Knights

The Tax Reform Act of 1986 generally preserves existing incentives that make ESOPs useful vehicles in connection with corporate acquisition and financing transactions, including white knight transactions.

Under existing law, eligible lenders financing the acquisition of a company by an ESOP of employer securities exclude from income 50 percent of interest received with respect to such a loan. A securities acquisition loan must be made either directly to an ESOP by the eligible lender or through a back-to-back loan by the eligible lender to the employer followed by a loan by the employer to the ESOP on substantially similar terms. The Code, as amended in 1986, in the case of a back-to-back loan, permits more rapid repayment of principal and interest with respect to the loan from the employer to the ESOP, provided that the terms of the loan from the eligible lender to the employer do not exceed seven years. However, legislation is pending in both the House and Senate to repeal the partial exclusion that certain qualified lenders enjoy with respect to interest paid on loans to ESOPs.

The Code allows a deduction for dividends paid with respect to shares held in the ESOP, including employer securities allocated to the accounts of ESOP participants and including dividends paid with respect to unallocated employer securities held by the ESOP, provided that such dividends are used to repay the ESOP loan and an appropriate number of shares are allocated to participants' accounts.

Although the Code provides that a reversion of excess assets upon termination of an overfunded pension plan is generally subject to a 15 percent excise tax in addition to the normal corporate income tax, an exception to both such taxes is provided for the transfer of excess assets from a terminating pension plan to an ESOP, provided that certain conditions are satisfied. The legislative history to this provision clarifies that an excess asset transfer to an ESOP is subject to general ERISA rules, including the "exclusive benefit" rule. The reversion provision applies generally with respect to amounts transferred after March 31, 1985 but ceased to apply with respect to terminations of pension plans occurring after December 31, 1988.

While the Code provides generally for a significant curtailment of net operating loss carry forwards following an acquisition, an exception, which will have the effect of aiding ESOP leveraged buyouts of loss companies, is provided for transactions resulting in an ESOP owning 50 percent or more of the value of the stock of the loss company.

VII. LITIGATION DEFENSES

A. General

The significance of takeover litigation has shifted dramatically away from the target's litigation attacks upon the raider's offer. In the absence of an antitrust showstopper or some other "smoking gun" type of defense, courts have shown a general reluctance to interfere with a raider's tender offer characterizing their refusal to intercede as deference to "the law of the marketplace." Recent decisions show that in the right circumstances, however, it is still possible to obtain an injunction against an illegal tender offer, even when the company is subject to competitive bids.

1. Caesars World

In *Caesars World, Inc.* v. *Sosnoff*, CV 87-1622 WJR (C.D. Cal. June 8, 1987) (order granting plaintiff's motion for preliminary injunction), the U.S. District Court for the Central District of California preliminarily enjoined a cash tender offer by Martin T. Sosnoff for up to 85.6 percent of the outstanding common shares of Caesars World, Inc. based upon a claim brought by Caesars under Section 7 of the Securities Exchange Act that Sosnoff's offer violated Regulation U of the Federal margin regulations. Sosnoff planned to finance the acquisition with a $500 million secured margin facility and the sale by his acquisition company of $475 million of Increasing Dividend Cumulative Exchangeable Preferred Stock. The court concluded that the preferred shares, which were exchangeable for subordinated notes, were actually debt instruments "due to the underlying and ultimate intentions of the issuer and the purchasers to create a creditor-debtor relationship." *Id.* at 3. The court then applied the Federal Reserve Board's interpretation of Regulation G and concluded that the preferred shares, being debt securities issued by a shell corporation to finance the acquisition of stock, were secured by the stock so acquired. Since the court concluded that both the margin facility and the preferred shares were secured by the stock to be acquired, pursuant to the tender offer, the purchase of such shares would violate Regulation U. The court also found that Caesars World had standing to bring an implied cause of action under Section 7 of the Exchange Act and Regulation U. *But see A. Copeland Enterprises* v. *Guste*, Civ. A. No. 88-4706 (E.D. La. Nov. 28, 1988) (court found that possible margin rule violations required disclosure of such possibility, but declined to address substantive margin claim), *aff'd mem.*, 865 F.2d 1264 (5th Cir. 1989); *West Point-Pepperell, Inc.* v. *Farley*, 711 F. Supp. 1088 (N.D. Ga. 1988) (finding no standing for target to bring margin regulation claims); *Amanda Acquisition Corp.* v. *Universal Foods Corp.*, 708 F. Supp. 984 (E.D. Wis. 1989) (same), *aff'd on other grounds*, 1989 U.S. App. LEXIS (7th Cir. May 24, 1989); *Duro-Test* v. *TCA-IV Ltd. Partnership*, No. 87-4418 (D.N.J. Dec. 10, 1987).

2. Burlington Industries

In *Burlington Industries, Inc.* v. *Edelman*, 666 F. Supp. 799 (M.D.N.C. 1987), *aff'd by sum. ord.*, [1987 Transfer Binder] Fed. Sec. L. Rep. (CCH)

¶ 93,339 (4th Cir. June 22, 1987), the United States District Court for the Middle District of North Carolina preliminarily enjoined a cash tender offer by a partnership controlled by Asher Edelman and Dominion Textile, Inc. for all outstanding shares of Burlington Industries at $77 per share. The court granted injunctive relief under the antifraud provisions of the Exchange Act based on Burlington's claim that James Ammeen, a former vice president of Burlington, disclosed confidential inside information to PaineWebber, who then together with Ammeen approached Dominion and Edelman with a plan to launch a hostile bid for Burlington. The court concluded that Burlington had demonstrated a likelihood of success on the merits in establishing the elements required under Section 14(e) of the Exchange Act, namely, standing, breach of duty, materiality, scienter, and injury. The court also concluded that it could not "sanction any purportedly curative disclosures—such as the release of Burlington's sensitive information to the public—which would have the attendant effect of exacerbating Burlington's injury."

As a condition of the injunctive relief, the court required Burlington to post a $500 million bond as security for the payment of costs and damages that the defendants might incur if it is later determined that they were wrongly enjoined. The bond requirement was subsequently lifted at the request of the Edelman group in order to secure an expedited appeal of the court's preliminary injunction before the Fourth Circuit Court of Appeals. However, the Fourth Circuit subsequently affirmed the entry of the preliminary injunction.

Compare *West Point-Pepperell* v. *Farley Inc.*, 711 F. Supp. 1088 (N.D. Ga. 1988), where the court rejected the argument that the raider's investment banker had breached a standstill agreement signed in connection with its evaluation of J.P. Stevens (now owned by West Point) in advising the raider in connection with the West Point bid and that, since confidential information had been obtained under the standstill, the current bid should be barred.

3. Koppers

In *Koppers Co.*v. *American Express Co.*, 689 F. Supp. 1371 (W.D. Pa. 1988), a case arising from Beazer's hostile tender offer for Koppers, the District Court granted the target an injunction against any attempt by the bidder to acquire any shares of the target's stock. The court determined that the bidder's tender offer disclosure was materially deficient because, among other things, it failed to disclose (1) that Shearson Lehman was a "bidder"; (2) what effect Shearson Lehman's projected equity position in Koppers would have on its status as a broker/dealer; (3) financial information with respect to Shearson Lehman; (4) how Shearson Lehman's interest in Koppers would be bought out; and (5) possible violations of the margin regulations.

B. Antitrust Defenses

1. Target Standing

The standing of targets to bring injunction actions against unsolicited takeovers under Section 7 of the Clayton Act has been called into question in recent years as a result of the decision in *Cargill, Inc.* v. *Monfort of Colorado, Inc.*, 479 U.S. 104 (1986). In the *Cargill* case, the Supreme Court held that plaintiffs seeking to enjoin a merger under Section 7 of the Clayton Act must show that they will suffer "antitrust injury" as a result of the merger (i.e., injury of the type which the antitrust laws were intended to prevent). Several lower courts have extended the reasoning of *Cargill* to hold that targets of unsolicited takeovers are unable to show antitrust injury and thus lack standing under Section 7. See *Consolidated Gold Fields, Inc.* v. *Minorco, S.A.*, 871 F.2d 252 (S.D.N.Y. Oct. 24, 1988); *Burnup & Sims, Inc.* v. *Posner*, 688 F. Supp. 1532 (S.D. Fla. 1988); *Burlington Industries, Inc.* v. *Edelman*, 666 F. Supp. 799 (M.D.N.C. 1987), *aff'd by sum. ord.*, [1987 Transfer Binder] Fed. Sec. L. Rep. (CCH) ¶ 93,339 (4th Cir. June 22, 1987).

The United States Court of Appeals for the Second Circuit has granted antitrust standing to a takeover target in a private action alleging a violation of Section 7 of the Clayton Act. *Consolidated Gold Fields, Inc.* v. *Minorco, S.A.*, [Current] Fed. Sec. L. Rep. (CCH) ¶ 94,342 (2d Cir. March 22, 1989). The Second Circuit also found that a 49 percent affiliate of the target had antitrust standing, affirming the lower court on that issue as well as the lower court's issuance of a preliminary injunction. The Second circuit reasoned that "Gold Fields will have lost one of the vital components of competition—the power of independent decision-making as to price and output." It concluded that it is hard to imagine an injury to competition more clearly under the proscription of the antitrust laws than "the elimination of a competitor's power to determine its price and output." The Second Circuit reversed the lower court, which had held that plaintiffs do not have standing merely because they will cease to exist as competitors after the acquisition. The lower court recognized that the Second Circuit, in *Grumman Corp.* v. *LTV Corp.*, had previously said that a target company is entitled to standing to preserve its separate existence as a competitor. The lower court, however, categorized that statement as dictum that has been undercut by reasoning of the United States Supreme Court in *Cargill, Inc.* v. *Monfort of Colorado, Inc.* The Second Circuit's decision in *Consolidated Gold Fields* has thus apparently resurrected the reasoning of *Grumman*, returning a potent tool to targets of hostile tender offers.

2. Federal Agency Enforcement

During the last few years, the Federal Trade Commission has become relatively more active in antimerger enforcement as compared with the early years of the Reagan administration. In the first six months of 1988, the FTC investigated numerous transactions and voted to seek preliminary injunctions against six mergers. Four of those transactions were abandoned before or during litigation. In the context of an unsolicited tender offer or open market purchase of voting securities, the threat of a Federal Trade Commission investigation is sometimes enough to deter an acquiror unless the acquiror is prepared to negotiate a curative divestiture early in the premerger review process, as in West Point-Pepperell's acquisition of J.P. Stevens Co.

In *United States of America* v. *BNS, Inc.*, Civ. No. 88-01452 MR (C.D. Ca. Apr. 4, 1988), *modified*, 848 F.2d 945 (9th Cir. 1988), the Justice Department and BNS had agreed to the divestiture of one of Koppers' plants to avoid any potential antitrust problem in BNS's hostile tender offer for Koppers. Koppers, although only a participant and not a party to the proceeding, persuaded the District Court to grant an injunction against BNS acquiring a controlling interest in Koppers, which was not in issue under the proposed consent order. On appeal by both the Federal government and BNS, the Ninth Circuit (in a 2-1 decision) modified the injunction to permit BNS to acquire Koppers (subject to the then existing injunction in the Western District of Pennsylvania) so long as a trustee was appointed to take control of the offending plant. In dissent, Judge Beezer stated that the District Court had exceeded its authority by issuing an injunction under the relevant statutory provisions and that, even if it had not, Koppers had failed to meet the standard for a preliminary injunction. This case was one of a trio of court actions in which Koppers effectively delayed, but did not prevent, a hostile takeover.

3. State Attorneys General

Recent years have also seen a rise in the antimerger enforcement activity of State Attorneys General, and the promulgation of an alternative set of merger guidelines by the National Association of Attorneys General. Invoking both state and federal antitrust law, the Attorneys General of Pennsylvania, New York, North Carolina, South Carolina, Maine, and California have investigated several consensual mergers and unsolicited takeovers and in some cases have obtained consent decrees or other agreements from the parties—even in cases where the transaction has already been cleared by federal antitrust authorities. See *City of Pittsburgh* v. *The May Department Stores Co.*, 1986-2 Trade Cases (CCH) ¶ 67,304 (W.D. Pa. Sept. 24, 1986). The

State of California's victory in *California* v. *American Stores Co.*, CV 1988-2 Trade Cases (CCH) ¶ 68,258 (C.D. Cal. Sept. 29, 1988), represents the high watermark of state enforcement of Section 7 of the Clayton Act. This decision, which is on appeal, enjoined a supermarket merger even after the merging parties had obtained federal antitrust clearance pursuant to a consent decree negotiated with the Federal Trade Commission. Increasingly, investigations and threatened litigation from State Attorneys General can be significant deterrents to unsolicited takeovers.

C. Other Regulatory Defenses

Depending upon the specific nature of a target's business, various regulatory defenses may be available to defend against, or at least delay, a hostile bid.

1. Pillsbury/Tied House Statutes

Pillsbury has attempted to utilize "tied house" statutes, which prohibit a distiller from owning restaurants that serve liquor, in its defense against a hostile bid for Grand Metropolitan, plc. As of November 8, 1988, tied house litigation was ongoing in 14 states. In *Garland's, Inc.* v. *Pillsbury*, Civ. No. 88-17834 (Minn. D. Ct. Nov. 10, 1988), a Minnesota state court refused to require Pillsbury to redeem its Shareholders Rights Plan, but noted that the tied house statutes did not prohibit negotiations between the two companies, and issued a limited injunction prohibiting Pillsbury from raising the tied house issue to impede negotiations. In separate litigation, the Delaware Chancery Court noted that the decisions regarding the application of the tied house statutes should be left to the states involved. Grand Metropolitan had disclosed its intention to divest Pillsbury's liquor retailing subsidiaries. Pillsbury also attempted to utilize federal statutes which prohibit foreigners from owning American ships. Grand Metropolitan received a waiver from complying with the statute when it promised to sell the ships involved.

2. Consolidated Gold Fields/National Security

Consolidated Gold Fields attempted to block a takeover attempt by Minorco under an amendment to the Defense Production Act of 1950, which was part of the 1988 trade bill, granting the President the power to block takeovers judged harmful to United States national security. Minorco's offer expired, on its own terms, after being referred by the British government to the British Monopolies and Mergers Commission. Because of the expiration of the offer, President Reagan took no action to block it under the Act; however, the

United States Departments of Defense, Treasury, and Commerce did consider the issue, and the Treasury Department warned that action could be taken if Minorco renewed its bid.

Under the Exon-Florio amendment, the President of the United States (or his designee) is empowered to undertake an investigation to determine the effects on national security of any merger, acquisition, or takeover "by or with foreign persons which could result in foreign control of persons engaged in interstate commerce in the United States." This decision-making process has been delegated to the Committee on Foreign Investment in the United States ("CFIUS"). Such information is to remain confidential.

Following such an investigation, the President may take "appropriate" action to prohibit or suspend such acquisition, merger, or takeover, "so that such control will not threaten to impair national security." This action must occur within 15 days of the completion of such investigation. The President need only find "credible evidence" that national security may be impaired *and* that existing provisions of law do not provide "adequate and appropriate" authority to protect the national security with regard to such matters. The decision of the President is *not* subject to judicial review.

3. Farmers Group/Insurance Regulation

Farmers Group, a Los Angeles based insurer, relied on state insurance regulation in its attempt to block a hostile bid from BATUS, an American subsidiary of the British B.A.T. Industries plc. Nine states required BATUS to obtain prior approval of insurance regulators before purchasing more than 10 percent of Farmers, and regulators in four of those states ruled against the acquisition. See Franklin, "Big 'D' to the Rescue," *New York Law Journal*, Sept. 1, 1988. After a California court overturned a California state insurance ruling blocking the bid, Farmers Group agreed to be acquired. California represented a substantial amount of Farmers' 1987 insurance policies.

4. Foreign Investors

Certain acquisitions of United States companies by foreign investors are restricted by federal statutory and regulatory provisions. These acquisitions concern companies in the areas of communications, defense contracting, atomic energy, aviation, shipping, and commercial banking. Various states also restrict the activities of foreigners in banking, insurance, land use and ownership, and the development and exploitation of natural resources.

VIII. CASH OR STOCK ACQUISITIONS

A. General

A sometimes effective response to an unsolicited offer is a stock or cash acquisition by the target. Such an acquisition may change the nature of the business and financial picture of the target and may make it less desirable to the initial bidder. The acquisition might result in the creation of antitrust or other regulatory barriers to the acquisition of the target. The acquisition may have the effect of increasing the size of the target and thereby forcing the acquiror to alter its financing arrangements. Further, in the case of a cash acquisition, the use of the cash or the incurrence of debt by the target may make the target less desirable, especially if the bidder had intended to rely upon the assets of the target to repay its own financing. Finally, if the acquisition has resulted in increasing the target's price/earnings ratio, the bidder's balance sheet may no longer be able to withstand the dilution.

B. Johnson Controls

A negotiated acquisition in the face of a possible takeover threat by Victor Posner was upheld by a Wisconsin state court in *Wanvig* v. *Johnson Controls, Inc.*, No. 663-487 (Wis. Cir. Ct. Mar. 29, 1985), even though the issuance of stock in the acquisition, without a shareholder vote, risked delisting from the New York Stock Exchange. The court found no likelihood of success on the merits of a claim that the directors acted improperly in structuring the transaction as a "triangular merger," which required no shareholder vote, even though shares equaling over 40 percent of the presently outstanding shares would be issued in the merger. Slip op. at 7–9. The court stressed that the directors' decision was a "carefully thought out business decision which the directors believe[d] in good faith will be to Johnson Controls' long-term advantage." *Id.* at 16. The court also noted that, in considering whether to enter into the merger agreement, the directors could consider a perceived threat to the corporation by a large shareholder. The court found that, under the circumstances, the directors could reasonably believe that "repelling" that shareholder would be in the corporation's best interest. *Id.* at 15–16.

C. Time

In *Paramount Communications Inc.* v. *Time Incorporated*, C.A. No. 10866 (Del. Ch. July 14, 1989), *aff'd*, No. 279 (Del. Supr. July 24, 1989), in upholding Time's cash tender offer for Warner in the face of a hostile bid by Paramount, the court held that a corporation's long-term strategic plans can take precedence over short-term maximization of share prices. The court characterized Time's achievement of its long-term strategic plan of combining with Warner as "a most important corporate policy" and indicated that it was within the business judgment of the board, and not in the wishes of the majority of the shareholders, that the duty of achieving that policy lay. The court stated that

> under Delaware law, directors are under no obligation to act so as to maximize the immediate value of the corporation or its shares, except in the special case in which the corporation is in a "Revlon mode." Thus Delaware law does recognize that directors, when acting deliberately, in an informed way, and in the good faith pursuit of corporate interests, may follow a course designed to achieve long-term value even at the cost of immediate value maximization. (citations omitted)

The court was influenced heavily by the documented history of Time's long-term business and acquisition strategies, including the fact that Time had determined that Warner was the optimal merger partner long before Paramount had made its hostile bid, as well as Time's previous consideration and rejection of Paramount as a merger partner.

IX. PAC-MAN COUNTER TENDER OFFER

A. General

Pac-Man counter tender offers became an accepted defensive strategy during 1982. NLT-American General showed the efficacy of the counter tender offer to obtain a higher price. Martin Marietta's counter tender for Bendix was the key element in maintaining its independence. In 1984, Houston Natural's counter tender for Coastal was critical to its successful defense.

In the only two instances in which courts have ruled on the legitimacy of the counter tender offer defense, they have sustained the defense under the business judgment rule and have also ruled that the Pac-Man defense is not manipulative under Section 14(e) of the Williams Act. See *American General Co.* v. *NLT Corp.*, (1982 Transfer Binder) Fed. Sec. L. Rep. (CCH) ¶ 98,808 (S.D. Tex. July 1, 1982); *Martin Marietta Corp.* v. *The Bendix Corp.*, 549 F. Supp. 623, 633–34 (D. Md. 1982.

The Pac-Man defense, however, has certain limitations. First, as in the case of the self-tender, it may require a great many unencumbered assets or a large amount of free cash. Second, by making a counter tender offer, the target necessarily waives certain defenses such as antitrust and regulatory approval of change of control and implicitly acknowledges the desirability of a business combination (although only on its terms). Third, the counter tender offer can give rise to a confusing tangle of fiduciary obligations.

B. Martin Marietta

The court in *Martin Marietta Corp.* v. *The Bendix Corp.*, in declining to enjoin the Martin Marietta offer even though Bendix had purchased 70 percent of the Martin Marietta stock, cited Martin Marietta's fiduciary duty to its shareholders and the *shareholders* of Bendix—not the management or directors of Bendix. The court also concluded that as the majority shareholder of Martin Marietta, Bendix had a duty to the other Martin Marietta shareholders not to force abandonment of the Martin Marietta offer:

> By refusing to halt its offer, Marietta's board is permitting Bendix' shareholders to freely exercise their own judgment as to whether the Marietta offer is in their own best interests. Indeed, Bendix, as the majority shareholder of Marietta, owes fiduciary duties to Marietta's other shareholders not to force Marietta to abandon a desirable business opportunity. . . . Maryland law prohibits a controlling shareholder from using his control for some ulterior purpose adverse to the interests of the corporation and its stockholders. *Id.* at 634 (footnote omitted).

The situation was further tangled and complicated by proceedings in Delaware. The Delaware Chancery Court held that the bidder in defending against the counter offer may take steps designed to insure the success of its offer and the defeat of the target's counter offer. The Chancery Court upheld the call by Bendix of a special meeting of shareholders on the statutory minimum 10-day notice for the purpose of adopting shark repellants designed to prevent the removal of the Bendix directors by the written consent of the holder of a majority of the Bendix shares (i.e., Martin Marietta, assuming the success of its offer) and to require a supermajority shareholder vote to approve a merger with Martin Marietta. *Martin Marietta Corp.* v. *The Bendix Corp.*, Del. Ch., No. 6942 (Sept. 19, 1982). On appeal, the Delaware Supreme Court expressly reserved judgment on the legality of the proposed amendments and the procedure used by the Bendix board of directors in recommending the amendments to shareholders; the Court found that the Chancery Court had not abused its discretion in refusing to enjoin the Bendix shareholder meeting [*Martin Marietta Corp.* v. *The Bendix Corp.*, No. 298 (Del. Supr. Sept. 21, 1982)].

Perhaps as a result of the notoriety of the Bendix/Martin Marietta situation, counter tender offers were not prominent in subsequent years.

C. American Brands

In 1988, American Brands successfully used the Pac-Man defense to remain independent in the face of a hostile acquisition effort by E-II Holdings. E-II announced plans to acquire and dismantle American Brands, and American Brands responded with a cash tender offer for E-II. After American Brands raised its offer, E-II agreed to be acquired.

CHAPTER 24

TAKEOVER AND DEFENSE LAW IV: DISCLOSURE OF TAKEOVER NEGOTIATIONS

Martin Lipton
James H. Fogelson
Andrew R. Brownstein
Craig M. Wasserman
Wachtell, Lipton, Rosen & Katz

I. DISCLOSURE OF NEGOTIATIONS WITH POTENTIAL ACQUIRORS

Negotiations with potential white squires and white knights present a number of delicate practical and legal problems. Advance contact with potential white knights can lead to misunderstanding and, in certain cases, to an undesired takeover bid; on the other hand, contact delayed until the eleventh hour may be too late to permit a friendly deal to be negotiated. Moreover, while both the target and the potential white knight will generally desire to negotiate in secret, the federal securities laws may require disclosure of preliminary negotiations under certain circumstances. These same disclosure issues arise in almost every scenario where takeover negotiations occur, and both sides must study the implications of premature disclosure when deciding how such negotiations should be structured.

 This chapter is current through November 18, 1988 (with modifications through July 1989). David A. Katz and David M. Silk, associates of the firm, and many other members of Wachtell, Lipton, Rosen & Katz assisted in the preparation.

A. Schedule 14D-9

Any target making a solicitation or recommendation with respect to a tender offer is required to file a Schedule 14D-9 with respect to such solicitation or recommendation and to mail such schedule to its stockholders. The target must make its recommendation within 10 business days of the commencement of the tender offer. Exchange Act, Rule 14e-2(a). Schedule 14D-9 requires the target to disclose, among other things, whether or not any negotiation is being undertaken or is underway by the target in response to the tender offer which relates to or would result in certain types of transactions, including most white squire or white knight transactions. If no agreement in principle has been reached, however, the possible terms of any transaction or the parties thereto need not be disclosed if, in the opinion of the target's board of directors, such disclosure would jeopardize continuation of such negotiations and if the board has passed appropriate resolutions to that effect. In such event, disclosure that negotiations are being undertaken or are underway and are in the preliminary stages is probably sufficient (Schedule 14D-9, Item 7). In addition, a target has an ongoing obligation to update its 14D-9 or other disclosures by promptly disclosing to stockholders any material change in the information previously published or sent or given to stockholders. Exchange Act, Section 13(d) (2); Rule 14d-6(d).

1. Revlon

In a Schedule 14D-9 dated August 27, 1985 and filed in response to Pantry Pride's initial offer (see Chapter 22.I.F.3 and 22.II.A.1), Revlon stated that it "may undertake negotiations which relate to or could result in," among other things, a merger or a sale of a material amount of Revlon's securities. The Schedule 14D-9 also stated that, pursuant to a resolution of Revlon's Board of Directors, Revlon would not disclose the parties to, or possible terms of, any merger or any such sale, unless and until Revlon had reached an agreement in principle. Between the date of the Schedule 14D-9 and September 24, 1985, Revlon and its investment bankers supplied various persons, including Forstmann Little and Adler & Shaykin, with confidential business information and engaged in discussions with various persons, including Forstmann Little and Adler & Shaykin, regarding the possibility of entering into business combinations. On September 24, 1985, Revlon amended its Schedule 14D-9 in response to a second Pantry Pride offer. This amendment repeated in substance the statements made in the original Schedule 14D-9 that Revlon's Board "may undertake" negotiations relating to, or which could result in, a merger or sale of a material amount of assets.

In the evening of September 26, 1985, the Chairman of the Board of Revlon met with Theodore Forstmann and discussed the subject of equity participation of Revlon's management in a leveraged buyout led by Forstmann Little. Between September 26 and September 29, representatives of Revlon, Forstmann Little, Adler & Shaykin, and their respective counsel, held a number of meetings at which they discussed the nature of the businesses to be sold and the structure and timing of the acquisitions. On September 30 and October 1, Revlon, Forstmann Little, Adler & Shaykin, and their respective counsel, lenders, and financial advisors held additional meetings and exchanged drafts of acquisition agreements.

On October 2, Revlon filed a second amendment to its Schedule 14D-9 and issued a press release disclosing that its Board was considering several proposals, including an LBO with management participation for $54 per share, a new Pantry Pride $53 per share offer, the possible liquidation of Revlon, and a proposal by a major corporation to acquire Revlon. The possible parties to the LBO and the identity of the major corporation were not disclosed.

On October 3, Revlon again amended the Schedule 14D-9 to disclose the terms of a definitive merger agreement with Forstmann Little, an asset sale of a Revlon division by Revlon to Adler & Shaykin, and a sale of two additional Revlon divisions by Forstmann Little to American Home Products Corp. after the merger.

In *In re Revlon, Inc.*, Exch. Act Rel. No. 23320 [1986-87 Transfer Binder] Fed. Sec. L. Rep. (CCH) ¶84,006 (June 16, 1986), the SEC concluded that Revlon's failure to promptly disclose the discussions held with Forstmann Little and Adler & Shaykin between September 26 and September 29 violated Rule 14d-9(b), which requires that the subject company promptly disclose any material change in the information set forth in a Schedule 14D-9. The SEC concluded that Revlon's statement in the September 24 Schedule 14D-9 that Revlon "may undertake" negotiations implied "that no negotiations were then underway but that they might be undertaken in the future." Stating that the term "negotiations" includes "not only final price bargaining but also applies to substantive discussions between the parties or their legal and financial advisors concerning a possible transaction," the SEC concluded that "the discussions between and among Revlon, [Adler & Shaykin], and Forstmann Little constituted negotiations as of the time period from the evening of September 26 to September 29." The SEC concluded that:

> Compliance by Revlon with Rule 14d-9(b) required the filing of an amendment and the public dissemination of information disclosing the fact that negotiations were underway and were in the preliminary stages (but not the terms of the

> possible transactions or the parties thereto) as soon as practicable after negotiations had commenced. Under the circumstances of this case, Revlon should have disseminated the information at least before the market opened on September 30 and simultaneously amended its Schedule 14D-9 (¶84,006, at 88,147).

Thus, in *Revlon*, the SEC stated its view that when a previously filed Schedule 14D-9 states or indicates that no merger negotiations are underway, and such negotiations are subsequently commenced, the existence of such negotiations must be promptly disclosed.

2. Allied Stores/George Kern

In a Schedule 14D-9 filed on September 24, 1986 in response to a tender offer by Campeau Corp. (see Chapter 21.IV.B.4), Allied Stores stated that its Board had determined to "continue to explore and investigate, with the assistance and advice of Goldman Sachs," certain transactions, including a change in its present capitalization and the acquisition of the Company, or of one or more of its significant business segments or of certain of its assets, or a portion of its shares by another company or person. In *Allied Stores Corp. and George C. Kern*, Exch. Act Rel. No. 24648 [1987 Transfer Binder] Fed. Sec. L. Rep. (CCH) ¶84,142 (June 29, 1987), the SEC alleged that Allied Stores did not promptly amend its Schedule 14D-9 to disclose that (1) in response to Campeau's tender offer, negotiations were underway on September 25, 1986 with another party relating to or which would result in the sale or transfer by Allied Stores of a material amount of its assets and a material change in its capitalization, (2) in response to Campeau's amended tender offer, that negotiations were underway on September 30, 1986 with another party relating to a merger, and (3) an agreement in principle for the acquisition of Allied Stores had been reached and board resolutions had been passed on October 3, 1986 directing Allied Stores' management to execute a merger agreement subject to the acquiror obtaining the financial commitments contemplated by the merger agreement.

The SEC alleged that on September 25, 1986, representatives of Allied Stores and the Edward J. DeBartolo Corporation (DeBartolo) engaged in "negotiations" concerning the sale of Allied Stores shopping centers to DeBartolo and had agreed on a $405 million purchase price for six specified shopping centers, subject to a due diligence examination which was commenced by DeBartolo immediately following the meeting. The SEC further alleged that, following Campeau's increase in its tender offer price on September 29, 1986, Allied Stores determined not to pursue the sale of the shopping centers and commenced "negotiations" the following day with a partnership comprising DeBartolo and a private investor for the acquisition of the Company.

On October 3, 1986, the SEC alleged that the representatives of Allied Stores and the partnership reached an agreement in principle, subject to the approval of the Allied Stores' Board of Directors and the partnership's obtaining financial commitments, whereby the partnership would make a cash tender offer for all Allied Stores' common shares at $67 per share to be followed by a merger at the same price. Later that day, the Allied Stores' Board of Directors met and adopted a resolution directing the company's management to execute a merger agreement, subject to the partnership's obtaining financial commitments contemplated by the merger agreement. However, following the Board's action, the partnership encountered problems obtaining the necessary financing commitments and held discussions to resolve these problems with its lenders from October 3 to October 7. On October 7, 1986, after the partnership agreed to increase its equity contribution to the transaction, the partnership obtained the required financial commitments from its lenders, and the merger agreement was executed. On October 8, 1986, Allied Stores filed Amendment No. 1 to its Schedule 14D-9 to disclose, among other things, the October 3rd Board meeting and the execution of the merger agreement.

In an unprecedented action, the SEC also brought an administrative enforcement proceeding pursuant to Section 15(c)(4) of the Exchange Act against Allied Stores' principal outside counsel, George C. Kern, a Sullivan & Cromwell partner and a director of the company. The SEC alleged that Mr. Kern was a cause of Allied Stores' failure to comply, in a material respect, with Section 14(d)(4) of the Exchange Act and Rule 14d-9 thereunder, due to an act or omission that he knew or should have known would contribute to the company's failure to comply. While Allied Stores settled the administrative proceeding, neither admitting nor denying the findings but consenting to an order barring future violations, Sullivan & Cromwell has opposed the SEC's position. This would be the first litigated proceeding under Section 15(c)(4).

In *In re George C. Kern, Jr. (Allied Stores Corp.)*, Admin. Proc. File No. 3-6869 [1988–89 Transfer Binder] Fed. Sec. L. Rep. ¶84,342, the Chief Administrative Law Judge agreed with the Enforcement Division of the SEC that Kern caused Allied to fail to comply with Section 14(d)(4) of the Exchange Act and Rule 14d-9 thereunder by failing to promptly amend Allied's Schedule 14D-9. He found that (1) the commencement of negotiations relating to a sale or transfer by Allied Stores of a material amount of its assets was a "material change" in the information previously provided (as contemplated by *Basic, Inc. v. Levinson*; see Chapter 24.I.B.2); (2) the negotiations relating to a merger of Allied Stores were material on, if not before, October 2, 1986, at which point the parties possessed drafts of merger agreements and had agreed on price and other terms of the contemplated merger, but the proposed purchaser did not yet have firm financing commitments; and (3) those terms embodied in the "agreement in principle" and the Board Resolution should have been disclosed on October 3, and regardless of financing, no later than Monday, October 6. The ALJ made these findings despite the fact that four "leading practitioners and scholars in the field of securities law" all testified that in each of their opinions, Kern's disclosure decisions were "reasonable exercises of his professional judgment" (*Id.* at 39-40).

Section 15(c)(4) of the Exchange Act authorizes the SEC to issue a compliance order to any person who was a cause of a failure to comply with Section 14 of the Act "due to an act or omission the person knew or should have known would contribute to the failure to comply." The ALJ rejected Kern's argument that this statutory language calls for a knowing or reckless standard of culpability and settled instead on a negligence standard. The ALJ stated that a requirement of a showing greater than negligence would conflict with Congress' intent that Section 15(c)(4) would "provide the Commission with a quick means to obtain disclosures mandated by the Exchange Act" (*Id.* at 44). Moreover, the ALJ held that the SEC was not required to introduce expert testimony proving that Kern did not comply with accepted standards of legal practice (See *Id.* at 49), and that the *Revlon* decision should have alerted Kern to the SEC's disclosure philosophy. He concluded that Kern did not exercise the necessary level of due care and consideration to the need for amendment of Allied's Schedule 14D-9.

The ALJ did not, however, grant the SEC's request to issue an order pursuant to Section 15(c)(4) directing future compliance by Kern with Section 14(d)(4) of the Exchange Act and Rule 14d-9 thereunder. He found that, although the SEC had authority, if appropriate, to issue an order of future compliance requiring Kern to take steps necessary to effect compliance on the part of Allied, it did not have the authority to issue an order that Kern comply generally or take steps necessary to effect compliance by any other issuer that Kern might represent in the future. He also held that since Kern no longer had authority in regard to Allied's SEC filings or future compliance, an order requiring Kern to take steps to effect future compliance by Allied would be inappropriate (*Id.* at 58-59).

Both sides have stated they may appeal the ALJ's findings.

3. Kenner Parker Toys

The SEC staff has informally taken the position that a target's response to Item 7(a) of Schedule 14D-9 that it "may undertake discussions or negotiations" relating to certain extraordinary transactions and that it "intends to have discussions with third parties" to explore such alternatives to the tender offer is not fully responsive to Item 7(a) since it does not disclose either that negotiations are or are not taking place.

In New World Entertainment's bid for Kenner Parker Toys, Kenner Parker filed an amendment to its Schedule 14D-9, at a time that possible white knights were being contacted and several were entering into confidentiality agreements, which stated:

> The Company is continuing to work with its financial and legal advisors to explore the Company's alternatives with a view toward maximizing value for the Company's stockholders. In this connection, *the Company is in the preliminary stages of negotiation with parties concerning the possibility of an extraordinary transaction which could involve an acquisition or recapitalization of the Company*, having begun the process of furnishing information to certain of such parties, responding to due diligence inquiries, and entering into confidentiality agreements concerning the furnishing of such information. Members of management of the Company and the Company's advisors have met with certain of such parties and intend to meet with others. In accordance with the rules of the Securities and Exchange Commission and the previously reported resolution of the Company's Board of Directors, the Company does not intend to disclose the possible terms of any transaction or the parties thereto prior to an agreement in principle being reached because such disclosure would jeopardize continuation of such negotiations.
>
> There can be no assurance that any of the foregoing will result in a transaction being recommended to the Company's Board of Directors or that any transaction that may be recommended will be authorized or consummated. The continuation of such activities may be dependent upon the future actions of [the bidders] with respect to the Offer and the outcome of any litigation with respect to the Offer. Amendment No. 4 to Schedule 14D-9 filed by Kenner Parker Toys at 2–3 (emphasis supplied).

Pursuant to the instruction to Item 7(a), the names of the parties involved and the terms of any possible transactions as negotiations evolved did not need to be disclosed unless an agreement in principle was reached.

In response to New World's increased $47 per share bid, Kenner Parker disclosed in a further amendment to its Schedule 14D-9 that it was "actively engaged in negotiations with parties concerning an acquisition of the Company . . . [which] could result in a transaction in which the Company would be acquired at a price in excess of $47 per share" (Amendment No. 6 to Schedule 14D-9 filed by Kenner Parker Toys at 2–3). In light of such ongoing negotiations, Kenner Parker was unable to take a position with respect to the increased offer. The next amendment to Kenner Parker's Schedule 14D-9 disclosed that it had entered into a merger agreement to be acquired by Tonka Corp. at a price of $51 per share.

B. Rule 10b-5

Rule 10b-5 makes it illegal for any person in connection with a purchase or sale of a security "to make any untrue statement of any material fact or to omit to state a material fact necessary in order to make the statements made, in light of the circumstances under which they were made, not misleading," and section 14(3) contains almost identical language. The cases construing Rule 10b-5 have required that, to find liability, there must be either a duty to disclose or a material misstatement or omission. However, courts have overwhelmingly held that Rule 10b-5 does *not* "impose a general obligation for continuous and complete disclosure of material information."

Before the Supreme Court's recent decision in *Basic* v. *Levinson*, there was a clear split in the circuits as to whether the failure to disclose preliminary merger negotiations was actionable under Rule 10b-5. The issue has arisen primarily in two circumstances: first, where the target has made no disclosure as to the existence of preliminary merger negotiations; and second, where the target has not acknowledged the existence of the negotiations but has made some form of disclosure that either explicitly denies the existence of the negotiations or implies that no negotiations are occurring.

In *Greenfield* v. *Heublein, Inc.*, 742 F.2d 751 (3d Cir. 1984), *cert. denied*, 469 U.S. 1215 (1985), the Third Circuit Court of Appeals held that merger negotiations were immaterial as a matter of law because they were preliminary and that until an agreement in principle was reached "on price and structure," no disclosure was required, even though the corporation has made a public statement denying the existence of the negotiations (*Id.* at 756-59). The statement made by the target company, Heublein, was in response to a New York Stock Exchange inquiry resulting from a dramatic increase in the trading of Heublein stock. Despite the fact that Heublein had recently entered into "preliminary merger discussion[s]" with a potential friendly suitor, "a spokesman for Heublein, Inc. said the Company was aware of no reason that would explain the activity in its stock in trading on the NYSE today" (*Id.* at 754). The result in *Greenfield* that preliminary merger negotiations are immaterial as a matter of law until an agreement in principle on price and structure is reached, was based on belief that such negotiations were material only when the parties had agreed to the fundamental terms of the merger.

In a similar case in the Seventh Circuit, the court, in *Flamm* v. *Eberstadt*, 814 F.2d 1169 (7th Cir.), *cert. denied*, 108 S. Ct. 157 (1987), held that a target company's discussions with a potential white knight were not material information that had to be disclosed because there was no agreement by the parties on price and structure of any transaction and thus no violation of Rule 10b-5. However, in *Flamm*, unlike *Greenfield*, the defendant had remained silent and made no disclosure. The rationale of *Flamm* was that silence on preliminary merger negotiations would benefit most investors most of the time, until some agreement on price and structure was reached, because it made completion of a deal more likely.

1. Carnation

In *Carnation Co.*, Exch. Act Rel. No. 22214, [1984–85 Transfer Binder] Fed. Sec. L. Rep. (CCH) ¶ 83,801 (July 8, 1985), the SEC found that certain public statements by Carnation were materially false and misleading in violation of Section 10(b) of the Exchange Act and Rule 10b-5. On August 7, 1984, in a story appearing on the Dow Jones newswire, Carnation's treasurer had been quoted as saying, in reference to recent takeover rumors and unusual market activity in Carnation's stock, "there is no news from the company and no corporate developments that would account for the stock action." In fact, Carnation's senior management knew at that time that a major stockholder of Carnation had undertaken activities aimed at a sale of Carnation, that several contacts had occurred between senior management of Carnation and Nestle, S.A. concerning a possible acquisition of Carnation by Nestle, and that additional such contacts were planned for the near future. By August 21, 1984, additional meetings had been held between senior officers of Carnation and Nestle, a representative of Nestle had proposed an acquisition price of $75 per Carnation share (though that proposal had been rejected), Carnation had supplied Nestle with nonpublic information concerning its operations and future prospects, and discussions about the possible price and structure of a transaction were ongoing. Notwithstanding these facts, a Dow Jones newswire story on August 21 quoted Carnation's treasurer as having stated the previous day that Carnation knew "of no corporate reason for the recent surge in its stock price." The story also quoted the treasurer as having said that "to the best of [his] knowledge there [was] nothing to substantiate" recent rumors that Carnation was about to be acquired by Nestle or taken private in a leveraged buyout transaction and that "we are not negotiating with anyone."

The SEC concluded that Carnation's public statements on August 7 had been materially misleading and that Carnation's public statements on August 21 had been materially false and misleading. In the SEC's view, the omissions and misstatements were material because, had Carnation disclosed in those statements the contacts with Nestle and the activities of the major stockholder, "the reasonable Carnation shareholder would have considered that information to be significant in deciding whether to buy, sell or hold the stock" (*Id.* at 87,597). In coming to this conclusion, the SEC stated:

> Whenever an issuer makes a public statement or responds to an inquiry from a stock exchange official concerning rumors, unusual market activity, possible corporate developments, or any other matter, the statement must be materially accurate and complete. If the issuer is aware of nonpublic information concerning acquisition discussions that are occurring at the time the statement is made, the issuer has an obligation to disclose sufficient information concerning the discussions to prevent the statements made from being materially misleading. See *Schlanger* v. *Four-Phase Systems, Inc.*, *supra* (issuer statement denying knowledge of any corporate development which would account for market activity in its stock at a time when the company was engaged in preliminary merger discussions could be materially misleading).
>
> When an issuer makes a public statement, information concerning preliminary acquisition discussions is material and must be disclosed if the information assumes "actual significance in the deliberation of" and significantly alters "the total mix of information available [to]" the reasonable shareholder. *TSC Industries, Inc.* v. *Northway*, 426 U.S. 438 (1976). Thus, in the Commission's view, an issuer statement that there is no corporate development that would account for unusual market activity in its stock, made while the issuer is engaged in acquisition discussions, may be materially false and misleading. *Id.* at 87,595-96.

The SEC acknowledged the contrary result in *Heublein*, stating that it believed *Heublein* to have "wrongly decided" (*Id.* at 87,596, n. 8). *Carnation* thus states the SEC's view that a company faced with a request for public comment regarding confidential merger negotiations that are in their preliminary stages must either disclose the existence of negotiations or refuse to comment.

One provision of a takeover reform bill introduced in 1988 by Representatives Dingell and Markey would prohibit a company from refusing to respond to an SEC or stock exchange inquiry concerning a possible tender offer or other change of control transaction.

2. Basic v. Levinson

In *Basic, Inc.* v. *Levison*, 108 S. Ct. 978 (1988), the Supreme Court held that the test for when merger negotiations become material is the test set forth in *TSC Industries, Inc.* v. *Northway, Inc.*, 426 U.S. 438 at 449 (1976) ("[a]n omitted fact is material if there is a substantial likelihood that a reasonable shareholder would consider it important in deciding how to vote") and adopted the probability of occurrence and significance to the company test (first enunciated in *SEC* v. *Texas Gulf Sulphur Co.*, 401 F.2d 833, 849 (2d Cir. 1968)), *cert. denied*, 394 U.S. 976 (1969) for determining materiality of merger negotiations under Section 10(b) and Rule 10b-5. In this case, senior officers of Basic and of Combustion Engineering, Inc. engaged over the period between September 1976 and December 1978 in numerous meetings and telephone conversations regarding a possible business combination between the two companies. Basic, from time to time during this period, supplied Combustion with confidential forecasts and projections, and other confidential information, regarding Basic. On four occasions—the first on October 21, 1977 and the last on December 15, 1978—Basic issued public statements stating that it knew of no reason for recent abnormal market activity in Basic's stock. On December 20, 1978, Basic announced its approval of a Combustion tender offer to buy all of Basic's outstanding shares.

In *Basic*, the Supreme Court rejected the argument that it is not necessary to disclose merger negotiations until an agreement in principle is reached. See *Flamm* v. *Eberstadt*, 814 F.2d 1169 (7th Cir.), *cert. denied*, 108 S. Ct. 157 (1987); *Starkman* v. *Marathon Oil*, 772 F.2d 231 (6th Cir. 1985), *cert. denied*, 475 U.S. 1015 (1986); *Greenfield* v. *Heublein*, 742 F.2d 751 (3d Cir. 1984), *cert. denied*, 469 U.S. 1215 (1985).[1] On the other hand, the Court recognized that silence—which it stated in a footnote that a no comment position is equivalent to—is permissible during merger negotiations. In the same footnote, the Court endorsed the SEC position in the *Carnation* case and cited with approval the NYSE position that "premature public announcement may properly be delayed for valid business purposes where adequate security can be maintained."

In concluding the footnote discussed above, the Supreme Court articulated the basis for its position, possibly even recognizing that the disclosure of preliminary merger negotiations might have negative consequences for business: "[W]e think that creating an exception to a regulatory scheme founded on a prodisclosure legislative philosophy, because complying with the regulation might be 'bad for business,' is a role for Congress, not this Court."

The Supreme Court also refused to create two different standards of materiality depending on either who the plaintiff is or on whether insiders have profited, although it recognized that profitmaking by insiders might serve as an indication of materiality. See *SEC* v. *Ingram*, 694 F. Supp. 1347 (C.D. Cal. 1988). The Supreme Court also refused to distinguish materiality in situations where there was an obligation to disclose but the "disclosure duty had been breached" and the situation where there were "affirmative misrepresentations"

---

[1]Concerning the materiality of disclosure of the consideration of a spin-off in connection with a registered securities offering, the Second Circuit distinguished the line of cases involving nondisclosure of preliminary merger discussions, which the court interpreted as resting on a "policy exception," and found that in this case there was a triable question of materiality. *Kronfeld* v. *Trans World Airlines, Inc.*, 832 F.2d 726 (2d Cir. 1987), *cert. denied*, 108 S. Ct. 1470 (1988).

but no duty to disclose (although the Court noted that there was always a duty not to mislead). The Supreme Court stated that such a distinction "would effectively collapse the materiality requirement into an analysis of the defendant's disclosure duties." Thus the Supreme Court promoted a uniform materiality standard, although it did not articulate the disclosure obligations for preliminary merger discussions.

It is important to note that the Supreme Court made clear it was *not* addressing the issue of when disclosure with respect to preliminary merger negotiations must be made. Rather, *Basic* dealt only with the issue of inaccurate, and hence misleading, disclosure. Accordingly, while the *Basic* case makes advising on mergers more difficult, it does not address the timing of required disclosure. There are no clear guidelines. The Supreme Court recognized that there was no simple answer to deciding on materiality: "No particular event or factor short of closing the transaction need be either necessary or sufficient by itself to render merger discussions material." Each situation will require day-to-day monitoring. The tension will be strong between disclosure and the desire not to be put in play until there is an agreement.

The materiality of ongoing merger activity must be judged on the facts of each case; ongoing merger discussions may be material before an agreement in principle is reached, depending upon the significance the merger would have for the company and the likelihood of its occurrence. It is also important to recognize that the *Basic* test does not govern the line-item disclosure requirements of Schedule 14D-9, which controls in the context of the tender offer, timing of disclosure.

3. McLaury

In *McLaury* v. *Duff and Phelps, Inc.*, 691 F. Supp. 1090 (N.D. Ill. 1988), the United States District Court for the Northern District of Illinois used the holding in *Basic* to reject defendants' argument on a motion for summary judgment that merger or acquisition negotiations were not material until there was an agreement in principle on price and structure. McLaury, while an employee of Duff and Phelps, sold his stock back to the corporation, at its request, but the corporation did not disclose that it had engaged in merger negotiations which ultimately did not lead to a transaction. The court applied the materiality standard announced in *Basic* to find the preliminary merger negotiations material, stating: "Because of the significance of a buyout to a privately held corporation such as Duff and Phelps, negotiations regarding a buyout become material at an earlier stage than negotiations concerning other transactions." The court also noted that given the factual nature of an inquiry into materiality, such an inquiry could rarely be resolved at the summary judgment stage.

4. GM/EDS

The shareholder litigation arising out of GM's repurchase of the GM Class E stock by H. Ross Perot and three other EDS officers applied the *Basic* test to information deemed material. *In re General Motors Class E Stock Buyout Securities Litigation*, 694 F. Supp. 1119 (D. Del. 1988).

The Federal District Court in Delaware held, on the basis of a probability/magnitude analysis of materiality mandated by the recent Supreme Court decision in *Basic*, that alleged failures by GM to disclose information relating to its discussions with AT&T about a possible sale of EDS and with Perot relating to a possible buyback, were material. However, citing *Basic* for the proposition that "[s]ilence absent a duty to disclose is not misleading under Rule 10b-5," the Delaware District Court held that plaintiffs had not pleaded sufficient facts to demonstrate a duty to disclose the material information:

> The plaintiffs have pleaded no facts to support imposition of a duty to disclose upon Perot or the director defendants. There are no allegations of insider trading, rumors, or the need to correct inaccurate or misleading information [attributable to the company] ¶ 94,014 at 90,740 (footnote omitted).

5. Taylor

In *Taylor* v. *First Union Corp. of So. Carolina*, 857 F.2d 240 (4th Cir. 1988), *cert. denied*, 109 S. Ct. 1532 (1989), applying the "probability/magnitude" test enunciated by the Supreme Court in *Basic*, the court held that "highly tentative" merger discussions were not "material" for purposes of Rule 10b-5. Lacking other statements that would be rendered misleading by the failure to disclose the merger discussions, they did not have to be disclosed by a prospective acquiror to a shareholder of the target in connection with the potential acquiror's purchase of the shareholder's target stock.

The initial merger discussions took place in January 1984, the purchase occurred in February 1984, and the merger was announced in September 1985.

The court reiterated that silence absent a duty to disclose is not misleading. The Court found that there was no reasonable likelihood that a reasonable shareholder would have considered the undisclosed information material in deciding whether to sell his shares to the potential acquiror. While the Supreme Court in *Basic* rejected the "price/structure" test, the Court used the absence of agreement on price and structure as a factor in its decision. Also considered important were the facts that there was no board authorization or actual negotiations and no instructions to investment bankers to facilitate a merger, the Supreme Court had not ruled on the legality of the interstate banking statutes, and there was no local enabling legislation.

The court also stated that the potential acquiror had no duty to the shareholders of the target company, although if an officer or director of the target had been the purchaser, the Court stated that under South Carolina law there would have been a disclosure obligation for the shareholder-seller.

7. Kammerman

In a recent case, the United States District Court for the Southern District of New York ruled on a motion for summary judgment that weekend negotiations between a company and a large stockholder that continued on Monday, following an announcement by the large stockholder of a tender offer on the previous Friday, and which resulted in a stock repurchase and withdrawal of the tender offer after the market had closed on the following Monday, were not immaterial as a matter of law. *Kammerman* v. *Steinberg*, [1988–89 Transfer Binder] Fed. Sec. L. Rep. (CCH) ¶ 94,073 (S.D.N.Y. Oct. 27, 1988). The plaintiffs' claim was made on behalf of the class of individuals who purchased Disney stock on Monday in reliance on the large stockholder's public statements and amended Schedule 13D filing made the previous Friday, since it was not revealed until after the stock market closed on Monday that weekend negotiations between the two parties had resulted in the stock repurchase and withdrawal of the tender offer. The defendants argued that since, as of Monday morning, "standstill" agreements with the large stockholder had not been settled and the deal had not yet been approved by the Disney Board, no disclosure was mandated.

The court utilized the case-by-case approach adopted by the Supreme Court in *Basic* v. *Levinson* to analyze the materiality of the omitted disclosure:

> We think that the flexible standard adopted by the Court in *Basic* rebuts Defendants' claim that the weekend discussions cannot be considered legally material. That Disney's Board had yet to approve the deal and "standstill" agreements remained to be worked out do not render the negotiations immaterial as a matter of current law. The weekend talks [were] neither idle conversation nor mere exploratory overtures: a price was set and the important terms of the transaction agreed upon. As this Court has previously said, discussions between two parties over the sale of a large block of stock assume particular relevance when the stockholder's desire to sell represents a sharp break from his prior public positions. Having just announced a tender offer forty-eight hours before, the weekend negotiations between [defendant] and Disney have been especially significant to those Monday investors moving quickly to take advantage of [defendant]'s takeover bid . . . . This court believes that, under *Basic*, a jury could correctly find that a substantial likelihood existed that disclosure of the previous weekend's negotiations between Disney and [defendant] would have been significant to a reasonable investor deciding whether to purchase Disney stock on Monday, June 11, 1984. *Id.* at 91,029 (citations omitted).

The court found that in light of the disclosure made on Friday—"and the flurry of market activity it generated"—some announcement was required prior to the market's opening on Monday morning, to reflect the then-current state of affairs.

In addition, the court rejected the defendants' arguments that they fulfilled their disclosure obligations by filing their final amendment to Schedule 13D two days after the repurchase agreement was consummated and the tender offer was withdrawn, that this constituted a "prompt" amendment and therefore relieved the defendants of 10b-5 liability, and that to find otherwise would frustrate the purposes of the Williams Act. The court concluded by noting that "[i]t does no good to yell 'watch out!' after someone has fallen off the ledge" (*id.* at 91,032).

CHAPTER 25

TAKEOVER AND DEFENSE LAW V: LIABILITY AND INDEMNIFICATION

Martin Lipton
James H. Fogelson
Andrew R. Brownstein
Craig M. Wasserman
Wachtell, Lipton, Rosen & Katz

I. BACKGROUND

Although the business judgment rule (see Chapter 22.I) has been the primary source of protection against personal liability for directors responding to takeover bids, indemnification provisions and directors' and officers' liability insurance have long been the financial backstop on which directors relied. A severe curtailment in the availability of directors' and officers' liability insurance is a cause for great concern in that it will undoubtedly reduce the pool of those interested and willing to serve as directors of public companies and weaken the resolve of those who do serve to adopt the aggressive responses to takeover bids that are often the only available options to maximize shareholder value.

 This chapter is current through November 18, 1988 (with modifications through July 1989). David A. Katz and David M. Silk, associates of the firm, and many other members of Wachtell, Lipton, Rosen & Katz assisted in the preparation.

II. LIABILITY INSURANCE CRISIS

Many boards of directors confronted by a takeover bid can no longer rely on officers' and directors' liability insurance as a source of protection against personal liability for actions taken in good faith. The unavailability of meaningful directors' and officers' liability insurance is attributable to a number of factors, including developments in the law of director and officer liability that have changed the risk equation for insurance carriers (see discussion of *Smith* v. *Van Gorkom*, Chapter 22.I.C.1).

A. Effects of Liability Crisis

The effects of the "crisis" in the liability insurance industry have been widely felt in corporate boardrooms as insurance carriers have declined to renew D&O policies or have increased premiums to such an extent that the cost becomes prohibitive. See "Directors Insurance Drying Up," *The New York Times*, March 7, 1986, Sec. D, p. 1, col. 3; "Kibitzing from the Board Room," *Forbes*, February 10, 1986, p. 70 [hereinafter "Kibitzing"] (reporting that many premiums have increased 500 percent and some as much as 1,100 percent); and Olson and Morgan, "D&O Exclusions Extend to Takeover Context," *Legal Times*, March 10, 1986 [hereinafter "D&O Exclusions"] (noting increases in premiums and that a number of carriers have discontinued issuing D&O policies). Moreover, many policies no longer indemnify directors and officers personally, but only indemnify the company in the event that the company pays an indemnity to a director or officer. This restricts the protection of directors and officers to the areas where the company is permitted by law to indemnify them, whereas formerly, insurance covering nonindemnifiable liabilities could be obtained.

B. Takeover Exclusions in D&O Liability Insurance Contracts

Insurance carriers now routinely offer policies that exclude liabilities that arise from directors' and officers' actions in response to a takeover bid for a company. One carrier has gone so far as to cancel an existing policy when a takeover bid became imminent. See *Unocal Corp.* v. *Harbor Insurance Co.*, No. C550393 (Cal. Super. Ct., L.A. County, filed June 1985). *D&O Exclusions* provides a detailed analysis of the law related to policy cancellations. A typical policy now excludes from coverage, for both corporate reimbursement and direct reimbursement to directors and officers, losses in connection with claims "arising from, attributable to, or involving attempts, whether alleged or actual, successful or unsuccessful, by persons or entities to acquire securities of the company against the opposition of the Board of Directors of the company and claims arising from, attributable to, or involving the efforts, whether alleged or actual, successful or unsuccessful, by the company and/or its Directors to resist such attempts." Specimen Policy, National Union Fire Insurance Co. of Pittsburgh, Pa.

C. Impact on Corporations

The inability of a corporation to provide meaningful officer and director liability insurance has had a damaging effect on the ability of public corporations to recruit and retain corporate directors. See "Scarce Corporate Directors," *The New York Times*, January 7, 1986, Sec. D, p. 20, col. 1, and *Kibitzing*, which reports that currently two out of every three candidates approached by the Korn & Ferry recruiting firm decline board nominations, and that as a result of Control Data Corporation's inability to obtain a D&O policy, three of Control Data's directors resigned. Some commentators have argued that the absence of D&O policies makes a target corporation more vulnerable because without such protection directors will be less willing to take the legal risks necessary to mount a strong defense to enhance shareholder values. See Herzel & Harris, "Uninsured Boards Mount Weak Defense," *National Law Journal*, April 21, 1986, p. 19; see also *D&O Exclusions* at 28.

III. CORPORATE RESPONSES TO THE LIABILITY CRISIS

Substantially all state corporation statutes authorize a corporation to indemnify its officers and directors. See, e.g., Del. Gen. Corp. Law §145; N.Y. Bus. Corp. Law §721; and Cal. Corp. Code §317; see also §§8.51 and 8.56 of the Model Business Corporation Act. Moreover, many statutes provide that the indemnification provided by statute is not exclusive of other rights to indemnification to which an officer or director is entitled under any bylaw, agreement, vote of shareholders, or otherwise. Within this existing statutory framework, corporations can attempt to ameliorate the effect of the withdrawal of D&O insurance through amendments to their charter and bylaws and/or through indemnification agreements.

A. Charter and Bylaw Amendments

A corporation should examine its charter and bylaws to ensure that they provide for indemnification to the fullest extent permitted by law. Many corporations have recently adopted a charter provision that provides that indemnification is a contract right of the indemnified party.

B. Contracts

Several companies have entered into specific contracts with their officers and directors providing for indemnification to the fullest extent permitted by law. These may be particularly useful for companies whose jurisdiction of incorporation has not adopted statutes, such as the Delaware statute discussed below, limiting the scope of director liability. Although the enforceability of these contracts has not been tested and proven in litigation, their use may give directors and officers more comfort that their rights to indemnification will be enforceable. This may be particularly important in the acquisition context, where the acquiror may be able to amend the indemnification charter and/or bylaw provisions but may not abrogate an existing contract. To ensure that the officer or director will be covered in the event of a change of control, the contract should provide that the corporation shall require any successor corporation to assume the agreement.

IV. LEGISLATIVE SOLUTIONS

Many states have adopted some form of legislation designed to reduce the risk of directors' personal liability for money damages. Such remedial legislation for dealing with the D&O liability problem has generally followed one or more of seven different approaches. See generally Hanks, "Evaluating Recent State Legislation on Director and Officer Liability Limitation and Indemnification," 43 *Bus. Law.* 1207 (Aug. 1988).

A. Charter Option Statutes

The most popular form of legislation has been the charter option statute, which provides authorization for a charter or bylaw provision eliminating or limiting directors' personal liability for monetary damages, with certain exceptions. Delaware was the first state to enact a charter option statute, effective July 1, 1986.

In enacting the legislation, the Delaware legislature specifically noted the crisis in D&O liability insurance, the corresponding threat to the quality and stability of corporate governance, and the need for Delaware corporations to provide substitute forms of protection:

> Section 102(b)(7) and the amendments to Section 145 represent a legislative response to recent changes in the market for directors' liability insurance. Such insurance has become a relatively standard condition of employment for directors. Recent changes in that market, including the unavailability of the traditional policies (and, in many cases, the unavailability of any type of policy from the traditional insurance carriers) have threatened the quality and stability of the governance of Delaware corporations because directors have become unwilling, in many instances, to serve without the protection which such insurance provides and, in other instances, may be deterred by the unavailability of insurance from making entrepreneurial decisions. The amendments are intended to allow Delaware corporations to provide substitute protection, in various forms, to their directors and to limit director liability under certain circumstances.

As amended, §102(b)(7) of the Delaware General Corporation Law enables a Delaware corporation, through a provision in its certificate of incorporation, to partially limit or totally eliminate its directors' monetary liability for violations of their duty of care. The Delaware statute does not permit a corporation to eliminate or limit a director's liability for (1) breach of the director's duty of loyalty, (2) acts or omissions not in good faith or involving intentional misconduct or knowing violation of law, (3) unlawful payment of dividends or repurchases of stock out of other than lawfully available funds, or (4) for any transactions in which the director derives an improper personal benefit.

In addition to Delaware, other states that have adopted charter option statutes include Arizona, Arkansas, California, Colorado, Georgia, Idaho, Iowa, Kansas, Louisiana, Maryland, Massachusetts, Michigan, Minnesota, Montana, Nebraska, Nevada, New Jersey, New Mexico, New York, North Carolina, Oklahoma, Oregon, Pennsylvania, Rhode Island, South Dakota, Tennessee, Texas, Utah, Washington, and Wyoming. The principal difference among the various state charter option statutes is found in their exceptions. New York, for example, has the same exceptions as Delaware except that New York eliminates the exception for breach of duty of loyalty.

Charter option statutes apply only to liability for money damages and have no effect on the availability of equitable remedies, such as an injunction or rescission, for breach of the duty of care. Additionally, a director's duty of care is not changed by a charter option statute. However, the exculpatory provisions in the charter option statutes are not limited to derivative suits or suits by the corporation. Thus, stockholders suing directors in their own right would be barred from alleging duty of care violations.

B. Self-Executing Statutes

The most far reaching approach to director liability is direct alteration of the standard of liability necessary to recover monetary damages from directors by requiring proof of more than gross negligence. This self-executing approach was pioneered by Indiana and subsequently adopted by other states including Ohio, Florida, Wisconsin, and Maine.

The Indiana statute provides that a director is only liable for a breach of his duty of care if "the breach or failure to perform constitutes willful misconduct or recklessness" (Ind. Code Ann. §23-1-35-1). This limitation on liability applies to suits by third parties as well as by stockholders and includes both monetary damages and equitable relief.

The Ohio statute provides that a director will not be liable for monetary damages for any action he takes or fails to take as a director (but not for any act or omission in a capacity other than as a director) unless it is proved by "clear and convincing" evidence that his action or failure to act involved an act or omission undertaken with deliberate intent to cause injury to the corporation or with reckless disregard for the best interests of the corporation.

C. Cap on Money Damages

The Virginia statute, which became fully effective on July 1, 1987, provides a comprehensive approach to director and officer liability that combines the charter option and self-executing approaches in addition to providing a unique cap on monetary damages. There is a statutory standard of conduct that a director act "in accordance with his good faith business judgment of the best interests of the corporation," thereby eliminating the measurement of director conduct against a standard of an ordinary prudent person acting in a manner that he " reasonably" believes to be in the best interests of the corporation. A director acting in accordance with the good faith business judgment standard is statutorily protected from liability "for any action taken as a director, or any failure to take any action."

Even if a director is found to have acted in bad faith or to have breached his duty of loyalty to the corporation's interests, Virginia has a statutory cap on damages against a director or officer in a derivative suit or a suit by or on behalf of shareholders, except in cases of willful misconduct or knowing violations of criminal law. The cap is equal to the greater of (1) $100,000 or (2) the amount of cash compensation received by the officer or director from the corporation during the 12 months immediately preceding the act or omission. The statutory cap may also be reduced by action of the corporation's stockholders. The cap is not applicable in suits brought by the corporation with the approval of the board of directors.

While Virginia provides a statutory standard for indemnification, it also expressly authorizes a corporation, with the approval of its stockholders, to "make any further indemnity, including indemnity with respect to a proceeding by or in the right of the corporation, and to make additional provision for advances and reimbursement of expenses, to any director, officer, employee, or agent . . . except an indemnity against (1) his willful misconduct, or (2) a knowing violation of the criminal law." See King, *Director Protection Under Virginia Law*, 20 Securities & Commodities Regulation 129 (August 1987).

D. Expansion of Indemnification in Derivative Suits

States that have enacted statutes expanding the right of corporations to indemnify their directors for expenses, settlements, and/or adverse judgments in derivative suits include Arizona, Arkansas, California, Delaware, Florida, Georgia, Indiana, Kansas, Louisiana, Maine, Maryland, Michigan, Minnesota, Missouri, Nevada, New York, North Carolina, Utah, Wisconsin, and Wyoming.

The most far-reaching statutory developments affecting derivative suits are provisions that virtually eliminate the distinction between third-party and derivative suits and permit indemnification against judgments, settlements, and expenses for any director or officer who meets the general statutory standards for indemnification without the requirement of court approval. The typical statutory standards for indemnification are good faith and reasonable belief that the conduct was in the corporation's best interests.

Wisconsin now *requires* indemnification against liability in any proceeding unless the director's or officer's breach or failure to perform constitutes willful misconduct, improper personal profit, or a crime.

Under the New York statute, a corporation is permitted to indemnify a director or officer against settlements and expenses in derivative suits if he acted in good faith and for purposes he reasonably believed to be in the best interests of the corporation. However, the New York statute does not permit indemnification absent court approval for threatened or settled actions or for adverse judgments.

E. Expansion of Nonexclusivity Provisions

Many states have recently expanded the provisions of their indemnification statutes by permitting corporations to provide rights other than indemnification by charter, bylaw, board resolution, contract, or otherwise, thereby substantially expanding the ability of a corporation, with or without shareholder approval, to indemnify and advance expenses to its directors and officers. States that have made statutory indemnification provisions nonexclusive include Alabama, Alaska, Arizona, Arkansas, California, Delaware, District of Columbia, Florida, Hawaii, Idaho, Indiana, Iowa, Kansas, Kentucky, Louisiana, Maine, Maryland, Michigan, Mississippi, Missouri, Nevada, New Hampshire, New Jersey, New Mexico, New York, Ohio, Oklahoma, Oregon, Pennsylvania, Rhode Island, South Dakota, Tennessee, Utah, Virginia, Washington, Wisconsin, and Wyoming.

The broad form of nonexclusivity provision is typified by §145(f) of the Delaware General Corporate Law, which provides that statutory indemnification "shall not be deemed exclusive of any other rights to which those seeking indemnification or advancement of expenses may be entitled under any bylaw, agreement . . . or otherwise."

In contrast to Delaware, other states include express limits in their nonexclusivity provisions. For example, New York's statute prohibits indemnification if a judgment establishes that a director acted in bad faith or personally gained a benefit to which he was not legally entitled.

Nonexclusivity provisions offer an important opportunity for providing broad contractual protection for officers and directors in the event of a change in control. Under the nonexclusivity provisions, contracts can be drafted that contain all of the substantive rights (including advancement of expenses) to furnish the desired protection without the need to rely upon changeable charter or bylaw provisions.

F. Alternative Sources of Reimbursement

As conventional D&O liability insurance has become more expensive or unavailable at any price, several states have authorized reimbursement from alternative sources. Such states include Arizona, California, Colorado, Hawaii, Louisiana, Maine, Maryland, Nevada, New Jersey, New Mexico, Ohio, Pennsylvania, and Texas. Examples of alternative sources include captive insurance subsidiaries or associations formed by industry groups, trust funds, letters of credit, guaranties, and sureties. Virtually all of these devices amount to self-insurance, since the corporation remains the ultimate source of payment.

G. Nonstockholder Constituency Statutes

A different approach to the D&O liability crisis is exemplified by nonstockholder constituency statutes. Such statutes help shield directors from liability by expanding the criteria that directors may consider in reaching decisions on behalf of the corporation. States that have adopted nonstockholder constituency statutes include Arizona, Idaho, Illinois, Indiana, Kentucky, Maine, Minnesota, Missouri, Nebraska, New Mexico, New York, Ohio, Pennsylvania, and Wisconsin.

All of the statutes, except Missouri's and New York's, tie consideration of nonshareholder constituencies to consideration of the corporation's best interests. The New York statute provides that directors are "entitled to consider, without limitation, both the long-term and the short-term interests of the corporation and its shareholders."

Several of the new statutes specifically mention that a director may consider the possibility that nonstockholder interests may be best served by the continued independence of the corporation. In addition, Ohio specifically authorizes its corporations to resist a potential change in control if the directors determine that such a potential change would not be in the best interests of the corporation, its stockholders, and other nonshareholder constituencies.

CHAPTER 26

TAKEOVER AND DEFENSE LAW VI: REGULATORY INITIATIVES

Martin Lipton
James H. Fogelson
Andrew R. Brownstein
Craig M. Wasserman
Wachtell, Lipton, Rosen & Katz

I. OVERVIEW: THE POLICY DEBATE

Over the past decade, there has been a great transformation in the nature of corporate control transactions, a transformation to which public policy has yet to adjust. Until recently, shareholders of large public corporations provided corporate directors with significant autonomy, enabling directors to manage corporations for the long-term benefit of all corporate constituencies. Today, corporate directors cannot be assured of such shareholder "loyalty." Large institutional investors, whose investment decisions are typically controlled by aggressive portfolio managers interested in short-term performance, have become a powerful voice in the arena of corporate control contests. Arbitrageurs, with access to vast sums of capital, have also played a key role in pressuring corporate managements to adopt strategies focused on achieving short-term quick-fix results. Moreover, corporate "raiders" and even main-

---

 This chapter is current through November 18, 1988 (with modifications made through July 1989). David A. Katz and David M. Silk, associates of the firm, and many other members of Wachtell, Lipton, Rosen & Katz assisted in the preparation.

stream corporate acquirors, through use of hostile takeovers, have been able to bypass the board and even the proxy machinery and take their proposals for change of control of large corporate entities directly to the shareholders.

Free-market theorists have hailed this phenomenon. They argue that a board of directors' sole duty is to maximize share values and that if a board fails to do so it should be replaced. They believe that if a corporation's stock market value does not reflect the true value of a corporation's assets, management and the Board must be at fault, and someone else should have the unfettered ability to take control of such assets to use them more efficiently.

Many policy analysts, however, argue that unfettered takeover activity has been harmful to shareholders, other corporate constituencies, and the economy as a whole, and that a board of directors should resist a takeover attempt which it deems not to be in the best interests of constituent groups. They stress that the failure of government regulation to adjust to the changing nature of takeover activity has led to a proliferation of takeover abuses.

The courts, caught in the middle of this ideological debate, have been struggling to develop a coherent doctrine by which to judge the actions of directors in corporate control transactions (see Chapter 22.III). For the most part, the responsibility for formulating constraints on takeover techniques and defenses has fallen on the courts, as regulatory policies, with the notable exception of certain state legislative initiatives (see Chapter 26.III), designed to address the problems of hostile takeovers have failed to keep pace with the changing nature of takeover activity; and the courts have been extremely reluctant to set aside a raider's tactics (see Chapter 22.IV).

From time to time over the past ten years, attempts have been made to modify the corporate governance provisions of state corporation law and federal regulations of takeover activity. In 1978 the ALI embarked upon its "Corporate Governance Project" focusing debate on such topics as (1) the proper goals of directors in managing the corporation; (2) the appropriate governance structure of the corporation; and (3) the proper standards for regulating directorial behavior under the duty of care and duty of loyalty doctrines. The ALI's *Principles of Corporate Governance and Structure; Restatement and Recommendations* is currently in its eleventh draft and no consensus concerning major revisions of state corporate doctrines has been reached. In 1983 the SEC formed a Tender Offer Advisory Committee—consisting of representatives of a variety of constituencies, including corporations, shareholders, market professionals, lawyers, and investment bankers—to study changes in takeover practices and to make proposals for changes in the federal regulatory framework. While the Committee was divided on several major issues, including the propriety of federal regulation of certain defensive measures which, as some participants noted, would constitute a major intrusion of federal law into the traditional domain of state corporation law, the Committee made strong recommendations concerning the need for federal regulation to control certain abusive takeover practices. To date, no major regulatory innovations, either through federal legislation or SEC rulemaking, have resulted from the Advisory Committee report, although some technical rule changes regarding tender offers were enacted and other proposals have been made.

II. CONGRESSIONAL INITIATIVES

Prompted by the July 1983 report of the SEC's Tender Offer Advisory Committee and the recent insider trading scandals that have rocked the takeover arena, a number of "takeover reform" bills have been introduced in Congress over the last several years. Still, the opposition of the Reagan Administration to the contemplated reforms (see Council of Economic Advisors, 1985 Economic Report of the President ("further federal regulation of the market for corporate control would be premature, unnecessary, and unwise") at 216 (1985)) and the debate over state versus federal regulation of corporate governance responses to takeovers (see *Senate Approves Amendments to Require Shareholder Vote on Golden Parachutes*, 20 Sec. Reg. & L. Rep. 980-81 (1988)) both stymied efforts to enact federal legislation to address the problems posed by takeover abuses.

Since January 1987 there have been numerous congressional committee hearings on insider trading and hostile takeovers, and a number of significant bills were introduced in Congress to regulate takeover activity. Bills introduced in the House and Senate would have affected corporate control transactions by reducing the 10-day window period for Schedule 13D filings, reducing below 5 percent the threshold for triggering a 13D filing, restricting so-called "greenmail" stock repurchases, addressing perceived abuses in "street sweeps" and creeping acquisitions of control through open market purchases, increasing the period of time that a tender offer must remain open, altering the requirements for filings by acquirors under the HSR Act, regulating tender offer financing and the issuance of junk bonds, requiring stock listed on national securities exchanges to have uniform voting rights, requiring an independent appraisal before an LBO could be consummated, and restricting a target's ability to institute certain takeover defenses or issue golden parachutes once a bid is announced or without shareholder approval. Indeed, the most recent sessions of Congress have seen a number of different measures designed to address perceived problems in the field of corporate control transactions.

Much of the debate in the area of takeover regulation has focused on the problem of striking a balance between congressional action to address takeover abuses by reforming the federal securities laws and the traditional role of states in regulating corporate governance. It has not been an easy balance to strike, and little real progress in federal takeover reform legislation has ultimately occurred, often because takeover proponents have used preemption as a force with which to destroy the sought balance. One solution would be both to effect an overhaul of the federal securities laws, at times intruding into traditional state roles, and to implement a uniform state takeover statute as discussed below. Such an overhaul would include, among other things, the following proposals: (1) no more than 5 percent of a company's common stock could be purchased unless a tender offer for all of the company's common stock is made, except for investments up to 10 percent by purely passive institutional investors; (2) the time frame for tender offers would be extended to 120 calendar days; (3) a bidder would be required to have actual commitments for all the financing needed to consummate a transaction; (4) the target's shareholders (who had been shareholders for at least 60 days prior to announcement of the offer) would have the opportunity to vote on the proposed tender offer; (5) the tax code would be amended to eliminate the deductibility of interest on junk bonds issued to finance certain transactions; (6) the tax code would also be amended to impose a graduated tax, based on the holding period, of profits from substantial securities positions; (7) all publicly traded companies would be required to adhere to the one-share, one-vote concept; (8) staggered boards and other shark-repellent provisions would be proscribed; and (9) large shareholders would have free and equal access to the corporation's proxy machinery at the corporation's expense. See Lipton, *Corporate Governance in the Age of Finance Corporatism*, 136 U. Pa. L. Rev. 1, 62-69 (1987).

Much of the force behind the current takeover frenzy stems from cultural attitudes and economic factors beyond the reach of the federal securities laws, and responsible fiscal and tax policies are needed to stem the tide of leveraged transactions and remove the excess speculation and volatility from our capital markets. One proposal has been put forward by Warren E. Buffett to tax certain securities transactions as a means of encouraging long-term investment. Buffett has proposed a 100 percent tax on any profits derived from the sale of stock that the holder has owned for less than one year and that such tax should apply even to pension funds and other institutional investors that are not normally taxed. See Buffett, "How to Tame the Casino Society," *The Washington Post*, December 4, 1986, p. A23; see also Canellos, *The Overleveraged Acquisition*, 39 Tax Law 91 (Fall 1985). Nobel Laureate James Tobin has proposed a similar tax, as well as a transactions tax aimed at discouraging speculative transactions. Another approach has been seen in proposed legislation in Congress to limit the deduction for interest payments.

Following management's proposal to buy out the RJR Nabisco shareholders, a number of congressmen expressed a concern about the growing number and size of leveraged transactions and their potential costs. *See* Reich, *Leveraged Buyouts: America Pays the Price*, New York Times Magazine, Feb. 6, 1989, at 32. The 101st Congress is holding a number of hearings on the issue, and a variety of legislative proposals are likely to be introduced.

There is also increased concern about the amount of debt available in the financial markets. Currently, LBO loans make up a significant portion of the loans in commercial bank portfolios. Alan Greenspan has warned banks that they should be certain that their LBO loans are creditworthy. Recently, some banks have reported that they will cut back on their LBO financings because of recent losses. On February 16, 1989, the Board of Governors of the Federal Reserve sent letters to the officers in charge of supervision at each federal reserve bank discussing issues raised by highly leveraged financing. The letter encouraged stricter scrutiny of the borrower's financial position and the establishment of specific policies and practices that would effectively balance the trade-offs between risk and return. The letter included specific guidelines for examiners studying highly leveraged financing transactions. *See* Letter from Board of Governors of the Federal Reserve System to the Officer in Charge of Supervision at Each Federal Reserve Bank (Feb. 16, 1989).

The House Energy and Commerce Telecommunications and Financing Subcommittee, chaired by Representative Markey, is exploring legislation intended to ensure the fairness and integrity of the management buyout process. The following issues are being considered:

- prohibiting investment bankers providing fairness opinions from receiving greater compensation if the transaction is consummated;
- requiring management to detail the necessity for taking a company private in order to accomplish certain objectives;
- requiring management to provide the Board of Directors (and any special committee thereof) with all studies and analyses prepared by management and its advisors in connection with a possible buyout;
- requiring that all financing be in place prior to announcing any buyout;
- extending the expiration date for offers in management buyouts to require that the offer remain outstanding for at least 45 to 60 days (instead of the current 20 business days);
- requiring the company to continue to make public filings of financial information with the SEC following the going-private transaction; and
- expanding the coverage of Rule 13e-3 to all parties in a buyout and implementing civil penalties for violations of the rule.

There is legislation currently pending in the Senate that would narrow the 13(d) window for filing from ten days to one day and reduce the level required for filing from 5 percent to 4 percent. The same proposal would require that tender offers remain open for a minimum of 60 calendar days. Other proposals include requiring that golden parachutes and rights plans be made subject to shareholder approval and barring greenmail payments unless approved by a majority of the shareholders.

III. STATE TAKEOVER STATUTES

A. Overview

The takeover frenzy of the 1970s resulted in more than 35 states enacting laws to regulate tender offers by 1982. These first generation takeover statutes generally imposed more extensive disclosure requirements than the federal Williams Act and were designed to aid targets by delaying tender offers beyond the periods provided in the Williams Act. Additionally some of the first generation statutes vested power in a state official to make a determination regarding the fairness of the tender offer. As a result, these statutes posed significant federalism concerns, and in 1982 the Supreme Court invalidated as unconstitutional the first generation Illinois takeover statute. In the absence of federal regulation of takeovers in the wake of that decision, the states themselves developed a number of different types of second generation takeover statutes.

Three basic approaches have evolved in the second generation of state takeover regulation. Each is premised on the traditional role of the states in defining the framework for corporate governance. By framing statutes in terms of corporate governance, states have attempted to avoid the Williams Act preemption and Commerce Clause concerns that prompted the Court to overturn the first generation statutes. Maryland and a number of other states enacted statutes that tried to prevent the abuses of the two-tiered, front-end-loaded tender offer, and the creeping and partial tender offers frequently employed by raiders. Those statutes require a raider to pay at least as high a price in a second-step squeeze-out as the raider paid to acquire control in the first step of the acquisition. Ohio then enacted the first control share acquisition statute and was copied by a number of other states, including Indiana. The control share acquisition statutes typically deny voting rights to a purchaser who acquires in excess of 20 percent of the stock of the target, unless the raider first obtains permission of the target's shareholders at a special meeting. Focusing on voting rights and corporations with a true nexus with Indiana, the Indiana statute was validated by the Supreme Court in early 1987. New York and a number of other states have adopted a third type of second generation takeover statute. This type of statute provides that if a raider acquires a certain percentage of the target's stock (e.g., 10 percent), there cannot be, among other business combinations, a second-step merger for a fixed period of time (e.g., five years) after that acquisition, unless the target's board approved such a transaction prior to the triggering acquisition.

As a result of all these developments, there is now a melange of state takeover statutes of varying degrees of effectiveness. The variety and inconsistencies of the state takeover statutes support the arguments of those who are urging Federal preemption because they want the takeover frenzy to continue. The inescapable conclusion is that there must be a uniform state takeover law designed to remedy the problems of the current takeover environment.

A new wave of state statutes is also likely in response to recent case law developments in Delaware. Several states have adopted or are in the process of adopting statutes rejecting the heightened standard established under *Unocal* and affirming a company's right to reject and defend against inadequate offers.

B. Constitutionality of First Generation State Takeover Statutes

1. MITE

In *Edgar* v. *MITE Corp.*, 457 U.S. 624 (1982), the Supreme Court, by a five to four vote with a plurality opinion, held the Illinois Business Takeover Act unconstitutional under the Commerce Clause, concluding that the incidental burdens the Act placed on interstate commerce outweighed any putative local benefits.

The Illinois Act required that tender offers for target companies having certain defined relationships with Illinois (including certain companies that were not incorporated in Illinois) be registered with the Illinois Secretary of State. An offer became effective under the Act 20 days after a registration statement was filed with the Secretary of State, unless a hearing was called by the Secretary. The Secretary of State could call a hearing on his own and was required to call a hearing at the request of a majority of the target's outside directors of shareholders owning 10 percent of the class of securities subject to the offer. The Secretary could block an offer if he found that the offeror's disclosure was inadequate or that the offer was inequitable.

The Court held that the effects on interstate commerce of allowing the Secretary of State to block a nationwide tender offer were substantial and that Illinois' interest in protecting resident shareholders was insufficient to outweigh the burdens that the Act imposed on interstate commerce. The Court noted that the benefits that the Act provided resident shareholders were "for the most part, speculative."

Four Justices (White, J., Burger, C.J., Stevens and O'Connor, J.J.) found the Illinois Act unconstitutional as a direct regulation of interstate commerce, noting that the Act could prevent an offeror from making an offer and conducting interstate transactions not only with resident shareholders, but with shareholders having no connection with Illinois. The Justices noted in particular that on its face the Act could apply to a tender offer even if none of the target's shareholders were Illinois residents.

Three Justices (White, J., Burger, C.J. and Blackmun, J.) found that the Illinois Act was preempted by the Williams Act and therefore unconstitutional under the Supremacy Clause, while two Justices (Powell and Stevens, J.J.) disagreed with this conclusion. The remaining Justices did not address the question. Justice White's plurality opinion noted that in adopting the Williams Act, Congress intended to protect investors "while maintaining the balance between management and the bidder." Justice White, agreeing with the conclusion reached by the Seventh Circuit, found that the Illinois Act frustrated the objectives of the Williams Act, upsetting "the careful balance struck by Congress."

The plurality opinion identified three offending provisions of the Illinois Act: (1) the 20-day precommencement period, which provided "management with a powerful tool to combat tender offers"; (2) the hearing provisions of the Act, which permitted management to delay a tender offer, thus "favoring management at the expense of stockholders"; and (3) the provisions of the Act which allowed the Secretary of State to pass on the substantive fairness of an offer, which "offers investor protection at the expense of investor autonomy— an approach quite in conflict with that adopted by Congress. *Id.* at 640. Justices Stevens and Powell, disagreeing with the plurality opinion regarding the preemption issue, argued that "Congress' decision to follow a policy of neutrality in its own legislation" was not "tantamount to a federal prohibition against state legislation designed to provide special protection for incumbent management." *Id.* at 655.

2. Post-MITE Cases

Following *MITE* the Circuit Courts, playing on both the Commerce Clause and Preemption analysis set forth in *MITE*, invalidated a number of first generation statutes. See *Mesa Petroleum Co.* v. *Cities Service Co.*, 715 F.2d 1425 (10th Cir. 1983); *Telvest, Inc.* v. *Bradshaw*, 697 F.2d 576 (4th Cir. 1983); *Martin-Marietta* v. *The Bendix Corp.*, 690 F.2d 558 (6th Cir. 1982); *National*

City Lines, Inc.v. *LLC Corp*., 687 F.2d 1122 (8th Cir. 1982). More recently, in a case involving a first generation state takeover statute after the second generation Indiana statute was upheld by the Supreme Court in *CTS*, the First Circuit Court of Appeals in *Hyde Park Partners, L.P.* v. *Connolly,* 839 F.2d 837 (1st Cir. 1988), held that Section 3 of the Massachusetts Takeover Bid Regulation Act was preempted in its entirety by the Williams Act, and that the penalty provision of such section also probably violated the Commerce Clause.

Section 3 of the Massachusetts Takeover Bid Regulation Act required a prospective takeover bid "offeror" to disclose its intent to gain control of a target company before acquiring five percent of its stock (839 F.2d at 840 n.1). Failure to disclose such intent would preclude that offeror from making a takeover bid for that target for one year after the failure to disclose (*Id).*

The District Court for the District of Massachusetts issued a preliminary injunction against enforcement of the section on Commerce Clause grounds. (See 676 F. Supp. 391). The First Circuit, applying both the test articulated in *CTS* for Commerce Clause analysis and a balancing test that analyzes whether a statute's effects on interstate commerce are clearly excessive in relation to the putative local benefits, held that the one-year moratorium on purchasing shares was invalid since it directly prohibits the interstate sale of shares. 839 F.2d at 844-45, 847-48.

Turning to the preemption issue, the court noted that entities could comply with both the Williams Act and Section 3 (*Id*.at 849). The court stated that under *CTS*, the focus should be whether the disclosure provision of Section 3 is beneficial to the investors caught between management and an offeror (*Id*.at 850). After analyzing the terms and legislative history of the provision of the Williams Act requiring disclosure of intent after passing the 5 percent threshold, the court stated that Section 3 "in effect second-guesses the balance struck by Congress" (*Id*). In addition, since the disclosure and penalty provisions of Section 3 could be waived by management, the court held that Section 3 was not beneficial to shareholder interests.

Hyde Park Partners and the post-*MITE* and pre-*CTS* cases invalidating first generation anti-takeover statutes leave little room for effective deterrence of takeover bids through first generation statutes. This is not to say that the first generation statute is completely dead—a first generation statute recently survived a petition for preliminary injunction on constitutional grounds [see *CRTF Corp*. v. *Federated Department Stores*, 679 F. Supp. 731 (S.D. Ohio 1988), (denying preliminary injunction based on constitutional grounds)]—it is only to suggest that the first generation statutes ultimately offer little, if any, protection from a hostile bid.

C. Second Generation State Takeover Statutes

1. Control Share Acquisition Statutes

Following the *MITE* decision, a variety of "second generation" state takeover statutes were enacted. One form of such statute is the "control share acquisition" statute. Indiana's version of such statute was upheld by the Supreme Court (See 26.III.C.1.).

The Indiana Act (Ind. Code. Ann. §§23-1-42) provides that shares acquired in a "control share acquisition" automatically lose their voting rights unless and until voting rights are granted to such shares by the affirmative vote of a majority of shares of each class of stock, excluding shares owned by an acquiring person, an officer or employee director of the target corporation. A control share acquisition is defined as the direct or indirect acquisition of shares by any person that would bring such person's voting power in the target corporation to or above the 20 percent, 33⅓ percent or 50 percent threshold. A person who proposes to make or has made a control share acquisition has the right to request that a special shareholders' meeting be held (at his expense) within 50 days (and no sooner than 30 days if he so requests) to determine his voting rights. If the acquiring person's shares are not accorded voting rights (or if no request for a special meeting is made by an acquiror within 60 days) the corporation may, if authorized by its charter and bylaws prior to the control share acquisition, purchase the acquiring person's shares at their "fair value." If voting rights are approved and the acquiring person controls 50 percent or more of the voting power, all shareholders other than the acquiring person have dissenters' rights, which enable them to receive "fair value" for their shares. In both cases, "fair value" is not less than the highest price paid in the control share acquisition. The Indiana Act permits target corporations to opt out of the protections of the Act by adopting a bylaw or charter provision prior to a control share acquisition stating that the control share acquisition chapter shall not apply.

Other states had adopted statutes similar to the Indiana statute prior to the *CTS* decision, including Hawaii (Haw. Rev. Stat. §§416-171 to 172), Minnesota (Minn. Stat. Ann. §302A-671), Missouri (Mo. Ann. Stat. §351.407), Ohio (Ohio Rev. Code Ann. 1701.831), and Wisconsin (Wis. Stat. Ann. §180.69). The Hawaii statute was declared unconstitutional in *Terry* v. *Yamashita*, 643 F. Supp. 161 (D. Haw. 1986). The Minnesota statute was declared unconstitutional in *APL Ltd. Partnership* v. *Van Dusen Air, Inc.*, 622 F. Supp. 1216 (D. Minn. 1985). That decision was subsequently vacated after the case was settled, but the Minnesota statute was again declared unconstitutional in *Gelco Corp.* v. *Coniston Partners*, 652 F. Supp. 829 (D. Minn.

1986), *aff'd in part, vacated in part*, 811 F.2d 414 (1987). The Missouri statute was declared unconstitutional in *Icahn* v. *Blunt*, 612 F. Supp. 1400 (W.D. Mo. 1985). The Wisconsin statute was repealed effective April 22, 1986. The offending Minnesota and Missouri statutes were also repealed (although new versions were later effected). The Ohio statute was originally declared unconstitutional by the Court of Appeals in *Fleet Aerospace Corp.* v. *Holderman*, 796 F.2d 135 (6th Cir. 1986), *vacated*, 481 U.S. 1003, *vacated*, 481 U.S. 1026 (1987), *remanded*, 848 F.2d 7120 (6th Cir. 1988), but in light of *CTS* the Supreme Court vacated and remanded. The Sixth Circuit Court of Appeals, in turn, remanded to the district court to determine whether the constitutional challenge to the statute had been rendered moot by completion of the merger in question. In *Veere Inc.* v. *Firestone Tire & Rubber Co.*, 685 F. Supp. 1027 (N.D. Ohio 1988), the district court denied plaintiff's motion for a preliminary injunction enjoining enforcement of the Ohio statute. Following the Supreme Court's decision in *CTS*, a number of other states adopted control share acquisition statutes, including Arizona, Florida, Idaho, Kansas, Louisiana, Massachusetts, Michigan, Minnesota, Missouri, Nebraska, Nevada, New Hampshire, North Carolina, Oklahoma, Oregon, South Carolina, Tennessee, and Utah.

2. Supermajority/Fair Price Requirements

Several states have amended their corporate statutes to include a "supermajority/fair price" provision similar to those found in many corporate charters (see Chapter 23.I.A). These provisions are designed to combat perceived inequities resulting from front-end loaded partial tender offers by regulating the second step of a two-tier transaction. The provisions operate by imposing supermajority voting requirements for mergers, sales of assets, liquidations, and recapitalizations (but not tender offers) between a corporation incorporated in the relevant state and an "interested shareholder," unless the transaction meets statutory fair price requirements. An "interested shareholder" is generally defined to include a ten-percent-or-more beneficial owner of the corporation's voting securities. The statutory definitions of a fair price are complex and somewhat varied, but are typically designed to assure that shareholders receive, in the second or later stage of an acquisition a price, at least as high as the highest price paid by the interested shareholder for any shares within the past two years. If the fair price standards are not met, the statutes generally require an 80 percent vote of the outstanding shares and a 66⅔ percent vote of the shares held by disinterested shareholders. Generally a corporation may elect not to be governed by the statute if it secures approval for a charter amendment to that effect by the same supermajority vote.

Statutes of this type have been enacted in Arizona, California, Connecticut (Conn. Gen. Stat. Ann. §§33-374a to -374c), Florida, Georgia (Ga. Code Ann. §§14-2-232 to -234), Illinois (Ill. Ann. Stat. ch. 32, para. 7.85), Indiana, Kentucky (Ky. Rev. Stat. Ann. §§271A. 396.398), Louisiana (La. Rev. Stat. Ann. §§12:132-134), Maryland (Md. Corps. & Ass'ns Code Ann. §§3-601 to -603), Michigan (Mich. Comp. Laws Ann. §§450.1776-1784), Minnesota, Mississippi (Miss. Code Ann. §§79-25-1 to -7), Missouri, New Jersey, New York, North Carolina (95 percent supermajority for transactions with 20 percent stockholder), Pennsylvania (Pa. Bus. Corp. L. §409.1 (c)), Virginia (Va. Code Ann. §§13.1-725 to -728), Washington (Wash. Rev. Code §23A.08.425), and Wisconsin (Wis. Stat. Ann. §180.725).

3. Pennsylvania's Fair Value Statute

Pennsylvania has adopted an unusual approach to state takeover regulation, which is patterned after the appraisal rights traditionally accorded by state law to shareholders who dissent from a merger. The Pennsylvania statute (Pa. Bus. Corp. L. §910) requires persons acquiring 20 percent or more of the voting power of a Pennsylvania corporation to pay the remaining shareholders the "fair value" of their shares. The statute does not apply to corporations that amended their bylaws within 90 days of its enactment, or that subsequently amended their charters, in each case to provide explicitly that the statute does not apply.

In *Pennwalt Corp.* v. *Centaur Partners*, 710 F. Supp. 111 (E.D. Pa. 1989), a federal district court granted a preliminary injunction against the solicitation of consents to call a special meeting of shareholders. The court found that Centaur's consent solicitation was void by its terms since the consents would otherwise trigger the application of the Pennsylvania Fair Value Statute. The court ruled that consent solicitation would result in shareholders who held over 20 percent of Pennwalt's shares being deemed to be acting "in concert" for purposes of § 910 and would thus trigger application of the statute, allowing all other shareholders to put their shares to the group for "fair value." The court also found that the application of § 910 would not violate the Supremacy Clause of the Constitution nor would it impermissibly burden the solicitation of proxies under § 14(a) of the Exchange Act.

A statute providing redemption rights similar to the Pennsylvania fair value statute has been adopted in Maine (Me. Rev. Stat. Ann. tit. 13-A, §910). Utah had also adopted a similar statute but, following the *CTS* decision, the statute was repealed and a control share acquisition statute was adopted.

Pennsylvania has enacted a new Business Corporation Law taking effect October 1, 1989. Many of the changes were designed to conform Pennsylvania law to the Delaware General Corporation law to make Pennsylvania more attractive to corporations as a state in which to be incorporated. In addition, some of the advantages that the revised Pennsylvania law has over Delaware are that Pennsylvania allows greater flexibility in the redemption of shares; permits a board that is not classified to be protected by action of the shareholders against removal without cause; adjusts the share ownership threshold for commencement of a derivative action against a director or officer without security for costs of inflation by raising the fair market value to $200,000; authorizes boards of directors to effect a merger or consolidation without shareholder approval if the charter of the corporation and its previously outstanding shares are unaffected by the merger; and allows managements to reject hostile takeover bids without offering shareholders an alternative buyout or restructuring plan if they can show that they have an appropriate business reason. In addition, last year Pennsylvania enacted a statute authorizing Pennsylvania corporations to adopt rights plans.

4. Limitations on Certain Business Combinations

The New York statute (N.Y. Bus. Corp. Law §912) prohibits certain New York corporations from entering into a "business combination" with a 20 percent stockholder for five years after the 20 percent threshold is crossed, unless the board of directors approved the combination in advance of the 20 percent acquisition. Any business combination after the five-year period must be approved by a majority of the disinterested stockholders or must satisfy a fair price test. No business combination is permitted if the 20 percent shareholder acquires additional stock after crossing the 20 percent threshold, unless the additional shares are purchased at the fair price or in a fashion, prescribed by the statute, designed to allow all shareholders to share proportionately. The term "business combination" is broadly defined to include certain self-dealing transactions as well as mergers and consolidations. The statute applies to any New York corporation with its principal executive offices, significant business operations, and 10 percent of its beneficial shareholders located in New York. The statute does not apply to a corporation if the disinterested shareholders amend the bylaws so to provide. Similar statutes have been adopted in states including Arizona (Ariz. Rev. Stat. Ann. §§10-1221 to 10-1223), Connecticut, Delaware (see below), Georgia, Idaho, Indiana (Ind. Code Ann. §23-1-43-18), Kentucky (Ky. Rev. Stat. Ann. §271A.397), Maine, Minnesota, Missouri, Nebraska, New Jersey (N.J. Stat. Ann. §14A:10A-4), South Carolina, Tennessee, Virginia, Washington, and Wisconsin.

In January 1988, Delaware passed a weak variation of the New York statute. New Section 203 of the Delaware General Corporation Law prohibits a Delaware corporation from entering into a "business combination" with an "interested stockholder" for three years following the date that such person became an interested stockholder. "Business combination" is defined to include certain "self-dealing" transactions as well as mergers and consolidations. The definition of an interested stockholder includes any person who is the owner of 15 percent or more of the outstanding voting stock of the corporation (subject to certain limited exceptions). However, the prohibition against business combinations does not apply if, among other things, (1) the board of directors approves either the business combination or the transaction in which the person becomes an interested stockholder, (2) upon consummation of the transaction in which the person becomes an interested stockholder, the interested stockholder owns at least 85 percent of the voting stock of the corporation (excluding stock owned by persons who are directors and also officers or owned by certain types of employee stock plans), or (3) the business combination is approved by the board of directors and authorized at a meeting of stockholders by at least 66⅔ percent of the outstanding voting stock not owned by the interested stockholder.

The SEC has filed amicus curiae briefs in several cases involving challenges to business combination statutes on the grounds that they are unconstitutional under the Commerce Clause or preempted by the Williams Act.

D. Constitutionality of Second Generation State Takeover Statutes

1. CTS and Other Control Share Acquisition Statute Cases

In *CTS Corp.* v. *Dynamics Corp. of America*, 481 U.S. 69 (1987), the Supreme Court, by a six to three vote, upheld the Indiana Control Share Acquisition Statute (see 26.III.D.1), finding that the Indiana Act is not preempted by the Williams Act and does not discriminate against interstate commerce in violation of the Commerce Clause.

The Court stated that since it was possible for an acquiror to comply with both the Williams Act and the Indiana Act, the Act would be preempted only if it frustrates the purposes of the Williams Act. The Court concluded that the Indiana Act did not frustrate the purposes of, and thus was not preempted by, the Williams Act, even under the broad interpretation of the Williams Act contained in Justice White's plurality opinion in *MITE* (see 26.III.B.1). In fact, the Court stated the Act "furthers a basic purpose of the Williams Act, 'plac[ing] investors on an equal footing with the takeover bidder" (*id.*, at 82, citing *Piper* v. *Chris-Craft Industries, Inc.*, 430 U.S. 1, 30 (1977)), by giving shareholders the power to collectively consider the merits of a control share acquisition.

The Court distinguished the Indiana Act from the Illinois Act struck down in *MITE*, noting that the Indiana Act does not (1) give management or the offeror an advantage in communicating with shareholders about a tender offer, (2) impose an indefinite delay on tender offers, or (3) allow the state to impose its view of fairness on willing sellers of shares.

The court concluded that even if the Indiana Act did impose some additional delay on tender offers, the 50-day period established by the Act could not be deemed unreasonable since it was within the 60-day maximum period established by Congress for tender offers. The Court also noted that a variety of state corporate laws, such as those permitting staggered boards and cumulative voting, can delay the free exercise of voting power after a successful tender offer.

Rejecting the Commerce Clause challenge, the Court found that the Indiana Act does not discriminate against out-of-state offerors and does not subject activities in interstate commerce to potentially inconsistent regulation. The Court noted that the Indiana Act has the same effect on a tender offer whether or not the offeror is an Indiana resident or domiciliary, concluding that the Act "'visits its effects equally upon both interstate and local business"' *Id.* at 87, citing *Lewis* v. *BT Investment Managers, Inc.*, 447 U.S. 27, 36 (1980). The Court noted that "so long as each State regulates voting rights only in the corporations it has created, each corporation will be subject to the law of only one State" (*Id.*). The Court stressed that "state regulation of corporate governance is regulation of entities whose very existence and attributes are a product of state law," (*id.*), and that it "is an accepted part of the business landscape in this country for States to create corporations, to prescribe their powers, and to define the rights that are acquired by purchasing their shares" (*Id.* at 91).

The Court concluded that "[a] State has an interest in promoting stable relationships among parties involved in the corporations it charters, as well as in ensuring that investors in such corporations have an effective voice in corporate affairs." *Id.* The Court noted that:

> A change in management may have important effects on the shareholders' interests; it is well within the State's role as overseer of corporate governance to offer [shareholders an opportunity to decide collectively whether a change in voting control would be desirable] (*Id.*).

The Court also rejected the argument that Indiana had no legitimate interest in protecting nonresident shareholders. While recognizing that Indiana has no interest in protecting nonresident shareholders of nonresident corporations (referring to the Illinois Act in *MITE* that applied to certain out-of-state corporations), the Court stated that:

> We reject the contention that Indiana has no interest in providing for the shareholders of its corporations the voting autonomy granted by the Act. Indiana has a substantial interest in preventing the corporate form from becoming a shield for unfair business dealing. Moreover, unlike the Illinois statute invalidated in *MITE*, the Indiana Act applies only to corporations that have a substantial number of shareholders in Indiana. *Id.* at 93.

Finally, the Court stated that even assuming the Indiana Act will limit the number of successful tender offers,[1] its Commerce Clause analysis would not be substantially affected:

> We reiterate that this Act does not prohibit any entity—resident or nonresident—from offering to purchase, or from purchasing, shares in Indiana Corporations, or from attempting thereby to gain control. It only provides regulatory procedures designed for the better protections of the corporations' shareholders. *Id.*

Justice White, the author of the *MITE* decision, dissented, arguing that the Indiana Act is preempted by the Williams Act and that the Act prohibits interstate commerce in violation of the Commerce Clause. Justice White criticized the majority's approach, stating that the majority wrongly "equates protection of individual investors, the focus of the Williams Act, with the protection of shareholders as a group." *Id.* at 97. Justice White argued that "the Control Share Acquisitions Chapter will effectively prevent minority shareholders in some circumstances from selling their stock to a willing tender offeror. It is the practical impact of the Chapter that leads to the conclusion that it is preempted by the Williams Act." *Id.* at 99.

Justices Blackmun and Stevens joined Justice White's dissent with respect to the Commerce Clause, while Justice White was the sole dissenting voice with respect to the preemption issue.

Notwithstanding *CTS*, raiders have continued to challenge the constitutionality of control share acquisition statutes. In *Veere Inc.* v. *The Firestone Tire & Rubber Co.*, 685 F. Supp. 1027 (N.D. Ohio 1988), the plaintiff argued that the prohibition on the acquisition of shares under the Ohio Control Share Acquisition Statute without shareholder approval was not constitutional under *CTS*. The court concluded that this variance from the Indiana Act—the inability to obtain the economic benefits of tendered shares—was not sufficient to take the Ohio statute outside the holding in *CTS*, and refused to grant an injunction against enforcement of the Ohio statute.

---

[1]The Court noted that there is little evidence that this will occur.

2. Koppers/Staley/Interco: The Delaware Business Combination Statute

In the first case squarely[2] addressing the issue of the constitutionality of the Delaware Business combination statute, *BNS, Inc.* v. *Koppers Co.*, 683 F. Supp. 458 (D. Del. 1988), the court held that it was probably constitutional in an action for a preliminary injunction. The plaintiff argued that the Delaware statute was preempted by the Williams Act because it favors target company management over offerors and therefore frustrates the shareholder protection purpose of the Williams Act. In its analysis, the Court stated that "allowing [states] to deprive the tender offeror of . . . a business combination would permit a de facto frustration of the goals of the Williams Act," but that a statute would not be preempted "so long as hostile offers which are beneficial to target shareholders have a meaningful opportunity for success" (*Id.* at 468, 469). From its review of *CTS*, the court stated that four questions had to be considered in making a decision concerning preemption. It held that the statute protected independent shareholders by preventing certain dealings between an offeror and a target; that any advantage bestowed on incumbent management was not readily discernible (and that it could not find that that advantage outweighed the benefits to shareholders); that it imposed no delay on the actual purchase of shares; and that it did not interpose the state's view of fairness between willing buyers and sellers. The court stated:

> [E]ntrusting management to protect shareholders is the norm in current corporate law. Moreover, the heightened judicial scrutiny of management imposed by Delaware law in the takeover context no doubt also will apply to the decisions of boards with respect to proposed business combinations. Therefore, notwithstanding the pro management tilt of the Delaware statute, [it] more probably than not is within the sphere of constitutional state regulation of tender offers. *Id.* at 470 (citation omitted).

The court also applied *CTS* in rejecting the assertion that the Delaware statute is unconstitutional under the Commerce Clause. In so doing, the court determined that the Delaware statute does not discriminate against out-of-state offerors; does not create a risk of inconsistent regulation; and promotes stable corporate relationships and protects shareholders, both of which are valid state concerns (*Id.* at 472-73).

---

[2]In *Black & Decker Corp.*v. *American Standard Inc.*, 679 F. Supp. 1183 (D. Del. 1988), the court avoided reaching the constitutional issues by holding that Black & Decker was not entitled to an injunction against the Delaware statute because it could not prove that it would suffer irreparable harm if the injunction was not granted. See also, *Salant Acquisition Corp.* v. *Manhattan Industries, Inc.*, 682 F. Supp. 199 (S.D.N.Y. 1988) (same result in case involving New York Business Combination Statute).

In *RP Acquisition Corp.* v. *Staley Continental, Inc.*, 686 F. Supp. 476 (D. Del. 1988), the federal District Court of Delaware again refused to hold that the Delaware statute was most likely unconstitutional and denied a preliminary injunction. The court stated that in *CTS*, the Supreme Court had "accepted that states, in promoting shareholder protection, an aim consistent with the Williams Act, can to some extent at least affect the offeror-management neutrality, which the Williams Act proclaims" (*Id.* at 481). The court concluded, in its preemption analysis, in language equally applicable to other business combination statutes:

> The Supreme Court having advised thus that a two-year delay before an acquiror obtains "untrammeled authority" endures Supremacy Clause–Williams Act scrutiny, we are pressed to understand plaintiff's claim of the sudden unconstitutionality of the three-year delay which Section 203 imposes on "business combinations" (*Id.* at 486).

In rejecting the plaintiff's and the SEC's Commerce Clause argument that attempted to distinguish *CTS* on the grounds that the Indiana Act required certain additional Indiana contacts, the court concluded that "Delaware has a substantial, and constitutionally weighty, interest 'in preventing the corporate form [which Delaware itself has created] from being a shield for unfair business dealings.'" *Id.* at 488 (quoting *CTS*, 107 S. Ct. at 1651-52).

Yet again the district court denied a motion to preliminarily enjoin the Delaware statute on constitutional grounds in *City Capital Associates* v. *Interco*, 696 F. Supp. 1551 (D. Del. 1988). The court relied upon its previous decisions in *Koppers* and *Staley* to dispose of the Williams Act and Commerce Clause claims. The court observed that the limited opportunity that *Koppers* left for future constitutional challenges of §203 on the basis of statistical data (showing that the application of the statute harms shareholders by preventing a sufficient number of hostile tender offers) required, as in *Staley*, a much greater evidentiary showing than that which was presented by the plaintiff in *Interco*.

The only new argument the plaintiff presented was that §203 constituted an improper delegation of governmental authority to the boards of target companies and that it violated the due process clause of the Fourteenth Amendment, because the statute does not provide any guidelines for boards to determine whether or not to apply §203 in a given transaction.

In rejecting this novel constitutional claim, the court stated that §203 simply is not a delegation of governmental authority because a corporation can opt out of the statutory provision. Therefore, because the government does not have the authority to decide whether a particular business combination would benefit a particular corporation, the government "cannot delegate authority it does not possess."

3. Other Constitutional Cases

(a) West Point

In *West Point-Pepperell, Inc.* v. *Farley Inc.* 711 F. Supp. 1088–96 (N.D. Ga. 1989) the court considered constitutional challenges to the Georgia business combination statute (O.C.G.A. § 14-2-236), and, after a four day trial, found that there was insufficient evidence to find the statute unconstitutional. The Georgia statute prohibits certain Georgia corporations that have opted into coverage by the statute from engaging in any business combination with a 10 percent stockholder for 5 years following the date that such stockholder crossed the 10 percent threshold, unless (1) the board of directors approved the business combination prior to the stockholder's crossing the threshold; (2) the stockholder became a 90 percent (excluding stock held by officers, directors, their affiliates, subsidiaries of the issuer, and certain employee stock option plans) stockholder in the threshold-crossing transaction; or (3) after the stockholder acquired 90 percent of the outstanding shares of the corporation, holders of a majority of the remaining shares [with the same exclusions as in (2)] approve the business combination at an annual or special meeting.

The court determined that the Georgia statute did not violate the Supremacy Clause of the Constitution because the statute's requirements are not in direct conflict with the requirements of the Williams Act and do not frustrate the purposes of the Williams Act. The court, citing *CTS* and *Hyde Park*, reasoned that since neutrality was only a characteristic of the Williams Act, a statute such as Georgia's, which, in an effort to protect shareholders' interests, has some "incidental effect on the balance between offeror and target management does not *per se* contravene the purpose of the Williams Act." *Id.* at 1102. The court reasoned further that "so long as hostile offers which are beneficial to target shareholders enjoy a 'meaningful opportunity for success,'" (*id.* at 15 (citing *Koppers* and *Staley*)) statutes that have substantial deterrent effects on tender offers do not frustrate the goals of the Williams Act. The court held that Farley did not meet its burden of showing that the Georgia statute's exceptions (the 90 percent clauses) did not offer such meaningful opportunity for success. *Id.* at 1105.

The court next considered the Georgia statute's validity under the Commerce Clause and applied a three-part test to find that the Georgia statute (1) "does not favor in-state offerors over out-of-state offerors" (*id.* at 1107); (2) "does not subject interstate activities to an impermissible risk of inconsistent adjudication . . . [because] by its terms, [it] applies only to corporations created under Georgia law"; and (3) enables the state to govern the internal affairs of corporations enacted under its laws without explicitly denying hostile tender offers a meaningful opportunity to succeed.

(b) RTE

In *RTE Corp.* v. *Mark IV Industries, Inc.*, [1987–88 Transfer Binder] Fed. Sec. L. Rep. (CCH) ¶ 93,789 (E.D. Wis. May 6, 1988), *vacated*, No. 88-C-378 (E.D. Wis. June 22, 1988), the Wisconsin business combination statute was declared unconstitutional on Williams Act preemption grounds. Based on the New York model, the Wisconsin statute generally provides that a raider cannot engage in a business combination with the target company for three years, unless the transaction or the raider's becoming a 10 percent shareholder is approved by the target board of directors before the raider crosses the 10 percent mark.

The court's single paragraph analysis in *RTE* attempted to distinguish *CTS*, asserting that the Wisconsin statute, unlike the Indiana statute in *CTS*, "does not promote investor choice and instead gives to the management of target companies virtual veto power over the outcome of a tender offer contest" (Slip op. at 8). Among other things, the court failed to consider the Supreme Court's observation in *CTS* that numerous state laws, which may discourage tender offers by delaying a takeover bidder's acquisition of full authority over a target company, are not preempted by the Williams Act. The *RTE* decision has been vacated and establishes no precedent even as to Wisconsin law, because the same judge who issued the opinion later vacated it.

(c) Batus

In *Batus Inc.* v. *McKay*, 684 F. Supp. 637 (D. Nev. 1988), the court declared unconstitutional a peculiar Nevada Takeover Act requiring shareholders to deposit their shares, pursuant to a takeover bid, within 60 days from the date of the first invitation to deposit shares. The court held that the 60-day limit conflicted with the Williams Act because the Williams Act imposes no limit on how long a tender offer may remain open, and requires that a tender offer remain open for at least 10 business days after a price change is announced.

(d) Vernitron

In *Vernitron Corp.* v. *Kollmorgen Corp.*, 89 Civ. 241 (JES) (S.D.N.Y. Feb. 9, 1989) (transcript) the United States District Court for the Southern District of New York upheld the constitutionality of the New York Business Combination Statute. The plaintiff in *Vernitron* claimed that the New York statute was preempted by the Williams Act and that it violated the Commerce Clause of the United States Constitution. The *Vernitron* court, in denying a motion for summary judgment, rejected both claims, relying on the Supreme Court's decision in *CTS Corp.* v. *Dynamics Corp.*, 481 U.S. 69 (1987). The court held that "[i]t would be stretching the Williams Act beyond all rationality" to find that that Act preempted state regulation of corporate mergers. With respect to the Commerce Clause claim, the court ruled "that the Supreme Court contemplates the broadest possible power in the state to regulate its own corporations." The court also rejected the claim that the New York statute gives directors the "absolute" power to bar tender offers, noting that the statute gives New York corporations the right to opt out of its coverage and that New York corporate law gives shareholders the right to vote out a board that refuses to give approval under the statute.

(e) Universal Foods

In the first appellate decision to review the constitutionality of a state business combination statute that applies only to domestic corporations, the Seventh Circuit Court of Appeals has held that the Wisconsin Business Combination Act is constitutional. *Amanda Acquisition Corp.* v. *Universal Foods Corp.*, [Current] Fed. Sec. L. Rep. (CCH) ¶ 94,436 (7th Cir. May 24, 1989). The Wisconsin Act bans second step mergers with a 10 percent or greater shareholder for three years after the 10 percent position is acquired unless, prior to the 10 percent stock acquisition, the board of directors of the target gives its approval. The Wisconsin Act, like the New York Business Combination Statute, does not contain an exception for acquisitions of a specified percentage of shares pursuant to a tender offer, as, for example, the Delaware statute does.

The Seventh Circuit, through Circuit Judge Frank Easterbrook, rejected preemption and Commerce Clause challenges to the Wisconsin law. With respect to the preemption challenge, the Seventh Circuit held that only if the Williams Act "gives investors the right to be the beneficiary of [tender] offers could Wisconsin's law run afoul of the federal rule". But, said the Court, because "[i]nvestors have no right to receive tender offers" and the Williams Act "does not create a right to profit from the business of making tender offers," the Wisconsin law is not preempted.

In his Commerce Clause discussion, significantly, Judge Easterbrook, like the court below, rejected the "meaningful opportunity" test developed by the federal district court in Delaware in the *Koppers* case and followed in several other cases involving business combination statutes like the Delaware statute. The Seventh Circuit thus held that "[t]he Commerce Clause does not demand that states leave bidders a 'meaningful opportunity for success.'"

4. Takeover Statutes Regulating Foreign Corporations

In recent cases, district courts have struck down on constitutional grounds state antitakeover statutes regulating foreign corporations on constitutional grounds. In *TLX Acquisition Corp.* v. *Telex Corp.*, 679 F. Supp. 1022 (W.D. Okla.

1987), the Oklahoma Control Shares Acquisition Act was declared unconstitutional after *CTS* was decided. The decision addressed the constitutional limits to the applicability of the statute to corporations other than those incorporated in Oklahoma. In this case the target was a Delaware corporation with its principal place of business and over 10 percent of its shareholders located in Oklahoma. The court found that Oklahoma had no interest in protecting nonresident shareholders of nonresident corporations and that the statute posed "an impermissible risk of inconsistent regulation by different states." *Id.* at 1031; *LF Acquisition Corp.* v. *Linear Films, Inc.*, No. CIV-88-134-W (W.D. Okla., Feb. 3, 1988) (Oklahoma statute was "facially unconstitutional" as applied to a nondomestic corporation).

In *Campeau Corp.* v. *Federated Department Stores, Inc.*, 679 F. Supp. 735 (S.D. Ohio 1988), the court held that the Ohio Foreign Business Acquisitions Act, which purported to regulate only those acquisitions of resident corporations by certain statutorily defined foreign businesses, violated the Commerce Clause because, unlike the Indiana statute upheld in *CTS*, the Ohio statute was discriminatory on its face and created the risk of inconsistent state regulation.

In *Grand Metropolitan P.L.C.* v. *Butterworth*, Civ. A. No. 88-40317WS (N.D. Fla. Nov. 29, 1988), a federal district court in Florida enjoined Pillsbury and the Florida attorney general from enforcing Florida's "antitakeover" statutes. Grand Metropolitan claimed that the Florida statutes, one of which required special approvals for "affiliated transactions" and the second of which regulated control share acquisitions, were unconstitutional as applied to foreign corporations. The court found these statutes unconstitutional on Commerce Clause grounds, since they improperly "regulate[d] the internal affairs of out-of-state corporations" and subjected foreign corporations to inconsistent regulation in the different states.

In *Tyson Foods, Inc.* v. *McReynolds*, 700 F. Supp. 906 (M.D. Tenn. 1988) *aff'd*, 865 F.2d 99 (6th Cir. 1989), the district court granted a preliminary injunction preventing the enforcement of the Tennessee statutes regulating takeovers against foreign corporations. The court found these statutes unconstitutional on Commerce Clause grounds to the extent that they regulated the behavior of foreign corporations. The court found that the Tennessee statutes impermissibly regulated foreign corporations because the statutes (1) were direct regulation, while in *CTS*, the "burdens on interstate commerce created by the statute were merely incidental" to the exercise of legitimate state interests (*slip op.* at 9); (2) created a substantial risk of inconsistent regulation among the different states; (3) impermissibly protected incumbent management, not shareholders; and (4) resulted in minimal local benefits, which were far outweighed by the burdens placed on interstate commerce.

Both the Florida statute in *Grand Metropolitan* and the Tennessee statute in *Tyson* were struck down despite the fact that each statute contained a savings clause. These clauses were attempts to avoid the problem of inconsistent regulation among the different states. However, both courts rejected use of the savings clause, finding that in *CTS* the Supreme Court had ruled that one state could not simply implement regulations that would be effective only if another state had not already implemented regulations governing the same subject matter. In addition, the courts noted that a savings clause would not be effective in deciding among the different states attempting to regulate foreign corporations. It is still unclear the extent to which states may attempt to regulate takeovers of foreign corporations. *See Nomad Acquisition Corp.* v. *Damon Corp.*, 701 F. Supp. 10 (D. Mass. 1988).

E. Corporate Constituencies Statutes

A number of states have enacted statutes authorizing directors to consider a variety of constituency interests in addition to shareholder interests. These states include Arizona, Idaho, Illinois, Indiana, Kentucky, Maine, Minnesota, Missouri, Nebraska, New Mexico, New York, Ohio, Pennsylvania, and Wisconsin. A number of state statutes are broad enough to allow a board to consider all types of interests in evaluating a takeover bid.

For example, the Ohio statute (Ohio Rev. Code Ann. §1701.59) provides that for the purpose of performing his duties to the corporation:

> a director, in determining what he reasonably believes to be in the best interests of the corporation, shall consider the interests of the corporation's shareholders and, in his discretion, may consider any of the following:
>
> 1. The interests of the corporation's employees, suppliers, creditors, and customers,
> 2. The economy of the state and nation,
> 3. Community and societal considerations,
> 4. The long-term as well as short-term interests of the corporation and its shareholders, including the possibility that these interests may be best served by the continued independence of the corporation.

The Missouri statute (Mo. Rev. Stat. §351.347) also permits a target's board to consider a wide variety of constituencies when responding to a takeover proposal, including: (1) social, legal, and economic effects on employees, suppliers, customers, and others having similar relationships with the corporation, and the communities in which the corporation conducts its businesses; (2) the financial condition and earning prospects of the person making the acquisition proposal; and (3) the competence, experience, and integrity of the person making the acquisition proposal.

While all the constituency statutes do not reach as far as the Ohio and Missouri statutes, the statutes nonetheless should help boards examine the broad ramifications of a hostile bid, and lessen the pressure to accede to the short-term demands and views of the arbitrageurs and institutional investors in connection with a hostile bid.

Indiana recently enacted a progressive constituency statute that addresses many of the concerns directors must face when confronted with an acquisition proposal. Indiana explicitly permits a director, in considering the best interests of a corporation, to "consider the effects of any action on shareholders, employees, suppliers, and customers of the corporation, on communities in which offices or other facilities of the corporation are located, and any other factors the director considers pertinent." The statute states that in deciding whether a given action is in the best interests of the corporation, "directors are not required to consider the effects of a proposed corporate action on any particular corporate constituent group or interest as a dominant or controlling factor." In addition, the Indiana statute allows a board of directors, in taking or declining to take any action, or in making or declining to make any recommendation to shareholders, to use its discretion to consider "both the short-term and long-term best interests of the corporation, taking into account, and weighing as the directors deem appropriate, the effects thereof on the corporation's shareholders and the other corporate constituent groups and interests . . . as well as any other factors deemed pertinent by the directors."

The Indiana statute rejects application of the *Unocal* standard and limits director liability for actions taken as a director or any failure to take action to situations where "the director has breached or failed to perform the duties of the director's office . . . and the breach or failure to perform constitutes willful misconduct or recklessness." In addition, the statute provides that when a board makes a determination concerning whether it will take any action or make a recommendation to shareholders with "the approval of a majority of the disinterested directors of the board of directors, that determination shall conclusively be presumed to be valid unless it can be demonstrated that the determination was not made in good faith after reasonable investigation." This progressive constituency statute addresses in a comprehensive manner many of the difficult questions directors must face in the context of a hostile acquisition proposal and the Indiana statute should be the basis for reforms in other states.

Constituency statutes provide support for a "just say no" defense, *see, e.g., Amanda Acquisition Corp.* v. *Universal Foods Corp.*, No. 88-C-1296 (E.D. Wis. Mar. 18, 1989), and are often supported by legislative history indicating that the legislature rejects the heightened *Unocal* standard; *see, e.g.*, Indiana Code §23-1-35-1 (1989). They are often accompanied by statutes validating rights plans. *See* Section III.B.7.

New York recently adopted a weaker version of a constituency statute that does not alter directors' duties. Florida also recently adopted a constituency statute and a number of states are considering the adoption of constituency statutes. For a model provision, *see* Chapter 23.II.G.

F. Disclosure Statutes

A number of states have adopted first generation-type statutes (or have amended existing statutes) to require the filing of a disclosure statement with the state's securities agency upon the commencement of a tender offer. Such statutes are designed, for the most part, to avoid direct conflict with the Williams Act, although several statutes do provide for state agency review of the adequacy of the disclosure. States with disclosure or registration statutes include Alaska, Arkansas, Connecticut, Hawaii, Indiana, Iowa, Massachusetts, Minnesota, Mississippi, Missouri, Nevada, New Hampshire, New Jersey, New York, North Carolina, Ohio, Oklahoma, Pennsylvania, South Dakota, Tennessee, Virginia, and Wisconsin.

Public concern over LBOs and potential management conflicts of interest has been translated into legislation in California that is intended to combat abuses perceived to be inherent in management buyout transactions. Cal. Corp. Code § 1203 (1988). *See generally* Kraus, *Revised California Statute Requires Fairness Opinions*; Insights, Sept. 1988, at 24; *Bagley & Robertson, California Adds Rule to Protect Some Shareholders*, Nat'l Law J., Feb. 20, 1989, at 51. Section 1203 requires (1) an independent appraisal of the proposed offering price (*i.e.*, a fairness opinion); and (2) disclosure to, and consideration by, shareholders of competing offers prior to consummation of the management transaction. This statute applies to California corporations and certain foreign corporations with significant contacts with California. The statute covers tender offers and written proposals for a sale of substantially all assets, a merger, or an "exchange reorganization." The statute's requirements are triggered if the tender offer is by, or the written proposal is received from, an "interested party," which includes people who directly or indirectly control the target corporation and entities with material financial interests held by a director or executive officer of the target corporation.

G. A Proposed Uniform Third Generation State Takeover Statute

While Congress and the Administration remain at odds about the appropriateness of reform of the takeover process, the states obviously have responded with differing statutes designed to protect shareholders and other corporate constituencies from the effects of abusive hostile takeovers. It has been suggested that the adoption of a uniform state takeover law might be appropriate. The North American Securities Administrators Association has recommended a model statute based on the Indiana statute. However, that statute does not prevent, and may even create, incentives for a corporate raider to put a company in play.

An alternative would be a uniform state takeover statute based on the second generation share purchase rights plan. (see Chapter 23.II.E)

The uniform statute would apply to an acquiror who holds more than 1 percent of a company's shares and who, after enactment of the statute, acquired shares in excess of 1 percent without the approval of the company's board. Such an acquiror would be barred from engaging in a merger, liquidation, significant asset sale, significant stock issuance, or similar transaction with the company for five years from the date the acquiror crossed the 1 percent threshold.

The uniform statute would not bar any entity from buying in any manner—tender offer or open market—as many shares as it wished to buy. Nor would the statute affect voting or any other aspect of share ownership. An acquiror would remain free to purchase a controlling interest in a target and manage the target as it wished. The uniform statute would only bar a second-step transaction with an acquiror who exceeded the 1 percent threshold without the prior approval of the company's board. The statute would provide an exception to the 1 percent threshold for large shareholders with a pure investment motive, who would be permitted to go to a 5 percent threshold without incurring the five-year bar.

The 1 percent limitation deters (but does not prevent) two-tier takeovers and partial tender offers. The deterrence derives from the five-year bar to a second-step squeeze-out, which is an important limitation on the ability of corporate raiders to do bootstrap, junk bond, bust-up takeovers. The longer it takes for a raider to bust up the target to get the money to repay the bootstrap financing of the takeover bid, the more difficult it is for the raider to obtain the financing.

An acquiror who did not exceed the 1 percent threshold, or who holds more than 1 percent but did not acquire shares after enactment of the statute, and who makes or proposes to make a tender offer for all of the outstanding shares of the company for cash or securities, or a combination of cash and securities, would have the right to demand a shareholder referendum on its proposal. To obtain the referendum, the acquiror would have to have the financing or financing commitments for the cash portion of its offer. If the offer were for securities or partially for securities, the amount of debt securities to be issued in the transaction, together with the existing balance sheet debt of the acquiror and the target, could not be greater than three times the market equity of the acquiror at the time of the demand plus the value of any equity securities to be issued in the transaction.

The cash financing condition protects against corporate raiders putting companies in play without financing and on the basis of "highly confident" letters as to financing or vague descriptions of tentative financing plans, as they now may do under the SEC's view of federal tender offer regulation. The condition limiting the amount of debt securities to be issued in the transaction protects against the use of questionable securities and protects against the extremely high leverage common to almost all bootstrap, bust-up takeovers by corporate raiders using junk bonds.

The person demanding the shareholder referendum would be required to pay half the cost of the special meeting. This provision guards against indiscriminate use of the right to demand a special meeting. The special meeting would be required to be held within not more than 120 days after the demand.

Failure to meet the criteria for the shareholder referendum also would not prohibit or prevent whatever takeover tactics a raider may choose to pursue. It would only foreclose access to the shareholder referendum. Raiders would be free as at present to pursue any lawful takeover tactics, and companies could defend against them by any lawful means. Since a raider could proceed in any manner it chose independent of the shareholder referendum procedure, the statute would not proscribe the ability of companies to continue to adopt structural takeover defenses prior to a referendum being properly demanded.

Failure to meet the criteria for a shareholder referendum would, as both a practical matter and legal matter, strengthen the ability of the target's board to defend against such takeover tactics. Failure to follow the statutory procedure established to avoid takeover abuses would, in and of itself, be a sufficient basis for the target's board to reject such a takeover bid and take strong defensive actions. In addition, the uniform statute would confirm the right of the target's board, in making a determination with respect to a takeover bid, to take into account long-term shareholder interests and the interests of employees, customers, suppliers, and communities.

If a shareholder referendum were properly demanded, a majority of the target's outstanding shares could authorize the proposed takeover bid. After a referendum has been properly demanded, no defensive actions would be permitted other than (1) a restructuring designed to create share value at least approximately equal to the bid, (2) a white knight transaction at a price at least approximately equal to the bid, or (3) those defenses based on the substantive or procedural illegality of the bidder's proposal.

The referendum vote is independent of the election to tender or not tender into the raider's bid that the shareholders of a target must make whenever there is a hostile tender offer. The provision for a separate referendum removes one of the principal coercive aspects of tender offers—the uncertainty as to the response by other shareholders of the target, which leads shareholders to tender rather than risk being locked into a minority situation. Shareholders are free to vote "no" in the referendum while preserving their right to tender if the holders of a majority of the target's shares vote "yes" in the referendum.

The 120-day period would give the company a reasonable period to evaluate its situation, assess the restructuring or white knight alternatives, determine the position of its major shareholders and, if there is a basis therefor, test the legality of the offer. The 120-day period allows corporate decision making to proceed under conditions of normalcy, rather than the extraordinary pressures of the tender offer process. Under these conditions, even some institutional investors may be receptive to the arguments of the target's board in favor of its long-term plans, so that there will be enough diversity of opinion to prevent the institutions from forcing the target to restructure or find a white knight.

The uniform statute would encourage cash offers for all the shares of the target. The statute would discourage accumulations of more than 1 percent by nonpassive investors who seek 100 percent ownership. By assuring major companies willing to pay a full price for a synergistic acquisition of the ability to have a shareholder referendum, the statute would encourage true industrial-strategy mergers that add to productivity and employment. By making bootstrap takeovers more difficult, the statute would discourage junk bond bust-up takeovers that have such devastating effects on employees and communities.

The statute fulfills the policy objectives of allowing all shareholders to share equally in any takeover premium and of allowing the decision as to a company's future to reside ultimately in the hands of the shareholders. See Lipton, *Need for a Uniform State Takeover Law*, N.Y.L.J. Mar. 21, 1988.

V. PROGNOSIS

Takeover activity has been the subject of a unique dynamism as bidders and targets each add to their arsenal of weapons by way of tactic and countertactic. There is no reason this process will not continue.

CHAPTER 27

NONTAXABLE METHODS FOR MERGERS AND ACQUISITIONS

Marc D. Teitelbaum
Spengler Carlson Gubar Brodsky & Frischling
Neil A. Wassner
Wassner Mattingly and Company

In the last seven or so years, the predominant method by which one corporation acquires another corporation has been the fully taxable cash acquisition of a target corporation. The rise of the cash tender offer was fueled by the relative ease by which acquiring corporations could obtain financing from banks, leveraged buyout (LBO) funds, and of course, from the sale of junk bonds. However, such taxable methods may involve burdensome interest and debt costs.

On the other hand, nontaxable methods of acquisition generally provide an established acquiring corporation with a less costly form of acquiring a target corporation. Any form of nontaxable corporate acquisition will essentially require that at least 50 percent of the total consideration paid by the acquiring corporation will be the stock of the acquiring corporation (or its parent corporation). Therefore, if an acquiring corporation has acceptable equity securities or creates such securities, a nontaxable form of acquisition will save the acquiring corporation substantial funds. Although the shareholders of the target corporation are limited in the amount of

Note: Parts of this chapter have been derived from "Nontaxable Methods" by Neil A. Wassner in *Handbook of Mergers, Acquisitions and Buyouts*, edited by Steven James Lee and Robert Douglas Colman. (Englewood Cliffs, NJ: Prentice-Hall), 1981.

cash they can receive in a nontaxable transaction, there is little practical limitation upon such shareholders, if the target corporation is publicly traded, in selling the shares received at any time after the transaction. Thus, in the right circumstances, nontaxable methods of acquiring target corporations provide an extremely important acquisition financing technique. The tax consequences of this technique must be analyzed.

INTRODUCTION TO GENERAL RULES

The parties involved in any corporate merger or acquisition are the two corporations involved in the merger, as well as the shareholders and holders of other securities of the two corporations. In general, depending upon whether various requirements are satisfied, a merger or acquisition can be taxable or tax-free to both the acquired corporation and its shareholders, provided the equity consideration paid by the acquiring corporation (or its parent corporation) for the target corporation is a substantial part of the value of the target stock transferred. Before focusing on the details, it is important to understand the importance of the formal observance of the rules and the fact that a tax-free merger or acquisition involves tax deferral rather than tax elimination.

Formalisms and Tax Deferral at the Shareholder and Corporate Level

It would be possible, based on a substantive economic analysis, for a stock-for-stock merger or acquisition to be viewed as a "sale" resulting in the holders of securities in the acquired company "selling" their stock for stock of the acquiring corporation. If viewed as a "sale," the transaction should be taxed to the shareholders just as if they had sold their shares for cash, and the gain should be the difference between what the stock in the acquired corporation cost them and what the stock in the acquiring corporation is worth.

It is also possible to view the transaction not as a sale but as a continuation of the old investment in another form, thereby qualifying for tax-free treatment. Under this approach, there would be no taxable gain at the time of the exchange of stock, since the original investment would be viewed as being unliquidated and the tax would therefore be deferred until the investment was finally sold.

These two approaches, which are at the heart of the tax treatment of mergers and acquisitions, can perhaps best be seen by looking at two examples.

Y Airlines Inc. and X Airlines Inc. merged to form a new corporation—New Airlines, Inc. Common shareholders of each of the merging corporations received common shares of the new corporation. Assume that a shareholder of Y had owned 100 shares of Y common stock that he had purchased many years ago for $1,000. On the merger that formed New Airlines, the exchange ratio was 2.1 shares of New Airlines for each share of Y; so he would receive 210 shares of New Airlines for his 100 shares of Y. On the day of the merger, when New Airlines shares started trading, the shares sold for $6.88 per share; so the total value of the 210 shares that he received would be worth $1,444, or a profit of $444 over the cost of his original investment in Y.

A Mr. X, sole shareholder of the Z Corporation, a small local newspaper, "sold out" to a national newspaper chain whose shares are traded on the New York Stock Exchange. He received $1 million of stock in the national chain in exchange for his shares in his own corporation, which had cost him $25,000 when he purchased the corporation in the 1940's. Thus he had a profit of $975,000 on the transaction. Mr. X is no longer involved in the newspaper business; he has retired to Florida (where he reads the stock pages daily).

How should these two transactions be taxed? Clearly, it would seem, the first transaction should not be viewed as a sale. The shareholders of Y Airlines Inc. and the shareholders of X Airlines Inc. have not liquidated their investments but have merely "continued" their investments in a new form—that of the new New Airlines Inc. It would not appear to be appropriate to tax them at this time.

But what of Mr. Z, relaxing in Florida, living off his dividends in the national newspaper chain—is his situation the same? Has he "continued" his investment or has he, in effect, "cashed in his chips" by converting his investment into that of a liquid New York Stock Exchange company whose shares he can sell by merely picking up his phone and calling his broker? Is not the real effect of his transaction, as he no doubt tells his friends, that he "sold out" to the national chain rather than that he "merged" with the national chain?

Interestingly enough, if Mr. Z had structured his transaction properly, he will be treated in the same way as the shareholders of X and Y Airlines, that is, as a "continuing" investor in the company that merged with or acquired his corporation. That is because the tax statute that deals with mergers and acquisitions—the so-called "reorganization" provisions of the Internal Revenue Code—depend heavily on the *form* rather than the substance of the transactions that it governs. The position taken in each of the examples is that the shareholder should not be taxed at the time of the transaction; hence, the mergers and acquisitions that are structured to take advantage of these tax provisions are usually called "tax-free acquisitions" or "tax-free reorganizations" or "tax-free exchanges."

"Tax-Free"—A Misnomer

While the term "tax-free" is commonly applied to these transactions to distinguish them from "taxable exchanges," the term is really a misnomer. The relevant Internal Revenue Code provisions call for "tax deferral" not "tax elimination" in the transactions covered by these sections. This is accomplished by providing for a so-called "substituted basis" for shareholders in merger or acquisition situations treated as "reorganizations." The workings of the substituted basis provisions can best be seen by returning to our examples.

We have seen that the shareholder of Y Airlines, who had paid $1,000 for his investment, has received 210 shares of stock in New Airlines worth $6.88 per share. Since the transaction qualified as a "reorganization," he did not have to pay a tax on his gain of $444. However, suppose that several months after the exchange he wishes to sell 100 shares of New Airlines, which are now selling for $5.88 per share. How does he determine his gain or loss on the transaction? This is calculated by dividing his "substituted basis" of $1,000 among the 210 shares of New Airlines that he received, producing a basis of $4.76 per share of the New Airlines shares. Thus a sale of 100 of these shares for $5.88 per share results in a gain of $1.12 per share even though the shares have declined in value from the date that he received them at the time of the merger. This gain is taxable to him, at rates applicable to capital gains.

While the substituted basis rules tend to make "tax-free mergers" really "tax-deferred mergers," there is a circumstance under which the gain will not only be deferred but will go unrecognized forever. If Mr. Z, the retired newspaper owner, were to die before he sold any of his shares in the New York Stock Exchange-listed stock of his acquiror, his heirs, under current law, would inherit his stock at the value on the date of his death.

The concept of tax deferral also applies at the corporate level. The tax basis of the assets of Y Airlines and X Airlines is "carried over" to become the tax basis of the assets of New Airlines. If Y Airlines owned an airplane valued at $5 million with a $1 million tax basis, then such tax basis will be "carried over," and will become the tax basis of New Airlines in the airplane. Thus, if New Airlines sells the airplane for $5 million, it will realize a gain of $4 million, the gain that Y Airlines would have realized. The carryover basis system reflects the fact that the Internal Revenue Code analyzes the merger of Y Airlines into New Airlines as the continuation of Y Airlines' business in another form. In addition, the tax history of Y Airlines would be inherited by New Airlines. Thus, if Y Airlines has net operating losses, New Airlines would generally be able to utilize such net operating losses, subject to other rules and limitations.

The failure of a proposed merger, such as the merger of Y Airlines and X Airlines into New Airlines, to qualify as a tax-free reorganization would subject Y Airlines itself to a tax on the net appreciation of its assets and a second tax to be paid by its shareholders on the exchange of their shares of stock. The corporate level tax would not apply in non-asset acquisitions (e.g., a tender offer) where solely the stock of the target corporation is acquired by the acquiring corporation. The high cost of failure of an asset acquisition or a merger to qualify as a tax-free reorganization (i.e., a double tax) is in part attributable to the repeal of the General Utilities Doctrine under the Tax Reform Act of 1986.

The Importance of Satisfying Form

By now, it should be apparent that the "reorganization" provisions of the Internal Revenue Code are, by nature, liberal provisions. They define, in a sense, exceptions to the general rules that a taxpayer should pay a tax at the time he has received income, and income includes gains on the exchange of securities for other securities, unless an exception applies. Because the tax statute involved is essentially granting relief from the payment of tax, it is almost certain that the requirements for falling within the relief provisions will be set out in some detail with the taxpayer having the responsibility for following the form of the transaction as set out in order to be granted the relief. A taxpayer will want to be certain, prior to having entered the transaction, that he has, by obtaining appropriate counsel, properly followed the form dictated by the Code.

The detailed requirements for qualifying as a "reorganization," or tax-free transaction, are essentially set out in Section 368(a)(1) of the Internal Revenue Code. In addition, many court cases and Revenue Rulings have further defined these requirements, and most of this chapter will deal with the statutory, administrative, and court-imposed rules for a tax-free exchange. It should be apparent, particularly in this age of multibillion dollar mergers and acquisitions, that the stakes for following the rules are enormous, with hundreds of millions of dollars of taxes at stake in a transaction.

Of course, because of the huge potential taxes involved, if the transaction does not fit the Internal Revenue Service requirements, the legal and/or business considerations may have to give way to tax considerations, or, if this is not possible, the transaction may be aborted. Most tax practitioners are aware of many acquisitions that would have made good business sense but floundered because the tax rules could not be met. No doubt many businessmen are also aware of situations where the deal was changed to meet tax considerations and the acquisitions proved unsuccessful because of those changes!

Prior to taking a close look at the statutory language of the reorganization sections of the Internal Revenue Code, it is necessary to examine some of the requirements that are common to all transactions that wish to be classified as tax-free reorganizations. Some of these requirements are contained in the statute but others are gleaned from reading the court cases in this area. Regardless of whether the transaction is structured as a merger, a stock-for-stock exchange, or a stock-for-asset exchange, it is necessary to clear the hurdles of the continuity of proprietary interest test, the continuity of business enterprise test, the business purpose test, and the step-transaction doctrine.

RELEVANT NONSTATUTORY REQUIREMENTS

Continuity of Proprietary Interest

The continuity of proprietary interest requirement arose early in the history of reorganization taxation, and it should be easily understood from the examples that have been presented above. As we have seen, the essential tax philosophy in allowing a taxpayer to defer rather than pay his taxes is that his profit has not been realized in the reorganization. No sale has occurred; rather it is said that his investment has merely continued in another form. In an early court case, a corporation's assets were acquired in a transaction in which it received some cash and some short-term notes. The question arose as to whether this transaction qualified as a reorganization, because it met the statutory definition at that time. The court said no—since short-term notes did not represent a continuation of the interest in the new corporation. An ownership interest in assets was essentially converted into a creditor position by acquisition of short-term notes.

Over the years, many court cases have further clarified this requirement, so that today it can be said that what is required for tax-free reorganizations is that:

1. The transferor corporation or its shareholders retain a proprietary stake in the enterprise, represented by an equity interest in the transferee corporation,

2. Such retained interest represents a substantial part of the value of the property transferred.

As we will see in our consideration of stock-for-stock and stock-for-asset acquisitions, the statute defines quite precisely the type of security and the percentage that represents a "substantial part of the value of the property transferred." However, in the case of statutory mergers (the statute is silent on these points in general), the Internal Revenue Service will favorably rule that a transaction has the requisite continuity of proprietary interest if at least 50 percent of the consideration paid represents equity-type securities. It is for this reason that many corporate mergers today are made for 51 percent stock and 49 percent cash or debt.

For example, in the second step of an acquisition, Y Co. is merged into X Co. with each common shareholder of Y Co. receiving one share of a new X Co. convertible preferred stock for each share of Y Co. common stock. The new preferred stock has one-half vote, pays a dividend of $2.55 annually and is convertible into .375 shares of X Co. common stock. It had a market value when issued of $28 per share.

In the first step, X Co. had purchased, via a tender offer, 49 percent of Y Co. stock for cash of $28 per share. When the two transactions are viewed together, as required by the step-transaction doctrine discussed below, the merger was 51 percent for stock and 49 percent for cash.

Furthermore, the Internal Revenue Service and the courts agree that it is not necessary for voting rights to be present for the required proprietary interest to be found. Thus, nonvoting preferred stock is not an uncommon instrument in corporate mergers. Moreover, it is generally accepted that a sinking fund preferred stock with a mandatory redemption date can qualify as preferred stock and not be treated as a debt security, provided that the redemption date is more than 10 years from the date of issuance. (The formalism of the tax-free reorganization rules can be heightened by other formalistic tax rules.)

In addition, case law requires that the shares counted toward the continuity of proprietary interest test be held by former target shareholders who do not have a present intention of selling their shares. No definite holding period is required, and case law reflects that changed circumstances, such as a significant stock price movement, can provide an independent justification to sell, negating the assertion that the shareholder had the intention at the time of the merger to sell the shares of the acquiring corporation received pursuant to the reorganization. In publicly-traded corporations, this requirement is not enforced, except to the extent of significant "inside" shareholders.

Finally, it must be noted that the analysis of the continuity of proprietary interest assumes a set of facts regarding stock ownership that does not exist in publicly-traded companies. It is assumed that shareholders of the target corporation have a long-standing relationship with the target corporation such that continuing stock ownership by the former shareholders of the target corporation is one indication of operation of the same business in a different form. However, once a proposed merger or tender offer is announced, arbitrageurs take stock positions in the target corporation. Arbitrageurs, if they hold the shares at the merger time, intend to sell the shares received. As a result, there is some uneasiness as to satisfying this tax-free reorganization requirement in certain hotly contested merger situations. To date, no significant guidance exists as to the resolution of this issue, but we are not aware of the Internal Revenue Service challenging any such purported tax-free transaction on this ground.

Continuity of Business Enterprise

The continuity of business enterprise test requires that the acquiring corporation either continue the transferor's business or use a significant portion of the transferor's business assets if it does not continue the business. The Treasury Regulations do not require that all of the acquired corporation's business be continued, just a "significant" line of the acquired corporation's historic business. What constitutes a significant line of the acquired corporation's business or a significant portion of the acquired corporation's business assets may not always be clear. The continuity of business enterprise test applies to the acquired corporation, not the acquiring corporation. Therefore, the surviving corporate entity in a tax-free merger or an acquisition could be determined by deciding which form satisfies the continuity of business enterprise test.

Business Purpose

The business purpose test is not unique to the reorganization sections, but is applied by the courts throughout the tax law. In essence, the business purpose test requires a finding that the transaction entered into was not done primarily for the purpose of tax avoidance (e.g., to acquire net operating losses) but rather has a business purpose for the parties involved. It now seems clear that the business purpose looked to may be that of the corporation or the shareholder. Thus, if the transaction has a business purpose for either of the parties, it should pass muster. If the parties to the reorganization cease operating the combined business following a merger, it is likely that the transaction will be held to fail the business purpose test, and the transaction might be treated, for tax purposes, as a liquidation.

Step-Transaction Doctrine

The step-transaction doctrine often raises some of the most complex questions in the merger and acquisition area. In almost any corporate transaction of some complexity, certain significant corporate events occur prior to the transaction being examined and, of course, certain events occur after the transaction. They may be (or may appear to be) unrelated to the particular transaction. Yet in many cases the Internal Revenue Service or the taxpayer may argue that the prior or past occurrences should be viewed as a "step" in the entire transaction and thus change the nature of the particular deal.

If Buyer Inc. issues voting shares for all the shares of Seller Inc., this would appear to be a tax-free acquisition. But suppose on the day after the acquisition, Buyer Inc. buys back all of the shares issued to the shareholders of Seller Inc. for cash. Should the two steps be viewed as one, changing the transaction into one in which Buyer Inc. paid cash for all the shares of Seller Inc.? If so, the transaction clearly would fail to meet the continuity of proprietary interest test.

While it is often extremely difficult to determine when the step-transaction rule will be applied and when it will not, it is helpful to apply the so-called "but for" test in this area. If the Internal Revenue Service can show that the second step would not have occurred "but for" the first step, they will often try to argue, if it is in their interest to do so, that the two steps are not independent but should be viewed as one.

A's, B's and C's OF CORPORATE ACQUISITIONS

Even beginners in the world of the taxation of corporate mergers and acquisitions are probably familiar with the terms "A", "B" or "C" acquisitions although they may not know their precise meaning or the derivation of the terms. The meanings can be found in Section 368(a)(1) of the Internal Revenue Code, which defines reorganization as follows:

Type A Reorganization

Section 368(a)(1)(A) The Type A reorganization: "a statutory merger or consolidation."

Type B Reorganization

Section 368(a)(1)(B) The Type B reorganization: "the acquisition by one corporation, in exchange for all or part of its voting stock (or the voting stock of a parent corporation), of stock of another corporation, if the first corporation has control of the second immediately after the exchange."

Type C Reorganization

Section 368(a)(1)(C) The Type C reorganization: "the acquisition by one corporation, in exchange for all or part of its voting stock (or the voting stock of a parent corporation), of substantially all of the properties of another corporation."

Types D, E, F Reorganizations

The Code then goes on to define Types D, E, and F reorganizations. A Type D reorganization involves either a combination of directly or indirectly affiliated corporations or a split-up of an existing corporation. Types E and F deal essentially with changes in a single corporation, such as changes in its corporate structure or state of incorporation.

Mergers and acquisitions are covered primarily in the A, B, and C sections and thus we will deal with only those sections in this chapter.

STATUTORY MERGER OR CONSOLIDATION ("A" REORGANIZATIONS)

A Type "A" reorganization is defined in the Internal Revenue Code quite simply as "a statutory merger or consolidation"—nothing more, nothing less—and it is the simplicity of this definition, with the lack of specific technical requirements that makes the "A" and its derivatives (the *triangular* "A") the most flexible and the most often used of the merger and acquisition structures.

Description

A statutory merger or consolidation means that a combination is effected under the laws of the United States, or any state, territory, or the District of Columbia. The combinations thus occurs "by operation of law" after the vote of the shareholders or whatever else is necessary to merge the companies under the laws of whatever state has jurisdiction in the matter.

For example, X Co., a publicly-held oil exploration company, agrees to merge with Y Co., another publicly-held corporation in the same business.

According to documents filed with the SEC, the transaction was to occur as follows:

> X Co. will merge with and into Y Co. under the laws of Colorado. Y Co. will be the Surviving Corporation. At the effective date of the merger, the corporate existence of X Co. will cease and all of the business, properties, and assets of X Co. will vest in Y Co. as the Surviving Corporation, and Y Co., as the Surviving Corporation, will assume all of the liabilities, obligations, and debts of X Co. The Articles of Incorporation and Bylaws of Y Co. will continue to be effective following the merger . . . At the effective time of the merger, the 7,937,500 issued and outstanding shares of X Co. common stock . . . will automatically be converted into 8,731,250 shares of the Surviving Corporation's common stock . . . (and) the present holders of common stock of Y Co. will continue to hold 8,733,333 shares of Y Co., the Surviving Corporation.

The statute imposes no requirements other than a merger or consolidation under state law. The X Co.-Y Co. deal above was a merger, because one of the corporations survived. If the two corporations had merged into a newly formed third corporation and the two older corporations had ceased to exist, a consolidation would have occurred.

We have already seen that although the statute itself imposes little in the way of requirements for a valid "A" reorganization, the continuity of proprietary interest doctrine may be a substantial hurdle in the structuring of a valid transaction of this type. Suppose, for example, that X Co. shareholders had received not only common stock of Y Co. in this transaction, but had received a combination of 50 percent cash and 50 percent common, or a package of securities consisting of 50 percent cash, 25 percent nonvoting preferred stock, and 25 percent common stock. Flexibility is the major advantage of the type "A" transaction since it permits the use of liberal amounts of cash to be paid to dissenting shareholders who do not wish to go along with the merger, and it permits the use of the "exotic" types of securities that have become popular in recent years, such as nonvoting preferred stock.

Disadvantages of Type "A"

There are several disadvantages to a type "A" reorganization, and although they are essentially legal rather than tax matters, they should be briefly discussed here. First, since a merger combines all of both companies, it is generally not possible to avoid the assumption of contingent or unknown liabilities in a merger, because the surviving corporation automatically assumes all of the liabilities of the disappearing corporation.

Since a type "A" reorganization requires a valid transaction under state law, and since the laws of most states require appraisal rights for dissenters, it may be necessary for a merging corporation to provide a significant amount of cash for those shareholders who do not wish to go along with the transaction. Essentially, appraisal rights give the dissenter the opportunity to go to court to request cash equal to the value of his interest in the corporation.

A pragmatic problem with type "A" reorganizations is that the laws of most states require shareholder approval by both corporations that are parties to the merger. Thus, for example, if giant A&P were to merge with a corner grocer, it would be necessary for A&P shareholders to vote on the merger. This would require expensive SEC filings and other heavy costs associated with the calling of a shareholders meeting. While in a merger of two substantial companies a meeting would make sense, it should not be necessary for A&P shareholders to approve a merger with a minute corporation. Prior to 1968 the tax flexibility of an "A" reorganization often had to give way to the impracticability and cost of holding shareholder meetings for small acquisitions. Then in 1968, the Internal Revenue Code was amended to provide for a new merger form—the triangular "A." This was followed in 1971 by the *reverse triangular* "A."

Triangular "A"

The ABC Company was acquired by XYZ, Inc., a large food processing company. The transaction that effectuated this acquisition was the merger of ABC into a wholly-owned subsidiary of XYZ, with the shareholders of ABC receiving stock of XYZ in the merger. After the merger the subsidiary changed its name to The ABC Company.

The 1968 change in the Internal Revenue Code that allowed the development of the triangular merger was to permit the shareholders of ABC to receive stock of XYZ, rather than the stock of the acquiring subsidiary. Obviously, they would only want the stock of XYZ, a publicly-traded corporation, on the merger, but prior to 1968 it was clear that shareholders could not receive stock other than that of its direct merger partner on the combination.

The shareholders of ABC met and approved the merger. The shareholders of the acquiring subsidiary of XYZ approved the merger. This was accomplished by having the Board of Directors of XYZ approve the merger. And this, of course, was the reason for the structure in the first place. By allowing the directors, rather than the shareholders, of XYZ to vote on the merger, the company saved a substantial amount of expenses that would have been incurred in holding a shareholders' meeting. A further advantage of this structure is that XYZ does not become liable for the liabilities of ABC since they are not directly assumed by it in the merger. The liabilities become those of XYZ's acquiring subsidiary.

The requirements for a valid triangular "A" are that the merger would have been a valid "A" if it had been with the parent rather than the subsidiary, that no stock of the subsidiary be used in the transaction, and that the subsidiary must acquire "substantially all" of the assets of the acquired corporation.

This final point, the "substantially all" the assets test, presents most of the problems in this type of reorganization. This requirement springs from a similar rule long required in the stock-for-asset (or Type "C") reorganization and its discussion is deferred.

Reverse Triangular Merger

DEF, Inc., a major company in the steel business, was acquired by XYZ Co. The merger was structured as a reverse triangular merger with the shareholders of DEF becoming shareholders of XYZ Co. In actuality, what happened was that a subsidiary of XYZ, a newly formed wholly-owned subsidiary, was merged into DEF with DEF becoming the surviving corporation and its shareholders receiving XYZ stock on the combination.

Of course, the similarity with the triangular merger should be quickly apparent—but so should the difference! Instead of the newly formed subsidiary being the survivor, the reverse occurs. The acquired corporation survives as a wholly-owned subsidiary of the acquiror. Hence, the term "reverse triangular" merger. The advantage of the reverse triangular over the "A" reorganization is again the elimination of the need for a stockholders' meeting by the "true" acquiror, in our case XYZ Co. The advantage over the triangular merger is that the reverse triangular allows the legal attributes of the acquired company—leases, franchises, etc.—to survive the merger without having to be conveyed to another corporation. The acquired corporation is legally preserved in the reverse triangular merger.

Again, the price one pays for the advantages of the reverse triangular merger is the loss of some flexibility, for several requirements are imposed not present in the straight "A" reorganization. In addition to the "substantially all" requirement discussed above, only voting stock of the parent company can be issued in exchange for stock constituting control (80 percent) of the target company in the reverse triangular merger. Other types of consideration, such as cash, debt, or nonvoting stock, may be used to acquire the remaining 20 percent. As a result, those using the reverse triangular form are more restricted in the type of consideration that can be used than those using the "A" or straight triangular route. Some flexibility is provided by the fact that shares redeemed by the target corporation for cash are not counted as outstanding for this purpose.

STOCK-FOR-STOCK ACQUISITIONS (TYPE "B" REORGANIZATIONS)

In January of 1990, the X Corporation purchased approximately 8 percent of the stock of Y Corporation through market purchases on the New York Stock Exchange. In May of 1990, X and Y entered into merger negotiations and in July they agreed on terms. X would issue one share of a newly created voting preferred stock in exchange for each share of Y's common stock in an exchange offer that would be made to all of Y's shareholders. The offer was contingent upon acceptance by holders of 72 percent of the shares not already owned by X Corporation. In October, all the shares of Y Corporation were exchanged for shares of X Corporation pursuant to the exchange offer.

Issues and Problems

This transaction illustrates several of the key issues that arise in any discussion of stock-for-stock acquisitions ("B" reorganizations). The Internal Revenue Code requirement of a "B" reorganization is that the stock of the acquired corporation is obtained in exchange solely for either the acquiring corporation's or its parent's voting stock, provided that the acquiring corporation has control of the acquired corporation immediately after the acquisition.

Most of the problems that arise in stock-for-stock transactions involve difficulties in one of the two areas stressed above, so it is therefore necessary to examine both of these requirements more carefully.

"Solely" Voting Stock

It is the word "solely" that presents most of the trouble in the stock-for-stock acquisition area and makes this type of acquisition the least flexible and therefore least used of the tax-free acquisition routes. Only voting stock may be given in the exchange—any other consideration paid, whether it be cash, nonvoting securities, or even stock warrants, will cause the transaction to be taxable to all parties, even those receiving only voting stock. The Supreme Court and many circuit courts have stated that the word solely provides "no leeway" in the type of consideration that can be exchanged for the acquired company's stock. While the requirement is obviously very strict, a small exception has been recognized in the cases. It allows cash to pay for fractional shares where the exchange ratio of the stock-for-stock transaction leaves some shareholders with less than a full share of the acquiring company's stock.

The difficulties in this area can arise in several ways. Most troublesome is the question of expenses of the acquisition. The payment by the acquiring corporation of expenses that should clearly be those of the target company's shareholders, such as independent legal counsel or financial advisors, would constitute additional nonvoting stock consideration and would destroy the tax-free nature of the transaction. Often, expenses of a transaction cannot clearly be allocated among the parties, and since, theoretically, $1 of cash consideration can thwart the transaction, the risks are enormous.

However, cash paid by the target corporation as part of the reorganization does not violate the "solely for voting" stock requirement because it is not paid by the acquiring corporation. As long as the cash paid by the target corporation is not merely an indirect payment of cash by the acquiring corporation, there should not be any problem with the former target shareholders receiving cash from the target corporation as part of the stock-for-stock reorganization.

Another problem sometimes arises when the acquiring corporation enters into an employment agreement with the shareholder-managers of the target company. The Internal Revenue Service has argued, on occasion, that payments under the employment contract were really disguised payments of cash for the stock, and has challenged the reorganization. Clearly, where bonuses are to be paid to shareholder-managers in proportion to their share ownership rather than to their salary and performance, a challenge from the Internal Revenue Service can be expected.

The Control Requirement

The "control" requirement in the stock-for-stock acquisition differs considerably from the common understanding of the term—enough votes to be able to elect a Board of Directors. Control in the "B" reorganization sense, and in many other areas of the Code, means ownership of stock possessing at least 80 percent of total combined voting power of all classes of stock entitled to vote, plus at least 80 percent of the total number of shares of all other classes of stock. Assume a corporation had outstanding 100 shares of Class A common stock (voting); 100 shares of Class B common stock (voting); and 100 shares of nonvoting preferred stock. The ownership of 70 shares of Class A, 90 shares of Class B, and 80 shares of preferred would meet the requirement since 160 shares of A and B represents 80 percent of the total "combined" voting power present in 200 shares (assuming Class A and B have equal weight).

In the example at the start of this section, the transaction is conditioned on X Corporation obtaining 72 percent of Y Corporation on the offer so that, immediately after the exchange, X Corporation will own 80 percent of Y Corporation. But the example is meant to illustrate a common problem in the stock-for-stock cases—that of so-called "creeping-control." If the purchase in January on the open market, for cash, is viewed as part of the same transaction as the stock-for-stock exchange in October, then the transaction will fail because the cash consideration paid in January would violate the solely for voting stock requirement. If, however, the transactions can be viewed as separate from the cash purchase, then the stock-for-stock exchange should be tax-free if X Corporation also meets the control test.

Step Transactions

While we have seen in the discussion of the step-transaction doctrine that it is not always clear when transactions will be considered to be part of a single plan, in the "B" reorganization area, the Internal Revenue Service will generally view any transaction occurring within one year of the reorganization as part of the reorganization, although the taxpayer may be able to prove the transactions were in fact unrelated. In our example, the one-year rule of thumb would destroy the "B" reorganization. Interestingly, sometimes it is the taxpayer who wishes the step-transaction rule to be applied. Assume, for example, that X Corporation has acquired 8 percent of Y Corporation for voting stock, not cash, in January. Here application of the doctrine would make the January transaction tax-free as part of the subsequent reorganization, while failure to apply the doctrine would make the January transaction taxable, because the 8 percent purchase would not satisfy the "control" test.

STOCK-FOR-ASSETS ("C" REORGANIZATION)

Miniconglomerate Corp. has grown through acquisitions in the 1980s and, in 1990 was negotiating to be acquired by the much larger Conglomerate Corp. Miniconglomerate was composed of 7 successful operating companies, one of which was in the same business as one of the businesses of Conglomerate. It was clear from discussions with the Justice Department that a merger of Miniconglomerate with Conglomerate would be attacked on antitrust grounds. Conglomerate was willing to proceed with the acquisition even if it could not acquire the new competing company, but the shareholders of Miniconglomerate insisted on a tax-free transaction.

Description

This example provides an opportunity to examine the stock-for-asset or "C" reorganization. This type of reorganization contemplates the acquisition by one corporation of substantially all of the properties of another corporation in exchange solely for voting stock of the acquiring corporation or its parent, or in exchange for such voting stock and a limited amount of money or property. In a "C" reorganization, the stock of the acquiring corporation is required to be distributed to the shareholders of the acquired corporation in liquidation of the acquired corporation.

The stock-for-asset acquisition usually results in the assets of the transferor corporation becoming a division of the acquiring corporation. This result is similar to the one attained when a statutory merger takes place, but it is unlike a stock-for-stock acquisition where a parent-subsidiary relationship results. Since a newly formed subsidiary can issue its parent's stock in a "C" reorganization, it is possible, however, to structure a "C" so as to create a parent-subsidiary relationship.

"Substantially All of the Properties"

The major complication in the stock-for-asset transaction is the question of what represents substantially all of the properties. In our example, let us assume that the division of Miniconglomerate that will not be sold to Conglomerate (because of the likely antitrust challenge) has assets worth $20 million and liabilities of $10 million, for a net worth (at fair market value, not cost) of $10 million. In total, Miniconglomerate has assets worth $100 million and liabilities of $60 million, or a "net worth" of $40 million. Does the conveyance of all of the assets and liabilities of the other 6 divisions of Miniconglomerate to Conglomerate represent substantially all of the properties of Miniconglomerate?

For purposes of issuing favorable rulings, the Internal Revenue Service holds that "substantially all" means at least 90 percent of the fair market value of the net assets and at least 70 percent of the fair market value of the gross assets held by the target corporation immediately preceding the transfer. Thus, in our example, the proposed reorganization will fail to be tax-free; while $80 million of the $100 million (or 80 percent) of the gross assets will be transferred, only $30 million of the $40 million (or 75 percent) of the net assets will be conveyed.

Since fair market value of the assets rather than historical cost is the key, it is not possible to determine merely from observing a company's balance sheet whether the "C" will succeed. Further, the use of fair market value can lead to significant "second guessing" by the Internal Revenue Service, whose appraisers can challenge appraisals made by the taxpayer. Courts have used a much more flexible standard, looking to whether substantially all of the operating assets have been transferred, rather than the numerical safe harbor test adopted by the Internal Revenue Service. For example, court decisions have held that intangibles, such as goodwill, should be considered in applying the substantially all test, and a court permitted the target company to retain investment assets making up 14 percent of total properties in an important case in this area.

Some Cash or Other Property as Consideration (20% or Less)

Prior to 1954, only voting stock was permitted to be paid in a stock-for-asset acquisition. The 1954 Internal Revenue Code liberalized the type "C" reorganization by permitting some cash or other property to be used in this type of acquisition, as long as 80 percent or more of the fair market value of the property acquired is acquired for voting stock.

In applying this 80 percent test, it is necessary to include liabilities assumed as part of the purchase price if $1 of property or cash is paid, making the 1954 liberalization less flexible than might first appear. Thus, for example, if the target company has assets of $100 million and liabilities of $10 million, all of which are to be assumed in the acquisition, then the acquiror cannot pay more than $10 million in cash or property as part of the purchase price. Since fair market value is used in applying the rule, the taxpayer again runs the risk of being second-guessed by the IRS. In our example above, if the assets thought to be worth $100 million are worth less, the reorganization would fail since the liabilities assumed and the cash paid will exceed 20 percent of the fair market value of the properties acquired.

Principal Advantage: Only Specified Liabilities Assumed

The principal advantages of the stock-for-asset acquisition are that only the liabilities specifically assumed become the liabilities of the acquiror and that no dissenting shareholders of the transferor corporation become shareholders of the acquiring corporation. Further, as we have seen in the Miniconglomerate-Conglomerate example, unwanted assets can be withheld, to some degree, from the exchange.

Principal Disadvantage: Legally Burdensome and Costly

The principal disadvantages of the stock-for-asset transaction are that it is more burdensome for the attorneys to convey all of the assets to be acquired and hence may be more costly to accomplish and that the business and legal identity of the transferor corporation is not transferred to the acquiror. While the acquiror may transfer the assets of the transferor corporation to a newly formed subsidiary and change its name to the same name as the transferor company—to preserve business continuity and goodwill—the loss of legal identity can be more profound. Such assets as leases, franchises, and licenses may not be transferable by their terms, and therefore a stock-for-asset transaction may be precluded. A stock-for-stock or a reverse triangular corporate merger may be mandatory under these conditions.

CONTINGENT PAY-OUT ARRANGEMENTS

After months of negotiations, the officers of Buyer, Inc. and Seller Corp. seemed to be getting nowhere in their merger discussions. Buyer, Inc. was convinced it was offering a fair price of 10 times Seller's 1988 earnings of $15 million, or $150 million of Buyer, Inc. common stock in a stock-for-stock acquisition. This represented 15 million shares at Buyer's current price of $10 per share. Seller Corp. did not disagree that 10 was a reasonable multiple, but they did disagree on the earnings base period. Seller was convinced that its future earnings would greatly exceed $10 million per year and, after all, wasn't Buyer really buying the future rather than the past? While Buyer saw merit in Seller's case it was not prepared to pay in advance for earnings that might not materialize. Suppose, for example, that the newly wealthy officer-shareholders of Seller quit their jobs after the acquisition. Could Seller reach its earnings goals without these key people? Late into the night a compromise began to develop. Buyer could pay Seller $100 million in stock now. Then, after three years, the average earnings of Seller would be calculated. If they exceeded $10 million, Buyer would pay Seller more stock, at the then current price of its stock, equal to 5 times the average earnings in excess of $10 million. The lower multiple was in recognition of the fact that, to some extent, Buyer would be helping Seller to achieve its goals.

Seller Corp. shareholders were happy with the opportunity to "earn" more shares after the acquisition. Buyer, Inc., while recognizing that it might have to pay more than originally anticipated, liked the idea that this type of transaction gave the officer-shareholders of Seller an incentive to remain with the company for three years and to work hard to achieve its goals. Buyer did feel, however, that prudence required that a limit be placed on the total number of additional shares that could be issued. Otherwise a combination of high earnings by the Seller subsidiary and a falling stock price of Buyer common stock could result in Seller's former shareholders controlling Buyer! After some more negotiations, a ceiling of 8 million additional shares was agreed to.

The above scenario has occurred numerous times in merger negotiations. The compromise solution—whether called "contingent pay-out" or "earn-out" or "kicker" transaction—is both a logical way to resolve differences between forward-looking sellers and backward-looking buyers, and a way to provide incentives for shareholder-management to work as hard for someone else as they did for themselves.

Two-Fold Tax Question

The tax question that arises in our transaction is two-fold: first, is the payment of 15 million shares in 1989 tax-free to the Seller shareholders; and second, is the payment in 1992 of up to 8 million additional shares, based upon earnings in the 1989-1991 period, tax-free to these shareholders? The Internal Revenue Service has not been unreasonable in this area. When these transactions began to proliferate in the "go-go" 1960s, the Internal Revenue Service adopted a ruling policy, modified in 1977 and 1984, that tried to reconcile the Service's desire for finality and definiteness in tax matters with the taxpayer's requirements to postpone a final accounting until the contingency period had run.

The Six Requirements For Tax-Free Status

The result was an Internal Revenue Service statement that it would issue favorable rulings in this area if six requirements were met. The requirements, insofar as relevant, can be examined in the context of our example.

The *first* requirement is that all the shares that will be issued must be issued within 5 years of the date of the initial distribution. Our 3-year contingency period clearly meets this test.

The *second* requirement is more subjective—that a valid "business reason" must exist for not issuing all of the stock immediately. Presumably, both resolving a difference in the valuation of Seller's worth and providing an incentive to Seller's shareholder-managers would meet this test.

The *third* requirement is that the maximum number of shares which may be issued must be stated in the agreement of the parties, and the *fourth* requirement is that at least 50 percent of the maximum number of shares of each class of stock which could be issued must be issued initially. By providing a maximum total of 23 million shares and issuing 15 million shares initially, the Buyer, Inc.-Seller Corp. transaction has no trouble with these requirements.

The *fifth* requirement for a favorable advance ruling by the Internal Revenue Service is that the contingent right to additional stock must not be assignable, except by operation of law or, if assignable, the right must not be marketable or evidenced by a negotiable certificate of any kind. Since, in our transaction, Seller, Inc. has few shareholders, this is not a problem. In a public company, the failure of a shareholder to be able to sell his contingent rights when, for example, he sells his stock in the acquiring company, is a problem.

The *sixth* and final requirement that the Internal Revenue Service imposes is that the right to additional stock must be only with respect to stock of the acquiring corporation or a corporation in control of the corporation. This presents no problem in our example.

Escrow Agreements

Some of the problems that can arise in the contingent payout area may be resolved by the use of an appropriate escrow agreement. For example, interest must generally be imputed on transactions involving a deferred delivery of shares. The Internal Revenue Service has been liberal in its interpretation of when stock is "issued" so that shares placed in escrow are considered "issued" for purposes of these Internal Revenue Service requirements. Thus no imputed interest need be calculated on escrowed shares.

TAXATION OF PARTIES TO A REORGANIZATION

We have examined numerous examples of corporate acquisition—some real and some imagined—to determine whether they qualify as "reorganizations" under the Internal Revenue Code. It now remains to examine the Federal income tax consequences to the various parties to the reorganization, assuming that the transaction does qualify for the favorable income tax treatment of the reorganization provisions.

As we have seen, there are usually three parties to a reorganization—the corporation whose stock or assets are acquired (the acquired or transferor corporation), the corporation which issues its stock to make an acquisition (the acquiring corporation), and the shareholders of the acquired or transferor corporation. The shareholders of the acquiring corporation are not parties since they do not exchange their interests in the transaction. Of course, in a statutory consolidation, shareholders of both corporations will be viewed as shareholders of an acquired corporation.

Treatment of Transferor Corporation

A transferor corporation recognizes neither gain nor loss when it transfers property for stock or securities of another corporation, a "party to a reorganization," if the exchange is pursuant to a "plan of reorganization." While the terms "party to a reorganization" and "plan of reorganization" are terms of art, they contemplate all of the various types of acquisitions discussed in this chapter. Where stock or securities are the only consideration issued in an acquisition, the result is clear. Suppose, however, that Corp. A issues $120 million of voting stock and $10 million of cash to acquire all the assets of Corp. B, a corporation with $10 million of liabilities, which are assumed by Corp. A. As we have seen from our discussion of stock-for-asset acquisitions, this transaction qualifies as a tax-free "C" reorganization, because the voting stock represents 80 percent or more of the consideration paid.

Presently, the Internal Revenue Code provides that a transferor corporation will not be subject to tax on any exchange pursuant to a plan of reorganization. The transferor corporation is not taxed, because it is essentially a conduit. The transferor's corporation business is continued by the acquiring corporation. Under all the forms of reorganization involving mergers or asset acquisitions, the transferor corporation must liquidate. The former shareholders of the transferor corporation hold new securities and maybe some boot (i.e., cash, property, or non-qualifying securities). The transferor corporation, however, will be required to recognize gain (not loss) on the distribution of appreciated property that was retained by the transferor corporation. The transferor corporation is also permitted to transfer to its creditors tax-free stock or securities received pursuant to the reorganization.

Treatment of Acquiring Corporation

The nonrecognition of gain or loss to an acquiring corporation that issues its stock in exchange for property of a second corporation is not covered by the reorganization provisions of the Internal Revenue Code but by another section of the Code, which states that a corporation does not recognize gain or loss on the issuance of its own shares.

It is only the basis rules that are really of interest to the acquiring corporation. Here the rules call for a carryover basis. The acquiring corporation obtains a basis in the property equal to the basis that the transferor corporation had in the property, increased by any gain recognized by the transferor on the transaction. Corp. A has a tax basis of $50 million in its assets and such assets have a gross fair market value of $130 million. Assume that Corp. A transfers all of its assets to Corp. B for $10 million cash, $10 million assumption of liabilities, and $110 million of voting stock of Corp. B., and thereafter liquidates. This transaction qualifies as a "C" reorganization, because more than 80 percent of total consideration was voting stock of the acquiring corporation. Corp. B will get a basis of $50 million in the property, equal to Corp. A's $50 million basis, even though Corp. B paid $10 million in cash and assumed $10 million of Corp. A's debt obligation. If Corp. B were to later sell the property for its presumed value of $130 million, its gain would be $80 million.

Treatment of Stockholders

The Internal Revenue Code provides that an exchanging stockholder in a reorganization recognizes neither gain nor loss if stock or securities in a corporation that is a "party to a reorganization" are exchanged "solely" for stock or securities in another corporation that is a "party to a reorganization", if the exchange is pursuant to a "plan of reorganization".

The Code provides that if there is boot in the transaction (i.e., cash or other property), the gain recognized will be limited to the amount of boot that is received by the exchanging shareholder. For example, Z is a 50 percent shareholder of Corp. A which, as discussed above, was merged into Corp. B. Z held Corp. A stock worth $60 million (50 percent of Corp. A's gross fair market value of $130 million reduced for debt of $10 million) and had a tax basis of $10 million in the A shares. (Note that there is no correlation between a shareholder's tax basis in the stock of the target corporation, and the target corporation's tax basis in its assets). Z will receive $55 million of Corp. B stock plus $5 million in cash. Z's realized gain is $50 million, but Z will be required to recognize only $5 million of such gain at the time of the reorganization. One problem that frequently arises in this area, the question of whether the gain to be recognized is taxed as dividend income or as a capital gain, can be illustrated by the following example.

Smallco is a corporation owned equally by two individuals and one corporation. Largeco proposes to form a subsidiary to enter into a "triangular merger" with Smallco, issuing $40 million of its stock and $10 million in cash to each of the three Smallco shareholders for their stock, in which each shareholder has a basis of $20 million. As we have seen from our previous discussions of "triangular mergers" and "continuity of interest," the transaction should qualify as a valid "A" reorganization. Further, it should be apparent that the $10 million in cash received by each shareholder is taxable boot, resulting in a realized gain of $30 million and a recognized gain of $10 million to each shareholder. The remaining question is whether the $10 million gain should be taxed as a capital gain or as a dividend.

Generally, capital gain treatment results from the "sale or exchange" of property that is a "capital asset"—a term which includes corporate stock. If the Smallco shareholders had sold their shares for $50 million cash, the gain would unquestionably have been capital. However, by bringing the transaction within the purview of the reorganization provisions of the Code, we are faced with a rule that provides that if the exchange has the "effect of the distribution of a dividend," the taxpayer's gain must be so treated. Since a dividend, for this purpose, can be payable only out of "earnings and profits" of a corporation (a highly complex tax term beyond the scope of this chapter but generally referring to corporation's earnings since 1913—the year the Income Tax was enacted), it is possible that only a portion of the gain could be taxed as a dividend with the remainder taxed as a capital gain.

How then can an exchange have the "effect of a distribution of a dividend"? If we return to our three shareholders, we may find a clue. Suppose that immediately prior to the acquisition of Smallco by Largeco, the shareholders had the corporation declare a $30 million cash dividend and that Largeco had then acquired Smallco for only $120 million in stock. The shareholders would be in no different position under either example. Yet in this latter example, the $10 million cash they each receive would clearly be a dividend. Why then, the Internal Revenue Service essentially is saying, should a capital gain result in the former example?

For a time, tax authorities were of the opinion that boot received in a tax-free exchange would "automatically" give rise to dividend treatment (the so-called "automatic dividend" rule), if "earnings and profits" were present. Recent cases, however, have changed this view by testing the dividend effect of the boot as if each of the three shareholders received only stock and then a portion of their stock was redeemed. As a result, each transaction is presently tested on its facts to determine whether the boot received has the "effect of a distribution of a dividend." A recent Supreme Court case approved the analysis of the hypothetical stock redemption of stock assumed to be received in the acquiring corporation. Under such an approach, a capital gain result is more likely to be obtained.

Whether the boot is treated as capital gain income or ordinary income will generally be of little concern to the two individual Smallco shareholders. The federal income tax rates applicable to capital gain income and ordinary income are presently the same. State tax rates, however, may not be the same, and the characterization of the boot may be important. On the other hand, the one corporate shareholder of Smallco will be very interested in a determination that the $10 million in boot received is a dividend. Corporate shareholders are taxed at a 34 percent rate on capital gains income. Thus, the Smallco corporate shareholder will pay taxes of $3.4 million (i.e. 34 percent × $10,000,000). Corporate shareholders are also taxed at a 34 percent rate on ordinary dividend income, but, in addition, they can usually claim a deduction in the amount of 70 percent of dividends received. Thus, the Smallco corporate shareholder will pay taxes of $1,020,000 [i.e., (10,000,000 − 7,000,000) × 34 percent].

Once it is established how much gain is to be recognized on the transaction, it is necessary to determine the basis that the shareholders receive in the stock of the acquiring corporation. Here the rule is that the basis of the stock received is equal to the basis of the property transferred increased by the amount of any gain recognized (whether capital gain or dividend) and decreased by the fair market value of any boot received.

Returning to our three Smallco shareholders, each has a basis of $20 million in Smallco, each had a recognized gain of $10 million and each received $10 million of boot. Thus their basis in Largeco will be $20 million. If they sold Largeco stock for $40 million, its presumed value, they would recognize $20 million of further gain. Once again, the logic of the basis rules should be clear—$20 million of gain was deferred in the initial exchange and that gain is now picked up when the stock received is sold.

THE FUTURE

As a result of the revision of substantial portions of the Internal Revenue Code, Congress has asked the U.S. Treasury Department to prepare a report on Subchapter C of the Code, to determine, in light of the amendments made and problems that existed already, what amendments may be required. Subchapter C includes the reorganization provisions affecting nontaxable mergers and acquisitions. Therefore, we can expect the reorganization provisions of the Internal Revenue Code to be amended in the near future. "Stay tuned to your counsel for further news bulletins."

CHAPTER 28

ACCOUNTING CONSIDERATIONS FOR MERGERS, ACQUISITIONS, AND RESTRUCTURINGS

H Ronald Weissman
Timothy P. Kane
Arthur Andersen & Co.

Business combinations involve two principal accounting issues—determining what method to use to give effect to the combination and how to apply it.[1]

TWO BASIC METHODS

Two basic methods are used to account for business combinations—pooling-of-interests and purchase accounting. For any given business combination, these methods are not alternatives; only one will be appropriate to the circumstances.

Purchase Accounting

In the purchase method, the combination is viewed as one company acquiring another, and the required accounting closely parallels that used in the purchase

[1] Accounting issues and treatments, particularly those in this chapter, can be quick to evolve. As discussed in Chapter 24 of Volume 1, several different organizations can change accounting principles, or the way they are applied to specific transactions, often with little notice. Thus material herein, though accurate at the time of its writing (1989 Summer), should be verified with professionals if significant to any contemplated transaction.

of assets in the ordinary course of business. The purchase price of the acquired company is allocated to the net assets obtained. A difference between the cost of an acquired company and the sum of the fair values of tangible and identifiable intangible assets, less the fair value of liabilities, is recorded as goodwill (the "residual"). The incomes of the entities are combined only for periods after the acquisition date, with the income of the acquired company being adjusted to recognize depreciation and amortization on the revised net asset values.

Pooling of Interests

In the pooling-of-interest method, the transaction is viewed as a merger (pooling) of the ownership interests into a single entity as though that entity and its combined shareholder groups had always existed. The assets and liabilities of the constituent companies are carried forward at their previously recorded or historical amounts, and the incomes of the enterprises, before and after the date of the transaction, are combined with no change.

APB Opinions 16 and 17

APB (Accounting Principles Board, predecessor to the Financial Accounting Standards Board [FASB]) Opinion Nos. 16 and 17 specify the accounting practices to be followed in accounting for mergers and acquisitions.

APB 16 provides specific guidelines to be used when accounting for a business combination as a purchase or a pooling of interests.

APB 17 specifies the accounting required for goodwill arising in a business combination accounted for as a purchase, as well as the accounting required for other acquired intangibles. In particular, APB 17 requires that goodwill and other acquired intangibles be (1) amortized over a period not in excess of 40 years and (2) not be written off in the period of acquisition.

APB 16 and 17 were adopted amid much controversy. The accounting issues in these areas had been under consideration for many years, and debate on them had been lengthy and heated. The resulting opinions reflect numerous compromises. For example, APB 16 created many arbitrary rules to be met if the pooling-of-interests method is to be used. These rules have been extremely difficult to implement. In recent years, of course, purchase transactions have become more prevalent and have given rise to many purchase price allocation issues.

SEC Restrictions

In addition to the arbitrariness of the Opinions, the Securities and Exchange Commission (SEC) has been quite restrictive on the use of pooling-of-interests accounting for business combinations. In some cases, the SEC staff interprets the pooling rules literally; in other cases, it emphasizes substance over form. The result: further confusion over the accounting rules and the need for frequent consultation with accounting advisers and the SEC about the appropriate accounting.

Chapter Overview

The following discussion summarizes the major requirements of APB 16 and 17; the actual Opinions, however, should be referred to with respect to specific transactions, and professional advice should always be sought. Later sections discuss certain special application problems, and examples of pooling and purchase accounting are included at the end of the chapter.

PURCHASE ACCOUNTING RULES

Accounting for a business combination by the purchase method follows accounting principles normally applicable under historical cost accounting. It applies whether the acquisition involves an entire entity or a portion of an entity; whether stock is acquired or assets are purchased; and whether the consideration given is in the form of cash, other assets, debt, equity securities (unless pooling-of-interests conditions are met), or a combination of these forms.

There are three basic steps in applying the purchase method:

- Determining the acquiror
- Determining the cost, or purchase price, of the acquired company
- Recording the assets acquired and the liabilities assumed (or allocating the purchase price)

Determining the Acquiror

When nonstock consideration (e.g., cash, other assets, or debt) is offered, the offeror is clearly the acquiror. When stock is issued, regardless of the extent, the acquiror is usually evident from the facts and circumstances.

If the acquiror is not clearly evident, the general presumption is that the acquiror is the one whose shareholders end up owning the majority of the voting control of the combined enterprise. This may not be the case if, for example, voting restrictions are imposed on the "majority's" stock, if the board of directors and management of the combined entity are from the "minority," if the market value of the shares issued to the minority is greater than that of the shares issued or retained by the majority, or if the assets, revenues, and earnings of the company previously owned by the minority are greater than those of the company owned by the majority. In such cases the company whose shareholders own the majority of the voting stock may not necessarily be deemed the acquiring company.

Careful consideration, then, should be given to situations where an acquisition is to be made of a target of comparable size. The determination of the acquiror can have a dramatic effect on the resultant financial reporting, particularly if the market value of one of the companies is equal to or below its book value while the market value of the other company is substantially in excess of its book value, or the relative price/earnings multiples of the two companies are significantly different. Careful structuring of the transaction could (1) eliminate all or a portion of the "step-up" in value (discussed below) or the recording of goodwill and (2) reduce the impact of the related amortization on earnings if the target is deemed to be the acquiror for accounting purposes.

If a new corporation is formed to issue stock to effect a business combination to be accounted for as a purchase, one of the existing companies should be deemed the acquiror based on an evaluation of the facts described above. SEC Staff Accounting Bulletin No. 24 discusses this problem in more detail.

Determining the Cost of the Acquired Company

The second step under the purchase method is determining the cost of the acquired company. This determination should normally be made as of the date the business combination is consummated. This is normally the date assets are received and other assets are given or securities are issued. However, it also is acceptable to use an earlier date for the sake of accounting convenience if the terms of the combination are fixed and if effective control was obtained by the acquiror at that date. This, however, requires adjusting the cost of the acquired company and recognizing income related to the acquired company as of the earlier date. To compensate for recognizing income before consideration is transferred, interest on the consideration given should be imputed for the period from the transfer date to the control date.

Fair Value

The cost of the acquired company generally should be measured by the fair value of the consideration surrendered. When traded equity securities are issued, their fair value should be based on current market prices. When the securities carry restrictions, however, their value generally is less than the market price—sometimes substantially less. In other situations, a thin market for the securities may exist, or individual blocks may be significant in relation to normal trading; in such cases, discounts from quoted market price also may be appropriate. In situations like this, or when no market exists, accountants look to investment bankers or others experienced in such valuations to help determine the fair value.

In rare cases, when the fair value of the consideration issued is not clearly evident, the cost of the acquisition should be determined by valuing the acquired net assets. Goodwill normally would not be recognized in such instances.

Contingent Consideration

A purchase agreement may provide for the issuance of additional shares of a security or the transfer of cash or other consideration contingent upon specified events or transactions in the future. For example, additional consideration may be contingent upon maintaining or achieving specified earnings levels in future periods, or may be contingent upon the market price of a specified security issued to effect a business combination.

Contingent consideration that is determinable beyond a reasonable doubt should be recorded at the acquisition date and included in the cost of the target entity. Contingent consideration not determinable beyond a reasonable doubt should be included in the cost of the acquired entity when the contingency is resolved. This normally creates additional goodwill, which should be accounted for prospectively, not retroactively.

Only in rare instances are contingencies based on earnings determinable beyond a reasonable doubt. Therefore, this value is usually not included in the purchase price at the acquisition date unless it is immaterial.

Market Price Guarantee

If the purchase agreement provides for a market price guarantee through the issuance of additional securities, the cost initially recorded for the acquired entity should be the greater of (1) the guaranteed amount of the consideration, or (2) the fair value of the securities originally issued. This amount should be recorded when the combination is consummated. Any additional consideration given at a later date should not affect the acquisition cost, but should be treated as an adjustment to paid-in capital or debt discount/premium accounts, where appropriate.

Acquisition Costs

Direct acquisition costs (finder's and investment banking fees, legal and accounting fees, etc.) are considered part of the cost of an acquisition and must be included as part of the cost assigned to the acquired assets. Indirect costs (generally expenses incurred internally by an acquiring company) must be expensed. Financing fees and expenses should be deferred and amortized to expense over the life of the related loans.

Recording the Assets Acquired and the Liabilities Assumed

The third step under the purchase method is allocating the acquisition cost.

All Assets and Liabilities—Intangible As Well As Tangible

In order to assign the purchase cost to individual assets acquired in a purchase transaction, all tangible and intangible assets must be identified and individually valued. This identification process should also include consideration of overfunded or underfunded pension plans, favorable or unfavorable debt, leases and other contracts, undervalued inventories due to use of the LIFO method, undervalued fixed assets, and other unrecorded assets and liabilities. Similarly, liabilities for postemployment benefits need to be recorded, although the required accounting currently varies. The purchase cost plus the fair value of liabilities assumed or incurred must then be allocated to the acquired assets based on their individual fair values.

Goodwill and Negative Goodwill

If the aggregate purchase cost exceeds the total fair value of the identifiable assets acquired less the fair value of liabilities assumed, that excess or "residual" amount must be allocated to goodwill. If there is an excess of fair value of net assets acquired over the purchase cost, the values assigned to noncurrent assets (such as land, buildings, machinery and equipment, intangible and other assets, but excluding long-term investments in marketable securities) must be reduced proportionately to a basis of zero, if necessary, before recording negative goodwill. If an excess of fair value over cost still exists after reducing the basis of noncurrent assets to zero, it should be assigned to negative goodwill. Negative goodwill normally should be amortized in the same manner as goodwill.

Accounting and Tax Differences

In many cases, the final amounts assigned to individual assets or liabilities will differ for accounting and tax purposes due to the differing valuation and allocation practices that are prescribed for each purpose. In these instances, under APB 16, the resulting allocation differences would be considered an inherent part of the accounting valuation process (see below for impact of SFAS No. 96 on this section).

For example, if an amount allocated to a particular asset for accounting purposes is greater than the tax-basis allocation, the final value to be used for accounting purposes would be reduced in recognition of the lower tax value of that asset or tax effect of that difference. This would be accomplished by reducing the accounting cost allocated to the asset by the effective loss of tax benefit resulting from the lower tax valuation (commonly referred to as the "net-of-tax" approach). Generally, the amount of the reduction would be assigned to goodwill or noncurrent assets. When measuring the impact of tax effects assigned to individual assets and liabilities, the timing of the tax effects may be important in certain cases. (Discounting of the tax effects, while not common in practice, was acceptable in certain instances under APB 16.)

In December 1987, the FASB issued Statement of Financial Accounting Standards No. 96 entitled "Accounting for Income Taxes" (SFAS 96). Companies are required to adopt the accounting rules therein for the first fiscal year beginning after December 15, 1990, although earlier adoption is encouraged. SFAS 96 precludes companies from following the net-of-tax approach described above. Instead, the "liability" method will be required under which a deferred tax asset (if considered realizable) or liability will be recognized for the tax effects of differences between assigned values and tax bases of assets that are acquired and liabilities that are assumed. No deferred taxes will be recognized for a difference in the book and tax basis of goodwill, the amortization of which will continue to be a permanent difference. Applying the liability method rather than the net-of-tax method generally will not change net income, goodwill, or net assets (except to the extent that deferred tax assets are not considered to be realizable). However, it will change the individual financial statement accounts affected (e.g., property and equipment, inventory, cost of sales, depreciation, and provision for income taxes). In addition, SFAS 96 will preclude the discounting of deferred tax assets and liabilities arising in a purchase business combination.

Present Value of Liabilities

Liabilities assumed should be recorded at the present value of amounts to be paid, determined by using appropriate current interest rates. This may result in the creation of debt discount or premium. Recording a discount reduces the amount assigned to goodwill, if any, or other noncurrent assets by a corresponding amount. This generally has a negative effect on reported earnings in the initial years after the combination, since debt discount must be amortized by charges to earnings over the term of the related debt, and that term is frequently shorter than the period for goodwill or for other noncurrent assets. The converse is true if debt premium results.

Unresolved Pre-acquisition Contingencies

Unresolved contingencies (other than contingent consideration) may exist at the date of acquisition. These contingencies, called "pre-acquisition contingencies," include unsettled litigation, contractual disputes, renegotiation proceedings, and contested tax assessments. The fair value of any pre-acquisition contingency should be included in the allocation of the purchase price when determinable (i.e., "probable" and "estimable"). However, if this determination is made generally beyond one year from the acquisition date, the difference between the estimate used in allocating the purchase price and the actual amount of the contingency should be included in net income in that period. Because of this requirement, care should be taken in identifying and estimating the impact of contingent matters, and reference should be made to SFAS 96—"Accounting for Pre-acquisition Contingencies of Purchased Enterprises."

Changes in other estimates used in allocating the purchase price normally should also be included in net income if they occur after a reasonable period of time (the "allocation period," which normally extends to one year after the date of acquisition).

Unused Tax Credits

Under APB 11 and until SFAS 96 is adopted, unused investment tax credits acquired may not be recognized as an asset at the acquisition date. Instead, they should be recorded as an adjustment to goodwill in the period in which they are utilized.

Net Operating Loss Carryforwards

Net operating loss carryforwards (NOLs) acquired would normally not be recognized at the acquisition date under the APB 11 tax accounting rules, unless realization is assured beyond a reasonable doubt. This will rarely occur. Subsequent realization of NOLs that were unrecorded at the acquisition date would be recorded as a retroactive adjustment of goodwill. (Once goodwill is reduced to zero, any subsequently realized NOLs would reduce noncurrent assets—excluding long-term investments in marketable securities—to zero;

negative goodwill would be created for the remainder.) If not material, the goodwill adjustment can be reported prospectively.

SFAS 96, discussed above, also sets forth new rules for recognizing carryforward benefits existing at the acquisition date of both the acquired and acquiring company. Under SFAS 96, in those unusual situations under the tax code where a loss or credit carryforward of the acquired company could reduce the actual taxes payable of the other companies in future periods, those benefits would generally be recognized at the acquisition date as a reduction of the other company's deferred tax liability. To the extent either company's deferred tax liability is reduced, goodwill would be reduced until zero, other noncurrent assets (except long-term investments in marketable securities) would be reduced until zero, and negative goodwill would be created for the remainder. Where such tax benefit carryforwards of the acquired company are not recognized at the acquisition date, they would, when subsequently realized, first reduce goodwill (until zero) and other noncurrent intangible assets related to the acquisition (until zero), and then reduce income tax expense.

Amortization of Goodwill and Other Intangibles Required

Goodwill and other intangibles must be amortized over a period not exceeding 40 years. They cannot be written off in the period of acquisition. Intangibles should be amortized over their estimated useful life if less than 40 years. Legal and regulatory aspects, contractual provisions, renewal provisions, competition, and obsolescence should be considered in establishing the amortization period, and a periodic review of the amortization period should be made to determine if later events warrant revision in the original amortization period. The straight-line method of amortization normally is required.

The SEC has become more active in reviewing the lives assigned to goodwill in certain industries, particularly high tech related, and they have required amortization periods of 25 years for financial institutions and 10 years or less for software companies and other high tech industries.

The trend toward very large purchase combinations involving significant premiums over net tangible asset value has caused acquirors to become more aggressive in identifying short-lived, tax deductible intangibles. For accounting purposes, however, acquirors prefer to either assign such premiums to nondeductible goodwill—the amortization of which over 40 years does not as adversely impact future earnings or amortize the identified intangibles over a period longer for accounting purposes than for tax purposes. Thus, an inherent conflict exists between tax and accounting objectives. The general presumption should be that identified intangibles have comparable lives for both financial reporting and tax purposes, unless statutory requirements or other such facts and circumstances justify differences.

Disclosure Requirements

Complete details of a purchase transaction should be disclosed, and summary pro forma results of operations should be shown for the current period (and for the prior period if comparative statements are issued) as though the companies had combined at the beginning of the period.

Acquisition of Minority Interests

Acquisitions of minority interests should be accounted for under the purchase method. The consideration paid should be allocated as previously discussed. This accounting would apply whether the parent buys publicly traded shares of a subsidiary itself, or has the subsidiary do so as a treasury stock acquisition.

Push-Down Accounting

When substantially all of the common stock of a company is acquired in one or a series of purchase transactions, the SEC generally requires that the purchase price be "pushed down" to the acquired company's (subsidiary) financial statements if those statements are included in an SEC filing (e.g., an initial public offering).

Push-down accounting reflects the allocation of purchase price adjustments to assets and liabilities in the financial statements of the acquired (subsidiary) entity. Retained earnings are generally not carried forward by the acquired entity after applying push-down accounting. Unless the acquisition debt of the acquiror is also pushed down, the net effect of pushing down the purchase accounting adjustments is to increase (or, rarely, decrease) the equity of the acquired company to the purchase price.

The debt directly incurred by the acquiror to make the purchase is required, in SEC filings, to be pushed down to the financial statements of the acquired entity if such entity (1) guarantees the debt or pledges its assets as collateral, (2) assumes the debt either immediately or in a planned transaction, or (3) issues or plans to issue debt or equity securities of its own and will remit the proceeds to the parent to retire all or a part of the acquisition debt. The requirement to push down acquisition debt is independent of the requirement or election to push down the purchase price. Such debt need not be pushed down if the parent can borrow on an unsecured basis, pledge other assets of its pre-existing operations or, most commonly, pledge the *stock* of the acquired subsidiary rather than allow the lenders direct access to the *assets* of the subsidiary itself.

When push-down accounting is required in an SEC filing, the financial statements required normally include both the historic financial statements through the acquisition date, as well as those reflected on a push-down basis.

Leveraged Buyout

The SEC and the Emerging Issues Task Force of the FASB have developed guidelines for accounting for leveraged buyout transactions. The accounting is based upon whether the transaction can be considered a purchase or whether it is, in fact, a recapitalization (distribution to existing shareholders of cash and stock, without any real change in control). If it is determined that a purchase has occurred, purchase accounting, as discussed above, would at least partially apply. If, however, the transaction is considered a recapitalization, historical basis would carry over and any cash distribution would be treated like a dividend. The rules governing this are extremely detailed, and consultation with accounting experts is necessary for complex structures or whenever the equity holders in the acquiring company (usually a Newco) also held shares in the acquired company.

POOLING OF INTERESTS

The pooling-of-interests method is applicable to a business combination in which the ownership interests of two or more companies are united or combined solely by an exchange of the majority class of voting securities. Since the transaction occurs solely among the shareholders, neither assets nor liabilities are added or withdrawn from the companies themselves and no revaluation of the assets or liabilities of either company is reflected in the combined financial statements. Historical financial statements of companies qualifying for this accounting treatment are combined as though the two companies had always been commonly owned. Shareholders prospectively share risks and rewards in the company as they previously did in the separate companies. The pooling accounting concept is applicable to business combinations involving partnerships or proprietorships, as well as corporations.

Differences Between Pooling and Purchase Accounting

A pooling of interests is usually preferred when the purchase price exceeds the historical carrying amount of the net assets acquired, since the excess of the fair market value over the historical carrying amount of the assets acquired does not have to be recorded. Consequently, the surviving company can continue to amortize the historical cost amounts; extra depreciation of written-up fixed assets and amortization of goodwill will not exist to depress future earnings.

The other critical difference between pooling and purchase accounting is that in pooling accounting the surviving company reports the results of operations of both businesses combined for all periods presented in its consolidated financial statements, including pre-acquisition periods. In contrast, purchase accounting permits the results of operations of the acquired company to be included in the surviving company's financial statements only from the date of acquisition.

Pooling Accounting Rules

As discussed previously, APB 16 sanctions the use of both purchase and pooling-of-interests accounting but not as elective alternatives in any given business combination. Detailed conditions, rules, and criteria must be met if a business combination is to be eligible for pooling accounting. If these conditions are not met, the acquisition must be accounted for as a purchase. These conditions are extremely technical, and the discussion below is an attempt only to capture the flavor of the rules. The spirit of these rules is to prevent the use of pooling accounting in any case not involving a merging of the respective shareholder interests. For example, the use of cash, alterations of equity interests, redemptions, treasury stock transactions, extraordinary dividends, asset disposition, other changes in the merged entities, and similar actions change the shareholder groups in some way and prevent a true merging of interests.

Conditions for Pooling

The conditions necessary to record a business combination as a pooling of interests can be classified as (1) pre-acquisition attributes, (2) combining attributes, and (3) post-combination attributes.

Pre-acquisition Attributes

There are three pre-acquisition attributes that must be met in order to qualify the transaction for pooling-of-interests accounting:

- Another company cannot have owned over 50 percent of either company within two years before the pooling is initiated. Exceptions to this rule include a new company incorporated within the two-year period that is not a successor to another company, and a subsidiary or division being divested to comply with an order from a governmental authority.
- Each of the combining companies must be independent of the other. Neither may hold more than 10 percent of the voting common stock of the other at either initiation or consummation of the pooling (or at any time in between).
- Neither of the companies involved in the pooling can "alter the equity interests" of their voting common stock or of their relative shareholder interests in contemplation of the combination, either within two years before the plan is initiated or between the dates the combination is initiated and consummated. Any such alteration may be presumed to be in contemplation of the business combination and could preclude pooling. Changes made in contemplation of effecting the combination may include distributions to stockholders or additional issuance, exchange, or retirement of securities. Normal dividends are not considered changes. Generally, if a company sells a significant portion of its assets prior to combination, it will not qualify for pooling accounting; likewise, a spin-off of assets would disqualify pooling, because this would constitute a change in equity interests. The SEC has concluded that sales of a significant portion of a company's assets, occurring six to nine months prior to initiation of a pooling, are presumed to be in contemplation of the combination.

In some situations, factual evidence may support a contention that the "alterations" were not in contemplation of a business combination and, therefore, do not preclude pooling accounting. Such factual evidence must be clear; the closer the alteration is to the initiation of the combination, the more difficult it is for any factual evidence to be persuasive.

In the absence of persuasive evidence to the contrary, it is presumed that all treasury shares acquired within two years of a business combination and between initiation and consummation of the transaction were made in contemplation of the business combination and that pooling is, therefore, prohibited if such purchases exceed certain limits (see *Other Prohibitions* below). This prevents the indirect use of cash through acquisition of treasury shares just before and during the combination. In addition, significant greenmail transactions normally preclude pooling accounting if the limit noted is exceeded.

The SEC has issued detailed rules (Accounting Series Release Nos. 146 and 146A) that must be met to provide "persuasive evidence" that treasury shares were not acquired in contemplation of the combination. Exceptions to the rules include normal acquisitions to support option plans, stock purchase plans, or convertible securities; these shares, however, must be acquired in a systematic manner over the two-year period. In addition, exceptions include purchases made under agreements related to a shareholder's death, settlement of lawsuits, or other contractual obligations.

In view of these requirements, companies must use care when establishing stock reacquisition plans. Plans established to reduce capitalization, forestall later dilution of earnings per share, utilize available cash, buy shares at times when the stock market price is depressed, or defend against takeovers—as is often done in today's environment—will not meet the specified conditions and will instead produce "tainted" treasury shares.

Tainted shares are cured automatically two years after their acquisition. Tainted shares can also be cured through sale in the marketplace, through use of such shares in an unrelated business combination accounted for under the purchase method, or through other use in the ordinary course of business.

Combining Attributes

There are four combining attributes that must be met in order to qualify for pooling-of-interests accounting:

- The acquisition must be effected in a single transaction or in accordance with a specified plan within one year of the plan's initiation. The period may be longer than one year if the delay in completing the transaction is beyond the control of the companies because of litigation or proceedings of a governmental authority. A substantive change in the terms of a merger agreement is considered a new plan and, in that case, the one-year clock is restarted.
- The acquiring corporation can issue only common stock with rights identical to those of the majority of its outstanding voting common stock in exchange for substantially all the voting common stock of the acquired company. Substantially all the voting common stock means 90 percent or more; no pro rata distribution of cash is permitted. Cash, however, may be used to purchase fractional shares or shares held by dissenting stockholders, providing the 90 percent test is met. If

the company to be acquired has outstanding equity or debt securities other than voting common stock, the acquiring company normally can exchange cash, substantially identical securities, or its common stock for those securities, or retire the securities for cash or debt. Warrants, options, and other securities deemed "substantially equivalent" to voting common stock must be exchanged for common stock or comparable securities.

- Each individual common stockholder who exchanges his stock must receive a voting common stock interest exactly in proportion to his relative voting common stock interest before the combination.
- APB 16 requires purchase accounting when an earnings or market price contingency agreement is present in a business combination. However, the opinion does not prohibit certain types of contingency agreements in a pooling as long as they relate to a condition at consummation and not a post-combination contingency (e.g., do not represent earnings or market price contingency agreements). The most common types of contingency agreements not prohibited in a pooling are those related to specific contingencies, such as litigation and income tax disputes and "general management representations," which are present in nearly all business combinations. In general, contingency agreements related to specific contingencies may extend for the period during which the underlying contingencies are unresolved, while general management representation contingency arrangements should normally not extend beyond one year or the completion of the first audit of the combined operations after the merger, whichever is sooner.

Post-combination Attributes

There must be no planned transactions on the part of the combining companies to (1) agree, directly or indirectly, to retire or reacquire any of the common stock issued; (2) enter into any financial arrangements for the benefit of stockholders of the acquired company that in effect negate the pro rata exchange of equity securities, such as a guarantee of loans secured by stock issued in the acquisition; or (3) dispose of a significant part of the assets of the combined companies within two years of the combination, other than by disposals in the ordinary course of business or in order to eliminate duplicate facilities or excess capacity of the acquired company. Treasury stock transactions can occur subsequent to combination. However, to avoid the presumption that these transactions are considered "planned transactions," a waiting period of 30 to 90 days is suggested.

Other Prohibitions

If the sum of (1) intercorporate investments, (2) "tainted" treasury shares (expressed in equivalent shares of the acquired company), (3) shares acquired for cash (dissenter or fractional shares), and (4) minority interests of the acquired company remaining after the combination, exceeds 10 percent of the voting common stock of the acquired company, pooling accounting is precluded.

Recording Poolings

In a pooling, the historical carrying amounts of the net assets of both entities must be carried forward without change. Adjustments to conform the accounting practices of the combining entities are acceptable if these changes would otherwise have been appropriate for the separate entity. These adjustments should be made retroactively.

Combining Equity Accounts

The shareholders' equity accounts of the separate entities should be combined; retained earnings should represent the aggregate of both companies. When the par or stated value of the shares issued is less than the par or stated value of the acquired entity's stock, the differences should be assigned to additional paid-in capital. When the par or stated value of the shares issued exceeds that of the acquired company's stock, the excess should be assigned, first, to reduce or eliminate any additional paid-in capital of the acquired entity; second, to reduce or eliminate any additional paid-in capital of the issuing company to the extent permitted by law; and third, to reduce retained earnings.

Reporting Requirements

A pooling of interests should be recorded as of the date the combination is consummated. That date usually is the date of the legal closing of the transaction. A combination consummated after year-end but before the annual financial statements are issued should not be reflected in the earlier year's annual financial statements.

The combined entity should report results of operations for the period in which the combination occurs as though the entities had been combined as of the beginning of the period. Financial statements presented for prior periods should be restated on a combined basis as if the entities had always been one enterprise. However, if the operations acquired are immaterial, prior periods do not have to be restated.

Costs incurred to effect a pooling of interests—such as registration fees, costs of furnishing information to stockholders, and legal (finders and consultants') fees—should be charged to expense. Costs incurred to integrate the continuing operations and to eliminate or mitigate existing inefficiencies also should be charged to expense as they are incurred.

Disclosure Requirements

APB 16 provides for significant disclosures relating to pooling combinations. Among other requirements, revenue, extraordinary items, and net income of each company should be disclosed separately for the period from the beginning of the year to the date of combination. A reconciliation of revenue and earnings previously reported by the acquiring company to the restated combined amounts currently presented in financial statements and summaries should be provided.

Reconciliation of Accounting and Tax Requirements

Both accounting and tax rules governing business combinations set forth specific requirements that must be met to achieve a pooling of interests or a tax-free reorganization. Those transactions not complying completely with the specified rules are to be accounted for as a purchase for accounting purposes and as partially or fully taxable transactions.

Tax-Free and Taxable Transactions

In most business combinations, a pooling of interests will also be a tax-free transaction, and a taxable transaction will normally be reported as a purchase for accounting purposes. There are, however, exceptions to this general rule. Although the financial and tax accounting rules for business combinations are similar in many respects, close scrutiny reveals many subtle, and often extremely significant, differences. It is essential, therefore, to review in depth the specific technical criteria that companies must meet to achieve the desired accounting and tax treatment. It should not be assumed automatically that a tax-free transaction qualifies as a pooling or that a purchase is necessarily a taxable transaction. (See Chapter 27.)

Conflicts Between Accounting and Tax Considerations

A sound understanding of the advantages and disadvantages of taxable purchases, as contrasted with those of tax-free poolings, also is necessary in deciding which method is best for any given transaction. One of the most difficult reconciliation processes occurs when the net assets of the company being acquired have a low accounting and tax basis in relation to the price being paid. For accounting purposes, it normally is desirable to use pooling accounting. This treatment avoids charging future earnings with the amortization and depreciation of the stepped-up amounts that would result from purchase accounting. However, for the buyer's tax purposes, it may be desirable to structure the transaction in a fashion to obtain future tax deductions on a stepped-up basis of the assets acquired. Reconciling these conflicting objectives is often difficult, particularly when other business objectives may be in conflict or when the seller's objective is to make the transaction tax-free, which is often the case. A situation like this could also have serious Alternative Minimum Tax consequences.

The differences between tax-free poolings and taxable purchases, and the advantages and disadvantages of each method, are too numerous to discuss here. However, companies must consider all factors—tax, accounting and others—together with the objectives of individual buyers and sellers to arrive at the most appropriate structure for a combination transaction.

ACCOUNTING FOR DIVESTITURES

The accounting method for divestitures in the financial statements of the divesting company depends on whether the unit being divested qualifies as a "segment of a business."

If a Segment

If a divestiture qualifies as a segment of a business, the results of operations of the divested entity should be retroactively deconsolidated and reported separately from income from continuing operations as a component of income before extraordinary items. This is discussed in greater detail below.

If Not a Segment

If the divestiture does not qualify as a segment of a business, the results of operations and assets and liabilities are still deconsolidated, but prospectively rather than retroactively. In addition, results of these operations cannot be reported separately as a discontinued business. Instead, they must be reported as part of income from continuing operations. If material, any gain/loss on the sale of such business should be disclosed separately as a component of income from continuing operations.

Accounting for the Disposal of a Segment of a Business

APB 30 provides specific guidelines for accounting and reporting the effects of the disposal of a segment of a business. A "segment of a business" refers to a component of an entity whose activities represent a separate major line of business or class of customer. A segment may be in the form of a subsidiary, a division, or a department, provided that its assets, results of operations, and activities can be clearly distinguished—physically, operationally, and for financial reporting purposes—from other assets, results of operations, and activities of the entity.

Deconsolidation

Operations of a segment that have been or will be sold or discontinued should be retroactively "deconsolidated" and reported separately from "income from continuing operations" on the face of the income statement as a "discontinued business" component of "income before extraordinary items." See the example in Figure 1.

The assets and liabilities of the divestiture should also be deconsolidated and reported net in one or several summary lines in the balance sheet.

FIGURE 1
Deconsolidating a Divestiture Income Statement Reporting Form

Income from continuing operations before income taxes	$	
Provision for income taxes	———	
Income from continuing operations		$
Discontinued operations (Note 0):		
Income (loss) from operations of discontinued Division X (less applicable income taxes of $)	$	
Loss of disposal of Division X, including provision of $ for operating losses during phaseout period (less applicable income taxes of $)	———	———
Net Income		$

Losses

The actual or estimated loss from disposal of a segment, including operating losses during the phase-out period, should be included in the reported results of operations of the segment in the year in which the divestiture plan is formally adopted. Any changes in estimates of the eventual loss should be recorded when they become known.

Gains

Estimated gains should not be recorded until actually realized, although operating losses during the phase-out period may be deferred (i.e., capitalized) until the eventual sale of the business as long as an overall net gain is anticipated.

Gain recognition may be precluded or limited, even after closing of the sale, if the buyer is a highly-leveraged Newco formed to purchase the business being sold. If that is the case, when the seller's consideration received includes debt or equity securities of the buyer, or if the seller guarantees some or all of the buyer's acquisition debt, any gain would have to be deferred if its realization is dependent upon the successful operation of the business being sold. In other words, gain would be recorded only when cash was realized on the debt or equity securities received (or the guarantee of the buyer's debt was removed).

Allocating Interest

It is acceptable, but not mandatory, to allocate interest to discontinued operations. The maximum amount of interest allocated is limited to the total of (1) interest on debt of the discontinued operation assumed by the buyer and (2) an allocation of other consolidated interest that is not directly attributable to other operations of the enterprise. General corporate overhead may not be allocated to discontinued operations. The SEC will expect registrants to clearly disclose their accounting policy and the amount allocated in (1) the reclassified profit or loss from discontinued operations for periods prior to the decision to divest and (2) the operating profit or loss incurred between decision date and the disposal date that was included in the calculation of the gain or loss on disposal.

Dispositions in Form Only

Discontinued operations treatment should not be applied to the disposition of an operation when the risks of ownership have not, in substance, been transferred. This may be the case when (1) there is continuing involvement by the seller after disposal, (2) the principal consideration is debt of the buyer with repayment dependent on the success of future operations, or (3) significant debt or other performance guarantees are made by the seller.

These situations differ from the discussion of gain deferral in the previous section in that the seller continues to have continuing performance obligations, such as buying the entity's product or supplying it with materials at favorable prices. Whereas the aforementioned scenario leads to deferral of gain but otherwise allows the application of discontinued operations accounting (e.g., restatement of prior income statements), if the disposition is determined to be in form only, discontinued operations treatment is also prohibited until all uncertainties are resolved.

Disclosure Requirements

APB 30 provides for significant disclosures relating to the disposal of a segment of a business. The disclosure requirements include the identity of the segment, expected disposal date, manner of disposal, a description of any remaining assets and liabilities of the segment at the balance sheet date, income taxes applicable to the results of discontinued operations, and the gain or loss and any proceeds expected from the disposal of the segment as of the balance sheet date.

Expenses Related to a Divestiture

Under the provisions of APB 30, costs and expenses directly associated with the decision to dispose of a segment, which may include severance pay, additional pension costs, employee pension expenses, and so on, must be charged to income as part of the results of operations of the discontinued business.

RESTRUCTURING TECHNIQUES

The wave of corporate restructuring in the past several years has spawned so many innovative structures that no listing could be complete. Three common techniques are discussed herein; many of the variations involve the same accounting principles. In addition, the issue of whether, at the completion of a transaction, one entity may have to consolidate another entity, carry it on the equity method or as a cost-basis investment can be critical.

Spin-offs

The term "spin-off" is one used by many different people to refer to varying transactions, but we will define it here as the distribution of shares of a subsidiary by a parent company on a pro rata basis to the parent's own shareholders. In such a case, for at least an instant, the owners of the two companies are identical.

Such a transaction, which requires no cash or financing to accomplish, is specifically required by the accounting literature to be recorded at the historical carrying value of the subsidiary by the parent. Thus, the parent records no gain or loss on the distribution regardless of the fair market value of the subsidiary being spun-off. Likewise, the subsidiary opens business (as a separate company) with its assets on the same basis, including pre-existing goodwill, if any, as that at which it was previously carried in the consolidated financial statements. The sole exception exists in that if the assets of the subsidiary are not realizable through its operations, they must be written-down to net realizable value before the spin-off (i.e., a parent cannot use a spin-off to avoid taking a write-off that it otherwise would have had to record).

Partial Sales of Subsidiaries

For a variety of reasons, ranging from the need for cash to the desire to bring a particular subsidiary to the public's attention in order to show its hidden value, a company may sell off a minority interest in a subsidiary. If this is accomplished via a direct sale by the parent of some of the shares it owns, a gain is recorded as simply the difference between the proceeds realized and the pro rata portion of the carrying amount (in the consolidated financial statements) of the subsidiary whose shares were sold. This method results in a taxable transaction, however, so an alternative has become popular. Substantially the same result can be obtained by having the subsidiary sell new shares directly. Whether the subsidiary remits the proceeds to the parent (generally in advance by borrowing) or not, the parent will benefit whenever the per share sale price of the subsidiary's offering is greater than the consolidated per share carrying amount of the subsidiary. Under an SEC Staff Accounting Bulletin (No. 51), a gain (or, rarely, a loss) is recordable for this benefit in the consolidated financial statements. This gain or loss can be taken through income or directly to the shareholders' equity account.

Joint Venturing

The third common restructuring technique to be discussed in this section is the establishment of a joint venture using an operation already owned. The variations on this technique are numerous, and can include both venturers contributing assets (or businesses) for shares; one or the other contributing cash while the other puts in assets; one or the other contributing a smaller asset plus some cash to even out the venture; having the venture borrow to buy the assets from one or both venturers; having one or both venturers leverage their assets before contributing to the venture; and many, many more.

The accounting for the multitude of structures that can be developed can be complex, and different accounting answers can be obtained for what appear to be virtually identical end results; further, this is an area in which the accounting rules are not clear and accountants often disagree. Careful analysis of all the facts, risks, and rewards of each party is necessary, and consultation with accounting experts is essential.

Nonetheless, several general rules tend to be relevant in most cases: first, a company putting an asset (or business) and the related debt, if any, into a joint venture will get them off balance sheet as long as it does not control the venture and have to consolidate (see Volume I, Chapter 25 for consolidation criteria); second, a company contributing assets into a venture, even if off balance sheet accounting is achieved, will not be able to recognize any gain unless it receives cash; and, third, even if cash is received, no gain is recordable if the venture must be consolidated. With respect to the issue of how much gain can be recorded, accountants currently disagree. Some maintain than only pro rata gain is recordable as long as the company owns an equity interest in the venture (i.e., you cannot record a gain by selling something to yourself); others would allow more than pro rata gain to be recorded if cash was received in excess of the sum of parents' historical carrying amount for the subsidiary and the pro rata gain. The FASB's Emerging Issues Task Force attempted to resolve this controversy in its Issue No. 89-7, but failed to reach a consensus.

Subsidiaries Sold to the Public or Spun Off (Carveout Accounting)

When shares of a subsidiary (or a segment of a business that is subsequently incorporated) are initially sold to the public or spun off, or when debt securities are initially sold to the public by a subsidiary, the SEC requires that the financial statements of the subsidiary in the prospectus include all expenses incurred by the parent on the subsidiary's behalf. To the extent that they have not been charged to the subsidiary in the past, the expenses must be retroactively reflected with the offsetting credit recorded in paid-in capital. The SEC's policy also applies to credits allocable to the subsidiary (e.g., management fees to the subsidiary in excess of the underlying cost of the services rendered). In such cases, the adjustment would be treated as a dividend to the parent.

The SEC also requires disclosure in the notes to the financial statements of management's estimates of what the expenses of the subsidiary would have been on a stand-alone basis when such expenses are significantly different from those reflected in the statements. Such estimates, however, should not be recorded in the historical statements. Further, it requires that the pro forma statements reflect or disclose (1) a separate return income tax provision, (2) the effects of terminated or revised agreements with the parent, (3) dividends declared after the date of the balance sheet, and (4) certain other adjustments. Lastly, in certain cases, historical earnings per share are not permitted; and, when the entity was not a legal entity, retained earnings prior to incorporation may not be carried forward.

EXAMPLES OF PURCHASE AND POOLING-OF-INTERESTS ACCOUNTING

The following examples of pooling and purchase accounting illustrate the principal differences between the two methods.

Assumptions used in Examples are as follows:

- ABC Co. acquired XYZ Co. at the close of business on December 31, 19X8. Both companies utilize the calendar year as their financial reporting year. XYZ Co. was liquidated immediately upon closing of the acquisition.
- The total consideration for the acquisition of XYZ Co. was ABC Co. stock with a value of $2 million.
- Inventory turns over in one year.
- The historical balance sheets of ABC Co. at December 31, 19X8, together with the fair values at that date of the net assets of XYZ Co., are shown in Figure 2.
- The income statements of ABC Co. and XYZ Co. for the year ending December 31, 19X9, assuming that no acquisition had taken place, are shown in Figure 3.
- Book and tax bases of the assets and liabilities are the same on the date of the transaction.

FIGURE 2

Balance Sheet—December 31, 19X8

	ABC Co. Historical	XYZ Co. Historical	XYZ Co. Fair Market Value	XYZ Co. Difference
		(amounts in thousands)		
Cash	$200	$50	$50	$—
Receivables	700	200	200	—
Inventory	600	300	350	50
Prepaid assets	80	50	50	—
	1,580	600	650	50
Fixed assets, net	950	400	1,050	650
Patents	—	—	300	300
Goodwill	—	—	305	305
	$2,530	$1,000	$2,305	$1,305
Payables	$600	$100	$100	$—
Accruals	250	75	75	—
Income tax payable	200	80	80	—
	1,050	255	255	—
Long-term debt	380	50	50*	—
Capital and surplus	1,100	695	2,000	1,305
	$2,530	$1,000	$2,305	$1,305

*Would be adjusted if rate of interest did not approximate current rate of interest.

FIGURE 3

Statements of Income—19X9(Assuming no acquisition)

	ABC Co.	XYZ Co.
	(amounts in thousands)	
Sales	$2,500	$700
Cost of sales	(1,500)	(420)
Gross profit	1,000	280
Selling, general and administrative expenses	(500)	(140)
Income from operations	500	140
Federal Income tax*	(250)	(70)
Net income	$250	$70
Return on sales	10%	10%

*Assumes a 50% statutory tax rate.

Example I: Pooling-of-Interests Accounting

Example I in Figure 4 reflects tax-free, pooling-of-interests accounting. The financial statements presented reflect the financial accounting theory underlying pooling accounting—that all financial reports be presented on the basis that the companies had been combined since their respective incorporation dates.

Example I-A reflects the pooled balance sheet of two combined companies. The corresponding historical accounts of the two companies are combined without adjustment or recognition of the relative current fair values of the assets acquired or the consideration exchanged in the transaction.

Example I-B reflects post-acquisition operating results, also accomplished by a combination of separate company operating results. Depreciation charges against income are based on historical accounts with no recognition being given to current fair values.

Example II: Purchase Accounting

Example II in Figure 5 contrasts pooling accounting with the recorded purchase transactions. The example assumes the same facts as assumed in Example I, except that the transaction does not meet the requirements of a pooling. In a purchase, the fair value of the price paid must be allocated to all assets acquired. After recording fair values, the accounting fair values are adjusted for differences between financial and tax allocation practices.

As shown in Example II-B, the financial operating results of subsequent periods are charged with the depreciation and amortization of the written-up amounts and adjusted for the net effect of the difference between the accounting and tax-cost basis. Example II is calculated by using the principles described as "net-of-tax" accounting in the preceding section of this chapter.

Example II-C reconciles the results of purchase versus pooling accounting.

As was discussed, SFAS 96 significantly affects the examples reflected herein. Examples III-A and III-B in Figure 6 contrast the purchase accounting adjustment necessary under the old accounting rules (APB 11) with that which is required under SFAS 96.

FIGURE 4
Example I: Tax-Free Pooling

Example I-A
Combined Balance Sheet December 31, 19X8

	ABC Co. Historical	*XYZ Co. Historical*	*Combined ABC/XYZ on Basis of Tax-Free Pooling*
		(amounts in thousands)	
Cash	$ 200	$ 50	$ 250
Receivables	700	200	900
Inventory	600	300	900
Prepaid assets	80	50	130
	1,580	600	2,180
Fixed assets	950	400	1,350
Patents	—	—	—
Goodwill	—	—	—
	$2,530	$1,000	$3,530
Payables	$ 600	$ 100	$ 700
Accruals	250	75	325
Income tax payable	200	80	280
	1,050	255	1,305
Long-term debt	380	50	430
Capital and surplus	1,100	695	1,795
	$2,530	$1,000	$3,530

Example I-B
Combined Statements of Income—Year Ending December 31, 19X9

	ABC Co.	*XYZ Co.*	*Combined*
		(amounts in thousands)	
Sales	$2,500	$700	$3,200
Cost of sales	(1,500)	(420)	(1,920)
Gross profit	1,000	280	1,280
Selling, general and administrative expenses	(500)	(140)	(640)
Income from operations	500	140	640
Federal Income tax*	(250)	(70)	(320)
Net income	$250	$70	$320
Return on sales	10%	10%	10%

*Assumes a 50% statutory rate.

FIGURE 5
Example II: Purchase Accounting

EXAMPLE II-A

Combined Balance Sheet, December 31, 19X8 (Prior to Adoption of SFAS 96)

	Combined ABC/XYZ on Basis of Tax-Free Pooling (Example I)	*XYZ Co. Market Value Writeup (Figure 2)*	*XYZ Co. Effect of Tax Allocation of Excess(2)*	*Combined ABC/XYZ on Basis of Purchase*
		(amounts in thousands)		
Cash	$ 250	$ —	$ —	$ 250
Receivables	900	—	—	900
Inventory	900	50*	(9)	941
Prepaid assets	130	—	(1)	129
	2,180	50	(10)	2,220
Fixed assets	1,350	650*	(28)	1,972
Patents	—	300*	(8)	292
Goodwill	—	305 (1)	46	351
	$3,530	$1,305	$ —	$4,835
Payables	$ 700	$ —	$ —	$ 700
Accruals	325	—	—	325
Income tax payable	280	—	—	280
	1,305	—	—	1,305
Long-term debt	430	—	—	430
Capital and surplus	1,795	1,305	—	3,100
	$3,530	$1,305	$ —	$4,835

Notes:

[1]Residual value calculated as follows:

Purchase price	$2,000
XYZ Co. historical capital and surplus	(695)
Excess to be allocated	1,305
Less: Revaluation of identifiable assets to fair market value	(1,000)*
Allocated to goodwill	$ 305

[2] Required due to the fact that the tax basis of the assets acquired cannot be written up to the full market value of such assets acquired; as a result, the tax allocation of these purchased assets differs from the accounting or financial statement allocation and such accounting or financial statement allocation must be reduced to reflect the lack of full tax benefit reflected therein.

FIGURE 5—*Continued*

EXAMPLE II-B

Combined Statements of Income—Year Ending December 31, 19X9

	Combined ABC/XYZ on Basis of Tax-Free Pooling (Example 1-B)	*Combined ABC/XYZ on Basis of Purchase (Pre-SFAS 96)*
	(amounts in thousands)	
Sales	$3,200	$3,200
Cost of sales	(1,920)	(1,920)
Plus (minus) additional depreciation, net (see below)	—	(91)
Inventory adjustment, net of difference in tax basis	—	(41)
Gross profit	1,280	1,148
Selling, general and administrative expenses	(640)	(640)
Plus, prepaid adjustment, net of difference in tax basis	—	1
Goodwill amortization	—	(9)
Income from operations	640	500
Federal Income tax	(320)	(262)
Net income	$ 320	$ 238
Return on sales	10%	7%

EXAMPLE II-C

Reconciliation of Pooling and Pre-SFAS 96 Purchase Accounting Results

		Financial Results (amounts in thousands)
Pretax Income based on historical costs (Example 1-B)		$640
Add: Roll-through of step-down adjustment to current assets		10
Less: Additional amortization and depreciation due to fair market value write up of –		
Fixed assets (10 years)	(62)	
Patents (10 years)	(29)	
		(91)
Goodwill		(9)
Roll-through of inventory step-up		(50)
Net pretax income after purchase accounting		500

FIGURE 6
Example III: Purchasing Accounting: Contrasting Old and New Rules

EXAMPLE III-A
Combined Balance Sheets

	Pre-SFAS 96 (Example II-A)	*Under SFAS 96 (Note 1)*	*Difference*
Cash	$ 250	$ 250	$—
Receivables	900	900	—
Inventory	941	950	9
Prepaid assets	129	130	1
	2,220	2,230	10
Fixed assets	1,972	2,000	28
Patents	292	300	8
Goodwill	351	351	—
	$4,835	$4,881	$46
Payables	$ 700	$ 700	$—
Accruals	325	325	—
Income tax payable	280	280	—
	1,305	1,305	—
Deferred income taxes	—	46	46
Long-term debt	430	430	—
Capital and surplus	3,100	3,100	—
	$4,835	$4,881	$46

Note 1—Under SFAS 96, the "liability method" requires recognition of tax effects of differences between assigned values and tax bases of the net assets acquired as deferred income tax assets or liabilities, rather than as basis adjustments following the "net-of-tax" approach reflected in Example II-A. While this Example does reflect deferred tax liabilities in accordance with SFAS 96, it does not reflect any deferred tax assets since assigned values exceed tax bases. Were this not the case, under SFAS 96, the initial recording of deferred tax assets resulting from tax bases exceeding fair values might be precluded as a result of SFAS 96's stringent criteria for recording deferred tax assets. (Such amounts might have been recorded under the "net-of-tax" method contained in APB Opinion No. 11.)

FIGURE 6—*Continued*

Example III-B
Combined Statements of Income

	Pre-SFAS 96 (Example II-B)	*Under SFAS 96*
Sales	$3,200	$3,200
Cost of sales	(1,920)	(1,920)
Additional depreciation, net	(91)	(95)
Inventory adjustment, net of difference in tax basis	(41)	(50)
Gross profit	1,148	1,135
Selling, general, and administrative expenses	(640)	(640)
Prepaid adjustment, net of difference in tax basis	1	—
Goodwill amortization over 40 years	(9)	(9)
Income from operations	500	486
Federal income taxes	(262)	(248)
Net income	$ 238	$ 238
Effective tax rate analysis (Note 1):		
Income from operations	$ 500	$ 486
Plus: Nondeductible goodwill	9	9
	$ 509	$ 495
Statutory rate	50%	50%
Statutory tax	$ 255	$ 248
Actual tax	262	248
Difference	$ (7)	$ (0)

Note 1—SFAS 96 results in an effective tax rate more reflective of the statutory rate than the old accounting method.

PART 4

THE DEAL-MAKING PROCESS

CHAPTER 29

THE DEAL-MAKING PROCESS I: STRUCTURE AND STRATEGY

Robert Lawrence Kuhn

My purpose for writing these two chapters on deal making is to express some personal ideas about the most important process of investment banking in which negotiating transactions is an everyday obsession.[1] Deal making is so important to investment banking that it has come to epitomize the field, even to caricature it. The perceived image of the rapacious shark is a distortion of the truth and a disservice to the industry. The best deal makers combine optimal information and analytical skills with artistic intuition and human sensitivity. People make deals, and these two chapters focus on people.

I am an independent investment banker. I arrange mergers and acquisitions, restructure organizations, and develop new businesses. My doctorate is in brain science. I hold academic positions in corporate strategy and creative management. This background, I believe, helps me make the hurly-burly world of deal making understandable. Marketplace deals are what I do. Practical advice is what I give.

In many ways I see life as a deal. To live life is to make deals. Deal making is in constant session. From boardrooms to bedrooms, you can't avoid

[1]Editor's Note: This chapter has been derived from *DEALMAKER: All the Negotiating Skills and Secrets You Need*, Robert Lawrence Kuhn, copyright ©1988 by John Wiley & Sons. Reprinted by permission of John Wiley & Sons, Inc. No one doubts that deal making is a vital part of investment banking, but too often we think too much about technical finance and too little about human relations. My decision to include two substantial chapters on the deal-making process expresses my commitment to the importance of people and their behavior. Pardon an author's bias, but I believe that DEALMAKER's concepts are real, relevant, and permanent, and that teaching such interpersonal skills can advance the industry.

doing deals. You can either do them poorly or do them well. These chapters are about doing them well.

Every aspect of deal making is exhilarating—the thrill of a new deal beginning, the satisfaction of a good deal closing. Making deals intrigues and inspires: the electric sparks of planning creating, nurturing, and achieving. Nothing is as satisfying as a good deal well done (well, almost nothing).

What makes a deal "do-able?" How to do good deals? These are two crucial questions we address. The first asks how to recognize deals that can close, so that your time is spent efficiently. The second asks how to shift deals to your favor, so that your work is done effectively.

It's not all roses and medals. Some transactions are bombs—good deals that never closed and bad deals that sadly did. Why do good ones fall apart? Why do bad ones come together? One learns from failure as well as success. Vital principles are at work here. What the best deal makers do, often by the feel of their gut, can be grasped, absorbed, and applied. To be a great deal maker, you need perspective, insight, and techniques. So I must be provocative, impatient, and brusque. Intensity and guts must amplify strategy and structure.

The chapter is not a mystery, so there is no suspense in which to keep you. Right up front I'll tell you the punch lines. Don't be fooled by their simplicity. The more you dig, the more profound they get.

- *You must like deal making.*
- *You must like people.*

Like them both and you're off to a good start.

STRUCTURE OF THE CHAPTERS

There is logic in the order; it is based on the step-by-step sequence of parts and pieces of the deal-making process.

Chapter 29: The Deal-making Process I: Structure and Strategy

We introduce the basic attitudes and concepts of deals and good deals, and the personality traits of good deal makers. They lay out the general framework for making good deals. They develop the foundation for formulating, evaluating, and implementing proper strategy and tactics.

Chapter 30: The Deal-making Process II: Elements of Negotiations

Here we dissect out the elements and components of deal making. Collectively, they describe all aspects of transactions and negotiations, and by considering each one individually, we gain insight into the entire process. Disaggregating the whole into its constituent parts is an important mechanism for building deep understanding. These elements and components present key issues of initial position, organization, composition, characters, and assessment. They reveal the kinds of broad maneuvers and operations, offensive and defensive, implicit in all bargaining activity. They expose the kinds of detailed machinations and techniques that comprise the nitty gritty of making deals and conducting negotiations. They illustrate games and gambits, plots and ploys, schemes and stratagems. Describing deal elements and components requires analogies of chess, sports, sex, and war.

Bored with my simple agenda? No problem. Bothered by the linear layout? No worry. If you are so bored or bothered, forget my outline and devise your own. *Ignore* the structure I describe and access these bite-sized sections randomly, tackling them in order of personal preference, not author number. Enter and exit any place you like. Skip ahead and around. These chapters are not short stories: There is no harm in jumping to later sections if that's the subject on your mind. Learning is best when motivation is highest.

DEAL FALLACIES

Let's start in reverse. What common assumptions about deal making are just plain wrong? What is real deal making *not?*

Not Just Edge Getting

The popular press harangues us with getting-the-edge indoctrination. Predatory propaganda is the way of our world. If you don't know "the craft of negotiation," you're a dolt and a doormat. If you don't "conquer through intimidation," you're a pushover and a placemat. If you don't "watch out for Number One," you're a flake and a dish rag. No one wants to be a blockhead or a pansy or a nerd with a wet noodle for a backbone, so we are all compelled, actually bullied, to play the one-upmanship game.

But it's all so fugitive, so short-sighted. Today's quick buck chokes off a thousand tomorrow. Streams of dollars that could flow in the future are never seen. The irony, of course, is that what is not seen is not known; no negative reinforcement ever occurs, no long-term consequences of short-term actions are ever appreciated. Self-impressed edge-getters go blithely their devious ways, smug that they have mastered the craft of negotiation, conquered through intimidation, and watched out for Number One—whereas, in reality, they have flubbed the deal, blown the negotiations, and flattened Number One.

Not Just Negotiations

What constitutes a deal? Clever negotiations, if you believe popular wisdom. True—but not the whole truth. Deal making requires greater talent and demands broader technique. Deal making means more than negotiating. Learning how to do deals means more than learning how to negotiate them. How to get what you want in trading and haggling is only part of our story.

"Deal making" describes the whole process, whereas "negotiating" defines specific skills. Deal making involves far more than is usually assumed, and if you begin with techniques of negotiations, you've already conceded half the battle. Negotiations, if you think about them, start in the middle, taking for granted that a certain deal should or must be made. But *which* deal should or must be made? How do you know? It makes no sense to negotiate in a make-believe world, however nice the imagined fairyland. *It is better, I tell you, to negotiate the right deal badly than the wrong deal well.* Think about that.

Not Just Tactics

Deal making is strategy as well as tactics, how to plan ahead as well as how to carry out. It is creative choice as well as shrewd manipulation. Choosing the right deal—knowing in advance which deals are "do-able" and which are not—is more important than negotiating that deal. You need to be much more than a good negotiator to be a good deal maker.

Not a clever negotiator? Not to worry. You don't need to be one to be a good deal maker. Surprised? Read on. Certainly the skills of adroit bargaining are valuable. We will discuss them in detail—adding a few twists and turns sure to delight even the most jaded negotiator. But the facts are that one can be a good deal maker *without* being especially wily in negotiations, and that a smart negotiator may be winning minor victories on the wrong battlefield.

DEAL MAKING IN THE BIBLE

The Bible is a rich case book of famous deals:

- God giving Adam and Eve the Garden-of-Eden paradise with the one condition being not to eat from the forbidden tree.
- God's covenant with Abraham to make of him a great nation in exchange for his obedience and, well, a very small piece of very sensitive skin ("You want what. . ?!" "That's the deal, Abe, it's my best offer").
- Jacob wrestling with God and refusing to let go until receiving a blessing.
- God at Mount Sinai offering ancient Israel blessings for obedience and cursings for disobedience.
- God granting David a choice of punishment for his sins (he chose to fall into the hands of God and receive a plague rather than fall into the hands of man and flee from enemies).
- God allowing even the most wicked king (Manasseh) to repent and be forgiven.

Some deals worked for these biblical deal makers, such as when Jacob bought his brother Esau's birthright for a bowlful of porridge. And some deals did not work, such as when Sarah gave Haggar (her handmaiden) to Abraham (her husband) in hopes of having the promised son through this surrogate mother (a particularly modern issue, only back then the insemination process was natural not artificial).

DEFINING A DEAL

What, actually, *is* a deal? Let's frame some basic definitions. A little precision can't hurt. *A deal is an exchange of value and consideration among two or more parties.*

- *Value* means anything whatsoever that at least one side thinks has some kind of worth.
- *Consideration* means whatever things are used to purchase that value. A tangible or intangible "something" must change hands.[2]

---

[2]Value and consideration can be *tangible* (i.e., items that have physical substance) such as property, plant, equipment, and inventory; and they can be *intangible* (i.e., items that lack physical substance) such as copyrights, brand names, customer lists, and licenses.

- *Parties* means the participants in the deal.

The value and consideration of the exchange may include goods, services, assets, liabilities, cash, cash equivalents, promissory notes, stock ownership of all kinds, patents, rights, royalties, responsibilities, or commitments. Each side seeks to achieve specific objectives and may include any combination of tangible and intangible value and consideration in the deal.

In a traditional corporate deal, one party exchanges cash or notes to purchase the stock or assets of a company. In a less traditional corporate deal, a weak business might be exchanged solely for the assumptions of its liabilities.[3]

In a traditional personal deal, an employee gives his or her work time and effort to a company and receives a salary and other benefits in exchange. In a less traditional personal deal, an indicted criminal plea bargains for a less severe punishment in exchange for admitting guilt and/or cooperating with authorities.

DEAL COMPLEXITY

Complexity is a killer in deal making. It sucks time and saps strength. Deal makers should fear its ominous advance.

There is an *inverse* relationship between complexity of deals and probability of closure. This means that the more complicated the deal structure the less likely it is to work. The KISS principal—Keep it Simple, Stupid—is as valid with giant corporate transactions as it is with small personal arrangements. (In fact, small deals are no easier to make than big deals. Sometimes they are even harder, since personality and ego can more easily foul up the air and choke off progress.)

Transactions may be disarmingly simple or tortuously complex. A purchasing agent and a vendor can agree on price without need for written confirmation. Some corporate mergers cannot close without consuming hundreds of turgid legal documents. But a deal is a deal is a deal, and every point in every transaction must be sifted and selected, dissected and analyzed, considered and decided, no matter how large or small the numbers.

---

[3]Assumptions of liabilities to acquire businesses can be worse for the acquiror than paying an equivalent amount of cash since it introduces more uncertainty and risk.

DEAL COMPONENTS

Stripped to basics, all deals are similar. Simple or complex, all deals look the same inside and underneath. Reaching agreement with your kids on their weekly allowances is analogous in structure to hammering out terms of a line of credit with your bank—both of which parallel discussing a raise with your boss.

All deals have common components: distinct parties with differing interests, value and consideration to be exchanged, terms and conditions to be discussed, a process of negotiation, a closure or consummation event, and an execution or implementation of the agreed-upon terms and conditions.

Mutual agreement is the key idea. Easy to say. Hard to do. Determining terms and conditions is the crux of most deals. It is the area of greatest conflict, yet it offers the most opportunity for dynamic creativity—for bridging unbridgeable gaps and climbing unclimbable cliffs.

A first step in devising good deal terms and conditions is to understand their composition. We present the seven components needed to establish deal terms and conditions, followed by two example applications, one corporate and one personal.

The Seven Component Questions

Question 1. What Kind of Stuff?

What is the nature and character of the value and consideration being exchanged in the transaction? This means the specific types of goods, services, assets, liabilities, ownerships, intangibles, rights, responsibilities, commitments, and the like.

Question 2. How Much of the Stuff?

What are the amounts of the value and consideration being exchanged? This means the precise number of the things, tangible and intangible, changing hands in the transaction.

Question 3. What's the Stuff Really Worth?

What is the relative benefit of the value and consideration being exchanged? How does each side of the transaction relate to the other?

Question 4. What's the Stuff Really Like?

What promises and assurances (representations and warranties) are given to the value and consideration? These are the legal declarations about the state of the value and consideration being exchanged: the mutual promises by the respective parties, their rights to make the transaction, and the like.

Question 5. What's for Sure and What's Not?

Which terms and conditions cannot change (noncontingent) and which can change (contingent)? Contingent aspects of transactions depend on future events or conditions (such as income in later years in an acquisition). Noncontingent aspects are set forth absolutely and cannot be altered.

Question 6. How to Assure Compliance?

How to provide for each side living up to its end of the bargain? These are the mechanisms for generating confidence in deal completion by fulfilling the terms and conditions through security interests, guarantees, performance requirements, and the like.

Question 7. What's the Timing?

What is the schedule for completing the transaction? This describes the sequence of events for executing and activating each aspect of the terms and conditions, the time frame when exchanges and transfers of value and consideration all happen.

Example of a Corporate Transaction

Assume Company A is buying a small subsidiary of Company B (call it "SmallCo"). How would each of the components fit and apply? The following is a simplified summary of the terms and conditions organized in answer to the seven questions.

Question 1. What Kind Of Stuff?

Company A purchases from Company B all the assets and current liabilities of SmallCo for cash, notes, and profit participations; Company B keeps SmallCo's long-term debt and stock.

Question 2. How Much Of the Stuff?

It costs $12 million, to be paid as follows: $2 million in cash at closing, $2 million in Company A stock, $5 million in promissory notes to be paid $1 million per year for five consecutive years, and $3 million in Company A stock to be paid as a percentage of future profits of the SmallCo division.

Question 3. What's the Stuff Really Worth?

The $2 million cash is easy; cash is cash. Company A stock is more difficult—it can be valued at market value if Company A is public, if the stock has a ready market, if there are no restrictions, and if there is reasonable stability in the stock—a lot of "ifs." The $1 million for five consecutive years must be discounted to present value if no interest is being paid. Thus the $5 million of face value on the promissory notes would be only worth about $3.6 million (using a 12 percent discount factor). The $3 million based on profit participation is worth substantially less than its face value, because, in addition to the present value discount, its ultimate valuation is completely dependent on indeterminable elements: SmallCo's future prospects when controlled by other parties, and the double doubt of uncertain profits in the SmallCo division and uncertain valuation of Company B stock.

Question 4. What's the Stuff Really Like?

Company B asserts that all assets and liabilities being transferred are in good condition. Company A provides an acceptable method for determining the division's future profitability. Each company assures the other of its legal right to do the transaction.

Question 5. What's For Sure and What's Not?

All but the profit participation is certain (noncontingent); the profit participation is dependent on uncertain events (and is highly contingent).

Question 6. How To Assure Compliance?

The $1 million per year for five years can carry the corporate guarantee of Company A. It may also be backed up by security interests in the assets being sold or even the independent guarantee of a financial institution (e.g., a letter of credit).

Question 7. *What's the Timing?*

The schedule for transfer of ownership of Company B value (SmallCo's assets) is stated clearly (usually at closing), as is the schedule for transfer of consideration (the various payments of cash and stock at closing and over time).

Example of a Personal Transaction

These same components exist in every deal, although in smaller, more personal transactions, several are more implicit than explicit. For example, watch the seven components at work in a deal between you and your boss regarding last year's bonus.

Question 1. What Kind Of Stuff?
You transfer to your employer last year's work product and the implied promise of next year's work product in exchange for certain financial consideration.

Question 2. How Much Of the Stuff?
The length of your implied employment arrangement, say, one year. The quantity of each type of financial consideration is specified for your bonus, say, $60,000 in cash and $80,000 worth of stock options.

Question 3. What's the Stuff Really Worth?
A logical relationship should relate work performance to financial bonus.

Question 4. What's the Stuff Really Like?
Assertions are more assumed than stated. Each side (you and your boss) agrees to the exchange of bonus for continued work.

Question 5. What's For Sure and What's Not?
The bonus is generally certain (noncontingent) for the previous year. It is usually uncertain (contingent) for the coming year (i.e., it is based on specific or unspecific factors such as the company's profitability, the relative performance of your division or department, your own personal productivity, and, often, the whim and caprice of your boss).

Question 6. How to Assure Compliance?
Confidence in receiving the bonus is often its verbal promise; confidence in your continued work effort is assumed. (However, it becomes problematic if you deem the bonus to be too low.)

Question 7. What is the Timing?
The schedule for bonus payment is based on corporate tradition (e.g., at the end of the year when performance can be assessed).

DEAL DOMAINS

Different deals have different traits, and different traits require different strategies. Deals can be viewed from various perspectives, or "cut" from various angles. Seeing deals from complementary viewpoints gives insight into their nature and character. To give sense to viewing (or cutting) deals from various perspectives (or angles), we present three approaches: Deal Participants, Deal Locus, and Deal Sectors. Mood and feeling, the fuzzies and tinglies, are at issue. Make no mistake: How your stomach is churning influences how your head is working.

Deal Participants

What's a "Deal Participants" perspective? Here, we look at the composition, numbers, and organization of the human characters on each side of the proposed transaction:

One versus One
For example, discussions between husbands and wives or peers and friends, or negotiations between buyers and sellers of personal property.

One versus Group
For example, a spouse dealing with an ex-spouse's law firm, or a person buying a car from an automobile dealer.

Group versus Group
For example, law firm against law firm in corporate litigation, or marketing department against manufacturing over new product responsibility.

One versus Institution
For example, a veteran fighting for promised benefits from his military service, or an inventor trying to free up corporate funds for high-risk research and development.

Group versus Institution
For example, individual investors planning to take over a public company, or union organizers seeking formal recognition.

Institution versus Institution
For example, the daily commerce of corporate buying and selling of goods and services, or an acquisition battle for a desired target company.

Deal Locus

What's a "Deal Locus" perspective? Here, we look at the proposed transaction from the individual deal maker's vantage point. Where in one's own personal life spectrum, we ask, is the transaction taking place? On the job in the course of normal business. On the job affecting career potential (e.g., promotion opportunity). Within the family altering relationships. Concerning one's private life (e.g., personal finance).

Deals in each different locus take on different auras and atmospheres. For example, deal making on the job is studied and professional. When one's career is on the line, count on overtones of tension and insecurity. Within the family, there's less inhibition and social restraint (e.g., screaming becomes an easy way to make your point more strongly). Concerning one's private life, never forget that you're still doing deals.

Deal Sector

What's a "Deal Sector" perspective? Here, we look at the proposed transaction from the organization's vantage point. Where in society, we ask, is the transaction taking place. In commercial companies (i.e., the private sector). Government agencies (i.e., the public sector). Not-for-profit institutions (e.g., universities and charities). Ideological institutions (e.g., religious and political movements).

From this perspective, the issues are goals and strategies; that is, where we are going and how we are going to get there. In each sector, deals have their own special character and cast—influencing attitudes, objectives, and priorities. For example, in commerce, it's often money, career, and power. In politics, career and power. In not-for-profit institutions, organizational mission. In ideological institutions, transcendental mission (and, all too often, an unhealthy dose of power, career, and money thrown in for bad measure).

WHAT'S A GOOD DEAL?

Good deal making is like good love making: When both parties are satisfied, each party enjoys it more—and wants to do it again! Being satisfied, however, does not require being satisfied at the same time, to the same degree, or in the same manner—on either side of the analogy. Deal making, again, like love making, involves a complex mingling of personality and passion, a mysterious mixture of ego and desire.

A good deal means different things to different parties: To a company enjoying high growth, a good deal might mean a 25 percent or more annual return on investment. To a company threatened with bankruptcy, a good deal might mean selling off inventory at a loss to generate survival cash. To an independent consultant, a good deal might mean selling services at low-ball fees in order to establish a reputation in the market. To a governmental agency, a good deal might mean speeding up spending to justify a larger budgetary appropriation.

Larry Hagman (J.R.) gets paid bundles for each original episode of *Dallas*, but shares none of the residual income from the reruns of the hit series. Lorimar, the production company, loses substantial money on each first-run episode but amasses fat profits from syndication of those reruns. It's a good deal for both sides. The actors take no risks and pocket their cash up front; the producers take high risks (since most series are not hits and losses are never recovered) and hope to score big later. That's the nature of deal making: lower risk for lower reward and higher risk for higher reward. (Although here, the actor's "lower" reward is hardly skimpy!)

In the short run, a good deal is whatever makes *you* happy. In the long run, a good deal is whatever makes *everyone* happy. Short run boosts egos, long run promotes careers. In making deals, one often chooses between ego and career. It's a tough call: Conceit never likes second place.

WHEN "BAD" MEANS "GOOD"

In the language of the street, "bad" means "good"—something tough and strong; and "good" means mediocre—something soft and weak. The same reverse sense applies in evaluating deal making. A "good" deal maker is often glamorized as a ruthless manipulator, a cold-blooded predator of the concrete jungle who devours all without mercy.

By some quirk of character, evolutionary or social, we admire the tough guy. Macho is cool. The masculine image is steel and ice, not satin and silk. The feminine image is warm and sensitive, and few deal makers have the ego strength to survive such compliments.

How to win accolades and respect in this media-blasted world of saber-toothed virility? Pressure and squeeze the other side. Better yet, pummel and pulverize them. To trick your opponents and seize more for yourself is the touchstone of success, the proverbial pot of deal-making gold at the end of the shrewd tactician's rainbow. Building the business takes a backseat when personal ego does the driving.

Too many business people pride themselves on besting their buddies. They must twist an advantage to feel productive. You know the type. A fair price is never fair. Grinding never stops. Agreements are changed constantly. Power plays never end. An agreed-upon deal is altered on signing. Payment is delayed deliberately. Simple meaning is confounded by calculated obfuscation and legal pyrotechnics. The pounding is relentless.

Some of these characters browbeat and coerce. Others prefer to dupe and deceive—the former like to see you squirm; the latter enjoy the painless slice. Priorities are always inverted, objectives pulled inside out, goals flipped upside down. "Getting the edge" is the goal, and shaving points is the game. Edge-getters are often haughty and swell-headed ("legends in their own minds"), with more vanity and arrogance than acumen and smarts. When these types fancy themselves deal makers, they are often more addicted to the clever kill than to the extra meat. What counts is not the spending power of the bigger payoff but the puffing power of the smoother stroke. It's the edge itself that's sought, not necessarily the amount, the intoxicating elixir of Darwinian dominance brewed with sublimated sexuality.

Cutting a deal with a 1 percent nick is almost as gratifying as one with a 10 percent gouge. But whatever the hit, the entire deal becomes more tenuous and closure less sure. Commitment is weakened, confidence is shaken, and time is lost. Problems can erupt; days are wasted, deals delayed, relationships ruptured and reputations ruined—all silly sacrifices on the high altar of ego worship and gamesmanship.

Morality is not the issue here. Straight pragmatics is what we promote. We count numbers and keep score, with no special points given for being "fair" or "nice." Know, however, that the race we run is a marathon—our time frame extends well beyond the close of the current deal—and what will be remembered as a good deal tomorrow defines what must be considered as a good deal today.

DESCRIBING A GOOD DEAL

A deal is good when it optimizes objectives. This general definition means that solutions must be found for most problems under consideration. But "optimal" is different for each party and for the deal as a whole. From each side's separate viewpoint, a good deal fulfills most of that side's wants and needs—irrespective of the impact on the other side. In other words, as long as your side is content, it matters not a whit how the other side comes out.

A "best" deal, then, is the maximum you can reasonably expect to get combined with the minimum you can reasonably expect to give. This is what you "give" in deals:

- The value and consideration, the cash and stuff you paid or received.
- The risks assumed, such as the potential default by the other side.

- The opportunity costs incurred, such as the lost chances to do other deals.

When both sides of the deal are assessed at the same time, a deal is good when it optimizes objectives of both parties. A deal is "best" when it achieves the maximum total goals of every side while sustaining minimum risks all around. Using this collective definition, a "good deal" is not all that common and a "best deal" is indeed a rare commodity. Most deals have uneven value to the opposing parties. A best deal for one side is likely to be only a good deal for the other.

Good deal making is a means to an end, not an end in itself. Though it is satisfying to do good deals, the source of that satisfaction should be the higher goals being attained—not a showcase for advancing ego. All parties to a deal should be satisfied on signing, enthusiastic during execution, delighted on completion, and pleased on reflection. Solution sets that achieve nonconflicting objectives are always present in deals and should be sought aggressively.

A deal can be considered good when it fulfills at least minimum goals of all participants. A good deal is as good 10 months after closing as it is after 10 minutes. Good deals should stand the test of time and be remembered fondly 10 years hence.

UNEQUAL ROLES IN GOOD DEALS

Don't misunderstand. We build no safety nets under weaker parties. Social support has no place in this definition. Bleeding hearts we bar. The toughness of the marketplace must dominate. Deal makers must consider the other side simply because it makes smart business sense in the long run—not because it is a nice thing to do. This point is vital.

Unequal outcomes result from unequal positions. Each side is seeking good, better, and best for itself. The contest is adversarial and "win-lose" (i.e., if one side gets more the other side has less). The rules of the game, even when known, are not always fair. You play deal maker, therefore, very much at your own risk. Final decisions are yours alone.

A good deal does not require each party to play an equal role, to achieve the same degree of success, or even to make money. Natural power is distributed according to pre-existing patterns. For example, if a liquidator buys end-of-the-season merchandise below cost, the manufacturer seems to lose money. But if the manufacturer's overall costs are covered, the conversion of the unsalable inventory into ready cash produces a profit.

In another example, when a company with a tax-loss carryforward and low profits pays a whopping price to purchase a company with substantial profits, the deal can be good for both sides. The buyer thinks in terms of the acquired company's pretax income (which it shelters from tax) and the seller thinks in terms of receiving top dollar.

How about a more extreme example? Assume you are able to purchase a company in serious financial trouble by assuming only part of its outstanding liabilities. The previous owners wind up with residual debt and a negative worth. Is this a good deal by our definition? The answer is "yes," if it is the arrangement the sellers can construct under the circumstances. (In these dire situations, good deal makers like to give something positive to the other side. Here a multi-year, personal consulting contract is one possibility.)

RELATIVITY MAKES DEALS GOOD

Variety in deals is endless. No two are exactly alike. Good deals, however, have one facet in common: Comparisons are always made and assessments are always relative. Satisfaction is achieved to the extent that each party feels relatively positive about the outcome. The key word is "relatively." To find out what it means, we explore a peculiar aspect of human nature.

Human beings are creatures of comparison. We react emotionally to recent events, even when it makes no sense to do so. Consider the following situation.

You own 1000 shares of a stock selling for months at $20 per share. On Monday you hope but don't expect the price to rise. Suddenly, on Tuesday, there is a rumor of an unfriendly takeover and the stock shoots up to $30. You are elated. You are also $10,000 richer, at least on paper. You tell your spouse, kids, relatives, friends, perhaps plan some long-wanted pleasure purchase—you're a hero. Then, on Thursday, the target company sues and the raider backs off. While there may be other suitors, no one surfaces and the stock drops to $24 where it closes on Friday.

You are depressed. *Even though you are $4000 richer on Friday than you were on Monday,* you feel terrible—after all, you just "lost" $6,000. This emotional relativity is what we mean by saying that humans are creatures of comparison. Your mental attitude with the stock at $24 is controlled by your mental attitude when the stock was $30 (however momentary the event) and not when it was languishing at $20.

Now, for the sake of argument, we make the middle of the week disappear. There is no dramatic announcement of an unfriendly raid. Rumors of merger or acquisition build slowly. The company states it might begin negotiations. The stock moves smoothly from $20 to $24 over the course of the week. And on Friday, you are feeling fine—after all, you just "made" $4000.

The same relative emotions dominate in deal making. Absolute assessment of transactions carries less weight than logic would suggest. "Good" is appraised, consciously or unconsciously, in relation to other real or imagined alternatives. The closer you think your deal is to the best deal, the better you feel. The better you feel, the likelier you are to make that deal.

There is another, invidious kind of comparison skulking around deal making. This is the comparison *between or among* parties. All too often, one side blows a superb deal simply because it feels that the opposing side is getting a "better" deal. The truth or falsity of the attitude is irrelevant. Judging motivations of the other side is impossible. Furthermore, it doesn't matter how successful the other side is if your objectives are achieved. Nixing a deal because of ego imbalance is akin to cutting off your nose to spite your face. Good deal makers evaluate what *they* get, not what others get. They like their noses uncut.

WHY DEALS GET DONE

At first blush, doing deals seems unlikely. How can human nature allow it? Agreement on terms and conditions appear impossible. Yet dozens of healthy-sized deals, hundreds of mid-sized deals, and thousands of smaller ones are consummated every day. Deals get done because, ultimately, each side comes to believe that it is getting more than it is giving. Making each side believe that it is emerging as a winner is the critical essence of doing good deals.

WHY WORK GOOD DEALS

Good deal making is the way of dynamic action, potent growth, competitive edge. This is the frontier, the comparative advantage for contemporary business people. Good deal making is intense, gutsy, spirited, aggressive. Good deal making, in short, propels companies and catapults careers.

Edge-getters, however, often wind up with few deals and fewer friends. They can be found spinning endless hero stories of long-forgotten transactions. In deal making, if you will pardon one more lovemaking analogy, you can play by yourself but it just isn't as much fun.

WHAT'S A GOOD DEAL MAKER?

Inherited talent is not a necessity. Desire is important, no, *very* important. So is intensity. And never forget dedication and persistence. (Don't worry, I won't let you.)

Attitude. Substance. Skill. These are the three pillars that support good deal makers. *Attitude* is personality of the deal maker. *Substance* is content of the deal. *Skill* is deal-making technique.

What's the classic picture of a superb deal maker? What image pops into your mind's eye? Probably a sophisticated banker type, a denizen of New York's financial district, bedecked with three-piece suit, expensive jewelry, styled haircut, and big cigar.

Despite the visual sterotype, many of these folks are truly outstanding deal makers. They have to be. Whatever their external appearance, they know how to cut a deal—exacting maximum value and consideration while risking minimum fracture and rupture. They are intense, smart, single-minded, committed. Investment banking is a deal-making profession, with the largest financial stakes on earth, and those who rise to the top are the cream of the crop. How these deal makers conduct their craft and how they work their wonders, forms the foundation for the chapter.

A sharp business person is a sharp deal maker—someone who formulates, evaluates, and implements various transactions, someone who works with sensitivity and finesse. Such a person plans, organizes, strategizes, and structures the interchange of products, services, and financial considerations between companies and people. Such an animal, common wisdom assumes, survives in the marketplace jungle by wit and scheme—these being claw and fang—with only raw cunning providing protective cover. Yet the best business people live by reputation, the evidence of past deals done well, and the image of personal integrity long lasting.

Good deal makers defy stereotype. They cannot be easily classified. They can be female, minority, young or old. They can be doctoral graduates or high school dropouts. They can work in large companies or off by themselves. The sole distinguishing characteristic is their capability and compulsion to do good deals. To fulfill this one passion, they are united by drive and determination.

Good deal makers want the other side to know what they're doing. They want to involve the senior decision maker intimately in the process. If your opponents aren't knowledgeable and personally involved, it is more likely they can back out later—after you've expended money and effort and, most costly of all, forfeited other opportunities.

This rule, as you might expect, has exceptions. The idea of intimately involving the chief decision maker of the other side applies only when your property is first rate. Your stuff is hot and you won't waste time with lookers and tire kickers. However, when you are trying to unload, shall we say, inferior merchandise, you play a different game.

If the top guy gets involved too soon, the deal could be history. The "Sunk Cost" principle applies here. You want the other side to "invest" their time, money, effort, and ego in examining the deal. Nothing dishonest, mind you. Just let them sell themselves. Let them take their time. Then, with higher costs already "sunk," they may not scuttle the junk. They're less likely to fold the hand and more likely to stay in the pot and see the next card. After all, they have to justify their already-gone investment. More about Sunk Costs later.

ACTION PRINCIPLES FOR GOOD DEAL MAKERS

I like *four* action principles that mark good deal makers: choosing deals wisely, developing common interests, achieving personal objectives, and building personal careers.

Choose Your Deals Wisely

Don't squander your efforts. The most critical moment in making good deals is often overlooked. The decisive point comes up front, right at the beginning, *before* you start negotiating. I've said it once and I'll say it again: *It is better to do a good deal poorly than a poor deal well.* Your chances of success are affected dramatically by the type and nature of the deal you've chosen to do. Sensing "do-ability" of a deal is an art developed through insight and experience. (We promote the former with principles and with cases.) Time, too, is a valuable resource and it cannot be squandered on unlikely prospects. The tick of the clock is a professional deal maker's primary asset. Time allocated is the highest cost of doing business.

Develop Common Interests

Don't ignore the needs and wants of the other side. The best deal makers have a keenly developed sense of "people assessment." They just seem to know where that elusive bottom line falls—the absolute minimum that various parties must have for the deal to happen. They can differentiate necessity from desire. They can decide when to give something to their opponents and when not to. The ability to so distinguish is not limited to assessing the other side.

Power relationships shift as deals develop, and you must be able to make similar judgments—necessity versus desire—for your own side as well.

Achieve Your Objectives

Don't polish your ego at the expense of doing your deal. The best deal makers keep their goals clearly in mind and never allow personality conflict or narcissistic intrusion to deflect a straight run for the gold. Don't worry what others get; don't worry what others think. Just know what you want to accomplish. Keep your eye on that ball and don't allow extraneous pressures to distract you. A good deal maker is constantly enhancing his or her perceived power. The trick is track record. Everyone wants to associate with a winner.

Build a Career, Not a Caper

Don't misjudge the point of good deal making. It's not about personal puff before peers or press. It's not about gambits and games, strokes and schemes, sophistry and duplicity. It is about accomplishment and triumph, winning big and winning long. Constructing a career is a long-term program; copping a caper is a short-term heist. If you plan only one deal, go read the one-upmanship books and play the intimidation game. A fast-talking huckster, said to be veneer all the way through, was fabulous at one deal, and maybe a second, but inevitably the bubble would burst and his deals would self-destruct.

HOW TO LEARN THE SKILLS

Consider three steps in learning to use deal-making skills:

1. *Understand.* Understanding the deal-making skills and secrets means more than reading the words. It means knowing the essence. Picture how each would be worked by professional deal makers. Play with the skill or secret. Examine how it behaves under different deal conditions (e.g., when the stakes are large or small) and explore how it affects diverse deal situations (e.g., when negotiating with good guys or bad guys).

2. *Image.* Imaging the deal-making skills and secrets means picturing how you would put each one into productive use in your own deal-making life. Project yourself into potential negotiations and watch yourself employing each specific skill or secret smoothly and suavely. Feel comfortable and free, wholly at ease. See the actual image in your mind's eye and hear the actual dialogue in your mind's ear. Construct give-and-take exchanges; gauge your responses and monitor your emotions. (This process of pretending is called "simulation," doing something, as it were, without actually doing it.)[4]

3. *Utilize.* Utilizing the deal-making skills and secrets means literally putting each one into practice. Don't fear failure—learn from it. Fear is the only thing to fear. Sure, you'll feel awkward at first, but just as with learning a foreign language, you must use it to know it. Concentrate on two or three skills or secrets at a time, no more. If any don't work, figure out why—and then try it again. The more you use them, remember, the better they work.

FIVE IDEA-SKILLS FOR DEAL MAKING

The following five deal-making idea-skills discussed here set apart leading negotiators from haggling hacks. They should live inside you and form the core of your natural deal-making instincts. These idea-skills should become second nature, loading automatically into your subconscious whenever you commence deal-making behavior.

Know the Attitudes and Elements Of Deal Making

Knowledge builds confidence and competitive edge. Your effectiveness in using each deal skill and secret will increase as you appreciate the structure of the deal-making process. Picture this image: each deal skill and secret is a tree and the deal-making process is a forest. Your task is to see how each tree builds and blends with the entire forest and how the forest gives context to the tree. Seat-of-the-pants deal making is fine for some sharpies, but most mortals need some assistance in grasping the subjective aspects of each deal skill and secret.

Know What You Want to Achieve

It's self defeating to judge by comparison. Jealousy and envy are diversions for deal makers. They erect obstacles for making good business. Worry about yourself, and let the other side worry about itself. Don't get hot over what

---

[4]Simulation is used by pilots to practice realistic flying while grounded safely on solid earth. They use computer-controlled trainers that create the entire effect with all the right sights, sounds and shakes. Simulation of a different kind is used by professional athletes, such as tennis players and golfers, to image their strokes and improve their game.

your opponents get, and don't be bugged by their apparent satisfaction. Be pleased with what your side gets, and be content with your own satisfaction.

Good deal makers can segregate their own needs and wants from those of others. However, to do so, you need preparation and self-confidence. For instance, if you sell your business at the price and with the terms you want, you should have no gripe when the buyer makes even more money over time.

Discern What the Other Side Wants to Achieve

Project yourself to the other side of the table. Float down into the seats of those with whom you are dickering. What are their real requirements? What's on their "wish list"? What are they looking for in the deal—bottom line—and how important is it? Most critically, what are their priorities?

Often, giving others what they want will *not* take away from what you can get for yourself. But gaining such insight does not come quickly or easily: You must develop sensitivity to people and awareness of situations. For example, if the owner of a closely held company wants to sell out in order to retire, there is meaning beyond money. Maximum price can become secondary to special terms and conditions. Such an owner might well sell the business—a beloved "baby"—to a buyer offering a lower price, if the owner believed that these new managers would take better care of the family legacy (including employees, products, customers, community, and reputation) than those offering a higher price. The best deal makers always go for the emotional heart of the other side's interest—especially when it's not price.

Seek "Win-Win" Solutions

Search for areas where each side can achieve certain of its goals without adversely affecting the other side. In the language of "game theory," such sectors are called "win-win," since one side is not compelled to "lose" (i.e., give up something it likes) whenever the other side "wins" (i.e., gets something it likes).

How to find a win-win solution? Establishing common ground is key. Examine each aspect, element, and component of the deal. Go through all the pieces and particulars of the transaction several times—you never know where these optimal regions will turn up. Win-win intersections can be surprisingly broad if one has the foresight to search for them, the insight to develop them, the perception to recognize them, and the resolution to employ them. When one structures deals with innovation and intelligence, win-win solutions emerge constantly.

For example, a company acquiring a family business might replace some of the cash purchase price with its own equity stock. Such a modification may "win" for the selling parties by giving them a sense of participation and continuance, and "win" for the buying parties by diminishing the amount of cash they must dish up and fork over. What happens here can happen often: In a very real sense, the buyer pays less and the seller receives more.

Think Alternatives and Solution Sets

The best deal makers multiply their options. They think on several levels at the same time; they plan for contingencies. The unexpected they expect; the unimagined they imagine. They are constantly watching over their shoulder with one eye and over the horizon with the other.

Experienced negotiators keep diverse alternatives ready, like having several relief pitchers always warming up in the bullpen. They play "what-if" scenario games, devising creative responses to dummied-up problems. Expecting surprise at all times, professional deal makers are never surprised. They know how to hit curve balls even while waiting for sliders.

"Solution sets" suggest a family of related ideas available for bridging gaps and resolving conflicts. No professional ever relies solely on one "perfect" solution to negotiating disputes. Perfection is impossible in the crazy-quilt world of human bargaining. Total control can never be exercised in deal making. There are too many issues, too many people, too many agendas—many of which can be hidden and all of which can be contentious. Deal makers who think in terms of solution sets are better able to fine tune their deal structures. Optimizing the interests of both buyer and seller is the objective. That's the meaning of win-win.

THE SECRETS OF GOOD DEAL MAKING

What are the "secrets" in deal making? I like the concept. It stresses knowing and doing, remembering and applying. More particularly, it underscores the *active* accumulation of deal-making knowledge, and the internal storing of fresh ideas. Practice, not theory, cuts ice.

You must feel it inside. Often there's just no time for studied response. If you stop to think, you're stopped forever. If you hesitate, you could be lost. Deal makers must be driven by instinct to react properly under all circumstances. How to train those instincts? You need the right reflexes. That's the message here.

In a deal-making context, the word "secret" has two meanings. First, since the ideas presented here are often ignored by our deal-making populace they are, in a sense, "secret." Second, you can gain relative advantage over other deal makers, especially in the long run, by keeping these ideas "secret."

Following are seven deal-making "secrets" to train your instincts for rapid response.

Be Fair But Be Frank

Some of the toughest business people are also some of the fairest. Getting the upper hand should be gotten out of your head. But *conceding* the upper hand should be stricken from your mind. Don't seek personal domination. But don't appear frail, fragile, feeble, or flimsy, either. Remember, doormats get stepped on; placemats, eaten on; dishrags, wiped with. None of these textile-types do good deals (the soles of shoes, bottoms of plates, and dirt from dinner don't build negotiating strength).

Being fair does not mean being weak. Weakness, in fact, disrupts deals by tempting the other side to expand expectations and swell demands. Creating false hopes—building appetite without satisfaction—is not conducive to good deal making.

Let the other side realize that you know the nature of their game, the way they change the rules, and what their players have in mind. For example, if you decide to do business with a certain company regardless of price, be sure that they know that you know the score. If that supplier thinks they've pulled a fast one this time, they will try to pull a faster one next time. The price, already high, will go even higher. (As in the jungle, weakness is attacked mercilessly, and the nick will swell to a gouge.)

However, if the supplier realizes that you know what's going on—that you've decided to do business *in spite* of the high price (for whatever reason, say quick delivery), they will respect your strength. You may get a more reasonable price the next go-round. Respect encourages fairness.

Heave Hype

Hype helps? Well, that depends. Hype can sometimes sell a first deal, but never a second. (Fool me once, shame on you; fool me twice, shame on me!)

Exaggeration is a short-term, rapidly depleting asset—and a long-term, quickly accruing liability. Hype is usually either a bad habit or a desperate act. Be advised, neither is good for deal making. Just try negotiating again with someone you've jiggled. The French Resistance was no tougher than what you'll face.

If all you have is one deal to make, be my guest, make my day—have at it. Though I admit I've done it myself, I don't recommend hyping it; nor have I ever met a person who has only one deal to do. So give hype the old heave ho.

Be Conservative

Always be moderate in projecting your most likely results. Make reasonable and restrained public pronouncements. Aim forecasts below center. Strive to exceed to pessimistic projection rather than fall behind an optimistic one.

Develop Alternative Scenarios

Allow the other side choices in assessing your analysis. (This transfers some of the burden.) Give them room—and keep your options open.

What impact would various internal surprises or external shocks have on your company? For example, what might happen to cash flow if sales rose or fell 10 percent? 20 percent? 30 percent? What if competition pressured prices? What if interest rates escalated? What if two surprises or shocks hit simultaneously? Such "sensitivity analysis" is particularly apt for buyers and sellers of businesses and for lenders and borrowers of debt.

Sensitivity analysis should also be used to examine the position on the other side of the table. Such appraisal will probably be qualitative in character, more descriptive than numerical, providing more insight than facts. What are best guesses of your opponent's current position and possible options? Are they really at the wall or can they be coaxed just a bit further back?

Admit Uncertainty

Don't be afraid to profess doubt about parts of your package. Point out, for example, where some of your numbers or statements may be slightly suspect. Business information cannot be that perfect or that precise. Honesty enhances credibility, and careful admissions can be most disarming. (Try using such high-powered honesty when battling a cynic; it can melt the most hard-bitten deal maker.)

In preparing a proposal for bank financing, for example, a company should enumerate all assumptions precisely, pointing out areas of difficulty or ambiguity. Potential problems should be exposed by design, rather than be hidden by default. The honesty shown will be a potent force for augmenting confidence.

I'm not advocating, of course, spilling the beans, singing like a canary, hauling skeletons out of the closet, picking through your garbage, turning over all the rocks (and other such tattletale cliches). Taking truth serum is not the idea here. Improving credibility is.

You don't have to tell the whole truth, but be sure that whatever you do tell is in fact true. Deal makers are grownups. The rules of the game assume each side carries its own weight.

Address Questions Nobody Asked

Use this one deal-making secret for surprise. But use it cautiously. Few moves are more impressive than when one side brings up sensitive subjects regarding its own position that the other side has not considered. It enhances believability enormously—not to mention how the shock value can disorient the other side.

Such superfrank actions are good counterattacks to credibility problems. Say the company has fallen behind its sales projections and as a result its bank is beginning to question everything. A daring technique is to show your account officers something *else* they missed about the company, say a collection problem with minor accounts. Such "credibility enhancers" can become "credit enhancers." (This technique, be advised, is a bit of brinkmanship; there is danger that your new admission will undercut an already shaky house.)

One must be careful not to go overboard. Most people are conditioned to assume that their deal-making opponents aren't telling the whole truth anyway. Some deal makers always shave ("haircut") projections by 10 to 30 percent. By giving a pessimistic reading as your most likely case, you run the risk of having this low-ball projection subjected to the same financial clippers. A double haircut you don't need; baldness in transactions does not mean deal-making virility.

Think Image Not Ego

Act as if your deal opponents are your public relations agents. In a way, they will be. No matter how confidential the negotiations, no matter how secret the deal, other people will hear about it. Regardless of how you envision yourself, what circulates about you is how others see you. Your reputation is cast by the look in their eyes when your name is mentioned. Deal makers' reputations are their most valuable asset. Such an asset is not to be hidden away but made manifest openly.

It's in poor taste to parade your supposed superiority. Such conceit will boomerang and slap you on the backside. Whatever you dish out, so will you be dished. It comes down to this: What's your thing, getting the edge and puffing your ego, or building the business and promoting your career? You can "win" the battle of making one deal, and still lose the war of making many.

HOW TO FIND DEAL IDEAS

"Finding a new deal is like looking for my lunch," the street-smart cab driver informed me. "I know it's somewhere, maybe in the fridge, maybe in the microwave—I'll spot it if I just keep moving."

Some people assume that deal making is a black art, draped in secrecy and cloaked with mystery. Many novices, it seems, are on a search for dark sayings, the one special incantation for wrapping up negotiations and finishing up deals. The quest for deal making's holy grail is, regrettably, a vain one.

Never underestimate the difficulty of doing a deal. Closing a contract, even a small one, can be frightfully complex. So many things can misfire: changing conditions can trigger valuation disputes; personality clashes can incite emotional conflict; new options can cause second thoughts.

Always be on guard. Gremlins abound to muck up the works. Assume there are legions of deal-smashing demons lurking around. Most are not rational, but all are out to get you. Anything that can go wrong, says a famous lawmaker, probably will. Deals rupture with the slightest provocation. Busted transactions are more rule than exception.

The window for completing a deal is often small, and narrows quickly. I'm often asked to estimate the probability of making a particular deal happen. My answer usually hovers in the 10 to 20 percent region *if* all parties have already agreed to *all* significant terms and conditions! Surprised it's so low? (Note that we speak of a time *before* attorneys become involved, which, by the way, explains part of the high failure rate.)

I'm often amused to watch amateur deal makers splitting the spoils of undone deals. They deplete energy, waste time, and strain ego arguing over who gets what percentage—when the transaction itself hasn't a hope of actually working. Believe me, if you're ever tempted to call any deal "easy," bite your tongue.

The most important part of deal making comes right up front, *before* any negotiations begin. When you start negotiating a specific deal, you've already made your biggest decision. Choosing which deals to try and which to pass determines the end result more than all other factors combined.

How do you pick the best deals? The first step is to procure more prospects. Efficiency in deal making means selecting the most "do-able" deals. Such efficiency is increased by enjoying a large number of possible transactions. Multiple choices means higher efficiency. So, expand opportunities, augment alternatives, multiply options.

Finding deals is fun. You always await the next lead with eager anticipation. It is also frustrating. You get to run, it seems, all the blind alleys.

Generating ideas for new deals is not as important as recognizing them when they smack you in the face. It's easy to seek a certain deal, and not so easy to find what you seek. And if you do, perchance, discover the end of your rainbow, what spate of arrogance makes you think you'll negotiate reasonable terms?

Major investment banks, representing corporate clients, use sophisticated methods to screen merger and acquisition candidates.[5] However, comprehensive computer searches can just generate paper, not to mention fees. Better, in our tightly wired world, is the grapevine.

Who's around and what's happening? The more you talk, the more you find out. Lawyers and accountants are a good source of tips and leads; they keep close touch with their clients and know who could be ready to deal. Whenever you hear something that might have potential, don't hesitate—follow it up. The worst you can get is a cold "no, thanks." But even a negative reply can lead to "Its's not for me, but I'll keep you in mind . . ." Or, better yet, "I'm not interested, but I'll tell you who is . . ."

The game is called "networking;" it really works, and you should learn the rules. Networking is not just for big-time executives and lawyers on the one hand or for ex-hippies and swinging singles on the other. It is a generic technique that simply makes sense. The more people you know, the more people who know you, the greater your chances for making something happen.

Kinds of Ideas: Whether Buy or Sell Side

Generating fresh ideas is the key for multiplying options in deal making. The more alternatives from which you can choose, the greater your chances to make good choices. When jousting in the deal-making arena, flexibility means strength.

Good deal makers are effective and efficient when

- Choosing which deal to do and
- Using skills and secrets to do the deal.

---

[5]Computerized databases now contain virtually every conceivable number on every industry, every public company, and many private companies. It is possible to set extraordinarily specific criteria, generate a list of potential candidates, and have the hard copy on your desk in minutes. For example, you can call up all firms that do 50 percent or more of their business in health care, have revenues between $20 million and $150 million, have at least two years profitability above 5 percent (pretax) but below 15 percent (to keep the price down,), have minimal inside control (below 5 percent of the voting stock), and are located in California or the Northeast.

The key here is to provide real alternatives. Don't get caught with one deal being a critical necessity. Be independent and a bit remote. Such autonomy and distance is a spine-stiffener and bully-stopper, a bulwark against high-pressure shakedown.

Buyers and sellers have different attitudes about the sale. When selling something, whether a company asset such as a factory or a personal possession such as a house, the more potential buyers the merrier. After all, enlarging your net and extending its reach increases the odds of catching the biggest fish.

But when sellers attract numerous proposals, how close in price are the offers? Usually they fall within a tight range of one another. Almost inevitably, however, one or two bidders will ante up additional chips. Why do they stretch? For diverse reasons, from business necessity to personal interest—but none of them matter. What does matter is locating these premium players.

As a seller, the more you listen the more you learn. There is no substitute for up-to-the-minute, in-the-trenches marketplace information. But there is a point of diminishing returns. Progressively more input produces progressively less output. Once you've learned what you can learn, efficiency craters.

The same principles hold true on the buy side. Shopping around, "kicking the tires" of various deals and getting a feel for current conditions, is vital.

Receptivity to New Ideas

Original ideas have two purposes in deal making:

- Discovering new deals.
- Discerning new ways to do old deals.

Fresh thinking enhances each element of the deal-making process. Always be ready to intervene with a new thought to break a deadlock, bridge a gap, change an attitude, or shift the power.

At this stage of deal making, it is important not to over analyze or dismiss any notion too quickly. When multiplying options, allow no negative thoughts. Admit no worry about working. If you don't devise some "off the wall" ideas now, you're shooting too low. (See Volume I, Chapter 11 for a discussion of the creative process in investment banking.)

New ideas mean nothing in themselves. What's the sense of coming up with novel thoughts if nobody will listen to them? Being receptive to new ideas sounds simple. It is not. Much of our social conditioning fights flux and change. Old ideas have high inertia. It takes a strong force to put them in motion and an even stronger force to throw them out. We are brought up to fear "being wrong." An error is an insult. Such defensiveness is devastating to creativity and counterproductive to deal making. Being wrong is the natural result of being creative. Being wrong is not bad. Being scared to be is.

Improving receptivity to new ideas, then, is an important aspect of deal making.

The following methods will help.[6] They apply whether the new ideas are discussed on your side alone or with both sides together.

Paraphrasing

Paraphrasing is a method through which the listener uses his or her own words to repeat the new idea back to the original speaker. Stay faithful to the essence of the idea and the important specifics. Check your understanding with the speaker ("Let me see if I grasp your point . . ."). Keep the paraphrase free of evaluation or opinion. The task here is two-fold: (1) to define a mutual starting place, and (2) to keep the idea and its originator actively engaged.

Developmental Response

The development response technique guides the new, raw idea toward a more workable solution. First, state the pros of the idea—the elements you want to preserve. Next, explain how each pro is useful. Be specific and genuine, listing at least one pro more than comes easily. Often a valuable contribution comes from this last, hard-to-give pro. Then state the cons, phrasing each one to invite solution. As you consider and correct each con separately, the modification process will transform the original idea. The final solution may not even resemble the original suggestion. No matter what the outcome, give initial innovators credit, whichever side they're on.

Expert Sessions

Expert sessions, which were pioneered by Innotech[7], use specialists from widely divergent fields to brainstorm issues and problems. For example, a session searching for a painless blood sampling device included experts on

---

[6]See "Techniques for Fostering Innovation," by Richard Harriman, in *Handbook for Creative and Innovative Managers,* Robert Lawrence Kuhn, editor in chief (New York: McGraw-Hill, 1987). Mr. Harrison is chief executive officer of Synectics, Inc., a creativity and innovation company located in Cambridge, Massachusetts.

[7]Innotech is a creativity-facilitating company located in Turnbull, Connecticut. See "Toolbox for Practical Creativity," by R. Don Gamache, in *Handbook for Creative and Innovative Managers,* Robert Lawrence Kuhn, editor in chief (New York: McGraw-Hill, 1987).

mosquitos, acupuncture, magic, hypnosis, and electronics—medical doctors, and nurses, pointedly, were left out.

The creative sessions ask developing questions about new ideas ("What's good about it?"). Generally the most sparking gems are not noticed or appreciated when they appear. The ideas generated must be sifted and weighed afterwards like small nuggets of gold buried in heavy beds of mud.

Nonexpert Ideas

We are all too quick to reject simple-sounding words from simple-sounding people. Listening to nonexperts takes effort. Why should we pay attention to inexperienced folk who don't know anything about the subject? The history of human knowledge tells a quite different tale. Many radical breakthroughs were made by nonexperts shattering tradition. Remember, a nonexpert is not encumbered by years of entrenched thought patterns, nor burdened down with predictable approaches to obstinate issues. When a deal is stymied by technical problems, say inventory evaluation or financial matters, a nonexpert can sometimes find a novel solution.

Ideas Couched in Question Form

This technique recognizes that people frequently float queries as "trial balloons." Questions are a comfortable way to introduce radical ideas that may sound absurd. The pattern occurs because people have been burned by harsh rejection of new thoughts. They are gun-shy. You must draw out the ideas from behind these questions. By being sensitive to such suggestions, and by encouraging the questioner to develop the idea further, you can tap into creative gold.

HOW TO CHOOSE THE RIGHT DEALS

How do you "know" whether a deal is likely to work? How can you develop your deal-making "nose" to sniff out do-able deals? There is only one answer: wisdom and insight undergirded by knowledge and experience.

The key to selecting the best deals is rigorous evaluation—the tough, tight analysis of the deal ideas, alternatives, and options. Some criteria for deal evaluation are discussed here.

Evaluation Question to Ask

Efficiency in deal making means choosing those deals most "do-able." *It's better to do the right deal wrong than the wrong deal right.* This is the first principle of good deal making (I told you I'd say it again). The following series of test questions address the deal strictly from your side's viewpoint:

- Is the deal identifiable and clear, easily understood, and readily explainable? (Deals should be simple.)
- Does the deal seem workable and practical, able to be put into practice with a minimum of hurdles to jump? (Deals should begin uncomplicated; even the plain ones become complex enough.)
- Does the deal take advantage of any competitive advantage; does it maximize any distinctive competencies or play up any special capacities? (If not, where's your edge?)
- Is the deal internally consistent with your side's goals, strengths and weaknesses, functional capacities, financial capital, human resources, and timing requirements? (Lack of internal consistency is the prime killer of deals.)
- Are the personal values and aspirations of your side's senior players being satisfied? Will the deal stimulate managerial effort and engender corporate commitment? (Good deals light your fire.)
- Does the deal consider the diverse participants of your side? (You don't need dissension when doing deals.)
- Can the deal be consummated and executed with the present organizational structure? If not, can the required alteration be handled? (You must assess the consequences of closing, as well as how to get the deal closed.)
- How does the proposed deal affect other deals currently being negotiated? What about any deals already consummated? (Deals that adversely affect each other are a double negative.)
- What is the risk/reward trade-off? Are the risks acceptable in economic and personal terms? (What are the consequences, for example, of a deal well bungled?)
- Can doing the deal trigger any unpleasant side effects, say a price war from competing bidders? (Deals that can kick back need a long second look.)
- Can the deal be assessed up front? Can its viability be checked? Can you forecast the effect of a closed deal *before* you actually close? Can you discern early indicators of results, such as market reaction? (Good deals reduce uncertainty.)
- Is the time sequencing of the deal elements realistic? (Good deals need clear deal-making paths.)

- Is the deal flexible enough to adapt to changing conditions arising during negotiations? How much are you locked in? (Good deals are malleable, able to meet new situations.)
- Are you "betting the company"—or your own career—on the success of the deal? (The rewards of good deals must far exceed their risks.)

Evaluation Techniques to Use

Consider a powerful "rejection rule" for deal evaluation: Any strategy or deal that does not either create or exploit an asymmetry in the environment constituting an advantage for the firm or the individual must be rejected. There are four "tests" in the evaluation procedure:[8] the Consistency test, the Importance test, the Structure test, and Smell test.

The Consistency Test

Is the deal internally consistent? Any deal that contains any conflicting or contradictory goals, objectives, or implications must be rejected. Thus, deals that require more cash than the company can pay, or will change the direction of the company in undesirable directions, are not good choices.

The Importance Test

Does the deal concern areas of relevance? Any deal that does not involve major and meaningful goals must be rejected. The relevance test highlights the consequences of issues—not the solving of problems. One must be sure that the deal involves the "right" values and consideration. Discriminating between importance and unimportance is the essence of deal-making wisdom. Thus, deals that enhance a company's current market share are more important than those that develop totally new businesses.

---

[8] I like to apply Richard Rumelt's rules for strategy evaluation to deal evaluation (to assess both which deal to do and how to do each deal). He stresses discovering "asymmetries," the lack of equality and evenness, in the environment. Under conditions of absolute equality, he says, "no one can predict which of two identical armies or corporations [or competing deal makers] will prevail . . . the winning strategy is always the same—play only those games in which you have an advantage . . . . one wins games by exploiting asymmetries that make a difference." Richard Rumelt, "Strategy Evaluation," in Dan Schendel and Charles Hofer, editors, *Strategic Management* (Boston: Little, Brown, 1979).

The Structure Test

Is the deal properly organized to enable successful completion? Any deal that is too diffuse or too constrained must be rejected. Unless there's real potential for completing the deal to your liking, trying to force it is wishful thinking and wasting time. Deals hung out as bait should be avoided.

The Smell Test

Is the deal likely to work? Any deal that is not likely to close must be rejected. Use your nose. For example, deals offered by deal makers with reputations for obstinacy or disruption are "smellier" than those offered by deal makers known for their reasonableness. Take a deep breath before plunging into a deal opportunity.

HOW TO SET THE GOALS

Where to go determines how to get there. Goals are the most discussed and least understood part of making deals. When deal makers plan their transactions, goals are often overlooked as obvious and simple and not worth worry or concern. Strategy and tactics are studied, but strategy and tactics to accomplish what? The setting of deal-making goals, not so obvious and not so simple, drive the deal-making process.

What Are Goals?

Goals are planned positions. They are results to be achieved, desired situations to be attained. By definition or default, deal makers must have goals. If a deal maker does not set formal goals, they are set nonetheless by default. A smart deal maker always sets formal goals. Figure 1 lists some characteristics that distinguish good goals from bad goals. From a corporate viewpoint, goals serve several purposes at the same time. For example, they

- Serve as guidelines for directing strategy.
- Function as guidelines for suggesting tactics.
- Assign team players to specific tasks.
- Focus the team on coordinating its efforts.
- Motivate the team and guide its behavior.
- Act as yardsticks with which to measure results.
- Provide the basis for feedback and control.

FIGURE 1
Goal Content Characteristics

Good Goals Are		*Bad Goals Are*
Clear	←——→	Vague
Specific	←——→	General
Focused	←——→	Diffuse
Contained	←——→	Boundless
Difficult	←——→	Easy
Consistent	←——→	Inconsistent
Measurable	←——→	Unmeasurable
Achievable	←——→	Unachievable

Deal Goals

Deal makers bring diverse goals into a negotiation. Some are more productive than others.

- *Satisfying your own needs.* This is a healthy, productive goal. You know your own bottom line—the minimum requirements you demand. Seek to get them or better them.
- *Thwarting the other side's needs.* This one is not so healthy or productive. Success is defined in the negative—stopping the other side cold. Your mission is to prevent them from achieving their bottom-line needs. Sometimes, of course, you can't help it, such as in adversary proceedings (e.g., when creditors seek to liquidate bankrupt companies).
- *Maximizing your desires.* A sound approach. Go for highest personal benefit. Seek to exceed minimum requirements. Start by establishing hard-to-reach goals.
- *Optimizing the other side's desires.* The best approach. Going for highest mutual benefit. Even in bankruptcies, both creditors and debtors gain from a successful turnaround.
- *Getting a bargain.* An emotional approach to goals. Few can resist a bargain—even when it's something they don't want and can't afford. Some deal makers will only buy a bargain. They will not close a transaction unless they believe they've gotten "such a deal" that they can't refuse. What's a bargain to these birds? Getting the lowest price around. Getting a hefty price reduction (forgetting where the price began). Getting the last item (it must be good). Getting something else "thrown in" free (whether you want it or not). Finally, the comparative test: if someone else says you got a bargain then you got a bargain.

Goal Components

Consider the various parts of a goal. Being conscious of each element helps set good goals.

Position (Where does the goal fit in the corporate or personal hierarchy?)

Content (What is the nature of the goal?)

Measure (What is the criterion of the goal?)

Level (What is the amount of the goal?)

Period (What is the time constraint of the goal?)

The following example shows how this "goal dissection" works. Here, the situation is (1) a search for the right acquisition candidate and (2) the proper negotiation of the deal. The acquiring company is a large conglomerate that seeks to strengthen one of its divisions, a medium-sized manufacturer of telecommunications equipment. Figure 2 shows how each component contributes to, and defines, the whole goal. Observe how the goals guide which deal to do and how to structure each deal. The five goals are picked by position in the corporate hierarchy.

- A *corporate* goal might be a financial return of 20 percent per year on shareholders' investment. (This suggests a certain price limit, below a specific price-earnings multiple, and possibly a certain debt structure, allowing leverage of equity.)
- A *divisional* goal might be an increasing amount of contribution income of $1 million every year. (This suggests certain revenue expansion and/or cost reduction opportunities.)
- A *marketing* goal might be an increasing market share of 5 percent in the first season by incorporating the new acquisition (raising total market share from 30 to 35 percent). (This suggests that new and old companies must not cannibalize each other's sales.)
- A *manufacturing* goal might be increasing the utilization rate of current facilities by 15 percent (from 75 to 90 percent) within 18 months, thereby absorbing additional overhead burden. (This suggests purchasing the target company's products and marketing resources, but not buying its manufacturing plants and equipment—an important, if difficult, negotiating strategy.)
- A *research and development* goal might be developing innovation synergy between the companies by technology transfer of four new products over 24 months. (This suggests that the R & D capabilities of the target company must be included in the deal.)

FIGURE 2
Goal Components of an Acquisition

Deal Component	*1*	*2*	*3*	*4*	*5*
Position	Corporate	Divisonal	Marketing	Manufacturing	Research and Development
Content	Financial return	Absolute dollars	Product scope and control	Facility use and overhead absorbtion	Innovation synergy
Measure	Return on equity investment	Contributional income	Increase in market share	Increase in utilization rate	Technology transfer of new products
Level	20%	\$1 million (increasing)	5% (30 ⟶35%)	15% (75 ⟶90%)	4
Period	Year	Year	Season	18 months	24 months

By so dissecting your goals, you could have a clearer image of what you want to achieve. You may not get all you want, but you'll understand what you want, and thereby come closer to your ideal.

Politics of Goal Setting

Goals would seem to be logical statements. In the real world, this is not necessarily so. Gone is the fiction that goals are set rationally and logically.

Good procedures include general commitment, especially by principals; belief in the meaningfulness of the outcome; easy communication up and down the deal-team hierarchy; feedback of results; healthy and spirited competition among peers.

But often, deal-making goals are set on the basis of power and position—just like other business decisions. The general rule is that each person or area seeks to maintain (or increase) his, her, or its relative strength and authority. Corporate politics (i.e., which individual or department will exercise control) is a major factor in setting deal-making goals.

Whoever has the boss' ear has a good grip on the company soul. Jockeying position and maneuvering people is the corporate bargaining game, and it's played hard and tough in deal making where the stakes are high and the prestige is powerful.

Individual Politics

Familiar with the organizational politician? We all know him (or her). What makes him tick? At the top of the list, this person fancies himself a deal maker, influencing goal setting whenever possible. He has consummate knowledge of company systems and people—not how they work on paper but how they work in reality, the informal relationships. He tracks opinion of superiors, senior managerial successors, even current sleeping arrangements. His favorite position? Controlling the flow of information. He's not too hot on authority; responsibility too soon can get you knocked out early. He's always seen with the right people (lunches are visible), and the "CEO-secretary game" he plays well. He chooses his tasks carefully, selecting only those that will work and win.

Departmental Politics

Departments, too, are creatures of politics. They act as if animate. Mere boxes on organizational charts, they have an uncanny sense of their own existence. It doesn't matter who's operating the shop, managers can come and go, there is constant pressure to sustain power and position, to maintain the established routine, and to keep the status quo. Departments will do anything to maintain their mystical being.

Deal making is both the greatest threat and the strongest ally of organizations. Deals are disruptive. They alter power and position, break up the established routine, and demolish the status quo. Organizations, or sub-groups within organizations, will kill to control deals and the deal-making process.

How Expectations Affect Goals

Power of Expectations

What you expect will happen influences what in fact does happen. The strength of what you anticipate alters both your strategy and the commitment with which you carry it out.

Changing Expectations

When anticipations change, deal making becomes less sure. Confidence in goals is shaken, strategy becomes unstable, and enthusiasm is sapped.

When Expectations Differ

A deal-making team with different goals is both weaker and stronger. Weaker in that strategies may conflict and dissension overflow. Stronger in that there is spirited discussion of issues, and "group think" (when everyone supports the same wrong-headed policy) is less likely.

HOW TO PLAN THE STRATEGIES

Strategy in deal making is a directed plan. It defines the approach. It links overall goals with operational tactics. It has specific, clear-cut objectives and describes the actions and reactions of decision makers to the shifts and changes of conditions. Strategy for a deal maker is like a hammer for a handyman or a bat for a baseball player. It is the tool that gets the job done. The better your strategy, the better your deals.

In this sense, strategy is the search for *competitive advantage,* for areas of relative strength that can coax, coddle or coerce favorable outcomes. Competitive advantage seeks to capitalize on your *distinctive competencies,* those aspects of the deal-making process where your side excels or can excel compared with the other side.

Assessing mutual strengths and weaknesses is the key to devising the best deal-making strategy. Compare your strengths and weaknesses to those of your opponent in the context of the deal issues. The result of this assessment is a series of alternative strategies. These various options for deal-making direction are then evaluated for probable outcomes, and the best are chosen to be put into action.

- *Creativity* promotes strategy formulation.
- *Consistency* directs strategy evaluation.
- *Structure* controls strategy implementation.

Scope of Strategy

Strategic thinking works for individuals as well as for companies. People can apply the thought processes for making personal decisions and planning personal deal making. For example, you can use the strategic method to resolve whether to push for a still higher salary at a prospective job or to negotiate a better position at your current job.

An honest assessment of your strengths and weaknesses in light of the employment opportunities and threats (e.g., the prospective versus current job) can be a critical part of the process. Careful consideration of diverse alternatives in light of overall lifetime goals is certainly worth the effort. (One would not, of course, need strategic thinking to make the vast majority of daily deals. Lifetime goals are irrelevant for buying a car or settling time-to-bed arguments with kids.)

When Planning Strategy

What to do first when planning your strategy? When negotiating or structuring a deal, do *not* focus on conjuring up tricky tactics. Gimmicks do not achieve goals. Plots sicken as they thicken.

Devising the *plan* must come first. Where do you want to go, and how will each step of the process help get you there? See ends from beginnings. Have a clear vision of the proposed path—even though that path will twist and turn often. Keep ultimate results in current focus. After each step of the deal, try to reconstruct your objectives. Are you proceeding on target? Or have you drifted? If you've strayed off course, can you get back on? Or should you now consider altering your objectives to conform to the new reality? Negotiating deals is a continuous series of course corrections and target shifts.

Strategic Attitudes

There are three general kinds of strategic attitudes in deal making. They are: (1) simple and direct, (2) press and push, and (3) cool and aloof.

Simple and Direct

Come right to the point. Say what you mean. The straightforward approach may be startlingly effective, disarming the other side and driving to quick resolution. Go "simple and direct" when you've worked with the other side before, the deal is bogging down, or immediate closure is a goal.

Press and Push

Here's where the shoving starts. Sensitive points are squeezed. To be effective, the pressing and pushing should be subtle. If the other side thinks that you are twisting arms, they will become resentful. Pressure is not some evil, alien torture. It is often the mechanism to get a deal closed.[9] "Press and push" when your side is stronger, the other side needs a quick close, or you want to assess limits.

Cool and Aloof

This approach uses reverse psychology. Play hard to get. Let the other side sell themselves. It can be marvelously effective. If you give points too quickly, if you're too compromise-minded, the other side may worry that they've undershot their potential. (I've been there, kicking myself when the positive response came a mite too easily.) Avoid tempting your opponents: Awakening latent greed is not smart. The key here is making the other side work when exacting the concession. Be "cool and aloof" when the other side is stronger, your side is under time pressure, or you have other alternative deals.

TACTICS TO CONSIDER

Attitudes and approaches to negotiating vary. In some situations, the "drip" is preferred, letting out demands little by little so as not to scare off the other

[9]On arrival in the United States, my father-in-law had to be "pressured" and "tricked" by a real estate agent to make an excellent purchase of a small apartment building. Having been buffeted by the business ways of his old country, my father-in-law was highly skeptical of everyone. There's no doubt that, left unpressured and untricked, he would have never bought anything. His investment of $15,000 grew to over $400,000 in 15 years, not to mention all the years of income, free rent, and meaningful work.

side. In different situations, the "drop" is preferred, with the whole load being dumped at once. The following 12 tactics are used commonly in negotiations. If you choose to use them, know how to thrust. If they're used against you, know how to parry. Consistency is vital here: Tactics must be matched to strategy.

Patience. You wait. However anxious, you don't show it. Patience is a devastating weapon when the other side is highly volatile. When you set the pace, you control the deal.

Slow Agony. The deal moves at a crawl. Every issue takes inordinate amounts of time. Delays are frequent. Slow agony never says "no"; the deal never actually stalls. This is an interesting defense against high pressure.

Apathy. Overt concern is minimal. Whether the deal goes or blows appears immaterial. You request without energy and respond without passion. Apathy defends against high pressure.

Empathy/Sympathy. Concern is shown for the other side. This is a powerful tactic for breaking deadlocks and bridging gaps. Such feelings should be genuine. Do not feign personal concern; compassion as a ruse is off limits. Use empathy/sympathy when you mean it.

Sudden Shifts. Whim and caprice do not build solid reputation. Consistency is important, but sometimes it equals sluggishness, even obstinacy. When talks are turgid and momentum has dissipated, unexpected changes can dislodge blockage and overcome obstacles. You have nothing to lose by shaking the tree.

Faking. Deal makers are like football halfbacks, able to feint one way and run the other. Faking is more trading than lying. Fake when you want to protect a particular point. For example, you might insist on all cash in selling your home (or business)—just to be able to maintain your price when you finally "concede" some seller financing—which you planned to "concede" all along.

Walking. Closing your briefcase and leaving the room. A dead deal. This tactic is less extreme than it looks. After all, you can always reopen negotiations (though some of your credibility is lost). Walking works when the other side has more basic power and has pushed too hard too long. Quitting is the ultimate leveler.

Fait Accompli. The threat to take unilateral action. The deal, or something about it, would be irrevocably changed. For example, when a finacially troubled company negotiates with creditors, each side can threaten to file bankruptcy proceedings—which would put all decisions in the hands of the court. Use *fait accompli* when you control a critical issue—but use it cautiously.

Salami. Cut a little here, a little there, and soon the salami is all gone. Some negotiators grind for small gain—but they never stop. The deal's never done. You must stop these people. Strict limits are the antidote for salami tactics.

Limits. Allow the other side to go so far but no farther. Setting boundaries can be imposing, even riveting. Don't do it often, but always make it count. Set your limits once and stick to them. Use this tactic when the other side keeps pushing.

Deadlines. Countdowns are contentious. Calendar pressure is troublesome. One must never make a hasty decision under time constraint. Try to force yourself to go even a bit slower than normal. If the deal evaporates, it evaporates. It's far better to pass a dozen good deals than to make one bad one.

Antagonism. Not a good tactic. More is accomplished by seeking personal harmony even during professional disputes. Nonetheless, people are antagonistic, some deliberately as a technique, others because that's just the way they are. Disarm the antagonist by side-steps, not body blocks, by leveraged angles, not frontal assaults. Direct confrontation rarely works. Try gentle correction, tinged with humor. "I see the new day hasn't brought forth a new attitude." "I can't toughen my position because you can't get more upset."

HOW TO BUILD THE STRUCTURES

So you've set glorious goals and plotted dynamic strategies. Feeling pretty powerful? Well, now comes the hard part: making those strategies work and reaching those goals. This is the moment of truth when words and papers are transformed into deeds and action. This is when machinery gets rolling and hands get dirty.

Structure in both process and content is needed to make the deal work. Thus, in deal making, structure has two meanings: It is the mechanism for putting the strategy into action during negotiations (process), and it is the actual way the deal is put together, the terms and conditions as they ultimately turn out (content).

Structure Your Strategy

Structure is to strategy as form is to function. The relationship is symbiotic: Each is dependent on the other. Each can cause the other. Start with a specific strategy, and the structure needed to implement it is defined. And if you start with a specific structure, the proper strategy is described.

Watch for strategy-structure relationships in deal making. For example, if a seller's strategy calls for an exceptionally high purchase price, then the deal's structure will probably have to include some noncash consideration (e.g., contingent future payments or seller financing). If, however, the deal's structure demands all cash, then the strategy must allow for a lower price.

The principles are parallel for personal deal making. Take salary negotiations. If your strategy is to absolutely maximize the amount of money you could conceivably put in your pocket, your structure might require a lower base salary coupled with a higher incentive bonus. If your structure requires a higher guaranteed amount, your strategy would have to be to accept a lower ceiling.

Structuring Your Negotiations

The stages of negotiation are important. They form a structural foundation. Though seemingly static, stages modulate pace and control direction. Good deal makers understand stages; they recognize where they fall and what should be done in each. The boundaries between these periods can be indistinct. Nevertheless, any negotiation can be dissected into five independent stages.

Stage 1: Deciding

Don't jump into the middle of a battle without choosing the right war. Too many people forget the preliminaries and lose the game before it begins. Determining whether and what to negotiate usually controls more of the outcome than all the strategies and tactics combined together (Deal Skills 6 and 7). What are your long-term goals and short-term objectives? Verbalizing what seems to be "obvious" may reveal elements that are not so obvious.

Stage 2: Preparing

Good lawyers write detailed briefs. Good scientists plan careful experiments. Doing your homework is essential. Maximum data should be accumulated early on, condensed down into concise information, and then transformed into critical knowledge—all before actual negotiating sessions are begun.

Understand the other side's positions and postures. Separate superficial stances from fundamental necessities. Get your hands on all possible information—numbers, public reports and statements, press clippings, even private opinions. Do a self-analysis as if from your opponent's point of view.

Note the distinction between "data" (raw facts), "information" (facts that are organized and categorized), and "knowledge" (facts that have meaning and implications). The problem in organizations is often too much data, not too little. The need is for better data reduction, not more data collection.

Stage 3: Initiating

At the beginning of negotiations, positions are presented and images are portrayed. Healthy self-interest demands proper mutual respect. Good deal makers put priority on establishing good rapport at the outset. Power plays of meeting location, seating arrangements, first proposals, and instant deadlines are common. These opening gambits are generally more irritating than effective. What you want to establish is common ground.

Stage 4: Continuing

Keep going, and don't despair. Persistence and patience are assets in protracted deal-making discussions. Progress will never zip along in straight lines, so don't expect the impossible. Watch out for emotional ploys, feints of sudden disruption (or sympathy-attracting weakness), and trumped-up issues. Remember, neither high speed nor straight direction is quite in the cards. Be satisfied with minor movement.

Good deal makers can overcome frustration. Obstacles can be circled, hurdles can be jumped. Go back to the beginning and ask why you are there. Reiterate your initial objectives. Sticking points are often the result of artificial ego hindrances. "Saving face" often means losing deals. Novelty is an effective win-win tactic. Try generating fresh sets of alternatives to overcome inertia, especially when negotiations stall.

Stage 5: Concluding

Have the good sense to finalize when finished. Many deals have been ruptured after having been made because one side did not stop pressing for advantage (which is often more cosmetic than substantial).

What is your attitude when seeing your opponent fulfill needs and achieve goals? This is a marvelous test for the professional deal maker. If you can kick yourself for not asking more, you're still in the amateur ranks. If you feel genuine satisfaction, you're well on your way to making it in the pros.

Structuring Your Deals

The Other Side's Price

"Your price, my terms," is a classic phrase attributed to various legendary deal makers. Essentially, this saying sums up an entire philosophy about structure in four easy words. It speaks volumes about deal making.

A seasoned buyer likes to give people "their price." Why? Not good-heartedness, though compassion is no vice. By delivering their price, you know you can beat competition and make your deal—and that's surely a virtue. Price is a solid number, easily remembered and simply repeated. When getting their price (or close to it), people feel good about themselves, because they achieved their goal. The fact that terms of payment weren't exactly as anticipated is no major matter—especially when the story is recounted to friends over drinks at the club.

Your Side's Terms

A seasoned buyer also likes to provide substantial margins of safety. You like to maintain maximum flexibility—time to work in the new operation and room to maneuver if things should go awry. Good deal makers are usually willing to pay more in exchange for postponed payments. If sellers wait, they get more; if they can't or (won't), they get less—this is the rule of the deal-making jungle. The buyer is happy to pay interest. Where else can you get a non–asset-supported, nonguaranteed loan on a risky business? And it is especially true when the future payments are contingent on performance.

Good deal makers will always give up a good portion of the upside to gain real protection on the downside. Proportion is not the issue here. It's worth much to a buyer to make a deal less likely to crater. The difference between major success and modest success is small compared to the vast difference between minor success and major failure. A deal maker likes to sleep at night.

Mutual Victory

Structuring deals is the best route to win-win resolution. It is the mechanism by which opposing interests have a chance at harmony. When I'm asked to "structure a deal," I focus on how or where can I get more for my side without taking away a similar amount from the other side. My opponent's hide is the last place I look to gouge (or slice). Improving the deal is infinitely easier when both sides gain, even if one side (my side) gains a little more.

For example, if you are buying some products from a vendor, look for other products offered by the same firm that you might need. Determine prices for each item separately, giving the impression that if you buy anything at all, it'll be one or the other, certainly not both. After working the best price for each individually, and maybe walking away for a while to show the serious possibility of buying nothing, then suggest buying both together. What's the additional discount, you inquire? It must be healthy, for sure. Vendor reaction to your surprise request, even more than their specific answer, gives insight into how much play really remains in the price.

Strategic Change

A private investment company was locked in a severe strategic dispute that threatened to incite senior resignations and organizational fracture. The aging founder (still CEO) was maintaining an absolutely indefensible position, keeping the firm rigidly adhered to a faltering philosophy. I was sitting with the top management group listening to the CEO's prime protector of current policy present a series of tortuously complex arguments that I was sure no one followed, much less understood. Yet the older conservative executives, the keepers of the moribund status quo (those whose loyalty to the founder was really a self-protective mechanism), revelled in watching the younger liberal executives, the proponents of constructive shift, finally being put down. "Well, that takes care of them," smirked a senior manager after the sinuous presentation. "We won't hear from that crowd again."

I was furious. The subject cut to the core of company mission. To keep the old ways would invite organizational collapse. So, corraling my overactive emotions and restraining any sarcasm in my voice, I put a question to this smug senior manager, "Of all the excellent arguments defending our current strategy, which did you think was the very best?"

The older manager, who couldn't possibly have understood what he had heard much less repeat any of it, fumbled a bit, then admitted, "You know, I never could follow anything that man ever said." Slinking away, he never discussed the matter again. Well-chosen words, even a few of them, can cut a sharp edge.

CHAPTER 30

THE DEAL-MAKING PROCESS II: ELEMENTS OF NEGOTIATIONS

Robert Lawrence Kuhn

Deal making pervades investment banking.[1] No individual goes unaffected; no organization is immune. Since you must play the game, you should play it well. You should also have fun. How to have fun? Having fun means being good. How to be good? Know the elements of negotiations and understand their applications.

Compare the process to playing poker. Don't ante up unless you know the rules. That means *all* the rules, especially the crafty ones. The difference between a cough and a comment may be as important as between a flush and a straight.

DEAL-MAKING ELEMENTS

The 39 deal elements presented in this chapter are pithy and pungent. The multiple nibbles are designed to make digestion easier: Each element is

[1]Editor's Note: This chapter has been derived from *DEALMAKER: All the Negotiating Skills and Secrets You Need*, Robert Lawrence Kuhn, copyright ©1988 by John Wiley & Sons. Reprinted by permission of John Wiley & Sons, Inc. No one doubts that deal making is a vital part of investment banking, but too often we think too much about technical finance and too little about human relations. My decision to include two substantial chapters on the deal-making process expresses my commitment to the importance of people and their behavior. Pardon an author's bias, but I believe that DEALMAKER's concepts are real, relevant, and permanent, and that teaching such interpersonal skills can advance the industry.

a complete capsule, a tasty morsel able to be savored in one sitting or, depending on appetite, devoured in one gulp.

Each element portrays one specific aspect of the deal-making process, showing what it means and how it applies. Useful practice is stressed. Cases and concepts are interwoven to mold the heart as well as school the head.

Scan the 39 deal elements. Sense their motion, direction, relation. Appreciate how we peel apart the deal-making process, and how, step by step, this dissection improves your deal-making proficiency. By appreciating the microstructure of each deal component individually, you gain confidence in the macrostructure of the entire deal-making process collectively.

These elements may not be mystical or arcane—but don't let their familiarity breed your contempt. Sometimes the obvious choice is the biggest mystery and the most-known idea is the best-kept secret.

1. BALANCING THE POWER

In physics, power is the energy needed to do work. In deal making, power is the force needed to shift odds and skew results. Skew—it's what you want to do; it means weighting outcomes in your favor. Everyone wants advantage. No one wants equality—not unless starting out behind. Power gives one the capacity to create advantage, or if one is behind, to catch up quickly.

Power is the essence of deal making. Power is strength. Power is control. It establishes the opening positions, and it determines the end game. Power means winning.

How do you assess power in deal making? Not easily. Strength and control are not simple judgments. Much lurks beneath the surface. The bigger, brawnier side may not have all the marbles.

Power is Relative

A young, single friend of mine, a successful investment banker, reasonably good looking and not without charm, found himself sitting beside an attractive young woman on an airplane. He was returning from a trip where he held the "power" to do or undo a $200 million transaction. The young woman was also single, a struggling artist working as a waitress in a backwater restaurant. For the entire three hour flight, though my buddy tried every imaginable negotiating ploy, he could not get that woman's last name (much less her phone number). He just didn't have the "power."[2]

Power is determined by balance, how much on one side versus how much on the other. Negotiations between corporations over terms of a joint venture have a similar power structure to discussions between children over which movie to see. When assessing power, the critical issue is which side has more.

Absolute levels of power mean nothing. Relative power is all that counts. If your side's got it, exploit it (but, as we'll see, carefully). If your side doesn't have it, figure out how to foul up your opponent. Real power players don't put on parades. Show offs show out. Crass displays of power bristle backs, stiffening, not softening, resolve. Real power players get their way quietly before anyone realizes what's happening.

Symbols of Power

People look to assert power—over things, events, and other people. Power is a primary human motive. To some, the substance of power is all that matters. To others, the appearance is the shining crown.

"Power symbols" are more appearance than substance. It's fun to consider power dressing, power eating, power puffing, power living, and power talking—although they really have minimum impact. More than ever in investment banking, substance prevails over form.[3]

---

[2]Robert Meisel, an officer of TSG Holdings Inc., was rather ambivalent about pinning his name to this little story. At the author's goading, he finally put social amusement over macho power—a brave decision for any investment banker.

[3]*Power Dressing* is asserting personal strength with clothing. In the world of high finance, elegant suits, preferably three-piece or double-breasted, are required. So are shirts with white collars and cuffs, a small accent of expensive (but not-too-ostentatious) jewelry, and, in some circles, bright suspenders. (I like the suits and shirts, not the jewelry or suspenders.)

Power Eating means where to dine to see and be seen. For example, in New York it's the Regency Hotel for breakfast, Four Seasons for lunch, Lutece, among others, for dinner. Each industry has its own hangouts.

Power Puffing is smoking large, imported cigars—clearly superior to munching small, crunchy apples.

Power Living means aboding on the right side of the tracks. Park or Fifth Avenue in New York whips First, Second, Third, or Lexington, and absolutely stomps anything on the West Side. In the arts, however, West Side wins.

Power Talking means using industry jargon and clever language. "Taking" meetings in Hollywood. Putting companies "in play" on Wall Street.

Pieces of the Power Puzzle

Power in deal making is not calculated without complication. There are at least 15 pieces of the power puzzle. Identifying which are most important and assessing their relative strength is tricky. Traditional factors alone can be misleading. For example, a bankrupt company may threaten a fire-sale liquidation in negotiating with creditors—and thus tip the balance of power. In the same way, an employee can threaten to quit a vital job—and gain the upper hand in dealing with a boss.

To assess power in deal making, pay attention to the following power pieces. Be subtle when applying power: When you've got it, use it; when you haven't, hide it. Power in deals promotes your side and retards the other side. It is always being weighed and balanced, tested and shifted. Power, remember, skews deals.

Size Power

Which side is bigger? The larger side has more power, if only psychologically, since size is always a threat. Size is the clearest indicator of potential force, whether that size be financial, legal, market, or the like. If you're on the bigger side, don't flaunt your girth. Size Power looms larger if veiled—the most powerful arrow is the one still in the quiver. If you're on the smaller side, exploit the slowness, sloth, or stodginess of your opponents. Try quick changes to rattle their cage. (A flea can make life more difficult for a dog than a dog can for a flea.)

Need Power

Which side requires the deal more? The party that has greater necessity to do the deal is weaker throughout the process. A small vendor supplying a critical part to a large manufacturer can demand and receive a healthy premium.

Priority Power

Which side considers the deal more important? The party that puts higher emphasis on doing the deal is stronger, especially in competitive situations. When doing deals, put a premium on the top of the list. If doing multiple deals, think like a computer and "time share"; each deal gets your full, undivided attention, as if it were the only deal on your plate, for short bursts of time.

Focus Power

Which side is concentrating more on the deal? The party that zeros in more intently on this one deal is stronger. Dispersed, fragmented interests sap deal-making strength.

Passion Power

Which side likes the deal more? The party that has more desire to make the transaction is weaker. When an acquiring company's chief executive officer is enamored with your business (or your industry), hold out for more goodies. When the CEO buys by the numbers and has a wide selection of acquisition candidates, get what you can—take the money and run.

Resource Power

Which side has greater muscle? The party that can throw more dollars, people, and lawyers at the deal is stronger. When confronted by greater resources, strive for straightforward simplicity and sure-footed speed. "Let's keep these eggs unscrambled," is your line. When the greater resources are in your pocket, don't mind some foot dragging and omelette eating.

Sunk Power

Which side has made the larger investment? The party that has "sunk" more costs into the deal—time, money, effort, ego, image—is weaker. If you are a private company and your opponent is public, a premature press release describing the deal, especially if glowing, puts more pressure on them. In some cases, Sunk Power can be used to encourage the other side to "invest" in the deal-making process by holding meetings, analyzing data, visiting factories, retaining accountants, and cranking up lawyers. (Note: Sunk Power and Focus Power can pull in opposite directions. This illustrates the complexity of power analysis.)

Flexibility Power

Which side has more options? The party that can shift and move in more directions is stronger. A deal maker with only one way to work is forever running up hill.

Unity Power

Which side is more together? The party that has greater internal agreement is stronger. There is nothing more disrupting than lack of unity among a deal-making team.

Personal Power

Which side has the better people and personalities? The team that has more knowledgeable players is stronger. Knowledge in deal making includes: content data, legal technicalities, tax expertise, negotiating techniques, and the like.

Political Power

Which side wields more influence? The party that can bring greater external forces to bear on the deal is stronger. If a negotiator on one side knows the boss of the negotiator on the other side, he has implicit Political Power. (This type of power is there even if never used—especially if never used, since it's probably more perceived than real.)

Reward Power

Which side can help the other more? The party that can aid the other to a greater degree in affairs beyond this one deal is stronger. If your company can provide additional business to the company with which you're negotiating, whether directly through additional orders or indirectly through recommendations, you've got a leg up.

Punishment Power

Which side can hurt the other more? The party that can inflict higher relative damage—be it economic injury or insult to prestige—is the stronger. When one side is a heavy customer of the other side, there is an implicit commercial threat of general cancellation. Even a weak company can command high ground by supplying a difficult-to-replace product or service. If your opponent can tarnish your reputation more than you can blacken theirs, they are stronger. Poison, sadly, is easy to spread.

Knowledge Power

Which side has more information and understanding? The party that has more relevant data and deal-specific comprehension is stronger. If you've got it, use it. Knowledge is a powerful intimidator.

Logic Power

Which side has more sensible arguments? The party whose points are more defensible is stronger. The careful, concentrated use of good reasoning, without a cocky, know-it-all attitude, can effectively control deals.

2. PEGGING THE PARTIES

The "parties" to the deal are the entities making it. Good deal makers understand who and what they are up against. They know how to classify the other side of the deal. They can distinguish among diverse parties—who they each are, what they are each about, what they each want, and how they each act. The objective is to know how best to handle each type, how to match strategy choice to party type. We consider three ways to classify the other side of the deal, to "peg the parties": identifying the entity, assessing the need, and locating the key decision maker.

Identifying the Entity

What parties are participating in the transaction? Their nature and composition can suggest purposes to fulfill and "hot buttons" to push.

Individuals
Solitary people have complex motives. They are driven by various factors: mission, wealth, ego, and power. When individuals are party to the deal, be sensitive to the relative strength of their driving motives.

Groups
Groups are individuals who band together to achieve specific objectives. Motivation can become less complex as the group grows larger. When working with groups, either close the deal by targeting the central objectives or confuse the deal by appealing to fragmentary issues.

Companies

A company is a profit-making entity whose goal is to increase earnings and equity. Yet, though the principal in the transaction is a company, never forget that you deal only with people—and people think as individuals. When negotiating with companies, understand the profit objectives, but don't ignore people purposes. For example, assume you are purchasing several products from a distributor. You can probably lower your overall costs by buying some slower-moving items in exchange for additional discounts on your primary products. The salesman becomes a hero and you save some bucks.

Institutions

Not-for-profit organizations strive to accomplish specific missions. When dealing with such institutions—whether religious (churches), humanitarian (charities), or cultural (museums)—any hint of goal agreement can facilitate your deal making. But don't be sickeningly sweet.

Governments

These bureaucratic organizations seek survival and status quo. When dealing with public sector agencies or entities, assume they are risk averse, protective of the current state, and upset by disruptions. There is high inertia to change; lots of force is needed to alter the existing way of doing things. Government employees, remember, can fail more easily than they can succeed.

Assessing the Need

As we've seen, need power is a critical power piece. The relative strength of each party's need should be assessed.

Anxious Parties are what you like to see sitting on the other side of the table. They want the deal done more than you do. Fearing failure, they are desperate. Any reasonable costs are acceptable. But you can only push anxious opponents so far. Be careful: These types can be volatile; push them over the edge and they'll blow off.

Interested Parties want to do the deal—but not at any cost. Here, you have to use more logic than pressure to coax the deal to closure. Remember, these people can walk without worry.

Indifferent Parties can take it or leave it. They have other alternatives and will spring only for a good deal. Patience is a virtue here. You can't be overly aggressive with indifferents. Try playing "hard to get" to induce them to do the chasing.

Browsing Parties are time eaters—the worst of the bunch. They are lookers, professional tire kickers, deal-making hobbyists who might check out 100 situations and not do one of them. Browsers are the bane of a deal maker's life. They sap energy and destroy efficiency. Develop your nose: Sniff out these temporal parasites and give them short shrift.

Locating the Decision Maker

Deals are closed when some person or group from each side gives a final thumbs-up. You know the key person or persons on your side. The trick is to find him, her, or them on the other side. It's always helpful to find the desk on which the buck stops.

Table Person

When the key decision maker is active and visible in the negotiations, assessment is simple. You look the decision maker in the eye, make your moves, and see who blinks.

Closet Person

Here, the deal maker is not present. He or she is "hiding," as it were, in the closet, never visible but always there. Sometimes you know who the person is and sometimes you do not. The people at the table are basically messengers. How to handle this situation? Smoking out a closet person may be helpful, though it may be better to allow the other side comfort in their little secret. Don't knock the ploy of leaving the decision maker in the closet. Since it is an effective way to avoid making instant decisions, it may be a good strategy for your side. This is why a president and chairman should rarely be in the same deal-making meeting at the same time. Each provides the other with a convenient "re-entry." When both are present, each is on the spot.

Heavenly Group

In this decision-making structure, only a high-level group, such as an executive committee or a board of directors, can give final approval. Life is difficult for deal makers on both sides. Here, the people with whom you are negotiating are not in control of the deal content or process. Be sensitive to their frustrations.

Amorphous Group

This is the worst case. Disasterville. No one is responsible and no one can take responsibility. This situation is characteristic of government bureaucracies and commercial companies in organizational transition. What are the signs of amorphous decision making? Watch for uncertainty in response time, vacillation in response content, mixed signals on deal points, contradictions in terms, and open disagreement among same-side participants. If you are faced with an amorphous group, try to determine if different or disputing forces are involved. Then play directly to those who seek the deal more avidly. For example, if one signal demands a higher price, and the other requires complex conditions, try countering with an upgraded price and even simpler conditions.

3. PSYCHING THE CHARACTERS

Personalities of deal makers vary dramatically and influence how they make deals. Learn to recognize the traits and types of deal-making characters and thus plan your strategies. Even when parties to transactions are large organizations, particular (and sometimes peculiar) human beings make those deals happen.

How to assess personality traits of deal makers? How to match strategic response to personality types? Effective deal makers must be good judges of character. They make quick studies of people. Getting a good sense of personality helps the proper planning of strategy.

How to classify the people with whom you deal? Categorize each character according to a basic understanding of makeup and manner. Use the "Character Scales" discussed in the following sections. Most people fall somewhere in the middle of each category. Don't take this "rating system" too seriously. Try it a few times, just to get the hang of it. Normally, your assessments will be rather informal.

Top Banana or Errand Boy/Girl

What kinds of decisions can the person make on his or her own? How much independence does an individual have? In other words, are you dealing with a principal who can make decisions or an agent who can only transmit them?

Good deal makers play principals and agents differently. For example, irritation or outrage is only rarely expressed to a principal. It's just not done unless circumstances are extreme. Hitting an agent hard, however, is perfectly acceptable (as long as social decorum is maintained). You know full well that the message will be reported back to the boss accurately and quickly. Hot buttons of top bananas, the ones you push to get results, are normally greased with vanity.

Veteran or Virgin

How experienced is the person? Does he or she have a long track record of making deals, or are you initiating a greenhorn? Is your opposite a grizzled-old buzzard or a fuzzy-faced fledgling? With veterans, you play it straight—and you watch for tricks. They are usually either forthright and direct or cunning and crafty.

Novices are noisome, virgins the pits. Both hide their inexperience behind a facade of awkward toughness. They think flint-headedness, even rudeness to other people, portrays fortitude and confidence. They are wrong, but you must still deal with these upstarts.

With virgins, there are two approaches. The first allows them to bolster their weak self-image through bluster; they may calm down into good deal makers. The second approach is to pull them up short. Let them know that you know the script and can read their lines. Tell them that bravado is not bravura. Show them carrot and stick. They can either make or break the deal, and bask in the former or give account for the latter.

Egotistical or Action-Centered

What's the person's primary objective? Is it accomplishing the task of puffing the self? Egotists who fancy themselves consummate deal makers can be spotted in a nanosecond. Some telltale signs: the number of "I's" in their conversations and the ring of constant condescension in their tone. Check how they speak in meetings, act in front of others, handle subordinates, even write their names or answer the phone.

How to deal with egotists? Direct confrontation is a last resort. It can always be tried, but if it flubs all other efforts end.[4] Instead, you can deflect the egotist by appealing to his or her baser instincts. Give the braggart something to crow about. Skew part of the deal to puff the person, as long as it costs you nothing. For example, trade away public recognition (with no authority), additional features thrown in (cosmetics only), an inflated purchase price (watered way down with extended payments and little interest), or a hefty special payment (subtracted from the real purchase price).

---

[4]Taking a finesse in bridge is an apt analogy. It may or may not work, so you try other alternatives first. Then, if all else fails and you need the finesse to make the hand, you have nothing to lose by trying it.

Action-centered people are fulfilled by closing good deals; they seek the straightest and clearest route to success, irrespective of personal prestige. Don't be followed by their pleasant manner. They work hard and tough and can be smooth and slippery. You can give away more than you should and feel good about it. Deal making is not philanthropy. Be on guard here.

Self-Willed or Team Player

Does the person play ball with a group, or is he or she a loner? Can he or she share responsibility, authority, and credit? Self-willed principals should be handled one-on-one. Don't worry about alienating the team; they don't count, anyway.

Self-willed agents are messy for both sides, and are likely to cause confusion. If you've got an uncontrollable ego representing the decision maker, communicate directly with the principals. (But don't antagonize the overblown messenger.)

Team-playing principals tend to rely on one or two special associates. Determine the favorite counselors and find their hot buttons.

It's a mistake to assume that team players are all good news and self-willed types are all bad. Self-willed principals can make fast decisions, even ones to your liking, and not wait around for others to critique them. Team players, however, may be indecisive and waste everyone's time while they grope with their group.

Intense or Relaxed

Is the person uptight or at ease in the deal-making setting? Intense people show little patience and drive linearly for clear objectives. They are less flexible in thought and deed. Relaxed people are apt to find more creative solutions. They tend to take themselves less seriously and don't mind looking a little foolish as they search for new answers. Your task, in general, is to induce a more unruffled, easygoing atmosphere, to encourage a calm, positive posture in the deal-making process.

Innovative problem solving is nurtured when parties are less high-strung. Humor is a good technique, especially good-natured kidding of opponents combined with light deprecation of oneself. Try comments like, "We're acting like this deal's important. A million years from now, who'll care?" Or, "Nothing kills a good deal like hard heads on stiff necks—on both sides."

Objective or Subjective

Is the person influenced more by logic or emotion? Will he or she conform to the traditional solutions or seek the unusual? Which appeals more, converging to a solution or diverging with more options?

Objective types are more analytical, rational, and focused. They generally conform to traditional ways of thinking and behaving. They like to converge ever closer to stark solutions. Proceed step-by-step with these folks.

Subjective types are more passionate, abstract, and daring. They are generally more nontraditional and iconoclastic. They seek to explore new areas even if confusing and risky. This type of personality is often more flexible in deal making.

Subjective types are great at bridging gaps and breaking deadlocks. They are not great, however, at closing deals. It's hard for them to come to a final agreement because they can always find something else novel or better. In order to consummate a deal, objective types should be in control. To do good deals, especially if they're complex, it's a good idea to have both objectives and subjectives on your team.

Consistent or Capricious

Is the person reliable in both promise and practice? Can he or she be trusted to follow a predictable path? You can deal directly with consistent thinkers. Moves can be planned well ahead. When dealing with capricious thinkers, you must focus more on the present. Nail down agreements in detail, even on small points, before moving on to new subjects. With capricious personalities, sit lightly and never rest. Always expect change.

When there's a real impasse in a deal, however, roles may reverse. Capricious types are often better at unblocking problems. They can jump higher hurdles, though you can never predict how, where, or when they will land. Consistent types, those who think step-by-step, have a harder time overcoming obstacles.

Likers or Haters

How does the person see people—as individuals to know or as objects to exploit? Likers see the good in people and forgive their faults. Haters see the bad and carry grudges. Likers enjoy doing deals with friends. Haters prefer getting even with foes. Likers and haters are polar opposites, and the look on their faces is often a dead giveaway.

Doing business with haters is no fun. You never know when you've tripped their tightly strung wires. Disarming a hater is like defusing a bomb. Confrontation, while tempting, is the technique of last resort. You might consider showing that you do not take yourself, or the deal, too seriously. It's hard to hate someone who just doesn't care. Make small talk. Try to establish a relationship. Friendliness can be contagious.

Normal or Strange

Once in a while you come across a head case (more often, I'm afraid, in investment banking than in other industries). Be careful. Normal rules of the road don't apply. Deal making as a profession attracts diverse characters. A few are real oddballs. You expect to contest large egos, and you learn to handle them (if not like them). But occasionally you'll meet an ego so massive that it's almost comical. You never know when that mental mass is going to explode. An innocent remark taken wrong, an inadvertent slight blown out of proportion, and we have a fireball.

It's hard to prescribe proper response, short of a graduate degree in abnormal psychology. Your primary task is to recognize what you are dealing with, and to take care not to react strongly to any provocation. If you are patient, it may be possible to make your deal. But if it works it will probably come in an unexpected manner.

4. SURVEYING THE TURF

How do settings of deals affect their substance? How does environment influence the way deals get done? In deal making, signals are always being sent. Your side sends them. The other side sends them; even the setting sends telltale signs. Conscious awareness may or may not be involved. You may not recognize these hidden communications. Like infrared or ultraviolet light, however, they are always there. The medium is part of the message.

Metamessages

Signals are "metamessages," nonverbal feelings, projections, impressions, connotations, and influences. They bias the actual messages with their subliminal tugs and pulls. Consider the following examples:

When a principal will not speak without an attorney beside him, you begin to wonder. The literal message is that your opponent is one careful person. The metamessage may be that your opponent is uncertain, unsure, nervous, worried, or frightened. (Ask yourself what he or she is so afraid of.)

When one side of the deal volunteers to take a crack at writing a first draft of an agreement, the literal message is "We'll do the work and cover the expense." The metamessage is, "We know the deal better than you do, so we will control procedure from now on."

The following sections are metamessages regarding "turf," subliminal signals about the setting of deals. Watch for these subtleties.

Home Court Advantage

There are two general rules of thumb regarding meeting place. The first describes relative power: Home court gives control; meeting location indicates positional strength. The second describes relative desire: The one who wants, walks; the "beseecher" travels to the territory of the "beseechee." (Accountants and advertising executives, for example, usually meet at their clients' offices.)

Often, the meeting venture is a matter of mutual convenience, not game-playing tricks. However, be aware that some deal makers deliberately use the home court advantage. I prefer to concede place of meeting and have the other side assume that I come in a weaker position. (I like defying convention when it comes to power.) I also like to see the home grounds of my opponents. You never know what you can learn. For example, if there are lots of vacated offices, this could mean that the business may not be as rosy as it's being pictured.

On a personal note, I hold many meetings in my home. The atmosphere is private and relaxed. It is always conducive to serious business with a creative touch. I never thought of this practice in terms of any psychological advantage until a foreign dignitary told a friend that I must be exceedingly important since I had invited him to come to see me. Indeed, by agreeing to meet at my home, rather than at his hotel, the dignitary was reaffirming my preeminence in his mind.

Seating Arrangements

Remember how long it took just to decide the *shape* of the negotiating table at the Vietnam Peace Conference? In your deal, does the primary principal take the head seat? If not, does that indicate real dominance and high confidence? If the principal is not present, who takes the chief spot—and does that person take the lead? Either way you gain insight about the "power behind the throne."

A curious thing happens in organizations. You sometimes find that meeting rooms fill up in reverse, from the rear forward, so that the last one in must take the uppermost seat. Such an external show of meekness can be more artificial pretense than true humility. It can also mask a political conflict boiling below the surface.

Telephone

Where would investment bankers be without telephones? I am fascinated by their power. You can get to "see" people by phone whose offices you could never even approach. An urgent meeting with a person who might have traveled across the country can be interrupted by a casual call from across the street.[5]

When asked whether I like to travel, my snappy answer is, "Sure, by telephone." Phone calls—especially conference calls—are highly efficient. They compress time and promote a get-down-to-business attitude. Actual geography is becoming less relevant for business. When I'm staying on the West Coast, I can often do my East Coast business better. My day starts earlier, twenty-minute phone calls replace two-hour meetings, and efficiency is much improved. (Don't tell the phone companies, but communication costs are one of the best bargains in contemporary society.)

Telephone talk doesn't work in all situations. For example, it's too easy for the other part to say "No" to the mouthpiece; the impersonality makes for an easier turndown. The medium also promotes rapid-fire response—not a positive if you want the other side to reflect on your ideas or proposals.

There is no slighting direct contact in deal making. You often need to see reactions and expressions. This factor is especially important when making and responding to proposals. The telephone cannot communicate body language.

Deal making on the telephone has special character. For example, advantage is achieved, however slight, by the one who makes the call. Readiness is key. The caller is obviously ready; the one who receives the call is obviously not. Some people just do not take many calls, preferring to return calls at their discretion. Secretaries and answering machines are good filters. If, after a secretary asks your name and says "Just a moment," you are told that the person you are calling is "unavailable," become suspicious. But you always

[5]Why is the telephone so invasive? I think it's the mystery of the sudden ring, the arresting intrusion of the unknown, perhaps the easy access to instant gratification. Something's happening, you don't know what, but to find out all you do is pick up that piece of light plastic. It's intoxicating.

learn something, even the fact that your opponent is not ready to speak with you.

As another example, facts are more literal on the phone. The specific details of offers and counteroffers are uncolored by atmosphere and aura. Sometimes this is good for your side, sometimes not. It depends on your current position and intended strategy.

Telephone tricks are common. Lawyers like to bill out a minimum of seven to twelve minutes of their time for each call made for clients, irrespective of whether the call was much shorter or even whether the person was actually there. Since these "calls" can average well under a minute, such a lawyer can rack up several "hours" worth of billings in less than 60 real minutes. (Some would call this system "efficient"; others would use a less kind word.)

Ducking calls is a required skill; to some it's a new art form. Let's say you want to avoid giving a final answer to a prospective buyer because you'd rather test some other offers first. But you don't want to turn them off, since they indeed might be making the best deal. If you talk, and if they catch you before you're ready, you're in Trouble City. It's like the proverbial mouthful of scalding soup; the next thing you do must be wrong. You don't want to say "yes" (you want to check those other offers), you can't say "no" (theirs may prove to be the best offer), and any hesitation will betray your fence sitting. The situation is a delicate one. Calling back during low likelihood office hours—such as lunch time or early evening—is a favorite technique for slipping people without making it too obvious. Using secretaries to leave messages is another. Ducking can't work for long, of course, but it might buy a few precious days.

Informal Settings

While deals get consummated in more formal settings, they usually commence in more informal ones. Business meals are a favorite. Watch protocol here. Signals are sent by what restaurant is chosen and who picks up the bill. It is inappropriate, for example, for a start-up entrepreneur to cavort with investors at an expensive nightspot. Likewise it doesn't sit well for a struggling company to entertain its bankers at a swanky watering hole.

I often apply a story my father told me. In the go-go 1960s, when his private apparel company was being courted by a conglomerate, my father was invited to lunch at an extravagant restaurant by the division president. The big executive made lofty promises with great fanfare and flamboyant gestures; but when it came to check-paying time, his hands developed sudden rigor mortis—as did, I might add, his deal.

Sporting events, spectator and participatory, are good catalysts for building relationships. People get to know each other as individuals instead of objects. Emotions are less inhibited by social convention and you get a glimpse of the real person hiding beneath the three-piece suit.

Such personal knowledge is invaluable in understanding the characters in the deal-making process, and it is essential if the deal involves a continuing relationship. The golf course is a legendary place for making deals. The relaxed atmosphere stimulates expansive thinking. (You also get to see how the other fellow functions in the rough, in the traps, and when four-putting a short green.)

5. GAUGING THE SIZE

Remember back when $100,000 salaries were the stratosphere for sports superstars? It seems that a certain well-known athlete was offered $100,001. When asked if the extra dollar was symbolic, he reputedly answered, "Hell no, a buck is a buck."

How Size Influences Deals

Why is size important? What aspects of the deal-making process are affected by the amplitude, volume, and weight of transactions? No doubt the number of dollars exchanged is critical—size is surely measured in green. But there are other colors to the deal-making rainbow—size counts in more ways than one.

Size can sway the intensity of negotiations, the length of discussions, and the difficulty of agreement. It can slant the visibility of outcomes, the public image of results, and the reputation of participants. It can determine the level of management doing the negotiating, the attention paid by senior executives, and the orchids or onions reserved for the deal makers.

Relativity

Size, as most things in business, must be judged by comparison. Relative balance is more important than absolute standard.

Deal size may relate to the size of the parties making the deal. It is nonsense to speak of $20 million as a "large" deal. To General Motors Corporation, it's microscopic. To Paul's Pontiac dealership, it's mammoth.

Deal size also relates to other options available to the parties. A $50 million deal would have been small to Carl Icahn when he was contemplating taking over Trans World Airlines. Similarly, a $100 million suit against Texaco would not have made much of a ripple when they were busy appealing the $10 *billion* judgment for Pennzoil.

Factors of Size

What parts of a deal determine its size? Dollar value is the obvious answer. But must a $10 million deal always be ten times larger than a $1 million deal? Not necessarily. The fact is that the latter, even in the same company, can be even bigger than the former. Remember, there is more to size than numbers.

Positive Kick

A small deal with a large customer may be a test case. Upside potential can be enormous; the future can dwarf the present. Do a good job on this one, and the sky's the limit. In some industries, for example, where expertise is hard to judge up front, smaller contracts are generally given before larger ones. Likewise, this is true with government programs such as public finance, where confidence must be built slowly.

Negative Kick

Mess up a smaller deal with a current customer and you foul up an on-going relationship. Downside danger can be serious; the present can disrupt the future. A small acquisition from a major customer may deserve more attention than a larger acquisition from a smaller customer.

Visibility

The public presence of a transaction, inside or outside the company, influences its magnitude. Raising capital for a high-profile R&D partnership for a company may be more important for an investment bank than for a large, plain vanilla debt offering from that same company. Similarly, a corporate defense assignment, no matter how small the company, risks nasty public relations if mishandled.

Strategic Value

A small deal that helps achieve your longer-term objectives can exceed in size a larger deal that is not so relevant. A $20 million commercial paper offering by an investment bank seeking entry into this market may be "larger" than a $200 million bond offering. Sure, the $200 million means higher fees—but that may be a one-shot deal. The commercial paper deal may build expertise that could produce continuous profits. (Give a hungry man a fish and you feed him for a day; teach him how to fish and you feed him forever.)

Symbolic Value

What a deal means affects how it is perceived. A small matter with large implications can be a big deal. A company that talks innovation, yet funds tradition digs credibility gaps. Nothing speaks louder than the movement of money, and a pilot project in a risky new area looms large in the corporate consciousness.[6]

Strategies of Size

So you can gauge the size of your deal—big deal! Now what? How does such knowledge help make better deals? Certain strategies work better under different size conditions. Several follow.

What To Do When a Deal is Large

The following should be done when a deal is big: Put your best people on the case. Focus on the deal—don't be distracted by trivia. Provide proper resources; recognize that investment is necessary; and don't skimp on legal, accounting, and consulting fees. Pay attention to details; small points in large deals can cost bundles. Build human relationships; a light touch can ease protracted negotiations with heavy stakes. The high tension in huge mergers and acquisitions is reduced when opposing sides eat pepperoni pizzas together in all-night sessions.

What To Do When a Deal is Small

The following should be done when a deal is little: Prime your negotiating team—it's easy to go into small deals unprepared. Be sure your people do not consider the job beneath them; look for ways to show your team the

---

[6]Symbolism is especially critical in religious organizations. In a certain Bible-believing group the observance of a specific holy day was changed from Monday to Sunday; the move was enormous, as was the prior controversy, since it represented biblical fidelity and a willingness to admit error, both of which were claimed as vital group attributes.

importance of the deal. Stay alert even if you aren't excited. Give credit to your deal makers; it's often just as hard to pull off a small deal as a large one.

What To Do When a Corporate Deal is Mismatched

Consider a situation where a large public corporation is negotiating to buy a small private company. When you're the larger corporation, don't bully or condescend; treat your potential deal partners with dignity—after all, you want what they've got. When you're the smaller company, don't cower or show anxiety; handle your suits with equality—after all, you've got what they want.[7]

What To Do When a Personal Deal is Mismatched

Consider the relationship when superiors and subordinates make deals in the workplace; for example, the negotiation of salary or position. Each side must maintain its mutual dignity. The superior's tactics must not intimidate or humiliate, and the subordinate's tactics must not embarrass or beguile. When you're the superior, use questions to draw out ideas, showing real interest in your subordinate's opinions. When you're the subordinate, offer ideas and information, asserting confidence in your convictions. Be careful that criticism is always constructive; the superior should not feel compelled to pull rank, the subordinate should not fear to be firm. Each side should lead through proper example.

6. VALUING THE STUFF

Vincent van Gogh produced over 800 paintings, but during his entire lifetime he could sell only one—for $25. Recently, one of those unsold paintings sold for $40 million. So much for absolute value.

"Stuff" is the value and consideration being traded in a transaction. Stuff is all kinds of things; in fact, it's anything changing hands in a deal. How you value stuff is important.

If beauty is in the eye of the beholder, then worth is in the wallet of the holder. Cash is about the only thing with a fixed value. The value of virtually

---

[7]Bullying and cowering provoke equal and opposite reactions and are not conducive to making good deals. Bullying raises resisting hackles; cowering invites aggressive attack.

everything else depends on who is the owner or potential owner, what are the conditions, and who is the judge. Absolute value is a myth.

Principles of Relative Value

Value is a moving target—subjective and ever changing. When, as well as who, affects outcome. Scarcity, need, and social values all contribute to the perception of worth. I am reminded of Woody Allen's incisive insight in *Stardust Memories*. Allen plays an enormously successful filmmaker who has become rich and famous from making funny movies (semiautobiographical). When he meets a childhood friend who drives a cab, Woody consoles him by saying something like: "So our society puts high value on humor. If we were Apache Indians, I'd be at the bottom of the totem pole—jokes weren't important when chasing buffalo—and I can't ride a horse. . ."

I like to define "value" relatively, in comparison with other things. In this sense, the real value of your stuff can be defined by the value of the other side's stuff. "How much is some 'X' worth?" is not the best question. I prefer, "Which would you rather have, the stuff you're giving or the stuff you're getting?"

A good technique for valuing stuff is to ask yourself constantly which side of the trade you like better. Ask the question every time the deal changes. Another objective is to discover your "indifference point"—that special place where it doesn't matter whether you do the deal.

Remember, too, that relative value affects each side differently. One side may look simply at financial data—the generally accepted market value—while the other side may consider what business advantages it can gain by ownership.

Your task is to assess relative value on both sides. Get at underlying motivations. First understand how your side values the stuff. Then perceive how the other side does its valuing.

Polarity of Value

In general, there are two categories for assigning value: What are the positive benefits to be achieved by getting hold of this stuff? (Obvious.) What are the negative costs that can be avoided by getting rid of this stuff? (Less obvious.)

Each category has its own subtleties. Positive value means that you want to do the deal because, if you do, the stuff will increase your worth or wealth. A company whose high-growth division could command a massive multiple of earnings would sell for a premium price. Negative value means that you want to do the deal because, if you do not, the stuff will decrease your worth or wealth. A company whose cash-hungry division could drive it into bankruptcy would sell for a discounted price.

Desire, greed, and lust differ from fear, anxiety, and dread. Would you do a deal if you had 99 chances in 100 to make 20 times your annual salary but had 1 chance in 100 to lose your right arm? Most people would refuse (even lefties). What about 50 times your salary? A hundred times? A thousand times?

Most people are "risk averse," that is they would rather play it safer than mere odds would suggest. Avoiding negative impact, therefore, carries heavy weight in valuations.

Valuation Under Competition

Bidding in auctions can be dangerous to your financial health. When a joint venture between Phillips Petroleum and Chevron won offshore drilling rights in 1981, they were shocked to discover that they paid more than double the next highest bid. The four other bids ranged from under $1 million to $161 million. These pros paid $333.6 million—$170 million more than necessary—and suffered what has become known as the "winners curse" among oil lease auction victors.

Research has shown that bidders are usually overconfident about their ability to assess value, often generating a huge gap between the highest and next highest bids. The phenomenon is strongest when involving unproven values (e.g., defense contracts for new technologies, leases in new shopping malls, mineral rights). Factors affecting price, in addition to true value, include the number of bidders and the structure of the auction. Sealed bids with many bidders induce the wildest frenzy.

Appraisal Process

Few things have an unconditionally fair value. Lots of values may be "fair," although some may be more fair than others. It depends on whom you are asking and why you are asking them. In general, beware of the appraisal process.

Appraisers have notorious reputations for skewing valuations according to their client's objectives. Purposes affect outcomes. Whether the appraisal is for sale purposes (on the upper hand) or tax purposes (on the lower hand) will influence how a real estate appraiser values a piece of property. When the government appropriates forest lands from a company, appraisers for each side make their best case. You can be sure the government's appraisers assign a far lower worth per acre than do the company's, even though both appraisers may be expert and honest. (Reverse the clients and watch those appraisals flip.) You get, it seems, what you pay for.

Kinds of Corporate Valuations

I represented an excellent company that wanted to sell. How much should they ask? How should they establish the right purchase price?

We analyzed the business and categorized five kinds of buyers who would be interested in an acquisition—each would have a different number, each would use a different method.

The "Cash Flow" Buyer would look at the profits generated, targeting the "net free cash"; they wouldn't care one whit about the products, process, or people. They might offer $40 million for the steady stream of dollars.

The "Asset-Based" Buyer would assess the fair market value for the company's net assets—the dollar amount of all assets sold off in orderly fashion minus all liabilities. They could offer $25 million for the liquidation rights.

The "Replacement Value" Buyer would consider what it would cost them to set up an equivalent facility, the production plants, and marketing organization that they needed. They could offer $50 million for fast and cheap entry into the business.

The "Synergy" Buyer would view what they could do with the company by integrating it into their own company, how the new entity would enjoy increased market share and lower average costs. They might offer $55 million for the increased effectiveness, efficiency, and market dominance.

The "Defensive" Buyer would envision what their rivals might do with the new business, controlling the market and driving others out. They could offer $60 million to keep competitors at bay. (Need I say which one we accepted?)

Kinds of Personal Valuations

Let's go close to home—setting your salary. Consider the following methods of valuation. (Compare these categories with those in the corporate example.)

A Net Dollar Value Salary is pegged to the incremental gross profit—the fresh bottom-line dollars—that you bring into the company. A merger and acquisition "rainmaker" who can bring in tens of millions of dollars in fees is worth seven figures.

A Market Value Salary is a collective valuation of what people with your general skills and experience could expect to command in your field or industry. This valuation is *not* individual.

A Replacement Value Salary is the company's total cost of finding and paying someone else to do your job if you were no longer working. Job-interruption costs (down-time on your tasks), job-disruption costs (interference with the tasks of others), search expenses, and subsequent salary must be included.

A Synergy Value Salary is what a company would pay you considering the added benefits that other aspects of the company could derive from your talents and participation. For example, a corporate finance banker who has good relationships with corporate treasurers might also be able to bring in some M&A business.

A Competitive Value Salary is what a competitor might pay you to join their firm. Your presence would not only help the new firm, your absence would also hurt the old one. Investment bankers thank competitive valuation: This is what keeps salaries sky high.

7. APPRAISING THE STAKES

Stakes very high or stakes very low make deals very tricky. Everything you do in deals is colored by relative significance. When stakes are high you act one way, when low, another way. The gravity dictates attitudes and approaches.

Stakes are high when deal success would contribute dramatically to company progress or personal career. Stakes are also high when failure would severely undermine organizational viability or professional path.

Anxiety and Stakes

Anxiety is a good indicator of stress and stakes. The degree of apprehension can signal the level of the deal's importance. Anxiety is a general sense of foreboding, an unspecific fear of the future. You are afraid, but you are not sure of what. Anxious behavior includes over-eager reactions, exaggerated responses, and inappropriate demeanor.

People function best with moderate levels of anxiety, and worse with very high or very low levels.[8] High levels of anxiety disturb and distract.

[8]Research in various areas of human performance, from athletic events to academic exams, shows that moderate levels of anxiety are better than either high or low levels.

Low levels allow ramble and roam. Moderate anxiety is ideal. It is enough to maintain and preserve interest but not enough to sabotage and subvert attention.

Stakeholder Analysis

Stakeholder analysis is a technique that helps analyze how each side views the deal. Uniformity is out. Neither "side" is considered homogenous; the parties are not all cut from the same cloth. Instead, each side is seen to be composed of individuals with special motives and interests. Thus each person has his or her own private agenda, a committed interest (or "stake") that each group member maintains (or "holds"). Your task is to discern the special stake of each individual in order to determine the group's overall thrust. Organizational behaviorists believe that stakeholder analysis—getting at personal motivations—is vital for understanding why groups act they way they do.

How to Judge the Stakes

Certain signals help in evaluating the stakes in deal making. Knowing these signs can give your side an advantage.

Level of Key Person. How high in the organization is the prime negotiator? The higher the person the higher the stakes.

Focus of Key Person. How much attention does the prime negotiator give the deal? The greater the focus the higher the stakes.

Level of Activity. How responsive is the other side? Are your phone calls returned quickly? Are requests for information fulfilled promptly?

Frequency of Meetings. How often are meetings scheduled? When are the next steps planned? Do days float by without concrete progress?

Degree of Pushiness. Which side is setting the time schedules and deadlines? The active party generally has higher stakes.

Conscious Behavior. Are there any obvious signs of stress and anxiety, such as exaggerated reactions, hair-trigger tempers that are out of character, or wide (and wild) swings of moods?

Unconscious Behavior. Are there any telltale signs of stress and anxiety? Fidgety, nervous habits and rapid, high-pitched speech suggest very high or low stakes. (By the way, don't forget to monitor—and mask—your own reactions. The other side might have read this chapter, too.)

When Stakes Are High

When you play "bet the company" or "wager the career" on a particular deal, mental attitudes are complex. You are tough because the deal is important; you are soft because you fear the deal won't happen. Your posture can be volatile, with violent shifts in moods and positions.

As a result, you are likely to react quickly and simplistically to tricks and trades by the other side. It is hard to be cool when your feet are on fire.

When negotiating a high stakes deal, concentrate on reducing your levels of stress and anxiety (if only their outward show). Slow down your speech. Do physical exercise to soak up that awkward energy. Use breathing exercises to induce relaxation. Try faking calmness; artificial serenity can induce real serenity.

Stakes in a deal can be reduced by finding another option outside the deal. Assume the deal is broken and consider what to do next. Don't actually do anything, but think of alternative action. If you can develop independent choices, stakes decline, anxiety drops, and deal-making behavior improves.

When Stakes Are Low

When you do not care about a deal, you get sloppy. Lack of attention breeds mistakes of fact and errors of judgment. Control slips away and advantage is lost.

When deals degenerate, deals disrupt. Sometimes, in a belated attempt to salvage a decaying deal, the negotiator will make a sudden shift in position. Unfortunately, the surprise move may trigger outright rupture.

When negotiating a deal where the stakes are low, concentrate on raising your levels of stress and anxiety (if only their outward show). Speed up lazy speech. Force yourself to pay strict attention to details. Don't dawdle over issues. Try faking fervor; artificial intensity can induce real intensity.

However, if you find it impossible to generate even modest anxiety, you may be the wrong person for the job. Find another person to negotiate this deal and find another deal for yourself.

Pennzoil-Texaco

How about playing some high-stakes corporate poker? At the table we find Pennzoil and Texaco squaring off. The game is five-card stud, four cards up, one hidden in the hole. Pennzoil is showing three of a kind; Texaco is flaunting a possible flush. They're head to head, taunting and bluffing each other.

Pennzoil's legal judgment against Texaco for interrupting its deal with Getty was about $10 billion in claims and damages, the largest verdict in corporate history. Tough talk of huge security demands blasted forth from Pennzoil. Dark threats of bankruptcy filings emanated from Texaco. Relativity played a role here, and the game was an artful one. For Pennzoil, it was a bonanza, the issue was how big. For Texaco, it was life and death, the issue was survival.

Strangely, the interests of both companies should have suggested settling the suit long before they actually did. Both sides had too much to lose by not agreeing out of court. Texaco was not without resources, nor was Pennzoil without fear. Let's see why.[9]

If Pennzoil did not settle, one of two things could happen: (1) Texaco could declare bankruptcy, and Pennzoil would become just one of many unsecured creditors embroiled in a legal miasma, or (2) a subsequent judicial appeal could overturn the verdict and Pennzoil would wind up with nothing. Furthermore, it was unlikely that Pennzoil would ever get everything. So Pennzoil should have been motivated to settle, not gamble.

If Texaco did not settle, Pennzoil could have won the appeal and extracted the full $10 billion plus accumulated interest, virtually gobbling up Texaco in the process. Even if this worst case scenario would not have happened, it was likely that Pennzoil would have gotten more through the courts than in a settlement. So Texaco, too, should have been highly motivated to settle, not gamble.

Following the failure of final negotiations between Texaco and Pennzoil, including face-to-face meetings between their chief executives, Texaco filed for protection from all creditors under Chapter 11 of the Federal Bankruptcy Code. Texaco, America's eighth largest industrial company and its third largest oil company, had become the largest bankruptcy in history. The court

---

[9]The situation is illustrative of "game theory" in action. Game theory is a method of using formal mathematical analysis to select the best available strategy in order to maximize one's potential gain and/or minimize one's potential losses under various circumstances and conditions. Applications range from battlefield strategy in warfare to pricing strategy in business.

proceedings were monstrously complex, the legal maneuverings tortured and twisted. Whereas all reason had demanded mutual agreement, the two oil giants were reduced to trading charges of greed and arrogance while the stock of both companies plummeted. There is no doubt that each firm was suddenly worse off—Texaco's business was debilitated and Pennzoil scrambled to protect their rights in the overwhelmed courts. Logic had screamed "Settle!"—both companies would have been better served. (In a Chapter 11, often the only real victors are the lawyers.) But logic, as we've seen, does not reign freely in organizations. Suffice it to say that managerial ego upstaged stockholder interests on both sides. There is no other conclusion. No matter the ultimate outcome—the $3 billion settlement—the risks were just not worth the rewards for either side. Pennzoil had consumed enormous fees, time, and energy. Texaco was teetering on the brink of takeover.

8. ESTABLISHING THE POSITIONS

Most positions are predictable. An athlete coming off a brilliant season makes noises about contract problems. TASS, the Soviet Union's news service, reports the American position to be "reactionary and imperialistic." The White House considers the Soviet position to be "propaganda and nothing new."

Establishing position is the opening engagement in a negotiating campaign. First posture is like an "imprint," a permanent pattern of behavior. It sets the stage for subsequent conduct. Relationships are formed early. Once imprints are stamped, they are difficult to alter.

Establishing deal-making positions for humans is akin to securing territorial control for animals. Consider a dominion battle between two male chimpanzees for regional rule (the area being marked off by urine). Who will take the lead? Who will mate the females? Once dominance and submissiveness are set, each chimp maintains its assigned role. (Now I do not mean to imply that deal makers are apes, but those not-too-infrequent "pissing contests" among lawyers do make one wonder.)

Positioning the Other Side

Establishing proper initial position is critical. It sets a mood that generally does not change during the rest of the negotiations. Initial positions are not set in the dark. Deals are not blind dates. Each side considers the other before going into the first meeting. It is important to know your opponents, understand their relationship to you, and have a general sense of how you are going to act with them.

When Dealing With Equals. Be open and direct. Build subtle dominance by aggressive concern for mutual interests (such as schedule, procedure, etc.) Control is achieved more easily by process assistance (e.g., setting the agenda) than by position assertion (e.g., insisting on your price).

When Dealing With Superiors. Confident respect is the key here. Your power is inferior and, face facts, it will remain so. A forced aggressiveness is, at best, shallow and, at worst, silly. A strong, friendly attitude is what you want to project.

When Dealing With Subordinates. Be respectful and listen seriously. Draw them out when they are not communicating forthrightly. Avoid haughty disdain or put-on deference. Maximize your superior position by not making it obvious.

When Dealing With Clients and Customers. Here's heresy: The power of the buyer is overrated. The buyers' job is to buy. If they don't buy, they lose their job. After all, their firm needs what your firm has. Your relationship with buyers should be viewed this way: You enable buyers to keep their jobs.

When Dealing With Sellers, Vendors, and Suppliers. Now you write the check. You wield the "Big Pencil," that fabled instrument of order-writing fame. You need to know your relative power versus that of other customers. However strong you are, never bully. A hand on the shoulder always beats a twist of the arm. Show your vendor the importance of the relationship. Dangling this carrot—confidence in continuing business—will improve your position.

Personality colors deals. Friendly, personable stances usually work better. Remember first names. Effective deal makers don't take themselves too seriously. Attitude is especially important when setting forth initial positions.

After You, Please

A good rule for deal making is *"Always let the other side move first."* Maybe, if you're the buyer, the seller will set an initial price lower than what you would have offered. Maybe, if you're the seller, the buyer will offer an initial price higher than you would have set. You'll never know if you go first. You can't lose by not going first. If the other side's number is ludicrously out of line, you can always dismiss it with a laugh. This flips the question back to them.

Another good rule is, "*Never bid against yourself.*" Anxious buyers often get caught in the trap of increasing their offers when there are no other serious players in the game. The best antidote for this poison is patience. Wait a while before responding to a rejection of your last bid. Don't be quick to modify and change. Good sellers make an art of encouraging qualified buyers to up their offers.

Aim for the Best Deal

You can't get across the street without walking across the road. Sometimes naive buyers get a better price than "experts"—they don't know what they can't do. And they're not afraid to ask. Asking is easy, it's cheap—and you can always say you were kidding. Too many people forget to ask.

There's another side to this tactic. If you take too aggressive an initial position, you run the risk of scaring off the other side. Sometimes buyers bid so far from reality that sellers think that the buyers are either (1) incapable of evaluating the situation and therefore not worth wasting time with, or (2) downright insulting and not worth doing business with.

There are two ways of balancing these two extremes: (1) Know the other side—the characters, their desire for the deal, and their other alternatives. (2) Ask high, but do it with a "twinkle." Make that an enigmatic twinkle. Put a pixyish sparkle in your eyes, a Mona Lisa smile on your lips. A quixotic grin can mean either "Don't take me too seriously" (if the offer is outrageous) or "You can really hit this pitch" (if the offer is in the ballpark).

When You Must Go First

Sometimes you can't avoid making the first offer. So maximize the positive benefits of going first. You control the opening issues and attitudes. It is in your power to decide what matters will be discussed and where initial negotiations will focus. In an acquisition, for example, if you make an offer that allows something other than full cash payment up front, it makes a statement.

When You Can Go Second

Counterpunching is always easier than throwing the first blow. You can see the specific interests of the other side. You now have great insight into their approach. For example, if they play lowball, you have a choice of responses: highball (an equal and opposite reaction); a mild laugh (as if to say, "That's funny, now let's get serious"); or a more formal dismissal ("There's no sense in countering").

If their first offer is reasonable, you again have a choice: You can play hardball and pretend that the offer is lowball, choose from the above responses, and await further developments; maybe they'll go up. Or you can respond in kind. This is a better tactic. You want to make many deals, not exact every last cent from one deal. After all, you might be back for another bite.[10]

When You're Exploring Boundaries

Making deal proposals that push limits must be done with care. You must avoid antagonism and quick rupture of relationships. A good approach is to vary one part of the deal at a time, while holding all others constant. Try to frame your offer in the context of honest inquiry.

For example, after discussing a complex deal that has many elements of consideration to be paid over long periods of time, switch to all cash: "Let's say we would pay everything in hard dollars. How much could you reduce the price if we all-cash at closing?" This gives insight into the importance of cash and the lowest possible price within reason.

Conversely, a seller might switch from insistence on all cash at closing to very favorable terms. How much could the seller raise prices by giving such advantageous conditions? If the buyer can and will give acceptable guarantees, and if the seller does not need as much cash, such a deal could be better for both buyer and seller.

When in Competition

As Buyer

Buyers have two simple objectives: not getting knocked out early, and smoking out competitors' offers. When you're a buyer competing with others, offer a fat price—but with the open understanding that your numbers are subject to further analysis and checking. The seller has nothing to worry about because if everything turns out as claimed, the higher price will be justified. (In real-

---

[10]I like the other side to do well. It's not pleasurable for me to find, after making a deal, that the other side paid too much as a buyer. If the other side received too little as a seller, well, I must admit, that bothers me less. Why the double standard? When a buyer pays too much, they have the continuing burden of making the damn thing work. When a seller gets too little, that's a one-time event with few subsequent pains. I'm not sure my thinking's logical but that's the way I feel.

ity, you can always find something wrong.) Your juicy offer will keep you actively in the game, and may even scare off some competitors.

As Seller

Sellers, too, have two simple objectives: keeping as many bidders as active as possible, and discovering the hottest candidates. Sellers might consider proposing a slightly lower price and then observing the reactions of potential buyers. If the price is like chum before sharks, and buyers start swirling around you in a craze, then you know you can really land a big one—and at an inflated price. Again, do not deceive. Put out your offer in a contingent manner: "Suppose we set a price of X, what would be your reaction?" You can then inform buyers that, on further reflection, your "trial" price was low. You hope that the blood-dazed piranhas hardly notice the difference.

When You Really Mean It

Have no illusions: No one is going to believe that your first offer is your final offer. It's like bluffing in poker. You must go all the way a few times before anyone will take you seriously. Once in a while, you must stick to your guns.

Assume you have no flexibility whatsoever on a particular deal point. How can you build credibility if you've already modified other deal points? One strategy might be to tackle another, rather minor issue first and prove to the other side that you really mean it when you say that your first offer is "all she wrote."

9. GETTING YOUR PRICE

When asked why he was making more money than the president of the United States, Babe Ruth replied, "I had a better year." Price is the crux of all deals. It is the way we all keep score. Although price seems simple, straightforward, and easy to evaluate, it is not.

Getting Your Price as Seller

How to Determine Price

The market generally sets the prices, but you do not have to be straitjacketed by the market. (Sure, if you're selling a commodity, the exact same stuff everyone else is selling, the market governs.) First, determine the selling price for products like yours. Next, you must position your specific stuff.

Some aspects to compare are firm reputation in the area, special features, responsiveness, and the like. Perceived value (e.g., Porsche 928S versus Ford Mustang) makes for higher pricing.

How to Differentiate Your Product

Your goal is to sustain maximum market share within a limited market. Seek control of a niche. In other words, be a big fish in a little pond. The way to do this is to make your stuff different. If you're the same, you get the same price. If your product is recognizably different, you can get a better price.

The key to making your products different is "segmentation"—carving out a particular area where you can claim uniqueness. Any uniqueness. It doesn't matter whether you differentiate by size, category, distribution system, varieties, quality, or customer. It doesn't matter which you choose. Any difference, if perceived to be important to the buyer, can command a higher price. Products must be tailored tightly to the market.

How to Stimulate Bids

Shopping around without revealing your game is the best way to stimulate bids. Don't give the impression of handling picked-over merchandise. When it becomes known in Hollywood that a script is making the rounds of the studios no one will touch it—after all, who wants to be last in line? The same is true when selling a business. Pick your targets carefully.

When working with interested parties, get a bid—any bid. The only way to find the market is with real numbers. Your objective is to get the highest number on the table. Thus, prospective buyers should be told that their bids should assume "everything presented is perfectly true." These bids are not morally or legally binding. Buyers can do their detailed analysis later and make any changes they want.

How to Raise Prices

A positive change in your product should be made at the same time you raise the price.[11] The change doesn't have to be big, but customers and prospective buyers should feel that they are getting something for their extra cash. For example, 2 percent of a 7 percent price increase should be plowed back into the product in a visible way (e.g., quicker response, slight redesign, a little extra service).

---

[11]The opposite is devastating. Every time a favorite restaurant kicks up prices, it seems, food quality falls flat. Is it my imagination? I think the same profit squeeze that triggers the price hike also provokes cost cuts. Unfortunately, you taste the latter while paying the former.

How to Improve Terms
Is it worth trading off a lower price for better terms? For example, if a buyer is allowed to reduce the cash payment in a corporate sale, the seller can boost the effective price. The seller must be compensated for the cost of money and the additional burden of carrying the note.

How to Get Your Price as Buyer

How to Determine Price
Shop around. The market is key. Compare all aspects of the products, not just the price. The least costly products are not always the cheapest. Low price is often more complex than simple numbers. For example, when comparing competing investment banking bids for a corporate project, a buyer's cost comparison should include a probability-of-closing discount as well as the traditional underwriters' or M&A commissions.

How to Make Your Bids
Make an offer that you would love to be accepted. Judge the situation. If you're hot for the deal, make a reasonable first offer. If you're unsure, throw out a red herring. You never know who may bite. Don't be afraid to discuss your offer over and over again. The more you talk the more you learn.

How to Adjust Prices
Every offer is made subject to appropriate due diligence. Deals should be bid as if everything presented is absolutely correct. Thus, a fat first offer encourages the seller that the bidder is a prime candidate. The process may even drive out some competitors. Then, after making a detailed analysis, you can always change your mind ("take a haircut" or "move South" in deal-making parlance).

How to Improve Terms
"Your price, my terms" is a deal maker's maxim. Deal terms are as important as price to the buyer.[12] The opposite is often true (at least psychologically) for the seller. Sellers like to brag about the price they got. Cater to this tendency: Trade off higher prices for better terms.

When Parties Compete

Competition is great when you're a seller; not so when you're a buyer. The same tricks, I'm pleased to report, work in both situations.

---

[12]You'd be happy to pay a full asking price as long as it required little money down, all financed by the seller, and all cash payments to come from the company. If you could buy a business strictly from the cash flow of that business, say within four years, then no price, if you think about it, is too high.

When Buying

As buyer, never bid against yourself. Many have upped their offers when no other parties were even in the running. Look for situations where the sellers will acknowledge that your party is the only bidder. "Let's do a negotiated deal," you would say. "Let's proceed in good faith. If we can't reach a good deal for both of us, we'll back off with nothing lost." If necessary, agree to a time limit. Stretch as far as possible to eliminate competition.

When Selling

As seller, try to deal with several interested (or, better yet, anxious) suitors simultaneously. Having other options around makes you a more confident negotiator. Alternatives stiffen backbones. Furthermore, there's a strange phenomenon in the buying and selling game. The great majority of offers cluster, as you'd expect, within a tight range. But then there are usually one or two outliers, parties who for their own reasons bid significantly higher. Your task is to find these fine folks.

Buying and Selling in Auctions

Bidding Theory

Recent research has confirmed what canny traders have known for some time: Most bidders in auctions harbor inflated opinions of their own judgment of value. Though they may do detailed analyses, the bottom line is that they generally go with their intuitions. Instincts lead the charge, and more often than not, it's a slaughter for the buyer (and a windfall for the seller).

New theory in bidding psychology shows that the structure of auctions molds strategies and influences behavior.[13] Major companies are monitoring the progress.

---

[13]Generating the highest bids from the seller's viewpoint depends on the characteristics of the assets being auctioned. If demand is not sensitive to price (inelastic), the highest price is produced by a normal auction in which the highest bidder pays the price he offered. If, however, demand is highly sensitive to price (elastic), then a "second-price" auction is recommended for the seller's benefit. Here the top bidder pays the price offered by the runner up. Buyer psychology encourages inflating the price since each buyer knows that he will not have to pay his own high price if he wins. Since all buyers think the same, the overall price pushes up. To demonstrate that different auction structures produce different results, Charles Plott of the California Institute of Technology auctioned off a dollar bill. How to get more than 100 cents? If the dollar is given to the highest bidder, but the second highest must pay for it, bidding skyrocketed (above $1.00!) since everyone had an incentive to outbid rivals.

How to Handle Auctions as Sellers

Which deals do you auction? When you have an especially hot property, the rules change. Now you're in the driver's seat. Make wide contacts. Establish a date for bids to be submitted.

A seller's optimum auction strategy for soliciting bids includes the following steps:

1. Encourage the maximum number of bidders; the greater the number of participants the higher the winning bid.
2. Make available before the auction as much information as possible about the object or asset to be auctioned. Trust the marketplace to squeeze out any windfall profits—but only if all relevant data is widely distributed to all potential bidders.
3. Do not give away any information about the bidders before the auction. Avoid all actions that will reveal the number, nature, or strategies of the rival bidders (e.g., use no "prequalification" procedures. Keep your bidders totally blind).
4. Do not give away any information after the auction. Avoid giving bidders any hint of their competitors' strategies. (This applies both to second-round bids or future auctions.)
5. Consider a second round. This is delicate. Allow those bidders that came close to "sweeten" their offers. Since the first round winner would scream like hell, don't announce who won. Do not disclose the winning bid, either. However, a new "floor" for the final round should be established.

How to Handle Auctions as Buyers

When do you participate in auctions? Auctions should be avoided whenever possible. Only bid when you have specific competitive advantage. For example, an operating company that knows it can bring substantial new business to the firm being auctioned has an edge over an investment company looking purely at that firm's current cash flow. The operating company can afford to make a higher offer and still generate a similar return.

A buyer's optimum auction strategy for making bids includes the following steps:

1. Only participate when the number of bidders is relatively small. Some companies will not even enter auctions with more than five hats in the ring.

2. Seek some competitive edge in the bidding. For example, look for synergies with your current operations. Or try to get special information about the object or asset to be auctioned. If you cannot go into the auction with some sort of comparative advantage, forget it.
3. Learn as much as possible before the auction about the number, nature, or strategies of the rival bidders. Put yourself in their shoes and plan alternative scenarios.
4. Learn as much as possible after the auction about your competitors' strategies. This will prove useful when bidding against the same rivals again, and it will be a benchmark against which to judge your own pre-auction evaluation techniques.

Making Sure Buyers and Sellers Can Deliver

The most frustrating experience is to cut a good deal with a party that can't produce. You must establish confidence in the other side's credibility. Sometimes, the parties with the lowest credibility offer the best deals. This is logical since weaker buyers must offer sellers something special to compensate for the uncertainty. Don't dismiss these flakes too quickly. They may be hungry enough to belly up to the table.

You always want to know how much the buyer can pay. It's like children selling candy to each other. "How much does the Mars Bar cost?" asked the wide-eyed six year old. "How much do you have in your pocket?" answered the street-smart eight year old.

10. LEARNING THE OPENING GAME

What marvelous analogies come from Chess! "Chess is life," expound the grandmasters, who speak of the "essence of a bishop" and the "elegance of a sacrifice." No grandmaster, it is said, has ever lost a game when feeling well.

Chess games are divided into three parts: the opening game, the middle game, and the end game. Each part, with its special attributes, teaches specific lessons about deal making. Each will be discussed in its own section.

The Opening Game is the first few moves in which all the pieces are put into play. Good opening-game strategy is characterized by well-prepared themes and variations.

The Middle Game is the play with the major pieces on the board. Good middle-game strategy is characterized by plans projected out many moves deep, positional strength, combinations, sacrifices, and mating attacks.

The End Game begins when the major pieces come off the board. Here, through the promotion of pawns to queens, small advantages are transformed into winning positions. Good end-game strategy is characterized by precise calculations of tempo and timing.

Kinds of Chess Openings

In chess, openings are patterns of moves. There are dozens of different openings with wonderfully colorful names.[14] There are also hundreds of variations, which sport their own personalities.[15] Each of these patterns of moves has clear advantages and disadvantages—with the boundary between brilliance and blunder often being subtle. The same is true of deal making.

"Gambits" are important in both chess and deal making. A gambit gives up something, such as a pawn (in essence a fetal queen), to gain position and mobility. A gambit is a risk, trading something tangible for something intangible. If there's little compensation, if your opponent's pawn advantage is maintained to the end, you face a lost position.

Surprise is an important opening ploy. Shock can often overwhelm a superior system. Say your opponent chooses an older, inferior opening. If you haven't prepared for it and your opponent has, you could be in trouble. See an analogy to deal making?

Principles of the Opening Game

There are certain ideas behind good chess openings. These principles correspond directly to deal making.

Develop Pieces Efficiently

Each move should bring out a new piece. Developing your pieces by attacking your opponent's pieces is efficient. If your opponent must defend after each move, he or she is less likely to develop an attack. Good deal makers optimize their resources.

---

[14] Names are given for people (e.g., Morphy Attack, Evans Gambit, Reti Opening, Colle System, Falkbeer Counter-Gambit), countries (e.g., English Opening, Sicilian Defense, French Defense), and positions (e.g., Giuoco Piano, King's and Queen's Indian, King's Gambit, Queen's Gambit Declined, Hypermodern).

[15] For example, the Sicilian Defense has numerous variations, including the Dragon, the Moscow, the Najdorf, the Scheveningen, and the Nimzowitsch.

Put Pieces on Good Squares

Positioning of pieces is vital. Maximize move-making mobility.[16] Know the value of each piece in your arsenal. Good deal makers understand how best to take advantage of their capabilities.

Pieces Should Work Together

Synergy is important.[17] Good deal makers appreciate how their resources combine for maximum effectiveness.

Control the Center

Center control is the most important early principle. The greater your control of the center, the greater space for your pieces, and the more constricted the space for your opponent's. An offensive posture is always more desirable. Good deal makers know that control of central issues is a critical factor for success.

Protect the King

The king is your vital piece. Lose it and you lose the game. What cannot be lost must be constantly protected. Good deal makers never forget or neglect their bottom-line vulnerability.[18]

---

[16]Knights, for example, should be positioned near the center, not the edge of the board (since they can jump over other pieces). Bishops, on the other hand, can rake the board from edges, and should not be blocked by pawns.

[17]For example, lining up or "connecting" rooks reinforces their strength. Bishop pairs on long diagonals can skewer opposing pieces and dominate the board. Pawns should support one another on adjacent files.

[18]Try the following openings of the deal-making game. (I've had some fun with these.) *Ronald Reagan Center Game*: Friendly and compelling. Moves are made for show and image, not content and substance. *Cary Grant Suave Game*: Cultured and urbane. Moves are made to develop an atmosphere of graciousness and charm. *Jackie Kennedy Onassis System*: Elegant and refined. Moves are made for polished manners and social standing. *Carl Sagan System*: Erudite and understandable. Moves are made to make hard concepts easy to digest. *Don Rickles Attack*: Insulting and cutting. Moves are made to irritate and offend. *Charles Bronson Attack*: Brutal and solitary. Moves are made to blow you away. *Mr. T. Attack*: Intimidating and coercive. Moves are made to bounce you around. *J. R. Ewing Gambit*: Tough and sneaky. Moves are made behind your back. *Muammar Khaddafy Gambit*: Wild and dangerous. Moves are made without concern for consequences. *Sylvester Stallone Gambit*: Powerful but superficial. Moves are made to accomplish simple purposes. *Yogi Berra Counter-Gambit*: Odd and wise. Moves are made that appear silly but contain real insight. *Woody Allen Counter-Gambit*: Witty and wise. Moves are made to convey profound truth in a lighthearted manner. *Johnny Carson Defense*: Light and easy. Moves are made to put you to sleep. *Leonid Brezhnev Defense*: Stoic and blunt. Moves are made to maintain an iron curtain. *Nikita Khrushchev Defense*: Boorish and uncouth. Moves are made to irritate and affront. *Rodney Dangerfield Defense*: Hesitant and self-conscious. Moves are made with worry and uncertainty—sure not to get any respect.

11. IMAGING THE MIDDLE GAME

Let's start with a surprise: The trick in good deal making is often not what tactic you use but how well you use it. Specific strategy sometimes doesn't matter. Making that strategy work is what counts. It's like the middle game in chess where there are numerous strategies from which to choose. How well you execute the strategy is more important than which one you pick. Implementation, in other words, is more critical than formulation.

The current world champion of chess, Gari Kasparov of the Soviet Union, is a dynamic player known for explosive attacks that border on the reckless. The former world champion, Anatoly Karpov, also of the Soviet Union, is a positional player known for a suffocating style that has been likened to that of a boa constrictor. Kasparov is electrifying but erratic. Karpov is dull but consistent. The "Super Ks" are, without doubt, the two best players in the world. Their strategies differ widely, yet both are world-class. Likewise in deal making: First-rate deal makers evince diversity of strategy but commonality of excellence.

Strategies for the Middle Game

The following strategic ideas fit the middle game. The general idea is to meld consistency and creativity in driving toward success. Most of these strategies can work together.

Complete Development

Finish the process begun in the opening. Get all your pieces activated; get all your issues on the table. Get all your resources working as a unit. Be sure all moves support a clear plan.

Plan an Attack

Determine the best approach for mounting an offensive, whether a direct assault against the opponent's primary sticking point (such as price) or an indirect foray on an opposing flank (such as timing). In chess, the strategic decision is when to go after the king. In deal making, it's whether to go after vital or peripheral issues first.

Combinations

Look for ways and means to combine your resources. Moves must be thought through carefully. In chess, take advantage of the particular attribute of each piece. In deal making, it's the special character of each issue. Discover how several separate issues might be solved in one overall solution.[19]

Sacrifices

In chess, watch for unique opportunities where giving up a valuable piece can produce quick victory, normally by exposing the King's defensive position. The victory needs to be swift, since you are now down substantial material and would eventually lose if the position becomes simplified. In deal making, sacrifices are strategic concessions. Watch for unique opportunities where giving something up can induce swift closure on favorable terms. Maybe a sudden swing on price can cut through a morass of tangled problems.

Develop Complications

If you have the superior position, seek ways to increase complexity. In chess, a superior position is better placed pieces, more focused resources, and more board control. In deal making, it's less necessity to make the deal, larger size, and lower stakes. Here, for example, you should add additional issues and factors. Do not allow simplification.

Simplify the Position

If you have the inferior position, seek ways to decrease complexity. In chess, an inferior position is poorly placed pieces, dispersed resources, and less board control. In deal making, it's greater necessity to make the deal, smaller size, and higher stakes. Here, for example, you should eliminate current issues by exchanging or trading them off. Do not allow complications.

Prepare for the End Game

Few grandmaster matches end in the middle game. Few deals are consummated here, either. A concluding handshake with a room full of issues is rare. Instead, the preparations that begin in the middle of negotiations are what win the close. The key is to think out where you want to end up. Imaging the future is vital.

---

[19]For example, consider a deal where the buyer does not want to pay the seller's price of $105 million, and the seller does not like taking back $20 million (of the $105) in long-term, high-risk notes. A proposed solution is to lower the amount to $92.5 million and make it all in cash. The buyer is pleased to save $12.5 million in value; the seller is pleased to get an extra $7.5 million in cash.

Deal Tactics of the Middle Game

Relative Value of Pieces[20]

Understand the comparative value of your issues and resources, strengths and weaknesses, so that you can trade them to your advantage. In deal making, however, there is no nice point system to count on your fingers. However, if you think in terms of relative value of issues, it can guide the trading process.

Patterns and Positions[21]

Familiarity with various deal positions is vital. Develop (1) a sense of circumstance and (2) limits around critical problems. Avoid being suckered by high pressure.

Deep Calculations[22]

Determining moves in deals is much the same as in chess. You consider (1) a move, (2) your opponent's possible replies, and (3) your possible answers to each of those replies, and so on. You must learn to weed out the least likely scenarios quickly and concentrate on the most likely.

Active People[23]

You want your people to be hard workers, and doing all the things of which they are capable. Each element of deal making should be used where it works

---

[20]*Relative Value of Pieces*. In chess it's easy; there's a "point count" to help: Queens, 9; Rooks, 5; Bishops, 3 1/4; Knights, 3; Pawns, 1. You would therefore exchange your Queen and one Knight (which total 12 points) for your opponent's two Rooks and one Bishop (13 1/4), but not your rook and two pawns (7) for two knights (6).

[21]*Patterns and Positions*. Familiarity with various positions of pieces is vital. Develop a sense of position. Look for "mating nets" around the opposite king. Avoid "fool's mate" on your king.

[22]*Deep Calculations*. Determining moves in chess is simple to say, hard to do. What do I do, you ask yourself, if I make move "X" and my opponent makes move "Y"? You consider a move, then consider the various possible replies of your opponent, then your possible responses to each of those replies, and so on. The variations branch rapidly and become impossibly complex. Assume that there are 10 reasonable moves for each side on every turn. This means, since each side must move on each turn, that considering your options just *six* moves out requires analyzing 10^{12} positions, or one *trillion* possible positions. (Incredibly, there are over 10^{115} possible 40-move games, far greater than the number of atomic particles in the universe.) The only solution is to limit drastically the options that you consider. Look at only the most likely. Which to study and which to ignore? This is where experience comes in.

[23]*Active Pieces*. Knights, remember, jump over other pieces, so they're especially valuable when the board is crowded. Bishops skewer like a sword, and work well with wide-open spaces. Rooks love to connect, especially on the seventh rank deep in your opponent's camp.

best, flexibility in the opening to build rapport, complexity in the middle game to add opportunity, and firmness in the end game to close the deal.

Multiple Attacks[24]
Applying "multiple attacks" to deal making can stimulate creativity. Two examples: "Pins," finding issues that your opponent can't be tough on for fear of uncovering a worse situation (e.g., a selling company might readily agree to pay extra money to eliminate a liability exposure for fear that the actual liability may be far more extensive); "double attacks," simultaneously addressing more than one issue (e.g., giving your kids a weekly allowance can eliminate all disputes over financing their movies, new clothes, parties, etc.). Remember the strategy here: Whenever you find a "pinned" issue, attack it! Whenever you can handle two issues at once, do it!

12. CALCULATING THE END GAME

In deal making, closing is what counts. You can be brilliant in finding, selecting, and structuring deals—but none of that matters if you can't finish them off. In chess, the end game begins when all the heavy pieces (queens and rooks) are off the board. In deal making, the end game begins when most major issues are resolved. End game play takes on a different character. It must be very precise.

Ideas for the End Game

Wins occur when you have clear superiority in material or position. At this point, it's all a matter of technique. In chess, exchange pieces—since the fewer pieces on the board the larger your advantage becomes. In deal making, trade out all remaining issues quickly. Press your advantage with care. In deals, winning positions can be blown by a high-handed manner.

---

[24]*Multiple Attacks.* Pins, forks, double attacks, and discovered checks are chess tactics. A "pin" is when a piece can't move because, if it does, a more valuable piece will be lost (the strategy is to attack a pinned piece). A "double attack" is when a piece attacks two valuable pieces at the same time (and often it is impossible to defend them both). A "fork" is when a knight is the double attacker. A "discovered check" is a direct attack on the king by a piece that occurs when an interfering piece is moved out of the way. A discovered check is very powerful since it allows the moving piece a "free" move (say to attack a queen) since the king must be protected on the next move. In chess you are always on search for multiple attacks—to attack with or defend against.

Forced Wins occur when you totally control the situation no matter what the other side does. In chess, it's just a matter of demonstrating your checkmate. In deal making, such occurrences are exceedingly rare, and flaunting your position can ruin it.

Draws occur when the game is ended even. In chess, draws are declared when one side offers and the other accepts. (Protocol dictates that the side with the slight advantage should offer the draw.) Draws are usually duds in chess, though important when needed to clinch match victory. In deal making, draws occur when negotiations end in a tie. Draws are not duds in deals: If they mean closure, they are good; however, you may be disappointed if you sought more gain than you got.

Forced Draws[25] occur when any of the following happen: (1) all issues are resolved; (2) positions are repeated continuously without compromise or movement; (3) neither side can alter its position without conceding basic points; (4) a long period of time elapses without progress.

Zugzwang is a German word meaning "move compulsion." It occurs when one side cannot make a move without giving away something important.[26] In chess, you have to move. In deals, you do not.

Deal Strategies for the End Game

Precise Calculations are needed to determine the exact sequence and timing of your final moves in negotiations. In chess, victory or loss is often measured in the tempo of a single move: Whoever would make the next move would win (generally by the promotion of a pawn to a queen). In deal making, completion or disruption is often calculated in terms of the resolution of a single issue.

Mobility is critical. In chess, it's position and timing: The king needs to shepherd its pawns down the board to become a queen. In deal making, it's attitude and issues: Deal makers need to shepherd their final points down to closing.

---

[25]In chess, forced draws are when any of the following happen: (1) material is exchanged down so that checkmate is impossible (such as a king and a bishop against a king); (2) a position is repeated three times consecutively; (3) one side cannot move without moving into check; (4) neither side has captured a piece or moved a pawn after 50 moves.

[26]In chess, these positions occur only in end games, and are usually when pawns must move forward into being captured.

Sacrifice in the end game is more apparent than real, since you know exactly what you are getting for what you are giving. In chess, the benefits of an end-game sacrifice must happen in short order.[27] In deal making, the reason for the sacrifice is usually a quick trade to reach final agreement.

How to Become an Expert

Developing world-class expertise is exceedingly difficult. One prominent management researcher—who did much of his work with chess grandmasters—believes that such expertise requires 10 years of concentrated experience and some 50,000 "chunks" of information.[28]

What's a chunk? A good bit more than a byte. A chunk is an integrated concept of knowledge—whole experiences—complete patterns of awareness that become the foundation for evaluating new situations. A chess example is a repeatable pattern of pieces. A deal example is handling an irritating personal affront.

Chess Lingo

I am fascinated by the jargon of chess players. The talk sounds violent, yet has a whimsical touch. Some examples that relate to deal making follow.

Hopelessly Lost: In chess, the winner is identified by default. If a player is winning, he is not declared a "sure victor"; rather his opponent is described as being "hopelessly lost." In deal making, it's when one side just gives up the fight.

Blunders: Clear mistakes—very bad moves made by very good players. A blunder to a grandmaster might be a decent move for normal mortals. We all blunder, even in deal making. Examples of the latter include giving away too much too soon and not compromising for ego's sake. Remember what chess players say about blunders: It's not the first mistake that kills you, but the second—the fatal flaw is often made while worrying over that initial,

---

[27] An example offensive sacrifice is when you give up two pawns for one so that another of your pawns can queen first. An example defensive sacrifice is when you are behind in material and trade your last minor piece (bishop or knight) for an opponent's last pawn, thereby assuring a draw.

[28] Herbert Simon, "Understanding Creativity and Creative Management," in *Handbook for Creative and Innovative Managers*: Robert Lawrence Kuhn, editor in chief (New York, McGraw-Hill, 1987).

often minor, error. The message is clear: Don't fret about past failures; just concentrate on current issues.

Stalemate: A forced draw—and a wonderful word. In chess, it's a would-be, should-be checkmate that has gone "stale." Stalemates often occur when one side has a winning advantage and gets sloppy. Deal makers who have negotiated a good deal must maintain full focus and not allow a minor issue to disrupt the transaction.

Perpetual Check: In chess, when one side can continuously check the other side but never actually pull the mate. In deal making, when one side can keep the other side constantly off balance, say, by harping on a sensitive subject. Perpetual check, in chess and in deals, is done by the weaker side and draws by repetition of moves.

Adjournments: In chess, after 40 moves are made without victory, the players may take a recess to the next day—and all the strict rules of the game evaporate. Players are expected to work hard analyzing the numerous variations of the adjourned position. This is not like a take-home examination in college. There is no honor code to uphold. You may consult every expert, use every tool, boot up every computer. Similarly, in deal making, when negotiations are adjourned, it is vital to rethink strategy and plan your next moves carefully.

"Always Check, It May Be Mate": This is my favorite chess maxim. There are two points here: (1) you never know the impact of a strategy until you try it, and (2) you should always give luck a chance to weave its serendipitous magic.

When to Take Risks in Chess and Deals

In both personal and business deal making, as in chess, you take risks when your position is either very good or very poor. In either position, a gamble can result in a profitable payoff. In chess, whether in the middle game or end game, you take risks under two, quite opposite conditions: (1) When you have a superior position with greater control of board space or better mobility for your pieces (risk here may assure a quick victory), and (2) when your position is desperate and you have little to lose by trying (risk here may salvage a lost position).

Superior Corporate Position

Assume you are discussing a promotion with your boss. You have just created a successful sales campaign (which gives you superior position) and have personally opened up several major accounts (which gives you greater control of space). As a result, several competitors are making attractive bids for your services (which gives you better mobility). What to do? Now is the time to go for that promotion; the game is stacked in your favor.

Inferior Corporate Position

If you are in a poor position, you can afford to take the same kind of risk because you have little to lose. Suppose, for example, your department was decimated by budget cuts. Your boss has been fired and it is rumored that you are next. What to do? It can't hurt to take an aggressive posture here. March right into the division head's office, assert your positive contribution to the company, and state with confidence that you would like to be transferred to another department. At worst, you may be fired today instead of Friday. At best, you may be viewed as a take-charge person and a loyal employee.

Superior Personal Position

Your mother-in-law has been bugging you for years. Not much of a provider, she laments. Not good enough for her daughter, she carps. Finally, you get a healthy raise. What to do? Time to take a risk and put the lady linebacker in her place.

Inferior Personal Position

Your marriage is falling apart, fighting is on the increase, divorce is in the winds. What to do? Time to take a risk and put more adventure in the bedroom.

13. STRESSING THE STRENGTHS

Build strengths; avoid weaknesses—a "good balance" I like to avoid. The arena for doing deals is fiercely combative. Deal makers must show their best stuff or be thrown out on their rears. It is better to be great at some things and poor at others than average at everything. Mediocrity just doesn't hold tough in competitive deal making.

Strength and Weakness Assessment

Good deal makers must know their own strengths and weaknesses, aptitudes and limitations. This holds true whether assessing one's firm or one's self. Check your personal balance sheet: What are your assets and liabilities?

The self-assessment process is tricky because it is so biased.[29] Thus, the definition of one's strengths and weaknesses cannot be divorced from one's position and responsibility. Objective analysis is difficult, and one should never assume otherwise. However, performing the assessment in a comparative context can help.

Inside Analysis

First, go internal. Compare your various departments or attributes among one another. For a company example, which is your firm's stronger division, marketing or manufacturing? For a personal example, which is your own better talent, technical or people skills?

Outside Analysis

Next, go external. Compare your various departments or attributes to those of competitors. For a company example, how does your firm's distribution system compare to those of marketplace opponents? For a personal example, how good are you at outselling your rivals?

Techniques for Maximizing Strengths

The following areas of deal-making strengths are matched with appropriate tactics to take advantage of these strengths.

Size. When your side is larger (and has more resources), take your time, strive for complexity, allow no pressure. Above all, however, treat the other side as equals. Do not condescend. Do not chance antagonism.

Power. When your side has more force (see Deal Secret 1), be slow to change on demand, quick to press agreement on your terms, and willing to allow face-saving concessions.

Flexibility. When your side is more adaptable, add complexities, alter issues, change agendas, move schedules, postpone meetings.

Needs. When your side has less demand for the deal, go slower, avoid pressure, be meticulous.

---

[29] A research study asked corporate executives to judge their firm's strengths and weaknesses. The results were startling: The assessment was based more on these executives' kind of job and level in the hierarchy than on the actual strengths and weaknesses of their particular company. In other words, perception had more influence than reality! Thus, personnel and financial concerns (whether considered strength or weakness) peak at senior management, while marketing and technical concerns peak at middle management—*irrespective of the firm involved*! Senior managers all saw about the same strengths and weaknesses, as did all financial managers, as did all foremen—and it didn't matter which company employed them. Howard H. Stevenson, "Defining Corporate Strengths and Weaknesses," *Sloan Management Review*, Spring, 1976.

Expertise. When your side is more knowledgeable, use the impact of your advantage quietly. The less overt your content superiority, the stronger your influence.

People. When your side has stronger negotiators, have more face-to-face contact. Encourage larger, more frequent meetings. Discourage written communications.

Time. When your side has less schedule pressure, proceed properly. Do not slow the pace deliberately or you may infuriate the other side.

Insight. Sometimes you just "know" what to do; other times you just take a chance. Deal-making wisdom is the product of experience, natural gift, and trusting your own judgment.[30] Intuition can contradict logic. When you feel it, use it; when you believe it, do it.

Corporate Example

Assume that you are representing a large conglomerate and have become embroiled in a competitive bidding battle to purchase a spin-off division of another conglomerate. The purchase is critical for one of your client's divisions. You've already reached the price limit set by the board's executive committee. You cannot go higher and you cannot win at this price. How can the offer be sweetened without violating the corporate rules?

Go with your strengths. Both conglomerates consist of large corporate groups with many diverse subsidiaries. In all likelihood, one of your company's other divisions can do business with one of the seller's other divisions. It may be worth a substantial amount to the selling corporation to secure a large, multi-year contract for its products. It may even be enough to give your group the acquisition as part of a larger deal.

14. SKIRTING THE WEAKNESSES

Improve your strengths—not your weaknesses. Deal making is not school. Bury those wobbly areas; never give in to them. When you haven't got it, hide it—don't improve it. (Why not strengthen your weaknesses? It's too expensive!)

---

[30]Not trusting my own insight, to be frank, has occasionally held me back from making dynamic advances. It's tough when you've been trained to respect quantitative, legal, or scientific reasoning to go forward with ideas that you cannot fully support.

Techniques for Minimizing Weaknesses

The following areas of deal-making weaknesses are matched with appropriate tactics to downplay these weaknesses.

Size. When your side is smaller (and has less resources), propel the process, strive for simplicity, appeal to fairness. Above all, treat the other side as equals. Do not fawn.

Power. When your side has less force (see Deal Secret 1), be careful when conceding points. Be sure every concession really counts and that your concessions become progressively smaller. Try toughness as a surprise.

Flexibility. When your side is less adaptable, strive to simplify, contain issues, maintain agendas, keep to schedules.

Needs. When your side needs the deal more, try not to show it. Move the deal along without evincing nervousness. Showing anxiety is a serious lapse.

Expertise. When your side is less knowledgeable, try to learn quickly. Use your lack of information or experience as a negotiating ploy. "Now you can't expect me to understand you 'city boys' right away. . ."

People. When your side has weaker negotiators, have less face-to-face contact. Encourage smaller, less frequent meetings. Communicate more in writing.

Time. When your side has more schedule pressure, move the deal along without showing anxiety. (Express nervous concern and you will be attacked like a wounded animal.)

Insight. When your side has less understanding of the deal, you can either let the other side lead and learn as you go or boldly suggest "naive" ideas and see what happens.

Attitudes When Weak

Never succumb to weakness. Never evince resignation. A sullen, depressed demeanor invites stagnation; and rudeness, surliness, and sarcasm induce disruption. Consider the following: Be hopeful, in outward attitude if not inward spirit. Speak clearly and directly, not muffled and askance. Sit erect and look well pulled together. Don't give yourself away with slumping, dejected posture—a slithering body conveys feebleness. Eye contact is important. Don't fear glances colliding across the table. Indeed, search out your opponents' pupils. You'll feel awkward at first, then good.

Weakness Can Be a Strength

Used circumspectly, a "help me" posture can evoke concessions. Even investment bankers can fall prey to compassion. The key is to appeal to your opponents' human nature—not to their competitive instincts. (Naturally, when you're on the stronger side, beware of this tactic.) Some people, sadly, have a sadistic bent, and any side of weakness will just encourage their rapacious behavior.

Finally, recall President Kennedy's words: "Let us never negotiate out of fear. But let us never fear to negotiate." We tend to overlook what he said beforehand: "So let us begin anew—remembering on both sides that civility is not a sign of weakness, and sincerity is always subject to proof."

15. DRIVING THE OFFENSE

Forward movement is vital for deal success. Stalling is as dangerous in making deals as it is in flying aircraft. Your object is to "drive the offense" without being offensive. Be a "killer" for the cause.

A deal is never over, in Yogi Berra's immortal words, till it's over. Never be satisfied with good movement and proper direction. Never rest until papers are signed, money changes hands, and the deal is closed. Never be complacent.

Deals can stall because of inattention. Everyone, especially attorneys, pays more attention to those who complain. So growl, grumble, and grouse. Wail, lament, and moan. Talk to your people every day. Keep things hopping. If squeaky wheels get greased, then *squawk*, don't just squeak.

Tips for Breaking Crises

There is a critical point in most deals. It occurs when initial enthusiasm meets contentious disagreement. Progress slows, discouragement grows, and many deals abort. The problem has two solutions: Break through the crisis by resolving the issues, or close the deal before it reaches the crisis point. Following are techniques for achieving crisis breakthrough.

Multiplying Options

Advancing is easiest when you have a choice of direction and method. The more alternatives you have, the more likely you'll find one that will work. Multiplying options is one of my major themes. The constant assessment of situations and the frequent search for new ideas facilitates breakthrough.

Using the Team

It is not desirable for principals to confront each other too often. The top brass should get together only to resolve final issues. Other members of the negotiating team should be used for the nitty-gritty. Divide up duties—this technique allows communication to proceed at all levels.

Going Off the Record

In "off the record" conversations, ideas can be suggested and opinions expressed without commitment. Don't misunderstand—there's no deception here; rarely are such discussions really off the record. Each side knows the technique, and both sides like using it. Off the record discussions give all parties a low-pressure opportunity to explore alternatives and fresh approaches.

Setting Time Limits

There comes a moment when you know the deal is not happening. At that certain point you must crank up the heat. For example, if your offer as buyer is being shopped around or if your offer as seller is being delayed, you must increase pressure. Let the other side know your displeasure, that you're up to their tricks, that you have other options, and that you're prepared to take a walk.

Using Written Communications

No matter what the circumstances or relationships, the agreement should always be put in writing. (See Deal Secret 36.) This puts the issues into clear view and reveals any hidden problems that must be resolved before the deal can get done.

Timing is important here. If the problems emerge too soon, they can kill the deal. For example, introducing technical difficulties early on might slow down momentum and cut off progress. The intrusions can divert energy and fragment focus. The solution is to reach agreement on the broad business matters before getting down to the details.

Which Side Should Go First? Generally the side that wants to control the deal will draw up the document. Then, any changes go on that side's original form (and word processor). However, if there are some points of uncertainty, you might let the other side prepare the first draft. Perhaps they recollect the questionable areas in ways more favorable to you. Another approach is to draw up the memo or letter with blanks left for the key deal numbers.

Memoranda of Understanding highlight all the primary deal points and are excellent instruments for moving a deal from talk to action. These memos are designed to confirm mutual understanding and are often composed by the parties involved—not their attorneys (however, an attorney should probably read over the memo). Since such memos are not legally binding, they enable both sides to express their thinking. Clear disclaimers are included and they need not be signed.

Letters of Intent are more serious. They are signed instruments drawn up by attorneys. Both sides now affirm that they are committed to go ahead with the transactions according to the specified terms and conditions. You can still back out, but it's getting harder—and it might cost you something.

Doing Nothing

Doing nothing is the hardest thing to do well. But often, there is no stronger offense. Going silent puts tremendous pressure on the other side, especially if they've invested time and effort in the deal ("sunk costs") and need to get it done. Furthermore, as you may recall, silence protects your side from talking too much—a disease that can cause you to bid against yourself when there's no one else in the running.

Wooing and Wowing

Time for charm. Don't laugh. Everyone likes to be complimented, even flattered. If you're a buyer, tell the other side how well they've done with their business; if you're a seller, explain why they'll be satisfied owners.

Also, everyone likes to associate with a winner. If the deal involves any continuing relationship between the parties, you should build your side's image in the eyes of the other side. You want to show, without being overt, that the association will be good for them.

16. BUTTRESSING THE DEFENSE

"The best defense is a good offense" sounds great. When it works, this is nice. When a weak spot is attacked, don't defend, attack back. For example: If the other side demands that certain guarantees must be strengthened, tell them you are considering cutting them down further. If your boss claims you are not spending enough time traveling to see customers, say, "What about those additional expense allowances you promised?"

Good strategy? Sure. The problem is that offense doesn't always work. Following are some ideas for counteracting adverse negotiating conditions.

Counterpunching

Let the other side make the first proposals. It is easier to respond than to offer when defending a position. According to military theory, an attacking army needs far more soldiers than does a defending army. When you are the "proposee," you have time for considered response. You learn more, too.

Substitute Players

Put in some new folks. They may help, even if only slowing the process and shifting momentum. This tactic is like calling a timeout to make a substitution in basketball—often used to break the other team's hot streak.

Good-Guy/Bad-Guy

Playing "good-guy/bad-guy" is always worth a shot. In deal making, this is also known as the "black-hat/white-hat" ritual. Note that taking the bad-guy/black-hat role means disagreeing—not being disagreeable. Creating a bad guy is often valuable because it makes the good guy stand out by contrast. He or she is someone with whom the other side can talk and in whom they can confide. Good guys can sometimes perform magic. This technique can be effective even if the other side is fully aware of your ploy.

Stonewalling

Just say no. However much the facts demand change in your position, simply refuse to budge. Be obstinate. Keep a straight face and be stubborn and inflexible—mulish and bullheaded. Obviously the strength of your stone and the height of your wall depends on the relative power of the parties. If your side is the more powerful, stonewalling is easy to implement (though not necessarily good strategy). If your side is the less powerful, stonewalling adds a touch of the irrational, which isn't all bad.[31]

Perhaps the most positive benefit of stonewalling is its impact. It can't be ignored. Furthermore, when you finally do make a change, however modest, the importance of the concession becomes exaggerated. Your efforts are much appreciated. The key is timing and relativity: People assess current events by comparing them with recent events.

The Art of Bluffing

Bluffing is a common business practice. It is easy to do, but hard to do well. It's also dangerous, especially if the parties involved know your style; repeatable patterns are sensed quickly. If you bluff, you must be prepared to carry through with your threats.

---

[31] Watch how irrationality helps the weaker side. Assume you're the stronger. How do you deal with people who won't make a decision that is clearly in their own best interest (as well as in yours)? How do you handle situations where normal logic, power, and persuasion won't work? It can be disorienting, and sometimes you make a quick, "unnecessary" concession just to get the thorn out of your flesh. When deal makers, however strong, confront illogical reaction, they may bend if they really want the deal.

When Fighting Time

Take charge of the process. Schedule meetings. Set agendas. Energize attorneys. Produce paperwork. In other words, you assume responsibility for movement. If the other side continues to delay, they either don't want to make a fair deal (in which case you'd rather know it sooner than later) or their effort to use time as a weapon is exposed.

Here's another, less traditional approach. If the other side thinks it has you in a time squeeze, then perhaps you should shock them by slowing negotiations yourself. It can disrupt their strategy and work to your advantage.

When Fighting Bullies

Handling toughs and tyrants is risky because all options hold dangers. Pushing back hard can expose their cowardliness—but it may also trigger a blowout. Playing meek and defenseless can disarm the other side—but it may also invite mayhem. The best tactic is to side-step ruffians. Allow their abuse to bounce off harmlessly, like a hot laser off a shiny mirror. If you don't react, their assaults don't penetrate.

When Fighting Authority

Understand the character of the command structure you face and make your appeal accordingly. If the authority is based on merit and achievement, use logic and fact. If the authority is based on politics and gamesmanship, use ego and emotion. The critical factor for manipulating authority is to show that taking your suggestions will enhance their leadership control, while not doing so will undermine their personal position.

When Fighting Coercion

When the other side keeps trying to muscle you into making concessions, it is a mistake to assume that they will stop. They won't stop until you stop them.

When Doing Nothing is the Best Defense

Fickleness frustrates. Indecision can blunt the strongest attack. So be wishy-washy. Force your opponent to try cornering you. Become loose like Jello—attempting to nail Jello to the wall can be nerve-wracking. Doing nothing is sometimes the most aggressive move you can make.

Consider a protected negotiating session where the other side, at the end of a long day, throws their "final proposal" at you. If that proposal is still well off the mark, perhaps you should just "do nothing." Be unable to schedule the next meeting. Be unavailable for personal chats. Be polite but vague during phone calls. The contrast will be sharp and the pressure maddening.

Generally, you don't have to do nothing for long to make your point. Nothing, remember, is not nothing.

17. SURMOUNTING THE SETBACKS

So you've had a setback. You're down. You're flat on your back. A setback is not the end of the world—or the deal. Maybe you've had to make some concessions. You're discouraged. The other side is pressing for more give. Your tendency is to let up, resign, and stay flat on your back.

Don't! Don't give in and don't succumb. Above all, don't make hasty decisions that can compound your first error. Recall the chess maxim about the second mistake, the one you make when lamenting the first mistake? It happens all the time in deal making. The first fall hurts, the second kills.

Contain and Circle the Problem

The first step is containment. Confine your losses to one location. Isolate the issue. Treat the setback as if it were an independent, water-tight compartment on a ship. The ship won't sink if one compartment ruptures.[32]

The next step is shifting the focus away from the problem. Once having isolated the problem, you must break away from it. Change directions. Break stride. Make alterations of any kind. Pick yourself up and scout the lay of the land. Move the theatre of operations. You have several good options. For example: Put new players on your negotiating team; their freshness provides a convenient excuse to retard the pace or change the pattern of current negotiations. Set a strange meeting time, perhaps later in the day; such a switch suggests that you have more important activities earlier in the day. Invite the other side out to a nice restaurant to continue talking; this shows confidence in your position. Start talking about other issues; pick an area where the other side is weak, or one that has not yet been discussed, or

[32]In fact, such a provision is a standard clause in most legal documents: If one provision of the contract is proven to be unenforceable, the other provisions are not affected.

one in which the other side has a keen interest (e.g., if they've wanted to get a hands-on look at your plants, arrange the trip).

Ultimatums

Declaring ultimatums is never an easy tactic to use or face. Too much self-image is involved, and logic is often overrun by emotion. Yet few deals get done without a bit of brinkmanship.

Try this tactic right after a setback. It's the most unexpected moment. The threat may seem irrational, but not idle. It may scare the other side into worrying whether you'll trash the deal. That's not so bad. Let them trade their iron mallet for kid gloves.

Turning Lemons Into Lemonade

No matter what happens, you can always improve the situation. Often, the embryo of a vital, new approach is buried within the carcass of the old approach. Being a little naive never hurts. If you don't know something can't be done, you might go out and do it.

18. BREAKING THE DEADLOCKS

Every deal reaches an impasse somewhere along the line. Breaking through that impasse is what you have to do. Stopping the standoff is what turns good deal makers into great ones. Crack the tension, not your head.

Tips for Breaking Deadlocks

The following list describes various deadlock-breaking techniques.

Change the Pace. Switch topics, shift agendas, move meetings, or take a break. (Remember the time-out in basketball.)

One-on-one Meetings. Interrupt a larger meeting and go head-to-head with the other side's principal. Get the old, cynical attorneys and young, intense MBAs out of the room. Maybe out of the building.

Play Mediator. Take the "good guy" role and put yourself in the middle. Try seeing the deal from both sides. (Play Solomon without the crown.)

Bring in New Factors. Generate fresh ideas. Introduce new concerns, matters, points, and problems. Reduce the importance of deadlocked issues by surrounding them with other issues. Substitute people. Bring in new people (someone "off the bench"—that substitute in basketball.)

Go Senior. A last resort. If you're not already dealing with the most senior person, reach up. Recognize that you are antagonizing your peers. Now they can't look good, no matter the outcome. If the deal works, the boss gets the credit; if the deal doesn't work, your peers get the blame.

Do Nothing. Often, the safe solution is to stand still. Be patient. When in doubt, don't do the wrong thing. Something can always be done tomorrow. You only lose your options when you use them.

Art of Compromise

If you think compromise is "splitting the difference"—dividing negotiating positions evenly—you think wrong. Carving issues down the middle do not make the best deals. Compromise is a complex and surprisingly precarious process. Used properly, it closes deals. Used improperly, it causes disaster.

Compromise is the art of getting both sides to agree to a resolution that neither side likes. As long as everybody is unhappy, goes one adage, the deal is a fair one. The following principles should be used in making compromises.

Don't be the First to Concede a Major Issue

Being the first to accept a substantial compromise is a sign of weakness. It can induce aggressive behavior across the table. The more you give, if given in the wrong way, the more they want. Feeding the greed only breeds greater appetite.

Suggest Only Minor Compromises First

Offering minor compromises first is fine. It is a good way to encourage a reasonable solution. This tactic does not bring out the shark in your opponent.

Don't Compromise Near Deadlines

Don't give the impression of caving in to pressure. Compromise should always be combined with confidence. Offering a concession when a deadline approaches smacks of concern and collapse. Instead, you might inform the other side that you are ready to offer some new ideas—*after* their deadline has expired.

Concede the Right Way

It is vital that the other side interpret your concessions properly. You must communicate, in fact more than in statement, that your offers are minor and getting smaller. If your opposites think they can get more, they will push for more. That's the nature of negotiations. (Sometimes, being human means playing by jungle rules.)

Milk Concessions

When you've made a concession, no matter how small, make the most of it. Use your compromise to show your willingness to get the deal done. Use it to show what nice people you are. Talk about it seriously and with good humor. ("Now look how much you've squeezed out of us!")

Skewing the Split

Splitting the difference, please note, does not necessarily mean hacking the issue in half, nor must it always relate to price. Deals can be "split," even though skewed to one side. A critical criterion is the test of "mutually and relatively equal *un*happiness." All issues are subject to such compromises, from features of product to terms of payment.

Finding the Right Angles

If we assume that the two sides are 180 degrees opposed on outstanding issues, a 90 degree switch for both sides—each one moving half way towards the other side—sounds ideal. This would be true if we were limited to two dimensions. Since we aren't limited, the best solution might lie in three dimensions.

For example, if Company A (the seller) insists that it must receive $10 million all cash for a certain division, whereas Company B (the buyer) asserts that it will only pay $8 million cash, they must negotiate. Assume the difference lies in disputed forecasts of next year's earnings. An even, split-the-difference compromise—which neither side will like and either may reject—is to pay $9 million cash. However, there is a better way. A three-dimensional solution would involve (1) paying $8 million cash on closing and (2) an additional $2 million based on future earnings. A formula tied directly to those earnings will allocate the additional payments plus interest. Both sides should be happy. If the earnings will materialize, as the seller maintains, the buyer will be pleased to pay the full $10 million. If the earnings are not there, $8 million was the right price and the seller has no complaint.

Careful Concessions

Be cautious with concessions; they can cut both ways.

When to Offer Concessions

It is best to offer a concession when you are strong.[33] Concessions should be well chosen and restrained—not arbitrary and unbounded. If the deal can be consummated with a final concession, go for it. A desperate concession to keep a deal alive generally has little value (but if you are desperate to do the deal. . . .)

How to Offer Concessions

Proper style depends on underlying motivation. If you pull back your position out of strength, make a big deal of it. If out of weakness, underplay it. If you make a move that finalizes the deal, make it obvious that your offer benefits both sides.

When to Accept Concessions

It rarely hurts to accept concessions, unless some return action is expected or implied.

How to Accept Concessions

Don't gloat about them. Don't dwell on them. No one likes to make concessions, and the other side may be harboring second thoughts. It's a mistake to rub your opponent's nose in his or her weakness. Treat concessions as "creative contribution" rather than as erosions of strength.

19. BRIDGING THE GAPS

What's the difference between "breaking the deadlocks" and "bridging the gaps"? The former concerns *process*, the means to get deals done, while the latter concerns *content*, the matter and substance of deals. This section discusses specific mechanisms for spanning chasms in deal making. Bridges are man-made links.

---

[33]This was why President Sadat of Egypt could not attempt to make peace with Israel until after he had regained Egypt's pride with the semivictory of the 1973 Yom Kippur War.

Give Both Sides Something

A bridge must have two sides; you can't cross a river without being anchored on both banks. It is surprising how many negotiators ignore the importance of giving something to the other side. Ignore? They avoid it like a disease. To give is to fail, some deal makers mistakenly believe. Concession is sacrilege, heresy, the unpardonable sin against the deal-making god. Such twisted thinking is nothing but the triumph of ego over action. In deal-making terms, you get more when you give a little. Always try to couple what your side wants to get with something the other side can receive in return.

Seek Fresh Ideas

Even the appearance of newness is important. If nothing else, innovation is a face-saving device. If you attempt to exact concessions through brute force, you will breed resistance. No one wants to cave in. However, if you convince the other side that your approach is original, it is easier for them to concede.

Critical Issues

Critical issues make or break deals. They either build up or break up blockage. What you do with them depends on circumstances.

When to Address Critical Issues

Sometimes you go right for the jugular. The deal is made or missed right here. You must have high confidence in the likelihood of success—or be under extreme pressure—to take this tactic.

When to Avoid Critical Issues

It is more likely that you will skirt the major problems for a while. Get the other side into the habit of agreeing. Resolve the light issues first, then lay into the heavies.

Eliminate Misunderstandings

Opposing sides view complex issues from opposite perspectives. Take, for example, the evaluation of inventory, a crucial part of most business acquisitions. A buyer may consider the downside scenario—what happens if the company goes out of business—and arrive at a low value. The seller, of course, takes inventory at full value. How to resolve the dispute? If the seller can demonstrate firm orders for most of the inventory, that would clear up the problem.

When to eliminate misunderstandings is a judgment call. You shouldn't do it too soon. Trying to mitigate a problem often exacerbates it. Attempting to cool down a smoldering altercation can actually flame it up. Open debate allows events to take their own course—actions and reactions become neither predictable nor controllable. Better let "sleeping dogs lie," at least while working on other issues. When a major misconception stops a deal cold, you must handle it. Other times, take care.

When dealing with explosive situations, never slam the door shut. The risk is too high, the reward too low. For example, when negotiating ground rules for a hostile press interview, the attorney for a controversial organization was careful never to be the one actually stopping the interview, which was exactly what he wanted to do. By engaging in elaborate discussions, primarily by written correspondence, he was able to get the reporter to tire of the process and drop the story. A directly belligerent approach would have invoked wrath and ensured a real hatchet job.

Use a Contingency Formula

When a problem just cannot be solved, a "contingent" formula can give both sides what they seek. The unpleasant side effect of this strategy is the added complexity. For example, when the buyer of a business insists that $12 million is the maximum they will pay, and the seller of that business insists that $15 million is the minimum they will accept, a compromise must be reached. Perhaps a deal can be structured as follows: a $12 million floor, a $15 million ceiling, and the $3 million difference contingent on something (e.g., collection of the seller's receivables).

The formulas, procedures, and policing methods needed to structure a contingent-based deal must be established. This is easier said than done. Often, the contingent proposal bridges the gap, but is ultimately eliminated as being too complicated.

Use Options

Try to give the other side alternatives. Allow them flexibility to choose from among various possibilities. As long as all of the available choices are good for you, you have nothing to lose and much to gain.

Array various options. The intent you show is more important than the specifics you offer. You evince serious interest to find solutions, to meet the other side's needs. This attitude creates an atmosphere conducive for making deals.

Change Criteria

Whenever possible, consider the way you evaluate issues and problems. Can you reexamine your major needs? Have any shifted since the start of negotiations? Sometimes, resolution of one issue can help resolve another issue. For example, establishing an "escrow" account to cover any inventory shortfalls (which may be a minor concern) may be the solution to a heated dispute about the quality of receivables.

Change Value or Consideration

Reconsider the material being transferred in the deal. If the sides are very far apart, try changing some basic assumptions. Altering the deal stuff—modifying what is being sold and/or how it is being bought—may give each side a fresh perspective.

Acquisition Example

As a seller of some unusual personal property, you have been negotiating with one buyer for weeks. Price is the only issue to resolve, but it seems an insurmountable one. A wide gulf remains between the maximum he will offer and the minimum you will accept. Your problem is that the property is so specialized that it will be difficult to attract other buyers. What to do?

Make a valiant attempt to traverse the gulf between you and the buyer through a combination of fresh ideas. Give the buyer a choice of novel alternatives for bridging the price gap. For example: paying the disputed amount over time. Paying the disputed amount with assets other than cash. Binding arbitration with third-part appraisers. Appraising the property at some later date to determine today's fair market value with hindsight. The key here is the choice: You allow the buyer to pick the option he prefers. At best, he will select one of your alternatives. At worst, he will come back with a new offer. Perhaps his will be more complicated. So what, it will get negotiations moving again.

20. TAKING THE CONTROL

Leadership is vital for deal making. The process is both fascinating and subtle. What's going on over the table may mask what's going on below it. Managing how things happen means mastering what things happen.

Regulate how a deal gets made and you influence what deal gets done. In other words, the deal-making process controls the deal-doing content.

Control is not a simple function of power, however. Even though the most powerful player starts out with greater control, the control can shift with subsequent events. Control is elusive and hard to pin down. Following are various techniques for asserting leadership of deals, for taking the control.

Effect a Compromise

The point here is progress and process. Substance doesn't matter—the issue may be major or minor. It is vital for your side to initiate and effect some sort of compromise. You must be the catalyst—that's how you take charge of the process. (Strangely, it is often better to effect a compromise than to receive a concession. The latter is a single event, the former a recurring attitude.)

Get a Concession

Getting or giving a concession affects other issues. Movement in your direction is great, and you should strive to achieve such positive action irrespective of issue or importance. Better to get a minor concession during negotiations than to start out with a major agreement.

However, if the other side has greater power, minimal largess, and only one concession to grant, don't squander the opportunity. Forget false pride and take what you can get.

Set or Reject an Ultimatum

Ultimatums take charge. Little else is relevant once deal-busting conditions enter the scene. Setting an ultimatum is a powerful tactic. A typical case is declaring a time limit for concluding the deal: "Gentlemen: We have 48 hours to reach a conclusion—or we walk."

Refusing to succumb to an ultimatum is just as powerful. When confronted with a buyer reducing his price, a wily seller deadpanned, "May I assume your lower offer voids my moral commitment not to speak with other buyers?"

Sustain the Momentum

Having momentum means having control. If you've got it, preserve it. Keep doing what you're doing. Avoid disruption. Go with the flow. If you've lost it, the other side's probably got it. If that's the case, get it back. Try disruption, any break in the action. Again, the basketball "time out"—usually called by the team that's falling behind. Break their rhythm and reverse momentum.

Change the Schedule

It's amazing how deal schedules control deal momentum. Changing the schedule can be as simple as postponing a meeting for a day to as serious as recommending a week's hiatus. It can also include requesting a shift from verbal discussions to written communications.

Change the Deal

Changing deal terms is never pleasant. But "retrading" is always expected. It establishes control at the same time it risks rupture. The other side is ticked off: They thought they had an agreement—suddenly they don't.

Altering prices is the obvious move. More often, price changes are couched in other terms. A buyer may delay payments or demand more features, while a seller may require faster payments or give fewer features.

Bring In New Troops

In most deal-making situations, the participants become too familiar with one another. Sometimes you can break stride and take control by changing the players. For example: Bringing in an unknown senior person with full decision-making authority can be quite disrupting. New relationships need to be formed. In some ways, it's as if negotiations must be reset and started afresh. Trotting in new professionals, say your attorneys, accomplishes the same thing. The cozy negotiating group is suddenly invaded by aliens. Everyone has to back up in order to bring the new people up to date. As a result, the entire process slows to your speed.

Request New Information

A call for additional data does more than give you further knowledge. It subtly communicates your lack of confidence in current direction and your need for verification. Since your side is doing the asking, the other side is put under pressure. (Calling for something substantial, like an in-depth audit, is a much more serious request and risks problems.)

If the information you request turns out to be unavailable or difficult to get, do not slough it off as unimportant. Doing so will send the wrong messages. Not only will it imply that the request was frivolous, but also that you are shaky and unsure.

Criticize Constructively

Constructive criticism of the other side can be effective. Before voicing the criticism, however, try to recognize a positive contribution they made, such as an insightful observation or a thoughtful suggestion. This creates the proper atmosphere.

Good deal makers make points when they offer a helpful critique. The action demonstrates a commitment to truth and a sincere desire to get the deal done. Made in the proper manner, criticism can build the other side's confidence in your personal integrity. "Do not reprove a scorner, lest he hate you; rebuke a wise man, and he will love you."[34]

Investment Example

You are representing a company that wants to co-invest with a venture partner in a leveraged buyout. Negotiations have stalled over several issues. Your required equity investment seems well secured. A primary problem is that although financial returns should be excellent over the life of the investment, you cannot afford to have assets deployed that do not generate income in the short run. But your venture partner maintains that cash cannot be paid by the debt-laden leveraged buyout for several years. How to make the investment?

Effect a compromise, giving both sides something. Since cash is not as important to your side as reported income, you make your investment as a "zero coupon note," which generates income for your profit and loss statement, but does not pay cash until the note matures in several years. At that time you have the option of converting your note to the appropriate amount of stock.

21. FOLLOWING THE LOGIC

Start with logic no matter where you end up. Logic is a thought process in which each step dictates the next. Such thinking is built on facts, not opinion;

---

[34]Proverbs 9:8

truth, not belief. Well, that's the theory. But facts and truth in science are one thing; in deal making, they are something else again.

Recall the prototypical example of logic: If all people are honest, and all deal makers are people, then all deal makers are honest. But if some deal makers are honest, and some honest people are investment bankers, it does *not* follow from logic that some deal makers are investment bankers (though they are) or that the investment bankers you know are honest (though they probably are).

How Logic Works

The scientific method is the application of logic to analyzing data and drawing conclusions. It seeks to understand how the world works from what can be observed. Proof involves the repeated testing of hypotheses against evidence, and the rejecting of those explanations that do not fit the facts. Theories are modified to match the findings as the process is repeated. Such repetition is essential.

Deal making follows a similar pattern: First, in deal selection, you repeatedly test which of several possible deals looks better. Second, in deal negotiations, you repeatedly assess how well you can achieve your goals based on feedback from the other side. Third, as a result of such regular reassessments, you constantly modify your goals and strategies.

How Logic Is Used

Logic is used to accomplish the following objectives:

Demonstrating Correctness

Logic can show why your position is the right one; why, for example, the price you're asking for your car, considering its fine bodywork, is appropriate.

Demonstrating Incorrectness

Logic can also show why the other side's position is not right; why, to flip sides in the car-selling example, the price is *not* appropriate since, although the bodywork looks good, the structure was damaged in a major accident.

Moving Ahead

Logic is a powerful device for getting and keeping deals going forward. "Let's stick to the facts."

How Logic Is Abused

To canonize logic is to deify a computer. A machine can be taught to assess mechanical truth but not to discern whole truth. There is more to making deals than accurate analysis.

People make deals, arguments do not. Logic has its place, but not the whole place. People are motivated by feelings and emotions; they do what they want, and logic may not change their attitudes. An owner of a business may not sell to the highest bidder just because she didn't like their negotiating tactics. Not logical? Though *Star Trek's* Mr. Spock wouldn't approve, it doesn't matter. No deal.

Proving your point with logic can even break a deal, if in the process the other side gets, to use the vernacular, "ticked off." Logic is often a battle winner and war loser. Using logic, you can be "right" and still be "wrong"—right in your analysis of facts and wrong in how you used them.

The worst application of logic in deal making is to put down the other side. It can be tempting. Suddenly, after hours of contentious dispute, you find the winning argument or piercing fact—and you jam it right down those bastards' throats. It makes you feel good, sure, but it hurts more than helps your deal. Your opponents may concede that one point but they will resist you more intensely on every other point.

Be careful when proving someone wrong in a meeting, especially a superior in front of subordinates. Consider presenting your argument in private. It will save face, and you will be appreciated.

Techniques of Logic

The following are good ways to apply logic.

Be a Good Listener

You can't use logic's full strength unless you understand fully the other side's position. Concentrate on what your opponent says.

Paraphrase

Repeat back to the speaker in your own words what you think he or she is saying. Do it without judgment or critique. You make progress when you show that you really understand an opposing position.

Fact Association

Organize your information. Relate the data and ideas to the other side's argument. Look for those facts that undermine or subvert the opposing argument. There is a major difference between facts that do not confirm an argument and facts that destroy it. The former are common; the latter, rare.

Coax, Don't Insult

Unless you can blow the other side's argument out of the water, which is unlikely, proceed with caution. Take heed: You don't want to alienate the opposition—only thwart their attacks. Imagine yourself a surgeon, excising only those parts of the argument that are "diseased." Start with positives before negatives. Approach the argument as one ripe for mutual improvement instead of coming on like gangbusters. Use developmental phrases such as, "What happens if we modify. . . ."

Location of Logic

When Logic is on Your Side

With a winning position, you don't want to muck it up with bad feelings. The idea is to make your point and gain respect in the process. Don't make the other side look bad. Your mental image is "mutual victory over faulty logic."

When Logic Is on the Other Side

When your side has presented a failing argument, try to cloud the issue and lessen its impact. But avoid anxiety and obvious obfuscation. Heavy smoke screens are dead giveaways. Look for an excuse to move on to other topics. If the other side fumbles in explanation, be understanding. Your mental image is "a minor matter of no consequence."

Eyeball to Eyeball

Two legendary corporate deal makers were negotiating the sale of a large division from one to the other. "I like the deal you're offering," said buyer to seller. "The companies are excellent—dominant market share, fine brand recognition, high quality, superb distribution, nice cash flow. I've only got one problem: If you're selling at a price, why should I be buying at that price? I've never known you to leave much on the plate." What to do?

Forget price. It's not the issue here. Seller motivation is what counts. The seller should give the buyer convincing reasons why he needs to divest the businesses. Perhaps the division to be disposed of doesn't fit a new strategic posture; perhaps debt needs to be paid down; perhaps another cash-hungry acquisition has just been made; perhaps. . . .

22. FEELING THE EMOTION

Emotion in deals is kingmaker, tipping the balance. It often decides issues at the end, even if it does not initiate them at the beginning. Emotion is not shameful; it is noble, worthy, and valid. Emotion, never forget, makes deals.

How Emotion Works

Emotions are nonrational, unplanned feelings. They are private knowledge, sensations we know ourselves but cannot demonstrate to others. They are outside the orbit of logic but do not contradict it. "Intellect [logic] is to emotion as our clothes are to our bodies," said Alfred North Whitehead. "We could not very well have civilized life without clothes, but we would be in a poor way if we had only clothes without bodies."

How Emotion Is Used

Emotion affects the atmosphere of deal making, casting positive or negative spells, invoking spirits that uplift or depress. Good deal makers encourage honest emotional expression. As long as respectful, nonthreatening behavior is maintained, there is nothing wrong with putting some volume behind your words. If you're upset, show it. If you're bothered, say it. What you are seeking is candid communication, and displaying emotion is part of that candor. In this sense, deal making is like group therapy; problems are discussed openly and emotion is expressed without shame.

How Emotion is Abused

Faking or flaunting emotions, on the other hand, is counterproductive. Fibbing or fabrication leads to more tricks than treats, and boisterous exhibitionism detracts from deal-closing solutions. Emotion shown should be sincere, or not shown at all. Don't plot artificial emotion, but don't be embarrassed to express the genuine variety.

Kinds of Emotion

In what environment are you working? The deal-making atmosphere influences the deal makers' attitudes. Following are some descriptions of deal-making climates. The further you can move to the left, with no political pun intended, the better for getting deals done.

Cooperative—Competitive. Is the environment collaborative or cut-throat?

Equality—Superiority. Are the parties content with parity, or do they seek dominance?

Factual—Judgmental. Do the parties stick with simple data and information, or do they evaluate motives and imagine hidden agendas?

Spontaneous—Calculating. Do the parties react naturally to situations and events, or do they plot and scheme to get their way?

Issue Exploring—Self-Certain. Do the parties concentrate on examining points and solving problems, or are they arrogant and cocky in their private appraisals?

Problem Sharing—Self-Protective. Are the parties open and honest in investigating issues, or are they secretive and uncommunicative in their daily dealings?

Solution Oriented—Ego Oriented. Do the parties focus on resolving issues, or are they consumed by posturing and vanity?

Empathetic—Callous. Do the parties genuinely relate to the concerns of the other side, or are they cold-hearted and insensitive?

Techniques of Emotion

The following are good ways to use emotions.

Set a Baseline. Get some sense of the normal emotional state of all deal participants. People are different—some are highly charged, others are low key. Good deal makers come in all shades.

Be a Good Listener. Hear the nonverbal sounds—the tones and pitches of voices—being communicated. Receive the "metamessages."

Be a Good Watcher. Observe body language of the people on both sides. Note how people interact with one another.

Control Your Own Emotions. Control does not mean repress. Use your emotions to underscore meaning and intensity.

Note Changes. Any emotional shift may indicate a reaction to the current state of the deal. No matter what words are being said, whether the other side is conceding or stonewalling, emotional change indicates something's afoot.

Character of Emotions

Emotions can influence deals. Once you understand what's happening, you can use it to your advantage.

Assess Commitment. The depth of the other side's commitment to its stated position is the best clue to how hard you can push and how far you can go. An emotional upswing suggests increasing commitment while an emotional downswing indicates decreasing commitment.

When Emotion Is High. Substantial emotion can cause deal volatility. Heightened intensity can either (1) help take control of the deal-making process or (2) disrupt progress. High emotion is like a catalyst in a chemical reaction: Whatever is supposed to happen will happen more swiftly. This can mean higher efficiency or a bigger explosion.

When Atmosphere is Too Tense. High emotion generates tension, but tension itself is not bad. Moderate tension may even be beneficial. Excessive tension, however, should be diffused since it puts everyone on edge. Try humor, especially the self-deprecating kind. ("If I weren't such a masochist, I'd enter a more relaxed profession, like arbitrage.")

When Atmosphere Is Too Relaxed. Looseness and sloth do not close deals. A serene, untroubled environment is generally conducive to making deals, but sometimes a little zip is needed to prod things along. How to add zip? Try injecting some competition for your deal, or at least the threat of it.

23. CHANGING THE ATTITUDES

Good or bad attitudes mean good or bad deals. Deal making begins under every conceivable circumstance. You never know what to expect when you first walk into the room: The other side may be desperate or unconcerned, ready to peel you apart or determined to play it straight. Your side also brings along a mixed bag of interests and attitudes.

Attitude is a frame of mind, within which the entire picture of deals is portrayed. The right attitude maximizes the chances of making a good deal. Even if the deal opens well, you must work at keeping it that way. Good attitudes must be maintained throughout all of the deal's problems. This requires constant attention. Bad attitudes must be changed from natural competition to mutual cooperation. This takes special talent.

Types of Changes in Attitude

The following are the different types of changes that occur in attitudes.

Incremental Change

This type of attitude alteration is generally positive. It is a gradual, almost imperceptible shift. No major movement is noticed, but after a while you can see the change. Positive changes are usually incremental.

Sudden Change

This type of attitude alteration is more rare. It is usually triggered by a particular event that either destroys or enhances the party's confidence in the deal. For example, if something you said was true is proven false, trust is shattered. Conversely, a sudden step for the better can occur if the other side realizes it made a judgmental error. For example, if they thought you were holding back financial information, only to discover that their accountants had it all the time, their attitudes could mellow as a form of penance.

Self-Induced Change

Sometimes attitudes seem to improve by themselves. This can happen as confidence grows in the deal's progress. In this case, you don't interfere, but simply maintain the momentum.

Your attitude is a potent tool. The aura you project affects the strategy you plan. Your attitude toward the other side influences their attitude toward you. Smiling, for example, is contagious; it's also simple, cheap, and effective.

Techniques for Changing Attitude

The following are good ways to change attitudes.

Build Trust

Since the common assumption is that you will say anything and do anything to win your point, the only way to build trust is by being truthful and consistent. Trust is elusive in deal making. It takes time to build—and no time to destroy.

Reduce Resentment

Few deals start out with an overload of animosity, although many wind up that way. Resentment is resilient and resourceful and extraordinarily hard to eradicate. If your deal is so afflicted, perhaps you can signal a change in attitude by reapproaching the issue from a different angle. Find the root of the problem. If it's a misunderstanding, be open about it. If it's real, work around it.

Reduce Seriousness

The best deal makers work seriously but do not take themselves that way. A bloated sense of personal importance will antagonize, not impress. A light touch is the strongest pressure.

Transfer Credit

It is remarkable how much can be accomplished if you are willing to give others the recognition. In one organization where change was vital, I was the only one who really knew what to do, but I was too young to do it myself. I had to work through the senior leadership, getting several executives to internalize my ideas and present them as their own. I didn't mind because I was deeply committed to that organization (normally I would mind!). Its success was all that mattered to me. You can change the world as long as you don't need the credit.

Build Relationships

The more impersonal and unapproachable you seem, the harder it will be to modify attitudes. Try looking and acting human, with problems as well as positions. Perfect, you're not.

Use Informality

Social settings are good environments to break ice and reduce tension. Sometimes, inviting your counterpart to an informal meal can melt metal.

Use Humor

It is hard to get mad at someone funny. A good sense of humor is a marvelous asset in high-tension deal making. No tactic is better.

Personal Example

After serving in World War II, my father decided to start his own business. He had been a successful men's outerwear salesman before the War, but feared following in the footsteps of Willy Loman in Arthur Miller's "Death of A Salesman."[35] My father had saved $5000, and with another $5000 borrowed from his new brother-in-law, he set up his new company. He wasn't starting cold, however, having amassed a sizable amount of initial orders from loyal customers. The business would flourish, if the merchandise could be delivered. The problem was money. How to get the clothing financed? How to pay for the raw materials, labor, manufacture, shipping, and the like until receiving payment? A bank loan was essential. But a new company with little capital? Which bank would loan such a fledgling firm so much exposed cash?

One major bank did make the loan and the business grew into one of the largest in its industry segment. Why that bank took the gamble is the point of this case. It seems that when these august bankers were inspecting my father's meager facilities, they noted that he would always turn out the lights when leaving each room. When in later years they recounted their critical observation, my father remarked: "But I didn't even pay for the electricity; that was part of the rent!" The banker smiled: "We knew that—that's why we made the loan. If you took that much care of your landlord's money, we figured you would do no less with ours."

---

[35]How my father entered the apparel trade is a different kind of deal-making story. He had been an excellent athlete, an all-city center fielder. Though academically talented, finishing high school at 16, he had to support his immigrant family. A jewelry job paying $8 a week was all he could land. Well, those were the days when union sports leagues were serious business, and so the garment union discovered my father's bat and arm, offering him $16 a week if he would play ball for their team. They hinted that he wouldn't need to work too hard, or for that matter have to show up at all. (I call it the Depression's version of an "athletic scholarship.") My father accepted the "deal," but fooled them by not only going to work but working very hard.

24. SENSING THE CHANGES

Deal making is an environment of constant flux. Everything is waxing and waning, altering and being altered. These changes may be for better or worse. It either case, they affect the deal.

Signs of Change

The following events suggest deal shift and movement.

Pregnant Questions

Questions are self-protecting mechanisms that allow negative responses without loss of face. It's better to test waters with tiny toes before jumping in with large bodies. For example, if you want to break a deal deadlock by lowering your asking price, you might ask "What could we trade off if I were to reduce the price a bit?" This approach shows neither weakness nor concession.

Trial Balloons

"Trial balloons" allow you to float ideas without actually committing to them. You test your thought by observing the reaction. If good, you can make it official. If not, you've learned another idea that won't work. The prime objective here is self protection. You certainly don't want to make a concession and then have it refused.

Trial balloons are released in numerous ways. For example, the lower-level parties on your team can speak off the record to their peers on the other side. (Nothing, you must assume, is ever really off the record.) Alternatively, principals can go one-on-one and use a Pregnant Question.

Mood Shifts

Most deal people aren't good poker players. Their moods are read easily. For example, I'd be concerned if a person's mood plummets when I've made a concession or we've concluded the deal. I'd wonder if there's more here than meets the eye.

Tone Or Body Shifts

Your sixth sense can tell you when the other side is more relaxed or more tense, more responsive or more obstinate, more inclined to compromise or more steadfast to stonewall. The way things are moving is more important than the way things are.

Changes in voice tone and body language are the signals. You only have to listen and watch. Note fluctuations of voice and body, the subtle sounds and movements. For example, are the words more calming or cutting, the tones more comforting or sarcastic, the pitch more pleasant or high-strung? Are the torsos more straight or slumped, the hands more steady or shaky, the faces more open or crimped? Direction of change, remember, is the key.

Increased Humor

A witty spirit cannot come forth from a sullen soul. Even a small, unfunny joke from a generally dour person is a positive sign. Conversely, silence from a generally ebullient sort screams a warning. If parties on the other side evince an uptick in humor, whether telling detailed jokes or making off-the-cuff drollery, you're making progress. I like to encourage humor during deal making. It makes the process more enjoyable; more important, it's a positive influence on emotions and outcomes.

Indirect Expressions of Attitude

If some of the participants on their side are freely mixing with peers on your side, that's a good sign. If the sides maintain strict formality around the negotiating table in meeting after meeting, that's a bad sign. (If the latter, you might try breaking the spell by pulling up a chair on their side: "Thought I'd like to see how the deal looks from this side of the board.") Telephone calls are another sign. Some people strictly obey protocol regarding who calls whom. Any changes here should be noted.

Increased Informality and Personal Rapport

If your opposite invites you to a business meal, gym workout, or a weekend social visit, that's positive movement. During the deal-making process, such outings are a sign of success. The results for both sides might even be good enough to build a long-term relationship.[36] When a union official told Denys Henderson that he was "friendly, fair, but bloody hard," the chairman of Imperial Chemical Industries (the United Kingdom's largest manufacturing firm) was flattered. "I would rest content with that on my gravestone," he noted.

---

[36]In doing deals, you strive to build relationships. If friendship is budding with any of your opposites, that's good. It gives me great pleasure when someone with whom I've dealt requests that, should the parties do another deal together, they'd like me to again be sitting on the other side of the table. (Also nice is when opponents ask me to represent *them* in their next deal.)

Change Within Organizations

Massive change is never made without turmoil and disruption, and deal making energizes the process. What happens to deal making within organizations beset by fundamental flux? The subject is a personal passion. It focuses on how changes are made within organizations in transition. The key is *commitment*, which I define as "the link between personal meaning and organizational mission." How to study commitment? Much can be learned under conditions of extreme religious fervor. The results show remarkable parallels between business and religion.[37]

Change In Business and Religion

Which pieces of the past do you honor? Which are so sacrosanct that they are forever above challenge? Such questions are addressed at critical times during the life cycles of both religious and business organizations, and the sets of answers that emerge have much in common.

Framing the issue for religion, when are doctrines and dogmas still fluid? When do they solidify? When do they ossify? How do beliefs define the boundary of spiritual groups, and what happens to internal deal making when some of those beliefs must change?

Framing the issue for business, when are strategies and policies still fluid? When do they solidify and ossify? How do corporate goals define the boundary of commercial groups, and what happens to internal deal making when some of those goals must change?

The Lifestyle of Change

One might consider the issue of doctrinal or strategic change within the context of an organization's life cycle. In the early days of a religious movement or business company, there is generally free discussion between the founder and his first followers or employees. Doctrines or strategies are hammered out freely and openly, with opposing views vying for dominance.

---

[37]George Geis of UCLA and I examined organizations embroiled in fundamental transition while studying "commitment," the psychic knot that binds individuals and institutions. Our approach was that commitment could best be studied in extreme religious groups, such as apocalyptic sects and cults that believe in a near-term end-of-the-world. We investigated several such groups, building a model for commitment. We then derived principals that "build" or "break" commitment, techniques that can be applied to strengthening business organizations. See *The Firm Bond: Linking Meaning and Mission in Business and Religion* (New York: Praeger, 1984).

Yet something happens as an organization matures. Doctrines or strategies stiffen, then harden. What was once considered loyal somehow becomes disloyal. Whereas at first it was supportive to challenge and prune, later it becomes supportive to defend and preserve. The more success an organization has, the more immobile its positions become. The cycle turns on itself since such doctrinal or strategic rigidity facilitates fracture. The character of internal deal making changes in the process.

25. SENDING THE PROBES

Often, searching questions—probes—are needed to communicate serious intent in deal making. Probes explore limits and boundaries without risking insult and alienation. They are the best way to discover how far you can go in a deal.

Objective of Probes

The following are some purposes of probes.

Solicit Information. Get new knowledge from the other side: "How old is the building?"

Transmit Information. Give new knowledge to the other side: "Did you know that our building was remodelled two years ago?"

Project an Attitude. Show the other side your mood: "Could you assist me in understanding these numbers?" is beseeching. "When are you going to stop retrading the deal?" showing irritation.

Stimulate Reflection. Encourage the other side to do some thinking: "Assuming we can come close to your price, how much do you really need in cash up front?"

Focus Attention. Make the other side concentrate on a fundamental issue: "If you refuse to do any seller financing, is it worth continuing discussions?"

Finalize the Deal. Bring the other side to a conclusion: "If I agree to your final point, can we close in 30 days?"

Probes That Make Progress

These questions usually help. They inform and instruct, thus encouraging the deal-making process.

Fact Probes. Questions to gather data and information for building knowledge—asked with neutral emotions: "How current is your inventory? What is the discount on your bonds?"

No Limits Probes. Questions that cannot be answered by a simple "yes" or "no": "What do you think the future strategy of the business should be? What is your opinion of current management?"

Sequential Probes. Inquiries that are part of a step-by-step train of thought: "If we were to solve the question of price, which issue would then become most important to you?"

Conclusion-Suggesting Probes. Leading questions of the variety not allowed in court: "You wouldn't have made such an absurd offer if my client weren't in Chapter 11, now would you?"

Introspective Probes. Queries that peer into the inner sanctum of one's mind: "How do you feel about selling your business after 25 years? Would you like to consider a consulting contract after you sell?"

Solicitous Probes. Questions that express an attitude of supplication and appeal: "Would you mind if I ask your accountant for help in understanding these schedules?"

"What If . . ." Probes. The easy entry for trial balloons. It's hard to get angry at a "What if. . . ." It conveys personal uncertainty and mutual respect: "What if we were to reduce your cash at closing but more than make it up within two years?"

Questions That Deflect. Bounce the ball of inquiry back to sender: "Why should I accept less cash up front?"

Probes That Retard Progress

These questions usually don't help. They intimidate and alienate, thus fouling up the deal-making process.

Deceptive Probes. Any answer is wrong: The classic, "When did you stop beating your wife?" Or in business, "When did you stop manipulating that stock?"

Bristle Probes. The only purpose is to antagonize: "Having made a public fool of yourself, don't you think you should apologize to your peers?"

Insulting Probes. The respondent is put on the defensive: "How dare you charge such an exorbitant fee for virtually no work? What prompts you to make such an insolent offer?"

Spot-Putting Probes. The respondent is put in an awkward or embarrassing situation: "Since your boss is here now, tell him to his face why you said that his price was a sham."

Intimidating Probes. Confrontation, not information, is the objective: "How can your projections be so perfect? Why do you think you're so much smarter than we are?"

Coercive Probes. Forcing an answer to agree with your opinion: "I think that your company is really falling behind, don't you?"

Responding to Probes

People answer questions in different ways from complete truths to outright lies to clever evasions. Generally, the best way to answer is with targeted, unembroidered information. When you tell the truth you never have to remember what you said.

Lies may solve the immediate problem, but they can cause bigger problems later. But what happens when you just can't answer a question? Sidestepping direct probes is difficult. Try using polite answers that convey sincerity and interest but little substance or information (e.g., "I know how you feel," or "I hear you").

26. LIGHTING THE SPARKS

In deals, as in forests, there are two kinds of sparks: controlled and uncontrolled. Controlled and used properly, sparks can start small fires that keep you warm. Uncontrolled and used improperly, sparks can ignite large conflagrations that scorch and destroy.

Sparks That Warm

Helpful sparks are elusive to define and difficult to use. There's the ever-present danger of the fledgling flame flying out of control. In deal making, your intent can be taken out of context and blown out of proportion. Take care when making these sparks. You really are playing with fire.

Kidding and Ribbing

You can often say humorously what you cannot say seriously. Jest is a marvelous form of communication, as long as you avoid sarcasm and sensitive subjects. A joshing remark can convey an important message. Be sure to sprinkle your humor with a healthy dose of self-mockery.

Chiding and Chastening

This is a cross between constructive criticism and general kidding. The tone is sharper, but the spirit is still good-natured. Such remarks are intended to make a point. You can say, for example, "You are focusing so much on the tax issues that you are forgetting about the business. How about taking that trip to the plants?"

Deadlines and Ultimatums

Used carefully, setting deadlines and giving ultimatums can push deals to conclusions. They remind everyone there's movement to be made. After all, you can't negotiate forever. Closure must happen or deals must collapse. Put the bad news nicely: "Well, my boss has given me the word. It we don't sign by next Tuesday, we're going to have to solicit other efforts."

Sparks That Burn

Harmful sparks are generated in two ways. Some people fly off the handle with minor provocation. Sometimes it's words they don't mean; sometimes it's words they do mean but shouldn't say. Other people plot and plan their rudeness. Thinking they can control the deal through coarse dominance, their malice is both insidious and premeditated.

Outbursts and Rudeness

Loud disruptions and temper tantrums are very unpleasant. They might take control for a time, but they hardly create the proper climate. "Negotiating with terrorists" only encourages more terror. Don't reinforce the offensive behavior. Don't cater to it. Don't give in to it. Just wait with a slightly annoyed, slightly bored look gracing your face.

Sarcasm and Insults

Slurs and accusations heat emotions and compel retaliation. Try to avoid this natural reaction and encourage the decibel-producing party to calm down. If the ranting maniac does not cool off, the deal is over, anyway. You have nothing to lose by not jumping into the gutter.

Clashes and Confrontations

These types of attacks are disagreeable, but they can be constructive. There is an issue to fight about. Try to get the other side to explain their position in detail. Ask complex questions about their views. It's hard to be analytical and scream at the same time.

Threats and Warnings

These are the most disgraceful of all. Here you are being browbeaten and coerced and perhaps intimidated and frightened. You are being accosted by lurid statements of what the other side is going to do to you if you do not agree to their terms. The threats, which are generally vague, should be taken seriously—irrespective of whether they are in fact serious. If the threats are real, it is better to back off from a deal than to stir such hostility. If the threats are only a ruse, you will force the other side to confront the unpleasant consequences of their inappropriate ploy.

27. DEFUSING THE BOMBS

There is a fine line between equilibrium and explosion. Deal makers operate near the flash point, where spontaneous combustion is an ever-present threat. Disaster is never far way as any disturbance can trigger a rapid rise in temperature.

Deadlines

Once a deadline is set, there's no going back. One of three things must happen: (1) The deal gets done despite adverse conditions for the party not setting the deadline. (2) The deadline is postponed, putting the setter of the deadline in an adverse position. (3) The deadline passes and the deal aborts. Touch choice!

Ultimatums

Ultimatums in deals focus on specific issues. Here, there are three possible outcomes: (1) The ultimatum is met and the deal progresses. (2) The ultimatum is not met and the deal collapses. (3) The ultimatum is not met but conditions are changed.

Some examples of ultimatums are: from buyer to seller—"Either guarantee the quality of your receivables or we reduce the price 50 cents on a dollar." Or from seller to buyer—"Put up $200,000 good faith money by Friday or we're history."

Verbal Attacks

When engulfed by a tidal-wave tirade, the issue is how to maintain personal dignity while not conceding deal control.[38] You have a choice of response tactics: answer softly, allowing the insults to wash on by, or answer in kind, confronting strength with strength. The Proverbs[39] explain both sides of the question: *Answer not a fool according to his folly, lest you be like him; answer a fool according to his folly, lest he be wise in his own conceit.*

Defusing Attitudes

Attitude more than technique determines how to smooth the situation.

Keep Perspective

How important is the overall deal? How important is the contentious point? Weigh relative values. Compare current pressure with desired results. Decouple the other side's behavior from your side's needs and wants. If the deal is still good for you in spite of any deadlines, ultimatums, or verbal attacks, go for it.

Look for Negotiating Gain

Can the deadline be met? Is the ultimatum workable? Even if the answer to both questions is yes, try to exact concessions from the other side. After all, they threw down the gauntlet and might be feeling a bit badly. Before succumbing too quickly to their pressure, try to gain some deal trade-offs.

Never Judge the Motivation of Others

You never know why other people do what they do. You don't know all their problems and pressures. It's tough enough to keep track of your own reasons for doing things. We tend to judge others as if they should be saints while

---

[38]See Deal Element 26.

[39]Proverbs 26:4-5.

giving ourselves every benefit of every doubt. Consider the boy with old shoes, who felt deprived until he saw a boy with no shoes, who felt deprived until he saw a boy with no feet.

Don't Take Yourself Too Seriously

Throughout the struggle, remember that this is just one deal. It's not your life. Salvation is not at stake. If you find yourself becoming overwhelmed by emotion, call a time out.

Techniques for Defusing

The following tactics reduce the likelihood of deal detonation.

Deflate the Pressure

Try to throw the ball right back into your opponent's court. Say something like "If my answer has to be now, my answer has to be 'no'."

Switch Issues

Substitute a viable option for a troublesome condition. For example, instead of guaranteeing all receivables as demanded by the buyer, you as the seller might suggest putting some of the purchase price into an escrow account to cover any possible shortfall. This satisfies the buyer while it limits your exposure. As another example, if a seller demands substantial "good faith money" from you as the buyer, you might try softening the terms rather than reducing the amount. The idea is that you should have so many "outs" that it's hardly worth the seller's effort.

Puncture Seriousness

Relieve the tension of the moment by injecting a little humor. Coaxing a smile from your opponent's face can facilitate a favorable trade-off. Get the other side to see themselves as human beings. Sure, they are professionals doing work, but they should also be people having fun. Humor is the most potent weapon to disarm the dreary.

Give a "Fair Reading"

Restate the other side's ultimatum or deadline to reflect a position with which you could live. You are not being deceptive by modifying their statements—you are overtly trying to make it a livable offer. Assume the seller gives you a "firm and final" three weeks to close the deal. A "fair reading" might be, "As long as our financial institution, as an independent third party, takes to complete its due diligence"—a more flexible time period. If they want to break off the deal, nothing will stop them. But if they really want to make the deal, they'll listen to your "fair reading."

28. PLAYING THE TRICKS

I'm going to describe several deal-making gambits. Learn how they work, how to recognize them when they're being played against you, and what you can do to thwart their impact. The following "tricks" are designed to be like karate moves—killers that are best used for self defense. As in fencing, parry is what I offer, not thrust.

Lowball: Buyer's Version

As the buyer, keep a straight face and test the market by offering the lowest possible price. You never know, you might get lucky—recall the chess adage, "Give a check, it may be mate." The seller will scream, but how loud and how shrill will tell you where the deal is going. The greater your relative power the more serious lowball becomes. This is especially true when the seller is under time pressure.

Lowball: Seller's Version

As the seller, lowball is less common. The object here is to attract as many potential buyers as possible in hopes that some will become seriously interested. This way, more parties will be around when you raise the price. If a lot of buyers are smoked out, it may pay to go into a formal auction.

Highball: Buyer's Version

As the buyer, highball is a competitive trick. The key here is to get the first shot at the deal and keep other bidders blocked out. Try entering into an arrangement with the seller that limits negotiations to you. Once you get all the inside information, you can make your actual proposal.

Highball: Seller's Version

As the seller, you start by setting the highest possible price while still within the realm of reason. Test the market. Again, give luck a chance—give that "check." Buyers will complain, but how strong and how long will tell you where the deal is going. The greater your relative power, the more serious the game. This is especially true when you have no time pressure.

Bait and Switch

The intent of the gambit is to attract—no, *entice*—the other side with a deal they can't refuse. Once they're hooked, the gloves come off and the real offer is made. In a sense, this is similar to a buyer's game of highball and a seller's game of lowball.

Bluffing

Bluffing is saying one thing and meaning another. Up to a point, it is an accepted part of deal making. For example, a buyer may tell a seller that the offer will only stay on the table for 48 hours. The buyer hopes to shut off other bids and prevent the seller from shopping the deal. A seller may tell the buyer that other bidders are offering more in hopes of getting the buyer to bid against himself or herself.

Bluffing is deception but not lying (although I am struggling to explain why not). It is easier to define where bluffing ends and lying begins. Giving false financials, for example, is clearly a lie. Speeding up last month's good reports while slowing down this month's bad reports—just as the deal is being consummated—is borderline. Perhaps a good analogy is that bluffing is pretending you've got great cards while lying is stacking the deck.

Sandbagging

In sandbagging, one party strings the other side along, allowing (encouraging) them to think that they have a deal at their price. Only after they have invested substantial effort and resources (sunk costs)—really hooking themselves on the deal—are actual prices sprung.

If you find yourself on the receiving end of this trick, if you sense sandbags piling up, make the other side be as explicit as possible. Stop and confirm your understanding at every step, preferably in writing.

Sting Operation

This is more dangerous. It involves the collusion of two or more parties who are conspiring to get the best of you. As buyers, their tactics may involve one of these set-ups to drive down your price: one party lowballing the price to give the other feedback; one party highballing the price and then suddenly dropping out to disorient you; one party giving you discouraging reports to intimidate you into accepting a compatriot's offer.

New Entrant

As a deal moves toward completion, the other side introduces a new wrinkle to disrupt the deal. Often, the wrinkle is an actual person who has suddenly materialized to conduct the negotiations. The relationships carefully built up over the course of the discussions are shaken. Since you seem so close to closure, and you've sunk so much into the deal, there may be a tendency to give a little extra to placate this new person. (It's like paying an insurance premium.)

Sometimes, the new wrinkle is a fictitious party who has "unexpectedly" made a better offer. The other side professes to be embarrassed, moaning about their fiduciary responsibility to accept the best offer. Although there is no binding contract, they avow a "moral" responsibility to you—consequently they will give you the option of matching the new offer. Keep your wits about you. The whole scene may be a ruse—the new entrant may be a bluff.

Appeal to Authority

Blaming an uncontrollable force is a favorite ploy. If the person doesn't have the authority, a better offer cannot be made. This tactic is especially useful when an intangible such as "the budget" is the target of the appeal. For example, what can you do if a prospective corporate treasurer claims that your retainer fee "is just not in my budget"? The answer lies in devising creative proposals. Suggest splitting your price, for instance, so that whatever cannot be included in this year's budget can be included in next year's. Just make sure that your contract is enforceable and carrying costs are included.

Executive Search

You are being recruited by an executive search firm for a high-level banking position that you really want. There are five other finalists for the position. Credentials and experience seem about equal. One issue is compensation. What, you are asked, are your requirements? At your level the industry scale is very broad. What to do?

If you play highball, you could be deemed expensive or arrogant. If you play lowball, you could be judged cheap or insecure. So try a combination: Play lowball and highball at the same time. Be willing to take an absolute minimal guaranteed salary, near the bottom end of the scale, and a relatively short contract. But couple it with a performance-based contingency that can produce the highest total compensation in your class. This way, they have the least risk—and you radiate confidence.

29. HAGGLING THE TRADES

There is an old Spanish proverb about getting rich: Buy from those who go to be executed, since they don't care how cheap they sell; and sell to those who go to be married, since they don't care how dear they buy. Unfortunately, we can rarely choose so carefully with whom we trade.

Trading is the essence of deal making. One side gives something. The other side gives something. Both give a little. Both get a little. Bargains are struck. Agreements are made.

Dora in the Souk

Middle Eastern markets, such as the "souk" in Old Jerusalem, are classic examples of nitty gritty trading. This give-and-take maelstrom of swapping, exchanging, and bargaining can define the term. In dickering to buy an old knife from a shopkeeper there, my wife Dora (who speaks some Arabic) learned of the knife's "long history in the Sinai" and of the "terrible consequences" for selling such a priceless relic so far under cost. The deal miraculously materialized when my wife agreed to buy *two* knives at that same "horrendously low" price (which was, I think, about one-third the original asking price). Why if the shopkeeper was losing so much money selling one, he was so delighted selling two, my wife never asked.

Some deal makers find the trading game more enjoyable than the results. Another shopkeeper in that same souk complained to us that the previous tourist had paid the original sticker price and departed without so much as a disgruntled sound or exasperated gesture. (After my wife would leave, he would yearn for the serenity of that previous tourist.) When haggling trades, whether over ancient relics in crowded markets or modern products in splendid offices, certain principles are universal.

Value is Relative

If you get what you want, don't worry about what the other side gets. My wife wanted those knives, both of them, in fact, from the beginning. They were ornate, well made, and decorative; they were reminiscent of her childhood, and most important they would go well in our living room. Whether that sixteenth century Bedouin chieftain really used those bejeweled blades in heroic exploits, or more likely his far-removed descendent just made them last week, was quite irrelevant.

Only you can judge whether you are getting a good deal. It's difficult for anyone else to label your deal "good" or "bad". One just doesn't know another's reasons and motives. Generally, if both sides get what they want, then the values are equivalent.

Making Trades Count

When making trades, make them count. Surprisingly, much of what's offered in deals is often more meaningful to the side giving it away than to the side receiving it. Thus, to make good trades, it is imperative to know what's important to your opponents. Hit these hard. For example, if the seller needs cash, you can probably cut a better price by cutting a quick check. A cash-rich seller, however, might be happier with taking back part of the purchase price in high interest-bearing notes. Finding and pushing "hot buttons" is more art than science. It involves the senses of touch and smell more than sight and sound. It demands thinking the unusual.

First Offers

The original price of the knife that my wife bought in the souk had, shall we say, a healthy gross margin. At least two-thirds of the sticker was "reserve." But, in this case, the buyer and seller knew the same rules and both made a good deal.

Most people do not give their best offer up front. No one expects them to. It's just not done. You can't swim upstream, so you might as well start in a range where you can make some movement.

Corporate America is not much different from the Old Jerusalem souk. The percentage of "reserves" in deals may differ but the principle is the same. A prominent financier told me, "There's always 10 percent in every deal, maybe more."

All Cards on the Table

Complicated deals contain so many issues that it's easy to fall prey to the salami technique. Each slice doesn't take too much off, but after many cuts you've lost a lot of meat. Getting "nickel-and-dimed to death" is a variation on the same theme. Here each little coin seems trivial, but the process never ends. Such deals can rupture more for the annoyance they cause than for the amount they lose.

The solution to the problem is to get all the issues out on the same table. Whenever I sense a salami slicer (especially if I hear the jiggle of small change in his pockets), I stop discussing any minor matter, no matter how minor. "We are going to get all the issues out on the table," I proclaim, "and solve them all together, not one at a time; simultaneously, not sequentially." I stress that although every issue may be negotiable, they are only negotiable collectively, not individually. I must see the entire puzzle before altering any particular piece. (Gathering all points together is especially important when dealing with those most infamous of Salami carvers—lawyers.)

Playing the Game

In each deal-making situation you must play according to the rules. In the souk, you must at some point begin to walk out, even if you have no intentions of leaving. If you worry, "But I really want to buy," you're an easy mark amateur.

Never forget that the buyer is the one spending the money. The buyer can walk out—and come back again. My wife made three forays out the shop door, one of which brought her 10 yards down the road, before being frantically called back to bargain. She swapped stories with the shopkeeper, each accompanied by verbal exuberance and visual flamboyance. He told her of all the fierce battles won by these knives, interspersed with heart-rending accounts of sick parents and hungry children. She told him of just seeing 10 duplicates of the same "one-of-a-kind" knives in other stores at half the price (her lie was innocent, his a little less so).

Each deal follows its own path to completion. If you go through the required ritual and play the game, the deal will probably work out. Some corporate deal makers use tough-talking attorneys to get in some additional whacks. Others blame faraway executives or nameless committees. Preserving the honor of principals is always a primary objective.

Playing the deal-making game should be fun. My wife and the shopkeeper both enjoyed their 30-minute negotiation. I liked the show so much I almost gave the man a tip.

Corporate Exchanges

In one M&A transaction, the parties were about $10 million apart in a $50 million transaction. Negotiations had proceeded as far as possible without resolution. Here were two of the canniest traders in U.S. commerce; neither had budged in weeks and both had run out of ideas. What to do?

Suddenly, in the course of a casual conversation, it was discovered that the buyer, not in the real estate business, had a money-losing property that he was trying to dump. The property was worth, to the buyer, under $5 million. The seller, with a large real estate operation, could easily run such a property with minimal additional overhead. To the seller, the property was worth above $10 million. You guessed the outcome; the property was thrown in as additional payment and the deal made.

30. MANAGING THE TIME

Strength in sports means nothing without timing. In swinging, throwing, shooting, and hitting, "when" is more important than "how hard." The same is true for deal doing. Time is a deal maker's most valuable resource.

Functions of Time

Time serves various functions in deals. It is the standard of progress against which milestones are measured. It is an ally of the less pressured side and an enemy of the more pressured side. It is a resource to be conserved and spent wisely.

Every deal has a critical period. There's a strange spirit in a deal, a mutual feeling of movement that engenders positive feelings. However, pass the critical period and trouble ensues—up emotions swing down and the entire transaction becomes less likely to happen.

To make deals, various things must be timed to happen simultaneously. When you are negotiating to buy a business, for example, you must reach agreement, arrange the financing, coordinate the legal work, audit the financial statements, and plan for future operations—not to mention maintain harmony and focus within your own organization.

Principles of Timing

The following are specific suggestions for using timing in deals.

Assign Specific Functional Responsibility

Be sure that one individual is answerable for each independent activity (e.g., for M&A: accounting due diligence, working with management, plant visits, appraisals, bank negotiations, etc.).

Assign Specific Timing Coordination

Be sure that one individual is responsible for coordinating all independent activity. Whenever possible, this person should be the principal deal maker.

Monitor Progress Regularly

Keep in close touch with the key people in each functional area of responsibility. Keep in touch on a regular basis. Require each area leader to maintain and update a specific timetable of milestones and accomplishments. Using a personal computer can aid such project-planning activities.[40]

Deadlines

Deadlines add volatility to a deal and kick a series of events into motion. Your side may set the deadlines. You may need to force a "fish or cut bait" decision (also known as "____ or get off the pot"). If the other side sets the firm time limit, you must decide whether it's in your best interest. If it is, fine. If it isn't, what will happen if the deadline is not met?

A deadline must always be taken seriously. *Never* give the impression that you think it is a charade. You must convey the gravity of the act to the other side. Deadline setters must confront the consequences of their actions. However, if you are unsure about just how firm the deadline is, test its resilience. Ask a question such as: "Our bank can't close until three days after the deadline expires—so what can we do to bridge the time gap?" The answer will give you the clue you are looking for.

Slowdowns

Slowdowns are one side's deliberate effort to stall. They may be playing out an alternative opportunity because they think it is better. They may be using a coercive tactic because they suspect you are under heavy pressure. It doesn't really matter. The bottom line is that the deal is not going anywhere.

What to do when faced with a slowdown? The best tactic may be an ultimatum. If the other side is working another deal, you'll put them on the spot—right where they belong. If they're trying to pressure you to make concessions, they'll find out that the tables have been turned.

---

[40]See George T. Geis and Robert L. Kuhn, *Micromanaging: Transforming Business Leaders With Personal Computers* (Englewood Cliff, N.J.: Prentice Hall), 1987.

Making Meetings Efficient

Time is a precious commodity—especially in deal making. Since deal makers must monitor their time, they should follow these caveats: Meetings need reasons. Brief telephone calls can replace long meetings. Everyone doesn't have to be at every meeting. Specialists (e.g., lawyers and accountants) can meet with their counterparts alone. A smaller team can often accomplish more in a shorter time than a larger team can in a longer time.

Perhaps most important, your team's chief deal maker must stay personally in touch with all participants working with the other side. Reports, even if brief, should be given after every meeting.

31. MAINTAINING THE MOMENTUM

Recall the frustration of a faltering deal? We've all felt the fizzle. Suddenly, the spirit seems sapped. Both sides lose enthusiasm in the process and confidence in the outcome. Commitment unravels. You don't know what went wrong. Deadlocks and gaps abound—but that's normal for deals. What happened here? Momentum was lost.

Momentum is the essence of deal making, giving impetus and generating action. It's what happens when the dead weight of inertia is overcome through the application of constant force. Momentum is exciting. Once started, it's hard to stop. Once stopped, it's hard to start.

Deal-making momentum is the exhilarating sense of energized activity. The payoff is twofold: (1) making the buy or closing the sale and (2) obtaining the personal pleasure of being a winner.

Momentum is more attitude than action. When seeking momentum, never be satisfied with the status quo and always be on search for new ideas: new methods to bridge gaps, new ways to break deadlocks, new approaches to solve problems.

Momentum is movement. Progress is a step or steps toward an acceptable goal. Either can be present without the other. However, momentum without progress is too wild and progress without momentum is too tame. In deal making, momentum without progress runs the risk of running rampant and progress without momentum may falter short of the goal.

Methods for Maintaining Momentum

Momentum won't maintain itself. That's contrary to the laws of physics. Momentum requires force, force needs energy, and energy demands effort.

It's no different in deal making. Three elements for maintaining momentum follow.

Reach for Attainable Objectives.

Two concepts reside here: "reach for," meaning exceeding current grasp; and "achievable," meaning within your capacity to get done. Nothing slows momentum more than objectives too easy or objectives too hard. If you do not stretch, overconfidence sets in, or worse, boredom. If you do not believe in the likelihood of success, discouragement sets in, or, worse, depression. Both stuck out needed energy and momentum stops.

Always Keep Moving

Momentum has an odd cumulative quality. Once it begins to slow, it is hard to speed up. Just as a bicycler must begin pedaling faster when approaching a steep hill, deal makers must work harder when approaching sticky situations. So, it is your job to keep the action going.

Always have the next step planned before the last step ends. If you can't make progress on central issues, work on peripheral issues. If there are no easy problems to solve, look for odd ones or make some up. Sometimes the illusion of progress is enough to keep the deal rolling toward completion.

Consider the old airline joke where the pilot announces, "I have good news and bad news. The good news is that we're making excellent time. The bad news is that we're lost." While making excellent-time-though-lost is not too cool for a pilot, it isn't so bad for a deal maker. Maintaining the atmosphere of forward motion contributes to the problem-solving spirit needed to handle those knotty, axial issues.

Bypass Problems, Then Circle Back

It is not easy to keep moving forward, especially when unexpected obstacles crop up. If a seemingly insoluble problem arises, don't despair. Go on to simpler matters instead. You can always return to the thorny one later. In fact, it is often easier to resolve an open issue when it is the last one remaining on the table. Furthermore, the bare passage of time solves many problems by making them irrelevant.[41]

---

[41]When I do not know what to do with some papers, I put them in a pile that sits for a while, perhaps several weeks, on, under, or over my desk. When I return to these little annoyances, the time having past, I usually find about half the issues are no longer relevant and much of the other half can be classified quickly.

Conveying Interest

How to show the other side that you really want to move the deal along—without looking like a supplicant? The following subtle actions can sustain momentum.

Roll Up Your Sleeves. Get to work. Dig into figures. As buyer, investigate what you'll receive. As seller, assist the buyer in making the investigation.

Go Kick the Tires. Get out of the office and into the field. See the stuff.

Compromise Hints. Float trial balloons. Use pregnant questions. Offer tentative suggestions. Go off the record.

Informal Occasions. Invite the other side to more informal settings—meals, sporting events, or social activities.

32. MAKING THE CLOSE

Negotiating deals and not closing is like getting married and not mating. You can't be a good deal maker unless you're a good deal closer. You can be weak in any of the other elements—but not this one. You must be able to put that final knot on the noose, that final nail in the coffin (Ugh!—I like love-making analogies far better).

Good deal closers focus on the desired outcomes. They see their goals clearly and keep them always in mind. Closing the deal takes a bit of bravado: You need guts to go for it—and the smarts to know when and how. You need not await a magical moment. You can end it all at any point. You can make the winning touchdown from any place on the playing field.

Smell the Close

The best sign that a deal is ready to close is a suggested compromise on the critical outstanding issue. The offer should be made on the most contentious problem, the one that was most resistant to solution. Furthermore, it doesn't matter whether there are other unresolved issues still outstanding.

Other signs are certain telegraphic phrases; for example, "I think we can work this out," in response to any offer you make; or "We need to rock this baby to sleep."

Watch for a lower tension level. A signal can be a change in tone of voice. Even before the final points are decided, conversation becomes more relaxed and informal, and humor picks up. Often, you can test the waters by initiating such relaxed conversation yourself. If you do not get back reciprocal relaxation, you know you're not ready to close. Even if you get a positive response, you must judge whether you're really ready to close or the other person is just being friendly.

Isolate Final Points

Closing deals means obtaining agreement on every issue. This is a formidable task. There are two general approaches: (1) Attack the major issues head on and leave the minor ones for later mop up, or (2) solve all the minor issues first and then confront the now isolated majors.

Which approach you choose depends on circumstances. When the deal looks relatively simple, or when the parties are not terribly far apart on the primary issues (such as price), you can go for a quick close by negotiating the major issues up front. When the deal is more complex, or when the parties remain far apart on the primary issues, then it is smarter to surround the problem by resolving the minor issues first.

Who Makes the Push

Making the first move toward closure scares some deal makers. They imagine it to be a sign of weakness. It isn't, although the possibilities of being rebuffed can be daunting.

I like to take the initiative. If it fails to get proper results for whatever reason (timing, offer, etc.), I make sure that the rejection does not affect my own self-image.

Knowing When to Stop

There are two kinds of "stops" in deal making. Although they are opposite in intent, the same principle—sensing when to cease and desist—applies to both situations.

When to Stop Pushing For More

Work your tail off trying to maximize your value, but when you're finished, be finished. Some deal makers never cease scheming. They're still retrading as they sign the final documents. The sure sign of reaching the limit is an escalation of irritation on the other side. When you've gotten what you can get, call off the show.

When to Stop Trying To Close

Recognize that some deals never will be ready for signature. But some deal makers press obliviously forward—annoying the other side and frustrating themselves. If at first you don't succeed, sure, try again—but not again and again, at least not in the same way.

Looking Good

Human beings seek admiration in the eyes of their peers. There is no principle more fundamental in making deals. Remembering it makes you wise. Applying it makes you win.

Always strive to give the other side something they can repeat with pride to others. Consider their reactions as you plan the close. Think how they'll explain the deal to superiors, subordinates, even friends and family. A small concession, especially a cosmetic one, can work wonders.

Problem Types

Lots of characters are deal makers. Some give headaches by not being able to close. One type always wants to excise more flesh, to perpetually nibble your hide. These characters keep grinding for gain.

Nervous types are also unable to close deals. They are too scared to complete a transaction, worrying constantly about all the things that could go wrong. These characters keep looking for loopholes.

How to handle problem types? Nibblers must be smacked on the snout. A hard shot, this they understand. Just tell them categorically that "If you want to close, close; if you want more, you're history." The frightened types are more difficult to handle. Pressure will alienate, not coerce. You must give them room.

After the Deal Closes

Good deal makers do more than pack up their briefcases after the deal is done. They look for ways to express their appreciation for both the deal and the people doing it. Maintain contact for a while. Consider giving some needed assistance that is not covered in the contract.

The final point is what *not* to do. Never boast about besting. Even if you did get the better of the deal, forget it. Never make the other side feel beaten. If anything, do the opposite—show the other side some additional benefits of the transaction.

These actions will boost your reputation. They will also encourage the next deal. Good deal makers view every just-completed deal as the forerunner of a yet-to-be-started deal.

33. EMPLOYING THE PROS

Attorneys are predisposed to break deals. This is not a slur; it is just fact. Negative attitudes of lawyers are as much a natural law of commerce as parental love for children is a natural law of biology. I cast no blame. They can't help it. It's the way the system is designed. Attorneys, you see, don't profit from deals that get done. But they sure take the heat for deals that get undone.

Listening to lawyers can turn optimists into pessimists, pollyannas into cynics. There are problems behind every deal point; there is no issue without peril. No deal, it can seem, should ever be made.

Deals, by definition, have risk. You accept risk in order to seek reward. The amount of reward must match the degree of risk, with the former well exceeding the latter. Attorneys and accountants explain the risk. Only you know the reward.

Use Independent Judgment

Push your professionals to their limit. Ask them to go over the deal from top to bottom. Maximize the full extent of their expertise. Encourage them to be rough and tough, vigorous and vicious. Throw them raw meat. Exhort them to exercise independent judgment, to disagree with you and your deal. If they do anything less, they're not doing their job. "I am counting on you," I inform my attorneys and accountants solemnly, "to unearth all the issues I've missed. Excavate and exhume if you must, but ferret out those problems."

Due Diligence

"Due diligence" is the name given to the procedure that transpires between negotiating the deal and closing it. The process involves checking all books and records to determine if what has been represented to be true is indeed true. Normally, the buyer's team conducts due diligence on the seller's property. (The seller may conduct some due diligence if they are taking any of their consideration for the deal in buyer stock or notes.)

Risk assessment—lurking dangers and potential threats—is the primary role of attorneys and accountants. The due diligence process searches for skeletons; for example: undisclosed liabilities such as underfunded pension funds or contingent guarantees; overvalued assets such as inflated inventories or improperly reserved receivables; long-term contracts to sell goods and services priced below market or cost; potential legal insults such as product liability suits not covered by insurance; tax problems.[42]

Finding the problems is fine. But you should also ask the pros to suggest possible solutions. You do not want to change the deal more than once.

Hidden Opportunities

While your attorneys and accountants are conducting their due diligence, prompt them to keep an eye out for hidden opportunities. Some examples: low cost debt such as industrial revenue bonds; LIFO (last-in first-out) inventories with a buried layer of low-cost raw materials; law suits against vendors, customers, or insurance companies with likelihood of collection; overfunded pension funds that can generate cash; fully depreciated assets that have significant value; raw land carried on the books at minuscule long-ago costs; investment assets such as minority ownership of other companies that have appreciated above book carrying costs.

It's Your Deal

After the professionals have found all the problems (and then some), it's your turn. Remember, they work for you, not you for them. Never forget the big picture—why you wanted to do the deal in the first place. Although the deal may now look like a technical jungle—a thicket of legal thorns and tax bristles—don't despair. Instead, weigh the original benefits of the deal against just how problematic the issues are, whether there are solutions to these problems, and whether you think the deal is still worth doing.

---

[42]One issue in acquisitions is the question of buying assets or stock. Generally the buyer likes to purchase assets, since they thereby avoid any undisclosed problems (e.g., tax, legal, and the like) associated with the prior company. Sometimes stock purchase is more desirable, such as with tax carryforwards, lease arrangements, and, most of the time, seller wishes.

Balance the risks turned up by the pros against the rewards of the original idea. It is, after all, your deal and your decision. (If you decide to get out of the deal, the pros are your best resource. They can always find convincing reasons to back out.)

Using Consultants

Consultants are freelance experts in a particular field; they are well positioned to give an unbiased assessment of the deal. (Their only bias is to recommend, as part of the first study, that you should continue with a second study.)

Consultants, it is said, will fly across the country to give a speech, but won't walk across the street to hear one. A less kind definition frames consultants as people who, having been fired from a previous job, can't seem to find a present one. The point is to be selective. There are numerous consultants around. Few are really good, but some are outstanding.

In appraising a potential deal (normally an acquisition), consultants should bring three strengths to the table: experience and expertise in the specific industry or field, a good nose for sniffing out opportunities and threats, and true independence of judgment.

Getting the most out of consultants means using them for highly specific purposes. Consultants are excellent for technical analysis of products and markets; assessing distinctive competencies of companies; estimating competitive advantages of firms; formulating alternative strategies; and evaluating diverse scenarios.

A good analysis of a business should include detailed information on every critical aspect from product technology to cost structure to distribution systems. The more general the assignment the more nebulous the product. If you are not satisfied with a consultant's work, the blame should often fall on those who structured the task.[43]

34. COACHING THE TEAM

Leverage in mechanics is the ability of a small force to move a large object. Leverage in finance is the ability of a small amount of equity to control a large amount of assets. Leverage also applies to deal making. Here, it is the

[43]Finally, my favorite lawyer joke: Why are medical researchers replacing white mice with lawyers in their experiments? First, there are more lawyers than white mice. Second, they breed faster. Third, you don't get so attached to them. Fourth, there are just some things that white mice won't do!

ability of good deal makers to multiple themselves by working with a group of key individuals. Just like a good surgeon uses assistants to "open" and "close," a good deal maker uses assistants to handle various matters.

Team Roles

Deal making has various parts, some of which should be delegated to members of your team. There is no sense having everyone do everything. There's no leverage in that.

Always staff for strength. Use each team member's talents for your advantage. Never allocate effort to improve weaknesses. Team members will vary in ability, experience, and interest. Give each one what he or she likes and does best. For instance, some people excel at the initial scouting of possible deals, others enjoy the due diligence process, and still others like coordinating the flow of activities.

Seek balance in assignment structure. Make your tasks too loose and you lose focused motivation and personal commitment of the individuals. Make your tasks too rigid and you lose innovative interaction and brainstorming dynamism of the group. Deal making is both art and science, and you need both creative types and analytical types on the team. You also need someone who knows where each type belongs.

Team Coordination

One person should be responsible for assuring that all tasks are running in proper sequence and schedule. That person should be the principal deal maker, or someone close to the key person. Progress should be monitored regularly. Few days should pass without communication.

Ego and Attitude

There is one cardinal rule for deal teams: Never air your differences in public. (Exception: when the "differences" are part of a planned strategy.)

People who make deals have notoriously active egos. They think much of themselves, often more highly than they ought. They have strong opinions about things, and if those opinions are rejected, they may suffer or sulk.

Caring for a deal-making team can require the temperament of an opera impresario. Prima donnas abound—you never know when they will go manic or depressive. Deal-making types may be pampered and protected, though they shouldn't be coddled or spoiled.

Shuffling the Team

Let's say you're in deal-making purgatory: Deadlocks can't be broken; gaps can't be bridged; momentum has stopped; and the deal has stalled. Worse, emotions have frayed on both sides and sparks are beginning to fly. You need to do something fast.

Try something different: Rotate your team. Break the accustomed relationships. Make each member of your side work with a new member of the other side. Go as far as having nonattorneys work with attorneys. The change in perspective can only be beneficial. After all, you have little left to lose.

35. FIGURING THE NUMBERS

Figures lie, it is said, and liars figure. Numbers often appear to be statements of absolute truth. This is illusion. In doing deals, you must understand where numbers come from and how they are calculated. Equally important—and often forgotten—are the numbers that aren't available. Fooling around with numbers is really rather easy. Counting counts, but not too much.

Profits and Cash

Many a bankrupt company had a stellar record of steady profits until the day it filed Chapter 11. There have been companies, for example, that booked sales as "revenues" even though all they ever received for their products were uncollectible accounts receivable that eventually had to be written off as worthless. The "profits" were always on the books—but the cash was never in the bank.[44]

When evaluating companies, stock analysts have come to realize that cash is king, and that watching the statements of changes in financial position, especially as they relate to cash flow, can be more important than tracking profitability. This is often proven by leveraged buyouts that may never show

---

[44]For companies, there is a great deal of difference between profits and cash. This is not so for individuals, who can calculate their personal profit for the year by simply adding up all the money they received and subtracting all that they spent. Businesses operate on the "accrual" system, which means that revenues and expenses are booked "when realized"—which is not when cash payments are received and disbursed. Furthermore, when a company buys new equipment, it is "capitalized" and therefore not an "expense"—although you can be sure that real payment was in cash or cash equivalents.

profits (due to high interest and depreciation)—but can eventually be sold for huge capital gains.

Equivalent Value

The key for understanding all financial numbers, especially in deals, is "present value." All deal makers must understand this pivotal concept that relates all future dollars back to a dollar value today. The process is simply the compounding of interest, either backward or forward in time. However, it become complex quickly. Deal makers must be able to operate a financial calculator—or have someone handy who does.

Return on Investment

Return on investment (ROI) over time is a trap for naive deal makers. ROI demands more awareness and insight than many might think. Consider a deal where an investor group would loan $7 million at 13 percent interest and receive 25 percent of the company equity as an incentive "kicker." The company would like to have the option of buying out the loan and equity for $9 million (plus interest) at the end of the year. The return for the year comes to almost 42 percent. Spectacular, you say. But ROI is more than numbers, and herein lies the problem.

There's high risk in the deal. Now the degree of risk in investments relates directly to the required rates of return. For example, venture capital deals must have very high returns in order to compensate for their very high risks—many of these business start-ups fail completely and the investors lose all their money. Therefore, returns of 40 percent or better for many years are needed on successful deals.

Furthermore, those returns must be compounded over many years to make the absolute number of dollars worthwhile. I'd much rather get 30 percent per year for three years than 42 percent for one year. In the above case, the profit over and above the 13 percent interest would be $5.6 million for the 30 percent over three years, and $2 million for the 42 percent over one year.

Payout Perceptions

Assume that you have agreed to sell your business to a qualified seller. Part of the offer is $1 million now or $5 million in 10 years. How can you compare the alternatives? (For simplicity, we leave out tax considerations—but they really must be included.) What to do?

How to compare the equivalent value of $1 million paid today with $5 million paid in 10 years? You have to ask, in essence, how many dollars do I have to invest today, and at what interest rate (called the "discount rate"), in order to generate $5 million 10 years from now? Obviously, it depends on what interest rate you assume. If you use 7 percent interest, that $5 million out there is worth about $2.5 million back here. If you assume 10 percent, it's worth almost $2 million; if 17.5 percent, it's worth about the same $1 million; and if the interest rate is higher than 17.5 percent, then that glorious $5 million is actually worth less than $1 million is today.

How to determine a proper discount rate to use? You must add a risk premium to the riskless market rate (i.e., Treasuries). A 17.5 percent interest rate compounded for 10 years seems like a terrific investment opportunity in today's world. Why not grab it? Be cautious. Proper determination of your required rate of return should include an evaluation of intangibles as well as present value cash equivalents. For instance, how do you know the company will be around in 10 years? What will happen to its market, its customers, its competitors? Then there's the issue of time itself: Do you really want to wait 10 years to collect? Believe me, as a seller I'll take my sure million right now. As a buyer, I'll try all day to convince you that you're walking away from a great deal.

36. CRAFTING THE WORDS

So you have a deal. Talking, you've done lots of. Writing, precious little. Now that you have an oral agreement, it's time to put the understanding into words on paper. It's amazing how different the deal looks in black and white.

Document Authorship

Who prepares the documents? Which side takes the first cut? There are two approaches here. Generally, when you draw up the first draft, it's your outline and structure that controls the contract process. Thus, it is better to prepare the document and have the other side offer suggestions for change.

However, if there are still some ambiguities in the deal, you face a dilemma. If your side prepares the papers, you might antagonize the other side—or give away something unnecessary. In this case, it might be better to have the other side write the first draft. Perhaps they'll state the ambiguity in your favor. If not, you can always discuss the matter. And, if you aren't happy with their draft, you can always rewrite it. If you do so, include at least some of their language to avoid a battle of wills among the lawyers.

When to Start Writing

Not Too Late

Sometimes it is wise to write up the deal elements at various stages of negotiations. Doing so can prevent misunderstandings from solidifying. By spelling out the deal points, you uncover problems not resolved and even issues not discussed.

Not Too Early

Be aware, however, that a written document can highlight—even exacerbate—any real gaps between the parties. Sometimes it is better for such gaps to go unnoticed for a while. If focused on too soon, they may retard momentum and disrupt the deal. If ignored, these gaps might be narrowed through later discussions, or at least not interfere with the resolution of other issues.

Types of Documents

Term Sheets

Term sheets are two to three page summaries of deals. They are drawn up to confirm an oral agreement and only stress the major issues. Term sheets are generally not morally or legally binding. Thus, they are rarely signed.

I find term sheets extremely useful in making deals—all parties can focus on each deal point without ambiguity or personality influence. Term sheets are so important that I write them myself—not trusting them to attorneys. Often there are good vibes and strong momentum at this stage, and lawyers can slow the process and confound the issues.

Don't misunderstand. Attorneys are essential for deals—but not for this function. The legal issues lawyers bring up are necessary and you'll be in thick soup if you ignore them—but term-sheet-time is not the time to address these technicalities. Term sheets are tools for confirming agreement on the cardinal issues, and you don't want minutia impeding progress.

Memoranda of Understanding (or Letters of Agreement)

Memoranda of understanding (MOUs) are more official statements of the agreement between the parties. MOUs, which can run more than 10 pages, describe all essential elements of the deal. They facilitate the preparation of contracts by exposing most of the issues. It is often stated explicitly that the MOU must be replaced by a formal contract to be binding. Nonetheless, MOUs are often signed, and the parties can begin to act as if the deal were in effect. Lawyers must prepare and critique MOUs.

Formal Contracts

Formal contracts are the last step. Good attorneys shelter the principals from the ritual and tedium, but they always report any business change or difference from the expected structure, no matter how small. Attorneys from both sides generally work together to smooth the logistics of closing. "Preclosings" are often necessary to coordinate all the paperwork. Simply getting all of the signatures on all of the documents—some of which, we'd predict, will just have been changed—can take hours.

Document Style

Documents can be prepared in many ways, depending on what position you're in. If you feel that the deal is good for your side and should be done quickly, then go for documents that are straight, specific, simple, clear, and fast. If there are still some points that need to be resolved and if delay is to your benefit, then aim for documents that are tricky, general, complex, turgid, and slow. You can always trade off the ambiguity in a final give and take.

Keep in mind that turnaround time for documents is important in maintaining momentum. When you have an agreed deal, you must have a "killer instinct" to close it. More than one deal has died between lawyers' edits and choking word processors.

37. AVOIDING THE PITFALLS

"Don't cough up the ball," coaches implore their teams. Football games are often determined by which side makes the fewer turnovers. The same is true in deal making: Whichever side makes the fewer mistakes is likely to achieve its objectives more easily.

Some common pitfalls are summarized here. (Several have been discussed in prior sections.) Your goal is to understand these deal-making traps, watch for them, recognize them—and avoid them.

Faulty Information

Errors of fact are an inexcusable gaffe. Any information used as a basis for a negotiating position should be both accurate and appropriate.[45]

---

[45]Note that information can be either accurate or appropriate without being the other. An example of being appropriate and not accurate is when an appraisal of a property fails to take new zoning laws into consideration. An example of being accurate and not appropriate is when that appraisal is made of the land and not the building, when the deal is for the building and not the land.

Premature Threats

Demands and ultimatums, whether blatant or subtle, are part of the deal-making process. But timing is critical. Shooting too soon looks ridiculous and has little effect. Worse, it ruins the potential power of these tactics at a later stage.

Unplanned Anger

Showing anger without objective can adversely affect both the deal and your reputation. All deal makers get a little hot at times. Frankly, it's not necessarily bad to show some viscera—it warns the other side that this stuff is important. But rage without reason does more harm than good.[46]

Personal Insults

As for me, I never do it. I don't like to intimidate, and I refuse to humiliate. No deal is that important. Also, it never works, not in the long run. Even if everything you say is true, you're building up resentment. What goes around, comes around.

People Antagonisms

Friction between the sides sets up barriers to making deals. The only people you dislike, if you think about it, are the people you know. With big stakes involved (ego above all), it's easy to project your frustrations on to the other side, to blame them for your faults.[47] Control your personal feelings and get the job done.

---

[46]Do not jump to the opposite conclusion. I'm not advising you to "plan" your anger, to calculate your "fury" in advance as if playing some trick (though this may work on occasion). Rather, whenever your ire is triggered, be sure to consider the consequences of your actions and then direct your heat toward those goals.

[47]For example, my daughter just overslept and was late for work. At first, she blamed me for not answering her phone when her employer called. I wasn't answering any phones that day, not even my own, since the feared deadline of this manuscript was fast approaching.

Cozy Relations

Getting too friendly with the other side can lead to conflicts of interest. These may not be immoral or illegal, but they still could be a detriment to doing good deals. Avoid even the appearance of potential conflict or compromise.[48]

Talking Too Much

A big mouth can lead to big trouble. Never forget that the other side is the opposing and you must watch what you say to them. You can be forthright, sure, but don't be foolish. You should be friendly, you can be informal, but always control your tongue. Everything said should be planned. (When reconsidering an investment after several months, an analyst on the other side confided that he thought the company was worse now than it was then. Well, I was 70 percent negative then, so his offhanded comment short-circuited my revaluation.)

Fear of the Unknown

Never worry your way into deals. Concern about specifics can be helpful, but general agitation is detrimental. Good preparation is the best antidote against fear.

Showing Anxiety[49]

Showing nervousness among deal makers is like spilling blood among sharks. Neither is recommended for continued well-being. Such apparent weakness invites aggressiveness.

Feeling Inferior

This problem is more in the head than around the table. You may have less knowledge than the other side, or wield less power, but at the bargain-

[48] Occasionally during long negotiations, real friendships develop between members of opposing camps. Be careful to protect professional integrity. If business relationships develop, that's even worse. Co-investing in an unrelated deal, for example, is going too far.

[49] Anxiety is the outward expression of inner concern, an unspecific dread of the future, an uncontrollable consternation about upcoming events. It bespeaks a lack of confidence in outcomes. It reflects pressures that cannot be relieved.

ing table all are equal. Everyone has the same ultimate weapon: The word is "no."

Early Weakness

It's almost never good to show weakness in deal making, but it's disastrous at the outset. The emotional imprint for the entire negotiating process is formed up front. Even if your side has less power and control, hide it at first. Throw in some confusing signs, some swagger and brag if you must. You might even threaten an early abort.

Being Nibbled

Giving up little by little can quickly turn into giving up more than you ever intended to concede. This "salami" technique of getting slivered by small slices must be avoided. State that all ideas and proposals will be considered, but simultaneously—not sequentially.

Excessive Logic

When your head rules your heart, you can focus too much on facts and too little on feelings. People make deals for personal reasons. You can be right and still be wrong, winning battles while losing wars. Too much rational analysis of deals may slight the human factors. Too much numerical emphasis, too much quantitative decision making, can inhibit or destroy the insight and intuition needed to do deals. You can structure brilliantly, but if you don't also persuade pleasantly, you can lose what you should have won. Never forget, deal making is a people-intensive process.

Excessive Emotion

When your heart rules your head, you may ignore facts and make emotional deals. Getting too attached to deals can lead to volatile decisions. Too much emphasis on intuition can dissipate or negate the detailed examinations needed to do a good job. Never make an emotional deal without knowing the logic behind it. Overriding logic with gut feelings is fine—as long as you remain fully aware of what you are doing. Never forget, deal making involves value and consideration measured in dollars and cents.

Too Little Principle

A good reputation takes many years to build and a few minutes to destroy. Think about that in every deal you do.[50]

Too Much Principle

Too much principle can also thwart a deal. Can't be "too principled," you say, just like you can't be "too rich or too thin?" Well, that depends on definitions.

Having too much principle is clearly better than having too little. This is certain. Still, some people set standards that are spuriously high only because they seek to sustain their own lofty self image. Ego, remember, is the great killer of good deals.

38. DOING THE WORK

Work doesn't exist—not unless you would rather be doing something else. People do not suffer because of hard work; they break down due to worry, fear, tension, and anxiety.

The work of good deal making is exhilarating. It invigorates the soul while engaging the mind. But have no illusions. Good deal making is hard—rigorous, arduous, strenuous, demanding, exacting, enervating, and exhausting. It is concentrated and intense, requiring both mental effort and social grace. It taxes all your resources, demanding people perception as well as technical precision. Doing deals is real work.

We're almost finished. We're almost through the 39 deal elements. We've said so much about deal making that you may be a little shell-shocked. Relax. You don't have to memorize everything we've said. Absorbing the ideas and experiencing the stories doesn't mean instant recall of every point. Your subconscious is getting it, even if you feel a bit overwhelmed.

---

[50]A lack of principle can ruin a deal, or even a career, and doing hard time in the slammer isn't impossible (as several ex-Wall Streeters wouldn't be happy to confirm). Some deal makers are steeped in conflicts of interest all the time. They know no other way. They represent one group overtly while participating in another group covertly. All their actions must be suspect. A typical example: purchasing agents receiving "appreciation" from vendors, however subtle the form of payment. Insider trading is but the latest, grotesque expression of one of the world's two oldest professions (which, by the way, have much in common).

Perhaps it's like a first lesson in golf or tennis. The instructor tells you how, where, and when to move each limb. You can't remember it all, much less coordinate it together. But with practice, the diverse movements all begin to fall into place.

So take a deep breath and a step back. What follows is summary. If you remember and put these principles into practice, you'll be a good maker of deals.

Be Committed and Focused

You must be dedicated, persevering, and intense. Good deal makers are single-minded in pursuit of their clear goals. They have great desire to succeed and always seek new solutions to old problems. They make better deals because they focus on objectives.

Keep Flexible With Multiple Options

You must have various alternative deals from which you can select. Good deal makers know that the most critical decision is often made up front, deciding in advance which deals are most "do-able." They know that maintaining other possible deals outside the current transaction improves negotiating strength. They are creative in devising innovative strategies, structures, and bargaining ideas. They make better deals because they have greater choices.

Shoot Rifles, Not Shotguns

You must hit the trunk of the tree, not fool with the branches. Good deal makers go for the jugular, not to kill, but to close. They know what issues are critical to resolve, what both sides need and want, what techniques bridge gaps and break deadlocks. They know where to find regions of win-win arrangements. They aim straight and true. They make better deals because they select the right problems to solve.

Seek Progress, Not Puff

You must concentrate on doing the deal, not building your image. Good deal makers focus on resolving issues, not enhancing power. They are socially aware, keeping track of characters and personalities on both sides of the table. They make better deals because personal ego is subservient to collective benefit.

Have Fun

You must like the action, not just the results. Good deal makers love what they do as well as appreciate what they get. They relish the deal-making process and look forward to every new opportunity. They make better deals because everything about them stimulates and excites. Deal-doing work, above all else, requires deal-doing fun. Doing the work means having the fun.

39. HAVING THE FUN

If work is whatever you need to get done, then fun is whatever you like to be doing. Deal making must be both fun and work: You should like doing whatever you need to be doing.

A wealthy investment banker was asked why he continued working so hard into his late 70s. "My friends play golf," he said, keeping his eyes glued to obscure financial notes, "I make deals." He explained that he likes to do what he's reasonably good at doing—a category that did not include driving, chipping, or putting.

Good deal makers have fun doing their deals. What's to enjoy in deal making? How to have fun amidst the tension? The following attitudes should help.

Relax

Manner and demeanor are important. How you feel governs how you act. Don't allow pressures to overwhelm emotions. No deal is that vital. Cool beats hot. But the deal's getting away, you say? Don't be anxious. If a horse runs away, says a proverb, don't fret; if it's your horse, it will come back; if it's not, you don't want it back.

Being relaxed doesn't contradict being focused and committed. You can be dedicated to deal making and work with ferocious intensity. The key is not to take yourself too seriously.

Anticipate Newness

There's one special quality about doing deals that makes it exciting. Making deals is always new, always changing, always refreshing. Nothing is ever humdrum. Being bored is never a concern. So savor the ever-present novelty.

When searching for new deals, look forward to each fresh possibility as if it were your first. Be eager. Sense the uniqueness, the expectation of surprise. What will the next deal bring? From where will it come? How will you do it?

When doing a particular deal, take pleasure in addressing each new problem. Problems have solutions. Solutions can be better or worse, and your task is to find those that are better. Make the search scintillating, invigorating, rejuvenating. Psych yourself and expect results!

Keep Score

Whether your game is golf, tennis, chess, bridge, or Scrabble, keeping score keeps your interest. You need a benchmark against which to judge performance. Winning may not be the only thing, but constant improvement helps maintain momentum. You don't practice your strokes or study your moves without testing them in live action. Part of the fun is charting your progress.

Enjoy the People

To be a good deal maker, you must like people. This is the first half of the bottom line. Good deal makers enjoy engaging different personalities and handling different characters. They savor constructing deals in which the other side is satisfied. Good deal makers never build resentment. New friendships, these they build often.

Enjoy the Process

To be a good deal maker, you must also like deal making. This is the second half of the bottom line. You must like what you do while you are doing it. The process should be pleasurable.

You can't really relish everything—conflicting opinions and stalled progress do not spark your spirit, nor do personality conflicts and disruptive threats give you belly laughs. But even the aggravation can be fun if you view obstacles as challenges and problems as opportunities.

How to handle friction and strife? The trick is to see all action as part of a bigger picture. Keep end results in mind: Visualizing where you want to go facilitates how you are going to get there. Appreciate the quandaries and predicaments. Consider trouble the tests of your mettle—the chance to devise creative solutions.

Do What You Enjoy

A favorite story involves an exchange between two high school friends meeting after many years. One has become an enormously successful investment banker, doing megadeals daily. The other remains an economic basketcase, teaching part time in a small college, philosophizing with friends, and generally enjoying life.

"Why don't you get a real job?" asks the suave investment banker.

"Why should I?" answers the disheveled professor.

"Look, if you get a real job, you can make money."

"But why do I want to make money?"

"With money you can buy a business."

"But why do I want to buy a business."

"Then you can make even more money."

"But why do I want to make even more money?"

"So you can buy a bigger business."

"But why do I want to buy a bigger business?"

"So you can amass a huge amount of money."

"But why do I want to amass a huge amount of money?"

"Because then you can retire and do what you want!"

"But that's what I'm doing right now!"

INDEX

A

C

D

E

H

N

O

P

T

U

V

W

Y

Z